S0-AFD-119

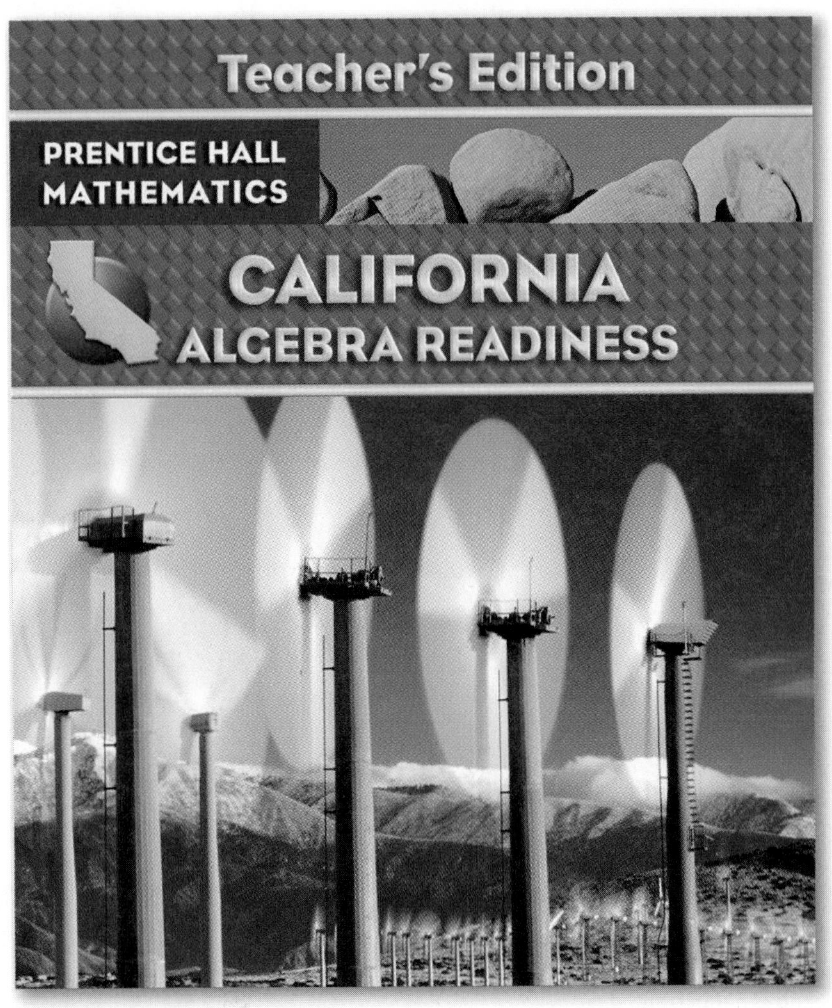

Randall I. Charles
Mark Illingworth
Darwin Mills
Bonnie McNemar
Alma Ramirez
Andy Reeves

Boston, Massachusetts
Upper Saddle River, New Jersey

Acknowledgments appear on p. T481, which constitute an extension of this copyright page.

ISBN-13: 978-0-13-350027-1
ISBN-10: 0-13-350027-6
1 2 3 4 5 6 7 8 9 10 11 10 09 08 07

Prentice Hall Algebra Readiness Teacher's Edition Contents

California Mathematics Teacher Handbook

California Student Edition With Teacher Notes

Authors

Series Author

Randall I. Charles, Ph.D., is Professor Emeritus in the Department of Mathematics and Computer Science at San Jose State University, San Jose, California. He began his career as a high school mathematics teacher, and he was a mathematics supervisor for five years. Dr. Charles has been a member of several NCTM committees and is the former Vice President of the National Council of Supervisors of Mathematics. Much of his writing and research has been in the area of problem solving. He has authored more than 75 mathematics textbooks for kindergarten through college. *Scott Foresman-Prentice Hall Mathematics Series Author Kindergarten through Algebra 2.*

Authors

Mark Illingworth has taught in both elementary and high school math programs for more than 20 years. During this time, he received the Christa McAuliffe sabbatical to develop problem solving materials and projects for middle grades math students, and he was granted the Presidential Award for Excellence in Mathematics Teaching. Mr. Illingworth's specialty is in teaching mathematics through applications and problem solving. He has written two books on this subject and has contributed to math and science textbooks at Prentice Hall.

Bonnie McNemar is a mathematics educator with more than 30 years' experience in Texas schools as a teacher, administrator, and consultant. She began her career as a middle school mathematics teacher and served as a supervisor at the district, county, and state levels. Ms. McNemar was the director of the Texas Mathematics Staff Development Program, now known as TEXTEAMS, for five years, and she was the first director of the Teachers Teaching with Technology (T^3) Program. She remains active in both of these organizations as well as in several local, state, and national mathematics organizations, including NCTM.

Darwin Mills, an administrator for the public school system in Newport News, Virginia, has been involved in secondary-level mathematics education for more than 14 years. Mr. Mills has served as a high school teacher, a community college adjunct professor, a department chair, and a district-level mathematics supervisor. He has received numerous teaching awards, including teacher of the year for 1999–2000 and an Excellence in Teaching award from the College of Wooster, Ohio, in 2002. He is a frequent presenter at workshops and conferences. He believes that all students can learn mathematics if given the proper instruction.

Alma Ramirez is co-director of the Mathematics Case Project at WestEd, a nonprofit educational institute in Oakland, California. A former bilingual elementary and middle school teacher, Ms. Ramirez has considerable expertise in mathematics teaching and learning, second language acquisition, and professional development. She has served as a consultant on a variety of projects and has extensive experience as an author for elementary and middle grades texts. In addition, her work has appeared in the 2004 NCTM Yearbook. Ms. Ramirez is a frequent presenter at professional meetings and conferences.

Andy Reeves, Ph.D., teaches at the University of South Florida in St. Petersburg. His career in education spans 30 years and includes seven years as a middle grades teacher. He subsequently served as Florida's K–12 mathematics supervisor, and more recently he supervised the publication of *The Mathematics Teacher, Mathematics Teaching in the Middle School,* and *Teaching Children Mathematics* for NCTM. Prior to entering education, he worked as an engineer for Douglas Aircraft.

California Mathematics Program Advisors

Prentice Hall wishes to thank the following educators for their ongoing advice in the development of this California Edition of Prentice Hall Mathematics. Their valuable insights have helped ensure that this mathematics series meets the needs of California students and their teachers.

Danelle Almaraz
Pre-Algebra Teacher
East Whittier City School District
Whittier, California

Catherine Barker
Algebra Teacher
Los Angeles USD
Long Beach, California

Eric Bitter
Pre-Algebra & Algebra Teacher
Clovis USD
Clovis, California

Joe Brumfield
Consultant
Pasadena, California

Lynn Cevallos
Consultant
Hacienda Heights, California

Manuel E. Chavez
AP Calculus Teacher/Math Coach
Los Angeles USD
Huntington Park, California

Edward Ford
Consultant
Escondido, California

Courtney Glass
Algebra 2 & Pre-Calculus Teacher
Monrovia City USD
Monrovia, California

Bernice Levens
Former Teacher/Consultant
Hacienda Heights, California

Sia Lux
Algebra & Calculus Teacher
Coachella Valley USD
Indio, California

Christy McAloney
Algebra & Calculus Teacher
Grossmont Union High School District
Spring Valley, California

Brian McElfish
Pre-Algebra & Algebra Teacher
Saddleback Valley USD
Lake Forest, California

Paul Dennis McLaughlin
Algebra Teacher
Walnut Valley USD
Walnut, California

Shawn Neal
Pre-Algebra & Algebra Teacher
Visalia USD
Visalia, California

Jason Rose
Algebra Teacher
Temple City USD
Temple City, California

Keith Smith
Pre-Algebra & Algebra Teacher
Grant Joint USD
Sacramento, California

Sarah Thomson
Calculus Teacher & Math Coach
San Bernardino City USD
San Bernardino, California

Vocabulary Development Consultants

Kate Kinsella, Ed.D., is a faculty member in the Department of Secondary Education at San Francisco State University. A specialist in second-language acquisition and adolescent literacy, she teaches coursework addressing language and literacy development across the secondary curricula. Dr. Kinsella earned her master's degree in TESOL from San Francisco State University and her Ed.D. in Second Language Acquisition from the University of San Francisco.

Kevin Feldman, Ed.D., is the Director of Reading and Early Intervention with the Sonoma County Office of Education (SCOE) and an independent educational consultant. At the SCOE, he develops, organizes, and monitors programs related to K–12 literacy. Dr. Feldman has a master's degree from the University of California, Riverside, in Special Education, Learning Disabilities, and Instructional Design. He earned his Ed.D. in Curriculum and Instruction from the University of San Francisco.

Variables and Algebraic Expressions

Student Support

 California Check System

Check Your Readiness 2
CA Standards Check 5, 8, 9, 15, 20, 21, 27, 31
Checkpoint Quiz 12, 24

New Vocabulary 4, 8, 20, 26, 30
Vocabulary Builder 19, 25
Vocabulary Tip 20, 26
Vocabulary Review 38, 40

Online

Homework Video Tutor 6, 10, 16, 22, 28, 32
Active Math 4, 14
MathXL 6, 10, 16, 22, 28, 32
Lesson Quizzes 7, 11, 18, 23, 29, 33
Vocabulary Quiz 38
Chapter Test 40

California Standards

Number Sense
NS 1.2

Algebra and Functions
AF 1.1, AF 1.3

Mathematical Reasoning
MR 2.1, MR 2.5, MR 2.6, MR 2.7

Standards Mastery and Assessment

Page 18

Integers and Exponents

Student Support

California Check System

GO Online

California Standards

Number Sense
NS 1.2

Algebra and Functions
AF 1.3, AF 2.1

Mathematical Reasoning
MR 2.5, MR 3.1, MR 3.3

Algebra 1
Alg1 2.0

Standards Mastery and Assessment

Page 58

Equations and Applications

Student Support

California Check System

GO Online

California Standards

Number Sense
NS 1.2

Algebra and Functions
AF 1.1, AF 1.3, AF 4.1

Measurement and Geometry
MG 3.3

Mathematical Reasoning
MG 2.6, MG 3.1

Algebra 1
Alg1 2.0

Standards Mastery and Assessment

Page 107

Rational Numbers

Student Support

 California Check System

Check Your Readiness 130
CA Standards Check 132, 133, 136, 137, 142, 143, 148, 149, 154, 155
Checkpoint Quiz 140, 152

New Vocabulary 132, 136, 142, 148, 154
Vocabulary Builder 160
Vocabulary Tip 136, 155
Vocabulary Review 162, 165

GO Online

Homework Video Tutor 134, 138, 145, 150, 156
Active Math 133, 155
MathXL 134, 138, 145, 150, 156
Lesson Quizzes 135, 139, 146, 151, 157
Vocabulary Quiz 162
Chapter Test 164

California Standards

Number Sense
NS 1.2, NS 1.3, NS 1.5

Algebra and Functions
AF 2.1

Mathematical Reasoning
MR 1.1, MR 2.2, MR 2.4, MR 3.3

Standards Mastery and Assessment

Page 154

Rational Number Operations

Student Support

California Check System

Check Your Readiness 168
CA Standards Check 171, 172, 176, 177, 182, 183, 186, 187, 190, 191, 196, 197, 203
Checkpoint Quiz 181, 200

New Vocabulary 186, 196
Vocabulary Builder 201
Vocabulary Tip 203
Vocabulary Review 208, 211

GO Online

Homework Video Tutor 173, 179, 184, 188, 192, 198, 204
Active Math 187
MathXL 173, 178, 184, 188, 192, 198, 204
Lesson Quizzes 174, 180, 185, 189, 193, 199, 205
Vocabulary Quiz 208
Chapter Test 210

California Standards

Number Sense
NS 1.2, NS 1.3, NS 1.5, NS 2.1

Algebra and Functions
AF 1.1, AF 1.3, AF 2.1, AF 4.1

Mathematical Reasoning
MR 2.1, MR 2.4, MR 2.5, MR 2.7, MR 3.2

Algebra 1
Alg1 2.0

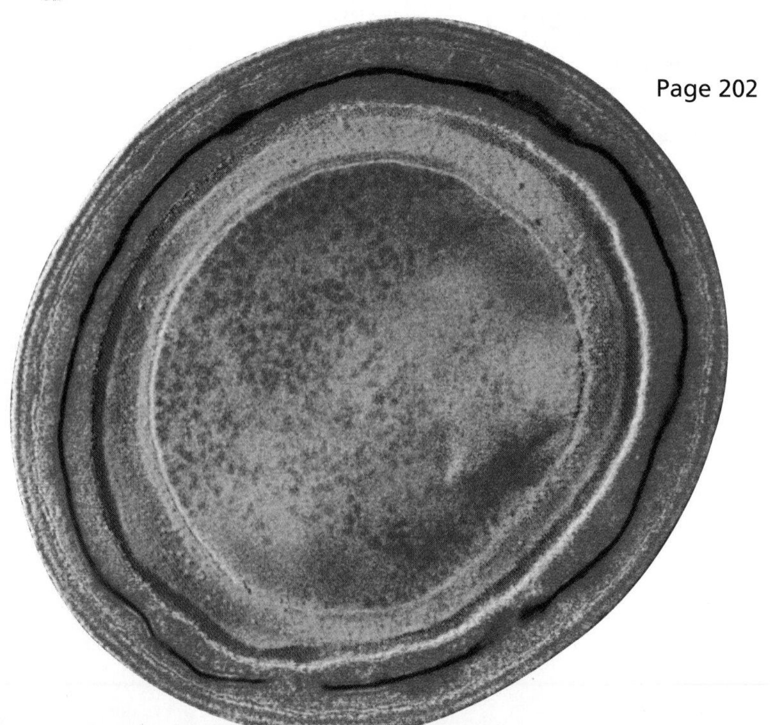
Page 202

Rates and Proportions

Student Support

 California Check System

Check Your Readiness 214
CA Standards Check 216, 217, 220, 221, 226, 227, 230, 231, 235, 236
Checkpoint Quiz 224, 234

New Vocabulary 216, 220, 226, 235
Vocabulary Builder 225
Vocabulary Tip 227
Vocabulary Review 244, 247

GO Online

Homework Video Tutor 218, 222, 228, 232, 238
Active Math 216, 235
MathXL 218, 222, 228, 232, 238
Lesson Quizzes 219, 223, 229, 233, 239
Vocabulary Quiz 244
Chapter Test 246

California Standards

Algebra and Functions
AF 4.2

Measurement and Geometry
MG 1.3

Mathematical Reasoning
MR 1.1, MR 2.5

Page 220

Table of Contents

Applications of Percent

Student Support

 California Check System

 Vocabulary

 Online

California Standards

Number Sense
NS 1.3

Mathematical Reasoning
MR 2.7, MR 3.1, MR 3.2

Standards Mastery and Assessment

Page 266

Linear Functions and Graphing

Student Support

 California Check System

Check Your Readiness 286
CA Standards Check 289, 292, 293, 298, 299, 302, 303, 311, 316, 317
Checkpoint Quiz 296, 315

Vocabulary

New Vocabulary 288, 298, 302, 310, 316
Vocabulary Tip 288, 292, 299
Vocabulary Review 322, 325

 Online

Homework Video Tutor 290, 294, 300, 305, 312, 318
Active Math 289, 303, 310
MathXL 290, 294, 300, 305, 312, 318
Lesson Quizzes 291, 295, 301, 306, 313, 319
Vocabulary Quiz 322
Chapter Test 324

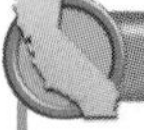

California Standards

Algebra and Functions
AF 1.1, AF 3.3, AF 3.4, AF 4.2

Measurement and Geometry
MG 3.3

Mathematical Reasoning
MR 1.1, MR 2.3, MR 2.4, MR 3.2

Standards Mastery and Assessment

Page 310

Table of Contents

Inequalities

Student Support

California Check System

Check Your Readiness 328
CA Standards Check 330, 331, 335, 341, 345, 349, 350
Checkpoint Quiz 338, 348

Vocabulary

New Vocabulary 330, 334, 340, 344
Vocabulary Builder 338
Vocabulary Tip 331, 334, 335
Vocabulary Review 358, 361

GO Online

Homework Video Tutor 332, 336, 342, 346, 352
Active Math 345
MathXL 332, 336, 342, 346, 351
Lesson Quizzes 333, 337, 343, 347, 353
Vocabulary Quiz 358
Chapter Test 360

California Standards

Number Sense
NS 1.2

Algebra and Functions
AF 1.1, AF 4.1

Mathematical Reasoning
MR 2.4, MR 2.6, MR 3.3

Standards Mastery and Assessment

Page 349

Exponents and Equations

Student Support

 California Check System

Check Your Readiness 364
CA Standards Check 366, 367, 370, 371, 375, 380, 381, 386, 387, 392, 393
Checkpoint Quiz 378, 391

New Vocabulary 374, 380
Vocabulary Builder 378
Vocabulary Tip 366, 370, 374, 380
Vocabulary Review 400

GO Online

Homework Video Tutor 368, 372, 376, 382, 389, 394
MathXL 368, 372, 376, 382, 389, 394
Lesson Quizzes 369, 373, 377, 383, 390, 395
Vocabulary Quiz 400
Chapter Test 402

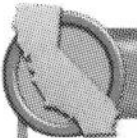

California Standards

Number Sense
NS 2.1

Algebra and Functions
AF 1.1, AF 2.1

Mathematical Reasoning
MR 2.5, MR 2.6, MR 3.3

Algebra 1
Alg1 2.0, Alg1 4.0, Alg1 5.0

Standards Mastery and Assessment

Page 374

Table of Contents

Learning the California Standards

Your *Prentice Hall Algebra Readiness* textbook is designed to help you fully understand and learn the California Mathematics Standards. Here are some features of your textbook that will support your learning throughout the year.

 for Help: Math Companion

Look for references throughout every lesson that direct you to the **Math Companion**. This resource helps support your in-class learning – so you can be successful with each day's lesson.

California Check System

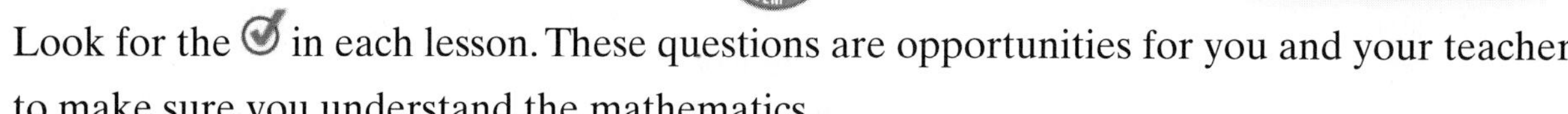

Look for the ✓ in each lesson. These questions are opportunities for you and your teacher to make sure you understand the mathematics.

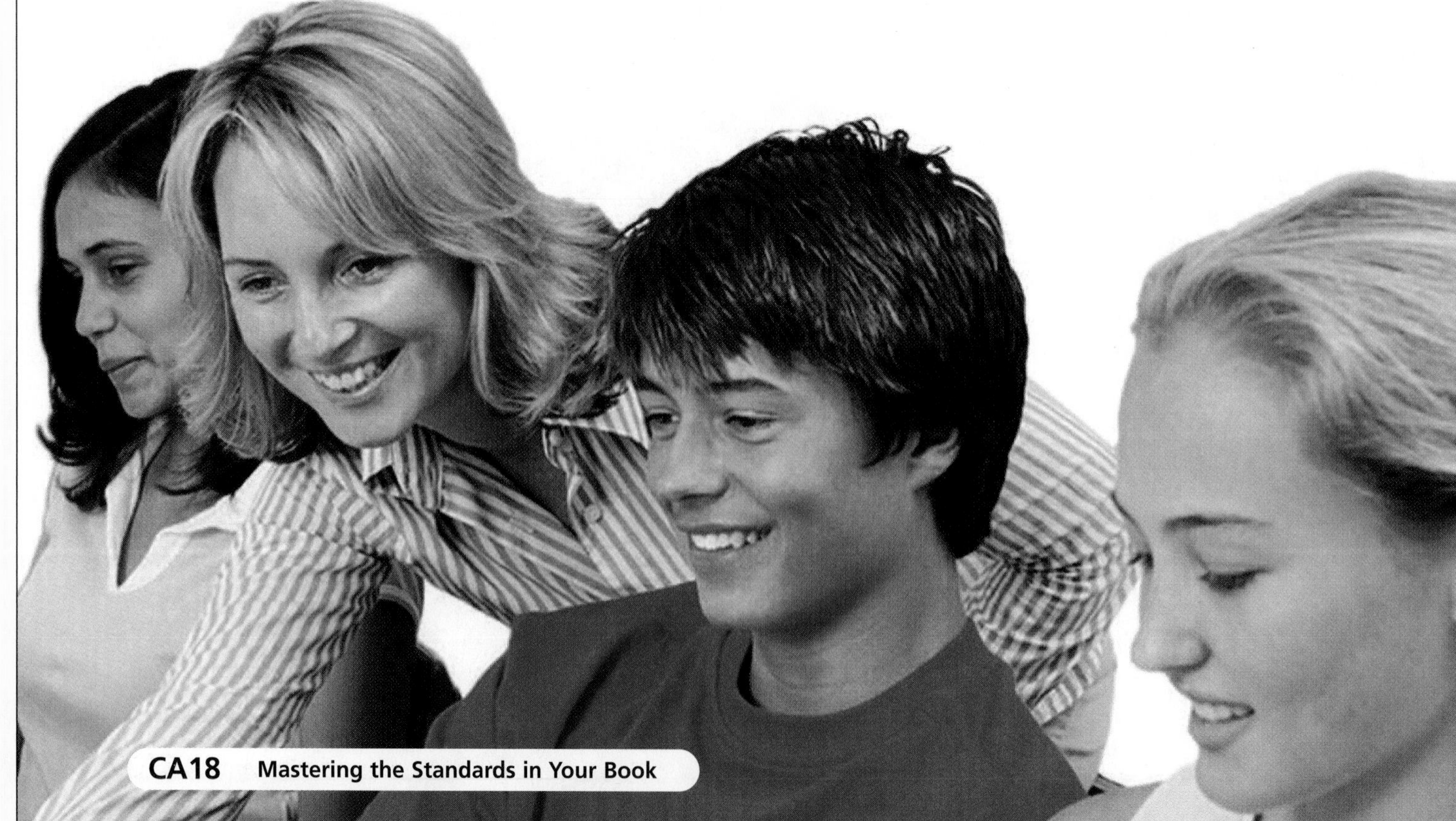

Get Ready to Learn

California Content Standards

Your textbook identifies which California standards you'll be covering each day.

Check Skills You'll Need

Go to your Math Companion to review important skills you'll need to be successful with this lesson.

Vocabulary

New vocabulary words are listed for every lesson. Go to your **Math Companion** to build your understanding of these new vocabulary words and to review previously learned words.

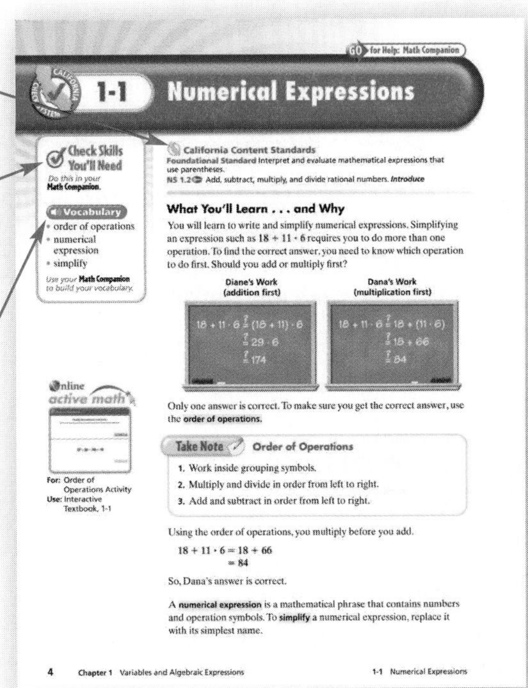

GO for Help: Math Companion

1-1 Numerical Expressions

Check Skills You'll Need
Do this in your **Math Companion.**

Vocabulary
- order of operations
- numerical expression
- simplify

Use your **Math Companion** *to build your vocabulary.*

California Content Standards
Foundational Standard Interpret and evaluate mathematical expressions that use parentheses.
NS 1.2 Add, subtract, multiply, and divide rational numbers. *Introduce*

What You'll Learn . . . and Why

You will learn to write and simplify numerical expressions. Simplifying an expression such as $18 + 11 \cdot 6$ requires you to do more than one operation. To find the correct answer, you need to know which operation to do first. Should you add or multiply first?

Diane's Work (addition first)	Dana's Work (multiplication first)
$18 + 11 \cdot 6 \stackrel{?}{=} (18 + 11) \cdot 6$	$18 + 11 \cdot 6 \stackrel{?}{=} 18 + (11 \cdot 6)$
$\stackrel{?}{=} 29 \cdot 6$	$\stackrel{?}{=} 18 + 66$
$\stackrel{?}{=} 174$	$\stackrel{?}{=} 84$

Only one answer is correct. To make sure you get the correct answer, use the **order of operations.**

Online active math
For: Order of Operations Activity
Use: Interactive Textbook, 1-1

Take Note Order of Operations
1. Work inside grouping symbols.
2. Multiply and divide in order from left to right.
3. Add and subtract in order from left to right.

Using the order of operations, you multiply before you add.

$$18 + 11 \cdot 6 = 18 + 66$$
$$= 84$$

So, Dana's answer is correct.

A **numerical expression** is a mathematical phrase that contains numbers and operation symbols. To **simplify** a numerical expression, replace it with its simplest name.

4 Chapter 1 Variables and Algebraic Expressions 1-1 Numerical Expressions

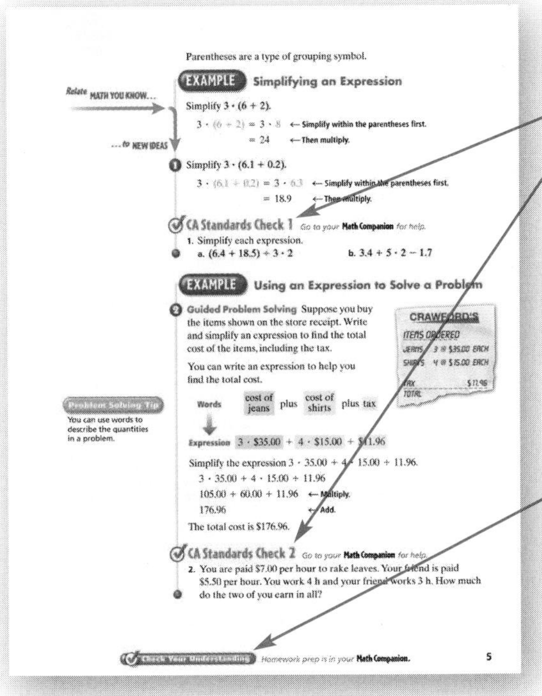

Parentheses are a type of grouping symbol.

EXAMPLE Simplifying an Expression

Relate MATH YOU KNOW...

Simplify $3 \cdot (6 + 2)$.

$3 \cdot (6 + 2) = 3 \cdot 8$ ← Simplify within the parentheses first.
$= 24$ ← Then multiply.

... *to* NEW IDEAS

1 Simplify $3 \cdot (6.1 + 0.2)$.

$3 \cdot (6.1 + 0.2) = 3 \cdot 6.3$ ← Simplify within the parentheses first.
$= 18.9$ ← Then multiply.

CA Standards Check 1 *Go to your* **Math Companion** *for help.*
1. Simplify each expression.
   a. $(6.4 + 18.5) \div 3 \cdot 2$ b. $3.4 + 5 \cdot 2 - 1.7$

EXAMPLE Using an Expression to Solve a Problem

2 **Guided Problem Solving** Suppose you buy the items shown on the store receipt. Write and simplify an expression to find the total cost of the items, including the tax.

CRAWFORD'S
ITEMS ORDERED
JEANS 3 @ $35.00 EACH
SHIRTS 4 @ $15.00 EACH
TAX $11.96
TOTAL

You can write an expression to help you find the total cost.

Problem Solving Tip
You can use words to describe the quantities in a problem.

Words: cost of jeans plus cost of shirts plus tax

Expression: $3 \cdot \$35.00 + 4 \cdot \$15.00 + \$11.96$

Simplify the expression $3 \cdot 35.00 + 4 \cdot 15.00 + 11.96$.

$3 \cdot 35.00 + 4 \cdot 15.00 + 11.96$
$105.00 + 60.00 + 11.96$ ← Multiply.
176.96 ← Add.

The total cost is $176.96.

CA Standards Check 2 *Go to your* **Math Companion** *for help.*
2. You are paid $7.00 per hour to rake leaves. Your friend is paid $5.50 per hour. You work 4 h and your friend works 3 h. How much do the two of you earn in all?

Check Your Understanding *Homework prep is in your* **Math Companion.** 5

CA Standards Check

These questions, after every example, help you and your teacher make sure you understand the example – and the California Standards being taught. Go to your **Math Companion** for help.

Check Your Understanding

Go to your **Math Companion** to review what you've just learned and make sure you're ready for homework success.

Standards Mastery in Your Book

Practicing the California Standards

Your *Prentice Hall Algebra Readiness* textbook gives you plenty of opportunities to practice, with plenty of homework help along the way.

GO for Help: *MathXL*

Your MathXL CD-ROM gives you personalized homework help. With step-by-step exercises and tutorials, it's like having your own at-home tutor.

Standards Practice

Each lesson's Standards Practice gives you different levels of exercises.

- **A** Practice by Example: These exercises give you practice with the examples you just learned. Go for Help points you back to the example for easy reference. Plus, the first exercises are always started for you.
- **B** Apply Your Skills: These exercises give you a chance to practice everything you learned in the day's lesson.
- **C** Challenge: This problem extends your learning and gives you a more challenging problem.

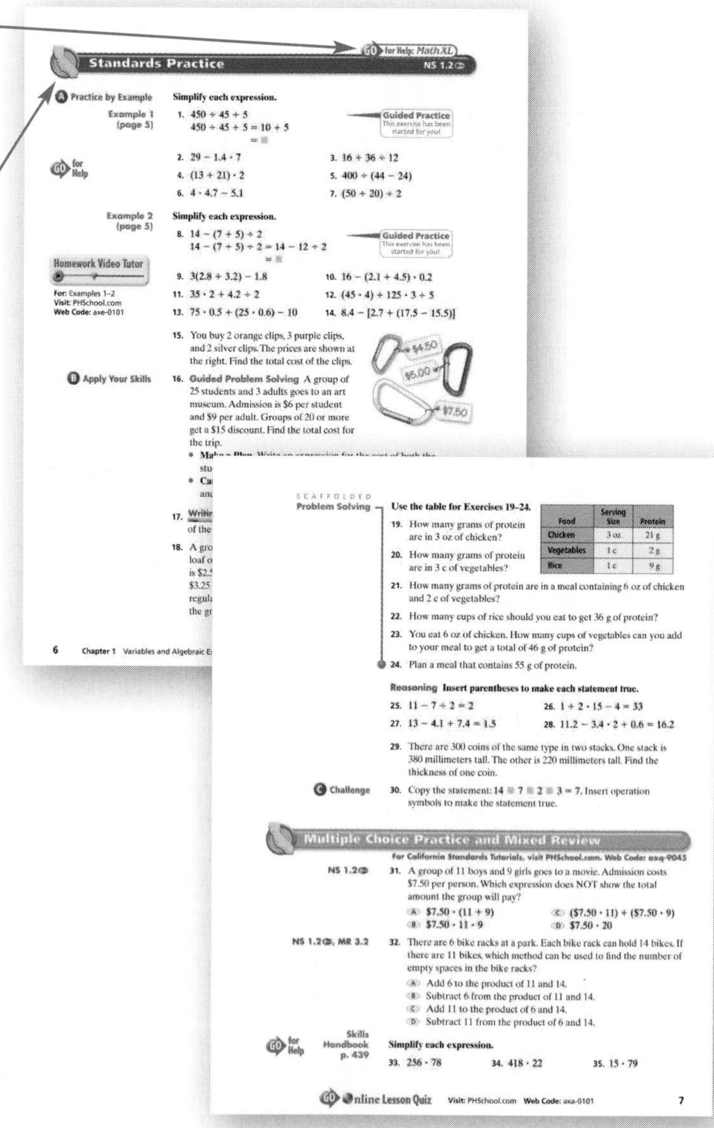

GO for Help: *MathXL*

Standards Practice NS 1.2

A Practice by Example

Example 1 (page 5)

Simplify each expression.

1. $450 \div 45 + 5$
   $450 \div 45 + 5 = 10 + 5$
   $= ■$

Guided Practice: This exercise has been started for you!

GO for Help

2. $29 - 1.4 \cdot 7$
3. $16 + 36 \div 12$
4. $(13 + 21) \cdot 2$
5. $400 \div (44 - 24)$
6. $4 \cdot 4.7 - 5.1$
7. $(50 + 20) \div 2$

Example 2 (page 5)

Simplify each expression.

8. $14 - (7 + 5) \div 2$
   $14 - (7 + 5) \div 2 = 14 - 12 \div 2$
   $= ■$

Guided Practice: This exercise has been started for you!

Homework Video Tutor
For: Examples 1–2
Visit: PHSchool.com
Web Code: axe-0101

9. $3(2.8 + 3.2) - 1.8$
10. $16 - (2.1 + 4.5) \cdot 0.2$
11. $35 \cdot 2 + 4.2 \div 2$
12. $(45 \cdot 4) + 125 \cdot 3 \div 5$
13. $75 \cdot 0.5 + (25 \cdot 0.6) - 10$
14. $8.4 - [2.7 + (17.5 - 15.5)]$
15. You buy 2 orange clips, 3 purple clips, and 2 silver clips. The prices are shown at the right. Find the total cost of the clips.

B Apply Your Skills

16. **Guided Problem Solving** A group of 25 students and 3 adults goes to an art museum. Admission is $6 per student and $9 per adult. Groups of 20 or more get a $15 discount. Find the total cost for the trip.

6 Chapter 1 Variables and Algebraic E

SCAFFOLDED Problem Solving

Use the table for Exercises 19–24.

Food	Serving Size	Protein
Chicken	3 oz	21 g
Vegetables	1 c	2 g
Rice	1 c	9 g

19. How many grams of protein are in 3 oz of chicken?
20. How many grams of protein are in 3 c of vegetables?
21. How many grams of protein are in a meal containing 6 oz of chicken and 2 c of vegetables?
22. How many cups of rice should you eat to get 36 g of protein?
23. You eat 6 oz of chicken. How many cups of vegetables can you add to your meal to get a total of 46 g of protein?
24. Plan a meal that contains 55 g of protein.

Reasoning **Insert parentheses to make each statement true.**

25. $11 - 7 \div 2 = 2$
26. $1 + 2 \cdot 15 - 4 = 33$
27. $13 - 4.1 + 7.4 = 1.5$
28. $11.2 - 3.4 \cdot 2 + 0.6 = 16.2$
29. There are 300 coins of the same type in two stacks. One stack is 380 millimeters tall. The other is 220 millimeters tall. Find the thickness of one coin.

C Challenge

30. Copy the statement: 14 ■ 7 ■ 2 ■ 3 = 7. Insert operation symbols to make the statement true.

Multiple Choice Practice and Mixed Review

For California Standards Tutorials, visit PHSchool.com. Web Code: axq-9045

NS 1.2

31. A group of 11 boys and 9 girls goes to a movie. Admission costs $7.50 per person. Which expression does NOT show the total amount the group will pay?
    - A $7.50 · (11 + 9)
    - B $7.50 · 11 · 9
    - C ($7.50 · 11) + ($7.50 · 9)
    - D $7.50 · 20

NS 1.2, MR 3.2

32. There are 6 bike racks at a park. Each bike rack can hold 14 bikes. If there are 11 bikes, which method can be used to find the number of empty spaces in the bike racks?
    - A Add 6 to the product of 11 and 14.
    - B Subtract 6 from the product of 11 and 14.
    - C Add 11 to the product of 6 and 14.
    - D Subtract 11 from the product of 6 and 14.

GO for Help Skills Handbook p. 439

Simplify each expression.

33. $256 \cdot 78$
34. $418 \cdot 22$
35. $15 \cdot 79$

GO Online Lesson Quiz Visit: PHSchool.com Web Code: axa-0101 7

Homework Video Tutor

Need more help with your homework? These tutorials show real teachers reviewing every example. Your Prentice Hall textbook gives you a unique source for more help – called Homework Video Tutors. Log on to PHSchool.com and enter the Web Code provided – you'll get the homework help you need!

Standards Mastery in Your Book

Mastering the California Standards

Your *Prentice Hall Algebra Readiness* textbook provides opportunities for you to ensure you've mastered the standards after every lesson and every chapter in your textbook.

Standards Mastery After Every Lesson

Multiple Choice Practice and Mixed Review

The final part of each day's exercises includes practice with multiple choice problems and a chance to review skills you learned earlier in your course. This will help keep your skills sharp and help you receive lots of practice with multiple choice questions. All questions are correlated to the California Standards.

The Go for Help arrow points to the lesson you can review. You can also go online and take a lesson quiz – another chance to make sure you've mastered the California Standards you learned.

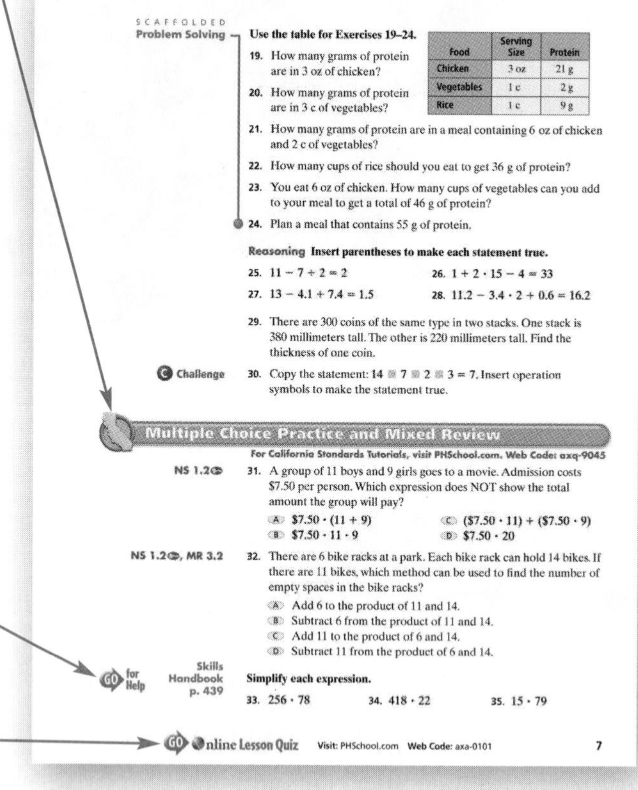

SCAFFOLDED Problem Solving

Use the table for Exercises 19–24.

Food	Serving Size	Protein
Chicken	3 oz	21 g
Vegetables	1 c	2 g
Rice	1 c	9 g

19. How many grams of protein are in 3 oz of chicken?
20. How many grams of protein are in 3 c of vegetables?
21. How many grams of protein are in a meal containing 6 oz of chicken and 2 c of vegetables?
22. How many cups of rice should you eat to get 36 g of protein?
23. You eat 6 oz of chicken. How many cups of vegetables can you add to your meal to get a total of 46 g of protein?
24. Plan a meal that contains 55 g of protein.

Reasoning **Insert parentheses to make each statement true.**

25. $11 - 7 \div 2 = 2$
26. $1 + 2 \cdot 15 - 4 = 33$
27. $13 - 4.1 + 7.4 = 1.5$
28. $11.2 - 3.4 \cdot 2 + 0.6 = 16.2$
29. There are 300 coins of the same type in two stacks. One stack is 380 millimeters tall. The other is 220 millimeters tall. Find the thickness of one coin.

Challenge

30. Copy the statement: 14 ■ 7 ■ 2 ■ 3 = 7. Insert operation symbols to make the statement true.

Multiple Choice Practice and Mixed Review

For California Standards Tutorials, visit PHSchool.com. Web Code: axq-9045

NS 1.2

31. A group of 11 boys and 9 girls goes to a movie. Admission costs \$7.50 per person. Which expression does NOT show the total amount the group will pay?
    - A \$7.50 · (11 + 9)
    - B \$7.50 · 11 · 9
    - C (\$7.50 · 11) + (\$7.50 · 9)
    - D \$7.50 · 20

NS 1.2, MR 3.2

32. There are 6 bike racks at a park. Each bike rack can hold 14 bikes. If there are 11 bikes, which method can be used to find the number of empty spaces in the bike racks?
    - A Add 6 to the product of 11 and 14.
    - B Subtract 6 from the product of 11 and 14.
    - C Add 11 to the product of 6 and 14.
    - D Subtract 11 from the product of 6 and 14.

GO for Help Skills Handbook p. 439

Simplify each expression.

33. $256 \cdot 78$
34. $418 \cdot 22$
35. $15 \cdot 79$

GO Online Lesson Quiz Visit: PHSchool.com Web Code: axa-0101

7

Standards Mastery after Every Chapter

After every chapter, Standards Mastery Cumulative Practice provides an opportunity to demonstrate your understanding of all the California Standards covered so far.

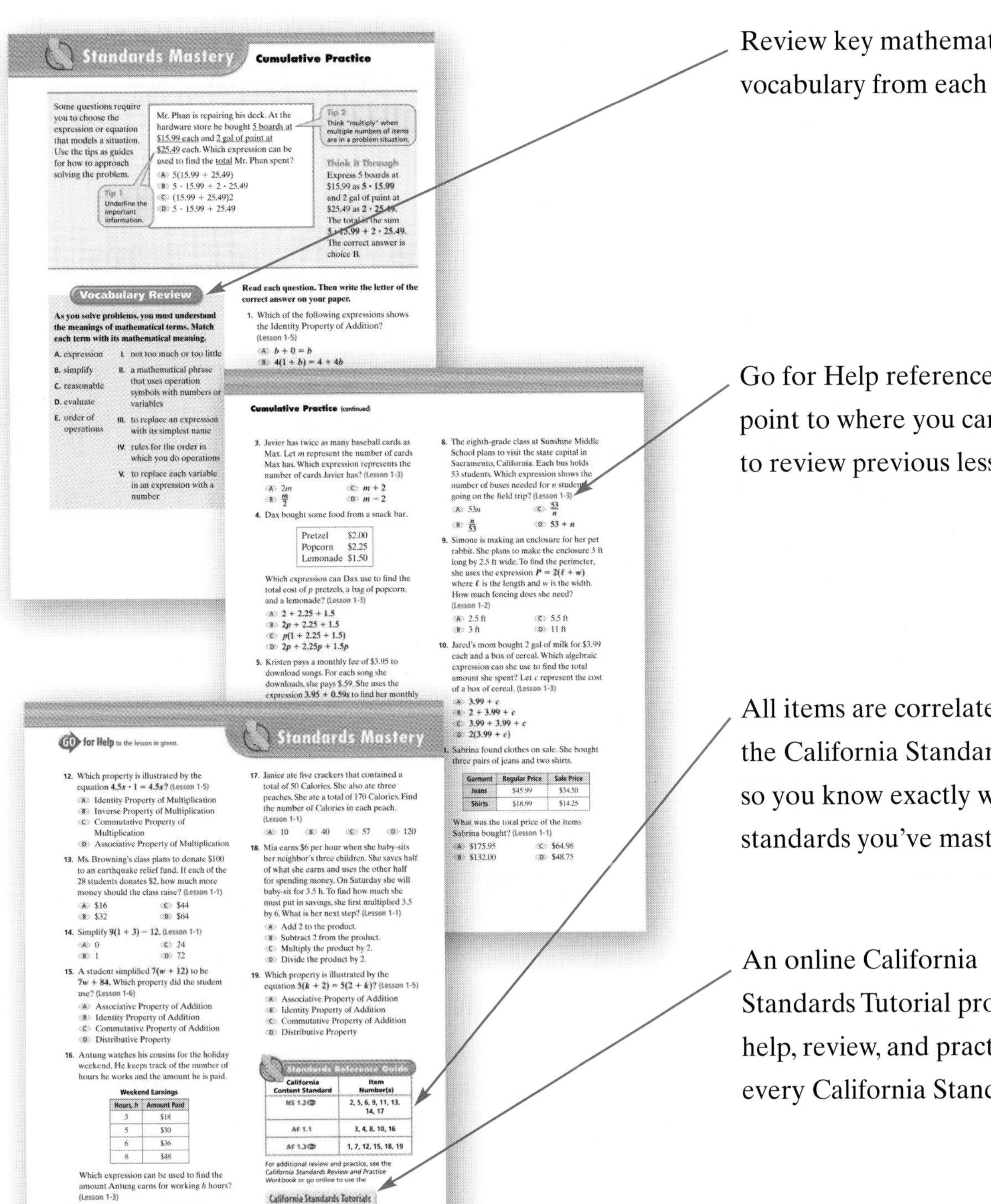

Standards Mastery **Cumulative Practice**

Some questions require you to choose the expression or equation that models a situation. Use the tips as guides for how to approach solving the problem.

Mr. Phan is repairing his deck. At the hardware store he bought 5 boards at \$15.99 each and 2 gal of paint at \$25.49 each. Which expression can be used to find the total Mr. Phan spent?

Ⓐ $5(15.99 + 25.49)$
Ⓑ $5 \cdot 15.99 + 2 \cdot 25.49$
Ⓒ $(15.99 + 25.49)2$
Ⓓ $5 \cdot 15.99 + 25.49$

Tip 1: Underline the important information.

Tip 2: Think "multiply" when multiple numbers of items are in a problem situation.

Think It Through: Express 5 boards at \$15.99 as $5 \cdot 15.99$ and 2 gal of paint at \$25.49 as $2 \cdot 25.49$. The total is the sum $5 \cdot 15.99 + 2 \cdot 25.49$. The correct answer is choice B.

Vocabulary Review

As you solve problems, you must understand the meanings of mathematical terms. Match each term with its mathematical meaning.

A. expression — I. not too much or too little
B. simplify — II. a mathematical phrase that uses operation symbols with numbers or variables
C. reasonable — III. to replace an expression with its simplest name
D. evaluate — IV. rules for the order in which you do operations
E. order of operations — V. to replace each variable in an expression with a number

Read each question. Then write the letter of the correct answer on your paper.

1. Which of the following expressions shows the Identity Property of Addition? (Lesson 1-5)
Ⓐ $b + 0 = b$
Ⓑ $4(1 + b) = 4 + 4b$

Cumulative Practice (continued)

3. Javier has twice as many baseball cards as Max. Let m represent the number of cards Max has. Which expression represents the number of cards Javier has? (Lesson 1-3)
Ⓐ $2m$ Ⓑ $\frac{m}{2}$ Ⓒ $m + 2$ Ⓓ $m - 2$

4. Dax bought some food from a snack bar.

Pretzel	\$2.00
Popcorn	\$2.25
Lemonade	\$1.50

Which expression can Dax use to find the total cost of p pretzels, a bag of popcorn, and a lemonade? (Lesson 1-3)
Ⓐ $2 + 2.25 + 1.5$
Ⓑ $2p + 2.25 + 1.5$
Ⓒ $p(1 + 2.25 + 1.5)$
Ⓓ $2p + 2.25p + 1.5p$

5. Kristen pays a monthly fee of \$3.95 to download songs. For each song she downloads, she pays \$.59. She uses the expression $3.95 + 0.59s$ to find her monthly

8. The eighth-grade class at Sunshine Middle School plans to visit the state capital in Sacramento, California. Each bus holds 53 students. Which expression shows the number of buses needed for n students going on the field trip? (Lesson 1-3)
Ⓐ $53n$ Ⓑ $\frac{n}{53}$ Ⓒ $\frac{53}{n}$ Ⓓ $53 + n$

9. Simone is making an enclosure for her pet rabbit. She plans to make the enclosure 3 ft long by 2.5 ft wide. To find the perimeter, she uses the expression $P = 2(\ell + w)$ where ℓ is the length and w is the width. How much fencing does she need? (Lesson 1-2)
Ⓐ 2.5 ft Ⓑ 3 ft Ⓒ 5.5 ft Ⓓ 11 ft

10. Jared's mom bought 2 gal of milk for \$3.99 each and a box of cereal. Which algebraic expression can she use to find the total amount she spent? Let c represent the cost of a box of cereal. (Lesson 1-3)
Ⓐ $3.99 + c$
Ⓑ $2 + 3.99 + c$
Ⓒ $3.99 + 3.99 + c$
Ⓓ $2(3.99 + c)$

11. Sabrina found clothes on sale. She bought three pairs of jeans and two shirts.

Garment	Regular Price	Sale Price
Jeans	\$45.99	\$34.50
Shirts	\$18.99	\$14.25

What was the total price of the items Sabrina bought? (Lesson 1-1)
Ⓐ \$175.95 Ⓑ \$132.00 Ⓒ \$64.98 Ⓓ \$48.75

GO for Help to the lesson in green.

Standards Mastery

12. Which property is illustrated by the equation $4.5x \cdot 1 = 4.5x$? (Lesson 1-5)
Ⓐ Identity Property of Multiplication
Ⓑ Inverse Property of Multiplication
Ⓒ Commutative Property of Multiplication
Ⓓ Associative Property of Multiplication

13. Ms. Browning's class plans to donate \$100 to an earthquake relief fund. If each of the 28 students donates \$2, how much more money should the class raise? (Lesson 1-1)
Ⓐ \$16 Ⓑ \$32 Ⓒ \$44 Ⓓ \$64

14. Simplify $9(1 + 3) - 12$. (Lesson 1-1)
Ⓐ 0 Ⓑ 1 Ⓒ 24 Ⓓ 72

15. A student simplified $7(w + 12)$ to be $7w + 84$. Which property did the student use? (Lesson 1-6)
Ⓐ Associative Property of Addition
Ⓑ Identity Property of Addition
Ⓒ Commutative Property of Addition
Ⓓ Distributive Property

16. Antung watches his cousins for the holiday weekend. He keeps track of the number of hours he works and the amount he is paid.

Weekend Earnings

Hours, h	Amount Paid
3	\$18
5	\$30
6	\$36
8	\$48

Which expression can be used to find the amount Antung earns for working h hours? (Lesson 1-3)
Ⓐ $6h$ Ⓑ $8h$ Ⓒ $h + 12$ Ⓓ $h + 15$

17. Janice ate five crackers that contained a total of 50 Calories. She also ate three peaches. She ate a total of 170 Calories. Find the number of Calories in each peach. (Lesson 1-1)
Ⓐ 10 Ⓑ 40 Ⓒ 57 Ⓓ 120

18. Mia earns \$6 per hour when she baby-sits her neighbor's three children. She saves half of what she earns and uses the other half for spending money. On Saturday she will baby-sit for 3.5 h. To find how much she must put in savings, she first multiplied 3.5 by 6. What is her next step? (Lesson 1-1)
Ⓐ Add 2 to the product.
Ⓑ Subtract 2 from the product.
Ⓒ Multiply the product by 2.
Ⓓ Divide the product by 2.

19. Which property is illustrated by the equation $5(k + 2) = 5(2 + k)$? (Lesson 1-5)
Ⓐ Associative Property of Addition
Ⓑ Identity Property of Addition
Ⓒ Commutative Property of Addition
Ⓓ Distributive Property

Standards Reference Guide

California Content Standard	Item Number(s)
NS 1.2	2, 5, 6, 9, 11, 13, 14, 17
AF 1.1	3, 4, 8, 10, 16
AF 1.3	1, 7, 12, 15, 18, 19

For additional review and practice, see the *California Standards Review and Practice Workbook* or go online to use the

California Standards Tutorials

Visit: PHSchool.com, Web Code: axq-9045

California Standards Mastery Cumulative Practice 43

Review key mathematical vocabulary from each chapter.

Go for Help references point to where you can go to review previous lessons.

All items are correlated to the California Standards, so you know exactly which standards you've mastered.

An online California Standards Tutorial provides help, review, and practice for every California Standard.

Mastering the California Standards

There are other types of features in your *Prentice Hall Algebra Readiness* textbook that will help you learn the mathematics and be successful in your class.

Activity Lab

These features provide opportunities for you to engage with the mathematics being taught. Each feature states the California Standards being covered.

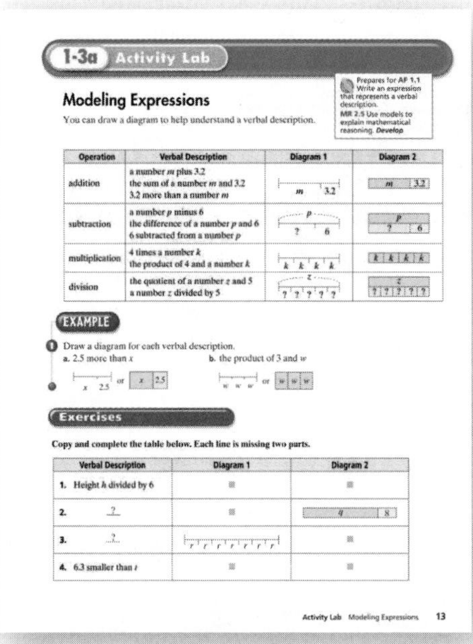

1-3a Activity Lab

Modeling Expressions

You can draw a diagram to help understand a verbal description.

Prepares for AF 1.1 Write an expression that represents a verbal description.
MR 2.5 Use models to explain mathematical reasoning. *Develop*

Operation	Verbal Description	Diagram 1	Diagram 2
addition	a number m plus 3.2 the sum of a number m and 3.2 3.2 more than a number m	m, 3.2	m, 3.2
subtraction	a number p minus 6 the difference of a number p and 6 6 subtracted from a number p	p; ?, 6	p; ?, 6
multiplication	4 times a number k the product of 4 and a number k	k, k, k, k	k, k, k, k
division	the quotient of a number z and 5 a number z divided by 5	z; ?, ?, ?, ?, ?	z; ?, ?, ?, ?, ?

EXAMPLE

1 Draw a diagram for each verbal description.
a. 2.5 more than x — b. the product of 3 and w

Exercises

Copy and complete the table below. Each line is missing two parts.

Verbal Description	Diagram 1	Diagram 2
1. Height h divided by 6	■	■
2. ?	■	q, 8
3. ?	r, r, r, r, r, r, r	■
4. 6.3 smaller than t	■	■

Activity Lab Modeling Expressions 13

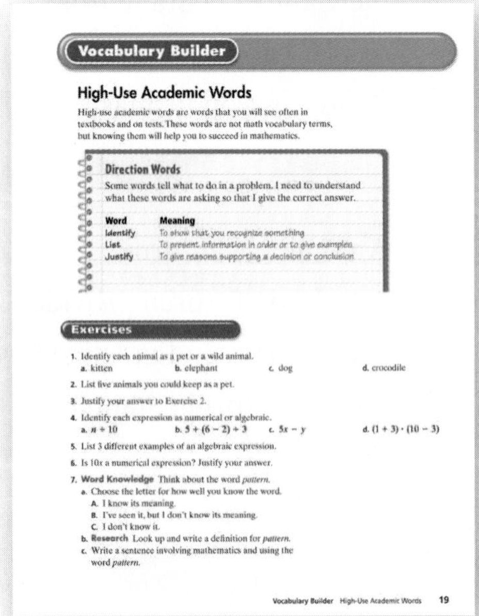

Vocabulary Builder

High-Use Academic Words

High-use academic words are words that you will see often in textbooks and on tests. These words are not math vocabulary terms, but knowing them will help you to succeed in mathematics.

Direction Words

Some words tell what to do in a problem. I need to understand what these words are asking so that I give the correct answer.

Word	Meaning
Identify	To show that you recognize something
List	To present information in order or to give examples
Justify	To give reasons supporting a decision or conclusion

Exercises

1. Identify each animal as a pet or a wild animal.
   a. kitten b. elephant c. dog d. crocodile
2. List five animals you could keep as a pet.
3. Justify your answer to Exercise 2.
4. Identify each expression as numerical or algebraic.
   a. $n + 10$ b. $5 + (6 - 2) + 3$ c. $5x - y$ d. $(1 + 3) \cdot (10 - 3)$
5. List 3 different examples of an algebraic expression.
6. Is $10x$ a numerical expression? Justify your answer.
7. **Word Knowledge** Think about the word *pattern*.
   a. Choose the letter for how well you know the word.
      A. I know its meaning.
      B. I've seen it, but I don't know its meaning.
      C. I don't know it.
   b. **Research** Look up and write a definition for *pattern*.
   c. Write a sentence involving mathematics and using the word *pattern*.

Vocabulary Builder High-Use Academic Words 19

Vocabulary Builder

Understanding mathematical vocabulary is an important part of your success in any mathematics class. These features give you even more practice and support in learning these vocabulary words.

GPS Guided Problem Solving

These features give you more support in becoming a good problem solver.

- We provide a great model for talking through the problem-solving process.
- "Think It Through" questions get more in-depth.

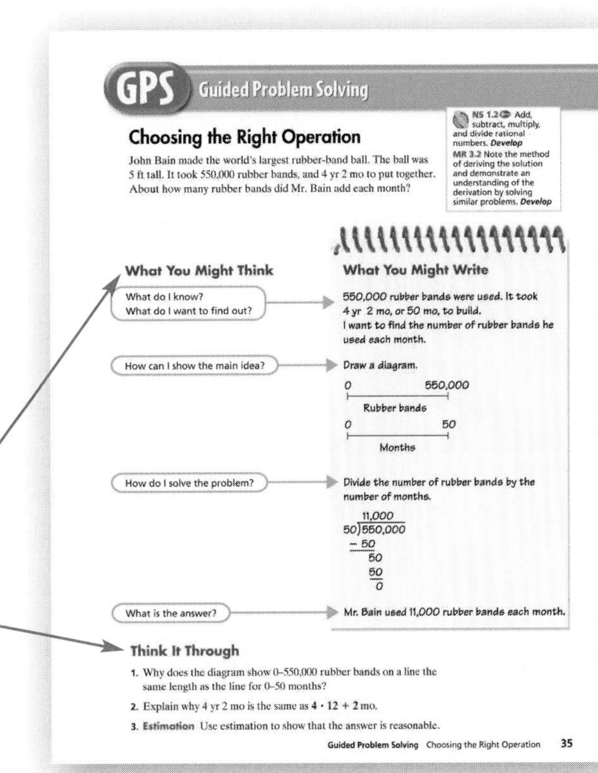

GPS Guided Problem Solving

Choosing the Right Operation

John Bain made the world's largest rubber-band ball. The ball was 5 ft tall. It took 550,000 rubber bands, and 4 yr 2 mo to put together. About how many rubber bands did Mr. Bain add each month?

NS 1.2 Add, subtract, multiply, and divide rational numbers. *Develop*
MR 3.2 Note the method of deriving the solution and demonstrate an understanding of the derivation by solving similar problems. *Develop*

What You Might Think	What You Might Write
What do I know? What do I want to find out?	550,000 rubber bands were used. It took 4 yr 2 mo, or 50 mo, to build. I want to find the number of rubber bands he used each month.
How can I show the main idea?	Draw a diagram. 0 — 550,000 Rubber bands; 0 — 50 Months
How do I solve the problem?	Divide the number of rubber bands by the number of months. 50)550,000 = 11,000; − 50, 50, 50, 0
What is the answer?	Mr. Bain used 11,000 rubber bands each month.

Think It Through

1. Why does the diagram show 0–550,000 rubber bands on a line the same length as the line for 0–50 months?
2. Explain why 4 yr 2 mo is the same as **4 · 12 + 2** mo.
3. **Estimation** Use estimation to show that the answer is reasonable.

Guided Problem Solving Choosing the Right Operation 35

- The first two exercises present the steps you should take to solve the problem. They often contain a visual model of the problem.
- The remaining exercises provide independent practice.

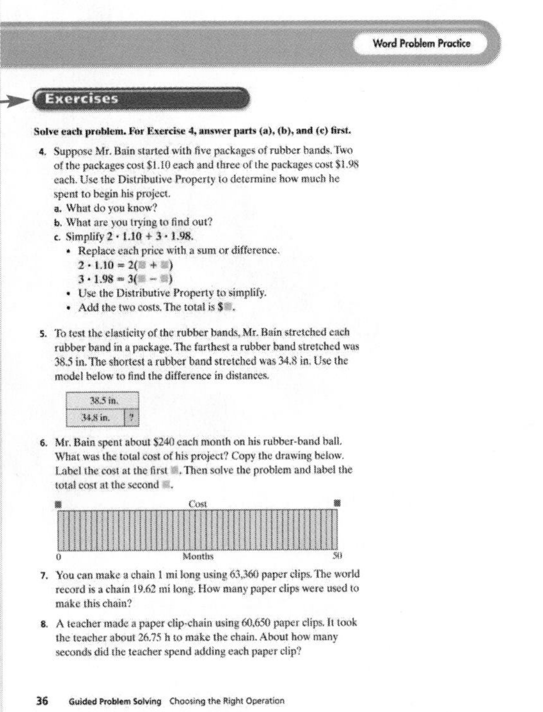

Word Problem Practice

Exercises

Solve each problem. For Exercise 4, answer parts (a), (b), and (c) first.

4. Suppose Mr. Bain started with five packages of rubber bands. Two of the packages cost $1.10 each and three of the packages cost $1.98 each. Use the Distributive Property to determine how much he spent to begin his project.
   a. What do you know?
   b. What are you trying to find out?
   c. Simplify **2 · 1.10 + 3 · 1.98.**
      - Replace each price with a sum or difference.
        2 · 1.10 = 2(■ + ■)
        3 · 1.98 = 3(■ − ■)
      - Use the Distributive Property to simplify.
      - Add the two costs. The total is $■.
5. To test the elasticity of the rubber bands, Mr. Bain stretched each rubber band in a package. The farthest a rubber band stretched was 38.5 in. The shortest a rubber band stretched was 34.8 in. Use the model below to find the difference in distances.

6. Mr. Bain spent about $240 each month on his rubber-band ball. What was the total cost of his project? Copy the drawing below. Label the cost at the first ■. Then solve the problem and label the total cost at the second ■.

7. You can make a chain 1 mi long using 63,360 paper clips. The world record is a chain 19.62 mi long. How many paper clips were used to make this chain?
8. A teacher made a paper clip-chain using 60,650 paper clips. It took the teacher about 26.75 h to make the chain. About how many seconds did the teacher spend adding each paper clip?

36 Guided Problem Solving Choosing the Right Operation

Standards Mastery in Your Book

Standards Mastery in Your Book

California
Student Center

Your Prentice Hall Student Center is your one-stop spot for reviewing the math you learned in class and completing your homework.

Interactive Text

Your complete textbook – electronically!
Also includes:

- Stepped examples for you to review
- Activities and Videos to review your lesson
- Self-Check tests to make sure you're on the right track.

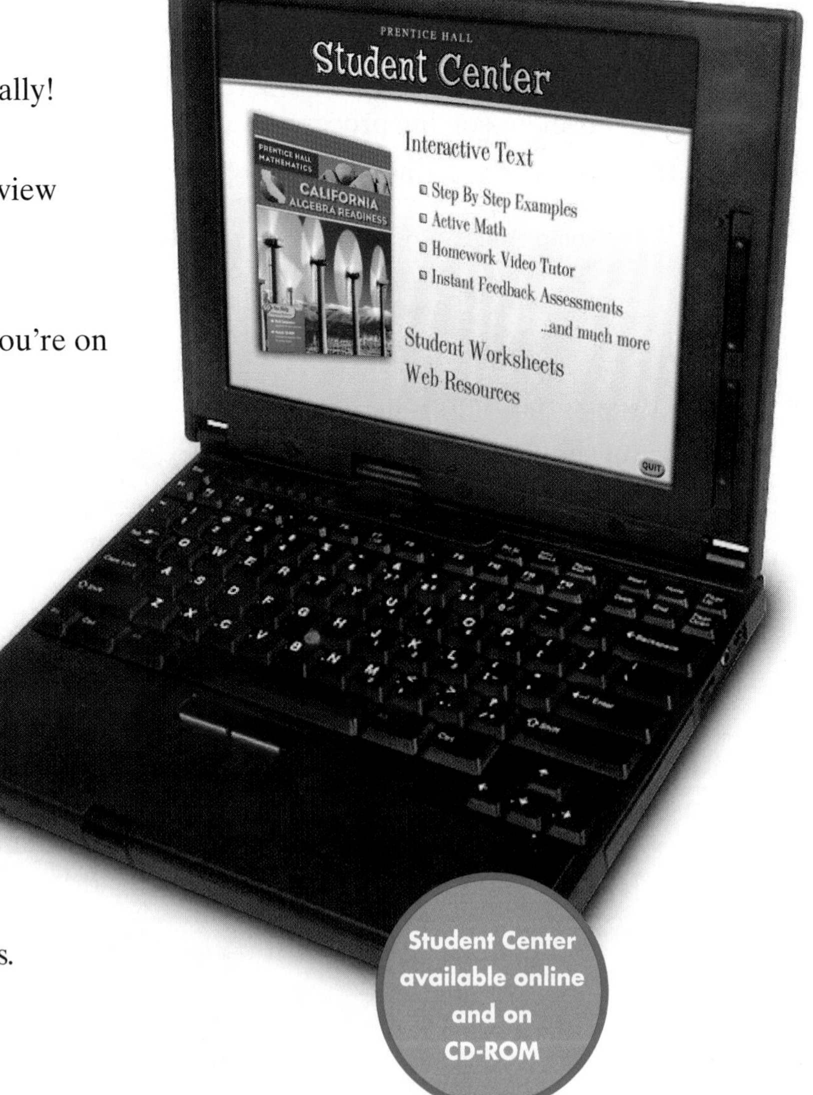

Student Worksheets

All the additional resources your teacher might assign you to extend your learning.

Web Resources

Links out to helpful sites to extend your understanding of math concepts.

Throughout this book you will find links to the Prentice Hall Web site. Use the Web Codes provided with each link to gain direct access to online material. Here's how to *Go Online*:

1. **Go to PHSchool.com**
2. **Enter the Web Code**
3. **Click Go!**

Lesson Web Codes

Lesson Quiz Web Codes: There is an online quiz for every lesson. Access these quizzes with Web Codes axa-0101 through axa-1006 for Lesson 1-1 through Lesson 10-6.

Lesson Quizzes
Web Code format: axa-0204 02 = Chapter 2 04 = Lesson 4

Homework Video Tutor Web Codes: For every lesson, there is additional support online to help students complete their homework. Access the Homework Video Tutors with Web Codes axe-0101 through axe-1006 for Lesson 1-1 through Lesson 10-6.

Homework Video Tutor
Web Code format: axe-0605 06 = Chapter 6 05 = Lesson 5

Chapter Web Codes

Chapter	Vocabulary Quizzes	Chapter Tests	Chapter Projects	California Standards Tutorial
1	axj-0151	axa-0152	axd-0161	axq-9045
2	axj-0251	axa-0252	axd-0261	axq-9045
3	axj-0351	axa-0352	axd-0361	axq-9045
4	axj-0451	axa-0452	axd-0461	axq-9045
5	axj-0551	axa-0552	axd-0561	axq-9045
6	axj-0651	axa-0652	axd-0661	axq-9045
7	axj-0751	axa-0752	axd-0761	axq-9045
8	axj-0851	axa-0852	axd-0861	axq-9045
9	axj-0951	axa-0952	axd-0961	axq-9045
10	axj-1051	axa-1052	axd-1061	axq-9045

Additional Web Codes

Video Tutor Help:
Use Web Code axe-0775 to access engaging online instructional videos to help bring math concepts to life.

Data Updates:
Use Web Code axg-9041 to get up-to-date government data for use in examples and exercises.

Standards Mastery in Your Book

Your Guide to the Standards

California Mathematics Content Standards

Here is a complete list of the Mathematics Content Standards for Algebra Readiness. The standards are organized around five major strands: Number Sense; Algebra and Functions; Measurement and Geometry; Algebra 1; and Mathematical Reasoning. Use this section as a reference guide as you explore the topics in each chapter.

Number Sense

1.2 Add, subtract, multiply, and divide rational numbers (integers, fractions, and terminating decimals) and take positive rational numbers to whole-number powers.

1.3 Convert fractions to decimals and percents and use these representations in estimations, computations, and applications.

1.5 Know that every rational number is either a terminating or a repeating decimal and be able to convert terminating decimals into reduced fractions.

2.1 Understand negative whole-number exponents. Multiply and divide expressions involving exponents with a common base.

What It Means to You

In Chapter 5, you will learn to solve problems like the one below involving various forms of rational numbers.

A student has \$56.75 in her bank account. This is \$5 more than $2\frac{1}{2}$ times as much as her brother has in his bank account. How much money does the student's brother have in his account?

Where You'll Learn This

You will study these standards in Chapters 1, 2, 3, 4, 5, 7, and 10.

Algebra and Functions

1.1 Use variables and appropriate operations to write an expression, an equation, an inequality, or a system of equations or inequalities that represents a verbal description (e.g., three less than a number, half as large as area A).

1.3 Simplify numerical expressions by applying properties of rational numbers (e.g., identity, inverse, distributive, associative, commutative) and justify the process used.

2.1 Interpret positive whole-number powers as repeated multiplication and negative whole-number powers as repeated division or multiplication by the multiplicative inverse. Simplify and evaluate expressions that include exponents.

What It Means to You

In Chapter 3, you will learn to use variables and equations to solve problems such as the one below.

A bag of rice costs \$1.99. You buy one bag of rice and six cans of black beans for a total cost of \$7.33. If you have \$8.25, can you buy another can of beans? Explain.

Where You'll Learn This

You will study these standards in Chapters 1, 2, 3, 4, 5, and 10.

Algebra and Functions (continued)

3.3 Graph linear functions, noting that the vertical change (change in y-value) per unit of horizontal change (change in x-value) is always the same and know that the ratio ("rise over run") is called the slope of the graph.

3.4 Plot the values of quantities whose ratios are always the same (e.g., cost to the number of an item, feet to inches, circumference to diameter of a circle). Fit a line to the plot and understand that the slope of the line equals the ratio of the quantities.

4.1 Solve two-step linear equations and inequalities in one variable over the rational numbers, interpret the solution or solutions in the context from which they arose, and verify the reasonableness of the results.

4.2 Solve multistep problems involving rate, average speed, distance, and time or a direct variation.

What It Means to You

In Chapter 8, you will learn to use graphs to describe the relationship between two quantities, as in the problem below.

The graph at the right shows the relationship between pounds of lunchmeat purchased x and the total cost y. How much does the lunchmeat cost per pound?

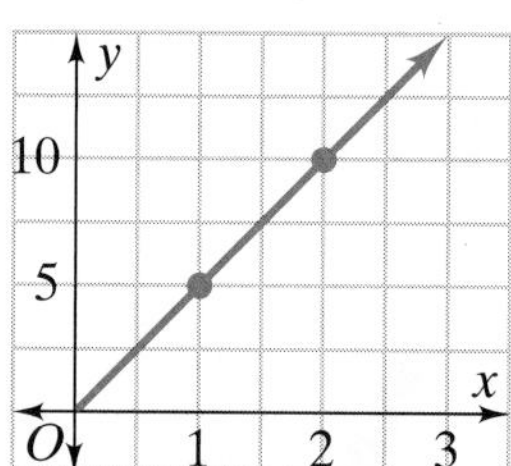

Where You'll Learn This

You will study these standards in Chapters 3, 5, 6, 8, and 9.

Measurement and Geometry

1.3 Use measures expressed as rates (e.g., speed, density) and measures expressed as products (e.g., person-days) to solve problems; check the units of the solutions; and use dimensional analysis to check the reasonableness of the answer.

3.3 Know and understand the Pythagorean theorem and its converse and use it to find the length of the missing side of a right triangle and the lengths of other line segments and, in some situations, empirically verify the Pythagorean theorem by direct measurement.

What It Means to You

In Chapter 6, you will learn to solve problems involving rates such as the problem below.

A boat travels downstream at 10 mi/h for 1.5 h. Then the speed of the current increases and the boat travels for 1 h at a speed 5 mi/h faster than before. What distance does the boat travel?

Where You'll Learn This

You will study these standards in Chapters 3, 6, and 8.

Your Guide to the Standards

Algebra 1

2.0 Students understand and use such operations as taking the opposite, finding the reciprocal, and taking a root. They understand and use the rules of exponents.

4.0 Students simplify expressions before solving linear equations in one variable, such as $3(2x - 5) + 4(x - 2) = 12$.

5.0 Students solve multistep problems, including word problems, involving linear equations in one variable and provide justification for each step.

What It Means to You

In Chapter 10, you will learn Algebra 1 skills such as solving multi-step problems like the one below.

A chef and his assistant are making ravioli. The assistant can make 2 ravioli per minute and the chef can make 5 ravioli per minute. The chef starts making ravioli $\frac{1}{4}$ h after the assistant. How long after the assistant starts making ravioli have they both made the same number of ravioli?

Where You'll Learn This

You will study these standards in Chapters 2, 3, 5, and 10.

Mathematical Reasoning

1.0 Students make decisions about how to approach problems.

1.1 Analyze problems by identifying relationships, distinguishing relevant from irrelevant information, identifying missing information, sequencing and prioritizing information, and observing patterns.

1.2 Formulate and justify mathematical conjectures based on a general description of the mathematical question or problem posed.

1.3 Determine when and how to break a problem into simpler parts.

What It Means to You

Throughout *Algebra Readiness*, you will use problem-solving strategies such as *Look for a Pattern* to solve problems like the one below.

A high school student has started a new job. He plans to save $1 in the first week, $2 in the second week, $4 in the third week, and $8 in the fourth week. If this pattern of savings could continue, how much would he save in the tenth week?

Where You'll Learn This

You will study these standards throughout *Algebra Readiness*.

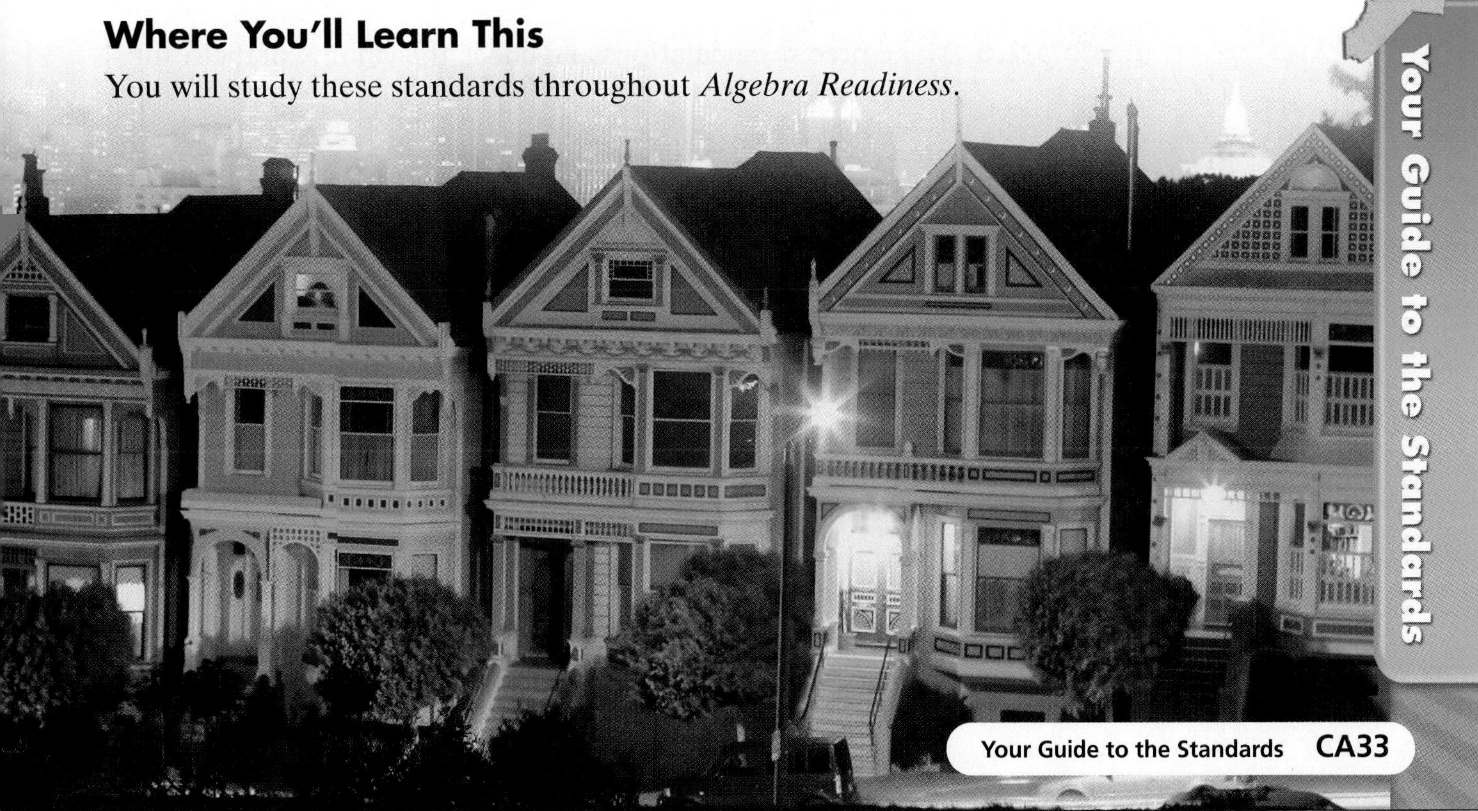

Your Guide to the Standards

Mathematical Reasoning (continued)

2.0 Students use strategies, skills, and concepts in finding solutions.

2.1 Use estimation to verify the reasonableness of calculated results.

2.2 Apply strategies and results from simpler problems to more complex problems.

2.3 Estimate unknown quantities graphically and solve for them by using logical reasoning and arithmetic and algebraic techniques.

2.4 Make and test conjectures by using both inductive and deductive reasoning.

2.5 Use a variety of methods, such as words, numbers, symbols, charts, graphs, tables, diagrams, and models, to explain mathematical reasoning.

2.6 Express the solution clearly and logically by using the appropriate mathematical notation and terms and clear language; support solutions with evidence in both verbal and symbolic work.

2.7 Indicate the relative advantages of exact and approximate solutions to problems and give answers to a specified degree of accuracy.

2.8 Make precise calculations and check the validity of the results from the context of the problem.

What It Means to You

You will use mathematical reasoning skills throughout *Algebra Readiness* to solve problems like the one below.

A tailor has a section of material that is $28\frac{1}{2}$ ft long. He wants to cut it into pieces, each one $1\frac{1}{2}$ ft long. How many cuts will he have to make?

Where You'll Learn This

You will study these standards throughout *Algebra Readiness*.

Mathematical Reasoning (continued)

3.0 Students determine a solution is complete and move beyond a particular problem by generalizing to other situations.

3.1 Evaluate the reasonableness of the solution in the context of the original situation.

3.2 Note the method of deriving the solution and demonstrate a conceptual understanding of the derivation by solving similar problems.

3.3 Develop generalizations of the result obtained and the strategies used and apply them to new problem situations.

What It Means to You

Throughout *Algebra Readiness*, you will apply problem solving strategies such as *Try, Test, Revise* to new problems like the one below.

You can buy balloons in packages of 25 or packages of 75. Suppose you buy 8 packages and have 450 balloons in all. How many packages of each size do you buy?

Where You'll Learn This

You will study these standards throughout *Algebra Readiness*.

Your Guide to the Standards

California Algebra Readiness Progression and Background

The list of standards on these two pages, as identified by the California Department of Education, serve as the Foundational Skills and Concepts for Algebra Readiness. They are identified by grade level and strand (NS – Number Sense, AF – Algebra and Functions, MG – Measurement and Geometry). They are also organized by seven key topics: Whole Numbers, Operations on Whole Numbers, Rational Numbers, Operations on Rational Numbers, Symbolic Notation, Equations and Functions, and the Coordinate Plane.

Topic 1 Whole Numbers	
Grade 3—NS 1.3:	Identify the place value for each digit in numbers to 10,000.
Grade 3—NS 1.5:	Use expanded notation to represent numbers (e.g., $3{,}206 = 3{,}000 + 200 + 6$).
Topic 2 Operations on Whole Numbers	
Grade 2—AF 1.1:	Use the commutative and associative rules to simplify mental calculations and to check results.
Grade 3—AF 1.5:	Recognize and use the commutative and associative properties of multiplication (e.g., if $5 \times 7 = 35$, then what is 7×5? And if $5 \times 7 \times 3 = 105$, then what is $7 \times 3 \times 5$?).
Grade 4—NS 3.1:	Demonstrate an understanding of, and the ability to use, standard algorithms for the addition and subtraction of multidigit numbers.
Grade 4—NS 3.2:	Demonstrate an understanding of, and the ability to use, standard algorithms for multiplying a multidigit number by a two-digit number and for dividing a multidigit number by a one-digit number; use relationships between them to simplify computations and to check results.
Grade 5—AF 1.3:	Know and use the distributive property in equations and expressions with variables.
Topic 3 Rational Numbers	
Grade 5—NS 1.4:	Determine the prime factors of all numbers through 50 and write the numbers as the product of their prime factors by using exponents to show multiples of a factor (e.g., $24 = 2 \times 2 \times 2 \times 3 = 2^3 \times 3$).
Grade 6—NS 1.1:	Compare and order positive and negative fractions, decimals, and mixed numbers and place them on a number line.
Topic 4 Operations on Rational Numbers	
Grade 6—NS 1.4:	Calculate given percentages of quantities and solve problems involving discounts at sales, interest earned, and tips.
Grade 6—NS 2.0:	Students calculate and solve problems involving addition, subtraction, multiplication, and division.
Grade 6—NS 2.1:	Solve problems involving addition, subtraction, multiplication, and division of positive fractions and explain why a particular operation was used for a given situation.
Grade 6—NS 2.2:	Explain the meaning of multiplication and division of positive fractions and perform the calculations (e.g., $\frac{5}{8} \div \frac{15}{16} = \frac{5}{8} \times \frac{16}{15} = \frac{2}{3}$).

Topic 5 Symbolic Notation
Grade 4—AF 1.2: Interpret and evaluate mathematical expressions that now use parentheses.
Grade 4—AF 1.3: Use parentheses to indicate which operation to perform first when writing expressions containing more than two terms and different operations.
Grade 5—AF 1.0: Students use variables in simple expressions, compute the value of the expression for specific values of the variable, and plot and interpret the results.
Grade 6—AF 1.0: Students write verbal expressions and sentences as algebraic expressions and equations; they evaluate algebraic expressions, solve simple linear equations, and graph and interpret their results.
Grade 6—AF 1.1: Write and solve one-step linear equations in one variable.

Topic 6 Equations and Functions
Grade 4—AF 1.5: Understand that an equation such as $y = 3x + 5$ is a prescription for determining a second number when a first number is given.
Grade 4—AF 2.0: Students know how to manipulate equations.
Grade 4—AF 2.1: Know and understand that equals added to equals are equal.
Grade 4—AF 2.2: Know and understand that equals multiplied by equals are equal.

Topic 7 The Coordinate Plane
Grade 4—MG 2.0: Students use two-dimensional coordinate grids to represent points and graph lines and simple figures.
Grade 4—MG 2.1: Draw the points corresponding to linear relationships on graph paper (e.g., draw 10 points on the graph of the equation $y = 3x$ and connect them by using a straight line).
Grade 4—MG 2.2: Understand that the length of a horizontal line segment equals the difference of the *x*-coordinates.
Grade 4—MG 2.3: Understand that the length of a vertical line segment equals the difference of the *y*-coordinates.
Grade 5—AF 1.4: Identify and graph ordered pairs in the four quadrants of the coordinate plane.

Algebra Readiness Standards Progression and Background

Grade 7
Number Sense
Standard 1.2

1.2 Add, subtract, multiply, and divide rational numbers and take positive rational numbers to whole-number powers.

Progression

Prior Grade Level Standards
Students compare, order, add, subtract, multiply, and divide positive rational numbers and integers.

This Year's Standards
Students expand their operations work to include negative rational numbers.

Where the Standards Are Leading
In later courses, students extend their knowledge of rational numbers and real numbers to include complex numbers.

Background

A **rational number** is any number you can write as a quotient $\frac{a}{b}$ of two integers, where b is not zero. The rational numbers include both positive and negative fractions and decimals, as well as the integers. This is because every integer can be written as a fraction. The integer a is equal to the fraction $\frac{a}{1}$.

By the time students complete sixth grade they should understand computation using positive rational numbers and integers. Negative rational numbers are introduced in this course. Students will graph negative rational numbers on a number line and evaluate rational expressions for negative values of the variables.

EXAMPLE In three plays, a football team gained 5 yd, lost 12 yd, and gained 10 yd. Which integer represents the change in yards?

A −12 **B** 3
C 5 **D** 10

Answer: B

Standards 1.3 and 1.5

1.3 Convert fractions to decimals and percents and use these representations in estimations, computations, and applications.

1.5 Know that every rational number is either a terminating or repeating decimal and convert terminating decimals into reduced fractions.

Progression

Prior Grade Level Standards
Students know decimal and percent equivalents for fractions and compare and order fractions and decimals.

This Year's Standards
Students differentiate between rational and irrational numbers and convert terminating decimals to fractions.

Where the Standards Are Leading
In later math courses, students will extend their understanding of real numbers to complex numbers.

Background

An **irrational number** is a number that can be represented by a nonrepeating, nonterminating decimal. An example of an irrational number is π. While π is an exact number, it is not exactly equal to 3.14.

In this course, students will learn the difference between rational and irrational numbers. Show students how to construct a nonrepeating decimal such as 3.454454445444445. . . .

Students also learn the difference between terminating and repeating decimals and can convert from fractions to decimals and vice versa.

EXAMPLE Which decimal is equivalent to $\frac{12}{15}$?

A 0.15 **B** 0.25
C $0.\overline{3}$ **D** 0.8

Answer: D

Key Standards =

Number Sense (continued)

Standard 2.1

2.1 Understand negative whole-number exponents. Multiply and divide expressions involving exponents with a common base.

Progression

Prior Grade Level Standards
Students compute positive integer powers.

This Year's Standards
Students extend their understanding of powers to negative integer exponents and to multiply and divide expressions involving exponents.

Where the Standards Are Leading
In algebra, students will extend their use of exponents to include rational exponents.

Background

An **exponent** is a number that shows how many times a base is used as a factor. For 3^4, 3 is the base and 4 is the exponent.

$3^4 = 3 \cdot 3 \cdot 3 \cdot 3$

To multiply powers with the same base, add the exponents.

$3^2 \cdot 3^4 = 3^{2+4} = 3^6$

$a^m \cdot a^n = a^{m+n}$ for positive integers m and n

To define the zero exponent, x^0, use the first law of exponents.

$x^m \cdot x^0 = x^{m+0} = x^m$

If $x \neq 0$, multiply each side of the equation by the reciprocal, $\frac{1}{x^m}$.

$\frac{1}{x^m} \cdot x^m \cdot x^0 = \frac{1}{x^m} \cdot x^m$ or $1 \cdot x^0 = 1$

The definition of the zero exponent is:

If $x \neq 0$, then $x^0 = 1$.

This means that $5^0 = 1$ and $10^0 = 1$.

EXAMPLE Simplify 5^{-3}.

A -125 **B** $-\frac{1}{125}$

C $\frac{1}{125}$ **D** 125

Answer: C

Algebra and Functions

Standard 1.1

1.1 Use variables and appropriate operations to write an expression, an equation, an inequality, or a system of equations or inequalities that represents a verbal description.

Progression

Prior Grade Level Standards
Students write expressions and equations.

This Year's Standards
Students extend their knowledge of writing expressions and equations to writing expressions and equations for real-world situations and to writing systems of equations and finding the solutions of systems of equations and inequalities by graphing.

Where the Standards Are Leading
In later math courses and advanced science courses, students will use the systems of equations and inequalities for real-world applications.

Background

A **variable** is a letter that stands for a number. A **variable expression** is a mathematical phrase that uses variables, numerals, and operation symbols. An **equation** is a mathematical sentence with an equal sign. An **inequality** is a mathematical sentence that contains $>$, $<$, $\geq$, $\leq$ or $\neq$.

Two or more linear equations form a **system of equations.** Any ordered pair that is a solution of all of the equations in the system is a solution of the system. One way to solve a system of equations is by graphing the equations and finding the point or points of intersection of the graphs.

Two or more linear inequalities form a **system of inequalities.**

Equations and inequalities come from everyday situations, from business, and from sciences. Having the ability to translate these situations into equations and inequalities, gives students tools for understanding these situations.

EXAMPLE Which description matches the expression $\frac{n}{3} + 5$?

A five more than three times a number
B three times a number increased by five
C five less than a number divided by three
D the sum of five and a number divided by three

Answer: D

Algebra Readiness Standards Progression and Background (continued)

Algebra and Functions (continued)

Standard 1.3

1.3 Simplify numerical expressions by applying properties of rational numbers (e.g., identity, inverse, distributive, associative, commutative) and justify the process used.

Progression

Prior Grade Level Standards
Students apply order of operations and identify the commutative, associative, and distributive properties.

This Year's Standards
Students extend their ability to evaluate algebraic expressions to include expressions that contain exponents and extend their use of properties to include the identity and inverse properties and to evaluate expressions.

Where the Standards Are Leading
Students multiply and factor algebraic expressions and use properties in geometric proofs.

Background

Simplifying numerical expressions by applying the properties of rational numbers gives students a foundation in abstract thinking. Students will use this foundation to make sense of complex situations. They will use the inverse properties to solve equations.

Students evaluate expressions that contain more than one operation, for example, $3(2x + 5)^2$ for $x = 0$. For an algebraic expression involving two or more operations, you need to know which operation to do first, second, and so on.

EXAMPLE Which property justifies the statement $\frac{1}{6} \cdot 6g = g$?

A Associative Property of Multiplication
B Commutative Property of Multiplication
C Inverse Property of Multiplication
D Identity Property of Multiplication

Answer: D

Standard 1.5

1.5 Represent quantitative relationships graphically and interpret the meaning of a specific part of a graph in the situation represented by the graph.

Progression

Prior Grade Level Standards
Students use graphs to solve problems involving rates and proportions.

This Year's Standards
Students extend their use of graphs to show the solutions of equations with two variables, systems of equations, and inequalities and to interpret the meaning of a specific part of a graph.

Where the Standards Are Leading
Students will build on their understanding of the meaning of graphs and use linear programming to find an optimal solution to a problem.

Background

An equation with two variables, such as $y = x - 4$, has many solutions. One way to show these solutions is to graph them. A **linear equation** is any equation whose graph is a line. The equation $y = x - 4$ is a linear equation.

To graph the solutions of $y = x - 4$, find a minimum of two ordered pairs that make the equation true, graph the ordered pairs, then draw a line through the points. It is best to find more than two solutions as a check for accuracy.

x	y	(x, y)
0	−4	(0, −4)
1	−3	(1, −3)
2	−2	(2, −2)

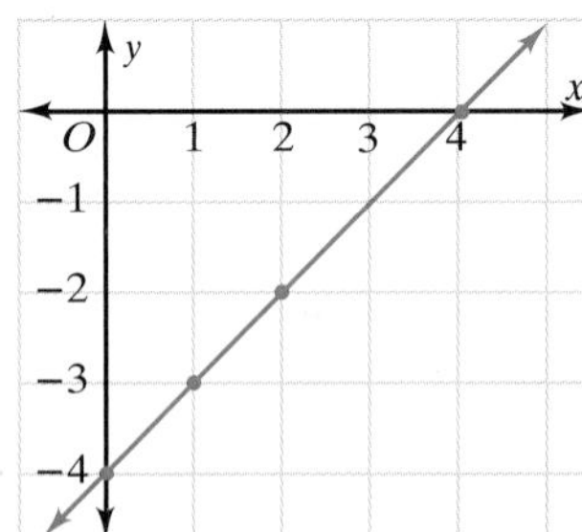

Test another point on the line. Test (4, 0). Is the equation true when $x = 4$ and $y = 0$?

$y = x - 4$
$0 \stackrel{?}{=} 4 - 4$
$0 = 0$

Algebra and Functions (continued)

Standard 2.1

2.1 Interpret positive whole-number powers as repeated multiplication and negative whole-number powers as repeated division or multiplication by the multiplicative inverse. Simplify and evaluate expression that include exponents.

Progression

Prior Grade Level Standards
Students take positive integers to whole-number powers.

This Year's Standards
Students extend the use of exponents to include 0 and negative exponents.

Where the Standards Are Leading
In later courses students use fractional powers and relate them to roots and complex numbers.

Background

You can use exponents to show repeated multiplication.

5^3 means $5 \times 5 \times 5 = 125$

5^{-3} means $\frac{1}{5^3} = \frac{1}{5 \times 5 \times 5} = \frac{1}{125}$

EXAMPLE Alyssa wrote the prime factorization of 180 as $2 \cdot 2 \cdot 3 \cdot 3 \cdot 5$. How can Alyssa write this product using exponents?

A $2^2 \cdot 3^2 \cdot 5$ **B** $4 \cdot 9 \cdot 5$

C $2^2 \cdot 3^3 \cdot 5$ **D** $2 \cdot 6 \cdot 15$

Answer: A

Standards 3.3 and 3.4

3.3 Graph linear functions, noting that the vertical change per unit of horizontal change is always the same and know that the ratio is called the slope of a graph.

3.4 Plot the values of quantities whose ratios are always the same. Fit a line to the plot and understand that the slope of the line equals the quantities.

Progression

Prior Grade Level Standards
Students solve problems involving linear functions with integer values and graph the resulting ordered pairs of integers on a grid.

This Year's Standards
Students extend their knowledge of one-step linear equations to graphing linear functions and understanding slope.

Where the Standards Are Leading
An understanding of slope and linear equations is crucial to understanding calculus and analysis.

Background

The ratio that describes the tilt of a line is its slope. If a line slants upward from left to right, it has a positive slope. If it slants downward, it has a negative slope. To calculate slope, use this ratio:

$$\text{slope} = \frac{\text{vertical change}}{\text{horizontal change}} = \frac{\text{rise}}{\text{run}}$$

Rise shows vertical change. Up is positive; down is negative. Run shows horizontal change. Right is positive; left is negative.

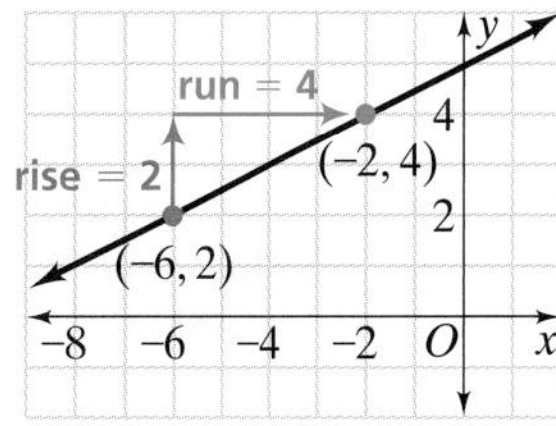

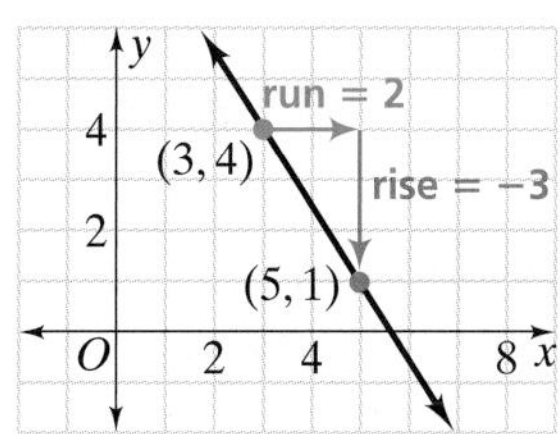

$\text{slope} = \frac{\text{rise}}{\text{run}} = \frac{2}{4} = \frac{1}{2}$ $\text{slope} = \frac{\text{rise}}{\text{run}} = \frac{-3}{2} = -\frac{3}{2}$

You can use two points on the line to find the slope.

$$\text{slope} = \frac{\text{difference in } y\text{-coordinates}}{\text{difference in } x\text{-coordinates}}$$

Students can use slope to describe the incline of a ramp, the slant of a roof, or the grade of a road or to determine whether two lines are parallel.

Algebra Readiness Standards Progression and Background (continued)

Algebra and Functions (continued)

Standards 4.1 and 4.2

4.1 Solve two-step linear equations and inequalities in one variable over the rational numbers, interpret the solution or solutions in the context from which they arose, and verify the reasonableness of the results.

4.2 Solve multistep problems involving rate, average speed, distance, and time or a direct variation.

Progression

Prior Grade Level Standards
Students solve one-step linear equations.

This Year's Standards
Students extend their ability to solve one-step equations to solve two-step equations, inequalities, and multistep problems.

Where the Standards Are Leading
Students solve polynomial equations, many of which arise in calculus.

Background

A **linear equation** in one variable is an equation equivalent to an equation in the form $ax + b = 0$, where a and b are constants and $a \neq 0$. You solve a linear equation using inverse operations and the properties of equality to get the variable alone on one side of the equation.

Students use two-step equations and inequalities to solve multistep problems in real-world situations. Many of these situations involve rates or direct variations. One application of direct variation is converting units of measurement.

EXAMPLE A school group is taking a trip to the state capital. The cost is \$50 for the bus driver plus \$2.50 per mile for gasoline and maintenance of the bus. The total cost is \$67.50. How many miles did the group travel?

A 5 mi **B** 6 mi
C 7 mi **D** 8 mi

Answer: C

Measurement and Geometry

Standard 1.3

1.3 Use measures expressed as rates and measures expressed as products to solve problems; check the units of the solutions; and use dimensional analysis to check the reasonableness of the answer.

Progression

Prior Grade Level Standards
Students use appropriate units of measure for two- and three-dimensional objects.

This Year's Standards
Students extend the use of units of measure to comparing units of measure within and between systems and use rates to solve problems.

Where the Standards Are Leading
Students understand applications of units in problem solving, science, business, and trigonometry.

Background

A **rate** is a ratio that compares quantities in different units. A **unit rate** is a rate that has a denominator of 1. Examples of unit rates include unit prices, gas mileage, and speed.

You can use dimensional analysis to choose conversion factors for converting rates.

Convert 10 mi/h to feet per minute.

$$10 \text{ mi/h} = \frac{\overset{1}{\cancel{10}}\ \cancel{\text{mi}}}{1\ \cancel{\text{h}}} \cdot \frac{\overset{880}{\cancel{5{,}280}}\ \text{ft}}{1\ \cancel{\text{mi}}} \cdot \frac{1\ \cancel{\text{h}}}{\underset{\underset{1}{\cancel{6}}}{\cancel{60}}\ \text{min}}$$

$$= 880 \text{ ft/min}$$

Use conversion factors that convert miles to feet and hours to minutes.
Divide the common factors and units.

EXAMPLE Which of the following stores has the lowest price per box of juice?

A Corner Store: 4 boxes for \$1.52
B Joe's Grocery: 10 boxes for \$3.60
C Fast Mart: 8 boxes for \$2.80
D Mandy's Market: 5 boxes for \$1.85

Answer: C

Measurement and Geometry (continued)

Standard 3.3

3.3 Know and understand the Pythagorean theorem and its converse and use it to find the length of the missing side of a right triangle and the lengths of other line segments and, in some situations, empirically verify the Pythagorean theorem by direct measurement.

Progression

Prior Grade Level Standards
Students draw triangles from given information about them.

This Year's Standards
Students extend their knowledge of triangles to knowing and using the Pythagorean theorem and its converse and using it to find the length of the missing side of right triangle.

Where the Standards Are Leading
The Pythagorean theorem is used extensively in trigonometry.

Background

The Pythagorean Theorem:

In any right triangle, the sum of the squares of the lengths of the legs is equal to the square of the length of the hypotenuse.

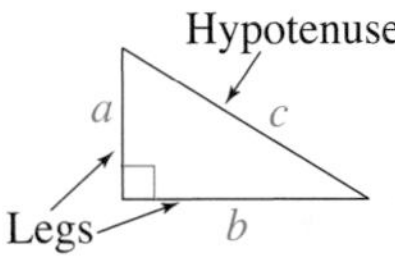

$a^2 + b^2 = c^2$

The Converse of the Pythagorean Theorem:

Given the measurement of three sides, if $a^2 + b^2 = c^2$, the triangle is a right triangle.

EXAMPLE Refer to the triangle. Which equation is true?

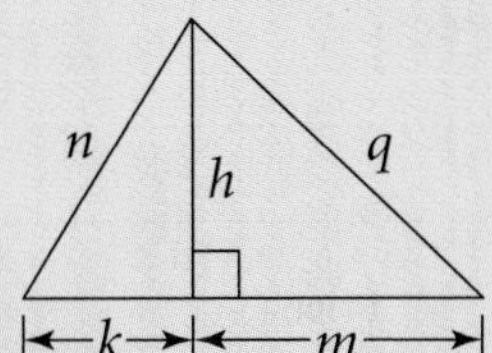

A $k^2 + n^2 = h^2$ **B** $h^2 + n^2 = m^2$

C $h^2 + m^2 = q^2$ **D** $m^2 + q^2 = h^2$

Answer: C

Mathematical Reasoning

Standards 1.0, 1.1, 1.2, and 1.3

1.0 Students make decisions about how to approach problems.

1.1 Analyze problems by identifying relationships, distinguishing relevant from irrelevant information, identifying missing information, sequencing and prioritizing information, and observing patterns.

1.2 Formulate and justify mathematical conjectures based on a general description of the mathematical question or problem posed.

1.3 Determine when and how to break a problem into simpler parts.

Progression

Prior Grade Level Standards
Same as this year's

This Year's Standards
Students identify relationships, distinguish relevant or missing information, and observe patterns. They formulate conjectures and determine how to break a problem into simpler parts.

Where the Standards Are Leading
Students become adept at problem solving.

Background

Students need many opportunities to analyze relationships. In addition to analyzing numerical relationships, they will analyze geometrical relationships. Understanding how one problem relates to another helps students develop problem solving skills.

Distinguishing relevant or missing information in problems helps prepare students for real-world problem situations. Since solving problems is often overwhelming, students should be shown how to approach complex problems by breaking them into simpler parts.

There are many patterns in everyday life, so students need to be given different types of mathematical patterns to observe. Students need to practice analyzing, continuing, and finding rules for patterns.

Algebra Readiness Standards Progression and Background (continued)

Mathematical Reasoning (continued)

Standards 2.0, 2.1, and 2.2

2.0 Students use strategies, skills, and concepts in finding solutions.

2.1 Use estimation to verify the reasonableness of calculated results.

2.2 Apply strategies and results from simpler problems to more complex problems.

Progression

Prior Grade Level Standards
Same as this year's

This Year's Standards
Students use estimation to verify the reasonableness of results and apply strategies from simpler problems to more complex ones.

Where the Standards Are Leading
Students will use the strategies from arithmetic to simplify algebraic expressions and solve algebraic equations.

Background

Number sense and estimation can be used to determine whether answers are reasonable.

These are different estimation strategies that students should use:

For a front-end estimate, the front-end digits are added. Then the remaining digits are rounded and combined to estimate the sum. A front-end estimate can sometimes be closer to the exact sum than an estimate found by rounding.

Clustering can be used to estimate the sum of several numbers that are close to one value. You can replace all of the numbers with a single number close to them that is easy to multiply. Then multiply. For example, estimate $26.7 + 26.2 + 24.52 + 25.25 + 23.9$. Since the values cluster around 25, multiply $5 \cdot 25$.

Compatible numbers are used to estimate quotients. Compatible numbers are numbers that are easy to divide mentally. When you estimate a quotient, first round the divisor, and then round the dividend to a compatible number.

Good estimation skills are important as students become consumers.

Standards 2.3 and 2.4

2.3 Estimate unknown quantities graphically and solve for them by using logical reasoning and arithmetic and algebraic techniques.

2.4 Make and test conjectures by using both inductive and deductive reasoning.

Progression

Prior Grade Level Standards
Students estimate unknown quantities graphically and solve them by using logical reasoning and arithmetic and algebraic techniques.

This Year's Standards
Students make and test conjectures by using both inductive and deductive reasoning.

Where the Standards Are Leading
Students explain the difference between inductive and deductive reasoning and identify and provide examples of each.

Background

One application of estimating quantities graphically is using scatter plots to look for trends and to make predictions.

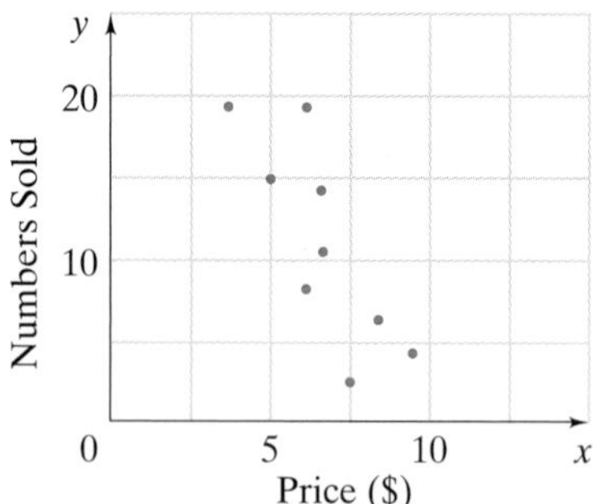

This scatter plot shows the relationship between price and number of items sold. The trend shown is that as the price increases fewer items are sold.

Inductive reasoning is making conclusions based on patterns you observe. A conclusion by inductive reasoning is a conjecture. An example that proves a statement false is a counterexample. You only need one counterexample to prove that a conjecture is incorrect.

Deductive reasoning is the process of reasoning logically from given facts to a conclusion.

Mathematical Reasoning (continued)

Standards 2.5 and 2.6

2.5 Use a variety of methods, such as words, numbers, symbols, charts, graphs, tables, diagrams, and models to explain mathematical reasoning.

2.6 Express the solution clearly and logically by using the appropriate mathematical notation and terms and clear language; support solutions with evidence in both verbal and symbolic work.

Progression

Prior Grade Level Standards
Same as this year's

This Year's Standards
Students use a variety of methods to explain mathematical reasoning and use appropriate mathematical notation and language.

Where the Standards Are Leading
Students need language skills to explain their thinking. They need to be able to express mathematical reasoning using tables, graphs, diagrams, and models.

Background

For students to achieve a high level of mathematical understanding, they need to be able to show their reasoning in different ways. Since no single method of showing reasoning is best or most appropriate in all situations, students need a variety of methods to choose from. Also, the best methods of reasoning will vary among students. However, it is still important to discuss with them what methods work best for different situations. Students need to be able to use tables, charts, and graphs to show mathematical thinking and solutions to problems.

In order to evaluate whether students understand concepts rather than only being able to use computational and procedural skills, students need to be able to explain their thinking.They must be able to express their solutions clearly and support these solutions with verbal and symbolic notation.

Standards 2.7 and 2.8

2.7 Indicate the relative advantages of exact and approximate solutions to problems and give answers to a specified degree of accuracy.

2.8 Make precise calculations and check the validity of the results from the context of the problem.

Progression

Prior Grade Level Standards
Same as this year's

This Year's Standards
Students indicate the advantages of exact and approximate solutions and check the validity of their results from the context of the problem.

Where the Standards Are Leading
Students understand that their solutions depend upon the context of the problem and are able to analyze possible solutions.

Background

Some real-world problems require only an estimate for an answer. Others require an exact answer. It is important for students to understand when approximations are valuable or when exact values are needed. For example, if you are reading a newspaper you may only need an estimate of the distance from Earth to the moon. However, a scientist working on a moon landing project would need to know the exact distance.

It is also important for students to determine if an answer is reasonable. They should know that $1\frac{1}{2}$ people or $3\frac{3}{4}$ buses are not reasonable answers. Have students get in the habit of checking the validity of their answer in the context of the original problem.

Algebra Readiness Standards Progression and Background (continued)

Mathematical Reasoning (continued)

Standards 3.0 and 3.1

3.0 Students determine a solution is complete and move beyond a particular problem by generalizing to other situations:

3.1 Evaluate the reasonableness of the solution in the context of the original situation.

Progression

Prior Grade Level Standards
Same as this year's

This Year's Standards
Students check the reasonableness of a solution by using the context of the original situation.

Where the Standards Are Leading
Students understand that some solutions that are mathematically correct are not solutions in the context of a situation.

Background

Estimating can be used along with the context of the problem to determine whether a solution is reasonable.

In 1998, there were 748 drive-in movie screens in the United States. This was only about 21% of the number in 1980. About how many drive-in screens were there in 1980?

$$\frac{21}{100} = \frac{748}{n}$$
$$21n = 100(748)$$
$$\frac{21n}{21} = \frac{100(748)}{21}$$
$$n \approx 3{,}560$$

There were about 3,560 screens in 1980.

Is the answer reasonable? The original problem says that the number of screens in 1998 was 21% of the number in 1980.

Check by estimating:

21% of 3,560 $\approx 0.2 \times 3{,}600 = 720$, which is close to 748, the number for 1998. So the answer is reasonable.

Standards 3.2 and 3.3

3.2 Note the method of deriving the solution and demonstrate a conceptual understanding of the derivation by solving similar problems.

3.3 Develop generalizations of the results obtained and the strategies used and apply them to new problem situations.

Progression

Prior Grade Level Standards
Same as this year's

This Year's Standards
Students understand how to solve a problem and apply the same steps to solving similar problems.

Where the Standards Are Leading
Students will be able to apply the strategies they know to other problem solving situations.

Background

This course will give students opportunities to apply the strategies and concepts that they used to solve one problem to a similar problem. It is through these connections that students become powerful problem solvers. As students solve problems they will realize how math concepts are connected and how mathematics is connected to their lives and to the real world.

We often use multiple strategies to solve problems. The more strategies students learn, the more they use the strategies, and the more connections they can make between problems, the better equipped they will be to solve problems.

Algebra 1

Standard 2.0

2.0 Students understand and use such operations as taking the opposite, finding the reciprocal, taking a root, and raising to a fractional power. They understand and use the rules of exponents.

Progression

Prior Grade Level Standards
Students use operations such as taking the opposite, finding the reciprocal, finding a square root, and raising to an integer power. Students understand negative integer exponents.

This Year's Standards
Students' knowledge of exponents is expanded to include rational exponents.

Where the Standards Are Leading
In later courses, students use exponential and logarithmic functions.

Background

Before students begin this course they have found opposites and reciprocals of rational numbers. In this course they extend these skills to include variables. While using variables is not new to students, their use is more extensive in algebra.

EXAMPLE Simplify $3 + \sqrt{25} - \sqrt[3]{8}$.

A 5.17
B 6
C 10
D 12.83

Answer: B

Standard 4.0

4.0 Students simplify expressions before solving linear equations and inequalities in one variable, such as $3(2x - 5) + 4(x - 2) = 12$.

Progression

Prior Grade Level Standards
Students simplify numerical expressions by applying properties of rational numbers (e.g., identity, inverse, distributive, associative, commutative).

This Year's Standards
Students extend their knowledge of simplifying expressions to include multiple grouping symbols, the inverse of a sum property, rational expressions, and radical expressions.

Where the Standards Are Leading
In advanced algebra, students will add, subtract, multiply, divide, reduce, and evaluate rational expressions with monomial and polynomial denominators and simplify complicated rational expressions, including those with negative exponents in the denominators.

Background

Students have been simplifying expressions since fifth grade. In this course, students will be simplifying more complex expressions. Parentheses, brackets, and braces are grouping symbols that are used in algebra. When an expression contains more than one grouping symbol, the computations in the innermost grouping symbols are done first.

$$\text{Simplify: } 9 - [7 - (13 + 4)] = 9 - [7 - 17] = 9 - [-10] = 19$$

EXAMPLE Simplify: $8(3x - 2) - 5(2x - 3)$

A $14x + 1$
B $34x - 31$
C $34x + 31$
D $14x - 1$

Answer: D

Algebra Readiness Standards Progression and Background (continued)

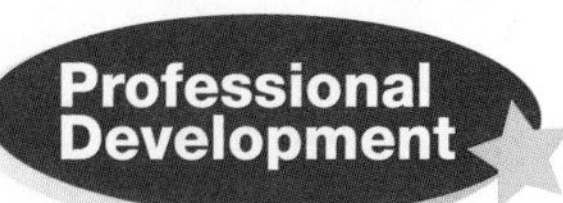

Algebra 1 (continued)

Standard 5.0

5.0 Students solve multistep problems, including word problems, involving linear equations and linear inequalities in one variable and provide justification for each step.

Progression

Prior Grade Level Standards

Students solve multistep problems involving rate, average speed, distance, and time or a direct variation.

This Year's Standards

Students expand their ability to solve multistep problems to include applications besides speed, distance, and time involving linear equations and inequalities.

Where the Standards Are Leading

In later math courses, students solve multistep problems involving nonlinear equations and inequalities.

Background

When solving a multi-step equation, first combine like terms to simplify the expression on each side of the equation. You may also need to use the Distributive Property to simplify the equation.

However, the word problems are more complex. Emphasize finding a key relationship and expressing it as a word equation.

To solve an inequality, you utilize the same steps as solving an equation, with one important difference: when you multiply or divide by a negative number, you must *reverse* the direction of the inequality symbol.

EXAMPLE What value makes the equation $2x + 16 = -4x + 4$ true?

A -20 **B** -2
C 2 **D** 20

Answer: B

California Standards Correlation

This chart shows the lessons in which each standard is introduced, developed, and mastered. Next to each lesson is a brief description of the concept(s) addressed in that lesson. The estimated times given in the third column for the target standards provide an approximate number of days it will take to cover each given standard. Key standards for Grade 7 are denoted by 🔑.

Foundational Skills and Concepts

Math Content Standard	Prentice Hall Algebra Readiness Math Lessons
Topic 2 Operations on Whole Numbers	
Grade 2—AF 1.1: Use the commutative and associative rules to simplify mental calculations and to check results.	**1-5** Properties of Numbers
Grade 3—AF 1.5: Recognize and use the commutative and associative properties of multiplication.	**1-5** Properties of Numbers
Grade 5—AF 1.3: Know and use the distributive property in equations and expressions with variables.	**1-6** The Distributive Property
Topic 3 Rational Numbers	
Grade 5—NS 1.4: Determine the prime factors of all numbers through 50 and write the numbers as the product of their prime factors by using exponents to show multiples of a factor.	**4-1** Prime Factorization **4-2** Greatest Common Divisor
Grade 6—NS 1.1: Compare and order positive and negative fractions, decimals, and mixed numbers and place them on a number line.	**4-3** Equivalent Fractions **4-5** Comparing and Ordering Rational Numbers
Topic 4 Operations on Rational Numbers	
Grade 6—NS 1.4: Calculate given percentages of quantities and solve problems involving discounts at sales, interest earned, and tips.	**7-2** Finding a Percent of a Number **7-5** Applications of Percent
Grade 6—NS 2.0: Students calculate and solve problems involving addition, subtraction, multiplication, and division.	**2-2** Adding Integers **2-3** Subtracting Integers **2-4** Multiplying Integers **2-5** Dividing Integers
Grade 6—NS 2.1: Solve problems involving addition, subtraction, multiplication, and division of positive fractions and explain why a particular operation was used for a given situation.	**5-1** Adding Rational Numbers **5-2** Subtracting Rational Numbers **5-3** Multiplying Rational Numbers **5-4** Dividing Rational Numbers
Topic 5 Symbolic Notation	
Grade 4—AF 1.2: Interpret and evaluate mathematical expressions that now use parentheses.	**1-1** Numerical Expressions
Grade 5—AF 1.0: Students use variables in simple expressions, compute the value of the expression for specific values of the variable, and plot and interpret the results.	**1-2** Algebraic Expressions **8-1** Graphing in the Coordinate Plane
Grade 6—AF 1.0: Students write verbal expressions and sentences as algebraic expressions and equations; they evaluate algebraic expressions, solve simple linear equations, and graph and interpret their results.	**1-2** Algebraic Expressions **1-3** Writing Expressions

Foundational Skills and Concepts (continued)

Math Content Standard	Prentice Hall Algebra Readiness Math Lessons
Grade 6—AF 1.1: Write and solve one-step linear equations in one variable.	**3-1** Solving Addition Equations **3-2** Solving Subtraction Equations **3-3** Solving Multiplication and Division Equations **5-5** Solving Equations by Adding and Subtracting **5-6** Solving Equations by Multiplying and Dividing
Topic 6 Equations and Functions	
Grade 4—AF 1.5: Understand that an equation such as $y = 3x + 5$ is a prescription for determining a second number when a first number is given.	**8-3** Functions
Topic 7 The Coordinate Plane	
Grade 4—MG 2.0: Students use two-dimensional coordinate grids to represent points and graph lines and simple figures.	**8-1** Graphing in the Coordinate Plane
Grade 4—MG 2.1: Draw the points corresponding to linear relationships on graph paper.	**8-4** Graphing Linear Functions
Grade 4—MG 2.2: Understand that the length of a horizontal line segment equals the difference of the *x*-coordinates.	**8-2** Length in the Coordinate Plane
Grade 4—MG 2.3: Understand that the length of a vertical line segment equals the difference of the *y*-coordinates.	**8-2** Length in the Coordinate Plane
Grade 5—AF 1.4: Identify and graph ordered pairs in the four quadrants of the coordinate plane.	**8-1** Graphing in the Coordinate Plane

Grade 7
Number Sense

	Math Content Standard	Prentice Hall Algebra Readiness Math Lessons	Estimated Time
NS 1.2	Add, subtract, multiply, and divide rational numbers (integers, fractions, and terminating decimals) and take positive rational numbers to whole-number powers.	**1-1** Numerical Expressions **1-2** Algebraic Expressions **1-4** Estimating for Reasonableness **2-2** Adding Integers **2-3** Subtracting Integers **2-4** Multiplying Integers **2-5** Dividing Integers **2-6** Positive Exponents **3-5** Square Roots **3-6** The Pythagorean Theorem **3-7** Using the Pythagorean Theorem **4-1** Prime Factorization **4-2** Greatest Common Divisor **4-3** Equivalent Fractions **5-1** Adding Rational Numbers **5-2** Subtracting Rational Numbers **5-3** Multiplying Rational Numbers **5-4** Dividing Rational Numbers	36 days
NS 1.3	Convert fractions to decimals and percents and use these representations in estimations, computations, and applications.	**4-4** Equivalent Forms of Rational Numbers **4-5** Comparing and Ordering Rational Numbers **5-1** Adding Rational Numbers **7-1** Fractions, Decimals, and Percents **7-2** Finding a Percent of a Number **7-3** Percents and Proportions **7-4** Percent of Change **7-5** Applications of Percent	16 days
NS 1.5	Know that every rational number is either a terminating or repeating decimal and be able to convert terminating decimals into reduced fractions.	**4-4** Equivalent Forms of Rational Numbers **5-2** Subtracting Rational Numbers **5-4** Dividing Rational Numbers	6 days
NS 2.1	Understand negative whole-number exponents. Multiply and divide expressions involving exponents with a common base.	**5-7** Zero and Negative Exponents **10-1** Properties of Exponents **10-2** Power Rules	6 days

Algebra and Functions

Math Content Standard		Prentice Hall Algebra Readiness Math Lessons	Estimated Time
AF 1.1	Use variables and appropriate operations to write an expression, an equation, an inequality, or a system of equations or inequalities that represents a verbal description (e.g., three less than a number, half as large as area A).	**1-3** Writing Expressions **3-1** Solving Addition Equations **3-2** Solving Subtraction Equations **3-3** Solving Multiplication and Division Equations **3-4** Solving Two-Step Equations **5-5** Solving Equations by Adding or Subtracting **5-6** Solving Equations by Multiplying **8-3** Functions **9-1** Writing Inequalities **9-2** Solving Inequalities by Adding or Subtracting **9-3** Solving Inequalities by Dividing **9-4** Solving Inequalities by Multiplying **9-5** Solving Two-Step Inequalities **10-4** Simplifying Algebraic Expressions	28 days
AF 1.3	Simplify numerical expressions by applying properties of rational numbers (e.g., identity, inverse, distributive, associative, commutative) and justify the process used.	**1-5** Properties of Numbers **1-6** Distributive Property **2-2** Adding Integers **3-1** Solving Addition Equations **3-2** Solving Subtraction Equations **3-3** Solving Multiplication and Division Equations **5-5** Solving Equations by Adding or Subtracting **5-6** Solving Equations by Multiplying	16 days
AF 2.1	Interpret positive whole-number powers as repeated multiplication and negative whole-number powers as repeated division or multiplication by the multiplicative inverse. Simplify and evaluate expressions that include exponents.	**2-6** Positive Exponents **4-1** Prime Factorization **5-3** Multiplying Rational Numbers **5-7** Zero and Negative Exponents **10-1** Properties of Exponents **10-2** Power Rules	12 days
AF 3.3	Graph linear functions, noting that the vertical change (change in *y*-value) per unit of horizontal change (change in *x*-value) is always the same and know that the ratio ("rise over run") is called the slope of a graph.	**8-4** Graphing Linear Functions **8-5** Slope **8-6** Slope and Direct Variation	6 days
AF 3.4	Plot the values of quantities whose ratios are always the same (e.g., cost to the number of an item, feet to inches, circumference to diameter of a circle). Fit a line to the plot and understand that the slope of the line equals the ratio of the two quantities.	**8-4** Graphing Linear Functions **8-5** Slope **8-6** Slope and Direct Variation	6 days
AF 4.1	Solve two-step linear equations and inequalities in one variable over the rational numbers, interpret the solution or solutions in the context from which they arose, and verify the reasonableness of the results.	**3-4** Solving Two-Step Equations **5-6** Solving Equations by Multiplying **9-5** Solving Two-Step Inequalities	6 days
AF 4.2	Solve multistep problems involving rate, average speed, distance, and time or a direct variation.	**6-2** Rates **6-4** Applications of Rates **8-6** Slope and Direct Variation	6 days

Key Standards =

Measurement and Geometry

	Math Content Standard	Prentice Hall Algebra Readiness Math Lessons	Estimated Time
MG 1.3	Use measures expressed as rates (e.g., speed, density) and measures expressed as products (e.g., person-days) to solve problems; check the units of the solutions; and use dimensional analysis to check the reasonableness of the answer.	**6-2** Rates **6-3** Dimensional Analysis **6-4** Applications of Rates **6-5** Proportions	8 days
MG 3.3	Know and understand the Pythagorean theorem and its converse and use it to find the length of the missing side of a right triangle and the lengths of other line segments and, in some situations, empirically verify the Pythagorean theorem by direct measurement.	**3-6** The Pythagorean Theorem **3-7** Using the Pythagorean Theorem **8-2** Length in the Coordinate Plane	6 days

Mathematical Reasoning

	Math Content Standard	Prentice Hall Algebra Readiness Math Lessons
MR 1.0	Students make decisions about how to approach problems.	**2-5** Dividing Integers **4-3** Equivalent Fractions **6-5** Proportions **7-3** Percents and Proportions **8-3** Functions
MR 1.1	Analyze problems by identifying relationships, distinguishing relevant from irrelevant information, identifying missing information, sequencing and prioritizing information, and observing patterns.	**4-3** Equivalent Fractions **4-4** Equivalent Forms of Rational Numbers **6-5** Proportions **8-3** Functions
MR 1.2	Formulate and justify mathematical conjectures based on a general description of the mathematical question or problem posed.	**2-2** Adding Integers **2-3** Subtracting Integers **2-4** Multiplying Integers **3-7** Using the Pythagorean Theorem
MR 1.3	Determine when and how to break a problem into simpler parts.	**6-4** Applications of Rates **7-4** Percent of Change **7-5** Applications of Percent
MR.2.0	Students use strategies, skills, and concepts in finding solutions.	**1-3** Writing Expressions **2-5** Dividing Integers **3-4** Solving Two-Step Equations **4-3** Equivalent Fractions **5-2** Subtracting Rational Numbers **6-5** Proportions **7-3** Percents and Proportions **8-4** Graphing Linear Functions **9-5** Solving Two-Step Inequalities **10-5** Solving Multi-Step Equations

Mathematical Reasoning (continued)

Math Content Standard		Prentice Hall Algebra Readiness Math Lessons
MR 2.1	Use estimation to verify the reasonableness of calculated results.	**1-4** Estimating for Reasonableness **3-3** Solving Multiplication and Division Equations **3-4** Solving Two-Step Equations **5-6** Solving Equations by Multiplying **10-2** Power Rules
MR 2.2	Apply strategies and results from simpler problems to more complex problems.	**1-5** Properties of Numbers **3-2** Solving Subtraction Equations **4-5** Comparing and Ordering Rational Numbers **9-5** Solving Two-Step Inequalities **10-4** Simplifying Algebraic Expressions
MR 2.3	Estimate unknown quantities graphically and solve for them by using logical reasoning and arithmetic and algebraic techniques.	**8-4** Graphing Linear Functions **8-6** Slope and Direct Variation
MR 2.4	Make and test conjectures by using both inductive and deductive reasoning.	**2-4** Multiplying Integers **3-3** Solving Multiplication and Division Equations **4-2** Greatest Common Divisor **5-1** Adding Rational Numbers **9-3** Solving Inequalities by Multiplying
MR 2.5	Use a variety of methods, such as words, numbers, symbols, charts, graphs, tables, diagrams, and models, to explain mathematical reasoning.	**1-3** Writing Expressions **1-5** Properties of Numbers **1-6** Distributive Property **2-2** Adding Integers **2-3** Subtracting Integers **3-2** Solving Subtraction Equations **3-4** Solving Two-Step Equations **5-1** Adding Rational Numbers **6-5** Proportions **10-4** Simplifying Algebraic Expressions **10-5** Solving Multi-Step Equations
MR 2.6	Express the solution clearly and logically by using the appropriate mathematical notation and terms and clear language; support solutions with evidence in both verbal and symbolic work.	**1-5** Properties of Numbers **1-6** Distributive Property **3-3** Solving Multiplication and Division Equations **9-5** Solving Two-Step Inequalities **10-5** Solving Multi-Step Equations
MR 2.7	Indicate the relative advantages of exact and approximate solutions to problems and give answers to a specified degree of accuracy.	**1-4** Estimating for Reasonableness **5-2** Subtracting Rational Numbers **7-2** Finding a Percent of a Number
MR 2.8	Make precise calculations and check the validity of the results from the context of the problem.	**3-1** Solving Addition Equations **6-3** Dimensional Analysis **10-6** Solving Equations With Variables on Both Sides
MR 3.0	Students move beyond a particular problem by generalizing to other situations.	**7-2** Finding a Percent of a Number
MR 3.1	Evaluate the reasonableness of the solution in the context of the original situation.	**3-4** Solving Two-Step Equations **7-4** Percent of Change
MR 3.2	Note the method of deriving the solution and demonstrate a conceptual understanding of the derivation by solving similar problems.	**7-2** Finding a Percent of a Number
MR 3.3	Develop generalizations of the results obtained and the strategies used and apply them in new problem situations.	**2-2** Adding Integers **4-3** Equivalent Fractions **9-4** Solving Inequalities by Multiplying

Algebra 1

Math Content Standard		Prentice Hall Algebra Readiness Math Lessons	Estimated Time
Alg1 2.0	Students understand and use such operations as taking the opposite, finding the reciprocal, taking a root, and raising to a fractional power. They understand and use the rules of exponents [*excluding fractional powers*].	**2-1** Integers and Absolute Value **2-3** Subtracting Integers **3-5** Square Roots **3-6** The Pythagorean Theorem **3-7** Using the Pythagorean Theorem **5-4** Dividing Rational Numbers **10-1** Properties of Exponents **10-2** Power Rules **10-3** Exploring Roots	18 days
Alg1 4.0	Students simplify expressions before solving linear equations and inequalities in one variable, such as $3(2x - 5) + 4(x - 2) = 12$ [*excluding inequalities*].	**10-4** Simplifying Algebraic Expressions **10-5** Solving Multi-Step Equations **10-6** Solving Equations with Variables on Both Sides	6 days
Alg1 5.0	Students solve multistep problems, including word problems, involving linear equations and linear inequalities in one variable and provide justification for each step [*excluding inequalities*].	**10-5** Solving Multi-Step Equations **10-6** Solving Equations with Variables on Both Sides	5 days

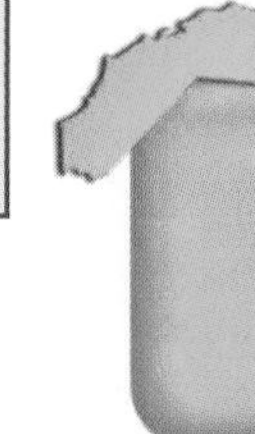

Algebra Readiness Leveled Pacing Chart

This chart is provided as a guide to help you customize your course and to provide for differentiated instruction. This chart covers the content of this book.

The suggested number of days of instruction for each chapter is based on a traditional 45-minute class period and on a 90-minute block period. The total of 160 days of instruction leaves time for assessments, projects, assemblies, or other special days that vary from school to school.

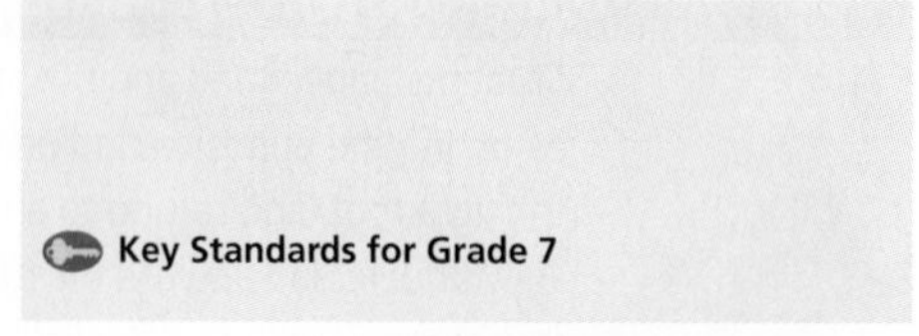

Universal Access

	California Standards	Foundational	Targeted
Chapter 1 Variables and Algebraic Expressions Traditional 14 Block 7			
1-1 Numerical Expressions	NS 1.2	✓	
1-2 Algebraic Expressions	NS 1.2	✓	
1-3 Writing Expressions	AF 1.1, MR 2.0, MR 2.5	✓	✓
1-4 Estimating for Reasonableness	NS 1.2, MR 2.1, MR 2.7	✓	✓
1-5 Properties of Numbers	AF 1.3, MR 2.2, MR 2.5, MR 2.6	✓	✓
1-6 The Distributive Property	AF 1.3, MR 2.5, MR 2.6	✓	✓
Chapter 2 Integers and Exponents Traditional 14 Block 7			
2-1 Integers and Absolute Value	NS 1.2, Alg1 2.0	✓	✓
2-2 Adding Integers	NS 1.2, AF 1.3, MR 1.2, MR 2.5, MR 3.3	✓	✓
2-3 Subtracting Integers	NS 1.2, Alg1 2.0, MR 2.0, MR 2.5	✓	✓
2-4 Multiplying Integers	NS 1.2, MR 1.2, MR 2.4	✓	✓
2-5 Dividing Integers	NS 1.2, MR 1.0, MR 2.0	✓	✓
2-6 Positive Exponents	NS 1.2, AF 2.1		✓
Chapter 3 Equations and Applications Traditional 16 Block 8			
3-1 Solving Addition Equations	AF 1.1, AF 1.3, MR 2.8	✓	✓
3-2 Solving Subtraction Equations	AF 1.1, AF 1.3, MR 2.2, MR 2.5	✓	✓
3-3 Solving Multiplication and Division Equations	AF 1.1, AF 1.3, MR 2.1, MR 2.4, MR 2.6	✓	✓
3-4 Solving Two-Step Equations	AF 1.1, AF 4.1, MR 2.0, MR 2.1, MR 2.5, MR 3.1		✓
3-5 Square Roots	NS 1.2, Alg1 2.0		✓
3-6 The Pythagorean Theorem	NS 1.2, MG 3.3, Alg1 2.0		✓
3-7 Using the Pythagorean Theorem	NS 1.2, MG 3.3, Alg1 2.0, MR 1.2		✓
Chapter 4 Rational Numbers Traditional 12 Block 6			
4-1 Prime Factorization	NS 1.2, AF 2.1	✓	✓
4-2 Greatest Common Divisor	NS 1.2, MR 2.4	✓	
4-3 Equivalent Fractions	NS 1.2, NS 1.5, MR 1.0, MR 1.1	✓	
4-4 Equivalent Forms of Rational Numbers	NS 1.3, NS 1.5, MR 1.1		✓
4-5 Comparing and Ordering Rational Numbers	NS 1.3, MR 2.2	✓	✓

	California Standards	Foundational	Targeted
Chapter 5 Rational Number Operations Traditional 21 Block 10			
5-1 Adding Rational Numbers	NS 1.2, NS 1.3, MR 2.5	✓	✓
5-2 Subtracting Rational Numbers	NS 1.2, NS 1.5, MR 2.7	✓	✓
5-3 Multiplying Rational Numbers	NS 1.2, AF 2.1	✓	✓
5-4 Dividing Rational Numbers	NS 1.2, NS 1.5, Alg1 2.0	✓	✓
5-5 Solving Equations by Adding or Subtracting	AF 1.1, AF 1.3	✓	✓
5-6 Solving Equations by Multiplying	AF 1.1, AF 1.3, AF 4.1, MR 2.1	✓	✓
5-7 Zero and Negative Exponents	NS 2.1, AF 2.1	✓	✓
Chapter 6 Rates and Proportions Traditional 12 Block 6			
6-1 Ratios	AF 3.4, AF 4.2	✓	
6-2 Rates	AF 4.2, MG 1.3	✓	✓
6-3 Dimensional Analysis	MG 1.3, MR 2.8	✓	✓
6-4 Applications of Rates	AF 4.2, MG 1.3, MR 1.3	✓	✓
6-5 Proportions	MG 1.3, MR 1.0, MR 1.1, MR 2.0, MR 2.5	✓	✓
Chapter 7 Applications of Percent Traditional 12 Block 6			
7-1 Fractions, Decimals, and Percents	NS 1.3	✓	✓
7-2 Finding a Percent of a Number	NS 1.3, MR 2.7, MR 3.2	✓	✓
7-3 Percents and Proportions	NS 1.3, MR 1.0, MR 2.0	✓	✓
7-4 Percent of Change	NS 1.3, MR 1.3, MR 3.1	✓	✓
7-5 Applications of Percent	NS 1.3, MR 1.3	✓	✓
Chapter 8 Linear Functions and Graphing Traditional 18 Block 9			
8-1 Graphing in the Coordinate Plane	AF 3.3	✓	
8-2 Length in the Coordinate Plane	MG 3.3	✓	✓
8-3 Functions	AF 1.1, MR 1.0, MR 1.1	✓	✓
8-4 Graphing Linear Functions	AF 3.3, AF 3.4, MR 2.3, MR 2.4	✓	✓
8-5 Slope	AF 3.4, AF 3.4		✓
8-6 Slope and Direct Variation	AF 3.3, AF 3.4, AF 4.2, MR 2.3		✓
Chapter 9 Inequalities Traditional 15 Block 8			
9-1 Writing Inequalities	AF 1.1	✓	✓
9-2 Solving Inequalities by Adding or Subtracting	AF 1.1, AF 4.1	✓	✓
9-3 Solving Inequalities by Dividing	AF 1.1, AF 4.1, MR 2.4	✓	✓
9-4 Solving Inequalities by Multiplying	AF 1.1, AF 4.1, MR 3.3	✓	✓
9-5 Solving Two-Step Inequalities	AF 1.1, AF 4.1, MR 2.0, MR 2.2, MR 2.6		✓
Chapter 10 Exponents and Equations Traditional 18 Block 9			
10-1 Properties of Exponents	NS 2.1, AF 2.1, Alg1 2.0		✓
10-2 Power Rules	NS 2.1, AF 2.1, Alg1 2.0		✓
10-3 Exploring Roots	Alg1 2.0		✓
10-4 Simplifying Algebraic Expressions	AF 1.1, Alg1 4.0, MR 2.5		✓
10-5 Solving Multi-Step Equations	Alg1 4.0, Alg1 5.0, MR 2.0, MR 2.5, MR 2.6		✓
10-6 Solving Equations With Variables on Both Sides	Alg1 4.0, Alg1 5.0, MR 2.8		✓

Aligning with the California Standards and Framework

Prentice Hall Mathematics California Algebra Readiness was developed specifically for California, so you can be confident that mastery of the *California Mathematics Standards for Algebra Readiness* is at the core of the program. The following pages describe some of the ways *Prentice Hall Mathematics California Algebra Readiness* meets and exceeds the Evaluation Criteria outlined by the state:

- Mathematics Content/ Alignment with the standards
- Program Organization
- Universal Access
- Assessment
- Instructional Planning and Support

Mathematics Content/Alignment with the Standards

Prentice Hall California Algebra Readiness is aligned with and addresses 100% of the *California Mathematics Standards for Algebra Readiness*. The following resources will help acquaint you with the program and the way it assures complete and thorough mastery of the Standards.

Support in your California Teacher Edition

These comprehensive correlation charts and content background ensure coverage and understanding of California Standards.

California Standards Correlation

This chart details how the California Content Standards are thoroughly covered. The chart shows the lesson in which each standard is introduced, developed, and mastered. Key standards and foundational standards are denoted as well.

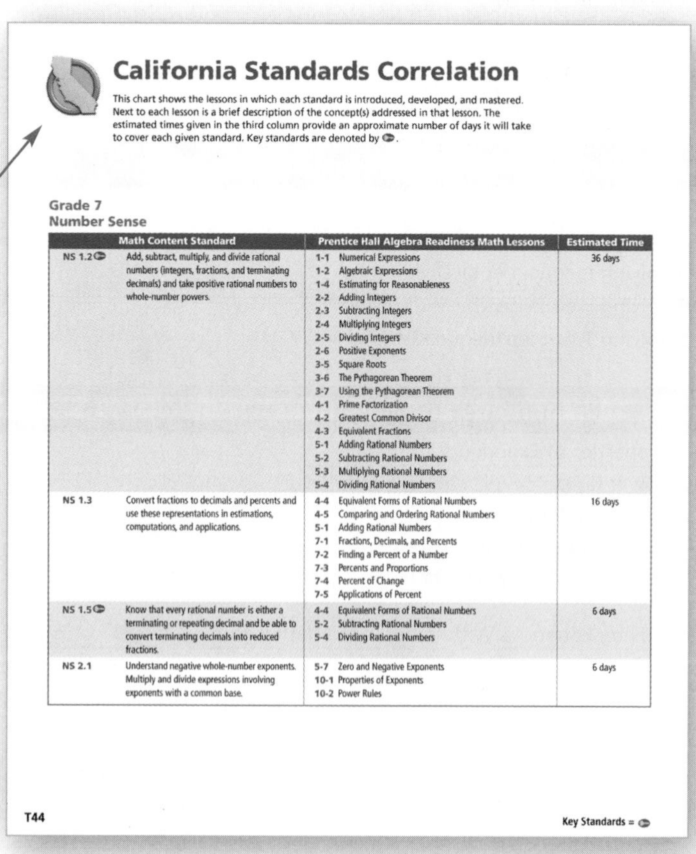

California Standards Correlation

This chart shows the lessons in which each standard is introduced, developed, and mastered. Next to each lesson is a brief description of the concept(s) addressed in that lesson. The estimated times given in the third column provide an approximate number of days it will take to cover each given standard. Key standards are denoted by ●.

Grade 7
Number Sense

Math Content Standard		Prentice Hall Algebra Readiness Math Lessons	Estimated Time
NS 1.2 ●	Add, subtract, multiply, and divide rational numbers (integers, fractions, and terminating decimals) and take positive rational numbers to whole-number powers.	1-1 Numerical Expressions 1-2 Algebraic Expressions 1-4 Estimating for Reasonableness 2-2 Adding Integers 2-3 Subtracting Integers 2-4 Multiplying Integers 2-5 Dividing Integers 2-6 Positive Exponents 3-5 Square Roots 3-6 The Pythagorean Theorem 3-7 Using the Pythagorean Theorem 4-1 Prime Factorization 4-2 Greatest Common Divisor 4-3 Equivalent Fractions 5-1 Adding Rational Numbers 5-2 Subtracting Rational Numbers 5-3 Multiplying Rational Numbers 5-4 Dividing Rational Numbers	36 days
NS 1.3	Convert fractions to decimals and percents and use these representations in estimations, computations, and applications.	4-4 Equivalent Forms of Rational Numbers 4-5 Comparing and Ordering Rational Numbers 5-1 Adding Rational Numbers 7-1 Fractions, Decimals, and Percents 7-2 Finding a Percent of a Number 7-3 Percents and Proportions 7-4 Percent of Change 7-5 Applications of Percent	16 days
NS 1.5 ●	Know that every rational number is either a terminating or repeating decimal and be able to convert terminating decimals into reduced fractions.	4-4 Equivalent Forms of Rational Numbers 5-2 Subtracting Rational Numbers 5-4 Dividing Rational Numbers	6 days
NS 2.1	Understand negative whole-number exponents. Multiply and divide expressions involving exponents with a common base.	5-7 Zero and Negative Exponents 10-1 Properties of Exponents 10-2 Power Rules	6 days

T44

Key Standards = ●

California Leveled Pacing Chart

This chart is provided as a guide to help you customize your course or provide for differentiated instruction. The chart covers the content for the entire book.

California Standards Progression and Background

The California Content Standards flow smoothly from grade level to grade level. Seeing the big picture and understanding the goal of the Standards will help you as you guide your students through the year.

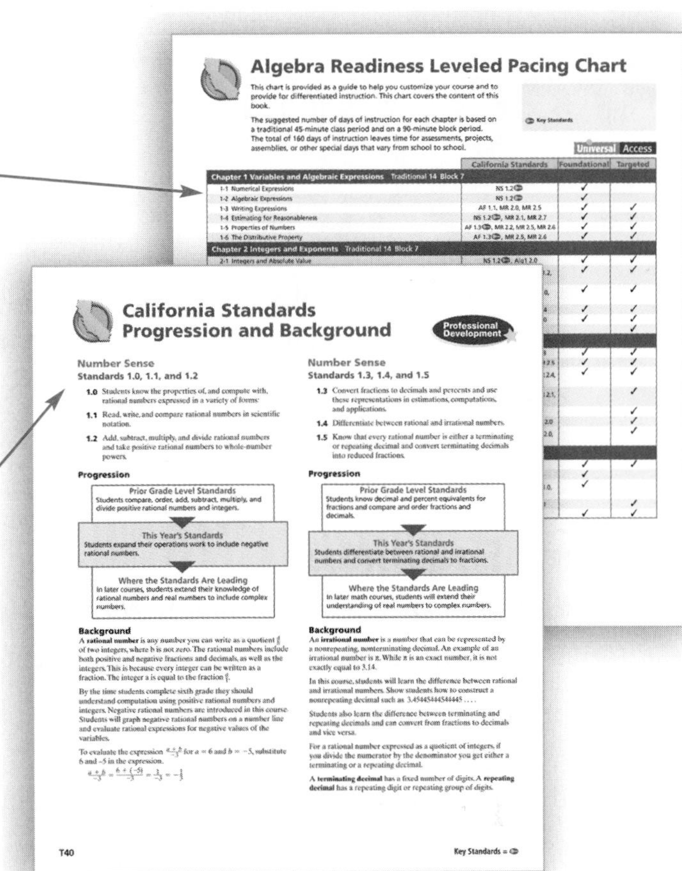

Algebra Readiness Leveled Pacing Chart

This chart is provided as a guide to help you customize your course and to provide for differentiated instruction. This chart covers the content of this book.

The suggested number of days of instruction for each chapter is based on a traditional 45-minute class period and on a 90-minute block period. The total of 160 days of instruction leaves time for assessments, projects, assemblies, or other special days that vary from school to school.

Key Standards

Universal Access

	California Standards	Foundational	Targeted
Chapter 1 Variables and Algebraic Expressions Traditional 14 Block 7			
1-1 Numerical Expressions	NS 1.2	✓	
1-2 Algebraic Expressions	NS 1.2	✓	
1-3 Writing Expressions	AF 1.1, MR 2.0, MR 2.5	✓	✓
1-4 Estimating for Reasonableness	NS 1.2, MR 2.1, MR 2.7	✓	✓
1-5 Properties of Numbers	AF 1.3, MR 2.2, MR 2.5, MR 2.6	✓	✓
1-6 The Distributive Property	AF 1.3, MR 2.5, MR 2.6	✓	✓
Chapter 2 Integers and Exponents Traditional 14 Block 7			
2-1 Integers and Absolute Value	NS 1.2, Alg1 2.0	✓	✓

California Standards Progression and Background

Professional Development

Number Sense
Standards 1.0, 1.1, and 1.2

1.0 Students know the properties of, and compute with, rational numbers expressed in a variety of forms:

1.1 Read, write, and compare rational numbers in scientific notation.

1.2 Add, subtract, multiply, and divide rational numbers and take positive rational numbers to whole-number powers.

Progression

Prior Grade Level Standards
Students compare, order, add, subtract, multiply, and divide positive rational numbers and integers.

This Year's Standards
Students expand their operations work to include negative rational numbers.

Where the Standards Are Leading
In later courses, students extend their knowledge of rational numbers and real numbers to include complex numbers.

Background

A **rational number** is any number you can write as a quotient $\frac{a}{b}$ of two integers, where b is not zero. The rational numbers include both positive and negative fractions and decimals, as well as the integers. This is because every integer can be written as a fraction. The integer a is equal to the fraction $\frac{a}{1}$.

By the time students complete sixth grade they should understand computation using positive rational numbers and integers. Negative rational numbers are introduced in this course. Students will graph negative rational numbers on a number line and evaluate rational expressions for negative values of the variables.

To evaluate the expression $\frac{a+b}{-3}$ for $a = 6$ and $b = -5$, substitute 6 and −5 in the expression.

$$\frac{a+b}{-3} = \frac{6+(-5)}{-3} = \frac{1}{-3} = -\frac{1}{3}$$

Number Sense
Standards 1.3, 1.4, and 1.5

1.3 Convert fractions to decimals and percents and use these representations in estimations, computations, and applications.

1.4 Differentiate between rational and irrational numbers.

1.5 Know that every rational number is either a terminating or repeating decimal and convert terminating decimals into reduced fractions.

Progression

Prior Grade Level Standards
Students know decimal and percent equivalents for fractions and compare and order fractions and decimals.

This Year's Standards
Students differentiate between rational and irrational numbers and convert terminating decimals to fractions.

Where the Standards Are Leading
In later math courses, students will extend their understanding of real numbers to complex numbers.

Background

An **irrational number** is a number that can be represented by a nonrepeating, nonterminating decimal. An example of an irrational number is π. While π is an exact number, it is not exactly equal to 3.14.

In this course, students will learn the difference between rational and irrational numbers. Show students how to construct a nonrepeating decimal such as 3.454454445444445 . . . .

Students also learn the difference between terminating and repeating decimals and can convert from fractions to decimals and vice versa.

For a rational number expressed as a quotient of integers, if you divide the numerator by the denominator you get either a terminating or a repeating decimal.

A **terminating decimal** has a fixed number of digits. A **repeating decimal** has a repeating digit or repeating group of digits.

T40 Key Standards =

Support in your California Student Edition

These features ensure your students know the standards for which they will be accountable and have support using their math textbook for success.

Your Guide to the Standards

This feature includes a complete list of the mathematics content standards, an example problem that involves the math standards, and chapter references where students can expect to study these concepts. An additional section, **Standards Mastery in Your Book**, shows students the special features in the textbook that will help them master the content standards.

Identification of the Standard being covered

Each lesson also includes a point-of-use reference to the content standard covered in that lesson. Furthermore, it also notes whether that standard is being Introduced, Developed, or Mastered.

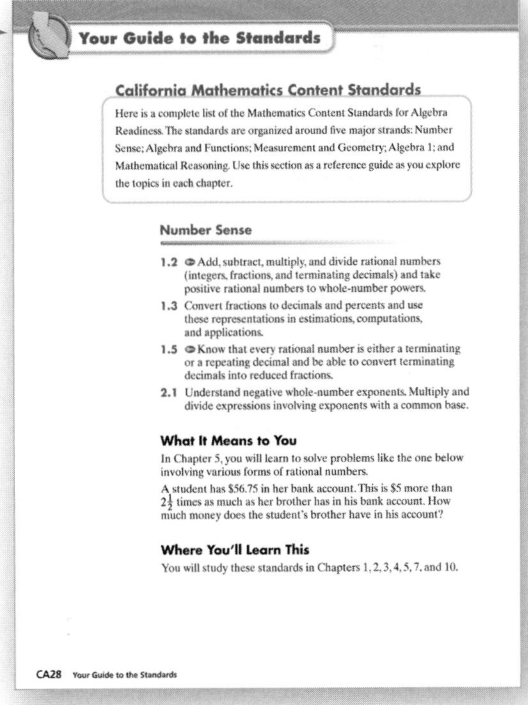

Your Guide to the Standards

California Mathematics Content Standards

Here is a complete list of the Mathematics Content Standards for Algebra Readiness. The standards are organized around five major strands: Number Sense; Algebra and Functions; Measurement and Geometry; Algebra 1; and Mathematical Reasoning. Use this section as a reference guide as you explore the topics in each chapter.

Number Sense

1.2 Add, subtract, multiply, and divide rational numbers (integers, fractions, and terminating decimals) and take positive rational numbers to whole-number powers.

1.3 Convert fractions to decimals and percents and use these representations in estimations, computations, and applications.

1.5 Know that every rational number is either a terminating or a repeating decimal and be able to convert terminating decimals into reduced fractions.

2.1 Understand negative whole-number exponents. Multiply and divide expressions involving exponents with a common base.

What It Means to You

In Chapter 5, you will learn to solve problems like the one below involving various forms of rational numbers.

A student has $56.75 in her bank account. This is $5 more than $2\frac{1}{2}$ times as much as her brother has in his bank account. How much money does the student's brother have in his account?

Where You'll Learn This

You will study these standards in Chapters 1, 2, 3, 4, 5, 7, and 10.

CA28 Your Guide to the Standards

Program Overview

Program Organization

The goal of your *Prentice Hall California Mathematics* textbook is to ensure coverage and mastery of the *California Mathematics Standards*. The sequence of the content, the structure of the daily lesson, and the teacher support provided for each lesson all help achieve this goal.

Content Sequence

Prentice Hall Mathematics California Algebra Readiness is organized with the goal of addressing all of the *California Mathematics Standards*, building concept upon concept and skill upon skill in an order that is pedagogically sound. The Table of Contents shows the smooth flow of the book, with prerequisite skills and concepts presented before the more complex topics that depend on them. Foundational standards are addressed and incorporated throughout every chapter. This allows teachers to cover these important foundational standards when necessary.

Starting the Chapter

Every chapter begins by reviewing the previous *California Mathematics Standards* that have been learned and the standards that will be covered in the chapter. New Vocabulary is identified to prepare students for the chapter. Finally, Check Your Readiness assesses student understanding of necessary prerequisite skills and identifies which lesson they can go to for any necessary remediation.

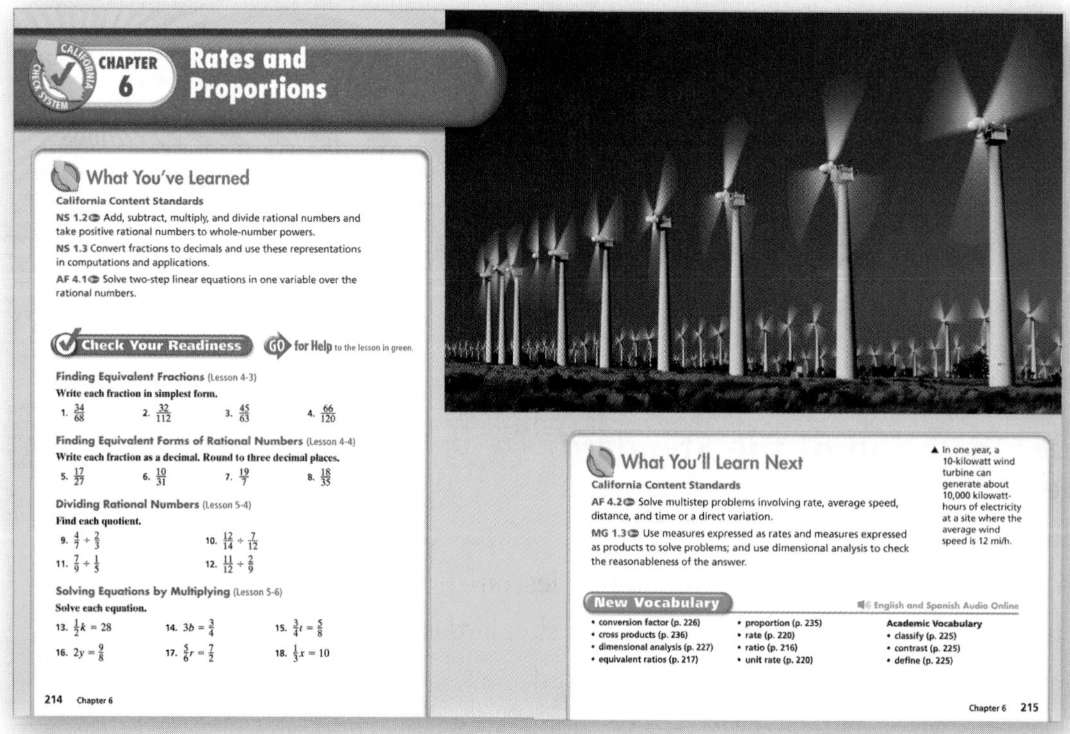

CALIFORNIA CHECK SYSTEM

CHAPTER 6 **Rates and Proportions**

What You've Learned

California Content Standards

NS 1.2 Add, subtract, multiply, and divide rational numbers and take positive rational numbers to whole-number powers.

NS 1.3 Convert fractions to decimals and use these representations in computations and applications.

AF 4.1 Solve two-step linear equations in one variable over the rational numbers.

Check Your Readiness GO for Help to the lesson in green.

Finding Equivalent Fractions (Lesson 4-3)

Write each fraction in simplest form.

1. $\frac{34}{68}$ 2. $\frac{32}{112}$ 3. $\frac{45}{63}$ 4. $\frac{66}{120}$

Finding Equivalent Forms of Rational Numbers (Lesson 4-4)

Write each fraction as a decimal. Round to three decimal places.

5. $\frac{17}{27}$ 6. $\frac{10}{31}$ 7. $\frac{19}{7}$ 8. $\frac{18}{35}$

Dividing Rational Numbers (Lesson 5-4)

Find each quotient.

9. $\frac{4}{7} \div \frac{2}{3}$ 10. $\frac{12}{14} \div \frac{7}{12}$

11. $\frac{7}{9} \div \frac{1}{5}$ 12. $\frac{11}{12} \div \frac{2}{9}$

Solving Equations by Multiplying (Lesson 5-6)

Solve each equation.

13. $\frac{1}{2}k = 28$ 14. $3b = \frac{3}{4}$ 15. $\frac{3}{4}t = \frac{5}{8}$

16. $2y = \frac{9}{8}$ 17. $\frac{5}{6}r = \frac{7}{2}$ 18. $\frac{1}{3}x = 10$

214 Chapter 6

What You'll Learn Next

California Content Standards

AF 4.2 Solve multistep problems involving rate, average speed, distance, and time or a direct variation.

MG 1.3 Use measures expressed as rates and measures expressed as products to solve problems; and use dimensional analysis to check the reasonableness of the answer.

▲ In one year, a 10-kilowatt wind turbine can generate about 10,000 kilowatt-hours of electricity at a site where the average wind speed is 12 mi/h.

New Vocabulary English and Spanish Audio Online

- conversion factor (p. 226)
- cross products (p. 236)
- dimensional analysis (p. 227)
- equivalent ratios (p. 217)
- proportion (p. 235)
- rate (p. 220)
- ratio (p. 216)
- unit rate (p. 220)

Academic Vocabulary

- classify (p. 225)
- contrast (p. 225)
- define (p. 225)

Chapter 6 215

Lesson Organization

The daily lesson is structured and presented in a consistent format that enables you to effectively present the content and monitor student understanding. Furthermore, students know exactly what they will learn and parents can help in the learning process.

- Each lesson identifies the *California Mathematics Standards* being addressed in that lesson, focusing students' attention on the content that will be covered. It is also noted whether the standard is being *Introduced*, *Developed*, or *Mastered* in that lesson.

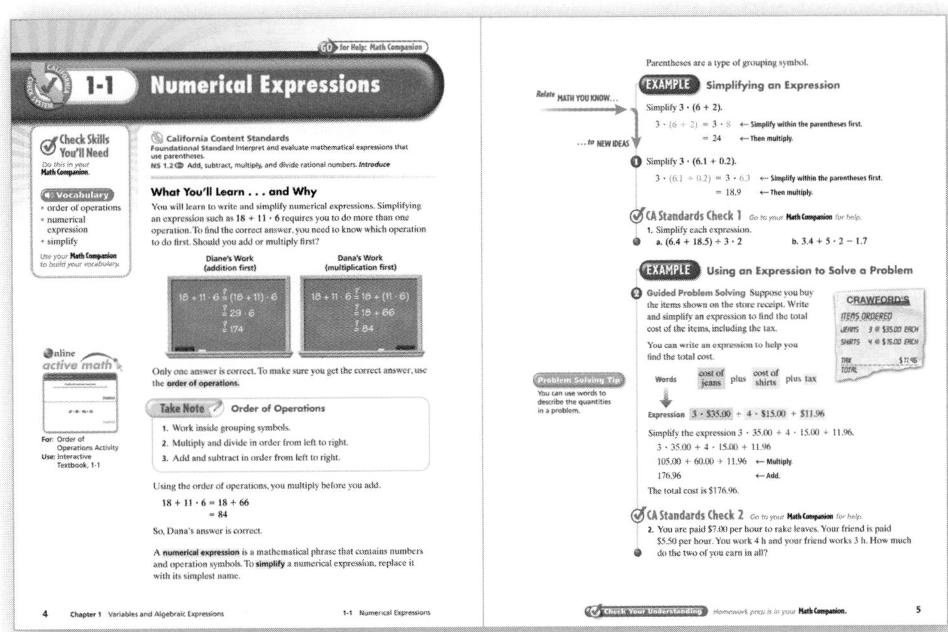

GO for Help: Math Companion

1-1 Numerical Expressions

Check Skills You'll Need
Do this in your **Math Companion**.

Vocabulary
- order of operations
- numerical expression
- simplify

Use your **Math Companion** *to build your vocabulary.*

California Content Standards
Foundational Standard Interpret and evaluate mathematical expressions that use parentheses.
NS 1.2 Add, subtract, multiply, and divide rational numbers. *Introduce*

What You'll Learn . . . and Why

You will learn to write and simplify numerical expressions. Simplifying an expression such as $18 + 11 \cdot 6$ requires you to do more than one operation. To find the correct answer, you need to know which operation to do first. Should you add or multiply first?

Only one answer is correct. To make sure you get the correct answer, use the **order of operations.**

Take Note Order of Operations

1. Work inside grouping symbols.
2. Multiply and divide in order from left to right.
3. Add and subtract in order from left to right.

Using the order of operations, you multiply before you add.

$$18 + 11 \cdot 6 = 18 + 66 = 84$$

So, Dana's answer is correct.

A **numerical expression** is a mathematical phrase that contains numbers and operation symbols. To **simplify** a numerical expression, replace it with its simplest name.

Online active math
For: Order of Operations Activity
Use: Interactive Textbook, 1-1

4 Chapter 1 Variables and Algebraic Expressions 1-1 Numerical Expressions

Parentheses are a type of grouping symbol.

Relate MATH YOU KNOW... ...to NEW IDEAS

EXAMPLE Simplifying an Expression

Simplify $3 \cdot (6 + 2)$.

$3 \cdot (6 + 2) = 3 \cdot 8$ ← Simplify within the parentheses first.
$= 24$ ← Then multiply.

1 Simplify $3 \cdot (6.1 + 0.2)$.

$3 \cdot (6.1 + 0.2) = 3 \cdot 6.3$ ← Simplify within the parentheses first.
$= 18.9$ ← Then multiply.

CA Standards Check 1 *Go to your* **Math Companion** *for help.*

1. Simplify each expression.
a. $(6.4 + 18.5) \div 3 \cdot 2$ b. $3.4 + 5 \cdot 2 - 1.7$

EXAMPLE Using an Expression to Solve a Problem

2 **Guided Problem Solving** Suppose you buy the items shown on the store receipt. Write and simplify an expression to find the total cost of the items, including the tax.

You can write an expression to help you find the total cost.

Words: cost of jeans plus cost of shirts plus tax
Expression: 3 · $35.00 + 4 · $15.00 + $11.96

Simplify the expression $3 \cdot 35.00 + 4 \cdot 15.00 + 11.96$.

$3 \cdot 35.00 + 4 \cdot 15.00 + 11.96$
$105.00 + 60.00 + 11.96$ ← Multiply.
176.96 ← Add.

The total cost is $176.96.

Problem Solving Tip
You can use words to describe the quantities in a problem.

CA Standards Check 2 *Go to your* **Math Companion** *for help.*

2. You are paid $7.00 per hour to rake leaves. Your friend is paid $5.50 per hour. You work 4 h and your friend works 3 h. How much do the two of you earn in all?

Check Your Understanding *Homework prep is in your* **Math Companion.** 5

- **California Check System** is a system of assessments that helps ensure standards mastery. It is comprised of assessments to use before, during, and after instruction to easily and effectively monitor student understanding. Throughout the Student Edition, students are directed to their **Math Companion** to complete these assessments. This provides support throughout every lesson to focus on mastering the standards covered in the lesson.
  —Each lesson begins with *Check Skills You'll Need* to ensure students have the necessary prerequisite skills for success in the lesson. A *Go for Help* reference directs them to a previous lesson if remediation is necessary.
  —*CA Standards Check* questions after every single example provide a way to check student understanding during instruction.
  —*Check Your Understanding* questions are placed prior to independent practice to ensure students are prepared for homework.
  —Finally, *Checkpoint Quizzes* occur throughout the chapter to continually monitor student progress.

- **Daily Standards Practice** is provided with a comprehensive exercise set following every lesson. Each exercise set is leveled to ensure a variety of practice. **Multiple Choice Practice and Mixed Review** ensure students also have a daily opportunity to practice concepts and skills previously mastered.

Concluding the Chapter

The following features conclude each chapter, providing opportunities for students to review all standards and demonstrate mastery. These regular opportunities for review and practice ensure focus on and mastery of the Standards.

Chapter Review

The Chapter Review serves as a chapter study guide for students by reviewing the key concepts covered in each lesson and providing an opportunity to practice. In addition, key vocabulary is reviewed.

Chapter Test

Students demonstrate their understanding of the entire chapter by completing this practice chapter test.

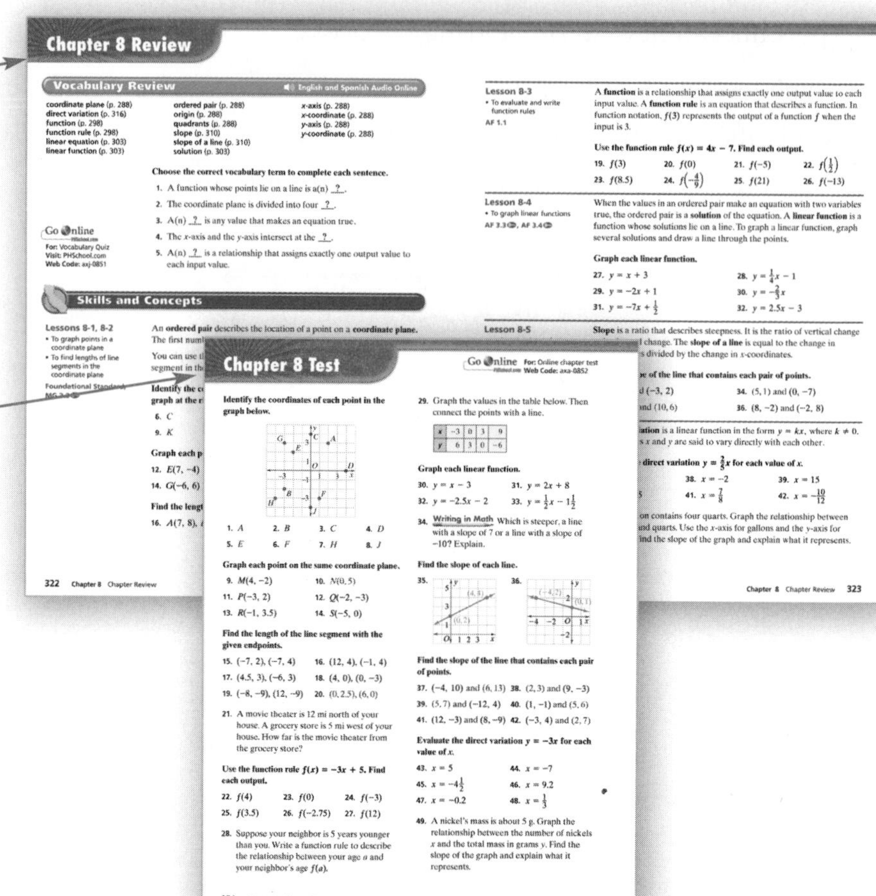

Standards Mastery Cumulative Practice

This provides a regular opportunity for students to practice and demonstrate mastery of all the California Standards that have been covered. If remediation is necessary, students are directed to previous lesson where each concept was taught. A reference chart correlates every practice item to the California Standard it assessed.

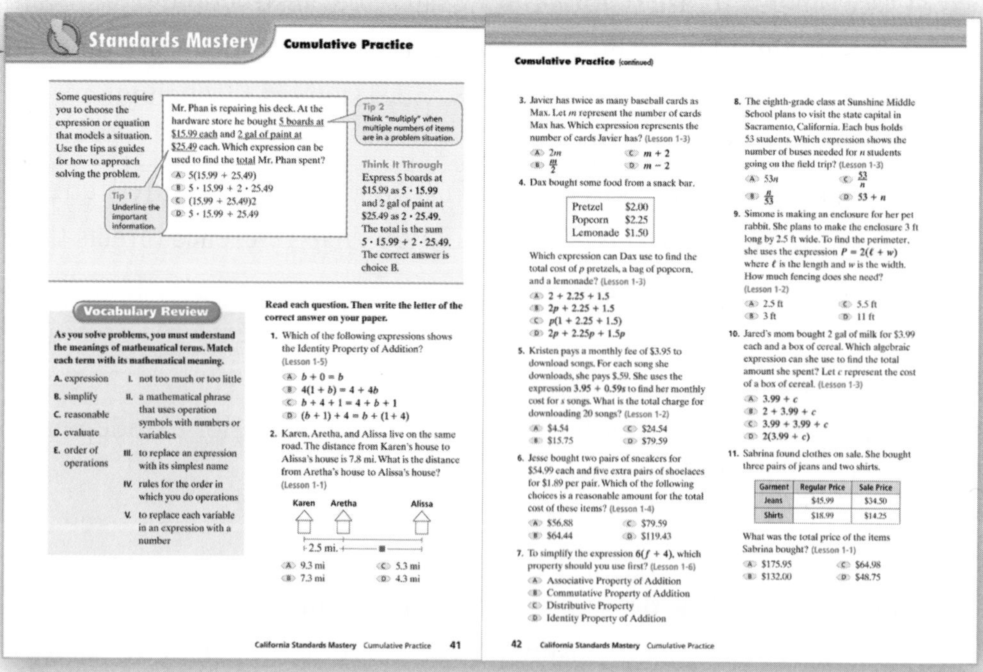

Extending the Learning

Additional feature pages exist in each chapter to deepen students' understanding of the *California Mathematics Standards*. The Student Edition Table of Contents provides an at-a-glance overview of where these feature pages occur in each chapter. Each feature page includes the *California Mathematics Standard* being addressed.

Guided Problem Solving

These features provide scaffolded support in solving problems. The student walks through how to solve one representative problem, focusing on both the reasoning and the computation that must be done.

Activity Labs

These features provide students with an opportunity to complete more in-depth problems and apply the mathematical content they're learning.

Vocabulary Builders

Understanding mathematical and academic vocabulary is an important part of mastering the standards. These feature pages provide an opportunity to focus on key vocabulary terms.

Mathematical Reasoning

Although coverage of Mathematical Reasoning standards is woven throughout the entire program, these feature pages provide students with opportunities to apply what they've learned and focus on the Mathematical Reasoning standards.

Math Companion Workbook

This innovative resource for students provides complete in-class support for learning the Standards. It was designed to work with the Student Edition by providing a place to practice the concepts, skills, and vocabulary from each lesson. Consistent references throughout the Student Edition direct students when to use the Math Companion, including:

- **Check Skills You'll Need**—Students use their Math Companion to review the skills needed to be successful with each lesson.
- **Vocabulary**—Building math vocabulary is an important part of mastering the standards. Students use their Math Companion to learn and understand the vocabulary words for each lesson.
- **California Standards Check**—Students use their Math Companion to check understanding of each of the examples from their Student Edition. This provides an opportunity to practice the standards being taught.
- **Check Your Understanding**—Students use their Math Companion to make sure they're ready to tackle homework.

Assessment

Assessment is integral to mathematics instruction. Assessment should occur often and with a variety of different measures. *Prentice Hall California Mathematics* provides an ongoing assessment strand that addresses assessment for learning and assessment of learning. The formative assessment features – before and during instruction – offer a variety of methods for teachers to assess student understanding of the *California Mathematics Standards* being taught and to help inform future instruction. The summative assessment features – after instruction – document student mastery of the *California Mathematics Standards*.

California Check System—Ongoing Assessment in each lesson

This unique feature of *Prentice Hall California Mathematics* ensures students make progress every day, in every lesson. A feature in every lesson, it helps teachers assess necessary prerequisite skills and monitor student understanding throughout instruction. The California Check System assessments include:

- Check Your Readiness—Assesses prerequisite skills before each chapter
- Check Skills You'll Need—Assesses prerequisite skills for each lesson
- CA Standards Check—Assesses student understanding after every example in the book

California Progress Monitoring Assessments

This comprehensive teacher support resource contains all the program assessments needed to evaluate student understanding, monitor student progress, and inform future instruction. The following assessments are included:

Formative Assessments

- **Screening Test**—checks student readiness at the beginning of the school year
- **California Benchmark Tests**—monitor student progress on targeted California math content standards at regular intervals
- **Test-Taking Strategy Practice Masters**—provide opportunities to improve problem-solving skills

Summative Assessments

- **Quarter Tests**—regular and below level versions
- **Mid-Course Tests**—regular and below level versions
- **Final Tests**—regular and below level versions

California Standards Review and Preparation Workbook

This workbook contains review lessons and multiple-choice practice items for each of the California Math Content Standards for Algebra Readiness, providing regular assessment and monitoring of standards mastery.

Using Assessment Technology

Technology can greatly ease the assessment process for teachers and also improve its quality. *Prentice Hall California Mathematics* includes technology products that generate assessments, calculate results, and provide remediation.

Teacher Center: Exam*View*® CD-ROM

The Teacher Center: **Exam***View*® test generator allows teachers to create customized tests from banks of thousands of questions. The test bank questions are based on content covered in the Student Editions and are all aligned to the *California Mathematics Content Standards*. Questions can be sorted by many criteria, including California standards, difficulty levels, textbook objectives – even by textbook examples to provide leveled quizzes and tests for universal access.

SuccessTracker

Prentice Hall's online Success Tracker™ provides comprehensive support for monitoring student progress and providing personalized remediation. SuccessTracker™ can:

- **Assess student progress**—Teachers can assign three types of built-in assessments:
  1) Diagnostic tests to assess student readiness,
  2) California Benchmark tests to assess student progress on the *California Mathematics Content Standards*, and
  3) Math topic tests to assess student understanding of specific mathematical strands.
- **Diagnose student strengths and weaknesses**—For each assessment, Success Tracker™ *automatically* diagnoses student mastery of each standard or skill.
- **Provide personalized remediation**—Based on each student's performance, SuccessTracker™ provides an individual remediation plan. Students complete their assessments online. Remediation activities assigned include videos, tutorials, games, audio, and worksheets.
- **Generate Reports**—Success Tracker™ generates comprehensive, color-coded reports showing test scores, California standards mastery, and class performance.

Universal Access

Universal Access can be fostered by modifying instruction to address individual needs. Lesson plans in the Teacher's Edition provide universal access strategies and suggest additional ancillary support. Below are some general instructions for modifying instruction for Special Needs students, English Language Learners, and Advanced students.

Instructional Support for providing Universal Access

Prentice Hall uses a consistent method for labeling and identifying resources and instructional support. This consistency helps you easily identify and choose the appropriate support for your students.

- L1 Special Needs
- L2 Below Level
- L3 All Students
- L4 Advanced Learners
- ELL English Language Learners

Daily Universal Access Teaching Notes

Daily teaching notes help you differentiate the lesson for all learners, including special needs, below level, Advanced and English Language Learners.

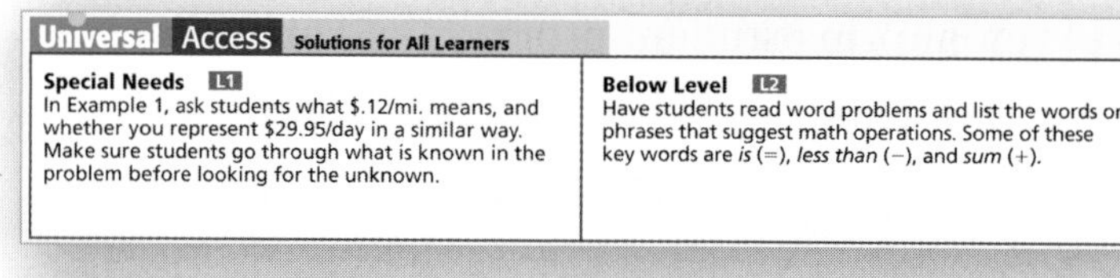

Universal Access Solutions for All Learners

Special Needs L1
In Example 1, ask students what $.12/mi. means, and whether you represent $29.95/day in a similar way. Make sure students go through what is known in the problem before looking for the unknown.

Below Level L2
Have students read word problems and list the words or phrases that suggest math operations. Some of these key words are *is* (=), *less than* (−), and *sum* (+).

Advanced Learners L4
Give students a variable equation. Have students write a word problem that can be solved by using the given equation.

English Learners EL
Translating words to algebraic equations is linguistically challenging. In Example 1, the words *two days* translate to *2*, not *2d*, while the rate *$29.95/day* translates to *29.95* not *$29.95d*.

Planning and Using Universal Access Resources

Chapter-level support pages provide you with an easy-to-read overview of the resources available and suggests ways in the instructional lesson to use the resources.

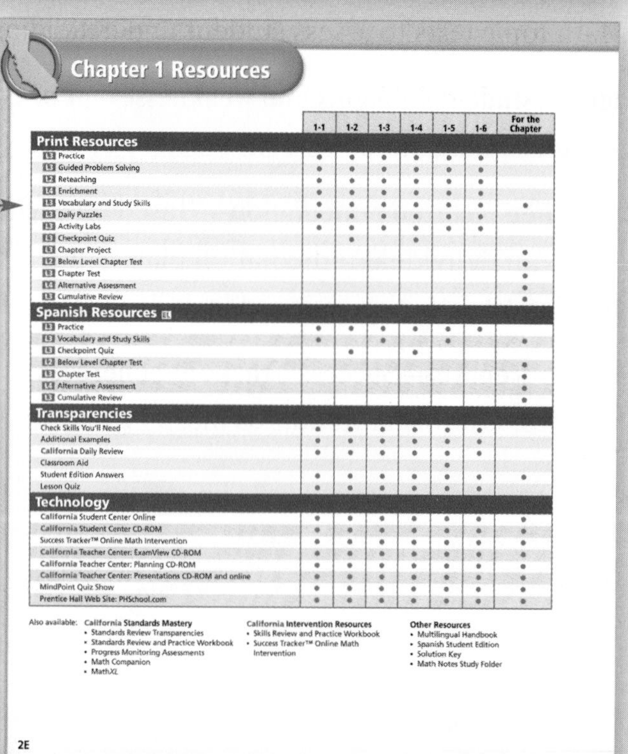

Chapter 1 Resources

	1-1	1-2	1-3	1-4	1-5	1-6	For the Chapter
Print Resources							
L3 Practice	•	•	•	•	•	•	
L3 Guided Problem Solving	•	•	•	•	•	•	
L2 Reteaching	•	•	•	•	•	•	
L4 Enrichment	•	•	•	•	•	•	
L3 Vocabulary and Study Skills	•	•	•	•	•	•	•
L3 Daily Puzzles	•	•	•	•	•	•	
L3 Activity Labs	•	•	•	•	•	•	
L3 Checkpoint Quiz		•		•			
L3 Chapter Project							•
L2 Below Level Chapter Test							•
L3 Chapter Test							•
L4 Alternative Assessment							•
L3 Cumulative Review							•
Spanish Resources EL							
L3 Practice	•	•	•	•	•	•	
L3 Vocabulary and Study Skills	•		•		•		•
L3 Checkpoint Quiz		•		•			
L2 Below Level Chapter Test							•
L3 Chapter Test							•
L4 Alternative Assessment							•
L3 Cumulative Review							•
Transparencies							
Check Skills You'll Need	•	•	•	•	•	•	
Additional Examples	•	•	•	•	•	•	
California Daily Review	•	•	•	•	•	•	
Classroom Aid					•		
Student Edition Answers	•	•	•	•	•	•	•
Lesson Quiz	•	•	•	•	•	•	
Technology							
California Student Center Online	•	•	•	•	•	•	•
California Student Center CD-ROM	•	•	•	•	•	•	•
Success Tracker™ Online Math Intervention	•	•	•	•	•	•	•
California Teacher Center: ExamView CD-ROM	•	•	•	•	•	•	•
California Teacher Center: Planning CD-ROM	•	•	•	•	•	•	•
California Teacher Center: Presentations CD-ROM and online	•	•	•	•	•	•	•
MindPoint Quiz Show	•	•	•	•	•	•	•
Prentice Hall Web Site: PHSchool.com	•	•	•	•	•	•	•

Also available:

California Standards Mastery
- Standards Review Transparencies
- Standards Review and Practice Workbook
- Progress Monitoring Assessments
- Math Companion
- MathXL

California Intervention Resources
- Skills Review and Practice Workbook
- Success Tracker™ Online Math Intervention

Other Resources
- Multilingual Handbook
- Spanish Student Edition
- Solution Key
- Math Notes Study Folder

2E

Resources for Specific Student Populations

Below is an overview of some of the resources that are a part of *Prentice Hall California Mathematics* to help meet the needs of all students during instruction.

Special Needs

Students with special education needs have unique cognitive needs, and need modifications to help support their learning. Set clear expectations and provide reasonable choices for students. Plan lessons with individual adaptations and modifications.

Student Workbook

Prentice Hall offers a Student Workbook to support students in practicing the lesson's mathematics. This workbook consists of:

- Practice for every lesson
- Guided problem solving pages for every lesson with scaffolded questions
- Vocabulary and study skills focusing on key mathematical vocabulary

English Learners

Students who are learning English require preteaching because they are more apt to have limited background knowledge and weak English vocabulary. Focusing on mathematical and academic vocabulary, along with visual presentation of the mathematics will help support their learning.

Prentice Hall Resources:

- **Spanish Program Resources**—Spanish Student Editions, Spanish Practice Workbooks, and Spanish Assessment Resources (including regular and below-level Chapter tests)
- **Multilingual Handbook**—Glossary of key terms in 7 different languages.
- **Vocabulary Worksheets**—Format of these worksheets include Visual Vocabulary, Graphic Organizers, and Vocabulary Review
- **Exam*View*® Assessment Suite**—Translates any test or practice sheet into Spanish automatically

Gifted and Talented Students And Advanced Learners

Gifted and talented students and advanced learners tend to understand complex concepts quickly, learn more rapidly, and comprehend in greater depth. Modify pacing to allow for exploring topics in depth.

Prentice Hall Resources:

- **Daily Challenge Exercises** in every lesson to stretch the thinking of students who would benefit from a challenge.
- **Chapter Projects** give your advanced students opportunities to broaden their understanding of the content covered in each chapter.
- **Daily Enrichment Worksheets** are available to extend their learning
- **Alternative Assessments**—These program assessments require higher-level thinking and a demonstration of a deep understanding of the mathematics.

Instructional Planning and Support

Prentice Hall California Mathematics was designed to provide you the tools needed to effectively and easily implement the program in your classroom.

A Road Map for Planning the Year

The Leveled Pacing Chart provided in your Teacher's Edition lays out a plan for teaching all the mathematics content required by the standards. It suggests time to spend on each chapter, and offers support for adjusting the instruction to meeting the pacing needs of all students.

Planning a Chapter

The Teacher's Edition begins each chapter with a series of planning pages. These pages provide an overview of the chapter and make it easy to determine how to individualize lessons for specific students. The chapter planning pages include:

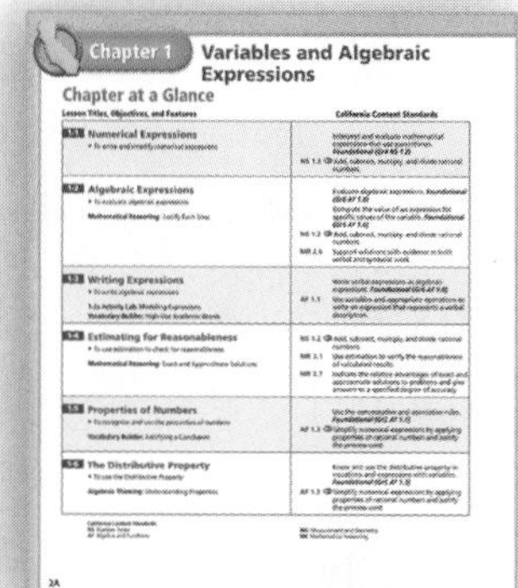

- **Chapter at a Glance—** This features lists the primary mathematics content standards for each lesson and the lesson objectives.

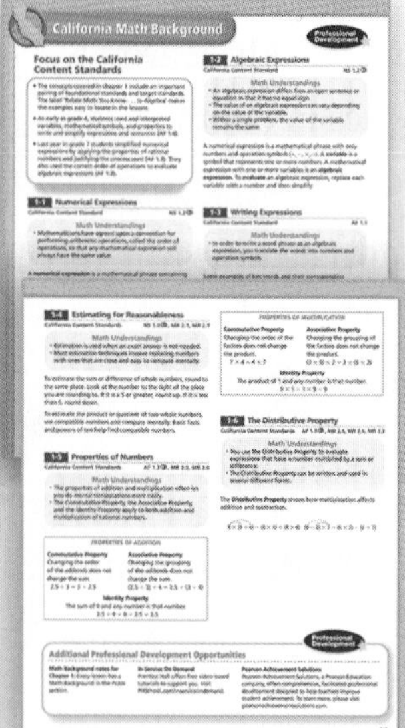

- **California Math Background—** This feature provides in-depth information about the mathematics content in each lesson. Especially useful for new teachers, these Background pages help support teachers' understanding of the content.

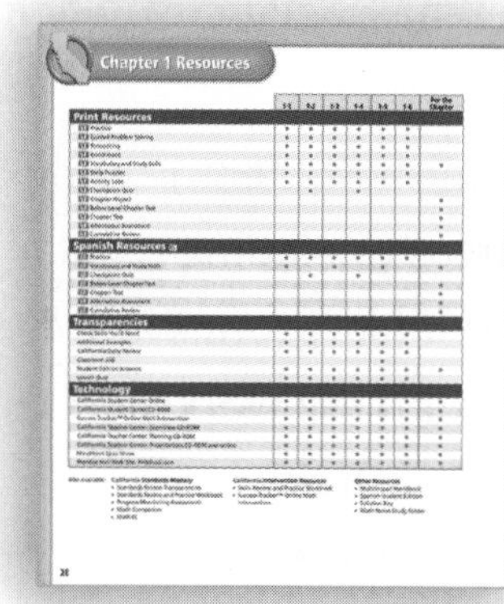

- **Chapter Resources—** This comprehensive spread provides a complete list of all the Print Resources, English Learner Resources, Transparencies, and Technology support for every lesson. This provides a one-stop place for teachers to see all the resources that exist to support them.

- **Where You can Use the Lesson Resources—**This chart provides support for using a 4-step teaching plan (Plan, Teach, Practice, and Assess/Reteach) and provides an overview of how to achieve Universal Access by using the resources available to you.

Planning Daily Instruction

Teachers can use a variety of program materials to organize their teaching. The primary planning tools are the California Teacher's Edition and the Teacher Center Planning Tools CD-ROM. The Teacher's Edition includes step-by-step, daily support for directing instruction. Support is organized around a 4-step teaching plan of Plan, Teach, Practice, and Assess/Reteach.

Using Technology for Teacher Support—Technology can aid teachers in numerous ways:

- Working with electronic lesson plans can save time
- Teacher can obtain instant access to teaching resources
- Online links can provide quick opportunities for professional growth
- Technology provides tools that enhance lessons
- Electronic Assessment tools improve teachers' opportunities to plan, teach and assess the California standards

The Teacher Center Planning Tools CD-ROM is a key tool for lesson planning. This product includes worksheets and other materials integrated with the content in the Student and Teacher's Editions. It enables teachers to align content with standards, track standards coverage, address universal access, and view teaching resources electronically.

In-Service On Demand

To further support you as you plan your instruction, Prentice Hall offers In-Service On Demand to help you learn the resources and technology that are a part of *Prentice Hall California Mathematics*. In-Service On Demand is a collection of easy-to-use online tutorials, that you can access any time at PHSchool.com.

Using the Problem Solving Plan

Throughout this text, students will be encouraged to use the four-step problem-solving plan that is outlined in this lesson. This approach gives students a simple yet effective framework for organizing their work in the process of solving a problem. Rather than having students haphazardly approach the task of problem solving, this four-step plan gives them an organized procedure to follow for a wide range of problems.

Guided Instruction

Students should remember these key phrases: Understand the Problem; Make a Plan; Carry out the Plan; Check for Reasonableness.

Call attention to the list of problem-solving strategies in the text. Ask for an example of each.

Have students brainstorm strategies that they can use to solve real-world problems such as Make a Table. Write up their ideas on poster board and display them in the room for students' reference.

Error Prevention!

Students often focus on one condition of a problem and forget another. Stress the importance of checking that a proposed solution satisfies all the conditions of the problem.

California Standards

MR 3.2 Note the method of deriving the solution and demonstrate a conceptual understanding of the derivation by solving similar problems. ***Develop***

MR 3.3 Develop generalizations of the results obtained and the strategies used and apply them to new problem situations. ***Develop***

Using the Problem Solving Plan

One of the most important skills you can have is the ability to solve problems. An integral part of learning mathematics is how adept you become at unraveling problems and looking back to see how you found the solution. Maybe you don't realize it, but you solve problems every day—some problems are easy to solve, and others are challenging and require a good plan of action. In this Problem Solving Handbook, you will learn how to work through mathematical problems using a simple four-step plan:

THE 4-STEP PLAN

1. **Understand** **Understand the problem.**
   Read the problem. Ask yourself, "What information is given? What is missing? What am I being asked to find or to do?"

2. **Plan** **Make a plan to solve the problem.**
   Choose a strategy. As you use problem solving strategies throughout this book, you will decide which one is best for the problem you are trying to solve.

3. **Carry Out** **Carry out the plan.**
   Solve the problem using your plan. Organize your work.

4. **Check** **Check the answer to be sure it is reasonable.**
   Look back at your work and compare it against the information and question(s) in the problem. Ask yourself, "Is my answer reasonable? Did I check my work?"

Problem Solving Strategies

Creating a good plan to solve a problem means that you will need to choose a reasoning strategy. What is the best way to solve that challenging problem? Perhaps drawing a diagram or making a table will lead to a solution. A problem might seem to have too many steps. Maybe simplifying the problem is the key. There are a number of reasoning strategies to choose from. You must decide which strategy is most effective.

As you work through this book, you will encounter many opportunities to improve your problem solving and reasoning skills. Working through mathematical problems using this four-step process will help you to organize your thoughts, develop your reasoning skills, and explain how you arrived at a particular solution.

Putting this problem solving plan to use will allow you to work through mathematical problems with confidence. Getting in the habit of planning and strategizing for problem solving will result in success in future math courses and high scores on those really important tests!

THE STRATEGIES

Here are some examples of problem solving strategies. Which one will work best for the problem you are trying to solve?

- **Draw a Diagram**
- **Look for a Pattern**
- **Try, Test, Revise**
- **Simulate a Problem**
- **Make a Table**
- **Simplify a Problem**
- **Work Backward**
- **Write an Equation**

Good Luck!

Data Analysis Connection
Point out that problem-solving strategies are used to solve many types of problems, mathematical and non-mathematical.
Ask questions such as:

- *What are some real-world problems that scientists, mathematicians, professional athletes and coaches, or other professionals might need to analyze?* Accept all reasonable answers.

Universal Access

Visual Learners
To help students remember the four steps of the Problem-Solving Plan, display these phrases on a poster and have students suggest graphics to illustrate each. For instance, they might suggest a telescope to signal Check for Reasonableness.

Draw a Diagram

Draw a Diagram is a visual problem-solving strategy that helps students clarify what information is known and what information remains unknown.

Guided Instruction

Use a concrete model. Cut a piece of cardboard into a rectangular shape (for example, 3 ft long and 4 in. wide). Explain that this represents a board w (for whole) feet long. Mark the board as if to cut off a segment c feet (for cut off) long. Ask students to represent the length that is left after the cut with an algebraic expression. $w - c$.

Elicit the problem solving steps:

- Understand the Problem
- Make a Plan
- Carry Out the Plan
- Check the Answer

Error Prevention!

Drawing a picture can also help students check the reasonableness of their answers by using their picture to remember to which measurements their answers refer.

Universal Access

Tactile Learners

Have students make models similar to the one you may have used for the demonstration. Ask how long the leftover piece is. Then discuss how to apply this thinking to the kite problem.

MR 1.1 Analyze problems by identifying relationships. ***Develop***

MR 2.5 Use a variety of methods, such as diagrams, to explain mathematical reasoning. ***Develop***

Draw a Diagram

When to Use This Strategy Some word problems are hard to solve mentally. In such cases, you can *draw a diagram* of the problem.

The tail of a kite steadies the kite in the air. One of the longest kites is a Chinese dragon kite. The length of one dragon kite, including its tail, is 21 ft. If the tail is 15 ft longer than the kite body, how long is the body of the kite?

Understand The combined length of the kite tail and body is 21 ft. The tail is 15 ft longer than the kite body. The goal is to find the length of the kite body.

Plan *Draw a diagram* to show that the kite with its tail is 21 ft long and the tail is 15 ft longer than the body.

Carry Out The diagram shows that the total length of 21 ft is equal to 15 ft plus two body lengths.

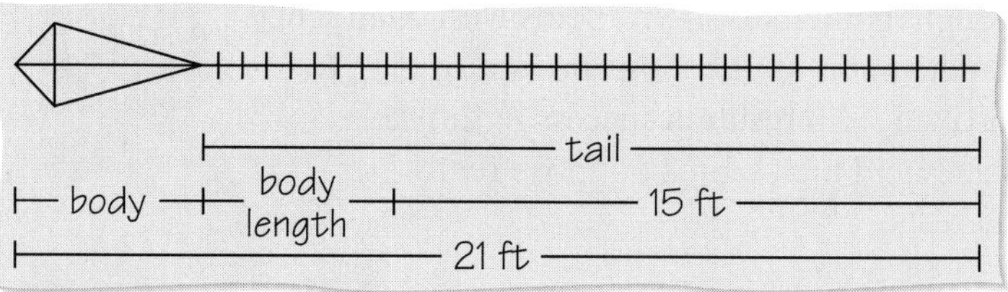

Subtracting 15 ft from 21 ft results in 6 ft, which is twice the body length. The kite's body length is 3 ft.

Check If the body is 3 ft, then the length of the tail is 3 ft + 15 ft = 18 ft. The length of the kite is then 3 ft + 18 ft = 21 ft. The answer checks.

Practice

1. Your aunt is building a garden in her backyard. She has 90 ft of fencing to surround it. If she wants the length to be 15 ft longer than the width, what should the dimensions of her garden be? **30 ft by 15 ft**
2. You bike 32 mi in two days. On the second day, you bike 9 mi more than on the first day. How many miles do you bike each day? **11.5 mi and 20.5 mi**
3. If you have 20 yd of ribbon and need to cut it into 2-yd lengths, how many cuts do you have to make? **9 cuts**

California Standards

MR 1.1 Analyze problems by observing patterns. ***Develop***
MR 2.4 Make and test conjectures by using both inductive and deductive reasoning. ***Introduce***

Look for a Pattern

When to Use This Strategy In problems where more objects are added, you can *look for a pattern* to solve the problem. When you make a conjecture based on a pattern, you are using *inductive reasoning*.

A rectangular table seats two people on each end and three on each side. How many seats are available if you push the ends of five tables together?

Understand There are five rectangular tables. Each table seats two people on each end and three on a side.

Plan To find the number of seats when five tables are pushed together, start by finding the number of seats when there are fewer tables.

Carry Out Start with 1, 2, and 3 tables.

1 table → 10 seats

2 tables → 16 seats

3 tables → 22 seats

Extend the pattern by adding six seats for each new table.

Number of Tables	1	2	3	4	5
Number of Seats	10	16	22	28	34

Check Five tables pushed together seat $5 \cdot 6$, or 30, people on the sides and 2 people on each end, or $30 + 2 + 2 = 34$.

Practice

1. A high school student has started a new job. He plans to save $1 in the first week, $2 in the second week, $4 in the third week, and $8 in the fourth week. If this pattern of savings could continue, how much would he save in the tenth week? **$512**

2. Your younger brother is pulling a sled up a hill. Each minute he moves forward 20 ft but also slides back 3 ft. How long will it take him to pull his sled 130 ft up the hill? **about 8 min**

Look for a Pattern

Look for a Pattern often "partners" with other problem-solving strategies. In this lesson, the partner is *Make a Table.*

Guided Instruction

Point out to students that they are also using the problem-solving strategy *Draw a Picture.* Have four student volunteers read the text aloud. Have each point out one problem-solving step.

- Understand the Problem
- Make a Plan
- Carry Out the Plan
- Check the Answer

Universal Access

Special Needs L1

Give students several blank 2-in.-by-3-in. cards. Have them label the 2-in. sides "2 seats" and the 3-in. sides "3 seats." Students use the cards to form the rectangle chains and calculate the number of available seats.

Try, Test, Revise

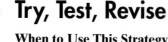

Guessing possible solutions to a problem may initially give students an entry point to understanding the problem, but they may feel discouraged if they don't begin to see relevant connections to the problem. Being systematic about their trials—making choices, knowing why they made those choices, recording their trials and observing any patterns that emerge, and checking their solutions—can help students make reasonable estimates and more accurately solve problems.

Guided Instruction

Have a volunteer read the problem.

Elicit the problem solving steps:

- Understand the Problem
- Make a Plan
- Carry Out the Plan
- Check the Answer

Teaching Tip
Encourage students to try different strategies to solve problems and compare approaches with other students.

Universal Access

Tactile Learners
Have students use coins to model and make sense of the problem.

California Standards

MR 1.2 Formulate and justify mathematical conjectures based on a general description of the mathematical question or problem posed. ***Develop***

MR 2.8 Make precise calculations and check the validity of the results from the context of the problem. ***Develop***

MR 3.1 Evaluate the reasonableness of the solution in the context of the original situation. ***Develop***

Try, Test, Revise

When to Use This Strategy Use *Try, Test, Revise* in situations where you can make a conjecture and then, based on the result, make a better conjecture.

Your friend used equal numbers of quarters and nickels in a vending machine to buy a drink for $1.20. How many quarters and how many nickels did your friend use?

Understand The drink cost $1.20. He paid with equal numbers of quarters and nickels. You need to find how many of each it will take to add up to $1.20.

Plan Use *Try, Test, Revise* to find the answer. Make a table to record your conjectures.

Carry Out Start the table with a conjecture. Suppose you use one quarter and one nickel. From the table, you can see how the result of each conjecture helps you make a better conjecture.

CONJECTURE Number, n	TEST $n \cdot \$.25 + n \cdot \$.05 =$	RESULT Compare to $1.20
1	$1 \cdot \$.25 + 1 \cdot \$.05 = \$.30$	too low
2	$2 \cdot \$.25 + 2 \cdot \$.05 = \$.60$	too low
5	$5 \cdot \$.25 + 5 \cdot \$.05 = \$1.50$	too high
4	$4 \cdot \$.25 + 4 \cdot \$.05 = \$1.20$	correct

You friend used four quarters and four nickels to make $1.20.

Check Another way to think about this problem is to consider that one quarter and one nickel are worth $.30. How many times does 30 go into 120? The answer is 4 times, so you need four of each coin.

Practice

1. A groomer clips the claws of 40 dogs and birds. There are 110 feet among them. How many dogs and how many birds are there? 15 dogs, 25 birds
2. You can buy balloons in packages of 25 or packages of 75. Suppose you buy 8 packages and have 450 balloons in all. How many packages of each size do you buy? 5 packages of 75, 3 packages of 25

MR 2.5 Use a variety of methods, such as models, to explain mathematical reasoning. ***Develop***

Simulate a Problem

When to Use This Strategy Sometimes the best way to solve a problem is to simulate the actions described in the problem.

Ten students stand in a circle. Starting with the first student, the teacher begins counting as follows: "One, two, three, four, five, six, out!" When a student is called out, he or she has to leave the circle. The teacher then continues until only one student is left. Which student is it?

Understand The teacher is counting out every seventh student as she goes around in a circle. The students are numbered 1 to 10. You need to find the number of the last student left in.

Plan Using 10 pennies, you can *simulate the problem* and see who wins.

Carry Out Arrange the pennies in a circle. Start counting, pointing at the pennies one at a time. Every time you reach seven, remove the penny you point to. When you are done counting, you are left with the ninth penny. The ninth student is left.

Check If you complete the table, you can get the same result.

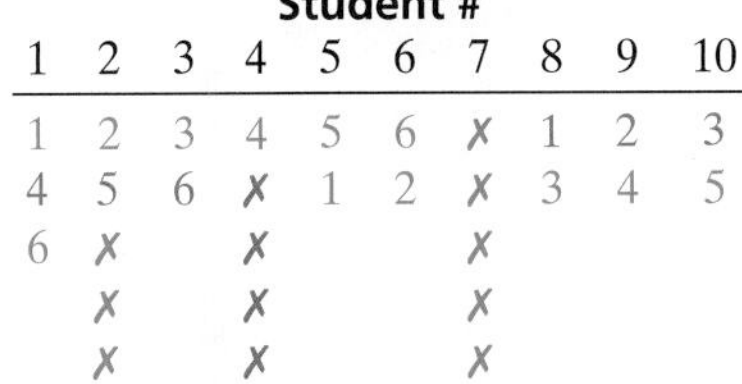

Student #

1	2	3	4	5	6	7	8	9	10
1	2	3	4	5	6	✗	1	2	3
4	5	6	✗	1	2	✗	3	4	5
6	✗		✗			✗			
	✗		✗			✗			
	✗		✗			✗			

Practice 1–3. See left.

1. If the teacher has 12 students and counts out every ninth student, which student will be left?
2. An uncle is giving some baseball cards away to five nieces and nephews. He decides the fairest way to do this is to give just one card to the first child, then two to the second, and so on. If everybody gets three turns, how many cards will each niece or nephew have?
3. Four robots stand in the corners of a four-by-four grid. All four robots are facing in the same direction. They move at the same time. If a robot sees another robot directly ahead, it takes one step forward, and if not, it stays in place but turns right. Where are the robots after three moves?

1. the second student
2. 18; 21; 24; 27; 30
3. Answers may vary. Sample:

Simulate a Problem

This strategy emphasizes the Carry Out the Plan step. It is effective where a strategy, such as completing a table or solving a simpler problem, are difficult or don't work. In many cases, it has the added benefit of increased classroom participation.

Guided Instruction

Have a student volunteer read the problem aloud. Have other students point out the problem-solving steps:

- Understand the Problem
- Make a Plan
- Carry Out the Plan
- Check the Answer

Universal Access

Special Needs L1

In order to make the Carry Out the Plan step easier for students to see, label each of the pennies from 1 to 10 using a small piece of tape.

Make a Table

The *Make a Table* strategy is useful for recording and organizing information. Tables also help students observe numerical patterns across rows or columns.

Guided Instruction

Have a volunteer read the problem. Discuss students' understanding of the goal.

Elicit the problem-solving steps:

- Understand the Problem
- Make a Plan
- Carry Out the Plan
- Check the Answer

Teaching Tip
Encourage students who have difficulty translating flat diagrams into three-dimensional models to also use the problem-solving strategies *Draw a Picture and Act It Out.* Have students model the problem with several different boxes, each starting with a piece of paper that is 9 in. by 12 in. Have them measure dimensions and compare volumes.

Connection to Geometry
Review with students the relationships between dimensions length and width, and volume of a three-dimensional figure. Review units associated with each.

MR 2.5 Use a variety of methods, such as tables, to explain mathematical reasoning. ***Develop***

Make a Table

When to Use This Strategy You can *make a table* to help you keep track of possible solutions to a problem. A table can help you organize your data and compare solutions.

A company makes boxes without tops by cutting squares out of the corners of rectangular sheets of cardboard. Each rectangular sheet is 7 in. by 10 in. Using whole-inch lengths only, find the dimensions of the box with the greatest possible volume.

Understand The goal is to find the dimensions of a box that will result in the greatest volume. The piece of cardboard used to make the box is 7 in. by 10 in.

Plan *Make a table* to organize the information in the problem. Start with square cuts 1 in. on each side. Then increase the size 1 in. at a time.

Carry Out Let x represent the size of the squares. The length of the box is represented by $10 - 2x$. The width of the box is represented by $7 - 2x$. The expression $x(10 - 2x)(7 - 2x)$ represents the volume.

Height (Size of Cut) x	Length $10 - 2x$	Width $7 - 2x$	Volume $x(10 - 2x)(7 - 2x)$
1 in.	8 in.	5 in.	40 in.^{3}
2 in.	6 in.	3 in.	36 in.^{3}
3 in.	4 in.	1 in.	12 in.^{3}

As the size of the square cut increases, the volume decreases. Square cuts of 1 in. result in the maximum volume of 40 in.^{3}.

Check A value of 4 for x makes the expression $(7 - 2x)$ negative, which is an impossible value for length. The possible lengths are 1, 2, and 3 in.

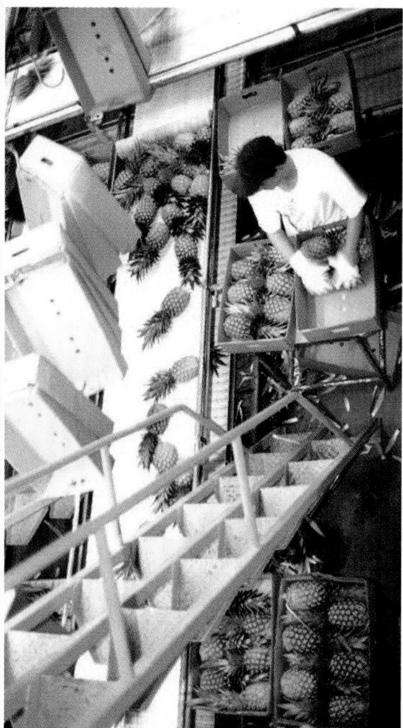

Practice

1. A dog owner has 200 ft of fencing and wants to enclose the greatest possible rectangular area for her dog. What dimensions should she use? **50 ft by 50 ft**
2. A customer gives a cashier a $100 bill for a $64 shirt. The customer will accept no more than six $1 bills. In what ways can the cashier give change using bills only? Assume that the cashier has no $2 bills. **See left.**

2.

$20	$10	$5	$1
1	1		6
1	1	1	1
1		3	1
1		2	6
	3	1	1
	3		6
	2	2	6
	2	3	1
	1	4	6
	1	5	1
		6	6
		7	1

California Standards

MR 1.3 Determine when and how to break a problem into simpler parts. ***Develop***

MR 2.2 Apply strategies and results from simpler problems to more complex problems. ***Develop***

Simplify a Problem

When to Use This Strategy Using simpler numbers can sometimes help you solve a difficult problem.

You tile a rectangular floor $17\frac{1}{2}$ ft by $13\frac{3}{4}$ ft. You are using square tiles that are $1\frac{1}{4}$ ft on each side. How many tiles do you need?

Understand The rectangular floor is $17\frac{1}{2}$ ft long and $13\frac{3}{4}$ ft wide. Each tile is a square with sides $1\frac{1}{4}$ ft long. You must find how many tiles are needed to cover the floor.

Plan First, *simplify the problem.* Then use the same approach to solve the harder problem. Multiply each number by 4 to remove the fractions. Replace $17\frac{1}{2}$ with $17\frac{1}{2} \cdot 4 = 70$. Replace $13\frac{3}{4}$ with $13\frac{3}{4} \cdot 4 = 55$, and $1\frac{1}{4}$ with $1\frac{1}{4} \cdot 4 = 5$.

Simpler Problem A rectangular floor is 70 ft by 55 ft. How many 5 ft-by-5 ft tiles do you need to cover the floor?

Carry Out For one row of tiles to cover the length of the room, you need $70 \div 5$, or 14, tiles. For enough rows to cover the width of the room, you need $55 \div 5$, or 11, rows. So you need $14 \cdot 11$, or 154, tiles.

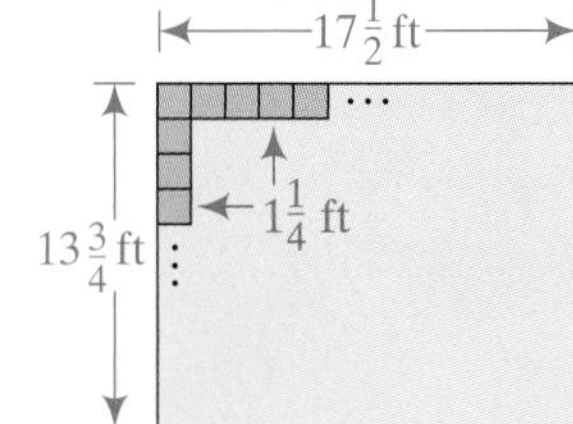

Now solve the original problem. For one row of tiles, you need $17\frac{1}{2} \div 1\frac{1}{4}$, or 14, tiles. For enough rows to cover the width, you need $13\frac{3}{4} \div 1\frac{1}{4}$, or 11, rows. So you need $14 \cdot 11$, or 154, tiles.

Check Because all the lengths in the simpler problem are four times as long, the answers to both problems should be the same. They are, so the answer checks.

Practice

1. On a school day, José spends $5\frac{1}{4}$ h in classes. Each class lasts $\frac{3}{4}$ h. How many classes does José have? **7 classes**

2. A tailor has a section of material that is $28\frac{1}{2}$ ft long. He wants to cut it into pieces, each one $1\frac{1}{2}$ ft long. How many cuts will he have to make? **18 cuts**

Simplify a Problem

Problems sometimes appear intimidating simply because they involve fractions, decimals, or greater whole numbers. In this lesson, students learn how to approach such problems by first considering numbers that are more manageable. With the "difficult" numbers temporarily set aside, students can focus their attention on making a plan for solving the problem.

Guided Instruction

Point out that using the strategy *Work a Simpler Problem* is useful when it is difficult to get started on a problem or the problem involves numbers that appear "difficult."

Elicit the problem-solving steps:

- Understand the Problem
- Make a Plan
- Carry Out the Plan
- Check the Answer

Tell students that they may need to use them for both the simpler problem and the original problem.

Work Backward

Some problems truly do not have enough information to solve them. However, most have bits of information that need to be pieced together like a puzzle. Working backward can help students make sense of the gaps in a situation, such as, when a final amount is given in addition to a few midway values or events.

Guided Instruction

Have a volunteer read the problem. Discuss the meanings of monetary terms, such as*withdrawal* and *initial amount.*

Elicit the problem solving steps:

- Understand the Problem
- Make a Plan
- Carry Out the Plan
- Check the Answer

Teaching Tip
Before students begin to calculate, help them understand the situation. Have students act out the situation and model the problem with paper money.

Connection to Geography
Have students locate Paris, Cairo, and Istanbul on a world map.

California Standards

MR 1.1 Analyze problems by sequencing and prioritizing information. ***Develop***

MR 2.5 Use a variety of methods, such as words and numbers, to explain mathematical reasoning. ***Develop***

Work Backward

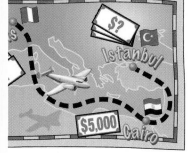

When to Use This Strategy Use the *Work Backward* strategy to solve problems that give only a final result and ask you to find an initial value.

At the start of a mission, international spy Rex King withdrew half of the money in his bank account in Paris. Later, he withdrew $5,000 in Cairo. In Istanbul, he withdrew half of the remaining money. He had $7,500 left. What amount did he have at the start of the mission?

Understand The goal is to find the initial amount. Rex withdrew half of the initial amount in Paris, $5,000 in Cairo, and half of the remaining amount in Istanbul. He had $7,500 left.

Plan *Work backward* by starting with what you know.

Carry Out Start with $7,500 and work backward.

- The final amount, $7,500, is half the amount in the bank before Rex went to Istanbul. So he had $15,000 when he arrived in Istanbul.
- He withdrew $5,000 in Cairo. So he left Paris with $20,000.
- At the start, he withdrew half of the amount he had. So at the start he had $40,000 in the bank account.

Check Start with $40,000 and work forward.

Paris		Cairo		Istanbul
$\frac{1}{2}$ of \$40,000 = \$20,000	→	\$20,000 − \$5,000 = \$15,000	→	$\frac{1}{2}$ of \$15,000 = \$7,500 ✔

Practice

1. You returned home from mowing lawns at 3:00 P.M. on Saturday. It took $1\frac{1}{2}$ h to mow the first lawn. It took twice as long to mow the next lawn. After a half-hour lunch break, it took $1\frac{1}{4}$ h to mow one more lawn. At what time did you start? **8:45 A.M.**

2. **Business** A salesperson bought a case of pens. On Monday, he sold $\frac{1}{2}$ of the pens. On Tuesday, he sold 30 more. On Wednesday, he sold $\frac{1}{3}$ of the pens that were left. On Thursday, he sold the remaining 40 pens. How many pens were originally in the case? **180 pens**

California Standards

MR 1.2 Formulate and justify mathematical conjectures based on a general description of the mathematical question or problem posed. ***Develop***

MR 2.5 Use a variety of methods, such as words, numbers, symbols and models, to explain mathematical reasoning. ***Develop***

Write an Equation

When to Use This Strategy You can *Write an Equation* when a real-world situation involves two related variables.

You plan a party at a restaurant. A buffet dinner costs \$15 per person. For dessert, you plan to buy a birthday cake for \$30. You have \$275 to spend. How much will you have left if there are 16 people at the party?

Understand Your goal is to find out how much money you will have left out of \$275. You must spend \$15 for each person plus an additional \$30 for the cake.

Plan *Write an equation* to represent the total cost of the party. Subtract the total cost from \$275 to see how much money you will have left.

Carry Out Write an equation to represent the total cost.

Words total cost is cost per person times number of people plus cost of cake

Let t = the total cost.

Let p = the number of people.

Equation $t \quad = \quad 15 \quad \cdot \quad p \quad + \quad 30$

$$t = 15p + 30$$

Substitute 16 for p. This gives $t = 15 \cdot 16 + 30 = 240 + 30 = 270$. Now subtract the total cost from \$275. This gives $\$275 - \$270 = \$5$.

Check Estimate. The cost for 20 people would be $\$300 + \$30 = \$330$, which is more than \$270. Similarly, the cost for 10 people would be $\$150 + \$30 = \$180$, which is less than \$270. A cost of \$270 is reasonable.

Practice

1. You buy a belt for \$10 and some socks. Each pair of socks costs \$3. The total shipping cost is \$3. What is the total cost if you buy 11 pairs of socks? \$46
2. You mix 8 oz of concentrate with 64 oz of water to make orange juice. If you need a total of 288 oz of juice, how much concentrate should you buy? 32 oz

Write an Equation

Writing an equation from a real-world situation is an important mathematical and algebraic skill. However, getting from the words to the symbols is often quite a challenge. Writing a sentence that can help identify important values, as well as graphing the situation, can help students make the transition.

Guided Instruction

Have a volunteer read the problem. Ask students to identify key quantities and identify letters to represent quantities that are unknown.

Elicit the problem solving steps:

- Understand the Problem
- Make a Plan
- Carry Out the Plan
- Check the Answer

Alternative Method
Have students identify which quantities in the problem depend on each other. Cost depends on number of people. Have students use those quantities as axes and graph the situation for a few hypothetical values. Noticing a linear relationship can help students visualize and make sense of the problem.

Universal Access

Visual Learners
Have students highlight different parts of the sentence in different colors to help them associate corresponding parts of the equation.

Entry-Level Assessment

This Entry-Level Assessment covers the Foundational Concepts and Skills outlined for Algebra Readiness. See pages T36 and T37 in this Teacher's Edition for the complete listing of these standards.

Question	Foundational Standard
1	Grade 2 AF 1.1
2	Grade 2 AF 1.1
3	Grade 3 NS 1.3
4	Grade 3 NS 1.3
5	Grade 3 NS 1.5
6	Grade 3 NS 1.5
7	Grade 3 AF 1.5
8	Grade 3 AF 1.5
9	Grade 4 NS 3.1
10	Grade 4 NS 3.1
11	Grade 4 NS 3.2
12	Grade 4 NS 3.2
13	Grade 4 AF 1.2
14	Grade 4 AF 1.3
15	Grade 4 AF 1.3
16	Grade 4 AF 1.5
17	Grade 4 AF 1.5
18	Grade 4 AF 2.1
19	Grade 4 AF 2.1
20	Grade 4 AF 2.2
21	Grade 4 AF 2.2
22	Grade 4 MG 2.1

Entry-Level Assessment

Read each question. Then write the letter of the correct answer on your paper.

1. What is the missing number?

   $(\blacksquare + 4) + 2 = 5 + (4 + 2)$ B

   Ⓐ 4
   Ⓑ 5
   Ⓒ 6
   Ⓓ 7

2. What is the missing number?

   $28 + 56 = 56 + \blacksquare$ D

   Ⓐ 84
   Ⓑ 56
   Ⓒ 29
   Ⓓ 28

3. The Mitchells' new house is 2,900 square feet. Which digit is in the hundreds place in the number 2,900? C

   Ⓐ 0 Ⓒ 9
   Ⓑ 2 Ⓓ 900

4. Which number has a 7 in the ones place and a 2 in the thousands place? C

   Ⓐ 2,089
   Ⓑ 7,102
   Ⓒ 32,477
   Ⓓ 72,532

5. One of the most populated cities in the world in Buenos Aires, Argentina. It has the population shown below. Write the population in standard form. D

   1 ten million + 3 million +
   8 hundred thousand +
   2 ten thousand +
   7 thousand + 2 hundred

   Ⓐ 30,827,200
   Ⓑ 31,872,200
   Ⓒ 31,827,200
   Ⓓ 13,827,200

6. Which is 40,807,060 in expanded notation? B

   Ⓐ 400,000,000 + 800,000 + 7,000 + 60
   Ⓑ 40,000,000 + 800,000 + 7,000 + 60
   Ⓒ 40,000,000 + 80,000 + 7,000 + 60
   Ⓓ 4,000,000 + 800,000 + 7,000 + 60

7. What is the missing number?

   $9 \times 8 = 8 \times \blacksquare$ D

   Ⓐ 2
   Ⓑ 7
   Ⓒ 8
   Ⓓ 9

8. Which expression shows how you can rewrite $4 \times 9 \times 25$ to make it easier to solve using mental math? A

   Ⓐ $(4 \times 25) \times 9$
   Ⓑ $(4 \times 25) + 9$
   Ⓒ $(4 + 25) \times 9$
   Ⓓ $(4 \times 9) \times 25$

9. Add.

   1,876 + 6,540 C

   Ⓐ 7,316
   Ⓑ 7,416
   Ⓒ 8,416
   Ⓓ 9,326

10. Subtract.

    5,291 − 348 B

    Ⓐ 4,147
    Ⓑ 4,943
    Ⓒ 5,157
    Ⓓ 5,953

11. Divide. Check your answer.

    $5\overline{)703}$ D

    Ⓐ 14 R3
    Ⓑ 104 R3
    Ⓒ 139 R8
    Ⓓ 140 R3

12. A pet store can keep 14 fish in each tank. To find the number of tanks needed for 338 fish, the store manager divided by 14 as shown.

$$14\overline{)338}\quad 24\text{ R2}$$

How can the manager check the result? B

- (A) Multiply 2 by 14, and then add 24.
- (B) Multiply 24 by 14, and then add 2.
- (C) Multiply 24 by 2, and then add 14.
- (D) Multiply 24 by 14. Then multiply by 2.

13. What is the value of the expression below?

$17 - (4 + 6)$ A

- (A) 7
- (B) 13
- (C) 19
- (D) 27

14. What is the value of x?

$(9 + 21) \div (7 - 2) = x$ B

- (A) 5
- (B) 6
- (C) 10
- (D) 30

15. Choose the number expression that matches the words.

A centipede can have 100 legs. A spider has 8 legs and a beetle has 6 legs. How many more legs does a 100-leg centipede have than a spider and a beetle combined? C

- (A) $100 + (8 + 6)$
- (B) $100 - (8 - 6)$
- (C) $100 - (8 + 6)$
- (D) $100 + (8 - 6)$

16. Use the equation below.

$6x + 4 = y$ D

If $x = 5$, what is the value of y?

- (A) 4
- (B) 6
- (C) 10
- (D) 34

17. The product of 8 and x is equal to y. If $x = 4$, which equation can be used to find y? C

- (A) $8 + 4 = y$
- (B) $y - 8 = 4$
- (C) $8 \times 4 = y$
- (D) $8 \div y = 4$

18. Which expression completes the equation?

$7 + 15 = 7 + \blacksquare$ B

- (A) $3 + 5$
- (B) 3×5
- (C) $5 - 3$
- (D) 7

19. If $h + 35 = j + 35$, which statement is true? C

- (A) $h = 35$
- (B) $h + j = 35$
- (C) $h = j$
- (D) $j < h$

20. What value of a makes the equation true?

$4 \times (7 + 23) = 4 \times a$ C

- (A) 7
- (B) 28
- (C) 30
- (D) 92

21. If $x = y$, which statement is true? A

- (A) $x \times 5 = y \times 5$
- (B) $x + 5 = y \times 5$
- (C) $x + 5 = y - 5$
- (D) $x \times 5 = y + 5$

22. The three points graphed below all lie on the same line. Which ordered pair names another point on the line? C

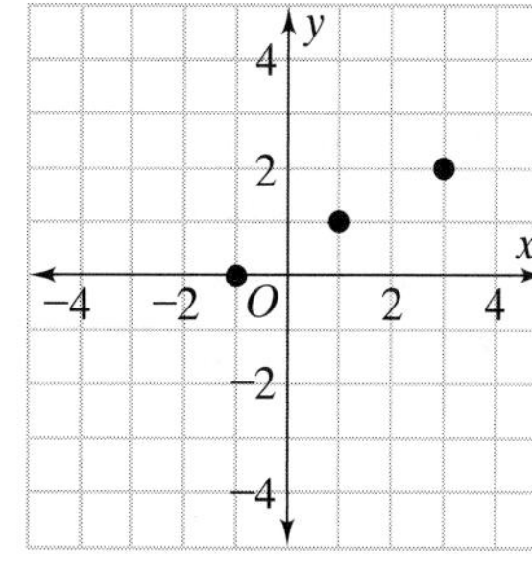

- (A) (0, 0)
- (B) (−1, −3)
- (C) (−3, −1)
- (D) (1, −3)

Question	Foundational Standard
23	Grade 4 MG 2.1
24	Grade 4 MG 2.2
25	Grade 4 MG 2.3
26	Grade 5 NS 1.4
27	Grade 5 NS 1.4
28	Grade 5 AF 1.3
29	Grade 5 AF 1.3
30	Grade 5 AF 1.4
31	Grade 5 AF 1.4
32	Grade 6NS 1.1
33	Grade 6NS 1.1
34	Grade 6NS 1.4
35	Grade 6NS 1.4
36	Grade 6NS 2.1
37	Grade 6NS 2.1
38	Grade 6NS 2.2
39	Grade 6NS 2.2
40	Grade 6AF 1.1
41	Grade 6AF 1.1

23. Which graph shows the function $y = 3x + 2$? B

Ⓐ 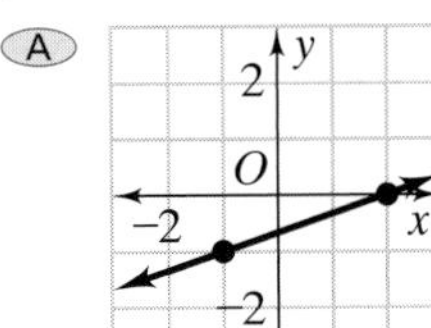

Ⓒ 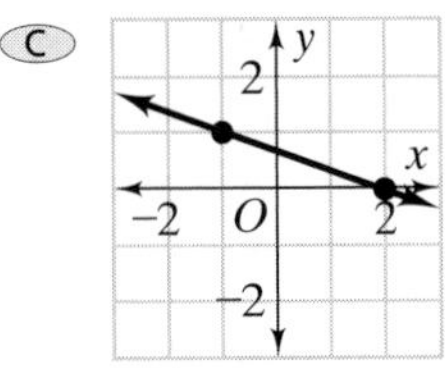

Ⓑ 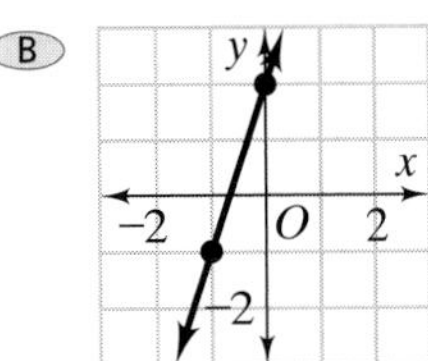

Ⓓ 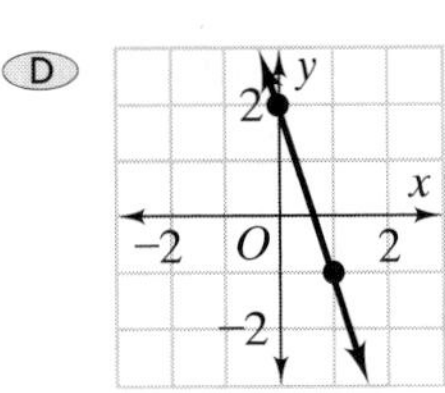

24. What is the length of the line segment joining the points (12, 1) and (0, 1)? D

Ⓐ 0
Ⓑ 1
Ⓒ 6
Ⓓ 12

25. What is the length of the line segment joining the points (3, 7) and (3, 2)? C

Ⓐ 1
Ⓑ 3
Ⓒ 5
Ⓓ 9

26. Which is the prime factorization of 120? B

Ⓐ $2^3 \times 15$
Ⓑ $2^3 \times 3 \times 5$
Ⓒ $2 \times 3^3 \times 5$
Ⓓ $2 \times 3^2 \times 5^2$

27. Why is $4 \times 5 \times 7$ NOT the prime factorization of 140? A

Ⓐ 4 is not a prime number.
Ⓑ 5 is not a prime number.
Ⓒ $5 \times 4 \times 7$ is more than 140.
Ⓓ $5 \times 4 \times 7$ is less than 140.

28. Which of the following is equivalent to the expression $4(6 + n)$? C

Ⓐ $(4 + 6) + (4 + n)$
Ⓑ $(4 + 6) \times (4 + n)$
Ⓒ $(4 \times 6) + (4 \times n)$
Ⓓ $(4 \times 6) \times (4 \times n)$

29. What value of x makes the equation true?

$3 \times 14 = (3 \times 10) + (3 \times x)$ B

Ⓐ 3
Ⓑ 4
Ⓒ 14
Ⓓ 30

30. Which point on the coordinate plane below has coordinates $(-3, 2)$? D

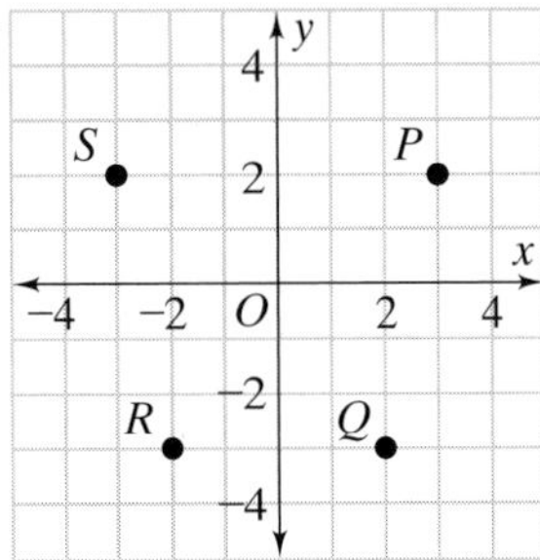

Ⓐ point P
Ⓑ point Q
Ⓒ point R
Ⓓ point S

31. What are the coordinates of point G on the coordinate plane below? B

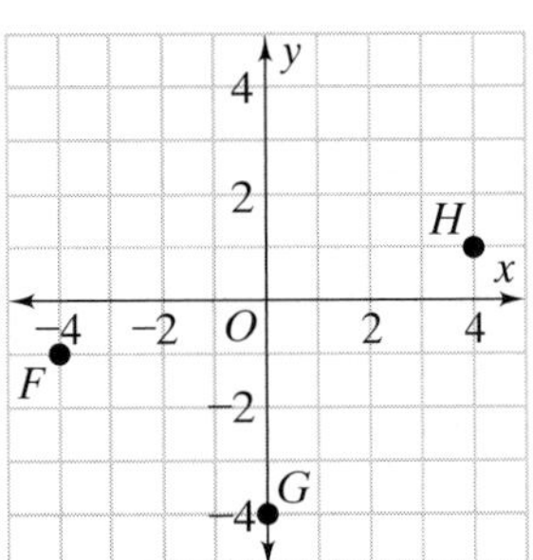

Ⓐ $(-4, 0)$
Ⓑ $(0, -4)$
Ⓒ $(0, 4)$
Ⓓ $(4, 0)$

32. Four students painted a mural on a concrete wall in the schoolyard. Maggie painted $\frac{3}{8}$ of the mural, Pedro painted $\frac{5}{16}$ of the mural, Laurel painted $\frac{1}{4}$ of the mural, and Zach painted $\frac{1}{16}$ of the mural. Which student did the most painting? A

Ⓐ Maggie
Ⓑ Pedro
Ⓒ Laurel
Ⓓ Zach

33. Which of the following lists of numbers is in order from least to greatest? D

Ⓐ $\frac{3}{5}, -3, 0, -\frac{2}{9}, 0.5$

Ⓑ $-\frac{2}{9}, \frac{3}{5}, 0.5, 0, -3$

Ⓒ $-3, 0, -\frac{2}{9}, 0.5, \frac{3}{5}$

Ⓓ $-3, -\frac{2}{9}, 0, 0.5, \frac{3}{5}$

34. Ana pays $22.75 for dinner. If she leaves a 15% tip, how much will she spend on dinner and the tip? D

Ⓐ $3.41 Ⓒ $22.90

Ⓑ $22.75 Ⓓ $26.16

35. Sue's bank account pays her a simple yearly interest rate of 4.8% on the money in her college savings account. She opens her account with $812. Which is the closest estimate of the amount of interest her account will have earned after one year? C

Ⓐ $30 Ⓒ $40

Ⓑ $32 Ⓓ $42

36. The table below shows the weight and length of three young manatees. About how much *total* weight did the manatees gain in the six-month period? A

Manatee Growth

Manatee	January 1		July 1	
	Weight (kg)	Length (m)	Weight (kg)	Length (m)
1	$35\frac{1}{2}$	$\frac{3}{4}$	$78\frac{1}{2}$	$1\frac{1}{2}$
2	$42\frac{3}{4}$	$\frac{7}{8}$	$85\frac{3}{4}$	$1\frac{3}{4}$
3	$41\frac{1}{3}$	$\frac{4}{5}$	$89\frac{1}{4}$	$1\frac{4}{5}$

Ⓐ 134 kg Ⓒ 186 kg

Ⓑ 139 kg Ⓓ 254 kg

37. Solve.

$\frac{5}{6} - \frac{2}{3}$ B

Ⓐ $\frac{1}{18}$ Ⓒ $\frac{2}{3}$

Ⓑ $\frac{1}{6}$ Ⓓ 1

38. Solve.

$\frac{1}{3} \div \frac{1}{4}$ D

Ⓐ $\frac{1}{12}$ Ⓒ 1

Ⓑ $\frac{3}{4}$ Ⓓ $1\frac{1}{3}$

39. In 1954, Roger Bannister was the first to break the four-minute mile. He completed four $\frac{1}{4}$-mile laps in 3 minutes $59\frac{4}{10}$ seconds. What was his average time per lap? C

Ⓐ $39\frac{17}{20}$ seconds

Ⓑ $49\frac{17}{20}$ seconds

Ⓒ $59\frac{17}{20}$ seconds

Ⓓ $69\frac{17}{20}$ seconds

40. Lou scored 18 points in the first basketball game of the season and p points in the second game. He scored a total of 32 points in these two games. Which equation would Lou use to find out how many points he scored in the second game? A

Ⓐ $18 + p = 32$

Ⓑ $18 - p = 32$

Ⓒ $32 - p = 32$

Ⓓ $32 + 18 = p$

41. Solve for n.

$\frac{n}{4} = 53.3$ D

Ⓐ 1.7 Ⓒ 13.3

Ⓑ 13.3 Ⓓ 213.2

Variables and Algebraic Expressions

Chapter at a Glance

Lesson Titles, Objectives, and Features	California Content Standards
1-1 Numerical Expressions • To write and simplify numerical expressions	Interpret and evaluate mathematical expressions that use parentheses. ***Foundational (Gr4 NS 1.2)*** **NS 1.2** Add, subtract, multiply, and divide rational numbers.
1-2 Algebraic Expressions • To evaluate algebraic expressions **Mathematical Reasoning:** Justify Each Step	Evaluate algebraic expressions. ***Foundational (Gr6 AF 1.0)*** Compute the value of an expression for specific values of the variable. ***Foundational (Gr5 AF 1.0)*** **NS 1.2** Add, subtract, multiply, and divide rational numbers. **MR 2.6** Support solutions with evidence in both verbal and symbolic work.
1-3 Writing Expressions • To write algebraic expressions **1-3a Activity Lab:** Modeling Expressions **Vocabulary Builder:** High-Use Academic Words	Write verbal expressions as algebraic expressions. ***Foundational (Gr6 AF 1.0)*** **AF 1.1** Use variables and appropriate operations to write an expression that represents a verbal description.
1-4 Estimating for Reasonableness • To use estimation to check for reasonableness **Mathematical Reasoning:** Exact and Approximate Solutions	**NS 1.2** Add, subtract, multiply, and divide rational numbers. **MR 2.1** Use estimation to verify the reasonableness of calculated results. **MR 2.7** Indicate the relative advantages of exact and approximate solutions to problems and give answers to a specified degree of accuracy.
1-5 Properties of Numbers • To recognize and use the properties of numbers **Vocabulary Builder:** Justifying a Conclusion	Use the commutative and associative rules. ***Foundational (Gr2 AF 1.1)*** **AF 1.3** Simplify numerical expressions by applying properties of rational numbers and justify the process used.
1-6 The Distributive Property • To use the Distributive Property **Algebraic Thinking:** Understanding Properties	Know and use the distributive property in equations and expressions with variables. ***Foundational (Gr5 AF 1.3)*** **AF 1.3** Simplify numerical expressions by applying properties of rational numbers and justify the process used.

California Content Standards
NS Number Sense
AF Algebra and Functions
MG Measurement and Geometry
MR Mathematical Reasoning

Correlations to Standardized Tests

All content for these tests is contained in *Prentice Hall Math, Algebra Readiness.* This chart reflects coverage in this chapter only.

	1-1	1-2	1-3	1-4	1-5	1-6
Terra Nova CAT6 (Level 18)						
Number and Number Relations	✔	✔	✔	✔	✔	✔
Computation and Numerical Estimation	✔	✔	✔	✔	✔	✔
Operation Concepts	✔	✔	✔	✔	✔	✔
Measurement						
Geometry and Spatial Sense						
Data Analysis, Statistics, and Probability						
Patterns, Functions, Algebra	✔	✔	✔	✔	✔	✔
Problem Solving and Reasoning	✔	✔	✔	✔	✔	✔
Communication	✔	✔	✔	✔	✔	✔
Decimals, Fractions, Integers, Percent	✔	✔	✔	✔	✔	✔
Order of Operations	✔	✔	✔			✔
Algebraic Operations	✔	✔	✔	✔	✔	✔
Terra Nova CTBS (Level 18)						
Decimals, Fractions, Integers, Percents	✔	✔	✔	✔	✔	✔
Order of Operations, Numeration, Number Theory	✔	✔	✔	✔	✔	✔
Data Interpretation						
Measurement						
Geometry						
ITBS (Level 14)						
Number Properties and Operations	✔	✔	✔	✔	✔	✔
Algebra	✔	✔	✔	✔	✔	✔
Geometry						
Measurement						
Probability and Statistics						
Estimation				✔		
SAT10 (Adv 1 Level)						
Number Sense and Operations	✔	✔	✔	✔	✔	✔
Patterns, Relationships, and Algebra	✔	✔	✔	✔	✔	✔
Data, Statistics, and Probability						
Geometry and Measurement						
NAEP						
Number Sense, Properties, and Operations	✔	✔	✔	✔	✔	✔
Measurement						
Geometry and Spatial Sense						
Data Analysis, Statistics, and Probability						
Algebra and Functions	✔	✔	✔		✔	✔

CAT6 California Achievement Test, 6th Ed. **CTBS** Comprehensive Test of Basic Skills **ITBS** Iowa Test of Basic Skills, Form M
SAT10 Stanford Achievement Test, 10th Ed. **NAEP** National Assessment of Educational Progress 2005 Mathematics Objectives

California Math Background

Focus on the California Content Standards

- The concepts covered in chapter 1 include an important pairing of foundational standards and target standards. The label 'Relate Math You Know . . . to Algebra' makes the examples easy to locate in the lessons.
- As early as grade 4, students used and interpreted variables, mathematical symbols, and properties to write and simplify expressions and sentences (**AF 1.0**).
- Last year in grade 7 students simplified numerical expressions by applying the properties of rational numbers and justifying the process used (**AF 1.3**). They also used the correct order of operations to evaluate algebraic expressions (**AF 1.2**).

1-1 Numerical Expressions

California Content Standard **NS 1.2**

Math Understandings

- Mathematicians have agreed upon a convention for performing arithmetic operations, called the order of operations, so that any mathematical expression will always have the same value.

A **numerical expression** is a mathematical phrase containing numbers and operation symbols. To **simplify** a numerical expression, replace it with its simplest name.

An incomplete order of operations is presented as follows:

Order of Operations

1. Work inside grouping symbols.
2. Multiply and divide in order from left to right.
3. Add and subtract in order from left to right.

1-2 Algebraic Expressions

California Content Standard **NS 1.2**

Math Understandings

- An algebraic expression differs fron an open sentence or equation in that it has no equal sign.
- The value of an algebraic expression can vary depending on the value of the variable.
- Within a single problem, the value of the variable remains the same.

A numerical expression is a mathematical phrase with only numbers and operation symbols (+, −, ×, ÷). A **variable** is a symbol that represents one or more numbers. A mathematical expression with one or more variables is an **algebraic expression.** To **evaluate** an algebraic expression, replace each variable with a number and then simplify.

1-3 Writing Expressions

California Content Standard **AF 1.1**

Math Understandings

- In order to write a word phrase as an algebraic expression, you translate the words into numbers and operation symbols.

Some examples of key words and their corresponding mathematical operations follow.

Operation	Key Words
Addition	sum, add, plus, increased by, more than
Subtraction	difference, subtract, minus, decreased by, less than
Multiplication	product, multiplied by, times
Division	quotient, divided by

1-4 Estimating for Reasonableness

California Content Standards **NS 1.2, MR 2.1, MR 2.7**

Math Understandings

- Estimation is used when an exact answer is not needed.
- Most estimation techniques involve replacing numbers with ones that are close and easy to compute mentally.

To estimate the sum or difference of whole numbers, round to the same place. Look at the number to the right of the place you are rounding to. If it is a 5 or greater, round up. If it is less than 5, round down.

To estimate the product or quotient of two whole numbers, use compatible numbers and compute mentally. Basic facts and powers of ten help find compatible numbers.

1-5 Properties of Numbers

California Content Standards **AF 1.3, MR 2.5, MR 2.6**

Math Understandings

- The properties of addition and multiplication often let you do mental computations more easily.
- The Commutative Property, the Associative Property, and the Identity Property apply to both addition and multiplication of rational numbers.

PROPERTIES OF ADDITION

Commutative Property
Changing the order of the addends does not change the sum.
$2.5 + 3 = 3 + 2.5$

Associative Property
Changing the grouping of the addends does not change the sum.
$(2.5 + 3) + 4 = 2.5 + (3 + 4)$

Identity Property
The sum of 0 and any number is that number.
$2.5 + 0 = 0 + 2.5 = 2.5$

PROPERTIES OF MULTIPLICATION

Commutative Property
Changing the order of the factors does not change the product.
$7 \times 4 = 4 \times 7$

Associative Property
Changing the grouping of the factors does not change the product.
$(3 \times 5) \times 2 = 3 \times (5 \times 2)$

Identity Property
The product of 1 and any number is that number.
$9 \times 1 = 1 \times 9 = 9$

1-6 The Distributive Property

California Content Standards **AF 1.3, MR 2.5, MR 2.6, MR 3.2**

Math Understandings

- You use the Distributive Property to evaluate expressions that have a number multiplied by a sum or difference.
- The Distributive Property can be written and used in several different forms.

The **Distributive Property** shows how multiplication affects addition and subtraction.

$8 \times (4 + 6) = (8 \times 4) + (8 \times 6)$ $(6 - 2) \times 7 = (6 \times 7) - (2 \times 7)$

Professional Development

Additional Professional Development Opportunities

Math Background notes for Chapter 1: Every lesson has a Math Background in the PLAN section.

In-Service On Demand
Prentice Hall offers free video-based tutorials to support you. Visit PHSchool.com/inserviceondemand.

Pearson Achievement Solutions
Pearson Achievement Solutions, a Pearson Education company, offers comprehensive, facilitated professional development designed to help teachers improve student achievement. To learn more, please visit pearsonachievementsolutions.com.

Chapter 1 Resources

	1-1	1-2	1-3	1-4	1-5	1-6	For the Chapter
Print Resources							
L3 Practice	●	●	●	●	●	●	
L3 Guided Problem Solving	●	●	●	●	●	●	
L2 Reteaching	●	●	●	●	●	●	
L4 Enrichment	●	●	●	●	●	●	
L3 Vocabulary and Study Skills	●	●	●	●	●	●	●
L3 Daily Puzzles	●	●	●	●	●	●	
L3 Activity Labs	●	●	●	●	●	●	
L3 Checkpoint Quiz		●		●			
L3 Chapter Project							●
L2 Below Level Chapter Test							●
L3 Chapter Test							●
L4 Alternative Assessment							●
L3 Cumulative Review							●
Spanish Resources EL							
L3 Practice	●	●	●	●	●	●	
L3 Vocabulary and Study Skills	●		●		●		●
L3 Checkpoint Quiz		●		●			
L2 Below Level Chapter Test							●
L3 Chapter Test							●
L4 Alternative Assessment							●
L3 Cumulative Review							●
Transparencies							
Check Skills You'll Need	●	●	●	●	●	●	
Additional Examples	●	●	●	●	●	●	
California Daily Review	●	●	●	●	●	●	
Classroom Aid					●		
Student Edition Answers	●	●	●	●	●	●	●
Lesson Quiz	●	●	●	●	●	●	
Technology							
California Student Center Online	●	●	●	●	●	●	●
California Student Center CD-ROM	●	●	●	●	●	●	●
Success Tracker™ Online Math Intervention	●	●	●	●	●	●	●
California Teacher Center: ExamView CD-ROM	●	●	●	●	●	●	●
California Teacher Center: Planning CD-ROM	●	●	●	●	●	●	●
California Teacher Center: Presentations CD-ROM and online	●	●	●	●	●	●	●
MindPoint Quiz Show	●	●	●	●	●	●	●
Prentice Hall Web Site: PHSchool.com	●	●	●	●	●	●	●

Also available:

California Standards Mastery
- Standards Review Transparencies
- Standards Review and Practice Workbook
- Progress Monitoring Assessments
- Math Companion
- Math*XL*

California Intervention Resources
- Skills Review and Practice Workbook
- Success Tracker™ Online Math Intervention

Other Resources
- Multilingual Handbook
- Spanish Student Edition
- Solution Key
- Math Notes Study Folder

Where You Can Use the Lesson Resources

Here is a suggestion, following the four-step teaching plan, for how you can incorporate Universal Access Resources into your teaching.

	Instructional Resources L3	Universal Access Resources
1. Plan		
Preparation Read the Math Background in the Teacher's Edition to connect this lesson with students' previous experience. **Starting Class** **Check Skills You'll Need** Assign these exercises from the Math Companion to review prerequisite skills. Review the full text of the student expectations and objectives covered in this lesson. **New Vocabulary** Help students pre-read the lesson by pointing out the new terms introduced in the lesson.	**California Math Background** **Math Understandings** **Transparencies & Presentations CD-ROM** Check Skills You'll Need California Daily Review **Resources** Vocabulary and Study Skills **Math Companion**	**Spanish Support** EL Vocabulary and Study Skills
2. Teach		
L3 **Guided Instruction** Use the Activity Labs to build conceptual understanding. Teach each Example. Use the Teacher's Edition side column notes for specific teaching tips, including Error Prevention notes. Use the Additional Examples found in the side column (and on transparency and PowerPoint) as an alternative presentation for the content. After each Example, assign the California Standards Check exercises for that Example to get an immediate assessment of student understanding. Utilize the support in the Math Companion to assist students with each Standards Check. Use the Closure activity in the Teacher's Edition to help students attain mastery of lesson content.	**Student Edition** Activity Lab **Resources** Math Companion Activity Lab **Transparencies & Presentations CD-ROM** Additional Examples Classroom Aids **Teacher Center: ExamView CD-ROM**	**Teacher's Edition** Every lesson includes suggestions for working with students who need special attention. L1 Special Needs L2 Below Level L4 Advanced Learners EL English Learners **Resources** **Multilingual Handbook** **Math Companion**
3. Practice		
Assignment Guide **Check Your Understanding** Use these questions from the Math Companion to check students' understanding before you assign homework. **Homework Exercises** Assign homework from these leveled exercises in the Assignment Guide. A Practice by Example B Apply Your Skills C Challenge California Multiple-Choice Practice and Mixed Review **Homework Quick Check** Use these key exercises to quickly check students' homework.	**Transparencies & Presentations CD-ROM** Student Answers **Resources** Math Companion Practice Guided Problem Solving Vocabulary and Study Skills Activity Lab Daily Puzzles **Teacher Center: ExamView CD-ROM** **Math *XL***	**Spanish Support** EL Practice EL Vocabulary and Study Skills **Resources** L4 Enrichment
4. Assess & Reteach		
Lesson Quiz Assign the Lesson Quiz to assess students' mastery of the lesson content. **Checkpoint Quiz** Use the Checkpoint Quiz to assess student progress over several lessons.	**Transparencies & Presentations CD-ROM** Lesson Quiz **Resources** Checkpoint Quiz	**Resources** L2 Reteaching EL Checkpoint Quiz Success Tracker™ **Teacher Center: ExamView CD-ROM**

KEY L1 Special Needs L2 Below Level L3 For All Students L4 Advanced, Gifted EL English Learners

Variables and Algebraic Expressions

Answers are in the back of the textbook.

For math intervention, direct students to:

Rounding
Skills Handbook, p. 436

Adding and Subtracting Decimals
Skills Handbook, p. 442

Multiplying Decimals
Skills Handbook, p. 443

Dividing Decimals by Whole Numbers
Skills Handbook, p. 445

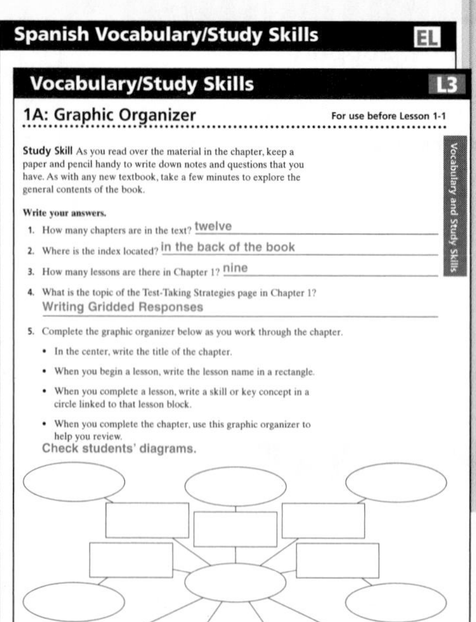

Spanish Vocabulary/Study Skills EL

Vocabulary/Study Skills L3

1A: Graphic Organizer — For use before Lesson 1-1

Study Skill As you read over the material in the chapter, keep a paper and pencil handy to write down notes and questions that you have. As with any new textbook, take a few minutes to explore the general contents of the book.

Write your answers.

1. How many chapters are in the text? twelve
2. Where is the index located? in the back of the book
3. How many lessons are there in Chapter 1? nine
4. What is the topic of the Test-Taking Strategies page in Chapter 1? Writing Gridded Responses
5. Complete the graphic organizer below as you work through the chapter.
   - In the center, write the title of the chapter.
   - When you begin a lesson, write the lesson name in a rectangle.
   - When you complete a lesson, write a skill or key concept in a circle linked to that lesson block.
   - When you complete the chapter, use this graphic organizer to help you review.

   Check students' diagrams.

Vocabulary and Study Skills

Variables and Algebraic Expressions

What You've Learned

California Content Standards

Foundational Standards

- Use the commutative and associative rules to simplify mental calculations and to check results.
- Recognize and use the commutative and associative properties of multiplication.
- Demonstrate an understanding of, and the ability to use, standard algorithms for the addition and subtraction of multidigit numbers.

to the lesson in green.

Rounding (Skills Handbook p. 436)

Round each number to the nearest ten.

1. 312 310 **2.** 7,525 7,530 **3.** 38 40 **4.** 1,989 1,990

Adding and Subtracting Decimals (Skills Handbook p. 442)

Find each sum or difference.

5. $0.0034 + 1.2$ 1.2034 **6.** $10.25 - 9.29$ 0.96 **7.** $8.1 - 0.81$ 7.29

8. $45.27 + 2.03$ 47.3 **9.** $4.55 - 2.67$ 1.88 **10.** $0.36 + 9.8$ 10.16

Multiplying Decimals (Skills Handbook p. 443)

Multiply.

11. $0.17 \cdot 4$ 0.68 **12.** $3.5 \cdot 4.2$ 14.7 **13.** $1.6 \cdot 9.7$ 15.52

14. $0.06 \cdot 0.23$ 0.0138 **15.** $7.5 \cdot 3.004$ 22.53 **16.** $8 \cdot 1.064$ 8.512

Dividing Decimals by Whole Numbers (Skills Handbook p. 445)

Divide.

17. $11.36 \div 2$ 5.68 **18.** $125.3 \div 14$ 8.95 **19.** $0.46 \div 5$ 0.092

California Content Standards for Chapter 1

Number Sense
NS 1.2

Algebra and Functions
AF 1.1, AF 1.3

Mathematical Reasoning
MR 2.1

Chapter 1 Overview

In this chapter, students work with numerical and algebraic expressions, using the order of operations to evaluate and simplify them. They write expressions and estimate to determine whether solutions are reasonable. They also learn and use the Commutative, Associative, Identity, and Distributive Properties.

Activating Prior Knowledge

In this chapter, students build on and extend their knowledge of numbers, properties, and operations to write, evaluate, and simplify numerical and algebraic expressions. Ask questions such as:

- *Is* $2 + 3 = 3 + 2$? yes
- *Is* $2 - 3 = 3 - 2$? no
- *Simplify* $4 + 6 \times 3$. 22

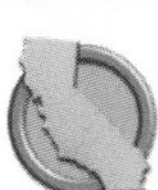

What You'll Learn Next

▲ You can use an algebraic expression to represent the cost of items you buy at a farmers' market.

California Content Standards

- **AF 1.1** Use variables and appropriate operations to write an expression that represents a verbal description.
- **AF 1.3** Simplify numerical expressions by applying properties of rational numbers and justify the process used.

New Vocabulary

English and Spanish Audio Online

- algebraic expression (p. 8)
- associative properties (p. 26)
- commutative properties (p. 26)
- compatible numbers (p. 21)
- Distributive Property (p. 30)
- evaluate (p. 9)
- identity properties (p. 26)
- numerical expression (p. 4)
- order of operations (p. 4)
- simplify (p. 4)
- variable (p. 8)

Academic Vocabulary

- identify (p. 19)
- justification (p. 25)
- justify (p. 19)
- list (p. 19)

1-1

1. Plan

California Content Standards

Interpret and evaluate mathematical expressions that use parentheses. *Foundational*

NS 1.2  Add, subtract, multiply, and divide rational numbers. *Introduce*

Professional Development

California Math Background

The order of operations for expressions involving parentheses (grouping symbols) and the four basic operations are presented in this lesson. The order of operations is accepted worldwide. Without agreement, simple expressions such as $5 + 3 \cdot 2$ could have two different answers ($5 + 6 = 11$ or $8 \cdot 2 = 16$). The order of operations ensures that everyone obtains the same result, which is 11 for this expression.

More Math Background: p. 2C

Lesson Planning and Resources

See p. 2E for a list of the resources that support this lesson.

...PRESENTATION CD-ROM
CD, Online, or Transparencies

Bell Ringer Practice

Check Skills You'll Need
Use student page, transparency, or PowerPoint.
See Math Companion.

California Standards Review
Use transparency or PowerPoint.

1-1 Numerical Expressions

Check Skills You'll Need

Do this in your **Math Companion.**

Vocabulary
- order of operations
- numerical expression
- simplify

Use your **Math Companion** *to build your vocabulary.*

California Content Standards

Foundational Standard Interpret and evaluate mathematical expressions that use parentheses.
NS 1.2 Add, subtract, multiply, and divide rational numbers. ***Introduce***

What You'll Learn . . . and Why

You will learn to write and simplify numerical expressions. Simplifying an expression such as $18 + 11 \cdot 6$ requires you to do more than one operation. To find the correct answer, you need to know which operation to do first. Should you add or multiply first?

Diane's Work (addition first)

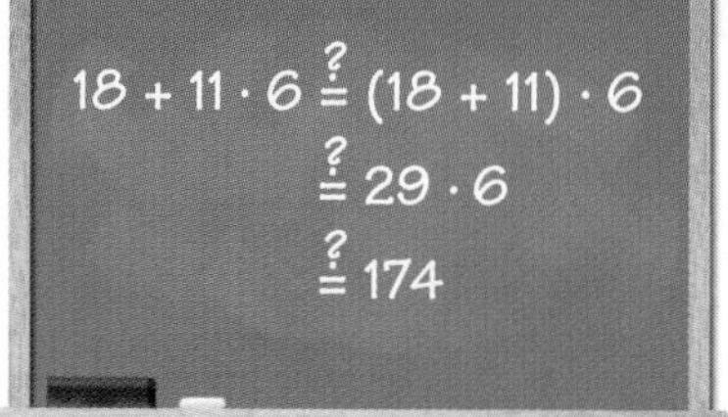

Dana's Work (multiplication first)

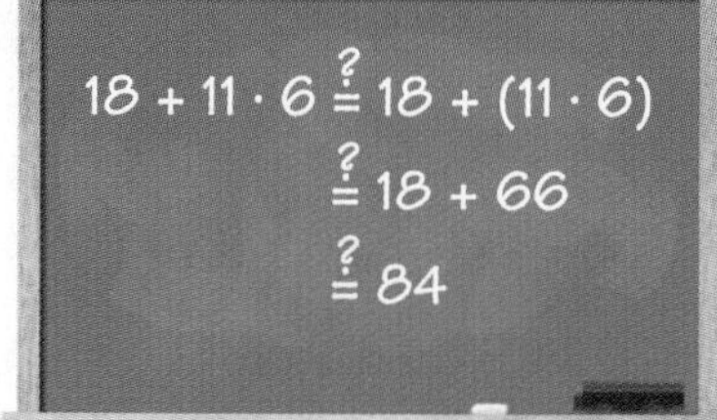

Only one answer is correct. To make sure you get the correct answer, use the **order of operations.**

Online active math

For: Order of Operations Activity
Use: Interactive Textbook, 1-1

Take Note — Order of Operations

1. Work inside grouping symbols.
2. Multiply and divide in order from left to right.
3. Add and subtract in order from left to right.

Using the order of operations, you multiply before you add.

$$18 + 11 \cdot 6 = 18 + 66$$
$$= 84$$

So, Dana's answer is correct.

A **numerical expression** is a mathematical phrase that contains numbers and operation symbols. To simplify a numerical expression, replace it with its simplest name.

Universal Access — Solutions for All Learners

Special Needs L1	**Below Level** L2
Have students rewrite, in shorthand, the order of operations. For example, **1.** ( ); **2.** × or ÷; **3.** + or −. They can keep this list on hand as they work through the problems in this lesson.	Discuss with students the importance of parentheses in this set of exercises. $(8 + 3) \cdot (4 - 2)$ 22 $(8 + 3) \cdot 4 - 2$ 42 $8 + (3 \cdot 4) - 2$ 18 $8 + 3 \cdot (4 - 2)$ 14

Parentheses are a type of grouping symbol.

Relate MATH YOU KNOW... ...*to* NEW IDEAS

EXAMPLE Simplifying an Expression

Simplify $3 \cdot (6 + 2)$.

$3 \cdot (6 + 2) = 3 \cdot 8$ ← **Simplify within the parentheses first.**

$= 24$ ← **Then multiply.**

1 Simplify $3 \cdot (6.1 + 0.2)$.

$3 \cdot (6.1 + 0.2) = 3 \cdot 6.3$ ← **Simplify within the parentheses first.**

$= 18.9$ ← **Then multiply.**

CA Standards Check 1 *Go to your* **Math Companion** *for help.*

1. Simplify each expression.

a. $(6.4 + 18.5) \div 3 \cdot 2$ 16.6 **b.** $3.4 + 5 \cdot 2 - 1.7$ 11.7

EXAMPLE Using an Expression to Solve a Problem

2 **Guided Problem Solving** Suppose you buy the items shown on the store receipt. Write and simplify an expression to find the total cost of the items, including the tax.

You can write an expression to help you find the total cost.

Problem Solving Tip

You can use words to describe the quantities in a problem.

Words	cost of jeans	plus	cost of shirts	plus	tax
Expression	$3 \cdot \$35.00$	$+$	$4 \cdot \$15.00$	$+$	$\$11.96$

Simplify the expression $3 \cdot 35.00 + 4 \cdot 15.00 + 11.96$.

$3 \cdot 35.00 + 4 \cdot 15.00 + 11.96$

$105.00 + 60.00 + 11.96$ ← **Multiply.**

176.96 ← **Add.**

The total cost is $176.96.

CA Standards Check 2 *Go to your* **Math Companion** *for help.*

2. You are paid $7.00 per hour to rake leaves. Your friend is paid $5.50 per hour. You work 4 h and your friend works 3 h. How much do the two of you earn in all? $44.50

Check Your Understanding *Homework prep is in your* **Math Companion.**

2. Teach

Guided Instruction

Example 1

Ask: *What do the parentheses in an expression indicate?* Operations in parentheses need to be done first.

Teaching Tip

You may want to share My Dear Aunt Sally with students so that they remember to Multiply, Divide, Add, and Subtract in that order.

PRESENTATION CD-ROM CD, Online, or Transparencies

Additional Examples

1 Find the value of $20 - 5 \times 8 \div 2$. 0

2 An Internet service provider charges $25 for a connection fee and then $16 per month. Write an expression to model the total cost for 5 months of Internet access and then evaluate the expression. $25 + 16 \times 5$; $105

Closure

- *What is a numerical expression?* a mathematical phrase that contains numbers and operation symbols
- *What is the order in which operations must be performed?* Do all operations within parentheses; multiply and divide in order from left to right; add and subtract in order from left to right.

Advanced Learners L4

Have students use 3 numbers, 2 operation symbols and 1 set of parentheses to write as many expressions as possible and simplify them. Sample: 12, 7, 2, +, −; $12 - (2 + 7) = 3$, and so on

English Learners EL

Make sure students understand that the expression $18 + 11 \times 6$ has just one (correct) value: $18 + 66 \neq 44$. The other solution (174) is an example of an incorrect simplification.

3. Practice

Assignment Guide

Check Your Understanding
See Math Companion.

Homework Exercises

A Practice by Example	1–15
B Apply Your Skills	16–29
C Challenge	30
California Multiple Choice Practice	31–32
Mixed Review	33–35

Homework Quick Check
To check students' understanding of key skills and concepts, go over Exercises 1, 10, 16, 17, 28.

Universal Access Resources

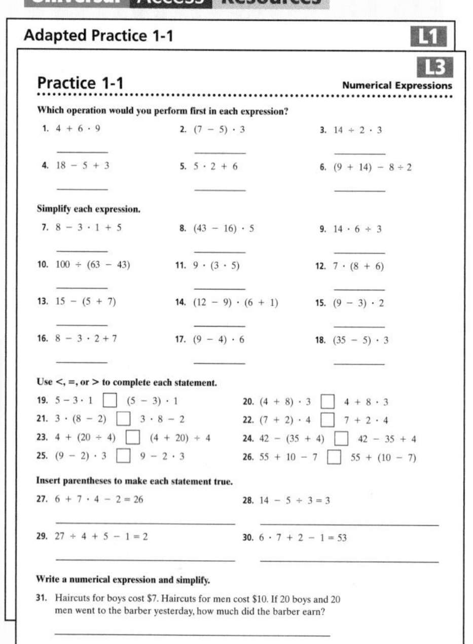

Adapted Practice 1-1 L1

L3

Practice 1-1 Numerical Expressions

Which operation would you perform first in each expression?

1. 4 + 6 · 9 2. (7 − 5) · 3 3. 14 ÷ 2 · 3
4. 18 − 5 + 3 5. 5 · 2 + 6 6. (9 + 14) − 8 ÷ 2

Simplify each expression.

7. 8 − 3 · 1 + 5 8. (43 − 16) · 5 9. 14 · 6 + 3
10. 100 ÷ (63 − 43) 11. 9 · (3 · 5) 12. 7 · (8 + 6)
13. 15 − (5 + 7) 14. (12 − 9) · (6 + 1) 15. (9 − 3) · 2
16. 8 − 3 · 2 + 7 17. (9 − 4) · 6 18. (35 − 5) · 3

Use <, =, or > to complete each statement.

19. 5 − 3 · 1 ☐ (5 − 3) · 1 20. (4 + 8) · 3 ☐ 4 + 8 · 3
21. 3 · (8 − 2) ☐ 3 · 8 − 2 22. (7 + 2) · 4 ☐ 7 + 2 · 4
23. 4 + (20 ÷ 4) ☐ (4 + 20) ÷ 4 24. 42 − (35 + 4) ☐ 42 − 35 + 4
25. (9 − 2) · 3 ☐ 9 − 2 · 3 26. 55 + 10 − 7 ☐ 55 + (10 − 7)

Insert parentheses to make each statement true.

27. 6 + 7 · 4 − 2 = 26 28. 14 − 5 + 3 = 3
29. 27 ÷ 4 + 5 − 1 = 2 30. 6 · 7 + 2 − 1 = 53

Write a numerical expression and simplify.

31. Haircuts for boys cost $7. Haircuts for men cost $10. If 20 boys and 20 men went to the barber yesterday, how much did the barber earn?

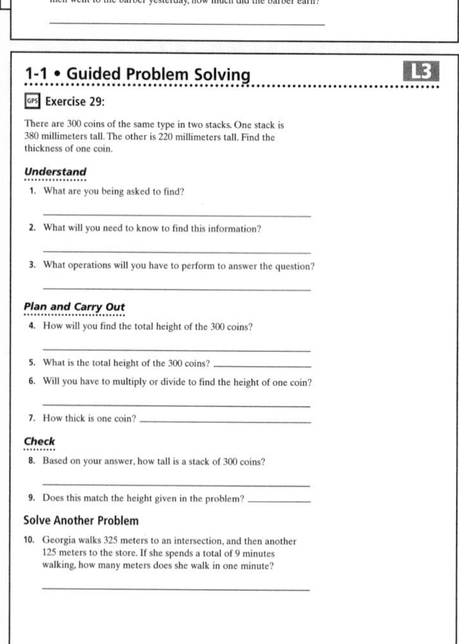

1-1 • Guided Problem Solving L3

Exercise 29:

There are 300 coins of the same type in two stacks. One stack is 380 millimeters tall. The other is 220 millimeters tall. Find the thickness of one coin.

Understand

1. What are you being asked to find?
2. What will you need to know to find this information?
3. What operations will you have to perform to answer the question?

Plan and Carry Out

4. How will you find the total height of the 300 coins?
5. What is the total height of the 300 coins?
6. Will you have to multiply or divide to find the height of one coin?
7. How thick is one coin?

Check

8. Based on your answer, how tall is a stack of 300 coins?
9. Does this match the height given in the problem?

Solve Another Problem

10. Georgia walks 325 meters to an intersection, and then another 125 meters to the store. If she spends a total of 9 minutes walking, how many meters does she walk in one minute?

Standards Practice

GO for Help: MathXL®

NS 1.2

A Practice by Example

Example 1 (page 5)

Simplify each expression.

1. $450 \div 45 + 5$ 15

   $450 \div 45 + 5 = 10 + 5$

   $= ■$

Guided Practice
This exercise has been started for you!

GO for Help

2. $29 - 1.4 \cdot 7$ 19.2
3. $16 + 36 \div 12$ 19
4. $(13 + 21) \cdot 2$ 68
5. $400 \div (44 - 24)$ 20
6. $4 \cdot 4.7 - 5.1$ 13.7
7. $(50 + 20) \div 2$ 35

Example 2 (page 5)

Simplify each expression.

8. $14 - (7 + 5) \div 2$ 8

   $14 - (7 + 5) \div 2 = 14 - 12 \div 2$

   $= ■$

Guided Practice
This exercise has been started for you!

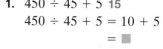

Homework Video Tutor

For: Examples 1–2
Visit: PHSchool.com
Web Code: axe-0101

9. $3(2.8 + 3.2) - 1.8$ 16.2
10. $16 - (2.1 + 4.5) \cdot 0.2$ 14.68
11. $35 \cdot 2 + 4.2 \div 2$ 72.1
12. $(45 \cdot 4) + 125 \cdot 3 \div 5$ 255
13. $75 \cdot 0.5 + (25 \cdot 0.6) - 10$ 42.5
14. $8.4 - [2.7 + (17.5 - 15.5)]$ 3.7
15. You buy 2 orange clips, 3 purple clips, and 2 silver clips. The prices are shown at the right. Find the total cost of the clips. $39

B Apply Your Skills

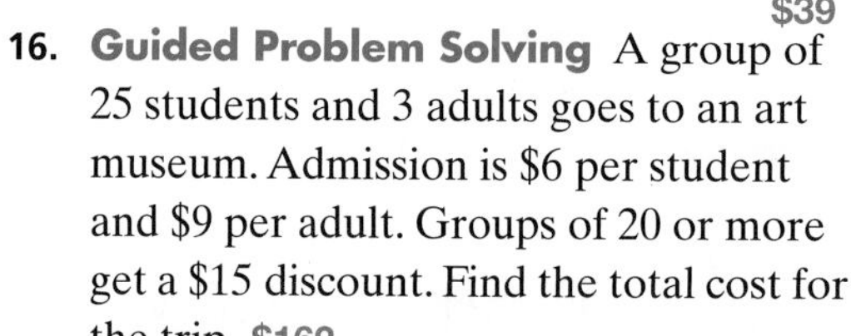

16. **Guided Problem Solving** A group of 25 students and 3 adults goes to an art museum. Admission is $6 per student and $9 per adult. Groups of 20 or more get a $15 discount. Find the total cost for the trip. $162
    - **Make a Plan** Write an expression for the cost of both the students and the adults. Next, find the total cost of the trip.
    - **Carry Out the Plan** An expression for the total cost for students and adults is 25 · $■ + 3 · $■ − $■.

17. First subtract the numbers in parentheses, then divide, then multiply, and finally add.

17. **Writing in Math** Explain the steps you would use to find the value of the expression $8 \div 4 \cdot 6 + (7 - 5)$. See left.

18. A grocery list is shown at the right. A loaf of bread costs $2. The price of milk is $2.50 per gallon. Peanut butter costs $3.25 per jar but is on sale for $1 off the regular price. What is the total cost of the groceries on the list? $8.75

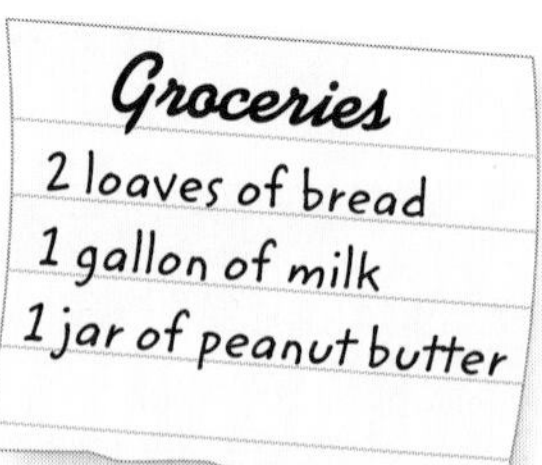

Groceries
2 loaves of bread
1 gallon of milk
1 jar of peanut butter

SCAFFOLDED
Problem Solving

Use the table for Exercises 19–24.

Food	Serving Size	Protein
Chicken	3 oz	21 g
Vegetables	1 c	2 g
Rice	1 c	9 g

19. How many grams of protein are in 3 oz of chicken? 21 g

20. How many grams of protein are in 3 c of vegetables? 6 g

21. How many grams of protein are in a meal containing 6 oz of chicken and 2 c of vegetables? 46 g

22. How many cups of rice should you eat to get 36 g of protein? 4 c

23. You eat 6 oz of chicken. How many cups of vegetables can you add to your meal to get a total of 46 g of protein? 2 c

24. Plan a meal that contains 55 g of protein. See left.

24. Answers may vary. Sample: 6 oz chicken, 2 c vegetables, 1 c rice

Reasoning **Insert parentheses to make each statement true.** 25–28. See left.

25. $11 - 7 \div 2 = 2$ **26.** $1 + 2 \cdot 15 - 4 = 33$

27. $13 - 4.1 + 7.4 = 1.5$ **28.** $11.2 - 3.4 \cdot 2 + 0.6 = 16.2$

25. $(11 - 7) \div 2 = 2$
26. $(1 + 2) \cdot (15 - 4) = 33$
27. $13 - (4.1 + 7.4) = 1.5$
28. $(11.2 - 3.4) \cdot 2 + 0.6 = 16.2$

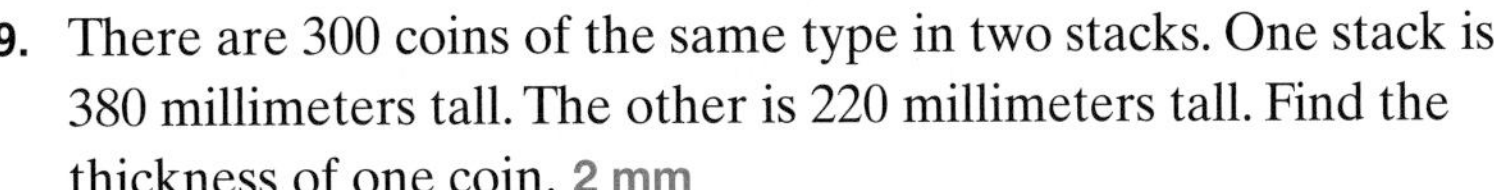

GPS **29.** There are 300 coins of the same type in two stacks. One stack is 380 millimeters tall. The other is 220 millimeters tall. Find the thickness of one coin. 2 mm

Challenge

30. Copy the statement: 14 ■ 7 ■ 2 ■ 3 = 7. Insert operation symbols to make the statement true. $14 \div 7 + 2 + 3 = 7$

Multiple Choice Practice and Mixed Review

For California Standards Tutorials, visit PHSchool.com. Web Code: axq-9045

NS 1.2

31. A group of 11 boys and 9 girls goes to a movie. Admission costs \$7.50 per person. Which expression does NOT show the total amount the group will pay? B

(A) $\$7.50 \cdot (11 + 9)$
(B) $\$7.50 \cdot 11 \cdot 9$
(C) $(\$7.50 \cdot 11) + (\$7.50 \cdot 9)$
(D) $\$7.50 \cdot 20$

NS 1.2, MR 3.2

32. There are 6 bike racks at a park. Each bike rack can hold 14 bikes. If there are 11 bikes, which method can be used to find the number of empty spaces in the bike racks? D

(A) Add 6 to the product of 11 and 14.
(B) Subtract 6 from the product of 11 and 14.
(C) Add 11 to the product of 6 and 14.
(D) Subtract 11 from the product of 6 and 14.

for Help

Skills Handbook p. 439

Simplify each expression.

33. $256 \cdot 78$ 19,968 **34.** $418 \cdot 22$ 9,196 **35.** $15 \cdot 79$ 1,185

Online Lesson Quiz Visit: PHSchool.com **Web Code:** axa-0101

Alternative Assessment

Have students bring to class various empty food containers that show nutritional information. They can use the information about protein, carbohydrates, vitamins, and so forth to create word problems similar to Exercises 19–24. Students can challenge classmates to solve their problems.

California Resources

Standards Mastery
- Standards Review Transparencies
- Standards Review and Practice Workbook
- Math Companion

Math Intervention
- Skills Review and Practice Workbook
- Math XL

4. Assess & Reteach

PRESENTATION CD-ROM
CD, Online, or Transparencies
Lesson Quiz

Evaluate each expression.

1. $9 + 5 \times 6 - 7$ 32

2. $(12 - 8) \times 10 \div 5$ 8

3. $(4 \times 62) + (4 \times 85)$ 588

4. $200 - (99 \div 3) \times 2$ 134

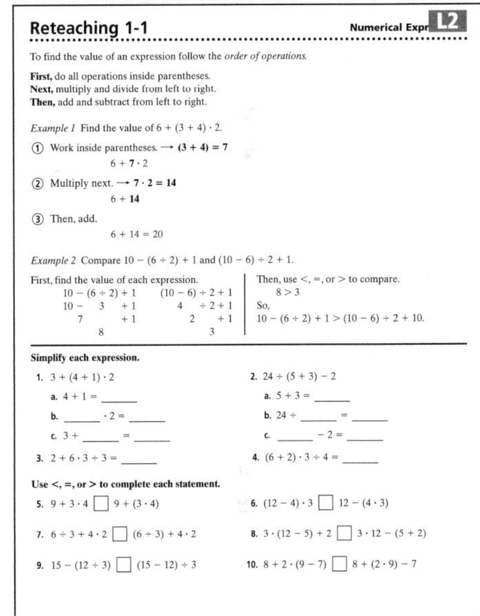

Reteaching 1-1 Numerical Expr L2

To find the value of an expression follow the *order of operations.*

First, do all operations inside parentheses.
Next, multiply and divide from left to right.
Then, add and subtract from left to right.

Example 1 Find the value of $6 + (3 + 4) \cdot 2$.

① Work inside parentheses. → $(3 + 4) = 7$
$6 + 7 \cdot 2$

② Multiply next. → $7 \cdot 2 = 14$
$6 + 14$

③ Then, add.
$6 + 14 = 20$

Example 2 Compare $10 - (6 \div 2) + 1$ and $(10 - 6) \div 2 + 1$.

First, find the value of each expression.

$10 - (6 \div 2) + 1$	$(10 - 6) \div 2 + 1$
$10 - 3 + 1$	$4 \div 2 + 1$
$7 + 1$	$2 + 1$
8	3

Then, use <, =, or > to compare.
$8 > 3$
So,
$10 - (6 \div 2) + 1 > (10 - 6) \div 2 + 10.$

Simplify each expression.

1. $3 + (4 + 1) \cdot 2$
   a. $4 + 1 =$ ____
   b. ____ $\cdot 2 =$ ____
   c. $3 +$ ____ $=$ ____
2. $24 \div (5 + 3) - 2$
   a. $5 + 3 =$ ____
   b. $24 \div$ ____ $=$ ____
   c. ____ $- 2 =$ ____
3. $2 + 6 \cdot 3 \div 3 =$ ____
4. $(6 + 2) \cdot 3 \div 4 =$ ____

Use <, =, or > to complete each statement.

5. $9 + 3 \cdot 4$ □ $9 + (3 \cdot 4)$
6. $(12 - 4) \cdot 3$ □ $12 - (4 \cdot 3)$
7. $6 \div 3 + 4 \cdot 2$ □ $(6 \div 3) + 4 \cdot 2$
8. $3 \cdot (12 - 5) + 2$ □ $3 \cdot 12 - (5 + 2)$
9. $15 - (12 \div 3)$ □ $(15 - 12) \div 3$
10. $8 + 2 \cdot (9 - 7)$ □ $8 + (2 \cdot 9) - 7$

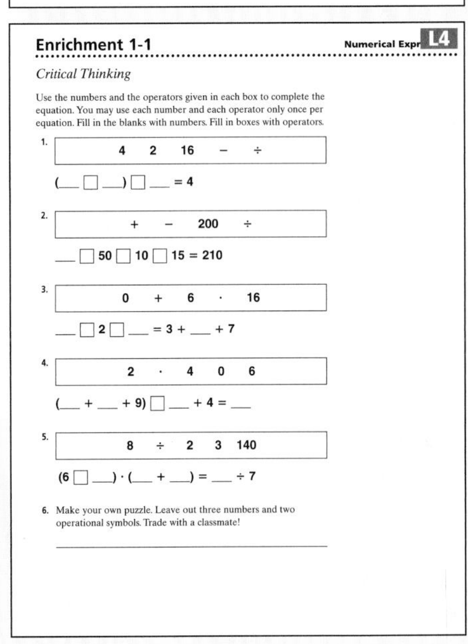

Enrichment 1-1 Numerical Expr L4

Critical Thinking

Use the numbers and the operators given in each box to complete the equation. You may use each number and each operator only once per equation. Fill in the blanks with numbers. Fill in boxes with operators.

1. 4 2 16 − ÷
   (__ □ __) □ __ = 4
2. + − 200 ÷
   __ □ 50 □ 10 □ 15 = 210
3. 0 + 6 · 16
   __ □ 2 □ __ = 3 + __ + 7
4. 2 · 4 0 6
   (__ + __ + 9) □ __ + 4 = __
5. 8 ÷ 2 3 140
   (6 □ __) · (__ + __) = __ ÷ 7
6. Make your own puzzle. Leave out three numbers and two operational symbols. Trade with a classmate!

GO for Help: Math Companion

1-2

1. Plan

California Content Standards

Evaluate algebraic expressions. *Foundational*

Compute the value of an expression for specific values of the variable. *Foundational*

NS 1.2 Add, subtract, multiply, and divide rational numbers. *Introduce*

California Math Background

You can use any letter to represent a variable, so it may help to choose a letter that relates to the meaning of the variable, such as *h* for the number of hours. An algebraic expression can be *simplified* without having any value for the variable. To *evaluate* an expression, a value for the variable is necessary.

More Math Background: p. 2C

Lesson Planning and Resources

See p. 2E for a list of the resources that support this lesson.

...PRESENTATION CD-ROM
CD, Online, or Transparencies

Bell Ringer Practice

Check Skills You'll Need
Use student page, transparency, or PowerPoint.
See Math Companion.

California Standards Review
Use transparency or PowerPoint.

1-2 Algebraic Expressions

Check Skills You'll Need
Do this in your **Math Companion.**

Vocabulary
- variable
- algebraic expression
- evaluate

Use your **Math Companion** *to build your vocabulary.*

California Content Standards
Foundational Standard Evaluate algebraic expressions.
Foundational Standard Compute the value of an expression for specific values of the variable.
NS 1.2 Add, subtract, multiply, and divide rational numbers. ***Introduce***

What You'll Learn . . . and Why

You will learn to evaluate algebraic expressions. Some types of technology use algebraic expressions. The title screen of a video game usually asks, "How many players?" The number of players is a variable. The game software uses your entry to set up the game.

A **variable** is a symbol that can represent one or more numbers. A mathematical expression with one or more variables is an **algebraic expression.** In the algebraic expressions at the right, d and x are variables.

5d 7x − 2
variables

You can draw diagrams to model algebraic expressions.

▫ represents 1. ▮ represents x.

Math Foundations
The expression $5x$ means "5 times a number x." It can also be written as $5 \times x$ and $5 \cdot x$.

EXAMPLE Modeling an Algebraic Expression

1 Model the expression $5x + 3$.

In this expression, there are five x's and three 1's.

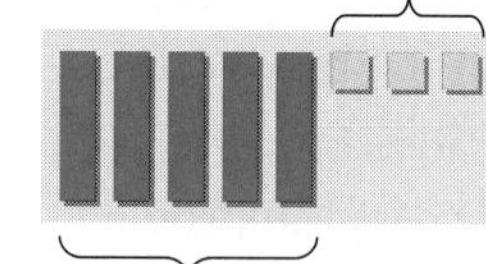

This part represents 3.
This part represents 5x.

CA Standards Check 1 *Go to your* **Math Companion** *for help.*

1. Model each expression. 1a–b. See above left.
   a. $x + 2$ b. $3x + 4$

1a. 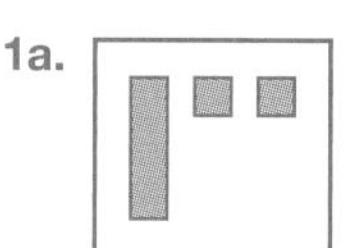

b. 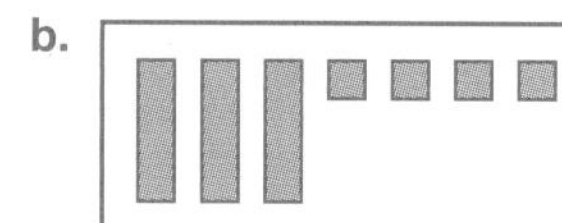

Universal Access Solutions for All Learners

Special Needs L1	**Below Level** L2
Have students model the numerical expression $3 + 2$ using objects. Then have them model $x + 2$ using diagrams. Ask what the difference is. We know the value fo 3 in 3 + 2, but we do not know the value of x.	Review *numbers, variables,* and *operation symbols.* Students provide examples of each. Then students write algebraic expressions using their examples.

To **evaluate** an algebraic expression, replace each variable with a number. Then use the order of operations to simplify the expression.

EXAMPLE Evaluating an Algebraic Expression

Relate MATH YOU KNOW...

What is the value of 2 · ■ − 8 when ■ = 11.2?

2 · ■ − 8 = 2 · 11.2 − 8 ← Replace ■ with 11.2.
= 22.4 − 8 ← Follow the order of operations. First multiply.
= 14.4 ← Then subtract.

... *to* ALGEBRA

2 Evaluate $2x - 8$ for $x = 11.2$.

$2x - 8 = 2 \cdot 11.2 - 8$ ← Replace *x* with 11.2.
$= 22.4 - 8$ ← Follow the order of operations. First multiply.
$= 14.4$ ← Then subtract.

CA Standards Check 2 *Go to your* **Math Companion** *for help.*

2. Evaluate each expression for $x = 7$.
   a. $56.8 - 4x$ 28.8
   b. $(3.7 + x) \div 5$ 2.14

You can evaluate an expression using more than one value. Make a table to organize the different values.

EXAMPLE Using a Table to Evaluate an Expression

3 **Guided Problem Solving** You work at a store that rents video games for $3. The expression 3*g* represents the amount the store earns when it rents *g* games. Copy and complete the table for the given number of games.

Video Game Earnings

Number of Games	Expression	Amount Earned	
g	3 · *g*	3*g*	← Substitute for *g*.
15	3 · ■	■	← 3 · 15 = 45
40	3 · ■	■	← 3 · 40 = 120
65	3 · ■	■	← 3 · 65 = 195

CA Standards Check 3 *Go to your* **Math Companion** *for help.*

3. Another store rents games for $4.50. The expression 4.5*g* represents the amount the store earns renting *g* games. Make a table to find the amount the store earns when 35, 50, or 60 games are rented.
See margin.

Check Your Understanding *Homework prep is in your* **Math Companion.**

2. Teach

Guided Instruction

Example 1
Ask: *What does the green tile represent?* a variable *What does a yellow tile represent?* 1

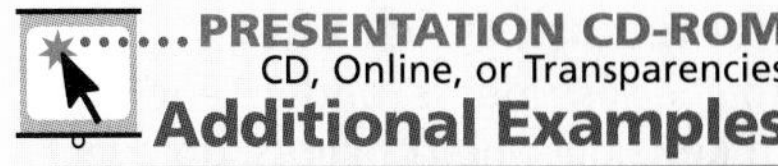

Additional Examples

1 Draw a diagram to model the expression $2x - 3$.

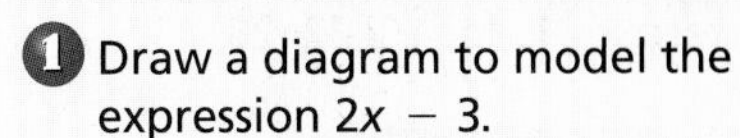

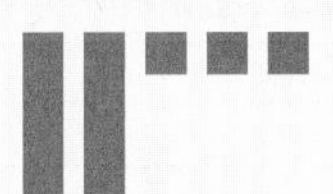

2 Evaluate $8x + 2$ for $x = 3$. 26

3 The cost to rent a canoe at the lake is a $6 basic fee plus $4 for each hour *h* the canoe is rented. The expression for the total cost of a canoe rental is $6 + $4*h*. Copy and complete the table.

Hours	Total Cost
h	6 + 4*h*
1	■ 10
2	■ 14
3	■ 18

Closure

- *What is a variable?* a symbol that represents an unknown
- What is an algebraic expression? a mathematical expression with at least one variable
- *What does it mean to evaluate an algebraic expression?* to replace each variable with a number and then simplify

Advanced Learners L4	**English Learners** EL
Students research the force of gravity on Mars and Venus and write an algebraic expression for weight on each of these planets.	Students often mistake a term like 3*g*, where the variable *g* stands for games, as 3 games. In Example 3, make sure students read 3*g* as *3 times the number of games*.

3. Practice

Assignment Guide

Check Your Understanding
See Math Companion.

Homework Exercises

A	Practice by Example	1–20
B	Apply Your Skills	21–31
C	Challenge	32
California Multiple Choice Practice		33–34
Mixed Review		35–37

Homework Quick Check
To check students' understanding of key skills and concepts, go over Exercises 1, 11, 19, 22, 28, 31.

Universal Access Resources

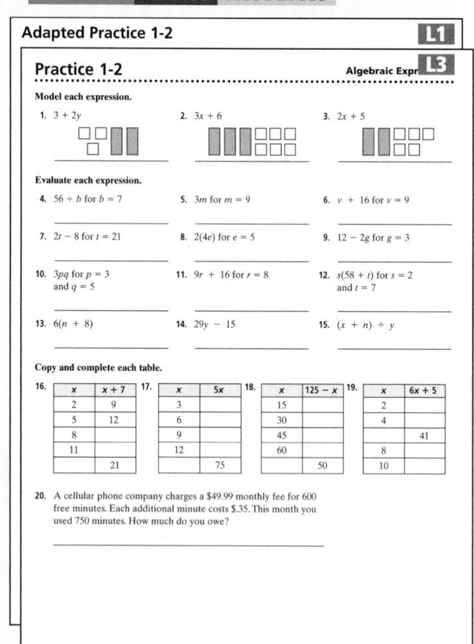
Adapted Practice 1-2 L1

Practice 1-2 L3 Algebraic Expr…

Model each expression.

1. $3 + 2y$ 2. $3x + 6$ 3. $2x + 5$

Evaluate each expression.

4. $56 \div b$ for $b = 7$ 5. $3m$ for $m = 9$ 6. $v + 16$ for $v = 9$

7. $2t - 8$ for $t = 21$ 8. $2(4e)$ for $e = 5$ 9. $12 - 2g$ for $g = 3$

10. $3pq$ for $p = 3$ and $q = 5$ 11. $9r + 16$ for $r = 8$ 12. $s(58 + t)$ for $s = 2$ and $t = 7$

13. $6(n + 8)$ 14. $29y - 15$ 15. $(x + n) \div y$

Copy and complete each table.

16.

x	$x + 7$
2	9
5	12
8	
11	
	21

17.

x	$5x$
3	
6	
9	
12	
	75

18.

x	$125 - x$
15	
30	
45	
60	
	50

19.

x	$6x + 5$
2	
4	
	41
8	
10	

20. A cellular phone company charges a $49.99 monthly fee for 600 free minutes. Each additional minute costs $.35. This month you used 750 minutes. How much do you owe?

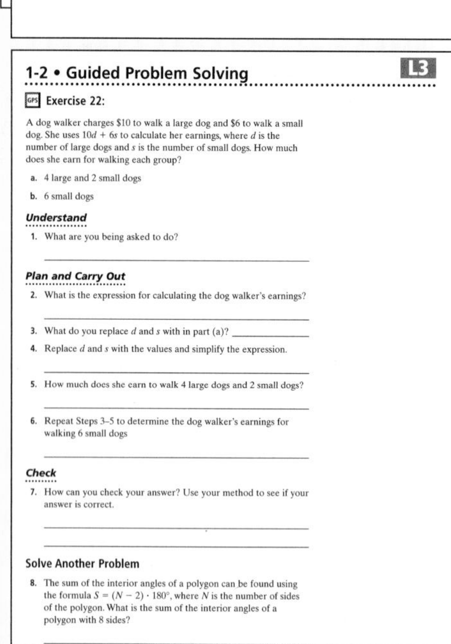
1-2 • Guided Problem Solving L3

GPS Exercise 22:

A dog walker charges $10 to walk a large dog and $6 to walk a small dog. She uses $10d + 6s$ to calculate her earnings, where d is the number of large dogs and s is the number of small dogs. How much does she earn for walking each group?

a. 4 large and 2 small dogs

b. 6 small dogs

Understand

1. What are you being asked to do?

Plan and Carry Out

2. What is the expression for calculating the dog walker's earnings?

3. What do you replace d and s with in part (a)?

4. Replace d and s with the values and simplify the expression.

5. How much does she earn to walk 4 large dogs and 2 small dogs?

6. Repeat Steps 3–5 to determine the dog walker's earnings for walking 6 small dogs

Check

7. How can you check your answer? Use your method to see if your answer is correct.

Solve Another Problem

8. The sum of the interior angles of a polygon can be found using the formula $S = (N - 2) \cdot 180°$, where N is the number of sides of the polygon. What is the sum of the interior angles of a polygon with 8 sides?

Standards Practice

GO for Help: *MathXL*

NS 1.2

A Practice by Example

Model each expression.

Example 1 (page 8)

1. $3x + 5$ 1–5. See below left.

Use ▮ for x. Use ▫ for 1.

Guided Practice: This exercise has been started for you!

GO for Help

2. $x + 3$ 3. 8 4. $x + 4$ 5. $4 + 2x$

6. $3x + 1$ 7. $5x$ 8. $1 + x$ 9. $2x + 6$

6–9. See margin.

Example 2 (page 9)

Evaluate each expression.

10. $24 \div d$ for $d = 3$ 8

$24 \div d = 24 \div 3$

$= ■$

Guided Practice: This exercise has been started for you!

Homework Video Tutor

For: Examples 1–3
Visit: PHSchool.com
Web Code: axe-0102

11. $p + 8$ for $p = 5$ 13

12. $8b - 12$ for $b = 2$ 4

13. $18 - 3y$ for $y = 3$ 9

14. $(g + 9) \div 3$ for $g = 6$ 5

15. $21 \div (t - 2)$ for $t = 9$ 3

16. $10m \div 5$ for $m = 1.5$ 3

Example 3 (page 9)

17. The rental fee for a bicycle is $5, plus $2 for each hour h the bike is rented. The expression for the total cost is $5 + 2h$. Copy and complete the table for the given number of hours.

Hour	Rental Fee	
h	$5 + 2h$	
1	■	7
2	■	9
3	■	11

1.

2.
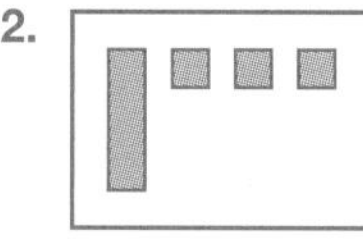

3.
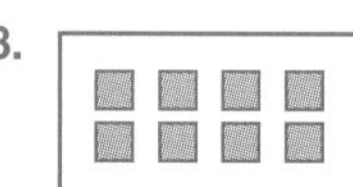

Copy and complete each table.

18.

x	$x + 6$	
1	7	
4	■	10
7	■	13

19.

x	$7x$	
2	■	14
4	■	28
6	■	42

20.

x	$100 - x$	
20	■	80
35	■	65
50	■	50

B Apply Your Skills

4.
5.
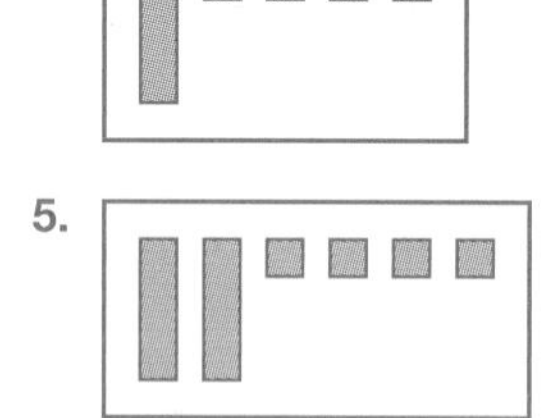

21. **Guided Problem Solving** The formula $P = 2\ell + 2w$ gives the distance around a rectangle with length ℓ and width w. Find P for a rectangle with length 7 cm and width 4 cm. 22 cm
- Replace each variable in the formula with the given values.
- Use the order of operations to simplify the expression.

GPS 22. A dog walker charges $10 to walk a large dog and $6 to walk a small dog. She uses $10d + 6s$ to calculate her earnings, where d is the number of large dogs and s is the number of small dogs. How much does she earn for walking each group?

a. 4 large and 2 small dogs $52 **b.** 6 small dogs $36

SCAFFOLDED
Problem Solving

A student sells balloons at the school fair. She starts with 100 balloons. Every hour, she counts the remaining balloons. The numbers are shown in the table below.

Hours Passed	1	2	3	4
Number of Balloons	90	80	70	60

23. How many balloons are remaining after 1 h? After 3 h? 90 balloons; 70 balloons

24. How many balloons does the student sell each hour? 10 balloons

25. Which expression can you use to find the number of balloons remaining after h hours? C

    (A) $10h$ (B) $100 - h$ (C) $100 - 10h$

26. Use the correct expression to predict the number of balloons that will be left after 6 h if the pattern continues. 40 balloons

27. If the pattern continues, after how many hours will the student run out of balloons? 10 h

28. The service charging $1 + 2n$ dollars; this service charges between \$3 and \$7, and the other charges between \$5 and \$7.

Supreme Taxi

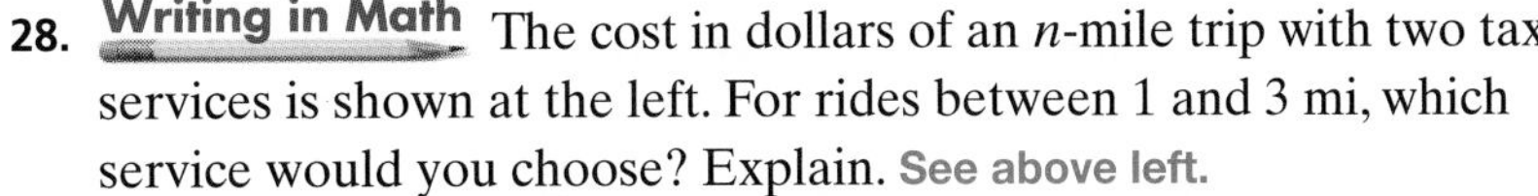

28. **Writing in Math** The cost in dollars of an n-mile trip with two taxi services is shown at the left. For rides between 1 and 3 mi, which service would you choose? Explain. See above left.

4 + n

Townie Taxi

Evaluate each expression for $a = 9$ and $b = 4$.

29. $11a - 6b$ 75

30. $2ab$ 72

31. $9b \div a + b$ 8

Challenge

32. Bob plays a game at the school fair. He starts with 0 points. He gets 25 throws. He wins 12 points for hitting the target and loses 8 points for each miss. Bob ends with a score of 0. How many hits and misses does Bob have? 10 hits, 15 misses

Multiple Choice Practice and Mixed Review

For California Standards Tutorials, visit PHSchool.com. Web Code: axq-9045

NS 1.2

33. Evaluate $w + w \div 2$ for $w = 14$. C

    (A) 7 (B) 14 (C) 21 (D) 28

NS 1.2

34. Mr. Vasquez can seat 200 people at his restaurant. So far tonight, Mr. Vasquez has seated 8 booths with 6 people each. How many empty seats are left in the restaurant? B

    (A) 48 seats (C) 198 seats
    (B) 152 seats (D) 248 seats

for Help

Lesson 1-1

Simplify each expression.

35. $(7.3 + 7.7) \div 3$ 5

36. $16 - 5 \cdot 2.2$ 5

37. $27 \div 3 + 6.8$ 15.8

Online Lesson Quiz Visit: PHSchool.com Web Code: axa-0102

California Resources

Standards Mastery
- Standards Review Transparencies
- Standards Review and Practice Workbook
- Math Companion

Math Intervention
- Skills Review and Practice Workbook
- Math XL

4. Assess & Reteach

PRESENTATION CD-ROM
CD, Online, or Transparencies

Lesson Quiz

1. Write an expression for the number of months in y years. $12y$

2. Evaluate your expression in Exercise 1 for 7 years. 84 months

3. Evaluate $5n - n \div 2$ for $n = 10$. 45

4. Evaluate $3c - 5$ for $c = 2, 4,$ and 6. 1, 7, 13

Alternative Assessment

Students work in pairs to write one-step algebraic expressions, such as $x + 4$ and $4x$, for each of the four operations. Together, partners use number sense to decide on a value for the variable in each expression and then evaluate the expression. When students show proficiency in evaluating simple expressions, vary the activity by having them write and evaluate expressions such as $4x - 3$ and $5x \div 4$.

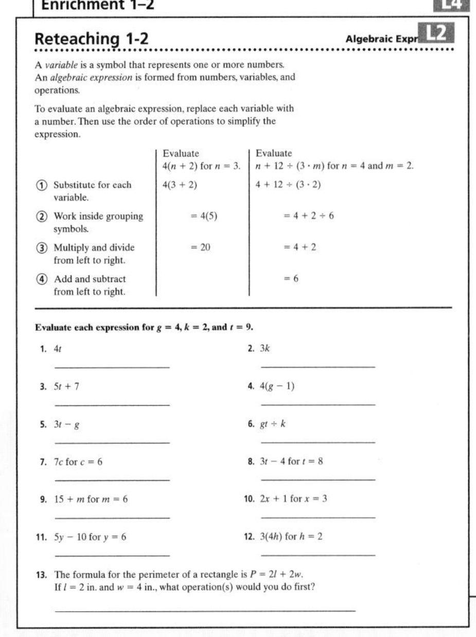

Enrichment 1–2 L4

Reteaching 1-2 Algebraic Expr L2

A *variable* is a symbol that represents one or more numbers. An *algebraic expression* is formed from numbers, variables, and operations.

To evaluate an algebraic expression, replace each variable with a number. Then use the order of operations to simplify the expression.

	Evaluate $4(n + 2)$ for $n = 3$.	Evaluate $n + 12 \div (3 \cdot m)$ for $n = 4$ and $m = 2$.
① Substitute for each variable.	$4(3 + 2)$	$4 + 12 \div (3 \cdot 2)$
② Work inside grouping symbols.	$= 4(5)$	$= 4 + 2 \div 6$
③ Multiply and divide from left to right.	$= 20$	$= 4 + 2$
④ Add and subtract from left to right.		$= 6$

Evaluate each expression for $g = 4$, $k = 2$, and $t = 9$.

1. $4t$ ______
2. $3k$ ______
3. $5t + 7$ ______
4. $4(g - 1)$ ______
5. $3t - g$ ______
6. $gt \div k$ ______
7. $7c$ for $c = 6$ ______
8. $3t - 4$ for $t = 8$ ______
9. $15 + m$ for $m = 6$ ______
10. $2x + 1$ for $x = 3$ ______
11. $5y - 10$ for $y = 6$ ______
12. $3(4h)$ for $h = 2$ ______
13. The formula for the perimeter of a rectangle is $P = 2l + 2w$. If $l = 2$ in. and $w = 4$ in., what operation(s) would you do first? ______

Use this Checkpoint Quiz to check students' understanding of the skills and concepts of Lessons 1-1 through 1-2.

Resources

- All-in-One Teaching Resources Checkpoint Quiz 1

Mathematical Reasoning

Justify Each Step

Students learn how justifying their steps to a solution can help them avoid reasoning mistakes.

Guided Instruction

Explain to students how writing out and justifying each step can be used to avoid mistakes and to explain their reasoning to someone else. For Exercises 2 and 3, ask students to write out each step as they simplify the expressions. Show them how to stack the steps vertically and line them up. Then ask them to write a justification to the right of each step.

Mathematical Reasoning

For Use With Lesson 1-2

NS 1.2 Add, subtract, multiply, and divide rational numbers. ***Develop***
MR 2.6 Support solutions with evidence in both verbal and symbolic work. ***Develop***

Justify Each Step

Some exercises ask you to justify your reasoning or explain each step in a solution. Supporting your solutions with words will help you to avoid reasoning mistakes.

1. A student simplified the expression $14.4 - (6.9 - 2.7) \cdot 2.5$ as shown below. Explain the student's mistake. **The student did add. before mult.**

$14.4 - (6.9 - 2.7) \cdot 2.5 = 14.4 - 4.2 \cdot 2.5$ Step 1 : Work within grouping symbols.
$= 10.2 \cdot 2.5$ Step 2 : Add from left to right.
$= 25.5$ Step 3 : Multiply from left to right.

2. Simplify the expression $14.4 - (6.9 - 2.7) \cdot 2.5$. Justify each step. **See margin.**

3. Evaluate the expression $13.3 - (t + 6.4) \div 2$ for $t = 4.2$. Justify each step. **See margin.**

Checkpoint Quiz 1

Lessons 1-1 through 1-2

Simplify each expression.

1. $6.2 \cdot 5.1 - 30.6$ **1.02**
2. $(1.2 + 23) \cdot 2.1$ **50.82**
3. $6.2 + 3.9 \div 3$ **7.5**
4. $15.5 - 12.3 + 9 \div 3$ **6.2**
5. A class goes on a field trip to the zoo. Admission costs \$9 for adults and \$6.50 for students. What is the total cost of admission for a class of 23 students and one teacher? **\$158.50**

Evaluate each expression for $x = 7$.

6. $8x$ **56**
7. $3(x - 4)$ **9**
8. $3 + (2x + 6)$ **23**
9. $4.2 + [x - (3x)]$ **−9.8**
10. A store has CDs on sale for \$7.50 each and DVDs on sale for \$12 each. The expression $7.5c + 12d$ gives the total cost for c CDs and d DVDs. Find the total cost of 4 CDs and 2 DVDs. **\$54**

1-3a Activity Lab

Modeling Expressions

You can draw a diagram to help understand a verbal description.

Prepares for **AF 1.1** Write an expression that represents a verbal description.
MR 2.5 Use models to explain mathematical reasoning. ***Develop***

Operation	Verbal Description	Diagram 1	Diagram 2
addition	a number m plus 3.2 the sum of a number m and 3.2 3.2 more than a number m	m 3.2	m | 3.2
subtraction	a number p minus 6 the difference of a number p and 6 6 subtracted from a number p	p ? 6	p ? | 6
multiplication	4 times a number k the product of 4 and a number k	k k k k	k | k | k | k
division	the quotient of a number z and 5 a number z divided by 5	z ? ? ? ? ?	z ? | ? | ? | ? | ?

EXAMPLE

1 Draw a diagram for each verbal description.

a. 2.5 more than x

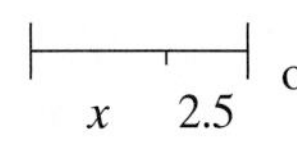

or

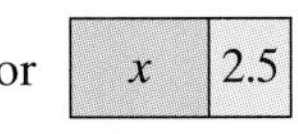

b. the product of 3 and w

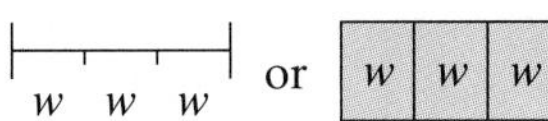

Exercises

Copy and complete the table below. Each line is missing two parts. 1–4. See back of book.

Verbal Description	Diagram 1	Diagram 2
1. Height h divided by 6	■	■
2. ?	■	q | 8
3. ?	r r r r r r r	■
4. 6.3 smaller than t	■	■

Activity Lab

Modeling Expressions

Students use diagrams to represent word phrases. This will allow students to more easily change words to algebraic expressions in Lesson 1-3.

Guided Instruction

Before beginning the Activity Lab, ask students for examples of diagrams they are familiar with that give a message. Ask questions such as:

- *What diagram indicates a school crossing?* Sample: a diagram of children crossing a street
- *What diagram represents a railroad crossing?* Sample: a diagram of tracks

Exercises

Have students work in pairs. For each line in Exercises 1–4, one partner can fill in one of the missing parts and the other partner can fill in the other missing part. Have them compare and discuss their work. Then have pairs write their own mathematical word phrase and draw a diagram for it.

Alternative Method

Some students may prefer to use algebra tiles to model word phrases.

GO for Help: Math Companion

1-3

1. Plan

California Content Standards

Write verbal expressions as algebraic expressions. ***Foundational***

AF 1.1 Use variables and appropriate operations to write an expression that represents a verbal description. ***Introduce***

California Math Background

An English phrase is a collection of words that form a cohesive unit, but the unit is less than a complete sentence. In a sense, expressions are the phrases of mathematics. That is, an expression is a collection of numbers, variables, and operation symbols that form a cohesive unit, but these units are less than a complete mathematical sentence.

More Math Background: p. 2

Lesson Planning and Resources

See p. 2 for a list of the resources that support this lesson.

PRESENTATION CD-ROM
CD, Online, or Transparencies

Bell Ringer Practice

Check Skills You'll Need
Use student page, transparency, or PowerPoint.
See Math Companion.

California Standards Review
Use transparency or PowerPoint.

1-3 Writing Expressions

Check Skills You'll Need

Do this in your **Math Companion.**

Vocabulary

Review:
- variable
- algebraic expression
- evaluate

Use your **Math Companion** *to build your vocabulary.*

California Content Standards

Foundational Standard Write verbal expressions as algebraic expressions.
AF 1.1 Use variables and appropriate operations to write an expression that represents a verbal description. ***Introduce***

What You'll Learn . . . and Why

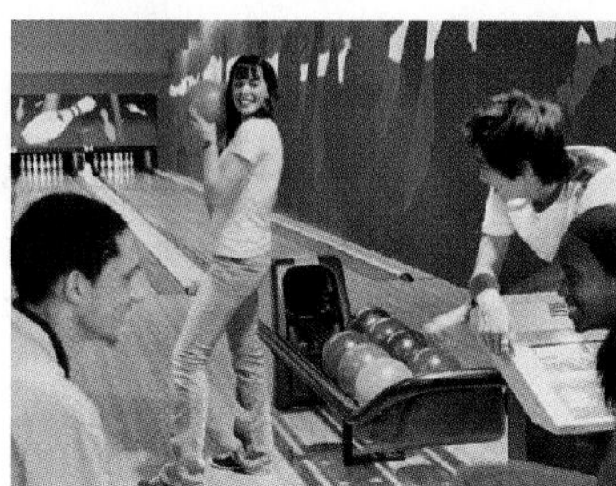

You will learn to write algebraic expressions. You can use an algebraic expression to represent the cost of a night out bowling with your friends.

You can use a model to help you translate a verbal description to an algebraic expression.

The model below represents *4.5 more than a number x.*

x	4.5

You can write this verbal description as $x + 4.5$.

The table below gives some examples of verbal descriptions written as algebraic expressions.

Operation	Verbal Description	Model	Algebraic Expression
Addition	• A number m plus 3.2 • The sum of a number m and 3.2 • 3.2 more than a number m	m | 3.2	$m + 3.2$
Subtraction	• A number p minus 6 • The difference of a number p and 6 • 6 less than a number p	p / ? | 6	$p - 6$
Multiplication	• 4 times a number k • The product of 4 and a number k	k | k | k | k	$4 \cdot k$ or $4k$
Division	• A number z divided by 5 • The quotient of a number z and 5	z / ? | ? | ? | ? | ?	$z \div 5$ or $\frac{z}{5}$

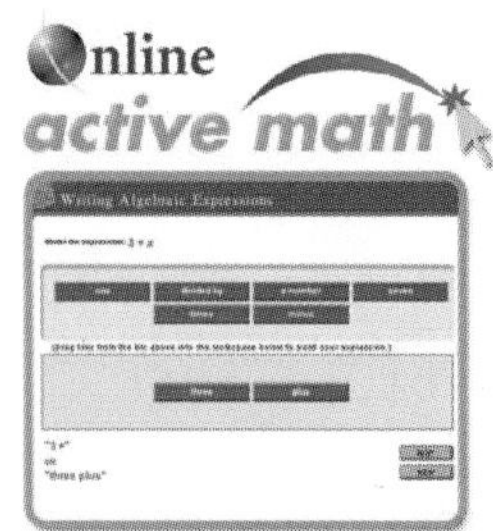

Online active math

For: Algebraic Expressions Activity
Use: Interactive Textbook, 1-3

Universal Access Solutions for All Learners

Special Needs L1
Show students several models that represent algebraic expressions. Have them write the expression that each model represents.

Below Level L2
Have students say word phrases for simple numerical expressions. For example:
$3 + 2$ 3 plus 2, the sum of 3 and 2
6×5 6 times 5, the product of 6 and 5

EXAMPLE From Words to Expressions

1 Write an expression for the verbal description *7 less than a number k.*

Use a model to help you write the expression.

k	
?	7

$k - 7$ ← **Use subtraction to represent *less than*.**

CA Standards Check 1 *Go to your* **Math Companion** *for help.*

1. Write an expression for each verbal description.

a. the product of 2 and x $2x$ **b.** q divided by 8 $q \div 8$

When you write an algebraic expression, remember to state what the variable represents.

EXAMPLE Writing an Algebraic Expression

Relate **MATH YOU KNOW...**

You go bowling and bowl three games. One game of bowling costs \$3. Shoe rental for the day is \$1.75. Find your total cost.

The model represents the situation.

Total Cost			
3	3	3	1.75

Since $3 + 3 + 3 + 1.75 = 10.75$, the total cost is \$10.75.

... to **ALGEBRA**

2 **Guided Problem Solving** You go bowling and bowl three games. Write an algebraic expression for the total cost for bowling three games at any cost per game. Include shoe rental of \$1.75.

Problem Solving Tip

When you choose a variable, use a letter that reminds you of what the variable stands for.

Let g = the cost of the game. ← **Choose a variable to represent the cost of one game.**

Total Cost			
g	g	g	1.75

Each g represents the cost of one game.

The total cost is $3g + 1.75$.

CA Standards Check 2 *Go to your* **Math Companion** *for help.*

2. Brandon is 28 years younger than his father. Write an expression using Brandon's age to describe his father's age. $b + 28$

2. Teach

Guided Instruction

Example 1

Use arrows to connect the corresponding words and symbols.

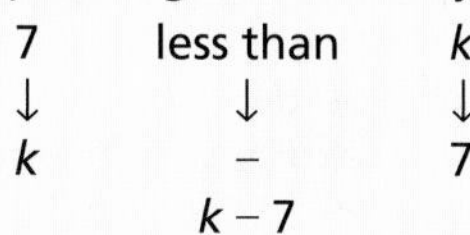

Error Prevention!

For Example 2, students might write $3 \times g$. Point out that the $\times$ symbol can be misread as the variable x, so it is generally avoided in algebraic expressions. Preferred forms include $3g$ and $3 \cdot g$.

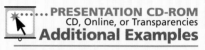

... PRESENTATION CD-ROM CD, Online, or Transparencies

Additional Examples

1 Write an expression for each word phrase.

a. 8 less than r $r - 8$

b. y is divided by 12 $y \div 12$

2 An ad reads, "Buy 3 T-shirts of the same kind, take \$5 off the total." Let t represent the cost of one T-shirt. Write an algebraic expression for the total cost of 3 T-shirts. $3t - 5$

Advanced Learners L4

Have students write several algebraic expressions for everday situations. Remind them to define the variable. **Sample: If I order *d* dozen cookies, the total number of cookies is 12*d*.**

English Learners EL

Ask students to translate the thinking in Luis's Method into a table. His input will be the number of minutes, and the output will be the cost. Translating words to a graphic organizer helps students develop comprehension skills.

Closure

- *How do you write a word phrase as an algebraic expression?* Sample: Identify a quantity that can be represented by a variable; look for words or phrases that suggest addition, subtraction, multiplication, or division.
- *How do you describe an algebraic expression in words?* Sample: You can write the words you say when you read the expression, or you can use a word or phrase that suggests the operation involved.
- *How do you evaluate an algebraic expression?* Replace each variable with a number and then simplify.

More Than One Way

A long distance call costs 10 cents, plus 4.5 cents for each minute. How much will an 8-minute call cost?

Tina's Method

I can let m represent the number of minutes. To find the cost of the call, I can use the algebraic expression $10 + 4.5m$. I will evaluate the expression for $m = 8$.

$10 + 4.5m = 10 + 4.5(8)$ ← **Replace *m* with 8.**

$= 10 + 36$ ← **Multiply 4.5 and 8.**

$= 46$ ← **Add 10 to 36.**

The telephone call will cost 46 cents.

Daryl's Method

If one minute costs 4.5 cents, then a two-minute call will cost 9 cents. Four minutes will cost 18 cents, and eight minutes will cost 36 cents. I need to add the 10 cents. So the total cost is 36 cents + 10 cents, or 46 cents.

Choose a Method

Another long-distance plan charges 5 cents per call, plus 6 cents for each minute. Find how much a 10-minute call costs with this plan. Describe your method and explain why you chose it. 65 cents; check students' work.

GO for Help: *MathXL*

Standards Practice

AF 1.1

A Practice by Example

Example 1 (page 15)

GO for Help

For: Examples 1–2
Visit: PHSchool.com
Web Code: axe-0103

Write an expression for each verbal description.

1. d more than 50 $50 + d$

Guided Practice This exercise has been started for you!

50	d

50 ■ d

2. 23 times q $23q$
3. 5 less than m $m - 5$
4. 7 decreased by b $7 - b$
5. p multiplied by 14 $14p$
6. f divided by 3 $f \div 3$
7. the sum of a and 6 $a + 6$
8. n less than 19 $19 - n$
9. 21 divided by w $21 \div w$

Homework prep is in your **Math Companion.**

Example 2 (page 15)

Write an expression for each verbal description.

10. the number of days in w weeks
    $7 \cdot$ ■ $7w$

Guided Practice
This exercise has been started for you!

11. the number of eggs n divided by 9 $n \div 9$
12. \$5 more than the price p $p + 5$
13. 8 lb less than the weight w $w - 8$
14. the number of students s plus 2 teachers $s + 2$
15. \$10 multiplied by h hours $10h$
16. 175 pages divided by d days $175 \div d$
17. Three brothers earn money by doing yard work. The brothers split the money equally. Write an expression that describes how much money each brother earns. $m \div 3$

B Apply Your Skills

18. **Guided Problem Solving** A hot-air balloon is at a height of 2,250 ft. It descends 150 ft per min. Find its height after 6, 8, and 10 min. 1,350 ft; 1,050 ft; 750 ft
    - Make a table to show the pattern of the balloon's height.
    - Write an expression for the balloon's height at m minutes.

Match each expression with its model.

A.

3	x

B.

x	x	x

C.

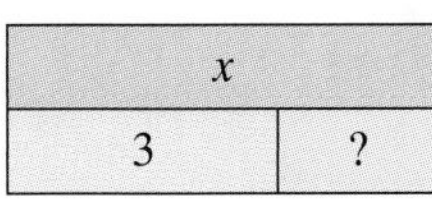

19. $3x$ B
20. $x - 3$ C
21. $3 + x$ A
22. **Writing in Math** Describe a situation you could model with the expression $y \div 3$. Check students' work.

SCAFFOLDED **Problem Solving**

Customers in a paint store use the table at the right to decide how much paint they need.

Area (ft.^{2})	Gallons
400	1
800	2
2,000	5
3,200	8

23. How much paint do you need to paint an area of 800 ft^2? 2 gal
24. How many square feet can you paint with each gallon of paint? 400 ft^2
25. Write an expression for the number of gallons of paint needed for an area of A ft^2. $A \div 400$
26. How much paint do you need to paint an area of 2,400 ft^2? 6 gal
27. Paint costs \$17.95 per gallon. Write an expression to find the cost of the paint needed for an area of A ft^2. $17.95 \cdot (A \div 400)$

3. Practice

Assignment Guide

Check Your Understanding
See Math Companion.

Homework Exercises

A	Practice by Example	1–17
B	Apply Your Skills	18–33
C	Challenge	34
California Multiple Choice Practice		35–37
Mixed Review		38–40

Homework Quick Check
To check students' understanding of key skills and concepts, go over Exercises 1, 11, 19, 22, 33.

Universal Access Resources

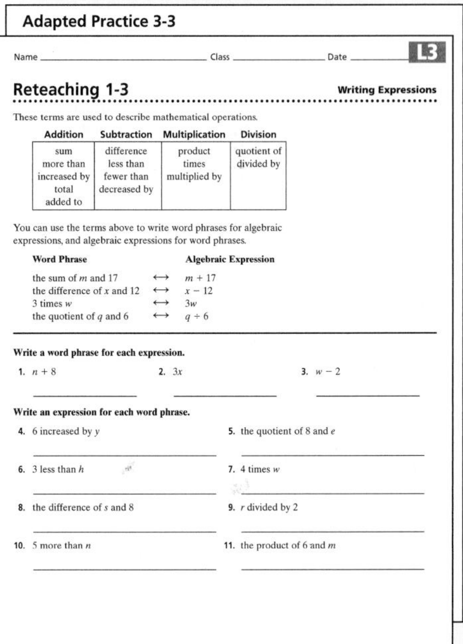
Adapted Practice 3-3

Name ______ Class ______ Date ______ L3

Reteaching 1-3 Writing Expressions

These terms are used to describe mathematical operations.

Addition	Subtraction	Multiplication	Division
sum more than increased by total added to	difference less than fewer than decreased by	product times multiplied by	quotient of divided by

You can use the terms above to write word phrases for algebraic expressions, and algebraic expressions for word phrases.

Word Phrase		Algebraic Expression
the sum of m and 17	⟷	$m + 17$
the difference of x and 12	⟷	$x - 12$
3 times w	⟷	$3w$
the quotient of q and 6	⟷	$q \div 6$

Write a word phrase for each expression.

1. $n + 8$
2. $3x$
3. $w - 2$

Write an expression for each word phrase.

4. 6 increased by y
5. the quotient of 8 and e
6. 3 less than h
7. 4 times w
8. the difference of s and 8
9. r divided by 2
10. 5 more than n
11. the product of 6 and m

Name ______ Class ______ Date ______ L3

1-3 • Guided Problem Solving

GPS **Exercise 29:**

a. An amusement park charges \$5 for admission and \$2 for each ride. Write an expression for the total cost of admission and r rides.

b. **Number Sense** How many rides can you go on if you have \$16?

Understand

1. What information is given in the problem?
2. What are you being asked to do?
3. What does it cost to enter the park? ______
4. What does a ride cost? ______

Plan and Carry Out

5. Write an expression for riding r rides costing \$2 each, after paying the cost for the admission.
6. Using your expression, how many rides can you go on with \$16?

Check

7. Is your expression reasonable? Does the expression check?

Solve Another Problem

8. A car-rental agency charges \$35 per day and \$.25 per mile. Write an expression for the cost of renting a car for one day and driving m miles. How many miles could you drive if you have only \$50?

4. Assess & Reteach

PRESENTATION CD-ROM
CD, Online, or Transparencies

Lesson Quiz

Write an expression for each word phrase.

1. a increased by 7 $a + 7$
2. 6 less than c $c - 6$

Alternative Assessment

Each student in a pair writes three word phrases similar to those in Exercises 1–5. Partners exchange papers and write the algebraic expression for each word phrase.

Name ______ Class ______ Date ______ **L2**

Reteaching 1-3 — **Writing Expressions**

These terms are used to describe mathematical operations.

Addition	Subtraction	Multiplication	Division
sum more than increased by total added to	difference less than fewer than decreased by	product times multiplied by	quotient of divided by

You can use the terms above to write word phrases for algebraic expressions, and algebraic expressions for word phrases.

Word Phrase		Algebraic Expression
the sum of m and 17	⟷	$m + 17$
the difference of x and 12	⟷	$x - 12$
3 times w	⟷	$3w$
the quotient of q and 6	⟷	$q \div 6$

Write a word phrase for each expression.

1. $n + 8$ ______
2. $3x$ ______
3. $w - 2$ ______

Write an expression for each word phrase.

4. 6 increased by y ______
5. the quotient of 8 and e ______
6. 3 less than h ______
7. 4 times w ______
8. the difference of s and 8 ______
9. r divided by 2 ______
10. 5 more than n ______
11. the product of 6 and m ______

Name ______ Class ______ Date ______ **L4**

Enrichment 1-3 — **Writing Expressions**

Algebra Patterns

For each math expression write the operation that undoes the expression. The first one is done for you.

1. twice the amount *one-half the amount*
2. 8 less than a number ______
3. the sum of x and 12 ______
4. 8 times the sum of 12 and x ______
5. one-third the amount ______
6. the product of x and 25 ______

After collecting data it is possible to represent the data using variables. Use this data for Exercises 7 and 8.

Total number of students in Algebra class	78
Total number of freshmen in Algebra class	55
Total number of athletes in Algebra class	31

7. If b is the number of boys taking Algebra, write an expression for the number of girls taking Algebra. ______
8. If s is the number of sophomores taking Algebra, write an expression for the number of juniors and seniors taking Algebra. ______
9. A textile pattern uses 24 feet of red yarn, 118 feet of blue, and y feet of yellow.
   a. Write an expression for the total amount of yarn you will use. ______
   b. Evaluate the expression to find the total amount of yarn if you use 46 feet of yellow. ______

28. The world's largest pan of lasagna weighed 3,477 lb. The length of the pan was ten times its width. The lasagna pan was 7 ft wide. Find the length of the pan. 70 ft

People spend over $11 billion per year at amusement parks in the United States.

GPS 29. a. An amusement park charges $5 for admission and $2 for each ride. Write an expression for the total cost of admission and r rides. $5 + 2r$
   b. **Number Sense** How many rides can you go on if you have $16? 5 rides

Use the table at the right to write an expression for the number of Calories in each situation.

Food	Calories
Peach	35
Banana	105
Bacon slice	37
Bread slice	65
Egg	75

30. p peaches $35p$
31. p peaches and n bananas $35p + 105n$
32. two slices of bread, b slices of bacon, and one egg $205 + 37b$
33. A store that personalizes shirts charges $20 for a shirt plus $.75 for each letter. Write an algebraic expression for the cost of t shirts using n letters each. $t \cdot (20 + 0.75n)$

Challenge

34. You have quarters, dimes, and nickels in a jar. There are twice as many quarters as nickels. Write an expression for the number of coins in the jar in terms of nickels and dimes. $3n + d$

Multiple Choice Practice and Mixed Review

For California Standards Tutorials, visit PHSchool.com. Web Code: axq-9045

AF 1.1

35. Dante bought three fewer than twice as many books as his sister bought. His sister bought b books. Which expression can you use to find the number of books Dante bought? D
   - A b
   - B $2b$
   - C $b - 3$
   - D $2b - 3$

NS 1.2

36. Simplify $5(3 - 2.5) + 9$. C
   - A 19.5
   - B 14.5
   - C 11.5
   - D 4.5

NS 1.2, MR 2.6

37. To find the area of a trapezoid with bases of 8 in. and 5 in. and a height of 6 in., you simplify the expression $\frac{1}{2}(8 + 5) \cdot 6$. Which step should you do first? A
   - A Add 8 and 5.
   - B Multiply 5 and 6.
   - C Divide 13 by $\frac{1}{2}$.
   - D Multiply $\frac{1}{2}$ and 6.

for Help — Lesson 1-2

Evaluate each expression for $w = 4$.

38. $6 + w \cdot 5$ 26
39. $9w - 6$ 30
40. $12 \div 3 \cdot w$ 16

Online Lesson Quiz Visit: PHSchool.com Web Code: axa-0103

California Resources

Standards Mastery
- Standards Review Transparencies
- Standards Review and Practice Workbook
- Math Companion

Math Intervention
- Skills Review and Practice Workbook
- Math XL

Vocabulary Builder

High-Use Academic Words

High-use academic words are words that you will see often in textbooks and on tests. These words are not math vocabulary terms, but knowing them will help you to succeed in mathematics.

Direction Words

Some words tell what to do in a problem. I need to understand what these words are asking so that I give the correct answer.

Word	Meaning
Identify	To show that you recognize something
List	To present information in order or to give examples
Justify	To give reasons supporting a decision or conclusion

Exercises

1. Identify each animal as a pet or a wild animal.
   a. kitten pet b. elephant wild animal c. dog pet d. crocodile wild animal
2. List five animals you could keep as a pet. Answers may vary. Sample: dog, cat, fish, bird, hamster
3. Justify your answer to Exercise 2. Check students' work.
4. Identify each expression as numerical or algebraic.
   a. $n \div 10$ algebraic b. $5 + (6 - 2) \div 3$ numerical c. $5x - y$ algebraic d. $(1 + 3) \cdot (10 - 3)$ numerical
5. List 3 different examples of an algebraic expression. Check students' work.
6. Is $10x$ a numerical expression? Justify your answer. No; numerical expressions do not contain variables.
7. **Word Knowledge** Think about the word *pattern*. 7a–c. Check students' work.
   a. Choose the letter for how well you know the word.
      A. I know its meaning.
      B. I've seen it, but I don't know its meaning.
      C. I don't know it.
   b. **Research** Look up and write a definition for *pattern.*
   c. Write a sentence involving mathematics and using the word *pattern.*

Vocabulary Builder

High-Use Academic Words

Students use a strategy for learning words that, while not math vocabulary terms, are important for success in mathematics and on tests.

Guided Instruction

Have students look through their texts for use of the terms *identify, list,* and *justify*. Ask the following questions:

- *Where do you find the term justify?* Sample: page xxx
- *What is another way to say "Order the decimals from least to greatest"?* Sample: List the decimals in order from least to greatest.
- *What direction could you write about even and odd numbers using the term* identify*?* Sample: Identify each number as even or odd.

Teaching Tip

Restate directions given in the text using *identify, list,* and *justify* as appropriate to familiarize students with these terms.

Universal Access

English Learners EL

Encourage students to write high-frequency academic words in their native language as needed.

1-4

1. Plan

California Content Standards

MR 2.1 Use estimation to verify the reasonableness of calculated results. ***Introduce***

NS 1.2 Add, subtract, multiply, and divide rational numbers. ***Introduce, Develop***

California Math Background

Whole numbers are rounded to the nearest 10, 100, and 1,000. You can round whole numbers to estimate sums, differences, and products. Two common estimation strategies are *rounding* and *compatible numbers*. Rounding is helpful when adding and subtracting numbers. Compatible numbers are used to estimate products and quotients.

More Math Background: p. 2C

Lesson Planning and Resources

See p. 2E for a list of the resources that support this lesson.

Bell Ringer Practice

Check Skills You'll Need
Use student page, transparency, or PowerPoint.
See Math Companion.

California Standards Review
Use transparency or PowerPoint.

1-4 Estimating for Reasonableness

Check Skills You'll Need

Do this in your **Math Companion.**

Vocabulary

- compatible numbers

Use your **Math Companion** *to build your vocabulary.*

California Content Standards

NS 1.2 Add, subtract, multiply, and divide rational numbers. ***Introduce, Develop***
MR 2.1 Use estimation to verify the reasonableness of calculated results. ***Introduce***

What You'll Learn . . . and Why

You will learn to use estimation to check for reasonableness. When you shop, estimation is useful for checking the total cost of the items you buy.

To estimate, you select numbers that are close to the exact numbers but are easier to use for computing. Rounding is one method you can use in estimation.

Round to the nearest: **One** **Hundred**

Look at the value to the right of the ones place. $7 \geq 5$ **so round up.**

Look at the value to the right of the hundreds place. $2 < 5$ **so round down.**

To estimate sums and differences, round each number to the same place before you add or subtract.

EXAMPLE Estimating by Rounding

1 Estimate 37 + 62 + 48. First round each number to the nearest ten.

37	$7 \geq 5$, so round up.	→	40
62	$2 < 5$, so round down.	→	60
+ 48	$8 \geq 5$, so round up.	→	+ 50
			150

So $37 + 62 + 48 \approx 150$.

Vocabulary Tip
The symbol ≈ means "is approximately equal to."

CA Standards Check 1 *Go to your* **Math Companion** *for help.*

1. Estimate. First round each number to the nearest ten.
   a. 22 + 97 + 48 about 170
   b. 94 − 32 − 41 about 20

Universal Access Solutions for All Learners

Special Needs L1	Below Level L2
Make sure students understand they are rounding to the nearest ten in Example 1. Have them circle the number they are rounding, and underline the number they will use to determine whether to round up or down.	Some students are confused by "unnecessary" digits. Have them circle the digit immediately to the right of the desired rounding place. Students can then cross out all other digits to the right of it.

Compatible numbers are numbers that are easy to compute mentally. They are particularly useful for estimating products and quotients.

EXAMPLE Estimating With Compatible Numbers

2 Estimate $298 \div 16$ using compatible numbers.

$$298 \div 16$$
$$\downarrow \quad \downarrow$$
$$300 \div 16 \qquad \leftarrow \text{Change 298 to 300 because 300 is easier to use mentally.}$$
$$\downarrow \quad \downarrow$$
$$300 \div 15 = 20 \qquad \leftarrow \text{Change 16 to 15 because 15 is compatible with 300.}$$

So $298 \div 16 \approx 20$.

CA Standards Check 2 *Go to your* **Math Companion** *for help.*

2. Estimate using compatible numbers.

a. $8 \cdot 39$ about 400 **b.** $672 \div 52$ about 14

When you shop, use estimation to verify the total cost of your purchase.

EXAMPLE Estimating for Reasonableness

Relate **MATH YOU KNOW...**

You buy a yard of fabric for \$5.75, a spool of thread for \$2.39, and a sewing pattern for \$8.37. Find the total cost of the items, including \$1.20 tax.

$$5.75 + 2.39 + 8.37 + 1.20 = 17.71 \qquad \leftarrow \text{Add the prices of all the items.}$$

The total cost is \$17.71.

...to **NEW IDEAS**

3 **Guided Problem Solving** You buy two yards of fabric for \$13.80, a pack of needles for \$3.93, and two spools of thread for \$2.59 each. The cashier says the total is \$29.82, including \$1.66 tax. Is this reasonable?

Estimate by rounding.

$$13.80 + 3.93 + 2 \cdot 2.59 + 1.66 \approx 14 + 4 + 2 \cdot 3 + 2$$
$$= 14 + 4 + 6 + 2 \qquad \leftarrow \text{Multiply.}$$
$$= 26 \qquad \leftarrow \text{Add.}$$

The estimate is \$26. Since the prices were all rounded up and \$29.82 is more than the estimate, the total from the cashier is not reasonable.

CA Standards Check 3 *Go to your* **Math Companion** *for help.*

3. You buy a book for \$13.79, a pen for \$3.59, and a hat for \$7.80. The cashier says the total is \$32.62, including \$1.83 tax. Is this reasonable? See left.

3. No; the estimate is \$28. This is significantly less than the cashier's estimate of \$32.62, so it is not reasonable.

Check Your Understanding *Homework prep is in your* **Math Companion.**

2. Teach

Guided Instruction

Before students estimate with compatible numbers, spend some time practicing how to identify compatible numbers. Emphasize the relationship between the numbers in basic division facts and in basic multiplication facts. Give students pairs of numbers. Ask:

- *Are 5 and 3 compatible numbers?* no
- *Are 6 and 2 compatible numbers?* Yes; 6 is divisible by 2.

...PRESENTATION CD-ROM
CD, Online, or Transparencies

Additional Examples

1 Estimate $97 - 21$ by rounding to the nearest ten. 80

2 Estimate $358 \div 9$ by using compatible numbers. 40

3 Jana buys a sandwich for \$4.64, a drink for \$3.12, and a snack for \$2.29. The cashier says the total is \$12.85, including \$.80 tax. Is this reasonable? Explain. No; the total should be close to \$11, so \$12.85 is not reasonable.

Closure

- *When is rounding appropriate to use?* when you estimate the sum or difference of numbers
- *When should you use compatible numbers to estimate?* when you estimate products and quotients

Advanced Learners L4	**English Learners** EL
Challenge students to explain why rounding might be inaccurate when estimating products or quotients. Use Example 2 to demonstrate.	Have students work in pairs. One partner should focus on explaining how to estimate by rounding using examples. The other partner should explain estimation using compatible numbers.

3. Practice

Assignment Guide

Check Your Understanding
See Math Companion.

Homework Exercises

A Practice by Example	1–16
B Apply Your Skills	17–30
C Challenge	31
California Multiple Choice Practice	32–33
Mixed Review	34

Homework Quick Check
To check students' understanding of key skills and concepts, go over Exercises 3, 11, 17, 29, 30.

Universal Access Resources

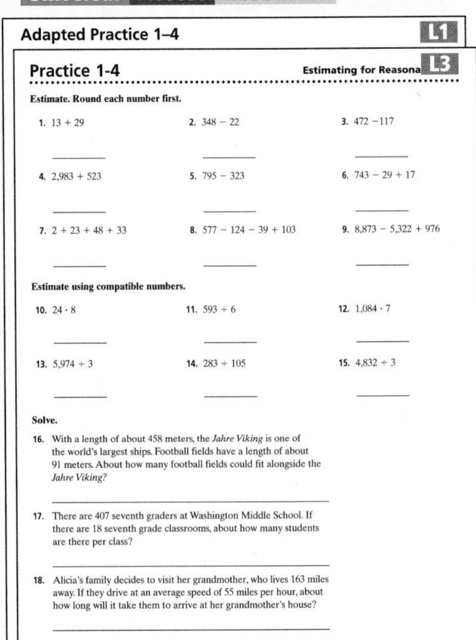
Adapted Practice 1–4 L1

Practice 1-4 — Estimating for Reasona[...] L3

Estimate. Round each number first.

1. 13 + 29
2. 348 − 22
3. 472 −117
4. 2,983 + 523
5. 795 − 323
6. 743 − 29 + 17
7. 2 + 23 + 48 + 33
8. 577 − 124 − 39 + 103
9. 8,873 − 5,322 + 976

Estimate using compatible numbers.

10. 24 · 8
11. 593 ÷ 6
12. 1,084 · 7
13. 5,974 ÷ 3
14. 283 ÷ 105
15. 4,832 ÷ 3

Solve.

16. With a length of about 458 meters, the *Jahre Viking* is one of the world's largest ships. Football fields have a length of about 91 meters. About how many football fields could fit alongside the *Jahre Viking?*
17. There are 407 seventh graders at Washington Middle School. If there are 18 seventh grade classrooms, about how many students are there per class?
18. Alicia's family decides to visit her grandmother, who lives 163 miles away. If they drive at an average speed of 55 miles per hour, about how long will it take them to arrive at her grandmother's house?

1-4 • Guided Problem Solving L3

GPS Exercise 23

The Chinese kwan note was used in the 1300s. It was about 34.1 cm long. The United States dollar bill is almost 15.6 cm long. About how many times longer was the kwan note?

Read and Understand

1. What information is given in the problem?
2. What is the problem asking you to determine?

Plan and Carry Out

3. Will you use rounding or compatible numbers to estimate the answer?
4. What estimate will you use for the length of the kwan note?
5. What estimate will you use for the length of the dollar bill?
6. What operation will you use to find how many times longer the kwan note was than the dollar bill?
7. Find about how many times longer the kwan note was.

Check

8. Multiply the length of a dollar bill by your answer. Compare it to the length of a kwan note.

Solve Another Problem

9. The mass of a dime is 2.268 g. The mass of a quarter is 5.670 g. About how many times heavier is a quarter than a dime?

Standards Practice

GO for Help: *MathXL*

NS 1.2, MR 2.1

A Practice by Example

Example 1 (page 20)

Estimate. Round each number first.

1. 48 + 22.8 + 2.3 about 73
   48 + 22.8 + 2.3 ≈ 48 + 23 + 2
   = ■

Guided Practice
This exercise has been started for you!

GO for Help

2. 653 − 295 about 350
3. 3.4 + 0.68 + 9.3 about 13
4. 59 + 2.6 − 2.3 about 60
5. 6,963 − 3,098 about 4,000
6. 804.3 + 598.3 about 1,400
7. 42 + 86 + 51 + 38 about 220

Example 2 (page 21)

Estimate using compatible numbers.

8. 2 · 3,978 about 8,000
   2 · 3,978 ≈ 2 · 4,000
   = ■

Guided Practice
This exercise has been started for you!

Homework Video Tutor

For: Examples 1–3
Visit: PHSchool.com
Web Code: axe-0104

9. 102 ÷ 25 about 4
10. 611 ÷ 58 about 10
11. 997 · 5 about 5,000
12. 1,089 ÷ 521 about 2
13. 4,978 ÷ 983 about 5
14. 48 · 41 about 2,000

Example 3 (page 21)

15. You buy a hat for $11.99, a sweatshirt for $23.65, and a pair of sneakers for $56.89. The total comes to $99.53. Is this reasonable? See margin.
16. You buy a sandwich for $2.65, a banana for $.75, and a bottle of juice for $1.29. The total comes to $4.69. Is this reasonable? See margin.

B Apply Your Skills

17. **Guided Problem Solving** You need $48.89 to buy a new video game. You earn $9.50 one week and $22.90 the next week. About how much more do you need to earn to buy the game? about $20
    - Do you need to find an exact answer?
    - About how much have you already earned?

18. A student has to buy all the equipment on the list at the right. The cashier charges him $92.70, including $5.83 tax. Is this reasonable? See margin.

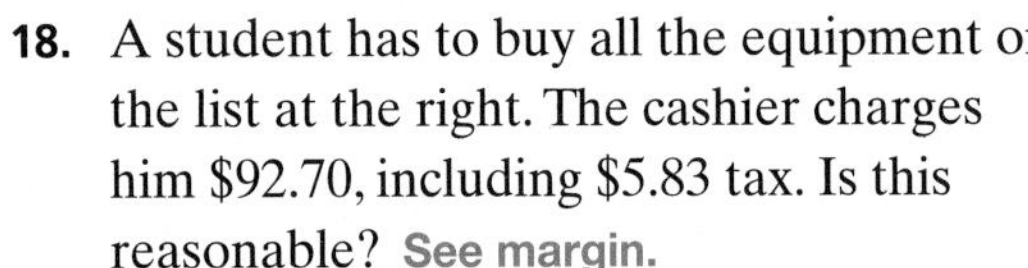

Soccer Equipment

Item	Price ($)
Ball	14.98
Cleats	18.99
Shin guards	11.75
Team socks	6.25
Team jersey	28.50

Choose a Method **Use either rounding or compatible numbers to estimate each answer.**

19. 429 + 88.9 about 500
20. 1,142 − 720 about 400
21. 551 ÷ 8.6 about 55
22. 0.36 · 99.8 about 36

GPS 23. The Chinese kwan note was used in the 1300s. It was 34.1 cm long. The United States dollar bill is almost 15.6 cm long. About how many times longer was the kwan note? about 2 times longer

The Chinese kwan note

SCAFFOLDED
Problem Solving

A clothing company sells T-shirts and sweatshirts. The prices are listed at the right.

T-Shirts and Sweatshirts For Sale

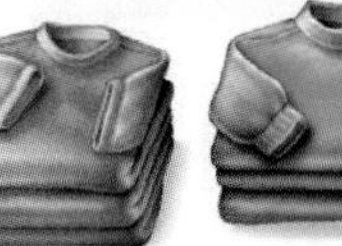

Adult T-shirt	Adult Sweatshirt
(M-XL) $15.00	(M-XL) $29.50
(XXL) $17.95	(XXL) $29.95

Child's T-shirt	Child's Sweatshirt
$12.50	$16.95

24. How much does an XXL adult T-shirt cost? $17.95

25. How much will it cost for three XL adult sweatshirts and four child's sweatshirts? $156.30

26. Suppose you buy one M adult T-shirt, three L adult sweatshirts, and two child's sweatshirts. Estimate the total cost. about $145

27. A field hockey coach buys three L adult sweatshirts, 12 child's T-shirts, and two child's sweatshirts. She is charged $302.40. Has the coach been overcharged? See left.

28. How many XXL adult sweatshirts can you buy with $160? 5 sweatshirts

29. **Writing in Math** The cost of four copies of a book is $37.64. Estimate the cost of one book. Is your estimate higher or lower than the book's actual cost? Explain. See left.

30. **Error Analysis** A classmate estimated that 29 + 42 + 37 is about 20 + 40 + 40. Explain your classmate's error. See left.

27. Yes; the total should be $272.40, not $302.40.

29. Answers may vary. Sample: $10; the estimate is higher than the actual because the total amount was rounded up to $40.

30. 29 should be rounded up to 30, not down to 20.

C Challenge

31. A ball has a mass of 238.8 g. A box holds 9 balls. The total mass of the balls and the box is 2,347.4 g. Estimate the mass of the box. about 200 g

Multiple Choice Practice and Mixed Review

For California Standards Tutorials, visit PHSchool.com. Web Code: axq-9045

NS 1.2

32. An auditorium has 10 rows with 22 seats in each row. There are 160 people seated. How many seats are empty? C

Ⓐ 100 seats Ⓒ 60 seats
Ⓑ 80 seats Ⓓ 40 seats

AF 1.1

33. Refer to the table. Which expression represents the cost of t tickets? B

Ⓐ $21.00 - 5.25t$
Ⓑ $5.25t$
Ⓒ $\frac{5.25}{t}$
Ⓓ $5.25 + t$

Tickets	Cost ($)
1	5.25
2	10.50
3	15.75
4	21.00

Lesson 1-3

34. A cable company charges a $25 setup fee and $34.95 per month for basic service. Write an expression to model these charges. Find the costs for 1, 3, and 6 mo. $25 + 34.95m$; $59.95, $129.85, $234.70

Online Lesson Quiz Visit: PHSchool.com Web Code: axa-0104

4. Assess & Reteach

PRESENTATION CD-ROM
CD, Online, or Transparencies
Lesson Quiz

Estimate. Round each number first.

1. 263 − 107 + 621 1,000

2. 37 + 21 60

Estimate using compatible numbers.

3. 898 × 51 45,000

4. 211 × 29 6,000

5. Rob received 39 e-mails yesterday. If he receives the same number every day, about how many e-mails will he receive in March? 1,200

Alternative Assessment

Students write an addition or subtraction problem in which they can use rounded numbers to estimate the answer. Then they write a multiplication or division problem in which they can use compatible numbers to estimate the answer. Students swap with a partner and solve each other's problems.

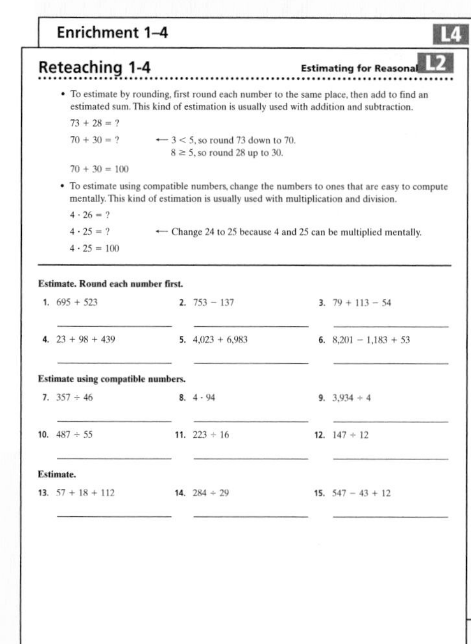

Enrichment 1–4 L4

Reteaching 1-4 Estimating for Reasonal L2

- To estimate by rounding, first round each number to the same place, then add to find an estimated sum. This kind of estimation is usually used with addition and subtraction.

  73 + 28 = ?
  70 + 30 = ? ← 3 < 5, so round 73 down to 70. 8 ≥ 5, so round 28 up to 30.
  70 + 30 = 100

- To estimate using compatible numbers, change the numbers to ones that are easy to compute mentally. This kind of estimation is usually used with multiplication and division.

  4 · 26 = ?
  4 · 25 = ? ← Change 24 to 25 because 4 and 25 can be multiplied mentally.
  4 · 25 = 100

Estimate. Round each number first.

1. 695 + 523 2. 753 − 137 3. 79 + 113 − 54
4. 23 + 98 + 439 5. 4,023 + 6,983 6. 8,201 − 1,183 + 53

Estimate using compatible numbers.

7. 357 ÷ 46 8. 4 · 94 9. 3,934 ÷ 4
10. 487 ÷ 55 11. 223 ÷ 16 12. 147 ÷ 12

Estimate.

13. 57 + 18 + 112 14. 284 ÷ 29 15. 547 − 43 + 12

California Resources

Standards Mastery
- Standards Review Transparencies
- Standards Review and Practice Workbook
- Math Companion

Math Intervention
- Skills Review and Practice Workbook
- Math XL

Mathematical Reasoning

Exact and Approximate Solutions

Students learn to distinguish problems that require exact solutions from those that require only approximate solutions.

Guided Instruction

Explain to students that some real-world problems may require only approximate solutions, which can make the computation easier. Discuss factors that make it likely that a problem will not require an exact solution: large numbers or long distances when a general idea is all that is needed (for example, driving distances between different states); discrete packages that render more specific information useless (for example, length of fabric that is only sold by the yard); conventions that determine number of significant digits (for example, dollars and cents). Discuss what might make an exact solution necessary: precise measurements used in construction, situations in which small differences are important, and problems with many detailed steps.

Use this Checkpoint Quiz to check students' understanding of the skills and concepts of Lessons 1-3 through 1-4.

All in One Resources

- Checkpoint Quiz 2

Mathematical Reasoning

For Use With Lesson 1-4

NS 1.2 Add, subtract, multiply, and divide rational numbers. ***Develop***

MR 2.7 Indicate the relative advantages of exact and approximate solutions to problems and give answers to a specified degree of accuracy. ***Develop***

Exact and Approximate Solutions

Some real-world problems require an exact solution. Other problems require only an approximate solution. For example, suppose you need to buy ice cream for a party. Rather than calculate the exact number of scoops, you can estimate the number of containers you will need.

For each situation, decide whether you need an exact or approximate solution. Explain your reasoning. 1–4. Answers may vary. Samples are given.

1. the number of cans of paint needed to paint a house
   Estimate; the area to be painted can be estimated.
2. the width of a pane of glass needed to fix a broken window
   Exact; the exact size is needed so the window will fit properly.
3. how much you can earn in a year delivering newspapers
   Estimate; earnings can be rounded to find a yearly approximate.
4. the driving distance from New York City to San Francisco
   Estimate; travel distances are estimated since different routes can be taken.
5. At a basketball tournament, each player will drink about 0.35 gal of sports drink. Determine the amount of sports drink needed for 22 players. Round your answer to the nearest gallon. about 8 gal

Checkpoint Quiz 2

Lessons 1-3 through 1-4

Write an algebraic expression for each verbal description.

1. the product of 3 and s $3s$
2. v divided by 12 $v \div 12$
3. d less than 17 $17 - d$
4. the quotient of m and 10 $m \div 10$
5. 4 more than f $f + 4$
6. 14 divided by q $14 \div q$
7. A mechanic charges \$168 for auto parts and \$35 per hour for labor. Write an expression to model the total charge for h hours of labor. Evaluate the expression to find the total charge for 3 h of labor. $168 + 35h$; \$273

Use rounding or compatible numbers to estimate each answer.

8. $55.3 - 38.5$ about 20
9. $5{,}964 + 3{,}088$ about 9,000
10. $108.5 \div 52.3$ about 2
11. You buy a magazine for \$4.15, a book for \$8.95, and a calendar for \$6.52. The cashier says the total is \$25.18, including \$1.18 for sales tax. Is this total reasonable? Explain. See margin.

Vocabulary Builder

Justifying a Conclusion

Some questions ask you to justify or to give a justification. To *justify* means to give reasons supporting a conclusion or process. A *justification* is a reason that supports the conclusion or process.

Prepares for **AF 1.3** Simplify numerical expressions by applying properties of rational numbers and justify the process used.
MR 2.5 Use words to explain mathematical reasoning. ***Develop***
MR 2.6 Support solutions with evidence in both verbal and symbolic work. ***Develop***

EXAMPLE

On Monday, a teacher announces that the class will go on a field trip in three days. A student concludes that the field trip will take place on Thursday. Which statement justifies the student's conclusion?

(A) Thursday is the best day for a field trip.
(B) Monday is the first day of the school week.
(C) Monday comes three days before Thursday.
(D) A trip planned for three days after Tuesday will take place on Friday.

All of the statements may be true, but they do not all support the conclusion. Monday comes three days before Thursday. So a field trip that takes place three days from Monday takes place on Thursday. The correct answer is choice C.

Exercises

Choose the correct justification for each conclusion.

1. December weather is usually colder in Canada than in Mexico. B
   (A) Canadians like cold weather.
   (B) Mexico is closer to the equator than Canada.
   (C) It snows frequently in Canada.
   (D) Mexico is far from Canada.

2. $5 + 6 + 7 = 6 + 5 + 7$ B
   (A) 7 is greater than 5 or 6.
   (B) Changing the order of addends does not change their sum.
   (C) $6 + 5 = 11$
   (D) According to the order of operations, you add 5 and 6 first.

3. While simplifying the expression $2 \cdot 13 \cdot 5$, a student first rewrites the expression as $2 \cdot 5 \cdot 13$. Give a justification for the conclusion that $2 \cdot 13 \cdot 5 = 2 \cdot 5 \cdot 13$. **Answers may vary. Sample: Changing the order of factors does not change their product.**

Vocabulary Builder

Justifying a Conclusion

Students define and use the words *justify* and *justification*. They practice justifying conclusions and identifying reasonable justifications.

Guided Instruction

Have students define *justify* and *justification* in their own words. Have them brainstorm related words, such as *justice*, *just*, and *justifiable*. Discuss the meanings of these words and how they relate to the meanings of *justify* and *justification*.

Teaching Tip
Make an effort to use the words *justify* and *justification* as you teach the next several lessons. Ask students the meaning of these words each time. This gives students, especially English learners, a chance to hear the words spoken correctly and in the correct context.

1-5

1. Plan

California Content Standards

Use the commutative and associative rules. *Foundational*

AF 1.3 Simplify numerical expressions by applying properties of rational numbers and justify the process used. *Introduce*

California Math Background

This lesson introduces the properties of addition and multiplication. The Commutative and Associative Properties of addition and multiplication state that the order and grouping of addends and factors make no difference to the result. The Identity Property states that a number added to or multiplied by the identity remains the same.

More Math Background: p. 2C

Lesson Planning and Resources

See p. 2E for a list of the resources that support this lesson.

PRESENTATION CD-ROM
CD, Online, or Transparencies

Bell Ringer Practice

Check Skills You'll Need
Use student page, transparency, or PowerPoint.
See Math Companion.

California Standards Review
Use transparency or PowerPoint.

1-5 Properties of Numbers

Check Skills You'll Need

Do this in your **Math Companion.**

Vocabulary

- commutative properties (addition and multiplication)
- associative properties (addition and multiplication)
- identity properties

Use your **Math Companion** *to build your vocabulary.*

California Content Standards

Foundational Standard Use the commutative and associative rules.
AF 1.3 Simplify numerical expressions by applying properties of rational numbers and justify the process used. ***Introduce***

What You'll Learn . . . and Why

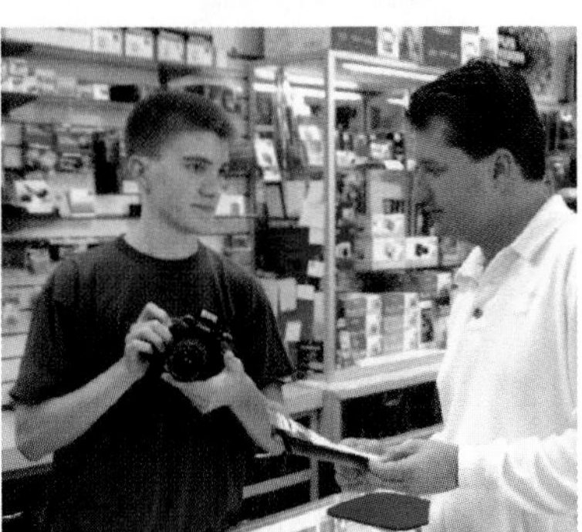

You will learn to recognize and use the properties of numbers. The properties of numbers can help you make calculations quickly when you are shopping.

You can add or multiply two numbers in any order and get the same result. You can also change the grouping of numbers before you add or multiply them.

You can apply the properties of numbers to both numerical and algebraic expressions.

Take Note Properties of Numbers

Commutative Properties: Addition and Multiplication

Arithmetic	Algebra
$7 + 12 = 12 + 7$	$a + b = b + a$
$7 \cdot 12 = 12 \cdot 7$	$a \cdot b = b \cdot a$

Associative Properties: Addition and Multiplication

Arithmetic	Algebra
$(4 + 7) + 3 = 4 + (7 + 3)$	$(a + b) + c = a + (b + c)$
$(4 \cdot 7) \cdot 3 = 4 \cdot (7 \cdot 3)$	$(a \cdot b) \cdot c = a \cdot (b \cdot c)$

Adding 0 and multiplying by 1 do not change the value of a number.

Vocabulary Tip

One meaning of *identity* is the state of remaining the same. The identity properties tell you a number stays the same when you add 0 or multiply by 1.

Take Note Identity Properties

Arithmetic	Algebra
$6 + 0 = 0 + 6 = 6$	$a + 0 = 0 + a = a$
$6 \cdot 1 = 1 \cdot 6 = 6$	$a \cdot 1 = 1 \cdot a = a$

Universal Access Solutions for All Learners

Special Needs L1
Students may need to "prove" that $9 + 5 = 5 + 9$ by adding the 9 and 5 and the 5 and 9 using counters. Have them try several addition or multiplication problems with counters to prove the Commutative Properties.

Below Level L2
Be sure students understand that addition and multiplication have different identity elements. For addition it is 0, but for multiplication it is 1. Give several examples of each orally.

Relate MATH YOU KNOW...

... *to* ALGEBRA

EXAMPLE Recognizing Properties

Which property does the equation $(3 + 8) + 7 = 3 + (8 + 7)$ illustrate?

The equation illustrates the Associative Property of Addition.

1 Which property does the equation $(3 + p) + 7 = 3 + (p + 7)$ illustrate?

Since the grouping of the numbers and variables changes, the equation illustrates the Associative Property of Addition.

CA Standards Check 1 *Go to your* **Math Companion** *for help.*

1. Name the property that each equation illustrates.

a. $w \cdot 5 = 5 \cdot w$ Comm. Prop. of Mult. b. $f + 0 = f$ Identity Prop. of Add.

You can use the properties of numbers to simplify expressions mentally.

EXAMPLE Using the Properties of Numbers

2 **Mental Math** You want to buy a camera and a camera case. The prices are shown below. Use mental math to find the total cost.

What you think

First I will think of 28 as 20 + 8. Next I will add 8 + 62 to get 70. 70 + 20 = 90. So 62 + 28 = 90.

Why it works

$62 + 28 = 62 + (20 + 8)$ ← Rewrite 28 as 20 + 8.

$= 62 + (8 + 20)$ ← Commutative Property of Addition

$= (62 + 8) + 20$ ← Associative Property of Addition

$= 70 + 20$ ← Order of operations

$= 90$ ← Simplify.

The total cost is $90.

CA Standards Check 2 *Go to your* **Math Companion** *for help.*

2. **Mental Math** Use mental math to simplify each expression.

a. $20 \cdot (13 \cdot 5)$ 1,300 b. $36 + 25 + 34$ 95 c. $4 \cdot 8 \cdot 25$ 800

Check Your Understanding *Homework prep is in your* **Math Companion.**

27

Advanced Learners L4	**English Learners** EL
Students write a set of questions about a property, with yes-or-no answers, that will lead to correct identification of the property.	Students write the addition symbol and the words *sum* and *addends* on a card to remind themselves that these go together. They write the multiplication symbol and the words *factors* and *product* on another card. They include examples of each term on the cards.

2. Teach

Guided Instruction

Example 2

Ask: *Why can you rewrite 28 as 20 + 8?* 28 in expanded form is 2 tens 8 ones or 20 + 8.

Error Prevention!

Help students identify properties by first asking them to carefully pronounce each name aloud, perhaps making a rhythmic song or poem. Suggest that they use these questions for identifying the property: 1) Is it all addition or all multiplication? 2) Is the order of the items changed? 3) Are the items grouped differently?

Students may differentiate between Commutative and Associative Properties by thinking of *commuters* as going back and forth each day and *associates* as groups of friends or colleagues.

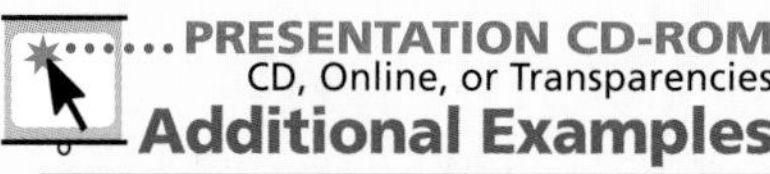

PRESENTATION CD-ROM
CD, Online, or Transparencies

Additional Examples

1 Which property does $3 \times (5 \times y) = (3 \times 5) \times y$ illustrate? Associative Property of Multiplication

2 Use mental math to find the total number of books in a carton that contains 43 math books, 15 history books, and 57 science books. 115 books

Closure

- Have students give examples for the Commutative, Associative, and Identity Properties of Addition and Multiplication. Sample answers:
$3 + 2 = 2 + 3$
$3 + (7 + 5) = (3 + 7) + 5$
$5 + 0 = 5$
$5 \times 4 = 4 \times 5$
$(2 \times 4) \times 3 = 2 \times (4 \times 3)$
$6 \times 1 = 6$

3. Practice

Assignment Guide

Check Your Understanding
See Math Companion.

Homework Exercises
A	Practice by Example	1–15
B	Apply Your Skills	16–28
C	Challenge	29
California Multiple Choice Practice		30–32
Mixed Review		33–35

Homework Quick Check
To check students' understanding of key skills and concepts, go over Exercises 3, 13, 19, 20, 27.

Universal Access Resources

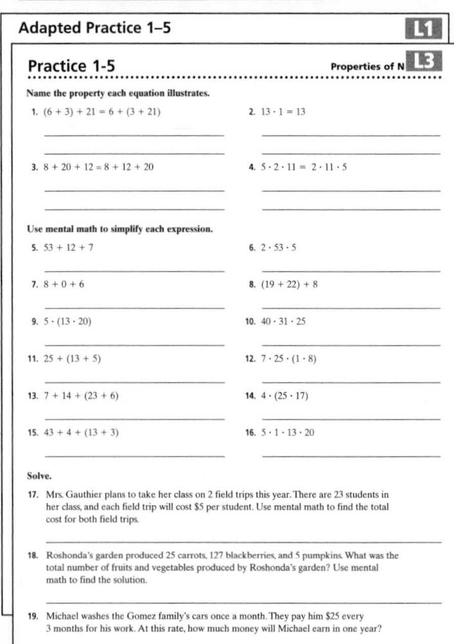
Adapted Practice 1–5 L1

Practice 1-5 Properties of N L3

Name the property each equation illustrates.

1. $(6 + 3) + 21 = 6 + (3 + 21)$
2. $13 \cdot 1 = 13$
3. $8 + 20 + 12 = 8 + 12 + 20$
4. $5 \cdot 2 \cdot 11 = 2 \cdot 11 \cdot 5$

Use mental math to simplify each expression.

5. $53 + 12 + 7$
6. $2 \cdot 53 \cdot 5$
7. $8 + 0 + 6$
8. $(19 + 22) + 8$
9. $5 \cdot (13 \cdot 20)$
10. $40 \cdot 31 \cdot 25$
11. $25 + (13 + 5)$
12. $7 \cdot 25 \cdot (1 \cdot 8)$
13. $7 + 14 + (23 + 6)$
14. $4 \cdot (25 \cdot 17)$
15. $43 + 4 + (13 + 3)$
16. $5 \cdot 1 \cdot 13 \cdot 20$

Solve.

17. Mrs. Gauthier plans to take her class on 2 field trips this year. There are 23 students in her class, and each field trip will cost $5 per student. Use mental math to find the total cost for both field trips.
18. Roshonda's garden produced 25 carrots, 127 blackberries, and 5 pumpkins. What was the total number of fruits and vegetables produced by Roshonda's garden? Use mental math to find the solution.
19. Michael washes the Gomez family's cars once a month. They pay him $25 every 3 months for his work. At this rate, how much money will Michael earn in one year?

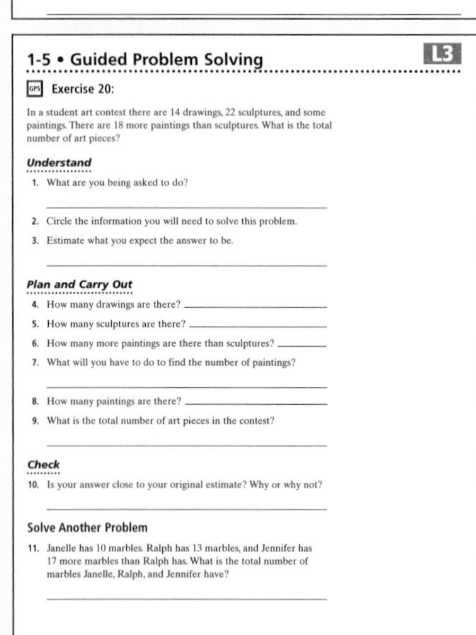
1-5 • Guided Problem Solving L3

GPS Exercise 20:

In a student art contest there are 14 drawings, 22 sculptures, and some paintings. There are 18 more paintings than sculptures. What is the total number of art pieces?

Understand

1. What are you being asked to do?
2. Circle the information you will need to solve this problem.
3. Estimate what you expect the answer to be.

Plan and Carry Out

4. How many drawings are there? ______
5. How many sculptures are there? ______
6. How many more paintings are there than sculptures? ______
7. What will you have to do to find the number of paintings?
8. How many paintings are there? ______
9. What is the total number of art pieces in the contest?

Check

10. Is your answer close to your original estimate? Why or why not?

Solve Another Problem

11. Janelle has 10 marbles. Ralph has 13 marbles, and Jennifer has 17 more marbles than Ralph has. What is the total number of marbles Janelle, Ralph, and Jennifer have?

Standards Practice

GO for Help: MathXL — AF 1.3

A Practice by Example

Example 1 (page 27)

Name the property each equation illustrates.

1. $k \cdot 5 \cdot 6 = 5 \cdot k \cdot 6$ Comm. Prop. of Mult.
The order of the factors changes, so the equation illustrates the _?_.

Guided Practice: This exercise has been started for you!

GO for Help

2. $1 \cdot h = h$ Identity Prop. of Mult.
3. $(e + d) + f = e + (d + f)$ Assoc. Prop. of Add.
4. $t + 7 + c = t + c + 7$ Comm. Prop. of Add.
5. $4(wx) = (4w)x$ Assoc. Prop. of Mult.
6. $ab = ba$ Comm. Prop. of Mult.
7. $m + 0 = m$ Identity Prop. of Add.

Example 2 (page 27)

Mental Math **Use mental math to simplify each expression.**

8. $5 \cdot 47 \cdot 2$ 470
$5 \cdot 47 \cdot 2 = 5 \cdot 2 \cdot 47$
$= ■$

Guided Practice: This exercise has been started for you!

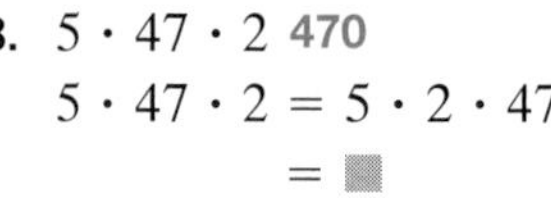

For: Examples 1–2
Visit: PHSchool.com
Web Code: axe-0105

9. $3.5 + 9 + 6.5$ 19
10. $70 \cdot 1 \cdot 4$ 280
11. $40 \cdot (33 \cdot 25)$ 33,000
12. $(17 + 24) - 18$ 23
13. $5.75 + 0 + 18.25$ 24
14. $20 \cdot 19 \cdot 5$ 1,900
15. A train started a trip pulling 9 cars. At the first stop, 17 cars were added to the train. At the second stop, 11 more cars were added. Use mental math to find the number of cars the train was pulling after the second stop. 37 cars

B Apply Your Skills

16. **Guided Problem Solving** Four running clubs raised money in a 24-hour relay race. Club A ran 183 mi, Club B ran 144 mi, Club C ran 117 mi, and Club D ran 146 mi. What was the total number of miles that all four clubs ran? 590 mi
    - Which pairs of numbers can you add easily using mental math?
    - What is the sum of each of those pairs?

Use <, =, or > to complete each statement.

17. $41 + 29$ ■ 70 =
18. $737 + 373$ ■ $4 \cdot 11 \cdot 25$ >
19. **Writing in Math** At the right is your friend's incorrect solution to a problem. Explain your friend's mistake. See left.

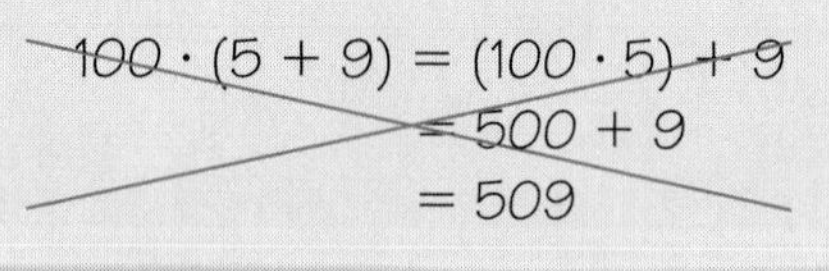

19. The assoc. prop. was applied but cannot be applied unless both operations are either addition or multiplication.

GPS 20. In a student art contest there are 14 drawings, 22 sculptures, and some paintings. There are 18 more paintings than sculptures. What is the total number of art pieces? 76

SCAFFOLDED
Problem Solving

A school lunch menu is shown at the right.

Lunch Menu	
Sandwich	\$1.95
Milk (carton)	\$.40
Banana	\$.60
Cookie	\$.25

21. How much does a carton of milk cost? \$.40
22. How much do a carton of milk and a banana cost? \$1.00
23. You buy a sandwich, a carton of milk, and a banana. How much do you spend? \$2.95
24. You have \$3. How much change do you get? \$.05
25. Your friend has \$4 to spend on lunch. She wants to buy a sandwich, a carton of milk, a banana, and a cookie. Does she have enough money? Explain. Yes; the total is \$3.20 and she has more money than this.
26. In a women's 4 × 100 m relay race, a team's times for the legs of the race are 11.92 s, 12.20 s, 12.08 s, and 11.86 s. How much slower is the team's total time than the world record of 41.37 s? 6.69 s
27. *To commute* means "to change places." How does this definition help to explain the commutative properties? See above left.
28. *To associate* means "to gather in groups." How does this definition help explain the associative properties? See above left.

C Challenge

29. Is subtraction commutative? Is division? Is either operation associative? Explain using examples. See above left.

27. The comm. properties show that you can change the places of the numbers without changing the values of an expression.
28. The assoc. properties show that you can change the grouping of numbers in an expression without changing the values of the expression.
29. No; no; no; examples may vary. Sample: $9 - 3 \neq 3 - 9$ and $9 \div 3 \neq 3 \div 9$; $(12 - 4) - 2 \neq 12 - (4 - 2)$ and $(12 \div 4) \div 2 \neq 12 \div (4 \div 2)$

Multiple Choice Practice and Mixed Review

For California Standards Tutorials, visit PHSchool.com. Web Code: axq-9045

AF 1.3

30. Which property does the equation $(x + y) + z = x + (y + z)$ illustrate? B
    - (A) Associative Property of Multiplication
    - (B) Associative Property of Addition
    - (C) Identity Property of Addition
    - (D) Commutative Property of Addition

NS 1.2

31. At a baseball game, Ben bought peanuts for \$3.25. He paid with a \$5 bill. How much change did Ben get? B
    - (A) \$1.25
    - (B) \$1.75
    - (C) \$2.25
    - (D) \$2.75

NS 1.2, MR 3.2

32. On a 100-point exam, you got 4 questions wrong. Each question was worth 5 points. What would you do to find your score? B
    - (A) Multiply and add.
    - (B) Multiply and subtract.
    - (C) Divide and subtract.
    - (D) Add and subtract.

Lesson 1-4

Estimate. Round each number first.

33. $56.7 + 12.2 + 5.9$ about 75
34. $502 - 397$ about 100
35. $42 + 15 + 72$ about 130

Online Lesson Quiz Visit: PHSchool.com Web Code: axa-0105

4. Assess & Reteach

PRESENTATION CD-ROM
CD, Online, or Transparencies

Lesson Quiz

1. Name the property that the equation illustrates.
   $25 \times (4 \times 19) = (25 \times 4) \times 19$
   Associative Property of Multiplication

Use mental math to find each sum.

2. $72 - 26 + 18$ 116
3. $113 + 25 + 207$ 345

Use mental math to find each product.

4. $5 \times 84 \times 20$ 8,400
5. $40 \times 13 \times 25$ 13,000

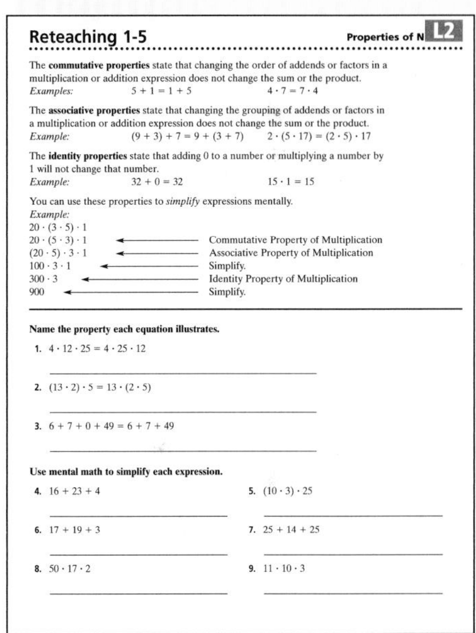

Reteaching 1-5 Properties of N L2

The **commutative properties** state that changing the order of addends or factors in a multiplication or addition expression does not change the sum or the product.
Examples: $5 + 1 = 1 + 5$ $4 \cdot 7 = 7 \cdot 4$

The **associative properties** state that changing the grouping of addends or factors in a multiplication or addition expression does not change the sum or the product.
Example: $(9 + 3) + 7 = 9 + (3 + 7)$ $2 \cdot (5 \cdot 17) = (2 \cdot 5) \cdot 17$

The **identity properties** state that adding 0 to a number or multiplying a number by 1 will not change that number.
Example: $32 + 0 = 32$ $15 \cdot 1 = 15$

You can use these properties to *simplify* expressions mentally.
Example:
$20 \cdot (3 \cdot 5) \cdot 1$
$20 \cdot (5 \cdot 3) \cdot 1$ ← Commutative Property of Multiplication
$(20 \cdot 5) \cdot 3 \cdot 1$ ← Associative Property of Multiplication
$100 \cdot 3 \cdot 1$ ← Simplify.
$300 \cdot 3$ ← Identity Property of Multiplication
900 ← Simplify.

Name the property each equation illustrates.

1. $4 \cdot 12 \cdot 25 = 4 \cdot 25 \cdot 12$ ____
2. $(13 \cdot 2) \cdot 5 = 13 \cdot (2 \cdot 5)$ ____
3. $6 + 7 + 0 + 49 = 6 + 7 + 49$ ____

Use mental math to simplify each expression.

4. $16 + 23 + 4$ ____
5. $(10 \cdot 3) \cdot 25$ ____
6. $17 + 19 + 3$ ____
7. $25 + 14 + 25$ ____
8. $50 \cdot 17 \cdot 2$ ____
9. $11 \cdot 10 \cdot 3$ ____

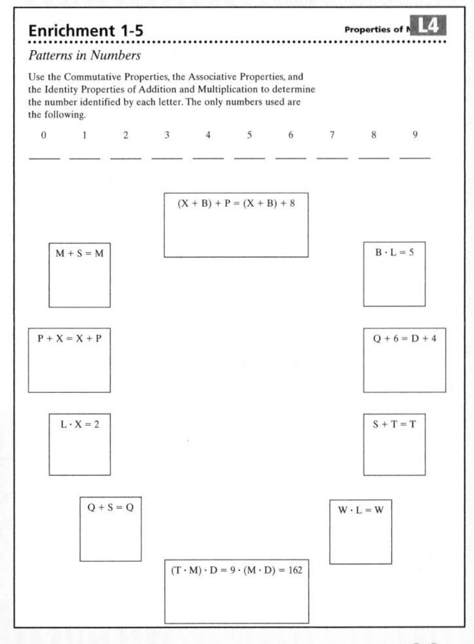

Enrichment 1-5 Properties of N L4

Patterns in Numbers

Use the Commutative Properties, the Associative Properties, and the Identity Properties of Addition and Multiplication to determine the number identified by each letter. The only numbers used are the following.

0	1	2	3	4	5	6	7	8	9
___	___	___	___	___	___	___	___	___	___

$(X + B) + P = (X + B) + 8$
$M + S = M$
$B \cdot L = 5$
$P + X = X + P$
$Q + 6 = D + 4$
$L \cdot X = 2$
$S + T = T$
$Q + S = Q$
$W \cdot L = W$
$(T \cdot M) \cdot D = 9 \cdot (M \cdot D) = 162$

Alternative Assessment

Students work in pairs and take turns. One student names a property. The partner gives a numerical example. Then students take turns writing a numerical example of a property and challenging the partner to name the property.

California Resources

Standards Mastery
- Standards Review Transparencies
- Standards Review and Practice Workbook
- Math Companion

Math Intervention
- Skills Review and Practice Workbook
- Math XL

1. Plan

California Content Standards

Know and use the distributive property in equations and expressions with variables. ***Foundational***

AF 1.3 Simplify numerical expressions by applying properties of rational numbers and justify the process used. ***Introduce***

California Math Background

The Distributive Property provides an important alternative when evaluating certain expressions. By the Distributive Property, an expression like $3 \times (10 + 8)$ is equivalent to $3 \times 10 + 3 \times 8$. Thus the value of $3 \times (10 + 8)$ can be found easily by calculating $3 \times 10 = 30$ and $3 \times 8 = 24$ and then performing the simple addition $30 + 24 = 54$.

More Math Background: p. 2C

Lesson Planning and Resources

See p. 2E for a list of the resources that support this lesson.

PRESENTATION CD-ROM
CD, Online, or Transparencies

Bell Ringer Practice

Check Skills You'll Need
Use student page, transparency, or PowerPoint.
See Math Companion.

California Standards Review
Use transparency or PowerPoint.

1-6 The Distributive Property

Check Skills You'll Need

Do this in your **Math Companion.**

Vocabulary

- Distributive Property

Use your **Math Companion** *to build your vocabulary.*

California Content Standards

Foundational Standard Know and use the distributive property in equations and expressions with variables.

AF 1.3 Simplify numerical expressions by applying properties of rational numbers and justify the process used. ***Introduce***

What You'll Learn . . . and Why

You will learn to use the Distributive Property. It can help you use mental math to quickly calculate your earnings from a summer job as a camp counselor.

The **Distributive Property** shows how multiplication affects addition or subtraction.

You can find the area of the shaded region below in two ways.

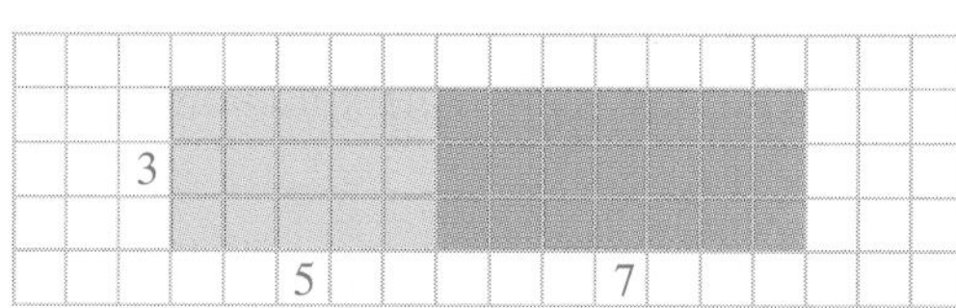

Math Foundations

The area of a rectangle is the product of its length and width.

Method 1 First add 5 + 7 to find the width of the combined region. Then multiply to find the area.

$$3(5 + 7) = 3(12) = 36$$

Method 2 First find the areas of the two smaller rectangles. Then add the two areas.

$$3 \cdot 5 + 3 \cdot 7 = 15 + 21 = 36$$

Both methods give an area of 36 m^2. This example illustrates the Distributive Property.

$$3(5 + 7) = 3 \cdot 5 + 3 \cdot 7$$

Take Note **Distributive Property**

Arithmetic	Algebra
$3(2 + 7) = 3 \cdot 2 + 3 \cdot 7$	$a(b + c) = ab + ac$
$(2 + 7)3 = 2 \cdot 3 + 7 \cdot 3$	$(b + c)a = ba + ca$
$5(8 - 2) = 5 \cdot 8 - 5 \cdot 2$	$a(b - c) = ab - ac$
$(8 - 2)5 = 8 \cdot 5 - 2 \cdot 5$	$(b - c)a = ba - ca$

Universal Access Solutions for All Learners

Special Needs L1
Students may have difficulty understanding how 6.90×8 translates to $(7 \times 8) - (0.90 \times 8)$. A model that shows $(7 - 0.10) \times 8$ placed under the 6.90×8 with arrows between corresponding numbers might help students see how the numbers are broken up.

Below Level L2
Give students several exercises like these orally to practice mental computations.

8×30 240	7×800 5,600
$360 + 12$ 372	$350 - 7$ 343

Relate MATH YOU KNOW...

... *to* ALGEBRA

EXAMPLE Using the Distributive Property

Simplify $8(9 + 14)$ using the Distributive Property.

$8(9 + 14) = 8 \cdot 9 + 8 \cdot 14$ ← Distributive Property
$= 72 + 112$ ← Multiply.
$= 184$ ← Simplify.

1 Simplify $8(n + 14)$ using the Distributive Property.

$8(n + 14) = 8n + 8 \cdot 14$ ← Distributive Property
$= 8n + 112$ ← Simplify.

CA Standards Check 1 *Go to your* **Math Companion** *for help.*

1. Simplify each expression.

a. $7(15 - h)$ $105 - 7h$ **b.** $(m + 3)6$ $6m + 18$

You can use the Distributive Property in mental calculations.

EXAMPLE The Distributive Property in Mental Math

2 **Guided Problem Solving** A summer job as an assistant camp counselor pays \$6.90 per hour. How much does the counselor earn for working 8 h?

What you think

I can think of 6.90 as $7 - 0.10$. Then I multiply both numbers by 8: $7 \cdot 8 = 56$ and $0.10 \cdot 8 = 0.80$. Now I subtract the two products: $56 - 0.80 = 55.20$.

Why it works

$6.90 \cdot 8 = (7 - 0.10)8$ ← Write 6.90 as 7 − 0.10.
$= (7 \cdot 8) - (0.10 \cdot 8)$ ← Distributive Property
$= 56 - 0.80$ ← Order of operations
$= 55.20$ ← Simplify.

The counselor earns \$55.20 for working 8 h.

CA Standards Check 2 *Go to your* **Math Companion** *for help.*

2. Mental Math Use the Distributive Property to answer each question.

a. A local bookstore charges \$2.80 for each used book. What is the charge for 5 used books? \$14

b. A teacher orders supply kits for a class of 20 students. Each kit costs \$5.90. What is the total cost? \$118

Homework prep is in your **Math Companion.**

Advanced Learners L4

Justify whether this statement is true or false.

$a + (b \cdot c) = (a + b) \cdot (a + c)$ Sample: false; $2 + (3 \cdot 4) = 14$; $(2 + 3) \cdot (2 + 4) = 30$; so $2 + (3 \cdot 4) \neq (2 + 3) \cdot (2 + 4)$

English Learners EL

Have students find the product \$6.90 × 8 two different ways: using the Distributive Property and multiplying using the traditional algorithm. Discuss which method made it easier to find the product, with less likelihood of errors.

2. Teach

Guided Instruction

Example 1
Students may forget to multiply the second number in the parenthesis by the multiplier. Suggest that before they begin to calculate, they draw arrows to pair the multiplier with each term in the parentheses.

Teaching Tip
Students might have difficulty with the term *distributive*. Ask: *What happens when a teacher distributes test papers to a class?* The teacher gives one test paper to each student in the class. Point out that, in a similar way, the number outside the parentheses "distributes" itself to each number inside the parentheses.

PRESENTATION CD-ROM
CD, Online, or Transparencies

Additional Examples

1 Find each product.

a. $7(t - 5)$ $7t - 35$

b. $(d + 23)(4)$ $4d + 92$

2 A student buys 11 CDs that cost \$6.10 each. How much do the CDs cost? \$67.10

Closure

- *Explain the Distributive Property.* Sample: When a sum or difference inside parentheses is multiplied by a number outside the parentheses, you can multiply each number inside the parentheses by the number outside, then add or subtract as indicated.
- *How does the Distributive Property differ from the other properties?* Sample: It always involves two operations and parentheses.

3. Practice

Assignment Guide

Check Your Understanding
See Math Companion.

Homework Exercises

A Practice by Example	1–24
B Apply Your Skills	25–38
C Challenge	39
California Multiple Choice Practice	40–42
Mixed Review	43–45

Homework Quick Check
To check students' understanding of key skills and concepts, go over Exercises 5, 16, 26, 29, 31, 37.

Universal Access Resources

Adapted Practice 3-8

Name ______ Class ______ Date ______ L3

Practice 1-6 The Distributive Property

Write an expression to represent the total area of each figure. Then use your expression to find the total area. Show all your work.

1. 3; 2, 8
2. 4; 4, 12
3. 5; 6, 12

Use the Distributive Property to find the missing numbers in the equations.

4. $8 \cdot (9 + 4) = (\square \cdot 9) + (8 \cdot \square)$
5. $(4 \cdot 7) + (4 \cdot 5) = 4 \cdot (\square + 5)$
6. $9 \cdot (7 - 1) = (9 \cdot \square) - (\square \cdot 1)$
7. $(5 \cdot 7) + (5 \cdot 6) = \square \cdot (7 + 6)$
8. $3 \cdot (7 + 9) = (\square \cdot 7) + (3 \cdot \square)$
9. $8 \cdot (9 - 6) = (8 \cdot \square) - (\square \cdot 6)$

Simplify each expression.

10. $8(m - 5)$
11. $3(t + 4)$
12. $(x + 3)9$

Use the Distributive Property to simplify each expression.

13. $7 \cdot 53$
14. $8 \cdot 97$
15. $5 \cdot 402$

16. The auditorium at the School for the Arts has 7 rows of seats, and each row has 102 seats in it. Use the Distributive Property to find the number of seats in the auditorium.

17. The largest television screen ever made was featured at the Tsukuba International Exposition near Tokyo, Japan, in 1985. The screen was called the Sony JUMBOtron and measured 40 meters by 25 meters. Use the Distributive Property to find the area of the screen.

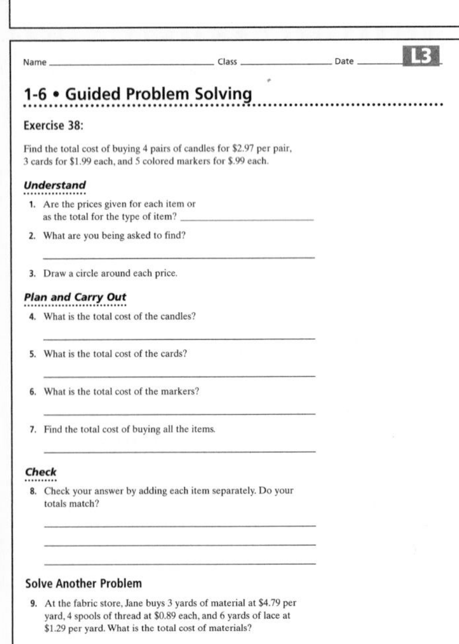

Name ______ Class ______ Date ______ L3

1-6 • Guided Problem Solving

Exercise 38:

Find the total cost of buying 4 pairs of candles for $2.97 per pair, 3 cards for $1.99 each, and 5 colored markers for $.99 each.

Understand

1. Are the prices given for each item or as the total for the type of item?
2. What are you being asked to find?
3. Draw a circle around each price.

Plan and Carry Out

4. What is the total cost of the candles?
5. What is the total cost of the cards?
6. What is the total cost of the markers?
7. Find the total cost of buying all the items.

Check

8. Check your answer by adding each item separately. Do your totals match?

Solve Another Problem

9. At the fabric store, Jane buys 3 yards of material at $4.79 per yard, 4 spools of thread at $0.89 each, and 6 yards of lace at $1.29 per yard. What is the total cost of materials?

Standards Practice

GO for Help: MathXL

AF 1.3

A Practice by Example

Example 1 (page 31)

Simplify each expression.

1. $5(a + 6)$ $5a + 30$
   $5(a + 6) = 5 \cdot a + 5 \cdot 6$
   $= \blacksquare + \blacksquare$

Guided Practice This exercise has been started for you!

2. $7(b - 9)$ $7b - 63$
3. $4(t + 3)$ $4t + 12$
4. $(v - 2)9$ $9v - 18$

GO for Help

5. $(8 + r)4$ $32 + 4r$
6. $(11 + w)2$ $22 + 2w$
7. $12(6 - f)$ $72 - 12f$
8. $15(z + 3)$ $15z + 45$
9. $(m + 10)7$ $7m + 70$
10. $25(4 - q)$ $100 - 25q$
11. $2(p - 0.5)$ $2p - 1$
12. $1.5(d + 6)$ $1.5d + 9$
13. $(22 + j)4$ $88 + 4j$

Example 2 (page 31)

Mental Math Use the Distributive Property to simplify each expression.

14. $3 \cdot 2.9$ 8.7
    $3 \cdot 2.9 = 3 \cdot (3.0 - 0.1)$
    $= \blacksquare + \blacksquare$

Guided Practice This exercise has been started for you!

Homework Video Tutor

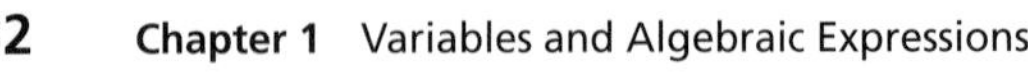

For: Examples 1–2
Visit: PHSchool.com
Web Code: axe-0106

15. $8 \cdot 28$ 224
16. $5 \cdot 63$ 315
17. $34 \cdot 4$ 136
18. $9.9 \cdot 6$ 59.4
19. $8.7 \cdot 3$ 26.1
20. $52 \cdot 6$ 312
21. $7.99 \cdot 5$ 39.95
22. $72 \cdot 8$ 576
23. $105 \cdot 9$ 945

24. Six students plan to go to a skating rink. The rink charges $4.50 per person. Find the total cost for the group. $27

B Apply Your Skills

25. **Guided Problem Solving** At the bakery, you want to buy 3 loaves of bread for $1.99 each and 2 muffins for $.89 each. You have $7 to spend. Do you have enough money? no
    - To find the cost of the bread, replace 1.99 with ■ − ■.
    - Multiply by 3 using the Distributive Property.

26. Your school plants 8 rows of trees. Each row has 27 trees. Find the total number of trees that the school plants. 216 trees

Plant a tree

Arbor Day

Use the Distributive Property to simplify each expression. Then evaluate the expression for $d = 5$.

27. $7(d - 2)$ $7d - 14; 21$
28. $(13 + d)2$ $26 + 2d; 36$
29. $18(9 + d)$ $162 + 18d; 252$

30. Your class is selling calendars for $2.90 each. How much money does your class collect for selling 8 calendars? $23.20

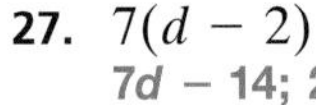

31. **Writing in Math** Explain how to use the properties of numbers to simplify $68 + 6 \cdot 99 + 32$. Answers may vary. Sample: First combine 68 and 32 to equal 100. Rewrite 99 as $100 - 1$ and distribute the 6. Then add and subtract from left to right.

SCAFFOLDED **Problem Solving**

32. Use the order of operations to simplify $5(3 + 5 + 7)$. 75

33. Use the order of operations to simplify $5 \cdot 3 + 5 \cdot 5 + 5 \cdot 7$. 75

34. Compare your answers for Exercises 32 and 33. Make a conjecture about how you can apply the Distributive Property to $5(3 + 5 + 7)$. See left.

35. Test your conjecture on $4(2 + 9 + 8)$. Check students' work.

36. Explain how you can apply the Distributive Property to an expression such as $5(a + b + c + d)$. Check students' work.

34. They are the same. Conjectures may vary. Sample: You can distribute the 5 to each number inside the parentheses.

37. **Reasoning** A student correctly simplified $8 \cdot 10.3 + 4.6$ as shown below. Write a justification for each step. See left.

Step 1: $8 \cdot 10.3 + 4.6$	$= 8(10 + 0.3) + 4.6$
Step 2:	$= 80 + 2.4 + 4.6$
Step 3:	$= 80 + 7$
Step 4:	$= 87$

37. Step 1: Write 10.3 as 10 + 0.3.; Step 2: Dist. Prop.; Step 3: Add.; Step 4: Simplify.

GPS 38. Find the total cost of buying 4 pairs of candles for \$2.97 per pair, 3 cards for \$1.99 each, and 5 colored markers for \$.99 each. \$22.80

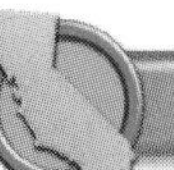 **Challenge**

39. A volunteer at a food bank is packing boxes with cans of fruit. Each box must weigh 20 lb or less. Can the volunteer put two dozen 15-oz cans in the box? Explain. (*Hint:* 1 lb = 16 oz) No; the weight will be greater than 20 lb.

Multiple Choice Practice and Mixed Review

For California Standards Tutorials, visit PHSchool.com. Web Code: axq-9045

AF 1.3

40. Which expression is NOT equivalent to the others? C

Ⓐ $(a \cdot c) + (b \cdot c)$ Ⓒ $b \cdot (c + a)$

Ⓑ $(b + a) \cdot c$ Ⓓ $(a + b) \cdot c$

AF 1.1

41. Marissa earned \$5 per hour baby-sitting. She worked for 4 h and then spent \$8.75 of her earnings. Which equation could be used to determine how much money, m, Marissa had left? B

Ⓐ $m = 4 \cdot (5 - 8.75)$ Ⓒ $m = 4 \cdot 5 + 8.75$

Ⓑ $m = 4 \cdot 5 - 8.75$ Ⓓ $m = 4 \cdot (5 + 8.75)$

NS 1.2, MR 2.1

42. Scarlet wants to buy 1 box of markers for \$3.49, 1 package of lined paper for \$1.19, and 2 packages of folders for \$.79 each. Which is a reasonable estimate for her total? C

Ⓐ \$3.50 Ⓑ \$5.50 Ⓒ \$6.30 Ⓓ \$7.00

 **Lesson 1-5**

Name the property each equation illustrates.

43. $12 + d = d + 12$ Comm. Prop. of Add.

44. $27(yc) = (27y)c$ Assoc. Prop. of Mult.

45. $1 \cdot p = p$ Identity Prop. of Mult.

 **Online Lesson Quiz** Visit: PHSchool.com **Web Code:** axa-0106

4. Assess & Reteach

 **PRESENTATION CD-ROM** CD, Online, or Transparencies

Lesson Quiz

Use the Distributive Property to rewrite each expression.

1. $8(a + 2)$ $8a + 16$
2. $-2(3x + 1)$ $-6x - 2$
3. $4 \cdot 3 \div 6 \cdot 3$ $(4 + 6)3$
4. $(6 - r)(-4)$ $-24 + 4r$
5. $5 \cdot 1 + 5 \cdot 9$ $5(1 + 9)$

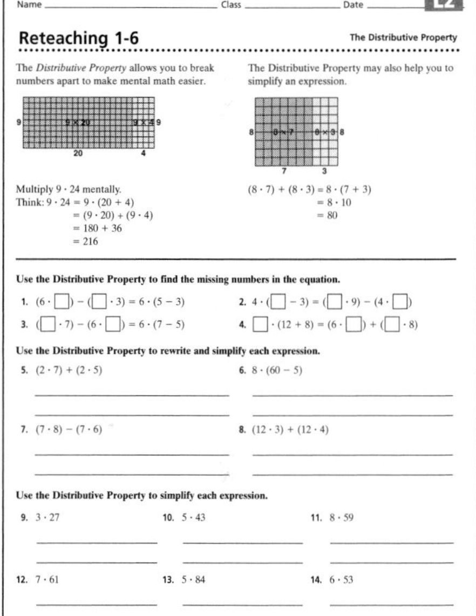

Name ______ Class ______ Date ______ L2

Reteaching 1-6 The Distributive Property

The *Distributive Property* allows you to break numbers apart to make mental math easier.

Multiply $9 \cdot 24$ mentally.

Think: $9 \cdot 24 = 9 \cdot (20 + 4)$
$= (9 \cdot 20) + (9 \cdot 4)$
$= 180 + 36$
$= 216$

The Distributive Property may also help you to simplify an expression.

$(8 \cdot 7) + (8 \cdot 3) = 8 \cdot (7 + 3)$
$= 8 \cdot 10$
$= 80$

Use the Distributive Property to find the missing numbers in the equation.

1. $(6 \cdot \square) - (\square \cdot 3) = 6 \cdot (5 - 3)$
2. $4 \cdot (\square - 3) = (\square \cdot 9) - (4 \cdot \square)$
3. $(\square \cdot 7) - (6 \cdot \square) = 6 \cdot (7 - 5)$
4. $\square \cdot (12 + 8) = (6 \cdot \square) + (\square \cdot 8)$

Use the Distributive Property to rewrite and simplify each expression.

5. $(2 \cdot 7) + (2 \cdot 5)$
6. $8 \cdot (60 - 5)$
7. $(7 \cdot 8) - (7 \cdot 6)$
8. $(12 \cdot 3) + (12 \cdot 4)$

Use the Distributive Property to simplify each expression.

9. $3 \cdot 27$
10. $5 \cdot 43$
11. $8 \cdot 59$
12. $7 \cdot 61$
13. $5 \cdot 84$
14. $6 \cdot 53$

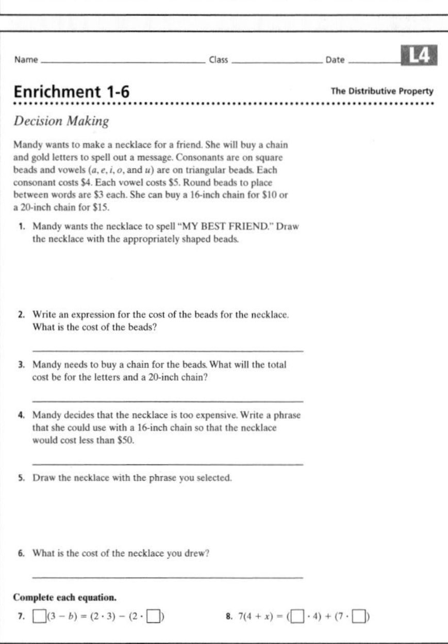

Name ______ Class ______ Date ______ L4

Enrichment 1-6 The Distributive Property

Decision Making

Mandy wants to make a necklace for a friend. She will buy a chain and gold letters to spell out a message. Consonants are on square beads and vowels ($a, e, i, o,$ and u) are on triangular beads. Each consonant costs \$4. Each vowel costs \$5. Round beads to place between words are \$3 each. She can buy a 16-inch chain for \$10 or a 20-inch chain for \$15.

1. Mandy wants the necklace to spell "MY BEST FRIEND." Draw the necklace with the appropriately shaped beads.
2. Write an expression for the cost of the beads for the necklace. What is the cost of the beads?
3. Mandy needs to buy a chain for the beads. What will the total cost be for the letters and a 20-inch chain?
4. Mandy decides that the necklace is too expensive. Write a phrase that she could use with a 16-inch chain so that the necklace would cost less than \$50.
5. Draw the necklace with the phrase you selected.
6. What is the cost of the necklace you drew?

Complete each equation.

7. $\square(3 - b) = (2 \cdot 3) - (2 \cdot \square)$
8. $7(4 + x) = (\square \cdot 4) + (7 \cdot \square)$

Alternative Assessment

Each student in a pair writes a multiplication problem similar to those in Exercises 8–14. Partners exchange papers and rewrite the expression using the Distributive Property. Students then simplify using mental math.

California Resources

Standards Mastery

- Standards Review Transparencies
- Standards Review and Practice Workbook
- Math Companion

Math Intervention

- Skills Review and Practice Workbook
- Math XL

Algebraic Thinking

Understanding Properties

Students use number properties as they learn to "think mathematically." Number properties will help them solve equations.

Guided Instruction

Example
Explain that the numbers in the Example are the same on each side of the equation. Only the order is changed, so the equation is true by the Commutative Property of Addition.

Exercises
Work through Exercises 1 and 2 as a class. For Exercise 1, students should note that multiplying by 0 always gives 0 as a result. For Exercise 2, students should use the Distributive Property.

Error Prevention!

Have students list the number properties on an index card and keep the list available as they do the Exercises.

Universal Access

Below Level L2
As students do Exercises 7–16, allow them to substitute several sets of numbers for the variables to get an idea of whether the statements are true.

Algebraic Thinking

For Use With Lesson 1-6

AF 1.3 Simplify expressions by applying properties of numbers. ***Develop***
MR 2.5 Use words to explain mathematical reasoning. ***Develop***
MR 2.6 Support solutions with evidence in verbal work. ***Develop***

Understanding Properties

Properties become more important as you "think algebraically." Understanding number properties and equality will help you solve algebraic equations.

EXAMPLE

Use a number property or number sense to determine whether the equation $8.8 + 12.5 + 1.2 = 1.2 + 8.8 + 12.5$ is true or false. Justify your reasoning.

$8.8 + 12.5 + 1.2 = 1.2 + 8.8 + 12.5$ ← The order of the numbers has changed. This is an example of the Commutative Property of Addition.

The equation is true. It uses the Commutative Property of Addition.

Exercises

Determine whether each equation is true or false. Do not compute with paper and pencil. Use number properties and mental math to decide. Justify your reasoning.

1. $3.78 + 14.95 + 0 = 3.78 + 14.95$
   true; Identity Prop. of Add.
2. $15.4 \cdot 10 = (15 \cdot 10) + (0.4 \cdot 10)$
   true; Distr. Prop.
3. $25.7 - (13 - 10) = (25.7 - 13) - 10$
   false; subtraction is not associative
4. $16 \cdot (3.8 \div 3.80) = 2 \cdot 8$
   true; Identity Prop. of Mult.
5. $60 \cdot 19.5 = 60 \cdot 2 - 60 \cdot 0.5$
   false; $19.5 \neq 2 - 0.5$
6. $321 \cdot 3 = 300 \cdot 3 + 21 \cdot 3$
   true; Dist. Prop.

Determine whether each statement is true for all numbers *a, b,* and *c.* Justify your reasoning.

7. $0 \cdot a = a$ false; Zero Prop. of Mult.
8. $0 \div a = a$ false; $0 \div a = 0$
9. $a - b + b = a$ true; Identity Prop. of Add.
10. $a \div 0 = 0$ false; cannot divide by 0
11. $a \cdot b = b \cdot a$ true; Comm. Prop. of Mult.
12. $b + a + c = bc + a$ false; $b + c \neq bc$
13. $a \cdot b \div c = b \cdot a \div c$ (if $c \neq 0$)
    true; Comm. Prop. of Mult.
14. $a \div b = b \div a$ (if $a, b \neq 0$)
    false; division is not commutative
15. $b \cdot 1 = b$ true; Identity Prop. of Mult.
16. $a \div a = b \div b$ (if $a, b \neq 0$) true; $1 = 1$
17. **Reasoning** If you use a calculator to compute $0 \div 5$, you will get 0. If you calculate $5 \div 0$, you will get an error message. Use multiplication to explain why $5 \div 0$ is not defined. You cannot multiply 0 by any number to get 5.

GPS Guided Problem Solving

Choosing the Right Operation

John Bain made the world's largest rubber-band ball. The ball was 5 ft tall. It took 550,000 rubber bands, and 4 yr 2 mo to put together. About how many rubber bands did Mr. Bain add each month?

NS 1.2 Add, subtract, multiply, and divide rational numbers. ***Develop***
MR 3.2 Note the method of deriving the solution and demonstrate an understanding of the derivation by solving similar problems. ***Develop***

What You Might Think	What You Might Write
What do I know? What do I want to find out?	550,000 rubber bands were used. It took 4 yr 2 mo, or 50 mo, to build. I want to find the number of rubber bands he used each month.
How can I show the main idea?	Draw a diagram. 0 —— 550,000 Rubber bands 0 —— 50 Months
How do I solve the problem?	Divide the number of rubber bands by the number of months. $\begin{array}{r} 11{,}000 \\ 50\overline{)550{,}000} \\ -50 \\ \hline 50 \\ 50 \\ \hline 0 \end{array}$
What is the answer?	Mr. Bain used 11,000 rubber bands each month.

Think It Through

1. Why does the diagram show 0–550,000 rubber bands on a line the same length as the line for 0–50 months? **because 550,000 rubber bands were used in 50 mo**
2. Explain why 4 yr 2 mo is the same as $4 \cdot 12 + 2$ mo. **See margin.**
3. **Estimation** Use estimation to show that the answer is reasonable. **Check students' work.**

GPS Guided Problem Solving

Choosing the Right Operation

In this feature, students identify what they know and what they are trying to find out. They show the main idea, decide which operation to use, estimate the answer, solve the problem, and check that their answer is reasonable.

Guided Instruction

Discuss with students the need to read the problem carefully. Students need to decide what information is relevant to the problem they are trying to solve.

Have a volunteer read the problem aloud. Ask:

- *What information is not needed to solve the problem?* **the dimensions of the ball, 5 feet tall**
- *How can you find the number of months?* **Multiply 4 years by 12 months per year and add the extra two months.**
- *How do you know to divide by 50?* **To find the average number per month, divide the total number by the number of months.**

Error Prevention!

Some students may have trouble deciding whether they used the right operation. Have them restate the problem using the answer they obtained to see if they used the correct operation. Sample: On average, Mr. Bain used 11,000 rubber bands each month. He worked 4 years, 2 months (or 50 months) to build the ball. So he used 50 × 11,000 or 550,000 bands in all.

Exercises

Have students do Exercises 4–7 independently. Then have them form groups to share, evaluate, and adjust answers.

Universal Access

English Learners EL

Ask: *What does "on average" in this problem mean?* Sample: It means that the number of bands used each month was about 11,000; it could have been a little more or less.

Exercises

Solve each problem. For Exercise 4, answer parts (a), (b), and (c) first.

4. Suppose Mr. Bain started with five packages of rubber bands. Two of the packages cost \$1.10 each and three of the packages cost \$1.98 each. Use the Distributive Property to determine how much he spent to begin his project. \$8.14
   a. What do you know?
   b. What are you trying to find out?
   c. Simplify $2 \cdot 1.10 + 3 \cdot 1.98$.
      - Replace each price with a sum or difference.
        $2 \cdot 1.10 = 2(■ + ■)$
        $3 \cdot 1.98 = 3(■ - ■)$
      - Use the Distributive Property to simplify.
      - Add the two costs. The total is \$■.

5. To test the elasticity of the rubber bands, Mr. Bain stretched each rubber band in a package. The farthest a rubber band stretched was 38.5 in. The shortest a rubber band stretched was 34.8 in. Use the model below to find the difference in distances. 3.7 in.

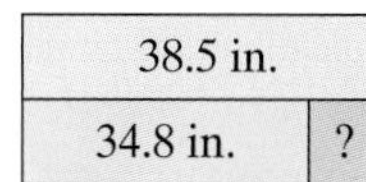

6. Mr. Bain spent about \$240 each month on his rubber-band ball. What was the total cost of his project? Copy the drawing below. Label the cost at the first ■. Then solve the problem and label the total cost at the second ■. \$12,000

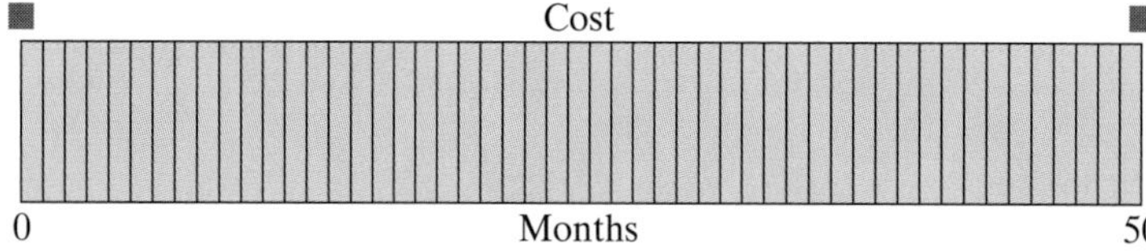

7. You can make a chain 1 mi long using 63,360 paper clips. The world record is a chain 19.62 mi long. How many paper clips were used to make this chain? 1,243,124 paper clips

8. A teacher made a paper clip-chain using 60,650 paper clips. It took the teacher about 26.75 h to make the chain. About how many seconds did the teacher spend adding each paper clip? 1.59 s

Finding Needed Information

Sometimes a problem asks you to find a missing piece of information. You can use the problem-solving plan to decide which information you need. Ask yourself, What do I know? and, How would I solve the problem?

EXAMPLE

Jenny stands on a scale while holding her dog. The scale reads 162 lb. What missing piece of information is needed to find the weight of Jenny's dog?

Ⓐ Jenny's height Ⓒ The time Jenny spends on the scale
Ⓑ The age of the dog Ⓓ Jenny's weight

What do you know?

You know the total weight of Jenny and her dog is 162 lb.

How would you solve the problem?

You can draw a diagram. You would subtract Jenny's weight from the total weight to find the dog's weight.

Total Weight	
Jenny	Dog

What missing piece of information do you need?

You need to know Jenny's weight.

The correct answer is choice D.

Multiple Choice Practice

Solve each problem by finding the missing piece of information.

NS 1.2, MR 1.1

1. A distributor had 3,000 games. It sent the same number of games to each store. What missing piece of information is needed to find how many games each store received? C

   Ⓐ The number of players Ⓒ The number of stores
   Ⓑ The distributor's location Ⓓ The cost of the game

NS 1.2, MR 1.1

2. A. J. bought three shirts, some socks, and a new tie. He paid with a \$50 bill. What missing piece of information is needed to find how much change A. J. should receive? D

   Ⓐ The number of pairs of socks Ⓒ The cost of one shirt
   Ⓑ The total number of items Ⓓ The total cost

Finding Needed Information

Students learn how to determine what information to use to solve a problem. They then choose the needed information from multiple choices.

Guided Instruction

Example

The example suggests subtracting Jenny's weight from the total.

Ask:

- *What word expression could you write for the situation?* **Total weight minus Jenny's weight equals dog's weight.**
- *If Jenny weighed 100 pounds, what equation could you use?* **162 − 100 = dog's weight**

Exercises

Have students write word expressions to help.

California Resources

Standards Mastery
- Math Companion
- Standards Review Transparencies
- Standards Review and Practice Workbook
- Progress Monitoring Assessments

Math Intervention
- Skills Review and Practice Workbook
- Math XL

Universal Access Resources
- Student Workbook
  - Vocabulary and Study Skills
  - Guided Problem Solving
- All-in-One Teaching Resources
  - Reteaching
  - Enrichment
- Spanish Practice Workbook L3
- Spanish Vocabulary and Study Skills 2A-F L3
- English/Spanish Glossary EL
- Multilingual Handbook EL
- Interactive Textbook Audio Glossary
- Online Vocabulary Quiz

Online at PHSchool.com

Spanish Vocabulary/Study Skills EL

Vocabulary/Study Skills L3

1F Vocabulary Review For use with the Chapter Review

Study Skill Review your class notes as soon as possible. This will help you identify any concepts in which you need additional explanation.

Match the term in Column A with its definition or example in Column B.

Column A	Column B
1. Identity Property of Multiplication E	A. decimals that represent the same amount
2. place value F	B. $7 + (3 + 9) = (7 + 3) + 9$
3. compatible numbers C	C. numbers that are easy to compute mentally
4. equivalent decimals A	D. $6 + 8 = 8 + 6$
5. Associative Property of Addition B	E. $8.3 \times 1 = 8.3$
6. Commutative Property of Addition D	F. value of a digit based on its location in a particular number

Match the term in Column A with its definition or example in Column B.

Column A	Column B
7. Identity Property of Addition L	G. $8 \cdot 4 = 4 \cdot 8$
8. Associative Property of Multiplication K	H. sum that shows the place and value of each digit
9. Commutative Property of Multiplication G	I. a number written using digits
10. expanded form H	J. mathematical phrase containing numbers and operations
11. standard form I	K. $8(7 \cdot 9) = (8 \cdot 7)9$
12. expression J	L. $4 + 0 = 4$

Vocabulary and Study Skills

38

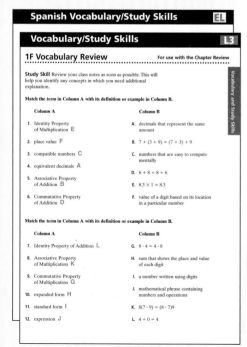

Chapter 1 Review

Vocabulary Review

English and Spanish Audio Online

algebraic expression (p. 8)
Associative Property of Addition (p. 26)
Associative Property of Multiplication (p. 26)
Commutative Property of Addition (p. 26)
Commutative Property of Multiplication (p. 26)
compatible numbers (p. 21)
Distributive Property (p. 30)
evaluate (p. 9)
Identity Property of Addition (p. 26)
Identity Property of Multiplication (p. 26)
numerical expression (p. 4)
order of operations (p. 4)
simplify (p. 4)
variable (p. 8)

Academic Vocabulary
identify (p. 19)
justification (p. 25)
justify (p. 19)
list (p. 19)

Go Online PHSchool.com
For: Vocabulary Quiz
Visit: PHSchool.com
Web Code: axj-0151

Choose the correct vocabulary term to complete each sentence.

1. An example of the _?_ is $5 + 0 = 5$. Ident. Prop. of Add.
2. $7 + 4 \cdot 2$ is a(n) _?_. numerical expression
3. A(n) _?_ contains one or more variables. algebraic expression
4. A(n) _?_ is a symbol that stands for a number. variable
5. Numbers that are easy to compute mentally are called _?_. compatible numbers

Skills and Concepts

Lesson 1-1
- To write and simplify numerical expressions

NS 1.2

A **numerical expression** is a mathematical phrase that contains numbers and operation symbols. You can use the **order of operations** to **simplify** an expression.

Simplify each expression.

6. $30.1 - 5 + 4 \cdot 3.2$ 37.9
7. $6.8 - (27 - 9) \div 3$ 0.8
8. $5.4 \cdot 8 + 4.6 \div 2$ 45.5
9. $7 \cdot 1.5 + 9 - 3$ 16.5

Lesson 1-2
- To evaluate algebraic expressions

NS 1.2

An **algebraic expression** is a mathematical expression with one or more **variables.** To **evaluate** an algebraic expression, replace each variable with a number and simplify.

Evaluate each expression.

10. $6y - 4$ for $y = 3$ 14
11. $d \div 7$ for $d = 28$ 4
12. $4v + 7$ for $v = 5$ 27
13. $8m + 9$ for $m = 2$ 25
14. Pies at a local bakery cost \$12. Use the expression $12p$, where p is the number of pies, to find the cost of 4 pies. \$48

Lesson 1-3

- To write algebraic expressions

AF 1.1

You can write a word phrase as an algebraic expression.

Write an expression for each word phrase.

15. x divided by 12 $x \div 12$ **16.** 2 times b $2b$ **17.** 3 more than k $k + 3$

18. Your school's basketball team scores five more points than the other team. Write an expression using the other team's score s to describe your team's score. $s + 5$

Lesson 1-4

- To estimate to check for reasonableness

NS 1.2, MR 2.1

You can round each number or use **compatible numbers** to estimate. Estimating calculations can help you check for reasonableness.

Estimate using rounding or compatible numbers.

19. $5{,}021 + 2{,}957$ about 8,000 **20.** $8{,}989 \div 3$ about 3,000 **21.** $1.9 \cdot 5.2$ about 10

22. You buy two greeting cards for $2.89 each and a roll of wrapping paper for $3.15. Is $8.93 a reasonable total for the purchase? yes

Lesson 1-5

- To recognize and use the properties of numbers

AF 1.3

The properties of numbers apply to both numerical and algebraic expressions. You can use the **commutative, associative,** and **identity properties** to help you add and multiply mentally.

Name the property each equation illustrates.

23. $s \cdot 1 = s$ Identity Prop. of Mult. **24.** $7 + h = h + 7$ Comm. Prop. of Add.

25. $(a + b) + 2 = a + (b + 2)$ Assoc. Prop. of Add. **26.** $n \cdot 36 = 36 \cdot n$ Comm. Prop. of Mult.

Mental Math Use mental math to find each sum or product.

27. $1 + 250 + 99$ 350 **28.** $2 \cdot 13 \cdot 5$ 130 **29.** $16 + 3 + 4 + 7$ 30

Lesson 1-6

- To use the Distributive Property

AF 1.3

You can use the **Distributive Property** to simplify an algebraic expression or do mental calculations.

Simplify each expression.

30. $3(p - 7)$ $3p - 21$ **31.** $(m + 4)8$ $8m + 32$ **32.** $5(2 + k)$ $10 + 5k$

Mental Math Use the Distributive Property to simplify each expression.

33. $7 \cdot 28$ 196 **34.** $5 \cdot 3.4$ 17 **35.** $11 \cdot 57$ 627

Alternative Assessment L4

Alternative Assessment Form C

Chapter 1

ALLOWANCE REQUEST

Antonio is 12 years old and in the sixth grade. He likes to play baseball, collect baseball cards, play catch with his dog, and play the trombone. He doesn't like to clean his room, set the table, take the dog for walks, or baby-sit his little brother.

One day Antonio found an article in *Zillions* magazine about allowances. He read that half of all students surveyed received an allowance. Most of the students (80%) had to do chores to get their allowances. The typical allowance for students between the ages of 11 and 14 was around $5. Most students used their allowances to buy things like snacks, gifts, magazines, games, sports supplies, CDs, and other "extras."

Antonio would like to have an allowance to earn, spend, and save, so he decided to write an "Allowance Request" to give to his parents. Copy and complete the request as if you were Antonio.

Allowance Request

1. I would like to request a weekly allowance of $5. I think this is a fair amount because

2. To earn the allowance, I will do the following chores. (I have marked what I think each chore is worth.)

Chore	Estimated Value	Times per Week	Total Earned

GRAND TOTAL

California Resources

Standards Mastery
- Teacher Center ExamView CD-ROM
- Math XL
- Progress Monitoring Assessments
- Online Chapter Test at PHSchool.com

Math Intervention
- Skills Review and Practice Workbook

Online at PHSchool.com

Universal Access Resources
- Chapter Test
- Alternative Assessment
- Spanish Chapter Test
- Spanish Alternative Assessment
- Teacher Center ExamView CD-ROM
  - Special Needs Test
  - Special Needs Practice Banks
  - Foundational Standards Practice Banks
- Online Chapter Test at www.PHSchool.com
- All-In-One Teaching Resources
  - Cumulative Review L3
- Spanish Assessment Resources
  - Cumulative Review L3

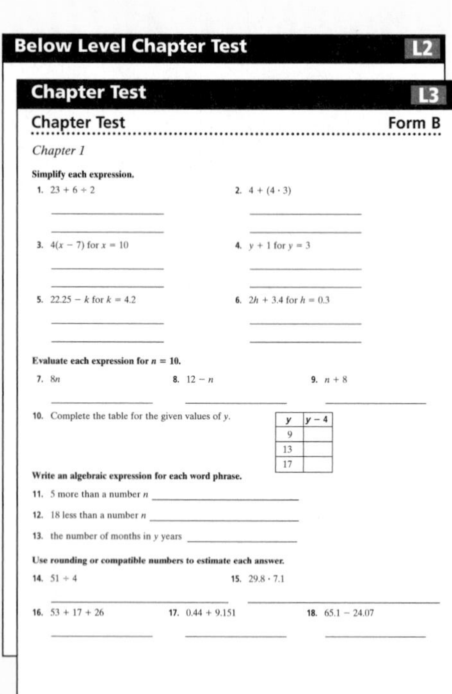

Below Level Chapter Test L2

Chapter Test L3

Chapter Test — Form B

Chapter 1

Simplify each expression.

1. $23 + 6 \div 2$
2. $4 + (4 \cdot 3)$
3. $4(x - 7)$ for $x = 10$
4. $y + 1$ for $y = 3$
5. $22.25 - k$ for $k = 4.2$
6. $2h + 3.4$ for $h = 0.3$

Evaluate each expression for $n = 10$.

7. $8n$
8. $12 - n$
9. $n + 8$
10. Complete the table for the given values of y.

y	$y - 4$
9	
13	
17	

Write an algebraic expression for each word phrase.

11. 5 more than a number n
12. 18 less than a number n
13. the number of months in y years

Use rounding or compatible numbers to estimate each answer.

14. $51 \div 4$
15. $29.8 \cdot 7.1$
16. $53 + 17 + 26$
17. $0.44 + 9.151$
18. $65.1 - 24.07$

Chapter 1 Test

Go Online — PHSchool.com — **For:** Online chapter test **Web Code:** axa-0152

Simplify each expression.

1. $16.8 \div (4.2 \cdot 4)$ 1
2. $8.3 - 4.8 \div 2$ 5.9
3. $5.6 + (32 - 16.1)$ 21.5
4. $5 \div (0.6 + 3.4)$ 1.25
5. $9.2 - 1 \cdot 3.3$ 5.9
6. $5.4 + 23 - 4.2$ 24.2

Evaluate each expression for $x = 12$.

7. $500 + (x - 8)$ 504
8. $2x - 3$ 21
9. $8 + x \div 2$ 14
10. $(16 + x) \div 4 - 3$ 4
11. Find the value of the expression for the given values of b in the table at the right.

b	$b + 7$	
8	■	15
12	■	19
20	■	27

12. Evaluate the expression $d + 4e$ for $d = 13$ and $e = 6$. 37

Write an algebraic expression for each word phrase.

13. c more than 4 $4 + c$
14. 8 less than $3s$ $3s - 8$
15. the sum of a number v and 18 $v + 18$
16. the product of m minutes and 5 $5m$
17. Gus is 8 yr younger than his brother, Alex. Alex is x years old. Write an algebraic expression that describes how old Gus is. $x - 8$
18. **Writing in Math** Write a word problem that could be described by the expression $d + 4$. Check students' work.
19. **Estimation** Suppose your savings account has a balance of \$238.52. You deposit \$42.56. Then you withdraw \$92.35. About how much is left in your savings account? about \$190

Use rounding or compatible numbers to estimate each answer.

20. $37 + 42 + 142$ about 220
21. $50.32 \cdot 22.1$ about 1,000
22. $4.63 \cdot 50.491$ about 250
23. $98 \div 24$ about 4
24. $1.01 + 2.89$ about 4
25. $622.85 - 24.12$ about 600
26. Five DVDs cost a total of \$72.25. Explain whether the cost of one DVD is greater or less than \$14. More than \$14; $5 \cdot 14 = 70$, so the cost for 1 DVD must be greater than \$14.

Name the property each equation illustrates.

27. $3(ck) = (3c)k$ Assoc. Prop. of Mult.
28. $7 + t = t + 7$ Comm. Prop. of Add.
29. $j \cdot 1 = j$ Identity Prop. of Mult.
30. $5 + h + 11 = h + 5 + 11$ Comm. Prop. of Add.

Mental Math **Use mental math to simplify each expression.**

31. $829 + 71$ 900
32. $24 + (76 + 60)$ 160
33. $25 \cdot 6 \cdot 4$ 600
34. $10 \cdot 7 \cdot 20$ 1,400
35. You buy movie tickets for yourself and three friends. Each ticket costs \$7. You pay with two twenty-dollar bills. How much change do you get back? \$12

Simplify each expression.

36. $12(p + 7)$ $12p + 84$
37. $(23 - r)4$ $92 - 4r$
38. $(t - 16)2$ $2t - 32$
39. $9(g + 15)$ $9g + 135$

Mental Math **Use the Distributive Property to simplify each expression.**

40. $8 \cdot 39$ 312
41. $6 \cdot 32$ 192
42. $4 \cdot 8.8$ 35.2
43. $9.8 \cdot 3$ 29.4
44. You buy five notebooks for \$.98 each. Use mental math to find the total cost. \$4.90

Cumulative Practice

Some questions require you to choose the expression or equation that models a situation. Use the tips as guides for how to approach solving the problem.

Mr. Phan is repairing his deck. At the hardware store he bought 5 boards at $15.99 each and 2 gal of paint at $25.49 each. Which expression can be used to find the total Mr. Phan spent?

(A) 5(15.99 + 25.49)
(B) 5 · 15.99 + 2 · 25.49
(C) (15.99 + 25.49)2
(D) 5 · 15.99 + 25.49

Tip 1
Underline the important information.

Tip 2
Think "multiply" when multiple numbers of items are in a problem situation.

Think It Through
Express 5 boards at $15.99 as 5 · 15.99 and 2 gal of paint at $25.49 as 2 · 25.49. The total is the sum 5 · 15.99 + 2 · 25.49. The correct answer is choice B.

Vocabulary Review

As you solve problems, you must understand the meanings of mathematical terms. Match each term with its mathematical meaning.

A. expression II
B. simplify III
C. reasonable I
D. evaluate V
E. order of operations IV

I. not too much or too little
II. a mathematical phrase that uses operation symbols with numbers or variables
III. to replace an expression with its simplest name
IV. rules for the order in which you do operations
V. to replace each variable in an expression with a number

Read each question. Then write the letter of the correct answer on your paper.

1. Which of the following expressions shows the Identity Property of Addition? A
(Lesson 1-5)
   (A) $b + 0 = b$
   (B) $4(1 + b) = 4 + 4b$
   (C) $b + 4 + 1 = 4 + b + 1$
   (D) $(b + 1) + 4 = b + (1 + 4)$

2. Karen, Aretha, and Alissa live on the same road. The distance from Karen's house to Alissa's house is 7.8 mi. What is the distance from Aretha's house to Alissa's house? (Lesson 1-1) C

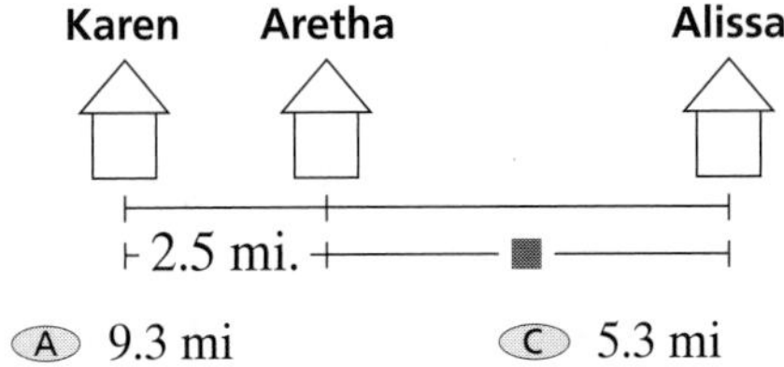

   (A) 9.3 mi
   (B) 7.3 mi
   (C) 5.3 mi
   (D) 4.3 mi

Standards Mastery

California Resources

Standards Mastery
- Teacher Center ExamView CD-ROM
- Math XL
- Progress Monitoring Assessments
- Online Chapter Test at PHSchool.com

Math Intervention
- Skills Review and Practice Workbook

- Teacher Center ExamView CD-ROM
  - Special Needs Test
  - Special Needs Practice Banks
  - Foundational Standards Practice Banks
- Online Chapter Test at www.PHSchool.com
- All-In-One Teaching Resources
  - Cumulative Review L3
- Spanish Assessment Resources
  - Cumulative Review L3

Success Tracker™
Online at PHSchool.com

Cumulative Practice (continued)

3. Javier has twice as many baseball cards as Max. Let m represent the number of cards Max has. Which expression represents the number of cards Javier has? (Lesson 1-3) A

   (A) $2m$ (C) $m + 2$
   (B) $\frac{m}{2}$ (D) $m - 2$

4. Dax bought some food from a snack bar.

Pretzel	$2.00
Popcorn	$2.25
Lemonade	$1.50

   Which expression can Dax use to find the total cost of p pretzels, a bag of popcorn, and a lemonade? (Lesson 1-3) B

   (A) $2 + 2.25 + 1.5$
   (B) $2p + 2.25 + 1.5$
   (C) $p(1 + 2.25 + 1.5)$
   (D) $2p + 2.25p + 1.5p$

5. Kristen pays a monthly fee of $3.95 to download songs. For each song she downloads, she pays $.59. She uses the expression $3.95 + 0.59s$ to find her monthly cost for s songs. What is the total charge for downloading 20 songs? (Lesson 1-2) B

   (A) $4.54 (C) $24.54
   (B) $15.75 (D) $79.59

6. Jesse bought two pairs of sneakers for $54.99 each and five extra pairs of shoelaces for $1.89 per pair. Which of the following choices is a reasonable amount for the total cost of these items? (Lesson 1-4) D

   (A) $56.88 (C) $79.59
   (B) $64.44 (D) $119.43

7. To simplify the expression $6(f + 4)$, which property should you use first? (Lesson 1-6) C

   (A) Associative Property of Addition
   (B) Commutative Property of Addition
   (C) Distributive Property
   (D) Identity Property of Addition

8. The eighth-grade class at Sunshine Middle School plans to visit the state capital in Sacramento, California. Each bus holds 53 students. Which expression shows the number of buses needed for n students going on the field trip? (Lesson 1-3) B

   (A) $53n$ (C) $\frac{53}{n}$
   (B) $\frac{n}{53}$ (D) $53 + n$

9. Simone is making an enclosure for her pet rabbit. She plans to make the enclosure 3 ft long by 2.5 ft wide. To find the perimeter, she uses the expression $P = 2(\ell + w)$ where ℓ is the length and w is the width. How much fencing does she need? (Lesson 1-2) D

   (A) 2.5 ft (C) 5.5 ft
   (B) 3 ft (D) 11 ft

10. Jared's mom bought 2 gal of milk for $3.99 each and a box of cereal. Which algebraic expression can she use to find the total amount she spent? Let c represent the cost of a box of cereal. (Lesson 1-3) C

   (A) $3.99 + c$
   (B) $2 + 3.99 + c$
   (C) $3.99 + 3.99 + c$
   (D) $2(3.99 + c)$

11. Sabrina found clothes on sale. She bought three pairs of jeans and two shirts.

Garment	Regular Price	Sale Price
Jeans	$45.99	$34.50
Shirts	$18.99	$14.25

   What was the total price of the items Sabrina bought? (Lesson 1-1) B

   (A) $175.95 (C) $64.98
   (B) $132.00 (D) $48.75

Spanish Cumulative Review EL

Cumulative Review L3

Name ________ Class ________ Date ________

Cumulative Review

Chapter 1

Multiple Choice. Choose the letter of the best answer.

1. Evaluate $4 \cdot (3 + 7)$.
   A. 19 B. 14
   C. 43 D. 40
2. Which word phrase best describes the expression $x + y$?
   A. a number plus itself
   B. twice a number
   C. a number more than two
   D. a number plus another number
3. Use mental math to solve $k - 4 = 9$.
   A. 5 B. 9
   C. 13 D. 36
4. Which is the value of $64 - 4 \cdot (2 + 13)$?
   A. 4 B. 34
   C. 47 D. 900
5. Use mental math to evaluate $4x - 9$ for $x = 6$.
   A. 14 B. 15
   C. 33 D. 37
6. Use mental math to evaluate $(24 + 86) \cdot 10$.
   A. 1,000 B. 1,010
   C. 1,100 D 1,110
7. Evaluate $9 \cdot 9 - 6 + 6$.
   A. 4.5 B. 12.5
   C. 45 D. 80
8. What would you *do first* if you had to evaluate the expression $5(9 - 4)$?
   A. $5 \cdot 9$ B. $5 \cdot 4$
   C. $(9 - 4)$ D. $5 \cdot 9 - 5 \cdot 4$
9. Estimate. $82{,}591 - 13{,}983$
   A. 7,000 B. 50,000
   C. 60,000 D. 70,000
10. Estimate. $5.3 \cdot 0.8$
   A. 0.40 B. 40
   C. 4 D. 48
11. Which sum is equivalent to $(3 + 4) + 12$?
   A. $(12 + 4) + (12 + 3)$
   B. $4 + 12 + 3$
   C. $(3 \cdot 4) \cdot 12$
   D. $(3 + 4) + (3 + 4) + (3 + 4)$
12. Evaluate $9 + 6 \div 3 \cdot 4$.
   A. 17
   B. 20
   C. 21
   D. 72
13. What is an expression for "45 less than twice a number"?
   A. $45 + 2n$ B. $2n - 45$
   C. $45 - 2n$ D. $(45 + n)^2$
14. Simplify. $9 + 7 \cdot 6 - (5 - 3)$
   A. 94 B. 49
   C. 47 D. 35

12. Which property is illustrated by the equation $4.5x \cdot 1 = 4.5x$? (Lesson 1-5) A

(A) Identity Property of Multiplication
(B) Inverse Property of Multiplication
(C) Commutative Property of Multiplication
(D) Associative Property of Multiplication

13. Ms. Browning's class plans to donate \$100 to an earthquake relief fund. If each of the 28 students donates \$2, how much more money should the class raise? (Lesson 1-1) C

(A) \$16 (C) \$44
(B) \$32 (D) \$64

14. Simplify $9(1 + 3) - 12$. (Lesson 1-1) C

(A) 0 (C) 24
(B) 1 (D) 72

15. A student simplified $7(w + 12)$ to be $7w + 84$. Which property did the student use? (Lesson 1-6) D

(A) Associative Property of Addition
(B) Identity Property of Addition
(C) Commutative Property of Addition
(D) Distributive Property

16. Antung watches his cousins for the holiday weekend. He keeps track of the number of hours he works and the amount he is paid.

Weekend Earnings

Hours, *h*	Amount Paid
3	\$18
5	\$30
6	\$36
8	\$48

Which expression can be used to find the amount Antung earns for working *h* hours? (Lesson 1-3) A

(A) $6h$ (C) $h + 12$
(B) $8h$ (D) $h + 15$

17. Janice ate five crackers that contained a total of 50 Calories. She also ate three peaches. She ate a total of 170 Calories. Find the number of Calories in each peach. (Lesson 1-1) B

(A) 10 (B) 40 (C) 57 (D) 120

18. Mia earns \$6 per hour when she baby-sits her neighbor's three children. She saves half of what she earns and uses the other half for spending money. On Saturday she will baby-sit for 3.5 h. To find how much she must put in savings, she first multiplied 3.5 by 6. What is her next step? (Lesson 1-1) D

(A) Add 2 to the product.
(B) Subtract 2 from the product.
(C) Multiply the product by 2.
(D) Divide the product by 2.

19. Which property is illustrated by the equation $5(k + 2) = 5(2 + k)$? (Lesson 1-5) C

(A) Associative Property of Addition
(B) Identity Property of Addition
(C) Commutative Property of Addition
(D) Distributive Property

Standards Reference Guide

California Content Standard	Item Number(s)
NS 1.2	2, 5, 6, 9, 11, 13, 14, 17
AF 1.1	3, 4, 8, 10, 16
AF 1.3	1, 7, 12, 15, 18, 19

For additional review and practice, see the *California Standards Review and Practice Workbook* or go online to use the

Visit: PHSchool.com, **Web Code:** axq-9045

Chapter 2 Integers and Exponents

Chapter at a Glance

Lesson Titles, Objectives, and Features	California Content Standards
2-1 Integers and Absolute Value • To find absolute values of integers **Vocabulary Builder:** High-Use Academic Words	**NS 1.2** Add and subtract rational numbers. **Alg 1 2.0** Understand taking the opposite.
2-2a Activity Lab: Modeling Addition of Integers **2-2 Adding Integers** • To add integers **Mathematical Reasoning:** Positive and Negative Decimals	**NS 1.2** Add rational numbers. **AF 1.3** Simplify numerical expressions by applying properties of rational numbers and justify the process used. **MR 2.5** Use models to explain mathematical reasoning.
2-3a Activity Lab: Modeling Subtraction of Integers **2-3 Subtracting Integers** • To subtract integers	Solve subtraction problems that use positive and negative integers. ***Foundational (Gr6 NS 2.3)*** **NS 1.2** Subtract rational numbers. **Alg 1 2.0** Understand and use such operations as taking the opposite. **MR 2.5** Use models to explain mathematical reasoning.
2-4 Multiplying Integers • To multiply integers	Solve multiplication problems that use positive and negative integers. ***Foundational (Gr6 NS 2.3)*** **NS 1.2** Multiply rational numbers.
2-5 Dividing Integers • To divide integers **Vocabulary Builder:** Using Take Note Boxes	Solve division problems that use positive and negative integers. ***Foundational (Gr6 NS 2.3)*** **NS 1.2** Divide rational numbers.
2-6 Positive Exponents • To write, simplify, and evaluate expressions involving exponents	**NS 1.2** Take positive rational numbers to whole-number powers. **AF 1.2** Interpret positive whole-number powers as repeated multiplication. Simplify and evaluate expressions that include exponents.

California Content Standards
NS Number Sense
AF Algebra and Functions
MG Measurement and Geometry
MR Mathematical Reasoning

Correlations to Standardized Tests

All content for these tests is contained in *Prentice Hall Math, Algebra Readiness.* This chart reflects coverage in this chapter only.

	2-1	2-2	2-3	2-4	2-5	2-6
Terra Nova CAT6 (Level 18)						
Number and Number Relations	✔	✔	✔	✔	✔	✔
Computation and Numerical Estimation		✔	✔	✔	✔	✔
Operation Concepts	✔	✔	✔	✔	✔	✔
Measurement						
Geometry and Spatial Sense						
Data Analysis, Statistics, and Probability						
Patterns, Functions, and Algebra	✔	✔	✔	✔	✔	✔
Problem Solving and Reasoning	✔	✔	✔	✔	✔	✔
Communication	✔	✔	✔	✔	✔	✔
Decimals, Fractions, Integers, Percent	✔	✔	✔	✔	✔	✔
Order of Operations						
Algebraic Operations	✔	✔	✔	✔	✔	
Terra Nova CTBS (Level 18)						
Decimals, Fractions, Integers, and Percents	✔	✔	✔	✔	✔	✔
Order of Operations, Numeration, Number Theory	✔	✔	✔	✔	✔	✔
Data Interpretation						
Measurement						
Geometry						
ITBS (Level 14)						
Number Properties and Operations	✔	✔	✔	✔	✔	✔
Algebra	✔	✔	✔	✔	✔	✔
Geometry						
Measurement						
Probability and Statistics						
Estimation						
SAT10 (Adv 1 Level)						
Number Sense and Operations	✔	✔	✔	✔	✔	✔
Patterns, Relationships, and Algebra	✔	✔	✔	✔	✔	✔
Data, Statistics, and Probability						
Geometry and Measurement						
NAEP						
Number Sense, Properties, and Operations	✔	✔	✔	✔	✔	✔
Measurement						
Geometry and Spatial Sense						
Data Analysis, Statistics, and Probability						
Algebra and Functions	✔			✔	✔	✔

CAT6 California Achievement Test, 6th Ed. **CTBS** Comprehensive Test of Basic Skills **ITBS** Iowa Test of Basic Skills, Form M
SAT10 Stanford Achievement Test, 10th Ed. **NAEP** National Assessment of Educational Progress 2005 Mathematics Objectives

California Math Background

Focus on the California Content Standards

- As early as grade 4, students began to investigate the concept of positive and negative numbers, using number lines and counting, as well as the application to temperature and "owing" (**NS 1.8**). Grade 5 standards introduced the computational aspect of integers with **NS 1.5** and **NS 2.1**. Grade 6 expanded the topic to solve computational and situational problems that use positive and negative integers (**NS 2.3**).
- The examples provided in the lessons of chapter 2 that include the 'Relate Math You Know . . . to New Ideas' will be especially helpful to students who struggle with computing with signed numbers.

2-1 Integers and Absolute Value

California Content Standards **NS 1.2, Alg 1 2.0**

Math Understandings

- Zero is the only integer that is its own opposite. Zero is neither positive nor negative. The absolute value of zero is zero.
- A number and its opposite have the same absolute value.

Numbers that are the same distance from zero on a number line but in opposite directions are **opposites,** where 0 is its own opposite. 4 and −4 are opposites. **Integers** are the set of whole numbers and their opposites.

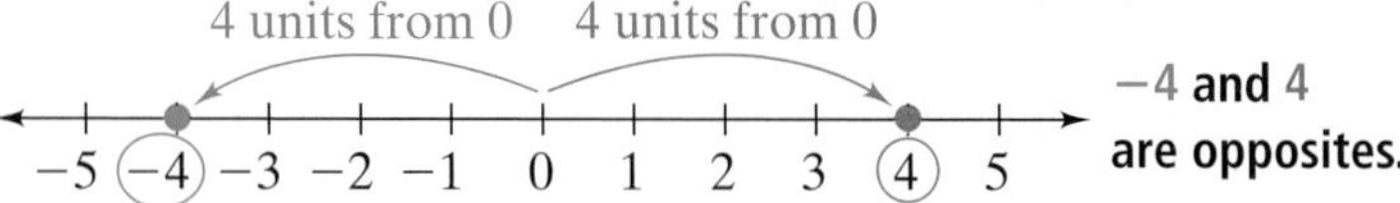

−4 and 4 are opposites.

A number's distance from zero on the number line is its **absolute value**. The absolute value of −4, written as $|-4|$, is 4 and $|4|$ is also 4.

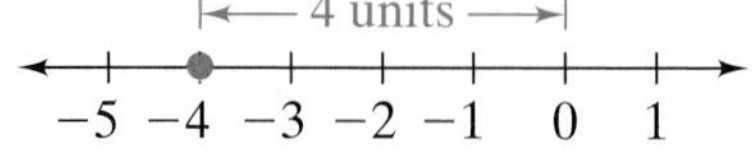

2-2 Adding Integers

California Content Standards **NS 1.2, AF 1.3, MR 2.5, MR 3.3**

Math Understandings

- Two numbers whose sum is 0 are additive inverses.
- The sum of two positive numbers is always positive.
- The sum of two negative numbers is always negative.

To add two numbers with different signs, find the absolute value of each integer. Then subtract the lesser absolute value from the greater absolute value. The sum has the sign of the integer with greater absolute value.

$|6| = 6$
$|-15| = 15$ ← **Find the absolute value of each integer.**
$15 - 6 = 9$ ← **Subtract 6 from 15 because $|6| < |-15|$.**
$6 + (-15) = -9$ ← **The sum has the same sign as −15.**

2-3 Subtracting Integers

California Content Standards **NS 1.2, MR 2.5, Alg 1 2.0**

Math Understandings

- You can rewrite subtracting a number as adding the opposite of that number.
- The opposite of the opposite of a number is the number itself.

Two numbers whose sum is 0 are **additive inverses**.

The number line below shows $3 + (-5)$.

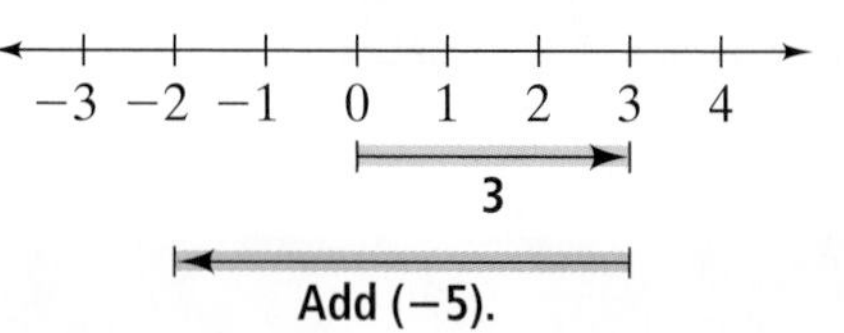

The number line below shows $3 - 5$.

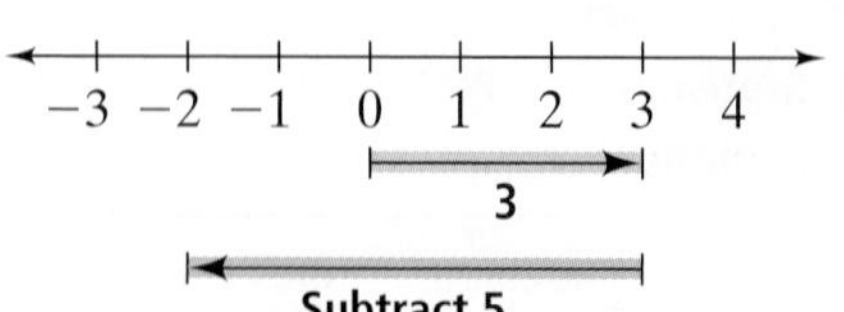

2-4 Multiplying Integers

California Content Standard **NS 1.2**

Math Understandings

- You can think of multiplication as repeated addition.
- The product of two positive numbers is positive.
- The product of two negative numbers is negative.
- The product of a positive number and a negative number is negative.

Example: -3×2 means the opposite of three groups of 2 each.

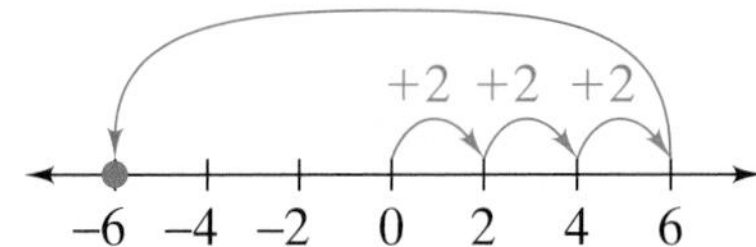

2-5 Dividing Integers

California Content Standards **NS 1.2, MR 3.1**

Math Understandings

- Inverse operations undo each other. Addition and subtraction are inverse operations. Multiplication and division are inverse operations.
- Dividing by a number is the same as multiplying by the reciprocal of that number.
- The rules for finding the sign of a quotient when dividing two integers are similar to the rules for finding the sign of a product when multiplying integers.

Take Note — Dividing Integers

The quotient of two integers with the same sign is positive.

Algebra:	$a \div b = a \div b$	$-a \div (-b) = a \div b$
Arithmetic:	$8 \div 2 = 4$	$-8 \div (-2) = 4$

The quotient of two integers with different signs is negative.

Algebra:	$a \div (-b) = -(a \div b)$	$-a \div b = -(a \div b)$
Arithmetic:	$12 \div (-6) = -2$	$-12 \div 6 = -2$

2-6 Positive Exponents

California Content Standards **NS 1.2, AF 2.1**

Math Understandings

- When you write a base with an exponent, you are using a mathematical operation that indicates repeated multiplication.
- An exponent applies only to its base, so $(-3)^2$ is 9 but -3^2 is -9.

An **exponent** tells you how many times a number, or **base,** is used as a factor.

$$5 \times 5 \times 5 \times 5 = 5^4$$ exponer / base

A number expressed using an exponent is called a **power**. The order of operations can be extended to include exponents.

Order of Operations

1. Work inside grouping symbols.
2. Simplify the powers.
3. Multiply and divide from left to right.
4. Add and subtract from left to right.

Professional Development

Additional Professional Development Opportunities

Math Background notes for Chapter 2: Every lesson has a Math Background in the PLAN section.

In-Service On Demand
Prentice Hall offers free video-based tutorials to support you. Visit PHSchool.com/inserviceondemand.

Pearson Achievement Solutions
Pearson Achievement Solutions, a Pearson Education company, offers comprehensive, facilitated professional development designed to help teachers improve student achievement. To learn more, please visit pearsonachievementsolutions.com.

Chapter 2 Resources

	2-1	2-2	2-3	2-4	2-5	2-6	For the Chapter
Print Resources							
L3 Practice	●	●	●	●	●	●	
L3 Guided Problem Solving	●	●	●	●	●	●	
L2 Reteaching	●	●	●	●	●	●	
L4 Enrichment	●	●	●	●	●	●	
L3 Vocabulary and Study Skills	●	●	●	●	●	●	●
L3 Daily Puzzles	●	●	●	●	●	●	
L3 Activity Labs	●	●	●	●	●	●	
L3 Checkpoint Quiz		●			●		
L3 Chapter Project							●
L2 Below Level Chapter Test							●
L3 Chapter Test							●
L4 Alternative Assessment							●
L3 Cumulative Review							●
Spanish Resources EL							
L3 Practice	●	●	●	●	●	●	●
L3 Vocabulary and Study Skills	●		●	●		●	●
L3 Checkpoint Quiz		●			●		
L2 Below Level Chapter Test							●
L3 Chapter Test							●
L4 Alternative Assessment							●
L3 Cumulative Review							●
Transparencies							
Check Skills You'll Need	●	●	●	●	●	●	
Additional Examples	●	●	●	●	●	●	
California Daily Review	●	●	●	●	●	●	
Classroom Aid	●	●	●	●	●	●	
Student Edition Answers	●	●	●	●	●	●	●
Lesson Quiz	●	●	●	●	●	●	
Technology							
California Student Center Online	●	●	●	●	●	●	●
California Student Center CD-ROM	●	●	●	●	●	●	●
Success Tracker™ Online Math Intervention	●	●	●	●	●	●	●
California Teacher Center: ExamView CD-ROM	●	●	●	●	●	●	●
California Teacher Center: Planning CD-ROM	●	●	●	●	●	●	●
California Teacher Center: Presentations CD-ROM and online	●	●	●	●	●	●	●
MindPoint Quiz Show	●	●	●	●	●	●	●
Prentice Hall Web Site: PHSchool.com	●	●	●	●	●	●	●

Also available:

California Standards Mastery
- Standards Review Transparencies
- Standards Review and Practice Workbook
- Progress Monitoring Assessments
- Math Companion
- Math*XL*

California Intervention Resources
- Skills Review and Practice Workbook
- Success Tracker™ Online Math Intervention

Other Resources
- Multilingual Handbook
- Spanish Student Edition
- Solution Key
- Math Notes Study Folder

Where You Can Use the Lesson Resources

Here is a suggestion, following the four-step teaching plan, for how you can incorporate Universal Access Resources into your teaching.

	Instructional Resources L3	Universal Access Resources
1. Plan		
Preparation Read the Math Background in the Teacher's Edition to connect this lesson with students' previous experience. **Starting Class** **Check Skills You'll Need** Assign these exercises from the Math Companion to review prerequisite skills. Review the full text of the student expectations and objectives covered in this lesson. **New Vocabulary** Help students pre-read the lesson by pointing out the new terms introduced in the lesson.	**California Math Background** **Math Understandings** **Transparencies & Presentations CD-ROM** Check Skills You'll Need California Daily Review **Resources** Vocabulary and Study Skills **Math Companion**	**Spanish Support** EL Vocabulary and Study Skills
2. Teach		
L3 Guided Instruction Use the Activity Labs to build conceptual understanding. Teach each Example. Use the Teacher's Edition side column notes for specific teaching tips, including Error Prevention notes. Use the Additional Examples found in the side column (and on transparency and PowerPoint) as an alternative presentation for the content. After each Example, assign the California Standards Check exercises for that Example to get an immediate assessment of student understanding. Utilize the support in the Math Companion to assist students with each Standards Check. Use the Closure activity in the Teacher's Edition to help students attain mastery of lesson content.	**Student Edition** Activity Lab **Resources** Math Companion Activity Lab **Transparencies & Presentations CD-ROM** Additional Examples Classroom Aids **Teacher Center: ExamView CD-ROM**	**Teacher's Edition** Every lesson includes suggestions for working with students who need special attention. L1 Special Needs L2 Below Level L4 Advanced Learners EL English Learners **Resources** **Multilingual Handbook** **Math Companion**
3. Practice		
Assignment Guide **Check Your Understanding** Use these questions from the Math Companion to check students' understanding before you assign homework. **Homework Exercises** Assign homework from these leveled exercises in the Assignment Guide. A Practice by Example B Apply Your Skills C Challenge California Multiple-Choice Practice and Mixed Review **Homework Quick Check** Use these key exercises to quickly check students' homework.	**Transparencies & Presentations CD-ROM** Student Answers **Resources** Math Companion Practice Guided Problem Solving Vocabulary and Study Skills Activity Lab Daily Puzzles **Teacher Center: ExamView CD-ROM** **Math *XL***	**Spanish Support** EL Practice EL Vocabulary and Study Skills **Resources** L4 Enrichment
4. Assess & Reteach		
Lesson Quiz Assign the Lesson Quiz to assess students' mastery of the lesson content. **Checkpoint Quiz** Use the Checkpoint Quiz to assess student progress over several lessons.	**Transparencies & Presentations CD-ROM** Lesson Quiz **Resources** Checkpoint Quiz	**Resources** L2 Reteaching EL Checkpoint Quiz Success Tracker™ **Teacher Center: ExamView CD-ROM**

KEY L1 Special Needs L2 Below Level L3 For All Students L4 Advanced, Gifted EL English Learners

Integers and Exponents

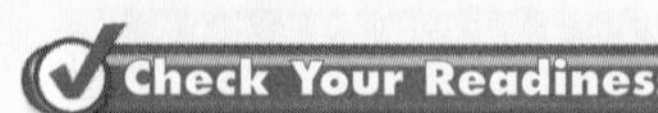

Answers are in the back of the textbook.

For math intervention, direct students to:

Numerical Expressions
Lesson 1-1

Algebraic Expressions
Lesson 1-2

Writing Expressions
Lesson 1-3

Properties of Numbers
Lesson 1-5

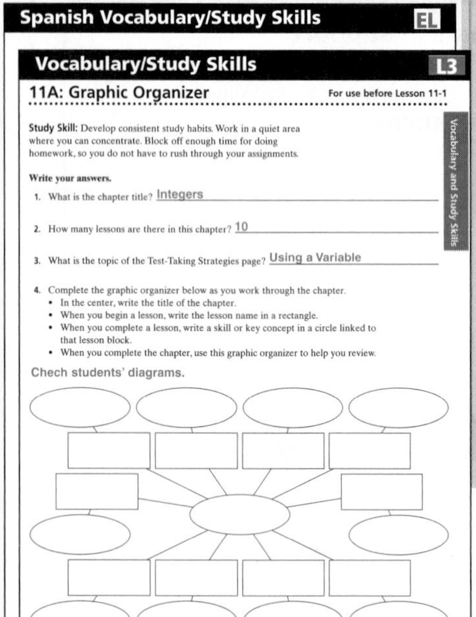

Spanish Vocabulary/Study Skills EL

Vocabulary/Study Skills L3

11A: Graphic Organizer — For use before Lesson 11-1

Study Skill: Develop consistent study habits. Work in a quiet area where you can concentrate. Block off enough time for doing homework, so you do not have to rush through your assignments.

Write your answers.

1. What is the chapter title? Integers
2. How many lessons are there in this chapter? 10
3. What is the topic of the Test-Taking Strategies page? Using a Variable
4. Complete the graphic organizer below as you work through the chapter.
   - In the center, write the title of the chapter.
   - When you begin a lesson, write the lesson name in a rectangle.
   - When you complete a lesson, write a skill or key concept in a circle linked to that lesson block.
   - When you complete the chapter, use this graphic organizer to help you review.

Chech students' diagrams.

Vocabulary and Study Skills

Integers and Exponents

What You've Learned

California Content Standards

AF 1.1 Use variables and appropriate operations to write an expression that represents a verbal description.

AF 1.3 Simplify numerical expressions by applying properties of rational numbers and justify the process used.

GO for Help to the lesson in green.

Simplifying Numerical Expressions (Lesson 1-1)

Simplify each expression.

1. $1.2 + 4.5 \cdot 7.1$ 33.15 **2.** $8.2(4.1 - 2.3)$ 14.76 **3.** $12 + 16.4 \div 4$ 16.1

Evaluating Algebraic Expressions (Lesson 1-2)

Evaluate each expression for $n = 4$.

4. $14(n + 2) - n$ 80 **5.** $3n + 4 \cdot 5$ 32

6. $81 \div (n + 5) \cdot n$ 36 **7.** $(9 + 7) \div n$ 4

Writing Expressions (Lesson 1-3)

Write an expression for each verbal description.

8. 12 more than a number a $a + 12$

9. a number y divided by 3.5 $y \div 3.5$

10. the product of a number t and 17.2 $17.2t$

Properties of Numbers (Lesson 1-6)

Mental Math **Use mental math and the properties of numbers to simplify each expression.**

11. $45 + 17 + 55$ 117 **12.** $20 \cdot 14 \cdot 5$ 1,400 **13.** $17 + 29 + 13$ 59

14. $25 \cdot 23 \cdot 4$ 2,300 **15.** $4 \cdot 2.99$ 11.96 **16.** $74 \cdot 6$ 444

▲ You can use the integer −1,500 to describe the change in feet of a hang glider's elevation.

What You'll Learn Next

California Content Standards

NS 1.2 Add, subtract, multiply and divide rational numbers and take positive rational numbers to whole-number powers.

AF 2.1 Interpret positive whole-number powers as repeated multiplication. Simplify and evaluate expressions that include exponents.

New Vocabulary

English and Spanish Audio Online

- absolute value (p. 46)
- additive inverses (p. 52)
- base (p. 73)
- exponent (p. 73)
- factor (p. 73)
- integers (p. 46)
- opposites (p. 46)
- power (p. 73)

Academic Vocabulary
- compare (p. 50)
- explain (p. 50)
- indicate (p. 50)

California Content Standards for Chapter 2

Number Sense
NS 1.2

Algebra and Functions
AF 1.3, AF 2.1

Chapter 2 Overview

In this chapter, students study integers and explore common applications of integers. First they examine integers and absolute value of integers using a number line. Next, they add, subtract, multiply, and divide integers. Finally, they use positive exponents to simplify and evaluate expressions.

Activating Prior Knowledge

In this chapter, students build on and extend their understanding of negative numbers (depths, temperatures below zero, golf scores) and knowledge of numbers and the number line to work with numbers less than zero. Ask questions such as:

- *What is the order of these temperatures from warmest to coldest: 15°F, 0°F, and 4°F?* 15°F, 4°F, 0°F

California Resources

Standards Mastery
- Teacher Center ExamView CD-ROM
- Math XL
- Progress Monitoring Assessments
- Online Chapter Test at PHSchool.com

Math Intervention
- Skills Review and Practice Workbook

Online at PHSchool.com

Universal Access Resources
- Chapter Test
- Alternative Assessment
- Spanish Chapter Test
- Spanish Alternative Assessment
- Teacher Center ExamView CD-ROM
  - Special Needs Test
  - Special Needs Practice Banks
  - Foundational Standards Practice Banks
- Online Chapter Test at www.PHSchool.com
- All-In-One Teaching Resources
  - Cumulative Review L3
- Spanish Assessment Resources
  - Cumulative Review 

Below Level Chapter Test L2

Chapter Test L3

Chapter Test Form B

Chapter 2

Name the opposite of each integer.

1. −17 2. −5 3. 140

Find each absolute value.

4. |−5| 5. |15| 6. |−9|

Write an integer to represent each situation. Then graph the integer on a number line.

7. 3° below zero 8. earnings of $6

Find each sum or difference.

9. −18 + (−5) 10. −25 + 17
11. −27 − 61 12. 84 − (−13)

Solve.

13. The building superintendent lives on the 9th floor. He goes up 6 floors to an apartment. Next he goes down 10 floors. Then he goes up 2 floors. What floor is he on?
14. Suppose you borrow $15 from each of 5 friends. Write an integer to express your debt.

Find each product or quotient.

15. 3 · 4 16. 5 · (−2) 17. −7 · (−6)
18. 18 ÷ 3 19. −25 ÷ 5 20. −27 ÷ (−9)

Chapter 2 Test

Go Online PHSchool.com **For:** Online chapter test **Web Code:** axa-0252

1. What integer represents 18 ft below sea level? −18

Name the opposite of each integer.

2. 89 −89
3. −100 100
4. −35 35
5. 0 0

Find each absolute value.

6. $|-13|$ 13
7. $|-717|$ 717
8. $|5|$ 5
9. $|-62|$ 62

10. Order the integers from least to greatest. 3, −1, −13, 5, 0 −13, −1, 0, 3, 5
11. **Writing in Math** Define *absolute value* and illustrate with a number line. See margin.

Find each sum.

12. $-14 + 60$ 46
13. $9 + (-4)$ 5
14. $71 + (-102)$ −31
15. $-12 + (-45)$ −57

16. Write an addition expression that can be modeled by the number line below.

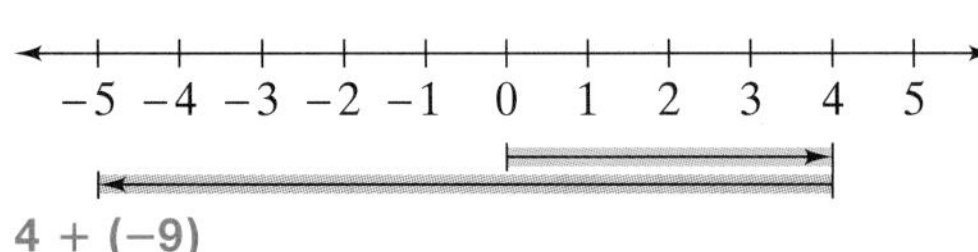

4 + (−9)

Find each difference.

17. $-2 - 8$ −10
18. $-3 - (-3)$ 0
19. $4 - 9$ −5
20. $44 - (-6)$ 50
21. $-11 - (-13)$ 2
22. $7 - 24$ −17

23. A football team gained 6 yd on a play. On the next play, the team lost 9 yd. What is the net yardage for the team? −3 yd
24. The temperature is 18°F at 1:00 A.M. The temperature falls 22 degrees by 6:00 A.M. Find the temperature at 6:00 A.M. −4°F
25. On a math quiz worth 50 points, a student misses 2 points on the first section, 3 points on the second, 2 points on the third, and 1 point on the last. Find the student's score. 42 points

Find each product.

26. $-4 \cdot 3$ −12
27. $-9 \cdot (-8)$ 72
28. $5 \cdot (-22)$ −110
29. $-2 \cdot 6$ −12
30. $-7 \cdot (-7) \cdot (-7)$ −343
31. $-12 \cdot 4 \cdot (-3)$ 144

Find each quotient.

32. $9 \div (-3)$ −3
33. $-5 \div (-5)$ 1
34. $-12 \div 4$ −3
35. $36 \div (-2)$ −18
36. $-121 \div (-11)$ 11
37. $-45 \div 15$ −3

Evaluate each expression for $m = -4$ and $p = 2$.

38. $mp - 6p$ −20
39. $(4p - m) \div 4$ 3
40. $(p - m + 3) \div 5$ 1.8
41. $m + p \cdot (-7)$ −18
42. **Number Sense** When does the product of two integers equal zero? When does the sum of two integers equal zero? See margin.

Write each expression using exponents.

43. $5 \cdot 5 \cdot 5 \cdot 5 \cdot 7 \cdot 7 \cdot 7 \cdot 7 \cdot 7 \cdot 7$ $5^4 \cdot 7^6$
44. $11 \cdot 11 \cdot b \cdot b \cdot b \cdot b \cdot b$ $11^2 \cdot b^5$

Simplify each power.

45. 5^3 125
46. $(-6)^2$ 36
47. -2^4 −16
48. $3^3 + 7^2$ 76
49. $4^2 \cdot 18$ 288
50. $(9 - 12)^2$ 9

Evaluate each expression for $c = 5$.

51. $c^2 + 2$ 27
52. $33 - 4 \cdot c^3$ −467
53. $(3 - c)^3 + 14$ 6
54. $(c^2 + 50) \div c^2$ 3

Some questions ask you to evaluate expressions. Read the question at the right. Then use the tips as guides for finding the answer.

Evaluate $2(11 - a)^2 \div 4$ for $a = 3$.

(A) 1
(B) 4
(C) 32
(D) 64

Tip 1
First substitute the correct value for the variable in the expression.

Tip 2
When simplifying the expression, write out each step to be sure you are using the correct order of operations.

Think It Through
Substitute 3 for a: $2(11 - 3)^2 \div 4$. Work within the grouping symbols first: $11 - 3 = 8$. Then simplify the power: $8^2 = 64$. Then multiply and divide from left to right: $2(64) \div 4 = 32$. The correct answer is C.

Vocabulary Review

As you solve problems, you must understand the meanings of mathematical terms. Match each term with its mathematical meaning.

A. integers II
B. opposites III
C. exponent V
D. additive inverses IV
E. absolute value I

I. the distance a number is from 0 on a number line
II. the set of whole numbers and their opposites
III. two numbers that are the same distance from zero but in different directions
IV. two numbers whose sum is 0
V. a number that tells how many times a number is used as a factor

Read each question. Then write the letter of the correct answer on your paper.

1. In three plays, a football team gained 5 yd, lost 12 yd, and gained 10 yd. Which integer represents the change in yards? (Lesson 2-2) B
   (A) −12
   (B) 3
   (C) 5
   (D) 10

2. Which property does the equation $(9f)g = 9(fg)$ illustrate? (Lesson 1-5) C
   (A) Identity Property of Multiplication
   (B) Distributive Property
   (C) Associative Property of Multiplication
   (D) Commutative Property of Multiplication

3. Which of the following is NOT a property of numbers? (Lesson 1-6) B
   (A) Commutative Property of Addition
   (B) Commutative Property of Subtraction
   (C) Commutative Property of Multiplication
   (D) Distributive Property

California Resources

Standards Mastery
- Teacher Center ExamView CD-ROM
- Math XL
- Progress Monitoring Assessments
- Online Chapter Test at PHSchool.com

Math Intervention
- Skills Review and Practice Workbook

Universal Access Resources
- Teacher Center ExamView CD-ROM
  - Special Needs Test
  - Special Needs Practice Banks
  - Foundational Standards Practice Banks
- Online Chapter Test at www.PHSchool.com
- All-In-One Teaching Resources
  - Cumulative Review L3
- Spanish Assessment Resources
  - Cumulative Review L3

4. Which expression has a value of 13? **(Lesson 2-6) B**

- (A) $(3 + 2)^2$
- (B) $3^2 + 2^2$
- (C) $3 + 2^2$
- (D) $3^3 + 2^2$

5. Which situation would NOT be represented by the integer -4? **(Lesson 2-1) D**

- (A) Four degrees below zero
- (B) Four dollars in debt
- (C) Four feet under sea level
- (D) Four children in a family

6. The table below shows Philip's and Miguel's ages over several years.

Philip's Age (*x* years)	Miguel's Age (*y* years)
3	6
4	7
5	8
6	9

Which expression best represents Miguel's age in terms of Philip's age? **(Lesson 1-3) A**

- (A) $x + 3$
- (B) $y + 3$
- (C) $3x$
- (D) $3y$

7. A hiker climbs up 415 ft and takes a break. Then the hiker continues to climb 322 ft before descending 119 ft to a lodge. How much higher than his starting position is the hiker? **(Lesson 2-2) C**

- (A) 856 ft
- (B) 737 ft
- (C) 618 ft
- (D) 26 ft

8. Which equation illustrates the Inverse Property of Addition? **(Lesson 2-2) B**

- (A) $a + b = b + a$
- (B) $a + (-a) = 0$
- (C) $a + a = 2a$
- (D) $(4 + a) + b = 4 + (a + b)$

9. Which integer is the opposite of 81? **(Lesson 2-1) A**

- (A) -81
- (B) -18
- (C) 9
- (D) 81

10. Which expression is equivalent to $7 \cdot 7 \cdot 7 \cdot 7 \cdot y \cdot y \cdot y \cdot y \cdot y \cdot y$? **(Lesson 2-6) D**

- (A) $7 + y$
- (B) $6y$
- (C) $4^7 6^y$
- (D) $7^4 y^6$

11. Erin lives in Alaska. She recorded the temperatures three times during the same day. By how many degrees did the temperature change between 6 A.M. and 6 P.M.? **(Lesson 2-3) C**

Temperature Changes

Time	Temperature (°F)
6 A.M.	−8
12 noon	6
6 P.M.	−2

- (A) −2°F
- (B) −4°F
- (C) 6°F
- (D) 10°F

12. Simplify $7^2 + 2^3$. **(Lesson 2-6) D**

- (A) 9
- (B) 20
- (C) 49
- (D) 57

13. A submarine starts at sea level. It dives 6 ft/min for 4 min and then stops. When the submarine stops, at what depth is it located? **(Lesson 2-4) A**

- (A) −24 ft
- (B) −6 ft
- (C) 0 ft
- (D) 6 ft

14. Alicia withdraws $20 from her bank account. Then she deposits $188. Which integer represents the change in the amount of money in her bank account? **(Lesson 2-2) D**

- (A) −188
- (B) −168
- (C) 20
- (D) 168

Spanish Cumulative Review EL

Cumulative Review L3

Cumulative Review

Chapters 1–2

Multiple Choice. Choose the letter of the best answer.

1. What is an expression for "four times a number, increased by six"?
   A. $4n + 6$ B. $6n + 4$ C. $(4n)(6)$ D. $6n - 4$
2. How many integers are there whose absolute value equals 5?
   A. zero B. two C. five D. ten
3. Which of the following expressions is equivalent to $-9 + (-8)$?
   A. $8 - 9$ B. $-9 + 8$ C. $-9 - 8$ D. $8 - (-9)$
4. Simplify. $9 + 7 \cdot (-6) - (5 - 3)$
   A. −94 B. −49 C. −47 D. −35
5. The average temperature in Caribou, Maine, is 18°C in July, and −12°C in January. What is the difference between these temperatures?
   A. 0°C B. 6°C C. 12°C D. 30°C
6. Polyus Nedostupnosti, Antarctica, is the coldest place in the world. Its annual mean temperature is 166°F colder than that of Dallol, Ethiopia, the world's hottest place, where the annual mean temperature is 94°F. What is the annual mean temperature of Polyus Nedostupnosti?
   A. −6°F B. −72°F C. 72°F D. 260°F
7. All of the following statements are true EXCEPT
   A. $12 \cdot (-3) + 6 = 12 \cdot 6 + (-3)$
   B. $8 + (-6) \cdot 5 = 8 + 5 \cdot (-6)$
   C. $78 \cdot (-7) = 70(-7) + 8(-7)$
   D. $24 \cdot (-6) = 20(-6) + 4(-6)$
8. What is $-6 + 3 + (-2)$?
   A. −3 B. 5 C. −5 D. −11
9. What integer is described by the following? The absolute value is 77 and the number is to the left of 0 on a number line.
   A. −7 B. 7 C. −77 D. 77
10. Add. $-23 + (-6)$
    A. 17 B. −17 C. 29 D. −29

15. The table below shows Xi's earnings for doing h hours of yardwork.

Time Worked (h hours)	Earnings (dollars)
2	10
3	15
4	20
6	30

Which expression best represents Xi's earnings for h hours of yardwork? (Lesson 1-3) C

A $h + 5$ C $5h$
B $h + 8$ D $8h$

16. Evaluate $(9 + d)^3 - 5$ for $d = -7$. (Lesson 2-6) B

A 1 C 25
B 3 D 338

17. Which expression describes the pattern in the table below? (Lesson 2-6) D

n	■
1	1
2	4
3	9

A n C $n + 3$
B $2n$ D n^2

18. Which two numbers are opposites? (Lesson 2-1) D

A 2 and 0.5 C −4 and −16
B −7 and 0 D −8 and 8

19. The water in a tide pool drops 12 in. in 3 h. What is the rate of change of the water level? (Lesson 2-5) A

A −4 in./h C 3 in./h
B −12 in./h D 4 in./h

20. You have \$6.00. You want to buy a hamburger that costs \$2.49, a drink that costs \$1.89, and cookies that cost \$.79 each. Which information do you need to determine if you have enough money? (Lesson 1-3) C

A The cost of French fries
B The weight of the meat in the hamburger
C The number of cookies
D The size of the drink

21. Which property does the equation $w + 0 = w$ illustrate? (Lesson 2-2) A

A Identity Property of Addition
B Associative Property of Addition
C Commutative Property of Addition
D Inverse Property of Addition

Standards Reference Guide

California Content Standard	Item Number(s)
NS 1.2	1, 5, 7, 11, 13, 14, 19, 20
AF 1.1	6, 15, 17
AF 1.3	2, 3, 8, 21
AF 2.1	4, 10, 12, 16
Alg1 2.0	9, 18

For additional review and practice, see the *California Standards Review and Practice Workbook* or go online to use the

Visit: PHSchool.com, **Web Code:** axq-9045

Review and Preparation Workbook

Cumulative Review

Chapters 1–2

11. Find $5^3 + 5^2$.

A. 25 B. 150
C. 3,125 D. 15,625

12. Simplify using exponents.
$7 \cdot x \cdot x \cdot x \cdot y \cdot 7 \cdot y \cdot y \cdot y$

A. $7^2x^3y^4$ B. $7x^37y^3$
C. $7xy^8$ D. $7x^3y^4$

13. Find $-24 + (3)(-5) - 1$.

A. −40 B. −10
C. 8 D. 70

14. Evaluate $4x^2 - (2 + y)^2$ where $x = 4$ and $y = 3$.

A. 0
B. 53
C. 39
D. 231

15. Simplify $(4 \cdot 2)^2 - 12$.

A. 24 B. 36
C. 48 D. 52

16. Express $4 \cdot 4 \cdot 4 \cdot 4 \cdot 4 \cdot 4 \cdot 4 \cdot 4$ using an exponent

A. 8^4 B. 2^8
C. 8^3 D. 4^8

17. In a football game, Mario gained 5 yards, then lost 12 yards, then gained another 15 yards. What was Mario's total yards gained?

A. −8 yards
B. 4 yards
C. 8 yards
D. 15 yards

18. What is $-13 - (-13)$?

A. −26 B. 0
C. 26 D. not here

19. The temperature dropped 15°F between 11:00 A.M. and 9:00 P.M. At 9:00 P.M. the temperature was −7°F. Which equation would you use to find t, the temperature at 11:00 A.M.?

A. $15t = -7$
B. $-7 = t - 15$
C. $-15t = -7$
D. $t + 15 = -7$

20. Stan is saving to buy a bicycle that costs \$225.00. If he wants to buy the bicycle in 6 weeks, how much does he need to put aside each week?

____

Chapter 3 Equations and Applications

Chapter at a Glance

Lesson Titles, Objectives, and Features	California Content Standards
3-1 Solving Addition Equations • To solve addition equations **Algebraic Thinking:** Understanding Equality	Write and solve one-step linear equations. ***Foundational (Gr6 AF 1.1)*** **AF 1.1** Use variables and appropriate operations to write an equation. **AF 1.3** Simplify expressions by applying properties of numbers.
3-2a Activity Lab: Modeling Equations **3-2 Solving Subtraction Equations** • To solve subtraction equations	See the Standards for Lesson 3-1.
3-3 Solving Multiplication and Division Equations • To solve multiplication and division equations **Mathematical Reasoning:** Using Deductive Reasoning	See the Standards for Lesson 3-1.
3-4a Activity Lab: Modeling Two-Step Equations **3-4 Solving Two-Step Equations** • To solve two-step equations	See the Standards for Lesson 3-1. **AF 4.1** Solve two-step linear equations, interpret the solution in context, and verify the reasonableness of the results.
3-5 Square Roots • To find square roots **Mathematical Reasoning:** Checking for Reasonableness	**NS 1.2** Take positive rational numbers to whole number powers. **Alg 1 2.0** Understand and use such operations as taking a root.
3-6 The Pythagorean Theorem • To use the Pythagorean Theorem to find the length of the hypotenuse of a right triangle	See the Standards for Lesson 3-5. **MG 3.3** Know and understand the Pythagorean Theorem and use it to find the length of the missing side of a right triangle.
3-7 Using the Pythagorean Theorem • To find the lengths of the legs of a right triangle and use the converse of the Pythagorean Theorem **37b Activity Lab:** Verifying Right Triangles	**NS 1.2** Take positive rational numbers to whole number powers. **MG 3.3** Understand the Pythagorean Theorem and its converse and use it to find the length of the missing side of a right triangle. **Alg 1 2.0** Understand and use such operations as taking a root.

California Content Standards
NS Number Sense
AF Algebra and Functions
MG Measurement and Geometry
MR Mathematical Reasoning

Correlations to Standardized Tests

All content for these tests is contained in *Prentice Hall Math, Algebra Readiness.* This chart reflects coverage in this chapter only.

	3-1	3-2	3-3	3-4	3-5	3-6	3-7
Terra Nova CAT6 (Level 18)							
Number and Number Relations					✔		
Computation and Numerical Estimation	✔	✔	✔	✔	✔		✔
Operation Concepts	✔	✔	✔				✔
Measurement							
Geometry and Spatial Sense			✔			✔	✔
Data Analysis, Statistics, and Probability							
Patterns, Functions, and Algebra	✔	✔	✔	✔	✔		
Problem Solving and Reasoning	✔	✔	✔	✔	✔	✔	✔
Communication	✔	✔	✔	✔	✔	✔	✔
Decimals, Fractions, Integers, and Percent	✔	✔	✔				
Order of Operations				✔			
Algebraic Operations	✔	✔	✔	✔			
Terra Nova CTBS (Level 18)							
Decimals, Fractions, Integers, Percents	✔	✔	✔	✔			
Order of Operations, Numeration, Number Theory	✔	✔	✔	✔	✔		
Data Interpretation							
Measurement							
Geometry						✔	✔
ITBS (Level 14)							
Number Properties and Operations	✔	✔	✔	✔	✔		
Algebra	✔	✔	✔	✔	✔		
Geometry						✔	✔
Measurement							
Probability and Statistics							
Estimation				✔			
SAT10 (Adv 1 Level)							
Number Sense and Operations	✔	✔	✔	✔	✔		
Patterns, Relationships, and Algebra	✔	✔	✔	✔	✔		
Data, Statistics, and Probability							
Geometry and Measurement						✔	✔
NAEP							
Number Sense, Properties, and Operations	✔			✔	✔		
Measurement							
Geometry and Spatial Sense						✔	✔
Data Analysis, Statistics, and Probability							
Algebra and Functions		✔	✔	✔	✔		

CAT6 California Achievement Test, 6th Ed. **CTBS** Comprehensive Test of Basic Skills **ITBS** Iowa Test of Basic Skills, Form M
SAT10 Stanford Achievement Test, 10th Ed. **NAEP** National Assessment of Educational Progress 2005 Mathematics Objectives

California Math Background

Focus on the California Content Standards

- Students' experiences with solving equations have links to math content standards in grades 3 through 7. As early as grade 3, students have been addressing the characteristics of equations in one variable through several key standards.
- In grade 3, students solved problems involving numeric equations (**AF 1.1**). In grade 4, students investigated how to manipulate equations through two key standards, **AF 2.1** and **AF 2.2**, that focused on equals added to equals or equals multiplied to equals are equal.
- The Guided Practice and Error Analysis exercises throughout the lessons in this chapter will be especially helpful to students who struggle with solving equations.

3-1 Solving Addition Equations

California Content Standards **AF 1.1, AF 1.3**

Math Understandings

- When you solve an equation, any operation that you do to one side you must also do to the other.
- Addition and subtraction are inverse operations.

A mathematical sentence with an equal sign is an **equation**. A **solution** to an equation is any value that makes the equation true. To find a solution of an equation, **isolate** the variable by using **inverse operations** (operations that undo each other) and the properties of equality.

Addition Property of Equality

If you add the same number to each side of an equation, the two sides remain equal.

Arithmetic	**Algebra**
$10 = 5(2)$, so $10 + 3 = 5(2) + 3$	If $a = b$ then $a + c = b + c$.

3-2 Solving Subtraction Equations

California Content Standards **AF 1.1, AF 1.3, MR 2.5**

Math Understandings

- Addition and subtraction are inverse operations.

Subtraction Property of Equality

If you subtract the same number from each side of an equation, the two sides remain equal.

Arithmetic	**Algebra**
$10 = 5(2)$, so $10 - 3 = 5(2) - 3$	If $a = b$ then $a - c = b - c$.

3-3 Solving Multiplication and Division Equations

California Content Standards **AF 1.1, AF 1.3, MR 2.4**

Math Understandings

- Multiplication and division are inverse operations.
- Division by zero is undefined.

PROPERTIES OF EQUALITY Arithmetic	Algebra
Multiplication Property of Equality	
$6 \div 2 = 3$, so $(6 \div 2) \times 2 = 3 \times 2$.	If $a = b$, then $a \cdot c = b \cdot c$.
Division Property of Equality	
$4 \times 2 = 8$, so $4 \times 2 \div 2 = 8 \div 2$.	If $a = b$ and $c \neq 0$, then $a \div c = b \div c$.

3-4 Solving Two-Step Equations

California Content Standards **AF 1.1, AF 4.1, AF 4.2, MR 2.5, MR 3.1**

Math Understandings

- A two-step equation has two operations, each of which must be undone by using an inverse operation and the properties of equality.

Students have already solved one-step equations, using the following infomation:

- Addition and subtraction are inverse operations that undo each other. Multiplication and division are also inverse operations that undo each other.
- When you solve an equation, any operation that you do to one side you must also do to the other.

When you solve a two-step equation, it is often easier to begin by undoing the addition or subtraction and then undoing the multiplication and division.

3-5 Square Roots

California Content Standards **NS 1.2, Alg 1 2.0**

Math Understandings

- The inverse of squaring is finding the square root.
- Mathematicians have agreed that the symbol $\sqrt{\ }$ indicates the nonnegative square root of a number.

A **square root** of a given number is a number that, when multiplied by itself, is the given number.

Example: Since 3×3 is 9, $\sqrt{9}$ is 3.

A **perfect square** is the square of a whole number.

Example: 1, 4, 9, 16, 25, 36, 49, 64, 81, and 100 are all perfect squares.

You can also estimate square roots of numbers that are not perfect squares.

Example: Tell which two consecutive whole numbers $\sqrt{5}$ is between.

$4 < 5 < 9$ ← Find the perfect squares close to 5.

$\sqrt{4} < \sqrt{5} < \sqrt{9}$ ← Write the square roots in order.

$2 < \sqrt{5} < 3$ ← Simplify.

3-6 The Pythagorean Theorem

California Content Standards **NS 1.2, MG 3.3, Alg 1 2.0**

Math Understandings

- The Pythagorean Theorem shows how the lengths of the sides in a right triangle are related.
- The labels *a, b,* and *c* are commonly used to label the unknown lengths of sides in right triangles (with *c* most often used for the hypotenuse).

In a right triangle, the two shorter sides are called **legs**. The longest side, which is opposite the right angle, is called the **hypotenuse**. If you know the lengths of the legs of a right triangle, you can use the Pythagorean Theorem to find the length of the hypotenuse.

Pythagorean Theorem

In any right triangle, the sum of the squares of the lengths of the legs (*a* and *b*) is equal to the square of the length of the hypotenuse (*c*).

$a^2 + b^2 = c^2$

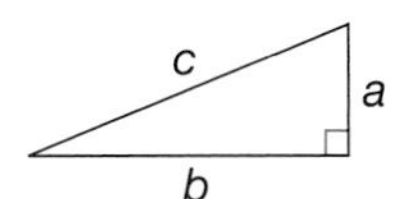

3-7 Using the Pythagorean Theorem

California Content Standards **NS 1.2, AF 1.1, MG 3.3, MR 3.2, Alg 1 2.0**

Math Understandings

- The converse of the Pythagorean Theorem is also true: A triangle with sides *a, b,* and *c* is a right triangle if the equation $a^2 + b^2 = c^2$ is true.
- In general, $\sqrt{a^2 + b^2}$ is not equal to $a + b$.

If you know the lengths of the hypotenuse and one leg of a right triangle, you can also use the Pythagorean Theorem to find the length of the other leg.

Professional Development

Additional Professional Development Opportunities

Math Background notes for Chapter 3: Every lesson has a Math Background in the PLAN section.

In-Service On Demand
Prentice Hall offers free video-based tutorials to support you. Visit PHSchool.com/inserviceondemand.

Pearson Achievement Solutions
Pearson Achievement Solutions, a Pearson Education company, offers comprehensive, facilitated professional development designed to help teachers improve student achievement. To learn more, please visit pearsonachievementsolutions.com.

Chapter 3 Resources

	3-1	3-2	3-3	3-4	3-5	3-6	3-7	For the Chapter
Print Resources								
L3 Practice	●	●	●	●	●	●	●	
L3 Guided Problem Solving	●	●	●	●	●	●	●	
L2 Reteaching	●	●	●	●	●	●	●	
L4 Enrichment	●	●	●	●	●	●	●	
L3 Vocabulary and Study Skills	●	●	●	●	●	●	●	●
L3 Daily Puzzles	●	●	●	●	●	●	●	
L3 Activity Labs	●	●	●	●	●	●	●	
L3 Checkpoint Quiz			●		●			
L3 Chapter Project								●
L2 Below Level Chapter Test								●
L3 Chapter Test								●
L4 Alternative Assessment								●
L3 Cumulative Review								●
Spanish Resources EL								
L3 Practice	●	●	●	●	●	●	●	
L3 Vocabulary and Study Skills	●		●	●		●		●
L3 Checkpoint Quiz			●		●			
L2 Below Level Chapter Test								●
L3 Chapter Test								●
L4 Alternative Assessment								●
L3 Cumulative Review								●
Transparencies								
Check Skills You'll Need	●	●	●	●	●	●	●	
Additional Examples	●	●	●	●	●	●	●	
California Daily Review	●	●	●	●	●	●	●	
Classroom Aid	●	●	●	●	●	●	●	
Student Edition Answers	●	●	●	●	●	●	●	●
Lesson Quiz	●	●	●	●	●	●	●	
Technology								
California Student Center Online	●	●	●	●	●	●	●	●
California Student Center CD-ROM	●	●	●	●	●	●	●	●
Success Tracker™ Online Math Intervention	●	●	●	●	●	●	●	●
California Teacher Center: ExamView CD-ROM	●	●	●	●	●	●	●	●
California Teacher Center: Planning CD-ROM	●	●	●	●	●	●	●	●
California Teacher Center: Presentations CD-ROM and online	●	●	●	●	●	●	●	●
MindPoint Quiz Show	●	●	●	●	●	●	●	●
Prentice Hall Web Site: PHSchool.com	●	●	●	●	●	●	●	●

Also available:

California Standards Mastery
- Standards Review Transparencies
- Standards Review and Practice Workbook
- Progress Monitoring Assessments
- Math Companion
- Math*XL*

California Intervention Resources
- Skills Review and Practice Workbook
- Success Tracker™ Online Math Intervention

Other Resources
- Multilingual Handbook
- Spanish Student Edition
- Solution Key
- Math Notes Study Folder

Where You Can Use the Lesson Resources

Here is a suggestion, following the four-step teaching plan, for how you can incorporate Universal Access Resources into your teaching.

	Instructional Resources L3	Universal Access Resources
1. Plan		
Preparation Read the Math Background in the Teacher's Edition to connect this lesson with students' previous experience. **Starting Class** **Check Skills You'll Need** Assign these exercises from the Math Companion to review prerequisite skills. Review the full text of the student expectations and objectives covered in this lesson. **New Vocabulary** Help students pre-read the lesson by pointing out the new terms introduced in the lesson.	**California Math Background** **Math Understandings** **Transparencies & Presentations CD-ROM** Check Skills You'll Need California Daily Review **Resources** Vocabulary and Study Skills **Math Companion**	**Spanish Support** EL Vocabulary and Study Skills
2. Teach		
L3 **Guided Instruction** Use the Activity Labs to build conceptual understanding. Teach each Example. Use the Teacher's Edition side column notes for specific teaching tips, including Error Prevention notes. Use the Additional Examples found in the side column (and on transparency and PowerPoint) as an alternative presentation for the content. After each Example, assign the California Standards Check exercises for that Example to get an immediate assessment of student understanding. Utilize the support in the Math Companion to assist students with each Standards Check. Use the Closure activity in the Teacher's Edition to help students attain mastery of lesson content.	**Student Edition** Activity Lab **Resources** Math Companion Activity Lab **Transparencies & Presentations CD-ROM** Additional Examples Classroom Aids **Teacher Center: ExamView CD-ROM**	**Teacher's Edition** Every lesson includes suggestions for working with students who need special attention. L1 Special Needs L2 Below Level L4 Advanced Learners EL English Learners **Resources** **Multilingual Handbook** **Math Companion**
3. Practice		
Assignment Guide **Check Your Understanding** Use these questions from the Math Companion to check students' understanding before you assign homework. **Homework Exercises** Assign homework from these leveled exercises in the Assignment Guide. **A** Practice by Example **B** Apply Your Skills **C** Challenge **California** Multiple-Choice Practice and Mixed Review **Homework Quick Check** Use these key exercises to quickly check students' homework.	**Transparencies & Presentations CD-ROM** Student Answers **Resources** Math Companion Practice Guided Problem Solving Vocabulary and Study Skills Activity Lab Daily Puzzles **Teacher Center: ExamView CD-ROM** **Math *XL***	**Spanish Support** EL Practice EL Vocabulary and Study Skills **Resources** L4 Enrichment
4. Assess & Reteach		
Lesson Quiz Assign the Lesson Quiz to assess students' mastery of the lesson content. **Checkpoint Quiz** Use the Checkpoint Quiz to assess student progress over several lessons.	**Transparencies & Presentations CD-ROM** Lesson Quiz **Resources** Checkpoint Quiz	**Resources** L2 Reteaching EL Checkpoint Quiz Success Tracker™ **Teacher Center: ExamView CD-ROM**

KEY **L1** Special Needs **L2** Below Level **L3** For All Students **L4** Advanced, Gifted **EL** English Learners

Equations and Applications

Answers are in the back of the textbook.

For math intervention, direct students to:

Numerical Expressions
Lesson 1-1

Adding Integers
Lesson 2-2

Multiplying Integers
Lesson 2-4

Positive Exponents
Lesson 2-6

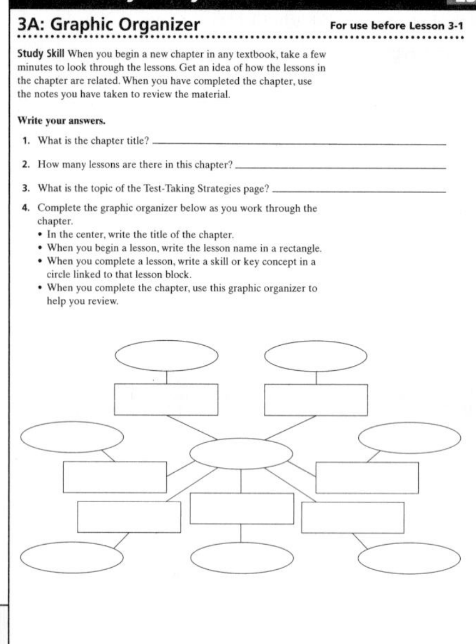

Spanish Vocabulary/Study Skills EL

Vocabulary/Study Skills L3

3A: Graphic Organizer — **For use before Lesson 3-1**

Study Skill When you begin a new chapter in any textbook, take a few minutes to look through the lessons. Get an idea of how the lessons in the chapter are related. When you have completed the chapter, use the notes you have taken to review the material.

Write your answers.

1. What is the chapter title? ______
2. How many lessons are there in this chapter? ______
3. What is the topic of the Test-Taking Strategies page? ______
4. Complete the graphic organizer below as you work through the chapter.
   - In the center, write the title of the chapter.
   - When you begin a lesson, write the lesson name in a rectangle.
   - When you complete a lesson, write a skill or key concept in a circle linked to that lesson block.
   - When you complete the chapter, use this graphic organizer to help you review.

Equations and Applications

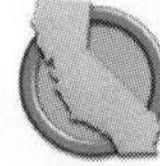

What You've Learned

California Content Standards

NS 1.2 Add, subtract, multiply, and divide rational numbers and take positive rational numbers to whole-number powers.

AF 1.3 Simplify numerical expressions by applying properties of rational numbers and justify the process used.

AF 2.1 Interpret positive whole-number powers as repeated multiplication. Simplify and evaluate expressions that include exponents.

for Help to the lesson in green.

Simplifying Numerical Expressions (Lesson 1-1)

Simplify each expression.

1. $3 \cdot 8 + 5$ 29
2. $3.6 + 6 \div 2$ 6.6
3. $48 - 6.5 \cdot 5$ 15.5
4. $(23 - 18) \cdot 0.6$ 3
5. $0.5 \cdot 2 - 1$ 0
6. $(3 \cdot 4.1) - 2 \cdot 5$ 2.3

Adding Integers (Lesson 2-2)

Find each sum.

7. $8 + 15 + (-25)$ −2
8. $6 + (-7) + 15$ 14
9. $-14 + 8 + (-8)$ −14
10. $12 + (-6) + 9$ 15

Multiplying Integers (Lesson 2-4)

Find each product.

11. $-12 \cdot 3$ −36
12. $-3 \cdot (-1)$ 3
13. $2(-2 - 5) \cdot 3$ −42
14. $6 \cdot (-2) \cdot 3$ −36
15. $4 \cdot (-4) \cdot 20$ −320
16. $-8 \cdot 3 \cdot (-6)$ 144

Simplifying Powers (Lesson 2-6)

Simplify each expression.

17. 6^2 36
18. 2^3 8
19. 10^5 100,000
20. 1^{14} 1
21. 5^4 625
22. 7^5 16,807

California Content Standards for Chapter 3

Number Sense
NS 1.2

Algebra and Functions
AF 1.1, AF 1.3, AF 4.1

Measurement and Geometry
MG 3.3

Algebra 1
Alg1 2.0

Chapter 3 Overview

In this chapter, students learn to solve equations using addition, subtraction, multiplication, and division. They use these skills to solve two-step problems. They learn to evaluate square roots of perfect squares and approximate square roots of integers. They use these skills to solve problems using the Pythagorean Theorem and its converse.

Activating Prior Knowledge

In this chapter, students will build on and extend their ability to solve one-step problems to solve two-step problems. They apply their knowledge of exponents to understanding square roots and solving problems using the Pythagorean Theorem and its converse. Ask questions such as:

- *What is a perfect square?* the result of multiplying a number by itself
- *What is a right triangle?* a triangle with exactly one right angle

What You'll Learn Next

▲ In Lesson 3-3, you will write an equation to find the number of teeth on the rear gear of a bicycle.

California Content Standards

AF 4.1 Solve two-step linear equations in one variable over the rational numbers, interpret the solution or solutions in the context from which they arose, and verify the reasonableness of the results.

MG 3.3 Know and understand the Pythagorean theorem and its converse and use it to find the length of the missing side of a right triangle.

New Vocabulary

English and Spanish Audio Online

- converse of the Pythagorean Theorem (p. 117)
- equation (p. 87)
- hypotenuse (p. 112)
- inverse operations (p. 87)
- isolate (p. 87)
- legs (p. 112)
- perfect square (p. 107)
- Pythagorean Theorem (p. 112)
- square root (p. 107)

Academic Vocabulary

- deductive reasoning (p. 100)

Understanding Equality

Students learn that the value on the left side of an equation must be the same as the value on the right. They use balance scales as a visual representation of equality.

Guided Instruction

Explain to students that an equation is a statement in which the value on the left side of the = symbol must be the same as the value on the right. For Exercises 1–4, ask students to explain why the number sentences are true or not true using number sense. Show them that solving equations is just a way to find the values for variables that make the equations true.

Foundational Standard Know and understand that equals added to equals are equal.
Foundational Standard Know and understand that equals multiplied by equals are equal.

Understanding Equality

The = symbol means that the value on the left side is the same as the value on the right side of the symbol. Balance scales are like equality statements.

EXAMPLES Understanding Equality

1 Is the number sentence $7 + 3.1 = 8 + 2.1$ true or false? Explain.

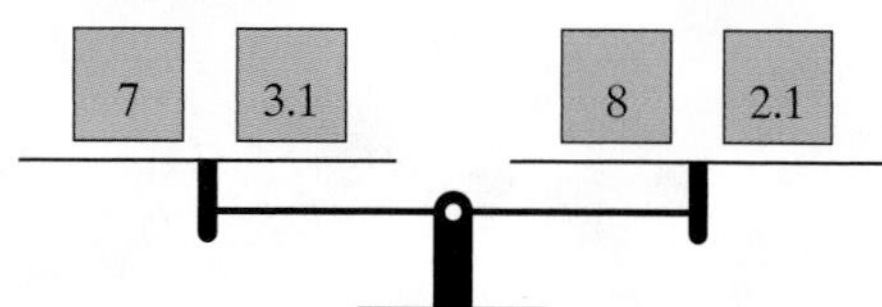

Compare the numbers on the left side to the numbers on the right.

Since 7 is one less than 8, and 3.1 is one more than 2.1, the weights on the left and right are equal. The scale is balanced.

The sentence is true.

2 Is the number sentence $(4 - 1.5) \cdot 6 = 2.5 \cdot 6$ true or false?

Since $(4 - 1.5)$ and 2.5 are equal, $4 - 1.5 = 2.5$. If you multiply each side of this sentence by 6, the two sides remain equal. The sentence is true.

Exercises

Find whether each number sentence is true. Explain your answer using logic and number sense. Do not compute. See margin.

1. $525 - 350 = 528 - 353$
2. $200 \cdot 2 \cdot 4 = 400 \cdot 2$
3. $(13 \cdot 10) \cdot 4 = 130 \cdot 4$
4. $48.2 + 28.2 = (38.1 + 10) + 18.2$

Use logic and number sense to find the value of x that makes each number sentence true.

5. $4 + 17.3 = 6 - 2 + x$ 17.3
6. $32 \cdot 15 = x \cdot 30$ 16
7. $(27 \div x) + 5 = 9 + 5$ 3
8. $73 - 21.5 = 83 - x - 21.5$ 10
9. $75 + 25 = 150 - x + 25$ 75
10. $100 \cdot 20 = 25 \cdot z$ 80

Each number sentence on the left is true. Use logic and number sense to answer the question on the right. Explain your reasoning.

11. $37.4 + 68.8 = 106.2$ — Does $(37.4 + 68.8) + 30 = 106.2 + 30$? yes
12. $224 \div 64 = 3.5$ — Does $(224 \div 64) \cdot 1.7 = 3.5 \cdot 1.7$? yes

GO for Help: Math Companion

3-1 Solving Addition Equations

Check Skills You'll Need

Do this in your **Math Companion.**

Vocabulary

- equation
- isolate
- inverse operations
- Subtraction Property of Equality

Use your **Math Companion** *to build your vocabulary.*

California Content Standards

Foundational Standard Write and solve one-step linear equations.

AF 1.1 Use variables and appropriate operations to write an equation that represents a verbal description. ***Develop***

AF 1.3 Simplify expressions by applying properties of numbers. ***Develop***

What You'll Learn . . . and Why

You will learn to solve addition equations. You can use equations to find the change in height or weight of things as they grow.

An **equation** is a mathematical sentence that has an equal sign, =.

To be in balance, a scale must have weights with the same total on each side.

$x + 2 = 5$ ← A true equation has equal values on each side of the equal sign.

The number 2 is added to the variable x in the equation $x + 2 = 5$. To solve the equation, you need to **isolate** the variable, or get it alone on one side of the equal sign.

To isolate the variable, you undo the operation. You undo adding 2 by subtracting 2. Operations that undo each other are **inverse operations.**

EXAMPLE Solving an Equation by Subtracting

1 Solve $x + 2 = 5$.

$x + 2 - 2 = 5 - 2$ ← Subtract 2 from each side to undo the addition and isolate x.

$x + 0 = 3$ ← Inverse Property of Addition

$x = 3$ ← Identity Property of Addition

Check $x + 2 = 5$ ← Check your solution in the original equation.

$3 + 2 \stackrel{?}{=} 5$ ← Substitute 3 for x.

$5 = 5$ ✔

Vocabulary Tip

Read the equation $3 + 2 \stackrel{?}{=} 5$ as the question, "Is 3 + 2 equal to 5?"

CA Standards Check 1 *Go to your* **Math Companion** *for help.*

1. a. Solve $w + 4.3 = 9.1$. 4.8 b. Solve $z + 6 = 12.9$. 6.9

Universal Access Solutions for All Learners

Special Needs L1
To "undo" an operation, get a number back to zero. Show students that $x + 4 - 4$ is the same as $x + 0$. Remind them to use the Identity Property, which tells them that $x + 0$ is really x. This is how to isolate x.

Below Level L2
Give students several addition and subtraction exercises like these to illustrate inverse operations.

32 + 6 38	28 − 7 21
38 − 6 32	21 + 7 28

3-1

1. Plan

California Content Standards

Write and solve one-step linear equations. ***Foundational***

AF 1.1 Use variables and appropriate operations to write an equation. ***Develop***

AF 1.3 Simplify expressions by applying properties of numbers. ***Develop***

California Math Background

An equation must have a verb (such as *equals* or *is*) just as a complete sentence must. Equations can be simplified and solved by undoing what has been done to the variable using inverse operations, such as undoing addition with subtraction. To maintain the balance, or truth, of an equation, the same operation must always be carried out on both sides of the equation.

More Math Background: p. 84C

Lesson Planning and Resources

See p. 84E for a list of the resources that support this lesson.

PRESENTATION CD-ROM
CD, Online, or Transparencies

Bell Ringer Practice

Check Skills You'll Need
Use student page, transparency, or PowerPoint.
See Math Companion.

California Standards Review
Use transparency or PowerPoint.

2. Teach

Guided Instruction

Example 1
Some students are better able to visualize the process of subtracting the same number from each side when the subtraction is performed vertically.

$$\begin{array}{rcr} x + 2 & = & 5 \\ -2 & = & -2 \\ \hline x & = & 3 \end{array}$$

Error Prevention!

Stress the importance of checking a proposed solution by substituting it for the variable *in the original equation.*

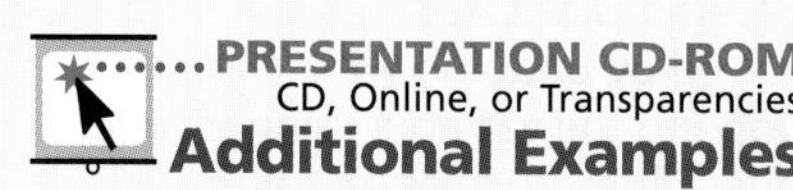
... PRESENTATION CD-ROM
CD, Online, or Transparencies
Additional Examples

1. Solve $h + 9 = 14$. 5
2. Today Anna discovered that she is 4 in. taller than she was last year at this time. Anna's height today is 51 in. What was Anna's height last year at this time? 47 in.

Closure

- *What are inverse operations?* operations that undo each other, such as addition and subtraction
- *How do you use subtraction to solve an equation?* Sample: For an equation like $y + 4 = 20$, subtract 4 from each side to undo the addition; then simplify to get $y = 16$.

When you solve problems using equations, drawing a diagram may help. The model indicates that the whole = part + part.

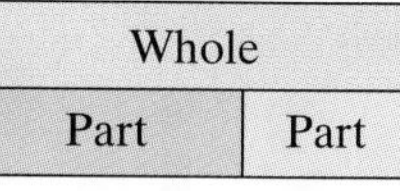

Relate **MATH YOU KNOW...**

EXAMPLE Writing an Addition Equation

A kitten weighed 15 oz. Over the next two years, it gained g ounces. Write an expression representing the new weight of the kitten.

Weight after 2 years	
15	g

... to ALGEBRA The expression $15 + g$ represents the new weight of the kitten.

2 Guided Problem Solving A kitten weighed 15 oz. After two years, the kitten had grown into a cat weighing 120 oz. How many ounces did the kitten gain?

Let g = the number of ounces gained.

120	
15	g

The equation $15 + g = 120$ represents this situation.

$$15 + g = 120$$
$$15 + g - 15 = 120 - 15 \quad \leftarrow \text{Subtract 15 from each side to undo the addition and isolate } g.$$
$$g = 105 \quad \leftarrow \text{Simplify.}$$

The kitten gained 105 oz.

CA Standards Check 2 *Go to your* **Math Companion** *for help.*

2. A cat has gained 1.8 lb in a year. It now weighs 11.6 lb. Write and solve an equation to find how much the cat weighed last year.
$g + 1.8 = 11.6$; 9.8 lb

When you use inverse operations to solve equations, you are using a mathematical property. The property you use in this lesson is called the Subtraction Property of Equality.

Take Note **Subtraction Property of Equality**

If you subtract the same value from each side of an equation, the two sides remain equal.

Arithmetic $2 \cdot 3 = 6$, so $2 \cdot 3 - 4 = 6 - 4$.
Algebra If $a = b$, then $a - c = b - c$.

Homework prep is in your **Math Companion.**

Advanced Learners L4
Only one of these equations has a solution. Which equation is it, and what is the solution? $n + n = 2$; 1

$$n + 2 = n$$
$$n + n = 2$$

English Learners EL
Have volunteers read the word problems in the Exercises before students are asked to work on them. Ask students to work in pairs to identify what they know and what they are trying to find. Have them come up with equations.

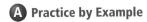

Standards Practice

AF 1.1, AF 1.3

A Practice by Example

Example 1 (page 87)

Homework Video Tutor

For: Examples 1–2
Visit: PHSchool.com
Web Code: axe-0301

Solve each equation. Check the solution.

1. $x + 46 = 72$
   $x + 46 - 46 = 72 - 46$
   $x = ■$ 26

Guided Practice This exercise has been started for you!

2. $d + 5 = 53$ 48
3. $v + 9 = -2$ −11
4. $n + 17 = 56$ 39
5. $m + 1.3 = 2.8$ 1.5
6. $h + 21 = -50$ −71
7. $14.7 = 5 + f$ 9.7
8. $y + 12 = 64$ 52
9. $p + 4.5 = 10.8$ 6.3

Example 2 (page 88)

Solve each equation. Check the solution.

10. $9.2 + d = 23.6$ 14.4
11. $-8.7 = k + 5.1$ −13.8
12. $1.3 + j = 0.4$ −0.9
13. $h + 6.7 = -6.7$ −13.4
14. $-12 = -6.4 + m$ −5.6
15. $y + 13.82 = 2.4$ −11.42
16. $-1.9 = g + (-0.4)$ −1.5
17. $10.5 + x = 9.7$ −0.8

Write and solve an equation for each problem. Then check the solution.

18–19. Equations may vary. Samples are given.

18. $x + 7 = 25$; 18

19. $x + 6 = 1{,}762$; 1756

18. You build 7 model airplanes during the summer. At the end of the summer, you have 25 model airplanes. How many model airplanes did you have before the summer? See left.

19. Wolfgang Amadeus Mozart wrote his first piano sonata in 1762, when he was 6 years old. In what year was Mozart born? See left.

B Apply Your Skills

20. **Guided Problem Solving** Jeans that were on sale last week now cost \$29.97. The savings were \$4.99. Write and solve an equation to find the former sale price of the jeans. $p + 4.99 = 29.97$; $p = \$24.98$
    - Let $p =$ the sale price of the jeans.
    - You can draw a diagram to help you write the equation.

Full price of jeans	
Sale price p	Savings \$4.99

22. Answers may vary. Sample: Joelle gave her sister \$8.40. Now her sister has \$11.55. How much money did Joelle's sister have to start?

23. No; after you subtract 27.6 from 31.8, the result will be much less than 59.4.

GPS 21. A collector sold a baseball card for \$9.30. This was \$3.75 more than the price he paid. How much did the collector pay for the card? \$5.55

22. **Writing in Math** Describe a problem that you can solve using the equation $a + 8.40 = 11.55$. See left.

23. **Reasoning** Is 59.4 a reasonable solution for the equation $x + 27.6 = 31.8$? Explain. See left.

3. Practice

Assignment Guide

Check Your Understanding

See Math Companion.

Homework Exercises

A	Practice by Example	1–19
B	Apply Your Skills	20–34
C	Challenge	35
	California Multiple-Choice Practice	36–38
	Mixed Review	39–41

Homework Quick Check

To check students' understanding of key skills and concepts, go over Exercises 2, 10, 18, 21, 22, 31.

Universal Access Resources

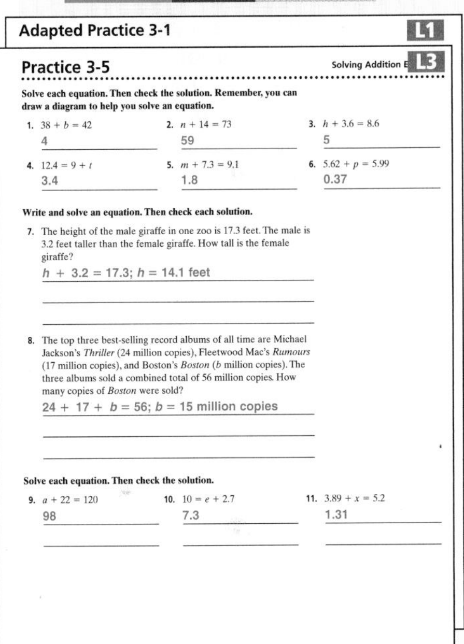

Adapted Practice 3-1 L1

Practice 3-5 Solving Addition E L3

Solve each equation. Then check the solution. Remember, you can draw a diagram to help you solve an equation.

1. $38 + b = 42$ 4
2. $n + 14 = 73$ 59
3. $h + 3.6 = 8.6$ 5
4. $12.4 = 9 + t$ 3.4
5. $m + 7.3 = 9.1$ 1.8
6. $5.62 + p = 5.99$ 0.37

Write and solve an equation. Then check each solution.

7. The height of the male giraffe in one zoo is 17.3 feet. The male is 3.2 feet taller than the female giraffe. How tall is the female giraffe?
   $h + 3.2 = 17.3$; $h = 14.1$ feet

8. The top three best-selling record albums of all time are Michael Jackson's *Thriller* (24 million copies), Fleetwood Mac's *Rumours* (17 million copies), and Boston's *Boston* (b million copies). The three albums sold a combined total of 56 million copies. How many copies of *Boston* were sold?
   $24 + 17 + b = 56$; $b = 15$ million copies

Solve each equation. Then check the solution.

9. $a + 22 = 120$ 98
10. $10 = e + 2.7$ 7.3
11. $3.89 + x = 5.2$ 1.31

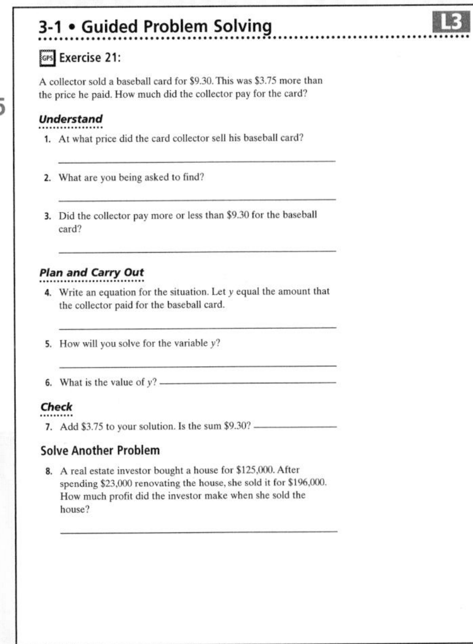

3-1 • Guided Problem Solving L3

GPS Exercise 21:

A collector sold a baseball card for \$9.30. This was \$3.75 more than the price he paid. How much did the collector pay for the card?

Understand

1. At what price did the card collector sell his baseball card?
2. What are you being asked to find?
3. Did the collector pay more or less than \$9.30 for the baseball card?

Plan and Carry Out

4. Write an equation for the situation. Let y equal the amount that the collector paid for the baseball card.
5. How will you solve for the variable y?
6. What is the value of y? ____

Check

7. Add \$3.75 to your solution. Is the sum \$9.30? ____

Solve Another Problem

8. A real estate investor bought a house for \$125,000. After spending \$23,000 renovating the house, she sold it for \$196,000. How much profit did the investor make when she sold the house?

4. Assess & Reteach

PRESENTATION CD-ROM
CD, Online, or Transparencies

Lesson Quiz

Solve each equation.

1. $18 + n = 40$ 22
2. $m + 3.5 = 6.7$ 3.2
3. $p + 0.99 = 4.15$ 3.16
4. $78 = q + 20$ 58

Alternative Assessment

Provide small groups of students with a balance scale, centimeter cubes, and several addition and subtraction equations that deal with whole numbers. Have students model the equations on the balance. For example, for the equation $x + 9 = 25$, have them place 9 cubes on one pan and 25 on the other. Then have them take away enough cubes from 25 so that the pans balance. Ask students to record the solution to each equation.

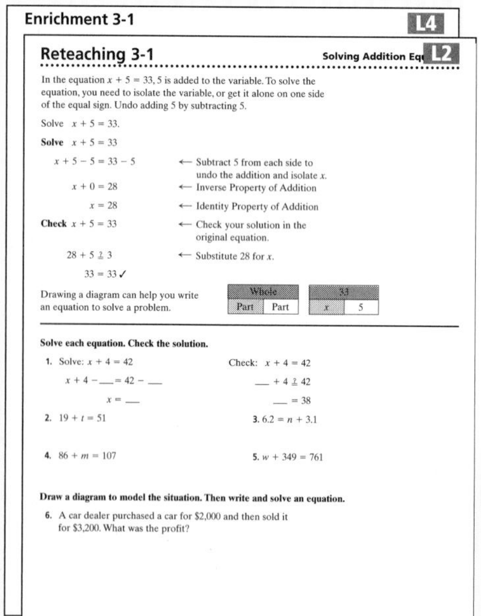

Enrichment 3-1 L4

Reteaching 3-1 **Solving Addition Eq** L2

In the equation $x + 5 = 33$, 5 is added to the variable. To solve the equation, you need to isolate the variable, or get it alone on one side of the equal sign. Undo adding 5 by subtracting 5.

Solve $x + 5 = 33$.

Solve $x + 5 = 33$

$x + 5 - 5 = 33 - 5$ ← Subtract 5 from each side to undo the addition and isolate x.

$x + 0 = 28$ ← Inverse Property of Addition

$x = 28$ ← Identity Property of Addition

Check $x + 5 = 33$ ← Check your solution in the original equation.

$28 + 5 \stackrel{?}{=} 3$ ← Substitute 28 for x.

$33 = 33$ ✓

Drawing a diagram can help you write an equation to solve a problem.

Whole	
Part	Part

33	
x	5

Solve each equation. Check the solution.

1. Solve: $x + 4 = 42$ Check: $x + 4 = 42$
   $x + 4 - \_\_ = 42 - \_\_$ $\_\_ + 4 \stackrel{?}{=} 42$
   $x = \_\_$ $\_\_ = 38$
2. $19 + t = 51$
3. $6.2 = n + 3.1$
4. $86 + m = 107$
5. $w + 349 = 761$

Draw a diagram to model the situation. Then write and solve an equation.

6. A car dealer purchased a car for $2,000 and then sold it for $3,200. What was the profit?

SCAFFOLDED **Problem Solving**

In a number square, the sum of the numbers in each row, column, and main diagonal is the same.

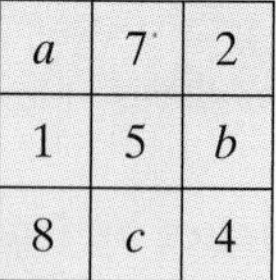

a	7	2
1	5	b
8	c	4

24. Find the sum of the number square at the right. 15
25. Use the equation $a + 7 + 2 = 15$ to find the value of a. 6
26. Which equation can you use to find the value of b? B
    Ⓐ $7 + b + 4 = 15$ Ⓑ $1 + 5 + b = 15$ Ⓒ $b = 2 + 4 + 15$
27. Find the value of b. 9
28. Write and solve an equation to find the value of c. See left.

28. $8 + c + 4 = 15$ or $7 + 5 + c = 15$; 3

29. Find the values of a, b, and c in the number square at the right. $a = -5$, $b = -3$, $c = 3$

2	b	−2
a	−1	c
0	1	−4

Population (thousands)
p
2,688
1950
2000
Topeka
Kansas

30. Between 1950 and 2000, the population of Kansas increased by 783,000. Use the graph at the left to find the population of Kansas in 1950. 1,905,000 people

Number Sense **Choose from −3, −2, −1, 0, 1, 2, and 3. Find all the numbers that are solutions of each equation.**

31. $|n| = 2$ −2 and 2
32. $-|n| = -3$ −3 and 3
33. $|n| + 1 = 2$ −1 and 1
34. $|n + 1| = 2$ −3 and 1

C Challenge

35. For what values of x is $x + 15 = x + 6 + 9$ true? Explain. See margin.

Multiple Choice Practice and Mixed Review

For California Standards Tutorials, visit PHSchool.com. Web Code: axq-9045

AF 1.1

36. The table shows the length and perimeter of different rectangles with a width of 3 cm. Which expression can be used to find the perimeter of a rectangle with a length of n units? D

Side Length	Perimeter
5 cm	16 cm
10 cm	26 cm
15 cm	36 cm

Ⓐ $n + 5$ Ⓑ $n + 10$ Ⓒ $n + 11$ Ⓓ $2n + 6$

AF 1.3

37. Use the Distributive Property to simplify the expression $25(4 + 5)$. C
    Ⓐ 100 Ⓑ 185 Ⓒ 225 Ⓓ 250

NS 1.2

38. A basketball team has 18 points. The team then scores six 2-point baskets and two 3-point baskets. What is the team's score? D
    Ⓐ 23 Ⓑ 26 Ⓒ 31 Ⓓ 36

GO for Help Lesson 2-5

Simplify each expression.

39. $-2 \cdot (-9) + 5$ 23
40. $16 - 5 \cdot (-2)$ 26
41. $-27 \div 3 \cdot 6$ −54

GO Online Lesson Quiz Visit: PHSchool.com Web Code: axa-0301

California Resources

Standards Mastery
- Standards Review Transparencies
- Standards Review and Practice Workbook
- Math Companion

Math Intervention
- Skills Review and Practice Workbook
- Math XL

3-2a Activity Lab

Modeling Equations

You can draw diagrams to model and solve equations.

 = +1 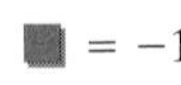 = −1 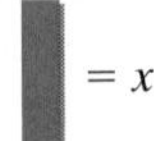 = x

To solve an equation, remove the same number of like-color units from each side or use zero pairs. A **zero pair** is a pair of units with a sum of zero.

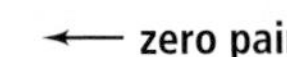 ← zero pair

Foundational Standard Solve one-step linear equations.
MR 2.5 Use diagrams and models to explain mathematical reasoning. *Develop*

EXAMPLE

1 Use a diagram to solve $x - 2 = 7$.

Model the equation. → 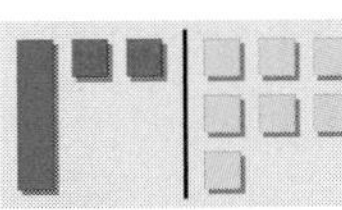 $x - 2 = 7$

Add 2 to each side, making two zero pairs on the left side. → 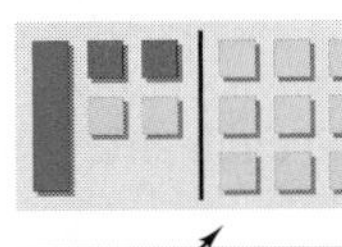 $x - 2 + 2 = 7 + 2$

Remove the zero pairs. → 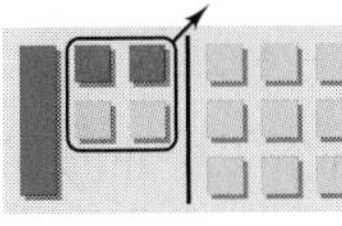 $x = 9$

Exercises

Use a diagram to solve each equation.

1. $x + 5 = 3$ −2
2. $x - 3 = -6$ −3
3. $x + 3 = -5$ −8
4. $x - 5 = 10$ 15
5. $x + 2 = 8$ 6
6. $x - 4 = 7$ 11
7. What operation do you use to solve a subtraction equation? addition
8. Write the equation that the model below represents. Then solve the equation. $x + 7 = 15$; 8

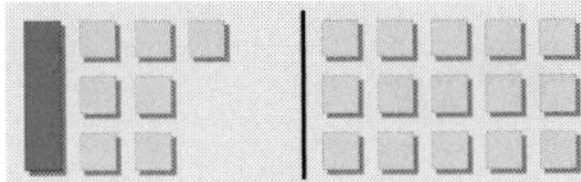

Activity Lab

Modeling Equations

The experience of using visual representations to model mathematical concepts helps many students to better understand the concept. In this activity, students solve addition and subtraction equations using diagrams.

Guided Instruction

Read the introduction with students. Be sure they know that the yellow units represent +1, the red units represent −1, and the long green units represent the variable, or "unknown," x.

Teaching Tip
Have student work in pairs as they draw diagrams as shown in Example 2. Ask: *Why are two +1 units placed on the left side of the equation?* **Sample: So the side with the variable has only zero pairs added to it.** *Why are two +1 units also placed on the right side of the equation?* **Sample: So the two sides are still equal.**

Universal Access
Auditory Learners
Have students explain their steps to their partners. Suggest that each person explains one example aloud.

GO for Help: Math Companion

3-2

1. Plan

California Content Standards

Write and solve one-step linear equations. ***Foundational***

AF 1.1 Use variables and appropriate operations to write an equation. ***Develop***

AF 1.3 Simplify expressions by applying properties of rational numbers. ***Develop***

California Math Background

An equation must have a verb (such as *equals* or *is*) just as a complete sentence must. Equations can be simplified and solved by undoing what has been done to the variable using inverse operations, such as undoing subtraction with addition. To maintain the balance, or truth, of an equation, the same operation must always be carried out on both sides of the equation.

More Math Background: p. 84C

Lesson Planning and Resources

See p. 84E for a list of the resources that support this lesson.

...PRESENTATION CD-ROM
CD, Online, or Transparencies

Bell Ringer Practice

Check Skills You'll Need
Use student page, transparency, or PowerPoint.
See Math Compation.

California Standards Review
Use transparency or PowerPoint.

3-2 Solving Subtraction Equations

Check Skills You'll Need
Do this in your **Math Companion.**

Vocabulary
- Addition Property of Equality

Use your **Math Companion** *to build your vocabulary.*

California Content Standards

Foundational Standard Write and solve one-step linear equations.

AF 1.1 Use variables and appropriate operations to write an equation that represents a verbal description. ***Develop***

AF 1.3 Simplify expressions by applying properties of rational numbers. ***Develop***

What You'll Learn . . . and Why

You will learn to solve subtraction equations. You can use an equation to find the nutritional contents of foods.

You learned to solve equations by subtracting the same amount from each side of an equation. You can also solve equations by using addition.

Take Note **Addition Property of Equality**

If you add the same value to each side of an equation, the two sides remain equal.

Arithmetic	$2 \cdot 3 = 6$, so $2 \cdot 3 + 4 = 6 + 4$.
Algebra	If $a = b$, then $a + c = b + c$.

Some equations have a number subtracted on one side. To isolate the variable, add the same number to each side of the equation.

Online active math

For: Equations Activity
Use: Interactive Textbook, 3-2

EXAMPLE Solving an Equation by Adding

1 Solve $c - 12 = 43$.

$$c - 12 = 43$$

$$c - 12 + 12 = 43 + 12 \quad \leftarrow \text{Isolate the variable. Use the Addition Property of Equality.}$$

$$c + 0 = 55 \quad \leftarrow \text{Inverse Property of Addition}$$

$$c = 55 \quad \leftarrow \text{Identity Property of Addition}$$

CA Standards Check 1 *Go to your* **Math Companion** *for help.*

1. Solve each equation.
   a. $n - 53 = 28$ 81
   b. $x - 4.3 = 12$ 16.3

Universal Access Solutions for All Learners

Special Needs L1
Model for students what happens if both sides of an equation do not balance. Draw a box for x number of apples and subtract 5 apples. Write $x - 5 = 8$. Then add 5 only on the left and write $x = 8$. Go back and draw 8 apples − 5 apples = 8 apples. That is not a true equation.
learning style: visual

Below Level L2
Have students line up problems vertically to solve. Example 1 could be solved as:

$$\begin{array}{rcr} c - 12 & = & 43 \\ +\,12 & = & +12 \\ \hline c & = & 55 \end{array}$$

learning style: visual

One way to model a real-world situation is to state the problem as simply as you can. Then use your statement to write an equation.

Relate **MATH YOU KNOW...**

EXAMPLE Writing Subtraction Equations

The amount of zinc in wheat flakes is 1.75 mg less than b, the amount of zinc in an energy bar. Write an expression for the amount of zinc in wheat flakes.

Words 1.75 less than amount in bar

Expression b  $-$ 1.75

...to ALGEBRA

The expression $b - 1.75$ represents the amount of zinc in wheat flakes.

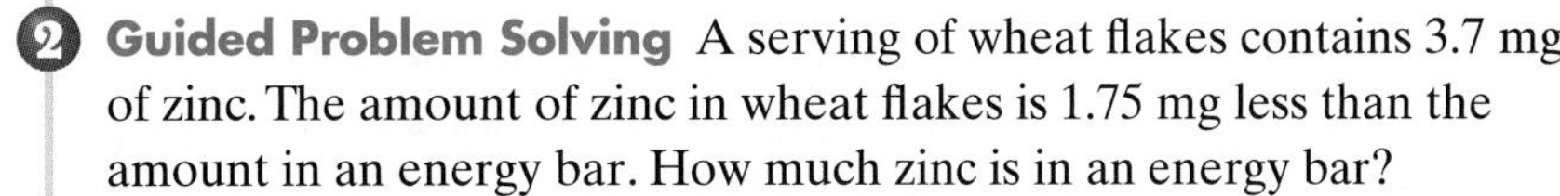

2 Guided Problem Solving A serving of wheat flakes contains 3.7 mg of zinc. The amount of zinc in wheat flakes is 1.75 mg less than the amount in an energy bar. How much zinc is in an energy bar?

Problem Solving Tip

Verbs such as *is, are, has,* and *was* show you where to place the equal sign, =.

Words amount in flakes is 1.75 less than amount in bar

Let b = the amount of zinc in an energy bar.

Equation $3.7 = b - 1.75$

$3.7 = b - 1.75$ ← **Write the equation.**

$3.7 + 1.75 = b - 1.75 + 1.75$ ← **Isolate the variable. Use the Addition Property of Equality.**

$5.45 = b$ ← **Simplify.**

The energy bar contains 5.45 mg of zinc.

CA Standards Check 2 *Go to your* **Math Companion** *for help.*

2. The temperature dropped 9°F between 7 P.M. and midnight. It was 54°F at midnight. Use an equation to find the temperature at 7 P.M. 63°F

Standards Practice

GO for Help: *MathXL* **AF 1.1, AF 1.3**

A Practice by Example

GO for Help **Example 1 (page 92)**

Solve each equation. Check the solution.

1. $x - 16 = 7.2$
   $x - 16 + ■ = 7.2 + ■$ 23.2

Guided Practice This exercise has been started for you!

2. $q - 2.4 = 1.8$ 4.2
3. $n - 297 = 18$ 315
4. $d - 68 = 40$ 108
5. $-37 = y - 2$ −35
6. $m - 15 = -31$ −16
7. $x - 5.7 = 5.7$ 11.4

Check Your Understanding *Homework prep is in your* **Math Companion.**

2. Teach

Guided Instruction

Example 2

Stress the importance of always indicating what quantity the variable represents.

Error Prevention!

Have students begin by drawing a circle around the variable for which they are solving. This may help to avoid confusion about which operation is needed to isolate the variable.

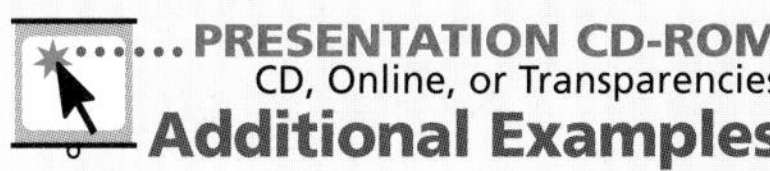

...PRESENTATION CD-ROM CD, Online, or Transparencies

Additional Examples

1. Solve $p - 22.3 = 5.08$. 27.38
2. The sale price of a CD is $11.49. This is $3.50 less than the regular price. What is the regular price? $14.99

Closure

- *How do you use addition to solve an equation?* Sample: For an equation like $m - 9 = 17$, add 9 to each side to undo the subtraction; then simplify to get $m = 26$.

Advanced Learners L4	**English Learners** EL
Have students answer the following. *A student said the solution to y − 1,214 = 31,214 is 30,000. Is this correct? If not, explain the error.* This is incorrect; the student subtracted 1,214 from 31,214 when it should have been added.	Be precise in the language you use to describe what happens when you add a value to both sides of the equation. Make sure students understand that they are undoing the subtraction on one side of the equation and compensating for it on the other side.

3. Practice

Assignment Guide

Check Your Understanding

See Math Companion.

Homework Exercises

A	Practice by Example	1–18
B	Apply Your Skills	19–37
C	Challenge	38
California Multiple-Choice Practice		39–41
Mixed Review		42–44

Homework Quick Check

To check students' understanding of key skills and concepts, go over Exercises 2, 8, 20, 30, 35.

Universal Access Resources

Adapted Practice 3-2 L1

Practice 3-2 Solving Subtraction Equa[tions] L3

Solve each equation. Check the solution. Remember, you can draw a diagram to help you solve an equation.

1. $x - 10 = 89$
2. $14 = y - 15$
3. $a - 10 = 3.4$
4. $12.3 = b - 7$
5. $n - 2.7 = 8.3$
6. $3.12 = d - 6.88$

Solve each equation.

7. The owner of a used music store bought a compact disc for $4.70. When she sold it, her profit was $4.75. What was the selling price?
8. Yesterday, Stephanie spent $38.72 on new shoes and $23.19 on computer software. When she was finished, she had $31.18. How much money did she have before she went shopping?

Solve each equation.

9. $x - 7 = 77$
10. $3.1 = r - 7.5$
11. $k - 5.13 = 2.9$
12. $h - 3.2 = -8$
13. $-9 = -1.2 + r$
14. $q - (-0.3) = -82.6$

3-2 • Guided Problem Solving L3

GPS **Exercise 35:**

You buy several posters. The total cost is $18.95. You have $7.05 left after you pay. Write and solve an equation to find how much money you had before this purchase.

Understand

1. What are you being asked to do?
2. What will the variable represent in the equation?
3. Circle the information you will need to solve.

Plan and Carry Out

4. How much did you pay for the posters? ______
5. Write an expression for the amount of money you had before the purchase minus the amount you paid for the posters. Choose any variable for the amount of money you had.
6. How much money did you have left after the purchase?
7. Write an equation comparing the amounts in Steps 5 and 6.
8. What do you do to both sides of the equation to isolate the variable?
9. Solve the equation.
10. How much money did you have before the purchase?

Check

11. Check your answer by substituting the result in step 10 into the equation you wrote in step 7. Does it check?

Solve Another Problem

12. Jim has saved $78. This is $23 less than his sister has saved. Write and solve an equation to find how much his sister has saved.

Example 2 (page 93)

Solve each equation.

8. $23 = j - 12$ 35
9. $b - 2 = 2$ 4
10. $0.6 = h - 2.9$ 3.5
11. $m - 24 = -5$ 19
12. $p - 5.9 = 15$ 20.9
13. $32.5 = v - 9$ 41.5
14. $k - 0.4 = 0$ 0.4
15. $w - 143.5 = -5.6$ 137.9
16. $54.9 = d - 7$ 61.9
17. $c - 6 = -0.5$ 5.5

Homework Video Tutor

For: Examples 1–2
Visit: PHSchool.com
Web Code: axe-0302

18. You withdraw $35 from your bank account. Use the information at the right. Write and solve an equation to find the original balance. $278

BANK
TIME 17:55
ATM NUMBER: 000856-3
CARD NUMBER: 2324XXXX
CHECKING WITHDRAWAL $35.00
NEW BALANCE $243.00
THANK YOU FOR BANKING WITH US AND HAVE A WONDERFUL DAY
BANK
DEBIT/CHECK CARD
5664 1400 2324 XXXX
CHARGE

B Apply Your Skills

19. **Guided Problem Solving** A healthy person has a normal temperature of 98.6°F. Suppose a sick person needs to decrease his temperature by 3.7°F to return to normal. Use an equation to find the sick person's temperature. 102.3°F
    - What equation will you use to model this problem?
    - What operation will you use to solve the equation?

29. The student should have subtracted 46 from each side rather than adding 46 to each side.

30. Add 4 to each side; 4 was subtracted from the variable *d*, so adding 4 will isolate the variable.

Solve each equation. Justify each step.

20. $w - 2.45 = 3.1$ 5.55
21. $h - (-7) = 4.3$ −2.7
22. $-12 = -6.4 + m$ −5.6
23. $g - (-4.56) = -8.5$ −13.06
24. $t - 7.9 = 17.9$ 25.8
25. $f - (-0.2) = -81.5$ −81.7
26. $-5.6 + q = 10.2$ 15.8
27. $55.6 = k - 0.9$ 56.5

28. In one weekend a student collected p pounds of cans to take to the recycling center. After delivering 5.2 lb of cans, the student still had 7.8 lb of cans. How many pounds of cans did the student collect? 13.0 lb

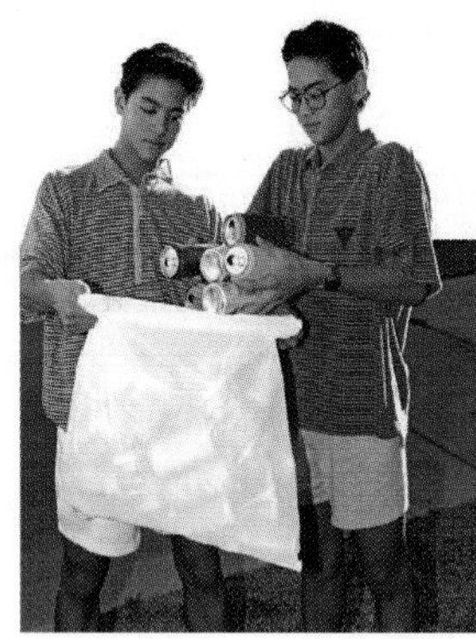

An aluminum beverage can weighs about half of an ounce.

29. **Error Analysis** A student estimated the solution to $45.9 + k = 1.1$ below. Explain why the student's estimate is not reasonable. See above left.

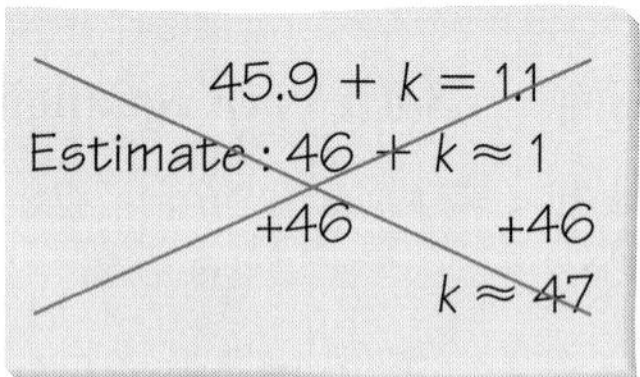

30. **Writing in Math** When solving the equation $d - 4 = -9$, should you add 4 or 9 to each side? Explain. See above left.

SCAFFOLDED
Problem Solving

An electronics store is having a sale on DVD players.

31. What is the sale price of the DVD player? $39.83

32. Let p be the original price of the DVD player. Write an equation you can use to find the original price. $p - 17.07 = 39.83$

33. What was the original price of the DVD player? $56.90

34. The following week, the DVD player is marked down another $5.50. Write and solve an equation to find the new sale price. $34.33

GPS 35. You buy several posters. The total cost is $18.95. You have $7.05 left after you pay. Write and solve an equation to find how much money you had before this purchase. $26

36. Susan saved $87.11. Susan's savings are $9.62 less than Dorinne's savings. How much has Dorinne saved? $96.73

37. Negative; if you add 9.7 to −10.5, the result will be negative.

37. **Number Sense** Will the solution to $x - 9.7 = -10.5$ be a positive number or a negative number? Explain. See left.

Challenge

38. Sue is 2 years older than Mary. Mary is 3 years younger than Bob. Sue is 13 years old. How old is Bob? 14 years old

Multiple Choice Practice and Mixed Review

For California Standards Tutorials, visit PHSchool.com. Web Code: axq-9045

AF 1.1

39. The gas tank in the Rivera family car can hold a maximum of 18.2 gal. After a trip, they filled the tank with 9.6 gal of gas. Which equation can they use to find how much gas was in the tank before it was filled? A

Ⓐ $18.2 - g = 9.6$
Ⓑ $18.2 + g = 9.6$
Ⓒ $9.6 - g = 18.2$
Ⓓ $18.2 + 9.6 = g$

Alg1 2.0

40. Which pair of numbers are opposites? C

Ⓐ 0, 10 Ⓑ 0, −10 Ⓒ 10, −10 Ⓓ 16, 61

NS 1.2

41. A student had $78. She then earned money baby-sitting. Now she has $116. How much did the student earn baby-sitting? C

Ⓐ −$38.00 Ⓑ $19.40 Ⓒ $38.00 Ⓓ $194.00

Lesson 1-1

Simplify each expression.

42. $24 \div 4 - 3 \cdot 2.5$ −1.5

43. $24 \div 3 - 2.5 \cdot 4$ −2

44. $24 \div (3 - 2.5) \cdot 4$ 192

Visit: PHSchool.com Web Code: axa-0302

4. Assess & Reteach

PRESENTATION CD-ROM
CD, Online, or Transparencies

Lesson Quiz

Solve each equation.

1. $m - 3.2 = 6.7$ 9.9
2. $z - 3.09 = 8.1$ 11.19
3. $7.9 = n - 0.35$ 8.25

Alternative Assessment

Students write two equations, each one involving subtraction. Students exchange papers with a partner, solve the equations, and then check each other's work.

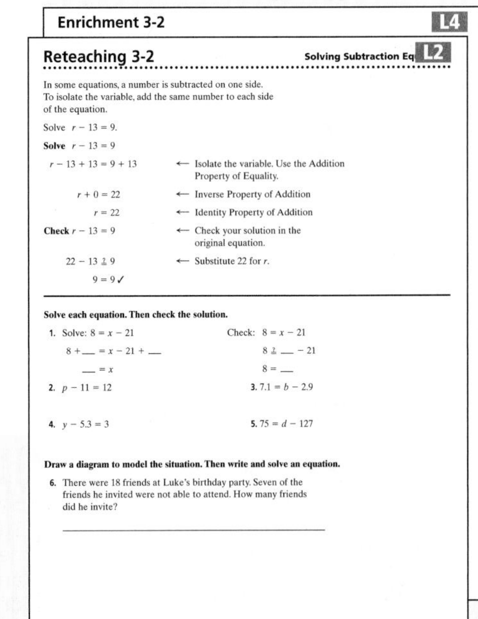

Enrichment 3-2 L4

Reteaching 3-2 Solving Subtraction Eq L2

In some equations, a number is subtracted on one side. To isolate the variable, add the same number to each side of the equation.

Solve $r - 13 = 9$.

Solve $r - 13 = 9$

$r - 13 + 13 = 9 + 13$ ← Isolate the variable. Use the Addition Property of Equality.

$r + 0 = 22$ ← Inverse Property of Addition

$r = 22$ ← Identity Property of Addition

Check $r - 13 = 9$ ← Check your solution in the original equation.

$22 - 13 \stackrel{?}{=} 9$ ← Substitute 22 for r.

$9 = 9$ ✓

Solve each equation. Then check the solution.

1. Solve: $8 = x - 21$ Check: $8 = x - 21$
   $8 + \_\_ = x - 21 + \_\_$ $8 \stackrel{?}{=} \_\_ - 21$
   $\_\_ = x$ $8 = \_\_$
2. $p - 11 = 12$
3. $7.1 = b - 2.9$
4. $y - 5.3 = 3$
5. $75 = d - 127$

Draw a diagram to model the situation. Then write and solve an equation.

6. There were 18 friends at Luke's birthday party. Seven of the friends he invited were not able to attend. How many friends did he invite?

California Resources

Standards Mastery
- Standards Review Transparencies
- Standards Review and Practice Workbook
- Math Companion

Math Intervention
- Skills Review and Practice Workbook
- Math XL

3-3

1. Plan

California Content Standards

Write and solve one-step linear equations. ***Foundational***

AF 1.1 Use variables and appropriate operations to write an equation. ***Develop***

AF 1.3  Simplify numerical expressions by applying properties of rational numbers. ***Develop***

Professional Development

California Math Background

Just as addition and subtraction are a pair of inverse operations, so too are multiplication and division. Students should note the principle that ties together the four properties of equality: If you perform the same operation on each side of an equation, the solution of the resulting equation is the same as the solution of the original equation. Students should also be aware of the restriction to the Division Property of Equality; that is, you cannot divide the sides of an equation by zero.

More Math Background: p. 84C

Lesson Planning and Resources

See p. 84E for a list of the resources that support this lesson.

...PRESENTATION CD-ROM
CD, Online, or Transparencies

Bell Ringer Practice

Check Skills You'll Need
Use student page, transparency, or PowerPoint.
See Math Companion.

California Standards Review
Use transparency or PowerPoint.

3-3 Solving Multiplication and Division Equations

Check Skills You'll Need
Do this in your **Math Companion.**

Vocabulary
- Division Property of Equality
- Multiplication Property of Equality

Use your **Math Companion** *to build your vocabulary.*

California Content Standards

Foundational Standard Write and solve one-step linear equations.
AF 1.1 Use variables and appropriate operations to write an equation. ***Develop***
AF 1.3 Simplify numerical expressions by applying properties of rational numbers. ***Develop***

What You'll Learn . . . and Why

You will learn to solve multiplication and division equations. You can use equations to find the cost of a single item that is normally sold as part of a carton, case, box, or bag of items. For example, plants are often sold in packages of six plants.

You can use the Division Property of Equality to solve equations involving multiplication.

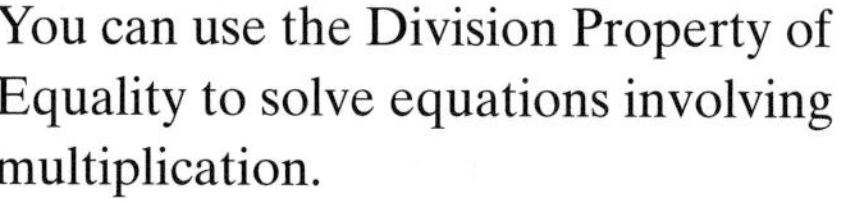

Take Note Division Property of Equality

If you divide each side of an equation by the same nonzero number, the two sides remain equal.

Arithmetic $4 \cdot 2 = 8$, so $4 \cdot 2 \div 2 = 8 \div 2$.

Algebra If $a = b$ and $c \neq 0$, then $a \div c = b \div c$.

Vocabulary Tip
The symbol $\neq$ means "does not equal."

Recall that $4n$ means 4 times n. To undo multiplication, divide by the same number. So $4n \div 4 = n$.

EXAMPLE Solving an Equation by Dividing

1 Solve $4n = 68$.

$4n = 68$

$\frac{4n}{4} = \frac{68}{4}$ ← **Isolate the variable. Use the Division Property of Equality.**

$n = 17$ ← **Simplify.**

Math Foundations
$\frac{4n}{4}$ means $4n \div 4$. The fraction bar represents division.

CA Standards Check 1 *Go to your* **Math Companion** *for help.*

1. Solve each equation.
   a. $0.8p = 32$ 40
   b. $3y = -12$ −4

Universal Access Solutions for All Learners

Special Needs L1	**Below Level** L2
Students may find diagramming the equations helpful. Assist them as needed, or ask them to pair up and generate ideas for useful diagrams before drawing.	Have students say aloud several multiplication and division exercises like these to illustrate inverse operations. 6×9 54 $88 \div 4$ 22 $54 \div 9$ 6 22×4 88

EXAMPLE Writing a Multiplication Equation

2 Guided Problem Solving You buy a package of six tomato plants. The total cost is \$17.94. Use an equation to find the cost of one plant.

Relate **MATH YOU KNOW...**

Let c = the cost of one tomato plant. Draw a diagram to model the situation.

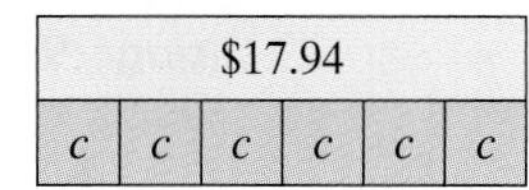

The equation $6c = \$17.64$ models this situation.

... to ALGEBRA

$6c = 17.64$ ← **Write the equation.**

$\frac{6c}{6} = \frac{17.64}{6}$ ← **Isolate the variable. Use the Division Property of Equality.**

$c = 2.94$ ← **Simplify.**

The cost of one tomato plant is \$2.94.

Check for Reasonableness Round 17.64 to 18. $18 \div 6 = 3$. Since 2.94 is close to 3, the answer is reasonable.

CA Standards Check 2 *Go to your* **Math Companion** *for help.*

2. A store sells each card at a \$.35 profit. The store's total profit is \$302.75. Use an equation to find the number of cards the store sold. 865 cards

You can use the Multiplication Property of Equality to solve equations involving division.

Take Note — Multiplication Property of Equality

If you multiply each side of an equation by the same number, the two sides remain equal.

Arithmetic $6 \div 2 = 3$, so $(6 \div 2) \cdot 2 = 3 \cdot 2$.

Algebra If $a = b$, then $a \cdot c = b \cdot c$.

EXAMPLE Solving an Equation by Multiplying

3 Solve $\frac{y}{-7} = 15$.

$-7 \cdot \left(\frac{y}{-7}\right) = 15 \cdot (-7)$ ← **Isolate the variable. Use the Multiplication Property of Equality.**

$y = -105$ ← **Simplify.**

CA Standards Check 3 *Go to your* **Math Companion** *for help.*

3. Solve each equation.

a. $\frac{t}{8} = -5$ −40

b. $\frac{w}{1.5} = 10$ 15

Homework prep is in your **Math Companion.**

2. Teach

Guided Instruction

Example 1

Present the following solution:

$$4n = 68$$
$$n \cdot 4 = 68$$
$$n \cdot 4 \div 4 = 68 \div 4$$
$$n = 17$$

Error Prevention!

Some students might apply the Division Property of Equality correctly but use the wrong number as the dividend. Suggest that they use this visual aid.

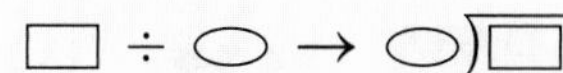

... PRESENTATION CD-ROM
CD, Online, or Transparencies

Additional Examples

1 Solve $6x = 144$. 24

2 The cost of a pay-per-view concert on television is \$39.95. Five friends decide to watch the concert together and split the cost equally. What amount will each friend pay? \$7.99

3 Solve $x \div 6 = 9$. 54

Closure

- *How do you use division to solve an equation?* Divide each side of an equation by the same nonzero number; then simplify.
- *How do you use multiplication to solve an equation?* Multiply each side of an equation by the same number; then simplify.

Advanced Learners L4

Use the properties of equality to solve $4z + 1.5 = 6.3$. Subtract 1.5 from each side to get $4z = 4.8$. Then divide each side by 4 to get $z = 1.2$.

English Learners EL

Help students attach language to equations they are solving. For example, in $5a = 100$, they can learn to say to themselves: *5 times a quantity a is equal to 100; or 5 groups of some number a are in 100; or 100 divided by 5 will tell me what the quantity a is.*

3. Practice

Assignment Guide

Check Your Understanding

See Math Companion.

Homework Exercises

A Practice by Example	1–21
B Apply Your Skills	22–38
C Challenge	39
California Multiple-Choice Practice	40–42
Mixed Review	43–45

Homework Quick Check

To check students' understanding of key skills and concepts, go over Exercises 3, 11, 15, 23, 25, 32, 38.

Universal Access Resources

Adapted Practice 3-3 L1

Practice 3-3 Solving Multiplication and Division Equations L3

Solve each equation. Check the solution.

1. $\frac{a}{-6} = 2$
2. $18 = \frac{v}{-1.8}$
3. $46 = 2.3m$
4. $-114 = -6k$
5. $0 = \frac{b}{19}$
6. $136 = 8y$
7. $0.6j = -1.44$
8. $28b = -131.6$
9. $\frac{n}{-9} = -107$
10. Skylar spent $90.65 on books that cost $12.95 each. How many books did Skylar buy?
11. Eugenio has five payments left to make on his computer. If each payment is $157.90, how much does he still owe?
12. Judy spent $83.86 to buy T-shirts for the 14 members of the Chess Club. How much did each T-shirt cost?
13. Lea drove 420 miles and used 20 gallons of gas. How many miles per gallon did her car get?
14. Ty spent $15 on folders that cost $3 each. How many folders did he buy?

3-3 • Guided Problem Solving L3

GPS **Exercise 38**

An elephant's height is about 5.5 times the length of her hind footprint. Use an equation to find the approximate height of an elephant whose hind footprint is 1.5 feet long.

Understand

1. What are you being asked to do?
2. Circle the information you will need to solve.
3. The phrase "*5.5 times*" tells you to perform what operation?

Plan and Carry Out

4. What is the length of the hind footprint of this particular adult female elephant?
5. Write an expression to represent the phrase "*5.5 times the length of the hind footprint.*"
6. Write an equation for the height of the elephant. ______
7. What is the height of the elephant? ______

Check

8. Explain how you can check your answer. Does your answer check?

Solve Another Problem

9. Angela makes 1.75 times the amount of money that Janet makes. If Janet makes $38,200, how much does Angela make? Write and solve an equation.

Standards Practice

GO for Help: *MathXL*

AF 1.1, AF 1.3

A Practice by Example

Example 1 (page 96)

Solve each equation. Check the solution.

1. $-6y = -30$

$\frac{-6y}{-6} = \frac{-30}{6}$

$y = ■$ 5

Guided Practice This exercise has been started for you!

GO for Help

2. $8k = 76$ 9.5 3. $7n = 11.9$ 1.7 4. $25h = 450$ 18

5. $0.4x = 1$ 2.5 6. $10b = 35$ 3.5 7. $64 = 4g$ 16

8. $20.4 = 12m$ 1.7 9. $14y = 7$ 0.5 10. $0.9c = 1.89$ 2.1

Example 2 (page 97)

11. An egg carton holds 12 eggs. A farmer gathers 8,616 eggs. Write and solve an equation to find how many cartons are needed for the eggs. 718 cartons

Example 3 (page 97)

Solve each equation. Check the solution.

12. $\frac{d}{10} = 64$

$10 \cdot \left(\frac{d}{10}\right) = 64 \cdot 10$

$d = ■$ 640

Guided Practice This exercise has been started for you!

Homework Video Tutor

For: Examples 1–3
Visit: PHSchool.com
Web Code: axe-0303

13. $12 = \frac{r}{9}$ 108 14. $\frac{a}{7} = 63$ 441 15. $\frac{w}{5} = 12$ 60

16. $\frac{k}{2.5} = -8$ −20 17. $1.4 = \frac{t}{0.3}$ 0.42 18. $7.5 = \frac{p}{10.2}$ 76.5

19. $\frac{x}{45} = 3.2$ 144 20. $120 = \frac{b}{19}$ 2,280 21. $\frac{e}{3.25} = 21.7$ 70.525

B Apply Your Skills

22. **Guided Problem Solving** A bicycle has 44 teeth on the front gear. This is four times the number of teeth on the rear gear. Write and solve an equation to find the number of teeth on the rear gear.
    - Translate the words into an equation.
      Words: Four times _?_ equals _?_.
      Equation: $4 \cdot ■ = ■$ 11 teeth

Use the picture at the left for Exercises 23 and 24.

23. You plan to buy the bodyboard nine weeks from now. How much money must you save per week? $5.56 per week

24. Your friend saves $10.50 per week. How many weeks will it take your friend to save enough to buy the bodyboard? 5 weeks

25. **Writing in Math** Explain why the Division Property of Equality includes the statement "$c \neq 0$." Answers may vary. Sample: Division by 0 is undefined.

26. Each volleyball team in a league needs 6 players, 2 alternates, and a coach. How many teams can be formed from 288 people? 32 teams

SCAFFOLDED
Problem Solving

A video store charges the same price to rent each movie. The line plot shows the number of movies rented from the store during one week.

Number of Movie Rentals

				✗
				✗
✗			✗	✗
✗			✗	✗
✗	✗		✗	✗
✗	✗	✗	✗	✗
✗	✗	✗	✗	✗
✗	✗	✗	✗	✗
M	T	W	T	F

27. How many movies were rented on Monday? 6 movies

28. What is the total number of movies rented from the store during the week? 27 movies

29. The store collected a total of \$80.73 for the week's rentals. Write an equation to represent the cost of renting one movie. $27r = 80.73$ or $80.73 \div r = 27$

30. What does it cost to rent one movie? \$2.99

31. Nine movies were returned one day late. The store collected \$4.95 in late fees for those 9 movies. What is the late fee for one movie? \$.55

Solve each equation. Justify each step and check the solution.

32. $65.13 = 13x$ 5.01
33. $-p = 29$ −29
34. $0.4f = 300$ 750
35. $-8.1 = \frac{r}{-5.2}$ 42.12
36. $-1 = \frac{-b}{7}$ 7
37. $\frac{y}{1.6} = 0.256$ 0.4096

GPS 38. An elephant's height is about 5.5 times the length of her hind footprint. Use an equation to find the approximate height of an elephant whose hind footprint is 1.5 feet long. about 8.25 ft

Challenge

39. Twice as many students go to the park as to the theater. Five more students go to the theater than to the museum. If 16 students go to the park, how many students go to the museum? 3 students

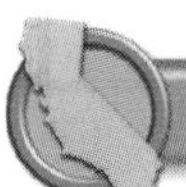

Multiple Choice Practice and Mixed Review

For California Standards Tutorials, visit PHSchool.com. Web Code: axq-9045

AF 1.1

40. Tickets to an event cost \$25 each. Which equation can you use to find the number of tickets t that you can buy with \$100? B

(A) $4t = 100$
(B) $25t = 100$
(C) $4 + t = 100$
(D) $25 + t = 100$

NS 1.2

41. Ashley bought a book for \$15.99. She now has \$32.12. How much money did Ashley have before she bought the book? D

(A) \$16.13
(B) \$17.13
(C) \$47.11
(D) \$48.11

AF 1.3

42. Which equation illustrates the Inverse Property of Addition? B

(A) $j + 0 = j$
(B) $-j + j = 0$
(C) $j + 0 = 0 + j$
(D) $(j + 0) + 1 = j + (0 + 1)$

Lesson 3-1

Solve each equation.

43. $g + 5.6 = 10$ 4.4
44. $-7 = k + 12$ −19
45. $9.2 + y = 34.5$ 25.3

Online Lesson Quiz Visit: PHSchool.com Web Code: axa-0303

Alternative Assessment

Provide pairs of students with red pencils. Each partner writes a multiplication and a division equation. Partners exchange papers and solve each other's equations, using the red pencils to write the inverse operations.

California Resources

Standards Mastery

- Standards Review Transparencies
- Standards Review and Practice Workbook
- Math Companion

Math Intervention

- Skills Review and Practice Workbook
- Math XL

4. Assess & Reteach

PRESENTATION CD-ROM
CD, Online, or Transparencies

Lesson Quiz

Solve each equation.

1. $6x = 156$ 26
2. $y \div 11 = 15$ 165
3. $3w = 13.5$ 4.5
4. $z \div 2.7 = 9$ 24.3

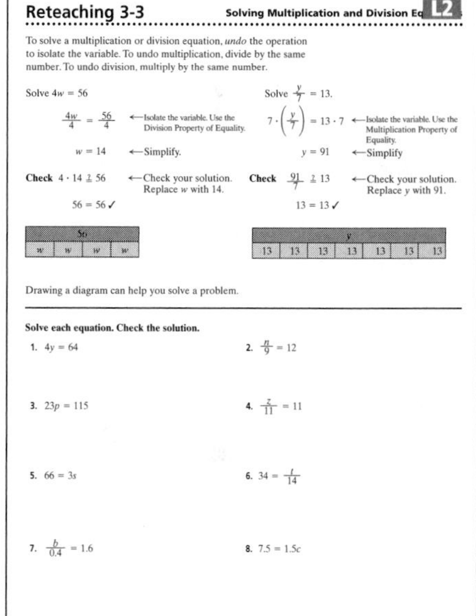

Reteaching 3-3 Solving Multiplication and Division Eq L2

To solve a multiplication or division equation, *undo* the operation to isolate the variable. To undo multiplication, divide by the same number. To undo division, multiply by the same number.

Solve $4w = 56$

$\frac{4w}{4} = \frac{56}{4}$ ← Isolate the variable. Use the Division Property of Equality.

$w = 14$ ← Simplify.

Check $4 \cdot 14 \stackrel{?}{=} 56$ ← Check your solution. Replace w with 14.

$56 = 56$ ✓

Solve $\frac{y}{7} = 13$.

$7 \cdot \left(\frac{y}{7}\right) = 13 \cdot 7$ ← Isolate the variable. Use the Multiplication Property of Equality.

$y = 91$ ← Simplify

Check $\frac{91}{7} \stackrel{?}{=} 13$ ← Check your solution. Replace y with 91.

$13 = 13$ ✓

56			
w	w	w	w

y						
13	13	13	13	13	13	13

Drawing a diagram can help you solve a problem.

Solve each equation. Check the solution.

1. $4y = 64$
2. $\frac{n}{9} = 12$
3. $23p = 115$
4. $\frac{z}{11} = 11$
5. $66 = 3s$
6. $34 = \frac{t}{14}$
7. $\frac{b}{0.4} = 1.6$
8. $7.5 = 1.5c$

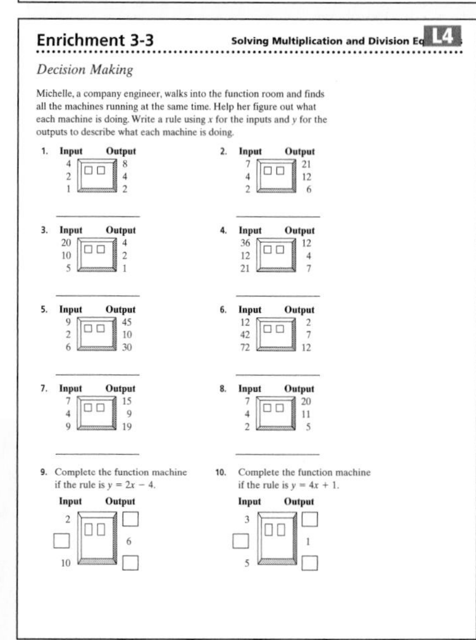

Enrichment 3-3 Solving Multiplication and Division Eq L4

Decision Making

Michelle, a company engineer, walks into the function room and finds all the machines running at the same time. Help her figure out what each machine is doing. Write a rule using x for the inputs and y for the outputs to describe what each machine is doing.

1. Input 4, 2, 1; Output 8, 4, 2
2. Input 7, 4, 2; Output 21, 12, 6
3. Input 20, 10, 5; Output 4, 2, 1
4. Input 36, 12, 21; Output 12, 4, 7
5. Input 9, 2, 6; Output 45, 10, 30
6. Input 12, 42, 72; Output 2, 7, 12
7. Input 7, 4, 9; Output 15, 9, 19
8. Input 7, 4, 2; Output 20, 11, 5
9. Complete the function machine if the rule is $y = 2x - 4$.
   Input 2, ☐, 10; Output ☐, 6, ☐
10. Complete the function machine if the rule is $y = 4x + 1$.
   Input 3, ☐, 5; Output ☐, 1, ☐

Mathematical Reasoning

Using Deductive Reasoning

Students learn to use deductive reasoning to solve equations by justifying each step with properties and definitions.

Guided Instruction

Explain to students that deductive reasoning is the process of reasoning logically from given facts to a conclusion. Point out that for each step in the Example, a reason is given. For Exercises 1–4, ask students to write out each step as they simplify the expressions. Show them how to stack the steps vertically and line them up. Then ask them to write a justification to the right of each step.

Use this Checkpoint Quiz to check students' understanding of the skills and concepts of Lessons 3-1 through 3-3.

All in One Resources

- Checkpoint Quiz 1

Mathematical Reasoning

For Use With Lesson 3-2

AF 1.3 Simplify expressions by applying properties of rational numbers and justify the process used. ***Develop***
MR 2.4 Make conjectures by using deductive reasoning. ***Introduce***

Using Deductive Reasoning

Deductive reasoning is the process of reasoning logically from given facts to a conclusion. You can use deductive reasoning to solve an equation. Justify each step with reasons such as properties and definitions.

EXAMPLE

Solve the equation $w - 3.5 = 18$. Justify each step.

$w - 3.5 = 18$	← Write the equation.
$w - 3.5 + 3.5 = 18 + 3.5$	← Isolate the variable. Use the Addition Property of Equality.
$w + 0 = 21.5$	← Inverse Property of Addition
$w = 21.5$	← Identity Property of Addition

Exercises

Solve each equation. Justify each step. 1–3. See margin.

1. $p + 12.3 = 45$
2. $15e = 120$
3. $67 = t - 9$
4. $\frac{k}{4.2} = 10$
5. **Reasoning** When solving the equation $h - (-5) = 245.6$, you can use either the Addition Property of Equality or the Subtraction Property of Equality. Explain. 4–5. See back of book.

Checkpoint Quiz 1

Lessons 3-1 through 3-3

Solve each equation.

1. $5 + x = 65$ 60
2. $32 = 1.6a$ 20
3. $n - 3.2 = 15$ 18.2
4. $4f = 28$ 7
5. $\frac{g}{3.8} = 10$ 38
6. $z + 6 = 8.2$ 2.2
7. $v - 4 = 3.7$ 7.7
8. $24.3 = \frac{t}{2}$ 48.6
9. You pay for refreshments at a movie theater with a $10 bill. The refreshments cost $5.73. How much change should you receive? $4.27
10. Your friend lives 0.75 mi from the school. You live five times as far from the school. How far from the school do you live? 3.75 mi

3-4a Activity Lab

Modeling Two-Step Equations

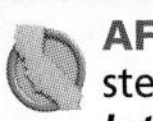

AF 4.2 Solve two-step linear equations. ***Introduce***

MR 2.5 Use diagrams and models to explain mathematical reasoning. ***Develop***

You can use diagrams to model and solve multi-step equations.

To solve a two-step equation, get the x-units alone on one side. Then divide each side into equal groups.

EXAMPLE

Use a diagram to solve $2x + 1 = -5$.

Model the equation. →

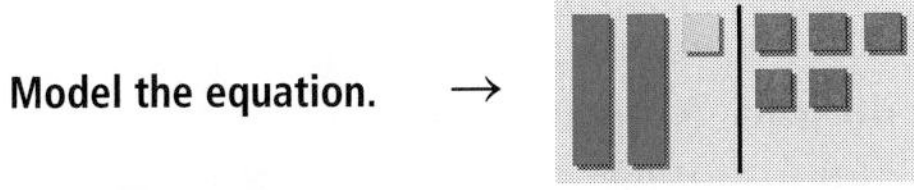

$2x + 1 = -5$

Add −1 to each side, creating a zero pair on the left side. →

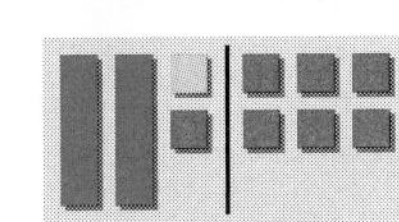

$2x + 1 + (-1) = -5 + (-1)$

Remove the zero pair. →

$2x = -6$

Divide each side into two equal groups. →

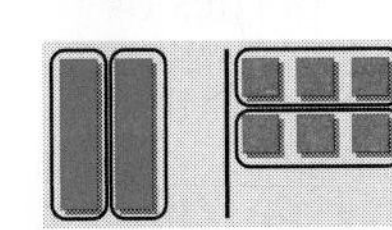

$\frac{2x}{2} = \frac{-6}{2}$

Remove one group from each side. →

$x = -3$

Exercises

Use a diagram to solve each equation.

1. $-2x + 5 = 3$ 1
2. $3x + 2 = -7$ −3
3. $2x - 4 = -2$ 1
4. $2x - 7 = 5$ 6
5. $1 + 2x = 5$ 2
6. $3x - 5 = -11$ −2
7. $-15 - 8x = 25$ −5
8. $16x + 36 = 100$ 4
9. $46 - 12x = -62$ 9
10. **Open-Ended** Write two different equations that have the solution modeled at the right. Answers may vary. Samples: $2x = 8$, $3x + 1 = 13$
11. Use a diagram to model and solve $2x + 5 = x - 1$. Describe each step. −6; check students' work.

Activity Lab

Modeling Two-Step Equations

By using diagrams, students can gain a visual understanding of what an equation is and what it means to find its solution.

Guided Instruction

Error Prevention!

Remind students that the size of the x-bar has no relationship to its value (for example, some students might think the value of x is 3 because 3 unit squares fit into one x-bar). Help students resist the urge to simply bring the unit representing 1 to the other side. Remind them that each side is equivalent and that what is done to one side must also be done to the other side. Have students draw a vertical line on their papers to better visualize the idea of two sides of an equation.

Universal Access

Visual Learners

As you work through the solution to the equation, guide students to see that adding a negative unit to each side to create a zero pair is equivalent to subtracting positive 1 from each side. As needed, remind students that they use inverse operations to "undo" operations when solving equations and that addition and subtraction are inverse operations.

3-4

1. Plan

California Content Standards

Write and solve one-step linear equations. ***Foundational***

AF 1.1 Use variables and appropriate operations to write an equation. ***Develop***

AF 4.1 Solve two-step linear equations, interpret the solution in context, and verify the reasonableness of the results. ***Introduce, Develop***

California Math Background

Two-step equations involve two distinct operations—either addition or subtraction for one step and multiplication or division for the other step. The goal in solving two-step equations is the same as in solving any equation: to get the variable alone on one side of the equation by using inverse operations.

More Math Background: p. 84C

Lesson Planning and Resources

See p. 84E for a list of the resources that support this lesson.

...PRESENTATION CD-ROM
CD, Online, or Transparencies

Bell Ringer Practice

Check Skills You'll Need
Use student page, transparency, or PowerPoint.
See Math Companion.

California Standards Review
Use transparency or PowerPoint.

GO for Help: Math Companion

3-4 Solving Two-Step Equations

Check Skills You'll Need

Do this in your **Math Companion.**

Vocabulary

Review:
- isolate
- properties of equality

Use your **Math Companion** *to build your vocabulary.*

California Content Standards

Foundational Standard Write and solve one-step linear equations.
AF 1.1 Use variables and appropriate operations to write an equation that represents a verbal description. ***Develop***
AF 4.1 Solve two-step linear equations, interpret the solutions in context, and verify the reasonableness of the results. ***Introduce, Develop***

What You'll Learn . . . and Why

You will learn to solve two-step equations. You can use a two-step equation to find the cost of adopting a puppy and buying dog food.

A two-step equation, such as $125 + 3b = 154.97$, is an equation that contains two operations.

To solve a two-step equation, you use inverse operations and the properties of equality to isolate the variable.

EXAMPLE Solving by Adding and Dividing

Relate MATH YOU KNOW...

Solve $y - 3 = 11$.

$y - 3 = 11$

$y - 3 + 3 = 11 + 3$ ← Addition Property of Equality

$y = 14$ ← Simplify.

...to ALGEBRA

1 Solve $2y - 3 = 11$.

$2y - 3 = 11$

$2y - 3 + 3 = 11 + 3$ ← Use the Addition Property of Equality to undo the subtraction.

$2y = 14$ ← Simplify.

$\frac{2y}{2} = \frac{14}{2}$ ← Use the Division Property of Equality to undo the multiplication.

$y = 7$ ← Simplify.

CA Standards Check 1 *Go to your* **Math Companion** *for help.*

1. Solve each equation.
   a. $5x - 2 = 18$ 4
   b. $3x - 4 = 23$ 9

Universal Access Solutions for All Learners

Special Needs L1
Have students use algebra tiles, when available, for Example 1 and CA Standards Check 1. When algebra tiles are not available, have students draw the algebra tiles for one example and cross out the tiles not needed as each operation is undone.

Below Level L2
Give students two-step expressions to evaluate for $x = 6$. Have students show their work.

$3x - 4$ $3(6) - 4 = 18 - 4 = 14$

$5x + 1$ $5(6) + 1 = 30 + 1 = 31$

$\frac{x}{2} + 7$ $\frac{6}{2} + 7 = 3 + 7 = 10$

EXAMPLE Solving by Subtracting and Multiplying

2 Solve $1.50 + \frac{v}{3} = 2.75$.

$$1.50 + \frac{v}{3} = 2.75$$

$$1.50 + \frac{v}{3} - 1.50 = 2.75 - 1.50 \quad \leftarrow \text{Subtraction Property of Equality}$$

$$\frac{v}{3} = 1.25 \quad \leftarrow \text{Simplify.}$$

$$3 \cdot \frac{v}{3} = 1.25 \cdot 3 \quad \leftarrow \text{Multiplication Property of Equality}$$

$$v = 3.75 \quad \leftarrow \text{Simplify.}$$

CA Standards Check 2 *Go to your* **Math Companion** *for help.*

2. Solve each equation.

a. $\frac{x}{3} + 2 = 5$ 9

b. $\frac{a}{2} + 4 = 8$ 8

EXAMPLE Writing a Two-Step Equation

3 **Guided Problem Solving** Suppose you adopt a dog from an animal shelter and buy 3 bags of dog food. The adoption fee is $125 and you spend a total of $154.97. How much does each bag of dog food cost?

Use a model to help write an equation.

Total cost $154.97	
Adoption fee $125	Bags $3b$

$$125 + 3b = 154.97 \quad \leftarrow \text{Write the equation.}$$

$$125 + 3b - 125 = 154.97 - 125 \quad \leftarrow \text{Subtraction Property of Equality}$$

$$3b = 29.97 \quad \leftarrow \text{Simplify.}$$

$$\frac{3b}{3} = \frac{29.97}{3} \quad \leftarrow \text{Division Property of Equality}$$

$$b = 9.99 \quad \leftarrow \text{Simplify.}$$

Each bag of dog food costs $9.99.

Check for Reasonableness Round 9.99 to 10. $3 \cdot 10 = 30$, and $125 + 30 = 155$. Since 155 is close to 154.97, the answer is reasonable.

CA Standards Check 3 *Go to your* **Math Companion** *for help.*

3. A phone plan costs $.70 per call and $.08 per minute. You pay $3.90 for a call. Write and solve an equation to find the length of the call.
40 min

Online active math

For: Two-Step Equations Activity
Use: Interactive Textbook, 3-4

2. Teach

Guided Instruction

Example 1
Emphasize that it is often easier to solve a two-step equation if students add or subtract before they multiply or divide. Solve CA Standards Check 1b by adding first and dividing second and then by dividing first and adding second to illustrate the point.

Error Prevention!

Help students rewrite $1.50 + \frac{y}{3} = 2.75$ in Example 2 as $1.50 + \frac{1}{3}y = 2.75$. In this form, students may better understand that they need to multiply by the reciprocal of $\frac{1}{3}$, or 3.

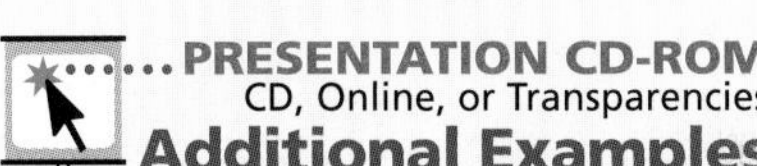

Additional Examples

1 Solve $6x - 14 = 16$. Check the solution. 5

2 Solve $2.25 + \frac{h}{5} = 8.5$ 31.25

3 The Science Club sells birdfeeders for $8 each. The club spends $32 in building materials. The club's profit is $128. How many birdfeeders did the club sell? Use b to represent the number of birdfeeders. Use the equation $8b - 32 = 128$. 20 birdfeeders

Advanced Learners L4
Explain that $7x - 2x = 5x$ and $7y + 2y = 9y$. Then have students solve these equations:

$7x - 4 = 2x + 6$ 2
$7y + 3 = 30 - 2y$ 3

English Learners EL
To help students with the equation in Example 3, write a heading on the board, such as *What We Know,* and list things like *the number of bags of dog food, the adoption fee*, and *the total cost*. Elicit the value of each of these from the students.

Closure

- *What is a two-step equation?* an equation that contains two operations
- *How do you solve a two-step equation?* Sample: Use inverse operations to get the variable alone on one side of the equation.
- *How can you check your solution?* Sample: Substitute the solution for the variable in the original equation and simplify. You should get the same value on both sides.
- *What is the difference between the two steps involved in solving a two-step equation?* The first step undoes the addition or subtraction; the second undoes the multiplication or division.

More Than One Way

Solve $2b - 18 = 34$.

Roberto's Method

First I add. Then I divide.

$2b - 18 = 34$

$2b - 18 + 18 = 34 + 18$ ← **Addition Property of Equality**

$2b = 52$ ← **Simplify.**

$\frac{2b}{2} = \frac{52}{2}$ ← **Division Property of Equality**

$b = 26$ ← **Simplify.**

Jasmine's Method

Since each number in the equation is an even number, I begin by dividing each side of the equation by 2.

$2b - 18 = 34$

$\frac{(2b - 18)}{2} = \frac{34}{2}$ ← **Division Property of Equality**

$b - 9 = 17$ ← **Divide $2b$, 18, and 34 by 2.**

$b - 9 + 9 = 17 + 9$ ← **Addition Property of Equality**

$b = 26$ ← **Simplify.**

Choose a Method

Solve $5p + 75 = 245$. Describe your method and explain why you chose it. 34; check students' work.

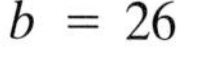

Standards Practice

GO for Help: *MathXL*

AF 1.1, AF 4.1

A Practice by Example

Example 1 (page 102)

GO for Help

Solve each equation. Check the solution.

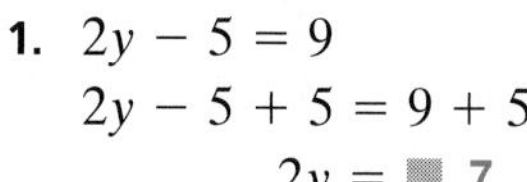

Guided Practice This exercise has been started for you!

1. $2y - 5 = 9$
   $2y - 5 + 5 = 9 + 5$
   $2y = \blacksquare$ 7
2. $-6b - 10 = 14$ −4
3. $15 = 3z - 6$ 7
4. $-14 + 2b = 28$ 21
5. $7r - 12 = 9$ 3
6. $23.7 = 9c - 12.3$ 4
7. $5j - 143 = -3$ 28
8. $-7 = 3x + 5$ −4
9. $625 = 8m + 345$ 35

Check Your Understanding *Homework prep is in your* **Math Companion.**

Example 2 (page 103)

Solve each equation. Check the solution.

10. $17 + \frac{b}{26} = 30$ 338
11. $\frac{m}{2} + 3 = -11$ −28
12. $\frac{x}{4} + 7 = 3$ −16
13. $-6 = 9 + \frac{a}{5}$ −75
14. $\frac{z}{12} + 63 = 3$ −720
15. $19 = 4 + \frac{h}{5}$ 75
16. $\frac{r}{11} - 13 = -2$ 121
17. $22 = \frac{d}{2} + 5$ 34
18. $\frac{w}{3} - 45 = 42$ 261
19. $\frac{t}{22} + 7 = 5$ −44
20. $\frac{n}{-13} - 27 = -14$ −169
21. $204 = 195 + \frac{c}{-25}$ −225

Homework Video Tutor

For: Examples 1–3
Visit: PHSchool.com
Web Code: axe-0304

Example 3 (page 103)

Write and solve an equation to answer each question. You may find a model helpful.

22. Anna Marie bought a notebook for \$1.19 and pencils for \$.39 each. The total cost was \$3.92. How many pencils did she buy? 7 pencils

23. You need to buy a pair of pants and three shirts. You have \$90 to spend on clothes. There is no sales tax. The pants you choose cost \$24. How much can you spend on each shirt? \$22 per shirt

B Apply Your Skills

24. **Guided Problem Solving** A bag of rice costs \$1.99. You buy one bag of rice and six cans of black beans for a total cost of \$7.33. If you have \$8.25, can you buy another can of beans? Explain.
    - What equation can you use to find c, the cost of a can of beans?
    - Knowing c, how can you determine whether you have enough money for another can of beans? See left.

24. Yes; using the equation $1.99 + 6b = 7.33$, the cost of each can of beans is \$.89. Since \$7.33 + \$.89 = \$8.22 is less than \$8.25, you can buy another can of beans.

Solve each equation.

25. $\frac{y}{3} - 9 = 30.3$ 117.9
26. $\frac{n}{1.4} + 1 = 10$ 12.6
27. $-8.2 + \frac{t}{-2} = 1.7$ −19.8
28. $12 = 6.9 - 3v$ −1.7
29. $1.2 = 3s - 1.8$ 1
30. $3q - 2.6 = 10$ 4.2

GPS 31. According to the Food and Drug Administration, the recommended daily intake of iron is 18 mg. This is 4 less than twice the recommended daily intake of zinc. What is the recommended daily intake of zinc? 11 mg

32. **Estimation** Use estimation to check whether 24.27 is a reasonable solution for $6p + 39.95 = 105.65$. Show your work. See left.

32. Answers may vary. Sample: Round 39.95 to 40 and round 105.65 to 100. Then $6p + 40 = 100$, so $6p = 60$ and $p = 10$. So 24.27 is not a reasonable solution.

For each table, write a rule that uses two operations. Then complete the table. (*Hint:* Multiply or divide first.)

33.

Input	Output
6	−6
9	−5
15	−3
30	■
63	■

output = input ÷ 3 − 8; 2, 13

34.

Input	Output
2	7
4	11
7	17
8	■
15	■

output = 2 · input + 3; 19, 33

3. Practice

Assignment Guide

Check Your Understanding

See Math Companion.

Homework Exercises

A Practice by Example	1–23
B Apply Your Skills	24–40
C Challenge	41
California Multiple-Choice Practice	42–44
Mixed Review	45–47

Homework Quick Check

To check students' understanding of key skills and concepts, go over Exercises 3, 10, 22, 25, 31, 33, 40.

Universal Access Resources

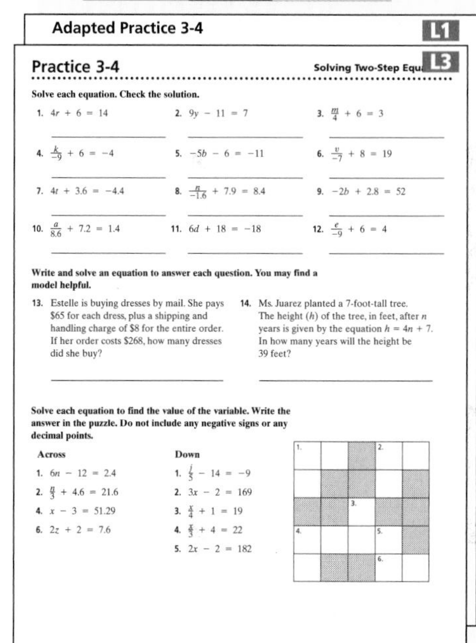
Adapted Practice 3-4 L1

Practice 3-4 Solving Two-Step Equ... L3

Solve each equation. Check the solution.

1. $4r + 6 = 14$
2. $9y - 11 = 7$
3. $\frac{m}{4} + 6 = 3$
4. $\frac{k}{-9} + 6 = -4$
5. $-5b - 6 = -11$
6. $\frac{v}{-7} + 8 = 19$
7. $4t + 3.6 = -4.4$
8. $\frac{n}{-1.6} + 7.9 = 8.4$
9. $-2b + 2.8 = 52$
10. $\frac{a}{8.6} + 7.2 = 1.4$
11. $6d + 18 = -18$
12. $\frac{e}{-9} + 6 = 4$

Write and solve an equation to answer each question. You may find a model helpful.

13. Estelle is buying dresses by mail. She pays \$65 for each dress, plus a shipping and handling charge of \$8 for the entire order. If her order costs \$268, how many dresses did she buy?

14. Ms. Juarez planted a 7-foot-tall tree. The height (h) of the tree, in feet, after n years is given by the equation $h = 4n + 7$. In how many years will the height be 39 feet?

Solve each equation to find the value of the variable. Write the answer in the puzzle. Do not include any negative signs or any decimal points.

Across

1. $6n - 12 = 2.4$
2. $\frac{n}{3} + 4.6 = 21.6$
4. $x - 3 = 51.29$
6. $2z + 2 = 7.6$

Down

1. $\frac{j}{5} - 14 = -9$
2. $3x - 2 = 169$
3. $\frac{x}{4} + 1 = 19$
4. $\frac{x}{3} + 4 = 22$
5. $2x - 2 = 182$

3-4 • Guided Problem Solving L3

GPS Exercise 31:

According to the Food and Drug Administration, the recommended daily intake of iron is 18 mg. This is 4 less than twice the recommended daily intake of zinc. What is the recommended daily intake of zinc?

Understand

1. What is the recommended daily intake of iron?
2. What are you being asked to find?
3. Will the recommended daily intake of zinc be more or less than that of iron?

Plan and Carry Out

4. Fill in the names of the minerals to help set up an equation.

   2 times ________ − 4 = ________

5. Write an equation, letting z represent the amount of zinc.
6. To solve the equation, what do you do first?
7. To solve for the recommended amount of zinc, what do you need to do to the equation?
8. What is the recommended daily intake of zinc? ________

Check

9. Does the answer check? Is twice 11 milligrams minus 4 milligrams the recommended daily intake of zinc?

Solve Another Problem

10. You spent \$10.50 at the fair. If it costs \$4.50 for admission and you rode 8 rides which all cost the same, how much does one ride ticket cost?

4. Assess & Reteach

PRESENTATION CD-ROM
CD, Online, or Transparencies

Lesson Quiz

Solve each equation.

1. $6a + 12 = 30$ 3
2. $\frac{b}{5} + 21 = 24$ 15
3. $4c - 40 = 28$ 17
4. $\frac{d}{7} + 15 = 22$ 49

Alternative Assessment

Provide algebra tiles to pairs of students. Partners use the tiles to model and solve exercises such as Exercises 1–5. Partners take turns recording each step of the solution process.

Reteaching 3-4 — Solving Two-Step Equ L2

Some equations contain two operations. To solve them, use inverse operations and the properties of equality to isolate the variable.

Solve $2d + 1 = 9$.

$2d + 1 = 9$	
$2d + 1 - 1 = 9 - 1$	Subtract 1 from each side to undo the addition.
$2d = 8$	Simplify.
$\frac{2d}{2} = \frac{8}{2}$	Divide each side by 2 to undo the multiplication.
$d = 4$	Simplify.
$2 \cdot 4 + 1 \stackrel{?}{=} 9$	Check your work by substituting 4 for d in the equation and solving.
$9 = 9$	Since $9 = 9$, the solution is correct.

1. Solve $7x - 5 = 16$.
   a. What must you first do to both sides? ______
   b. What must you next do to both sides? ______
   c. What is the solution? ______
2. Solve $12 = \frac{t}{5} + 8$.
   a. What must you first do to both sides? ______
   b. What must you next do to both sides? ______
   c. What is the solution? ______

Solve each equation. Check the solution.

3. $7y - 6 = 8$ ______
4. $81 = 3x - 6$ ______
5. $\frac{c}{8} + 10 = 15$ ______
6. $2f - 6 = 4$ ______
7. $2.4 + 3s = -0.6$ ______
8. $\frac{c}{5} + 100 = 120$ ______

Enrichment 3-4 — Solving Two-Step Equ L4

Problem Solving

Solve the equation $6x - 2 = 16$.

- Emma solved the equation by using inverse operations.

$$6x - 2 = 16$$
$$6x - 2 + 2 = 16 + 2$$
$$6x = 18$$
$$\frac{6x}{6} = \frac{18}{6}$$
$$x = \frac{18}{6}$$
$$x = 3$$

- Evan solved the equation by first dividing all terms by 6.

$$6x - 2 = 16$$
$$\frac{6x}{6} - \frac{2}{6} = \frac{16}{6}$$
$$x - \frac{2}{6} = \frac{16}{6}$$
$$x - \frac{2}{6} + \frac{2}{6} = \frac{16}{6} + \frac{2}{6}$$
$$x = \frac{18}{6}$$
$$x = 3$$

1. Did both students arrive at the same solution? ______
2. Compare the two approaches. Which one was easier? Explain. ______
3. Use Emma's method to solve the equation. $6x - 18 = 48$ ______
4. Use Evan's method to solve the equation. $6x - 18 = 48$ ______
5. Use Emma's method to solve the equation. $10x + 50 = 70$ ______
6. Use Evan's method to solve the equation. $10x + 50 = 70$ ______
7. When does dividing first work best? ______

SCAFFOLDED **Problem Solving**

Two students are both saving to buy the kayak shown at the right.

Kayak $600

35. One student starts with no money but earns \$9 per hour painting houses. Let x be the number of hours worked. Which equation represents the number of hours the student will have to work to buy the kayak? A
    (A) $9x = 600$ (B) $600 - x = 9$ (C) $600 - 9 = x$ (D) $600x = 9$
36. How many hours x of work will it take the student to save enough money to buy the kayak? 67 h
37. Another student starts with \$60 and rakes leaves for \$6 per hour. Write and solve an equation to find the number of hours this student will have to work to buy the kayak. $60 + 6x = 600$; 90 h
38. Which student will need to work more hours to save enough money for the kayak? How many more hours will be needed? the second student; 23 more hours
39. **Error Analysis** Explain the error in the student's work at the right. See left.

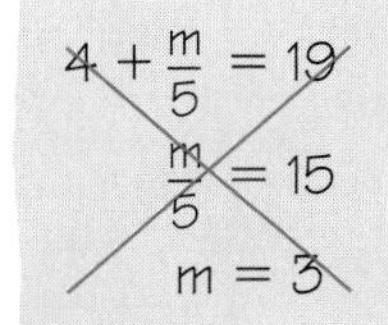

40. **Writing in Math** How is solving $16e - 32 = 176$ different from solving $16e = 176$? See left.

C Challenge

41. Multiply each side of the following equation by 10: $0.5x + 1.3 = 4.8$. Solve for x. How does this solution compare to the solution of the original equation? Explain why it is helpful to multiply by 10. See above left.

39. In the last step, the student should have multiplied each side by 5.
40. For the equation $16e - 32 = 176$, the first step is to add 32 to each side. Then you can divide each side by 16.
41. 7; multiplying each side by 10 removes all the decimal numbers.

Multiple Choice Practice and Mixed Review

For California Standards Tutorials, visit PHSchool.com. Web Code: axq-9045

AF 1.1 42. This year, 227 pets were adopted from a shelter. This is 35 fewer than twice the number of pets that were adopted last year. Which equation represents the number of pets adopted last year? A

(A) $n = \frac{227 + 35}{2}$ (B) $n = 2 \cdot 227 - 35$ (C) $n = \frac{227 - 35}{2}$ (D) $n = 2 \cdot 227 + 35$

AF 4.1 43. Solve $3.2 = 4t + 0.2$. A

(A) 0.75 (B) 0.85 (C) 1 (D) 4

AF 2.1 44. Simplify $4^5 - 3.5 \cdot 2$. C

(A) −3 (B) 13 (C) 1,017 (D) 2,041

GO for Help Lesson 2-6 **Simplify each expression.**

45. $5 - (-3)^2 \cdot 2$ −13
46. $(3 - 4)^3 + 11$ 10
47. $-4^4 + (-3)^2$ −247

 GO Online Lesson Quiz Visit: PHSchool.com Web Code: axa-0304

California Resources

Standards Mastery
- Standards Review Transparencies
- Standards Review and Practice Workbook
- Math Companion

Math Intervention
- Skills Review and Practice Workbook
- Math XL

GO for Help: Math Companion

3-5 Square Roots

Check Skills You'll Need

Do this in your **Math Companion.**

Vocabulary
- perfect square
- square root

Use your **Math Companion** *to build your vocabulary.*

California Content Standards

NS 1.2 Take positive rational numbers to whole number powers. ***Develop***

Alg1 2.0 Understand and use such operations as taking a root. ***Introduce, Develop***

What You'll Learn . . . and Why

You will learn to find square roots. You can use square roots to find the length of a square object or space, such as a garden, without measuring.

In the diagram below, 16 tiles form a square with 4 tiles on each side. A number such as 16 that is the square of an integer is a **perfect square.**

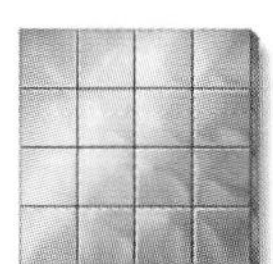

$4^2 = 16$

The inverse operation of squaring a number is finding its square root. The **square root** of a number is a number that when multiplied by itself is equal to the original number.

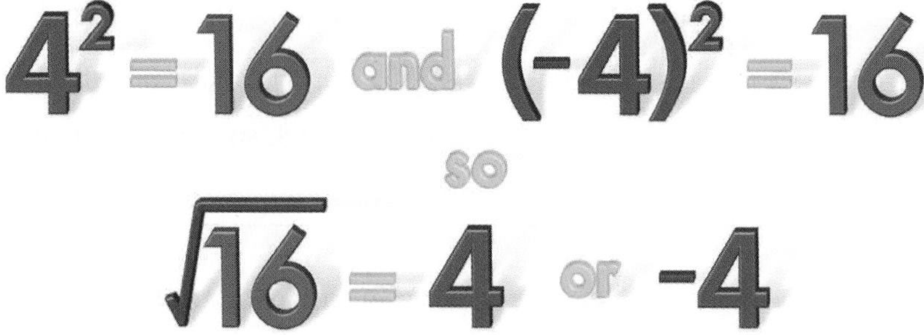

Since $4 \cdot 4 = 16$ and $-4 \cdot (-4) = 16$, the square roots of 16 are 4 and -4. Every positive number has two square roots. The two square roots of a number are opposites.

The symbol $\sqrt{}$ means the positive square root of a number. So $\sqrt{16}$ means the positive square root of 16, or 4, and $-\sqrt{16}$ means the opposite of the positive square root of 16, or -4.

Online active math

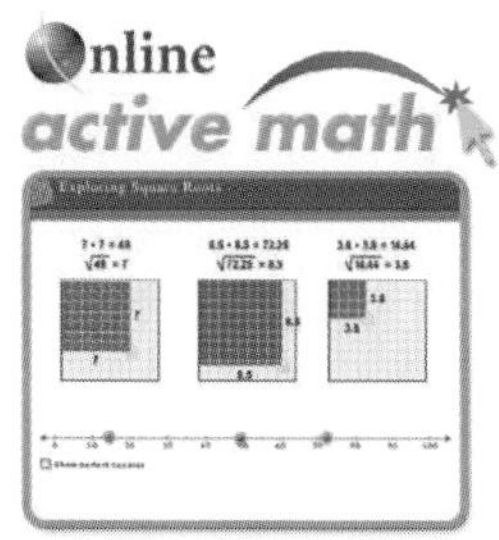

For: Square Root Activity
Use: Interactive Textbook, 3-5

Universal Access Solutions for All Learners

Special Needs L1
Using graph paper, have students draw squares with dimensions that are 1×1, 2×2, 3×3, 4×4, 5×5 and so on. Underneath each drawing, they should write the number represented (for example, 16) and its square root (4).

Below Level L2
Have students copy and continue this pattern to find the perfect squares from 1 to 100: 1, 4, 9, . . . , 100.

$1 \times 1 = 1$ $\sqrt{1} = 1$ $2 \times 2 = 4$ $\sqrt{4} = 2$
$3 \times 3 = 9$ $\sqrt{9} = 3$ $4 \times 4 = 16$ $\sqrt{16} = 4$

3-5

1. Plan

California Content Standards

NS 1.2 Take positive rational numbers to whole number powers. ***Develop***

Alg 1 2.0 Understand and use such operations as taking a root. ***Introduce, Develop***

California Math Background

The *square* of a number is the number multiplied by itself. A *square root* is a number that, when multiplied by itself, is equal to the given number. A *perfect square* is the square of a whole number. Square roots of perfect squares are also whole numbers.

The equation $x^2 = 9$ has two possible solutions: $x = 3$ and $x = -3$. However, there is only one solution to $x = \sqrt{9}$, $x = 3$. By convention, the radical sign, $\sqrt{}$, means the nonnegative square root only. *Nonnegative* describes all positive numbers and zero.

More Math Background: p. 84C

Lesson Planning and Resources

See p. 84E for a list of the resources that support this lesson.

PRESENTATION CD-ROM
CD, Online, or Transparencies

Bell Ringer Practice

Check Skills You'll Need
Use student page, transparency, or PowerPoint.
See Math Companion.

California Standards Review
Use transparency or PowerPoint.

2. Teach

Guided Instruction

Example 1
To help students recognize perfect squares, have them make a table showing the squares of integers from 2 through 25.

Error Prevention!

Students may confuse squaring a number with multiplying a number by 2. To clarify this, write 3^2 and $3 \cdot 2$ on the board. Elicit the fact that the first means $3 \cdot 3$, which is not the same as $3 \cdot 2$. Have students find the values for both expressions and write them on the board. $3^2 = 9$; $3 \cdot 2 = 6$

Additional Examples

1. Find the two square roots of 81. 9 and −9
2. A square tile has an area of 170 square inches. About how long is each side of the tile? about 13 inches

Closure

- *What is a square root? Give an example.* Sample: A number that, when multiplied by itself, is equal to the given number. $\sqrt{9}$ is 3.

Relate MATH YOU KNOW... ...*to* NEW IDEAS

EXAMPLE Finding Square Roots of Perfect Squares

Simplify $-8 \cdot (-8)$.

$-8 \cdot (-8) = 64$ ← same sign, positive product

1 Find the two square roots of 64.

$8 \cdot 8 = 64$
$-8 \cdot (-8) = 64$

Find each number that when multiplied by itself equals 64.

The square roots of 64 are 8 and −8.

CA Standards Check 1 *Go to your* **Math Companion** *for help.*

1. Find the square roots of each number.
   a. 36 6, −6 **b.** 49 7, −7

Problem Solving Tip
Knowing the first 12 perfect squares will help you make calculations more quickly.

The table below shows the first 12 perfect squares.

Perfect Squares

n	1	2	3	4	5	6	7	8	9	10	11	12
n^2	1	4	9	16	25	36	49	64	81	100	121	144

To estimate the square root of a number that is not a perfect square, use the square root of the nearest perfect square.

EXAMPLE Estimating Square Roots

2 **Guided Problem Solving** You need 60 ft^2 of land to plant a square garden. About how long will each side be?

Since 60 is not a perfect square, find the perfect square closest to 60.

$7^2 = 49$ and $8^2 = 64$, so $\sqrt{60}$ is between $\sqrt{49}$ and $\sqrt{64}$.

$\sqrt{49}$ (7) — $\sqrt{60}$ — $\sqrt{64}$ (8)

Since 60 is closer to 64 than to 49, $\sqrt{60}$ is closer to 8 than to 7.

Each side of the garden should be about 8 ft long.

CA Standards Check 2 *Go to your* **Math Companion** *for help.*

2. A square room has an area of 150 ft^2. About how long is each side of the room? about 12 ft

Homework prep is in your **Math Companion.**

Advanced Learners L4	**English Learners** EL
Solve each mystery digit problem. $\sqrt{AB} = B$ A = 2, B = 5 or A = 3, B = 6 $\sqrt{ZZY} = XY$ Z = 2, Y = 5, X = 1 or Z = 4, Y = 1, X = 2	Help students connect the words *square* and *square root* to the symbols ^{2} and $\sqrt{\ }$. Have them write several equations, such as $2^2 = 4$, $\sqrt{4} = 2$, $3^2 = 9$, $\sqrt{9} = 3$, $4^2 = 16$, and $\sqrt{16} = 4$. Then have them say each mathematical sentence aloud: "Two squared equals four; the square root of four equals two."

Standards Practice

GO for Help: MathXL

NS 1.2, Alg1 1.0

A Practice by Example

Find the square roots of each number.

Example 1 (page 108)

1. 25
   ■ · ■ = 25 5, −5

Guided Practice: This exercise has been started for you!

2. 1 1, −1
3. 81 9, −9
4. 9 3, −3
5. 4 2, −2
6. 16 4, −4
7. 100 10, −10
8. 400 20, −20
9. 121 11, −11
10. 169 13, −13
11. 144 12, −12
12. 10,000 100, −100
13. 625 25, −25

GO for Help

Estimate the value of each expression to the nearest integer.

Example 2 (page 108)

14. $\sqrt{3}$ 2
15. $\sqrt{15}$ 4
16. $-\sqrt{22}$ −5
17. $\sqrt{88}$ 9
18. $-\sqrt{54}$ −7
19. $\sqrt{105}$ 10
20. $-\sqrt{27}$ −5
21. $\sqrt{48}$ 7
22. $\sqrt{125}$ 11
23. $\sqrt{170}$ 13
24. $-\sqrt{390}$ −20
25. $\sqrt{10{,}050}$ 100

Homework Video Tutor

For: Examples 1–2
Visit: PHSchool.com
Web Code: axe-0305

26. The area of a square quilt is 40 ft^2. About how long is each side? about 6 ft
27. A square table has an area of 10 ft^2. Estimate the length of each side of the table to the nearest foot. about 3 ft

B Apply Your Skills

28. **Guided Problem Solving** A square patio has an area of 169 ft^2. What is the perimeter of the patio? 52 ft
    - **Make a Plan** Draw a picture. Find the side length of the square using square roots. Then find the perimeter.
    - **Check the Answer** How can you check to make sure you are using the correct side lengths for the patio?

29. A tile is shown at the right. The area of the larger square is 49 in.^{2}. Find the area of the smaller square. 9 in.^{2}

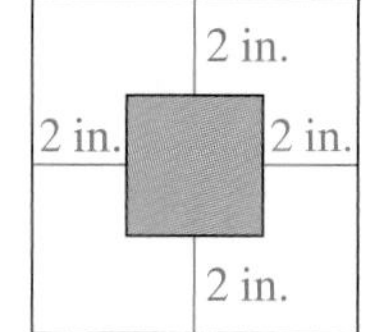

30. The area of a square boxing ring is 484 ft^2. What is the perimeter of the boxing ring? 88 ft

Simplify each expression for $x = 4$.

31. $3 + \sqrt{x}$ 5
32. $5\sqrt{x}$ 10
33. $4x + \sqrt{289}$ 33
34. $x - \sqrt{x}$ 2
35. $-2\sqrt{x} - 5$ −9
36. $x^2 + \sqrt{x}$ 18

37. **Writing in Math** Explain how you can approximate $\sqrt{30}$. See above left.

37. Answers may vary. Sample: $5^2 = 25$ and $6^2 = 36$. Since 30 is between 25 and 36, $\sqrt{30}$ is between 5 and 6. $\sqrt{30}$ is about 5.

GPS 38. The area of the square base of the Great Pyramid at Giza is 52,900 square meters. What is the length of each side of the base of the pyramid? 230 m

Great Pyramid at Giza

3. Practice

Assignment Guide

Check Your Understanding
See Math Companion.

Homework Exercises

A	Practice by Example	1–27
B	Apply Your Skills	28–50
C	Challenge	51
	California Multiple-Choice Practice	52–54
	Mixed Review	55–58

Homework Quick Check
To check students' understanding of key skills and concepts, go over Exercises 3, 14, 29, 31, 37, 38.

Universal Access Resources

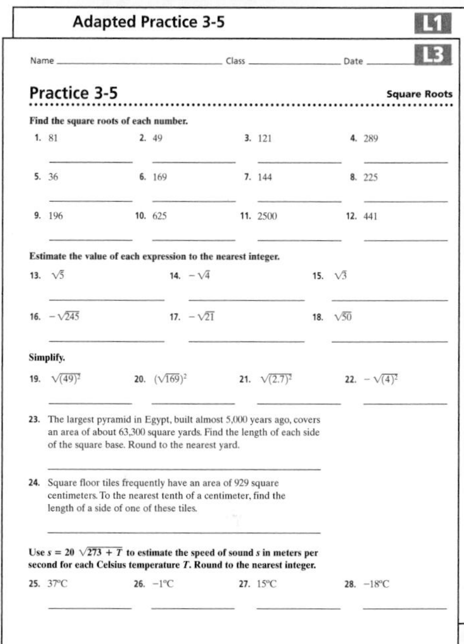

Adapted Practice 3-5 L1

Name ______ Class ______ Date ______ L3

Practice 3-5 — Square Roots

Find the square roots of each number.

1. 81 2. 49 3. 121 4. 289
5. 36 6. 169 7. 144 8. 225
9. 196 10. 625 11. 2500 12. 441

Estimate the value of each expression to the nearest integer.

13. $\sqrt{5}$ 14. $-\sqrt{4}$ 15. $\sqrt{3}$
16. $-\sqrt{245}$ 17. $-\sqrt{21}$ 18. $\sqrt{50}$

Simplify.

19. $\sqrt{(49)^2}$ 20. $(\sqrt{169})^2$ 21. $\sqrt{(2.7)^2}$ 22. $-\sqrt{(4)^2}$

23. The largest pyramid in Egypt, built almost 5,000 years ago, covers an area of about 63,300 square yards. Find the length of each side of the square base. Round to the nearest yard.

24. Square floor tiles frequently have an area of 929 square centimeters. To the nearest tenth of a centimeter, find the length of a side of one of these tiles.

Use $s = 20\sqrt{273 + T}$ to estimate the speed of sound s in meters per second for each Celsius temperature T. Round to the nearest integer.

25. 37°C 26. −1°C 27. 15°C 28. −18°C

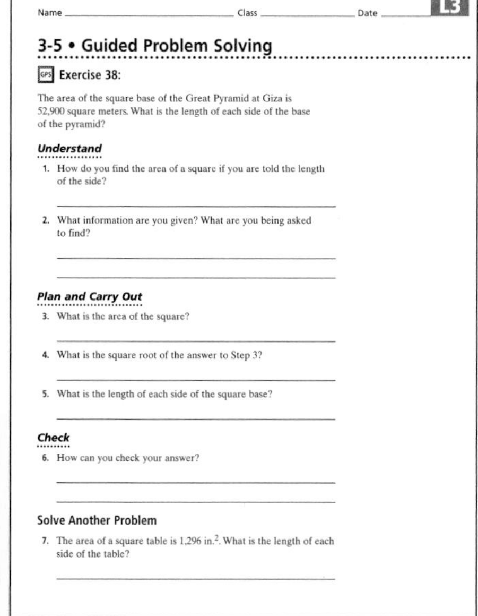

Name ______ Class ______ Date ______ L3

3-5 • Guided Problem Solving

GPS Exercise 38:

The area of the square base of the Great Pyramid at Giza is 52,900 square meters. What is the length of each side of the base of the pyramid?

Understand

1. How do you find the area of a square if you are told the length of the side?
2. What information are you given? What are you being asked to find?

Plan and Carry Out

3. What is the area of the square?
4. What is the square root of the answer to Step 3?
5. What is the length of each side of the square base?

Check

6. How can you check your answer?

Solve Another Problem

7. The area of a square table is 1,296 in.^{2}. What is the length of each side of the table?

4. Assess & Reteach

...PRESENTATION CD-ROM
CD, Online, or Transparencies

Lesson Quiz

Find each square root.

1. $\sqrt{49}$ 7
2. $\sqrt{81}$ 9
3. Find the two square roots of 400. 20 and −20
4. Estimate $\sqrt{34}$ to the nearest integer. 6
5. A square window has an area of 11 square feet. About how long is each side of the window? about 3 feet

---

Name ______ Class ______ Date ______ **L2**

Reteaching 3-5 — Square Roots

A *perfect square* is the square of a whole number. The number 81 is a perfect square because it is the square of 9.

You can also say that 9 is the *square root* of 81, or $\sqrt{81} = 9$. The inverse of squaring a number is finding its square root. The square root of a given number is a number that when multiplied by itself is equal to the original number.

Example 1

Find $\sqrt{9}$.

Since $3 \cdot 3 = 9$ and $-3 \cdot (-3) = 9$, the square roots of 9 are 3 and −3.

You can estimate square roots using perfect squares.

Example 2

Tell which two consecutive whole numbers $\sqrt{94}$ is between.

$81 < 94 < 100$ Find perfect squares close to 94.

$\sqrt{81} < \sqrt{94} < \sqrt{100}$ Write the square roots in order.

$9 < \sqrt{94} < 10$ Simplify.

$\sqrt{94}$ is between 9 and 10.

Determine if each number is a perfect square.

1. 24 ______ 2. 36 ______ 3. 49 ______ 4. 121 ______

Find the square roots of each number.

5. 9 ______ 6. 25 ______ 7. 4 ______
8. 100 ______ 9. 400 ______ 10. 2,500 ______
11. 576 ______ 12. 289 ______ 13. 2,401 ______
14. 900 ______ 15. 1,521 ______ 16. 324 ______

Estimate the value of each expression to the nearest integer.

17. $\sqrt{42}$ ______ 18. $\sqrt{88}$ ______ 19. $\sqrt{63}$ ______
20. $-\sqrt{75}$ ______ 21. $\sqrt{30}$ ______ 22. $-\sqrt{97}$ ______

Name ______ Class ______ Date ______ **L4**

Enrichment 3-5 — Square Roots

Building Bridges

A physics class was separated into groups. Each group was asked to build a bridge from balsa wood that would support a minimum of 600 pounds.

Edna, Kaya, and Chim used the expression $1000(99 - 70\sqrt{2})$ pounds to calculate the maximum safe load for the bridge they were building. They used 1.4 for $\sqrt{2}$ and decided that their bridge was a winner.

Complete the table below using different approximations for $\sqrt{2}$. Round your answer to the nearest thousandth.

	Approximation of $\sqrt{2}$	Maximum Safe Load of Bridge (in pounds)
1.	1.4	1,000.000
2.	1.41	
3.	1.414	
4.	1.4142	
5.	1.41421	
6.	1.414213	
7.	1.4142135	

8. Will the group's bridge support at least 600 pounds? Explain.
______

9. Why did the group's calculation appear to be accurate, but in actuality was not correct?
______

10. What do you notice about the calculated load as the approximation of $\sqrt{2}$ is rounded to a larger decimal value?
______

SCAFFOLDED
Problem Solving

40. 25; the square of the square root is the original number.
44. The square of the square root of a number is the original number.
46. The student squared 5 instead of finding the square root.
47. Yes; no; explanations may vary. Sample: Since $\sqrt{1} = 1$, $\sqrt{2}$ must be greater than 1. Since $\sqrt{4} = 2$, $\sqrt{2}$ must be less than 2.

---

39. Find $\sqrt{25}$. 5
40. Square your answer from Exercise 39. What do you notice? See left.
41. Simplify $(\sqrt{9})^2$. 9
42. Simplify $(\sqrt{16})^2$. 16
43. Simplify $(\sqrt{36})^2$. 36
44. **Patterns** Use inductive reasoning to make a conjecture about what happens when you square the square root of a number. See left.
45. Use your conjecture to find $(\sqrt{2})^2$. 2
46. **Error Analysis** Explain the student's error in the simplification at the right. See left.

$\sqrt{5} + 3 \cdot 2 = 25 + 3 \cdot 2$
$= 25 + 6$
$= 31$

47. **Number Sense** Is $\sqrt{2}$ greater than 1? Is $\sqrt{2}$ greater than 2? Explain. See left.
48. Aviators can calculate the distance to the horizon in miles by using the formula $d = 1.23\sqrt{h}$, where d represents the distance in miles you can see from h feet above ground. If a plane is at an altitude of 40,000 ft, what is the distance to the horizon? 246 mi
49. Find two perfect squares whose sum is 100. 36 and 64, or 0 and 100
50. **Reasoning** If $\sqrt{w}$ is an integer, how many values of w are between 20 and 120? 6

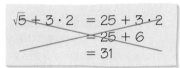

C Challenge

51. Explain how you know that the number 123,456,789,101,112 cannot be a perfect square. (*Hint:* What is the ones digit?)
No integer multiplied by itself ends in 2.

Multiple Choice Practice and Mixed Review

For California Standards Tutorials, visit PHSchool.com. Web Code: axq-9045

Alg1 2.0

52. The area of a square is 144 cm^2. How long is each side of the square? D
Ⓐ 72 cm Ⓒ 14 cm
Ⓑ 36 cm Ⓓ 12 cm

AF 2.1

53. Which of the following is equivalent to 6^4? B
Ⓐ $6 \cdot 4$ Ⓒ $4 \cdot 4 \cdot 4 \cdot 4 \cdot 4 \cdot 4$
Ⓑ $6 \cdot 6 \cdot 6 \cdot 6$ Ⓓ $\frac{4}{6}$

NS 1.2

54. Simplify 9^4. D
Ⓐ 13 Ⓑ 36 Ⓒ 162 Ⓓ 6,561

Lesson 3-3

Solve each equation.

55. $5x = 22.5$ 4.5 56. $90 = \frac{f}{8}$ 720 57. $\frac{r}{12} = 4$ 48 58. $13.2 = 6.6n$ 2

110  Visit: PHSchool.com Web Code: axa-0305

California Resources

Standards Mastery
- Standards Review Transparencies
- Standards Review and Practice Workbook
- Math Companion

Math Intervention
- Skills Review and Practice Workbook
- Math XL

Alternative Assessment

Each student in a pair writes a square root of a number that is not a perfect square. Then each partner decides which two whole numbers the other partner's value falls between.

Mathematical Reasoning

For Use With Lesson 3-4

Checking for Reasonableness

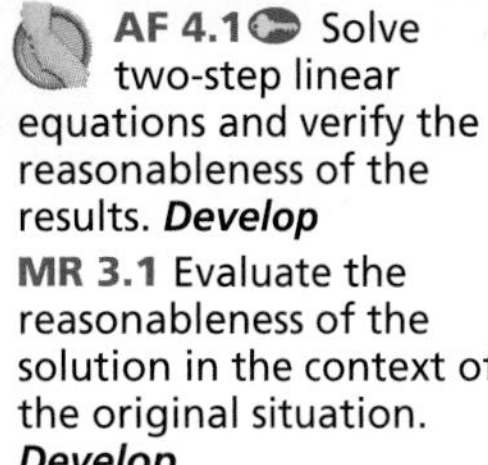

AF 4.1 Solve two-step linear equations and verify the reasonableness of the results. ***Develop***
MR 3.1 Evaluate the reasonableness of the solution in the context of the original situation. ***Develop***

When you solve real-world problems using equations, check whether your answer makes sense in the situation. Sometimes integers are the only reasonable solutions.

At a carnival, you pay \$2.75 for admission. You also pay \$1.50 for each ride. Suppose you have \$25. How many rides can you go on?

Use the equation $2.75 + 1.5r = 25$, where r is the number of rides.

$2.75 + 1.5r = 25$

$1.5r = 22.25$ ← **Subtract 2.75 from each side.**

$r = 14.8\overline{3}$ ← **Divide each side by 1.5.**

1. **Number Sense** Is $14.8\overline{3}$ a reasonable answer to the question? Explain. 1–3. See above right.
2. **Reasoning** Round $14.8\overline{3}$ to the nearest integer. Is this a reasonable answer to how many rides you can go on? Explain.
3. A bride and groom expect 123 people to attend their wedding. Each table seats 10 people. One table will be used for the 7 children who are attending. How many tables will they need at the wedding?

1. No; the number of rides must be a whole number.
2. 15; no, you have enough money for 14 rides, with some money left over.
3. 13 tables

Checkpoint Quiz 2

Lessons 3-4 through 3-5

Solve each equation.

1. $-7 + 2q = 4$ 5.5
2. $16 = -2v + 3.4$ −6.3
3. $-9 = 3b - 12$ 1
4. $\frac{m}{-2} + 7 = 21$ −28
5. $4.3 = 5a - 3.2$ 1.5
6. $32.3 = \frac{t}{2.5} + 19.5$ 32
7. You buy 6 roses for \$2.45 each, 12 carnations for \$.99 each, and 9 tulips. Your total cost is \$40.08. How much does each tulip cost? \$1.50

Find the square roots of each number.

8. 49 7, −7
9. 121 11, −11
10. 0 0
11. 64 8, −8
12. Estimate the value of $\sqrt{85}$ to the nearest integer. 9

111

Mathematical Reasoning

Checking for Reasonableness

Students learn to check their solutions for reasonableness based on what might make sense in a given problem.

Guided Instruction

Explain to students that solutions must make sense not only mathematically, but also in the context of a problem. There are some problems, like those that deal with discrete, real-world objects, for which the solutions must be integers. For instance, a question that asks for a number of cars as a solution requires an integer answer. Other problems might require solutions that are positive, but not necessarily integers (e.g., a question that asks for the amount of water in a pool). In Exercises 1 and 2, ask students what the solution $14.8\overline{3}$ represents. Then ask them whether rounding the solution up makes sense in the context. What restriction keeps them from rounding up? What should their final answer be?

Checkpoint Quiz

Use this Checkpoint Quiz to check students' understanding of the skills and concepts of Lessons 3-4 through 3-5.

All in One Resources

- Checkpoint Quiz 2

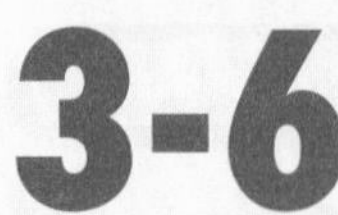

3-6

1. Plan

California Content Standards

NS 1.2 Take positive rational numbers to whole number powers. ***Develop***

MG 3.3 Know and understand the Pythagorean Theorem and use it to find the length of the missing side of a right triangle. ***Introduce, Develop***

Alg 1 2.0 Understand and use such operations as taking a root. ***Develop***

California Math Background

The Pythagorean Theorem states the relationship between the two shorter sides of a right triangle, called *legs*, and the longest side, or *hypotenuse*. The sum of the squares of the lengths of the legs (a and b) in any right triangle is equal to the square of the length of the hypotenuse (c): $a^2 + b^2 = c^2$. Given the lengths of two sides of a right triangle, you can always find the length of the third side.

More Math Background: p. 84C

Lesson Planning and Resources

See p. 84E for a list of the resources that support this lesson.

... PRESENTATION CD-ROM
CD, Online, or Transparencies

Bell Ringer Practice

Check Skills You'll Need
Use student page, transparency, or PowerPoint.
See Math Companion.

California Standards Review
Use transparency or PowerPoint.

3-6 The Pythagorean Theorem

Check Skills You'll Need

Do this in your **Math Companion.**

Vocabulary
- legs
- hypotenuse
- Pythagorean Theorem

Use your **Math Companion** *to build your vocabulary.*

California Content Standards

NS 1.2 Take positive rational numbers to whole number powers. ***Develop***
MG 3.3 Know and understand the Pythagorean theorem and use it to find the length of the missing side of a right triangle. ***Introduce, Develop***
Alg1 2.0 Understand and use such operations as taking a root. ***Develop***

What You'll Learn . . . and Why

You will learn to use the Pythagorean Theorem to find the length of the hypotenuse of a right triangle. You can use the Pythagorean Theorem to find the shortest distance from one corner of a rectangular park to the opposite corner.

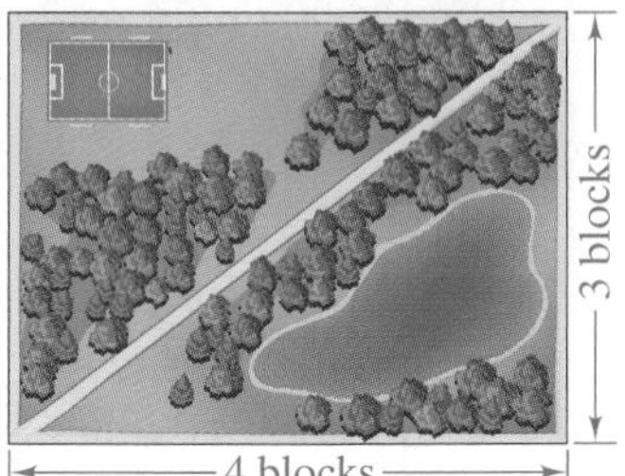

Recall that a right triangle has an angle measuring 90°. In a right triangle, the two shorter sides are called **legs.** The longest side, opposite the right angle, is called the **hypotenuse.**

The Pythagorean Theorem is an equation that shows the relationship between the legs and the hypotenuse of a right triangle.

Take Note **The Pythagorean Theorem**

In any right triangle, the sum of the squares of the lengths of the legs is equal to the square of the length of the hypotenuse.

Arithmetic	Algebra
Triangle with sides 5, 3, 4	Triangle with sides c, a, b
$3^2 + 4^2 = 5^2$	$a^2 + b^2 = c^2$

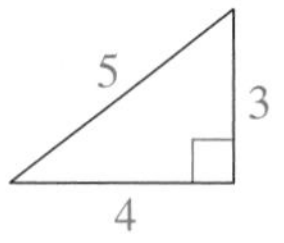

Online active math

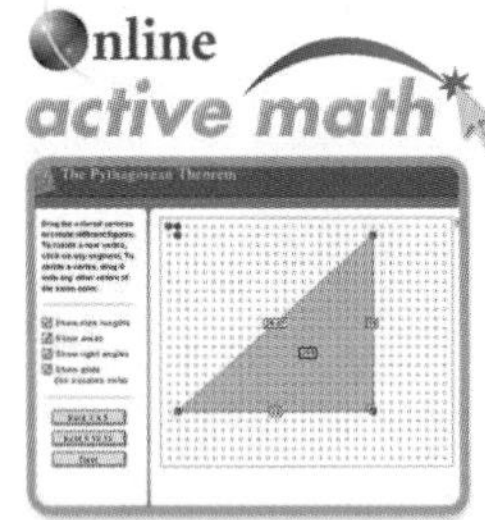

For: Pythagorean Theorem Activity
Use: Interactive Textbook, 3-6

Universal Access Solutions for All Learners

Special Needs L1	**Below Level** L2
Provide copies of Examples 1 and 2 for the students. Have them outline the triangles with the legs one color, and the hypotenuse a different color. They should label the legs a and b and label each hypotenuse c.	Draw several right triangles of different sizes and orientations. Help students identify the hypotenuse as the longest side and opposite the right angle. Have students label the sides a, b, and c, respectively.

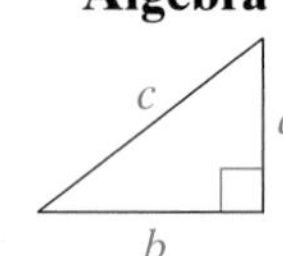

EXAMPLE Finding the Length of the Hypotenuse

1 Find the length of the hypotenuse of the triangle at the right.

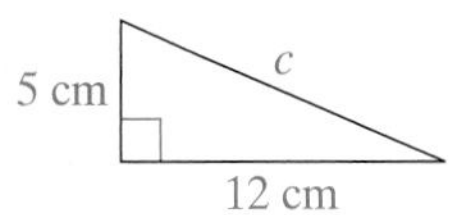

$$
\begin{aligned}
a^2 + b^2 &= c^2 && \leftarrow \text{Use the Pythagorean Theorem.}\\
5^2 + 12^2 &= c^2 && \leftarrow \text{Substitute 5 for } a \text{ and 12 for } b.\\
25 + 144 &= c^2 && \leftarrow \text{Simplify.}\\
169 &= c^2 && \leftarrow \text{Add.}\\
\sqrt{169} &= \sqrt{c^2} && \leftarrow \text{Find the positive square root of each side.}\\
13 &= c && \leftarrow \text{Simplify.}
\end{aligned}
$$

The length of the hypotenuse is 13 cm.

Math Foundations

Lengths are expressed as positive numbers. When you use the Pythagorean Theorem, find the positive square root.

CA Standards Check 1 *Go to your* **Math Companion** *for help.*

1. Find the length of the hypotenuse of each triangle.

a. 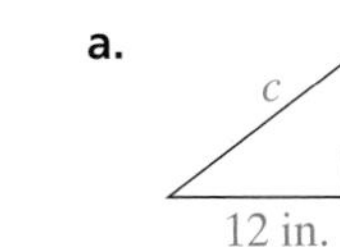 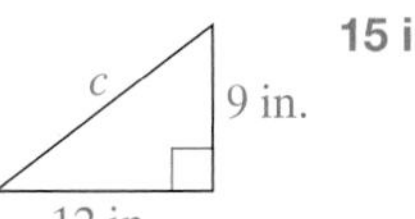

15 in.

b. 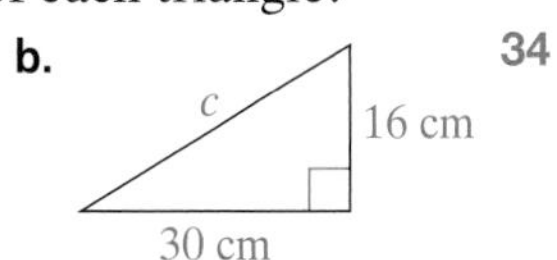

34 cm

EXAMPLE Using the Pythagorean Theorem

2 **Guided Problem Solving** A rectangular park is 8 blocks long and 12 blocks wide. Find the distance from one corner to the opposite corner.

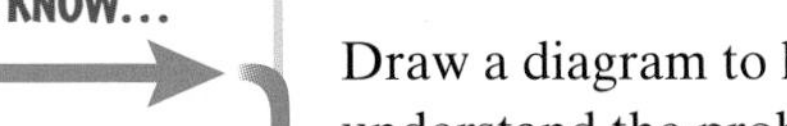

Draw a diagram to help you understand the problem.

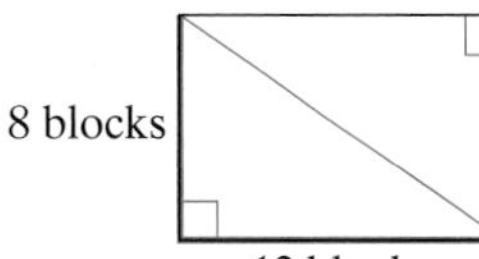

Find the length of the hypotenuse of the red right triangle.

...to ALGEBRA

$$
\begin{aligned}
a^2 + b^2 &= c^2 && \leftarrow \text{Use the Pythagorean Theorem.}\\
8^2 + 12^2 &= c^2 && \leftarrow \text{Substitute 8 for } a \text{ and 12 for } b.\\
208 &= c^2 && \leftarrow \text{Square 8 and 12. Then add.}\\
\sqrt{208} &= \sqrt{c^2} && \leftarrow \text{Find the positive square root of each side.}\\
\sqrt{208} &= c && \leftarrow \text{Simplify.}
\end{aligned}
$$

The distance is $\sqrt{208}$ or about 14.4 blocks.

Problem Solving Tip

If your answer is not a perfect square, you can leave the answer as a square root.

CA Standards Check 2 *Go to your* **Math Companion** *for help.*

2. Find the length of the hypotenuse of a triangle with legs that have lengths of 5 in. and 10 in. $\sqrt{125}$ in.

Homework prep is in your **Math Companion.**

2. Teach

Guided Instruction

Error Prevention!

Students may sometimes forget to find the square root of c^2. Point out that the hypotenuse is always the longest side and that $a + b$ must always be greater than c.

PRESENTATION CD-ROM
CD, Online, or Transparencies

Additional Examples

1 Find the hypotenuse of a right triangle whose legs are 6 ft and 8 ft. 10 ft

2 A wheelchair ramp leads into an apartment building doorway that is 5 feet above the ground. The horizontal distance from the entrance to the end of the ramp is 16 feet. What is the length in feet of the ramp? 16.8 ft

Closure

- *What does the Pythagorean Theorem state?* Sample: In a right triangle, the longest side squared equals the sum of the squares of the other two sides.
- *If you know the length of two legs of a right triangle, how would you find the hypotenuse?* Sample: Find the sum of the squares of the side lengths, and then take the square root.

Advanced Learners L4	**English Learners** EL
Have students explain whether the equation $(a + b)^2 = c^2$ is the same as $a^2 + b^2 = c^2$. Sample: No; exponents cannot be distributed over addition.	The words *Pythagorean, theorem,* and *hypotenuse* are difficult to pronounce for many English learners. Provide opportunities for students to practice saying them in a safe environment, with you or a partner, before requiring them to say the words in front of the whole class.

3. Practice

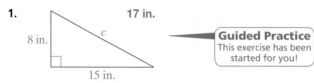

Assignment Guide

Check Your Understanding
See Math Companion.

Homework Exercises

A Practice by Example	1–14
B Apply Your Skills	15–26
C Challenge	27
California Multiple-Choice Practice	28–29
Mixed Review	30–33

Homework Quick Check
To check students' understanding of key skills and concepts, go over Exercises 4, 8, 21, 25, 26.

Universal Access Resources

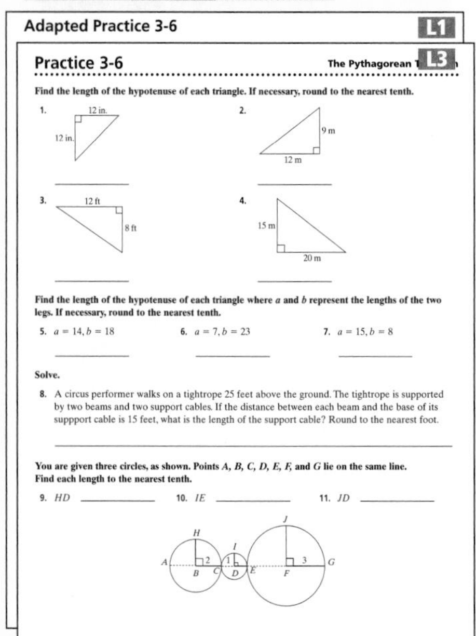

Adapted Practice 3-6 L1

Practice 3-6 The Pythagorean T[heorem] L3

Find the length of the hypotenuse of each triangle. If necessary, round to the nearest tenth.

1. 12 in., 12 in. ______
2. 9 m, 12 m ______
3. 12 ft, 8 ft ______
4. 15 m, 20 m ______

Find the length of the hypotenuse of each triangle where a and b represent the lengths of the two legs. If necessary, round to the nearest tenth.

5. $a = 14, b = 18$ ______
6. $a = 7, b = 23$ ______
7. $a = 15, b = 8$ ______

Solve.

8. A circus performer walks on a tightrope 25 feet above the ground. The tightrope is supported by two beams and two support cables. If the distance between each beam and the base of its suppport cable is 15 feet, what is the length of the support cable? Round to the nearest foot. ______

You are given three circles, as shown. Points A, B, C, D, E, F, and G lie on the same line. Find each length to the nearest tenth.

9. HD ______
10. IE ______
11. JD ______

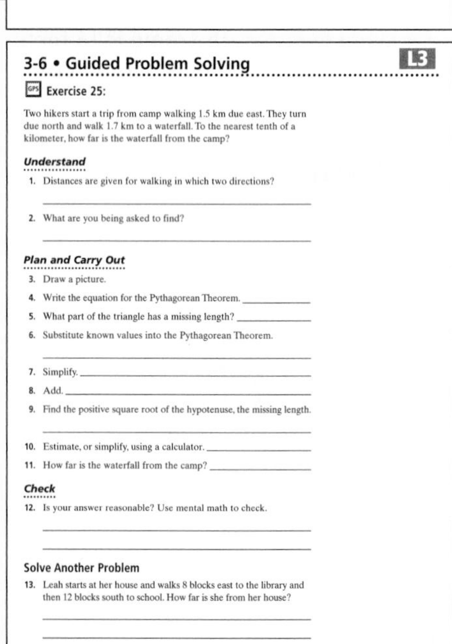

3-6 • Guided Problem Solving L3

GPS Exercise 25:

Two hikers start a trip from camp walking 1.5 km due east. They turn due north and walk 1.7 km to a waterfall. To the nearest tenth of a kilometer, how far is the waterfall from the camp?

Understand

1. Distances are given for walking in which two directions? ______
2. What are you being asked to find? ______

Plan and Carry Out

3. Draw a picture.
4. Write the equation for the Pythagorean Theorem. ______
5. What part of the triangle has a missing length? ______
6. Substitute known values into the Pythagorean Theorem. ______
7. Simplify. ______
8. Add. ______
9. Find the positive square root of the hypotenuse, the missing length. ______
10. Estimate, or simplify, using a calculator. ______
11. How far is the waterfall from the camp? ______

Check

12. Is your answer reasonable? Use mental math to check. ______

Solve Another Problem

13. Leah starts at her house and walks 8 blocks east to the library and then 12 blocks south to school. How far is she from her house? ______

Standards Practice

GO for Help: MathXL

NS 1.2, MG 3.3, Alg1 2.0

A Practice by Example

Example 1 (page 113)

GO for Help

Find the length of the hypotenuse of each triangle.

1. 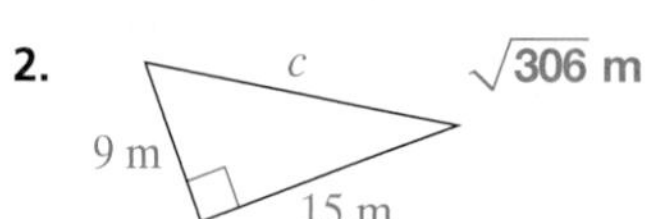

17 in.

Guided Practice: This exercise has been started for you!

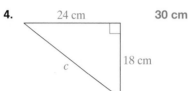

$8^2 + 15^2 = c^2$

2. c, 9 m, 15 m $\sqrt{306}$ m

3. 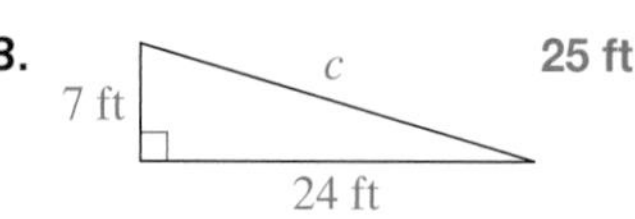

25 ft

4. 24 cm, 18 cm, c 30 cm

5. 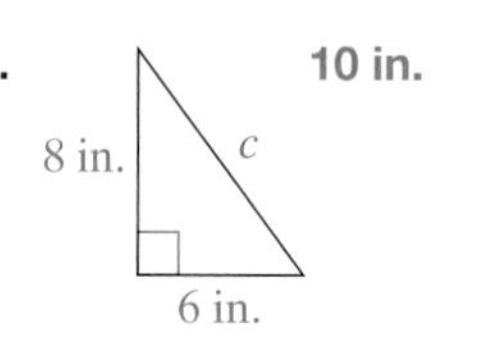

10 in.

6. 4.8 mi, 1.4 mi, c 5 mi

7. 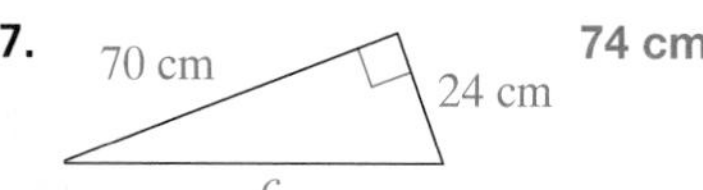

74 cm

Homework Video Tutor

For: Examples 1–2
Visit: PHSchool.com
Web Code: axe-0306

Example 2 (page 113)

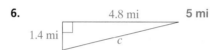

Find the length of the hypotenuse of each right triangle where a and b represent the lengths of the two legs.

8. $a = 21, b = 72$ 75
9. $a = 0.3, b = 0.4$ 0.5
10. $a = 1.2, b = 0.5$ 1.3
11. $a = 150, b = 200$ 250
12. $a = 20, b = 48$ 52
13. $a = 72, b = 54$ 90

14. A landscaper hammers a stake 9 ft from the base of a tree. A wire goes from the stake to a spot 40 ft up the trunk. How long must the wire be? 41 ft

40 ft

9 ft

B Apply Your Skills

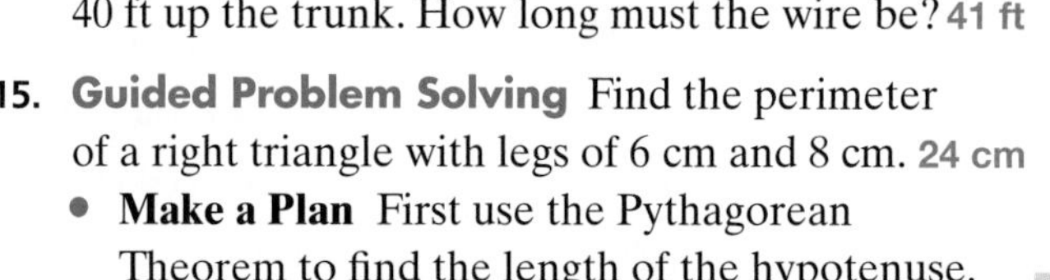

15. **Guided Problem Solving** Find the perimeter of a right triangle with legs of 6 cm and 8 cm. 24 cm
    - **Make a Plan** First use the Pythagorean Theorem to find the length of the hypotenuse. Then find the perimeter of the triangle.
    - **Carry Out the Plan** The hypotenuse is ■ cm long. The perimeter of the triangle is ■ cm.

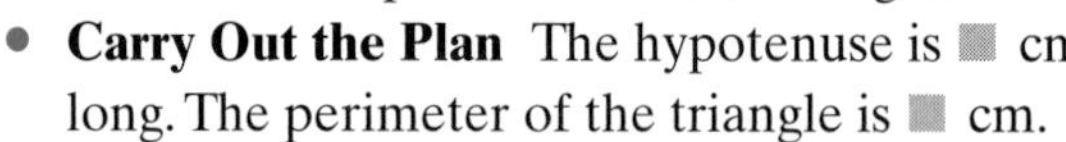

16. **Algebra** Use the Pythagorean Theorem. Write an equation to express the relationship between the legs and the hypotenuse of the triangle.

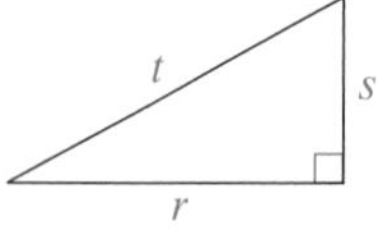

$r^2 + s^2 = t^2$

SCAFFOLDED
Problem Solving

20. Answers may vary. Sample: 8 in. by 26 in.

26. Answers may vary. Sample: Draw a line from B that is perpendicular to the 200-ft side. Then draw segment AB to form a right triangle with legs 100 ft and 200 ft − 50 ft, or 150 ft. Using the Pythagorean Theorem, the length of segment AB is $\sqrt{32{,}500}$, or about 180 ft long.

27. 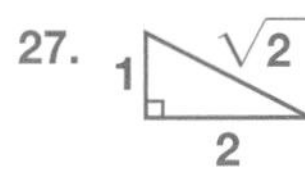

A television is measured by the diagonal dimension of its screen.

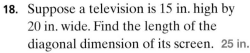

17. What is the diagonal dimension of the television at the right? 37 in.

18. Suppose a television is 15 in. high by 20 in. wide. Find the length of the diagonal dimension of its screen. 25 in.

19. A television screen is 16 in. high and 22 in. wide. What is its diagonal dimension to the nearest integer? 27 in.

20. Find the dimensions of a television screen that has the same diagonal measure as in Exercise 19, but a different height and width. See left.

Find the length of the hypotenuse of each right triangle where the two legs both have the given length. Round to the nearest tenth.

21. 5 cm 7.1 cm 22. 2 cm 2.8 cm 23. 10 in. 14.1 in. 24. 12 m 17.0 m

GPS 25. Two hikers start a trip from camp walking 1.5 km due east. They turn due north and walk 1.7 km to a waterfall. To the nearest tenth of a kilometer, how far is the waterfall from the camp? 2.3 km

26. **Writing in Math** Explain how you would find the distance AB across the lake at the right. Then find AB to the nearest foot. See left.

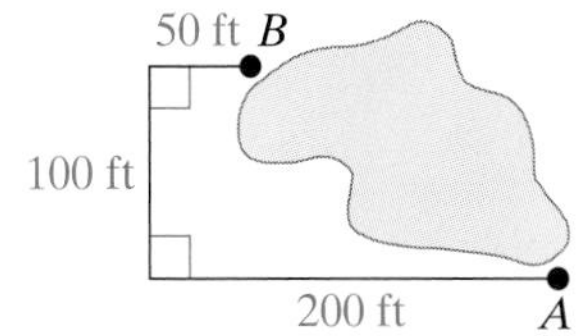

Challenge

27. Draw a triangle with a hypotenuse $\sqrt{2}$ in. long. See left.

Multiple Choice Practice and Mixed Review

For California Standards Tutorials, visit PHSchool.com. Web Code: axq-9045

MG 3.3

28. A carpenter is attaching a brace to the back of the frame shown at the right. What is the length, in inches, of the brace? B

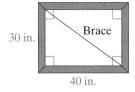

Ⓐ 70 in. Ⓒ $\sqrt{70}$ in.
Ⓑ 50 in. Ⓓ $\sqrt{50}$ in.

30 in. | Brace | 40 in.

AF 4.1, MR 2.1

29. Which number is a reasonable solution to the equation $3.2x + 15.9 = 43.2$? D

Ⓐ 59 Ⓒ 18
Ⓑ 27 Ⓓ 9

for Help Lesson 3-5

Find the square roots of each number.

30. 225 15, −15 31. 64 8, −8 32. 4 2, −2 33. 0.25 0.5, −0.5

Online Lesson Quiz Visit: PHSchool.com Web Code: axa-0306

California Resources

Standards Mastery
- Standards Review Transparencies
- Standards Review and Practice Workbook
- Math Companion

Math Intervention
- Skills Review and Practice Workbook
- Math XL

4. Assess & Reteach

PRESENTATION CD-ROM
CD, Online, or Transparencies

Lesson Quiz

Find the missing side length of each right triangle where a and b represent the length of the legs.

1. $a = ■$, $b = 24$, $c = 30$ 18
2. $a = 8$, $b = ■$, $c = 10$ 6
3. $a = 5$, $b = 3$, $c = ■$ 5.8

Alternative Assessment

Students in pairs take turns naming two of three lengths in a right triangle. The partner finds the missing length. Together they verify the results by showing that $a^2 + b^2 = c^2$.

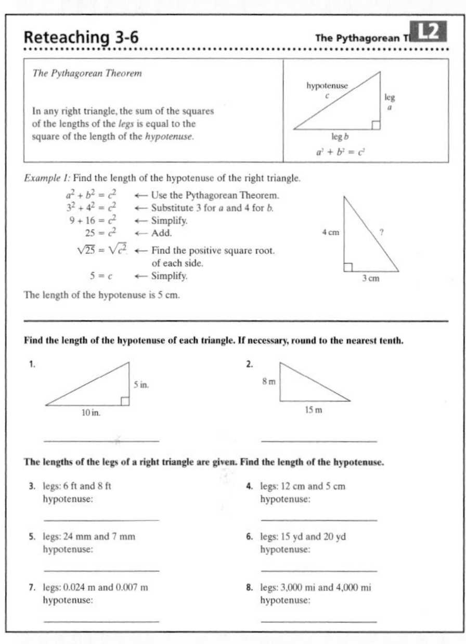

Reteaching 3-6 The Pythagorean T L2

The Pythagorean Theorem

In any right triangle, the sum of the squares of the lengths of the *legs* is equal to the square of the length of the *hypotenuse*.

Example 1: Find the length of the hypotenuse of the right triangle.

$a^2 + b^2 = c^2$ ← Use the Pythagorean Theorem.
$3^2 + 4^2 = c^2$ ← Substitute 3 for a and 4 for b.
$9 + 16 = c^2$ ← Simplify.
$25 = c^2$ ← Add.
$\sqrt{25} = \sqrt{c^2}$ ← Find the positive square root. of each side.
$5 = c$ ← Simplify.

The length of the hypotenuse is 5 cm.

Find the length of the hypotenuse of each triangle. If necessary, round to the nearest tenth.

1.

2.

The lengths of the legs of a right triangle are given. Find the length of the hypotenuse.

3. legs: 6 ft and 8 ft
hypotenuse: ______

4. legs: 12 cm and 5 cm
hypotenuse: ______

5. legs: 24 mm and 7 mm
hypotenuse: ______

6. legs: 15 yd and 20 yd
hypotenuse: ______

7. legs: 0.024 m and 0.007 m
hypotenuse: ______

8. legs: 3,000 mi and 4,000 mi
hypotenuse: ______

Enrichment 3-6 The Pythagorean T L4

Patterns in Geometry

If the three sides of a right triangle are integers, then the measures of those sides are called *Pythagorean Triples*. A common Pythagorean Triple is 3-4-5. You can use the Pythagorean Theorem to verify that the Pythagorean Triple is correct: $3^2 + 4^2 = 5^2$.

Use the Pythagorean Theorem to see if the following numbers are Pythagorean Triples. Write *yes* or *no*.

	Pythagorean Theorem	Pythagorean Triple
1. 7-24-25		
2. 20-21-29		
3. 9-25-27		
4. 8-15-17		

You can make other Pythagorean Triples by multiplying each number of a triple by the same integer. For example, 6-8-10 is a Pythagorean Triple because each number in the triple 3-4-5 has been multiplied by 2.

Write two other related Pythagorean Triples.

5. 3-4-5 ______
6. 20-21-29 ______
7. 7-24-25 ______
8. 8-15-17 ______

In a Pythagorean Triple, a, b, and c are also related in this way:

$a = m^2 - n^2$, $b = 2mn$, and $c = m^2 + n^2$

where m and n are relatively prime integers (their only common factor is 1) and $m > n$.

Complete this table of Pythagorean Triples.

	m	n	$a = m^2 - n^2$	$b = 2mn$	$c = m^2 + n^2$
9.	3	2			
10.	6	5			
11.	10	7			

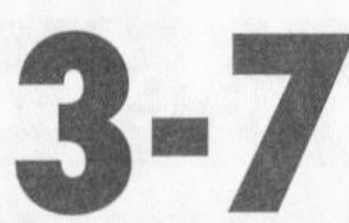

3-7

1. Plan

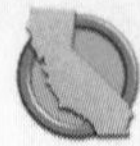

California Content Standards

NS 1.2 Take positive rational numbers to whole number powers. ***Develop***

MG 3.3 Understand the Pythagorean Theorem and its converse and use it to find the length of the missing side of a right triangle. ***Develop, Master***

Alg 1 2.0 Understand and use such operations as taking a root. ***Develop***

California Math Background

The Pythagorean Theorem gives the length of the hypotenuse for given lengths of legs in a right triangle, $a^2 + b^2 = c^2$. If you know the length of the hypotenuse and only one leg, you can find the other leg using this formula. A reasonable answer for the length of a leg will always be less than the hypotenuse.

More Math Background: p. 84C

Lesson Planning and Resources

See p. 84E for a list of the resources that support this lesson.

PRESENTATION CD-ROM
CD, Online, or Transparencies

Bell Ringer Practice

Check Skills You'll Need
Use student page, transparency, or PowerPoint.
See Math Companion.

California Standards Review
Use transparency or PowerPoint.

GO for Help: Math Companion

3-7 Using the Pythagorean Theorem

Check Skills You'll Need

Do this in your **Math Companion.**

Vocabulary

- converse of the Pythagorean Theorem

Use your **Math Companion** *to build your vocabulary.*

California Content Standards

NS 1.2 Take positive rational numbers to whole number powers. ***Develop***
MG 3.3 Understand the Pythagorean theorem and its converse and use it to find the length of the missing side of a right triangle. ***Develop, Master***
Alg1 2.0 Understand and use such operations as taking a root. ***Develop***

What You'll Learn . . . and Why

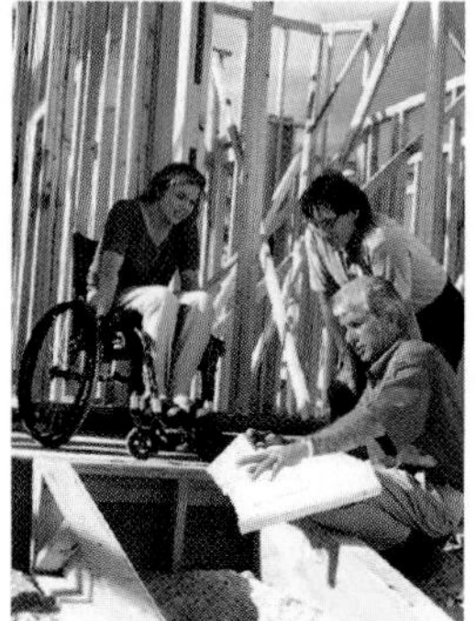

You will learn to find the length of the legs of a right triangle. You will also learn the converse of the Pythagorean Theorem. You can use the Pythagorean Theorem to find the height of objects such as ramps.

When you know the length of one leg and the hypotenuse of a right triangle, you can use the Pythagorean Theorem to find the length of the other leg.

EXAMPLE Finding the Length of a Leg

1 **Guided Problem Solving** A ramp forms a right triangle with the ground as shown below. How high is the top of the ramp?

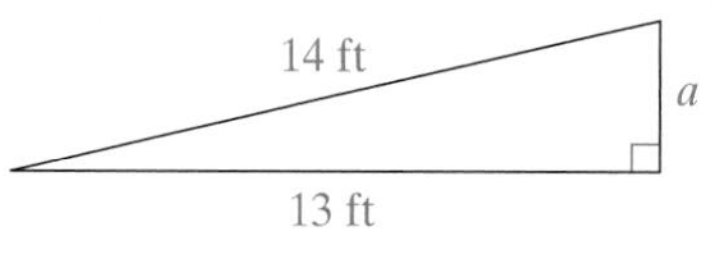

$a^2 + b^2 = c^2$ ← **Use the Pythagorean Theorem.**

$a^2 + 13^2 = 14^2$ ← **Substitute 13 for *b* and 14 for *c*.**

$a^2 + 169 = 196$ ← **Simplify.**

$a^2 = 27$ ← **Subtraction Property of Equality**

$\sqrt{a^2} = \sqrt{27}$ ← **Find the positive square root of each side.**

$a = \sqrt{27}$ ← **Simplify.**

The top of the ramp is $\sqrt{27}$ ft high. This is about 5.2 ft.

CA Standards Check 1 *Go to your* **Math Companion** *for help.*

1. An 11-ft ramp leading into a truck forms a right triangle with the ground. The base of the ramp is 10 ft from the truck. How high is the top of the ramp? **$\sqrt{21}$ ft or about 4.6 ft**

Universal Access Solutions for All Learners

Special Needs L1	**Below Level** L2
Students label the sides of each triangle *a*, *b*, and *c* so that they know which length corresponds to which variable. They may highlight or circle the leg whose length they need to find.	Students draw triangles and assign reasonable lengths for the hypotenuse and one leg. Then they set up the Pythagorean Theorem for each triangle and draw arrows from values in the equation to corresponding elements of their diagrams.

The converse of the Pythagorean Theorem is a property that allows you to use the Pythagorean Theorem to determine whether a triangle is a right triangle.

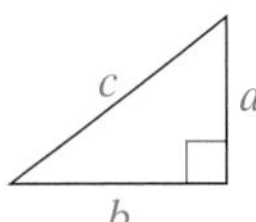

Take Note **Converse of the Pythagorean Theorem**

If a triangle has sides of length a, b, and c, and $a^2 + b^2 = c^2$, then the triangle is a right triangle with hypotenuse of length c.

To use the converse of the Pythagorean Theorem, substitute the lengths of the sides of a triangle into the equation $a^2 + b^2 = c^2$. If the equation is true, the triangle is a right triangle. If the equation is not true, the triangle is not a right triangle.

EXAMPLE Identifying a Right Triangle

Relate **MATH YOU KNOW...**

1 Find the length of the hypotenuse of a right triangle with legs of 8 in. and 15 in.

$a^2 + b^2 = c^2$ ← **Use the Pythagorean Theorem.**

$8^2 + 15^2 = c^2$ ← **Substitute 8 for *a* and 15 for *b*.**

$64 + 225 = c^2$ ← **Square 8 and 15.**

$289 = c^2$ ← **Simplify.**

$\sqrt{289} = \sqrt{c^2}$ ← **Find the positive square root of each side.**

$17 = c$ ← **Simplify.**

The hypotenuse is 17 in. long.

... *to* ALGEBRA

2 Is a triangle with sides 7 cm, 25 cm, and 24 cm a right triangle? Explain.

$a^2 + b^2 = c^2$ ← **Use the Pythagorean Theorem.**

$7^2 + 24^2 \stackrel{?}{=} 25^2$ ← **The longest side, 25 cm, is the hypotenuse. Substitute 7 for a, 24 for *b*, and 25 for c.**

$49 + 576 \stackrel{?}{=} 625$ ← **Square 7, 24, and 25.**

$625 = 625$ ✔ ← **Simplify.**

The equation is true, so the triangle is a right triangle.

CA Standards Check 2 *Go to your* **Math Companion** *for help.*

2. Determine whether the given lengths can be sides of a right triangle. Explain.

a. 15 yd, 35 yd, 40 yd
No; $15^2 + 35^2 \neq 40^2$.

b. 7 m, 15 m, 6 m
No; $7^2 + 6^2 \neq 15^2$.

Check Your Understanding *Homework prep is in your* **Math Companion.**

2. Teach

Guided Instruction

Alternative Method
Some students might prefer to see the value they want to find on the left side of the equals sign. To find a leg, rewrite the Pythagorean Theorem before substituting values: $a^2 = c^2 - b^2$.

PRESENTATION CD-ROM
CD, Online, or Transparencies

Additional Examples

1 The bottom of a 10-ft ladder is 2.5 ft from the side of a wall. How far, to the nearest tenth of a foot, is the top of the ladder from the ground? 9.7 ft

2 Is a triangle with sides 9 cm, 40 cm, and 41 cm a right triangle? Explain. Yes; the equation $9^2 + 40^2 = 41^2$ is true, so the triangle is a right triangle.

Closure

- *If you know the lengths of the hypotenuse and one leg of a right triangle, how would you find the other leg?* Sample: Subtract the square of the length of the hypotenuse from the square of the length of the leg and then take the square root.
- When you find the value of a leg given the hypotenuse and another leg, explain how you can check whether your answer is reasonable. Sample: The hypotenuse is the longest side, so the length of the leg should be less than the length of the hypotenuse.

Advanced Learners L4	**English Learners** EL
An isosceles right triangle has a hypotenuse of length 7. Use the Pythagorean Theorem to find the approximate lengths of its legs. both legs have length about 5	The exercises for this lesson require extensive reading, writing, and speaking skills. Students work in pairs on the exercises so that they can talk about what they understand and ask questions about what they do not understand.

3. Practice

Assignment Guide

Check Your Understanding
See Math Companion.

Homework Exercises
A Practice by Example 1–12
B Apply Your Skills 13–25
C Challenge 26
California Multiple-Choice Practice 27–29
Mixed Review 30–33

Homework Quick Check
To check students' understanding of key skills and concepts, go over Exercises 5, 6, 7, 16, 17, 21.

Universal Access Resources

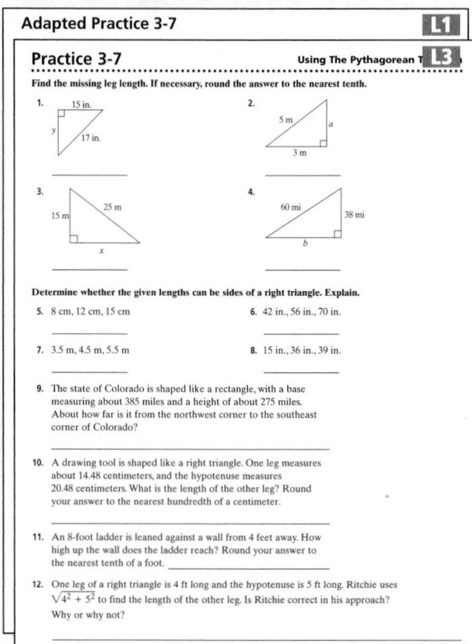
Adapted Practice 3-7 L1

Practice 3-7 Using The Pythagorean Theorem L3

Find the missing leg length. If necessary, round the answer to the nearest tenth.

1. (15 in., y, 17 in.)
2. (5 m, a, 3 m)
3. (15 m, 25 m, x)
4. (60 mi, 38 mi, b)

Determine whether the given lengths can be sides of a right triangle. Explain.

5. 8 cm, 12 cm, 15 cm
6. 42 in., 56 in., 70 in.
7. 3.5 m, 4.5 m, 5.5 m
8. 15 in., 36 in., 39 in.
9. The state of Colorado is shaped like a rectangle, with a base measuring about 385 miles and a height of about 275 miles. About how far is it from the northwest corner to the southeast corner of Colorado?
10. A drawing tool is shaped like a right triangle. One leg measures about 14.48 centimeters, and the hypotenuse measures 20.48 centimeters. What is the length of the other leg? Round your answer to the nearest hundredth of a centimeter.
11. An 8-foot ladder is leaned against a wall from 4 feet away. How high up the wall does the ladder reach? Round your answer to the nearest tenth of a foot.
12. One leg of a right triangle is 4 ft long and the hypotenuse is 5 ft long. Ritchie uses $\sqrt{4^2 + 5^2}$ to find the length of the other leg. Is Ritchie correct in his approach? Why or why not?

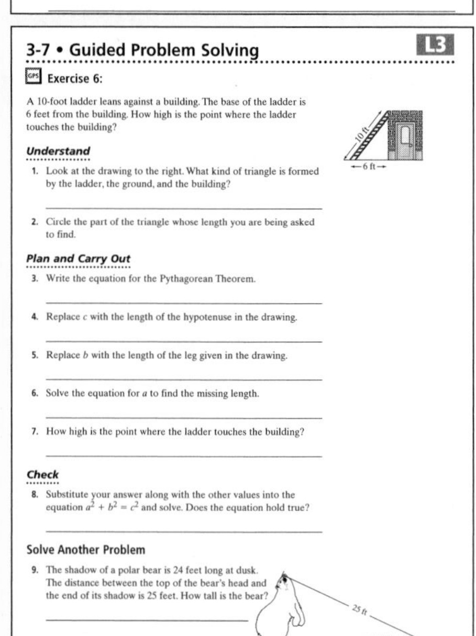
3-7 • Guided Problem Solving L3

GPS Exercise 6:

A 10-foot ladder leans against a building. The base of the ladder is 6 feet from the building. How high is the point where the ladder touches the building?

Understand

1. Look at the drawing to the right. What kind of triangle is formed by the ladder, the ground, and the building?
2. Circle the part of the triangle whose length you are being asked to find.

Plan and Carry Out

3. Write the equation for the Pythagorean Theorem.
4. Replace c with the length of the hypotenuse in the drawing.
5. Replace b with the length of the leg given in the drawing.
6. Solve the equation for a to find the missing length.
7. How high is the point where the ladder touches the building?

Check

8. Substitute your answer along with the other values into the equation $a^2 + b^2 = c^2$ and solve. Does the equation hold true?

Solve Another Problem

9. The shadow of a polar bear is 24 feet long at dusk. The distance between the top of the bear's head and the end of its shadow is 25 feet. How tall is the bear?

Standards Practice

GO for Help: MathXL

NS 1.2, MG 3.3, Alg1 2.0

A Practice by Example

Example 1 (page 116)

GO for Help

Find the missing leg length.

1. 12 ft

$a^2 + 16^2 = 20^2$

2. 27 m

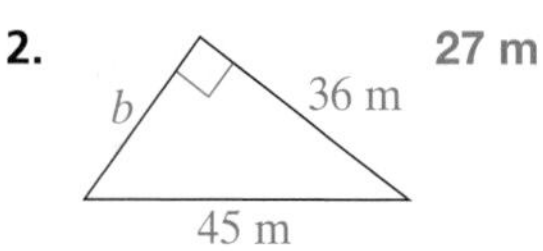

3. 24 in. (10 in., 26 in., a)

Homework Video Tutor

For: Examples 1–2
Visit: PHSchool.com
Web Code: axe-0307

4. 15 yd

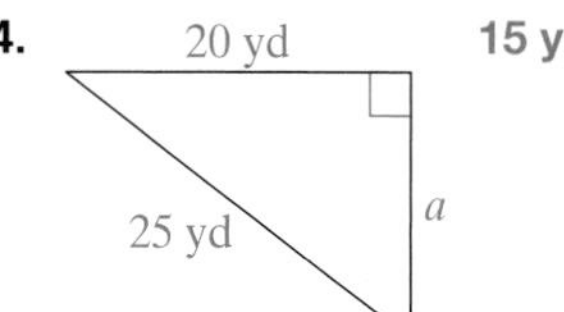

5. 12 cm (9 cm, 15 cm, b)

GPS 6. A 10-foot ladder leans against a building. The base of the ladder is 6 feet from the building. How high is the point where the ladder touches the building? 8 ft

Example 2 (page 117)

Determine whether the given lengths can be sides of a right triangle. Explain.

7. 1.5 in., 2.5 in., 3.5 in. No, $1.5^2 + 2.5^2 \neq 3.5^2$.
8. 6 cm, 10 cm, 8 cm Yes, $6^2 + 8^2 = 10^2$.
9. 39 m, 36 m, 15 m Yes, $36^2 + 15^2 = 39^2$.
10. 63 km, 16 km, 65 km Yes, $16^2 + 63^2 = 65^2$.
11. 75 ft, 100 ft, 125 ft Yes, $75^2 + 100^2 = 125^2$.
12. 96 mi, 40 mi, 105 mi No, $96^2 + 40^2 \neq 105^2$.

B Apply Your Skills

13. **Guided Problem Solving** A computer screen has a diagonal length of 17 in. and a height of 9 in. What is the area of the screen? about 130 in.^{2}
- What is the width of the computer screen?
- What is the formula for the area of a rectangle?

14. A large tent has an adjustable center pole. A rope 15 ft long connects the top of the pole to a peg 12 ft from the bottom of the pole. What is the height of the pole? 9 ft

15. **Number Sense** How do you know a triangle with side lengths $\sqrt{1}$, $\sqrt{2}$, and $\sqrt{3}$ is a right triangle? Explain. See left.

16. **Error Analysis** One leg of a right triangle is 3 cm and the hypotenuse is 4 cm. A student simplifies $\sqrt{3^2 + 4^2}$ to find the length of the other leg. What error did the student make? See left.

15. $(\sqrt{1})^2 + (\sqrt{2})^2 = 1 + 2 = 3$, and $(\sqrt{3})^2 = 3$, so $(\sqrt{1})^2 + (\sqrt{2})^2 = (\sqrt{3})^2$.

16. The student should have evaluated $\sqrt{4^2 - 3^2}$.

SCAFFOLDED
Problem Solving

17. Answers may vary. Sample: If d is the distance between the bases, write and solve the equation $d^2 + d^2 = 127.3^2$.

25. Yes; if $m = 3$, then $m^2 + (m + 1)^2 = 3^2 + 4^2 = 25$, and $(m + 2)^2 = 5^2 = 25$, so $m^2 + (m + 1)^2 = (m + 2)^2$.

The distance from home plate to second base is about 127.3 ft.

17. **Writing in Math** Explain how you would find the distance between the bases. See left.

18. **Estimation** Estimate the distance between the bases to the nearest foot. about 90 ft

19. Suppose you hit the ball and run from home to first base. How far do you run? about 90 ft

20. You run around all the bases for a home run. How far do you run? about 360 ft

Use the formula $\frac{1}{2}bh$ to find the area of a right triangle with a leg of length a and a hypotenuse of length c.

21. $a = 4$, $c = 5$ 6 m^2
22. $a = 8.6$, $c = 10$ about 21.9 m^2
23. $a = 7.3$, $c = 9.1$ about 19.8 m^2

24. A scuba diver swims 20 m under water to the anchor of a buoy that is 10 m below the surface of the water. On the surface, how far is the buoy located from the place where the diver started? about 17.3 m

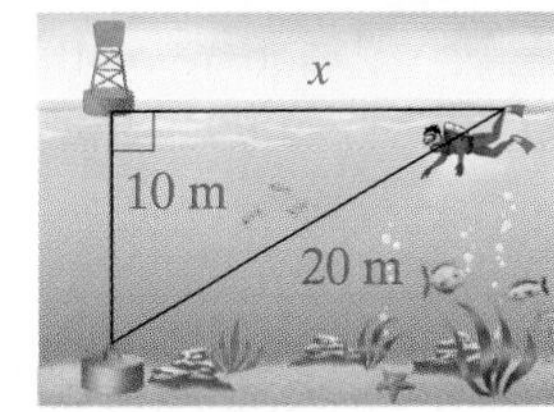

25. **Algebra** Is $m = 3$ a solution to $m^2 + (m + 1)^2 = (m + 2)^2$? Explain. See left.

C Challenge

26. The sides of a right triangle are labeled a, b, and c. Can $a + b = c$? Explain. No; if $a^2 + b^2 = c^2$, then $a + b \neq c$.

Multiple Choice Practice and Mixed Review

For California Standards Tutorials, visit PHSchool.com. Web Code: axq-9045

MG 3.3, MR 2.7

27. The top of a badminton net is 5 ft high. Ropes connect the top of each pole to stakes in the ground. The ropes are 8.5 ft long. Which estimate is closest to the distance from a stake to the base of a pole? B

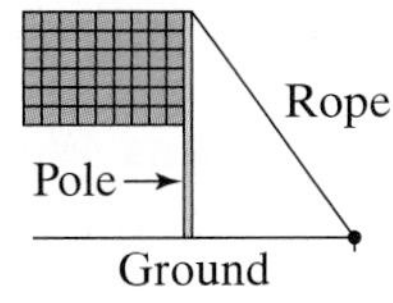

Ⓐ 4 ft Ⓑ 7 ft Ⓒ 9 ft Ⓓ 15 ft

Alg1 2.0

28. Which integer is closest to $\sqrt{10}$? B

Ⓐ 2 Ⓑ 3 Ⓒ 4 Ⓓ 5

NS 1.2

29. Oliver is buying three items that cost \$4.95, \$6.99, and \$1.05. He gives the cashier a \$20 bill. How much change should he receive? B

Ⓐ \$5.95 Ⓑ \$7.01 Ⓒ \$8.06 Ⓓ \$12.99

for Help Lesson 2-1

Find each absolute value.

30. $|0|$ 0
31. $|-3|$ 3
32. $|85|$ 85
33. $|-84|$ 84

Online Lesson Quiz Visit: PHSchool.com Web Code: axa-0307

4. Assess & Reteach

PRESENTATION CD-ROM CD, Online, or Transparencies

Lesson Quiz

1. A triangle has a hypotenuse of 17 in. and one of its legs is 8 in. What is the length of the other leg? 15 in.

2. The bottom of a 12-ft ladder is 4 ft from the side of a house. Find the approximate height of the top of the ladder above the ground. 11.3 ft

3. An artist is measuring a rectangular canvas. Its length is 30 in. The distance from one corner of the canvas to the other (along the diagonal) is 34 in. What is its width? 16 in.

4. A triangular window has sides of lengths 12 in., 16 in., and 20 in. Is the window a right triangle? Explain. Yes, the Pythagorean Theorem is true for $12^2 + 16^2 = 20^2$, so the window is a right triangle.

Alternative Assessment

Each student in a pair picks two different numbers. They use the greater number for the hypotenuse and the lesser number for a leg. Each partner uses the Pythagorean Theorem to solve for the other partner's missing leg length.

California Resources

Standards Mastery
- Standards Review Transparencies
- Standards Review and Practice Workbook
- Math Companion

Math Intervention
- Skills Review and Practice Workbook
- Math XL

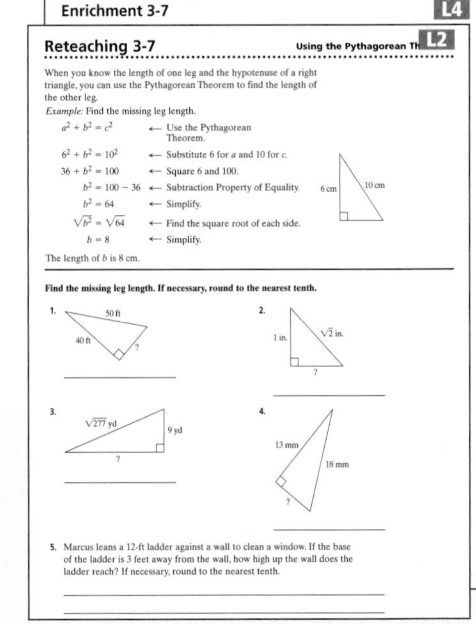

Enrichment 3-7 L4

Reteaching 3-7 Using the Pythagorean Th… L2

When you know the length of one leg and the hypotenuse of a right triangle, you can use the Pythagorean Theorem to find the length of the other leg.

Example: Find the missing leg length.

$a^2 + b^2 = c^2$ ← Use the Pythagorean Theorem.
$6^2 + b^2 = 10^2$ ← Substitute 6 for a and 10 for c.
$36 + b^2 = 100$ ← Square 6 and 100.
$b^2 = 100 - 36$ ← Subtraction Property of Equality.
$b^2 = 64$ ← Simplify.
$\sqrt{b^2} = \sqrt{64}$ ← Find the square root of each side.
$b = 8$ ← Simplify.

6 cm
10 cm

The length of b is 8 cm.

Find the missing leg length. If necessary, round to the nearest tenth.

1. 50 ft, 40 ft, ?
2. 1 in., $\sqrt{2}$ in., ?
3. $\sqrt{277}$ yd, 9 yd, ?
4. 13 mm, 18 mm, ?

5. Marcus leans a 12-ft ladder against a wall to clean a window. If the base of the ladder is 3 feet away from the wall, how high up the wall does the ladder reach? If necessary, round to the nearest tenth.

Verifying Right Triangles

Students use geometry to explore the basis of the Pythagorean Theorem. They use squares cut from grid paper to form the edges of a right triangle and analyze patterns in side lengths.

Guided Instruction

Before beginning the activity, students should review how squares are related to triangles and to exponents. Ask questions such as:

- *How many right triangles make up a square? How do the side lengths of the triangles compare to the side lengths of the square they make up?* 2; they are the same
- *What do you know about the angles of a right triangle?* one angle always measures 90°, the other two are less than 90°, they all add up to 180°
- *How do you find the area of a square?* "square" the length of a side

Universal Access

Special Needs L1

Help students identify the hypotenuse as the longest side and the side opposite the right angle. Draw several right triangles of different sizes and orientations on the board. Have students identify each hypotenuse.

Verifying Right Triangles

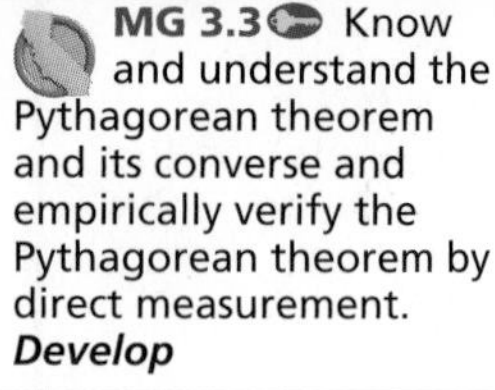

MG 3.3 Know and understand the Pythagorean theorem and its converse and empirically verify the Pythagorean theorem by direct measurement. ***Develop***

You can use graph paper or a ruler to verify the Pythagorean Theorem.

ACTIVITY

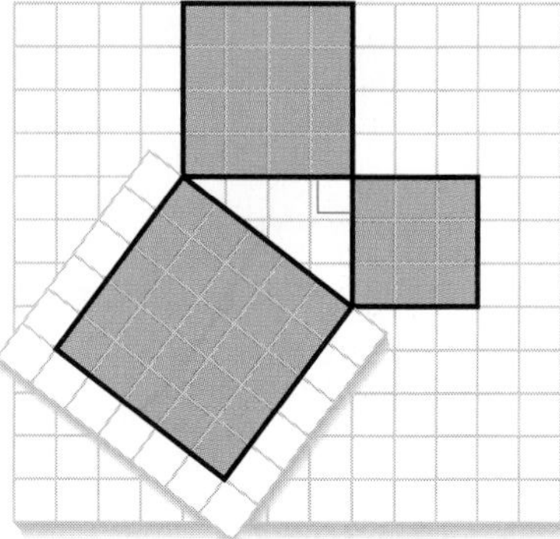

Step 1 Use centimeter graph paper to draw a right triangle with perpendicular sides that are 3 cm and 4 cm long.

Step 2 Draw squares that have the horizontal and vertical sides of the right triangle as sides.

Step 3 Use another piece of the graph paper to make a square on the side opposite the right angle, as shown at the right.

Exercises

1. What is the length of the side of the square opposite the right angle? 5 cm
2. What is the area of each of the three squares? 9 cm^2, 16 cm^2, 25 cm^2
3. Draw a right triangle on graph paper with perpendicular sides that are 8 cm and 15 cm long. Repeat Steps 2 and 3 from the Activity above for this triangle.
   a. What is the length of each side of the square made on the side opposite the right angle? 17 cm
   b. What is the area of each of the three squares? 64 cm^2, 225 cm^2, 289 cm^2
4. a. **Patterns** What seems to be the relationship of the areas of the smaller two squares and the third square made on the sides of a right triangle?
   b. Write an equation for each triangle that compares the areas of its squares.
   c. How does your equation relate to the Pythagorean Theorem?
   4a–c. See right.
5. Construct three squares on the sides of the triangle at the right. Is the triangle a right triangle? Explain.
   5. Yes; the squares have areas 36 unit^2, 64 units^2, and 100 units^2. It is a right triangle because $6^2 + 8^2 = 100 = 10^2$.

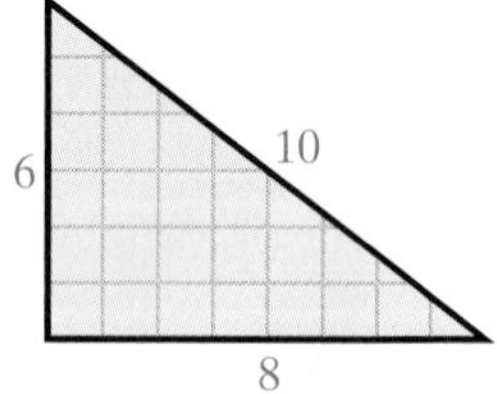

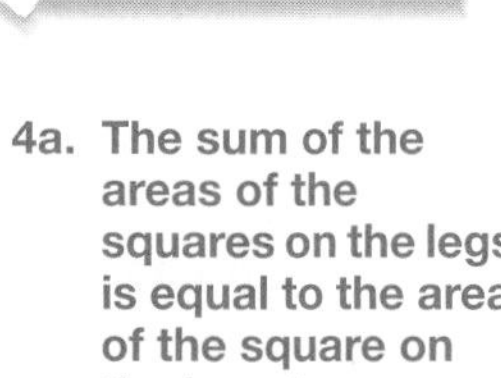

4a. The sum of the areas of the squares on the legs is equal to the area of the square on the hypotenuse.

b. Activity: $3^2 + 4^2 = 5^2$; Exercise 3: $8^2 + 15^2 = 17^2$

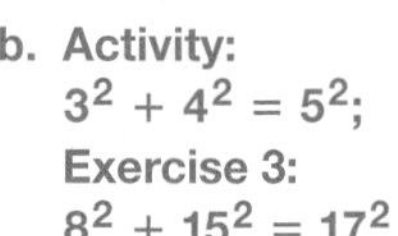

c. Each equation is a statement of the Pythagorean Theorem for the particular right triangle.

Writing Equations to Solve Problems

Around the World On March 4, 2005, Steve Fossett set a record by completing a nonstop solo jet flight around the world. He landed with 1,515 lb of fuel. A fuel leak caused a loss of 2,600 lb of fuel. He started with 18,100 lb of fuel. How much fuel did the jet use on the flight?

AF 1.1 Write an equation that represents a verbal description. ***Develop***
MR 3.2 Note the method of deriving the solution and demonstrate an understanding of the derivation by solving similar problems. ***Develop***

What You Might Think	What You Might Write
What do I know? What am I trying to find?	• Fuel remaining = 1,515 lb • Fuel lost = 2,600 lb • Total fuel at start = 18,100 lb • How much fuel (in pounds) was actually used on the flight?
How can I show the main idea?	Draw a diagram.
What equation can I write to show the problem?	$1{,}515 + 2{,}600 + x = 18{,}100$
How do I solve the equation?	$4{,}115 + x = 18{,}100$ $4{,}115 - 4{,}115 + x = 18{,}100 - 4{,}115$ $x = 13{,}985$
What is the answer?	A total of 13,985 lb of fuel was used on the flight.

Diagram:

18,100 lb		
1,515 lb	2,600 lb	x

Think It Through

1. Is the answer above reasonable? Explain.
2. Refer to the diagram above. How do you know that the section for x must be the largest section?
3. **Reasoning** Suppose the plane had not lost 2,600 lb of fuel. How much fuel would have been in the plane when it landed? 4,115 lb

1. Yes; using rounded values of 14,000 lb for fuel used, 1,500 lb for fuel remaining, and 2,600 lb for fuel lost, then $14{,}000 + 1{,}500 + 2{,}600 = 18{,}100$, which is the amount of fuel at the start.
2. Answers may vary. Sample: The amount accounted for is less than half of 18,100.

GPS Guided Problem Solving

Writing Equations to Solve Problems

Students use diagrams to show the relationships in problems and then write equations to solve the problems.

Guided Instruction

Discuss with students problems found in the real world and the need to solve them. Most real-world problems are posed in words, and students must extract information to solve them. They can draw a diagram to show relationships and then write an equation that reflects the same information.

Have a volunteer read the problem aloud. Ask:

- *What are the steps in the Problem-Solving Plan you'll use to solve this problem?* **Understand the Problem; Make a Plan; Carry Out the Plan; Check the Answer**
- *What information will allow you to find how much fuel was used?* **The amount of fuel started with, the amount of fuel lost, and the amount of fuel remaining**

Error Prevention!

Some students may have difficulty going from diagrams to equations. Review Activity Lab 1-3a on p. XXX with these students. Ask:

- *Why must the three quantities on the bottom of the diagram equal the quantity on the top?* **The used, lost, and remaining fuel must equal the total amount of fuel.**

Exercises

Have students work independently on the exercises. Have them form groups to share and evaluate their answers. Students should adjust their answers to reflect what they learn in the group.

Exercises

Solve each problem. For Exercise 4, answer parts (a), (b), (c), and (d) first.

4. The first flight around the world included stops. It was made by Lowell Smith and Alva Harvey in 1924. How many years passed between their flight and Fossett's flight? **81 yr**
   a. What do you know?
   b. What are you trying to find?
   c. Use the diagram below to write and solve an equation.

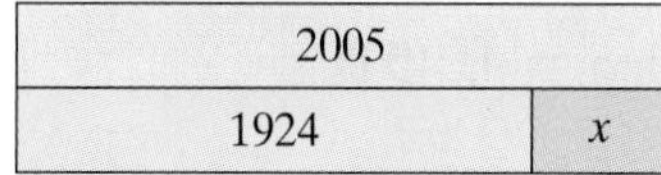

   d. Decide if the answer is reasonable. Explain.

5. The first altitude record was set in a hot-air balloon. It rose to 82 ft. Fossett's plane flew at 45,000 ft. How many times higher was Fossett's altitude than that of the hot-air balloon? Use the diagram below to write and solve an equation. Round your answer to the nearest tenth. **about 548.8 times greater**

45,000 ft			
82 ft	82 ft	82 ft	. . .

6. On October 3, 1967, William Knight flew an X-15 aircraft at 4,520 mi/h. This is 6.7 times the speed of sound. What is the speed of sound? Use the diagram at the right to help you write and solve an equation. Round your answer to the nearest tenth. **about 674.6 mi/h**

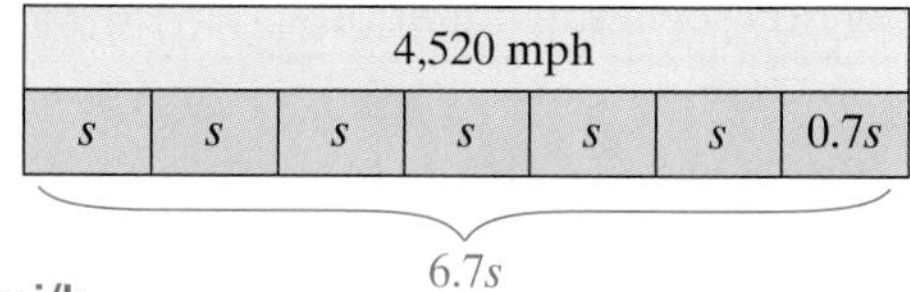

Write and solve an equation for each problem. You can draw a diagram to help you write an equation.

7. At one time the United States had the longest total length of railroad tracks in the world. The 149,129 mi of track could stretch around the world almost six times. What is the distance around the world? **about 24,854.8 mi**

8. In one year, London's Heathrow Airport had 44,262,000 passengers. In the same year, Germany's Frankfurt Airport had 27,546,000 passengers. How many more passengers were there in Heathrow Airport? **16,716,000 passengers**

Test-Taking Strategies

Working Backward

In multiple-choice questions, the correct answer is among the choices. To determine which answer is correct, you can use the problem solving strategy *Work Backward.*

EXAMPLES

1 A bus can hold 72 passengers. A school uses the expression $\frac{n}{72}$ to calculate the number of buses needed to transport n students. What is the greatest number of students 6 buses can hold?

Ⓐ 288 Ⓑ 360 Ⓒ 432 Ⓓ 504

You can substitute each answer choice for the variable until you find the solution.

Let $n = 288$. Then $\frac{288}{72} = 4$. Since $4 \neq 6$, choice A is wrong.

Let $n = 360$. Then $\frac{360}{72} = 5$. Since $5 \neq 6$, choice B is wrong.

Let $n = 432$. Then $\frac{432}{72} = 6$. Since $6 = 6$, the correct answer is choice C.

You do not need to try choice D.

2 Which expression is equivalent to $18 + 3x$?

Ⓐ $18(3x)$ Ⓑ $3(6 + x)$ Ⓒ $6(3 + x)$ Ⓓ $x(18 + 3)$

You can multiply each of the answer choices to answer the question.

$18(3x) = 54x$ This is not equal to $18 + 3x$, so choice A is wrong.

$3(6 + x) = 18 + 3x$ Choice B is correct.

You do not need to test the other two choices.

Multiple Choice Practice

NS 1.2 **1.** The expression $33g$ describes the number of miles a car can travel on g gallons of gas. How many gallons does it take to travel 297 mi? C

Ⓐ 4 gal Ⓑ 6 gal Ⓒ 9 gal Ⓓ 14 gal

NS 1.2 **2.** Jorge wants to run a half-marathon (13.1 mi). About how many miles per hour should he run to complete the half-marathon in 1.5 h? Use the equation $13.1 = 1.5r$. B

Ⓐ 5.2 mi/h Ⓑ 8.7 mi/h Ⓒ 9.6 mi/h Ⓓ 19.6 mi/h

Working Backward

In general, students can use the work-backward strategy effectively when they know a solution but need to find information that led to that solution. This feature guides students to work backward to solve multiple-choice questions.

Guided Instruction

Emphasize that students should stop checking answer choices once their substitution gives the desired result.

Discuss that eliminating some answer choices, by estimating or by using number sense, will increase their chances of success on that test question, whether they work backward or apply any other test-taking strategy.

Chapter 3 Review

California Resources

Standards Mastery
- Math Companion
- Standards Review Transparencies
- Standards Review and Practice Workbook
- Progress Monitoring Assessments

Math Intervention
- Skills Review and Practice Workbook
- Math XL

Universal Access Resources

- Student Workbook
  - Vocabulary and Study skills
  - Guided Problem Solving
- All-In-One Teaching Resources
  - Reteaching
  - Enrichment
- Spanish Practice Workbook L3
- Spanish Vocabulary and Study Skills 11A-F L3
- English/Spanish Glossary EL
- Multilingual Handbook EL
- Interactive Textbook Audio Glossary
- Online Vocabulary Quiz

Success Tracker™
Online at PHSchool.com

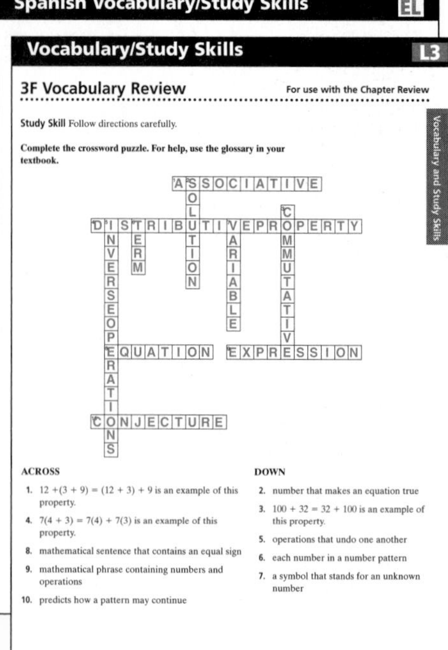

Spanish Vocabulary/Study Skills EL

Vocabulary/Study Skills L3

3F Vocabulary Review — For use with the Chapter Review

Study Skill Follow directions carefully.

Complete the crossword puzzle. For help, use the glossary in your textbook.

ASSOCIATIVE, DISTRIBUTIVE PROPERTY, EQUATION, EXPRESSION, CONJECTURE, INVERSE OPERATIONS, TERM, SOLUTION, VARIABLE, COMMUTATIVE

ACROSS
1. 12 + (3 + 9) = (12 + 3) + 9 is an example of this property.
4. 7(4 + 3) = 7(4) + 7(3) is an example of this property.
8. mathematical sentence that contains an equal sign
9. mathematical phrase containing numbers and operations
10. predicts how a pattern may continue

DOWN
2. number that makes an equation true
3. 100 + 32 = 32 + 100 is an example of this property.
5. operations that undo one another
6. each number in a number pattern
7. a symbol that stands for an unknown number

Chapter 3 Review

Vocabulary Review

English and Spanish Audio Online

Addition Property of Equality (p. 92)
converse of the Pythagorean Theorem (p. 117)
Division Property of Equality (p. 96)
equation (p. 87)
hypotenuse (p. 112)
inverse operations (p. 87)
isolate (p. 87)
legs (p. 112)
Multiplication Property of Equality (p. 97)
perfect square (p. 107)
Pythagorean Theorem (p. 112)
square root (p. 107)
Subtraction Property of Equality (p. 88)

Academic Vocabulary
deductive reasoning (p. 100)

For: Vocabulary Quiz
Visit: PHSchool.com
Web Code: axj-0351

Choose the correct vocabulary term to complete each sentence.

1. A(n) __?__ is a mathematical sentence with an equal sign. equation
2. A number such as 25, which is the square of a whole number, is a(n) __?__. perfect square
3. The __?__ is the longest side of a right triangle. hypotenuse
4. You can use the __?__ to determine whether a triangle is a right triangle. converse of the Pythagorean Theorem
5. The inverse of squaring a number is finding the __?__. square root

Skills and Concepts

Lessons 3-1, 3-2

- To solve addition and subtraction equations

AF 1.1, AF 1.3

You can use the **Addition Property of Equality** and the **Subtraction Property of Equality** to solve equations. Operations that undo each other are **inverse operations.**

Solve each equation.

6. $r - 1{,}078 = 4{,}563$ 5,614
7. $m + 8.4 = 15$ 6.6
8. $5.6 + x = 7$ 1.4
9. $d - 2.16 = 3.9$ 6.06
10. $v - 7 = 23.4$ 30.4
11. $6 = t + 3.7$ 2.3
12. Paulo is 2.7 lb heavier than Elizabeth. Paulo weighs 132.4 lb. How much does Elizabeth weigh? 129.7 lb
13. At a furniture store, a lamp costs \$15.50 less than a mirror. If a lamp costs \$36.99, how much does the mirror cost? \$52.49

Lessons 3-3, 3-4

- To solve multiplication and division equations
- To solve two-step equations

AF 1.1, AF 1.3, AF 4.1

You can use the **Multiplication Property of Equality** and the **Division Property of Equality** to solve equations.

Solve each equation.

14. $78x = 4{,}368$ 56
15. $\frac{h}{4} = -12$ −48
16. $7.2 = \frac{u}{1.5}$ 10.8
17. $4.5 = 5n$ 0.9
18. $1.2y + 3.5 = 6.5$ 2.5
19. $\frac{z}{5} - 9 = -8.6$ 2
20. John has five times as much money as Pen-Ying. John has $83.40. How much money does Pen-Ying have? $16.68

Lesson 3-5

- To find square roots

NS 1.2, Alg1 2.0

The square of an integer is a **perfect square.** The inverse of squaring a number is finding its **square root.**

Find the square roots of each number.

21. 81 9, −9
22. 196 14, −14
23. 1 1, −1
24. 49 7, −7
25. 144 12, −12
26. 0 0

Estimate the value of each expression to the nearest integer.

27. $\sqrt{52}$ 7
28. $-\sqrt{24}$ −5
29. $\sqrt{170}$ 13

Lessons 3-6, 3-7

- To use the Pythagorean Theorem to find the length of the hypotenuse of a right triangle
- To find the length of the legs of a right triangle and to use the converse of the Pythagorean Theorem

NS 1.2, MG 3.3, Alg1 2.0

The **Pythagorean Theorem** states that if a and b are the lengths of the legs of a right triangle, and c is the length of the hypotenuse, then $a^2 + b^2 = c^2$. Use the **converse of the Pythagorean Theorem** to determine whether a triangle is a right triangle.

Find the missing side length of each right triangle.

30. $a = 6$, $b = 8$, $c = ■$ 10
31. $a = 15$, $b = ■$, $c = 17$ 8
32. $a = 1$, $b = 2$, $c = ■$ $\sqrt{5}$ or 2.2
33. $a = ■$, $b = 6$, $c = 8$ $\sqrt{28}$ or 5.3
34. The base of a 24-ft ladder is 6 ft from the base of a house. How far up the house does the ladder reach? about 23 ft

Determine whether the given lengths can be sides of a right triangle.

35. 4 m, 6 m, 3 m no
36. 34 in., 16 in., 30 in. yes
37. $\sqrt{2}$ yd, $\sqrt{6}$ yd, $\sqrt{3}$ yd no
38. 0.5 ft, 0.3 ft, 0.4 ft yes

Alternative Assessment L4

Alternative Assessment Form C

Chapter 3

MOVING DAY

You are helping a friend move. You and your friend want to pack some boxes and then move several boxes that are already packed.

Items to Pack	Weight
50 books	$\frac{1}{2}$ lb per book
4 bookends	3 lb total
miscellaneous	m
CDs, 10 cases	6 lb per case
assorted tapes	x
tape cabinet	24 lb

Suppose you wanted to pack a box with several of the same item. How could you use mathematics to figure out how much the packed box weighs?

Suppose you knew the distance (d) and time (t) it took you to drive from one apartment to another. You want to find out the rate (r) you traveled. By what would you multiply both sides of the equation $d = rt$ to find the rate?

Show all your work on a separate sheet of paper.

1. Suppose you will pack the bookends and the miscellaneous items (m) in one box. Write an expression that tells how much the box will weigh.
2. If you decide to pack the bookends with some books, write an expression that tells how much a box will weigh if you pack the book ends and any number of books (b).
3. The box packed with the books and bookends weighs 24 pounds. How many books are in the box?

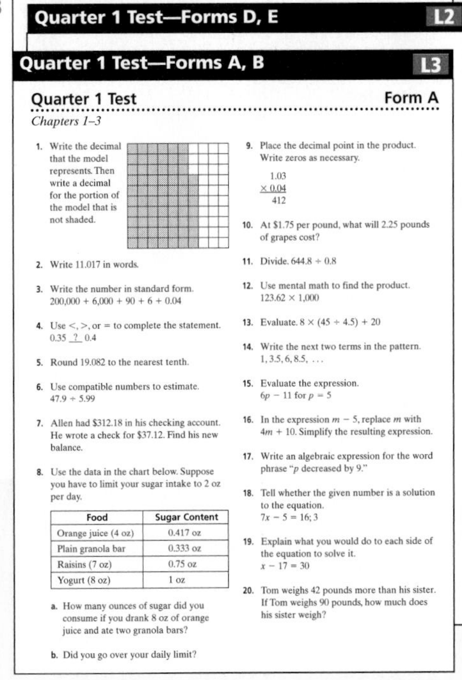

Spanish Quarter 1 Test—Forms A, B EL

Quarter 1 Test—Forms D, E L2

Quarter 1 Test—Forms A, B L3

Quarter 1 Test Form A

Chapters 1–3

1. Write the decimal that the model represents. Then write a decimal for the portion of the model that is not shaded.
2. Write 11.017 in words.
3. Write the number in standard form. 200,000 + 6,000 + 90 + 6 + 0.04
4. Use $<$, $>$, or = to complete the statement. 0.35 _?_ 0.4
5. Round 19.082 to the nearest tenth.
6. Use compatible numbers to estimate. 47.9 ÷ 5.99
7. Allen had $312.18 in his checking account. He wrote a check for $37.12. Find his new balance.
8. Use the data in the chart below. Suppose you have to limit your sugar intake to 2 oz per day.

Food	Sugar Content
Orange juice (4 oz)	0.417 oz
Plain granola bar	0.333 oz
Raisins (7 oz)	0.75 oz
Yogurt (8 oz)	1 oz

a. How many ounces of sugar did you consume if you drank 8 oz of orange juice and ate two granola bars?

b. Did you go over your daily limit?

9. Place the decimal point in the product. Write zeros as necessary.
   $1.03 \times 0.04 = 412$
10. At $1.75 per pound, what will 2.25 pounds of grapes cost?
11. Divide. 644.8 ÷ 0.8
12. Use mental math to find the product. 123.62 × 1,000
13. Evaluate. 8 × (45 ÷ 4.5) + 20
14. Write the next two terms in the pattern. 1, 3.5, 6, 8.5, ...
15. Evaluate the expression. $6p - 11$ for $p = 5$
16. In the expression $m - 5$, replace m with $4m + 10$. Simplify the resulting expression.
17. Write an algebraic expression for the word phrase "p decreased by 9."
18. Tell whether the given number is a solution to the equation. $7x - 5 = 16$; 3
19. Explain what you would do to each side of the equation to solve it. $x - 17 = 30$
20. Tom weighs 42 pounds more than his sister. If Tom weighs 90 pounds, how much does his sister weigh?

California Resources

Standards Mastery
- Teacher Center ExamView CD-ROM
- Math XL
- Progress Monitoring Assessments
- Online Chapter Test at PHSchool.com

Math Intervention
- Skills Review and Practice Workbook

Online at PHSchool.com

Universal Access Resources
- Chapter Test
- Alternative Assessment
- Spanish Chapter Test
- Spanish Alternative Assessment
- Teacher Center ExamView CD-ROM
  - Special Needs Test
  - Special Needs Practice Banks
  - Foundational Standards Practice Banks
- Online Chapter Test at www.PHSchool.com
- All-In-One Teaching Resources
  - Cumulative Review L3
- Spanish Assessment Resources
  - Cumulative Review L3

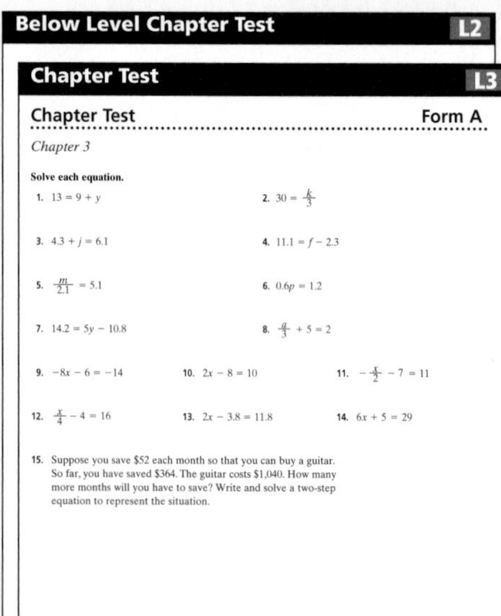
Below Level Chapter Test L2

Chapter Test L3

Chapter Test — Form A

Chapter 3

Solve each equation.

1. $13 = 9 + y$
2. $30 = \frac{k}{3}$
3. $4.3 + j = 6.1$
4. $11.1 = f - 2.3$
5. $\frac{m}{2.1} = 5.1$
6. $0.6p = 1.2$
7. $14.2 = 5y - 10.8$
8. $\frac{q}{3} + 5 = 2$
9. $-8x - 6 = -14$
10. $2x - 8 = 10$
11. $-\frac{x}{2} - 7 = 11$
12. $\frac{x}{4} - 4 = 16$
13. $2x - 3.8 = 11.8$
14. $6x + 5 = 29$
15. Suppose you save \$52 each month so that you can buy a guitar. So far, you have saved \$364. The guitar costs \$1,040. How many more months will you have to save? Write and solve a two-step equation to represent the situation.

Chapter 3 Test

Go Online — PHSchool.com — For: Online chapter test — Web Code: axa-0352

Solve each equation.

1. $n - 4 = 8.4$ 12.4
2. $25 + b = 138$ 113
3. $m - 45 = 10$ 55
4. $3x = -18$ −6
5. $\frac{a}{-2} = 2.5$ −5
6. $11t = 99$ 9
7. $2.8c = 1.4$ 0.5
8. $\frac{d}{3.6} = 14$ 50.4
9. $-25 = \frac{w}{4.5}$ −112.5
10. $-15s = 255$ −17
11. A baseball team sold greeting cards to raise money for uniforms. The team received \$.40 profit for each card sold. The total profit was \$302. How many cards did the team sell? 755 cards
12. A hiker begins a hike in Death Valley National Park at the park's lowest point. She climbs 11,331 feet to the park's highest point at 11,049 feet above sea level. Write and solve an equation to find the elevation of Death Valley's lowest point. 282 ft below sea level

Solve each equation.

13. $4u + 7 = 35$ 7
14. $6r - 4 = 20$ 4
15. $\frac{f}{3} + 5 = 20$ 45
16. $\frac{n}{8} - 2 = -1$ 8
17. $\frac{6z}{7} = -30$ −35
18. $-2c + 5 = 9$ −2
19. $\frac{r}{-5} - 3 = 14$ −85
20. $4m - 9 = 27$ 9
21. A quilter is making a quilt that will be 48 in. wide. The border will be 2 in. at each end. Each quilt square is 4 in. wide. How many quilt squares does the quilter need across the width of the quilt? 11 quilt squares
22. You buy 15 apples and a \$2.75 block of cheese. The bill is \$6.20. How much does each apple cost? \$.23
23. **Writing in Math** Describe how solving a two-step equation is similar to solving a one-step equation. Describe how it is different. See margin.

Find the square roots of each number.

24. 25 5, −5
25. 49 7, −7
26. 144 12, −12
27. 256 16, −16
28. 400 20, −20
29. 64 8, −8

Estimate the value of each expression to the nearest integer.

30. $\sqrt{60}$ 8
31. $-\sqrt{10}$ −3
32. $\sqrt{5}$ 2
33. $\sqrt{97}$ 10
34. $\sqrt{14}$ 4
35. $-\sqrt{150}$ −12

Find the missing side length of each right triangle, where *a* and *b* are the leg lengths and *c* is the hypotenuse length.

36. 15

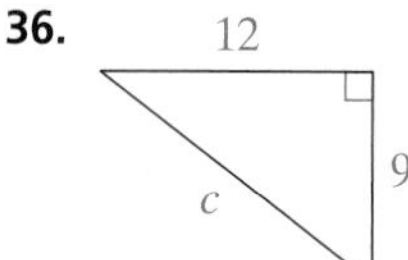

37. 45

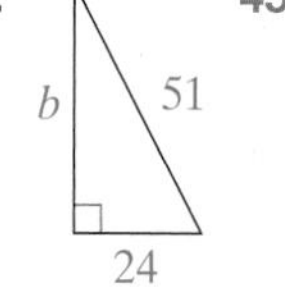

38. $c = 5,\ a = 3$ 4
39. $b = 30,\ c = 34$ 16
40. $a = 5,\ b = 12$ 13
41. $a = 48,\ c = 60$ 36
42. In the diagram of a sailboat at the right, the length of the luff is 17 ft. The length of the foot is 10 ft. What is the length of the leech to the nearest foot? 20 ft

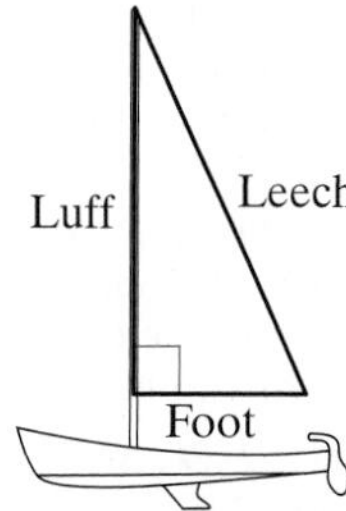

43. When you are given the side lengths of a right triangle, how do you know which side is the hypotenuse? See margin.

Determine whether the given lengths can be sides of a right triangle. Explain.

44. 9 ft, 12 ft, 15 ft Yes; $9^2 + 12^2 = 15^2$.
45. 2 m, 5 m, 4 m No; $2^2 + 4^2 \neq 5^2$.
46. 34 cm, 30 cm, 16 cm Yes; $16^2 + 30^2 = 34^2$.
47. 4 in., 4 in., 8 in. No; $4^2 + 4^2 \neq 8^2$.

Cumulative Practice

Some questions require you to use a formula or equation to find a quantity. Use the tips as guides for how to approach solving the problem.

The two legs of a right triangle have lengths of 6 m and 8 m. Use the Pythagorean Theorem to find the length of the hypotenuse.

Ⓐ 100 m
Ⓑ 50 m
Ⓒ 14 m
Ⓓ 10 m

Tip 1
To help you visualize the problem, draw a diagram of the triangle. This will help you find which quantity is unknown.

Tip 2
Write down the formula or equation you should use. Make sure you substitute the correct value for each variable.

Think It Through
To use the Pythagorean Theorem, use the equation $a^2 + b^2 = c^2$. Substitute 6 for a and 8 for b: $6^2 + 8^2 = c^2$. Now solve. The correct answer is choice D.

Vocabulary Review

As you solve problems, you must understand the meanings of mathematical terms. Match each term with its mathematical meaning.

A. equation V
B. hypotenuse IV
C. legs II
D. isolate I
E. perfect square III

I. to get the variable alone on one side of an equation
II. the two shorter sides of a right triangle
III. a number that is the square of an integer
IV. the longest side of a right triangle
V. a mathematical sentence with an equal sign

Multiple Choice

Read each question. Then write the letter of the correct answer on your paper.

1. Each of the 15 students in an orchestra was given 10 raffle tickets to sell. Which equation can be used to find the total number of tickets? **(Lesson 3-3) C**

   Ⓐ $15 + t = 10$ Ⓒ $\frac{t}{15} = 10$
   Ⓑ $15t = 10$ Ⓓ $t - 15 = 10$

2. Which square root is between 8 and 9? **(Lesson 3-5) C**

   Ⓐ $\sqrt{8.5}$ Ⓒ $\sqrt{75}$
   Ⓑ $\sqrt{10}$ Ⓓ $\sqrt{83}$

3. A car dealership sold 21 cars the first 3 months of the year. The dealership's goal is to sell 75 cars for the year. The equation $9n + 21 = 75$ can be used to find n, the number of cars that must be sold each of the last 9 months. How many cars must be sold each month? **(Lesson 3-4) B**

   Ⓐ 2.5 Ⓑ 6 Ⓒ 8 Ⓓ 10

Standards Mastery

California Resources

Standards Mastery
- Teacher Center ExamView CD-ROM
- Math XL
- Progress Monitoring Assessments
- Online Chapter Test at PHSchool.com

Math Intervention
- Skills Review and Practice Workbook

Universal Access Resources
- Teacher Center ExamView CD-ROM
  - Special Needs Test
  - Special Needs Practice Banks
  - Foundational Standards Practice Banks
- Online Chapter Test at www.PHSchool.com
- All-In-One Teaching Resources
  - Cumulative Review L3
- Spanish Assessment Resources
  - Cumulative Review L3

Success Tracker™
Online at PHSchool.com

4. A plane left the runway at the takeoff point shown below. By the time the airplane flew over the end of the runway, it was 3,500 ft in the air.

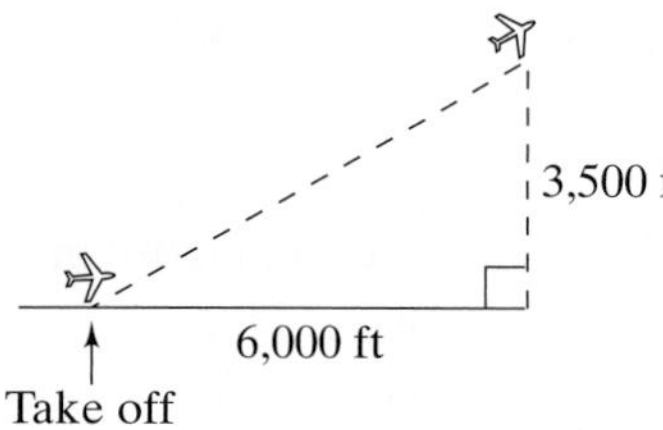

The horizontal distance the plane traveled along the runway was 6,000 ft. Which estimate is closest to the distance the plane traveled before it flew over the end of the runway? **(Lesson 3-6) C**

Ⓐ 5,300 ft
Ⓑ 6,000 ft
Ⓒ 7,000 ft
Ⓓ 10,500 ft

5. You buy notebooks for \$2.99 each and one pencil for \$.39. The total cost is \$9.36. How many notebooks did you buy? Use the equation $2.99x + 0.39 = 9.36$, where x is the number of notebooks. **(Lesson 3-4) B**

Ⓐ 0　Ⓒ 5
Ⓑ 3　Ⓓ 9

6. Which of the following is equivalent to 5^3? **(Lesson 2-6) B**

Ⓐ $5 \cdot 3$　Ⓒ 53
Ⓑ $5 \cdot 5 \cdot 5$　Ⓓ $3 \cdot 3 \cdot 3 \cdot 3 \cdot 3$

7. The high temperature on Monday was 12°F below zero. On Tuesday, the high temperature was 15°F. What integer represents the high temperature on Monday? **(Lesson 2-3) B**

Ⓐ 12　Ⓒ 15
Ⓑ −12　Ⓓ −15

8. Haley is 3 years younger than Miguel. If Haley is 7, which equation can be used to find Miguel's age? **(Lesson 3-2) C**

Ⓐ $7 - 3 = m$　Ⓒ $m - 3 = 7$
Ⓑ $m + 3 = 7$　Ⓓ $\frac{7}{3} = m$

9. Which figure represents a triangle with sides a, b, and c, where $a^2 + b^2 = c^2$? **(Lesson 3-6) C**

Ⓐ
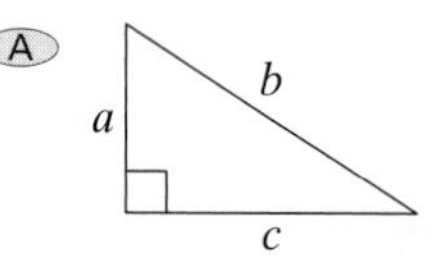

Ⓒ
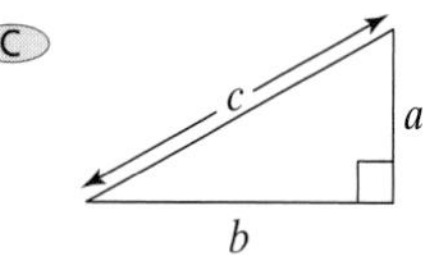

Ⓑ
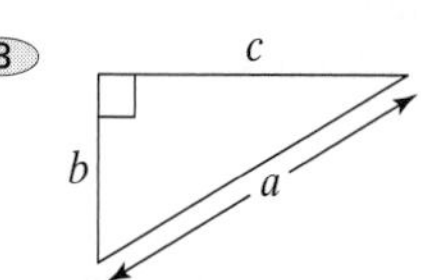

Ⓓ
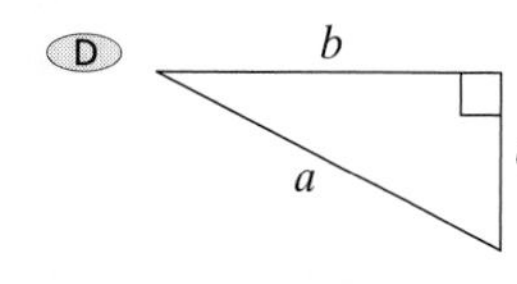

10. A submarine is 20 ft below the surface of the ocean. It is descending at a rate of 5 ft/min. After 15 min, how many feet below the surface is the submarine? **(Lesson 2-4) C**

Ⓐ 55 ft　Ⓒ 95 ft
Ⓑ 75 ft　Ⓓ 225 ft

11. According to Rosa, the distance between the top of her school and the top of a nearby flagpole is $\sqrt{109}$ yd. Which is the best estimate for $\sqrt{109}$? **(Lesson 3-5) B**

Ⓐ 8　Ⓑ 10　Ⓒ 36　Ⓓ 55

12. Which of the following groups of measurements could represent the side lengths of a right triangle? **(Lesson 3-7) B**

Ⓐ 3 ft, 5 ft, 6 ft　Ⓒ 17 ft, 5 ft, 16 ft
Ⓑ 12 ft, 13 ft, 5 ft　Ⓓ 9 ft, 9 ft, 18 ft

13. Which equation illustrates the Inverse Property of Addition? **(Lesson 2-2) A**

Ⓐ $3 + (-3) = 0$
Ⓑ $3 + 0 = 3$
Ⓒ $3 = 3$
Ⓓ $3 + (-3) = (-3) + 3$

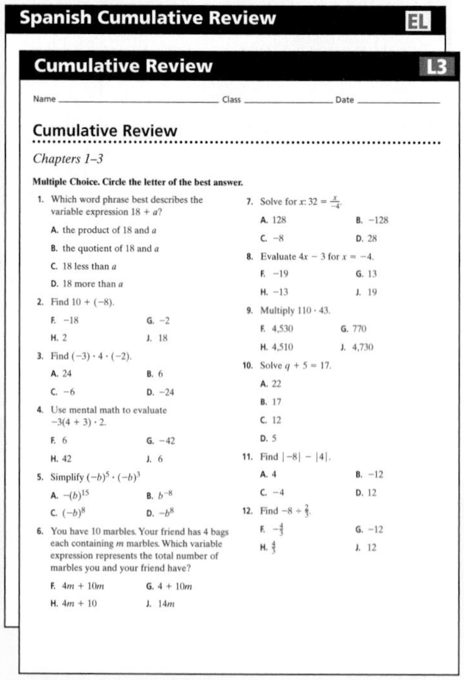

Spanish Cumulative Review EL

Cumulative Review L3

Name ______ Class ______ Date ______

Cumulative Review

Chapters 1–3

Multiple Choice. Circle the letter of the best answer.

1. Which word phrase best describes the variable expression $18 + a$?
   A. the product of 18 and a
   B. the quotient of 18 and a
   C. 18 less than a
   D. 18 more than a
2. Find $10 + (-8)$.
   F. −18　G. −2
   H. 2　J. 18
3. Find $(-3) \cdot 4 \cdot (-2)$.
   A. 24　B. 6
   C. −6　D. −24
4. Use mental math to evaluate $-3(4 + 3) \cdot 2$.
   F. 6　G. −42
   H. 42　J. 6
5. Simplify $(-b)^5 \cdot (-b)^3$
   A. $-(b)^{15}$　B. b^{-8}
   C. $(-b)^8$　D. $-b^8$
6. You have 10 marbles. Your friend has 4 bags each containing m marbles. Which variable expression represents the total number of marbles you and your friend have?
   F. $4m + 10m$　G. $4 + 10m$
   H. $4m + 10$　J. $14m$
7. Solve for x: $32 = \frac{x}{-4}$.
   A. 128　B. −128
   C. −8　D. 28
8. Evaluate $4x - 3$ for $x = -4$.
   F. −19　G. 13
   H. −13　J. 19
9. Multiply $110 \cdot 43$.
   F. 4,530　G. 770
   H. 4,510　J. 4,730
10. Solve $q + 5 = 17$.
    A. 22
    B. 17
    C. 12
    D. 5
11. Find $|-8| - |4|$.
    A. 4　B. −12
    C. −4　D. 12
12. Find $-8 \div \frac{2}{3}$.
    F. $-\frac{4}{3}$　G. −12
    H. $\frac{4}{3}$　J. 12

14. Which equation illustrates the Commutative Property of Multiplication? **(Lesson 1-5) A**

Ⓐ $5 \cdot 9 = 9 \cdot 5$
Ⓑ $(5 \cdot 6) \cdot 2 = 5 \cdot (6 \cdot 2)$
Ⓒ $5 \cdot (6 + 3) = 5 \cdot 9$
Ⓓ $5 \cdot 1 = 5$

15. What is the distance across Porridge Pond? **(Lesson 3-6) C**

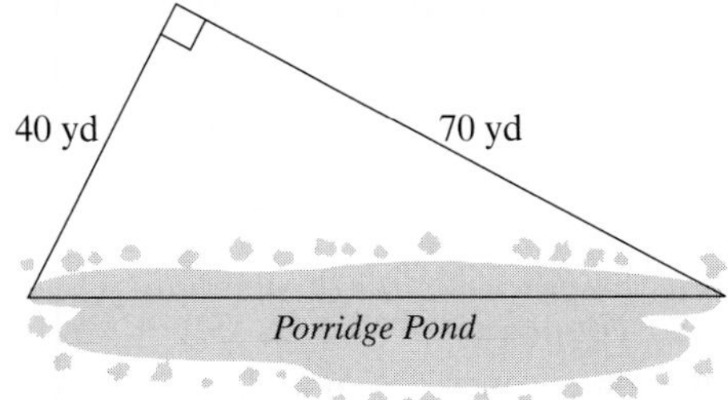

Ⓐ $\sqrt{3{,}300}$ yd
Ⓑ 80 yd
Ⓒ $\sqrt{6{,}500}$ yd
Ⓓ 110 yd

16. Simplify $3^3 + 5 \cdot 6^2$. **(Lesson 2-6) C**

Ⓐ 69
Ⓑ 927
Ⓒ 207
Ⓓ 1,152

17. The temperature outside is 58°F and rising 2.4 degrees per hour. After how many hours will the temperature be 67.6°F? Use the equation $67.6 = 58 + 2.4h$, where h is the number of hours that have passed. **(Lesson 3-4) A**

Ⓐ 4 h Ⓑ 9.6 h Ⓒ 28 h Ⓓ 52 h

18. A square section on a map has an area of 64 mi^2. What is the length of a side of the square? **(Lesson 3-5) C**

Ⓐ 32 mi Ⓑ 16 mi Ⓒ 8 mi Ⓓ 4 mi

19. Which expression is equivalent to $(6 \cdot 10) + (6 \cdot 7)$? **(Lesson 1-6) A**

Ⓐ $6 \cdot (10 + 7)$
Ⓑ $6 + (10 \cdot 7)$
Ⓒ $(6 + 6) \cdot (10 + 7)$
Ⓓ $(6 \cdot 6) + (10 \cdot 7)$

20. Hunter uses a 17-ft ladder to climb to the window of a building, as shown below. The base of the ladder is 5 ft from the building. To the nearest foot, how far is the windowsill from the ground? **(Lesson 3-6) B**

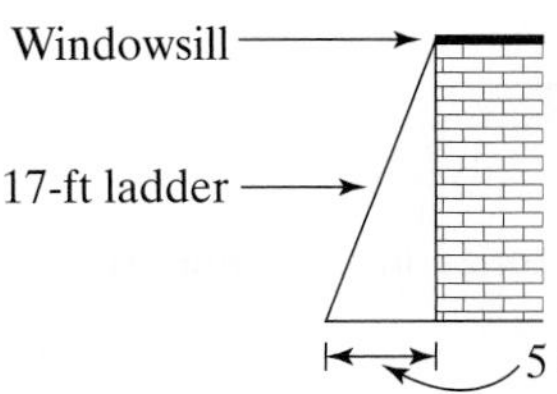

Ⓐ 12 ft Ⓑ 16 ft Ⓒ 18 ft Ⓓ 22 ft

21. Jaime makes a scale model of a chair. He uses the equation $0.08m = 3$ to find m, the height in inches of the full-sized chair. Find the height of the full-sized chair. **(Lesson 3-3) D**

Ⓐ 0.026 in.
Ⓑ 0.24 in.
Ⓒ 27 in.
Ⓓ 37.5 in.

Standards Reference Guide

California Content Standard	Item Number(s)
NS 1.2	7, 10, 21
AF 1.1	1, 8
AF 1.3	13, 14, 19
AF 2.1	6, 16
AF 4.1	3, 5, 17
MG 3.3	4, 9, 12, 15, 20
Alg1 2.0	2, 11, 18

For additional review and practice, see the *California Standards Review and Practice Workbook* or go online to use the

Visit: PHSchool.com, **Web Code:** axq-9045

Rational Numbers

Chapter at a Glance

Lesson Titles, Objectives, and Features	California Content Standards
4-1 Prime Factorization • To factor numbers and find the prime factorization of numbers	Write numbers as the product of their prime factors by using exponents to show multiples of a factor. ***Foundational (Gr5 NS 1.4)*** **NS 1.2** Multiply and divide rational numbers. **AF 2.1** Interpret positive whole-number powers as repeated multiplication.
4-2 Greatest Common Divisor • To find the greatest common divisor of two or more numbers **Mathematical Reasoning:** Divisibility Tests	Determine the prime factors of all numbers through 50. ***Foundational (Gr5 NS 1.4)*** Determine the greatest common divisor of whole numbers and use it to solve problems with fractions. ***Foundational (Gr6 NS 2.4)*** **NS 1.2** Multiply and divide rational numbers.
4-3a Activity Lab: Exploring Fractions **4-3 Equivalent Fractions** • To find equivalent forms of fractions **Algebraic Thinking:** Expressions With Fractions	Compare fractions and place them on a number line. ***Foundational (Gr6 NS 1.1)*** **NS 1.2** Add, subtract, multiply, and divide rational numbers. **NS 1.5** Convert terminating decimals into reduced fractions. **MR 1.1** Analyze problems by identifying relationships and observing patterns. **MR 3.3** Develop generalizations of strategies used and apply them to new problem situations.
4-4 Equivalent Forms of Rational Numbers • To convert rational numbers to equivalent forms **Mathematical Reasoning:** Repeating Decimals	**NS 1.3** Convert fractions to decimals. **NS 1.5** Know that every rational number is either a terminating or repeating decimal and convert terminating decimals into reduced fractions.
4-5a Activity Lab: Mixed Numbers **4-5 Comparing and Ordering Rational Numbers** • To compare and order rational numbers **Vocabulary Builder:** Using Concept Maps	Compare and order positive and negative fractions, decimals, and mixed numbers and place them on a number line. ***Foundational (Gr6 NS 1.1)*** **NS 1.3** Convert fractions to decimals and use these representations in estimations, computations, and applications. **MR 2.2** Apply strategies and results from simpler problems to more complex problems.

California Content Standards
NS Number Sense
AF Algebra and Functions
MG Measurement and Geometry
MR Mathematical Reasoning

Correlations to Standardized Tests

All content for these tests is contained in *Prentice Hall Math, Algebra Readiness.* This chart reflects coverage in this chapter only.

	4-1	4-2	4-3	4-4	4-5
Terra Nova CAT6 (Level 18)					
Number and Number Relations	✔	✔	✔	✔	✔
Computation and Numerical Estimation	✔	✔	✔	✔	✔
Operation Concepts					
Measurement					
Geometry and Spatial Sense					
Data Analysis, Statistics, and Probability					
Patterns, Functions, and Algebra	✔		✔		
Problem Solving and Reasoning	✔	✔	✔	✔	✔
Communication	✔	✔	✔	✔	✔
Decimals, Fractions, Integers, Percent	✔	✔	✔	✔	✔
Order of Operations			✔		
Algebraic Operations			✔		
Terra Nova CTBS (Level 18)					
Decimals, Fractions, Integers, and Percents	✔	✔	✔	✔	✔
Order of Operations, Numeration, Number Theory	✔	✔	✔	✔	✔
Data Interpretation					
Measurement					
Geometry					
ITBS (Level 14)					
Number Properties and Operations	✔	✔	✔	✔	✔
Algebra	✔		✔		
Geometry					
Measurement					
Probability and Statistics					
Estimation					
SAT10 (Adv 1 Level)					
Number Sense and Operations	✔	✔	✔	✔	✔
Patterns, Relationships, and Algebra	✔		✔		
Data, Statistics, and Probability					
Geometry and Measurement					
NAEP					
Number Sense, Properties, and Operations	✔	✔	✔	✔	✔
Measurement					
Geometry and Spatial Sense					
Data Analysis, Statistics, and Probability					
Algebra and Functions			✔		

CAT6 California Achievement Test, 6th Ed. **CTBS** Comprehensive Test of Basic Skills **ITBS** Iowa Test of Basic Skills, Form M
SAT10 Stanford Achievement Test, 10th Ed. **NAEP** National Assessment of Educational Progress 2005 Mathematics Objectives

California Math Background

Focus on the California Content Standards

- Three key topics presented in Chapter 4 are: prime factorization, equivalent fractions, and comparing and ordering. Lessons 4-1 and 4-2, with focus on factors and divisors, pair target standard **NS 1.2** with foundational standard **NS 1.4** from grade 5.
- Lessons 4-3 and 4-4 focus on equivalent forms of numbers. Students will find the 'More Than One Way' feature especially helpful if they struggle with deciding on a method for simplifying fractions.
- Lesson 4-5 brings the previous lessons together as students compare and order rational numbers, a concept they had experience with in grade 6 (**NS 1.1**).

4-1 Prime Factorization

California Content Standards **NS 1.2, AF 2.1**

Math Understandings

- A number that is divisible by *n* is also divisible by each factor of *n*. For example, any number divisible by 12 is also divisible by 2, 3, 4, and 6.
- The fundamental theorem of arithmetic states that every integer greater than 1 can be expressed as a product of prime factors in one and only one way, except for the order of the factors.
- The number 1 is neither prime nor composite.
- The number 2 is the only even prime number.

A number is **divisible** by a second number if the number can be divided by the second number with a remainder of 0. A **prime number** is a whole number greater than 1 with exactly two factors, 1 and the number itself. A **composite number** is a whole number greater than 1 with more than two factors.

A composite number written as a product of prime numbers is the **prime factorization** of the number.

4-2 Greatest Common Divisor

California Content Standards **NS 1.2, MR 2.4**

Math Understandings

- Two or more whole numbers may have several common divisors, but they have only one greatest common divisor.

A divisor that two or more numbers share is a **common divisor**. The **greatest common divisor (GCD)** of two or more numbers is the greatest divisor shared by all the numbers. You can find the GCD for two numbers by listing all the divisors, using a division ladder, or using factor trees.

4-3 Equivalent Fractions

California Content Standards **NS 1.2, NS 1.5, AF 2.1, MR 1.1, MR 3.3**

Math Understandings

- A fraction is a number representing some part of a whole and may be written in the form $\frac{a}{b}$, where $b \neq 0$.

Equivalent fractions are fractions that name the same amount. A fraction is in **simplest form** when the only common factor of the numerator and denominator is 1. One way to write a fraction in simplest form is to divide both the numerator and denominator by their greatest common divisor.

Example: Write $\frac{12}{16}$ in simplest form.

1. Find the greatest common divisor of 12 and 16.
   Divisors of 12: **1**, **2**, 3, **4**, 6, 12
   Divisors of 16: **1**, **2**, **4**, 8, 16
   The GCD is **4**.
2. Divide the numerator and denominator by 4.
   $\frac{12 \div 4}{16 \div 4} = \frac{3}{4}$

$\frac{3}{4}$ is $\frac{12}{16}$ in simplest form.

4-4 Equivalent Forms of Rational Numbers

California Content Standards **NS 1.3, NS 1.5, MR 1.1**

Math Understandings

- **Rational numbers** are numbers that can be written in the form $\frac{a}{b}$, where *a* and *b* are integers and *b* is not equal to 0.
- The set of rational numbers includes integers, fractions, terminating decimals, and repeating decimals.
- You can write any integer as a fraction with a denominator of 1, so all integers are rational numbers.
- You can write every rational number as either a terminating or a repeating decimal.

A **terminating decimal** is a decimal that stops. A decimal that repeats the same digit or group of digits forever is a **repeating decimal**.

Example: $\frac{1}{3} = 0.333\ldots = 0.\overline{3}$

$\frac{5}{12} = 0.41666\ldots = 0.41\overline{6}$

- To write a decimal as a fraction, write the fraction as you would say the decimal and simplify.
- When you write fractions as decimals, the decimal may continuously repeat one digit or a set of digits.

A fraction indicates division. To write a fraction as a decimal, divide the numerator by the denominator.

Example: $\frac{5}{6} = 6\overline{)5.000}$ (quotient $.833$) $= 0.8\overline{3}$

- One number can be written in many different forms, all of which are equivalent.

4-5 Comparing and Ordering Rational Numbers

California Content Standards **NS 1.2, NS 1.3, MR 1.1, MR 2.2**

Math Understandings

- If the denominators of two fractions are the same, the fraction with the greater numerator is greater.
- If the numerators are the same, the fraction with the lesser denominator has the greater value.
- If the denominators of two fractions are different, first rewrite the fractions with common denominators.
- You can always find a common denominator for two fractions by multiplying the two denominators, but the result may not be the least common denominator.

The **least common multiple (LCM)** of two or more numbers is the smallest multiple that is common to all of the numbers. The LCM of the denominators is called the **least common denominator (LCD)**. To add, subtract, or compare fractions, rewrite them with a common denominator.

Example: Find the LCD for $\frac{3}{10}$ and $\frac{5}{12}$.

For $\frac{3}{10}$ and $\frac{5}{12}$, the product of the denominators (120) is a common denominator. However, the least common multiple (LCM) of 10 and 12 is 60, so the LCD is 60.

Professional Development

Additional Professional Development Opportunities

Math Background notes for Chapter 4: Every lesson has a Math Background in the PLAN section.

In-Service On Demand
Prentice Hall offers free video-based tutorials to support you. Visit PHSchool.com/inserviceondemand.

Pearson Achievement Solutions
Pearson Achievement Solutions, a Pearson Education company, offers comprehensive, facilitated professional development designed to help teachers improve student achievement. To learn more, please visit pearsonachievementsolutions.com.

Chapter 4 Resources

	4-1	4-2	4-3	4-4	4-5	For the Chapter
Print Resources						
L3 Practice	●	●	●	●	●	
L3 Guided Problem Solving	●	●	●	●	●	
L2 Reteaching	●	●	●	●	●	
L4 Enrichment	●	●	●	●	●	
L3 Vocabulary and Study Skills	●	●	●	●	●	●
L3 Daily Puzzles	●	●	●	●	●	
L3 Activity Labs	●	●	●	●	●	
L3 Checkpoint Quiz		●		●		
L3 Chapter Project						●
L2 Below Level Chapter Test						●
L3 Chapter Test						●
L4 Alternative Assessment						●
L3 Cumulative Review						●
Spanish Resources EL						
L3 Practice	●	●	●	●	●	
L3 Vocabulary and Study Skills	●		●		●	●
L3 Checkpoint Quiz		●		●		
L2 Below Level Chapter Test						●
L3 Chapter Test						●
L4 Alternative Assessment						●
L3 Cumulative Review						●
Transparencies						
Check Skills You'll Need	●	●	●	●	●	
Additional Examples	●	●	●	●	●	
California Daily Review	●	●	●	●	●	
Classroom Aid					●	
Student Edition Answers	●	●	●	●	●	●
Lesson Quiz	●	●	●	●	●	
Technology						
California Student Center Online	●	●	●	●	●	●
California Student Center CD-ROM	●	●	●	●	●	●
Success Tracker™ Online Math Intervention	●	●	●	●	●	●
California Teacher Center: ExamView CD-ROM	●	●	●	●	●	●
California Teacher Center: Planning CD-ROM	●	●	●	●	●	●
California Teacher Center: Presentations CD-ROM and online	●	●	●	●	●	●
MindPoint Quiz Show	●	●	●	●	●	●
Prentice Hall Web Site: PHSchool.com	●	●	●	●	●	●

Also available:

California Standards Mastery
- Standards Review Transparencies
- Standards Review and Practice Workbook
- Progress Monitoring Assessments
- Math Companion
- Math*XL*

California Intervention Resources
- Skills Review and Practice Workbook
- Success Tracker™ Online Math Intervention

Other Resources
- Multilingual Handbook
- Spanish Student Edition
- Solution Key
- Math Notes Study Folder

Where You Can Use the Lesson Resources

Here is a suggestion, following the four-step teaching plan, for how you can incorporate Universal Access Resources into your teaching.

	Instructional Resources L3	Universal Access Resources
1. Plan		
Preparation Read the Math Background in the Teacher's Edition to connect this lesson with students' previous experience. **Starting Class** **Check Skills You'll Need** Assign these exercises from the Math Companion to review prerequisite skills. Review the full text of the student expectations and objectives covered in this lesson. **New Vocabulary** Help students pre-read the lesson by pointing out the new terms introduced in the lesson.	**California Math Background** **Math Understandings** **Transparencies & Presentations CD-ROM** Check Skills You'll Need California Daily Review **Resources** Vocabulary and Study Skills **Math Companion**	**Spanish Support** EL Vocabulary and Study Skills
2. Teach		
L3 **Guided Instruction** Use the Activity Labs to build conceptual understanding. Teach each Example. Use the Teacher's Edition side column notes for specific teaching tips, including Error Prevention notes. Use the Additional Examples found in the side column (and on transparency and PowerPoint) as an alternative presentation for the content. After each Example, assign the California Standards Check exercises for that Example to get an immediate assessment of student understanding. Utilize the support in the Math Companion to assist students with each Standards Check. Use the Closure activity in the Teacher's Edition to help students attain mastery of lesson content.	**Student Edition** Activity Lab **Resources** Math Companion Activity Lab **Transparencies & Presentations CD-ROM** Additional Examples Classroom Aids **Teacher Center: ExamView CD-ROM**	**Teacher's Edition** Every lesson includes suggestions for working with students who need special attention. L1 Special Needs L2 Below Level L4 Advanced Learners EL English Learners **Resources** **Multilingual Handbook** **Math Companion**
3. Practice		
Assignment Guide **Check Your Understanding** Use these questions from the Math Companion to check students' understanding before you assign homework. **Homework Exercises** Assign homework from these leveled exercises in the Assignment Guide. **A** Practice by Example **B** Apply Your Skills **C** Challenge **California** Multiple-Choice Practice and Mixed Review **Homework Quick Check** Use these key exercises to quickly check students' homework.	**Transparencies & Presentations CD-ROM** Student Answers **Resources** Math Companion Practice Guided Problem Solving Vocabulary and Study Skills Activity Lab Daily Puzzles **Teacher Center: ExamView CD-ROM** **Math *XL***	**Spanish Support** EL Practice EL Vocabulary and Study Skills **Resources** L4 Enrichment
4. Assess & Reteach		
Lesson Quiz Assign the Lesson Quiz to assess students' mastery of the lesson content. **Checkpoint Quiz** Use the Checkpoint Quiz to assess student progress over several lessons.	**Transparencies & Presentations CD-ROM** Lesson Quiz **Resources** Checkpoint Quiz	**Resources** L2 Reteaching EL Checkpoint Quiz Success Tracker™ **Teacher Center: ExamView CD-ROM**

KEY  L1 Special Needs L2 Below Level L3 For All Students L4 Advanced, Gifted EL English Learners

Rational Numbers

Answers are in the back of the textbook.

For math intervention, direct students to:

Place Value
Skills Handbook, p. 434

Comparing and Ordering Decimals
Skills Handbook, p. 435

Dividing Integers
Lesson 2-5

Positive Exponents
Lesson 2-6

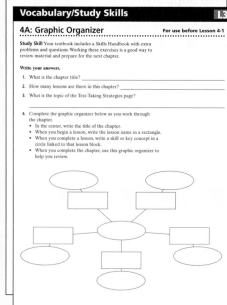

Spanish Vocabulary/Study Skills EL

Vocabulary/Study Skills L3

4A: Graphic Organizer — For use before Lesson 4-1

Study Skill Your textbook includes a Skills Handbook with extra problems and questions. Working these exercises is a good way to review material and prepare for the next chapter.

Write your answers.

1. What is the chapter title? ______
2. How many lessons are there in this chapter? ______
3. What is the topic of the Test-Taking Strategies page? ______
4. Complete the graphic organizer below as you work through the chapter.
   - In the center, write the title of the chapter.
   - When you begin a lesson, write the lesson name in a rectangle.
   - When you complete a lesson, write a skill or key concept in a circle linked to that lesson block.
   - When you complete the chapter, use this graphic organizer to help you review.

CALIFORNIA CHECK SYSTEM CHAPTER 4

Rational Numbers

What You've Learned

California Content Standards

AF 1.1 Use variables and appropriate operations to write an expression or an equation that represents a verbal description.

AF 4.1 Solve two-step linear equations in one variable.

MG 3.3 Know and understand the Pythagorean theorem and its converse.

Check Your Readiness

for Help to the lesson in green.

Decimals and Place Value (Skills Handbook p. 434)

Write each decimal in words.

1. 0.4 four tenths
2. 0.37 thirty-seven hundredths
3. 0.08 eight hundredths
4. 0.205 two hundred five thousandths
5. 0.0061 sixty-one ten-thousandths
6. 0.1502 one thousand five hundred two ten-thousandths

Comparing and Ordering Decimals (Skills Handbook p. 435)

Write the decimals in order from least to greatest.

7. 4.2, 4.02, 4.21 4.02, 4.2, 4.21
8. 0.3, 0.33, 0.033 0.033, 0.3, 0.33
9. 6.032, 6.302, 6.203 6.032, 6.203, 6.302
10. 9.013, 9.103, 9.13 9.013, 9.103, 9.13

Dividing Integers (Lesson 2-5)

Find each quotient.

11. $-12 \div 4$ -3
12. $25 \div (-5)$ -5
13. $-108 \div (-12)$ 9
14. $33 \div (-11)$ -3
15. $-54 \div (-9)$ 6
16. $-72 \div 24$ -3

Positive Exponents (Lesson 2-6)

Write each expression using exponents.

17. $3 \cdot 3 \cdot 3 \cdot 3$ 3^4
18. $5 \cdot 5 \cdot 5 \cdot 7 \cdot 7$ $5^3 \cdot 7^2$
19. $2 \cdot 2 \cdot 5 \cdot 5 \cdot 7$ $2^2 \cdot 5^2 \cdot 7$
20. $3 \cdot 3 \cdot 3 \cdot 3 \cdot 7 \cdot 11 \cdot 11 \cdot 11$ $3^4 \cdot 7 \cdot 11^3$

California Content Standards for Chapter 4

Number Sense
NS 1.2, NS 1.3, NS 1.5

Algebra and Functions
AF 2.1

Mathematical Reasoning
MR 1.1, MR 2.2, MR 2.4, MR 3.3

Chapter 4 Overview

In this chapter, students build on their knowledge of rational numbers as they learn about prime factorization, greatest common divisors, and least common multiples. They learn to simplify, convert, compare, and order rational numbers.

Activating Prior Knowledge

In this chapter, students build on and extend their knowledge of number theory, of decimals, and of properties of fractions in order to simplify fractions, to find equivalent fractions, and to express fractions as decimals.

Ask questions such as:

- *What do the following numbers have in common: 3, 11, 29, and 41?* **Samples: each is odd; each is divisible only by itself and 1; each is prime.**
- *What do these numbers have in common: 12, 18, 20, and 52?* **Samples: each is an even number; each is a multiple of 2; each is divisible by 2.**

▲ The notes you play on a musical instrument can be represented as fractions of a whole note.

What You'll Learn Next

California Content Standards

NS 1.3 Convert fractions to decimals and percents and use these representations in estimations, computations, and applications.

NS 1.5 Know that every rational number is either a terminating or a repeating decimal and be able to convert terminating decimals into reduced fractions.

New Vocabulary

English and Spanish Audio Online

- **composite number (p. 133)**
- **equivalent fractions (p. 142)**
- **greatest common divisor (p. 136)**
- **least common denominator (p. 155)**
- **least common multiple (p. 155)**
- **prime factorization (p. 133)**
- **prime number (p. 133)**
- **rational number (p. 148)**
- **repeating decimal (p. 149)**
- **simplest form (p. 143)**
- **terminating decimal (p. 149)**

Academic Vocabulary

- **concept map (p. 160)**
- **divisibility (p. 140)**

4-1

1. Plan

California Content Standards

Write numbers as the product of their prime factors by using exponents to show multiples of a factor. *Foundational*

NS 1.2 Multiply and divide rational numbers. ***Introduce, Develop***

AF 2.1 Interpret positive whole-number powers as repeated multiplication. ***Develop***

California Math Background

Every counting number greater than 1 either is a prime number, or can be written as the product of prime numbers. Writing a number (that is not prime) as the product of its prime factors is called *factoring* that number.

More Math Background: p. 130C

Lesson Planning and Resources

See p. 130E for a list of the resources that support this lesson.

PRESENTATION CD-ROM
CD, Online, or Transparencies

Bell Ringer Practice

Check Skills You'll Need
Use student page, transparency, or PowerPoint.
See Math Companion.

California Standards Review
Use transparency or PowerPoint.

4-1 Prime Factorization

Check Skills You'll Need

Do this in your **Math Companion.**

Vocabulary
- composite number
- prime number
- prime factorization

Use your **Math Companion** *to build your vocabulary.*

California Content Standards

Foundational Standard Write numbers as the product of their prime factors by using exponents to show multiples of a factor.

NS 1.2 Multiply and divide rational numbers. ***Develop***

AF 2.1 Interpret positive whole-number powers as repeated multiplication. ***Develop***

What You'll Learn . . . and Why

You will learn to factor numbers and find the prime factorization of numbers. You can use factors to arrange items or people in rows, like the rows of a marching band.

Recall that a factor is a whole number that divides a nonzero whole number with remainder 0. For example, 2 is a factor of 10 since $10 \div 2 = 5$. Divisibility rules can help you find factors.

EXAMPLE Finding Factors

Relate **MATH YOU KNOW . . .**

Solve $4 \cdot \blacksquare = 20$.

. . . *to* **NEW IDEAS**

Since $4 \cdot 5 = 20$, $\blacksquare = 5$.

1 **Guided Problem Solving** An instructor plans a dance routine for 20 dancers in rows. Each row has the same number of dancers. How many dancers can be in each row?

Look for pairs of factors of 20 to find the possible number of dancers in each row.

$1 \cdot 20$ ← **Write each pair of factors. Start with 1.**

$2 \cdot 10,\ 4 \cdot 5$ ← **2, 4, 5, and 10 are factors. Skip 3, since 20 is not divisible by 3.**

$5 \cdot 4$ ← **Stop when you repeat factors.**

The factors of 20 are 1, 2, 4, 5, 10, and 20. There can be 1, 2, 4, 5, 10, or 20 dancers in each row.

Quick Tip

When listing the factors of a number, begin with 1 and continue in order until a factor is repeated.

CA Standards Check 1

Go to your **Math Companion** *for help.*

1. You have 24 pears to put in a gift box. Each row must hold the same number of pears. How many pears can be in each row?
   1, 2, 3, 4, 6, 8, 12, 24

Universal Access Solutions for All Learners

Special Needs L1	**Below Level** L2
Students who have a difficult time drawing the branches on a factor tree can pair up with, and check the calculations of, students who can draw the trees.	Explain that a number divisible by 6 is also divisible by all other factors of 6: 1, 2, and 3. Have students test whether 30 is divisible by all the factors of 30 to reinforce the definition of *divisible*.

A **composite number** is a whole number greater than 1 with more than two factors. A **prime number** is a whole number with exactly two factors, 1 and the number itself. The numbers 0 and 1 are neither prime nor composite.

EXAMPLE **Prime and Composite Numbers**

2 Is 51 prime or composite? Explain.

Since 51 is divisible by 3, it has more than two factors. So 51 is composite.

CA Standards Check 2 *Go to your* **Math Companion** *for help.*

2. Is each number prime or composite? Explain.

a. 53 Prime; 53 has only two factors, 1 and 53.

b. 47 Prime; 47 has only two factors, 1 and 47.

c. 63 Composite; 1, 3, 7, 9, 21, and 63 are factors of 63.

A composite number written as a product of prime numbers is the **prime factorization** of the number. The written order of the factors does not matter. For example, the prime factorization $2 \cdot 3$ is the same as $3 \cdot 2$. Use exponents to express repeated factors.

$$12 = 2 \cdot 2 \cdot 3 = 2^2 \cdot 3$$

You can use a factor tree to find the prime factorization of a number.

EXAMPLE **Writing Prime Factorization**

3 Find the prime factorization of 54.

Use a factor tree. The number 54 is divisible by 2 because it is an even number. Begin the factor tree with $2 \cdot 27$.

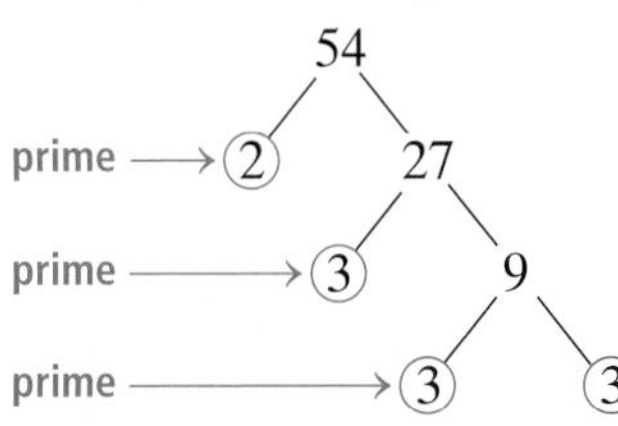

The prime factorization of 54 is $2 \cdot 3 \cdot 3 \cdot 3$, or $2 \cdot 3^3$.

Online active math

For: Prime Factorization Activity
Use: Interactive Textbook, 4-1

CA Standards Check 3 *Go to your* **Math Companion** *for help.*

3. Find the prime factorization of each number.

a. 99 $3^2 \cdot 11$ **b.** 84 $2^2 \cdot 3 \cdot 7$ **c.** 240 $2^4 \cdot 3 \cdot 5$

Homework prep is in your **Math Companion.**

2. Teach

Guided Instruction

Example 2
Connect the language of mathematics to the plain language that students use by explaining that x is divisible by y if y goes into x evenly, with nothing left over.

Error Prevention!

In listing the prime factors for a number (as in Example 3), students may omit one or more repetitions of a repeated factor. Have them check their work by multiplying the factors in the final list to verify that the product is equal to the original number.

Technology Tip
Students can also use calculators to investigate and verify the divisibility of one number by another.

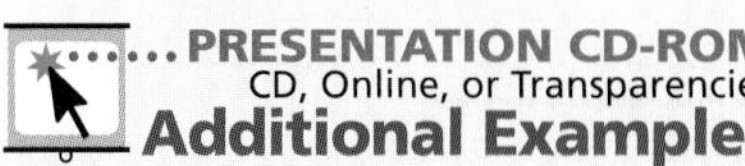

Additional Examples

1 You have 35 vegetable seeds to plant in your garden. The seeds must be planted in rows of equal length. How many seeds can be in each row?

2 Is each number prime or composite? Explain.

a. 61

b. 65

3 Find the prime factorization of 90.

Closure

- *What is the prime factorization of a number?* an expression that shows the number as a product of prime numbers

Advanced Learners L4	**English Learners** EL
Find all the whole numbers less than 50 whose only prime factors are 2 or 3. 2, 3, 4, 6, 8, 9, 12, 16, 18, 24, 27, 32, 36, 48	Ensure students can explain why, in Example 3, they start with 2 as a divisor. Explain that it is easier to find prime factors if they get one of the prime factors out of the way in the first division or first multiplication on the factor tree.

3. Practice

Assignment Guide

Check Your Understanding
See Math Companion.

Homework Exercises

A Practice by Example	1–33
B Apply Your Skills	34–49
C Challenge	50
California Multiple-Choice Practice	51–53
Mixed Review	54–56

Homework Quick Check
To check students' understanding of key skills and concepts, go over Exercises 8, 15, 25, 35, 43, 49.

Universal Access Resources

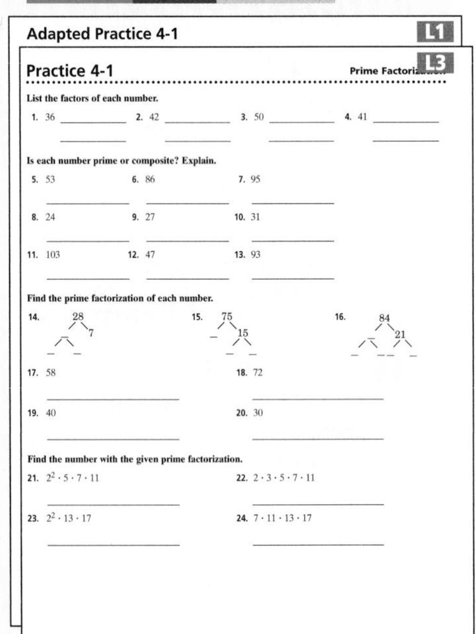
Adapted Practice 4-1 L1

Practice 4-1 Prime Factorization L3

List the factors of each number.

1. 36 2. 42 3. 50 4. 41

Is each number prime or composite? Explain.

5. 53 6. 86 7. 95
8. 24 9. 27 10. 31
11. 103 12. 47 13. 93

Find the prime factorization of each number.

14. 28 15. 75 16. 84
17. 58 18. 72
19. 40 20. 30

Find the number with the given prime factorization.

21. $2^2 \cdot 5 \cdot 7 \cdot 11$ 22. $2 \cdot 3 \cdot 5 \cdot 7 \cdot 11$
23. $2^2 \cdot 13 \cdot 17$ 24. $7 \cdot 11 \cdot 13 \cdot 17$

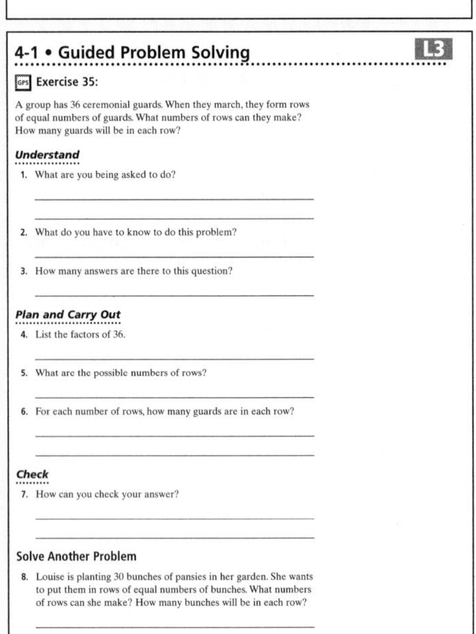
4-1 • Guided Problem Solving L3

GPS Exercise 35:

A group has 36 ceremonial guards. When they march, they form rows of equal numbers of guards. What numbers of rows can they make? How many guards will be in each row?

Understand
1. What are you being asked to do?
2. What do you have to know to do this problem?
3. How many answers are there to this question?

Plan and Carry Out
4. List the factors of 36.
5. What are the possible numbers of rows?
6. For each number of rows, how many guards are in each row?

Check
7. How can you check your answer?

Solve Another Problem
8. Louise is planting 30 bunches of pansies in her garden. She wants to put them in rows of equal numbers of bunches. What numbers of rows can she make? How many bunches will be in each row?

Standards Practice

GO for Help: MathXL
NS 1.2, AF 2.1

A Practice by Example

Example 1 (page 132)

List the factors of each number. 1–23. See margin.

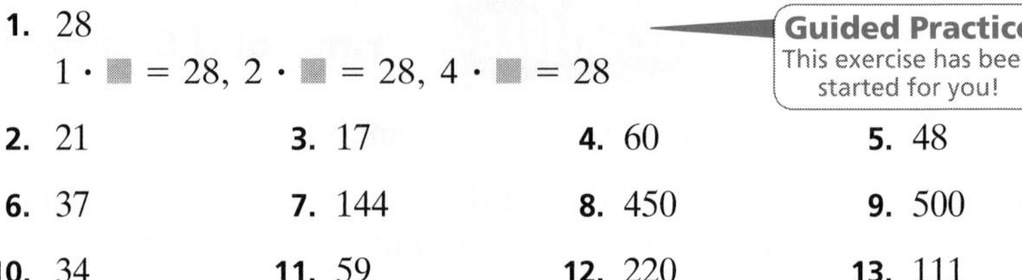
1. 28
$1 \cdot ■ = 28$, $2 \cdot ■ = 28$, $4 \cdot ■ = 28$

Guided Practice
This exercise has been started for you!

2. 21 3. 17 4. 60 5. 48
6. 37 7. 144 8. 450 9. 500
10. 34 11. 59 12. 220 13. 111

GO for Help

14. For a science project, you want to display 36 rocks in rows, with the same number of rocks in each row. How many rocks can you put in each row?

Example 2 (page 133)

Is each number prime or composite? Explain.

15. 19 16. 67 17. 57
18. 91 19. 48 20. 25
21. 73 22. 101 23. 250

Example 3 (page 133)

Find the prime factorization of each number.

24. 32 2^5
32 → ② and ■

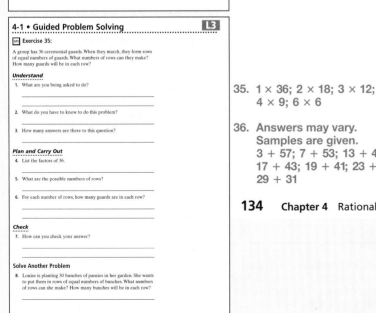

Guided Practice
This exercise has been started for you!

25. 42 $2 \cdot 3 \cdot 7$ 26. 75 $3 \cdot 5^2$ 27. 400 $2^4 \cdot 5^2$
28. 15 $3 \cdot 5$ 29. 56 $2^3 \cdot 7$ 30. 39 $3 \cdot 13$
31. 160 $2^5 \cdot 5$ 32. 1,000 $2^3 \cdot 5^3$ 33. 234 $2 \cdot 3^2 \cdot 13$

Homework Video Tutor
For: Examples 1–3
Visit: PHSchool.com
Web Code: axe-0401

B Apply Your Skills

34. **Guided Problem Solving** A yearbook editor must arrange 48 student photos on a page. Each row must have the same number of photos. What arrangements can the editor make? See left.
- **Make a Plan** What method can you use to find the factor pairs for 48?
- **Check the Answer** How do you know that you have found all the factor pairs?

34. 1×48; 2×24; 3×16; 4×12; 6×8

GPS 35. A group has 36 ceremonial guards. When they march, they form rows of equal numbers of guards. What numbers of rows can they make? How many guards will be in each row? See left.

35. 1×36; 2×18; 3×12; 4×9; 6×6

36. In 1742, the mathematician Christian Goldbach made a conjecture that every even number greater than 2 can be expressed as the sum of two prime numbers. Write the number 60 as the sum of two prime numbers. See left.

36. Answers may vary. Samples are given. $3 + 57$; $7 + 53$; $13 + 47$; $17 + 43$; $19 + 41$; $23 + 37$; $29 + 31$

SCAFFOLDED
Problem Solving

41. $2 = 2$; $3 = 3$; $4 = 2^2$; $6 = 2 \cdot 3$; $8 = 2^3$; $12 = 2^2 \cdot 3$; $24 = 2^3 \cdot 3$; each factor's prime factorization is a subset of the prime factorization of 24.

42. Find the products of all the combinations of the numbers in the prime factorization.

49. Composite; if p is a prime number greater than 2, then p is an odd number. So $p + 1$ is an even number, and the only even number that is prime is 2.

37. List the factors of 24. 1, 2, 3, 4, 6, 8, 12, 24

38. Find the prime factorization of 24. $2^3 \cdot 3$

39. One of the factors of 24 is 12. Find the prime factorization of 12. $2^2 \cdot 3$

40. Are all the prime factors of 12 also prime factors of 24? yes

41. Find the prime factorization for the other factors of 24 that are greater than 1. How is each factor's prime factorization related to the prime factorization of 24? See left.

42. Describe how you can use the prime factorization of a number to find the number's factors. See left.

Find the number with the given prime factorization.

43. $7 \cdot 11 \cdot 13$ 1,001

44. $2^2 \cdot 11$ 44

45. $2 \cdot 5^2 \cdot 17$ 850

46. $2^3 \cdot 5^2 \cdot 7 \cdot 11$ 15,400

47. **Number Sense** What is the greatest factor of any number? the number itself

48. **Algebra** Show that the expression $-x^2 + 7x + 7$ is a prime number when $x = 0$, $x = 2$, and $x = 3$. 7, 17, and 19 are prime

49. **Writing in Math** Suppose p is a prime number greater than 2. Does $p + 1$ represent a prime or a composite number? Explain. See above left.

C Challenge

50. Find all the pairs of prime numbers between 1 and 100 with a difference of two. 3, 5; 5, 7; 11, 13; 17, 19; 29, 31; 41, 43; 59, 61; 71, 73

Multiple Choice Practice and Mixed Review

For California Standards Tutorials, visit PHSchool.com. Web Code: axq-9045

AF 2.1

51. Simplify $2^4 \cdot 3$. D

Ⓐ 6　Ⓑ 18　Ⓒ 24　Ⓓ 48

NS 1.2

52. Three friends agree to split a dinner bill equally. The dinner costs \$33, and tax is an additional \$1.65. They leave a \$6 tip. How much does each person pay? B

Ⓐ \$11.65　Ⓑ \$13.55　Ⓒ \$36.05　Ⓓ \$40.65

AF 1.1

53. The table shows a sequence of terms. Which expression can be used to find the value of the term in position n? D

Position, n	Value of Term
1	3
2	6
3	9
n	■

Ⓐ $n + 2$　Ⓒ $n + 3$
Ⓑ $2n$　Ⓓ $3n$

for Help　**Lesson 3-1**

Solve each equation.

54. $m + 45 = 111$ 66

55. $17 + d = 4$ −13

56. $c + 6.2 = 13.8$ 7.6

Online Lesson Quiz　Visit: PHSchool.com　Web Code: axa-0401

4. Assess & Reteach

PRESENTATION CD-ROM
CD, Online, or Transparencies

Lesson Quiz

Write the prime factorization for each number.

1. 36 $2^2 \times 3^2$
2. 150 $2 \times 3 \times 5^2$
3. 99 $3^2 \times 11$
4. 225 $3^2 \times 5^2$

Alternative Assessment

Provide student pairs with several composite numbers such as 40, 72, 90, and 500. They are to find the prime factorization using factor trees. For 72, they might start with $8 \cdot 9$. One partner writes the factors for the first branch, 8, and the other writes the factors for the second branch, 9. Partners work together to write the prime factorization.

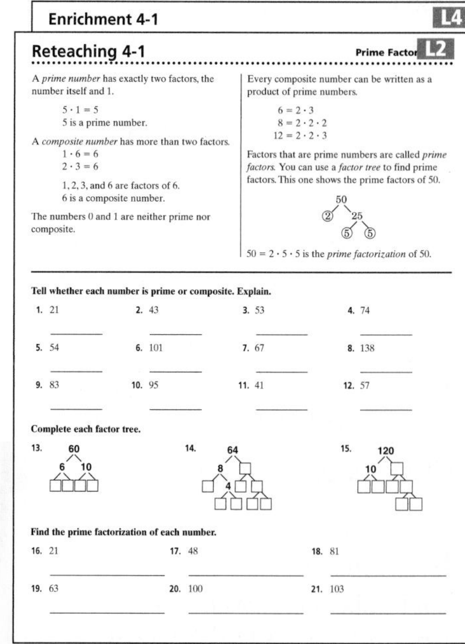

Enrichment 4-1 L4

Reteaching 4-1　Prime Factor L2

A *prime number* has exactly two factors, the number itself and 1.
$5 \cdot 1 = 5$
5 is a prime number.

A *composite number* has more than two factors.
$1 \cdot 6 = 6$
$2 \cdot 3 = 6$
1, 2, 3, and 6 are factors of 6.
6 is a composite number.

The numbers 0 and 1 are neither prime nor composite.

Every composite number can be written as a product of prime numbers.
$6 = 2 \cdot 3$
$8 = 2 \cdot 2 \cdot 2$
$12 = 2 \cdot 2 \cdot 3$

Factors that are prime numbers are called *prime factors*. You can use a *factor tree* to find prime factors. This one shows the prime factors of 50.

$50 = 2 \cdot 5 \cdot 5$ is the *prime factorization* of 50.

Tell whether each number is prime or composite. Explain.

1. 21　2. 43　3. 53　4. 74
5. 54　6. 101　7. 67　8. 138
9. 83　10. 95　11. 41　12. 57

Complete each factor tree.

13. 60　14. 64　15. 120

Find the prime factorization of each number.

16. 21　17. 48　18. 81
19. 63　20. 100　21. 103

California Resources

Standards Mastery

- Standards Review Transparencies
- Standards Review and Practice Workbook
- Math Companion

Math Intervention

- Skills Review and Practice Workbook
- Math XL

4-2

1. Plan

California Content Standards

Determine the prime factors of all numbers through 50. *Foundational*

Determine the greatest common divisor of whole numbers and use it to solve problems with fractions. *Foundational*

NS 1.2 Multiply and divide rational numbers. ***Introduce, Develop***

California Math Background

If two numbers are each divisible by a third number, the third number is a *common divisor* of the other two. In this lesson, students learn two methods for identifying the *greatest common divisor*, or the *GCD*.

More Math Background: p. 130C

Lesson Planning and Resources

See p. 130E for a list of the resources that support this lesson.

PRESENTATION CD-ROM
CD, Online, or Transparencies
Bell Ringer Practice

Check Skills You'll Need
Use student page, transparency, or PowerPoint.
See Math Companion.

California Standards Review
Use transparency or PowerPoint.

4-2 Greatest Common Divisor

Check Skills You'll Need

Do this in your **Math Companion.**

Vocabulary
- common divisor
- greatest common divisor (GCD)

Use your **Math Companion** *to build your vocabulary.*

Vocabulary Tip

The greatest common divisor (GCD) is sometimes called the greatest common factor (GCF).

California Content Standards

Foundational Standard Determine the prime factors of all numbers through 50.
Foundational Standard Determine the greatest common divisor of whole numbers and use it to solve problems with fractions.
NS 1.2 Multiply and divide rational numbers. ***Develop***

What You'll Learn . . . and Why

You will learn to find the greatest common divisor of two numbers. You can use the greatest common divisor to distribute items, such as sets of stamps or coins, evenly into groups.

A divisor that two or more numbers share is a **common divisor.** The **greatest common divisor (GCD)** of two or more numbers is the greatest divisor shared by all the numbers.

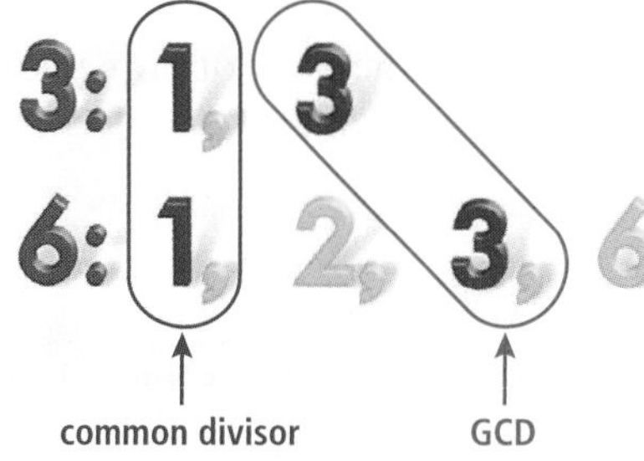

You can find the GCD of two numbers by listing their divisors.

EXAMPLE Using Lists of Divisors

1 Find the greatest common divisor of 18 and 30.

List the divisors of 18 and the divisors of 30. Circle the common divisors.

Divisors of 18: (1), (2), (3), (6), 9, 18
Divisors of 30: (1), (2), (3), 5, (6), 10, 15, 30

The common divisors are 1, 2, 3, and 6.

The greatest common divisor (GCD) is 6.

CA Standards Check 1 *Go to your* **Math Companion** *for help.*

1. Find the GCD of each pair of numbers by listing their divisors.
a. 6, 21 3 **b.** 18, 49 1 **c.** 14, 28 14

Universal Access Solutions for All Learners

Special Needs L1	**Below Level** L2
Some students may have difficulty drawing factor trees. If so, pair them with students who can draw the trees, while they say the numbers.	Have students find the GCD of pairs of numbers that are already in factored form. For example: $2 \times 2 \times 3$ and $2 \times 3 \times 7$: GCD = 6 $2 \times 3 \times 3 \times 5$ and $3 \times 3 \times 5 \times 5$: GCD = 45

You also can find the GCD of two or more numbers by using the prime factorization of the numbers.

You can use the greatest common divisor to divide sets of varying sizes evenly into groups. The largest number of groups the sets can be divided into is the GCD of the sizes of the sets.

EXAMPLE Using Prime Factorization

Relate **MATH YOU KNOW...**

Find the prime factorization of 18.

Make a factor tree.

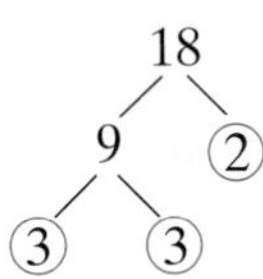

The prime factorization of 18 is $2 \cdot 3^2$.

... to **NEW IDEAS**

2 **Guided Problem Solving** The president of a collectors club evenly distributes 18 stamps, 27 coins, and 36 mineral samples to club members at a meeting. What is the greatest possible number of club members at the meeting?

To find the greatest possible number of club members present, find the GCD of 18, 27, and 36. Make a factor tree to find the prime factorization of each number.

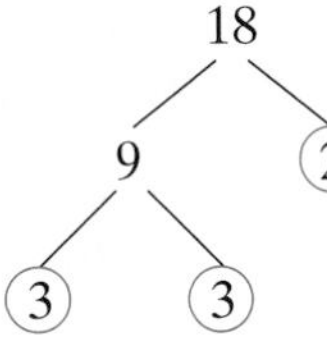

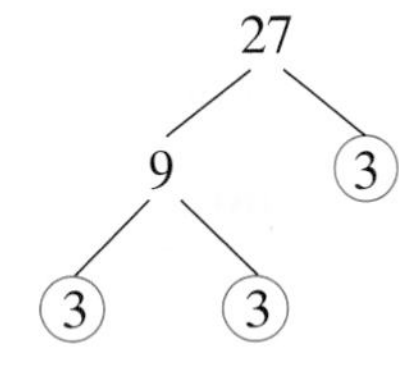

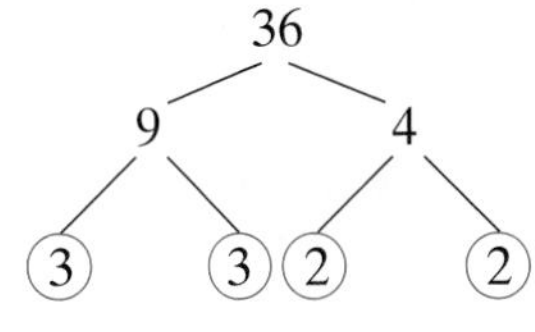

$18 = 3 \cdot 3 \cdot 2$
$27 = 3 \cdot 3 \cdot 3$
$36 = 3 \cdot 3 \cdot 2 \cdot 2$

Write the prime factorization for each number.

Identify common factors.

$3 \cdot 3 = 9$

The GCD of 18, 27, and 36 is 9. The greatest possible number of members is 9.

Problem Solving Tip

You can use one of the two methods shown in the examples to find the GCD. Then check your answer using the other method.

CA Standards Check 2 *Go to your* **Math Companion** *for help.*

2. Two pipes have lengths 63 ft and 84 ft. You cut both pipes into pieces of equal length with nothing left. What is the greatest possible length of the pieces? **21 ft**

Homework prep is in your **Math Companion.**

2. Teach

Guided Instruction

Example 2
Students can model the problem using three colors of tiles or cubes. One color can represent the set of 18 stamps, a second color can represent the set of 27 coins, and a third color can represent the set of 36 mineral samples.

Additional Examples

1 List the divisors to find the GCD of 48 and 64. **16**

2 Two ribbons have lengths of 28 cm and 42 cm. You cut both ribbons into pieces of equal length with nothing left over. What is the greatest possible length of the pieces? **14**

Closure

- Describe two ways to find the GCD. **1. List all the factors of each number. Find the greatest common divisor of all the numbers. 2. Use factor trees to find the prime factorization of each number. Multiply the prime factors common to all the numbers.**

Advanced Learners L4	**English Learners** EL
A number is a *perfect number* if the sum of all its factors (including 1) is equal to twice the number. Find all the perfect numbers in this list: 4, 6, 8, 14, 18, 34, 28, 32 **6, 28**	Assign groups to find the greatest common divisor of two numbers. Ask them to show how to do it using the two ways shown and *explain* the differences and similarities between the methods.

3. Practice

Assignment Guide

Check Your Understanding
See Math Companion.

Homework Exercises

A	Practice by Example	1–21
B	Apply Your Skills	22–35
C	Challenge	36
California Multiple-Choice Practice		37–39
Mixed Review		40–43

Homework Quick Check
To check students' understanding of key skills and concepts, go over Exercises 2, 12, 23, 27, 33.

Universal Access Resources

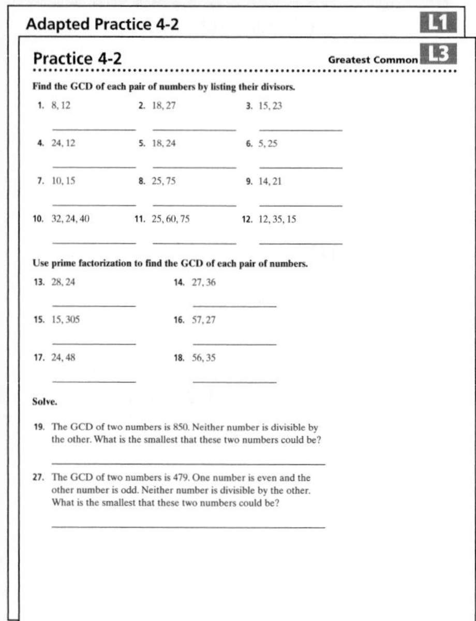

Adapted Practice 4-2 L1

Practice 4-2 Greatest Common L3

Find the GCD of each pair of numbers by listing their divisors.

1. 8, 12 2. 18, 27 3. 15, 23
4. 24, 12 5. 18, 24 6. 5, 25
7. 10, 15 8. 25, 75 9. 14, 21
10. 32, 24, 40 11. 25, 60, 75 12. 12, 35, 15

Use prime factorization to find the GCD of each pair of numbers.

13. 28, 24 14. 27, 36
15. 15, 305 16. 57, 27
17. 24, 48 18. 56, 35

Solve.

19. The GCD of two numbers is 850. Neither number is divisible by the other. What is the smallest that these two numbers could be?

20. The GCD of two numbers is 479. One number is even and the other number is odd. Neither number is divisible by the other. What is the smallest that these two numbers could be?

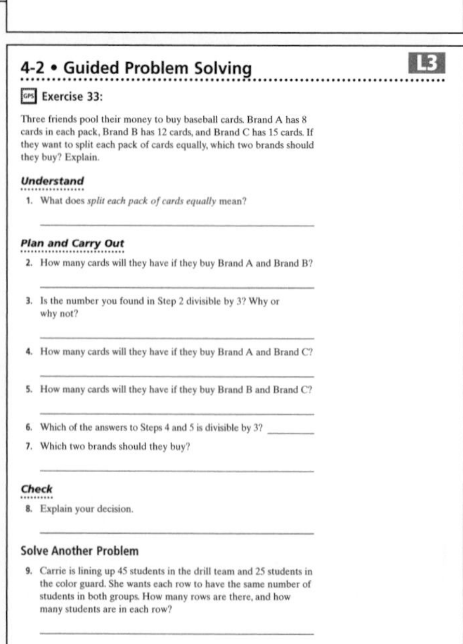

4-2 • Guided Problem Solving L3

Exercise 33:

Three friends pool their money to buy baseball cards. Brand A has 8 cards in each pack, Brand B has 12 cards, and Brand C has 15 cards. If they want to split each pack of cards equally, which two brands should they buy? Explain.

Understand

1. What does *split each pack of cards equally* mean?

Plan and Carry Out

2. How many cards will they have if they buy Brand A and Brand B?
3. Is the number you found in Step 2 divisible by 3? Why or why not?
4. How many cards will they have if they buy Brand A and Brand C?
5. How many cards will they have if they buy Brand B and Brand C?
6. Which of the answers to Steps 4 and 5 is divisible by 3?
7. Which two brands should they buy?

Check

8. Explain your decision.

Solve Another Problem

9. Carrie is lining up 45 students in the drill team and 25 students in the color guard. She wants each row to have the same number of students in both groups. How many rows are there, and how many students are in each row?

Standards Practice

GO for Help: *MathXL* NS 1.2

A Practice by Example

Example 1 (page 136)

Find the GCD of each pair of numbers by listing their divisors.

Guided Practice This exercise has been started for you!

1. 6, 32 2
   Divisors of 6: 1, 2, 3, 6
   Divisors of 32: 1, 2, 4, 8, 16, 32

GO for Help

2. 15, 54 3
3. 42, 72 6
4. 21, 63 21
5. 52, 78 26
6. 38, 82 2
7. 44, 68 4
8. 30, 50 10
9. 27, 30 3
10. 12, 11 1

Example 2 (page 137)

Use prime factorization to find the GCD of each pair of numbers.

For: Examples 1–2
Visit: PHSchool.com
Web Code: axe-0402

Guided Practice This exercise has been started for you!

11. 20, 60 20

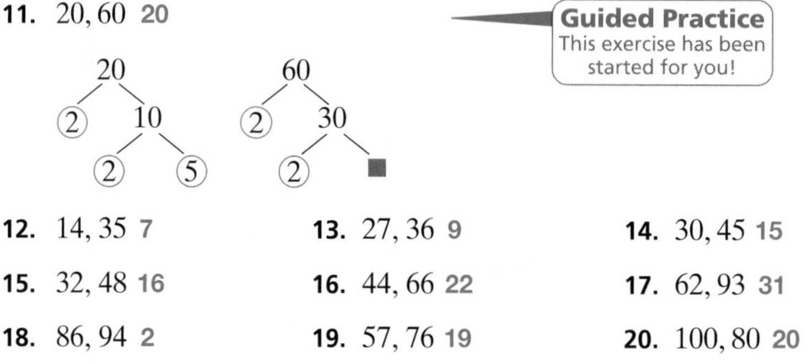

12. 14, 35 7
13. 27, 36 9
14. 30, 45 15
15. 32, 48 16
16. 44, 66 22
17. 62, 93 31
18. 86, 94 2
19. 57, 76 19
20. 100, 80 20

21. Students are cleaning a local park in groups. There are 50 boys and 75 girls. Each group has the same number of boys and the same number of girls. What is the greatest possible number of groups? 25 groups

B Apply Your Skills

22. **Guided Problem Solving** You are dividing a community garden that is 35 m long by 15 m wide into equal-sized square gardens. Find the greatest possible dimension of each square. 5 m by 5 m
    - **Make a Plan** Draw a picture to help you visualize the problem. Then find the GCD.
    - **Carry Out the Plan** The GCD is ■. The largest possible dimensions of each square are ■ m by ■ m.

Find the GCD of each set of numbers.

23. 22, 33, 44 11
24. 27, 45, −81 9
25. 12, −24, 36 12

26. The cafeteria has 144 bananas, 36 pears, and 72 apples. Each student gets the same number of pieces of each fruit. What is the greatest number of students who can receive fruit? 36 students

27. **Writing in Math** Nine people plan to share equally 24 stamps from one set and 36 stamps from another set. Explain why 9 people cannot share the stamps equally. 9 is not a divisor of 24.

SCAFFOLDED
Problem Solving

28. 1, 2, 3, 4, 5, 6, 8, 10, 12, 15, 20, 24, 30, 40, 60, 120

32. 13 boxes of markers, 4 packs of paper, and 9 sets of watercolors

33. Brand B and Brand C; 3 is a common divisor of 12 and of 15.

34. 48; its divisors are 1, 2, 3, 4, 6, 8, 12, 16, 24, and 48; any other number less than 50 has fewer than 10 divisors.

35. 1; since the divisors of a prime number are 1 and itself, the only common divisor for two different prime numbers is 1.

An art teacher hands out her entire inventory of art supplies, listed at the right.

paintbrushes 120
boxes of markers 78
packs of paper 24
sets of watercolors 54

28. List the divisors of the number of paintbrushes. See left.

29. Find the GCD of 120, 78, 24, and 54. 6

30. Each class gets the same number of each item. What is the greatest number of classes that can receive supplies? 6 classes

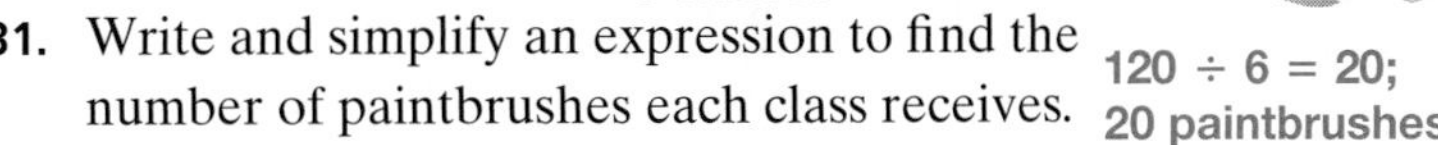

31. Write and simplify an expression to find the number of paintbrushes each class receives. $120 \div 6 = 20$; 20 paintbrushes

32. How many of the other items does each class get? See above left.

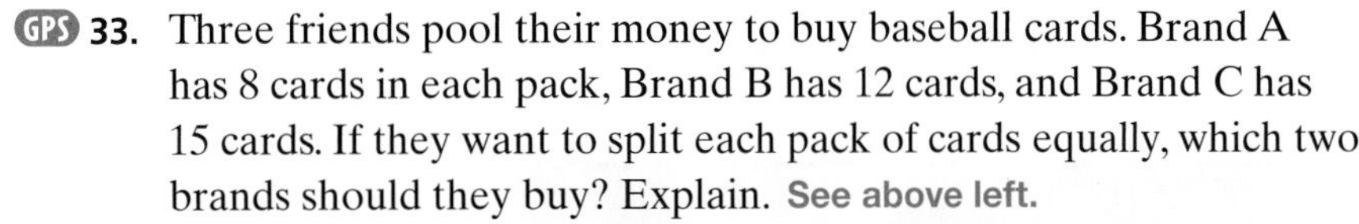

GPS 33. Three friends pool their money to buy baseball cards. Brand A has 8 cards in each pack, Brand B has 12 cards, and Brand C has 15 cards. If they want to split each pack of cards equally, which two brands should they buy? Explain. See above left.

34. **Number Sense** Which number greater than 0 and less than 50 has the most divisors? Justify your answer. See above left.

35. **Reasoning** What is the GCD of any two prime numbers? Explain. See above left.

C Challenge

36. There are four two-digit numbers that end with 6 and are less than 50. Find the GCD of the four numbers. 2

Multiple Choice Practice and Mixed Review

For California Standards Tutorials, visit PHSchool.com. Web Code: axq-9045

NS 1.2

37. A fishing lure is floating 6 ft below the surface of a pond. It sinks 3 ft. Which measurement describes the new position of the lure? A

A -9 ft B -6 ft C -3 ft D 3 ft

AF 1.3

38. Which equation illustrates the Inverse Property of Addition? C

A $x + (-x) = 1$
B $x + 1 = 1 + x$
C $x + (-x) = 0$
D $x + (x + 1) = (x + x) + 1$

MG 3.3

39. Sarah walks across a rectangular field as shown. Which is closest to the distance she walks? C

A 100 ft
B 90 ft
C 70 ft
D 50 ft

path
40 ft
60 ft

GO for Help Lesson 2-6

Simplify each expression.

40. 8^2 64 41. 2^4 16 42. $17 - (-2)^3$ 25 43. $(-4 + 7)^2$ 9

Online Lesson Quiz Visit: PHSchool.com Web Code: axa-0402

Alternative Assessment

Provide pairs of students with pairs of composite numbers such as those in Exercises 1–20. Each partner draws a factor tree to find the prime factorization for one of the composite numbers. Partners then work together to find the GCD of each set of numbers.

California Resources

Standards Mastery
- Standards Review Transparencies
- Standards Review and Practice Workbook
- Math Companion

Math Intervention
- Skills Review and Practice Workbook
- Math XL

4. Assess & Reteach

PRESENTATION CD-ROM
CD, Online, or Transparencies
Lesson Quiz

Find the GCD of each set of numbers.

1. 60, 80 20
2. 24, 57 3
3. 36, 48 12
4. 115, 70, 200 5

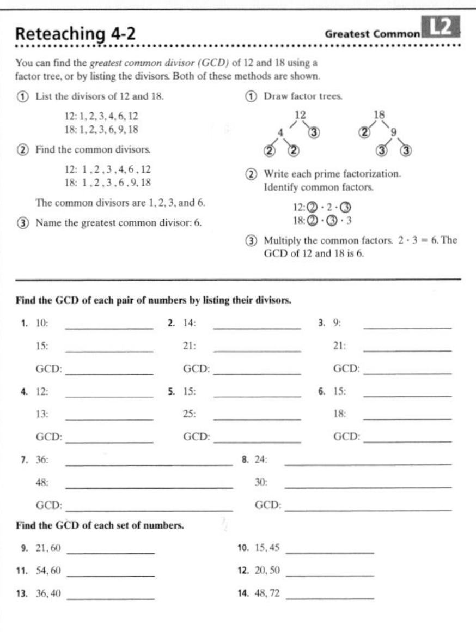

Reteaching 4-2 Greatest Common L2

You can find the *greatest common divisor (GCD)* of 12 and 18 using a factor tree, or by listing the divisors. Both of these methods are shown.

① List the divisors of 12 and 18.

12: 1, 2, 3, 4, 6, 12
18: 1, 2, 3, 6, 9, 18

② Find the common divisors.

12: 1, 2, 3, 4, 6, 12
18: 1, 2, 3, 6, 9, 18

The common divisors are 1, 2, 3, and 6.

③ Name the greatest common divisor: 6.

① Draw factor trees.

12 → 4, ③; 4 → ②, ②
18 → ②, 9; 9 → ③, ③

② Write each prime factorization. Identify common factors.

12: ② · 2 · ③
18: ② · ③ · 3

③ Multiply the common factors. $2 \cdot 3 = 6$. The GCD of 12 and 18 is 6.

Find the GCD of each pair of numbers by listing their divisors.

1. 10: ____ 15: ____ GCD: ____
2. 14: ____ 21: ____ GCD: ____
3. 9: ____ 21: ____ GCD: ____
4. 12: ____ 13: ____ GCD: ____
5. 15: ____ 25: ____ GCD: ____
6. 15: ____ 18: ____ GCD: ____
7. 36: ____ 48: ____ GCD: ____
8. 24: ____ 30: ____ GCD: ____

Find the GCD of each set of numbers.

9. 21, 60 ____
10. 15, 45 ____
11. 54, 60 ____
12. 20, 50 ____
13. 36, 40 ____
14. 48, 72 ____

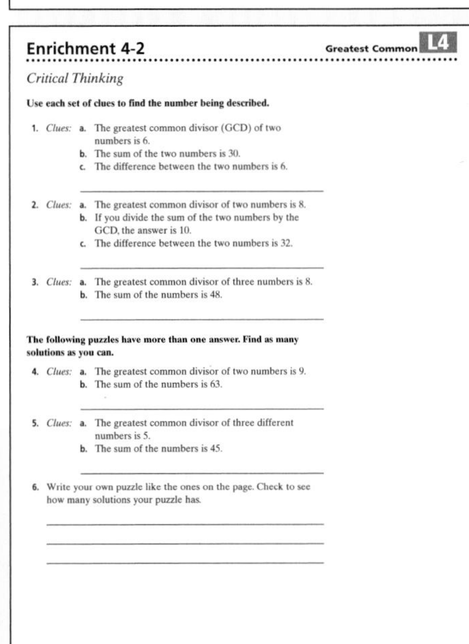

Enrichment 4-2 Greatest Common L4

Critical Thinking

Use each set of clues to find the number being described.

1. *Clues:* a. The greatest common divisor (GCD) of two numbers is 6.
b. The sum of the two numbers is 30.
c. The difference between the two numbers is 6.

____

2. *Clues:* a. The greatest common divisor of two numbers is 8.
b. If you divide the sum of the two numbers by the GCD, the answer is 10.
c. The difference between the two numbers is 32.

____

3. *Clues:* a. The greatest common divisor of three numbers is 8.
b. The sum of the numbers is 48.

____

The following puzzles have more than one answer. Find as many solutions as you can.

4. *Clues:* a. The greatest common divisor of two numbers is 9.
b. The sum of the numbers is 63.

____

5. *Clues:* a. The greatest common divisor of three different numbers is 5.
b. The sum of the numbers is 45.

____

6. Write your own puzzle like the ones on the page. Check to see how many solutions your puzzle has.

____

Mathematical Reasoning

Divisibility Tests

Students learn how to use divisibility tests to decide whether one number is divisible by another.

Guided Instruction

Explain that divisibility tests are most useful when working with large numbers because using divisibility tests is quicker than factoring large numbers.

Read the table with the students and have them suggest several large numbers. Try the tests out on numbers they suggest. Have students verify their results by dividing.

Checkpoint Quiz

Use this Checkpoint Quiz to check students' understanding of the skills and concepts of Lessons 4-1 through 4-2.

All in One Resources

- Checkpoint Quiz 1

Mathematical Reasoning

For Use With Lesson 4-2

NS 1.2 Divide rational numbers. ***Develop***
MR 2.4 Make and test conjectures by using deductive reasoning. ***Develop***

Divisibility Tests

A number is divisible by a second number if the number can be divided by the second number with a remainder of 0. You can use deductive reasoning and the divisibility tests shown below to easily decide if one number is divisible by another.

Divisible by	Divisibility Test
2	The ones digit is 0, 2, 4, 6, or 8.
3	The sum of the digits is divisible by 3.
4	The last two digits are divisible by 4.
5	The ones digit is 0 or 5.
9	The sum of the digits is divisible by 9.
10	The ones digit is 0.

Exercises

Is the first number divisible by the second? Explain. 1–9. See margin.

1. 48 by 4
2. 146 by 4
3. 122 by 6
4. 111 by 9
5. 12,304 by 2
6. 378 by 5
7. 5,780 by 10
8. 630,102 by 3

9. Reasoning Since 54 is divisible by 6, it is also divisible by 2 and 3. Explain.

Checkpoint Quiz 1

Lessons 4-1 through 4-2

Find the prime factorization of each number.

1. 42 $2 \cdot 3 \cdot 7$
2. 80 $2^4 \cdot 5$
3. 27 3^3
4. 1,000 $2^3 \cdot 5^3$

Find the GCD of each pair of numbers.

5. 45, 80 5
6. 24, 72 24
7. 18, 51 3
8. 9, 48 3

9. A photographer is arranging 105 students into rows for a class picture. She wants the same number of students in each row. What are the different arrangements of students she can make? 1×105; 3×35; 5×21; 7×15

140

4-3a Activity Lab

Exploring Fractions

A fraction is a number written in the form $\frac{a}{b}$, where a and b are integers, and b is not equal to zero. In the fraction $\frac{3}{4}$, 3 is the numerator and 4 is the denominator.

You can graph a fraction as a point on a number line.

Foundational Standard Compare and order fractions and place them on a number line.
MR 1.1 Analyze problems by identifying relationships and observing patterns. *Develop*

ACTIVITY

Find the position of $\frac{3}{4}$.

1. Draw a number line like the one shown below.

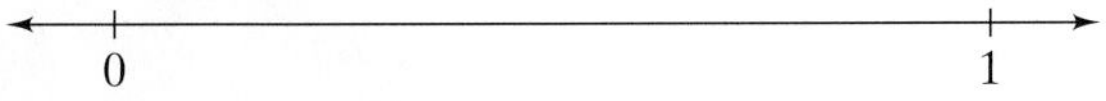

2. Divide the segment between 0 and 1 into four equal segments.
3. Start at 0 and count three segments to the right. Label the point $\frac{3}{4}$.

1–3.

Exercises

Write a fraction represented by each point on the number line below.

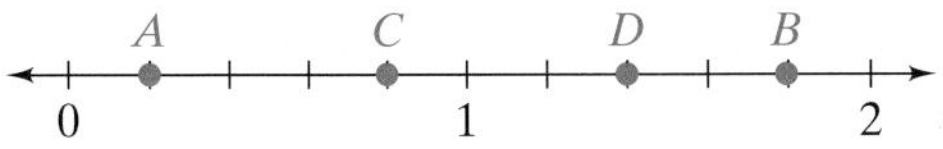

1. A $\frac{1}{5}$
2. B $\frac{9}{5}$
3. C $\frac{4}{5}$
4. D $\frac{7}{5}$

5. **Number Sense** Extend your number line from the activity above to 2. Divide the segment from 1 to 2 into four equal segments. Starting at 0, count eight segments to the right. Write a fraction for this point on the number line, using 4 as the denominator. What is another name for this point? $\frac{8}{4}$; 2

6. Copy the number line shown below. Into how many equal segments is the segment between each integer divided? 5 segments

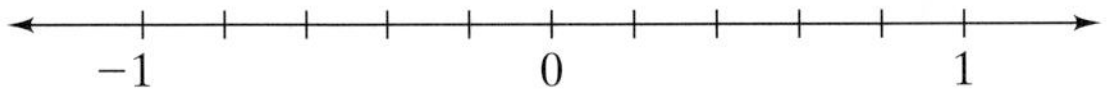

7. Graph $-\frac{2}{5}$ on the number line. Describe the process you used.

7.
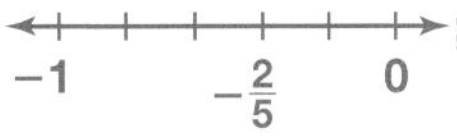

; Answers may vary. Sample: Divide the segment between −1 and 0 into five equal segments. Start at 0 and count two segments to the left.

8. **Reasoning** Suppose you are finding a fraction on a number line. Which part of the fraction tells you into how many equal segments to divide the segment between consecutive integers? Which part of the fraction tells you the number of segments away from 0 to move? the denominator; the numerator

Activity Lab

Exploring Fractions

In this Activity, students graph fractions as points on a number line.

Guided Instruction

Work through the Activity with the students. Then ask questions such as the following to check their understanding:

- Why do you divide the segment between 0 and 1 into four parts? Sample answer: because it takes 4 fourths to make a whole unit
- How many parts would you divide the segment between 0 and 1 into if the fraction were $\frac{3}{7}$? 7

Exercises 1–4

Have students work in pairs. This will help students who may have difficulty drawing the number lines.

4-3

1. Plan

California Content Standards

Compare fractions and place them on a number line. ***Foundational***

NS 1.2 Add, subtract, multiply, and divide rational numbers. ***Develop***

Preps for NS 1.5 Convert terminating decimals into reduced fractions.

California Math Background

Fractions that name the same amount are called *equivalent fractions.* You can find an equivalent fraction by either multiplying or dividing both numerator and denominator by the same number.

More Math Background: p. 130C

Lesson Planning and Resources

See p. 130E for a list of the resources that support this lesson.

PRESENTATION CD-ROM
CD, Online, or Transparencies

Bell Ringer Practice

Check Skills You'll Need
Use student page, transparency, or PowerPoint.
See Math Companion.

California Standards Review
Use transparency or PowerPoint.

GO for Help: Math Companion

4-3 Equivalent Fractions

Check Skills You'll Need

Do this in your **Math Companion.**

Vocabulary

- equivalent fractions
- simplest form

Use your **Math Companion** *to build your vocabulary.*

California Content Standards

Foundational Standard Compare and order fractions and place them on a number line.

NS 1.2 Add, subtract, multiply, and divide rational numbers. ***Develop***

Prepares for **NS 1.5** Convert terminating decimals into reduced fractions.

What You'll Learn . . . and Why

You will learn to find equivalent forms of fractions. You can use a fraction to describe a part of a whole, such as the number of empty seats on an airplane. Writing equivalent fractions often makes using fractions easier.

Equivalent fractions are fractions that name the same point on the number line. The fractions $\frac{2}{3}$ and $\frac{4}{6}$ are equivalent fractions.

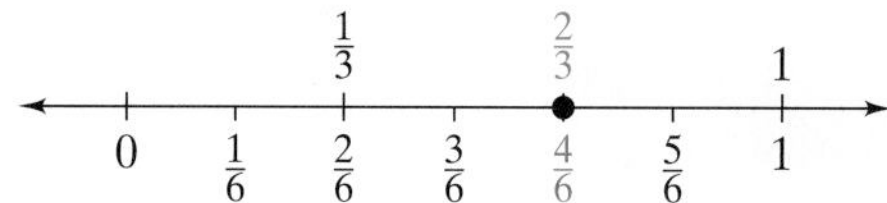

You can form equivalent fractions by multiplying or dividing the numerator and denominator of a fraction by the same nonzero number.

EXAMPLE Equivalent Fractions

1 Write two fractions equivalent to $\frac{6}{8}$.

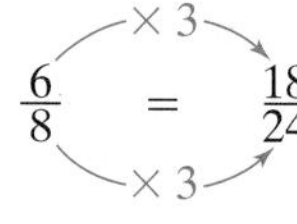

$\frac{6}{8} = \frac{18}{24}$ (× 3) ← **Multiply the numerator and denominator by 3.**

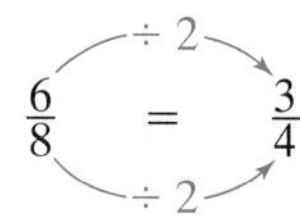

$\frac{6}{8} = \frac{3}{4}$ (÷ 2) ← **Divide the numerator and denominator by 2.**

So $\frac{3}{4} = \frac{6}{8} = \frac{18}{24}$.

CA Standards Check 1

Go to your **Math Companion** *for help.* **Answers may vary. Samples are given.**

1. Write two fractions equivalent to each fraction.

a. $\frac{4}{10}$ $\frac{2}{5}$, $\frac{6}{15}$ **b.** $\frac{5}{8}$ $\frac{10}{16}$, $\frac{15}{24}$ **c.** $\frac{1}{7}$ $\frac{2}{14}$, $\frac{3}{21}$

Universal Access Solutions for All Learners

Special Needs L1
Discuss the definition of simplest form, providing an example showing that a fraction is simplest form when you can no longer divide the numerator and denominator by the same number (other than 1).

Below Level L2
Have students identify groups of equivalent fractions represented by a set of fraction bars. For example:

$\frac{1}{2} = \frac{2}{4} = \frac{3}{6} = \frac{4}{8} = \frac{5}{10} = \frac{6}{12}$; $\frac{2}{3} = \frac{4}{6} = \frac{8}{12}$

A fraction is in **simplest form** when the only common divisor of the numerator and denominator is 1. A fraction in simplest form is often called a reduced fraction. You can write a fraction in simplest form by dividing both the numerator and the denominator by their greatest common divisor.

Relate **MATH YOU KNOW...** ... *to* **NEW IDEAS**

EXAMPLE Using the GCD to Simplify

Find the GCD of 20 and 28.

Divisors of 20: (1), (2), (4), 5, 10, 20
Divisors of 28: (1), (2), (4), 7, 14, 28
← The GCD is 4.

2 Write $\frac{20}{28}$ in simplest form.

The GCD of 20 and 28 is 4.

$$\frac{20}{28} = \frac{20 \div 4}{28 \div 4}$$ ← Divide the numerator and the denominator by the GCD.

$$= \frac{5}{7}$$ ← Simplify.

CA Standards Check 2 *Go to your* **Math Companion** *for help.*

2. Write each fraction in simplest form.

a. $-\frac{24}{32}$ $-\frac{3}{4}$ b. $\frac{50}{100}$ $\frac{1}{2}$ c. $\frac{27}{45}$ $\frac{3}{5}$

Math Foundations

A negative fraction can be written in three ways:

$-\frac{a}{b} = \frac{-a}{b} = \frac{a}{-b}$

You can represent parts of a whole or total with a fraction. The numerator shows how many parts the fraction represents. The denominator shows the number of parts that make a whole.

EXAMPLE Writing a Fraction

3 **Guided Problem Solving** On an airplane, 36 out of 120 seats are empty. In simplest form, what fraction of the seats are empty?

$\frac{36}{120}$ ← The numerator is the number of empty seats.
← The denominator is the total number of seats.

The GCD of 36 and 120 is 12.

$$\frac{36}{120} = \frac{36 \div 12}{120 \div 12}$$ ← Divide the numerator and the denominator by the GCD.

$$= \frac{3}{10}$$ ← Simplify.

Since $\frac{36}{120} = \frac{3}{10}$, $\frac{3}{10}$ of the seats are empty.

CA Standards Check 3 *Go to your* **Math Companion** *for help.*

3. In a parking lot, 24 of 84 vehicles are trucks. In simplest form, what fraction of the vehicles are trucks? $\frac{2}{7}$

2. Teach

Guided Instruction

Example 1
Relate the word *equivalent* to the word *equal. Equivalent fractions* are fractions that name *equal* amounts.

Alternative Method
For Example 3, students can also rewrite $\frac{36}{120}$ as $\frac{12 \cdot 3}{12 \cdot 10}$, which is $\frac{12}{12} \cdot \frac{3}{10}$ or $1 \cdot \frac{3}{10}$ or $\frac{3}{10}$.

Error Prevention!

Some students might multiply or divide the numerator and denominator of a fraction by different numbers. Encourage them to write the number by which they are multiplying or dividing.

Additional Examples

1 Write three fractions equivalent to $\frac{6}{9}$. Samples: $\frac{12}{18}$, $\frac{18}{27}$, $\frac{2}{3}$

2 Write $\frac{16}{40}$ in simplest form. $\frac{2}{5}$

3 A store stocks 12 types of blue pens, 6 types of black pens, and 2 types of red pens. In simplest form, what fraction of the pens are blue? $\frac{3}{5}$

Advanced Learners L4
Find all the fractions equivalent to $\frac{8{,}085}{14{,}553}$ in which both numerator and denominator are whole numbers less than 50. $\frac{5}{9}$, $\frac{10}{18}$, $\frac{15}{27}$, $\frac{20}{36}$, $\frac{25}{45}$

English Learners EL
Some students may have difficulty understanding when a fraction is in its simplest form. Make sure students understand that what makes a fraction in simplest form is that the numerator and denominator are evenly divisible only by 1.

Closure

- *What are equivalent fractions?* **fractions that name the same amount**
- *When is a fraction in simplest form?* **when the only common factor of the numerator and denominator is 1**

More Than One Way

Write $\frac{66}{165}$ in simplest form.

Daryl's Method

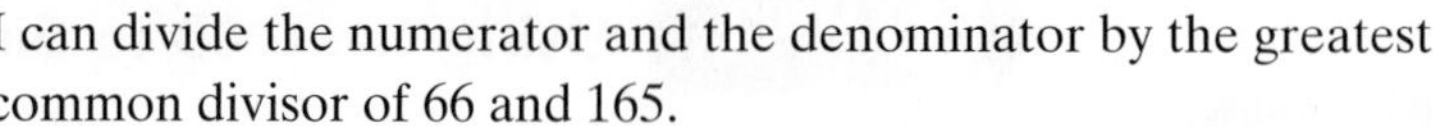

I can divide the numerator and the denominator by the greatest common divisor of 66 and 165.

Divisors of 66: 1, 2, 3, 6, 11, 22, 33, 66

Divisors of 165: 1, 3, 5, 11, 15, 33, 55, 165

The common divisors are 1, 3, 11, and 33.

The GCD of 66 and 165 is 33.

$\frac{66}{165} = \frac{66 \div 33}{165 \div 33}$ ← **Divide the numerator and the denominator by the GCD.**

$= \frac{2}{5}$ ← **Simplify.**

The fraction $\frac{66}{165}$ written in simplest form is $\frac{2}{5}$.

Michelle's Method

I can use the prime factorizations of the numerator and denominator to simplify the fraction. First I find the prime factorizations of 66 and 165. Then I divide the common factors to simplify.

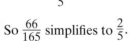

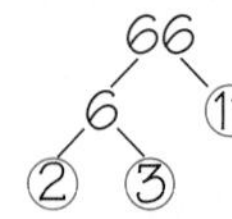

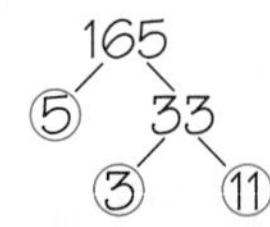

$\frac{66}{165} = \frac{2 \cdot 3 \cdot 11}{3 \cdot 5 \cdot 11}$ ← **Write the prime factorizations of the numerator and the denominator.**

$= \frac{2 \cdot \cancel{3}^{1} \cdot \cancel{11}^{1}}{\cancel{3}_{1} \cdot 5 \cdot \cancel{11}_{1}}$ ← **Divide the common factors.**

$= \frac{2}{5}$ ← **Simplify.**

So $\frac{66}{165}$ simplifies to $\frac{2}{5}$.

Choose a Method

Write $\frac{125}{250}$ in simplest form. Describe your method and explain why you chose it. **$\frac{1}{2}$; check students' work.**

Homework prep is in your **Math Companion.**

Standards Practice

GO for Help: MathXL

NS 1.2

A Practice by Example

Example 1 (page 142)

Write two fractions equivalent to each fraction. 1–9. Answers may vary. Samples are given.

1. $\frac{2}{4}$ $\frac{1}{2}, \frac{6}{12}$

$\frac{2}{4} = \frac{2 \cdot 3}{4 \cdot 3} = \frac{■}{■}$

Guided Practice
This exercise has been started for you!

GO for Help

2. $\frac{4}{11}$ $\frac{8}{22}, \frac{12}{33}$
3. $\frac{6}{7}$ $\frac{12}{14}, \frac{18}{21}$
4. $\frac{12}{18}$ $\frac{2}{3}, \frac{24}{36}$
5. $\frac{3}{16}$ $\frac{6}{32}, \frac{9}{48}$
6. $\frac{3}{5}$ $\frac{6}{10}, \frac{9}{15}$
7. $\frac{3}{9}$ $\frac{1}{3}, \frac{6}{18}$
8. $\frac{1}{20}$ $\frac{2}{40}, \frac{3}{60}$
9. $\frac{15}{20}$ $\frac{3}{4}, \frac{30}{40}$
10. $\frac{3}{10}$ $\frac{6}{20}, \frac{30}{100}$
11. $\frac{15}{30}$ $\frac{5}{10}, \frac{1}{2}$
12. $\frac{95}{105}$ $\frac{19}{21}, \frac{190}{210}$
13. $\frac{1}{3}$ $\frac{3}{9}, \frac{10}{30}$

Example 2 (page 143)

Write each fraction in simplest form.

14. $\frac{4}{6}$ $\frac{2}{3}$

$\frac{4}{6} = \frac{4 \div 2}{6 \div 2} = \frac{■}{■}$

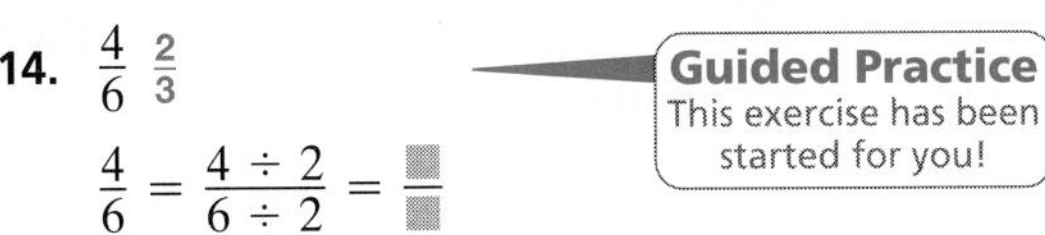
Guided Practice
This exercise has been started for you!

Homework Video Tutor

For: Examples 1–3
Visit: PHSchool.com
Web Code: axe-0403

15. $\frac{18}{81}$ $\frac{2}{9}$
16. $\frac{10}{35}$ $\frac{2}{7}$
17. $\frac{10}{20}$ $\frac{1}{2}$
18. $\frac{40}{50}$ $\frac{4}{5}$
19. $\frac{15}{45}$ $\frac{1}{3}$
20. $\frac{6}{8}$ $\frac{3}{4}$
21. $\frac{12}{18}$ $\frac{2}{3}$
22. $\frac{9}{21}$ $\frac{3}{7}$
23. $-\frac{4}{14}$ $-\frac{2}{7}$
24. $\frac{9}{45}$ $\frac{1}{5}$
25. $\frac{5}{13}$ $\frac{5}{13}$
26. $-\frac{12}{54}$ $-\frac{2}{9}$

Example 3 (page 143)

27. Over the last three seasons, a school football team has won 15 out of 25 games. In simplest form, what fraction of the games has the team won? $\frac{3}{5}$

B Apply Your Skills

28. **Guided Problem Solving** A store orders 105 greeting cards. The order includes 50 birthday cards, 30 get-well cards, and some anniversary cards. In simplest form, what fraction of the cards are anniversary cards? $\frac{5}{21}$
    - You can draw a diagram to model the situation.

105 cards in all		
50 birthday	30 get-well	■ anniversary

- Use the total number of cards as the denominator of the fraction.

29. Part of the sandwich at the right has been eaten. About what fraction of the sandwich is gone? Write your answer in simplest form. $\frac{1}{3}$

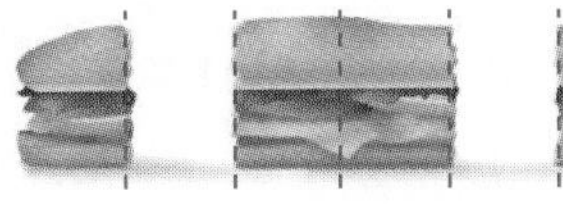

GPS 30. Two traffic engineers are writing about the average driving time between two towns. One engineer writes the time as 45, but the other writes it as $\frac{3}{4}$. What could explain the difference? See above left.

30. The first engineer is measuring time in minutes. The second engineer is measuring time in fractions of an hour.

3. Practice

Assignment Guide

Check Your Understanding
See Math Companion.

Homework Exercises

A Practice by Example	1–27
B Apply Your Skills	28–41
C Challenge	42
California Multiple-Choice Practice	43–45
Mixed Review	46–49

Homework Quick Check
To check students' understanding of key skills and concepts, go over Exercises 7, 15, 27, 30, 36, 40.

Universal Access Resources

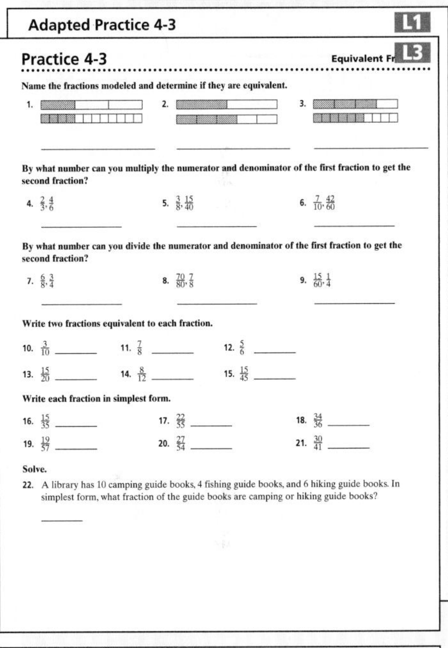

Adapted Practice 4-3 L1

Practice 4-3 Equivalent Fr L3

Name the fractions modeled and determine if they are equivalent.

1. 2. 3.

By what number can you multiply the numerator and denominator of the first fraction to get the second fraction?

4. $\frac{2}{3}, \frac{4}{6}$ 5. $\frac{3}{8}, \frac{15}{40}$ 6. $\frac{7}{10}, \frac{42}{60}$

By what number can you divide the numerator and denominator of the first fraction to get the second fraction?

7. $\frac{6}{8}, \frac{3}{4}$ 8. $\frac{70}{80}, \frac{7}{8}$ 9. $\frac{15}{60}, \frac{1}{4}$

Write two fractions equivalent to each fraction.

10. $\frac{3}{10}$ ____ 11. $\frac{7}{8}$ ____ 12. $\frac{5}{6}$ ____
13. $\frac{15}{20}$ ____ 14. $\frac{8}{12}$ ____ 15. $\frac{15}{45}$ ____

Write each fraction in simplest form.

16. $\frac{15}{35}$ ____ 17. $\frac{22}{55}$ ____ 18. $\frac{34}{36}$ ____
19. $\frac{19}{57}$ ____ 20. $\frac{27}{54}$ ____ 21. $\frac{30}{41}$ ____

Solve.

22. A library has 10 camping guide books, 4 fishing guide books, and 6 hiking guide books. In simplest form, what fraction of the guide books are camping or hiking guide books?

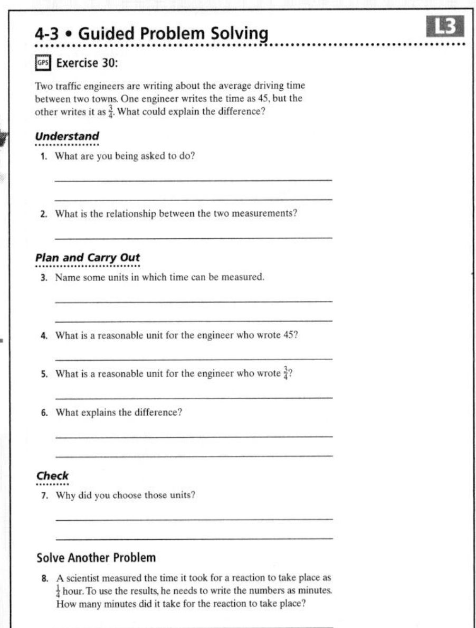

4-3 • Guided Problem Solving L3

GPS Exercise 30:

Two traffic engineers are writing about the average driving time between two towns. One engineer writes the time as 45, but the other writes it as $\frac{3}{4}$. What could explain the difference?

Understand

1. What are you being asked to do?
2. What is the relationship between the two measurements?

Plan and Carry Out

3. Name some units in which time can be measured.
4. What is a reasonable unit for the engineer who wrote 45?
5. What is a reasonable unit for the engineer who wrote $\frac{3}{4}$?
6. What explains the difference?

Check

7. Why did you choose those units?

Solve Another Problem

8. A scientist measured the time it took for a reaction to take place as $\frac{1}{4}$ hour. To use the results, he needs to write the numbers as minutes. How many minutes did it take for the reaction to take place?

4. Assess & Reteach

PRESENTATION CD-ROM
CD, Online, or Transparencies

Lesson Quiz

Write each fraction in simplest form.

1. $\frac{55}{100}$ $\frac{11}{20}$
2. $\frac{9}{12}$ $\frac{3}{4}$
3. $\frac{18}{20}$ $\frac{9}{10}$
4. $\frac{36}{72}$ $\frac{1}{2}$

Reteaching 4-3 — Equivalent Fr… L2

Equivalent fractions are fractions that name the same point on the number line.

To form equivalent fractions, multiply or divide the numerator and denominator by the same nonzero number.

$\frac{2}{5} = \frac{4}{10}$ (· 2) $\frac{4}{10} = \frac{2}{5}$ (÷ 2)

So, $\frac{2}{5} = \frac{4}{10}$.

To write a fraction in *simplest form*, divide the numerator and denominator by their greatest common divisor.

Example: Write $\frac{8}{12}$ in simplest form.

① Find the greatest common divisor.

8: 1, 2, **4**, 8
12: 1, 2, 3, **4**, 6, 12

The GCD is 4.

② Divide the numerator and denominator by the GCD.

$\frac{8}{12} = \frac{2}{3}$ (÷ 4)

$\frac{8}{12}$ in simplest form is $\frac{2}{3}$.

Write two fractions equivalent to each fraction.

1. $\frac{5}{6}$ ______ 2. $\frac{3}{7}$ ______ 3. $\frac{7}{8}$ ______
4. $\frac{3}{11}$ ______ 5. $\frac{3}{6}$ ______ 6. $\frac{1}{5}$ ______

Write each fraction in simplest form.

7. $\frac{12}{15}$ ______ 8. $\frac{8}{15}$ ______ 9. $\frac{15}{22}$ ______
10. $\frac{14}{30}$ ______ 11. $\frac{12}{24}$ ______ 12. $\frac{10}{200}$ ______
13. $\frac{56}{64}$ ______ 14. $\frac{3}{9}$ ______ 15. $\frac{130}{170}$ ______
16. $\frac{12}{16}$ ______ 17. $\frac{7}{49}$ ______ 18. $\frac{22}{33}$ ______
19. $\frac{30}{225}$ ______

20. There are 420 girls out of 1,980 people attending a state fair. In simplest form, what fraction of the people attending are girls?

______

Enrichment 4-3 — Equivalent Fr… L4

Patterns in Geometry

Graph fractions on a grid by plotting the numerator as x and the denominator as y. For example, the fraction $\frac{1}{3}$ can be plotted as the point (1, 3). Move one space to the right and three spaces up to plot the point.

1. Write four fractions that are equivalent to $\frac{1}{3}$. ______
2. Plot the equivalent fractions from Exercise 1.

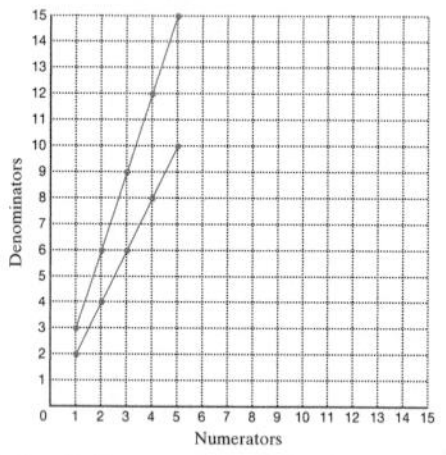

Denominators (0–15) / Numerators (0–15)

3. Connect the points. Describe the pattern that the graph makes.
4. Predict the pattern that will be made by fractions equivalent to $\frac{1}{2}$.
5. Write four fractions equivalent to $\frac{1}{2}$. Plot the five fractions on the grid above. Then connect the points. ______
6. Compare the two graphs to find another pattern.

SCAFFOLDED
Problem Solving

31. Write $\frac{4}{6}$ in simplest form. $\frac{2}{3}$
32. Evaluate $\frac{2a}{3a}$ for $a = 2$. Write the result as a fraction in simplest form. $\frac{2}{3}$
33. Evaluate $\frac{2a}{3a}$ for $a = 1$, 5, and 10. Write each result as a fraction in simplest form. $\frac{2}{3}, \frac{2}{3}, \frac{2}{3}$
34. **Reasoning** Suppose a is a nonzero whole number. What do you think the simplest form for $\frac{2a}{3a}$ is? Explain. See left.
35. Suppose b is any nonzero whole number. Write $\frac{5b}{7b}$ in simplest form. $\frac{5}{7}$

34. $\frac{2}{3}$; a is a common divisor of $2a$ and $3a$, so you can divide the numerator and denominator by a.

State whether each fraction is in simplest form. If the fraction is not, write it in simplest form.

36. $\frac{3}{6}$ no; $\frac{1}{2}$ 37. $\frac{1}{7}$ yes 38. $\frac{15}{18}$ no; $\frac{5}{6}$ 39. $\frac{17}{51}$ no; $\frac{1}{3}$

40. **Writing in Math** How can you use the GCD of the numerator and the denominator to write a fraction in simplest form? See left.

40. Answers may vary. Sample: Divide the numerator and the denominator by the GCD.

41. In the past 10 days, it has rained on $\frac{1}{5}$ of the days. On how many days has it rained? 2 days

Challenge

42. What fraction of 7,777 is the number 77? $\frac{1}{101}$

Multiple Choice Practice and Mixed Review

For California Standards Tutorials, visit PHSchool.com. Web Code: axq-9045

NS 1.2
43. The expression $-39 + 1.5(-24)$ gives an estimate of the wind chill in degrees Fahrenheit when the air temperature is -24°F and the wind speed is 20 mi/h. What is the wind chill? A
  (A) -75°F (B) -64.5°F (C) -3°F (D) 75°F

AF 1.1
44. Which problem situation matches the equation $x + 96 = 102$? D
  (A) Victoria rented two movies with run times of 96 min and 102 min. What is x, the time it took to watch both movies?
  (B) A class sells 96 concert tickets. They earn $102. What is x, the price of each ticket?
  (C) On her last two math exams, Hannah got scores of 96 and 102. What is x, her average?
  (D) Together, Joey and his cat weigh 102 lb. Alone, Joey weighs 96 lb. What is x, the weight of Joey's cat?

Alg1 2.0
45. Which pair of numbers is an integer and its opposite? C
  (A) 0, 1 (B) 13, -31 (C) -9, 9 (D) -2.4, 2.4

Lesson 4-1

Find the prime factorization of each number.

46. 55 $5 \cdot 11$ 47. 129 $3 \cdot 43$ 48. 240 $2^4 \cdot 3 \cdot 5$ 49. 990 $2 \cdot 3^2 \cdot 5 \cdot 11$

Online Lesson Quiz Visit: PHSchool.com Web Code: axa-0403

California Resources

Standards Mastery

- Standards Review Transparencies
- Standards Review and Practice Workbook
- Math Companion

Math Intervention

- Skills Review and Practice Workbook
- Math XL

Alternative Assessment

Students in pairs write fractions and exchange them with their partners. Partners state whether or not the fraction is in simplest form. If not, they rename the fraction in simplest form. After several turns, students should discuss how they made their decisions and explain their methods.

For Use With Lesson 4-3

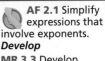

AF 2.1 Simplify expressions that involve exponents. ***Develop***
MR 3.3 Develop generalizations of strategies used and apply them to new problem situations. ***Develop***

Expressions With Fractions

Algebraic expressions can include fractions. In numerical and algebraic expressions, fraction bars are grouping symbols. For example, $\frac{3+2}{7} = (3 + 2) \div 7$.

When simplifying an expression with a fraction bar, use the order of operations. Simplify the numerator and denominator before simplifying the fraction.

EXAMPLE Evaluating Expressions With Fractions

You can find the radius of the arch in a doorway with the expression $\frac{s^2 + h^2}{2h}$. Find the radius of a doorway with dimensions $s = 4$ ft and $h = 2$ ft.

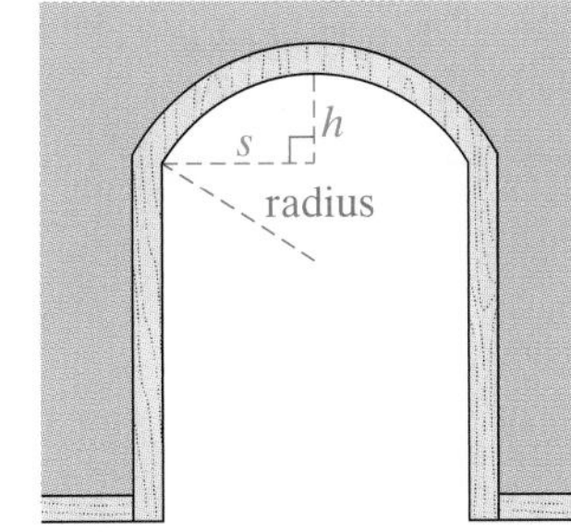

$$\frac{s^2 + h^2}{2h} = \frac{4^2 + 2^2}{2 \cdot 2}$$ ← **Substitute 4 for *s* and 2 for *h*.**

$$= \frac{16 + 4}{2 \cdot 2}$$ ← **Simplify the powers in the numerator.**

$$= \frac{20}{4}$$ ← **Simplify the numerator and denominator.**

$$= 5$$ ← **Simplify the fraction.**

The radius of the arch is 5 ft.

Exercises

1. Use the expression $\frac{s^2 + h^2}{2h}$ to find the radius of the arch in the doorway below. $5\frac{2}{3}$ m

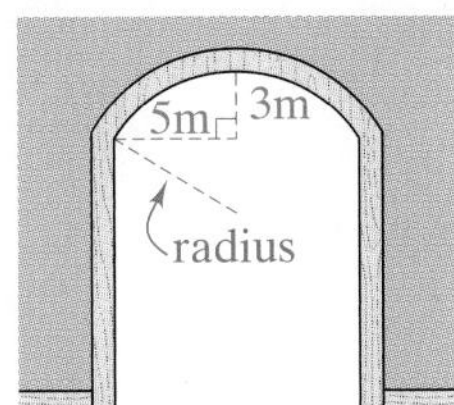

Evaluate each expression. Write your answer in simplest form.

2. $\frac{1 + a}{2b}$ for $a = 3$ and $b = -5$ $-\frac{2}{5}$
3. $\frac{x^2}{4y}$ for $x = 5$ and $y = 10$ $\frac{5}{8}$
4. $\frac{w^3 - 2}{24 + t}$ for $w = 2$ and $t = -6$ $\frac{1}{3}$
5. $\frac{1 - m}{2p - 4}$ for $m = 3$ and $p = 8$ $-\frac{1}{6}$
6. **Error Analysis** A student states that $\frac{6}{3} + \frac{12}{2}$ is equal to $\frac{6 + 12}{3 + 2}$. Is the student correct? Explain.
No; the student added the numerators and added the denominators. The correct sum is $\frac{6}{3} + \frac{12}{2} = 2 + 6 = 8$.

Expressions With Fractions

Students learn how to simplify algebraic expressions that include fractions using the order of operations.

Guided Instruction

As needed, begin this lesson with a review of the terms *algebraic expression* and *evaluate*. Write the order of operations on the board, and show students how the fraction bar fits into this order (a fraction bar is a grouping symbol, like parentheses).

4-4

1. Plan

California Content Standards

NS 1.3 Convert fractions to decimals. ***Introduce***

NS 1.5  Know that every rational number is either a terminating or repeating decimal and convert terminating decimals into reduced fractions. ***Introduce, Develop***

Professional Development

California Math Background

The name for the set of rational numbers comes from the fact that a **ratio**nal number can be expressed as a **ratio** of integers. All decimals are rational if they end or repeat a group of digits forever. They can be written as fractions with integers in both the numerator and the denominator.

More Math Background: p. 130C

Lesson Planning and Resources

See p. 130E for a list of the resources that support this lesson.

PRESENTATION CD-ROM
CD, Online, or Transparencies
Bell Ringer Practice

Check Skills You'll Need
Use student page, transparency, or PowerPoint.
See Math Companion.

California Standards Review
Use transparency or PowerPoint.

GO for Help: Math Companion

4-4 Equivalent Forms of Rational Numbers

Check Skills You'll Need

Do this in your **Math Companion.**

Vocabulary
- rational number
- terminating decimal
- repeating decimal

Use your **Math Companion** *to build your vocabulary.*

California Content Standards

NS 1.3 Convert fractions to decimals. ***Introduce***

NS 1.5 Know that every rational number is either a terminating or a repeating decimal and convert terminating decimals into reduced fractions. ***Introduce, Develop***

What You'll Learn . . . and Why

You will learn to convert rational numbers to equivalent forms. You can express rational numbers as both fractions and decimals. Fractions and decimals are used in statistics, such as baseball standings.

Team Standings

	W	L	PCT	GB
Los Angeles	24	14	.632	—
San Francisco	19	19	.500	5
San Diego	17	20	.459	$6\frac{1}{2}$
Arizona	17	20	.459	$6\frac{1}{2}$
Colorado	15	23	.395	9

A **rational number** is a number that can be written as the quotient $\frac{a}{b}$ of two integers where b is not 0. Any fraction that is a quotient of two integers is a rational number. You can write any integer as a fraction with a denominator of 1, so all integers are rational numbers. For example, $7 = \frac{7}{1}$.

Some decimals are rational numbers. To convert a decimal to a fraction, write the fraction as you would say the decimal. Then simplify.

Relate MATH YOU KNOW . . .

. . . *to* NEW IDEAS

EXAMPLE Converting a Decimal to a Fraction

Write 0.345 in words.

The 5 is in the thousandths place. In words, the number is three hundred forty-five thousandths.

1 Write 0.345 as a fraction in simplest form.

$$0.345 = \frac{345}{1{,}000}$$ ← Write "three hundred forty-five thousandths" as a fraction.

$$= \frac{345 \div 5}{1{,}000 \div 5}$$ ← Divide the numerator and the denominator by the GCD, 5.

$$= \frac{69}{200}$$ ← Simplify.

CA Standards Check 1 *Go to your* **Math Companion** *for help.*

1. Write each decimal as a fraction in simplest form.
   a. 0.822 $\frac{411}{500}$ **b.** 0.46 $\frac{23}{50}$

Universal Access Solutions for All Learners

Special Needs L1	**Below Level** L2
Review the place values of decimals with students: tenths, hundredths, thousandths, etc. Explain that, when converting a decimal to a fraction, the place value of the decimal tells you the correct denominator for the fraction.	Have students use long division to divide 1 by 3 $0.\overline{3}$; 2 by 3 $0.\overline{6}$; and 2 by 9 $0.\overline{2}$. Have students describe the quotients. Sample: In each example, the same digit repeats forever.

A fraction bar indicates division. You can write a fraction as a decimal by dividing the numerator by the denominator. If the division results in a decimal that stops, the decimal is called a **terminating decimal.**

0.375 6.2

Math Foundations

The symbol for a repeating decimal is a bar over the repeating digits. For example, $0.\overline{17} = 0.1717\ldots$

If the division results in a decimal with a digit or group of digits that repeats forever, the decimal is called a **repeating decimal.**

$$0.7777\ldots = 0.\overline{7}$$
$$0.8333\ldots = 0.8\overline{3}$$
$$0.4545\ldots = 0.\overline{45}$$

You can write every rational number as either a terminating or repeating decimal.

EXAMPLE Converting a Fraction to a Decimal

2 **Guided Problem Solving** In baseball, a player's batting average equals $\frac{\text{number of hits}}{\text{number of times at bat}}$. A batting average is written as a decimal rounded to three decimal places and is written without the leading 0. Find the batting average of a hitter with 36 hits in 125 times at bat.

$\frac{\text{number of hits}}{\text{number of times at bat}} = \frac{36}{125}$ ← **Use the formula to write the batting average as a fraction.**

$$\begin{array}{r} 0.288 \\ 125\overline{)36.000} \\ -250 \\ \hline 1100 \\ -1000 \\ \hline 1000 \\ -1000 \\ \hline 0 \end{array}$$

← **Divide 36 by 125.**

The player's batting average is .288.

CA Standards Check 2 *Go to your* **Math Companion** *for help.*

2. Find each batting average.
   a. 27 hits in 99 times at bat .273
   b. 39 hits in 85 times at bat .459

Check Your Understanding *Homework prep is in your* **Math Companion.**

2. Teach

Guided Instruction

Example 2

Remind the students that a number or an expression written as a fraction indicates division, so they can divide the numerator by the denominator to convert the fraction to a decimal.

Error Prevention!

Explain that a decimal that goes on forever can have a pattern and still not be a repeating decimal. For instance, in 0.121121112 ... you can predict the next digit, but there is no single group of digits that repeats.

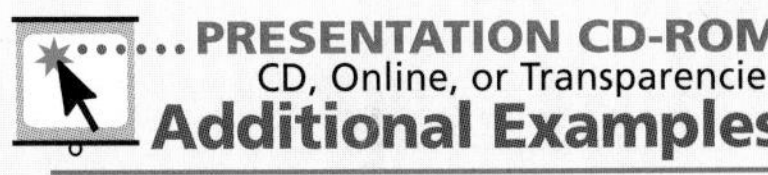

... PRESENTATION CD-ROM CD, Online, or Transparencies

Additional Examples

1. Write 0.225 as a fraction in simplest form. $\frac{9}{40}$
2. Write each batting average as a decimal.
   a. Joe made 4 hits in 20 times at bat. .200
   b. Pat made 6 hits in 33 times at bat. .182

Closure

- *Explain how to convert a decimal to a fraction.* **Write the fraction as you would say the decimal, and then simplify.**
- *Explain how to convert a fraction to a decimal.* **Divide the numerator by the denominator.**

Universal Access Solutions for All Learners

Advanced Learners L4

Have students write each fraction as a decimal using a bar to indicate repeating digits.

$\frac{1}{6}$ $0.1\overline{6}$ $\frac{1}{9}$ $0.\overline{1}$ $\frac{1}{11}$ $0.\overline{09}$

English Learners EL

Have students define the word *ratio* and then connect it to the term *rational number.*

3. Practice

Assignment Guide

Check Your Understanding

See Math Companion.

Homework Exercises

A Practice by Example	1–28
B Apply Your Skills	29–42
C Challenge	43
California Multiple-Choice Practice	44–46
Mixed Review	47–49

Homework Quick Check

To check students' understanding of key skills and concepts, go over Exercises 7, 16, 27, 30, 31, 41, 42.

Universal Access Resources

Adapted Practice 4-4 L1

Practice 4-4 Equivalent Forms of Rational N[umbers] L3

Write each number as a fraction in simplest form.

1. −5 ______ 2. 0.63 ______ 3. −0.9 ______ 4. 0.5 ______
5. 0.77 ______ 6. −0.375 ______ 7. −0.28 ______ 8. 0.195 ______
9. A baseball player averaged 0.375 last season. Express the batting average as a fraction. ______

Write each fraction as a decimal. Round to three decimal places, if necessary.

10. $\frac{7}{21}$ ______ 11. $-\frac{9}{21}$ ______ 12. $-\frac{2}{3}$ ______
13. $\frac{19}{6}$ ______ 14. $-\frac{39}{8}$ ______ 15. $\frac{47}{12}$ ______
16. $-\frac{51}{11}$ ______ 17. $\frac{55}{18}$ ______ 18. $-\frac{25}{18}$ ______
19. $-\frac{25}{9}$ ______ 20. $\frac{82}{15}$ ______ 21. $-\frac{74}{15}$ ______

Write each decimal as a fraction in simplest form.

22. 0.006 ______ 23. −0.8 ______ 24. 0.97 ______
25. 0.4 ______ 26. 0.05 ______ 27. −0.28 ______
28. 0.082 ______ 29. −0.41 ______ 30. 0.23 ______
31. 0.17 ______ 32. −0.031 ______ 33. 0.416 ______

Solve.

34. The eighth grade held a magazine sale to raise money for their spring trip. They wanted each student to sell subscriptions. After the first day of the sale, 25 out of 125 students turned in subscription orders. Write a rational number in simplest form to express the student response on the first day.

35. Pete wanted to win the prize for selling the most subscriptions. Of 240 subscriptions sold, Pete sold 30. Write a rational number in simplest form to express Pete's part of the total sales.

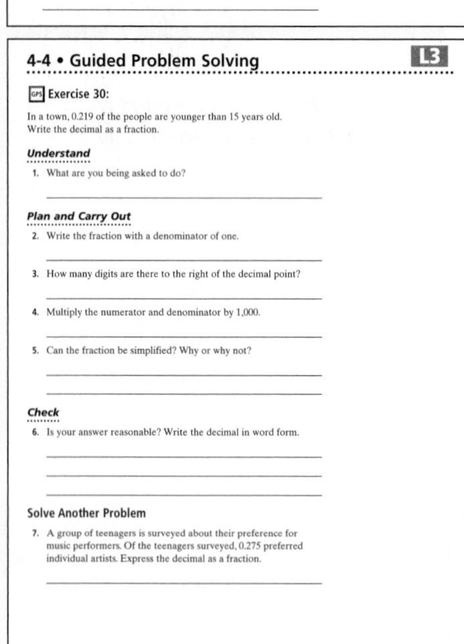

4-4 • Guided Problem Solving L3

GPS Exercise 30:

In a town, 0.219 of the people are younger than 15 years old. Write the decimal as a fraction.

Understand

1. What are you being asked to do?

Plan and Carry Out

2. Write the fraction with a denominator of one.
3. How many digits are there to the right of the decimal point?
4. Multiply the numerator and denominator by 1,000.
5. Can the fraction be simplified? Why or why not?

Check

6. Is your answer reasonable? Write the decimal in word form.

Solve Another Problem

7. A group of teenagers is surveyed about their preference for music performers. Of the teenagers surveyed, 0.275 preferred individual artists. Express the decimal as a fraction.

Standards Practice

GO for Help: MathXL

NS 1.3, NS 1.5

A Practice by Example

Example 1 (page 148)

Write each decimal as a fraction in simplest form.

1. 0.15

$0.15 = \frac{15}{100}$

$= \blacksquare$ $\frac{3}{20}$

Guided Practice: This exercise has been started for you!

GO for Help

2. 0.9 $\frac{9}{10}$ 3. 0.17 $\frac{17}{100}$ 4. 0.008 $\frac{1}{125}$ 5. 0.5 $\frac{1}{2}$
6. 0.25 $\frac{1}{4}$ 7. 0.149 $\frac{149}{1,000}$ 8. 0.075 $\frac{3}{40}$ 9. 0.32 $\frac{8}{25}$
10. 0.038 $\frac{19}{500}$ 11. 0.4 $\frac{2}{5}$ 12. 0.28 $\frac{7}{25}$ 13. 0.456 $\frac{57}{125}$

Example 2 (page 149)

Write each fraction as a decimal. Round to three decimal places, if necessary.

14. $\frac{5}{6}$ 0.833

$6\overline{)5.00}$ $\blacksquare$

Guided Practice: This exercise has been started for you!

Homework Video Tutor

For: Examples 1–2
Visit: PHSchool.com
Web Code: axe-0404

15. $\frac{4}{9}$ 0.444 16. $\frac{8}{25}$ 0.32 17. $\frac{17}{16}$ 1.063 18. $\frac{16}{17}$ 0.941
19. $-\frac{13}{7}$ −1.857 20. $\frac{9}{45}$ 0.2 21. $\frac{5}{13}$ 0.385 22. $-\frac{28}{35}$ −0.8
23. $\frac{25}{46}$ 0.543 24. $-\frac{1}{8}$ −0.125 25. $\frac{25}{40}$ 0.625 26. $-\frac{3}{20}$ −0.15

Find each batting average.

27. 34 hits in 102 times at bat .333
28. 24 hits in 96 times at bat .250

B Apply Your Skills

29. **Guided Problem Solving** At chili festivals over the past few years, Restaurant A won 56 out of 98 contests. Restaurant B won 84 out of 147 contests. Which restaurant has the better record? They have the same record.
    - What decimal represents the win record for Restaurant A?
    - What decimal represents the win record for Restaurant B?

GPS 30. In a town, 0.219 of the people are younger than 15 years old. Write the decimal as a fraction. $\frac{219}{1,000}$

Match each number with its location on the number line below.

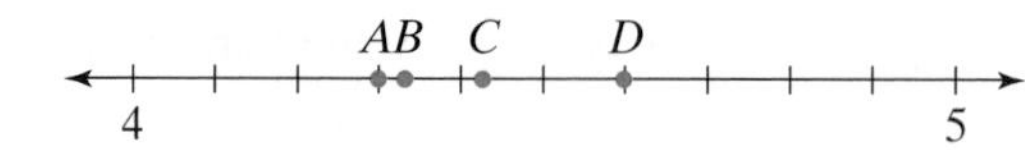

31. $4\frac{3}{5}$ D 32. 4.3 A 33. 4.43 C 34. $4\frac{1}{3}$ B

35. **Number Sense** Convert $\frac{2}{3}$, $\frac{3}{3}$, $\frac{4}{3}$, $\frac{5}{3}$, and $\frac{6}{3}$ to decimals. Describe when a denominator of 3 results in a repeating decimal.
$0.\overline{6}$; 1; $1.\overline{3}$; $1.\overline{6}$; 2; when the numerator is not a multiple of 3

SCAFFOLDED
Problem Solving

The circle graph at the right shows the sizes of the households in a city.

Households by Size

One person $\frac{1}{4}$; Four or more people $\frac{1}{4}$; Three people $\frac{1}{6}$; Two people $\frac{1}{3}$

36. What fraction of households have only one person? $\frac{1}{4}$

37. What decimal is equivalent to this fraction? 0.25

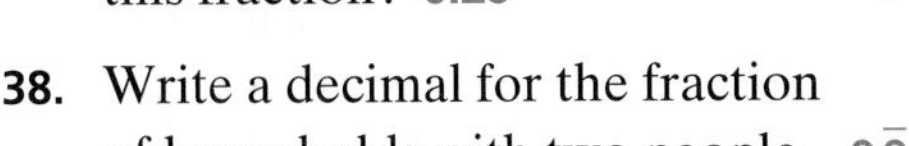

38. Write a decimal for the fraction of households with two people. $0.\overline{3}$

39. Is the decimal for the fraction of households with two people a repeating or terminating decimal? repeating

40. Write decimals for the fractions of households with three people and four or more people. $0.1\overline{6}$; 0.25

Refer to the cartoon.

THE LOCKHORNS

©1993 King Features Syndicate, Inc. World rights reserved.
HOEST & REINER 11-11
"SO I MISSED ONE OF YOUR BIRTHDAYS IN 25 YEARS OF MARRIAGE. WHAT'S WRONG WITH A .980 BATTING AVERAGE?"

41. If Leroy Lockhorn missed one of Loretta Lockhorn's birthdays in 25 yr, what would his "batting average" be? .960

42. **Writing in Math** Explain why, in 25 yr of marriage, Leroy Lockhorn could never have a "batting average" of .980. See left.

42. Answers may vary. Sample: $.980 = \frac{49}{50}$. It cannot simplify to a fraction with a denominator of 25.

C Challenge

43. Use the same digit in each blank to make $\frac{■6}{125} = 0.■08$ true. $\frac{26}{125} = 0.208$

Multiple Choice Practice and Mixed Review

For California Standards Tutorials, visit PHSchool.com. Web Code: axq-9045

NS 1.5 **44.** Which number is NOT rational? A

(A) $\sqrt{3}$ (B) 1.2 (C) 7 (D) $0.08\overline{3}$

NS 1.3, MR 3.2 **45.** Noah wants to write the fraction $\frac{5}{8}$ as a decimal. Which method should he use? C

(A) Write the decimal 0.58.
(B) Write the decimal 0.85.
(C) Divide 5 by 8.
(D) Divide 8 by 5.

AF 1.1 **46.** Yoel has 3 fewer coins than Selena. Selena has 15 coins. Which equation can be used to find k, the number of coins Yoel has? C

(A) $k = 3 \cdot 5$
(B) $k = 15 \div 3$
(C) $k = 15 - 3$
(D) $k = 15 + 3$

GO for Help **Lesson 2-3** **Find each difference.**

47. $-13 - (-6)$ -7 **48.** $-25 - 25$ -50 **49.** $19 - (-15)$ 34

Online Lesson Quiz Visit: PHSchool.com Web Code: axa-0404

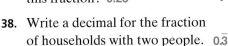

Alternative Assessment

In small groups, students choose digits from 1 to 9. Members use the digits to form a decimal to 3 places, such as 15.124. Then students work together to write the decimal as a fraction in simplest form. $15\frac{31}{250}$

California Resources

Standards Mastery
- Standards Review Transparencies
- Standards Review and Practice Workbook
- Math Companion

Math Intervention
- Skills Review and Practice Workbook
- Math XL

4. Assess & Reteach

PRESENTATION CD-ROM
CD, Online, or Transparencies

Lesson Quiz

1. Write $\frac{2}{16}$ as a decimal. 0.125

Write each decimal as a mixed number or fraction in simplest form.

2. 2.75 $2\frac{3}{4}$
3. 0.4 $\frac{2}{5}$

Reteaching 4-4 **Equivalent Forms of Rational Numbers** **L2**

A fraction is in simplest form when the *greatest common divisor* (GCD) of the numerator and denominator is 1.

Example 1: Write $\frac{24}{36}$ in simplest form.

Use prime factorization and circle the common factors.

$24 = (2) \cdot (2) \cdot 2 \cdot (3)$
$36 = (2) \cdot (2) \cdot 3 \cdot (3)$

So, $\frac{24}{36} = \frac{2}{3}$.

To write a fraction as a decimal:

① Divide numerator by denominator.
② Divide until the remainder is 0 or until the remainder repeats.
③ Use a bar to show digits repeating.

Example 2: Write $\frac{5}{6}$ as a decimal.

```
  0.833
6)5.000
 -48
   20
  -18
   20
  -18
    2  ← Remainder repeats.
```

So $\frac{5}{6} = 0.833\ldots$, or $0.8\overline{33}$.

To write a decimal as a fraction:

Example 3: Write 0.375 as a fraction.

① Write as a fraction with the denominator 1. $0.375 = \frac{0.375}{1}$
② Since there are 3 digits to the right of the decimal point, multiply the numerator and the denominator by 1,000. $= \frac{375}{1000}$
③ Divide the numerator and denominator by the GCD. $= \frac{375 \div 125}{1000 \div 125}$
④ Simplify. $= \frac{3}{8}$

So $0.375 = \frac{3}{8}$.

Write each fraction as a decimal. Round to three decimal places, if necessary.

1. $\frac{16}{64}$ ______ 2. $-\frac{30}{48}$ ______ 3. $\frac{42}{63}$ ______
4. $-\frac{32}{40}$ ______ 5. $-\frac{12}{28}$ ______ 6. $\frac{18}{27}$ ______
7. $\frac{7}{9}$ ______ 8. $-\frac{23}{7}$ ______ 9. $\frac{5}{9}$ ______
10. $\frac{38}{7}$ ______ 11. $\frac{4}{3}$ ______ 12. $\frac{1}{11}$ ______

Write each decimal as a fraction in simplest form.

13. 0.2 ______ 14. 0.16 ______ 15. 0.3 ______
16. .75 ______ 17. .52 ______ 18. 0.36 ______

Enrichment 4-4 **Equivalent Forms of Rational Nu...** **L4**

Critical Thinking

Place each number shown below in the correct column(s) in the table. Be careful: Some numbers might go into more than one column.

$\frac{4}{5}, \frac{9}{25}, 4, -50, -\frac{1}{2}, \frac{6}{20}, \frac{27}{10}, -\frac{19}{5}, 0.36, -1, 16, 0.8, 0.3, 2.7, -\frac{38}{10}, 25, -\frac{250}{5}$

1.

Whole Numbers	Integers	Rational Numbers

2. There are 6 pairs of equivalent rational numbers in the table. List them below in order from smallest to largest.

a. ______
b. ______
c. ______
d. ______
e. ______
f. ______

Mathematical Reasoning

Repeating Decimals

Students learn how to recognize the period of a repeating decimal.

Guided Instruction

Remind students that after determining the period of a repeating decimal, writing the decimal is done by placing a bar over the last set of the repeating digits.

Checkpoint Quiz

Use this Checkpoint Quiz to check students' understanding of the skills and concepts of Lessons 4-3 through 4-4.

All in One Resources

- Checkpoint Quiz 2

Mathematical Reasoning

For Use With Lesson 4-4

NS 1.5 Know that every rational number is either a terminating or a repeating decimal. ***Develop***

MR 1.1 Analyze problems by observing patterns. ***Develop***

Repeating Decimals

Recall that all rational numbers are either terminating or repeating decimals. A repeating decimal is a decimal in which the same digit or group of digits repeats forever. The period of a repeating decimal is the length of the group of digits that repeats. For example, the period of 0.145145145 . . . is 3.

Exercises

State the period of each repeating decimal.

1. 0.12121212 . . . 2
2. 0.4444444 . . . 1
3. 0.358358 . . . 3
4. 0.9123391233 . . . 5
5. 0.142857142857 . . . 6
6. 1.222222 . . . 1
7. Is 0.129012901390 . . . a rational number? Explain. No; the four digits "1290" do *not* repeat after the eighth digit.
8. **Number Sense** In the repeating decimal = 0.365365365 . . . , which digit is 100 places to the right of the decimal point? 3

Checkpoint Quiz 2

Lessons 4-3 through 4-4

Write each fraction in simplest form.

1. $\frac{8}{10}$ $\frac{4}{5}$
2. $\frac{15}{35}$ $\frac{3}{7}$
3. $\frac{7}{28}$ $\frac{1}{4}$
4. $\frac{11}{132}$ $\frac{1}{12}$

Write each decimal as a fraction in simplest form.

5. 0.56 $\frac{14}{25}$
6. 0.32 $\frac{8}{25}$
7. 0.85 $\frac{17}{20}$
8. 0.125 $\frac{1}{8}$
9. Convert $\frac{12}{36}$ to a decimal. $0.\overline{3}$
10. A baseball player gets 8 hits in 27 times at bat. Another player gets 10 hits in 30 times at bat. Which player has a higher batting average? Explain. See margin.

4-5a Activity Lab

Mixed Numbers

NS 1.3 Convert fractions to decimals. ***Develop***
MR 2.2 Apply strategies and results from simpler problems to more complex problems. ***Develop***

A mixed number shows the sum of a whole number and a fraction. For example, $6\frac{2}{3} = 6 + \frac{2}{3}$. You also can write a mixed number as an improper fraction. An improper fraction is a fraction with a numerator that is greater than or equal to its denominator.

The model shows that $6\frac{2}{3} = \frac{20}{3}$.

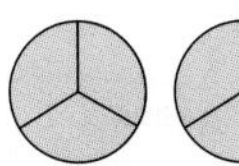 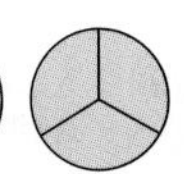 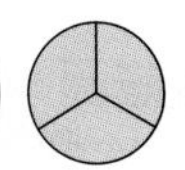 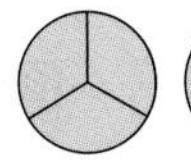 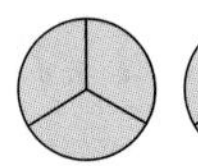 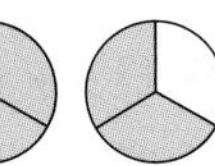

EXAMPLE Writing as an Improper Fraction

1 Write $6\frac{2}{3}$ as an improper fraction.

$6\frac{2}{3} = \frac{(3 \cdot 6) + 2}{3}$ ← **Multiply the whole number and the denominator. Then add the numerator.**

$= \frac{20}{3}$ ← **The denominator stays the same.**

To convert a mixed number to a decimal, first convert the fraction part to a decimal by dividing. Then add the decimal to the whole number.

EXAMPLE Converting to a Decimal

2 Convert $4\frac{1}{4}$ to a decimal.

$4\frac{1}{4} = 4 + \frac{1}{4}$ ← **Write the mixed number as a sum.**

$= 4 + 0.25$ ← **Convert the fraction to a decimal.**

$= 4.25$ ← **Simplify.**

Exercises

Write each mixed number as an improper fraction.

1. $2\frac{3}{8}$ $\frac{19}{8}$ **2.** $5\frac{1}{2}$ $\frac{11}{2}$ **3.** $1\frac{5}{9}$ $\frac{14}{9}$ **4.** $20\frac{4}{5}$ $\frac{104}{5}$

Convert each mixed number to a decimal.

5. $5\frac{1}{2}$ 5.5 **6.** $12\frac{5}{8}$ 12.625 **7.** $7\frac{10}{15}$ $7.\overline{6}$ **8.** $4\frac{8}{9}$ $4.\overline{8}$

9. Reasoning When writing a mixed number as an improper fraction, why do you multiply the whole number by the denominator? See margin.

Activity Lab

Improper Fractions

In this Activity, students write mixed numbers as improper fractions and convert mixed numbers to decimals.

Guided Instruction

Make sure students understand that each circle represents 1. If the model for a fraction involves more than one complete circle, the fraction is greater than 1.

Ask the following question to check students' understanding:

- *How does comparing the numerator to the denominator show whether a fraction is less than, equal to, or greater than 1?* Sample answer: If the numerator is less than the denominator, the fraction is less than 1. If the numerator and denominator are equal, the fraction is equal to 1. If the numerator is greater than the denominator, the fraction is greater than 1.

Explain that a number can be written in many different forms, all of which are equivalent. Being able to convert numbers to various forms enables you to compare numbers that are in different forms.

4-5

1. Plan

California Content Standards

Compare and order positive and negative fractions, decimals, and mixed numbers and place them on a number line. *Foundational*

NS 1.3 Convert fractions to decimals and use these representations in estimations, computations, and applications. *Develop*

California Math Background

When fractions have like denominators, you compare them by comparing numerators. For instance, $\frac{3}{5} > \frac{2}{5}$ because $3 > 2$.

When fractions have unlike denominators, comparing them involves rewriting the fractions with a common denominator. For instance, $\frac{1}{3} > \frac{1}{4}$ because $\frac{4}{12} > \frac{3}{12}$. Their *least common denominator,* or LCD, is the least common multiple (LCM) of their denominators. So, 12 is the LCM of 3 and 4, and 12 is the LCD of $\frac{1}{3}$ and $\frac{1}{4}$.

More Math Background: p. 130C

Lesson Planning and Resources

See p. 130E for a list of the resources that support this lesson.

...PRESENTATION CD-ROM
CD, Online, or Transparencies

Bell Ringer Practice

Check Skills You'll Need
Use student page, transparency, or PowerPoint.
See Math Companion.

California Standards Review
Use transparency or PowerPoint.

CALIFORNIA CHECK SYSTEM

4-5 Comparing and Ordering Rational Numbers

Check Skills You'll Need

Do this in your **Math Companion.**

Vocabulary

- least common multiple (LCM)
- least common denominator (LCD)

Use your **Math Companion** *to build your vocabulary.*

California Content Standards

Foundational Standard Compare and order positive and negative fractions, decimals, and mixed numbers and place them on a number line.

NS 1.3 Convert fractions to decimals and use these representations in estimations, computations, and applications. *Develop*

What You'll Learn . . . and Why

You will learn to compare and order rational numbers. You can compare rational numbers to see which recipe uses more of an ingredient.

Blueberry Muffins
$\frac{1}{2}$ cup unsalted butter
2 cups flour
$\frac{2}{3}$ cup sugar
2 tsp baking soda
$\frac{1}{4}$ tsp salt
Blueberry Muffins
$\frac{3}{4}$ stick unsalted butter
$\frac{3}{4}$ cup sugar
1 egg
$\frac{1}{3}$ cup whole milk
$\frac{1}{2}$ tsp salt

To order rational numbers, convert each fraction to a decimal. Then graph the decimals on a number line.

Relate MATH YOU KNOW... ...*to* NEW IDEAS

EXAMPLE Ordering Rational Numbers

Convert $\frac{4}{5}$ to a decimal.

$$\begin{array}{r} 0.8 \\ 5\overline{)4.0} \\ -40 \\ \hline 0 \end{array}$$ ← **Divide 4 by 5.**

1 Order $\frac{4}{5}$, -0.37, 1, $-\frac{29}{40}$, and 0.3 from least to greatest.

Write each fraction as a decimal.

$\frac{4}{5} = 0.8 \qquad -\frac{29}{40} = -0.725$

Then graph each decimal on a number line.

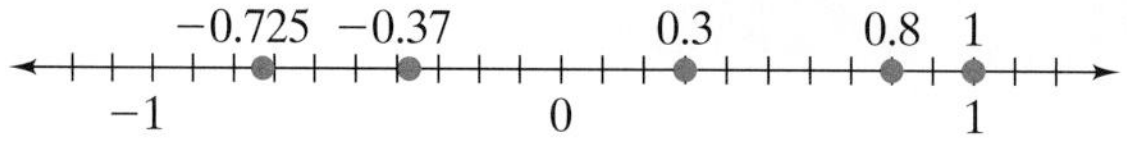

(Number line from −1 to 1 with points at −0.725, −0.37, 0.3, 0.8, 1.)

The number line shows that $-0.725 < -0.37 < 0.3 < 0.8 < 1$.
So $-\frac{29}{40} < -0.37 < 0.3 < \frac{4}{5} < 1$.

CA Standards Check 1 *Go to your* **Math Companion** *for help.*

1. Order each set of numbers from least to greatest.

a. $\frac{8}{5}$, $1\frac{1}{2}$, -0.625, $-\frac{7}{8}$, 1.61
$-\frac{7}{8}$, -0.625, $1\frac{1}{2}$, $\frac{8}{5}$, 1.61

b. $2\frac{5}{6}$, 0.375, $\frac{1}{3}$, 2.8, $1\frac{2}{3}$
$\frac{1}{3}$, 0.375, $1\frac{2}{3}$, 2.8, $2\frac{5}{6}$

Universal Access Solutions for All Learners

Special Needs L1	Below Level L2
Help students find the approximate locations of decimal numbers on a number line. Then have them characterize the numbers as less than zero, closest to 1, and so on, to help them grasp their relative value.	Have students cut 3 index cards into thirds, fourths, and eighths and compare to see that a greater denominator means a smaller part.

To compare fractions, you can find a common denominator. Multiply the numerator and denominator of each fraction by the denominator of the other fraction. Then compare the numerators.

EXAMPLE Comparing Fractions

2 **Guided Problem Solving** Recipe A uses $\frac{2}{3}$ c of sugar. Recipe B uses $\frac{3}{4}$ c. Which recipe uses more?

A common denominator of 3 and 4 is 3 · 4, or 12.

$$\frac{2}{3} = \frac{2 \cdot 4}{3 \cdot 4} = \frac{8}{12}$$
$$\frac{3}{4} = \frac{3 \cdot 3}{4 \cdot 3} = \frac{9}{12}$$
Write equivalent fractions with a denominator of 12.

Since $\frac{8}{12} < \frac{9}{12}$, $\frac{2}{3} < \frac{3}{4}$. Recipe B uses more sugar.

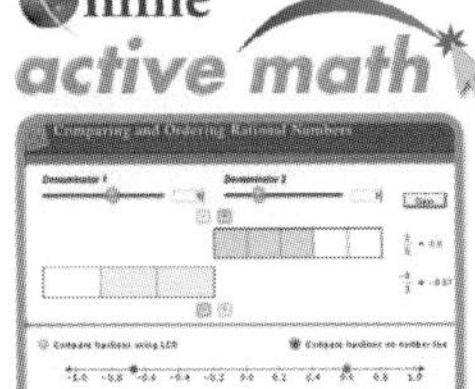

For: Rational Numbers Activity
Use: Interactive Textbook, 4-5

CA Standards Check 2 *Go to your* **Math Companion** *for help.*

2. Compare each pair of numbers. Use <, =, or >.

a. $\frac{6}{8}$ ■ $\frac{7}{9}$ < **b.** $\frac{1}{6}$ ■ $\frac{1}{10}$ >

The **least common multiple (LCM)** of two or more numbers is the least multiple shared by all of the numbers. The LCM of two denominators is called the **least common denominator (LCD).** You can use the LCD to compare fractions.

EXAMPLE Comparing Using the LCD

3 Compare $\frac{4}{9}$ and $\frac{5}{12}$ using their LCD. Use <, =, or >.

List multiples of each denominator to find their LCD.

Multiples of 9: 9, 18, 27, (36)
Multiples of 12: 12, 24, (36)
Stop when you find a multiple that is shared by both numbers.

The LCM of 9 and 12 is 36. So the LCD of the fractions is 36.

$$\frac{4}{9} = \frac{4 \cdot 4}{9 \cdot 4} = \frac{16}{36}$$
$$\frac{5}{12} = \frac{5 \cdot 3}{12 \cdot 3} = \frac{15}{36}$$
Use the LCD to write equivalent fractions.

Since $\frac{16}{36} > \frac{15}{36}$, $\frac{4}{9} > \frac{5}{12}$.

Vocabulary Tip

A multiple of a number is the product of that number and a nonzero whole number. For example, 6, 12, and 18 are multiples of 6.

CA Standards Check 3 *Go to your* **Math Companion** *for help.*

3. Compare each pair of numbers using their LCD. Use <, =, or >.

a. $\frac{9}{12}$ ■ $\frac{5}{6}$ < **b.** $\frac{4}{5}$ ■ $\frac{9}{15}$ >

Check Your Understanding *Homework prep is in your* **Math Companion.**

2. Teach

Guided Instruction

Example 3
Some students might observe that 5 > 4 and 12 > 9 and falsely conclude that $\frac{5}{12} > \frac{4}{9}$. Remind them that the fractions must have common denominators before they can compare numerators.

Alternative Method
Have students also compare fractions and decimals by converting all numbers to fractions.

PRESENTATION CD-ROM
CD, Online, or Transparencies
Additional Examples

1 Order −0.175, $\frac{2}{3}$, $-\frac{5}{8}$, 1.7, and −0.95 from least to greatest. −0.95, $-\frac{5}{8}$, −0.175, $\frac{2}{3}$, 1.7

2 The Eagles won 7 out of 11 games, while the Seals won 8 out of 12 games. Which team has the better record? Seals

3 Compare $\frac{7}{18}$ and $\frac{5}{12}$ using their LCD. $\frac{5}{12} > \frac{7}{18}$

Closure

- *How do you compare two rational numbers when the denominators are alike?* The greater number has the greater numerator.
- *How do you compare two rational numbers when the denominators are different?* Sample: Find a common denominator and compare numerators or change each fraction into a decimal and compare them on a number line.

Advanced Learners L4	**English Learners** EL
Have students quickly compare fractions by mentally comparing each fraction to $\frac{1}{2}$. $\frac{475}{910}$ ■ $\frac{395}{823}$ > $\frac{147}{299}$ ■ $\frac{161}{314}$ < $\frac{5,270}{9,615}$ ■ $\frac{30,421}{62,932}$ > $\frac{74}{136}$ ■ $\frac{21}{46}$ >	Have students read LCM and LCD as *least common multiple* and *least common denominator* to help them keep track of the meanings of the abbreviations.

3. Practice

Assignment Guide

Check Your Understanding
See Math Companion.

Homework Exercises
A Practice by Example 1–24
B Apply Your Skills 25–34
C Challenge 35
California Multiple-Choice Practice 36–38
Mixed Review 39–42

Homework Quick Check
To check students' understanding of key skills and concepts, go over Exercises 2, 10, 16, 32, 34.

Universal Access Resources

Adapted Practice 4-5 L1

Practice 4-5 Comparing and Ordering Rational Numbers L3

Compare each pair of numbers. Use <, =, or >.

1. $2\frac{14}{17}$ □ $1\frac{16}{17}$
2. $\frac{15}{21}$ □ $\frac{5}{7}$
3. $2\frac{7}{8}$ □ $2\frac{5}{6}$
4. $3\frac{15}{16}$ □ $3\frac{21}{32}$
5. $4\frac{7}{8}$ □ $3\frac{9}{10}$
6. $5\frac{9}{10}$ □ $5\frac{18}{20}$
7. $1\frac{19}{20}$ □ $2\frac{1}{20}$
8. $4\frac{5}{6}$ □ $5\frac{19}{20}$
9. $7\frac{3}{10}$ □ $7\frac{9}{30}$
10. $4\frac{19}{24}$ □ $4\frac{7}{12}$
11. $5\frac{19}{20}$ □ $6\frac{21}{22}$
12. $4\frac{15}{20}$ □ $4\frac{21}{28}$

Order each set of numbers from least to greatest.

13. $\frac{9}{10}, \frac{5}{6}, \frac{14}{15}$ ______
14. $1\frac{7}{8}, 1\frac{7}{12}, 1\frac{5}{6}$ ______
15. $\frac{14}{15}, \frac{9}{10}, \frac{11}{12}$ ______
16. $2\frac{1}{4}, 3\frac{7}{8}, 3\frac{5}{6}$ ______
17. $\frac{2}{3}, \frac{4}{5}, \frac{7}{30}, \frac{11}{15}$ ______
18. $2\frac{1}{6}, 1\frac{3}{4}, 3\frac{7}{8}, 2\frac{1}{10}$ ______
19. $\frac{5}{12}, \frac{17}{30}, \frac{3}{5}$ ______
20. $1\frac{5}{6}, 2\frac{1}{6}, 1\frac{11}{12}, 1\frac{11}{18}$ ______
21. $\frac{17}{20}, 1\frac{18}{25}, 2\frac{31}{36}$ ______

Compare each pair of numbers using their LCD. Use <, =, or >.

22. $\frac{1}{6}$ □ $\frac{1}{8}$
23. $\frac{8}{9}$ □ $\frac{8}{12}$
24. $\frac{1}{4}$ □ $\frac{1}{5}$
25. $\frac{3}{9}$ □ $\frac{3}{7}$
26. $\frac{5}{50}$ □ $\frac{1}{60}$
27. $\frac{9}{10}$ □ $\frac{10}{12}$
28. $\frac{1}{12}$ □ $\frac{1}{15}$
29. $\frac{5}{6}$ □ $\frac{3}{4}$
30. $\frac{1}{65}$ □ $\frac{3}{60}$

31. Four puppies measured $5\frac{1}{4}$ in., $5\frac{3}{8}$ in., $5\frac{5}{8}$ in., and $5\frac{5}{16}$ in. long at birth. Put the lengths in order from least to greatest.

______

4-5 • Guided Problem Solving L3

GPS **Exercise 34:**

Erika worked from 4:55 P.M. to 5:30 P.M. Maria worked $\frac{2}{3}$ of an hour. Who worked longer?

Understand

1. What information is given in the problem?
______
2. Underline the question.

Plan and Carry Out

3. How many minutes are in one hour? ______
4. How many minutes did Erika work? ______
5. Write an expression to represent the part of an hour that Erika worked.
______
6. What fraction of an hour did Erika work? ______
7. Compare the fraction of an hour Erika worked to the $\frac{2}{3}$ of an hour Maria worked.
______
8. Who worked longer, Erika or Maria? ______

Check

9. Is your answer reasonable? Determine how many minutes Maria worked.
______
______

Solve Another Problem

10. Anita swam from 3:25 P.M. to 4:05 P.M. Martin swam for $\frac{2}{5}$ of an hour. Who swam the greater part of an hour?
______
______

Standards Practice

GO for Help: MathXL NS 1.3

A Practice by Example

Order each set of numbers from least to greatest. 1–7. See margin.

Example 1 (page 154)

1. $\frac{10}{13}, \frac{15}{19}, 0.8, -3.13$

$\frac{10}{13} \approx 0.769 \quad \frac{15}{19} \approx 0.789$

Guided Practice This exercise has been started for you!

GO for Help

2. $\frac{1}{3}, \frac{3}{10}, 0.03, 0.33$
3. $0.7, 1\frac{2}{5}, 1.3, \frac{4}{9}$
4. $-4, -3.9, -\frac{2}{9}, \frac{2}{11}$
5. $\frac{5}{7}, \frac{5}{3}, \frac{5}{6}, \frac{5}{2}$
6. $1.5, \frac{1}{5}, 1\frac{1}{5}, \frac{15}{5}$
7. $-\frac{3}{7}, -3, -0.3, \frac{1}{3}$

Example 2 (page 155)

Compare each pair of numbers. Use <, =, or >.

8. $\frac{3}{5}$ ■ $\frac{5}{8}$ <

$\frac{3}{5} = \frac{3 \cdot 8}{5 \cdot 8} = \frac{24}{40}$

Guided Practice This exercise has been started for you!

Homework Video Tutor

For: Examples 1–3
Visit: PHSchool.com
Web Code: axe-0405

9. $\frac{3}{4}$ ■ $\frac{4}{5}$ <
10. $\frac{1}{2}$ ■ $\frac{7}{16}$ >
11. $\frac{5}{9}$ ■ $\frac{1}{4}$ >
12. $\frac{5}{7}$ ■ $\frac{12}{20}$ >
13. $\frac{5}{7}$ ■ $\frac{5}{6}$ <
14. $\frac{3}{11}$ ■ $\frac{1}{6}$ >
15. Tim ran $\frac{3}{4}$ mi. Naomi ran $\frac{7}{10}$ mi. Who ran farther? Tim

Example 3 (page 155)

Compare each pair of numbers using their LCD. Use <, =, or >.

16. $\frac{2}{9}$ ■ $\frac{4}{15}$ <
17. $\frac{15}{16}$ ■ $\frac{7}{8}$ >
18. $\frac{9}{24}$ ■ $\frac{3}{8}$ =
19. $\frac{1}{8}$ ■ $\frac{1}{4}$ <
20. $\frac{2}{3}$ ■ $\frac{4}{6}$ =
21. $\frac{7}{10}$ ■ $\frac{3}{5}$ >
22. $\frac{17}{18}$ ■ $\frac{13}{16}$ >
23. $\frac{4}{6}$ ■ $\frac{5}{7}$ <
24. $\frac{11}{20}$ ■ $\frac{15}{30}$ >

B Apply Your Skills

25. **Guided Problem Solving** A survey found that 13 out of 108 men and 23 out of 216 women were left-handed. Which group had the greater fraction of left-handed people? men
    - The fraction of men who were left-handed was ■.
    - The fraction of women who were left-handed was ■.

26. **Number Sense** If 1 is added to both the numerator and denominator of $\frac{5}{12}$, is the new number greater or less than $\frac{5}{12}$? Explain. Greater; the new fraction is $\frac{6}{13}$.

27. **Reasoning** Order $\frac{5}{3}$, $\frac{5}{8}$, $\frac{5}{4}$, and $\frac{5}{7}$ from least to greatest. Explain how you could order fractions with the same numerator *without* writing them as decimals or finding common denominators.

27. $\frac{5}{8}, \frac{5}{7}, \frac{5}{4}, \frac{5}{3}$; when the numerators are the same, the larger the denominator is, the smaller the value of the fraction.

SCAFFOLDED
Problem Solving

28. Compare $\frac{9}{20}$ and $\frac{7}{16}$. Use <, =, or >. >

29. The whole number parts of $12\frac{9}{20}$ and $12\frac{7}{16}$ are equal. The fractional parts are different. Which number is greater? $12\frac{9}{20}$

30. Two sports drinks have the same price. The cherry flavored drink contains $12\frac{9}{20}$ oz. The blueberry flavored drink contains $12\frac{7}{16}$ oz. Which drink is the better buy? the cherry flavored drink

31a. $\frac{1}{2}, \frac{1}{4}, \frac{1}{8}, \frac{1}{16}$

b. 

The "open" note symbol has the greatest value. The more flags the note has, the smaller the value of the note.

32. Answers may vary. Sample: Check to see if the numerator is greater or less than half of the denominator.

31. Musical notes are based on fractions of a whole note. See left.
   a. Order the fractions shown from greatest to least.
   b. **Patterns** Redraw the note symbols so they are in the order listed in part (a). Do the symbols change in a pattern? Explain.

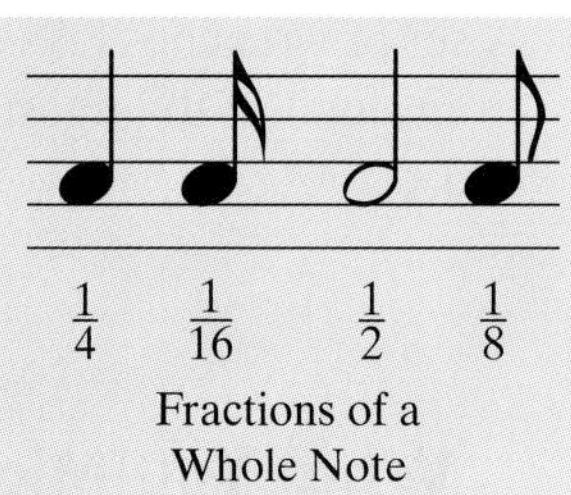

Fractions of a Whole Note

32. **Writing in Math** Explain how you can tell whether a fraction is greater than or less than $\frac{1}{2}$. See left.

33. In a video game, you successfully completed 30 out of 55 levels. Your friend completed all but 7 out of 46 levels of another game. Who completed the greater fraction of a game? your friend

GPS 34. Erika worked from 4:55 P.M. to 5:30 P.M. Maria worked $\frac{2}{3}$ of an hour. Who worked longer? Maria

Challenge

35. Find a whole number x such that $\frac{2}{3} < \frac{x}{8} < 1$. 6 or 7

Multiple Choice Practice and Mixed Review

For California Standards Tutorials, visit PHSchool.com. Web Code: axq-9045

NS 1.3 36. Which decimal is equivalent to $\frac{3}{8}$? B

Ⓐ 0.3 Ⓒ 0.38
Ⓑ 0.375 Ⓓ 0.8

AF 1.1 37. Nancy paid a membership fee of \$30 to use a skate park. Each time she skated, she paid \$2.50. Which equation can be used to find c, the cost of skating for s visits? A

Ⓐ $c = 2.5s + 30$ Ⓒ $c = 30s + 2.5$
Ⓑ $c = 30(s + 2.5)$ Ⓓ $c = 2.5(s + 30)$

Alg1 2.0 38. What is the opposite of −0.5? C

Ⓐ −2 Ⓑ −0.5 Ⓒ 0.5 Ⓓ 2

for Help **Lesson 4-2**

Find the GCD of each pair of numbers.

39. 48, 56 8 40. 15, 21 3 41. 42, 72 6 42. 300, 450 150

Online Lesson Quiz Visit: PHSchool.com Web Code: axa-0405

Alternative Assessment

Students write a paragraph identifying which method they prefer to use to compare fractions—using a least common denominator or using decimals. Then they justify their choice.

California Resources

Standards Mastery
- Standards Review Transparencies
- Standards Review and Practice Workbook
- Math Companion

Math Intervention
- Skills Review and Practice Workbook
- Math XL

4. Assess & Reteach

PRESENTATION CD-ROM
CD, Online, or Transparencies
Lesson Quiz

Compare. Use <, >, or =.

1. $\frac{5}{12}$ ■ $\frac{8}{15}$ < 2. $\frac{4}{5}$ ■ $\frac{8}{11}$ >
3. $\frac{15}{50}$ ■ $\frac{36}{120}$ = 4. $\frac{7}{20}$ ■ 0.35 =
5. Order 0.17, $\frac{1}{5}$, −0.3, 0, and $-\frac{1}{4}$ from least to greatest.
   $-0.3, -\frac{1}{4}, 0, 0.17, \frac{1}{5}$.
6. A survey found that 75 out of 125 men and 88 out of 136 women prefer comedy films over action films. Which group prefers comedy over action films more? women

Reteaching 4-5 Comparing and Ordering Rational Numbers L2

The *least common multiple* (LCM) of two or more numbers is the least multiple shared by all of the numbers. The LCM of two denominators is called the *least common denominator* (LCD).

To compare fractions that have the *same* denominator, compare their numerators.	To compare fractions with *different* denominators, rewrite the fractions using the LCD.
Compare $\frac{3}{4}$ and $\frac{1}{4}$. $3 > 1$ So, $\frac{3}{4} > \frac{1}{4}$.	Compare $\frac{2}{3}$ and $\frac{7}{9}$. Rewrite: $\frac{6}{9}$ $\frac{7}{9}$ $\frac{6}{9} < \frac{7}{9}$ So, $\frac{2}{3} < \frac{7}{9}$.

Determine which rational number is greater by rewriting each pair of fractions using their LCD.

1. $\frac{6}{7}, \frac{4}{5}$ 2. $\frac{5}{11}, \frac{8}{12}$ 3. $\frac{4}{8}, \frac{10}{12}$
4. $\frac{3}{4}, \frac{8}{10}$ 5. $\frac{2}{3}, \frac{3}{6}$ 6. $\frac{2}{4}, \frac{4}{5}$
7. $\frac{2}{8}, \frac{1}{5}$ 8. $\frac{5}{7}, \frac{9}{10}$ 9. $\frac{7}{8}, \frac{3}{4}$

Compare each pair of numbers. Use <, =, or >.

10. $\frac{8}{9}$ □ $\frac{1}{2}$ 11. $\frac{4}{9}$ □ $\frac{12}{27}$ 12. $\frac{12}{24}$ □ $\frac{9}{24}$
13. $\frac{1}{3}$ □ $\frac{1}{2}$ 14. $\frac{1}{9}$ □ $\frac{1}{3}$ 15. $\frac{1}{5}$ □ $\frac{1}{6}$
16. $\frac{12}{32}$ □ $\frac{3}{8}$ 17. $\frac{5}{9}$ □ $\frac{7}{12}$ 18. $\frac{1}{2}$ □ $\frac{3}{4}$
19. $\frac{3}{5}$ □ $\frac{3}{7}$ 20. $\frac{3}{10}$ □ $\frac{1}{5}$ 21. $\frac{5}{6}$ □ $\frac{2}{3}$

Enrichment 4-5 Comparing and Ordering Rational Numbers L4

Decision Making

An important thing to learn about fractions is that the size of the fraction is related to the size of the whole. For instance, $\frac{1}{2}$ of a large pizza is much larger than $\frac{1}{2}$ of a small pizza even though each is a half. A half of a dime is much less than a half of a dollar!

1. Would you rather have $\frac{1}{3}$ of two pounds of pennies or $\frac{1}{3}$ of one pound of silver dollars? Explain your reasoning.
2. Would you rather have $\frac{1}{2}$ of one million dollars or $\frac{1}{3}$ of two million dollars? Explain your reasoning.
3. Which would be more, $\frac{1}{2}$ of 3 dozen chocolate chip cookies or $\frac{1}{6}$ of 12 dozen chocolate chip cookies? How do you know?
4. Write a similar problem that has you compare the value of fractions. Trade problems with a classmate and solve.

GPS Guided Problem Solving

Practice Solving Problems

In this feature, students use their number sense and knowledge of equivalent fractions to order a set of wrenches by length from shortest to longest.

Guided Instruction

Discuss with students why someone might want to put the wrenches in order by length. Real-world problems such as this one often involve mathematics and since the wrench lengths are given in fractional parts of an inch, the problem involves ordering fractions.

Have a volunteer read the problem aloud. Ask:

- *How can you use number sense to start?* **Sample: Divide the set of wrenches into two parts so the ordering is easier.**
- *Why were some of the fractions changed from fractions with a denominator of 32 to equivalent fractions in the last step?* **so they would be in simplest form**

NS 1.2 Multiply and divide rational numbers. ***Develop***
MR 1.1 Analyze problems by observing patterns. ***Develop***

Practice Solving Problems

You can use number sense and equivalent fractions to order fractional amounts.

A set of wrenches falls out of its case. Arrange the wrenches by size from smallest to largest. The sizes, in inches, are $\frac{5}{16}$, $\frac{7}{8}$, $\frac{7}{32}$, $\frac{9}{16}$, $\frac{1}{2}$, $\frac{1}{8}$, and $\frac{21}{32}$.

What You Might Think	What You Might Write
How can I use number sense to get started?	Find the fractions that are less than $\frac{1}{2}$ and the fractions that are greater than $\frac{1}{2}$. Less than $\frac{1}{2}$: $\frac{5}{16}$, $\frac{7}{32}$, $\frac{1}{8}$ Greater than $\frac{1}{2}$: $\frac{7}{8}$, $\frac{9}{16}$, $\frac{21}{32}$
How can I order the fractions that are less than $\frac{1}{2}$? Greater than $\frac{1}{2}$?	Write the fractions with a common denominator (32). Less than $\frac{1}{2}$: $\frac{10}{32}$, $\frac{7}{32}$, $\frac{4}{32}$ Greater than $\frac{1}{2}$: $\frac{28}{32}$, $\frac{18}{32}$, $\frac{21}{32}$ $\frac{1}{2} = \frac{16}{32}$
What is the answer?	$\frac{4}{32}$, $\frac{7}{32}$, $\frac{10}{32}$, $\frac{16}{32}$, $\frac{18}{32}$, $\frac{21}{32}$, $\frac{28}{32}$ or $\frac{1}{8}$, $\frac{7}{32}$, $\frac{5}{16}$, $\frac{1}{2}$, $\frac{9}{16}$, $\frac{21}{32}$, $\frac{7}{8}$

Think It Through

1. **Number Sense** How did you decide which fractions were greater than $\frac{1}{2}$ and which fractions were less than $\frac{1}{2}$? **If a fraction is greater than $\frac{1}{2}$, then its numerator is more than half its denominator.**
2. **Reasoning** Without finding a common denominator, how can you use number sense to tell that $\frac{1}{8}$ is the least fraction and $\frac{7}{8}$ is the greatest fraction? **Using the results of Exercise 1, compare the fractions in each group two at a time.**

Exercises

3. Nail lengths, in inches, are given as mixed numbers. Arrange the nail lengths $2\frac{3}{4}$, $1\frac{3}{4}$, $1\frac{1}{2}$, $3\frac{1}{2}$, $3\frac{1}{4}$, 2, and $3\frac{3}{4}$ in order from least to greatest. (*Hint:* Start by grouping nails with the same whole-number part.) $1\frac{1}{2}$, $1\frac{3}{4}$, 2, $2\frac{3}{4}$, $3\frac{1}{4}$, $3\frac{1}{2}$, $3\frac{3}{4}$

4. **Patterns** Seven drill bits are arranged from smallest to largest in the table. They increase in size following a pattern. Find the diameters of the missing drill bits in simplest form. $\frac{7}{16}$; $\frac{9}{16}$

Drill Bits

Bit Number	1	2	3	4	5	6	7
Diameter (in.)	$\frac{5}{16}$	$\frac{3}{8}$	■	$\frac{1}{2}$	■	$\frac{5}{8}$	$\frac{11}{16}$

5. Two ships sail between New York and London. One makes a round trip in 12 d. The other takes 16 d to make a round trip. They both leave London today. In how many days will both ships leave on the same day again? 48 d

6. The thickness and width of two pieces of lumber are given below. Write two true statements comparing the measurements of these pieces of lumber. See right.

   Piece 1: $2\frac{1}{2}$ in. by $5\frac{1}{2}$ in. Piece 2: $1\frac{1}{4}$ in. by $7\frac{1}{4}$ in.

6. Answers may vary. Samples: The width of piece 1 is greater than that of piece 2. The length of piece 1 is less than that of piece 2.

7. You want to divide the field below into plots. The plots must be square and must all be the same size. Each plot must also have whole-number side lengths. What is the largest plot size you can use to divide the entire field? 12 ft × 12 ft

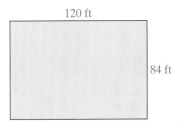

8. Your dog and cat both eat one can of food every day. Dog food comes in cases of 18 cans. Cat food comes in cases of 16 cans. What is the least number of cases of each that you can buy so that you have the same number of dog food cans and cat food cans?

9 cases of cat food and 8 cases of dog food

Error Prevention!

Some students may not understand why the fractions were put into sets of fractions less than $\frac{1}{2}$ and greater than $\frac{1}{2}$. These students may want to compare the fractions two by two.

Exercises

Have students work independently on the Exercises. Then have them form groups in which members share and evaluate their work. Students should make adjustments in their work based on their group discussion.

Universal Access

Advanced Learners L4

Ask: *What combinations of the nails in Exercise 3 could you use to lay out 5 inches of nails?* $1\frac{1}{2}$ and $3\frac{1}{2}$ nails, $1\frac{1}{4}$ and $3\frac{1}{4}$

Vocabulary Builder

Using Concept Maps

Students who grasp the precision of math vocabulary will improve their ability to understand and share mathematical ideas. In this feature, students learn a strategy for connecting new knowledge to existing knowledge.

Guided Instruction

Go over with students all of the parts of the sample concept map. Explain that the center rectangle represents a set and that the surrounding, attached shapes represent what is included in the set. The smallest shapes contain examples of what is included in the set. Ask questions such as the following:

- *What is the definition of a rational number?* **A number that can be written in the form $\frac{a}{b}$, where *a* and *b* are integers and *b* is not equal to 0.**
- *Explain why integers are included in the set of rational numbers.* **Any integer can be written as a fraction with 1 as the denominator.**
- *Explain why terminating and repeating decimals are included in the set of rational numbers.* **Any terminating or repeating decimal can be written as a fraction.**

Exercises

Have students work in pairs to do the Exercises. They should take turns pairing properties and examples and discussing the reasons for their choices.

Teaching Tip

Make an effort to use new math vocabulary often as you work through the textbook lessons. This practice gives students, particularly English learners, a chance to hear the words spoken correctly and in the right context.

Vocabulary Builder

Using Concept Maps

Concept maps are visual tools that show how you can relate different ideas and terms you have used. Connecting new knowledge to existing knowledge is important in understanding mathematics. To build a concept map, follow these steps:

- Place each concept or term inside a geometrical shape.
- Draw lines connecting the concepts or terms that are related.

EXAMPLE

In this chapter, you learned about different forms of rational numbers. You can show the relationships among these forms with the concept map below.

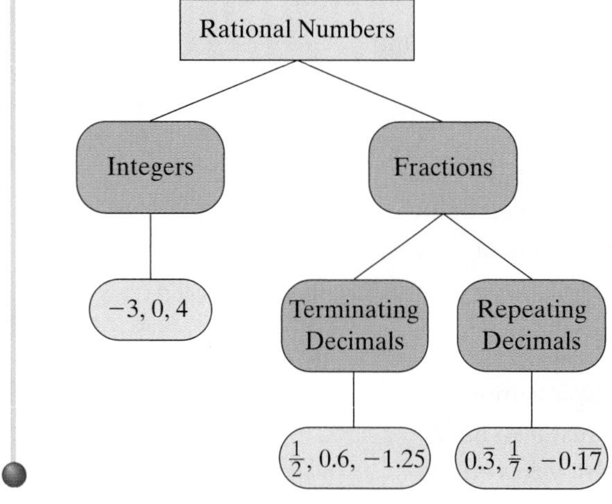

Exercises

1. Make a concept map for "Properties of Equality" using the following properties and examples from Chapter 3. **See margin.**
   - Addition Property of Equality
   - $12 = 4 \cdot 3$, so $\frac{12}{2} = \frac{4 \cdot 3}{2}$
   - $6 = 3 \cdot 2$, so $6 + 4 = 3 \cdot 2 + 4$
   - Multiplication Property of Equality
   - $6 = 3 \cdot 2$, so $6 - 4 = 3 \cdot 2 - 4$
   - Subtraction Property of Equality
   - Division Property of Equality
   - $4 = \frac{12}{3}$, so $3 \cdot 4 = 3 \cdot \frac{12}{3}$
2. Use the properties of numbers from Lesson 1-5 and 1-6. Make a concept map showing the relationships among the properties. **Check students' work.**

Choosing the Process

Not all questions ask you to find the solution to a problem. Some questions ask you to choose a process or strategy for solving a problem.

EXAMPLE

You want to fence 80 square feet of your backyard for your dog. You want the length and width of the fenced area, in feet, to be whole numbers. How can you find the possible dimensions of the fenced area?

Ⓐ Find the common multiples of 80.
Ⓑ Find the greatest common divisor of 80.
Ⓒ Find the factors of 80.
Ⓓ Find the least common multiple of 80.

The area formula for a rectangle is $A = \ell \cdot w$. To find the possible dimensions of the fenced area, you can list the pairs of numbers that equal 80 square feet when multiplied together. To list the pairs of numbers with 80 as a product, you can find the factors of 80. The correct answer is choice C.

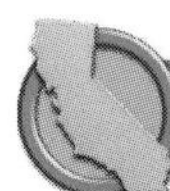

Multiple Choice Practice

NS 1.2, MR 3.2

1. Tina buys 2 loaves of bread and 6 muffins. Each loaf of bread costs \$2.29, and each muffin costs \$.77. To calculate the total cost, Tina first calculates 2 times \$2.29 and 6 times \$.77. What should she do next? **B**

Ⓐ Multiply the two products.
Ⓑ Add the two products.
Ⓒ Divide the first product by the second product.
Ⓓ Subtract the second product from the first product.

NS 1.3, MR 2.6

2. You want to convert the fraction $\frac{7}{12}$ to a decimal. What process can you use? **C**

Ⓐ Divide the denominator by the numerator.
Ⓑ Find the greatest common divisor of 7 and 12.
Ⓒ Divide the numerator by the denominator.
Ⓓ Find the prime factorization of the denominator.

Test-Taking Strategies

Choosing the Process

Students learn to choose a process or strategy to solve a problem. Then they can use the process to solve the problem.

Guided Instruction

Example

After students read the problem, remind them that they are choosing a process. They do not have to solve the problem. Ask:

- *What dimensions might make a good pen for a dog?* **Sample: Students might start with dimensions like 8 × 10, 5 × 16 and 4 × 20. Pens with smaller widths probably would not be good choices.**

Chapter 4 Review

California Resources

Standards Mastery
- Math Companion
- Standards Review Transparencies
- Standards Review and Practice Workbook
- Progress Monitoring Assessments

Math Intervention
- Skills Review and Practice Workbook
- Math XL

- Student Workbook
  - Vocabulary and Study Skills
  - Guided Problem Solving
- All-in-One Teaching Resources
  - Reteaching
  - Enrichment
- Spanish Practice Workbook L3
- Spanish Vocabulary and Study Skills 2A-F L3
- English/Spanish Glossary EL
- Multilingual Handbook EL
- Interactive Textbook Audio Glossary
- Online Vocabulary Quiz

Success Tracker™
Online at PHSchool.com

Spanish Vocabulary/Study Skills EL

Vocabulary/Study Skills L3

4F: Vocabulary Review Puzzle For use with the Chapter Review

Study Skill Combine clue words and pictures to prompt your memory.

Use the word list below to find hidden words in the puzzle. Once you have found a word, draw a circle around it and cross the word off in the word list. Words can be displayed forwards, backwards, up, down, or diagonally but they are always in a straight line.

divisible	prime factor	improper fraction	factor tree
multiple	composite number	equivalent fractions	least common multiple
mixed number	base	simplest form	common factor
fraction	power		

```
A Z E L P I T L U M N O M M O C T S A E L
C E B A S E W X T Y N U Z N A O G P H O E
O J V G R O T C A F N O M M O C S Q A P Q
M W A G H M L L I F H P F D O P O W E R U
P H P O W E R H E M N O B Q E R Y F Z I I
O I B P E L B I S I V I D C M X A R B M V
S K K G L L C R M E N D B I W C D A P E A
I X J K T S F J L U Q R X V T I V C D F L
T I Y W T D X P K R M E A O P U Y T O A E
E J Z U A E I F G Q D L R F A J E I G C N
N I V M E T R F L N Z T Q B C C T O Z T T
U B L X L K W M U I R D K X E Y Z N C O F
M W K U F E C M I E P A H S V B S T U R R
B N M V V O B U E X T J H M R W W N X A A
E U O I N E S D Z Y M U L T I P L E Q G C
R Y L Q R T P M R O F T S E L P M I S Y T
I M P R O P E R F R A C T I O N R S F Z I
K S I R B M T B Q A H O F M D G F H N I O
D A U C E W E N D O Z P V L Q L X A J C N
J T G U H S V G E P I C W R X M Z Y B K S
```

Vocabulary and Study Skills

Chapter 4 Review

Vocabulary Review

English and Spanish Audio Online

common divisor (p. 136)
composite number (p. 133)
equivalent fractions (p. 142)
greatest common divisor (GCD) (p. 136)
least common denominator (LCD) (p. 155)
least common multiple (LCM) (p. 155)
prime factorization (p. 133)
prime number (p. 133)
rational number (p. 148)
repeating decimal (p. 149)
simplest form (p. 143)
terminating decimal (p. 149)

Academic Vocabulary
concept map (p. 160)
divisibility (p. 140)

Go Online PHSchool.com
For: Vocabulary Quiz
Visit: PHSchool.com
Web Code: axj-0451

Choose the correct vocabulary term to complete each sentence.

1. The number 0.3589402 is a rational number and a(n) __?__. terminating decimal
2. The __?__ of 63 is $3^2 \cdot 7$. prime factorization
3. The fraction $\frac{3}{5}$ is in __?__. simplest form
4. Fractions that represent the same amount are __?__. equivalent fractions
5. The __?__ of 15 and 25 is 5. greatest common divisor

Skills and Concepts

Lesson 4-1

- To factor numbers and find the prime factorization of numbers

NS 1.2, AF 2.1

A **prime number** has exactly two factors, 1 and the number itself. A **composite number** has more than two factors. Writing a composite number as a product of prime numbers gives the **prime factorization** of the number.

Find the prime factorization of each number.

6. 28 $2^2 \cdot 7$
7. 250 $2 \cdot 5^3$
8. 378 $2 \cdot 3^3 \cdot 7$
9. 278 $2 \cdot 139$

10. A gardener wants to plant 36 tomato plants. Each row will have an equal number of plants. How many tomato plants can be in each row? 1, 2, 3, 4, 6, 9, 12, 18, 36

Lesson 4-2

- To find the greatest common divisor of two or more numbers

NS 1.2

The **greatest common divisor (GCD)** of two or more numbers is the greatest divisor shared by all the numbers.

Find the GCD of each pair of numbers.

11. 18, 28 2
12. 12, 62 2
13. 25, 35 5
14. 16, 40 8

15. There are 64 girls and 72 boys in the same grade. The principal divides the students into classes. Each class has the same number of boys and the same number of girls. What is the greatest possible number of classes? 8 classes

Lesson 4-3

- To find equivalent forms of fractions

NS 1.2

Equivalent fractions are fractions that name the same amount. A fraction is in **simplest form** when the only common divisor of the numerator and the denominator is 1.

State whether each fraction is in simplest form. If the fraction is not, write the fraction in simplest form.

16. $\frac{5}{20}$ no; $\frac{1}{4}$ **17.** $\frac{1}{3}$ yes **18.** $\frac{4}{6}$ no; $\frac{2}{3}$ **19.** $\frac{2}{9}$ yes

20. In a survey of a class of 35 students about favorite school subjects, 11 students liked math best. What fraction of the students in the class chose math as their favorite subject? $\frac{11}{35}$

Lesson 4-4

- To convert rational numbers to equivalent forms

NS 1.3, NS 1.5

A **rational number** is a number that can be written in the form $\frac{a}{b}$, where a and b are integers and b is not 0. Fractions and integers are rational numbers. To convert a fraction to a decimal, divide the numerator by the denominator. Every rational number is either a **terminating decimal** or a **repeating decimal.**

Write each decimal as a fraction in simplest form.

21. 0.98 $\frac{49}{50}$ **22.** 0.56 $\frac{14}{25}$ **23.** 0.82 $\frac{41}{50}$ **24.** 0.33 $\frac{33}{100}$

Write each fraction as a decimal. Round to three decimal places, if necessary.

25. $\frac{4}{12}$ 0.333 **26.** $\frac{2}{25}$ 0.08 **27.** $\frac{11}{30}$ 0.367 **28.** $\frac{21}{28}$ 0.75

29. A baseball player gets 22 hits in 89 times at bat. Find the player's batting average. .247

Lesson 4-5

- To compare and order rational numbers

NS 1.3

The **least common multiple (LCM)** of two or more numbers is the least multiple shared by all of the numbers. The **least common denominator (LCD)** of two or more denominators is the LCM of the denominators.

You can compare rational numbers by changing each fraction to a decimal or rewriting the fractions with a common denominator.

Order each set of numbers from least to greatest.

30. $-4, 3.25, \frac{7}{12}, -\frac{25}{6}, 0.54$
$-\frac{25}{6}, -4, 0.54, \frac{7}{12}, 3.25$

31. $2.7, \frac{12}{6}, 2.07, \frac{23}{10}, 2\frac{3}{5}$
$\frac{12}{6}, 2.07, \frac{23}{10}, 2\frac{3}{5}, 2.7$

Compare each pair of numbers. Use <, =, or >.

32. $\frac{3}{5}$ ■ $\frac{7}{9}$ < **33.** $-\frac{5}{8}$ ■ $-\frac{4}{7}$ < **34.** $\frac{2}{9}$ ■ $\frac{6}{27}$ =

Alternative Assessment L4

Alternative Assessment Form C

Chapter 4

THE PERFECT BIRDHOUSE

Did you know that birds will not move into just any birdhouse? A bird wants a house that fits; most prefer houses that are just big enough for them to squeeze into.

The drawing below shows an entrance hole that is just the right size for a downy woodpecker. The table beside it lists the right size hole for some other kinds of birds.

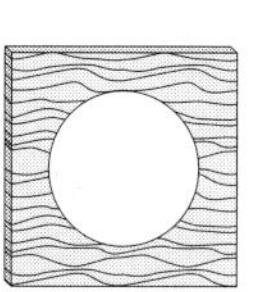
hole is not to scale

Bird	Minimum Diameter of Entrance Hole
Chickadee	$1\frac{1}{8}$ in.
House wren	$1\frac{1}{8}$ in.
Downy woodpecker	$1\frac{1}{4}$ in.
Hairy woodpecker	$1\frac{1}{2}$ in.
Red-headed woodpecker	2 in.
Great crested flycatcher	2 in.
Bluebird	$1\frac{1}{2}$ in.
Tree swallow	$1\frac{1}{2}$ in.
Purple martin	$2\frac{1}{2}$ in.
Screech owl	$3\frac{1}{4}$ in.

Show all of your work on a separate sheet of paper.

1. Why do you suppose birds are so particular about the size of the entrance hole to their house?
2. Make a circle that shows the size of the entrance hole you would need to make in a birdhouse for a chickadee. You can use a ruler and a compass to help you.
3. Three woodpeckers are pictured on the next page. One is a red-headed woodpecker, one is a downy woodpecker, and one is a hairy woodpecker. Next to each picture is the bird's length. Use the information in the table above to help you identify each woodpecker. Write the name of each under its correct drawing. Explain your thinking.

California Resources

Standards Mastery
- Teacher Center ExamView CD-ROM
- Math XL
- Progress Monitoring Assessments
- Online Chapter Test at PHSchool.com

Math Intervention
- Skills Review and Practice Workbook

Online at PHSchool.com

Universal Access Resources
- Chapter Test
- Alternative Assessment
- Spanish Chapter Test
- Spanish Alternative Assessment
- Teacher Center ExamView CD-ROM
  - Special Needs Test
  - Special Needs Practice Banks
  - Foundational Standards Practice Banks
- Online Chapter Test at www.PHSchool.com
- All-In-One Teaching Resources
  - Cumulative Review L3
- Spanish Assessment Resources
  - Cumulative Review L3

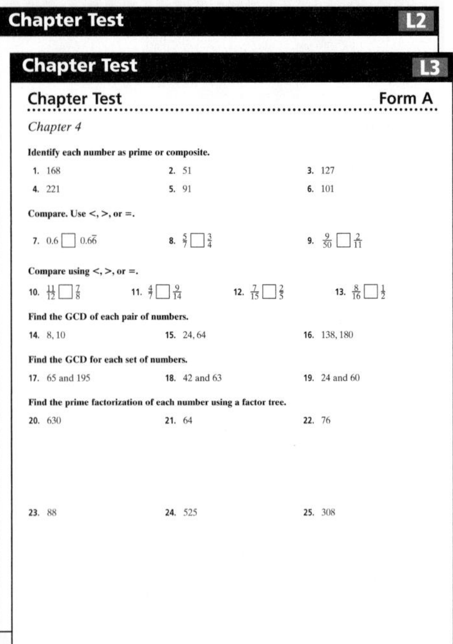
Chapter Test L2

Chapter Test L3

Chapter Test Form A

Chapter 4

Identify each number as prime or composite.

1. 168 2. 51 3. 127
4. 221 5. 91 6. 101

Compare. Use <, >, or =.

7. $0.6 \square 0.6\overline{6}$ 8. $\frac{5}{7} \square \frac{3}{4}$ 9. $\frac{9}{50} \square \frac{2}{11}$

Compare using <, >, or =.

10. $\frac{11}{12} \square \frac{7}{8}$ 11. $\frac{4}{7} \square \frac{9}{14}$ 12. $\frac{7}{15} \square \frac{2}{5}$ 13. $\frac{8}{16} \square \frac{1}{2}$

Find the GCD of each pair of numbers.

14. 8, 10 15. 24, 64 16. 138, 180

Find the GCD for each set of numbers.

17. 65 and 195 18. 42 and 63 19. 24 and 60

Find the prime factorization of each number using a factor tree.

20. 630 21. 64 22. 76

23. 88 24. 525 25. 308

Chapter 4 Test

Go Online PHSchool.com For: Online chapter test Web Code: axa-0452

State whether each number is prime or composite.

1. 48 composite
2. 39 composite
3. 51 composite
4. 67 prime

Find the prime factorization of each number.

5. 72 $2^3 \cdot 3^2$
6. 80 $2^4 \cdot 5$
7. 120 $2^3 \cdot 3 \cdot 5$
8. 432 $2^4 \cdot 3^3$
9. 141 $3 \cdot 47$
10. 280 $2^3 \cdot 5 \cdot 7$

Find the GCD of each pair of numbers.

11. 24, 36 12
12. 7, 19 1
13. 32, 48 16
14. 144, 192 48
15. 200, 164 4
16. 17, 34 17

17. For a writing workshop, 15 coaches and 35 students will be split into groups. Each group must have the same number of coaches and the same number of students. At most, how many groups can there be? 5 groups

Write two fractions equivalent to each fraction. 18–23. See margin.

18. $\frac{6}{18}$
19. $\frac{9}{24}$
20. $\frac{18}{20}$
21. $\frac{60}{100}$
22. $\frac{15}{42}$
23. $\frac{7}{11}$

Write each fraction in simplest form.

24. $\frac{5}{20}$ $\frac{1}{4}$
25. $\frac{9}{21}$ $\frac{3}{7}$
26. $\frac{34}{51}$ $\frac{2}{3}$
27. $\frac{35}{105}$ $\frac{1}{3}$

28. A runner has completed 4 mi of a 26-mi race. In simplest form, what fraction of the race has the runner completed? $\frac{2}{13}$ of the race

29. **Writing in Math** Explain how you can use the prime factorizations of a numerator and denominator to write a fraction in simplest form. Answers may vary. Sample: Write the prime factorization of the numerator and denominator and then divide by each factor that is common to both.

Write each decimal as a fraction in simplest form.

30. 0.04 $\frac{1}{25}$
31. 0.015 $\frac{3}{200}$
32. 0.875 $\frac{7}{8}$
33. 0.64 $\frac{16}{25}$
34. 0.471 $\frac{471}{1{,}000}$
35. 0.212 $\frac{53}{250}$

Write each fraction as a decimal. Round to three decimal places, if necessary.

36. $\frac{17}{40}$ 0.425
37. $\frac{8}{9}$ 0.889
38. $\frac{20}{5}$ 4
39. $\frac{6}{11}$ 0.545
40. $-\frac{7}{13}$ −0.538
41. $\frac{11}{35}$ 0.314
42. $-\frac{27}{8}$ −3.375
43. $\frac{19}{15}$ 1.267
44. $-\frac{3}{7}$ −0.429
45. $\frac{9}{20}$ 0.45

46. A baseball player gets 68 hits in 204 times at bat. Find the batting average of the player. .333

Order each set of numbers from least to greatest.

47. $1\frac{5}{6}, 1\frac{7}{9}, 1.67, \frac{35}{36}, 1\frac{3}{4}$ $\frac{35}{36}, 1.67, 1\frac{3}{4}, 1\frac{7}{9}, 1\frac{5}{6}$
48. $\frac{4}{12}, -0.39, -\frac{4}{12}, \frac{17}{9}, -1$ $-1, -0.39, -\frac{4}{12}, \frac{4}{12}, \frac{17}{9}$
49. $1, 2\frac{1}{8}, -0.79, -1.3, -\frac{3}{4}$ $-1.3, -0.79, -\frac{3}{4}, 1, 2\frac{1}{8}$

Compare each pair of numbers. Use <, =, or >.

50. $\frac{2}{5} \blacksquare \frac{4}{10}$ =
51. $\frac{15}{4} \blacksquare \frac{17}{5}$ >
52. $\frac{7}{14} \blacksquare \frac{1}{2}$ =
53. $\frac{3}{5} \blacksquare \frac{7}{11}$ <
54. $-\frac{1}{3} \blacksquare -\frac{5}{12}$ >
55. $-\frac{5}{11} \blacksquare -\frac{4}{9}$ <

56. Lee jogged $\frac{1}{2}$ mi, Orlando jogged $\frac{2}{3}$ mi, and Holden jogged $\frac{3}{8}$ mi. Who jogged the longest distance? Orlando

Cumulative Practice

Some questions ask you to convert rational numbers to equivalent forms. Read the question at the right. Then use the tips as guides for finding the answer.

In an orchard, 20 of the 80 fruit trees are apple trees. Which decimal is equivalent to the fraction of apple trees in the orchard?

Ⓐ 0.2 Ⓒ 0.80
Ⓑ 0.25 Ⓓ 2.8

Tip 1
First write the fraction described in the problem.

Tip 2
You can estimate the answer and eliminate some of the answer choices before finding the answer.

Think It Through
The fraction of the trees that are apple trees is $\frac{20}{80}$. To convert the fraction to a decimal, divide the numerator by the denominator: $20 \div 80 = 0.25$. The correct answer is choice B.

Vocabulary Review

As you solve problems, you must understand the meanings of mathematical terms. Match each term with its mathematical meaning.

A. rational number II
B. prime factorization IV
C. greatest common divisor III
D. least common multiple I

I. the least number that is a multiple of each number of a set
II. any number that can be written as the quotient of two integers, where the denominator is not 0
III. the greatest divisor shared by all numbers of a set
IV. writing a composite number as the product of prime numbers

Read each question. Then write the letter of the correct answer on your paper.

1. Oren needs to buy $\frac{3}{8}$ lb of sliced turkey. What is this fraction written as a decimal? (Lesson 4-4) B

Ⓐ 0.26 Ⓒ 0.38
Ⓑ 0.375 Ⓓ 0.425

2. The prime factorization of 1,400 is $2 \cdot 2 \cdot 2 \cdot 5 \cdot 5 \cdot 7$. How can this product be written using exponents? (Lesson 4-1) C

Ⓐ $8 \cdot 25 \cdot 7$
Ⓑ $2^3 + 5^2 + 7$
Ⓒ $2^3 \cdot 5^2 \cdot 7$
Ⓓ $(2 \cdot 3) + (5 \cdot 2) + 7$

3. For a birthday party, Maria buys some juice drinks for \$.95 each and a cake for \$12.99. She spends a total of \$24.39. How many juice drinks does Maria buy? (Lesson 3-4) C

Ⓐ 10 Ⓒ 12
Ⓑ 11 Ⓓ 13

California Resources

Standards Mastery
- Teacher Center ExamView CD-ROM
- Math XL
- Progress Monitoring Assessments
- Online Chapter Test at PHSchool.com

Math Intervention
- Skills Review and Practice Workbook

Universal Access Resources
- Teacher Center ExamView CD-ROM
  - Special Needs Test
  - Special Needs Practice Banks
  - Foundational Standards Practice Banks
- Online Chapter Test at www.PHSchool.com
- All-In-One Teaching Resources
  - Cumulative Review L3
- Spanish Assessment Resources
  - Cumulative Review L3

Online at PHSchool.com

4. Gabriela lives 3 mi east of the library and 4 miles north of Kyle's house. What is the direct distance from Kyle's house to the library? **(Lesson 3-6) B**

- (A) 3 mi
- (B) 5 mi
- (C) 16 mi
- (D) 25 mi

5. Which decimal is equivalent to $\frac{12}{15}$? **(Lesson 4-4) D**

- (A) 0.15
- (B) 0.25
- (C) $0.\overline{3}$
- (D) 0.8

6. Kwami takes 0.4 t of newspaper to the recycling plant. Which fraction is NOT equivalent to 0.4? **(Lesson 4-4) C**

- (A) $\frac{2}{5}$
- (B) $\frac{4}{10}$
- (C) $\frac{6}{14}$
- (D) $\frac{8}{20}$

7. Alyssa wrote the prime factorization of 180 as $2 \cdot 2 \cdot 3 \cdot 3 \cdot 5$. How can Alyssa write this product using exponents? **(Lesson 4-1) A**

- (A) $2^2 \cdot 3^2 \cdot 5$
- (B) $4 \cdot 9 \cdot 5$
- (C) $2^2 \cdot 3^3 \cdot 5$
- (D) $2 \cdot 6 \cdot 15$

8. A submarine starts at sea level. It dives 8 ft/min for 15 min and then stops. Which integer expresses the depth of the submarine when it stops? **(Lesson 2-4) A**

- (A) −120 ft
- (B) −23 ft
- (C) 23 ft
- (D) 120 ft

9. Amber has \$50 in her bank account. She deposits \$15 each week. After how many weeks will she have \$125 in her bank account? Use the equation $125 = 50 + 15w$, where w is the number of weeks. **(Lesson 3-4) C**

- (A) 1 wk
- (B) 3 wk
- (C) 5 wk
- (D) 15 wk

10. Which list shows the numbers in order from least to greatest? **(Lesson 4-5) A**

- (A) $-1, -\frac{1}{2}, -0.25, 0$
- (B) $-1, -0.25, -\frac{1}{2}, 0$
- (C) $0, -0.25, -\frac{1}{2}, -1$
- (D) $0, -\frac{1}{2}, -0.25, -1$

11. The figure below shows 7 shaded squares inside a larger square.

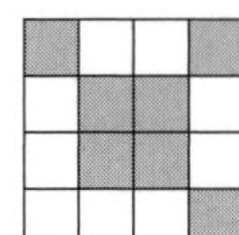

Which decimal is equivalent to the fraction of the larger square that is shaded? **(Lesson 4-4) B**

- (A) 0.16
- (B) 0.4375
- (C) 0.7
- (D) 7.16

12. Which number is NOT a rational number? **(Lesson 4-4) B**

- (A) −23
- (B) $\sqrt{7}$
- (C) $\frac{7}{8}$
- (D) 8.945

13. The triangle below is a right triangle.

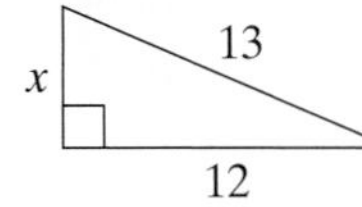

What is the value of x? **(Lesson 3-7) A**

- (A) 5
- (B) 12
- (C) 25
- (D) 144

14. You have \$4.75 in your pocket. You want to buy a sandwich and cookies. The sandwich costs \$3.25 and cookies cost \$.50 each. How many cookies can you buy? **(Lesson 3-4) D**

- (A) 0
- (B) 1
- (C) 2
- (D) 3

Spanish Cumulative Review EL

Cumulative Review L3

Cumulative Review

Chapters 1–4

Multiple Choice. Choose the letter of the best answer.

1. Find $-7 - (-7)$.
   A. 0 B. −7 C. −14 D. 14
2. The legs of a right triangle measure 6 ft and 8 ft. What is the length of the hypotenuse?
   A. 10 ft B. 14 ft C. 28 ft D. not here
3. A 17-foot ladder is leaning against a house. If the top of the ladder is 15 feet above the ground, how far from the house is the bottom of the ladder?
   A. 6 feet B. 7 feet C. 8 feet D. 9 feet
4. Evaluate $a^2 - b$ for $a = 3$ and $b = -5$.
   A. 1 B. 4 C. 11 D. 14
5. Which number is NOT a rational number?
   A. 0 B. $\frac{1}{3}$ C. $\sqrt{2}$ D. $|-6|$
6. Which number is equivalent to $-6.\overline{1}$?
   A. $-\frac{1}{6}$ B. $-6\frac{1}{9}$ C. $-\frac{6}{1}$ D. $-6\frac{1}{10}$
7. Which of the following is NOT true?
   A. $\frac{2}{3} < \frac{7}{4}$
   B. $1\frac{3}{4} < \frac{13}{8}$
   C. $\frac{2}{5} > \frac{2}{9}$
   D. $\frac{11}{5} > \frac{13}{7}$
8. Which decimal is equivalent to $\frac{15}{6}$?
   A. 0.25 B. 0.5 C. 2.05 D. 2.5
9. Give the prime factorization for 126.
   A. $2 \cdot 63$ B. $2 \cdot 7 \cdot 9$ C. $2 \cdot 3^2 \cdot 5$ D. $2 \cdot 3^2 \cdot 7$
10. Carl had 15 hits in 24 times at bat. What is his batting average? (A batting average is the ratio $\frac{\text{hits}}{\text{times at bat}}$.)
    A. 0.150 B. 0.625 C. 0.240 D. 0.325
11. Convert 0.36 to a fraction in simplest form.
    A. $\frac{3}{10}$ B. $\frac{36}{100}$ C. $\frac{9}{25}$ D. $\frac{4}{11}$
12. Which list shows the numbers in order from least to greatest?
    A. $\frac{5}{6}, \frac{24}{29}, 0.81$
    B. $0.81, \frac{24}{29}, \frac{5}{6}$
    C. $0.81, \frac{5}{6}, \frac{24}{29}$
    D. $\frac{5}{6}, 0.81, \frac{24}{29}$

15. In 20 d the level of a pond drops 10 in. What is the rate of change of the water level? (Lesson 2-5) C

Ⓐ −10 in./d
Ⓑ −5 in./d
Ⓒ −0.5 in./d
Ⓓ −1 in./d

16. Convert 0.98 to a fraction in simplest form. (Lesson 4-4) A

Ⓐ $\frac{49}{50}$ Ⓒ $\frac{49}{100}$
Ⓑ $\frac{98}{100}$ Ⓓ $\frac{4}{5}$

17. Which list shows the numbers in order from least to greatest? (Lesson 4-5) D

Ⓐ $0.56, \frac{3}{8}, 0.3, 1\frac{1}{8}$
Ⓑ $\frac{3}{8}, 0.3, 0.56, 1\frac{1}{8}$
Ⓒ $\frac{3}{8}, 1\frac{1}{8}, 0.3, 0.56$
Ⓓ $0.3, \frac{3}{8}, 0.56, 1\frac{1}{8}$

18. The outside temperature was 9°F. During the day it rose 2°F and then dropped 15°F. What was the temperature at the end of the day? (Lesson 2-3) B

Ⓐ −15°F Ⓒ 2°F
Ⓑ −4°F Ⓓ 26°F

19. In a math class, $\frac{2}{9}$ of the students are left-handed. Which decimal is equivalent to the fraction of left-handed students in the class? (Lesson 4-4) B

Ⓐ 0.2 Ⓒ $0.2\overline{9}$
Ⓑ $0.\overline{2}$ Ⓓ 2.9

20. Simplify $2^4 + (-31)$. (Lesson 2-6) B

Ⓐ −23 Ⓒ 39
Ⓑ −15 Ⓓ 47

21. Which number is NOT a rational number? (Lesson 4-4) B

Ⓐ $\frac{11}{23}$ Ⓒ −4
Ⓑ $\sqrt{1.34}$ Ⓓ $0.1\overline{5}$

22. A triangle has legs of length 18 m and 24 m. What is the length of the triangle's hypotenuse? (Lesson 3-6) A

Ⓐ 30 m Ⓒ 306 m
Ⓑ 42 m Ⓓ 900 m

23. Which fraction is equivalent to 0.45? (Lesson 4-4) B

Ⓐ $\frac{5}{10}$ Ⓒ $\frac{1}{2}$
Ⓑ $\frac{9}{20}$ Ⓓ $\frac{45}{10}$

Standards Reference Guide

California Content Standard	Item Number(s)
NS 1.2	8, 15, 18, 20
NS 1.3	1, 5, 10, 11, 17, 19
NS 1.5	6, 12, 16, 21, 23
AF 2.1	2, 7
AF 4.1	3, 9, 14
MG 3.3	4, 13, 22

For additional review and practice, see the *California Standards Review and Practice Workbook* or go online to use the

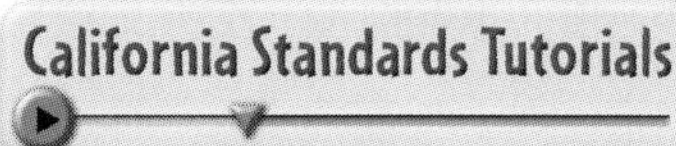

Visit: PHSchool.com, **Web Code:** axq-0945

Chapter 5 Rational Number Operations

Chapter at a Glance

Lesson Titles, Objectives, and Features	California Content Standards
5-1 Adding Rational Numbers • To add rational numbers **Mathematical Reasoning:** Adding Fractions	Solve problems involving addition of positive fractions. ***Foundational (Gr6 NS 2.1)*** **NS 1.2** Add rational numbers. **NS 1.3** Convert fractions to decimals and use these representations in estimations, computations, and applications.
5-2a Activity Lab: Estimating With Fractions **5-2 Subtracting Rational Numbers** • To subtract rational numbers	Solve problems involving subtraction of positive fractions. ***Foundational (Gr6 NS 2.1)*** **NS 1.2** Subtract rational numbers. **NS 1.5** Convert terminating decimals into reduced fractions.
5-3a Activity Lab: Modeling Fraction Multiplication **5-3 Multiplying Rational Numbers** • To multiply rational numbers and raise fractions to positive whole-number powers	Solve problems involving multiplication of positive fractions. ***Foundational (Gr6 NS 2.1)*** **NS 1.2** Multiply rational numbers and take positive rational numbers to whole-number powers. **AF 2.1** Interpret positive whole-number powers as repeated multiplication.
5-4 Dividing Rational Numbers • To find reciprocals and divide rational numbers	Solve problems involving division of positive fractions. ***Foundational (Gr6 NS 2.1)*** **NS 1.2** Divide rational numbers. **Alg1 2.0** Understand and use such operations as finding the reciprocal.
5-5 Solving Equations by Adding and Subtracting • To solve addition and subtraction equations with fractions	Write and solve one-step linear equations in one variable. ***Foundational (Gr6 AF 1.1)*** **AF 1.3** Simplify numerical expressions by applying properties of rational numbers and justify the process used.
5-6 Solving Equations by Multiplying • To solve multiplication and division equations with fractions **Algebraic Thinking:** Estimating Solutions	**AF 1.1** Use variables and appropriate operations to write an equation. **AF 1.3** See Lesson 5-5. **AF 4.1** Solve two-step linear equations in one variable.
5-7 Zero and Negative Exponents • To simplify and evaluate expressions with zero and negative exponents **5-7b Activity Lab:** Expanded Notations	**AF 2.1** Interpret negative whole-number powers as repeated division or multiplication by the multiplicative inverse. Simplify and evaluate expressions that include exponents.

California Content Standards
NS Number Sense
AF Algebra and Functions
MG Measurement and Geometry
MR Mathematical Reasoning

Correlations to Standardized Tests

All content for these tests is contained in *Prentice Hall Math, Algebra Readiness.* This chart reflects coverage in this chapter only.

	5-1	5-2	5-3	5-4	5-5	5-6	5-7
Terra Nova CAT6 (Level 18)							
Number and Number Relations	✔	✔	✔	✔	✔	✔	✔
Computation and Numerical Estimation	✔	✔	✔	✔	✔	✔	✔
Operation Concepts	✔	✔	✔	✔	✔	✔	✔
Measurement			✔	✔		✔	
Geometry and Spatial Sense							
Data Analysis, Statistics, and Probability							
Patterns, Functions, and Algebra	✔	✔	✔	✔	✔	✔	✔
Problem Solving and Reasoning	✔	✔	✔	✔	✔	✔	✔
Communication	✔	✔	✔	✔	✔	✔	✔
Decimals, Fractions, Integers, Percent	✔	✔	✔	✔	✔	✔	✔
Order of Operations							
Algebraic Operations			✔				✔
Terra Nova CTBS (Level 18)							
Decimals, Fractions, Integers, and Percents	✔	✔	✔	✔	✔	✔	✔
Order of Operations, Numeration, Number Theory	✔	✔	✔	✔	✔	✔	✔
Data Interpretation							
Measurement			✔	✔		✔	
Geometry							
ITBS (Level 14)							
Number Properties and Operations	✔	✔	✔	✔	✔	✔	✔
Algebra	✔	✔	✔	✔	✔	✔	✔
Geometry							
Measurement			✔	✔		✔	
Probability and Statistics							
Estimation		✔		✔			
SAT10 (Adv 1 Level)							
Number Sense and Operations	✔	✔	✔	✔	✔	✔	✔
Patterns, Relationships, and Algebra	✔	✔	✔	✔	✔	✔	✔
Data, Statistics, and Probability							
Geometry and Measurement			✔	✔		✔	
NAEP							
Number Sense, Properties, and Operations	✔	✔	✔	✔			✔
Measurement							
Geometry and Spatial Sense							
Data Analysis, Statistics, and Probability							
Algebra and Functions					✔	✔	✔

CAT6 California Achievement Test, 6th Ed. **CTBS** Comprehensive Test of Basic Skills **ITBS** Iowa Test of Basic Skills, Form M
SAT10 Stanford Achievement Test, 10th Ed. **NAEP** National Assessment of Educational Progress 2005 Mathematics Objectives

California Math Background

Professional
Development

Focus on the California Content Standards

- The first four lessons in Chapter 5 provide support for students who struggle with number sense skills involving fractions. The Guided Problem Solving examples in each of these lessons will be especially helpful to prepare students for lessons 5-5 and 5-6, where students apply their computation skills with fractions as they solve equations.
- Students bring experience in working with fractions from grade 6, when they calculated and solved problems involving addition, subtraction, multiplication, and division of positive fractions (**NS 2.0**, **2.1**, and **2.2**). The special Guided Problem Solving feature—Word Problem Practice—on pages 194 and 195 will serve as an effective formative assessment exercise.

5-1 Adding Rational Numbers

California Content Standards **NS 1.2, NS 1.3, MR 2.4, MR 2.5**

Math Understandings

- To find the sum of two fractions with unlike denominators, you first rewrite each fraction using a common denominator.
- Any common denominator may be used, but using the Least Common Denominator (LCD) may save steps and make it easier to simplify the final answer.

The least common multiple (LCM) of two or more numbers is the smallest multiple that is common to all of the numbers. The LCM of the denominators is called the least common denominator (LCD). To add fractions, rewrite them with a common denominator.

To add different forms of rational numbers, first write all the numbers in the same form, as fractions or as decimals.

Example: Find $8.8 + 7\frac{1}{8}$.

$8.8 + 7\frac{1}{8} = 8.8 + 7.125$	Write the mixed number as a decimal.
$= 15.925$	Add.

5-2 Subtracting Rational Numbers

California Content Standards **NS 1.2, NS 1.5, MR 2.7**

Math Understandings

- To find the difference of two fractions with unlike denominators, you first rewrite each fraction using a common denominator.
- Any common denominator may be used, but using the Least Common Denominator (LCD) may save steps and make it easier to simplify the final answer.

To subtract different forms of rational numbers, first write all the numbers in the same form, as fractions or as decimals.

Example: Find $8.8 - 7\frac{1}{8}$.

$8.8 + 7\frac{1}{8} = 8.8 - 7.125$	Write the mixed number as a decimal.
$= 1.675$	Subtract.

5-3 Multiplying Rational Numbers

California Content Standards **NS 1.2, AF 2.1**

Math Understandings

- To find the product of rational numbers that are fractions, multiply the numerators and multiply the denominators.
- You can multiply mixed numbers by writing each as an improper fraction.

An **exponent** tells how many times a number, or **base,** is used as a factor. An expression that uses a base and an exponent is called a **power**.

To raise a fraction to a power, raise the numerator and the denominator to the power.

Example: Simplify $\left(\frac{3}{5}\right)^4$.

$\frac{3}{5} \times \frac{3}{5} \times \frac{3}{5} \times \frac{3}{5} = \frac{81}{625}$

To multiply fractions, some students may find models useful. The model below shows $\frac{1}{2} \cdot \frac{5}{16}$.

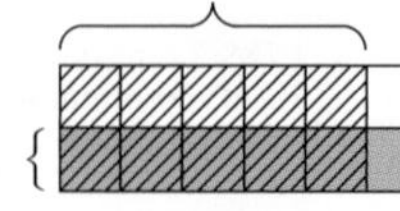
5/6 of the columns are shaded with diagonal lines.
1/2 the columns are shaded blue.
5 out of 12 of the squares include both types of shading.

5-4 Dividing Rational Numbers

California Content Standards **NS 1.2, NS 1.5, Alg1 2.0**

Math Understandings

- Two numbers are reciprocals if their product is 1.
- Dividing by a fraction is the same as multiplying by the reciprocal of the fraction.

The numbers $\frac{2}{3}$ and $\frac{3}{2}$ are **reciprocals**. Notice that the numerators and denominators are switched in fractions that are reciprocals. To divide by a fraction, multiply by the reciprocal of the fraction. You can remember this by thinking "invert and multiply."

Dividing Fractions	
Arithmetic	**Algebra**
$\frac{5}{8} \div \frac{1}{8} = \frac{5 \times 8}{8 \times 1} = \frac{8}{1}$	$\frac{a}{b} \div \frac{c}{d} = \frac{a}{b} \times \frac{d}{c}$ where b, c, and $d \neq 0$

5-5 Solving Equations by Adding and Subtracting

California Content Standards **NS 1.2, AF 1.1, AF 1.3, MR 3.2**

Math Understandings

- You solve an equation with fractions in the same way that you solve an equation with whole numbers: you **isolate**, or get the variable alone on one side of the equal sign using properties of equality and inverse operations.

You can solve equations with fractions and mixed numbers by applying the addition and subtraction properties of equality and inverse operations. Then write the answer in simplest form.

5-6 Solving Equations by Multiplying

California Content Standards **AF 1.1, AF 1.3, AF 4.1, MR 2.1**

Math Understandings

- You can use the Multiplication Property of Equality to multiply each side of an equation by the same number and write an equivalent simpler equation.
- You can use the **Inverse Property of Multiplication** to solve equations. The reciprocal of a number is also called its **multiplicative inverse**. Every nonzero number has a multiplicative inverse. The product of a number and its multiplicative inverse is 1.

Multiplication and division are inverse operations that undo each other.

5-7 Zero and Negative Exponents

California Content Standards **NS 2.1, AF 2.1**

Math Understandings

- An exponent that is a negative number indicates that you are to take a reciprocal.
- A zero exponent on a nonzero base means the power has a value of 1.
- To divide two powers with the same base, you keep the common base and subtract the exponent of the divisor from the exponent of the dividend to find the new exponent.

Zero as an Exponent
For any nonzero number a, $a^0 = 1$. **Example:** $9^0 = 1$ because $1 = \frac{x^a}{x^a} = x^{a-a} = x^0$, $x \neq 0$.

Negative Exponents
For any nonzero number a and integer n, $a^{-n} = \frac{1}{a^n}$. **Example:** $8^{-5} = \frac{1}{8^5}$

Professional Development

Additional Professional Development Opportunities

Math Background notes for Chapter 5: Every lesson has a Math Background in the PLAN section.

In-Service On Demand
Prentice Hall offers free video-based tutorials to support you. Visit PHSchool.com/inserviceondemand.

Pearson Achievement Solutions
Pearson Achievement Solutions, a Pearson Education company, offers comprehensive, facilitated professional development designed to help teachers improve student achievement. To learn more, please visit pearsonachievementsolutions.com.

Chapter 5 Resources

	5-1	5-2	5-3	5-4	5-5	5-6	5-7	For the Chapter
Print Resources								
L3 Practice	●	●	●	●	●	●	●	
L3 Guided Problem Solving	●	●	●	●	●	●	●	
L2 Reteaching	●	●	●	●	●	●	●	
L4 Enrichment	●	●	●	●	●	●	●	
L3 Vocabulary and Study Skills	●	●	●	●	●	●		●
L3 Daily Puzzles	●	●	●	●	●	●	●	
L3 Activity Labs	●	●	●	●	●	●	●	
L3 Checkpoint Quiz		●				●		
L3 Chapter Project								●
L2 Below Level Chapter Test								●
L3 Chapter Test								●
L4 Alternative Assessment								●
L3 Cumulative Review								●
Spanish Resources EL								
L3 Practice	●	●	●	●	●	●	●	●
L3 Vocabulary and Study Skills	●		●	●		●		●
L3 Checkpoint Quiz		●				●		
L2 Below Level Chapter Test								●
L3 Chapter Test								●
L4 Alternative Assessment								●
L3 Cumulative Review								●
Transparencies								
Check Skills You'll Need	●	●	●	●	●	●	●	
Additional Examples	●	●	●	●	●	●	●	
California Daily Review	●	●	●	●	●	●	●	
Classroom Aid	●	●	●	●	●	●	●	
Student Edition Answers	●	●	●	●	●	●	●	●
Lesson Quiz	●	●	●	●	●	●	●	
Technology								
California Student Center Online	●	●	●	●	●	●	●	●
California Student Center CD-ROM	●	●	●	●	●	●	●	●
Success Tracker™ Online Math Intervention	●	●	●	●	●	●	●	●
California Teacher Center: ExamView CD-ROM	●	●	●	●	●	●	●	●
California Teacher Center: Planning CD-ROM	●	●	●	●	●	●	●	●
California Teacher Center: Presentations CD-ROM and online	●	●	●	●	●	●	●	●
MindPoint Quiz Show	●	●	●	●	●	●	●	●
Prentice Hall Web Site: PHSchool.com	●	●	●	●	●	●	●	●

Also available: **California Standards Mastery**
- Standards Review Transparencies
- Standards Review and Practice Workbook
- Progress Monitoring Assessments
- Math Companion
- Math*XL*

California Intervention Resources
- Skills Review and Practice Workbook
- Success Tracker™ Online Math Intervention

Other Resources
- Multilingual Handbook
- Spanish Student Edition
- Solution Key
- Math Notes Study Folder

Where You Can Use the Lesson Resources

Here is a suggestion, following the four-step teaching plan, for how you can incorporate Universal Access Resources into your teaching.

	Instructional Resources L3	Universal Access Resources
1. Plan		
Preparation Read the Math Background in the Teacher's Edition to connect this lesson with students' previous experience. **Starting Class** **Check Skills You'll Need** Assign these exercises from the Math Companion to review prerequisite skills. Review the full text of the California Content Standards covered in this lesson. **New Vocabulary** Help students pre-read the lesson by pointing out the new terms introduced in the lesson.	**California Math Background** **Math Understandings** **Transparencies & Presentations CD-ROM** Check Skills You'll Need California Daily Review **Resources** Vocabulary and Study Skills **Math Companion**	**Spanish Support** EL Vocabulary and Study Skills
2. Teach		
L3 **Guided Instruction** Use the Activity Labs to build conceptual understanding. Teach each Example. Use the Teacher's Edition side column notes for specific teaching tips, including Error Prevention notes. Use the Additional Examples found in the side column (and on transparency and PowerPoint) as an alternative presentation for the content. After each Example, assign the California Standards Check exercises for that Example to get an immediate assessment of student understanding. Utilize the support in the Math Companion to assist students with each Standards Check. Use the Closure activity in the Teacher's Edition to help students attain mastery of lesson content.	**Student Edition** Activity Lab **Resources** Math Companion Activity Lab **Transparencies & Presentations CD-ROM** Additional Examples Classroom Aids **Teacher Center: ExamView CD-ROM**	**Teacher's Edition** Every lesson includes suggestions for working with students who need special attention. L1 Special Needs L2 Below Level L4 Advanced Learners EL English Learners **Resources** **Multilingual Handbook** **Math Companion**
3. Practice		
Assignment Guide **Check Your Understanding** Use these questions from the Math Companion to check students' understanding before you assign homework. **Homework Exercises** Assign homework from these leveled exercises in the Assignment Guide. A Practice by Example B Apply Your Skills C Challenge California Multiple-Choice Practice and Mixed Review **Homework Quick Check** Use these key exercises to quickly check students' homework.	**Transparencies & Presentations CD-ROM** Student Answers **Resources** Math Companion Practice Guided Problem Solving Vocabulary and Study Skills Activity Lab Daily Puzzles **Teacher Center: ExamView CD-ROM** **Math *XL***	**Spanish Support** EL Practice EL Vocabulary and Study Skills **Resources** L4 Enrichment
4. Assess & Reteach		
Lesson Quiz Assign the Lesson Quiz to assess students' mastery of the lesson content. **Checkpoint Quiz** Use the Checkpoint Quiz to assess student progress over several lessons.	**Transparencies & Presentations CD-ROM** Lesson Quiz **Resources** Checkpoint Quiz	**Resources** L2 Reteaching EL Checkpoint Quiz Success Tracker™ **Teacher Center: ExamView CD-ROM**

KEY L1 Special Needs L2 Below Level L3 For All Students L4 Advanced, Gifted EL English Learners

Rational Number Operations

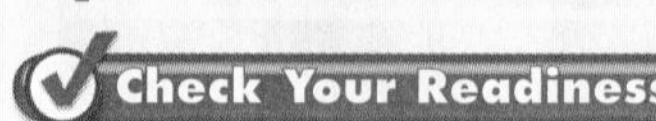

Answers are in the back of the textbook.

For math intervention, direct students to:

Subtracting Integers
Lesson 2-3

Positive Exponents
Lesson 2-6

Greatest Common Divisor
Lesson 4-2

Equivalent Fractions
Lesson 4-3

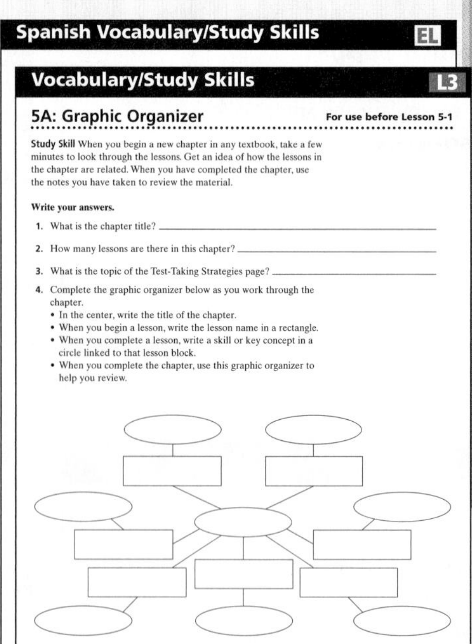

Spanish Vocabulary/Study Skills EL

Vocabulary/Study Skills L3

5A: Graphic Organizer — For use before Lesson 5-1

Study Skill When you begin a new chapter in any textbook, take a few minutes to look through the lessons. Get an idea of how the lessons in the chapter are related. When you have completed the chapter, use the notes you have taken to review the material.

Write your answers.

1. What is the chapter title? ____________
2. How many lessons are there in this chapter? ____________
3. What is the topic of the Test-Taking Strategies page? ____________
4. Complete the graphic organizer below as you work through the chapter.
   - In the center, write the title of the chapter.
   - When you begin a lesson, write the lesson name in a rectangle.
   - When you complete a lesson, write a skill or key concept in a circle linked to that lesson block.
   - When you complete the chapter, use this graphic organizer to help you review.

Rational Number Operations

What You've Learned

California Content Standards

NS 1.5 Know that every rational number is either a terminating or a repeating decimal and be able to convert terminating decimals into reduced fractions.

AF 1.1 Use variables and appropriate operations to write an expression or an equation that represents a verbal description.

MG 3.3 Know and understand the Pythagorean theorem and use it to find the length of the missing side of a right triangle.

to the lesson in green.

Subtracting Integers (Lesson 2-3)

Find each difference.

1. $-5 - 8$ -13
2. $16 - 29$ -13
3. $-23 - (-14)$ -9
4. $-36 - 11$ -47
5. $6 - (-12)$ 18
6. $-1 - 1$ -2

Writing Powers (Lesson 2-6)

Write each expression using exponents.

7. $5 \cdot 5 \cdot 5 \cdot 5$ 5^4
8. $w \cdot w \cdot w \cdot 3 \cdot 3$ $w^3 3^2$
9. $p \cdot p \cdot p \cdot p \cdot p \cdot p$ p^6
10. $19 \cdot 19 \cdot 19$ 19^3
11. $2 \cdot 2 \cdot 6 \cdot 6$ $2^2 6^2$
12. $10 \cdot 10 \cdot 10 \cdot 10$ 10^4

Finding the Greatest Common Divisor (Lesson 4-2)

Find the GCD of each pair of numbers.

13. 8, 36 4
14. 16, 54 2
15. 4, 24 4
16. 56, 96 8

Finding Equivalent Fractions (Lesson 4-3)

Write each fraction in simplest form.

17. $\frac{5}{10}$ $\frac{1}{2}$
18. $\frac{6}{15}$ $\frac{2}{5}$
19. $\frac{12}{16}$ $\frac{3}{4}$
20. $\frac{3}{33}$ $\frac{1}{11}$

California Content Standards for Chapter 5

Number Sense
NS 1.2, NS 1.3, NS 1.5, NS 2.1

Algebra and Functions
AF 1.1, AF 1.3, AF 2.1, AF 4.1

Mathematical Reasoning
MR 2.1, MR 2.4, MR 2.5, MS 2.7, MR 3.2

Algebra 1
Alg1 2.0

Chapter 5 Overview

In this chapter, students add and subtract rational numbers and fractions with unlike denominators. They multiply and divide rational numbers, raise fractions to positive whole-number powers, and find reciprocals. They solve addition, subtraction, multiplication, and division equations with fractions, and they also simplify and evaluate expressions with zero and negative exponents.

Activating Prior Knowledge

In this chapter, students build on and extend their knowledge of rational numbers to add, subtract, multiply, and divide fractions. They draw on their knowledge of the Properties of Equality to solve equations involving rational numbers, and they expand their understanding of exponents to include zero and negative exponents. Ask questions such as:

- *Write the mixed number $4\frac{4}{6}$ as an improper fraction in simplest form.* $\frac{14}{3}$
- *What is the GCD of 24 and 18?* 6
- *What is the LCM of 24 and 18?* 72
- *How can you simplify: (2x)(3x)?* $6x^2$

What You'll Learn Next

California Content Standards

NS 1.2 Add, subtract, multiply and divide rational numbers and take positive rational numbers to whole-number powers.

NS 2.1 Understand negative whole-number exponents.

AF 2.1 Interpret negative whole-number powers as repeated division or multiplication by the multiplicative inverse.

AF 4.1 Solve two-step linear equations in one variable over the rational numbers.

▲ In Lesson 5-3, you will multiply rational numbers to find the distance a flock of snow geese flies.

New Vocabulary

English and Spanish Audio Online

- multiplicative inverse (p. 196)
- reciprocals (p. 186)

Academic Vocabulary
- benchmark (p. 175)
- notation (p. 206)

Mathematical Reasoning

Adding Fractions

Students learn that adding fractions is similar to adding integers and that they can use a number line to add fractions just as they can with integers.

Guided Instruction

Explain to students how using a number line can help them add fractions as well as integers. For each of the exercises, ask students to make a number line starting at 0 and divided into equal lengths. Show them that they move along the line to the right to add a positive fraction and move along the line to the left to add a negative fraction. Ask them to write out each of their steps and to write a justification to the right of each step as they simplify the expressions.

Mathematical Reasoning

For Use With Lesson 5-1

NS 1.2 Add rational numbers. *Develop*

MR 2.4 Make and test conjectures by using inductive reasoning. *Develop*

MR 2.5 Use diagrams and models to explain mathematical reasoning. *Develop*

Adding Fractions

Adding fractions is similar to adding integers. You can use a number line to add fractions. Start at 0. Move right to add positive fractions. Move left to add negative fractions.

EXAMPLE

Add $\frac{5}{7} + \left(-\frac{1}{7}\right)$.

On a number line, divide the segment between 0 and 1 into 7 segments of equal length. Each small segment is $\frac{1}{7}$ unit long.

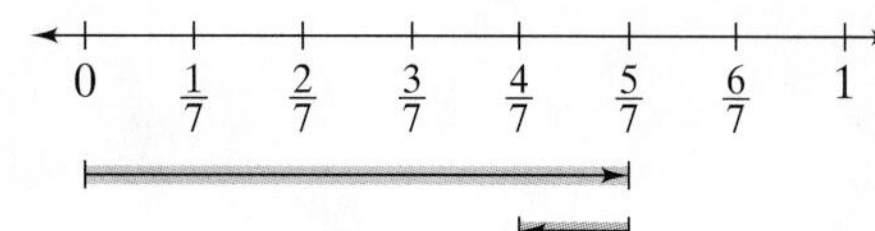

So $\frac{5}{7} + \left(-\frac{1}{7}\right) = \frac{4}{7}$.

Exercises

Find each sum using a number line.

1. $-\frac{1}{6} + \frac{4}{6}$ $\frac{3}{6}$ or $\frac{1}{2}$
2. $\frac{3}{8} + \frac{2}{8}$ $\frac{5}{8}$
3. $\frac{1}{3} + \left(-\frac{1}{3}\right)$ 0
4. $-\frac{3}{4} + \frac{1}{4}$ $-\frac{2}{4}$ or $-\frac{1}{2}$
5. $-\frac{2}{7} + \left(-\frac{2}{7}\right)$ $-\frac{4}{7}$
6. $\frac{2}{9} + \frac{5}{9}$ $\frac{7}{9}$
7. Write an addition problem that the diagram below can model.

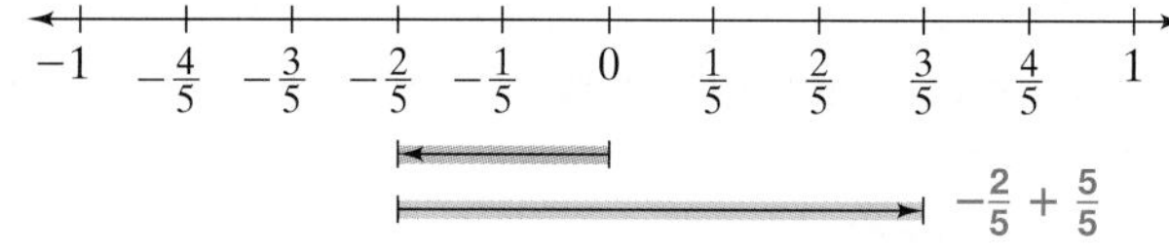

$-\frac{2}{5} + \frac{5}{5}$

8. **a.** Find $\frac{1}{5} + \left(-\frac{3}{5}\right)$. $-\frac{2}{5}$

   b. Find $-\frac{3}{5} + \frac{1}{5}$. $-\frac{2}{5}$

   c. Reasoning Use your number lines from parts (a) and (b) to make a conjecture about whether the Commutative Property of Addition is true for fractions. Test your conjecture with several other examples. The sums are the same so the Commutative Property of Addition holds true for fractions.

GO for Help: Math Companion

5-1 Adding Rational Numbers

 Check Skills You'll Need

Do this in your **Math Companion.**

 **Vocabulary**

Review:

- least common multiple (LCM)
- least common denominator (LCD)

Use your **Math Companion** *to build your vocabulary.*

California Content Standards

Foundational Standard Solve problems involving addition of positive fractions.

NS 1.2 Add rational numbers. ***Develop***

NS 1.3 Convert fractions to decimals and use these representations in estimations, computations, and applications. ***Develop***

What You'll Learn . . . and Why

You will learn to add rational numbers. Bakers add rational numbers to find how much of each ingredient they will need.

To add fractions with unlike denominators, first rewrite them with a common denominator. The method shown below works for adding any fractions.

Arithmetic		Algebra
$\frac{1}{2} + \frac{1}{3}$		$\frac{a}{b} + \frac{c}{d}$
$\frac{1 \cdot 3}{2 \cdot 3} + \frac{1 \cdot 2}{3 \cdot 2}$	← Write equivalent fractions with a common denominator. →	$\frac{a \cdot d}{b \cdot d} + \frac{c \cdot d}{d \cdot b}$
$\frac{3}{6} + \frac{2}{6}$	← Simplify. →	$\frac{ad}{bd} + \frac{bc}{bd}$
$\frac{5}{6}$	← Add the numerators. →	$\frac{ad + bc}{bd}$

EXAMPLE Adding With Unlike Denominators

1 Find $-\frac{1}{4} + \frac{2}{3}$.

$$-\frac{1}{4} = \frac{-1 \cdot 3}{4 \cdot 3} = \frac{-3}{12}$$
$$+\frac{2}{3} = \frac{2 \cdot 4}{3 \cdot 4} = +\frac{8}{12}$$

Multiply to find a common denominator.

$$\frac{5}{12}$$ ← Add the numerators.

Math Foundations

The rules for adding integers also apply to adding fractions.

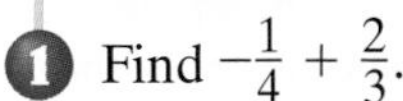

CA Standards Check 1 *Go to your* **Math Companion** *for help.*

1. Find each sum. Write your answer in simplest form.

a. $\frac{2}{15} + \frac{1}{10}$ $\frac{7}{30}$

b. $\frac{3}{5} + \frac{1}{7}$ $\frac{26}{35}$

5-1

1. Plan

California Content Standards

Solve problems involving addition of positive fractions. ***Foundational***

NS 1.2 Add rational numbers. ***Develop***

NS 1.3 Convert fractions to decimals and use these representations in estimations, computations, and applications. ***Develop***

California Math Background

In order to add fractions, the fractions must have the same denominator, known as a *common denominator.* The least common denominator (LCD) is the smallest denominator that is common to both fractions. Choosing the LCD may save the step of simplifying the sum. When adding fractions with unlike denominators, find a common denominator, write equivalent fractions with that denominator, add the numerators, and simplify as needed. To add different forms of rational numbers, first write all the numbers in the same form.

More Math Background: p. 168C

Lesson Planning and Resources

See p. 168E for a list of the resources that support this lesson.

PRESENTATION CD-ROM
CD, Online, or Transparencies

Bell Ringer Practice

Check Skills You'll Need
Use student page, transparency, or PowerPoint.
See Math Companion.

California Standards Review
Use transparency or PowerPoint.

Universal Access Solutions for All Learners

Special Needs L1
Before working on Examples 2 and 3, write a mixed number on the board and have students describe how to write this number as an improper fraction and as a decimal.

Below Level L2
Read aloud equivalent fractions like these. Have students explain how to find the missing numerators.

$\frac{3}{4} = \frac{■}{12}$ Multiply 3 by 3; 9.

$\frac{2}{3} = \frac{■}{12}$ Multiply 2 by 4; 8.

2. Teach

Guided Instruction

Teaching Tips
The greater number of the denominators is often the LCD. For $\frac{1}{2}$ and $\frac{3}{4}$, the LCD is 4.

If the denominators are one number apart, such as 3 and 4, and each of the fractions is in its simplest form, the LCD will be the product of the denominators. For $\frac{1}{4}$ and $\frac{2}{3}$, the LCD is 12.

Additional Examples

1. Find $-\frac{1}{3} + \frac{1}{2}$. $\frac{1}{6}$

2. A recipe calls for $\frac{1}{3}$ cup of white flour and $\frac{3}{4}$ cup of wheat flour. How many cups of flour do you need? $1\frac{1}{12}$ c

3. Find $6.75 + 8\frac{3}{10}$. 15.05

Closure

- *How do you add fractions with unlike denominators?* Write equivalent fractions with a like denominator. Then add numerators, keep the denominator, and simplify.
- *What do you need to do if the sum of rational numbers includes an improper fraction?* Change the improper fraction to a mixed number and add the whole numbers.

Quick Tip
To find the LCM, list the multiples of each number until you find a common multiple.

Sometimes it is easier to use the least common denominator (LCD) to add fractions with unlike denominators. Recall that the LCD of two or more fractions is the least common multiple (LCM) of their denominators.

EXAMPLE Adding Using the LCD

2 Guided Problem Solving A cake recipe calls for $\frac{5}{8}$ c of walnuts and $\frac{1}{2}$ c of pecans. How many cups of nuts do you need?

$$\frac{5}{8} = \frac{5}{8} = \frac{5}{8}$$
$$+\frac{1}{2} = \frac{1 \cdot 4}{2 \cdot 4} = +\frac{4}{8}$$
← The LCD is 8. Write the fractions with the same denominator.

$$= \frac{9}{8}$$
← Add the numerators.

You need $\frac{9}{8}$ c, or $1\frac{1}{8}$ c, of nuts.

CA Standards Check 2 *Go to your* **Math Companion** *for help.*

2. You exercise for $\frac{1}{2}$ h on Monday and $\frac{3}{4}$ h on Tuesday. How long did you exercise on Monday and Tuesday? $1\frac{1}{4}$ h

To add different forms of rational numbers, first write all the numbers in the same form. You can write all the numbers as fractions or you can write all the numbers as decimals.

EXAMPLE Adding Rational Numbers

Relate MATH YOU KNOW...

Write $6\frac{1}{5}$ as a decimal.

$6\frac{1}{5} = \frac{6 \cdot 5 + 1}{5}$ ← Write the mixed number as an improper fraction.

$= \frac{31}{5}$ ← Simplify.

$= 31 \div 5$ ← Divide the numerator by the denominator.

$= 6.2$ ← Simplify.

...to NEW IDEAS

3 Find $8.25 + 6\frac{1}{5}$.

$8.25 + 6\frac{1}{5} = 8.25 + 6.2$ ← Write the mixed number as a decimal.

$= 14.45$ ← Add.

CA Standards Check 3 *Go to your* **Math Companion** *for help.*

3. Find each sum.

a. $4\frac{2}{5} + 2.75$ 7.15

b. $9.6 + 4\frac{1}{4}$ 13.85

Homework prep is in your **Math Companion.**

Advanced Learners L4
Have students rewrite $\frac{1}{a} + \frac{1}{b}$ as a single fraction. Have students show their work and justify each step.

$$\frac{1}{a} + \frac{1}{b} = \frac{b}{ab} + \frac{a}{ab} = \frac{a+b}{ab}$$

English Learners EL
Discuss the prefix "un." Say: *When we see un in front of a word, it means "not" or "the opposite of." Unlike denominators are not like denominators. Because like denominators are common or the same, unlike denominators are different, or not the same.*

Standards Practice

NS 1.2, NS 1.3

3. Practice

Assignment Guide

Check Your Understanding

See Math Companion.

Homework Exercises

A Practice by Example	1–22
B Apply Your Skills	23–36
C Challenge	37
California Multiple-Choice Practice	38–39
Mixed Review	40–43

Homework Quick Check

To check students' understanding of key skills and concepts, go over Exercises 2, 9, 17, 28, 29, 32.

A Practice by Example

Example 1 (page 171)

Find each sum. Write your answer in simplest form.

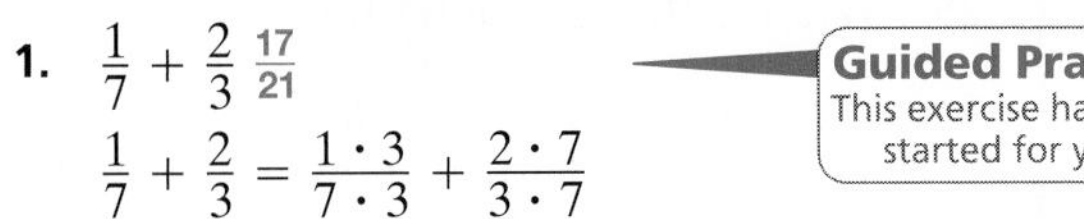

1. $\frac{1}{7} + \frac{2}{3}$ $\frac{17}{21}$

$\frac{1}{7} + \frac{2}{3} = \frac{1 \cdot 3}{7 \cdot 3} + \frac{2 \cdot 7}{3 \cdot 7}$

Guided Practice This exercise has been started for you!

2. $-\frac{7}{8} + \frac{1}{5}$ $-\frac{27}{40}$
3. $\frac{2}{7} + \frac{3}{4}$ $1\frac{1}{28}$
4. $\frac{2}{5} + \left(-\frac{5}{6}\right)$ $-\frac{13}{30}$
5. $\frac{3}{10} + \frac{5}{8}$ $\frac{37}{40}$
6. $-\frac{1}{3} + \frac{2}{7}$ $-\frac{1}{21}$
7. $\frac{11}{12} + \frac{1}{11}$ $1\frac{1}{132}$

Example 2 (page 172)

Find each sum using the LCD. Write your answer in simplest form.

8. $\frac{1}{3} + \frac{1}{6}$ $\frac{1}{2}$

$\frac{1}{3} + \frac{1}{6} = \frac{1 \cdot 2}{3 \cdot 2} + \frac{1}{6}$

Guided Practice This exercise has been started for you!

Homework Video Tutor

For: Examples 1–3
Visit: PHSchool.com
Web Code: axe-0501

9. $\frac{3}{5} + \frac{3}{20}$ $\frac{3}{4}$
10. $\frac{5}{12} + \frac{1}{3}$ $\frac{3}{4}$
11. $\frac{8}{9} + \frac{5}{6}$ $1\frac{13}{18}$
12. $\frac{1}{4} + \frac{5}{16}$ $\frac{9}{16}$
13. $-\frac{9}{10} + \frac{11}{12}$ $\frac{1}{60}$
14. $\frac{8}{25} + \left(-\frac{2}{100}\right)$ $\frac{3}{10}$
15. You have two baby hamsters. One weighs $\frac{1}{4}$ lb and the other weighs $\frac{3}{12}$ lb. What is the total weight of the hamsters? $\frac{1}{2}$ lb

Example 3 (page 172)

Find each sum.

16. $3.56 + \frac{3}{4}$ 4.31

$3.56 + \frac{3}{4} = 3.56 + 0.75$

Guided Practice This exercise has been started for you!

17. $\frac{1}{2} + 1.8$ 2.3
18. $0.23 + \frac{3}{10}$ 0.53
19. $5.5 + \left(2\frac{54}{100}\right)$ 8.04
20. $34.9 + 8\frac{2}{5}$ 43.3
21. $-10.6 + \frac{3}{5}$ −10
22. $-\frac{9}{8} + 0.15$ −0.975

B Apply Your Skills

23. **Guided Problem Solving** You skate $1\frac{1}{4}$ mi from your house to the park. The park has a path that is $2\frac{3}{10}$ mi long. You skate once around the path and then skate home. What is the total distance you skate? $4\frac{4}{5}$ mi
    - You can draw a diagram to model the problem.

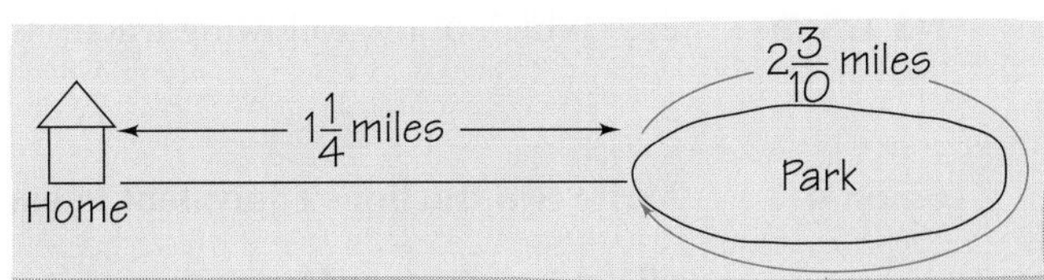

- Which distance do you skate twice?

Universal Access Resources

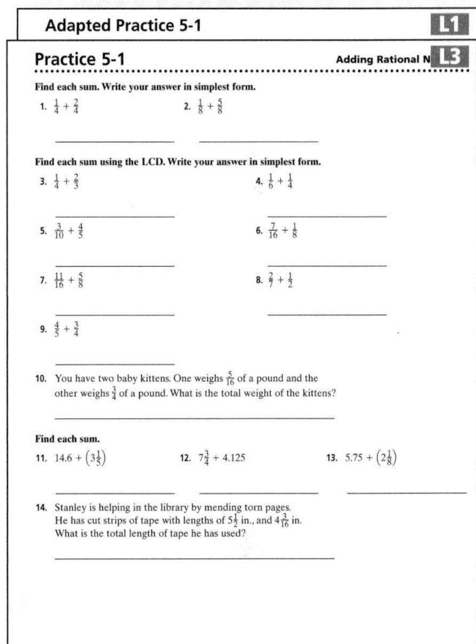

Adapted Practice 5-1 L1

Practice 5-1 Adding Rational N L3

Find each sum. Write your answer in simplest form.

1. $\frac{1}{4} + \frac{2}{4}$
2. $\frac{1}{8} + \frac{5}{8}$

Find each sum using the LCD. Write your answer in simplest form.

3. $\frac{1}{4} + \frac{2}{3}$
4. $\frac{1}{6} + \frac{1}{4}$
5. $\frac{3}{10} + \frac{4}{5}$
6. $\frac{7}{16} + \frac{1}{8}$
7. $\frac{11}{16} + \frac{5}{8}$
8. $\frac{2}{7} + \frac{1}{2}$
9. $\frac{4}{5} + \frac{3}{4}$
10. You have two baby kittens. One weighs $\frac{5}{16}$ of a pound and the other weighs $\frac{3}{4}$ of a pound. What is the total weight of the kittens?

Find each sum.

11. $14.6 + \left(3\frac{1}{5}\right)$
12. $7\frac{3}{4} + 4.125$
13. $5.75 + \left(2\frac{1}{8}\right)$
14. Stanley is helping in the library by mending torn pages. He has cut strips of tape with lengths of $5\frac{1}{2}$ in., and $4\frac{3}{16}$ in. What is the total length of tape he has used?

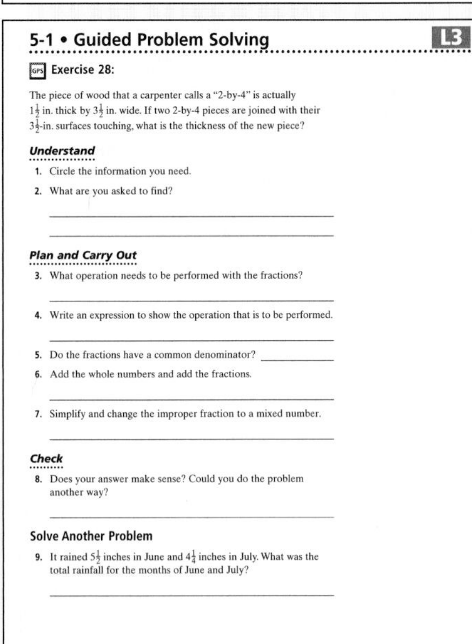

5-1 • Guided Problem Solving L3

GPS Exercise 28:

The piece of wood that a carpenter calls a "2-by-4" is actually $1\frac{1}{2}$ in. thick by $3\frac{1}{2}$ in. wide. If two 2-by-4 pieces are joined with their $3\frac{1}{2}$-in. surfaces touching, what is the thickness of the new piece?

Understand

1. Circle the information you need.
2. What are you asked to find?

Plan and Carry Out

3. What operation needs to be performed with the fractions?
4. Write an expression to show the operation that is to be performed.
5. Do the fractions have a common denominator? ______
6. Add the whole numbers and add the fractions.
7. Simplify and change the improper fraction to a mixed number.

Check

8. Does your answer make sense? Could you do the problem another way?

Solve Another Problem

9. It rained $5\frac{1}{2}$ inches in June and $4\frac{1}{4}$ inches in July. What was the total rainfall for the months of June and July?

4. Assess & Reteach

PRESENTATION CD-ROM
CD, Online, or Transparencies

Lesson Quiz

Find each sum.

1. $\frac{5}{8} + \frac{1}{12}$ $\frac{17}{24}$
2. $-\frac{13}{24} + \frac{3}{8}$ $-\frac{1}{6}$
3. $7.875 + 4\frac{5}{6}$ $12\frac{17}{24}$
4. It snowed $2\frac{1}{2}$ in. on top of 4.5 in. of snow already on the ground. How deep is the snow now? 7 in.

Reteaching 5-1 — Adding Rational Nu… L2

To add fractions with unlike denominators, rewrite them with a common denominator.

Example 1: Find $\frac{5}{6} + \frac{1}{2}$.

① Find the least common denominator of 6 and 2.

The LCD is 6.

② Write equivalent fractions using the LCD.

$\frac{5}{6} = \frac{5}{6}$ $\quad \frac{1}{2} = \frac{1 \cdot 3}{2 \cdot 3} = \frac{3}{6}$

③ Add. Write the sum in simplest form.

$\frac{5}{6} + \frac{1}{2} = \frac{5}{6} + \frac{3}{6} = \frac{5+3}{6} = \frac{8}{6} = \frac{4}{3} = 1\frac{1}{3}$

$\frac{5}{6} + \frac{1}{2} = 1\frac{1}{3}$

Example 2: Find $9.75 + 3\frac{1}{5}$.

① Write the fraction as a decimal.

$9.75 + 3.2$

② Add.

$9.75 + 3.2 = 12.95$

Find each sum.

1. $\frac{1}{2} + \frac{3}{4}$ ______
2. $\frac{1}{6} + \frac{1}{3}$ ______
3. $\frac{9}{10} + \frac{1}{2}$ ______
4. $\frac{2}{3} + \frac{5}{9}$ ______
5. $\frac{1}{2} + \frac{7}{10}$ ______
6. $\frac{5}{8} + \frac{1}{4}$ ______
7. $\frac{5}{6} + \frac{1}{3}$ ______
8. $\frac{3}{5} + \frac{1}{6}$ ______
9. $\frac{1}{12} + \frac{1}{10}$ ______
10. $6.7 + 5\frac{1}{4}$ ______
11. $3\frac{2}{5} + 5.6$ ______
12. $2.3 + 7\frac{3}{4}$ ______

Enrichment 5-1 — Adding Rational N… L4

Decision Making

You want to make a meat loaf. The only measuring cups in the house measure $\frac{1}{8}$ cup and $\frac{1}{4}$ cup. There are only $\frac{1}{8}$, $\frac{1}{4}$, and $\frac{1}{2}$ teaspoon measuring spoons. Since you don't want to continually wash and dry the measuring cups, you want to use certain ones for dry ingredients and the rest for wet ingredients.

Meat Loaf

$\frac{1}{2}$ lb ground beef
$\frac{1}{2}$ c ketchup
2 eggs
$\frac{1}{4}$ c tomato juice
$\frac{3}{4}$ c bran cereal
$1\frac{1}{2}$ tsp onion flakes
$\frac{1}{2}$ tsp Worcestershire sauce
$\frac{1}{2}$ tsp salt
$\frac{1}{8}$ tsp pepper

Topping
2 tsp mustard
$\frac{1}{4}$ c ketchup
2 tsp brown sugar

Mix ingredients in column 1. Place in 9 · 5 pan. Combine topping ingredients. Spread over meat loaf. Bake at 400° F for 45 minutes.

1. Identify the dry and wet ingredients in the recipe by placing a *D* beside the dry ingredients and a *W* beside the wet ingredients.
2. Which measuring cups and spoons will you use only for dry ingredients? Which for wet ingredients?
______
______
3. Show how you will measure each quantity using the measuring cups you decided to use in Exercise 2.
______
4. Rewrite the recipe so that it makes two meat loaves.
______

SCAFFOLDED
Problem Solving

24. $3\frac{1}{4}$ yd
25. 13 yd
26. 13.75 yd

Suppose you need the amounts of fabric shown in the table to make a flag.

Fabric Colors

Color	Length (yards)
Red	$3\frac{1}{4}$
White	$5\frac{1}{2}$
Blue	$4\frac{1}{4}$

24. How much red fabric do you need for the flag?
25. What is the total length of fabric you need?
26. Suppose you also buy 0.75 yd of green fabric for a shirt. What is the total length of fabric you need for the flag and the shirt?
27. All the fabric you buy costs \$5.50 per yard. How much do you spend on fabric? \$75.63

GPS 28. The piece of wood that a carpenter calls a "2-by-4" is actually $1\frac{1}{2}$ in. thick by $3\frac{1}{2}$ in. wide. If two 2-by-4 pieces are joined with their $3\frac{1}{2}$-in. surfaces touching, what is the thickness of the new piece? 3 in.

29. **Writing in Math** How can you use mental math to find $5\frac{1}{3} + 3\frac{4}{5} + 3\frac{2}{3} + 6\frac{1}{5}$? See margin.

Find each sum.

30. $\frac{5}{8} + \frac{9}{12} + \frac{1}{2}$ $1\frac{7}{8}$
31. $-7\frac{2}{5} + (-4.56) + \left(-3\frac{3}{10}\right)$ -15.26
32. $5^2 + 0.4 + 8\frac{1}{2}$ 33.9
33. $12\frac{1}{4} + 0.4^2 + \frac{8}{10}$ 13.21
34. $\frac{35}{10} + 7.9 + \left(-\frac{1}{2}\right)$ 10.9
35. $\frac{44}{8} + \frac{5}{25} + \left(-\frac{1}{4}\right)$ 5.45

36. Examples may vary. Sample: $\frac{1}{2} + \frac{1}{3} \neq \frac{1}{5}$.

37. 0.75; 0.875; 0.9375; never; the sum will always approach 1.

36. **Error Analysis** A student adds $\frac{1}{a} + \frac{1}{b}$ and says the sum is $\frac{1}{a+b}$. Give an example that shows the student is incorrect. See above left.

C Challenge

37. Find $\frac{1}{2} + \frac{1}{4}$. Then find $\frac{1}{2} + \frac{1}{4} + \frac{1}{8}$. Now find $\frac{1}{2} + \frac{1}{4} + \frac{1}{8} + \frac{1}{16}$. If this pattern continues, when will the sum be greater than 1? Explain. See above left.

Multiple Choice Practice and Mixed Review

For California Standards Tutorials, visit PHSchool.com. Web Code: axq-9045

NS 1.2

38. Shelly keeps track of the time she spends on her cellular phone. Today she made three calls that lasted 20 min 15 s, 3.2 min, and $12\frac{1}{2}$ min. How many minutes did Shelly spend on the phone today? D
 - Ⓐ 35.55 min
 - Ⓑ 35.75 min
 - Ⓒ 35.85 min
 - Ⓓ 35.95 min

NS 1.5

39. Which of the following fractions is equivalent to 0.25? B
 - Ⓐ $\frac{2}{5}$
 - Ⓑ $\frac{1}{4}$
 - Ⓒ $\frac{1}{25}$
 - Ⓓ $\frac{1}{2}$

GO for Help — Lesson 4-3

Write two fractions equivalent to each fraction. 40–43. Answers may vary. Samples are given.

40. $\frac{3}{8}$ $\frac{6}{16}, \frac{12}{32}$
41. $\frac{1}{6}$ $\frac{2}{12}, \frac{4}{24}$
42. $\frac{2}{5}$ $\frac{4}{10}, \frac{8}{20}$
43. $\frac{7}{10}$ $\frac{14}{20}, \frac{28}{40}$

GO Online Lesson Quiz Visit: PHSchool.com Web Code: axa-0501

Alternative Assessment

Each student in a pair writes several problems involving addition of rational numbers. Students exchange papers and write the sums in simplest form. Have partners record how they found the sums.

California Resources

Standards Mastery
- Standards Review Transparencies
- Standards Review and Practice Workbook
- Math Companion

Math Intervention
- Skills Review and Practice Workbook
- Math XL

5-2a Activity Lab

Estimating With Fractions

NS 1.2 Add and subtract rational numbers. ***Develop***
MR 2.7 Give answers to a specified degree of accuracy. ***Develop***

In some situations, you need to estimate with fractions. A *benchmark* is a convenient number used to replace fractions that are less than 1. The benchmarks 0, $\frac{1}{2}$, and 1 are particularly useful when estimating sums and differences of fractions. The table below can help you decide when to use each benchmark.

Description	Examples	Benchmark
Numerator is very small when compared to the denominator.	$\frac{1}{8}, \frac{3}{16}, \frac{2}{25}, \frac{9}{100}$	0
Numerator is about one half of denominator.	$\frac{3}{8}, \frac{9}{16}, \frac{11}{25}, \frac{52}{100}$	$\frac{1}{2}$
Numerator and denominator are close in value.	$\frac{7}{8}, \frac{14}{16}, \frac{23}{25}, \frac{95}{100}$	1

EXAMPLE Estimating Sums and Differences

Estimate $\frac{7}{12} + \frac{4}{5}$.

$\frac{7}{12} + \frac{4}{5} \approx \frac{1}{2} + 1$ ← **Replace each fraction with a benchmark.**

$= 1\frac{1}{2}$ ← **Add.**

Exercises

Estimate each sum or difference. Use the benchmarks 0, $\frac{1}{2}$, and 1.

1. $\frac{5}{13} + \frac{4}{25}$ about $\frac{1}{2}$ **2.** $\frac{17}{19} - \frac{2}{13}$ about 1 **3.** $\frac{70}{85} + \frac{32}{51}$ about $1\frac{1}{2}$ **4.** $\frac{11}{20} - \frac{2}{15}$ about $\frac{1}{2}$

5. Use the table at the right to estimate the total width of the coins. about $3\frac{1}{2}$ in.

U.S. Coins

Coin	Diameter (inches)
Dime	$\frac{141}{200}$
Penny	$\frac{3}{4}$
Nickel	$\frac{167}{200}$
Quarter	$\frac{191}{200}$

6. Number Sense You estimate $\frac{1}{8} + \frac{9}{16} + \frac{33}{32}$ using the benchmarks 0, $\frac{1}{2}$, and 1. Is your estimate less than or greater than the actual sum? Explain. The estimate is less than the actual sum because the actual numbers are greater than the estimate.

Activity Lab

Estimating With Fractions

Students estimate fractions using benchmarks, convenient numbers used to replace fractions that are less than 1. This will help them understand the advantages of exact and approximate solutions to problems later in the chapter.

Guided Instruction

Before beginning the Activity, have students compare a full sheet of notebook paper and a half sheet of notebook paper. Fold a third full sheet of paper in half three times so that it makes eight sections. Fold the paper in different ways to show various fractions of the whole, such as $\frac{1}{8}$ page, $\frac{2}{8}$ page, $\frac{3}{8}$ page, and so on. For each fold you make, ask the students what fraction of paper they see and whether the size is closer to one full sheet of paper or a half-sheet of paper. You might also consider folding it as small as possible to indicate that its size is closer to no paper (or zero sheets of paper) than to a half-sheet.

5-2

1. Plan

California Content Standards

Solve problems involving subtraction of positive fractions. *Foundational*

NS 1.2 Subtract rational numbers. *Develop*

NS 1.5 Convert terminating decimals into reduced fractions. *Develop*

California Math Background

Subtracting rational numbers is similar to adding rational numbers. In order to subtract fractions, you must make sure that the fractions have a common denominator. Using the LCD can eliminate the step of simplifying the difference. To subtract rational numbers in different forms, write the numbers in the same form.

More Math Background: p. 168C

Lesson Planning and Resources

See p. 168E for a list of the resources that support this lesson.

PRESENTATION CD-ROM CD, Online, or Transparencies

Bell Ringer Practice

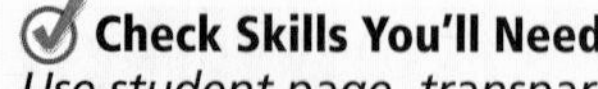

Check Skills You'll Need
Use student page, transparency, or PowerPoint.
See Math Companion.

California Standards Review
Use transparency or PowerPoint.

5-2 Subtracting Rational Numbers

Check Skills You'll Need

Do this in your **Math Companion.**

Vocabulary

Review:
- least common denominator (LCD)

Use your **Math Companion** *to build your vocabulary.*

California Content Standards

Foundational Standard Solve problems involving subtraction of positive fractions.
NS 1.2 Subtract rational numbers. *Develop*
NS 1.5 Convert terminating decimals into reduced fractions. *Develop*

What You'll Learn . . . and Why

You will learn to subtract rational numbers. Scientists subtract rational numbers when they compare measurements.

Subtracting fractions is similar to adding fractions. To subtract fractions with unlike denominators, first rewrite them with a common denominator. The rules for subtracting integers also apply to subtracting fractions.

EXAMPLE Subtracting With Unlike Denominators

Relate MATH YOU KNOW...

Find $\frac{1}{9} - \frac{5}{9}$.

$$\frac{1}{9} - \frac{5}{9} = -\frac{4}{9}$$ ← Subtract the numerators.

...to NEW IDEAS

1 Find $\frac{5}{9} - \frac{1}{2}$.

$$\frac{5}{9} = \frac{5 \cdot 2}{9 \cdot 2} = \frac{10}{18}$$
$$-\frac{1}{2} = -\frac{1 \cdot 9}{2 \cdot 9} = -\frac{9}{18}$$ Find a common denominator.

$$\frac{1}{18}$$ ← Subtract the numerators.

CA Standards Check 1 *Go to your* **Math Companion** *for help.*

1. Find each difference. Write your answer in simplest form.

a. $\frac{1}{10} - \frac{1}{4}$ $-\frac{3}{20}$ **b.** $\frac{2}{3} - \frac{7}{8}$ $-\frac{5}{24}$

Universal Access Solutions for All Learners

Special Needs L1
Students may need to review the rules for subtracting integers. A number line can help them understand how to apply the rules to rational numbers.

Below Level L2
Have students convert between mixed numbers and improper fractions, and describe how they did this, with exercises such as these:

$3\frac{1}{2}$ $\frac{7}{2}$ $5\frac{2}{3}$ $\frac{17}{3}$ $\frac{8}{3}$ $2\frac{2}{3}$

You can also use the least common denominator (LCD) to subtract fractions.

EXAMPLE Subtracting Using the LCD

2 Find $\frac{5}{6} - \frac{1}{4}$ using the LCD.

$$\frac{5}{6} = \frac{5 \cdot 2}{6 \cdot 2} = \frac{10}{12}$$
$$-\frac{1}{4} = -\frac{1 \cdot 3}{4 \cdot 3} = -\frac{3}{12}$$
$$\frac{7}{12}$$

The LCD is 12. Write the fractions with the same denominator.

← **Subtract the numerators.**

CA Standards Check 2 *Go to your* **Math Companion** *for help.*

2. Find each difference using the LCD.

a. $\frac{1}{6} - \frac{4}{9}$ $-\frac{5}{18}$

b. $\frac{7}{15} - \frac{1}{3}$ $\frac{2}{15}$

To subtract rational numbers, first rewrite them in the same form.

EXAMPLE Subtracting Rational Numbers

3 **Guided Problem Solving** A class grows plants for a science project. One student measures a plant to be 11.5 in. tall. Another student's plant is $7\frac{5}{6}$ in. tall. Find the difference in the heights of the plants.

First write both numbers in the same form.

$11.5 - 7\frac{5}{6} = 11\frac{1}{2} - 7\frac{5}{6}$ ← **Write the decimal as a mixed number.**

$= \frac{23}{2} - \frac{47}{6}$ ← **Write each mixed number as an improper fraction.**

$= \frac{23 \cdot 3}{2 \cdot 3} - \frac{47}{6}$ ← **Find the least common denominator.**

$= \frac{69}{6} - \frac{47}{6}$ ← **Simplify.**

$= \frac{22}{6}$ ← **Subtract.**

$= 3\frac{4}{6}$ ← **Write the improper fraction as a mixed number.**

$= 3\frac{2}{3}$ ← **Write the fraction in simplest form.**

One plant is $3\frac{2}{3}$ in. taller than the other plant.

Problem Solving Tip

Use estimation to check the reasonableness of your answer.

CA Standards Check 3 *Go to your* **Math Companion** *for help.*

3. One lion cub weighs $7\frac{1}{8}$ lb. Another cub weighs 5.75 lb. How much more does the heavier cub weigh? $1\frac{3}{8}$ lb or 1.375 lb

2. Teach

Guided Instruction

Example 1

Emphasize that you cannot subtract $\frac{1}{2}$ from $\frac{5}{9}$ without rewriting both fractions with the same denominator.

Example 3

To help visual learners, draw a vertical line segment on the board and label it 11.5 in. Label the bottom portion of the segment $7\frac{5}{6}$ in., and the remaining portion *t*.

PRESENTATION CD-ROM
CD, Online, or Transparencies

Additional Examples

1 Find $\frac{5}{8} - \frac{1}{6}$. $\frac{11}{24}$

2 Find $\frac{9}{10} - \frac{3}{4}$ using the LCD. $\frac{3}{20}$

3 A two-week-old panda bear weighed $\frac{3}{4}$ pound. At the age of one month, the cub weighed 2.3 pounds. How many pounds did it gain? $1\frac{11}{20}$ lb

Advanced Learners L4

Add a set of parentheses to each equation so that both expressions equal $\frac{1}{2}$.

$\frac{3}{4} - \left(\frac{1}{6} + \frac{1}{12}\right) = \frac{1}{2}\left(\frac{17}{18} - \frac{2}{3}\right) + \frac{2}{9} = \frac{1}{2}$

English Learners EL

For Example 3, help students write the correct equation by having them identify what they know and what they are trying to find. Have them ask themselves these same questions as they complete the next problem independently.

Closure

- *How do you subtract fractions with unlike denominators?* Write equivalent fractions with a like denominator. Then subtract numerators, keep the denominator, and simplify.
- *How do you subtract rational numbers that are written in different forms?* Write the numbers in the same form; then subtract.

More Than One Way

Suppose you catch two fish. The first fish is $9\frac{1}{8}$ in. long. The second fish is $7\frac{1}{4}$ in. long. How much longer is the first fish?

Kevin's Method

I need to subtract the lengths. Since $\frac{1}{8} < \frac{1}{4}$, I will rename $9\frac{1}{8}$.

$9\frac{1}{8} - 7\frac{1}{4} = 9\frac{1}{8} - 7\frac{2}{8}$ ← The LCD is 8. Write $\frac{1}{4}$ as $\frac{2}{8}$.

$= 8\frac{9}{8} - 7\frac{2}{8}$ ← Rename $9\frac{1}{8}$ as $8 + 1\frac{1}{8}$, or $8\frac{9}{8}$.

$= 1\frac{7}{8}$ ← Find the difference.

The first fish is $1\frac{7}{8}$ in. longer than the second fish.

Tina's Method

I need to subtract the lengths. I will change both mixed numbers to improper fractions with the same denominator.

$9\frac{1}{8} - 7\frac{1}{4} = \frac{73}{8} - \frac{29}{4}$ ← Write as improper fractions.

$= \frac{73}{8} - \frac{58}{8}$ ← Rename as equivalent fractions with a like denominator.

$= \frac{15}{8} = 1\frac{7}{8}$ ← Subtract. Write the difference in simplest form.

The first fish is $1\frac{7}{8}$ in. longer than the second fish.

Choose a Method

Find $10\frac{1}{3} - 7\frac{8}{9}$. Describe your method and explain why you chose it.
$2\frac{4}{9}$; check students' work.

GO for Help: *MathXL*

Standards Practice

NS 1.2, NS 1.5

A Practice by Example

Example 1 (page 176)

Find each difference. Write your answer in simplest form.

1. $\frac{3}{4} - \frac{2}{3}$ $\frac{1}{12}$

   $\frac{3}{4} - \frac{2}{3} = \frac{3 \cdot 3}{4 \cdot 3} - \frac{2 \cdot 4}{3 \cdot 4}$

Guided Practice This exercise has been started for you!

2. $\frac{3}{10} - \frac{3}{11}$ $\frac{3}{110}$
3. $\frac{5}{7} - \frac{2}{5}$ $\frac{11}{35}$
4. $\frac{4}{5} - \frac{2}{3}$ $\frac{2}{15}$
5. $\frac{3}{5} - \frac{1}{4}$ $\frac{7}{20}$
6. $\frac{5}{8} - \frac{2}{5}$ $\frac{9}{40}$
7. $\frac{5}{6} - \frac{1}{2}$ $\frac{1}{3}$

178  *Homework prep is in your* **Math Companion.**

Example 2 (page 177)

For: Examples 1–3
Visit: PHSchool.com
Web Code: axe-0502

Find each difference using the LCD.

8. $\frac{2}{3} - \frac{2}{9}$ $\frac{4}{9}$

$\frac{2}{3} - \frac{2}{9} = \frac{2 \cdot 3}{3 \cdot 3} - \frac{2}{9}$

Guided Practice This exercise has been started for you!

9. $\frac{3}{7} - \frac{11}{21}$ $-\frac{2}{21}$
10. $\frac{9}{10} - \frac{4}{5}$ $\frac{1}{10}$
11. $\frac{3}{10} - \frac{11}{15}$ $-\frac{13}{30}$
12. $\frac{5}{6} - \frac{4}{9}$ $\frac{7}{18}$
13. $\frac{3}{4} - \frac{1}{12}$ $\frac{2}{3}$
14. $\frac{5}{7} - \frac{3}{5}$ $\frac{4}{35}$
15. $\frac{5}{2} - \frac{7}{8}$ $1\frac{5}{8}$
16. $\frac{2}{3} - \frac{9}{12}$ $-\frac{1}{12}$
17. $\frac{10}{11} - \frac{4}{5}$ $\frac{6}{55}$

Example 3 (page 177)

Find each difference. Write your answer in simplest form.

18. $9\frac{4}{7} - 2.5$ $7\frac{1}{14}$

$9\frac{4}{7} - 2.5 = 9\frac{4}{7} - 2\frac{1}{2}$

Guided Practice This exercise has been started for you!

19. $\frac{3}{4} - 1.8$ $-1\frac{1}{20}$
20. $3.6 - 4\frac{2}{3}$ $-1\frac{1}{15}$
21. $0.75 - 12\frac{4}{9}$ $-11\frac{25}{36}$
22. $\frac{23}{4} - 3.5$ $2\frac{1}{4}$
23. $4\frac{1}{8} - 0.3$ $3\frac{33}{40}$
24. $11.7 - \frac{5}{4}$ $10\frac{9}{20}$
25. $25.37 - 4\frac{1}{4}$ $21\frac{3}{25}$
26. $0.99 - \frac{101}{100}$ $-\frac{1}{50}$
27. $\frac{15}{6} - 0.2$ $2\frac{3}{10}$
28. It snowed $6\frac{3}{5}$ in. during the first three months of the year. It did not snow again until December. The total snowfall for the year was 7.5 in. Find the December snowfall. $\frac{9}{10}$ in.

B Apply Your Skills

29. **Guided Problem Solving** You have a board that is 12 ft long. You cut two pieces from the board that are each $3\frac{7}{12}$ ft long. How much of the board is left? $4\frac{5}{6}$ ft
 - Draw a diagram to help you write an expression for the length left after you cut the two pieces.

12 ft		
$3\frac{7}{12}$ ft	$3\frac{7}{12}$ ft	x

 - Use estimation to check the reasonableness of your answer.

Evaluate each expression for $g = \frac{5}{8}$.

30. $g + \frac{9}{12} - \frac{1}{2}$ $\frac{7}{8}$
31. $12.35 - g + 3\frac{1}{4}$ $14\frac{39}{40}$
32. $2\frac{3}{4} + 8 - g$ $10\frac{1}{8}$
33. $g - 6\frac{1}{5} + 3.25 + 11\frac{3}{4}$ $9\frac{17}{40}$
34. $g + g + 6.5$ $7\frac{3}{4}$
35. $9.8 - g + \frac{1}{10}$ $9\frac{11}{40}$
36. A typical garden spider is $\frac{7}{8}$ in. long. A black widow spider is $\frac{3}{8}$ in. long. How much longer is the garden spider? $\frac{1}{2}$ in.

3. Practice

Assignment Guide

Check Your Understanding
See Math Companion.

Homework Exercises

A	Practice by Example	1–28
B	Apply Your Skills	29–42
C	Challenge	43
California Multiple-Choice Practice		44–46
Mixed Review		47–48

Homework Quick Check
To check students' understanding of key skills and concepts, go over Exercises 2, 10, 19, 30, 40, 42.

Universal Access Resources

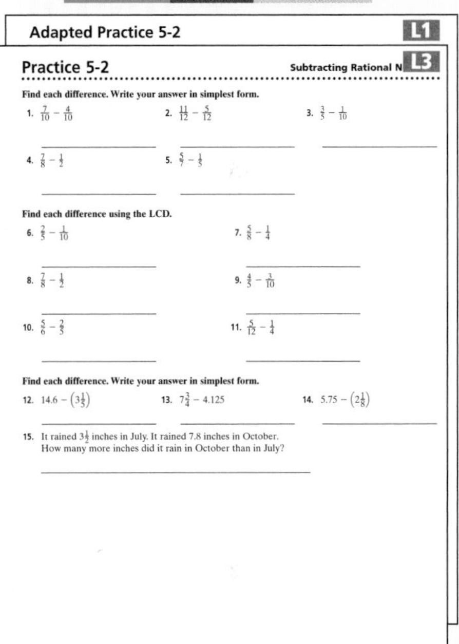
Adapted Practice 5-2 L1

Practice 5-2 Subtracting Rational N L3

Find each difference. Write your answer in simplest form.

1. $\frac{7}{10} - \frac{4}{10}$
2. $\frac{11}{12} - \frac{5}{12}$
3. $\frac{3}{5} - \frac{1}{10}$
4. $\frac{7}{8} - \frac{1}{2}$
5. $\frac{5}{7} - \frac{1}{5}$

Find each difference using the LCD.

6. $\frac{2}{5} - \frac{1}{10}$
7. $\frac{5}{8} - \frac{1}{4}$
8. $\frac{7}{8} - \frac{1}{2}$
9. $\frac{4}{5} - \frac{3}{10}$
10. $\frac{5}{6} - \frac{2}{5}$
11. $\frac{5}{12} - \frac{1}{4}$

Find each difference. Write your answer in simplest form.

12. $14.6 - \left(3\frac{1}{5}\right)$
13. $7\frac{3}{4} - 4.125$
14. $5.75 - \left(2\frac{1}{8}\right)$
15. It rained $3\frac{1}{2}$ inches in July. It rained 7.8 inches in October. How many more inches did it rain in October than in July?

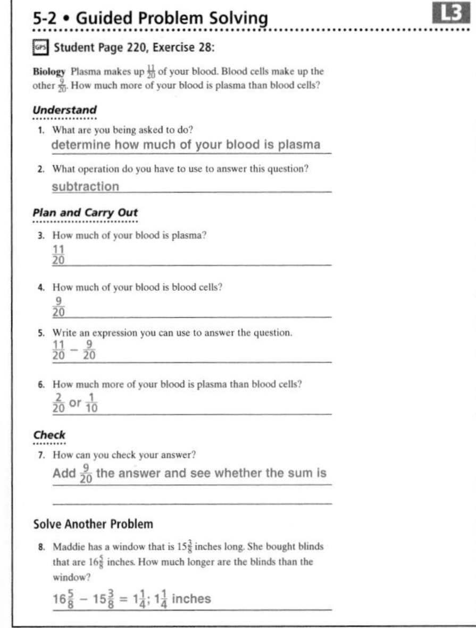
5-2 • Guided Problem Solving L3

Student Page 220, Exercise 28:

Biology Plasma makes up $\frac{11}{20}$ of your blood. Blood cells make up the other $\frac{9}{20}$. How much more of your blood is plasma than blood cells?

Understand

1. What are you being asked to do?
determine how much of your blood is plasma
2. What operation do you have to use to answer this question?
subtraction

Plan and Carry Out

3. How much of your blood is plasma?
$\frac{11}{20}$
4. How much of your blood is blood cells?
$\frac{9}{20}$
5. Write an expression you can use to answer the question.
$\frac{11}{20} - \frac{9}{20}$
6. How much more of your blood is plasma than blood cells?
$\frac{2}{20}$ or $\frac{1}{10}$

Check

7. How can you check your answer?
Add $\frac{9}{20}$ the answer and see whether the sum is

Solve Another Problem

8. Maddie has a window that is $15\frac{3}{8}$ inches long. She bought blinds that are $16\frac{5}{8}$ inches. How much longer are the blinds than the window?
$16\frac{5}{8} - 15\frac{3}{8} = 1\frac{1}{4}$; $1\frac{1}{4}$ inches

4. Assess & Reteach

PRESENTATION CD-ROM
CD, Online, or Transparencies

Lesson Quiz

Find each difference.

1. $\frac{8}{9} - \frac{5}{9}$ $\frac{1}{3}$
2. $\frac{1}{2} - \frac{7}{8}$ $-\frac{3}{8}$
3. $4\frac{5}{6} - 1.25$ $3\frac{7}{12}$
4. A black bear is about $5\frac{1}{4}$ ft tall. An Alaskan brown bear is about 7.5 ft tall. How much taller is an Alaskan brown bear than a black bear? $2\frac{1}{4}$ ft

Reteaching 5-2 — Fractions With Like Deno[minators] **L2**

Add: $\frac{1}{6} + \frac{3}{6}$

① Combine numerators over the denominator. $\frac{1}{6} + \frac{3}{6} = \frac{1+3}{6}$

② Add numerators. $= \frac{4}{6}$

③ Simplify, if possible. $= \frac{2}{3}$

$\frac{1}{6} + \frac{3}{6} = \frac{2}{3}$

Subtract: $\frac{7}{10} - \frac{2}{10}$

① Combine numerators over the denominator. $\frac{7}{10} - \frac{2}{10} = \frac{7-2}{10}$

② Subtract numerators. $= \frac{5}{10}$

③ Simplify, if possible. $= \frac{1}{2}$

$\frac{7}{10} - \frac{2}{10} = \frac{1}{2}$

Find each sum.

1. $\frac{1}{5} + \frac{3}{5}$ $\frac{4}{5}$
2. $\frac{4}{6} + \frac{1}{6}$ $\frac{5}{6}$
3. $\frac{3}{12} + \frac{3}{12}$ $\frac{1}{2}$
4. $\frac{6}{10} + \frac{5}{10}$ $1\frac{1}{10}$
5. $\frac{3}{10} + \frac{2}{10}$ $\frac{1}{2}$
6. $\frac{6}{12} + \frac{3}{12}$ $\frac{3}{4}$
7. $\frac{5}{8} + \frac{1}{8}$ $\frac{3}{4}$
8. $\frac{3}{8} + \frac{9}{8}$ $1\frac{1}{2}$
9. $\frac{3}{8} + \frac{6}{8}$ $1\frac{1}{8}$

Find each difference.

10. $\frac{6}{8} - \frac{3}{8}$ $\frac{3}{8}$
11. $\frac{9}{10} - \frac{3}{10}$ $\frac{3}{5}$
12. $\frac{3}{4} - \frac{1}{4}$ $\frac{1}{2}$
13. $\frac{7}{12} - \frac{1}{12}$ $\frac{1}{2}$
14. $\frac{8}{10} - \frac{6}{10}$ $\frac{1}{5}$
15. $\frac{4}{6} - \frac{2}{6}$ $\frac{1}{3}$
16. $\frac{5}{10} - \frac{1}{10}$ $\frac{2}{5}$
17. $\frac{7}{12} - \frac{6}{12}$ $\frac{1}{12}$
18. $\frac{9}{10} - \frac{4}{10}$ $\frac{1}{2}$

Find each sum or difference.

19. $\frac{2}{7} + \frac{2}{7} - \frac{1}{7}$ $\frac{3}{7}$
20. $\frac{10}{100} + \frac{20}{100} + \frac{90}{100}$ $1\frac{1}{5}$
21. $\frac{2}{5} - \frac{2}{5} + \frac{5}{5}$ 1
22. $\frac{10}{11} - \left(\frac{2}{11} + \frac{4}{11}\right)$ $\frac{4}{11}$
23. $\frac{8}{10} - \frac{2}{10} - \frac{1}{10}$ $\frac{1}{2}$
24. $\frac{62}{80} - \frac{10}{80} - \frac{5}{80}$ $\frac{47}{80}$
25. For school photos, $\frac{1}{5}$ of the students choose to have a blue background, $\frac{2}{5}$ of the students choose to have a purple background, and $\frac{1}{5}$ of the students choose to have a gray background. What portion of the students choose to have another background color? $\frac{1}{5}$

Enrichment 5-2 — Subtracting Rational N[umbers] **L4**

Critical Thinking

You can use multiplication to find sums and differences of fractions. Each of the examples below shows the same way to find $\frac{3}{4} - \frac{1}{2}$.

Find the cross products. Then write the sum (if adding) or difference (if subtracting) over the product of the denominators.

$\frac{3}{4} \times \frac{1}{2} = \frac{(3 \cdot 2) - (4 \cdot 1)}{4 \cdot 2} = \frac{6-4}{8} = \frac{2}{8} = \frac{1}{4}$

This can be written algebraically as

$\frac{a}{b} - \frac{c}{d} = \frac{(a \cdot d) - (b \cdot c)}{b \cdot d}$

and $\frac{a}{b} + \frac{c}{d} = \frac{(a \cdot d) + (b \cdot c)}{b \cdot d}$.

Write the fractions in the boxes. Multiply the denominator of each fraction by the numerator of the other fraction.

6 − 4; 3 × 2; 4 × 1

6	4	
3	1	2
4	2	8

Subtract: 6 − 4
Multiply: 4 × 2

So, $\frac{3}{4} - \frac{1}{2} = \frac{2}{8} = \frac{1}{4}$.

Subtract (or add) the products to find the numerator of the difference (or sum).

Multiply the two denominators to find the denominator of the difference (or sum).

Use cross products or boxes to find each sum or difference. Simplify if necessary.

1. $\frac{2}{8} + \frac{2}{3}$ ______
2. $\frac{5}{6} - \frac{3}{4}$ ______
3. $\frac{1}{4} + \frac{16}{25}$ ______
4. $\frac{13}{15} - \frac{3}{4}$ ______

Complete the boxes and write the answer in the blank. Simplify if necessary.

5. $\frac{2}{3} + \frac{1}{5} =$ ______
6. $\frac{9}{10} - \frac{5}{8} =$ ______
7. $\frac{5}{9} + \frac{3}{7} =$ ______

8. How are these methods alike? Which do you prefer? Why?

9. Try adding $1\frac{1}{2} + 2\frac{3}{4}$ using the cross products method. Does this method work with mixed numbers? Explain.

SCAFFOLDED **Problem Solving**

37. 24 ft $3\frac{1}{2}$ in.
38. 23 ft $8\frac{1}{4}$ in.
39. 11.57 in.

Women's Olympic Long Jump Winners

Year	Winner, Country	Distance
1988	Jackie Joyner-Kersee, United States	24 ft $3\frac{1}{2}$ in.
1992	Heike Drechsler, Germany	23 ft $5\frac{1}{4}$ in.
1996	Chioma Ajunwa, Nigeria	23 ft $4\frac{1}{2}$ in.
2000	Heike Drechsler, Germany	22 ft $11\frac{1}{4}$ in.
2004	Tatyana Lebedeva, Russia	23 ft $2\frac{1}{2}$ in.

SOURCE: *ESPN Sports Almanac*

37. How far did Jackie Joyner-Kersee jump to win in 1988?

38. Heike Drechsler came in second place in 1988. Her jump was 7.25 in. shorter than the winning jump. How far was Drechsler's jump?

39. Drechsler jumped 4.32 in. more than the third place athlete in 1988. How much farther did Jackie Joyner-Kersee jump than the third place finisher in 1988?

GPS **40.** Plasma makes up $\frac{11}{20}$ of your blood. Blood cells make up the other $\frac{9}{20}$. How much more of your blood is plasma than blood cells? $\frac{1}{10}$

41. The diameter of a golf ball is $1\frac{2}{3}$ in. The diameter of a hole is $4\frac{1}{4}$ in. Find the difference between the two diameters. $2\frac{7}{12}$ in.

42. Answers may vary. Sample: The denominators of the two forms are the same.

42. **Writing in Math** Explain why you do *not* have to change mixed numbers to improper fractions before you find the LCD. See left.

C Challenge

43. Solve the equation $x + 1\frac{2}{3} = 3\frac{1}{2}$. $1\frac{5}{6}$

Multiple Choice Practice and Mixed Review

For California Standards Tutorials, visit PHSchool.com. Web Code: axq-9045

NS 1.2

44. Larry spent $1\frac{3}{4}$ h doing math homework and $2\frac{1}{4}$ h reading. How many more hours did Larry spend reading? A

Ⓐ $\frac{1}{2}$ h Ⓑ $\frac{3}{4}$ h Ⓒ $1\frac{1}{2}$ h Ⓓ $1\frac{3}{4}$ h

AF 1.1

45. Anna spends $\frac{1}{2}$ of her savings on a new bike and $\frac{1}{3}$ of her savings on gifts for her family. Which expression gives the fraction of Anna's savings that is left? C

Ⓐ $\frac{1}{2} + \frac{1}{3}$

Ⓑ $\frac{1}{2} - \frac{1}{3}$

Ⓒ $1 - \left(\frac{1}{2} + \frac{1}{3}\right)$

Ⓓ $1 - \left(\frac{1}{2} - \frac{1}{3}\right)$

MG 3.3

46. A right triangle has side lengths of 6, 12, and x. Which of the following could be the length of the third side? C

Ⓐ 6 Ⓑ $\sqrt{72}$ Ⓒ $\sqrt{108}$ Ⓓ 12

Lesson 4-5

Order each set of numbers from least to greatest.

47. $0.8, \frac{1}{125}, 0.808, \frac{22}{25}$ $\frac{1}{125}, 0.8, 0.808, \frac{22}{25}$

48. $-2\frac{33}{50}, -2\frac{3}{50}, -2.006, -2.6$ $-2\frac{33}{50}, -2.6, -2\frac{3}{50}, -2.006$

Visit: PHSchool.com **Web Code:** axa-0502

California Resources

Standards Mastery
- Standards Review Transparencies
- Standards Review and Practice Workbook
- Math Companion

Math Intervention
- Skills Review and Practice Workbook
- Math XL

Alternative Assessment

Each student in a pair writes a mixed number and a decimal. Then partners use the numbers to write and solve four subtraction problems, each involving one mixed number and one decimal.

Checkpoint Quiz 1

Lessons 5-1 through 5-2

Find each sum or difference.

1. $\frac{3}{10} + \frac{5}{16}$ $\frac{49}{80}$
2. $-\frac{5}{6} - \frac{1}{3}$ $-1\frac{1}{6}$
3. $\frac{12}{13} - \frac{1}{9}$ $\frac{95}{117}$
4. $\frac{7}{12} + \left(-\frac{2}{3}\right)$ $-\frac{1}{12}$
5. $\frac{9}{10} - \frac{1}{3}$ $\frac{17}{30}$
6. $\frac{1}{7} + \frac{5}{14}$ $\frac{1}{2}$
7. $-\frac{17}{20} - \frac{3}{20}$ -1
8. $\frac{11}{12} + \left(-\frac{5}{6}\right)$ $\frac{1}{12}$
9. $\frac{5}{3} + \frac{1}{2}$ $2\frac{1}{6}$
10. In a class, $\frac{1}{6}$ of the students have blue eyes, and $\frac{7}{9}$ of the students have brown eyes. How much more of the class has brown eyes than blue eyes? $\frac{11}{18}$
11. You have two rolls of wrapping paper. One roll has 3.5 ft of paper. The other roll has $2\frac{3}{5}$ ft of paper. How much wrapping paper do you have? $6\frac{1}{10}$ ft

5-3a Activity Lab

Modeling Fraction Multiplication

Foundational Standard Explain the meaning of multiplication of positive fractions.

You can use grids to model fraction multiplication.

Use a model to find $\frac{3}{4} \cdot \frac{9}{10}$.

1. Draw a square that is 1 in. on each side. 1–2. Check students' work.
2. Divide the square into 4 rows of equal height. Then divide the square into 10 columns of equal width. See the model at the right.

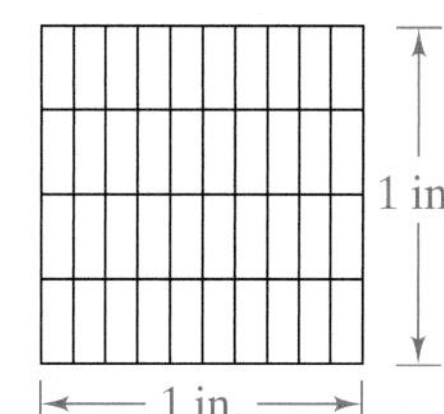

3. What fraction represents the height of each row? What fraction represents the width of each column? $\frac{1}{4}$; $\frac{1}{10}$
4. Explain why you can use the expression $\frac{1}{4} \cdot \frac{1}{10}$ to represent the area of each small rectangle in your model. 4. The length of each small rectangle is $\frac{1}{4}$ and the width is $\frac{1}{10}$.
5. Shade 3 out of 4 rows to model $\frac{3}{4}$. Shade 9 out of 10 columns to model $\frac{9}{10}$. Check students' work.
6. Explain why you can use the expression $\frac{3}{4} \cdot \frac{9}{10}$ to represent the area of the rectangles that are common to the two shaded regions. 6. The length of the shaded area is $\frac{3}{4}$ and the width is $\frac{9}{10}$.
7. To find the product $\frac{3}{4} \cdot \frac{9}{10}$, write a fraction comparing the number of shaded rectangles to the total number of rectangles. $\frac{27}{40}$

Checkpoint Quiz

Use this Checkpoint Quiz to check students' understanding of the skills and concepts of Lessons 5-1 through 5-2.

All in One Resources

- Checkpoint Quiz 1

Activity Lab

Modeling Fraction Multiplication

Students use rectangles drawn on grid paper to model fraction multiplication.

Guided Instruction

Example

Model the Example by sketching the 4-unit × 10-unit grid on the chalkboard. Use crosshatching in one direction to "shade" $\frac{3}{4}$ and crosshatching in another direction for $\frac{9}{10}$. The product is shown by the part of the rectangle that has crosshatching in both directions.

Universal Access

Visual Learners

Ask: *How does this model show that the product of two fractions less than 1 will always be less than 1?* Sample: When you shade both factors, the overlapping area will always be smaller than the whole rectangle, so it is less than 1.

5-3

1. Plan

California Content Standards

Solve problems involving multiplication of fractions. ***Foundational***

NS 1.2 Multiply rational numbers and take positive rational numbers to whole-number powers. ***Develop, Master***

AF 2.1 Interpret positive whole-number powers as repeated multiplication. ***Develop***

California Math Background

The familiar rule for multiplying two fractions as $\frac{a}{b} \cdot \frac{c}{d} = \frac{ac}{bd}$, provided that neither b nor d is zero. You can multiply any rational numbers in this form if you rewrite mixed numbers and decimals as improper fractions before multiplying. The rules for multiplying integers also apply to rational numbers. Raise a fraction to a power by raising the numerator and denominator to the power: $\left(\frac{a}{b}\right)^n = \frac{a^n}{b^n}$.

More Math Background: p. 168C

Lesson Planning and Resources

See p. 168E for a list of the resources that support this lesson.

PRESENTATION CD-ROM
CD, Online, or Transparencies

Bell Ringer Practice

Check Skills You'll Need
Use student page, transparency, or PowerPoint.
See Math Companion.

California Standards Review
Use transparency or PowerPoint.

5-3 Multiplying Rational Numbers

Check Skills You'll Need
Do this in your **Math Companion.**

Vocabulary
Review:
- exponent
- power

Use your **Math Companion** *to build your vocabulary.*

California Content Standards

Foundational Standard Solve problems involving multiplication of fractions.
NS 1.2 Multiply rational numbers and take positive rational numbers to whole-number powers. ***Develop, Master***
AF 2.1 Interpret positive whole-number powers as repeated multiplication. ***Develop***

What You'll Learn . . . and Why

You will learn to multiply rational numbers and raise fractions to positive whole-number powers. You can multiply rational numbers to find the length of materials used for building a model.

The model below shows $\frac{1}{2} \cdot \frac{5}{6}$.

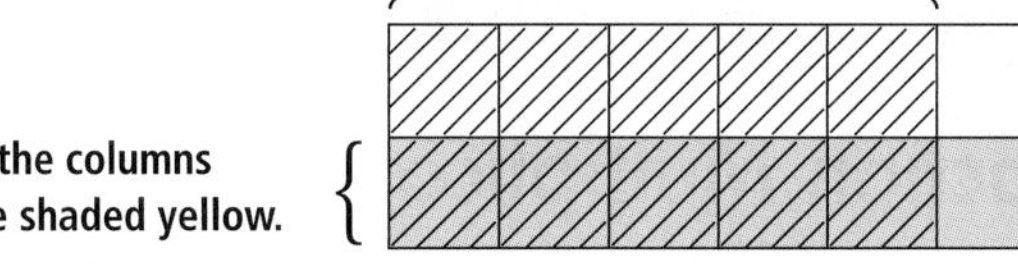

$\frac{5}{6}$ of the columns are shaded with diagonal lines.
$\frac{1}{2}$ the columns are shaded yellow.
5 out of 12 of the squares include both types of shading.

So $\frac{1}{2} \cdot \frac{5}{6} = \frac{5}{12}$. To find the product of rational numbers that are fractions, multiply the numerators and multiply the denominators. When the numerators and the denominators have a common factor, you can simplify before multiplying.

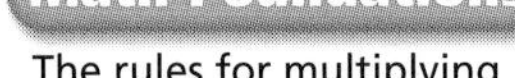

Math Foundations
The rules for multiplying integers also apply to multiplying fractions.

EXAMPLE Multiplying Fractions

1 Find $-\frac{3}{8} \cdot \frac{2}{5}$.

$-\frac{3}{8} \cdot \frac{2}{5} = \frac{-3 \cdot \overset{1}{\cancel{2}}}{\underset{4}{\cancel{8}} \cdot 5}$ ← Divide 8 and 2 by their GCD, 2.

$= \frac{-3 \cdot 1}{4 \cdot 5}$ ← Multiply the numerators. ← Multiply the denominators.

$= -\frac{3}{20}$ ← Simplify.

CA Standards Check 1 *Go to your* **Math Companion** *for help.*

1. Find each product. Write your answer in simplest form.

a. $-\frac{4}{5} \cdot \left(-\frac{3}{8}\right)$ $\frac{3}{10}$

b. $\frac{2}{9} \cdot \frac{5}{7}$ $\frac{10}{63}$

Universal Access Solutions for All Learners

Special Needs L1
Have students state the rules for multiplying integers and work in pairs to write them out. Each pair can then practice writing and solving multiplication problems involving integers, fractions, mixed numbers, and decimals.

Below Level L2
Give students several blank forms like the one below to use for organizing their work.

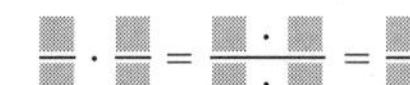

EXAMPLE Multiplying Rational Numbers

2 **Guided Problem Solving** You are building a model house. You have a piece of wood that is 2.5 in. long. You need another piece of wood that is $\frac{1}{3}$ as long. How long should you make the second piece of wood?

$$\frac{1}{3} \cdot 2.5 = \frac{1}{3} \cdot \frac{5}{2} \quad \leftarrow \text{Write 2.5 as an improper fraction.}$$

$$= \frac{5}{6} \quad \begin{array}{l} \leftarrow \text{Multiply the numerators.} \\ \leftarrow \text{Multiply the denominators.} \end{array}$$

The second piece of wood should be $\frac{5}{6}$ in. long.

CA Standards Check 2 *Go to your* **Math Companion** *for help.*

2. A baby alligator is $\frac{5}{6}$ ft long. An adult alligator is 12.5 times as long as the baby alligator. How long is the adult alligator? $10\frac{5}{12}$ ft

You can use fraction multiplication to raise a fraction to a power.

EXAMPLE Raising a Fraction to a Power

Relate MATH YOU KNOW...

Simplify 4^3.

$$4^3 = 4 \cdot 4 \cdot 4 \quad \leftarrow \text{The base is 4.}$$

$$= 64 \quad \leftarrow \text{Multiply.}$$

...to NEW IDEAS

3 Simplify $\left(\frac{4}{7}\right)^3$.

$$\left(\frac{4}{7}\right)^3 = \frac{4}{7} \cdot \frac{4}{7} \cdot \frac{4}{7} \quad \leftarrow \text{The base is } \tfrac{4}{7}.$$

$$= \frac{64}{343} \quad \begin{array}{l} \leftarrow \text{Multiply the numerators.} \\ \leftarrow \text{Multiply the denominators.} \end{array}$$

CA Standards Check 3 *Go to your* **Math Companion** *for help.*

3. Simplify each expression.

a. $\left(\frac{7}{10}\right)^2$ $\frac{49}{100}$ **b.** $\left(\frac{1}{3}\right)^4$ $\frac{1}{81}$

Example 3 suggests the following rule.

Take Note Raising Fractions to a Power

To raise a fraction to a power, raise the numerator and the denominator to the power.

Arithmetic $\left(\frac{3}{4}\right)^2 = \frac{9}{16}$ **Algebra** $\left(\frac{a}{b}\right)^n = \frac{a^n}{b^n}$

Check Your Understanding *Homework prep is in your* **Math Companion.**

2. Teach

Guided Instruction

Example 1
Review using the GCD to simplify or "cancel" fractions when multiplying.

Example 2
Remind students that rational factors must be in the same form before they can be multiplied and that mixed numbers must be rewritten as improper fractions.

Example 3
Review exponential notation: a positive whole-number exponent tells how many times the base is used as a factor.

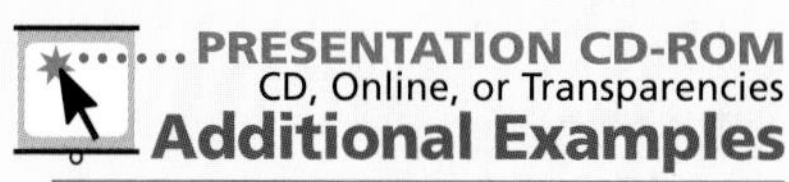

PRESENTATION CD-ROM
CD, Online, or Transparencies

Additional Examples

1 Find $\frac{5}{12} \cdot \left(-\frac{4}{7}\right)$. $-\frac{5}{21}$

2 A gear on a machine makes $\frac{2}{3}$ of a turn in one minute. How many turns does this gear make in 4.8 minutes? $3\frac{1}{5}$ turns

3 Simplify $\left(\frac{5}{6}\right)^3$. $\frac{125}{216}$

Closure

- *How do you multiply fractions?* Multiply the numerators, multiply the denominators, and simplify.
- *How do you raise a fraction to a power?* Raise both the numerator and denominator to the power.

Advanced Learners L4	**English Learners** EL
Find the product. Simplify before you multiply. $\frac{2}{3} \cdot \left(-\frac{9}{10}\right) \cdot \left(-\frac{5}{14}\right) \cdot \frac{7}{15}$ $\frac{1}{10}$	Have students use words, pictures, and symbols to explain why the product is less than the factors when multiplying two positive fractions less than 1. Have them explain why a power of a positive fraction less than 1 is less than the original fraction.

3. Practice

Assignment Guide

Check Your Understanding

See Math Companion.

Homework Exercises

A Practice by Example	1–33
B Apply Your Skills	34–46
C Challenge	47
California Multiple-Choice Practice	48–49
Mixed Review	50–53

Homework Quick Check

To check students' understanding of key skills and concepts, go over Exercises 3, 14, 22, 35, 41, 44.

Universal Access Resources

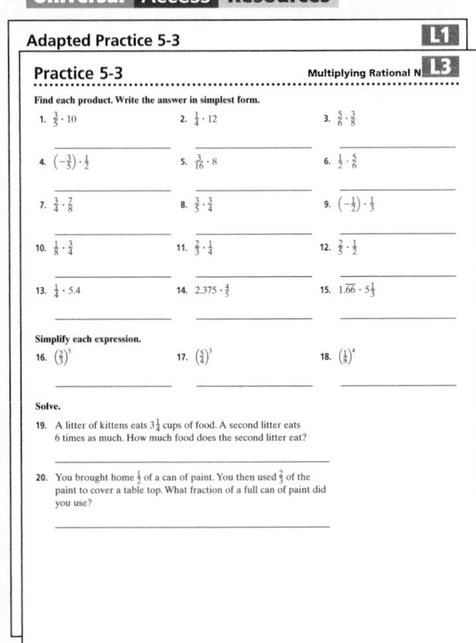

Adapted Practice 5-3 L1

Practice 5-3 — Multiplying Rational N L3

Find each product. Write the answer in simplest form.

1. $\frac{3}{5} \cdot 10$
2. $\frac{1}{4} \cdot 12$
3. $\frac{5}{6} \cdot \frac{3}{8}$
4. $\left(-\frac{3}{5}\right) \cdot \frac{1}{2}$
5. $\frac{3}{16} \cdot 8$
6. $\frac{1}{2} \cdot \frac{5}{6}$
7. $\frac{3}{4} \cdot \frac{7}{8}$
8. $\frac{3}{5} \cdot \frac{3}{4}$
9. $\left(-\frac{1}{2}\right) \cdot \frac{1}{3}$
10. $\frac{1}{8} \cdot \frac{3}{4}$
11. $\frac{2}{3} \cdot \frac{1}{4}$
12. $\frac{2}{5} \cdot \frac{1}{2}$
13. $\frac{1}{4} \cdot 5.4$
14. $2.375 \cdot \frac{4}{5}$
15. $1.\overline{66} \cdot 5\frac{1}{3}$

Simplify each expression.

16. $\left(\frac{2}{3}\right)^5$
17. $\left(\frac{5}{4}\right)^3$
18. $\left(\frac{1}{8}\right)^4$

Solve.

19. A litter of kittens eats $3\frac{1}{4}$ cups of food. A second litter eats 6 times as much. How much food does the second litter eat?
20. You brought home $\frac{1}{2}$ of a can of paint. You then used $\frac{2}{3}$ of the paint to cover a table top. What fraction of a full can of paint did you use?

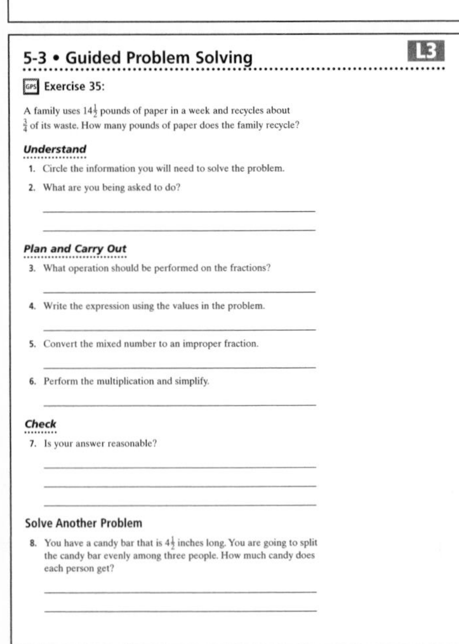

5-3 • Guided Problem Solving L3

GPS Exercise 35:

A family uses $14\frac{1}{2}$ pounds of paper in a week and recycles about $\frac{3}{4}$ of its waste. How many pounds of paper does the family recycle?

Understand

1. Circle the information you will need to solve the problem.
2. What are you being asked to do?

Plan and Carry Out

3. What operation should be performed on the fractions?
4. Write the expression using the values in the problem.
5. Convert the mixed number to an improper fraction.
6. Perform the multiplication and simplify.

Check

7. Is your answer reasonable?

Solve Another Problem

8. You have a candy bar that is $4\frac{1}{2}$ inches long. You are going to split the candy bar evenly among three people. How much candy does each person get?

Standards Practice

GO for Help: MathXL — NS 1.2, AF 2.1

A Practice by Example

Example 1 (page 182)

Find each product. Write your answer in simplest form.

1. $-\frac{4}{5} \cdot \left(-\frac{1}{2}\right)$ $\frac{2}{5}$

   $-\frac{4}{5} \cdot \left(-\frac{1}{2}\right) = \frac{-4 \cdot (-1)}{5 \cdot 2}$

   Guided Practice This exercise has been started for you!

GO for Help

2. $\frac{9}{10} \cdot \left(-\frac{2}{3}\right)$ $-\frac{3}{5}$
3. $-\frac{34}{35} \cdot \left(-\frac{7}{2}\right)$ $3\frac{2}{5}$
4. $\frac{3}{4} \cdot 20$ 15
5. $\frac{5}{6} \cdot \frac{1}{4}$ $\frac{5}{24}$
6. $\frac{8}{9} \cdot 6$ $5\frac{1}{3}$
7. $-\frac{1}{2} \cdot \frac{2}{3}$ $-\frac{1}{3}$
8. $-\frac{15}{4} \cdot \frac{6}{12}$ $-1\frac{7}{8}$
9. $\frac{17}{8} \cdot \frac{19}{34}$ 1
10. $-\frac{1}{30} \cdot \frac{33}{8}$ $-\frac{11}{80}$

Example 2 (page 183)

Find each product.

11. $-1.2 \cdot \frac{2}{3}$ $-\frac{4}{5}$

    $-1.2 \cdot \frac{2}{3} = -1\frac{1}{5} \cdot \frac{2}{3}$

    Guided Practice This exercise has been started for you!

12. $\frac{1}{4} \cdot 0.45$ $\frac{9}{80}$
13. $3.\overline{66} \cdot \frac{2}{9}$ $\frac{22}{27}$
14. $1.02 \cdot 3\frac{1}{6}$ $3\frac{23}{100}$
15. $0.11 \cdot \frac{1}{8}$ $\frac{11}{800}$
16. $27 \cdot \frac{4}{9}$ 12
17. $\frac{19}{4} \cdot 2.5$ $11\frac{7}{8}$
18. $\frac{3}{5} \cdot 21.7$ 13.02
19. $\frac{56}{22} \cdot 11$ 28
20. $1.89 \cdot \frac{2}{25}$ $\frac{189}{1,250}$

Homework Video Tutor

For: Examples 1–3
Visit: PHSchool.com
Web Code: axe-0503

21. A quilt pattern has squares with 7.5-in. sides. You want to make squares with side lengths that are $\frac{2}{3}$ of the pattern's sides. Find the new dimensions of a square in your quilt. 5 in. by 5 in.

Example 3 (page 183)

Simplify each expression.

22. $\left(\frac{2}{3}\right)^6$ $\frac{64}{729}$
23. $\left(\frac{1}{9}\right)^3$ $\frac{1}{729}$
24. $\left(\frac{5}{7}\right)^2$ $\frac{25}{49}$
25. $\left(\frac{3}{8}\right)^4$ $\frac{81}{4,096}$
26. $\left(\frac{4}{10}\right)^5$ $\frac{1,024}{100,000}$
27. $\left(\frac{1}{2}\right)^3$ $\frac{1}{8}$
28. $\left(\frac{5}{9}\right)^3$ $\frac{125}{729}$
29. $\left(\frac{4}{12}\right)^2$ $\frac{1}{9}$
30. $\left(\frac{11}{9}\right)^2$ $\frac{121}{81}$
31. $\left(\frac{5}{2}\right)^3$ $\frac{125}{8}$
32. $\left(\frac{1}{9}\right)^4$ $\frac{1}{6,561}$
33. $\left(\frac{22}{5}\right)^2$ $\frac{484}{25}$

B Apply Your Skills

34. **Guided Problem Solving** A carpenter has two 10-ft boards. The carpenter needs six pieces of wood $3\frac{1}{2}$ ft long. Does the carpenter have enough wood? Explain. See left.
    - What is the total length of wood needed?
    - What is the total length of wood the carpenter has?

34. No; he can get two $3\frac{1}{2}$-ft pieces from each 10-ft board. The remaining length of 3 ft is not enough for another piece. So, he has only enough wood for four pieces of wood $3\frac{1}{2}$ ft long.

GPS 35. A family uses $14\frac{1}{2}$ pounds of paper in a week and recycles about $\frac{3}{4}$ of its waste. How many pounds of paper does the family recycle? $10\frac{7}{8}$ lb

36. The school band uses 1.75 yd of blue fabric and $\frac{3}{8}$ yd of gold fabric to make one banner. How many yards of fabric does the band need to make five banners? $10\frac{5}{8}$ yd or 10.625 yd

SCAFFOLDED **Problem Solving**

The graph at the right describes Paulo's monthly spending.

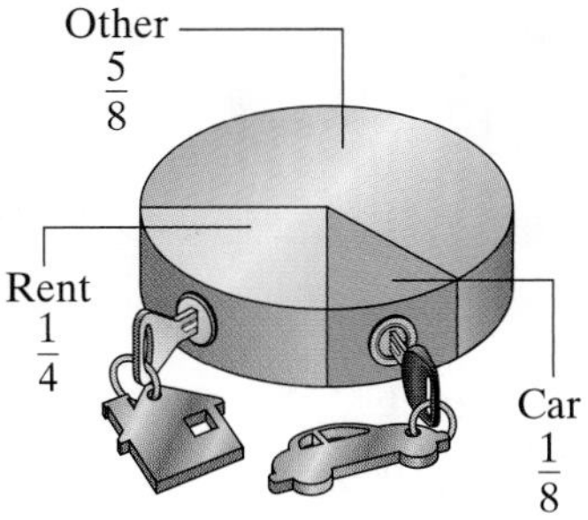

Other $\frac{5}{8}$

Rent $\frac{1}{4}$

Car $\frac{1}{8}$

37. What fraction of his income does Paulo spend on his car? $\frac{1}{8}$
38. Paulo makes $2,712.50 per month. How much does Paulo spend on his car? $339.06
39. How much does Paulo spend each month on his rent and car combined? $1,017.19
40. How much less does Paulo spend on his rent than he spends on his car and other things? $2,034.38

41. No; the denominator is the product of the two denominators.

41. **Writing in Math** Is it necessary to have a common denominator when you multiply two fractions? Explain. See left.
42. A flock of snow geese flies 83.3 km/h. The flock flies $4\frac{1}{2}$ h per day for 3 days each week. How far does the flock fly in two weeks? 2,249.1 km

Algebra **Evaluate each expression for $x = 1$, $y = 2$, and $z = 3$.**

43. $\left(x + \frac{x}{5}\right) \cdot \frac{1}{5}$ 0.24 or $\frac{6}{25}$
44. $\frac{x}{y}\left(\frac{y}{z} - x\right)^2$ $\frac{1}{18}$
45. $3\left(\frac{y}{z} - \frac{x}{yz}\right)$ 1.5 or $1\frac{1}{2}$
46. $\left(\frac{y}{z}\right)^3 + \left(\frac{x}{yz}\right)^2$ $\frac{35}{108}$

C Challenge

47. Your uncle has 36 coins in nickels and quarters. The value of his nickels is $\frac{1}{15}$ the value of his quarters. Find the number of nickels your uncle has. 9 nickels

Multiple Choice Practice and Mixed Review

For California Standards Tutorials, visit PHSchool.com. Web Code: axq-9045

NS 1.2

48. Simplify $3 \cdot \left(\frac{1}{2}\right)^3 + \frac{3}{4}$. C

Ⓐ $5\frac{1}{4}$ Ⓒ $1\frac{1}{8}$

Ⓑ $2\frac{1}{4}$ Ⓓ $\frac{1}{8}$

AF 1.1

49. Scott is twice as old as Ben. Donna is 6 years older than Ben. The sum of their ages is 34. Which expression can you use to represent the sum of their ages? D

Ⓐ $x + 2x - 6x$ Ⓒ $x + 2x + (x - 6)$

Ⓑ $x + 2x + 6x$ Ⓓ $x + 2x + (x + 6)$

Lesson 5-1 **Find each sum. Write your answer in simplest form.**

50. $\frac{5}{6} + \frac{1}{3}$ $1\frac{1}{6}$
51. $\frac{4}{5} + \frac{1}{2}$ $1\frac{3}{10}$
52. $\frac{7}{9} + \frac{3}{5}$ $1\frac{17}{45}$
53. $\frac{3}{10} + \frac{5}{8}$ $\frac{37}{40}$

 **Online Lesson Quiz** Visit: PHSchool.com Web Code: axa-0503

Alternative Assessment

Each student in a pair writes two rational numbers. Partners work together to multiply each possible pair of their numbers (6 possibilities). They then choose two fractions and raise each to the third power.

California Resources

Standards Mastery
- Standards Review Transparencies
- Standards Review and Practice Workbook
- Math Companion

Math Intervention
- Skills Review and Practice Workbook
- Math XL

4. Assess & Reteach

PRESENTATION CD-ROM CD, Online, or Transparencies

Lesson Quiz

Find each product. Simplify.

1. $-\frac{3}{5} \cdot \frac{5}{8}$ $-\frac{3}{8}$
2. $8.4 \cdot \frac{3}{4}$ 6.3
3. $\frac{5}{8} \cdot \left(-\frac{4}{5}\right)$ $-\frac{1}{2}$

Simplify each expression.

4. $\left(\frac{7}{9}\right)^2$ $\frac{49}{81}$
5. $\left(\frac{4}{5}\right)^4$ $\frac{256}{625}$

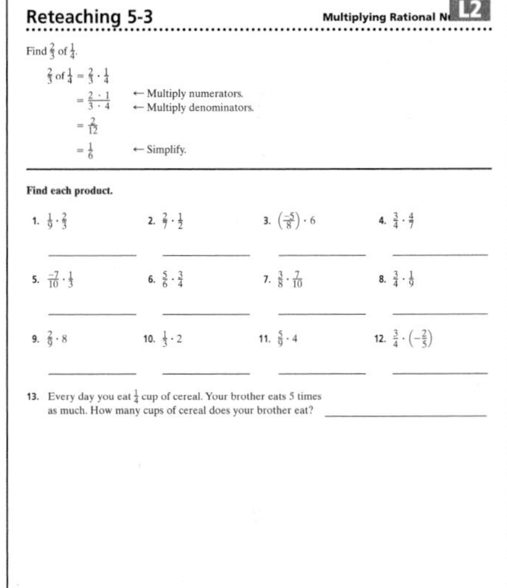

Reteaching 5-3 Multiplying Rational N... L2

Find $\frac{2}{3}$ of $\frac{1}{4}$.

$\frac{2}{3}$ of $\frac{1}{4} = \frac{2}{3} \cdot \frac{1}{4}$

$= \frac{2 \cdot 1}{3 \cdot 4}$ ← Multiply numerators. ← Multiply denominators.

$= \frac{2}{12}$

$= \frac{1}{6}$ ← Simplify.

Find each product.

1. $\frac{1}{9} \cdot \frac{2}{3}$
2. $\frac{2}{7} \cdot \frac{1}{2}$
3. $\left(\frac{-5}{8}\right) \cdot 6$
4. $\frac{3}{4} \cdot \frac{4}{7}$
5. $\frac{-7}{10} \cdot \frac{1}{3}$
6. $\frac{5}{6} \cdot \frac{3}{4}$
7. $\frac{3}{8} \cdot \frac{7}{10}$
8. $\frac{3}{4} \cdot \frac{1}{9}$
9. $\frac{2}{9} \cdot 8$
10. $\frac{1}{3} \cdot 2$
11. $\frac{5}{9} \cdot 4$
12. $\frac{3}{4} \cdot \left(-\frac{2}{5}\right)$
13. Every day you eat $\frac{1}{4}$ cup of cereal. Your brother eats 5 times as much. How many cups of cereal does your brother eat? ______

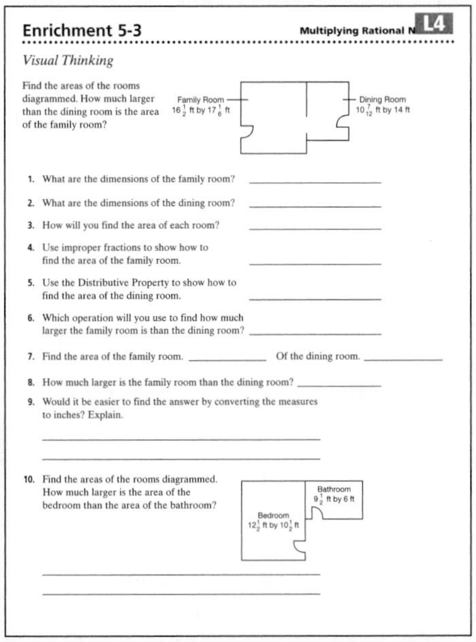

Enrichment 5-3 Multiplying Rational N... L4

Visual Thinking

Find the areas of the rooms diagrammed. How much larger than the dining room is the area of the family room?

Family Room $16\frac{1}{2}$ ft by $17\frac{1}{6}$ ft

Dining Room $10\frac{7}{12}$ ft by 14 ft

1. What are the dimensions of the family room? ______
2. What are the dimensions of the dining room? ______
3. How will you find the area of each room? ______
4. Use improper fractions to show how to find the area of the family room. ______
5. Use the Distributive Property to show how to find the area of the dining room. ______
6. Which operation will you use to find how much larger the family room is than the dining room? ______
7. Find the area of the family room. ______ Of the dining room. ______
8. How much larger is the family room than the dining room? ______
9. Would it be easier to find the answer by converting the measures to inches? Explain.
10. Find the areas of the rooms diagrammed. How much larger is the area of the bedroom than the area of the bathroom?

Bathroom $9\frac{1}{2}$ ft by 6 ft

Bedroom $12\frac{1}{2}$ ft by $10\frac{1}{2}$ ft

5-4

1. Plan

California Content Standards

Solve problems involving division of positive fractions. ***Foundational***

NS 1.2 Divide rational numbers. ***Develop, Master***

NS 1.5 Convert terminating decimals into fractions. ***Develop, Master***

Alg1 2.0 Understand and use such operations as finding the reciprocal. ***Introduce, Develop***

California Math Background

Algebraically, division is defined in terms of multiplication. The quotient $m \div n$ is defined as $m \times \frac{1}{n}$, where the divisor n is not zero. The number $\frac{1}{n}$ is the *reciprocal* of n. Dividing by a nonzero number is the same as multiplying by the reciprocal of that number. The reciprocal of a fraction $\frac{c}{d}$ is $\frac{d}{c}$. When division involves fractions, use the rule for dividing fractions: $\frac{a}{b} \div \frac{c}{d} = \frac{a}{b} \times \frac{d}{c}$, where b, c, and d are not zero. When dividing mixed numbers, first rewrite each number as an improper fraction.

More Math Background: p. 168C

Lesson Planning and Resources

See p. 168E for a list of the resources that support this lesson.

PRESENTATION CD-ROM
CD, Online, or Transparencies

Bell Ringer Practice

Check Skills You'll Need
Use student page, transparency, or PowerPoint.
See Math Companion.

California Standards Review
Use transparency or PowerPoint.

5-4 Dividing Rational Numbers

Check Skills You'll Need

Do this in your **Math Companion.**

Vocabulary

- reciprocal

Use your **Math Companion** *to build your vocabulary.*

California Content Standards

Foundational Standard Solve problems involving division of positive fractions.
NS 1.2 Divide rational numbers. ***Develop, Master***
NS 1.5 Convert terminating decimals into fractions. ***Develop, Master***
Alg1 2.0 Understand and use such operations as finding the reciprocal. ***Introduce, Develop***

What You'll Learn . . . and Why

You will learn to find reciprocals and divide rational numbers. You can divide $\frac{1}{2}$ by $\frac{1}{8}$ to find how many eighths you can cut from half of a pie.

You can use models to represent fraction division. The model below shows that there are four eighths in $\frac{1}{2}$. So $\frac{1}{2} \div \frac{1}{8} = 4$.

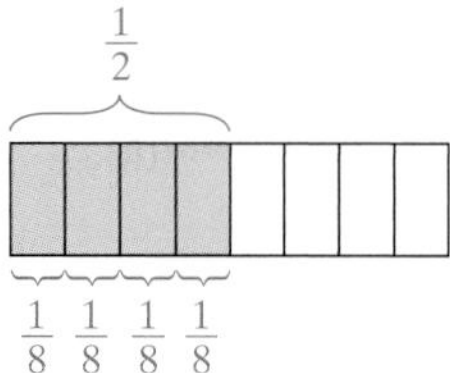

You can also use reciprocals to divide fractions. Two numbers with a product of 1 are called **reciprocals.** The reciprocal of $\frac{a}{b}$ is $\frac{b}{a}$, where $a \neq 0$ and $b \neq 0$. Notice that the numerators and denominators are switched in reciprocals such as $\frac{2}{3}$ and $\frac{3}{2}$.

EXAMPLE Finding a Reciprocal

1 Find the reciprocal of 9.

Since $9 \cdot \frac{1}{9} = 1$, the reciprocal of 9 is $\frac{1}{9}$.

CA Standards Check 1 *Go to your* **Math Companion** *for help.*

1. Find the reciprocal of each number.

a. $\frac{7}{8}$ $\frac{8}{7}$ **b.** $\frac{1}{7}$ 7

Universal Access Solutions for All Learners

Special Needs L1	**Below Level** L2
It is very easy to make errors when using the procedure for dividing fractions. When possible, allow students to draw a model or picture before they calculate so that they can make sense of their answers.	Give students several blank forms like the one below to use for organizing their work. $\frac{\square}{\square} \div \frac{\square}{\square} = \frac{\square}{\square} \cdot \frac{\square}{\square} = \frac{\square \cdot \square}{\square \cdot \square} = \frac{\square}{\square}$

You use reciprocals when dividing fractions.

Take Note **Dividing Fractions**

To divide by a fraction, multiply by the reciprocal of the fraction.

Arithmetic	Algebra
$\frac{3}{5} \div \frac{1}{3} = \frac{3}{5} \cdot \frac{3}{1}$	$\frac{a}{b} \div \frac{c}{d} = \frac{a}{b} \cdot \frac{d}{c}$, where b, c, and d are not 0.

Relate **MATH YOU KNOW...** **...to NEW IDEAS**

EXAMPLE Dividing Rational Numbers

Find $\frac{7}{1} \cdot \frac{3}{2}$.

$\frac{7}{1} \cdot \frac{3}{2} = \frac{21}{2}$ ← **Multiply the numerators.** ← **Multiply the denominators.**

$= 10\frac{1}{2}$ ← **Write $\frac{21}{2}$ as a mixed number.**

2 **Guided Problem Solving** A handbag designer has 15.5 yd of fabric. Each bag uses $\frac{7}{8}$ yd of fabric. How many bags can the designer make?

You need to find how many $\frac{7}{8}$-yd pieces there are in 15.5 yd. Divide 15.5 by $\frac{7}{8}$.

$15\frac{1}{2}$			
$\frac{7}{8}$	$\frac{7}{8}$	...	$\frac{7}{8}$

$15.5 \div \frac{7}{8} = \frac{31}{2} \div \frac{7}{8}$ ← **Write 15.5 as an improper fraction.**

$= \frac{31}{2} \cdot \frac{8}{7}$ ← **Multiply by $\frac{8}{7}$, the reciprocal of $\frac{7}{8}$.**

$= \frac{31}{\cancel{2}_1} \cdot \frac{\cancel{8}^4}{7}$ ← **Divide the numerator 8 and denominator 2 by their GCD, 2.**

$= \frac{124}{7}$ ← **Multiply.**

$= 17\frac{5}{7}$ ← **Write as a mixed number.**

Since you cannot make $\frac{5}{7}$ of a bag, the designer can make only 17 bags.

Check for Reasonableness Round 15.5 to 16 and $\frac{7}{8}$ to 1. Then $16 \div 1 = 16$, which is close to 17. The answer is reasonable.

Online active math

For: Dividing Mixed Numbers Activity
Use: Interactive Textbook, 5-4

CA Standards Check 2 *Go to your* **Math Companion** *for help.*

2. You have 7.5 c of birdseed. You use $\frac{2}{3}$ c of seed each day. How long will your birdseed last? $11\frac{1}{4}$ days or 11.25 days

Check Your Understanding *Homework prep is in your* **Math Companion.**

2. Teach

Guided Instruction

Example 1

Ask:

- *What is the product if you multiply a number and its reciprocal?* one

Error Prevention!

In the process of dividing rational numbers, students can use a checklist to remember the steps.

1. Rewrite mixed numbers as improper fractions.
2. Change the division to multiplication.
3. Write the reciprocal of the divisor.
4. Multiply the fractions.
5. Simplify the product.

Watch for students who multiply by the reciprocal of the dividend instead of the divisor.

PRESENTATION CD-ROM CD, Online, or Transparencies

Additional Examples

1 Write the reciprocal of each number.

a. $\frac{4}{9}$ $\frac{9}{4}$ b. 5 $\frac{1}{5}$

2 One bow takes $\frac{3}{4}$ yards of ribbon. How many bows could you make from a roll of ribbon that is $12\frac{1}{2}$ yards long? 16 bows

Closure

- *Explain how to rewrite division by a rational number using multiplication.* Sample: Dividing by a rational number is the same as multiplying by the reciprocal of that number, so rewrite the division as multiplication by the reciprocal.

Advanced Learners L4

Find the missing divisor.

$\frac{3}{8} \div \blacksquare = \frac{15}{16}$ $\frac{2}{5}$

$\frac{2}{8} \div \blacksquare = \frac{1}{16}$ 4

English Learners EL

Be aware that the word *reciprocal* is particularly difficult to pronounce. As students attempt to say the word, ensure that no one embarrasses them. While they master their pronunciation, allow students to use an abbreviation, like *recip.*

3. Practice

Assignment Guide

Check Your Understanding
See Math Companion.

Homework Exercises

A Practice by Example	1–24
B Apply Your Skills	25–38
C Challenge	39
California Multiple-Choice Practice	40–41
Mixed Review	42–44

Homework Quick Check
To check students' understanding of key skills and concepts, go over Exercises 5, 18, 24, 31, 37, 38.

Universal Access Resources

Adapted Practice 5-4 L1

Practice 5-4 Dividing Rational N... L3

Find the reciprocal of each number.

1. $\frac{7}{10}$ 2. 4 3. $\frac{-1}{3}$

Find each quotient.

4. $\frac{3}{10} \div \frac{4}{5}$ 5. $\frac{3}{8} \div 3$ 6. $\frac{1}{3} \div \frac{2}{7}$
7. $\frac{1}{4} \div \frac{1}{4}$ 8. $\frac{7}{8} \div \frac{2}{7}$ 9. $\frac{1}{4} \div \frac{1}{8}$
10. $\frac{1}{2} \div \frac{2}{5}$ 11. $\frac{8}{9} \div \frac{1}{2}$ 12. $3 \div \frac{3}{8}$
13. $1\frac{5}{7} \div \frac{2}{3}$ 14. $2\frac{1}{6} \div \frac{1}{3}$ 15. $1\frac{4}{9} \div \frac{6}{7}$
16. $3\frac{1}{4} \div (^-0.5)$ 17. $1\frac{5}{9} \div (0.25)$ 18. $\frac{8}{2} \div \frac{2}{3}$

Anna bought a strip of fabric 10 yd long. She needs a $1\frac{1}{3}$-yd piece to make a pillow.

19. How many pillows can Anna make?
20. Anna decides to make smaller pillows using $\frac{2}{3}$-yd pieces. How many small pillows can she make?

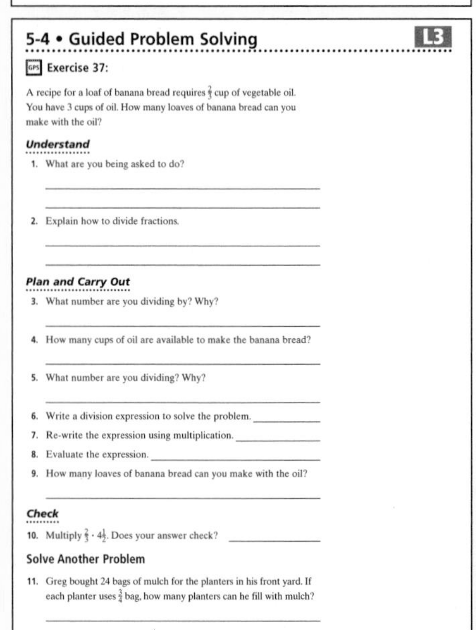

5-4 • Guided Problem Solving L3

GPS **Exercise 37:**

A recipe for a loaf of banana bread requires $\frac{2}{3}$ cup of vegetable oil. You have 3 cups of oil. How many loaves of banana bread can you make with the oil?

Understand

1. What are you being asked to do?
2. Explain how to divide fractions.

Plan and Carry Out

3. What number are you dividing by? Why?
4. How many cups of oil are available to make the banana bread?
5. What number are you dividing? Why?
6. Write a division expression to solve the problem.
7. Re-write the expression using multiplication.
8. Evaluate the expression.
9. How many loaves of banana bread can you make with the oil?

Check

10. Multiply $\frac{2}{3} \cdot 4\frac{1}{2}$. Does your answer check?

Solve Another Problem

11. Greg bought 24 bags of mulch for the planters in his front yard. If each planter uses $\frac{3}{4}$ bag, how many planters can he fill with mulch?

Standards Practice

GO for Help: MathXL

NS 1.2, NS 1.5, Alg1 2.0

A Practice by Example

Example 1 (page 186)

Find the reciprocal of each number.

1. $\frac{2}{5}$ $\frac{5}{2}$

$\frac{2}{5} \cdot ■ = 1$

Guided Practice This exercise has been started for you!

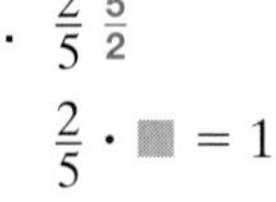

2. $\frac{9}{10}$ $\frac{10}{9}$
3. $\frac{1}{2}$ 2
4. $\frac{1}{12}$ 12
5. $\frac{5}{3}$ $\frac{3}{5}$
6. 15 $\frac{1}{15}$
7. $\frac{-5}{6}$ $-\frac{6}{5}$
8. $\frac{6}{13}$ $\frac{13}{6}$
9. 1 1
10. $\frac{25}{9}$ $\frac{9}{25}$
11. $\frac{17}{18}$ $\frac{18}{17}$
12. -25 $-\frac{1}{25}$
13. $\frac{1}{27}$ 27

Example 2 (page 187)

Find each quotient.

14. $7 \div \frac{3}{5}$ $11\frac{2}{3}$

$7 \div \frac{3}{5} = \frac{7}{1} \cdot \frac{5}{3}$

$= ■$

Guided Practice This exercise has been started for you!

15. $\frac{1}{2} \div \left(-\frac{3}{4}\right)$ $-\frac{2}{3}$
16. $-\frac{7}{9} \div \left(-\frac{9}{7}\right)$ $\frac{49}{81}$
17. $2\frac{1}{4} \div \frac{1}{4}$ 9
18. $\frac{8}{9} \div \frac{1}{3}$ $2\frac{2}{3}$
19. $\frac{2}{5} \div 6.2$ $\frac{2}{31}$
20. $3\frac{3}{5} \div (-9.1)$ $-\frac{36}{91}$
21. $\frac{43}{8} \div \frac{1}{4}$ $21\frac{1}{2}$
22. $25 \div \frac{1}{3}$ 75
23. $4.5 \div \frac{2}{9}$ $20\frac{1}{4}$

Homework Video Tutor

For: Examples 1–2
Visit: PHSchool.com
Web Code: axe-0504

24. You have $6\frac{2}{3}$ lb of raisins to divide evenly among 5 bags of trail mix. How many pounds of raisins will go in each bag? $1\frac{1}{3}$ lb

B Apply Your Skills

25. **Guided Problem Solving** Sunlight takes about $8\frac{1}{2}$ min to travel approximately 93 million miles from the sun to Earth. About how many miles does light travel in 1 min? 10,941,176.47 mi
    - **Understand the Problem** What operation should you use to find the number of miles light travels in 1 min?
    - **Check Your Answer** To check your answer, what values can you substitute in the problem?

26. **Error Analysis** Who is correct, Jocelyn or Annie? Explain. Annie; Jocelyn did not convert the mixed number $4\frac{1}{2}$ to its improper form correctly.

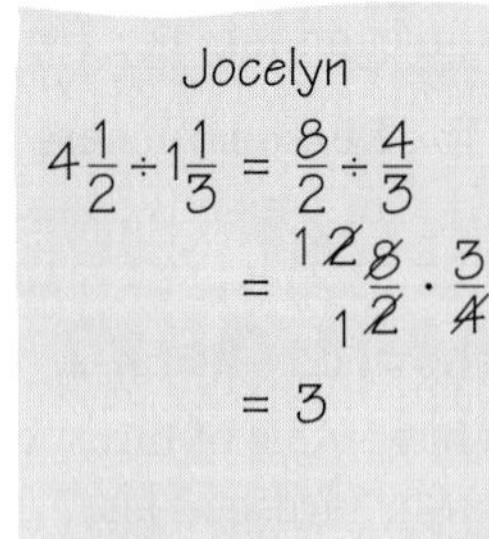

SCAFFOLDED **Problem Solving**

South American Population

Country	Portion of South America's Population
Brazil	$\frac{1}{2}$
Colombia	$\frac{1}{9}$
Argentina	$\frac{1}{10}$
Peru	$\frac{1}{13}$

SOURCE: U.S. Census Bureau. Go to **PHSchool.com** for a data update.
Web Code: axg-9041

27. What fraction of South America's population lives in Argentina? $\frac{1}{10}$

28. Suppose there are about 375,641,000 people in South America. About how many people live in Argentina? about 37,564,100 people

29. How many times as many people live in Brazil as in Argentina? 5 times

30. About how many times as many people live in Brazil than in Colombia, Argentina, and Peru combined? about 1.7 times

Algebra **Evaluate each expression for $a = \frac{1}{2}$, $b = \frac{1}{4}$, and $c = \frac{3}{8}$.**

31. $a \div b$ 2

32. $b \div c$ $\frac{2}{3}$

33. $c \div b \cdot a$ $\frac{3}{4}$

34. $(b + c) \div a$ $1\frac{1}{4}$

35. $(b + c) \div (a + b)$ $\frac{5}{6}$

36. $(a \div b) - (c \div b)$ $\frac{1}{2}$

GPS 37. A recipe for a loaf of banana bread requires $\frac{2}{3}$ cup of vegetable oil. You have 3 cups of oil. How many loaves of banana bread can you make with the oil? 4.5 loaves or $4\frac{1}{2}$ loaves

38. **Writing in Math** Explain the difference between dividing 10 by 4 and dividing 10 by $\frac{1}{4}$. Use diagrams to support your answer. See left.

38. Dividing 10 by $\frac{1}{4}$ is the same as multiplying 10 by 4, so the answer will be much greater than dividing 10 by 4. Check students' diagrams.

C Challenge

39. Simplify $\left(1\frac{1}{3}\right)^2 \div \left(\frac{5}{6}\right)^2$. $2\frac{14}{25}$

Multiple Choice Practice and Mixed Review

For California Standards Tutorials, visit PHSchool.com. Web Code: axq-9045

NS 1.2

40. Ali is tiling a bathroom that is $10\frac{1}{3}$ ft by $10\frac{1}{3}$ ft. How many tiles like the one at the right will fit along one side of the bathroom? C

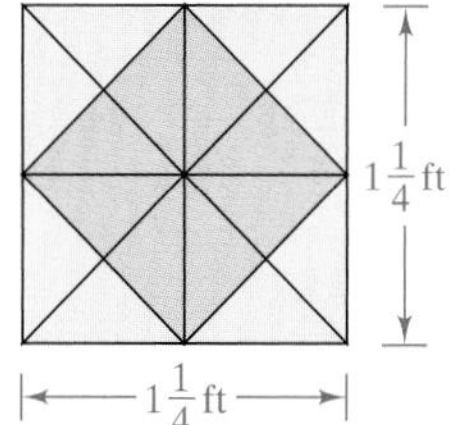

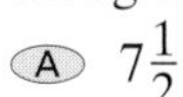 $7\frac{1}{2}$

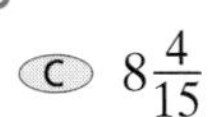 $8\frac{4}{15}$

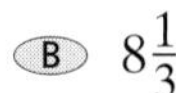 $8\frac{1}{3}$

D $12\frac{11}{12}$

NS 1.2, MR 1.3

41. Mr. Perez is driving 380 mi home from vacation at an average speed of 60 mi/h. Which method can Mr. Perez use to find how long it will take him to drive home? B

A Add 380 and 35.

B Divide 380 by 36.

C Multiply 380 by 60.

D Subtract 60 from 437.

Lesson 5-3

Simplify each expression.

42. $\left(\frac{3}{5}\right)^3$ $\frac{27}{125}$

43. $\left(\frac{7}{10}\right)^4$ $\frac{2,401}{10,000}$

44. $\left(\frac{1}{4}\right)^6$ $\frac{1}{4,096}$

Visit: PHSchool.com Web Code: axa-0504

4. Assess & Reteach

PRESENTATION CD-ROM
CD, Online, or Transparencies

Lesson Quiz

Write the reciprocal of each number.

1. $-\frac{4}{7}$ $-\frac{7}{4}$

2. 11 $\frac{1}{11}$

Find each quotient.

3. $-\frac{1}{6} \div \left(-\frac{3}{4}\right)$ $\frac{2}{9}$

4. $\left(-1\frac{7}{8}\right) \div (1.5)$ $-1\frac{1}{4}$

5. Megan has 3.5 quarts of punch. One serving is $\frac{1}{4}$ quart. How many servings does she have? 14

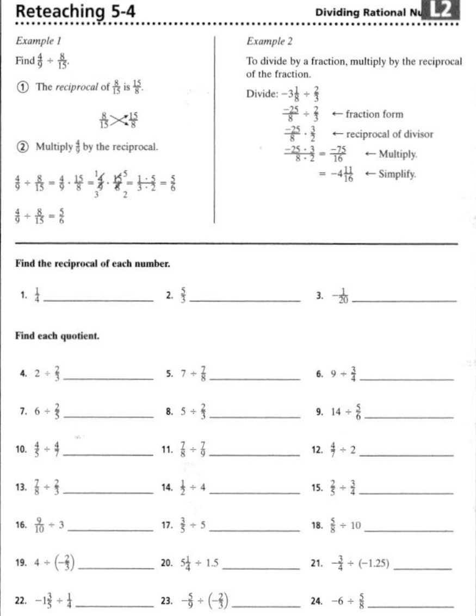

Reteaching 5-4 Dividing Rational Nu L2

Example 1

Find $\frac{4}{9} \div \frac{8}{15}$.

① The *reciprocal* of $\frac{8}{15}$ is $\frac{15}{8}$.

$\frac{8}{15} \times \frac{15}{8}$

② Multiply $\frac{4}{9}$ by the reciprocal.

$\frac{4}{9} \div \frac{8}{15} = \frac{4}{9} \cdot \frac{15}{8} = \frac{\overset{1}{\cancel{4}}}{\underset{3}{\cancel{9}}} \cdot \frac{\overset{5}{\cancel{15}}}{\underset{2}{\cancel{8}}} = \frac{1 \cdot 5}{3 \cdot 2} = \frac{5}{6}$

$\frac{4}{9} \div \frac{8}{15} = \frac{5}{6}$

Example 2

To divide by a fraction, multiply by the reciprocal of the fraction.

Divide: $-3\frac{1}{8} \div \frac{2}{3}$

$\frac{-25}{8} \div \frac{2}{3}$ ← fraction form

$\frac{-25}{8} \cdot \frac{3}{2}$ ← reciprocal of divisor

$\frac{-25 \cdot 3}{8 \cdot 2} = \frac{-75}{16}$ ← Multiply.

$= -4\frac{11}{16}$ ← Simplify.

Find the reciprocal of each number.

1. $\frac{1}{4}$ ______ 2. $\frac{5}{3}$ ______ 3. $-\frac{1}{20}$ ______

Find each quotient.

4. $2 \div \frac{2}{3}$ ______ 5. $7 \div \frac{7}{8}$ ______ 6. $9 \div \frac{3}{4}$ ______

7. $6 \div \frac{2}{5}$ ______ 8. $5 \div \frac{2}{3}$ ______ 9. $14 \div \frac{5}{6}$ ______

10. $\frac{4}{5} \div \frac{4}{7}$ ______ 11. $\frac{7}{8} \div \frac{7}{9}$ ______ 12. $\frac{4}{7} \div 2$ ______

13. $\frac{7}{8} \div \frac{2}{3}$ ______ 14. $\frac{1}{2} \div 4$ ______ 15. $\frac{2}{5} \div \frac{3}{4}$ ______

16. $\frac{9}{10} \div 3$ ______ 17. $\frac{3}{5} \div 5$ ______ 18. $\frac{5}{8} \div 10$ ______

19. $4 \div \left(-\frac{2}{3}\right)$ ______ 20. $5\frac{1}{4} \div 1.5$ ______ 21. $-\frac{3}{4} \div (-1.25)$ ______

22. $-1\frac{3}{5} \div \frac{1}{4}$ ______ 23. $-\frac{5}{9} \div \left(-\frac{2}{3}\right)$ ______ 24. $-6 \div \frac{5}{8}$ ______

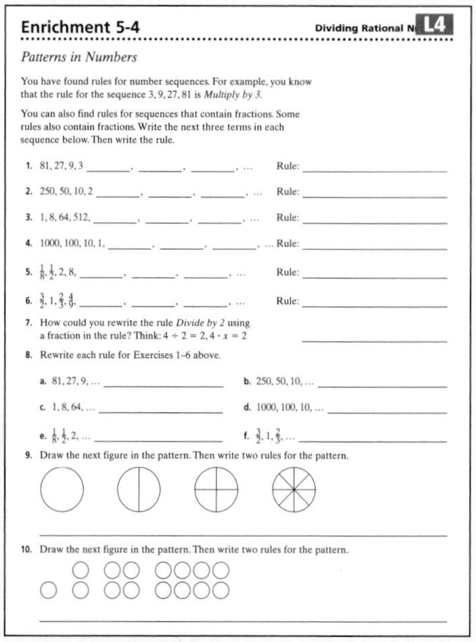

Enrichment 5-4 Dividing Rational N L4

Patterns in Numbers

You have found rules for number sequences. For example, you know that the rule for the sequence 3, 9, 27, 81 is *Multiply by 3.*

You can also find rules for sequences that contain fractions. Some rules also contain fractions. Write the next three terms in each sequence below. Then write the rule.

1. 81, 27, 9, 3 ______, ______, ______, … Rule: ______

2. 250, 50, 10, 2 ______, ______, ______, … Rule: ______

3. 1, 8, 64, 512, ______, ______, ______, … Rule: ______

4. 1000, 100, 10, 1, ______, ______, ______, … Rule: ______

5. $\frac{1}{8}, \frac{1}{2}$, 2, 8, ______, ______, ______, … Rule: ______

6. $\frac{3}{2}$, 1, $\frac{2}{3}, \frac{4}{9}$, ______, ______, ______, … Rule: ______

7. How could you rewrite the rule *Divide by 2* using a fraction in the rule? Think: $4 \div 2 = 2$, $4 \cdot x = 2$ ______

8. Rewrite each rule for Exercises 1–6 above.

a. 81, 27, 9, … ______ b. 250, 50, 10, … ______

c. 1, 8, 64, … ______ d. 1000, 100, 10, … ______

e. $\frac{1}{8}, \frac{1}{2}$, 2, … ______ f. $\frac{3}{2}$, 1, $\frac{2}{3}$, … ______

9. Draw the next figure in the pattern. Then write two rules for the pattern.

______

10. Draw the next figure in the pattern. Then write two rules for the pattern.

______

Alternative Assessment

Working in pairs, one partner writes a decimal greater than 1; the other writes a fraction. Together they first find the reciprocal of each number and then divide the decimal by the fraction. Students must agree on the solutions.

California Resources

Standards Mastery

- Standards Review Transparencies
- Standards Review and Practice Workbook
- Math Companion

Math Intervention

- Skills Review and Practice Workbook
- Math XL

5-5

1. Plan

California Content Standards

Write and solve one-step linear equations in one variable. *Foundational*

AF 1.1 Use variables and appropriate operations to write an equation. ***Develop***

AF 1.3 Simplify numerical expressions by applying properties of rational numbers and justify the process used. ***Develop***

California Math Background

You can solve equations with fractions in a manner similar to that of solving equations with whole numbers. To solve equations involving fractions and mixed numbers, you need to use the Addition Property of Equality or the Subtraction Property of Equality. These properties allow you to add the same number to, or subtract the same number from, both sides of an equation without changing the value of the equation.

More Math Background: p. 168C

Lesson Planning and Resources

See p. 168E for a list of the resources that support this lesson.

PRESENTATION CD-ROM
CD, Online, or Transparencies

Bell Ringer Practice

Check Skills You'll Need
Use student page, transparency, or PowerPoint.
See Math Companion.

California Standards Review
Use transparency or PowerPoint.

GO for Help: Math Companion

5-5 Solving Equations by Adding or Subtracting

Check Skills You'll Need

Do this in your **Math Companion.**

Vocabulary

Review:
- isolate

Use your **Math Companion** *to build your vocabulary.*

California Content Standards

Foundational Standard Write and solve one-step linear equations in one variable.

AF 1.1 Use variables and appropriate operations to write an equation that represents a verbal description. ***Develop***

AF 1.3 Simplify numerical expressions by applying properties of rational numbers and justify the process used. ***Master***

What You'll Learn . . . and Why

You will learn to solve addition and subtraction equations with fractions. You can use equations with fractions to find rainfall amounts.

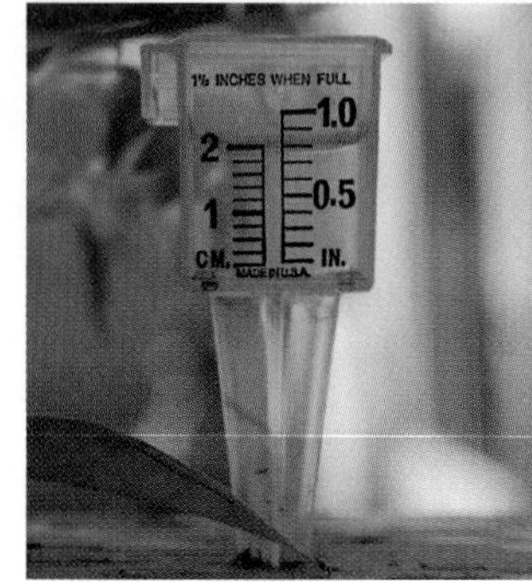

Solving equations with fractions is similar to solving equations with integers and decimals. Recall that to solve an equation, you isolate the variable.

Math Foundations

Remember to find a common denominator when you add or subtract fractions.

EXAMPLE Solving Equations With Fractions

1 Solve $x - \frac{1}{3} = \frac{5}{6}$.

$x - \frac{1}{3} = \frac{5}{6}$

$x - \frac{1}{3} + \frac{1}{3} = \frac{5}{6} + \frac{1}{3}$ ← Isolate the variable. Use the Addition Property of Equality.

$x + 0 = \frac{5}{6} + \frac{1}{3}$ ← Inverse Property of Addition

$x = \frac{5}{6} + \frac{1 \cdot 2}{3 \cdot 2}$ ← The LCD is 6. Write the fractions with the same denominator.

$x = \frac{5}{6} + \frac{2}{6}$ ← Simplify.

$x = \frac{7}{6}$ ← Add.

$x = 1\frac{1}{6}$ ← Simplify.

CA Standards Check 1 *Go to your* **Math Companion** *for help.*

1. Solve each equation.

   a. $n + \frac{1}{3} = \frac{11}{12}$ $\frac{7}{12}$

   b. $\frac{2}{5} - a = \frac{13}{20}$ $-\frac{1}{4}$

Universal Access Solutions for All Learners

Special Needs L1	**Below Level** L2
Assist students with different models to solve the equations in this lesson. Tiles and number lines can be useful models to use before students solve equations.	Write equations with like denominators for students to solve. $x - \frac{1}{9} = \frac{4}{9}$ $x = \frac{5}{9}$ $x + \frac{4}{8} = \frac{7}{8}$ $x = \frac{3}{8}$

You can use equations with fractions to solve real-world problems. Use estimation to check the reasonableness of your answer. Use the benchmarks 0, $\frac{1}{2}$, and 1 when estimating with fractions.

EXAMPLE Writing Equations With Fractions

Relate **MATH YOU KNOW...**

Solve $1 + r = 4$.

$$1 + r = 4$$
$$1 - 1 + r = 4 - 1 \quad \leftarrow \text{Subtraction Property of Equality}$$
$$r = 3 \quad \leftarrow \text{Subtract.}$$

***... to* ALGEBRA**

2 Guided Problem Solving During the first week of January, a rain gauge collected $\frac{1}{2}$ in. of rain. By the end of January, the total rainfall was $2\frac{3}{5}$ in. How much rain fell after the first week of January?

Problem Solving Tip

You can also use a model like the one below to represent the situation.

$2\frac{3}{5}$	
$\frac{1}{2}$	r

Words	rainfall during first week of January	plus	rainfall after first week of January	equals	total rainfall in January

Let r = the rainfall after the first week of January.

Equation	$\frac{1}{2}$	+	r	=	$2\frac{3}{5}$

$$\frac{1}{2} + r = 2\frac{3}{5}$$
$$\frac{1}{2} + r - \frac{1}{2} = 2\frac{3}{5} - \frac{1}{2} \quad \leftarrow \text{Isolate the variable. Use the Subtraction Property of Equality.}$$
$$r + 0 = 2\frac{3}{5} - \frac{1}{2} \quad \leftarrow \text{Inverse Property of Addition}$$
$$r = 2\frac{3 \cdot 2}{5 \cdot 2} - \frac{1 \cdot 5}{2 \cdot 5} \quad \leftarrow \text{The LCD is 10. Write the fractions with the same denominator.}$$
$$r = 2\frac{6}{10} - \frac{5}{10} \quad \leftarrow \text{Simplify.}$$
$$r = 2\frac{1}{10} \quad \leftarrow \text{Subtract.}$$

After the first week of January, $2\frac{1}{10}$ in. of rain fell.

Check for Reasonableness Round $2\frac{1}{10}$ to 2. Since $\frac{1}{2} + 2 = 2\frac{1}{2}$, and $2\frac{1}{2}$ is close to $2\frac{3}{5}$, the answer is reasonable.

CA Standards Check 2 *Go to your* **Math Companion** *for help.*

2. You hammer a nail $2\frac{3}{8}$ in. long through a board. On the other side, $\frac{5}{8}$ in. of the nail pokes through. How thick is the board? $1\frac{3}{4}$ in.

Check Your Understanding *Homework prep is in your* **Math Companion.**

2. Teach

Guided Instruction

Teaching Tip

Have students round their ages to the nearest whole number of months. Then have them divide by 12 and write the result as a mixed number in simplest form.

Example 1

Have students share with the class the methods they used to solve the Quick Check exercises.

PRESENTATION CD-ROM
CD, Online, or Transparencies

Additional Examples

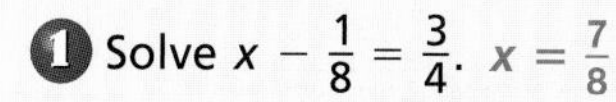

1 Solve $x - \frac{1}{8} = \frac{3}{4}$. $x = \frac{7}{8}$

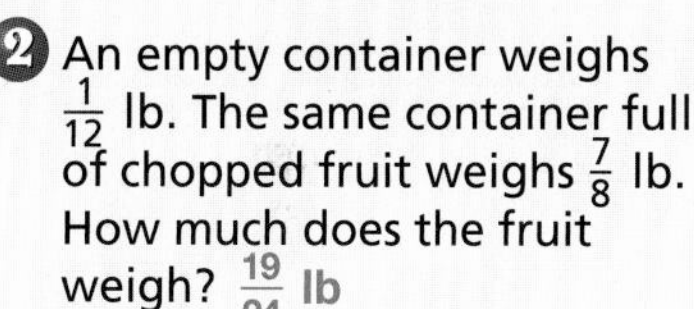

2 An empty container weighs $\frac{1}{12}$ lb. The same container full of chopped fruit weighs $\frac{7}{8}$ lb. How much does the fruit weigh? $\frac{19}{24}$ lb

Closure

- *How is solving equations with fractions similar to solving equations with whole numbers?* Sample: Both use the properties of equality to isolate variables.

Advanced Learners L4	**English Learners** EL
Write two one-step equations that have the solution $x = 5\frac{1}{9}$. Sample: $x - 1\frac{1}{3} = 3\frac{7}{9}$, $x + 5\frac{1}{6} = 10\frac{5}{18}$	A pictorial model for Example 2 would be helpful. For example, a number line can show what is being added to the rainfall after the first week, or the difference between $\frac{1}{2}$ and $2\frac{3}{5}$.

3. Practice

Assignment Guide

Check Your Understanding
See Math Companion.

Homework Exercises

A Practice by Example	1–16
B Apply Your Skills	17–33
C Challenge	34
California Multiple-Choice Practice	35–36
Mixed Review	37–39

Homework Quick Check
To check students' understanding of key skills and concepts, go over Exercises 6, 9, 16, 18, 26, 33.

Universal Access Resources

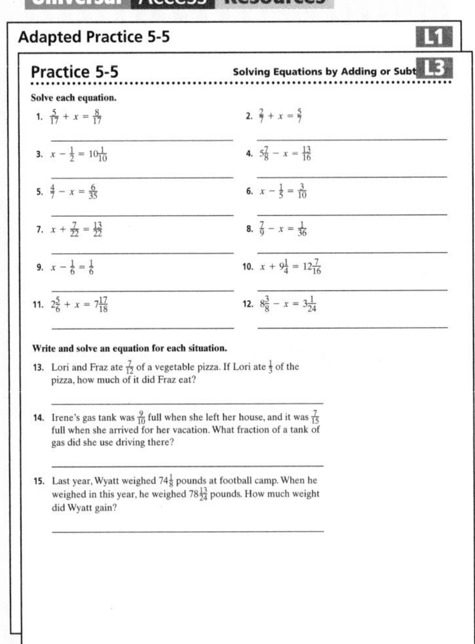

Adapted Practice 5-5 L1

Practice 5-5 Solving Equations by Adding or Subt L3

Solve each equation.

1. $\frac{5}{17} + x = \frac{8}{17}$
2. $\frac{2}{7} + x = \frac{5}{7}$
3. $x - \frac{1}{2} = 10\frac{1}{10}$
4. $5\frac{7}{8} - x = \frac{13}{16}$
5. $\frac{4}{7} - x = \frac{6}{35}$
6. $x - \frac{1}{5} = \frac{3}{10}$
7. $x + \frac{7}{22} = \frac{13}{22}$
8. $\frac{7}{9} - x = \frac{1}{36}$
9. $x - \frac{1}{6} = \frac{1}{6}$
10. $x + 9\frac{1}{4} = 12\frac{7}{16}$
11. $2\frac{5}{6} + x = 7\frac{17}{18}$
12. $8\frac{3}{8} - x = 3\frac{1}{24}$

Write and solve an equation for each situation.

13. Lori and Fraz ate $\frac{7}{12}$ of a vegetable pizza. If Lori ate $\frac{1}{3}$ of the pizza, how much of it did Fraz eat?
14. Irene's gas tank was $\frac{9}{10}$ full when she left her house, and it was $\frac{7}{15}$ full when she arrived for her vacation. What fraction of a tank of gas did she use driving there?
15. Last year, Wyatt weighed $74\frac{1}{8}$ pounds at football camp. When he weighed in this year, he weighed $78\frac{13}{24}$ pounds. How much weight did Wyatt gain?

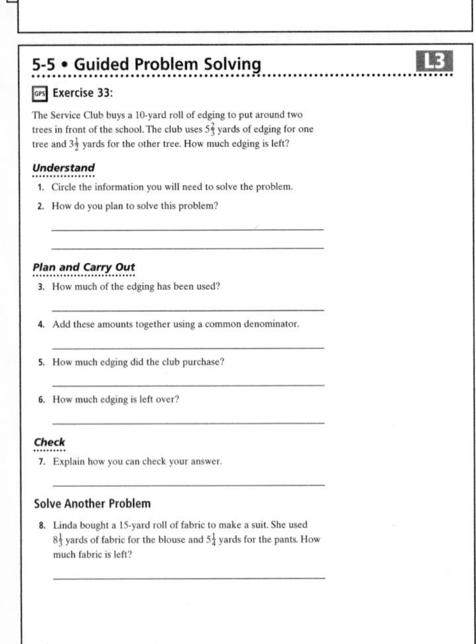

5-5 • Guided Problem Solving L3

GPS Exercise 33:

The Service Club buys a 10-yard roll of edging to put around two trees in front of the school. The club uses $5\frac{2}{3}$ yards of edging for one tree and $3\frac{1}{2}$ yards for the other tree. How much edging is left?

Understand

1. Circle the information you will need to solve the problem.
2. How do you plan to solve this problem?

Plan and Carry Out

3. How much of the edging has been used?
4. Add these amounts together using a common denominator.
5. How much edging did the club purchase?
6. How much edging is left over?

Check

7. Explain how you can check your answer.

Solve Another Problem

8. Linda bought a 15-yard roll of fabric to make a suit. She used $8\frac{1}{3}$ yards of fabric for the blouse and $5\frac{1}{4}$ yards for the pants. How much fabric is left?

Standards Practice

GO for Help: MathXL

AF 1.1, AF 1.3

A Practice by Example

Example 1 (page 190)

Solve each equation.

1. $x - \frac{5}{6} = \frac{7}{8}$ $1\frac{17}{24}$

   $x - \frac{5}{6} + \frac{5}{6} = \frac{7}{8} + \frac{5}{6}$

Guided Practice This exercise has been started for you!

GO for Help

2. $\frac{5}{24} + g = \frac{1}{3}$ $\frac{1}{8}$
3. $\frac{4}{9} = y - \frac{2}{5}$ $\frac{38}{45}$
4. $t - \frac{7}{9} = \frac{1}{3}$ $1\frac{1}{9}$
5. $\frac{2}{3} = n + \frac{11}{12}$ $-\frac{1}{4}$
6. $\frac{5}{8} = a + \frac{1}{3}$ $\frac{7}{24}$
7. $p - \frac{2}{5} = \frac{1}{9}$ $\frac{23}{45}$

Example 2 (page 191)

Solve each equation.

8. $3\frac{1}{5} = x - \frac{12}{25}$ $3\frac{17}{25}$
9. $y - 2\frac{8}{9} = \frac{5}{6}$ $3\frac{13}{18}$
10. $k - 4\frac{5}{6} = 2\frac{1}{4}$ $7\frac{1}{12}$
11. $9\frac{7}{8} + b = -\frac{3}{4}$ $-10\frac{5}{8}$
12. $\frac{16}{3} + a = \frac{5}{6}$ $-4\frac{1}{2}$
13. $w - \frac{11}{10} = \frac{5}{33}$ $1\frac{83}{330}$
14. $3\frac{2}{3} = m - 12.25$ $15\frac{11}{12}$
15. $6.7 = r + \frac{1}{2}$ $6\frac{1}{5}$
16. A costume designer has $15\frac{7}{8}$ yd of fabric. The designer uses $3\frac{1}{4}$ yd on a costume. How much fabric does the designer have left? $12\frac{5}{8}$ yd

Homework Video Tutor

For: Examples 1–2
Visit: PHSchool.com
Web Code: axe-0505

B Apply Your Skills

17. **Guided Problem Solving** You buy 12 lb of beef for a class picnic. You use $5\frac{1}{2}$ lb to make burgers and $4\frac{2}{3}$ lb to make tacos. Use an equation to find how much beef remains. $1\frac{5}{6}$ lb
    - Draw a diagram.

12		
$5\frac{1}{2}$	$4\frac{2}{3}$	b

    - What equation represents this situation?

18. **Writing in Math** Refer to the table. For this 1,600-m relay race, did the relay team beat their best total time of 6 min? Explain. Yes; their time was 5.875 s.
19. Your teacher asks the class to name one of the three primary colors for pigments. If $\frac{2}{5}$ of the class chooses yellow, and $\frac{1}{3}$ of the class chooses blue, what fraction of the class chooses red? $\frac{4}{15}$

Relay Times (minutes)

Kim	$1\frac{1}{2}$
Alison	$1\frac{3}{8}$
Laura	$1\frac{3}{4}$
Jamie	$1\frac{1}{4}$

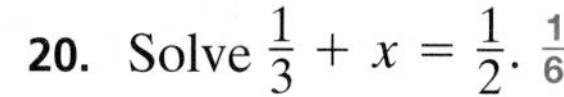
SCAFFOLDED
Problem Solving

22. Answers may vary. Sample: The solution is 1 over the product of the denominators or $\frac{1}{n(n+1)}$.

20. Solve $\frac{1}{3} + x = \frac{1}{2}$. $\frac{1}{6}$

21. Solve $\frac{1}{4} + x = \frac{1}{3}$. $\frac{1}{12}$

22. **Patterns** Make a conjecture about how the solution to the equation $\frac{1}{n+1} + x = \frac{1}{n}$ is related to $\frac{1}{n}$ and $\frac{1}{n+1}$. See left.

23. Does your conjecture hold true for the equation $\frac{1}{5} + x = \frac{1}{4}$? Check students' work.

24. Predict the solution of $\frac{1}{15} + x = \frac{1}{14}$. $\frac{1}{210}$

Brooklyn Bridge, New York

25. The Golden Gate Bridge in California is about $\frac{4}{5}$ mi long. It is about $\frac{1}{2}$ mi longer than the Brooklyn Bridge in New York. About how long is the Brooklyn Bridge? $\frac{3}{10}$ mi

(Algebra) Solve each equation for x when $a = \frac{1}{2}$, $b = \frac{1}{3}$, and $c = 0.25$. Write your answer in simplest form.

26. $a + x = 3$ $2\frac{1}{2}$

27. $2\frac{1}{6} + x = -b$ $-2\frac{1}{2}$

28. $c + x = \frac{1}{8}$ $-\frac{1}{8}$

29. $x - a = c$ $\frac{3}{4}$

30. $-5\frac{1}{2} + x = 2 + a$ 8

31. $x - 1\frac{1}{2} = b$ $1\frac{5}{6}$

32. **Number Sense** Which variable, m or n, has the greater value? n

$$m - \frac{3}{4} = \frac{37}{50} \qquad n - \frac{4}{5} = \frac{37}{50}$$

GPS 33. The Service Club buys a 10-yard roll of edging to put around two trees in front of the school. The club uses $5\frac{2}{3}$ yards of edging for one tree and $3\frac{1}{2}$ yards for the other tree. How much edging is left? $\frac{5}{6}$ yd

C Challenge

34. If $b = a + \frac{1}{3}$, what is the value of $b - 1$ in terms of a? $a - \frac{2}{3}$

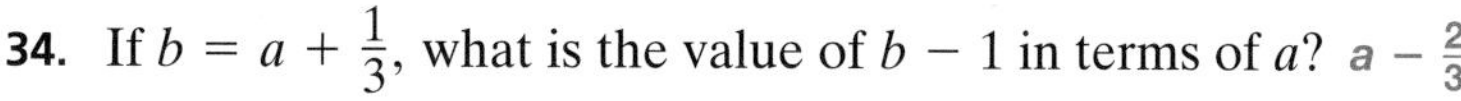
Multiple Choice Practice and Mixed Review

For California Standards Tutorials, visit PHSchool.com. Web Code: axq-9045

AF 1.3

35. Eli says $\frac{1}{3} + t - \frac{1}{3} = t + 0$. Which property justifies this statement? C
    - (A) Commutative Property of Addition
    - (B) Associative Property of Addition
    - (C) Inverse Property of Addition
    - (D) Distributive Property

AF 4.1

36. What is the solution to the equation $5x - 3.4 = 26.6$? C
    - (A) 4.64 (B) 5.32 (C) 6 (D) 6.35

GO for Help Lesson 5-4

Find each quotient.

37. $\frac{2}{7} \div \frac{1}{3}$ $\frac{6}{7}$

38. $4\frac{1}{2} \div \frac{7}{8}$ $5\frac{1}{7}$

39. $\frac{5}{9} \div \frac{11}{27}$ $1\frac{4}{11}$

GO Online Lesson Quiz Visit: PHSchool.com Web Code: axa-0505

Alternative Assessment

Have students work in pairs. One partner completes Exercises 6, 8, and 10 while the other completes Exercises 7, 9, and 11. Students explain to their partners how they found the solution to each equation.

California Resources

Standards Mastery
- Standards Review Transparencies
- Standards Review and Practice Workbook
- Math Companion

Math Intervention
- Skills Review and Practice Workbook
- Math XL

4. Assess & Reteach

PRESENTATION CD-ROM
CD, Online, or Transparencies

Lesson Quiz

Solve each equation.

1. $x + \frac{1}{3} = \frac{14}{15}$ $x = \frac{3}{5}$
2. $x + 10\frac{5}{8} = 16\frac{1}{4}$ $x = 5\frac{5}{8}$
3. $17\frac{3}{4} + x = 18\frac{1}{12}$ $x = \frac{1}{3}$
4. $x - \frac{9}{10} = 3\frac{7}{10}$ $x = 4\frac{3}{5}$

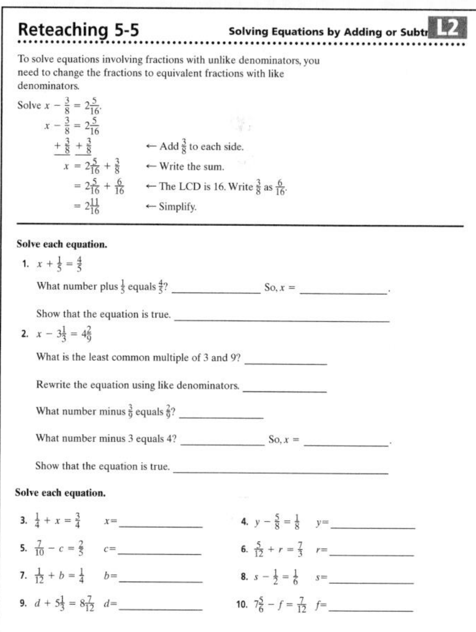
Reteaching 5-5 Solving Equations by Adding or Subtr L2

To solve equations involving fractions with unlike denominators, you need to change the fractions to equivalent fractions with like denominators.

Solve $x - \frac{3}{8} = 2\frac{5}{16}$.

$x - \frac{3}{8} = 2\frac{5}{16}$

$+\frac{3}{8} \quad +\frac{3}{8}$ ← Add $\frac{3}{8}$ to each side.

$x = 2\frac{5}{16} + \frac{3}{8}$ ← Write the sum.

$= 2\frac{5}{16} + \frac{6}{16}$ ← The LCD is 16. Write $\frac{3}{8}$ as $\frac{6}{16}$.

$= 2\frac{11}{16}$ ← Simplify.

Solve each equation.

1. $x + \frac{1}{5} = \frac{4}{5}$

   What number plus $\frac{1}{5}$ equals $\frac{4}{5}$? ______ So, x = ______.

   Show that the equation is true. ______

2. $x - 3\frac{1}{3} = 4\frac{2}{9}$

   What is the least common multiple of 3 and 9? ______

   Rewrite the equation using like denominators. ______

   What number minus $\frac{3}{9}$ equals $\frac{2}{9}$? ______

   What number minus 3 equals 4? ______ So, x = ______.

   Show that the equation is true. ______

Solve each equation.

3. $\frac{1}{4} + x = \frac{3}{4}$ x= ______
4. $y - \frac{5}{8} = \frac{1}{8}$ y= ______
5. $\frac{7}{10} - c = \frac{2}{5}$ c= ______
6. $\frac{5}{12} + r = \frac{7}{3}$ r= ______
7. $\frac{1}{12} + b = \frac{1}{4}$ b= ______
8. $s - \frac{1}{2} = \frac{1}{6}$ s= ______
9. $d + 5\frac{1}{3} = 8\frac{7}{12}$ d= ______
10. $7\frac{5}{6} - f = \frac{7}{12}$ f= ______

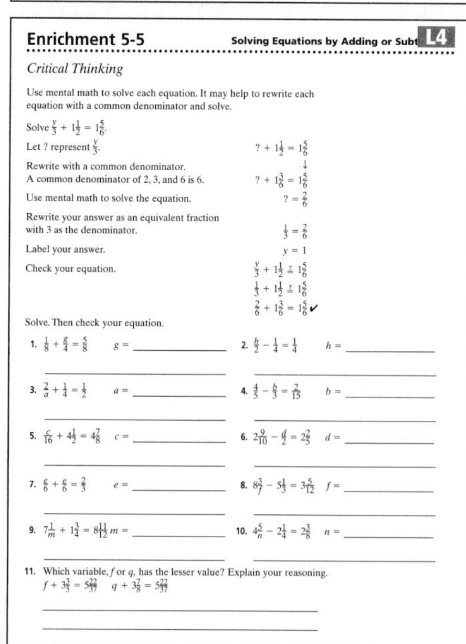
Enrichment 5-5 Solving Equations by Adding or Subt L4

Critical Thinking

Use mental math to solve each equation. It may help to rewrite each equation with a common denominator and solve.

Solve $\frac{y}{3} + 1\frac{1}{2} = 1\frac{5}{6}$.

Let ? represent $\frac{y}{3}$. $? + 1\frac{1}{2} = 1\frac{5}{6}$

Rewrite with a common denominator. A common denominator of 2, 3, and 6 is 6. $? + 1\frac{3}{6} = 1\frac{5}{6}$

Use mental math to solve the equation. $? = \frac{2}{6}$

Rewrite your answer as an equivalent fraction with 3 as the denominator. $\frac{1}{3} = \frac{2}{6}$

Label your answer. $y = 1$

Check your equation. $\frac{y}{3} + 1\frac{1}{2} \stackrel{?}{=} 1\frac{5}{6}$; $\frac{1}{3} + 1\frac{1}{2} \stackrel{?}{=} 1\frac{5}{6}$; $\frac{2}{6} + 1\frac{3}{6} = 1\frac{5}{6}$ ✔

Solve. Then check your equation.

1. $\frac{1}{8} + \frac{g}{4} = \frac{5}{8}$ g = ______
2. $\frac{h}{2} - \frac{1}{4} = \frac{1}{4}$ h = ______
3. $\frac{2}{a} + \frac{1}{4} = \frac{1}{2}$ a = ______
4. $\frac{4}{5} - \frac{b}{3} = \frac{2}{15}$ b = ______
5. $\frac{c}{16} + 4\frac{1}{2} = 4\frac{7}{8}$ c = ______
6. $2\frac{9}{10} - \frac{d}{2} = 2\frac{2}{5}$ d = ______
7. $\frac{e}{6} + \frac{e}{6} = \frac{2}{3}$ e = ______
8. $8\frac{3}{f} - 5\frac{1}{3} = 3\frac{5}{12}$ f = ______
9. $7\frac{1}{m} + 1\frac{3}{4} = 8\frac{11}{12}$ m = ______
10. $4\frac{5}{n} - 2\frac{1}{4} = 2\frac{3}{8}$ n = ______
11. Which variable, f or q, has the lesser value? Explain your reasoning.
    $f + 3\frac{3}{5} = 5\frac{22}{37}$ $q + 3\frac{7}{8} = 5\frac{22}{37}$

Practice Solving Problems

In this feature, students use diagrams to help them visualize the situation in each problem and then write and solve an equation for each problem.

Guided Instruction

Discuss with students that word problems with a lot of information are often difficult to visualize. Explain that drawing a diagram from the given information can make a problem easier to approach.

Have a volunteer read the example aloud. Ask:

- *What would you draw to represent the information in this problem?* boards of the dimensions described and one board with a variable for its width
- *What information is necessary to solve the problem?* the width of both boards, the total width of the wall
- *How can you find the value of the variable?* by adding the widths of the first two boards and subtracting that number from the total width

Practice Solving Problems

NS 1.2 Add, subtract, multiply, and divide rational numbers. *Develop*
AF 1.1 Use variables and appropriate operations to write an equation. *Develop*
MR 3.2 Note the method of deriving the solution and solve similar problems. *Develop*

You want to build a garden wall that is 36 in. tall. You place two $1\frac{1}{2}$ in.-by-$11\frac{1}{4}$ in. boards on top of each other. Each board is 5 ft long. How wide does the third board need to be to finish the wall?

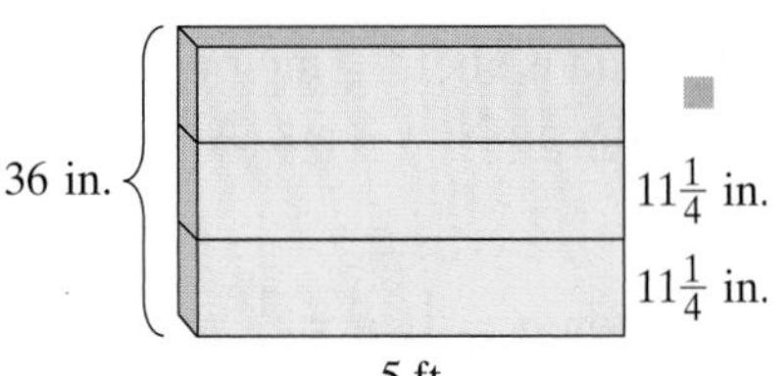
36 in.
$11\frac{1}{4}$ in.
$11\frac{1}{4}$ in.
5 ft

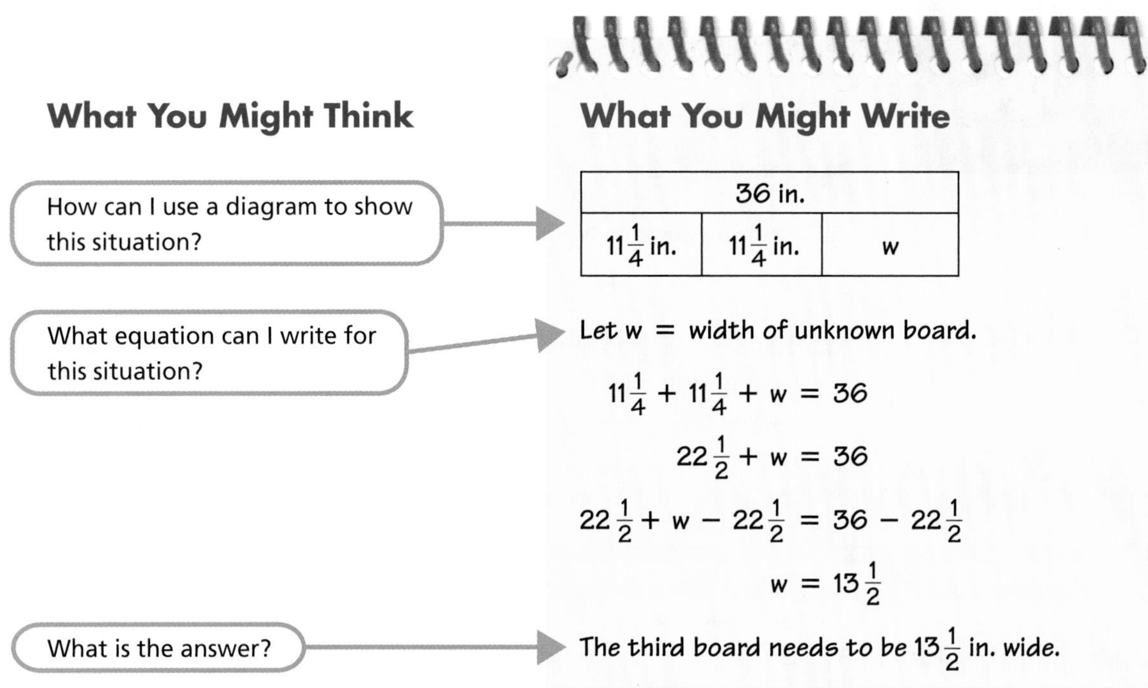
What You Might Think
What You Might Write
How can I use a diagram to show this situation?
What equation can I write for this situation?
What is the answer?

36 in.		
$11\frac{1}{4}$ in.	$11\frac{1}{4}$ in.	w

Let w = width of unknown board.

$$11\frac{1}{4} + 11\frac{1}{4} + w = 36$$

$$22\frac{1}{2} + w = 36$$

$$22\frac{1}{2} + w - 22\frac{1}{2} = 36 - 22\frac{1}{2}$$

$$w = 13\frac{1}{2}$$

The third board needs to be $13\frac{1}{2}$ in. wide.

Think It Through

1. Can you solve the equation $11\frac{1}{4} + 11\frac{1}{4} + x = 36$ by subtracting $11\frac{1}{4}$ from each side? Explain. See right.
2. **Estimation** How can you use rounding to decide whether the answer is reasonable? See margin.
3. **Reasoning** Which strategies can you use to determine which information in the problem is unnecessary? Check students' work.

1. Yes; answers may vary. Sample: you could subtract $11\frac{1}{4}$ from each side of the equation twice to get the variable alone on one side of the equation.

Exercises

4. Jack Earle starred in the 1924 movie *Jack & the Beanstalk.* He was 8 ft $6\frac{1}{2}$ in. tall. Trijntje Keever (1616–1633) was possibly the tallest woman ever at 8 ft $4\frac{1}{5}$ in. tall. How much shorter was Keever than Earle? **$2\frac{3}{10}$ in.**

5. A textbook is $1\frac{15}{16}$ in. thick. The front and back covers are each $\frac{1}{8}$ in. thick. How thick is the book without its covers? Use the diagram below to write and solve an equation. **$1\frac{11}{16}$ in.**

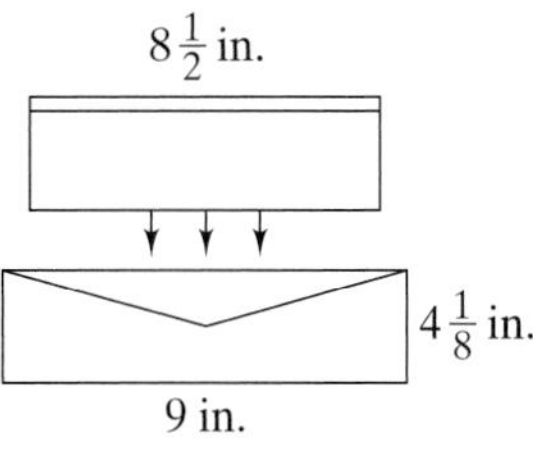

6. A standard business envelope is $4\frac{1}{8}$ in. high and 9 in. wide as shown at the right. An $8\frac{1}{2}$ in.-by-11 in. sheet of paper is folded and placed in the envelope. How much wider is the envelope than the paper? **$\frac{1}{2}$ in.**

7. An object needs to be shipped using one of the boxes in the table below. Either box is an appropriate length and width to fit the object. The object is $2\frac{3}{8}$ in. high. Which box would you use? How much extra space would there be? **the first box; $\frac{3}{16}$ in.**

Box Sizes (inches)

Length	Width	Height
$3\frac{3}{4}$	$3\frac{1}{2}$	$2\frac{9}{16}$
$3\frac{5}{8}$	$2\frac{11}{16}$	$2\frac{1}{4}$

8. What is the distance across the inside of the pipe shown at the right? **$2\frac{5}{8}$ in.**

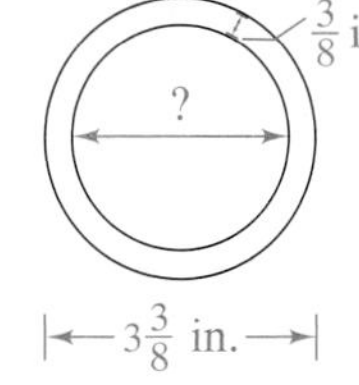

9. An A-10 envelope is 6 in. wide and $9\frac{1}{2}$ in. long. The inside of the envelope is $5\frac{3}{4}$ in. wide and $9\frac{1}{8}$ in. long. What is the difference between an A-10 envelope's outside and inside dimensions? **$\frac{1}{4}$ in.; $\frac{3}{8}$ in.**

10. **Writing in Math** Write a word problem that you can solve with the equation $1\frac{1}{2} + 1\frac{1}{2} + d = 10\frac{1}{2}$. Then solve your problem. **Check students' work; $7\frac{1}{2}$.**

Exercises

Have students work on the Exercises independently. Then review the answers as a class. Choose volunteers to give each answer and explain how they arrived at the solution.

Universal Access

Below Level 

Before beginning the Exercises, have students check the answer to the Example and label their diagrams with the value of *w*.

5-6

1. Plan

California Content Standards

AF 1.1 Use variables and appropriate operations to write an equation. ***Develop***

AF 1.3 Simplify numerical expressions by applying properties of rational numbers and justify the process used. ***Develop***

AF 4.1 Solve two-step linear equations in one variable. ***Develop***

California Math Background

In Lesson 3-3, students learned that an equation of the form $x \div a = b$ can be solved by applying the Multiplication Property of Equality. That is, they learned to solve for x by multiplying each side of the equation by a. Because a fraction bar represents division, the same method can be used to solve an equation that appears in the form $\frac{x}{a} = b$.

More Math Background: p. 168C

Lesson Planning and Resources

See p. 168E for a list of the resources that support this lesson.

... PRESENTATION CD-ROM
CD, Online, or Transparencies
Bell Ringer Practice

Check Skills You'll Need
Use student page, transparency, or PowerPoint.
See Math Companion.

California Standards Review
Use transparency or PowerPoint.

5-6 Solving Equations by Multiplying

Check Skills You'll Need

Do this in your **Math Companion.**

Vocabulary

- multiplicative inverse

Use your **Math Companion** *to build your vocabulary.*

California Content Standards

AF 1.1 Use variables and appropriate operations to write an equation that represents a verbal description. ***Develop***

AF 1.3 Simplify numerical expressions by applying properties of rational numbers and justify the process used. ***Master***

AF 4.1 Solve two-step linear equations in one variable. ***Develop***

What You'll Learn . . . and Why

You will learn to solve multiplication and division equations with fractions. You can use equations in projects involving measurements such as paneling a room.

Recall that reciprocals are numbers whose product is 1. The reciprocal of a number is also called its **multiplicative inverse.**

Take Note **Inverse Property of Multiplication**

Every nonzero number has a multiplicative inverse. The product of a number and its multiplicative inverse is 1.

Arithmetic	Algebra
$\frac{2}{3} \cdot \frac{3}{2} = 1$	$a \cdot \frac{1}{a} = 1$

You can use multiplicative inverses to solve equations.

Math Foundations

Multiplying by the multiplicative inverse of a number is the same as dividing by the number.

EXAMPLE Using the Multiplicative Inverse

1 Solve $6c = \frac{5}{7}$.

$\frac{1}{6} \cdot 6c = \frac{5}{7} \cdot \frac{1}{6}$ ← **Multiply each side by $\frac{1}{6}$, the multiplicative inverse of 6.**

$1c = \frac{5}{7} \cdot \frac{1}{6}$ ← **Inverse Property of Multiplication**

$c = \frac{5}{42}$ ← **Multiply.**

CA Standards Check 1 *Go to your* **Math Companion** *for help.*

1. Solve each equation.

a. $2f = \frac{4}{9}$ $\frac{2}{9}$ **b.** $5d = \frac{11}{13}$ $\frac{11}{65}$

Universal Access Solutions for All Learners

Special Needs L1	**Below Level** L2
Help students draw a picture for the problem in CA Standards Check 3. A number line using halves would be helpful. Have each student run a finger along the number line and count 1 inch every time it travels a distance of $4\frac{1}{2}$.	Review the Multiplication Property of Equality by having students solve several equations such as these. $k \div 4 = 9$ $k = 36$ $z \div 6 = 10$ $z = 60$

When fractions have common factors, simplify before you multiply.

EXAMPLE Solving Multiplication Equations

2 Solve $\frac{2}{3}x = 8$.

$\frac{3}{2} \cdot \frac{2}{3}x = 8 \cdot \frac{3}{2}$ ← Multiply each side by $\frac{3}{2}$, the multiplicative inverse of $\frac{2}{3}$.

$1x = \frac{8}{1} \cdot \frac{3}{2}$ ← Inverse Property of Multiplication

$x = \frac{\cancel{8}^{4}}{1} \cdot \frac{3}{\cancel{2}_{1}}$ ← Divide 8 and 2 by their GCD, 2.

$x = 12$ ← Multiply.

CA Standards Check 2 *Go to your* **Math Companion** *for help.*

2. Solve each equation.
   a. $\frac{7}{8}p = 42$ 48
   b. $\frac{4}{5}k = -\frac{9}{10}$ $-1\frac{1}{8}$

EXAMPLE Writing Multiplication Equations

3 **Guided Problem Solving** A contractor wants to cover a wall $59\frac{1}{2}$ in. wide with wood panels. Each wood panel is $4\frac{3}{8}$ in. wide. How many panels will the contractor need to cover the wall?

Relate **MATH YOU KNOW...** ... *to* **ALGEBRA**

Draw a diagram to model the situation.

$59\frac{1}{2}$ in.			
$4\frac{3}{8}$ in.	$4\frac{3}{8}$ in.	$4\frac{3}{8}$ in.	...

$4\frac{3}{8}p = 59\frac{1}{2}$ ← Let p represent the number of panels.

$\frac{35}{8}p = \frac{119}{2}$ ← Write each mixed number as an improper fraction.

$\frac{8}{35} \cdot \frac{35}{8}p = \frac{119}{2} \cdot \frac{8}{35}$ ← Multiply each side by the multiplicative inverse of $\frac{35}{8}$.

$p = \frac{\cancel{119}^{17}}{\cancel{2}_{1}} \cdot \frac{\cancel{8}^{4}}{\cancel{35}_{5}}$ ← Divide 2 and 8 by their GCD, 2. Divide 119 and 35 by their GCD, 7.

$p = \frac{68}{5}$ ← Multiply.

$p = 13\frac{3}{5}$ ← Write $\frac{68}{5}$ as a mixed number.

Since you cannot buy part of a panel, the contractor will need 14 panels.

CA Standards Check 3 *Go to your* **Math Companion** *for help.*

3. During a storm, the level of a river rose $10\frac{1}{2}$ in. in $4\frac{1}{2}$ h. How many inches per hour did the water level rise? $2\frac{1}{3}$ in./h

Check Your Understanding *Homework prep is in your* **Math Companion.**

2. Teach

Guided Instruction

Error Prevention!

In CA Standards Check 1b, students might calculate $\frac{11}{13} \times 5 = \frac{55}{13}$ and give the solution $x = 4\frac{3}{13}$. Stress the importance of checking the solution in the original equation.

PRESENTATION CD-ROM CD, Online, or Transparencies

Additional Examples

1. Solve $3c = \frac{4}{5}$. $c = \frac{4}{15}$
2. Solve $\frac{3}{4}m = 24$. Check the solution. $m = 32$
3. Mai Li worked $7\frac{1}{2}$ hours and earned \$150. What amount did she earn per hour? \$20 per hour

Closure

- Explain how to solve a fraction equation by multiplying. Sample: For an equation like $\frac{a}{5} = 20$, multiply each side by the denominator of the fraction. For an equation like $\frac{4}{5}b = 20$, multiply each side by the multiplicative inverse of the fraction.

Advanced Learners L4	**English Learners** EL
Solve mentally. $\frac{m}{12} = 4$, $m = 48$; $\frac{12}{n} = 4$, $n = 3$; $\frac{r}{3} = 6$, $r = 18$; $\frac{3}{s} = 6$, $s = 0.5$ or $\frac{1}{2}$	Remind students that they want the variable to be "alone," which means there is an implied (1) next to it. Because multiplying by a reciprocal yields a product of 1, they should multiply by the reciprocal to isolate the variable.

3. Practice

Assignment Guide

Check Your Understanding
See Math Companion.

Homework Exercises

A Practice by Example	1–27
B Apply Your Skills	28–40
C Challenge	41
California Multiple-Choice Practice	42–44
Mixed Review	45–47

Homework Quick Check
To check students' understanding of key skills and concepts, go over Exercises 4, 12, 18, 29, 34, 40.

Universal Access Resources

Adapted Practice 5-6 L1

Practice 5-6 Solving Equations by Multiplying L3

Solve each equation.

1. $\frac{n}{4} = \frac{1}{2}$ $n =$ ______
2. $\frac{x}{7} = 6$ $x =$ ______
3. $\frac{y}{19} = 3$ $y =$ ______
4. $\frac{m}{18} = 2$ $m =$ ______
5. $\frac{n}{8} = 1$ $n =$ ______
6. $\frac{n}{30} = \frac{3}{5}$ $n =$ ______
7. $\frac{3}{7}q = \frac{3}{8}$ $q =$ ______
8. $\frac{5}{14}c = \frac{1}{2}$ $c =$ ______
9. $\frac{3}{2}b = \frac{6}{7}$ $b =$ ______
10. $\frac{1}{4}n = 2$ $n =$ ______
11. $\frac{7}{8}t = 3$ $t =$ ______
12. $\frac{5}{12}h = \frac{3}{5}$ $h =$ ______
13. $\frac{4}{9}v = \frac{1}{4}$ $v =$ ______
14. $\frac{8}{25}h = 2$ $h =$ ______
15. $\frac{10}{7}h = \frac{1}{2}$ $h =$ ______
16. $\frac{2}{3}w = 3$ $w =$ ______
17. $\frac{8}{17}d = \frac{1}{3}$ $d =$ ______
18. $\frac{3}{2}v = \frac{1}{2}$ $v =$ ______

Solve.

19. The largest U.S. standard postage stamp ever issued has a width of about 1 inch, which was $\frac{3}{4}$ of the height of the stamp. Write and solve an equation to find the height of the stamp.
______
20. Candace said, "I'm thinking of a fraction. If I divide it by $\frac{1}{2}$, I get $\frac{3}{11}$." What fraction was Candace thinking of?
______

5-6 • Guided Problem Solving L3

GPS **Exercise 29:**

The price of a shirt is $\frac{5}{6}$ the price of a pair of pants. The shirt costs $12.50. How much do the pants cost?

Understand

1. What are you being asked to do?
______
2. Define a variable to represent the unknown.
______
3. Fill in the boxes with the correct information.
$\square \cdot \square = \square$

Plan and Carry Out

4. Write an expression for the phrase "$\frac{5}{6}$ the price of the pants" if the pants cost p dollars.
______
5. How much does the shirt cost? ______
6. Write an equation to solve the problem. ______
7. What do you do to both sides of the equation to solve for p?
______
8. Solve the equation. ______
9. How much did the pants cost? ______

Check

10. Determine if 12.50 is $\frac{5}{6}$ of 15.
______

Solve Another Problem

11. Lupe and Carlos are $\frac{1}{4}$ of the way done painting their new house. So far they have used $6\frac{2}{3}$ cans of paint. How many cans of paint will they use to paint the entire house?
______

Standards Practice

GO for Help: MathXL

AF 1.1, AF 1.3, AF 4.1

A Practice by Example

Example 1 (page 196)

Solve each equation.

1. $12x = \frac{1}{3}$ $\frac{1}{36}$

$\frac{1}{12} \cdot 12x = \frac{1}{3} \cdot \frac{1}{12}$

Guided Practice This exercise has been started for you!

GO for Help

2. $8a = \frac{5}{6}$ $\frac{5}{48}$
3. $3j = \frac{4}{5}$ $\frac{4}{15}$
4. $10g = \frac{1}{3}$ $\frac{1}{30}$
5. $6t = \frac{11}{15}$ $\frac{11}{90}$
6. $9s = \frac{3}{5}$ $\frac{1}{15}$
7. $5m = \frac{6}{11}$ $\frac{6}{55}$

Example 2 (page 197)

Solve each equation.

8. $\frac{3}{4}p = 9$ 12

$\frac{4}{3} \cdot \frac{3}{4}p = 9 \cdot \frac{4}{3}$

Guided Practice This exercise has been started for you!

Homework Video Tutor

For: Examples 1–3
Visit: PHSchool.com
Web Code: axe-0506

9. $\frac{2}{3}r = 10$ 15
10. $\frac{3}{5}n = \frac{9}{10}$ $1\frac{1}{2}$
11. $\frac{7}{8}b = 14$ 16
12. $\frac{3}{20}x = \frac{15}{17}$ $5\frac{15}{17}$
13. $\frac{3}{4}y = 21$ 28
14. $\frac{4}{5}v = \frac{9}{20}$ $\frac{9}{16}$
15. $\frac{21}{5} = \frac{7}{9}w$ $5\frac{2}{5}$
16. $\frac{34}{9}s = -2$ $-\frac{9}{17}$
17. $\frac{9}{14}t = \frac{36}{28}$ 2

Example 3 (page 197)

Solve each equation.

18. $1\frac{1}{3}w = -4\frac{1}{3}$ $-3\frac{1}{4}$
19. $-\frac{2}{7}b = 1\frac{1}{14}$ $-3\frac{3}{4}$
20. $-\frac{1}{3}u = 6\frac{1}{3}$ -19
21. $4\frac{5}{8}g = \frac{10}{16}$ $\frac{5}{37}$
22. $-\frac{3}{11} = -12\frac{3}{4}n$ $\frac{4}{187}$
23. $1\frac{3}{14} = -3\frac{6}{21}t$ $-\frac{17}{46}$
24. $\frac{9}{14}e = -7\frac{3}{7}$ $-11\frac{5}{9}$
25. $-\frac{8}{9} = 4\frac{1}{6}a$ $-\frac{16}{75}$
26. $-7\frac{1}{8}f = 13\frac{1}{12}$ $-1\frac{143}{171}$

27. The Sears Tower in Chicago is 1,450 ft tall. The height of the Sears Tower is about $1\frac{3}{7}$ the height of the U.S. Bank Tower in Los Angeles. Write and solve an equation to find the height of the U.S. Bank Tower. about 1,015 ft

B Apply Your Skills

28. **Guided Problem Solving** A student has $56.75 in her bank account. This is $5 more than $2\frac{1}{2}$ times as much as her brother has in his bank account. How much money does the student's brother have in his account? $20.70
    - Use a diagram to help you write an equation to represent the situation. Let b equal the amount of money her brother has.

$56.75	
$2\frac{1}{2}b$	$5

    - Is your equation a one-step or a two-step equation?

GPS 29. The price of a shirt is $\frac{5}{6}$ of the price of a pair of pants. The shirt costs $12.50. How much do the pants cost? $15

SCAFFOLDED
Problem Solving

You are making apple pies for a school fundraiser. You have the baskets of apples shown below.

12 apples 10 apples 11 apples

30. How many apples do you have all together? 33 apples

31. One apple fills about $\frac{1}{2}$ c. How many cups of apples do you have? $16\frac{1}{2}$ c

32. Each pie requires $3\frac{1}{5}$ c of apples. How many pies can you make? 5 pies

33. How many more apples do you need to make 10 pies? 31 apples

Solve each equation. Justify each step.

34. $3 + \frac{1}{5}z = 9$ 30

35. $\frac{6}{7} = -2d + \frac{1}{4}$ $-\frac{17}{56}$

36. $1\frac{3}{7} - \frac{4}{9}a = 8$ $-14\frac{11}{14}$

37. $2f - 5\frac{1}{6} = 3.625$ $4\frac{19}{48}$

38. $-\frac{1}{2}g + 7 = -2.6$ $19\frac{1}{5}$

39. $0.9c + \frac{7}{9} = 5\frac{3}{10}$ $5\frac{2}{81}$

40. Dividing each side by $\frac{2}{5}$ is the same as multiplying each side by the reciprocal, $\frac{5}{2}$.

40. **Writing in Math** To solve $\frac{2}{5}x = 6$, you multiply each side by $\frac{5}{2}$. Why is this the same as dividing each side by $\frac{2}{5}$? See left.

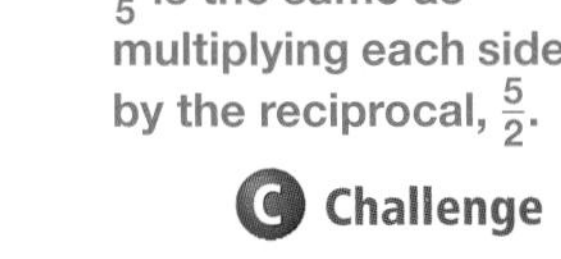

Challenge

41. Solve the equation $x^2 = \frac{36}{121}$. $\frac{6}{11}$ or $-\frac{6}{11}$

Multiple Choice Practice and Mixed Review

For California Standards Tutorials, visit PHSchool.com. Web Code: axq-9045

AF 4.1

42. Birgitta buys a bag of cashews for \$4.50. She also buys $\frac{1}{4}$ lb of peanuts. She spends a total of \$5.05. What is the cost per pound of the peanuts? B

  Ⓐ \$.55 Ⓑ \$2.20 Ⓒ \$3.05 Ⓓ \$5.05

NS 1.2

43. A student needs $1\frac{1}{4}$ yd of solid fabric and $4\frac{5}{8}$ yd of print fabric. About how much fabric does the student need in all? B

  Ⓐ 16 yd Ⓑ 6 yd Ⓒ 5 yd Ⓓ 1 yd

NS 1.2, MR 2.7

44. Suchin has three pieces of string to tie up newspapers for recycling. The lengths are 10 ft, 36 ft, and 22 ft. Estimate the amount of string Suchin has. C

  Ⓐ about 55 ft Ⓒ about 70 ft
  Ⓑ about 60 ft Ⓓ about 75 ft

GO for Help **Lesson 5-2**

Find each difference.

45. $15\frac{6}{9} - 13.4$ $2\frac{4}{15}$

46. $4.5 - 23\frac{2}{3}$ $-19\frac{1}{6}$

47. $26 - 4\frac{1}{9}$ $21\frac{8}{9}$

Online Lesson Quiz Visit: PHSchool.com Web Code: axa-0506

4. Assess & Reteach

PRESENTATION CD-ROM
CD, Online, or Transparencies

Lesson Quiz

Solve each equation.

1. $\frac{n}{4} = 6$ 24
2. $\frac{2}{5}p = 30$ 75
3. $\frac{3}{8}h = \frac{1}{4}$ $\frac{2}{3}$
4. $\frac{1}{6}k = 4$ 24

Alternative Assessment

Provide pairs of students with equations similar to those in Exercises 1–17. Before working together to solve each equation, have partners first discuss and list the steps they will take.

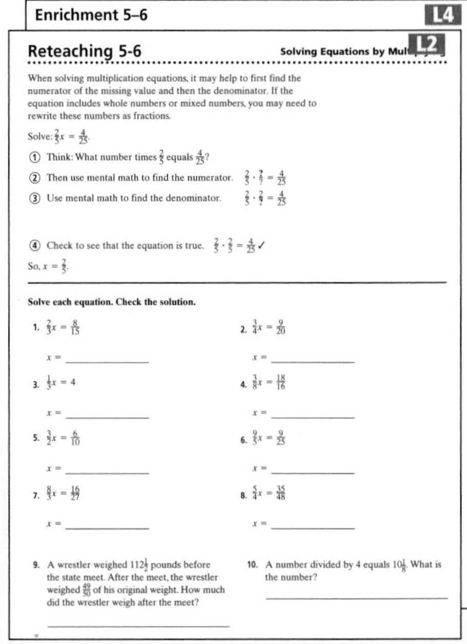

Enrichment 5–6 L4

Reteaching 5-6 Solving Equations by Mul... L2

When solving multiplication equations, it may help to first find the numerator of the missing value and then the denominator. If the equation includes whole numbers or mixed numbers, you may need to rewrite these numbers as fractions.

Solve: $\frac{2}{5}x = \frac{4}{25}$.

① Think: What number times $\frac{2}{5}$ equals $\frac{4}{25}$?

② Then use mental math to find the numerator. $\frac{2}{5} \cdot \frac{?}{?} = \frac{4}{25}$

③ Use mental math to find the denominator. $\frac{2}{5} \cdot \frac{2}{?} = \frac{4}{25}$

④ Check to see that the equation is true. $\frac{2}{5} \cdot \frac{2}{5} = \frac{4}{25}$ ✓

So, $x = \frac{2}{5}$.

Solve each equation. Check the solution.

1. $\frac{2}{3}x = \frac{8}{15}$ $x =$ ______
2. $\frac{3}{4}x = \frac{9}{20}$ $x =$ ______
3. $\frac{1}{3}x = 4$ $x =$ ______
4. $\frac{3}{8}x = \frac{18}{16}$ $x =$ ______
5. $\frac{3}{2}x = \frac{6}{10}$ $x =$ ______
6. $\frac{9}{5}x = \frac{9}{25}$ $x =$ ______
7. $\frac{8}{3}x = \frac{16}{27}$ $x =$ ______
8. $\frac{5}{4}x = \frac{35}{48}$ $x =$ ______
9. A wrestler weighed $112\frac{1}{2}$ pounds before the state meet. After the meet, the wrestler weighed $\frac{49}{50}$ of his original weight. How much did the wrestler weigh after the meet? ______
10. A number divided by 4 equals $10\frac{1}{8}$. What is the number? ______

California Resources

Standards Mastery

- Standards Review Transparencies
- Standards Review and Practice Workbook
- Math Companion

Math Intervention

- Skills Review and Practice Workbook
- Math XL

Algebraic Thinking

Estimating Solutions

In this Activity, students estimate solutions to equations. They can compare the estimates with the original equations' solutions to evaluate the solutions' reasonableness.

Guided Instruction

Discuss the Example with students.

Ask: *Why were the numbers not rounded to the nearest whole number, for example, 3, 32, and 628?* **Sample: It is easier to calculate with numbers rounded to the nearest ten, and the estimate is still reasonable.**

Special Needs L1

Review fractions that might reasonably be rounded to 1, such as $\frac{9}{10}$, $\frac{5}{6}$, $\frac{13}{16}$, and $\frac{2}{3}$. Review fractions that might be rounded to $\frac{1}{2}$, such as $\frac{6}{10}$, $\frac{5}{9}$, $\frac{4}{7}$, and $\frac{9}{20}$.

Checkpoint Quiz

Use this Checkpoint Quiz to check students' understanding of the skills and concepts of Lessons 5-3 through 5-6

All in One Resources

- Checkpoint Quiz 2

Algebraic Thinking

For Use With Lesson 5-6

AF 4.1 Solve two-step linear equations in one variable. ***Develop***
MR 2.1 Use estimation to verify the reasonableness of results. ***Develop***

Estimating Solutions

You can use rounding to check the reasonableness of the solution of an equation with fractions.

EXAMPLE

Your friend says the solution of the equation $3\frac{1}{4}x + 31\frac{2}{3} = 627\frac{5}{8}$ is $294\frac{3}{4}$. Is the solution reasonable?

$3x + 30 \approx 630$ ← **Round $3\frac{1}{4}$ to 3, $31\frac{2}{3}$ to 30, and $627\frac{5}{8}$ to 630.**

$3x \approx 600$ ← **Subtract 30 from each side.**

$x \approx 200$ ← **Divide each side by 3.**

The value of x is about 200. Your friend's solution is not reasonable.

Exercises

Is the solution to each equation reasonable? Explain.

1. $\frac{1}{4}y + 19\frac{1}{4} = 102\frac{3}{5}$; $y = 333\frac{2}{5}$ yes; $y \approx 320$
2. $3\frac{4}{5} - 39\frac{5}{6}z = -401$; $z = 1\frac{1}{6}$ no; $z \approx 10$
3. $\frac{t}{48} + 6 = 2\frac{9}{10}$; $t = -148\frac{8}{10}$ yes; $t \approx -150$
4. $\frac{6}{7}m - 34\frac{7}{8} = -21\frac{1}{3}$; $m = -56\frac{5}{24}$ no; $m \approx 15$

Checkpoint Quiz 2

Lessons 5-3 through 5-6

Find each product or quotient.

1. $\frac{5}{12} \cdot 36$ 15
2. $5\frac{1}{4} \cdot 4\frac{1}{2}$ $23\frac{5}{8}$
3. $24 \div \frac{3}{8}$ 64
4. $1\frac{1}{9} \div 6\frac{2}{3}$ $\frac{1}{6}$
5. $5\frac{1}{2} \cdot \frac{9}{14}$ $3\frac{15}{28}$
6. $-8 \div \frac{4}{5}$ 10

Solve each equation.

7. $d + \frac{5}{12} = \frac{4}{18}$ $-\frac{7}{36}$
8. $9\frac{1}{2} = s - \frac{5}{9}$ $10\frac{1}{18}$
9. $\frac{7}{8} = \frac{3}{16}k$ $4\frac{2}{3}$
10. $\frac{2}{3}x = 7$ $10\frac{1}{2}$
11. A 25-mi bicycle course has markers at the start, at the end, and at every $\frac{1}{2}$ mi. How many markers are on the course? 51 markers

200

Vocabulary Builder

Learning Vocabulary

Make your own mathematics dictionary in a notebook for new vocabulary terms. Use the following ideas to write your definitions.

- Write the vocabulary term and its definition. Include any symbols.
- If possible, draw a diagram.
- Give one or more examples of the term.
- Give one or more examples that do not satisfy the definition and explain how they are different.
- Include details, using other related terms you know.

Here is a possible entry for your dictionary.

Two numbers are reciprocals if their product is 1.

10 and $\frac{1}{10}$ are reciprocals, because their product is 1.

2 and −2 are not reciprocals, because their product is −4.

reciprocals

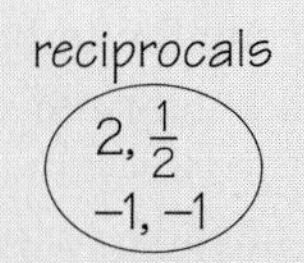

not reciprocals

2, 0.2
3, $-\frac{1}{3}$

1. Answers may vary. Sample: A rational number is a number in the form $\frac{a}{b}$, where $b \neq 0$.
2. Prime factorization can be written as the product of more than 2 factors. 1 is not a prime number.

EXAMPLE A Dictionary Entry

a. What term is being defined? *reciprocal*

b. Why do 10 and $\frac{1}{10}$ satisfy the definition? *Their product is 1.*

c. Why do 2 and −2 not satisfy the definition? *Their product is not 1.*

d. What does the diagram show? *It shows examples of numbers that are reciprocals and numbers that are not reciprocals.*

Exercises

1. Write a dictionary entry for *rational number.* 1–2. See above right.
2. **Error Analysis** A student wrote the definition for *prime factorization* at the right. Which parts are incorrect? Explain.

When a number is written in prime factorization, it is written as the product of two factors.

The prime factorization of 14 is 1 · 2 · 7 because 1, 2, and 7 are prime numbers.

The prime factorization of 20 is not 4 · 5, because 4 is not a prime number.

Vocabulary Builder

Learning Vocabulary

Students who grasp the precision of math vocabulary will improve their ability to understand and share mathematical ideas. In this feature, students learn a strategy for acquiring the new mathematics vocabulary they come across in their texts.

Guided Instruction

Call students' attention to the Table of Symbols and the Illustrated English/Spanish Glossary in the back of their texts.

Ask:

- *How will it help to show examples of reciprocals and examples that are not reciprocals?* Sample: to show more clearly what a reciprocal is.
- *Why are 3 and $-\frac{1}{3}$ not reciprocals?* Their product is −1. Reciprocals have a product of 1.

Teaching Tip

Make an effort to use new math vocabulary often as you work through the textbook lessons. This practice gives students, particularly English learners, a chance to hear the words spoken correctly and in the right context.

Exercises

Have students share dictionary entries with a partner. Invite pairs to discuss ways to improve each other's entries.

5-7

1. Plan

California Content Standards

NS 2.1 Understand negative whole-number exponents. ***Introduce, Develop***

AF 2.1 Interpret negative whole-number powers as repeated division or multiplication by the multiplicative inverse. Simplify and evaluate expressions that include exponents. ***Introduce, Develop***

California Math Background

Just as positive integer exponents represent repeated multiplication, negative exponents represent repeated division. Zero as an exponent represents no multiplication or division. These concepts can be expressed in two important rules:

$a^0 = 1$, for $a \neq 0$

$a^{-n} = \frac{1}{a^n}$, for $a \neq 0$

A negative exponent represents repeated multiplication by the multiplicative inverse of a number.

More Math Background: p. 168C

Lesson Planning and Resources

See p. 168E for a list of the resources that support this lesson.

PRESENTATION CD-ROM
CD, Online, or Transparencies

Bell Ringer Practice

Check Skills You'll Need
Use student page, transparency, or PowerPoint.
See Math Companion.

California Standards Review
Use transparency or PowerPoint.

GO for Help: Math Companion

5-7 Zero and Negative Exponents

Check Skills You'll Need

Do this in your **Math Companion.**

Vocabulary

Review:
- multiplicative inverse

Use your **Math Companion** *to build your vocabulary.*

California Content Standards

NS 2.1 Understand negative whole-number exponents. ***Introduce, Develop***

AF 2.1 Interpret negative whole-number powers as repeated division or multiplication by the multiplicative inverse. Simplify and evaluate expressions that include exponents. ***Introduce, Develop***

What You'll Learn . . . and Why

You will learn to simplify and evaluate expressions with zero and negative exponents. You can use negative exponents to write very small numbers, such as the diameter of a bacterium spore.

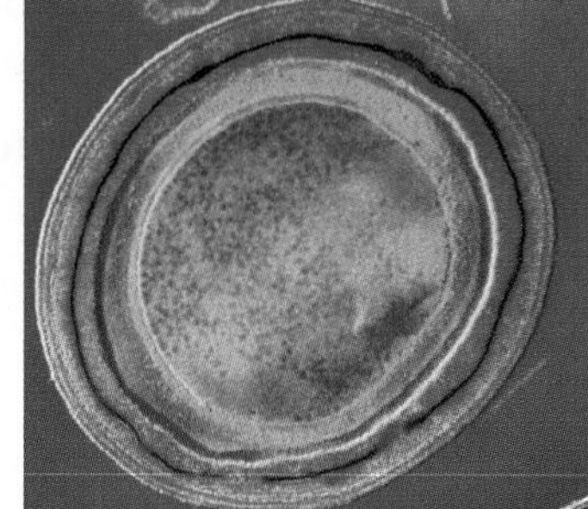

You can use negative exponents to represent repeated division. Observe the pattern in the examples below.

$$\frac{3^4}{3} = \frac{3 \cdot 3 \cdot 3 \cdot \cancel{3}}{\cancel{3}} = 3 \cdot 3 \cdot 3 = 3^3$$

$$\frac{3^3}{3} = \frac{3 \cdot 3 \cdot \cancel{3}}{\cancel{3}} = 3 \cdot 3 = 3^2$$

$$\frac{3^2}{3} = \frac{3 \cdot \cancel{3}}{\cancel{3}} = 3 = 3^1$$

Notice that decreasing the exponent by one is the same as dividing by 3. Continuing the pattern for 3^0 and 3^{-1} shows that $3^0 = 1$ and $3^{-1} = \frac{1}{3}$.

$$\frac{3^1}{3} = \frac{3}{3} = 1 = 3^0$$

$$\frac{3^0}{3} = \frac{1}{3} = \frac{1}{3^1} = 3^{-1}$$

The pattern suggests the following rule.

Take Note — **Zero and Negative Exponents**

Arithmetic	Algebra
$4^0 = 1$	$a^0 = 1$, for $a \neq 0$
$4^{-3} = \frac{1}{4^3}$	$a^{-n} = \frac{1}{a^n}$, for $a \neq 0$

Universal Access Solutions for All Learners

Special Needs L1
Students may need to review the rules for raising negative numbers to even and odd powers. Point out that negative numbers are also classified as even and odd. Thus, for example, $(-2)^{-2} = \frac{1}{4}$, while $(-2)^{-3} = -\frac{1}{8}$.

Below Level L2
When simplifying negative powers, students can break down the rule $a^{-n} = \frac{1}{a^n}$ into two steps:
1. Simplify a^n.
2. Write $\frac{1}{a^n}$.

EXAMPLE Simplifying Exponents

Relate MATH YOU KNOW... ...*to* NEW IDEAS

Simplify 10^6.

$10^6 = 10 \cdot 10 \cdot 10 \cdot 10 \cdot 10 \cdot 10$ ← The base is 10.
$= 1{,}000{,}000$ ← Simplify.

1 Guided Problem Solving A bacterium spore is about 10^{-6} m wide. Simplify 10^{-6}.

$10^{-6} = \frac{1}{10^6}$ ← Use the rule for negative exponents.
$= \frac{1}{1{,}000{,}000}$ ← Simplify the denominator.

CA Standards Check 1 *Go to your* **Math Companion** *for help.*

1. Simplify each expression.
   a. $(-2)^0$ 1
   b. 7^{-1} $\frac{1}{7}$

Recall that dividing by a number is the same as multiplying by the multiplicative inverse. So, you can use negative exponents to represent repeated multiplication by the multiplicative inverse of a number.

$$6^{-3} = \frac{1}{6^3} = \frac{1}{6} \cdot \frac{1}{6} \cdot \frac{1}{6}$$

$\frac{1}{6}$ is the multiplicative inverse of 6.

You can use multiplicative inverses to simplify fractions with negative exponents.

EXAMPLE Fractions and Negative Exponents

Vocabulary Tip

Remember that the multiplicative inverse of a number is its reciprocal.

2 Simplify $\left(\frac{2}{3}\right)^{-3}$.

$\left(\frac{2}{3}\right)^{-3} = \frac{3}{2} \cdot \frac{3}{2} \cdot \frac{3}{2}$ ← The multiplicative inverse of $\frac{2}{3}$ is $\frac{3}{2}$.
$= \frac{27}{8}$ ← Multiply.
$= 3\frac{3}{8}$ ← Simplify.

CA Standards Check 2 *Go to your* **Math Companion** *for help.*

2. Simplify each expression.
   a. $\left(\frac{1}{7}\right)^{-2}$ 49
   b. $\left(\frac{3}{5}\right)^{-4}$ $7\frac{58}{81}$

Check Your Understanding *Homework prep is in your* **Math Companion.**

2. Teach

Guided Instruction

Error Prevention!

Remind students that if $a \neq 0$, then $a^0 = 1$, not $a^0 = 0$.

Emphasize the fact that a negative power of a positive number is always positive. The sign of a negative power of a negative number depends on whether the exponent is even or odd.

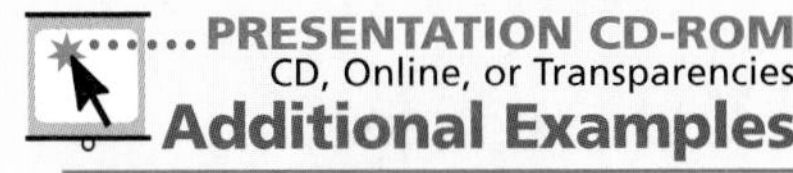

Additional Examples

1. Simplify $(-4)^{-3}$. $-\frac{1}{64}$
2. Simplify $\left(\frac{2}{3}\right)^{-5}$. $7\frac{19}{32}$

Closure

- *What is the value of any nonzero number with a zero exponent?* 1
- *How do you represent repeated multiplication of the multiplicative inverse of a number?* with a negative exponent

Advanced Learners L4	**English Learners** EL
Students compare the values of $-x^0$ and $(-x)^0$, where $x \neq 0$. −1 and 1	In Example 1, students may read 10^{-6} as 10 − 6 or 10(−6). Have them read the problem aloud and write out "ten to the negative six." They can practice by saying and writing out other expressions in words before simplifying.

3. Practice

Assignment Guide

Check Your Understanding
See Math Companion.

Homework Exercises
A Practice by Example 1–27
B Apply Your Skills 28–46
C Challenge 47
California Multiple-Choice Practice 48–50
Mixed Review 51–53

Homework Quick Check
To check students' understanding of key skills and concepts, go over Exercises.

Universal Access Resources

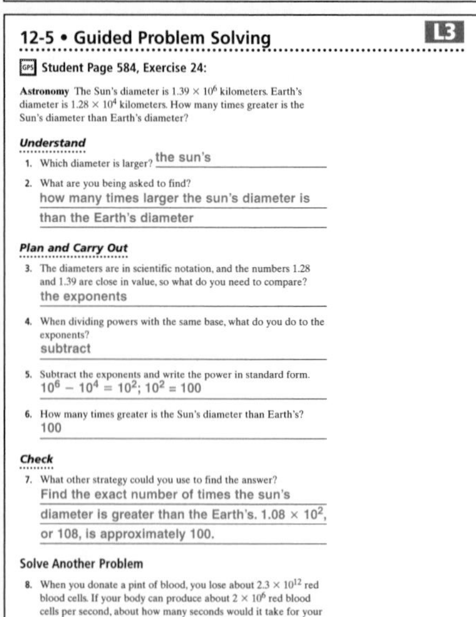
Adapted Practice 5-7 L1

Practice 12-5 Exponents and ... L3

12-5 • Guided Problem Solving L3

Student Page 584, Exercise 24:

Astronomy The Sun's diameter is 1.39×10^6 kilometers. Earth's diameter is 1.28×10^4 kilometers. How many times greater is the Sun's diameter than Earth's diameter?

Understand

1. Which diameter is larger? the sun's
2. What are you being asked to find? how many times larger the sun's diameter is than the Earth's diameter

Plan and Carry Out

3. The diameters are in scientific notation, and the numbers 1.28 and 1.39 are close in value, so what do you need to compare? the exponents
4. When dividing powers with the same base, what do you do to the exponents? subtract
5. Subtract the exponents and write the power in standard form. $10^6 - 10^4 = 10^2$; $10^2 = 100$
6. How many times greater is the Sun's diameter than Earth's? 100

Check

7. What other strategy could you use to find the answer? Find the exact number of times the sun's diameter is greater than the Earth's. 1.08×10^2, or 108, is approximately 100.

Solve Another Problem

8. When you donate a pint of blood, you lose about 2.3×10^{12} red blood cells. If your body can produce about 2×10^6 red blood cells per second, about how many seconds would it take for your body to replenish the red blood cells lost through donation? Write your answer in standard form. $10^{12} \div 10^6 = 10^6$; $10^6 = 1{,}000{,}000$ s

Standards Practice

GO for Help: MathXL

NS 2.1, AF 2.1

A Practice by Example

Example 1 (page 203)

Simplify each expression.

1. 8^{-4} $\frac{1}{4{,}096}$

$8^{-4} = \frac{1}{8^4}$

Guided Practice: This exercise has been started for you!

GO for Help

2. 4^0 1
3. y^{-12} $\frac{1}{y^{12}}$
4. 7^{-1} $\frac{1}{7}$
5. u^0 1
6. 15^{-2} $\frac{1}{225}$
7. 243^0 1
8. 6^{-3} $\frac{1}{216}$
9. 1^{-5} 1
10. 120^{-1} $\frac{1}{120}$
11. 0.5^0 1
12. 0.25^{-1} 4
13. 2.5^{-2} $\frac{4}{25}$
14. A nanometer is equal to 10^{-9} m. Simplify 10^{-9}. $\frac{1}{1{,}000{,}000{,}000}$

Example 2 (page 203)

Simplify each expression.

15. $\left(\frac{5}{8}\right)^{-4}$ $\frac{4{,}096}{625}$

$\left(\frac{5}{8}\right)^{-4} = \frac{8}{5} \cdot \frac{8}{5} \cdot \frac{8}{5} \cdot \frac{8}{5}$

Guided Practice: This exercise has been started for you!

Homework Video Tutor

For: Examples 1–2
Visit: PHSchool.com
Web Code: axe-0507

16. $\left(\frac{1}{2}\right)^{-6}$ 64
17. $\left(\frac{5}{12}\right)^{0}$ 1
18. $\left(\frac{3}{5}\right)^{-3}$ $\frac{125}{27}$
19. $\left(-\frac{2}{3}\right)^{-5}$ $\frac{243}{32}$
20. $\left(\frac{1}{8}\right)^{-2}$ 64
21. $\left(\frac{9}{20}\right)^{-3}$ $\frac{8{,}000}{729}$
22. $\left(\frac{6}{11}\right)^{0}$ 1
23. $\left(\frac{1}{7}\right)^{-3}$ 343
24. $-\left(\frac{10}{9}\right)^{-2}$ $-\frac{81}{100}$
25. $\left(\frac{8}{5}\right)^{-3}$ $\frac{125}{512}$
26. $\left(-\frac{8}{15}\right)^{-1}$ $-\frac{15}{8}$
27. $\left(-\frac{2}{5}\right)^{-4}$ $\frac{625}{16}$

B Apply Your Skills

28. **Guided Problem Solving** A spider web preserved in amber has strands that are 1.9 micrometers wide. A micrometer is 10^{-6} m. Write $1.9 \cdot 10^{-6}$ as a decimal. 0.0000019
   - Using the order of operations, which part of the expression should you simplify first?

Writing in Math **Is the statement true or false? Explain.**

29. $4^0 = 4^{-1}$ false; $4^0 = 1$ and $4^{-1} = \frac{1}{4}$
30. $8^{-1} = (-8)^1$ false; $8^{-1} = \frac{1}{8}$ and $(-8)^1 = -8$
31. $2^1 \cdot 2^{-1} = 2^0$ See left.
32. $(-2)^{-1} = 2$ false; $(-2)^{-1} = -\frac{1}{2}$

31. true; $2^1 \cdot 2^{-1} = 2 \cdot \frac{1}{2} = 1$ and $2^0 = 1$

GPS 33. **Error Analysis** A student simplified $2^{-2} \cdot (-3)^4$ as shown below. Find the student's error and simplify the expression correctly.

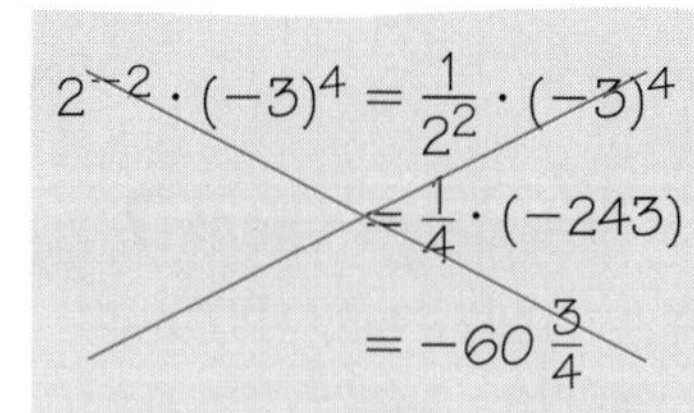

$2^{-2} \cdot (-3)^4 = \frac{1}{2^2} \cdot (-3)^4$
$= \frac{1}{4} \cdot (-243)$
$= -60\frac{3}{4}$

The student incorrectly simplified $(-3)^4$ to be -243; $2^{-2} \cdot (-3)^4 = \frac{1}{2^2} \cdot (-3)^4 = \frac{1}{4} \cdot 81 = 20\frac{1}{4}$

SCAFFOLDED
Problem Solving

34. Find 4^2. 16

35. Find 4^{-2}. $\frac{1}{16}$

36. Simplify $4^2 \cdot 4^{-2}$. 1

37. Simplify $6^3 \cdot 6^{-3}$. 1

38. **Patterns** Use inductive reasoning to make a conjecture about the relationship between a^n and a^{-n}. $a^n \cdot a^{-n} = 1$

39. Does your conjecture hold true for 2^5 and 2^{-5}? yes

Simplify each expression.

40. $3 \cdot 4^5 - 6^{-2}$ $3{,}071\frac{35}{36}$

41. $12 - 4^{-4} \cdot 5$ $11\frac{251}{256}$

42. $17^0 \cdot 3^{-2} + 16$ $16\frac{1}{9}$

43. $6^{-3} \div \frac{2}{3}$ $\frac{1}{144}$

44. $\left(\frac{1}{3}\right)^{-5} - 4^2$ 227

45. $9^2 \cdot 4^0 + \left(-\frac{3}{4}\right)^{-3}$ $78\frac{17}{27}$

46. Evaluate the expression $4r^2s^{-4}t^{-2}$ for $r = 9$, $s = 2$, and $t = -3$. 2.25 or $2\frac{1}{4}$

C Challenge

47. For which values of a does $\frac{a^5}{a^2} = a^3$? Explain. See above left.

47. Any value of a where $a \neq 0$; if you simplify $\frac{a \cdot a \cdot a \cdot a \cdot a}{a \cdot a}$, you get a^3.

Multiple Choice Practice and Mixed Review

For California Standards Tutorials, visit PHSchool.com. Web Code: axq-9045

AF 2.1

48. Which expression is equivalent to $\left(\frac{6}{7}\right)^{-4}$? B

   (A) $\frac{6}{7} \cdot \frac{6}{7} \cdot \frac{6}{7} \cdot \frac{6}{7}$
   (B) $\frac{7}{6} \cdot \frac{7}{6} \cdot \frac{7}{6} \cdot \frac{7}{6}$
   (C) $\frac{6}{7} \div \frac{6}{7} \div \frac{6}{7} \div \frac{6}{7}$
   (D) $\frac{7}{6} \div \frac{7}{6} \div \frac{7}{6} \div \frac{7}{6}$

NS 1.2, MR 2.4

49. Look for a pattern in the table at the right. Based on the pattern in the table, what value of x makes the statement $4^{15} = 2^x$ true? D

Powers of 4	Powers of 2
$4^2 = 16$	$2^4 = 16$
$4^3 = 64$	$2^6 = 64$
$4^4 = 256$	$2^8 = 256$
$4^5 = 1{,}024$	$2^{10} = 1{,}024$

   (A) 7.5
   (B) 15
   (C) 20
   (D) 30

AF 4.1

50. A company finds the cost c to install rain gutters on a house using the equation $c = 70 + 2n$, where n represents the number of feet of gutters needed. If the cost was \$262, how many feet of gutters were needed? B

   (A) 61 ft
   (B) 96 ft
   (C) 166 ft
   (D) 594 ft

Lesson 5-6

Solve each equation.

51. $\frac{3}{5}d = 27$ 45

52. $16 = \frac{4}{7}m$ 28

53. $\frac{11}{13}r = \frac{99}{100}$ $1\frac{17}{100}$

Online Lesson Quiz Visit: PHSchool.com **Web Code:** axa-0507

205

Alternative Assessment

Students work in pairs. One partner writes an integer a and a fraction b. The other partner writes a negative even integer m and a negative odd integer n. The partners work together to find the values of a^0, b^0, a^m, b^m, a^n, and b^n.

California Resources

Standards Mastery
- Standards Review Transparencies
- Standards Review and Practice Workbook
- Math Companion

Math Intervention
- Skills Review and Practice Workbook
- Math XL

4. Assess & Reteach

PRESENTATION CD-ROM
CD, Online, or Transparencies
Lesson Quiz

Simplify each expression.

1. 6^0 1

2. 4^{-2} $\frac{1}{16}$

3. $\left(\frac{1}{3}\right)^{-4}$ 81

4. $\left(-\frac{3}{7}\right)^{-3}$ $-12\frac{19}{27}$

5. $7^0 \times 5^3 + \left(-\frac{2}{3}\right)^{-2}$ $127\frac{1}{4}$

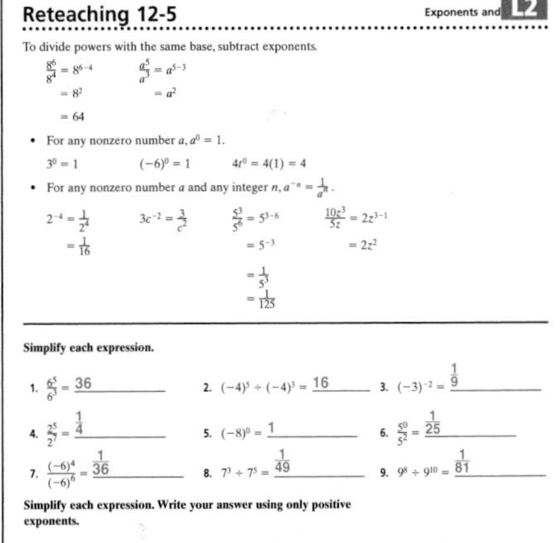

Reteaching 12-5 Exponents and L2

To divide powers with the same base, subtract exponents.

$\frac{8^6}{8^4} = 8^{6-4} = 8^2 = 64$ $\quad \frac{a^5}{a^3} = a^{5-3} = a^2$

- For any nonzero number a, $a^0 = 1$.

$3^0 = 1$ $\quad (-6)^0 = 1$ $\quad 4t^0 = 4(1) = 4$

- For any nonzero number a and any integer n, $a^{-n} = \frac{1}{a^n}$.

$2^{-4} = \frac{1}{2^4} = \frac{1}{16}$ $\quad 3c^{-2} = \frac{3}{c^2}$ $\quad \frac{5^3}{5^6} = 5^{3-6} = 5^{-3} = \frac{1}{5^3} = \frac{1}{125}$ $\quad \frac{10z^3}{5z} = 2z^{3-1} = 2z^2$

Simplify each expression.

1. $\frac{6^5}{6^3} =$ 36
2. $(-4)^5 \div (-4)^3 =$ 16
3. $(-3)^{-2} =$ $\frac{1}{9}$
4. $\frac{2^5}{2^7} =$ $\frac{1}{4}$
5. $(-8)^0 =$ 1
6. $\frac{5^0}{5^2} =$ $\frac{1}{25}$
7. $\frac{(-6)^4}{(-6)^6} =$ $\frac{1}{36}$
8. $7^3 \div 7^5 =$ $\frac{1}{49}$
9. $9^8 \div 9^{10} =$ $\frac{1}{81}$

Simplify each expression. Write your answer using only positive exponents.

10. $w^8 \div w^3 =$ w^5
11. $x^6 \div x^1 =$ x^5
12. $\frac{d^7}{d^3} =$ d^4
13. $\frac{w^2}{w^6} =$ $\frac{1}{w^4}$
14. $4c^5 \div c^8 =$ $\frac{4}{c^3}$
15. $\frac{8x^2}{4x^5} =$ $\frac{2}{x^3}$
16. $8a^4 \div 2a^2 =$ $4a^2$
17. $6w^2 \div 2w^5 =$ $\frac{3}{w^3}$
18. $\frac{6x^6}{3x^9} =$ $\frac{2}{x^3}$

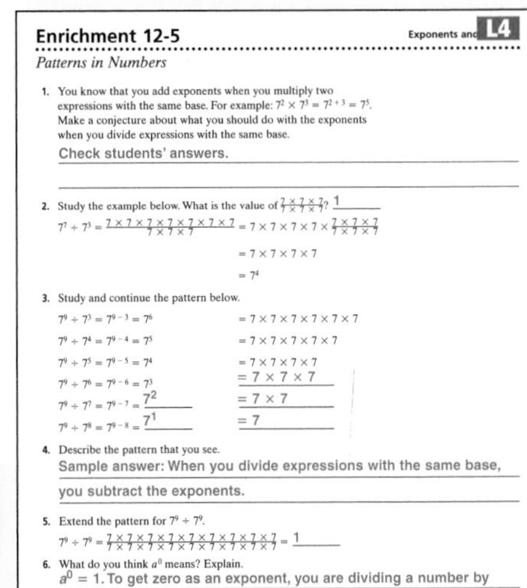

Enrichment 12-5 Exponents and L4

Patterns in Numbers

1. You know that you add exponents when you multiply two expressions with the same base. For example: $7^2 \times 7^3 = 7^{2+3} = 7^5$. Make a conjecture about what you should do with the exponents when you divide expressions with the same base.
   Check students' answers.

2. Study the example below. What is the value of $\frac{7 \times 7 \times 7}{7 \times 7 \times 7}$? 1
   $7^7 \div 7^3 = \frac{7 \times 7 \times 7 \times 7 \times 7 \times 7 \times 7}{7 \times 7 \times 7} = 7 \times 7 \times 7 \times 7 \times \frac{7 \times 7 \times 7}{7 \times 7 \times 7} = 7 \times 7 \times 7 \times 7 = 7^4$

3. Study and continue the pattern below.
   $7^9 \div 7^3 = 7^{9-3} = 7^6$ $\quad = 7 \times 7 \times 7 \times 7 \times 7 \times 7$
   $7^9 \div 7^4 = 7^{9-4} = 7^5$ $\quad = 7 \times 7 \times 7 \times 7 \times 7$
   $7^9 \div 7^5 = 7^{9-5} = 7^4$ $\quad = 7 \times 7 \times 7 \times 7$
   $7^9 \div 7^6 = 7^{9-6} = 7^3$ $\quad = 7 \times 7 \times 7$
   $7^9 \div 7^7 = 7^{9-7} = 7^2$ $\quad = 7 \times 7$
   $7^9 \div 7^8 = 7^{9-8} = 7^1$ $\quad = 7$

4. Describe the pattern that you see.
   Sample answer: When you divide expressions with the same base, you subtract the exponents.

5. Extend the pattern for $7^9 \div 7^9$.
   $7^9 \div 7^9 = \frac{7 \times 7 \times 7 \times 7 \times 7 \times 7 \times 7 \times 7 \times 7}{7 \times 7 \times 7 \times 7 \times 7 \times 7 \times 7 \times 7 \times 7} =$ 1

6. What do you think a^0 means? Explain.
   $a^0 = 1$. To get zero as an exponent, you are dividing a number by itself, such as $7^9 \div 7^9 = 7^{9-9} = 7^0 = 1$.

Activity Lab

Expanded Notation

Students learn to use expanded notation to show the place value of each digit in a number. Because numbers in expanded notation are written with exponents and powers of ten, students may find expanded notation convenient and easier when they have especially large or small numbers to multiply.

Guided Instruction

Make a table on the board to show students how expanded notation relates to place value. Work the Example and the first few Exercises with students and place them in the table. Line up each Exercise according to its place value so that all terms with 10^3 are in one column, all terms with 10^2 in the next, all terms with 10^1 in the next, and so on. Then label the table with the names for the place values: thousands, hundreds, tens, ones, etc.

Error Prevention!

Remind students of the meaning of a zero exponent. Have them work out $3 \times 10^0 = 3 \times 1 = 3$ to check their reasoning.

5-7b Activity Lab

Expanded Notation

Foundational Standard Use expanded notation to represent numbers.
AF 2.1 Simplify and evaluate expressions that include exponents.
Develop

Standard notation of numbers uses digits and place value. *Expanded notation* uses a sum to show the place value of each digit in a number. Expanded notation may also be called *expanded form.*

You can use exponents and powers of ten to write numbers in expanded notation. The number 287 is shown below in both standard and expanded notation.

Standard Notation	Expanded Notation
287	$(2 \cdot 10^2) + (8 \cdot 10^1) + (7 \cdot 10^0)$

EXAMPLE

Use expanded notation to write 23.472.

$23.472 = 20 + 3 + 0.4 + 0.07 + 0.002$ ← **First write out the place value of each digit.**

$= (2 \cdot 10) + (3 \cdot 1) + (4 \cdot 0.1) + (7 \cdot 0.01) + (2 \cdot 0.001)$ ← **Write each digit using a multiple of 10.**

$= (2 \cdot 10^1) + (3 \cdot 10^0) + (4 \cdot 10^{-1}) + (7 \cdot 10^{-2}) + (2 \cdot 10^{-3})$ ← **Use an exponent to write each multiple of 10 as a power.**

Exercises

Use expanded notation to write each number. 1–8. See margin.

1. 679
2. 43.67
3. 1,206.4
4. 9.03
5. 6.2367
6. 4,537.12
7. 0.731
8. 300.001

9. Write $(2 \cdot 10^3) + (1 \cdot 10^2) + (5 \cdot 10^1) + (6 \cdot 10^{-2})$ in standard notation. 2,150.06

Write each decimal in standard notation and expanded notation. 10–14. See right.

10. forty and nine thousandths
11. six hundred four millionths
12. The diameter of a white blood cell measures twelve ten-thousandths of a centimeter.
13. A marathon race is twenty-six and two tenths miles long.
14. **a.** Evaluate $3x^3 + 4x^2 + x + 3$ for $x = 10$.
    b. Reasoning How is this expression similar to expanded notation?

10. 40.009; $(4 \cdot 10^1) + (9 \cdot 10^{-3})$
11. 0.000604; $(6 \cdot 10^{-4}) + (4 \cdot 10^{-6})$
12. 0.0012; $(1 \cdot 10^{-3}) + (2 \cdot 10^{-4})$
13. 26.2; $(2 \cdot 10^1) + (6 \cdot 10^0) + (2 \cdot 10^{-1})$

14a. 3,413
b. The digits of the number are the same as the numbers multiplied by x in the expression.

Eliminating Answers

In a multiple-choice problem, you can often eliminate some of the answer choices.

EXAMPLE

A plant that you bought two years ago is 3 ft 2 in. tall. It was 1 ft 11 in. tall when you bought it. How many inches has the plant grown since you bought it?

Ⓐ 3 in. Ⓑ 11 in. Ⓒ 15 in. Ⓓ 61 in.

The plant is only 3 ft 2 in. tall. So it could not have grown 61 in. Eliminate choice D.

3 ft 2 in. is about 3 ft, and 1 ft 11 in. is about 2 ft. So the plant has grown about 1 ft, or 12 in. Eliminate choice A, which is much less than the estimate.

11 in. is less than 1 ft. So 11 in. + 1 ft 11 in. is less than 3 ft 2 in. Eliminate choice B.

The correct answer is choice C.

Multiple Choice Practice

Identify two choices that you can easily eliminate. Explain why. Then solve the problem.

NS 1.2 

1. A truck is carrying a load that weighs $15\frac{3}{5}$ t. The total weight of the truck and the load is $36\frac{1}{2}$ t. How many tons does the truck weigh? B

   Ⓐ $14\frac{9}{10}$ Ⓑ $20\frac{9}{10}$ Ⓒ $21\frac{1}{10}$ Ⓓ $52\frac{1}{10}$

NS 1.2

2. The height of a door is 86 in. A person standing in the doorway is 53 in. tall. Find the approximate distance in feet between the person's head and the top of the door. C

   Ⓐ 1 ft Ⓑ 2 ft Ⓒ 3 ft Ⓓ 4 ft

NS 2.1

3. A cell measures 10^{-5} mm in length. Which number represents this length as a decimal? B

   Ⓐ −50 Ⓑ 0.00001 Ⓒ 50 Ⓓ 100,000

Test-Taking Strategies

Eliminating Answers

This strategy alerts students to the fact that multiple-choice questions often have one or more answer choices that can be quickly discarded because they are unreasonable.

Guided Instruction

Emphasize that by eliminating unreasonable answers, students can greatly improve their chances on a multiple-choice test question. On tests that do not penalize incorrect answers, eliminating unreasonable answers to a question right away can improve students' chances when they have time left only to make a sensible guess.

Chapter 5 Review

California Resources

Standards Mastery
- Math Companion
- Standards Review Transparencies
- Standards Review and Practice Workbook
- Progress Monitoring Assessments

Math Intervention
- Skills Review and Practice Workbook
- Math XL

Universal Access Resources
- Student Workbook
  - Vocabulary and Study Skills
  - Guided Problem Solving
- All-in-One Teaching Resources
  - Reteaching
  - Enrichment
- Spanish Practice Workbook L3
- Spanish Vocabulary and Study Skills 2A-F L3
- English/Spanish Glossary EL
- Multilingual Handbook EL
- Interactive Textbook Audio Glossary
- Online Vocabulary Quiz

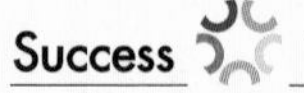

Online at PHSchool.com

Spanish Vocabulary/Study Skills EL

Vocabulary/Study Skills L3

6F: Vocabulary Review For use with the Chapter Review

Study Skill Take notes while you study. They will provide you with a helpful outline when you study for a quiz or test.

Complete the crossword puzzle. For help, use the glossary in your textbook.

ACROSS
1. a fraction whose numerator is greater than or equal to its denominator
3. a number that makes an equation true
5. fractions or decimals that name the same amount
7. a number that can be used to indicate part of a whole
9. a whole number greater than one with more than two factors
11. the top number in a fraction

DOWN
2. a whole number with only two factors—one and itself
4. factors that are the same for two or more numbers
6. one of two numbers whose product is 1
8. operations that undo one another
10. the bottom number in a fraction

Vocabulary Review

English and Spanish Audio Online

multiplicative inverse (p. 196)
reciprocal (p. 186)

Academic Vocabulary
benchmark (p. 175)
notation (p. 206)

Choose the correct vocabulary term to complete each sentence.

1. Two numbers whose product is 1 are called (opposites, reciprocals). reciprocals
2. The (multiplicative inverse, additive inverse) of 4 is $\frac{1}{4}$. multiplicative inverse
3. A(n) (exponent, reciprocal) tells how many times a base is used as a factor. exponent

PHSchool.com

For: Vocabulary Quiz
Visit: PHSchool.com
Web Code: axj-0551

Skills and Concepts

Lessons 5-1, 5-2
- To add rational numbers
- To subtract rational numbers

NS 1.2, NS 1.3, NS 1.5

To add or subtract fractions, write each fraction using a common denominator. Then add or subtract the numerators. To find a common denominator, you can multiply the denominators or you can use the least common denominator (LCD).

Find each sum or difference. Write your answer in simplest form.

4. $\frac{2}{5} + \frac{3}{5}$ 1
5. $-\frac{7}{8} - \frac{3}{4}$ $-\frac{13}{8}$ or $-1\frac{5}{8}$
6. $\frac{17}{24} - \left(-\frac{1}{6}\right)$ $\frac{7}{8}$
7. $5.6 + 2\frac{1}{3}$ $7\frac{14}{15}$
8. $-2\frac{4}{5} - \left(-1\frac{3}{10}\right)$ $-1\frac{1}{2}$
9. $\frac{12}{20} + 1.25 + 6.6$ 8.45 or $8\frac{9}{20}$
10. You rode your bicycle $\frac{2}{3}$ mi to school and $\frac{1}{5}$ mi to a friend's house. How far did you ride your bicycle? $\frac{13}{15}$ mi

Lesson 5-3
- To multiply rational numbers and raise fractions to positive whole-number powers

NS 1.2, AF 2.1

To multiply fractions, multiply the numerators and then multiply the denominators. To raise a fraction to a power, raise the numerator and the denominator to the power.

Find each product. Write your answer in simplest form.

11. $\frac{1}{2} \cdot \frac{3}{5}$ $\frac{3}{10}$
12. $\left(-\frac{12}{13}\right) \cdot \frac{1}{18}$ $-\frac{2}{39}$
13. $\frac{7}{9} \cdot 5\frac{1}{6}$ $4\frac{1}{54}$

Simplify each expression.

14. $\left(\frac{3}{10}\right)^6$ $\frac{729}{1{,}000{,}000}$
15. $\left(-\frac{1}{2}\right)^9$ $-\frac{1}{512}$
16. $\left(\frac{8}{15}\right)^2$ $\frac{64}{225}$
17. A recipe for fruit salad calls for $\frac{2}{3}$ c peaches. How many cups of peaches do you need to make $\frac{1}{2}$ of the original recipe? $\frac{1}{3}$ c

Lesson 5-4

- To find reciprocals and divide rational numbers

NS 1.2, NS 1.5, Alg1 2.0

Two numbers are **reciprocals** if their product is 1. The numbers $\frac{2}{3}$ and $\frac{3}{2}$ are reciprocals, as are $\frac{1}{5}$ and 5. To divide by a fraction, multiply by the reciprocal of the fraction.

Find the reciprocal of each number.

18. 9 $\frac{1}{9}$ 19. $\frac{7}{12}$ $\frac{12}{7}$ 20. $\frac{10}{17}$ $\frac{17}{10}$ 21. $\frac{1}{3}$ 3

Find each quotient. Write your answer in simplest form.

22. $8 \div \frac{1}{2}$ 16
23. $\frac{3}{11} \div \frac{3}{5}$ $\frac{5}{11}$
24. $\left(-\frac{18}{25}\right) \div 4\frac{2}{5}$ $-\frac{9}{55}$
25. $-3\frac{1}{2} \div -\frac{7}{8}$ 4

Lessons 5-5, 5-6

- To solve addition and subtraction equations with fractions
- To solve multiplication and division equations with fractions

AF 1.1, AF 1.3, AF 4.1

You can use properties of numbers to solve equations involving fractions. To solve equations in which a variable is multiplied by a fraction, multiply both sides of the equation by the **multiplicative inverse** of the fraction.

Solve each equation.

26. $\frac{5}{7} = p + \frac{2}{7}$ $\frac{3}{7}$
27. $q - 2\frac{1}{6} = 8\frac{8}{9}$ $11\frac{1}{18}$
28. $13\frac{3}{5} + h = 20$ $6\frac{2}{5}$
29. $\frac{5}{6}z = 3\frac{1}{3}$ 4
30. $\frac{4}{5}w = 1\frac{3}{5}$ 2
31. $3.5 + \frac{2}{3}a = 4\frac{4}{5}$ $1\frac{19}{20}$
32. A carpenter cuts a $7\frac{1}{2}$-ft board into $2\frac{1}{2}$-ft pieces. Write and solve an equation to find how many pieces the carpenter has. 3 pieces

Lesson 5-7

- To simplify and evaluate expressions with zero and negative exponents

NS 2.1, AF 2.1

You can use negative exponents to represent repeated division or repeated multiplication by the multiplicative inverse. For any nonzero number a, $a^{-n} = \frac{1}{a^n}$. Any number raised to the zero power equals 1.

Simplify each expression.

33. 5^{-6} $\frac{1}{15{,}625}$
34. $(-4)^{-6}$ $\frac{1}{4{,}096}$
35. 7^0 1
36. -3^{-3} $-\frac{1}{27}$
37. 19^0 1
38. 12^{-2} $\frac{1}{144}$
39. $\left(\frac{3}{5}\right)^{-4}$ $7\frac{58}{81}$
40. $\left(\frac{15}{25}\right)^0$ 1
41. $(-10)^{-9}$ $-\frac{1}{1{,}000{,}000{,}000}$
42. $\left(\frac{1}{8}\right)^{-2}$ 64
43. $4.5 + 6^{-2}$ $4\frac{19}{36}$
44. $(-3)^{-1} \cdot 7$ $-2\frac{1}{3}$

Alternative Assessment L4

Alternative Assessment Form C

Chapter 5

WORLD RECORDS

The Guinness Book of Records describes itself as "the world's most complete collection of astonishing authenticated facts and figures from around the globe."

Some records concern things that are especially large or small. For example, the world's largest dog is an Old English mastiff that weighs 343 pounds, stands 37 inches tall at the shoulder, and is 8 feet $3\frac{1}{4}$ inches long. The world's smallest dog is a miniature Yorkshire terrier that weighs 4 ounces, stands $2\frac{1}{2}$ inches tall, and is $3\frac{3}{4}$ inches long.

Show all of your work on a separate sheet of paper.

1. Using the numbers above, determine how much heavier, taller, and longer the mastiff is than the terrier. Show your work.
2. Some records concern things that people have done especially to get in the record books. For example, Reg Morris holds the world's crawling record. He crawled $28\frac{1}{2}$ miles on a measured course $1\frac{1}{2}$ miles long. To set the record, he crawled without stopping for $9\frac{1}{2}$ hours.

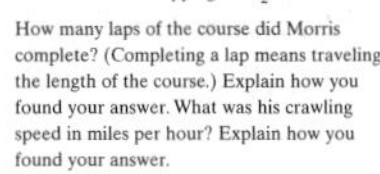

How many laps of the course did Morris complete? (Completing a lap means traveling the length of the course.) Explain how you found your answer. What was his crawling speed in miles per hour? Explain how you found your answer.

Spanish Quarter 2 Test—Forms A, B EL

Quarter 2 Test—Forms D, E L2

Quarter 2 Test—Forms A, B L3

Quarter 2 Test Form A

Chapters 4–6

1. Use mental math to determine whether 22,645 is divisible by 9.
2. Use a factor tree to find the prime factorization of 120. Write your answer using exponents.
3. Find the GCF of 24, 72, and 96.
4. If you were to plot the fractions $\frac{3}{12}$ and $\frac{1}{4}$ on the same number line, where would they be in relation to each other?
5. Write a fraction with a denominator of 18 that is equivalent to $\frac{2}{3}$.
6. Write $\frac{41}{6}$ as a mixed number.
7. Find the LCM of 18 and 30.
8. Order the mixed numbers from least to greatest. $3\frac{4}{5}, 3\frac{8}{15}, 3\frac{1}{3}$
9. Fill in the __?__ with <, >, or =. $\frac{23}{9}$ __?__ $2\frac{10}{18}$
10. Write 0.135 as a fraction in simplest form.
11. Write $6\frac{7}{20}$ as a decimal.
12. Write six and two fifths as a decimal.
13. The sum of two decimals is 1.2. One of the decimals is twice the other. What are the two decimals?
14. Round $11\frac{7}{12}$ to the nearest whole number.
15. Estimate $7\frac{3}{4} + 9\frac{1}{12}$ by first rounding to the nearest whole number.
16. Add. Write your answer in simplest form. $\frac{3}{20} + \frac{7}{20} - \frac{2}{20}$
17. Explain how you would add the fractions $\frac{1}{2}$ and $\frac{3}{4}$.
18. Sean rode his bicycle $4\frac{1}{2}$ miles on Saturday and $5\frac{2}{3}$ miles on Sunday. How many miles did he ride during the weekend?
19. Add. Write your answer in simplest form. $11\frac{1}{2} + 3\frac{3}{4} + 6\frac{1}{3}$
20. There are two boards leaning against the wall. The first board is $3\frac{2}{5}$ meters long and the second is $4\frac{1}{4}$ meters long. How much longer is the second board?

California Resources

Standards Mastery
- Teacher Center ExamView CD-ROM
- Math XL
- Progress Monitoring Assessments
- Online Chapter Test at PHSchool.com

Math Intervention
- Skills Review and Practice Workbook

Online at PHSchool.com

Universal Access Resources
- Chapter Test
- Alternative Assessment
- Spanish Chapter Test
- Spanish Alternative Assessment
- Teacher Center ExamView CD-ROM
  - Special Needs Test
  - Special Needs Practice Banks
  - Foundational Standards Practice Banks
- Online Chapter Test at www.PHSchool.com
- All-In-One Teaching Resources
  - Cumulative Review L3
- Spanish Assessment Resources
  - Cumulative Review L3

Below Level Chapter Test L2

Chapter Test L3

Chapter Test — Form A

Chapter 6

Estimate each product or quotient.

1. $9\frac{2}{3} \times 2\frac{1}{5}$ 20
2. $11\frac{3}{4} \div 1\frac{5}{6}$ 6
3. $29\frac{7}{8} \div 5\frac{1}{6}$ 6
4. $4\frac{1}{8} \times 10\frac{2}{3}$ 44

Find each product or quotient.

5. $\frac{5}{9} \div \frac{5}{6}$ $\frac{2}{3}$
6. $\frac{2}{5}$ of 35 14
7. $1\frac{8}{11} \div \frac{1}{3}$ $5\frac{2}{11}$
8. $\frac{1}{2} \times \frac{3}{4}$ $\frac{3}{8}$
9. $2\frac{1}{5} \times 1\frac{1}{3}$ $2\frac{14}{15}$
10. $18 \div \frac{1}{8}$ 144
11. $7\frac{4}{5} \div 3$ $2\frac{3}{5}$
12. $3 \times 4\frac{5}{7}$ $14\frac{1}{7}$

Solve.

13. Kisha plans to double a recipe for cookies. The original recipe calls for $1\frac{3}{8}$ cups of flour. How much does she need for the doubled recipe? Write as a mixed number in simplest form. $2\frac{3}{4}$ cups
14. Sammy wants to make a half portion of a recipe that calls for $1\frac{1}{3}$ cups of milk. How much milk does she need for the half portion? $\frac{2}{3}$ cup
15. You want to cut a 10-foot board into $2\frac{1}{2}$-foot lengths. How many pieces will you have? 4 pieces

Match the object in the left column with the most appropriate unit of measurement in the right column.

16. length of a person's ear b
17. weight of an elephant a
18. amount of shampoo in a bottle c
19. length of an airport runway e
20. weight of a penny d
21. amount of water in a reflecting pool f

a. tons
b. inches
c. fluid ounces
d. ounces
e. miles
f. gallons

Chapter 5 Test

Go Online PHSchool.com — For: Online chapter test — Web Code: axa-0552

Find each sum or difference. Write your answer in simplest form.

1. $-\frac{3}{5} - \frac{1}{3}$ $-\frac{14}{15}$
2. $\frac{5}{12} + \frac{5}{9} + 0.5$ $1\frac{17}{36}$
3. $3\frac{1}{4} - 2\frac{2}{3}$ $\frac{7}{12}$
4. $23.25 + \frac{11}{12} + \frac{3}{4}$ $24\frac{11}{12}$
5. $\frac{6}{10} - \left(-\frac{1}{4}\right) + 19.7$ $20\frac{11}{20}$
6. $\frac{1}{5} - \frac{1}{3} - (-3.6)$ $3\frac{7}{15}$
7. You need $\frac{3}{8}$ ft of lumber to fix a fence and $\frac{3}{4}$ ft of lumber to fix a shed. How much lumber do you need? $1\frac{1}{8}$ ft
8. Daniella ran $\frac{5}{6}$ mi. Sol ran $\frac{7}{8}$ mi.
   a. How much farther than Daniella did Sol run? $\frac{1}{24}$ mi
   b. What was their combined distance? $1\frac{17}{24}$ mi
9. How much did Sophia's hair grow during the month of May? $\frac{3}{16}$ in.

Sophia's Hair Length

May 1	$8\frac{1}{8}$ in.
May 31	$8\frac{5}{16}$ in.

Find each product or quotient. Write your answer in simplest form.

10. $-2\frac{3}{4} \cdot \frac{8}{9}$ $-2\frac{4}{9}$
11. $\frac{3}{8} \cdot 32$ 12
12. $-\frac{2}{5} \div \frac{7}{20}$ $-1\frac{1}{7}$
13. $\frac{5}{6} \cdot \frac{12}{25}$ $\frac{2}{5}$
14. $\frac{5}{8} \div \left(-\frac{1}{2}\right) \cdot 3.2$ -4
15. $-1\frac{1}{4} \div \frac{5}{12} \div 2.5$ -1.2 or $-1\frac{1}{5}$
16. A log cabin has walls built with 12 logs stacked horizontally on top of one another. If each log is $\frac{3}{4}$ ft thick, how high is each wall? 9 ft
17. Jolene weighs 96 lb. Jolene's father weighs $1\frac{7}{8}$ times as much as she does. How much does her father weigh? 180 lb
18. A runner jogs on a $\frac{1}{4}$-mi track. How many miles does the runner jog in 18 laps? 4.5 mi

Simplify each expression.

19. $\left(\frac{2}{5}\right)^3$ $\frac{8}{125}$
20. $\left(\frac{1}{7}\right)^2$ $\frac{1}{49}$
21. $\left(\frac{3}{4}\right)^4$ $\frac{81}{256}$
22. $\left(\frac{1}{10}\right)^7$ $\frac{1}{10{,}000{,}000}$
23. $\left(\frac{3}{8}\right)^3$ $\frac{27}{512}$
24. $\left(\frac{2}{3}\right)^6$ $\frac{64}{729}$
25. A cube has sides of length $\frac{3}{5}$ cm. What is the volume of the cube? Use the formula $V = s^3$, where s is the length of each side. $\frac{27}{125}$ cm^3

Solve each equation.

26. $\frac{6}{9} = \frac{1}{3} + g$ $\frac{1}{3}$
27. $4\frac{3}{4} + v = 17\frac{1}{8}$ $12\frac{3}{8}$
28. $13\frac{2}{3} = k - 10\frac{7}{9}$ $24\frac{4}{9}$
29. $y - \frac{4}{5} = -\frac{11}{20}$ $\frac{1}{4}$
30. $\frac{1}{3}x = -30$ -90
31. $\frac{2}{3}c = \frac{7}{24}$ $\frac{7}{16}$
32. $-\frac{4}{5} = 14 + \frac{10}{12}z$ $-17\frac{19}{25}$
33. $\frac{3}{7}m - \frac{9}{10} = \frac{1}{6}$ $2\frac{22}{45}$
34. At a party, there are $1\frac{1}{3}$ times as many girls as there are boys. If there are 18 boys, how many people are at the party? 24 people
35. A white spruce tree cone is $3\frac{7}{8}$ in. shorter than a Norway spruce tree cone. A Norway spruce tree cone is $5\frac{1}{2}$ in. long. How long is the white spruce tree cone? $1\frac{5}{8}$ in.

Simplify each expression.

36. 2^0 1
37. 9^{-4} $\frac{1}{6{,}561}$
38. $\left(\frac{1}{4}\right)^{-5}$ 1,024
39. 10^{-5} $\frac{1}{100{,}000}$
40. $\left(\frac{15}{16}\right)^0$ 1
41. x^{-4} $\frac{1}{x^4}$
42. **Writing in Math** Write what you would say to a classmate who asked you to explain why 5^0 is equal to 1. See margin.
43. The wavelength of red light is $7.6 \cdot 10^{-7}$ m. Write this number as a decimal. 0.00000076

Cumulative Practice

Some questions require you to add, subtract, multiply, or divide rational numbers. Use the tips as guides for solving the problem at the right.

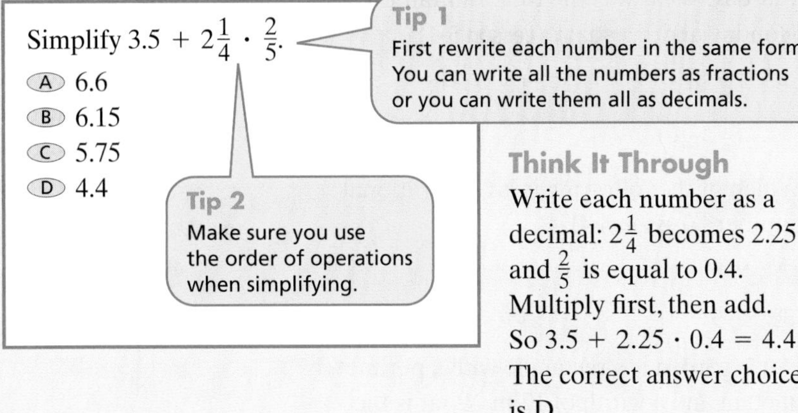

Simplify $3.5 + 2\frac{1}{4} \cdot \frac{2}{5}$.
A 6.6
B 6.15
C 5.75
D 4.4
Tip 1
First rewrite each number in the same form. You can write all the numbers as fractions or you can write them all as decimals.
Tip 2
Make sure you use the order of operations when simplifying.

Think It Through

Write each number as a decimal: $2\frac{1}{4}$ becomes 2.25 and $\frac{2}{5}$ is equal to 0.4. Multiply first, then add. So $3.5 + 2.25 \cdot 0.4 = 4.4$. The correct answer choice is D.

Vocabulary Review

As you solve problems, you must understand the meanings of mathematical terms. Match each term with its mathematical meaning.

- **A.** denominator V
- **B.** rational number I
- **C.** reciprocals IV
- **D.** isolate III
- **E.** multiplicative inverse II

- **I.** any number written as the quotient of two integers where the denominator is not zero
- **II.** also called the reciprocal of a number
- **III.** to get the variable alone on one side of an equation
- **IV.** two numbers whose product is 1
- **V.** the number on the bottom of a fraction

Read each question. Then write the letter of the correct answer on your paper.

1. Miles has $2\frac{1}{2}$ yd of fabric. He will use the fabric to make 3 pillows that require a total of $1\frac{1}{8}$ yd of fabric. How much fabric will Miles have left after making the pillows? (Lesson 5-2) C

- A 1 yd
- B $1\frac{1}{8}$ yd
- C $1\frac{3}{8}$ yd
- D $1\frac{3}{4}$ yd

2. A student is folding a square paper along the diagonal. Which formula can she use to find the length of the diagonal? (Lesson 3-6) B

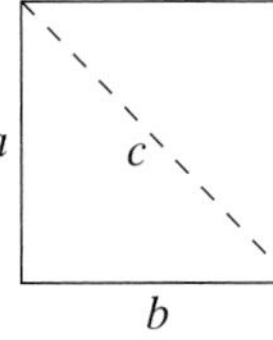

- A $a + b = c$
- B $a^2 + b^2 = c^2$
- C $a - b = c$
- D $a^2 - b^2 = c^2$

3. Simplify $\left(\frac{2}{3}\right)^4$. (Lesson 5-3) B

- A $\frac{2}{81}$
- B $\frac{16}{81}$
- C $\frac{8}{12}$
- D $\frac{16}{3}$

California Resources

Standards Mastery

- Teacher Center ExamView CD-ROM
- Math XL
- Progress Monitoring Assessments
- Online Chapter Test at PHSchool.com

Math Intervention

- Skills Review and Practice Workbook

Universal Access Resources

- Teacher Center ExamView CD-ROM
  - Special Needs Test
  - Special Needs Practice Banks
  - Foundational Standards Practice Banks
- Online Chapter Test at www.PHSchool.com
- All-In-One Teaching Resources
  - Cumulative Review L3
- Spanish Assessment Resources
  - Cumulative Review L3

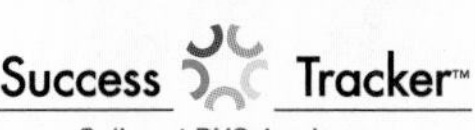

Online at PHSchool.com

4. It rained $3\frac{1}{8}$ in. on Monday and 4.75 in. on Tuesday. What was the total rainfall for Monday and Tuesday? (Lesson 5-1) A

   Ⓐ $7\frac{7}{8}$ in. Ⓑ $7\frac{1}{2}$ in. Ⓒ $7\frac{1}{8}$ in. Ⓓ 7 in.

5. Which of the following is NOT a rational number? (Lesson 4-4) D

   Ⓐ 9.3 Ⓑ $\sqrt{9}$ Ⓒ $\frac{9}{3}$ Ⓓ $\sqrt{3}$

6. Dan's garden is a rectangle with a perimeter of 60 m and a width of 12 m. What is the length of the garden? Use the formula $P = 2w + 2\ell$. (Lesson 3-4) B

   Ⓐ 5 m Ⓑ 18 m Ⓒ 24 m Ⓓ 36 m

7. The high and low temperatures for four cities in a particular month are shown in the table below. Which city had the greatest temperature change? (Lesson 2-3) A

Temperature Extremes

City	High (°F)	Low (°F)
Anchorage, Alaska	18	–12
Denver, Colorado	48	20
Rockland, Maine	22	–7
Amarillo, Texas	55	28

   Ⓐ Anchorage Ⓑ Denver Ⓒ Rockland Ⓓ Amarillo

8. A pet ID microchip can be as small as $2 \cdot 10^{-3}$ m in length. Which of the following is equivalent to $2 \cdot 10^{-3}$? (Lesson 5-7) B

   Ⓐ 0.0002 Ⓑ 0.002 Ⓒ 200 Ⓓ 2,000

9. Which property justifies the statement $\frac{1}{6} \cdot 6g = g$? (Lesson 5-6) C

   Ⓐ Associative Property of Multiplication
   Ⓑ Commutative Property of Multiplication
   Ⓒ Inverse Property of Multiplication
   Ⓓ Identity Property of Multiplication

10. Which fraction is equivalent to 0.375? (Lesson 4-4) B

    Ⓐ $\frac{1}{3}$ Ⓑ $\frac{3}{8}$ Ⓒ $\frac{3}{4}$ Ⓓ $\frac{5}{6}$

11. A pilot flies a plane 195 mi east from San Angelo to Waco, Texas. He then flies north 275 mi to Oklahoma City. About how far will he travel if he takes a direct route back to San Angelo? (Lesson 3-6) B

    Ⓐ 160 mi Ⓑ 337 mi Ⓒ 372 mi Ⓓ 470 mi

12. Kari solved the equation $\frac{3}{5} + 2d = 4\frac{1}{2}$. Which solution is reasonable? (Lesson 5-6) C

    Ⓐ 3.95 Ⓑ 2.95 Ⓒ 1.95 Ⓓ 0.95

13. Garrett buys a pair of shoes for $18. The price is $\frac{1}{4}$ off the original price. What decimal represents the discount? (Lesson 5-3) C

    Ⓐ 0.14 Ⓑ 0.20 Ⓒ 0.25 Ⓓ 0.40

14. Which of these is equivalent to the expression $5m \cdot 1$? (Lesson 1-5) C

    Ⓐ 1 Ⓑ 5 Ⓒ $5m$ Ⓓ $6m$

15. A chef's recipe for cooking ribs includes marinating the ribs for $2\frac{1}{3}$ h. Next he bakes the ribs for $6\frac{2}{3}$ h. Then he grills the ribs for 1.25 h. What is the total time the chef spends making ribs? (Lesson 5-1) C

    Ⓐ 9 h Ⓑ 9.25 h Ⓒ 10.25 h Ⓓ 10.75 h

Spanish Cumulative Review EL

Cumulative Review L3

Cumulative Review

Chapters 1–5

Multiple Choice. Choose the letter of the best answer.

1. You have a $10 bill and want to go to the movies for $5.50, buy popcorn for $2.45, and a drink for $1.95. How much change will you get?
   A. none
   B. $.10
   C. $.25
   D. $10 is not enough
2. Simplify $5 \cdot (9 + 8)$.
   A. 22 B. 53
   C. 85 D. 360
3. Find the product $1.82 \cdot 0.4$.
   A. 1.728
   B. 1.0728
   C. 0.728
   D. 0.0728
4. Five notebooks cost $4.65. What is the price for two notebooks?
   A. $.93
   B. $2.32
   C. $1.50
   D. $1.86
5. Solve $12z = 144$.
   A. 12
   B. 72
   C. 132
   D. 1,728
6. Solve. $\frac{1}{6}x = 4$
   A. $x = \frac{2}{3}$ B. $x = 10$
   C. $x = 2$ D. $x = 24$
7. Solve. $\frac{5}{8}y = \frac{1}{6}$
   A. $y = \frac{5}{6}$ B. $y = \frac{8}{30}$
   C. $y = \frac{4}{15}$ D. $y = 6\frac{5}{8}$
8. Multiply.
   $\frac{5}{8} \cdot \frac{16}{20}$
   A. 10 B. $\frac{25}{32}$
   C. $\frac{1}{2}$ D. 0
9. Which of the following numbers is NOT rational?
   A. 15.2615 B. $\sqrt{168}$
   C. 2.2525 D. -3
10. A pet store charges $12 for each dog collar and $3 for shipping and handling. Anna paid $51 for some dog collars. How many did she buy?
    A. 2
    B. 3
    C. 4
    D. 5
11. Find the prime factorization of 72.
    A. $2 \cdot 2 \cdot 3 \cdot 3$ B. $2^3 \cdot 3^2$
    C. $2 \cdot 3 \cdot 6$ D. $2 \cdot 6^2$
12. Aaron opened a savings account with a $25.45 deposit. He deposited $2.25 weekly for three weeks and then withdrew $6.38. What is his current balance?
    A. $25.45
    B. $38.58
    C. $25.08
    D. $25.82

16. A hiker is climbing a trail. After she has hiked 130 ft along the trail, her elevation has increased 50 ft as shown below.

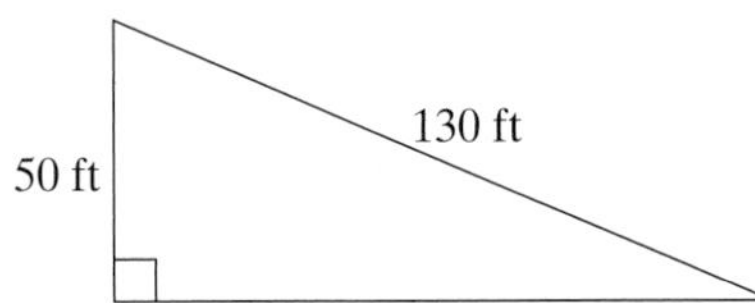

What is the horizontal distance the hiker has traveled? (Lesson 3-7) B

Ⓐ 80 ft   Ⓒ 140 ft
Ⓑ 120 ft   Ⓓ 180 ft

17. Simplify $\left(\frac{5}{9}\right)^{-2}$. (Lesson 5-7) A

Ⓐ $\frac{81}{25}$ Ⓒ $-\frac{25}{81}$
Ⓑ $\frac{25}{81}$ Ⓓ $-\frac{81}{25}$

18. Which equation has a solution of 3? (Lesson 3-4) D

Ⓐ $3x + 9 = 12$ Ⓒ $5x + 3 = 12$
Ⓑ $3x - 9 = 12$ Ⓓ $5x - 3 = 12$

19. Which property should you use to simplify the expression $3(4 + j)$? (Lesson 1-6) A

Ⓐ Distributive Property
Ⓑ Commutative Property of Addition
Ⓒ Identity Property of Addition
Ⓓ Associative Property of Addition

20. Akio deposited $\frac{1}{4}$ of his paycheck into a savings account. He donated $\frac{1}{10}$ of his paycheck to a charitable organization. How much of his paycheck does Akio have left? (Lesson 5-3) D

Ⓐ $\frac{2}{40}$ Ⓒ $\frac{7}{20}$
Ⓑ $\frac{1}{6}$ Ⓓ $\frac{13}{20}$

21. Which of the following is equivalent to 0.00027? (Lesson 5-7) C

Ⓐ $2.7 \cdot (-4)$ Ⓒ $2.7 \cdot 10^{-4}$
Ⓑ $2.7 \cdot (-3)$ Ⓓ $2.7 \cdot 10^{-3}$

22. This year, 4 more than $2\frac{1}{2}$ times as many people tried out for a city softball team as tried out last year. If 39 people tried out this year, how many people tried out last year? (Lesson 5-6) C

Ⓐ 4   Ⓑ 10   Ⓒ 14   Ⓓ 35

23. Which of the following are possible side lengths of a right triangle? (Lesson 3-7) C

Ⓐ 3 in., 5 in., 7 in.   Ⓒ 5 yd, 12 yd, 13 yd
Ⓑ 5 m, 7 m, 13 m   Ⓓ 9 ft, 12 ft, 20 ft

24. For a vacation, the Chans budget $200 in spending money plus $150 each day for a hotel. How many vacation days can they take on a budget of $1,100? Use the equation $150n + 200 = 1{,}100$, where n is the number of vacation days. (Lesson 3-4) B

Ⓐ 5 days   Ⓒ 7 days
Ⓑ 6 days   Ⓓ 8 days

Standards Reference Guide

California Content Standard	Item Number(s)
NS 1.2	1, 3, 4, 7, 14, 20
NS 1.5	5, 10, 13
NS 2.1	8, 17, 21
AF 1.3	9, 14, 19
AF 4.1	6, 12, 18, 22, 24
MG 3.3	2, 11, 16, 23

For additional practice, see the *California Standards Review and Practice Workbook* or go online to use the

Visit: PHSchool.com, **Web Code:** axq-9045

Chapter 6 Rates and Proportions

Chapter at a Glance

Lesson Titles, Objectives, and Features	California Content Standards
6-1 Ratios • To write and simplify ratios	Interpret and use ratios using appropriate notations. ***Foundational (Gr6 NS 1.2)*** **AF 3.4** Plot the values of quantities whose ratios are always the same. **AF 4.2** Solve multistep problems involving rate, distance, and time.
6-2 Rates • To use rates and unit rates **6-2b Activity Lab:** Simplifying Rates **Vocabulary Builder:** High-Use Academic Words	**AF 4.2** Solve multistep problems involving rate, average speed, distance, and time. **MG 1.3** Use measures expressed as rates to solve problems.
6-3 Dimensional Analysis • To convert units and use dimensional analysis	**MG 1.3** Use measures expressed as rates and measures expressed as products to solve problems; check the units of the solutions; and use dimensional analysis to check the reasonableness of the answer.
6-4 Applications of Rates • To solve multi-step rate problems	**AF 4.2** Solve multistep problems involving rate, average speed, distance, and time or a direct variation. **MG 1.3** Use measures expressed as rates to solve problems; check the units of the solutions; and use dimensional analysis to check the reasonableness of the answer.
6-5 Proportions • To identify and solve proportions. **Mathematical Reasoning:** Proportional Reasoning **Algebraic Thinking:** Similar Figures and Proportions	Use proportions to solve problems. ***Foundational (Gr6 NS 1.3)*** **MG 1.3** Use measurements expressed as rates to solve problems. **MR 1.1** Analyze problems by identifying relationships, identifying missing information, and observing patterns.

California Content Standards
NS Number Sense
AF Algebra and Functions
MG Measurement and Geometry
MR Mathematical Reasoning

Correlations to Standardized Tests

All content for these tests is contained in *Prentice Hall Math, Algebra Readiness.* This chart reflects coverage in this chapter only.

	6-1	6-2	6-3	6-4	6-5
Terra Nova CAT6 (Level 18)					
Number and Number Relations	✔	✔	✔	✔	✔
Computation and Numerical Estimation	✔	✔	✔	✔	✔
Operation Concepts	✔	✔	✔	✔	✔
Measurement		✔	✔	✔	✔
Geometry and Spatial Sense					
Data Analysis, Statistics, and Probability					
Patterns, Functions, and Algebra	✔	✔	✔	✔	✔
Problem Solving and Reasoning	✔	✔	✔	✔	✔
Communication	✔	✔	✔	✔	✔
Decimals, Fractions, Integers, Percent	✔	✔	✔	✔	✔
Order of Operations					
Algebraic Operations					
Terra Nova CTBS (Level 18)					
Decimals, Fractions, Integers, Percents	✔	✔	✔	✔	✔
Order of Operations, Numeration, Number Theory	✔	✔	✔	✔	✔
Data Interpretation					
Measurement		✔	✔	✔	✔
Geometry					
ITBS (Level 14)					
Number Properties and Operations	✔	✔	✔	✔	✔
Algebra	✔	✔	✔	✔	✔
Geometry					
Measurement		✔	✔	✔	✔
Probability and Statistics					
Estimation				✔	
SAT10 (Adv 1 Level)					
Number Sense and Operations	✔	✔	✔	✔	✔
Patterns, Relationships, and Algebra	✔	✔	✔	✔	✔
Data, Statistics, and Probability					
Geometry and Measurement		✔	✔	✔	✔
NAEP					
Number Sense, Properties, and Operations	✔	✔	✔	✔	
Measurement		✔	✔		
Geometry and Spatial Sense					
Data Analysis, Statistics, and Probability					
Algebra and Functions					✔

CAT6 California Achievement Test, 6th Ed.
SAT10 Stanford Achievement Test, 10th Ed.
CTBS Comprehensive Test of Basic Skills
NAEP National Assessment of Educational Progress 2005 Mathematics Objectives
ITBS Iowa Test of Basic Skills, Form M

California Math Background

Focus on the California Content Standards

- Students bring some experience with the concepts presented in Chapter 6 from their math study in Grade 6. They interpreted and used ratios in different contexts to show the relative sizes of two quantities, using appropriate notation such as *a*:*b* (**NS 1.2**). They used proportions to solve problems (**NS 1.3**) as well.
- The 'Check Your Readiness' exercises provided at the beginning of this chapter (page 214) as well as the 'Check Skills You'll Need' exercises presented in the ***Math Companion*** will be especially helpful to maintain the level of proficiency with the vocabulary and computation skills that students need in order to be successful in working with ratios and proportions.

6-1 Ratios

California Content Standards **AF 3.4, AF 4.2**

Math Understandings

- A ratio compares two similar measures by means of division.
- All ratios can be written in fraction form.
- Equivalent ratios can be generated using multiplication or division, just as with fractions.

A **ratio** is a comparison of two numbers by division. Each number in a ratio is called a *term*. Each of the following ratios are read "six to two."

Three Ways to Write a Ratio		
In Words	**With a Symbol**	**As a Fraction**
6 to 2	6 : 2	$\frac{6}{2}$

Two ratios that name the same number are **equivalent ratios**. You can find equivalent ratios by multiplying or dividing each term of a ratio by the same nonzero number.

Example: Write two different ratios equivalent to $\frac{4}{6}$.

$$\frac{4}{6} = \frac{4 \div 2}{6 \div 2} = \frac{2}{3} \text{ and } \frac{4}{6} = \frac{4 \times 3}{6 \times 3} = \frac{12}{18}$$

6-2 Rates

California Content Standards **AF 4.2, MG 1.3**

Math Understandings

- Rates and unit rates are special types of ratios.
- You can easily make price comparisons for products of different package sizes by finding the unit cost for each.

A **rate** is a ratio that compares quantities measured in different units, such as miles to gallons or feet to seconds. A **unit rate** is the rate for one unit of a given quantity. The unit rate of an item for sale, called the unit cost, is useful when you compare to find the best buy.

Example: Find the unit rate for typing 114 words in 3 minutes.

$$\frac{\text{words}}{\text{min}} = \frac{114 \text{ words}}{3 \text{ min}}$$
$$= 38 \text{ words/min}$$

6-3 Dimensional Analysis

California Content Standards **MG 1.3**

Math Understandings

- Units can give a feeling for the size of the quantity.
- You can change from one unit of measure to another by multiplying by a conversion factor.
- When you use a conversion factor, you are multiplying by 1, which results in an equivalent expression.

Length	Weight	Capacity
12 in. = 1 ft	16 oz = 1 lb	8 fl oz = 1 cup
36 in. = 1 yd	2,000 lb = 1 t	2 cups = 1 pt
3 ft = 1 yd		4 cups = 1 qt
5,280 ft = 1 mi		2 pt = 1 qt
		4 qt = 1 gal

The rates $\frac{3 \text{ ft}}{1 \text{ yd}}$ and $\frac{1 \text{ yd}}{3 \text{ ft}}$ are **conversion factors**, which are rates equal to 1. **Dimensional analysis** is the process of analyzing units to decide which conversion factor(s) to use. Sometimes you need to use two or more conversion factors.

Example: Use dimensional analysis to find an equal rate in inches per minute.

$$\frac{15 \text{ ft}}{1 \text{ s}} = \frac{15 \text{ ft}}{1 \text{ s}} \cdot \frac{12 \text{ in}}{1 \text{ ft}} \cdot \frac{60 \text{ s}}{1 \text{ min}} = 10{,}800 \text{ in./min}$$

6-4 Applications of Rates

California Content Standards AF 4.2, MG 1.3

Math Understandings

- A rate is a ratio that compares quantities measured in different units; you can use rates to solve problems such as determining distance traveled given a rate and time.
- Average speed is calculated by dividing the total distance traveled by the total amount of time.

You can use **rates** to determine a total distance traveled.

To find a distance d, use the formula $d = rt$, where r is the rate of travel and t is the amount of travel time.

$$\text{total distance} = 35\,\frac{\text{mi}}{\cancel{\text{h}}} \cdot 1\,\cancel{\text{h}} + 50\,\frac{\text{mi}}{\cancel{\text{h}}} \cdot 1.5\,\cancel{\text{h}} = 110\text{ mi}$$

$$\text{total time} = 1\text{ h} + 1.5\text{ h} = 2.5\text{ h}$$

$$\text{average speed} = \frac{\text{total distance}}{\text{total time}}$$ ← **Average speed is total distance divided by total time.**

$$= \frac{110\text{ mi}}{2.5\text{ h}}$$ ← **Substitute the values for total time and total distance.**

$$= 44\,\frac{\text{mi}}{\text{h}}$$ ← **Simplify.**

If a problem involves more than one rate, find the distance traveled at each rate, and then find the sum of the individual distances.

Example: A light rail train departing a station travels 5 meters per second for 10 seconds, and 8 meters per second for 35 seconds. Find the total distance the train has traveled.

$\frac{5\text{ meters}}{\text{second}} \times 10\text{ seconds} = 50\text{ meters};$

$\frac{8\text{ meters}}{\text{second}} \times 35\text{ seconds} = 280\text{ meters}$

$50 + 280 = 330\text{ meters}$

6-5 Proportions

California Content Standards MG 1.3

Math Understandings

- Ratios that are equal form a proportion.
- The Cross Products Property is true because of the Multiplication Property of Equality.

A **proportion** is an equation stating that two ratios are equal. For two ratios, the **cross products** are found by multiplying the denominator of each ratio by the numerator of the other ratio.

Cross Products Property

For two ratios, the cross products are found by multiplying the denominator of each ratio by the numerator of the other ratio.

Arithmetic	Algebra
$\frac{6}{10} = \frac{9}{15}$	$\frac{a}{b} = \frac{c}{d}$, where $b \neq 0$ and $d \neq 0$
$6 \cdot 15 = 10 \cdot 9$	$ad = bc$

$$\frac{4}{5} = \frac{12}{15}$$ ← **Start with a proportion.**

$$\frac{4}{5} \cdot 5 \cdot 15 = \frac{12}{15} \cdot 5 \cdot 15$$ ← **Multiply each side by the values in the denominators.**

$$\frac{4}{\cancel{5}_1} \cdot \cancel{5}^1 \cdot 15 = \frac{12}{\cancel{15}_1} \cdot 5 \cdot \cancel{15}^1$$ ← **Divide the common factors.**

$$(4 \cdot 15) = (12 \cdot 5)$$ ← **Simplify.**

$$60 = 60$$ ← **The cross products are equal.**

Professional Development

Additional Professional Development Opportunities

Math Background Notes for Chapter 6: Every lesson has a Math Background in the PLAN section.

In-Service On Demand
Prentice Hall offers free video-based tutorials to support you. Visit PHSchool.com/inserviceondemand.

Pearson Achievement Solutions
Pearson Achievement Solutions, a Pearson Education company, offers comprehensive, facilitated professional development designed to help teachers improve student achievement. To learn more, please visit pearsonachievementsolutions.com.

Chapter 6 Resources

	6-1	6-2	6-3	6-4	6-5	For the Chapter
Print Resources						
L3 Practice	●	●	●	●	●	
L3 Guided Problem Solving	●	●	●	●	●	
L2 Reteaching	●	●	●	●	●	
L4 Enrichment	●	●	●	●	●	
L3 Vocabulary and Study Skills	●	●	●	●	●	●
L3 Daily Puzzles	●	●	●	●	●	
L3 Activity Labs	●	●	●	●	●	
L3 Checkpoint Quiz		●		●		
L3 Chapter Project						●
L2 Below Level Chapter Test						●
L3 Chapter Test						●
L4 Alternative Assessment						●
L3 Cumulative Review						●
Spanish Resources EL						
L3 Practice	●	●	●	●	●	
L3 Vocabulary and Study Skills Worksheets	●		●	●		●
L3 Checkpoint Quiz		●		●		
L2 Below Level Chapter Test						●
L3 Chapter Test						●
L4 Alternative Assessment						●
L3 Cumulative Review						●
Transparencies						
Check Skills You'll Need	●	●	●	●	●	
Additional Examples	●	●	●	●	●	
California Daily Review	●	●	●	●	●	
Classroom Aid				●		
Student Edition Answers	●	●	●	●	●	●
Lesson Quiz	●	●	●	●	●	
Technology						
California Student Center Online	●	●	●	●	●	●
California Student Center CD-ROM	●	●	●	●	●	●
Success Tracker™ Online Math Intervention	●	●	●	●	●	●
California Teacher Center: ExamView CD-ROM	●	●	●	●	●	●
California Teacher Center: Planning CD-ROM	●	●	●	●	●	●
California Teacher Center: Presentations CD-ROM and online	●	●	●	●	●	●
MindPoint Quiz Show	●	●	●	●	●	●
Prentice Hall Web Site: PHSchool.com	●	●	●	●	●	●

Also available:

California Standards Mastery
- Standards Review Transparencies
- Standards Review and Practice Workbook
- Progress Monitoring Assessments
- Math Companion
- Math*XL*

California Intervention Resources
- Skills Review and Practice Workbook
- Success Tracker™ Online Math Intervention

Other Resources
- Multilingual Handbook
- Spanish Student Edition
- Solution Key
- Math Notes Study Folder

Where You Can Use the Lesson Resources

Here is a suggestion, following the four-step teaching plan, for how you can incorporate Universal Access Resources into your teaching.

	Instructional Resources L3	Universal Access Resources
1. Plan		
Preparation Read the Math Background in the Teacher's Edition to connect this lesson with students' previous experience. **Starting Class** **Check Skills You'll Need** Assign these exercises from the Math Companion to review prerequisite skills. Review the full text of the student expectations and objectives covered in this lesson. **New Vocabulary** Help students pre-read the lesson by pointing out the new terms introduced in the lesson.	**California Math Background** **Math Understandings** **Transparencies & Presentations CD-ROM** Check Skills You'll Need California Daily Review **Resources** Vocabulary and Study Skills **Math Companion**	**Spanish Support** EL Vocabulary and Study Skills
2. Teach		
L3 **Guided Instruction** Use the Activity Labs to build conceptual understanding. Teach each Example. Use the Teacher's Edition side column notes for specific teaching tips, including Error Prevention notes. Use the Additional Examples found in the side column (and on transparency and PowerPoint) as an alternative presentation for the content. After each Example, assign the California Standards Check exercises for that Example to get an immediate assessment of student understanding. Utilize the support in the Math Companion to assist students with each Standards Check. Use the Closure activity in the Teacher's Edition to help students attain mastery of lesson content.	**Student Edition** Activity Lab **Resources** Math Companion Activity Lab **Transparencies & Presentations CD-ROM** Additional Examples Classroom Aids **Teacher Center: ExamView CD-ROM**	**Teacher's Edition** Every lesson includes suggestions for working with students who need special attention. L1 Special Needs L2 Below Level L4 Advanced Learners EL English Learners **Resources** **Multilingual Handbook** **Math Companion**
3. Practice		
Assignment Guide **Check Your Understanding** Use these questions from the Math Companion to check students' understanding before you assign homework. **Homework Exercises** Assign homework from these leveled exercises in the Assignment Guide. **A** Practice by Example **B** Apply Your Skills **C** Challenge California Multiple-Choice Practice and Mixed Review **Homework Quick Check** Use these key exercises to quickly check students' homework.	**Transparencies & Presentations CD-ROM** Student Answers **Resources** Math Companion Practice Guided Problem Solving Vocabulary and Study Skills Activity Lab Daily Puzzles **Teacher Center: ExamView CD-ROM** **Math *XL***	**Spanish Support** EL Practice EL Vocabulary and Study Skills **Resources** L4 Enrichment
4. Assess & Reteach		
Lesson Quiz Assign the Lesson Quiz to assess students' mastery of the lesson content. **Checkpoint Quiz** Use the Checkpoint Quiz to assess student progress over several lessons.	**Transparencies & Presentations CD-ROM** Lesson Quiz **Resources** Checkpoint Quiz	**Resources** L2 Reteaching EL Checkpoint Quiz Success Tracker™ **Teacher Center: ExamView CD-ROM**

KEY L1 Special Needs L2 Below Level L3 For All Students L4 Advanced, Gifted EL English Learners

Rates and Proportions

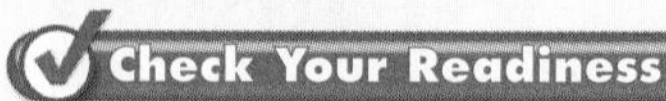

Answers are in the back of the textbook.

For math intervention, direct students to:

Equivalent Fractions
Lesson 4-3

Equivalent Forms of Rational Numbers
Lesson 4-4

Dividing Rational Numbers
Lesson 5-4

Solving Equations By Multiplying
Lesson 5-6

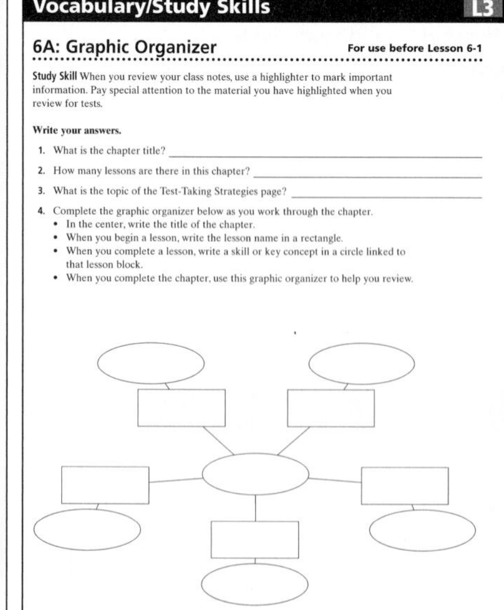

Spanish Vocabulary/Study Skills EL

Vocabulary/Study Skills L3

6A: Graphic Organizer — For use before Lesson 6-1

Study Skill When you review your class notes, use a highlighter to mark important information. Pay special attention to the material you have highlighted when you review for tests.

Write your answers.

1. What is the chapter title? ____
2. How many lessons are there in this chapter? ____
3. What is the topic of the Test-Taking Strategies page? ____
4. Complete the graphic organizer below as you work through the chapter.
   - In the center, write the title of the chapter.
   - When you begin a lesson, write the lesson name in a rectangle.
   - When you complete a lesson, write a skill or key concept in a circle linked to that lesson block.
   - When you complete the chapter, use this graphic organizer to help you review.

Rates and Proportions

What You've Learned

California Content Standards

NS 1.2 Add, subtract, multiply, and divide rational numbers and take positive rational numbers to whole-number powers.

NS 1.3 Convert fractions to decimals and use these representations in computations and applications.

AF 4.1 Solve two-step linear equations in one variable over the rational numbers.

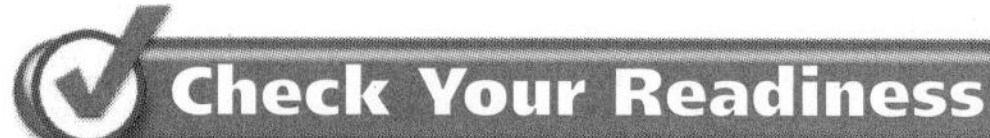

for Help to the lesson in green.

Finding Equivalent Fractions (Lesson 4-3)

Write each fraction in simplest form.

1. $\frac{34}{68}$ $\frac{1}{2}$
2. $\frac{32}{112}$ $\frac{2}{7}$
3. $\frac{45}{63}$ $\frac{5}{7}$
4. $\frac{66}{120}$ $\frac{11}{20}$

Finding Equivalent Forms of Rational Numbers (Lesson 4-4)

Write each fraction as a decimal. Round to three decimal places.

5. $\frac{17}{27}$ 0.630
6. $\frac{10}{31}$ 0.323
7. $\frac{19}{7}$ 2.714
8. $\frac{18}{35}$ 0.514

Dividing Rational Numbers (Lesson 5-4)

Find each quotient.

9. $\frac{4}{7} \div \frac{2}{3}$ $\frac{6}{7}$
10. $\frac{12}{14} \div \frac{7}{12}$ $1\frac{23}{49}$
11. $\frac{7}{9} \div \frac{1}{5}$ $3\frac{8}{9}$
12. $\frac{11}{12} \div \frac{2}{9}$ $4\frac{1}{8}$

Solving Equations by Multiplying (Lesson 5-6)

Solve each equation.

13. $\frac{1}{2}k = 28$ 56
14. $3b = \frac{3}{4}$ $\frac{1}{4}$
15. $\frac{3}{4}t = \frac{5}{8}$ $\frac{5}{6}$
16. $2y = \frac{9}{8}$ $\frac{9}{16}$
17. $\frac{5}{6}r = \frac{7}{2}$ $4\frac{1}{5}$
18. $\frac{1}{3}x = 10$ 30

What You'll Learn Next

California Content Standards

AF 4.2 Solve multistep problems involving rate, average speed, distance, and time or a direct variation.

MG 1.3 Use measures expressed as rates and measures expressed as products to solve problems; and use dimensional analysis to check the reasonableness of the answer.

▲ In one year, a 10-kilowatt wind turbine can generate about 10,000 kilowatt-hours of electricity at a site where the average wind speed is 12 mi/h.

New Vocabulary

English and Spanish Audio Online

- conversion factor (p. 226)
- cross products (p. 236)
- dimensional analysis (p. 227)
- equivalent ratios (p. 217)
- proportion (p. 235)
- rate (p. 220)
- ratio (p. 216)
- unit rate (p. 220)

Academic Vocabulary

- classify (p. 225)
- contrast (p. 225)
- define (p. 225)

California Content Standards for Chapter 6

Algebra and Functions
AF 4.2

Measurement & Geometry
MG 1.3

Mathematical Reasoning
MR 1.1, MR 2.5

Chapter 6 Overview

In this chapter, students learn to write ratios and to use rates and unit rates. In addition, they learn to convert units and use dimensional analysis, solve multi-step rate problems, and identify and solve proportions.

Activating Prior Knowledge

In this chapter, students build on their knowledge of rational numbers, of transformations, and of writing and solving equations to further investigate ratios. They also learn to write and solve proportions in order to solve a variety of problems. Ask questions such as:

- *Write the following in order from least to greatest:* $-3, 6, 4\frac{1}{2}, -1.5$. $-3, -1.5, 4\frac{1}{2}, 6$
- *Which of the following fractions is expressed in simplest form?* $\frac{4}{6}, \frac{8}{21}, \frac{3}{12}, \frac{9}{36}$ $\frac{8}{21}$
- *What is n in* $3n = 42$? $n = 14$

6-1

1. Plan

California Content Standards

Interpret and use ratios using appropriate notations. ***Foundational***

AF 3.4 Plot the values of quantities whose ratios are always the same.

AF 4.2 Solve multistep problems involving rate, distance, and time.

California Math Background

A *ratio* is a comparison of two quantities. A ratio can be expressed in three different ways: *a* to *b*, *a* : *b*, and $\frac{a}{b}$. Two ratios that name the same number are *equivalent ratios*. You can find equivalent ratios by multiplying both terms of the ratio by the same non-zero number. Using equivalent ratios, you can write ratios in simplest form.

More Math Background: p. 214C

Lesson Planning and Resources

See p. 214E for a list of the resources that support this lesson.

PRESENTATION CD-ROM
CD, Online, or Transparencies

Bell Ringer Practice

Check Skills You'll Need
Use student page, transparency, or PowerPoint.
See Math Companion.

California Standards Review
Use transparency or PowerPoint.

6-1 Ratios

Check Skills You'll Need

Do this in your **Math Companion.**

Vocabulary

- ratio
- equivalent ratios

Use your **Math Companion** *to build your vocabulary.*

California Content Standards

Foundational Standard Interpret and use ratios in different contexts to show the relative sizes of two quantities, using appropriate notations.

Prepares for **AF 3.4** Plot the values of quantities whose ratios are always the same.

Prepares for **AF 4.2** Solve multistep problems involving rate, distance, and time.

What You'll Learn . . . and Why

You will learn to write ratios. You can use ratios to compare the quantities of each ingredient in a recipe.

PARTY MIX
Makes 6 cups
4 cups cereal
2 cups pretzels
3 tbsp Worcestershire sauce

A **ratio** is a comparison of two quantities by division. You can write the ratio of cups of cereal to cups of pretzels as 4 to 2, $\frac{4}{2}$, or 4 : 2. All three ratios are read "four to two."

Take Note **Ratio**

A ratio is a comparison of two quantities by division. You can write a ratio in three ways.

Arithmetic	Algebra
4 to 2 $\frac{4}{2}$ 4 : 2	a to b $\frac{a}{b}$ $a : b$ where $b \neq 0$

Ratios can compare one part to another part or a part to the whole.

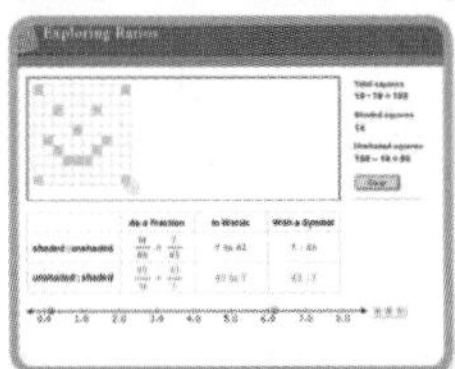

For: Exploring Ratios Activity
Use: Interactive Textbook, 6-1

EXAMPLE **Writing a Ratio**

1 **Guided Problem Solving** Use the party mix recipe above. Write the ratio of cups of cereal to cups of pretzels in three ways.

The recipe calls for 4 cups of cereal and 2 cups of pretzels.

cereal to pretzels →   4 to 2 $\frac{4}{2}$ 4 : 2

CA Standards Check 1 *Go to your* **Math Companion** *for help.*

1. Use the recipe above. Write each ratio in three ways.

a. cups of pretzels to cups of party mix
2 to 6; $\frac{2}{6}$; 2 : 6

b. cups of pretzels to cups of cereal
2 to 4; $\frac{2}{4}$; 2 : 4

Universal Access Solutions for All Learners

Special Needs L1	**Below Level** L2
Have students draw 2 bats and 3 balls and circle the picture. Then have them draw the same picture 3 more times. Show them that in the entire diagram there are now 8 bats and 12 balls, but the ratio of 2 to 3 has remained constant in each circle.	Help students understand that they can form equivalent fractions by multiplying or dividing a fraction by fractional forms of 1, such as $\frac{5}{5}$. $\frac{3}{4} \times \frac{5}{5} = \frac{15}{20}$ $\frac{15}{20} \div \frac{5}{5} = \frac{3}{4}$

Two ratios that name the same number are **equivalent ratios.** You can find equivalent ratios by multiplying or dividing each term of a ratio by the same nonzero number.

EXAMPLE Writing Equivalent Ratios

2 Write two different ratios equivalent to 4 : 6.

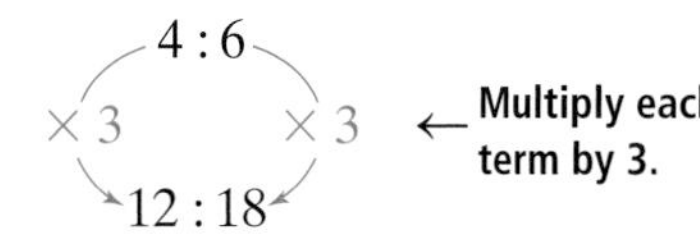

Two ratios equivalent to 4 : 6 are 2 : 3 and 12 : 18.

CA Standards Check 2 *Go to your* **Math Companion** *for help.*

2a–c. Answers may vary. Samples are given.
a. $\frac{2}{7}$ and $\frac{20}{70}$
b. 4 : 1 and 24 : 6
c. 4 to 11 and 16 to 44

2. Write two different ratios equivalent to each ratio. See left.

a. $\frac{10}{35}$ **b.** 12 : 3 **c.** 8 to 22

To write ratios in simplest form, you can divide the terms of the ratio by their greatest common divisor (GCD).

EXAMPLE Writing a Ratio in Simplest Form

Relate **MATH YOU KNOW...**

Write $\frac{4}{6}$ in simplest form.

$\frac{4}{6} = \frac{4 \div 2}{6 \div 2} = \frac{2}{3}$ ← **Divide the numerator and denominator by the GCD, 2.**

... to **NEW IDEAS**

3 Write the ratio of bats to balls in simplest form.

There are 8 bats and 12 balls, so the ratio of bats to balls is 8 to 12.

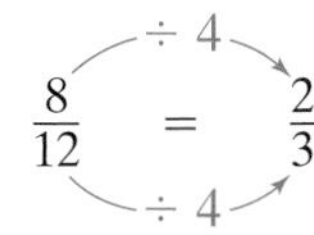

$\frac{8}{12} = \frac{2}{3}$ (÷ 4) ← **Write the ratio in simplest form.**

In simplest form, the ratio of bats to balls is $\frac{2}{3}$ or 2 to 3.

CA Standards Check 3 *Go to your* **Math Companion** *for help.*

3. At the grocery store you buy 12 green apples and 9 red apples. Write the ratio of green apples to red apples in simplest form.
4 to 3 or 4 : 3 or $\frac{4}{3}$

Check Your Understanding *Homework prep is in your* **Math Companion.**

2. Teach

Guided Instruction

Example 2

Ask: *How many equivalent ratios can you write for $\frac{4}{5}$?* infinitely many

Error Prevention!

Students may try to simplify a ratio, for instance, writing $\frac{3}{2}$ as a mixed number. Remind students that a ratio is a comparison that is easy to see when the ratio is written as a fraction, even an improper fraction.

... PRESENTATION CD-ROM CD, Online, or Transparencies

Additional Examples

1 During a school trip, there are 3 teachers and 25 students on each bus. Write the ratio of teachers to students in three ways. 3 to 25 or 3 : 25 or $\frac{3}{25}$

2 Write two different ratios equivalent to 24 : 8. Sample: 3 : 1 and 12 : 4

3 Write each ratio in simplest form.
a. 121 to 11 11 to 1
b. 28 : 16 7 : 4

Closure

- *What is a ratio?* a comparison of two quantities by division
- *What are equivalent ratios?* Sample: two ratios that name the same quantity

Advanced Learners L4

Students complete the table below to find ratios equivalent to 40 : 60.

40	20	8	4	12	5
60	30	12	6	18	7.5

English Learners EL

Make sure students understand that, although they can write a ratio like a fraction, fractions are not written in the other two ratio forms. They also are not customarily read like ratios. Ask them to practice "reading" ratios correctly.

3. Practice

Assignment Guide

Check Your Understanding
See Math Companion.

Homework Exercises

A	Practice by Example	1–26
B	Apply Your Skills	27–40
C	Challenge	41
California Multiple-Choice Practice		42–44
Mixed Review		45–48

Homework Quick Check
To check students' understanding of key skills and concepts, go over Exercises 2, 7, 20, 33, 39, 40.

Universal Access Resources

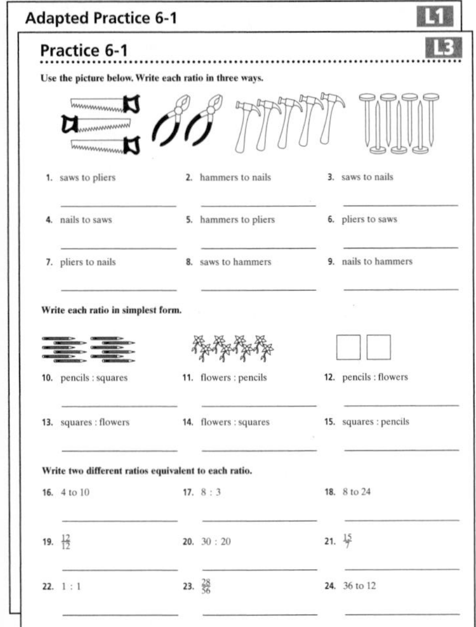
Adapted Practice 6-1 L1

Practice 6-1 L3

Use the picture below. Write each ratio in three ways.

1. saws to pliers	2. hammers to nails	3. saws to nails
4. nails to saws	5. hammers to pliers	6. pliers to saws
7. pliers to nails	8. saws to hammers	9. nails to hammers

Write each ratio in simplest form.

10. pencils : squares	11. flowers : pencils	12. pencils : flowers
13. squares : flowers	14. flowers : squares	15. squares : pencils

Write two different ratios equivalent to each ratio.

16. 4 to 10	17. 8 : 3	18. 8 to 24
19. $\frac{12}{12}$	20. 30 : 20	21. $\frac{15}{7}$
22. 1 : 1	23. $\frac{28}{56}$	24. 36 to 12

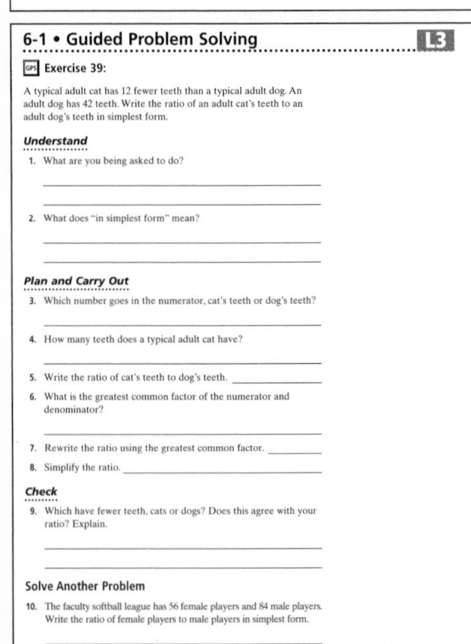
6-1 • Guided Problem Solving L3

GPS Exercise 39:

A typical adult cat has 12 fewer teeth than a typical adult dog. An adult dog has 42 teeth. Write the ratio of an adult cat's teeth to an adult dog's teeth in simplest form.

Understand

1. What are you being asked to do?
2. What does "in simplest form" mean?

Plan and Carry Out

3. Which number goes in the numerator, cat's teeth or dog's teeth?
4. How many teeth does a typical adult cat have?
5. Write the ratio of cat's teeth to dog's teeth. ______
6. What is the greatest common factor of the numerator and denominator?
7. Rewrite the ratio using the greatest common factor. ______
8. Simplify the ratio. ______

Check

9. Which have fewer teeth, cats or dogs? Does this agree with your ratio? Explain.

Solve Another Problem

10. The faculty softball league has 56 female players and 84 male players. Write the ratio of female players to male players in simplest form.

GO for Help: *MathXL*

Standards Practice

A Practice by Example

Example 1 (page 216)

For: Examples 1–3
Visit: PHSchool.com
Web Code: axe-0601

Use the picture below. Write each ratio in three ways.

1. red sandals to total number of sandals
   2 to 6 $\quad \frac{■}{6} \quad$ ■ : ■ 2 to 6; $\frac{2}{6}$; 2 : 6

   Guided Practice This exercise has been started for you!
2. blue sunglasses to total number of sunglasses 2 to 5; $\frac{2}{5}$; 2 : 5
3. sunglasses to sandals 5 to 6; $\frac{5}{6}$; 5 : 6
4. blue items to total number of items 4 to 11; $\frac{4}{11}$; 4 : 11
5. red sandals to red sunglasses 2 to 3; $\frac{2}{3}$; 2 : 3
6. green sandals to red sandals 2 to 2; $\frac{2}{2}$; 2 : 2

Example 2 (page 217)

Write two different ratios equivalent to each ratio. 7–15. See margin.

7. 6 to 18	8. $\frac{4}{14}$	9. 8 : 10
10. $\frac{30}{40}$	11. 3 : 5	12. 100 to 400
13. 9 to 7	14. $\frac{12}{24}$	15. 5 : 2

Example 3 (page 217)

Write each ratio in simplest form.

16. $\frac{6}{15}$ $\frac{2}{5}$

    $\frac{6}{15} = \frac{6 \div 3}{15 \div 3} = \frac{■}{■}$

    Guided Practice This exercise has been started for you!

17. 40 : 30 4 : 3	18. 8 to 36 2 to 9	19. $\frac{14}{42}$ $\frac{1}{3}$
20. 9 to 81 1 to 9	21. $\frac{18}{12}$ $\frac{3}{2}$	22. 75 : 15 5 : 1
23. $\frac{2}{26}$ $\frac{1}{13}$	24. 32 : 96 1 : 3	25. 17 to 34 1 to 2

26. You use 3 c of popcorn kernels to make 96 c of popcorn. Write the ratio of the amount of kernels to the amount of popcorn in simplest form. 1 to 32

B Apply Your Skills

27. **Guided Problem Solving** A jar contains 20 white marbles, 30 black marbles, and some red marbles. Half of the marbles are black. Find the ratio of white marbles to red marbles. 20 : 10 or 20 to 10 or $\frac{20}{10}$
    - How many marbles are in the jar?
    - How can you find the number of red marbles?
28. Find the ratio of the number of vowels to the number of consonants in your full name. Write the ratio in simplest form.
    Check students' work.

SCAFFOLDED **Problem Solving**

Your class is participating in a science fair. Of the 30 students in the class, 12 are growing plants, 8 are making model volcanoes, and the rest are doing other projects.

29. What is the ratio of the number of students making model volcanoes to the number of students growing plants? Write the ratio in simplest form. 2 : 3 or 2 to 3 or $\frac{2}{3}$

30. How many students are doing other projects? 10 students

31. What is the ratio of the number of students doing other projects to the total number of students? Write the ratio in simplest form. 1 : 3 or 1 to 3 or $\frac{1}{3}$

32. The ratio of the number of students growing bean plants to the total number of students growing plants is 1 : 2. How many students are growing bean plants? 6 students

Find the value that makes each pair of ratios equivalent.

33. 6 to 9, ■ to 3 2 **34.** 32 : 90, 16 : ■ 45 **35.** ■ to 96, 4 to 6 64

36. $\frac{■}{20}, \frac{50}{50}$ 20 **37.** 50 : 150, 75 : ■ 225 **38.** $\frac{72}{24}, \frac{■}{6}$ 18

GPS **39.** A typical adult cat has 12 fewer teeth than a typical adult dog. An adult dog has 42 teeth. Write the ratio of an adult cat's teeth to an adult dog's teeth in simplest form. 5 : 7 or 5 to 7 or $\frac{5}{7}$

40. 16 to 12 or 4 to 3; yes; in three years the ratio of their ages will be 19 to 15.

40. **Writing in Math** Your friend is 16 years old and her sister is 12 years old. What is the ratio of their ages? In three years, will the ratio of their ages be different? Explain. See left.

C Challenge

41. Write $8x : 16x$ in simplest form. Assume $x \neq 0$. 1 : 2

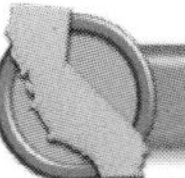

Multiple Choice Practice and Mixed Review

For California Standards Tutorials, visit PHSchool.com. Web Code: axq-9045

NS 1.5

42. Convert 0.35 to a fraction in simplest form. D

Ⓐ $\frac{35}{100}$ Ⓑ $\frac{35}{10}$ Ⓒ $\frac{7}{100}$ Ⓓ $\frac{7}{20}$

AF 1.3

43. Which equation illustrates the Associative Property of Multiplication? C

Ⓐ $3(a + b) = 3a + 3b$ Ⓒ $3(ab) = (3a)b$

Ⓑ $3(ab) = (ab)3$ Ⓓ $3(a + b) = (a + b)3$

NS 1.3

44. Which decimal is equivalent to $\frac{6}{25}$? A

Ⓐ 0.24 Ⓑ 0.25 Ⓒ 0.30 Ⓓ 0.6

for Help **Lesson 5-3**

Find each product. Write the answer in simplest form.

45. $\frac{2}{5} \cdot \frac{3}{7}$ $\frac{6}{35}$ **46.** $\frac{3}{4} \cdot \frac{5}{8}$ $\frac{15}{32}$ **47.** $\frac{1}{6} \cdot \frac{3}{5}$ $\frac{1}{10}$ **48.** $\frac{3}{16} \cdot \frac{16}{21}$ $\frac{1}{7}$

Online Lesson Quiz Visit: PHSchool.com Web Code: axa-0601

Alternative Assessment

Each student in a pair writes five different ratios in words. Partners exchange papers and write each ratio three ways. They then write each ratio in simplest form and write a second equivalent ratio.

California Resources

Standards Mastery
- Standards Review Transparencies
- Standards Review and Practice Workbook
- Math Companion

Math Intervention
- Skills Review and Practice Workbook
- Math XL

4. Assess & Reteach

PRESENTATION CD-ROM
CD, Online, or Transparencies

Lesson Quiz

A drama club has 14 females and 8 males. Write each ratio in three ways.

1. males to females
   8 to 14, 8 : 14, $\frac{8}{14}$
2. females to males
   14 to 8, 14 : 8, $\frac{14}{8}$
3. Write two different ratios equivalent to 4 : 8.
   Sample answer: 1 : 2; 5 : 10

Write each ratio in simplest form.

4. $\frac{8}{12}$ $\frac{2}{3}$ 5. 10 : 6 5 : 3

Reteaching 6-1 L2

A *ratio* is a comparison of two numbers by division. Each number in a ratio is called a *term*. You can write a ratio in three different ways. For example, the ratio 4 to 5 can be written:

4 to 5

4 : 5

$\frac{4}{5}$

Equivalent ratios name the same number.

- To find equivalent ratios, multiply *or* divide each term of a ratio by the same nonzero number.

Find a ratio equivalent to $\frac{4}{7}$.

$\frac{4}{7} = \frac{4 \cdot 2}{7 \cdot 2} = \frac{8}{14}$ ← Multiply each term by 2.

$\frac{8}{14}$ is equivalent to $\frac{4}{7}$.

Find the simplest form for the ratio $\frac{16}{20}$.

$\frac{16}{20} = \frac{16 \div 4}{20 \div 4} = \frac{4}{5}$ ← Divide each term by 4.

$\frac{4}{5}$ is the simplest form for $\frac{16}{20}$.

Write three different ratios equivalent to each ratio.

1. $\frac{2}{5}$ 2. 1 : 3 3. 3 to 4 4. 5 : 8

5. 2 to 7 6. $\frac{1}{5}$ 7. 12 to 20 8. 6 : 16

Write each ratio in simplest form.

9. 32 : 16 10. $\frac{14}{24}$ 11. $\frac{36}{50}$ 12. 60 : 25

13. $\frac{25}{40}$ 14. 60 : 180 15. $\frac{75}{120}$ 16. 80 : 20

Find the value that makes each pair of ratios equivalent.

17. 3 : 4, ? : 16 18. 20 to 25, 40 to ?

19. 7 : 10, ? : 100 20. 1 to 8, ? to 24

21. 5 : 100, 25 : ? 22. $\frac{7}{56}, \frac{?}{280}$

Enrichment 6-1 L4

Critical Thinking

The ratios below describe a set of polygons. Use the ratios to find the number of polygons in the set. All ratios are written in simplest form.

- Right triangles to obtuse triangles is 2 to 3.
  Obtuse triangles to acute triangles is 6 : 5.
- Triangles to rectangles is $\frac{5}{4}$.
- Rhombuses to trapezoids is 3 : 5.
- Quadrilaterals to triangles is $\frac{4}{3}$.

1. List the order in which you will find the number of polygons in the set. Explain.
   a. First ____ b. Second ____
   c. Third ____ d. Fourth ____
   e. Fifth ____ f. Sixth ____
2. What is the fewest number of polygons that can be in the set?
   a. Right triangles ____ b. Obtuse triangles ____
   c. Acute triangles ____ d. Triangles ____
   e. Rectangles ____ f. Rhombuses ____
   g. Trapezoids ____ h. Quadrilaterals ____
3. Show the number of polygons in another set that has the same ratios.
   a. Right triangles ____ b. Obtuse triangles ____
   c. Acute triangles ____ d. Triangles ____
   e. Rectangles ____ f. Rhombuses ____
   g. Trapezoids ____ h. Quadrilaterals ____

6-2

1. Plan

California Content Standards

AF 4.2 Solve multistep problems involving rate, average speed, distance, and time. ***Introduce***

MG 1.3 Use measures expressed as rates to solve problems. ***Introduce***

California Math Background

A *rate* is a type of ratio in which two quantities are measured in different units, such as 50 miles per hour. Miles per hour is an example of a *unit rate* because it is a rate for one unit of a given quantity (hours). So, unit rates are commonly expressed as decimals or whole numbers instead of fractions with a denominator of 1.

More Math Background: p. 214C

Lesson Planning and Resources

See p. 214E for a list of the resources that support this lesson.

PRESENTATION CD-ROM
CD, Online, or Transparencies

Bell Ringer Practice

Check Skills You'll Need
Use student page, transparency, or PowerPoint.
See Math Companion.

California Standards Review
Use transparency or PowerPoint.

6-2 Rates

Check Skills You'll Need

Do this in your **Math Companion.**

Vocabulary

- rate
- unit rate

Use your **Math Companion** *to build your vocabulary.*

California Content Standards

AF 4.2 Solve multistep problems involving rate, average speed, distance, and time. ***Introduce***

MG 1.3 Use measures expressed as rates to solve problems. ***Introduce***

What You'll Learn . . . and Why

You will learn to find and use rates and unit rates. You can use rates to describe the speed of a car or to predict the distance a car can travel on a certain amount of gasoline.

A **rate** is a ratio that compares two quantities measured in different units, such as miles to gallons or feet to seconds. A **unit rate** is the rate for one unit of a given quantity.

If a car travels 120 mi on 4 gal of gasoline, then the rate is $\frac{120 \text{ mi}}{4 \text{ gal}}$. The unit rate is $\frac{30 \text{ mi}}{1 \text{ gal}}$, or 30 mi/gal.

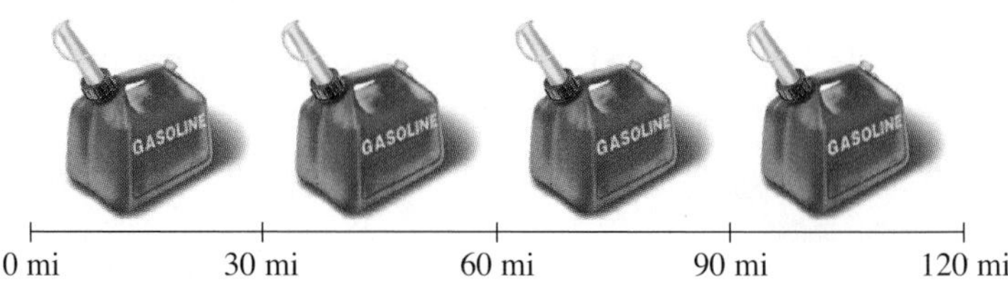

EXAMPLE Finding a Unit Rate

1 A team finishes a 200-lap bicycle race in 2 h and 4 min, or about 2.07 h. Find the unit rate of laps per hour.

$$\frac{\text{number of laps}}{\text{number of hours}} = \frac{200 \text{ laps}}{2.07 \text{ h}}$$ ← **Write a rate comparing laps to hours.**

$$\approx 96.6 \text{ laps/h}$$ ← **Divide. Round to the nearest tenth.**

The unit rate is about 96.6 laps per hour.

CA Standards Check 1 *Go to your* **Math Companion** *for help.*

1. Find each unit rate.

a. 52 deliveries in 8 h
6.5 deliveries/h

b. 420 Calories in 6 servings
70 Calories/serving

Universal Access Solutions for All Learners

Special Needs L1
On the board, write a (1) next to *oz* in the unit rates used in Example 3. Make sure students understand that dividing $2.99 by 64 ounces gives them the cost for one ounce.

Below Level L2
Have students make a table of miles traveled for each gallon of gasoline used for the model on page 220.

Gallons	1	2	3	4	5	6
Miles	30	60	90	120	150	180

You can use a unit rate to solve a problem by finding an equivalent ratio.

Relate **MATH YOU KNOW...**

EXAMPLE Using a Unit Rate

Write a fraction equivalent to $\frac{30}{1}$.

$$\frac{30}{1} \overset{\times 8}{=} \frac{240}{8}$$

← **Multiply the numerator and denominator by the same number.**

... to **NEW IDEAS**

2 Guided Problem Solving A car travels about 30 mi per gallon of gasoline. About how far can the car travel on 8 gal?

Write the unit rate. Then find an equivalent ratio.

$$\frac{30 \text{ miles}}{1 \text{ gallon}} \overset{\times 8}{=} \frac{240 \text{ miles}}{8 \text{ gallons}}$$

← **Multiply each term by 8.**

The car can travel about 240 mi on 8 gal of gasoline.

Problem Solving Tip

To write a whole number as a fraction, write the whole number in the numerator and 1 in the denominator.

CA Standards Check 2 *Go to your* **Math Companion** *for help.*

2. You can type 25 words per minute. Find the number of words you can type in each time period.

a. 10 min 250 words **b.** 1 h 1,500 words

A unit rate that gives the cost per unit is a unit cost. You can use unit costs to compare prices.

EXAMPLE Comparing Unit Costs

3 Which size bottle of juice is the better buy?

Find the unit cost for each bottle.

$\frac{\$2.99}{64 \text{ oz}} \approx \$.05/\text{oz}$

$\frac{\$1.59}{12 \text{ oz}} \approx \$.13/\text{oz}$

The 64-oz bottle has the lower unit cost. It is the better buy.

Check For Reasonableness $\$.05 \cdot 64 = \$3.20$ and $\$3.20 \approx \$2.99$. Also, $\$.13 \cdot 12 = \$1.56$ and $\$1.56 \approx \$1.59$. The answers are reasonable.

CA Standards Check 3 *Go to your* **Math Companion** *for help.*

3. The cost of a 20-oz box of cereal is \$4.29. A 12-oz box of the same cereal costs \$3.59. Which box of cereal is the better buy? 20-oz box

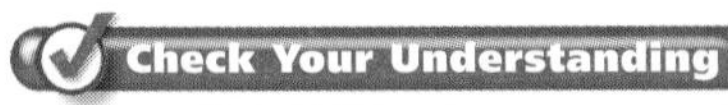

Check Your Understanding *Homework prep is in your* **Math Companion.**

Advanced Learners L4

One office space costs \$143,500 and has 1,825 ft². Another office space is \$129,799 and has 1,625 ft². Which looks like a better buy? 1,825 ft² office is slightly less per ft²

English Learners EL

One common linguistic misconception is that *better* means more or bigger. Make sure students understand that a *better buy* means you get *more* quantity for less *money.* Sometimes the *better buy* is the smaller quantity.

2. Teach

Guided Instruction

Example 3

Show students how multiplying both numerator and denominator by 8 is really multiplication by 1.

$$\frac{25 \text{ mi}}{1 \text{ gal}} \cdot \frac{8}{8} = \frac{25 \text{ mi} \cdot 8}{1 \text{ gal} \cdot 8} = \frac{200 \text{ mi}}{8 \text{ gal}}$$

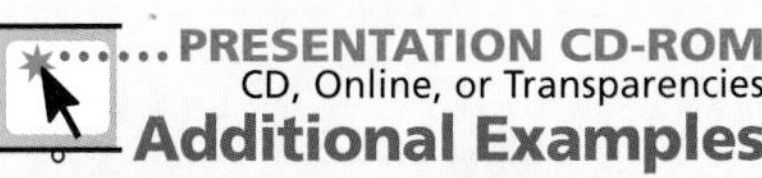

PRESENTATION CD-ROM CD, Online, or Transparencies

Additional Examples

1 Find the unit rate for typing 145 words in 5 minutes. 29 words per min

2 Apples cost \$1.49 for 1 pound. How much do 5 pounds of apples cost? \$7.45

3 The same brand of pretzels comes in two sizes: a 10-ounce bag for \$.99, and an 18-ounce bag for \$1.49. Which size is a better buy? Round each unit cost to the nearest cent. 10-oz: \$10, 18-oz: \$.08; The 18-oz bag is a better buy.

Closure

- *What is a rate?* Sample: A rate is a ratio that compares quantities of different units.
- *How can you compare the cost of two items that are different sizes?* Sample: Find the unit price for each item. The lesser unit price is the better buy.

3. Practice

Assignment Guide

Check Your Understanding
See Math Companion.

Homework Exercises

A	Practice by Example	1–18
B	Apply Your Skills	19–28
C	Challenge	29
California Multiple-Choice Practice		30–32
Mixed Review		33–35

Homework Quick Check
To check students' understanding of key skills and concepts, go over Exercises 5, 9, 15, 20, 28.

Universal Access Resources

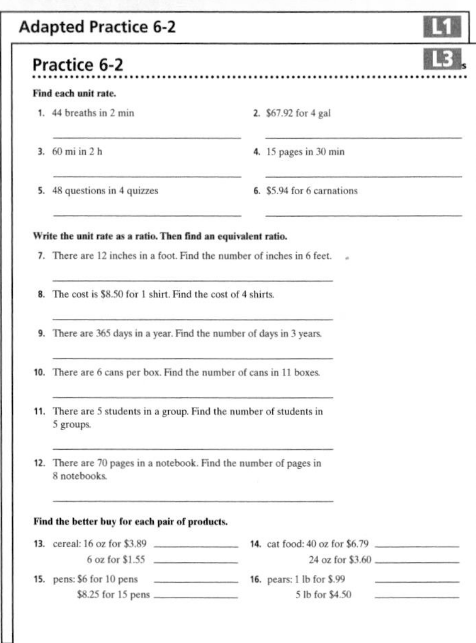
Adapted Practice 6-2 L1

Practice 6-2 L3

Find each unit rate.

1. 44 breaths in 2 min ________
2. $67.92 for 4 gal ________
3. 60 mi in 2 h ________
4. 15 pages in 30 min ________
5. 48 questions in 4 quizzes ________
6. $5.94 for 6 carnations ________

Write the unit rate as a ratio. Then find an equivalent ratio.

7. There are 12 inches in a foot. Find the number of inches in 6 feet. ________
8. The cost is $8.50 for 1 shirt. Find the cost of 4 shirts. ________
9. There are 365 days in a year. Find the number of days in 3 years. ________
10. There are 6 cans per box. Find the number of cans in 11 boxes. ________
11. There are 5 students in a group. Find the number of students in 5 groups. ________
12. There are 70 pages in a notebook. Find the number of pages in 8 notebooks. ________

Find the better buy for each pair of products.

13. cereal: 16 oz for $3.89 ________
6 oz for $1.55 ________
14. cat food: 40 oz for $6.79 ________
24 oz for $3.60 ________
15. pens: $6 for 10 pens ________
$8.25 for 15 pens ________
16. pears: 1 lb for $.99 ________
5 lb for $4.50 ________

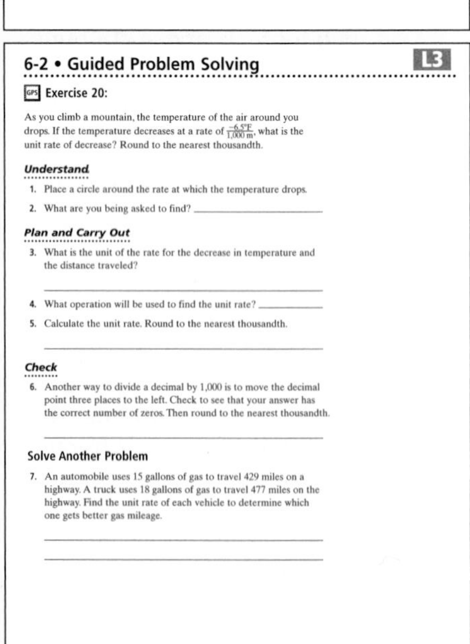
6-2 • Guided Problem Solving L3

GPS Exercise 20:

As you climb a mountain, the temperature of the air around you drops. If the temperature decreases at a rate of $\frac{-6.5°F}{1,000 \text{ m}}$, what is the unit rate of decrease? Round to the nearest thousandth.

Understand

1. Place a circle around the rate at which the temperature drops.
2. What are you being asked to find? ________

Plan and Carry Out

3. What is the unit of the rate for the decrease in temperature and the distance traveled? ________
4. What operation will be used to find the unit rate? ________
5. Calculate the unit rate. Round to the nearest thousandth. ________

Check

6. Another way to divide a decimal by 1,000 is to move the decimal point three places to the left. Check to see that your answer has the correct number of zeros. Then round to the nearest thousandth. ________

Solve Another Problem

7. An automobile uses 15 gallons of gas to travel 429 miles on a highway. A truck uses 18 gallons of gas to travel 477 miles on the highway. Find the unit rate of each vehicle to determine which one gets better gas mileage. ________

Standards Practice

GO for Help: MathXL

AF 4.2, MG 1.3

A Practice by Example

Example 1 (page 220)

For: Examples 1–3
Visit: PHSchool.com
Web Code: axe-0602

Find each unit rate.

1. 36 gal in 12 min
$\frac{36 \text{ gal}}{12 \text{ min}} = \blacksquare$ gal/min 3 gal/min

Guided Practice: This exercise has been started for you!

2. $42 for 3 books $14/book
3. 300 ft in 48 s 6.25 ft/s
4. $21.60 for 12 roses $1.80/rose
5. 200 m in 16 s 12.5 m/s
6. 676 mi in 13 h 52 mi/h
7. 45°F in 5 min 9°F/min
8. A water pump moves 330 gal of water in 22 min. Find the unit rate of gallons per minute. 15 gal/min

Example 2 (page 221)

Find the number of feet in each run by a football player. (3 ft = 1 yd)

9. 15 yd 45 ft
10. 30 yd 90 ft
11. 2 yd 6 ft
12. The density of water is 1 g/mL. Find the mass of the water, in kilograms, in the container at the right. 0.25 kg

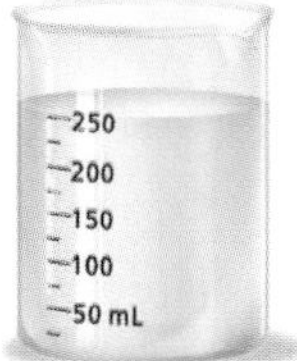

13. Five buses leave on field trip. There are about 45 students per bus. About how many students are on the 5 buses? about 225 students

Example 3 (page 221)

Find the better buy for each pair of products.

14. crackers: 16 oz for $2.39
20 oz for $3.19 16 oz
$\frac{\$2.39}{16 \text{ oz}} = \$\blacksquare$ per oz $\frac{\$3.19}{20 \text{ oz}} = \$\blacksquare$ per oz

Guided Practice: This exercise has been started for you!

15. juice: 48 fl oz for $2.07
32 fl oz for $1.64 48 fl oz
16. apples: 3 lb for $1.89
1 lb for $.79 3 lb
17. yogurt: 32 oz for $2.69
40 oz for $3.39 32 oz
18. bread: $2.75 for 1 loaf
$4.99 for 2 loaves 2 loaves

B Apply Your Skills

19. **Guided Problem Solving** *Apollo 11* traveled about 237,000 mi to the moon in about 103 h. *Apollo 12* made the same trip in about 123 h. Find the difference in the rates of travel of the two spacecraft. Round to the nearest whole number. 374 mi/h
   - What ratio represents the rate of *Apollo 11*?
   - What ratio represents the rate of *Apollo 12*?

GPS 20. As you climb a mountain, the temperature of the air around you drops. If the temperature decreases at a rate of $\frac{-6.5°C}{1,000 \text{ m}}$, what is the unit rate of decrease? Round to the nearest thousandth. −0.007°C/m

SCAFFOLDED
Problem Solving

You earn \$70.56 in 9 h. Your friend earns \$83.40 in 12 h.

21. What is your unit rate of pay? \$7.84/h
22. Is your friend's unit rate of pay greater than or less than your unit rate of pay? less than
23. How much will you earn if you work 40 h? \$313.60
24. Suppose you earn \$7.84 per hour for the first 40 h that you work, and \$9.25 per hour for each additional hour. If you work 52 h, how much will you earn? \$424.60

25. Answers may vary. Sample: About 28 mi/gal; round 279.9 mi to 280 mi and 9.8 gal to 10 gal. Then find the unit rate $\frac{280 \text{ mi}}{10 \text{ gal}}$ or 28 mi/gal.

25. **Estimation** A car travels 279.9 mi on 9.8 gal of gasoline. Estimate the car's unit rate of miles per gallon of gasoline. Explain how you found your estimate. See left.
26. During a 7.5-h drive, a car's mileage indicator starts at 18,560 mi and ends at 18,980 mi. What is the car's rate of travel? 56 mi/h
27. The results at the right show the number of words students typed during a 5-min typing test. To get an A, a student must type at a rate of 25 or more words per minute. Which students received an A on the test? Oscar and Monica

Oscar	130
Ana	110
Monica	149
Sean	102

28. Yes; the speed limit is posted as mi/h or km/h, which are unit rates.

28. **Writing in Math** Is the speed limit on a highway an example of a unit rate? Explain. See left.

Challenge

29. An airplane flies 2,750 mi in 5 h. Find the unit rate in miles per second. Round your answer to the nearest hundredth. 0.15 mi/s

Multiple Choice Practice and Mixed Review

For California Standards Tutorials, visit PHSchool.com. Web Code: axq-9045

MG 1.3

30. Ryan mows a 2,000-ft^2 lawn in 30 min. Which is closest to the number of square feet Ryan cuts in 1 min? B

    A $66\frac{1}{3}$ ft^2 B $66\frac{2}{3}$ ft^2 C $67\frac{1}{3}$ ft^2 D $66\frac{2}{3}$ ft^2

MG 3.3

31. What is the length of the missing leg of the triangle shown at the right? B

    A 9 m C 24 m
    B 18 m D 324 m

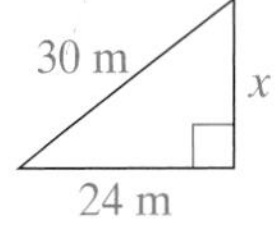

AF 1.1

32. Brian has four fewer than twice as many sports cards as Miles, who has c cards. Write an expression for the number of cards Brian has. A

    A $2c - 4$ B $4c + 2$ C $-4 - 2c$ D $4 - 2c$

Lesson 5-4 **Find each quotient.**

33. $4\frac{2}{3} \div 1\frac{3}{4}$ $2\frac{2}{3}$
34. $6\frac{1}{4} \div 2\frac{1}{2}$ $2\frac{1}{2}$
35. $2\frac{2}{5} \div 7\frac{1}{5}$ $\frac{1}{3}$

Online Lesson Quiz Visit: PHSchool.com Web Code: axa-0602

Alternative Assessment

Each student in a pair writes the size and cost for two different quantities of the same product. Partners exchange papers and find each unit price to determine the better buy.

California Resources

Standards Mastery
- Standards Review Transparencies
- Standards Review and Practice Workbook
- Math Companion

Math Intervention
- Skills Review and Practice Workbook
- Math XL

4. Assess & Reteach

PRESENTATION CD-ROM
CD, Online, or Transparencies
Lesson Quiz

Find the unit rate for each situation.

1. 18 in. in 3 years 6 in. per yr
2. 9 calls in 3 min 3 calls per min
3. Carli walked 16 miles in 5 hours. Find the unit rate. 3.2 mi/h
4. A 21-oz bottle of shampoo costs \$2.80. A 12-oz bottle costs \$1.35. Which bottle is the better buy? 12-oz bottle

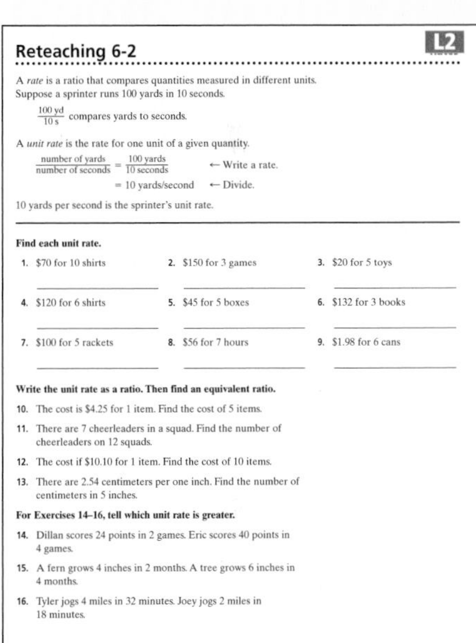

Reteaching 6-2 L2

A *rate* is a ratio that compares quantities measured in different units. Suppose a sprinter runs 100 yards in 10 seconds.

$\frac{100 \text{ yd}}{10 \text{ s}}$ compares yards to seconds.

A *unit rate* is the rate for one unit of a given quantity.

$\frac{\text{number of yards}}{\text{number of seconds}} = \frac{100 \text{ yards}}{10 \text{ seconds}}$ ← Write a rate.

$= 10$ yards/second ← Divide.

10 yards per second is the sprinter's unit rate.

Find each unit rate.

1. \$70 for 10 shirts
2. \$150 for 3 games
3. \$20 for 5 toys
4. \$120 for 6 shirts
5. \$45 for 5 boxes
6. \$132 for 3 books
7. \$100 for 5 rackets
8. \$56 for 7 hours
9. \$1.98 for 6 cans

Write the unit rate as a ratio. Then find an equivalent ratio.

10. The cost is \$4.25 for 1 item. Find the cost of 5 items.
11. There are 7 cheerleaders in a squad. Find the number of cheerleaders on 12 squads.
12. The cost if \$10.10 for 1 item. Find the cost of 10 items.
13. There are 2.54 centimeters per one inch. Find the number of centimeters in 5 inches.

For Exercises 14–16, tell which unit rate is greater.

14. Dillan scores 24 points in 2 games. Eric scores 40 points in 4 games.
15. A fern grows 4 inches in 2 months. A tree grows 6 inches in 4 months.
16. Tyler jogs 4 miles in 32 minutes. Joey jogs 2 miles in 18 minutes.

Enrichment 7-2 L4

Decision Making

Melissa is planning on attending college next year. She has decided to go to the University of Maryland, the University of Colorado, or UCLA. She made the table below to help her decide which college will cost the least based on her options.

	University of Maryland	University of Colorado	UCLA
Per Credit	\$556	\$503	\$179
Meal Plan	\$2,925	–	–
Housing	\$4,176	\$3,336	\$8,604

1. The University of Maryland is in session for 34 weeks.
   a. If Melissa eats 3 meals a day while school is in session, what is the per meal cost? How much does she pay each day for meals? about \$4.10 per meal; about \$12.29 per day
   b. How much per day does student housing cost? about \$17.55 per day
2. At the University of Colorado and UCLA, the cost of the meal plan is included in the cost of housing.
   a. School is in session for 31 weeks at the University of Colorado. What is the cost per day of housing and meals? about \$15.37 per day
   b. School is in session for 33 weeks at UCLA. What is the cost per day of housing and meals? about \$37.25 per day
   c. Compare the cost per day of housing and meals at the University of Colorado and UCLA. Which is the least expensive? Are there other issues besides cost that Melissa should consider? Explain your thinking. University of Colorado; Sample answers: tuition, quality of housing, number of meals she may eat off campus.
3. Melissa wants to compare the cost of meals and housing at the University of Maryland to the University of Colorado. How can she use unit rates to do this? Which is least expensive? Add together the cost per day for meals and for housing at Maryland, compare to the cost per day at Colorado. Colorado is still the least expensive.

Activity Lab

Simplifying Rates

Students explore ratios and rates that involve amounts expressed as fractions. This activity teaches students to write a ratio involving fractions in simplest form.

Guided Instruction

Before beginning the Activity Lab, review with students the process of writing equivalent ratios and writing ratios in simplest form. Then ask:

- *Write two ratios equivalent to $\frac{3}{8}$.* Sample answers: $\frac{6}{16}$ and $\frac{9}{24}$
- *Write the ratio 16 : 40 in simplest form.* 2 : 5

Checkpoint Quiz

Use this Checkpoint Quiz to check students' understanding of the skills and concepts of Lessons 6-1 through 6-2.

All in One Resources

- Checkpoint Quiz 1

6-2b Activity Lab

MG 1.3 Use measures expressed as rates to solve problems. *Develop*

Simplifying Rates

A ratio or rate may involve amounts expressed as fractions. To write a ratio involving fractions in simplest form, multiply both numbers in the ratio by the same number to get whole numbers.

$$\frac{3}{4} : 1\frac{1}{2} = \frac{\frac{3}{4}}{1\frac{1}{2}} \quad \leftarrow \text{Write the ratio as a fraction.}$$

$$= \frac{\frac{3}{4} \cdot 4}{1\frac{1}{2} \cdot 4} \quad \leftarrow \text{Multiply each number by 4.}$$

$$= \frac{3}{6} = \frac{1}{2} \quad \leftarrow \text{Multiply and simplify.}$$

5. Convert $\frac{1}{12}$ ft to 1 in. Then the unit rate is $2/in.

Exercises

Write each ratio as a fraction in simplest form.

1. $11\frac{1}{3} : 50\frac{2}{3}$ $\frac{17}{76}$
2. $5\frac{1}{4} : 20\frac{3}{4}$ $\frac{21}{83}$
3. $28\frac{1}{2} : 30\frac{1}{4}$ $\frac{114}{121}$
4. You run 3 mi in $\frac{1}{2}$ h. Find your unit rate of travel. 6 mi/h
5. **Reasoning** Explain how you can find a unit rate by changing units in the rate $2 : $\frac{1}{12}$ ft. See above right.

Checkpoint Quiz 1

Lessons 6-1 through 6-2

1. Write the ratio 18 : 41 in two different ways. 18 to 41 and $\frac{18}{41}$
2. In your aquarium, you have 5 red fish and 2 black fish. What is the ratio of the number of red fish to the number of black fish? 5 : 2 or 5 to 2 or $\frac{5}{2}$

Write each ratio in simplest form.

3. 48 to 70 24 to 35
4. $\frac{81}{27}$ $\frac{3}{1}$
5. 90 : 15 6 : 1
6. $\frac{25}{90}$ $\frac{5}{18}$

Find each unit rate.

7. $84 for 7 books $12/book
8. 96 m in 8 s 12 m/s
9. 57 gal in 19 min 3 gal/min
10. 232 mi in 29 h 8 mi/h
11. Cereal costs $.19 per ounce. How much does 15 oz of cereal cost? $2.85

Vocabulary Builder

High-Use Academic Words

High-use academic words are words that you will see often in textbooks and on tests. These words are not math vocabulary terms, but knowing them will help you to succeed in mathematics.

Direction Words

Some words tell what to do in a problem. I need to understand what these words are asking so that I give the correct answer.

Word	Meaning
Define	To give an accurate meaning with sufficient detail
Classify	To assign things to different groups based on their characteristics
Contrast	To show how two things are different; to include details or examples

Exercises

1. Define *salad.* Check students' work.
2. Classify each object as a fruit or a vegetable.
   a. apple fruit b. carrot vegetable c. lettuce vegetable d. banana fruit e. corn vegetable
3. Contrast a fruit salad and a vegetable salad. See below right.
4. Define *ratio.* See below right.
5. Classify each pair of ratios as equal or unequal.
   a. $\frac{1}{2}, \frac{3}{6}$ equal b. $\frac{2}{5}, \frac{4}{10}$ equal c. $\frac{5}{6}, \frac{1}{12}$ unequal d. $\frac{1}{3}, \frac{3}{9}$ equal
6. **Word Knowledge** Think about the word *comparison.*
   a. Choose the letter for how well you know the word.
      A. I know its meaning.
      B. I've seen it, but I don't know its meaning.
      C. I don't know it.
   b. **Research** Look up and write the definition of *comparison.*
   c. Use the word in a sentence involving mathematics.
   6a–c. Check students' work.

3. Answers may vary. Sample: A fruit salad contains fruit such as apples and bananas.
4. Answers may vary. Sample: A ratio is a comparison of two numbers by division.

Vocabulary Builder

High-Use Academic Words

Students become familiar with words that are frequently used in academic contexts.

Guided Instruction

These word are not strictly mathematical but students may find them in texts or tests.

Explain to students why understanding these words is helpful to them when they study math. Ask questions such as:

- *If you wanted to compare fractions and decimals and discuss their differences, what word might you use?* contrast
- *How else could you state "What is the meaning of* octagon*?"* Sample: Define *octagon.*

Use these words frequently as you teach to help students become familiar with their meanings.

Universal Access

Advanced Learners L4

Encourage students to write sentences containing these words that do not relate to math.

6-3

1. Plan

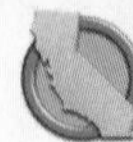

California Content Standards

MG 1.3 Use measures expressed as rates and measures expressed as products to solve problems; check the units of the solutions; and use dimensional analysis to check the reasonableness of the answer. ***Introduce, Develop***

California Math Background

Unit conversions are especially common in the sciences. Conversions are needed when anyone wants to change between and within systems of units. For instance, when changing from inches to feet, you multiply the given measurement in inches by the ratio $\frac{1 \text{ ft}}{12 \text{ in.}}$. Because 1 ft = 12 in., $\frac{1 \text{ ft}}{12 \text{ in.}}$ is a rate equal to 1 and is an example of a conversion factor. You can convert from one unit to another by multiplying a given measure by the corresponding conversion factor, which always equals 1.

More Math Background: p. 214C

Lesson Planning and Resources

See p. 214E for a list of the resources that support this lesson.

PRESENTATION CD-ROM
CD, Online, or Transparencies

Bell Ringer Practice

Check Skills You'll Need
Use student page, transparency, or PowerPoint.
See Math Companion.

California Standards Review
Use transparency or PowerPoint.

6-3 Dimensional Analysis

Check Skills You'll Need

Do this in your **Math Companion.**

Vocabulary

- conversion factor
- dimensional analysis

Use your **Math Companion** *to build your vocabulary.*

California Content Standards

MG 1.3 Use measures expressed as rates and measures expressed as products to solve problems; check the units of the solutions; and use dimensional analysis to check the reasonableness of the answer. ***Introduce, Develop***

What You'll Learn . . . and Why

You will learn to convert units and use dimensional analysis. You can use dimensional analysis to check units when finding amounts, such as how long it will take to finish a construction project.

The table below shows equivalent measures for units of length, weight, and capacity.

Length	Weight	Capacity
12 in. = 1 ft	16 oz = 1 lb	8 fl oz = 1 cup
36 in. = 1 yd	2,000 lb = 1 t	2 cups = 1 pt
3 ft = 1 yd		4 cups = 1 qt
5,280 ft = 1 mi		2 pt = 1 qt
		4 qt = 1 gal

A **conversion factor** is a rate equal to 1. For example, 12 in. = 1 ft, so $\frac{12 \text{ in.}}{1 \text{ ft}} = \frac{1 \text{ ft}}{12 \text{ in.}} = 1$. You can change one unit of measure to another by multiplying by a conversion factor. Since conversion factors equal 1, multiplying by them does not change the value of a measurement.

EXAMPLE Converting Units

1 Convert 1.2 mi to feet.

Since 5,280 ft = 1 mi, use the conversion factor $\frac{5{,}280 \text{ ft}}{1 \text{ mi}}$.

$$1.2 \text{ mi} = \frac{1.2 \cancel{\text{mi}}}{1} \cdot \frac{5{,}280 \text{ ft}}{1 \cancel{\text{mi}}}$$ ← **Multiply by the conversion factor and divide the common units.**

$$= 6{,}336 \text{ ft}$$ ← **Simplify.**

Problem Solving Tip

Choose the conversion factor with the units in the numerator and denominator that will allow you to divide common units.

CA Standards Check 1

Go to your **Math Companion** *for help.*

1. Convert each measurement.
   a. $2\frac{1}{4}$ lb to ounces 36 oz
   b. 3.5 c to fluid ounces 28 fl oz

Universal Access Solutions for All Learners

Special Needs L1	**Below Level** L2
Make sure students understand that "m" stands for meters in Example 2. Show them a meter stick, and remind them that it takes 1,000 meter sticks to cover a 1-kilometer distance.	Students find the reciprocals of $\frac{2}{3}$ $\frac{3}{2}$, 4 $\frac{1}{4}$, and $\frac{1}{2}$ 2, then multiply $\frac{3}{4}$ by $\frac{2}{3}$ $\frac{1}{2}$, 5 by $\frac{3}{5}$ 3, and $1\frac{1}{2}$ by $\frac{1}{2}$ $\frac{3}{4}$. Remind them to write mixed numbers as improper fractions.

You can multiply a rate by a conversion factor to find a unit rate in the desired units.

EXAMPLE Converting Units in a Rate

Relate MATH YOU KNOW...

Find the unit rate for traveling 2,000 m in 17.4 min.

$\frac{2{,}000 \text{ m}}{17.4 \text{ min}} \approx 114.9 \text{ m/min}$ ← Divide. Round to the nearest tenth.

... to NEW IDEAS

2 A rowing team completes a 2,000-m race in 17.4 min. Find the team's rate in meters per second.

$\frac{2{,}000 \text{ m}}{17.4 \text{ min}} = \frac{2{,}000 \text{ m}}{17.4 \text{ min}} \cdot \frac{1 \text{ min}}{60 \text{ s}}$ ← Write the rate and multiply by the conversion factor.

$= \frac{2{,}000 \text{ m}}{17.4 \not{\text{min}}} \cdot \frac{1 \not{\text{min}}}{60 \text{ s}}$ ← Divide the common units.

$\approx 1.9 \text{ m/s}$ ← Simplify. Write the correct units.

CA Standards Check 2 *Go to your* **Math Companion** *for help.*

2. You run 2 mi in 13.5 min. Find your rate of travel in feet per minute. 782.2 ft/min

Dimensional analysis is a method of determining the proper units of measure for a quantity. You can use dimensional analysis to check the reasonableness of an answer.

EXAMPLE Using Dimensional Analysis

Vocabulary Tip

You can use a hyphen to write the product of two units. For example, write *persons times hours* as "person-hours."

3 **Guided Problem Solving** A construction job takes 120 worker-hours to complete. How many hours does the job take 5 workers to finish? Use dimensional analysis to check the reasonableness of your answer.

$\frac{120}{5} = 24$ ← Divide the worker-hours by the number of workers.

The job takes 24 h.

Check for Reasonableness Use dimensional analysis to check the units of the answer.

$\frac{\not{\text{worker}} \cdot \text{hours}}{\not{\text{worker}}} = \text{hours}$ ← Divide the common units and simplify.

The question asked for the number of hours, so the answer is reasonable.

CA Standards Check 3 *Go to your* **Math Companion** *for help.*

3. You are planning a community service project that will take 50 person-hours. The project must be completed in 10 h. How many persons do you need? Use dimensional analysis to check the reasonableness of your answer. 5 persons

Check Your Understanding *Homework prep is in your* **Math Companion.**

2. Teach

Guided Instruction

Example 1

Explain that the conversion factor will have the unit of the desired measurement in the numerator and the given measurement in the denominator so the unit *miles* cancels.

PRESENTATION CD-ROM
CD, Online, or Transparencies

Additional Examples

1 Convert 0.7 mi to ft. 3,696 ft

2 A wilderness group completes a 15,000-meter hike in 5.2 hours. Find the group's rate in meters per minute. ≈ 48.1 m/min

3 The director of a political campaign has a project that will take 90 volunteer-hours. The project must be completed in 6 hours. How many volunteers will the director need? Use dimensional analysis to check the units of your answer. 15 volunteers; $\frac{\text{volunteers} \times \text{hours}}{\text{hours}} = \text{volunteers}$

Closure

- Explain how to choose a conversion factor when you use dimensional analysis. Sample: Choose a conversion factor (a rate that equals 1) that causes the units you have to cancel and the units you want to remain.

Advanced Learners L4

Students find unit rates in minutes for their heartbeat and breath. They count the number of beats or breaths in 15 seconds and use that ratio to calculate unit rates per minute.

English Learners EL

For Example 1, ask: *Since you are converting 1.2 miles to feet, will the resulting number be greater or less than 1.2?* Greater Have students explain their reasoning.

3. Practice

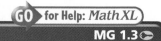

Assignment Guide

Check Your Understanding
See Math Companion.

Homework Exercises
A Practice by Example 1–20
B Apply Your Skills 21–33
C Challenge 34
California Multiple-Choice Practice 35–37
Mixed Review 38–41

Homework Quick Check
To check students' understanding of key skills and concepts, go over Exercises 2, 13, 18, 22, 28, 33.

Universal Access Resources

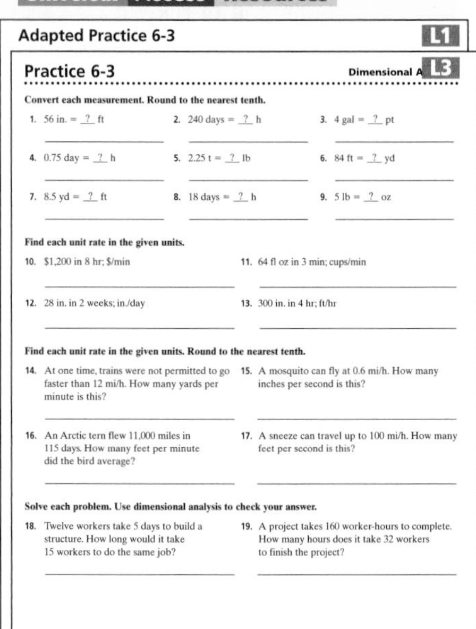

Adapted Practice 6-3 L1

Practice 6-3 Dimensional A L3

Convert each measurement. Round to the nearest tenth.

1. 56 in. = _?_ ft
2. 240 days = _?_ h
3. 4 gal = _?_ pt
4. 0.75 day = _?_ h
5. 2.25 t = _?_ lb
6. 84 ft = _?_ yd
7. 8.5 yd = _?_ ft
8. 18 days = _?_ h
9. 5 lb = _?_ oz

Find each unit rate in the given units.

10. $1,200 in 8 hr; $/min
11. 64 fl oz in 3 min; cups/min
12. 28 in. in 2 weeks; in./day
13. 300 in. in 4 hr; ft/hr

Find each unit rate in the given units. Round to the nearest tenth.

14. At one time, trains were not permitted to go faster than 12 mi/h. How many yards per minute is this?
15. A mosquito can fly at 0.6 mi/h. How many inches per second is this?
16. An Arctic tern flew 11,000 miles in 115 days. How many feet per minute did the bird average?
17. A sneeze can travel up to 100 mi/h. How many feet per second is this?

Solve each problem. Use dimensional analysis to check your answer.

18. Twelve workers take 5 days to build a structure. How long would it take 15 workers to do the same job?
19. A project takes 160 worker-hours to complete. How many hours does it take 32 workers to finish the project?

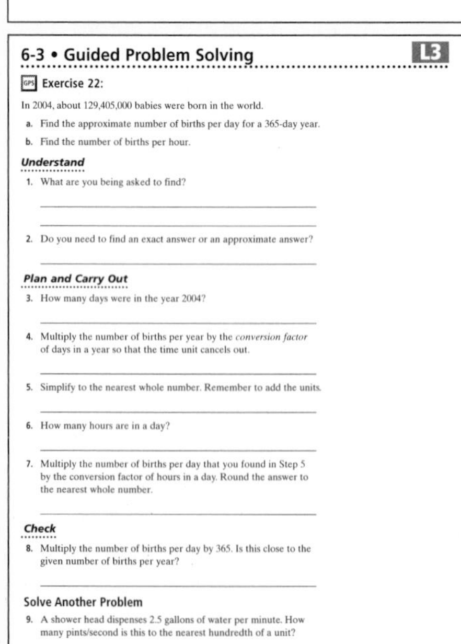

6-3 • Guided Problem Solving L3

GPS Exercise 22:

In 2004, about 129,405,000 babies were born in the world.

a. Find the approximate number of births per day for a 365-day year.
b. Find the number of births per hour.

Understand

1. What are you being asked to find?
2. Do you need to find an exact answer or an approximate answer?

Plan and Carry Out

3. How many days were in the year 2004?
4. Multiply the number of births per year by the *conversion factor* of days in a year so that the time unit cancels out.
5. Simplify to the nearest whole number. Remember to add the units.
6. How many hours are in a day?
7. Multiply the number of births per day that you found in Step 5 by the conversion factor of hours in a day. Round the answer to the nearest whole number.

Check

8. Multiply the number of births per day by 365. Is this close to the given number of births per year?

Solve Another Problem

9. A shower head dispenses 2.5 gallons of water per minute. How many pints/second is this to the nearest hundredth of a unit?

Standards Practice

GO for Help: MathXL MG 1.3

A Practice by Example

Example 1 (page 226)

Convert each measurement.

1. 6 qt = ■ pt 12 pt

$\frac{6\text{ qt}}{1} \cdot \frac{2\text{ pt}}{1\text{ qt}} = ■$

Guided Practice This exercise has been started for you!

GO for Help

2. 32 in. = ■ ft $2\frac{2}{3}$ ft
3. 125 min = ■ h $2\frac{1}{12}$ h
4. 6 lb = ■ oz 96 oz
5. 3 mi = ■ ft 15,840 ft
6. 136 pt = ■ qt 68 qt
7. 3.5 yd = ■ ft 10.5 ft
8. 5,500 lb = ■ t 2.75 t
9. 24 c = ■ gal 1.5 gal
10. 9 fl oz = ■ qt $\frac{9}{32}$ qt

Example 2 (page 227)

Find each unit rate in the given units.

11. 270 in. in 3 min; ft/min 7.5 ft/min

$\frac{270\text{ in.}}{3\text{ min}} \cdot \frac{1\text{ ft}}{12\text{ in.}} = ■$ ft/min

Guided Practice This exercise has been started for you!

12. $145 in 16 h; $/min $.15/min
13. 28 cm in 3 weeks; cm/day $1\frac{1}{3}$ cm/day
14. 24 qt in 2.5 min; gal/min 2.4 gal/min
15. 546 oz in 3 yr; lb/yr 11.375 lb/yr
16. 35 lb in 8 s; oz/s 70 oz/s
17. 243 yd in 9 h; ft/h 81 ft/h

Homework Video Tutor

For: Examples 1–3
Visit: PHSchool.com
Web Code: axe-0603

Example 3 (page 227)

Solve each problem. Use dimensional analysis to check your answer.

18. Research for a group project will take 12 person-hours. If 4 persons in the group do research, how many hours will the project take? 3 h
19. Setting up the chairs in an auditorium takes 75 person-minutes. You have 15 min to set up. How many persons are needed to set up the chairs? 5 persons
20. Six workers take 3 days to do a construction job. How long will 9 workers take to do the same job? 2 d

B Apply Your Skills

21. **Guided Problem Solving** You and two friends are painting a house. It will take 45 person-hours. If you and your friends work 5 h per day, how many days will painting the house take? 3 d
    - How many hours will the painting take you and your friends?
    - What conversion factor can you use to convert hours to days?

22. (GPS) In 2004, about 129,405,000 babies were born in the world.
    a. Find the approximate number of births per day for a 365-day year. about 355,000 births/d
    b. Find the number of births per hour. about 15,000 births/h

23. (Algebra) You can use the equation $3x = y$ to convert feet to yards, or yards to feet. Which unit of length is represented by each of the variables x and y? Explain. See left.

23. x represents yd and y represents ft since 1 yd = 3 ft.

SCAFFOLDED **Problem Solving**

A costume designer is making figure-skating costumes.

24. The designer needs two 27-in. strips of fabric for each costume. How many yards of fabric does the designer need for each costume? 1.5 yd

25. The fabric costs $6.25 per yd. How much does the fabric for one costume cost? $9.38

26. The designer uses 1.5 yd of sequin trim for each yard of fabric. How many yards of trim does the designer use in each costume? 2.25 yd

27. The designer has 40 yd of sequin trim. How many costumes can the designer make? 17 costumes

Convert each measure to a unit rate. Round to the nearest tenth.

28. $1\frac{1}{2}$ mi/h = ■ ft/day 190,080 ft/d

29. $64\frac{2}{3}$ yd/h = ■ in./s 0.6 in./s

30. $14\frac{1}{6}$ gal/min = ■ pt/s 1.9 pt/s

31. $2\frac{7}{8}$ lb/in. = ■ oz/ft 552 oz/ft

32. A $5\frac{1}{2}$ lb; B 9 lb; C 15 lb

33. Answers may vary. Sample: Count the number of times you blink in one minute, then multiply by $\frac{60 \text{ minutes}}{1 \text{ hour}}$, $\frac{24 \text{ hours}}{1 \text{ day}}$, and $\frac{7 \text{ days}}{1 \text{ week}}$.

32. Use the drawing at the right to find the weight of each block.

33. **Writing in Math** Explain how you would estimate the number of times you blink your eyes in a day or in a week.

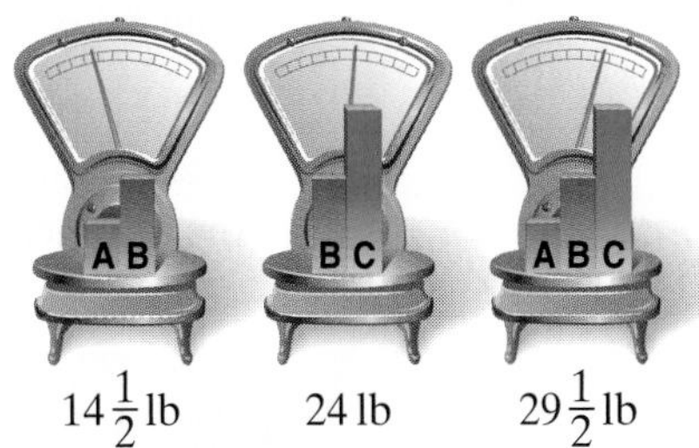

C Challenge

34. Simplify 8 qt 1 c − 6 qt 1 pt. Write the answer in simplest form. 1 qt 1 pt 1 c

Multiple Choice Practice and Mixed Review

For California Standards Tutorials, visit PHSchool.com. Web Code: axq-9045

MG 1.3

35. Four people take three days to paint a house. How long will two people take to paint another house of the same size? C

   (A) 2 d (B) 4 d (C) 6 d (D) 12 d

NS 1.3

36. Which decimal is equivalent to $\frac{6}{24}$? B

   (A) 0.24 (B) 0.25 (C) 0.3 (D) 0.6

AF 1.1

37. Sally was 30 yr old when her daughter Amy was born. Which equation can be used to find Amy's age a, using Sally's age s? C

   (A) $a = s + 30$ (C) $a = s - 30$

   (B) $s = a - 30$ (D) $s = 30a$

GO for Help **Lesson 4-3**

Write two fractions equivalent to each fraction. 38–41. See margin.

38. $\frac{2}{8}$ 39. $\frac{7}{12}$ 40. $\frac{9}{21}$ 41. $\frac{1}{11}$

Online Lesson Quiz Visit: PHSchool.com Web Code: axa-0603

4. Assess & Reteach

PRESENTATION CD-ROM
CD, Online, or Transparencies

Lesson Quiz

1. Convert 0.75 hours to seconds. 2,700 seconds
2. $150 per hour is how much per minute? $2.50 per min
3. A downhill skier travels 2,640 feet in 2 minutes. Find the skier's rate of travel in feet per second. 22 feet per second

Alternative Assessment

Pairs of students measure the length of a school corridor in yards. They convert that length to feet, and then to meters. They repeat the activity with other objects and units of measure.

California Resources

Standards Mastery

- Standards Review Transparencies
- Standards Review and Practice Workbook
- Math Companion

Math Intervention

- Skills Review and Practice Workbook
- Math XL

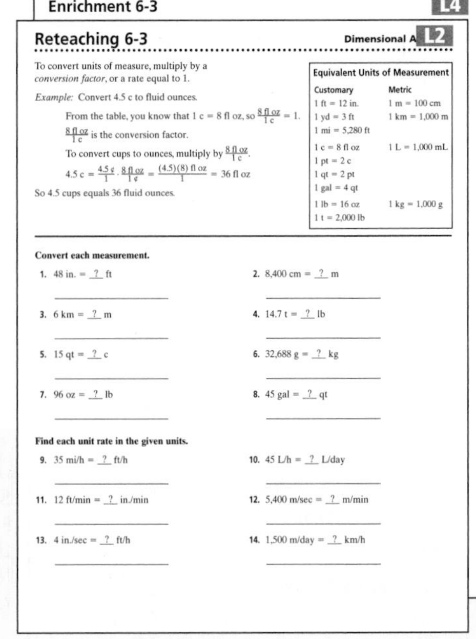

Enrichment 6-3 L4

Reteaching 6-3 Dimensional A L2

To convert units of measure, multiply by a *conversion factor*, or a rate equal to 1.

Example: Convert 4.5 c to fluid ounces.

From the table, you know that 1 c = 8 fl oz, so $\frac{8 \text{ fl oz}}{1 \text{ c}} = 1$.

$\frac{8 \text{ fl oz}}{1 \text{ c}}$ is the conversion factor.

To convert cups to ounces, multiply by $\frac{8 \text{ fl oz}}{1 \text{ c}}$.

$4.5 \text{ c} = \frac{4.5 \text{ c}}{1} \cdot \frac{8 \text{ fl oz}}{1 \text{ c}} = \frac{(4.5)(8) \text{ fl oz}}{1} = 36 \text{ fl oz}$

So 4.5 cups equals 36 fluid ounces.

Equivalent Units of Measurement	
Customary	Metric
1 ft = 12 in.	1 m = 100 cm
1 yd = 3 ft	1 km = 1,000 m
1 mi = 5,280 ft	
1 c = 8 fl oz	1 L = 1,000 mL
1 pt = 2 c	
1 qt = 2 pt	
1 gal = 4 qt	
1 lb = 16 oz	1 kg = 1,000 g
1 t = 2,000 lb	

Convert each measurement.

1. 48 in. = ? ft
2. 8,400 cm = ? m
3. 6 km = ? m
4. 14.7 t = ? lb
5. 15 qt = ? c
6. 32,688 g = ? kg
7. 96 oz = ? lb
8. 45 gal = ? qt

Find each unit rate in the given units.

9. 35 mi/h = ? ft/h
10. 45 L/h = ? L/day
11. 12 ft/min = ? in./min
12. 5,400 m/sec = ? m/min
13. 4 in./sec = ? ft/h
14. 1,500 m/day = ? km/h

6-4

1. Plan

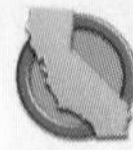

California Content Standards

AF 4.2 Solve multistep problems involving rate, average speed, distance, and time or a direct variation. ***Introduce, Develop***

MG 1.3 Use measures expressed as rates to solve problems; check the units of the solutions; and use dimensional analysis to check the reasonableness of the answer. ***Develop***

California Math Background

A *rate* is a ratio that compares quantities in different units, such as 5 gallons : 3 minutes or 50 miles : 2 hours.

A *unit rate* is the rate for one unit of a given quantity, such as 3 meters per second. This gives the rate for one unit of time (seconds).

More Math Background: p. 214C

Lesson Planning and Resources

See p. 214E for a list of the resources that support this lesson.

PRESENTATION CD-ROM
CD, Online, or Transparencies

Bell Ringer Practice

Check Skills You'll Need
Use student page, transparency, or PowerPoint.
See Math Companion.

California Standards Review
Use transparency or PowerPoint.

GO for Help: Math Companion

6-4 Applications of Rates

Check Skills You'll Need

Do this in your **Math Companion.**

Vocabulary

Review:
- rate
- unit rate

Use your **Math Companion** *to build your vocabulary.*

California Content Standards

AF 4.2 Solve multistep problems involving rate, average speed, distance, and time or a direct variation. ***Introduce, Develop***

MG 1.3 Use measures expressed as rates to solve problems; check the units of the solutions; and use dimensional analysis to check the reasonableness of the answer. ***Develop***

What You'll Learn . . . and Why

You will learn to solve multi-step rate problems. You can use rates to find total distances, such as the distance you ride your bike.

Some problems involve more than one rate. To find a total distance, first find the distance traveled at each rate. Then add the individual distances.

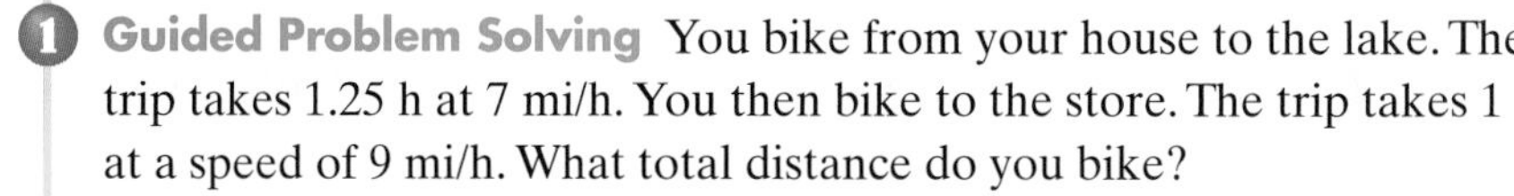

EXAMPLE Finding Total Distance

1 **Guided Problem Solving** You bike from your house to the lake. The trip takes 1.25 h at 7 mi/h. You then bike to the store. The trip takes 1 h at a speed of 9 mi/h. What total distance do you bike?

First find the distance of each part of the trip.

$$\text{distance to lake} = \text{rate to lake} \cdot \text{time to lake}$$
$$= 7\,\frac{\text{mi}}{\cancel{\text{h}}} \cdot 1.25\,\cancel{\text{h}}$$
$$= 8.75 \text{ mi}$$
$$\text{distance to store} = \text{rate to store} \cdot \text{time to store}$$
$$= 9\,\frac{\text{mi}}{\cancel{\text{h}}} \cdot 1\,\cancel{\text{h}}$$
$$= 9 \text{ mi}$$
$$\text{total distance} = 8.75 \text{ mi} + 9 \text{ mi} \quad \leftarrow \text{Add the two distances.}$$
$$= 17.75 \text{ mi} \quad \leftarrow \text{Simplify.}$$

You bike a total of 17.75 mi.

Math Foundations

To find a distance d, use the formula $d = rt$, where r is the rate of travel and t is the amount of travel time.

CA Standards Check 1

Go to your **Math Companion** *for help.*

1. A boat travels 10 mi/h for 15 min and 12 mi/h for 5 min. What total distance does the boat travel? 3.5 mi

Universal Access Solutions for All Learners

Special Needs L1	**Below Level** L2
For Example 1, have students draw a diagram showing the house, the lake, and the store, and label the lengths between these places with the rate and travel time.	For Example 1, have students use dimensional analysis to check the reasonableness of their answers. Ask them to describe how they know the answer is correct.

To find an average speed, divide the total distance traveled by the total amount of time.

EXAMPLE Finding Average Speed

2 A car travels 35 mi/h for 1 h. It then travels 50 mi/h for 1.5 h. What is the car's average speed over the total distance?

$$\text{total distance} = 35\,\frac{\text{mi}}{\cancel{\text{h}}} \cdot 1\,\cancel{\text{h}} + 50\,\frac{\text{mi}}{\cancel{\text{h}}} \cdot 1.5\,\cancel{\text{h}} = 110 \text{ mi}$$

$$\text{total time} = 1 \text{ h} + 1.5 \text{ h} = 2.5 \text{ h}$$

$$\text{average speed} = \frac{\text{total distance}}{\text{total time}}$$ ← **Average speed is total distance divided by total time.**

$$= \frac{110 \text{ mi}}{2.5 \text{ h}}$$ ← **Substitute the values for total time and total distance.**

$$= 44\,\frac{\text{mi}}{\text{h}}$$ ← **Simplify.**

The car's average speed is 44 mi/h.

CA Standards Check 2 *Go to your* **Math Companion** *for help.*

2. A bird flies 16.5 mi/h for 2 h and 10 mi/h for 1.25 h. What is the bird's average speed? 14 mi/h

If a unit rate stays the same, the two quantities in the rate vary directly.

EXAMPLE Using a Unit Rate

Relate **MATH YOU KNOW...**

Find the unit rate of 13.5 in. to 6 lb.

$$\frac{13.5 \text{ in.}}{6 \text{ lb}} = 2.25\,\frac{\text{in.}}{\text{lb}}$$ ← **Write a rate and divide to find the unit rate.**

... to **NEW IDEAS**

3 The distance a spring stretches varies directly with the force applied to it. A 6-lb weight stretches a spring 13.5 in. How far will a 9-lb weight stretch the spring?

$$\frac{13.5 \text{ in.}}{6 \text{ lb}} = 2.25\,\frac{\text{in.}}{\text{lb}}$$ ← **Find the unit rate.**

$$9 \cdot 2.25 = 20.25$$ ← **Multiply the weight by the unit rate.**

A 9-lb weight will stretch the spring 20.25 in.

Check for Reasonableness Use dimensional analysis to check the units: $\cancel{\text{lb}} \cdot \frac{\text{in.}}{\cancel{\text{lb}}} = \text{in.}$ The question asked for inches, so the answer is reasonable.

CA Standards Check 3 *Go to your* **Math Companion** *for help.*

3. a. The cost of 4 shirts is $22. How much do 7 shirts cost? $38.50

b. Eight bottles cost $6. Find the cost of 11 bottles. $8.25

Check Your Understanding *Homework prep is in your* **Math Companion.**

Advanced Learners L4
Have students estimate the distance they live from school and the amount of time it takes for them to travel from home to school. Then have them use these estimated values to calculate the average speed they travel.

English Learners EL
Make sure that students understand that rates such as "30 miles per hour" and "30 mi/h" are the same as the unit rate $\frac{30 \text{ miles}}{1 \text{ hour}}$.

2. Teach

Guided Instruction

Example 2
Show students the importance of working in steps to reach the final answer. Explain that they must first find the total distance traveled and total travel time before calculating the average speed.

PRESENTATION CD-ROM
CD, Online, or Transparencies

Additional Examples

1 A bus drives from the center of a city to its first stop. The trip takes 0.25 hours at 15 mi/h. The bus then continues on the highway to a park-and-ride station. The trip takes 0.50 hours at a speed of 56 mi/h. What is the total distance traveled by the bus? 31.75 miles

2 A speed skater travels 8 meters per second for 30 seconds, and then travels 6 meters per second for 18 seconds. What is the skater's average speed over the total distance? 7.25 meters per second

3 At a poster store, the shipping cost of a poster varies directly with its width. A poster that has a width of 16 inches costs $12 to ship. What is the shipping cost of a poster that has a width of 20 inches? $15

Closure

- *Explain how you can use dimensional analysis to check the reasonableness of answers to problems involving rates.* Since rates involve quantities in different units, you can use dimensional analysis to ensure that the operations used in solving the problem reduce the units from the rate to the correct units in the answer.

3. Practice

Assignment Guide

Check Your Understanding

See Math Companion.

Homework Exercises

A Practice by Example	1–12
B Apply Your Skills	13–21
C Challenge	22
California Multiple-Choice Practice	23–25
Mixed Review	26–28

Homework Quick Check

To check students' understanding of key skills and concepts, go over Exercises 3, 8, 14, 20, 21.

Universal Access Resources

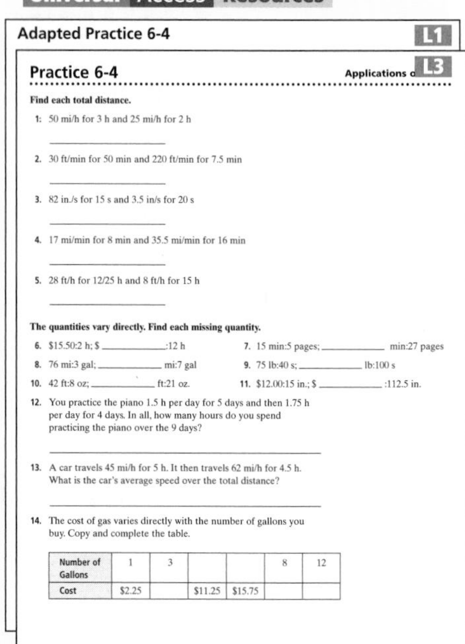

Adapted Practice 6-4 L1

Practice 6-4 — Applications o… L3

Find each total distance.

1. 50 mi/h for 3 h and 25 mi/h for 2 h ______
2. 30 ft/min for 50 min and 220 ft/min for 7.5 min ______
3. 82 in./s for 15 s and 3.5 in/s for 20 s ______
4. 17 mi/min for 8 min and 35.5 mi/min for 16 min ______
5. 28 ft/h for 12/25 h and 8 ft/h for 15 h ______

The quantities vary directly. Find each missing quantity.

6. \$15.50:2 h; \$ ______ :12 h
7. 15 min:5 pages; ______ min:27 pages
8. 76 mi:3 gal; ______ mi:7 gal
9. 75 lb:40 s; ______ lb:100 s
10. 42 ft:8 oz; ______ ft:21 oz.
11. \$12.00:15 in.; \$ ______ :112.5 in.
12. You practice the piano 1.5 h per day for 5 days and then 1.75 h per day for 4 days. In all, how many hours do you spend practicing the piano over the 9 days? ______
13. A car travels 45 mi/h for 5 h. It then travels 62 mi/h for 4.5 h. What is the car's average speed over the total distance? ______
14. The cost of gas varies directly with the number of gallons you buy. Copy and complete the table.

Number of Gallons	1	3			8	12
Cost	\$2.25		\$11.25	\$15.75		

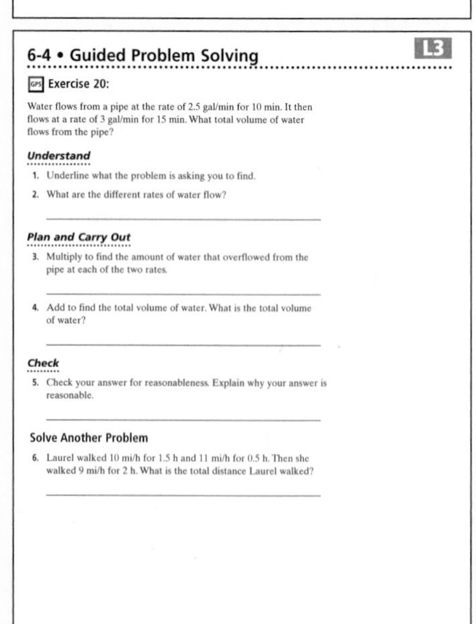

6-4 • Guided Problem Solving L3

GPS Exercise 20:

Water flows from a pipe at the rate of 2.5 gal/min for 10 min. It then flows at a rate of 3 gal/min for 15 min. What total volume of water flows from the pipe?

Understand

1. Underline what the problem is asking you to find.
2. What are the different rates of water flow? ______

Plan and Carry Out

3. Multiply to find the amount of water that overflowed from the pipe at each of the two rates. ______
4. Add to find the total volume of water. What is the total volume of water? ______

Check

5. Check your answer for reasonableness. Explain why your answer is reasonable. ______

Solve Another Problem

6. Laurel walked 10 mi/h for 1.5 h and 11 mi/h for 0.5 h. Then she walked 9 mi/h for 2 h. What is the total distance Laurel walked? ______

GO for Help: MathXL

Standards Practice

AF 4.2, MG 1.3

A Practice by Example

Example 1 (page 230)

Find each total distance.

1. 45 mi/h for 2 h and 32 mi/h for 5 h
   $45\ \frac{\text{mi}}{\cancel{\text{h}}} \cdot 2\ \cancel{\text{h}} = 90\text{ mi} \qquad 32\ \frac{\text{mi}}{\cancel{\text{h}}} \cdot 5\ \cancel{\text{h}} = 160\text{ mi}$
   total distance = ■ mi + ■ mi 250 mi

Guided Practice This exercise has been started for you!

GO for Help

2. 36 m/s for 20 s and 14 m/s for 6 s 804 m
3. 7.9 ft/min for 4 min and 12 ft/min for 3.5 min 73.6 ft
4. You drive 35 mi/h for $\frac{1}{2}$ h. You then drive 25 mi/h for $\frac{1}{5}$ h. How far do you drive in all? 22.5 mi

Example 2 (page 231)

5. You walk 2 mi/h for 0.75 h and 2.5 mi/h for 1 h. What is your average speed over the total distance? 2.3 mi/h
6. A caterpillar crawls 2 ft/min for 4 min and 1.25 ft/min for 2 min. What is the caterpillar's average speed over the total distance? 1.75 ft/min

Example 3 (page 231)

The quantities vary directly. Find each missing quantity.

7. 85 mi : 4 gal; ■ mi : 12 gal
   $\frac{85\text{ mi}}{4\text{ gal}} = 21.25\ \frac{\text{mi}}{\text{gal}}$
   $21.25\ \frac{\text{mi}}{\cancel{\text{gal}}} \cdot 12\ \cancel{\text{gal}} = ■\text{ mi}$ 255

Guided Practice This exercise has been started for you!

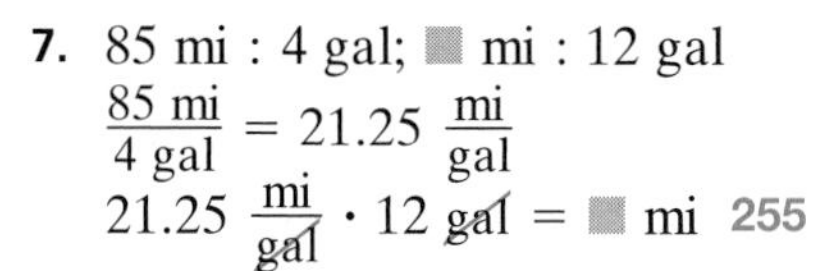

For: Examples 1–3
Visit: PHSchool.com
Web Code: axe-0604

8. \$58.50 : 13 books; \$■ : 16 books 72
9. 40 ft : 25 min; ■ ft : 55 min 88
10. 12 lb : 3 in.; ■ lb : 4.5 in. 18
11. 25 oz : 75 s; ■ oz : 125 s $41\frac{2}{3}$
12. The cost of 3 qt of milk is \$6.75. How much will 7 qt of milk cost? \$15.75

B Apply Your Skills

13. **Guided Problem Solving** A boat travels downstream at 10 mi/h for 1.5 h. Then the speed of the current increases and the boat travels for 1 h at a speed 5 mi/h faster than before. What distance does the boat travel? 30 mi
    - What is the speed of the boat on the second part of the trip?
    - What distance does the boat travel on each part of the trip?
14. Your pay varies directly with the number of hours you work. Copy and complete the table at the right. See margin.

Hours	1	■	4	6	■	■
Pay (Dollars)	5	10	■	■	35	50

15. You read for 3 h per day for 2 days, and then for 1.5 h per day for 4 days. Then you read for 2.5 h per day for 3 days. In all, how many hours do you spend reading over the 9 days? 19.5 h

SCAFFOLDED
Problem Solving

Copy and complete the table below.

Car	Rate	Time	Distance
A	45 mi/h	3 h	■
B	52 mi/h	2.5 h	■
C	■	t	■

16. How far does Car A travel? 135 mi

17. Which car travels a greater distance, Car A or Car B? Explain. See left.

17. Car A; Car A travels 135 mi and Car B travels 130 mi, so Car A travels farther.

18. Car C travels at a rate of 40 mi/h. It goes the same distance as Car A. Write and solve an equation to find t, the length of time Car C travels. $40t = 135$; 3.375 h

19. Car C then travels an additional 0.75 h at 20 mi/h. What is Car C's average speed? 36.36 mi/h

GPS 20. Water flows from a pipe at a rate of 2.5 gal/min for 10 min. It then flows at a rate of 3 gal/min for 15 min. What total volume of water flows from the pipe? 70 gal

21. **Writing in Math** Describe how you can use dimensional analysis to check for reasonableness when you find an average speed. See left.

21. Answers may vary. Sample: average speed = total distance ÷ total time, so answer should have a unit of distance divided by a unit of time.

C Challenge

22. You bike 6 mi/h from your house to a friend's house and arrive in 30 min. You leave your friend's house at 4:40 P.M. At what rate do you have to bike to be home by 5:00 P.M.? 9 mi/h

Multiple Choice Practice and Mixed Review

For California Standards Tutorials, visit PHSchool.com. Web Code: axq-9045

AF 4.2

23. The distance a spring stretches varies directly with the weight applied to it. A 12-oz weight stretches a spring 2.4 in. How far will a 9-oz weight stretch the spring? B

    (A) 0.2 in. (B) 1.8 in. (C) 2.4 in. (D) 9 in.

MG 1.3

24. Matt can type 216 words in 6 min. Lya can type 128 words in 4 min. Which statement is supported by the information? A

    (A) Matt can type faster than Lya.
    (B) Lya can type faster than Matt.
    (C) In 20 min, Matt can type 88 more words than Lya.
    (D) Matt can type 400 words in 10 min.

NS 1.2

25. Find the sum $-7.3 + 4.9 + (-3.4)$. B

    (A) -15.6 (B) -5.8 (C) 5.8 (D) 15.6

Lesson 4-3 **Write each fraction in simplest form.**

26. $\frac{4}{36}$ $\frac{1}{9}$ 27. $\frac{28}{7}$ 4 28. $\frac{24}{30}$ $\frac{4}{5}$ 29. $\frac{121}{550}$ $\frac{11}{50}$

Online Lesson Quiz Visit: PHSchool.com Web Code: axa-0604

Alternative Assessment

Students work in small groups and use stopwatches to record the amount of time it takes to walk a fixed distance, such as across the classroom. They then use this data to calculate their average walking speed.

California Resources

Standards Mastery
- Standards Review Transparencies
- Standards Review and Practice Workbook
- Math Companion

Math Intervention
- Skills Review and Practice Workbook
- Math XL

4. Assess & Reteach

...PRESENTATION CD-ROM
CD, Online, or Transparencies
Lesson Quiz

Find each total distance.

1. 55 mi/h for 1.5 hours and 60 mi/hr for 0.75 hours
   127.5 miles
2. 8 meters per second for 2.5 seconds and 6 meters per second for 1.8 seconds
   30.8 meters

Find the missing quantities. Each of the following quantities vary directly.

3. 53 miles : 2 gallons; ■ miles : 5 gallons 132.5
4. 16 feet : 2.5 seconds; ■ feet : 5.6 seconds 35.84

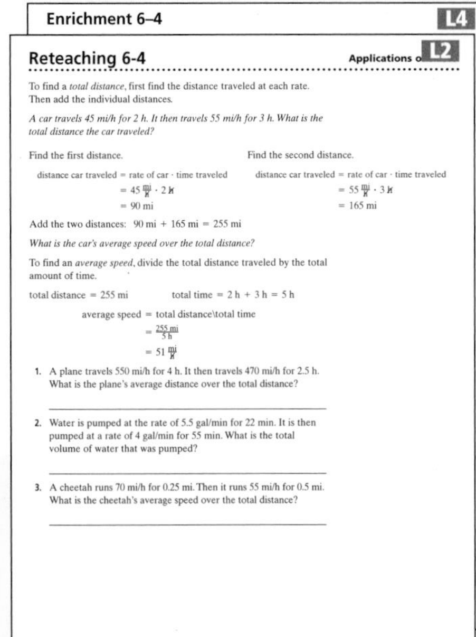

Enrichment 6–4 L4

Reteaching 6-4 Applications o L2

To find a *total distance*, first find the distance traveled at each rate. Then add the individual distances.

A car travels 45 mi/h for 2 h. It then travels 55 mi/h for 3 h. What is the total distance the car traveled?

Find the first distance.

distance car traveled = rate of car · time traveled
$= 45 \frac{mi}{h} \cdot 2 h$
$= 90$ mi

Find the second distance.

distance car traveled = rate of car · time traveled
$= 55 \frac{mi}{h} \cdot 3 h$
$= 165$ mi

Add the two distances: 90 mi + 165 mi = 255 mi

What is the car's average speed over the total distance?

To find an *average speed*, divide the total distance traveled by the total amount of time.

total distance = 255 mi total time = 2 h + 3 h = 5 h

average speed = total distance\total time
$= \frac{255 \text{ mi}}{5 \text{ h}}$
$= 51 \frac{mi}{h}$

1. A plane travels 550 mi/h for 4 h. It then travels 470 mi/h for 2.5 h. What is the plane's average distance over the total distance?

2. Water is pumped at the rate of 5.5 gal/min for 22 min. It is then pumped at a rate of 4 gal/min for 55 min. What is the total volume of water that was pumped?

3. A cheetah runs 70 mi/h for 0.25 mi. Then it runs 55 mi/h for 0.5 mi. What is the cheetah's average speed over the total distance?

Checkpoint Quiz

Use this Checkpoint Quiz to check students' understanding of the skills and concepts of Lessons 6-3 through 6-4.

All in One Resources

- Checkpoint Quiz 2

Mathematical Reasoning

Proportional Reasoning

Students learn to use visual models to write equivalent ratios and solve problems.

Guided Instruction

Explain to students how visual models can be used to represent fractions. Show that a circle divided into 4 equal sections with 1 section shaded can represent the ratio 1 : 4. Make sure students do not misunderstand the model by comparing shaded to unshaded sections. For Exercise 3, have students compare the methods they used to show that the ratios are equivalent.

Checkpoint Quiz 2

Lessons 6-3 through 6-4

Convert each measurement. If necessary, round to the nearest tenth.

1. 1.2 h = ■ min 72 min
2. 9 oz = ■ lb $\frac{9}{16}$ lb or 0.5625 lb
3. 5 yd = ■ in. 180 in.
4. 16 gal = ■ qt 64 qt
5. 2.5 ft = ■ in. 30 in.
6. 4.2 pt = ■ gal 0.525 gal
7. A construction job takes 35 person-hours to complete. If 5 people work on the job, how many hours will the job take? 7 h
8. You buy six beverages for $2.97. Find the cost of 16 beverages. $7.92
9. You bike 4 mi/h for 0.5 h and 9 mi/h for 0.25 h. What is your average speed over the total distance? 5.7 mi/h

Mathematical Reasoning

For Use With Lesson 6-5

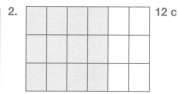

MG 1.3 Use measures expressed as rates to solve problems. ***Develop***

MR 2.5 Use diagrams to explain mathematical reasoning. ***Develop***

Proportional Reasoning

A recipe for fruit punch calls for 4 parts of apple juice for every 2 parts of grape juice. How much apple juice is needed to make 18 c of punch?

ACTIVITY

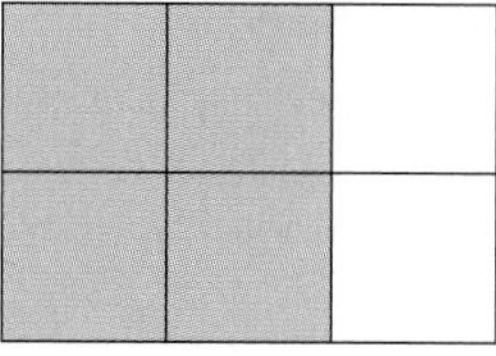

1. Use the diagram at the right to write a ratio comparing the amount of apple juice to the amount of punch. $\frac{4}{6}$

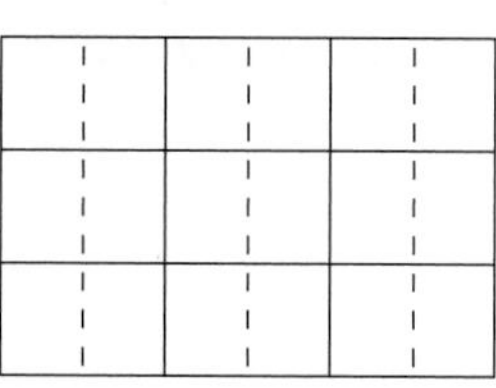

2\.

12 c

2. Copy the diagram at the right. Shade the same ratio of the diagram as in Exercise 1 to find the number of cups of apple juice needed to make 18 c of punch.
3. Are the ratios shown in the diagrams for Exercises 1 and 2 equivalent? Explain. Yes; both ratios simplify to $\frac{2}{3}$.
4. **Reasoning** Use equivalent ratios to find the number of cups of apple juice needed to make 9 c of punch. Draw a diagram to support your reasoning. 6 c; check students' diagrams.

GO for Help: Math Companion

6-5 Proportions

Check Skills You'll Need

Do this in your **Math Companion.**

Vocabulary

- proportion
- cross products

Use your **Math Companion** *to build your vocabulary.*

California Content Standards

MG 1.3 Use measurements expressed as rates to solve problems. ***Develop, Master***

What You'll Learn . . . and Why

You will learn to identify and solve proportions. You can use proportions and exchange rates to convert U.S. dollars to euros.

A **proportion** is an equation stating that two ratios are equal. The rectangles below have the same amount shaded, because the ratios $\frac{12}{32}$ and $\frac{3}{8}$ are equal. The equation $\frac{12}{32} = \frac{3}{8}$ is a proportion.

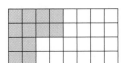

$\frac{12}{32}$ ← shaded / ← total

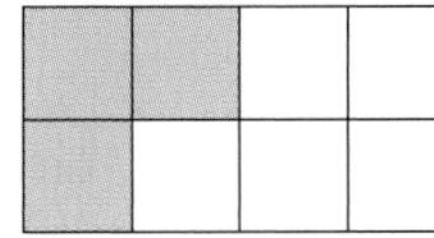

$\frac{3}{8}$ ← shaded / ← total

Take Note — Proportion

Ratios that are equal form a proportion.

Arithmetic	Algebra
$\frac{12}{32} = \frac{3}{8}$	$\frac{a}{b} = \frac{c}{d}$, where $b \neq 0$ and $d \neq 0$

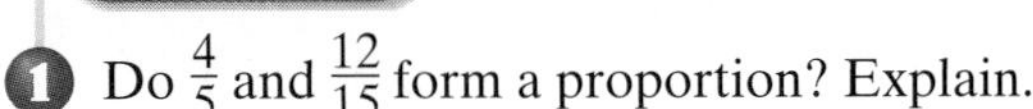

EXAMPLE Identifying Proportions

1 Do $\frac{4}{5}$ and $\frac{12}{15}$ form a proportion? Explain.

$\frac{4}{5} \stackrel{?}{=} \frac{12}{15}$ ← **Write as a proportion.**

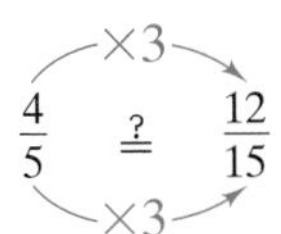

$\frac{4}{5} \stackrel{?}{=} \frac{12}{15}$ (×3 top and bottom) ← **Use number sense to find a common multiplier.**

Since $\frac{4}{5} = \frac{12}{15}$, they form a proportion.

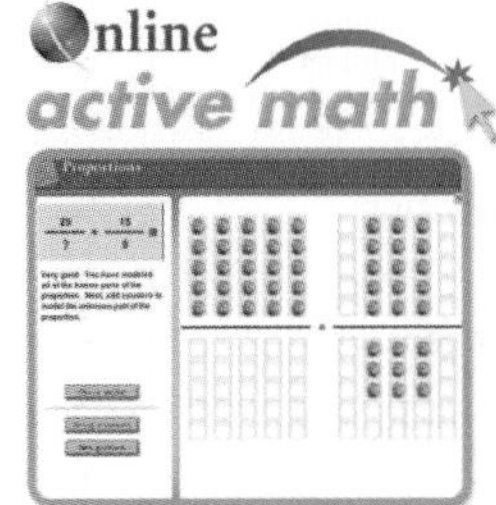

Online active math

For: Proportions Activity
Use: Interactive Textbook, 6-5

CA Standards Check 1

Go to your **Math Companion** *for help.*

1. Do the ratios form a proportion? Explain.

a. $\frac{6}{7}, \frac{23}{28}$ no; $\frac{6}{7} \neq \frac{23}{28}$

b. $\frac{16}{20}, \frac{74}{100}$ no; $\frac{16}{20} \neq \frac{74}{100}$

Universal Access Solutions for All Learners

Special Needs L1
After Example 1, give students a drawing of two congruent rectangles. (One rectangle is divided into 7 equal columns, the other into 7 equal columns and 4 equal rows.) Have them shade $\frac{6}{7}$ of the first rectangle, and $\frac{24}{28}$ of the second rectangle. Ask: *Is the same amount shaded?* yes

Below Level L2
Students use cross products to verify that ratios are equivalent with examples such as these.

$\frac{2}{3} = \frac{4}{6}$ $\qquad$ $\frac{10}{2} = \frac{5}{1}$

$2 \cdot 6 = 3 \cdot 4$ $\qquad$ $10 \cdot 1 = 2 \cdot 5$

6-5

1. Plan

California Content Standards

MG 1.3 Use measurements expressed as rates to solve problems. ***Develop, Master***

Professional Development

California Math Background

A proportion is a comparison between ratios, in the form $\frac{a}{b} = \frac{c}{d}$, where *a, b, c,* and *d* are rational numbers. To show students why it is necessary to state that *b* and *d* cannot equal zero in the general statement of a proportion, remind them that, for instance, in $\frac{10}{0} = x$, there is no value for *x* that will make 0 times *x* equal to 10.

More Math Background: p. 214C

Lesson Planning and Resources

See p. 214E for a list of the resources that support this lesson.

PRESENTATION CD-ROM
CD, Online, or Transparencies

Bell Ringer Practice

Check Skills You'll Need
Use student page, transparency, or PowerPoint.
See Math Companion.

California Standards Review
Use transparency or PowerPoint.

2. Teach

Guided Instruction

Math Tip
Explain to students that when you write the proportion in Example 1, you are testing whether or not the two ratios are really equal. So you must put a question mark over the equal sign until you are sure that the cross products have the same value.

Teaching Tip
Make sure students realize that they could write the proportion in Example 2 in a different form, such as $\frac{d}{250} = \frac{1}{0.7822}$ or $\frac{0.7822}{250} = \frac{1}{d}$, and get the same result. Help students keep track of what they are comparing by having them indicate the units.

Additional Examples

1. Do $\frac{4}{9}$ and $\frac{8}{18}$ form a proportion? Explain. Since $\frac{4}{9}$ and $\frac{8}{18}$ are equal, they form a proportion.

2. The fixed rate of conversion is 1 euro = 0.7876 Irish pounds. How many euros would you receive for 125 Irish pounds? 158.71 euros

Problem Solving Tip
You can use cross products to identify a proportion. If the cross products of two ratios are equal, then the ratios are equal and they form a proportion.

You find the **cross products** of two ratios by multiplying the numerator of each ratio by the denominator of the other ratio. The cross products of a proportion are always equal.

$$\frac{4}{5} = \frac{12}{15} \quad \leftarrow \text{Start with a proportion.}$$

$$\frac{4}{5} \cdot 5 \cdot 15 = \frac{12}{15} \cdot 5 \cdot 15 \quad \leftarrow \text{Multiply each side by the values in the denominators.}$$

$$\frac{4}{\cancel{5}_1} \cdot \cancel{5}^1 \cdot 15 = \frac{12}{\cancel{15}_1} \cdot 5 \cdot \cancel{15}^1 \quad \leftarrow \text{Divide the common factors.}$$

$$4 \cdot 15 = 12 \cdot 5 \quad \leftarrow \text{Simplify.}$$

$$60 = 60 \quad \leftarrow \text{The cross products are equal.}$$

Take Note **Cross-Products Property**

The cross products of a proportion are always equal.

Arithmetic	Algebra
$\frac{4}{5} = \frac{12}{15}$	$\frac{a}{b} = \frac{c}{d}$, where $b \neq 0$ and $d \neq 0$
$4 \cdot 15 = 5 \cdot 12$	$ad = bc$

You can use cross products to solve a proportion.

Relate MATH YOU KNOW... ...to ALGEBRA

EXAMPLE **Solving Proportions Using Cross Products**

You exchange 250 euros for \$319.61. Find the unit rate of exchange.

$$\frac{250 \text{ euros}}{\$319.61} \approx 0.7822 \text{ euro/dollar} \quad \leftarrow \text{Write the rate and divide.}$$

2 **Guided Problem Solving** Use the exchange rate 0.7822 euros = 1 dollar to find the number of dollars you receive for exchanging 250 euros.

Let d = the number of dollars.

$$\frac{0.7822}{1} = \frac{250}{d} \quad \leftarrow \text{Write a proportion using the ratio } \frac{\text{euros}}{\text{dollars}}.$$

$$0.7822 \cdot d = 1 \cdot 250 \quad \leftarrow \text{Write the cross products.}$$

$$\frac{0.7822d}{0.7822} = \frac{250}{0.7822} \quad \leftarrow \text{Isolate the variable. Use the Division Property of Equality.}$$

$$d \approx 319.61 \quad \leftarrow \text{Simplify. Round to the nearest cent.}$$

You receive \$319.61.

CA Standards Check 2 *Go to your* **Math Companion** *for help.*

2. Use the exchange rate 10.912 pesos = 1 dollar to find the number of dollars you receive for exchanging 250 pesos. \$22.91

Advanced Learners L4	**English Learners** EL
Ask: *What is the cost of a T-shirt marked 15 euros if the current exchange rate is \$.95 = 1 euro?* \$14.25	Discuss Jasmine's method. Why did Jasmine write $\frac{\$5.60}{16 \text{ batteries}}$? \$5.60 is the cost for 16 batteries. Dividing \$5.60 by 16 gives the unit cost for 1 battery.

More Than One Way

A store is having a sale on batteries for the price shown in the ad below.

However, the store has run out of 16-packs. The manager agrees to sell you 10-packs of AA batteries at the same unit price. About how much should a 10-pack of batteries cost?

Eric's Method

I'll set up a proportion and use the Cross-Products Property to solve it.

Let $x =$ the cost of 10 batteries.

$$\frac{16 \text{ batteries}}{\$5.60} = \frac{10 \text{ batteries}}{x \text{ dollars}}$$

$$16 \cdot x = 5.6 \cdot 10$$

$$16x = 56$$

$$\frac{16x}{16} = \frac{56}{16}$$

$$x = 3.5$$

A 10-pack of batteries should cost $3.50.

Jasmine's Method

I'll find the unit rate for the cost of one battery. Then I'll multiply to find the cost of 10 batteries.

$$\frac{\text{price}}{\text{number of batteries}} = \frac{\$5.60}{16 \text{ batteries}}$$

$$= \$.35 \text{ per battery}$$

The unit rate is $.35 per battery. So 10 batteries cost $10 \cdot \$.35 = \$3.50$. A 10-pack of batteries should cost $3.50.

Choose a Method

An ad for a video store says "3 movies for $18." At that rate, what is the cost of 5 movies? Describe your method and explain why you chose it.
$30; check students' work.

Check Your Understanding *Homework prep is in your* **Math Companion.**

Guided Instruction

Alternative Method

The method of solving proportions using a common multiplier is sometimes called the "factor of change" method. You can scale a ratio up or down to an equivalent ratio by multiplying its terms by a common multiplier, just as you can generate equivalent fractions by multiplying the numerator and denominator of a fraction by a common multiplier.

Error Prevention!

Remind students why you can only use cross multiplication with a proportion and not when adding (as in $\frac{1}{3} + \frac{2}{4}$) or multiplying (as in $\frac{3}{4} \cdot \frac{1}{6}$) fractions.

Closure

- *Explain how to solve a proportion.* **Sample: Find the cross products and then divide each side of the equation by the number that is the multiplier of the variable.**

3. Practice

Assignment Guide

Check Your Understanding

See Math Companion.

Homework Exercises

A Practice by Example	1–20
B Apply Your Skills	21–35
C Challenge	36
California Multiple-Choice Practice	37–39
Mixed Review	40–42

Homework Quick Check

To check students' understanding of key skills and concepts, go over Exercises 6, 11, 27, 34, 35.

Universal Access Resources

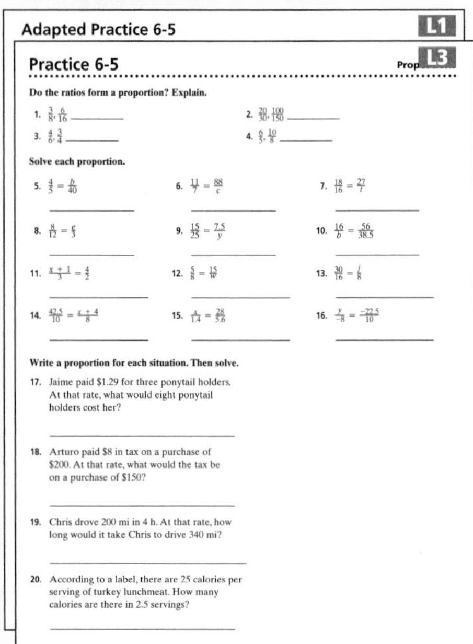

Adapted Practice 6-5 L1

Practice 6-5 Prop L3

Do the ratios form a proportion? Explain.

1. $\frac{3}{8}, \frac{6}{16}$ ______
2. $\frac{20}{30}, \frac{100}{150}$ ______
3. $\frac{4}{6}, \frac{3}{4}$ ______
4. $\frac{6}{5}, \frac{10}{8}$ ______

Solve each proportion.

5. $\frac{4}{5} = \frac{b}{40}$
6. $\frac{11}{7} = \frac{88}{c}$
7. $\frac{18}{16} = \frac{27}{t}$
8. $\frac{8}{12} = \frac{c}{3}$
9. $\frac{15}{25} = \frac{7.5}{y}$
10. $\frac{16}{b} = \frac{56}{38.5}$
11. $\frac{x+1}{3} = \frac{4}{2}$
12. $\frac{5}{8} = \frac{15}{w}$
13. $\frac{30}{16} = \frac{j}{8}$
14. $\frac{42.5}{10} = \frac{x+4}{8}$
15. $\frac{x}{1.4} = \frac{28}{5.6}$
16. $\frac{y}{-8} = \frac{-22.5}{10}$

Write a proportion for each situation. Then solve.

17. Jaime paid $1.29 for three ponytail holders. At that rate, what would eight ponytail holders cost her?
18. Arturo paid $8 in tax on a purchase of $200. At that rate, what would the tax be on a purchase of $150?
19. Chris drove 200 mi in 4 h. At that rate, how long would it take Chris to drive 340 mi?
20. According to a label, there are 25 calories per serving of turkey lunchmeat. How many calories are there in 2.5 servings?

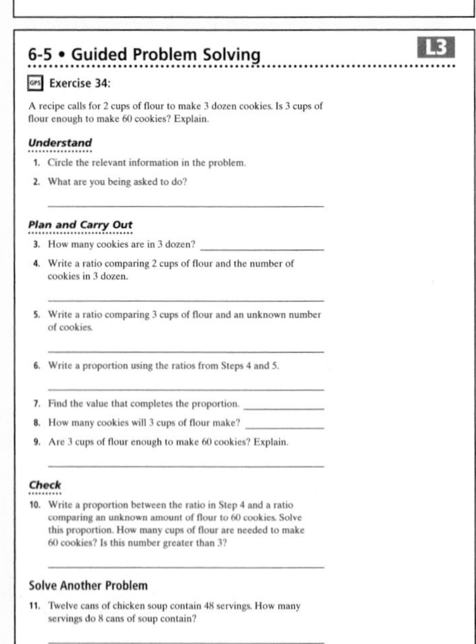

6-5 • Guided Problem Solving L3

GPS Exercise 34:

A recipe calls for 2 cups of flour to make 3 dozen cookies. Is 3 cups of flour enough to make 60 cookies? Explain.

Understand

1. Circle the relevant information in the problem.
2. What are you being asked to do?

Plan and Carry Out

3. How many cookies are in 3 dozen? ______
4. Write a ratio comparing 2 cups of flour and the number of cookies in 3 dozen.
5. Write a ratio comparing 3 cups of flour and an unknown number of cookies.
6. Write a proportion using the ratios from Steps 4 and 5.
7. Find the value that completes the proportion. ______
8. How many cookies will 3 cups of flour make? ______
9. Are 3 cups of flour enough to make 60 cookies? Explain.

Check

10. Write a proportion between the ratio in Step 4 and a ratio comparing an unknown amount of flour to 60 cookies. Solve this proportion. How many cups of flour are needed to make 60 cookies? Is this number greater than 3?

Solve Another Problem

11. Twelve cans of chicken soup contain 48 servings. How many servings do 8 cans of soup contain?

Standards Practice

GO for Help: MathXL

MG 1.3

A Practice by Example

Example 1 (page 235)

Do the ratios form a proportion? Explain. 1–9. See margin.

1. $\frac{1}{4}, \frac{2}{10}$

$$\frac{1}{4} \overset{\times 2}{=} \frac{2}{\blacksquare}$$

Guided Practice This exercise has been started for you!

GO for Help

2. $\frac{1}{2}, \frac{50}{100}$
3. $\frac{10}{20}, \frac{30}{40}$
4. $\frac{4}{12}, \frac{6}{8}$
5. $\frac{42}{6}, \frac{504}{72}$
6. $\frac{9}{11}, \frac{63}{77}$
7. $\frac{72}{27}, \frac{8}{3}$
8. $\frac{16}{27}, \frac{4}{9}$
9. $\frac{3}{2}, \frac{22}{16}$

Example 2 (page 236)

Solve each proportion.

10. $\frac{2}{9} = \frac{10}{a}$

$2a = 9 \cdot 10$ 45

$a = \blacksquare$

Guided Practice This exercise has been started for you!

Homework Video Tutor

For: Examples 1–2
Visit: PHSchool.com
Web Code: axe-0605

11. $\frac{k}{4} = \frac{21}{12}$ 7
12. $\frac{45}{15} = \frac{y}{1}$ 3
13. $\frac{12}{t} = \frac{8}{6}$ 9
14. $\frac{20}{b} = \frac{15}{9}$ 12
15. $\frac{12}{9} = \frac{w}{12}$ 16
16. $\frac{x}{63} = \frac{9}{14}$ 40.5
17. $\frac{3}{p} = \frac{5}{9}$ 5.4
18. $\frac{20}{6} = \frac{c}{12}$ 40
19. $\frac{h}{2} = \frac{3}{16}$ 0.375

20. You are visiting friends in Estonia. Suppose the exchange rate is 12.213 kroons = 1 dollar. If you exchange $120, how many Estonian kroons will you receive? 1,465.56 kroons

B Apply Your Skills

21. **Guided Problem Solving** You enlarge a photo that is 5 in. wide and 7 in. long. The sides of the new photo are in proportion to the original. The new photo is 14 in. wide. Find the length of the new photo. 19.6 in.
    - **Understand the Problem** You can *draw a diagram* to see the problem.
    - **Make a Plan** You can use a proportion. Write the widths in the numerator and the lengths in the denominator.

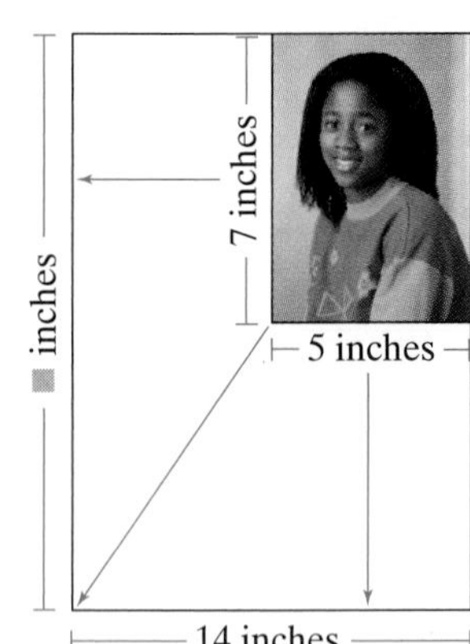

22. **Choose a Method** A car can travel 54 mi on 3 gal of gasoline. Find how far the car can travel on 8 gal. Explain why you chose the method you used. 144 mi; methods may vary.

SCAFFOLDED
Problem Solving

26. Yes; in one proportion, $ay = bx$. In the other proportion, $bx = ay$. These are the same.

23. Do $\frac{3}{15}$ and $\frac{2}{10}$ form a proportion? Yes; the cross products are equal.

24. Do the reciprocals of $\frac{3}{15}$ and $\frac{2}{10}$ form a proportion? yes

25. **Algebra** Compare the cross products of $\frac{a}{b} = \frac{x}{y}$ to the cross products of $\frac{b}{a} = \frac{y}{x}$. $ay = bx$ and $bx = ay$; they are the same.

26. **Reasoning** If the ratios $\frac{a}{b}$ and $\frac{x}{y}$ form a proportion, do the reciprocals $\frac{b}{a}$ and $\frac{y}{x}$ also form a proportion? Explain. See above left.

33. The student did not write the second rate in the correct order. It should be $\frac{3}{14} = \frac{h}{25}$.

34. No; 3 c will only make 54 cookies.

35. Answers may vary. Sample: x will only equal $x + z$ when z is 0.

Solve each proportion.

27. $\frac{x+3}{2} = \frac{5}{4}$ −0.5
28. $\frac{6}{9} = \frac{c+4}{12}$ 4
29. $\frac{h}{22.3} = \frac{4}{55}$ 1.62
30. $\frac{-1.5}{r} = \frac{3}{4.97}$ −2.485
31. $\frac{1.5}{-3} = \frac{-7.5}{d+1}$ 14
32. $\frac{3.21}{k - 1.3} = \frac{6}{8.2}$ 5.687

33. **Error Analysis** In 3 h, a student can walk 14 mi. To find the time he would take to walk 25 mi, the student wrote the proportion $\frac{3}{14} = \frac{25}{h}$. Explain the student's error. See above left.

GPS 34. A recipe calls for 2 cups of flour to make 3 dozen cookies. Is 3 cups of flour enough to make 60 cookies? Explain. See above left.

35. **Writing in Math** The ratios $\frac{x}{y}$ and $\frac{x+z}{y}$ form a proportion only when $z = 0$. Explain why. See above left.

Challenge

36. The scale shown at the right is balanced when $a : y = b : x$. Suppose a 50-lb weight rests 29 in. from the fulcrum. How far from the fulcrum must a 30-lb weight be placed to maintain balance? 48.3 in.

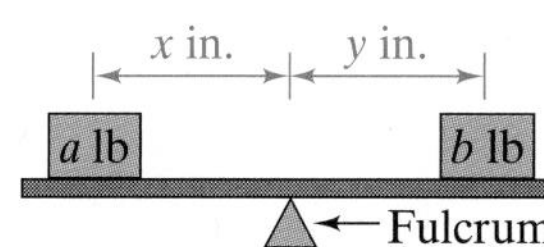

Multiple Choice Practice and Mixed Review

For California Standards Tutorials, visit PHSchool.com. Web Code: axq-9045

MG 1.3 37. You charge $11 to baby-sit for 2 h. Last night you earned $38.50. How long did you baby-sit? D

Ⓐ 2 h Ⓑ 3.5 h Ⓒ 4.5 h Ⓓ 7 h

Alg1 2.0 38. Which number is the opposite of −1.8? C

Ⓐ −8.1 Ⓑ −1.8 Ⓒ 1.8 Ⓓ 8.1

AF 4.1 39. If $-2m + 10 = 1.6$, what is the value of m? C

Ⓐ −5.8 Ⓑ −4.2 Ⓒ 4.2 Ⓓ 5.8

Lesson 2-2 **Find each sum.**

40. $-12 + (-22) + 4$ −30
41. $-7 + 9 + (-3)$ −1
42. $73 + (-24) + 1$ 50

Online Lesson Quiz Visit: PHSchool.com Web Code: axa-0605

Alternative Assessment

Pairs of students invent a new country, name the currency, and decide on an exchange rate to dollars that is not 1 : 1. They determine how much of the new currency they would receive for $1, $5, $10, $20, and $100.

California Resources

Standards Mastery

- Standards Review Transparencies
- Standards Review and Practice Workbook
- Math Companion

Math Intervention

- Skills Review and Practice Workbook
- Math XL

4. Assess & Reteach

PRESENTATION CD-ROM
CD, Online, or Transparencies

Lesson Quiz

1. Is $\frac{5}{8}$ is proportional to $\frac{10}{24}$? Explain. No, because the fractions are not equal.

Solve each proportion.

2. $\frac{w}{12} = \frac{3}{4}$ 9
3. $\frac{4}{5} = \frac{20}{r}$ 25
4. Suppose the exchange rate for dollars to Indian rupees is 0.02. How many rupees should you receive for $100? 5,000 rupees

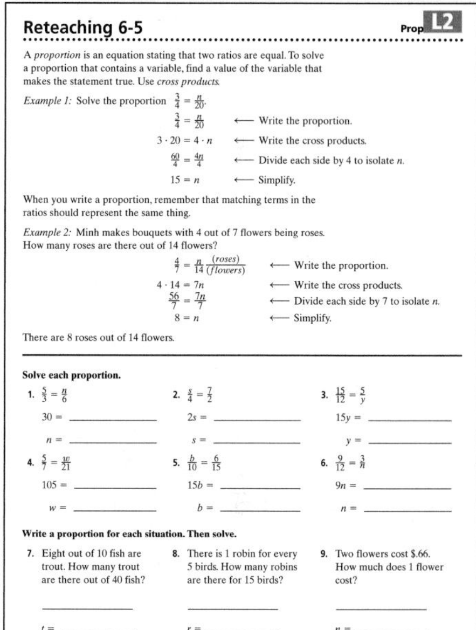

Reteaching 6-5 Prop L2

A *proportion* is an equation stating that two ratios are equal. To solve a proportion that contains a variable, find a value of the variable that makes the statement true. Use *cross products.*

Example 1: Solve the proportion $\frac{3}{4} = \frac{n}{20}$.

$\frac{3}{4} = \frac{n}{20}$ ⟵ Write the proportion.
$3 \cdot 20 = 4 \cdot n$ ⟵ Write the cross products.
$\frac{60}{4} = \frac{4n}{4}$ ⟵ Divide each side by 4 to isolate n.
$15 = n$ ⟵ Simplify.

When you write a proportion, remember that matching terms in the ratios should represent the same thing.

Example 2: Minh makes bouquets with 4 out of 7 flowers being roses. How many roses are there out of 14 flowers?

$\frac{4}{7} = \frac{n}{14}\frac{(roses)}{(flowers)}$ ⟵ Write the proportion.
$4 \cdot 14 = 7n$ ⟵ Write the cross products.
$\frac{56}{7} = \frac{7n}{7}$ ⟵ Divide each side by 7 to isolate n.
$8 = n$ ⟵ Simplify.

There are 8 roses out of 14 flowers.

Solve each proportion.

1. $\frac{5}{3} = \frac{n}{6}$ $30 =$ ____ $n =$ ____
2. $\frac{s}{4} = \frac{7}{2}$ $2s =$ ____ $s =$ ____
3. $\frac{15}{12} = \frac{5}{y}$ $15y =$ ____ $y =$ ____
4. $\frac{5}{7} = \frac{w}{21}$ $105 =$ ____ $w =$ ____
5. $\frac{b}{10} = \frac{6}{15}$ $15b =$ ____ $b =$ ____
6. $\frac{9}{12} = \frac{3}{n}$ $9n =$ ____ $n =$ ____

Write a proportion for each situation. Then solve.

7. Eight out of 10 fish are trout. How many trout are there out of 40 fish? ____ $t =$ ____
8. There is 1 robin for every 5 birds. How many robins are there for 15 birds? ____ $r =$ ____
9. Two flowers cost $.66. How much does 1 flower cost? ____ $n =$ ____

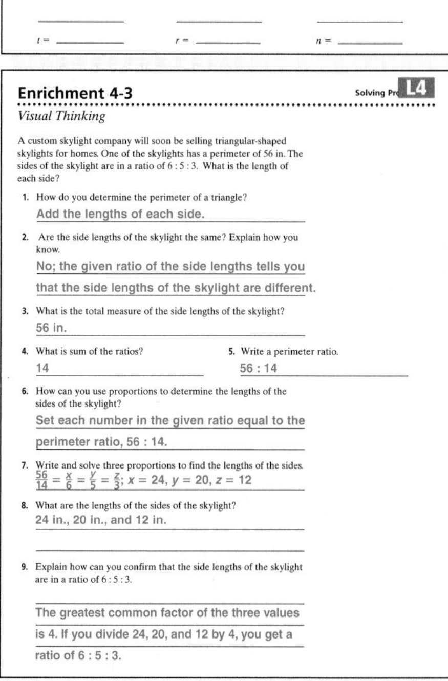

Enrichment 4-3 Solving Pr L4

Visual Thinking

A custom skylight company will soon be selling triangular-shaped skylights for homes. One of the skylights has a perimeter of 56 in. The sides of the skylight are in a ratio of 6 : 5 : 3. What is the length of each side?

1. How do you determine the perimeter of a triangle?
Add the lengths of each side.
2. Are the side lengths of the skylight the same? Explain how you know.
No; the given ratio of the side lengths tells you that the side lengths of the skylight are different.
3. What is the total measure of the side lengths of the skylight?
56 in.
4. What is sum of the ratios?
14
5. Write a perimeter ratio.
56 : 14
6. How can you use proportions to determine the lengths of the sides of the skylight?
Set each number in the given ratio equal to the perimeter ratio, 56 : 14.
7. Write and solve three proportions to find the lengths of the sides.
$\frac{56}{14} = \frac{x}{6} = \frac{y}{5} = \frac{z}{3}$; $x = 24$, $y = 20$, $z = 12$
8. What are the lengths of the sides of the skylight?
24 in., 20 in., and 12 in.
9. Explain how can you confirm that the side lengths of the skylight are in a ratio of 6 : 5 : 3.
The greatest common factor of the three values is 4. If you divide 24, 20, and 12 by 4, you get a ratio of 6 : 5 : 3.

Algebraic Thinking

Similar Figures and Proportions

Students compare the lengths of sides of similar triangles. They find and use the ratios of these measurements to write and solve proportions and find unknown lengths.

Guided Instruction

Before beginning the activity, review similar figures with students. Ask: *What are equal in similar figures?* measures of corresponding angles *What are proportional in similar figures?* lengths of corresponding sides *How can you tell which sides or measurements correspond to each other?* Place figures in the same orientation and compare lengths, widths, or distances between corresponding endpoints.

Activity

Help students keep track of the quantities they are comparing by having them write the category next to the numerators and denominators of their ratios. For example, $\frac{\text{length } A}{\text{length } B} = \frac{2}{4} = \frac{1}{2}$.

Alternative Method

Some students may find it easier to write the ratio of the known sides in simplest form before calculating the cross products.

Algebraic Thinking

For Use With Lesson 6-5

Foundational Standard Use proportions to solve problems (e.g., find the length of a side of a polygon similar to a known polygon).
MR 1.1 Analyze problems by identifying relationships, identifying missing information, and observing patterns.
Develop

Similar Figures and Proportions

Similar figures have the same shape but not necessarily the same size. If two figures are similar, then the lengths of corresponding sides are in proportion. To find the length of missing sides of similar figures, you can write and solve a proportion.

EXAMPLE

In the figure at the right, $\triangle ABC$ is similar to $\triangle DEC$. Find the length of x.

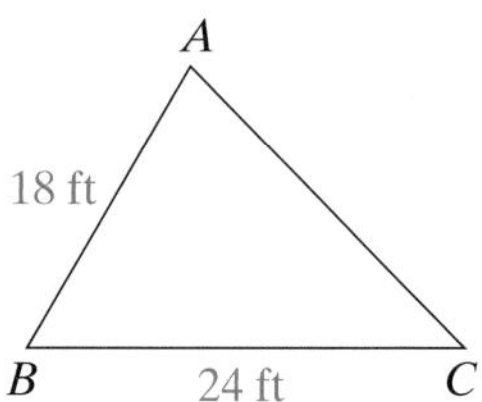

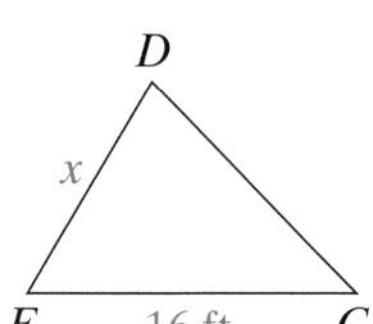

Write a proportion using corresponding sides of the triangles.

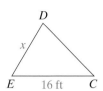

$\frac{18}{x} = \frac{24}{16}$ ← **Write a proportion.**

$18 \cdot 16 = 24 \cdot x$ ← **Write the cross products.**

$288 = 24x$ ← **Simplify.**

$\frac{288}{24} = \frac{24x}{24}$ ← **Division Property of Equality**

$12 = x$ ← **Simplify.**

The length of x is 12 ft.

Exercises

The figures in Exercises 1–3 are similar. Find the unknown lengths.

1. 5

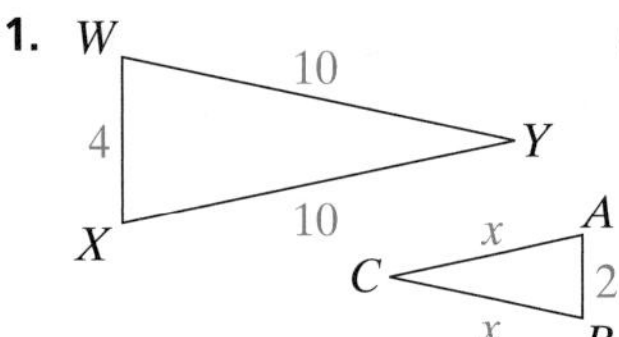

2. 32

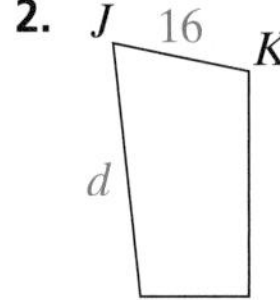

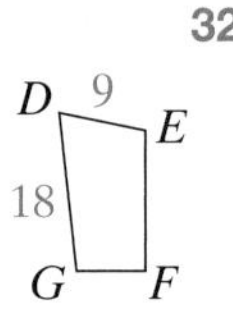

3. 42

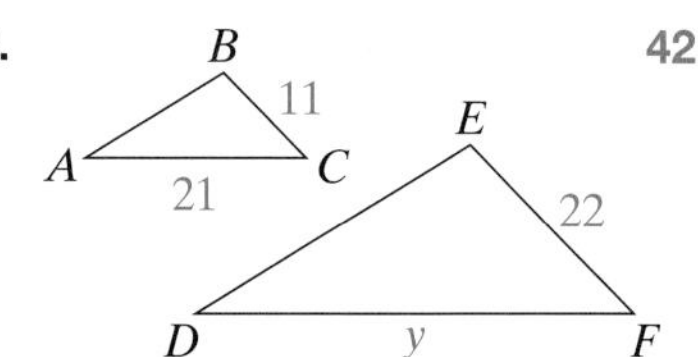

4. A frame of a movie film is 35 mm wide and 26.25 mm high. The film projects an image 8 m wide. How high is the image? 6 m

5. **Patterns** $\triangle MNO$ and $\triangle PQR$ at the right are similar. Find the ratio of corresponding sides and the ratio of the perimeters. Compare the two ratios.
Sides: 1 to 4; perimeters: 1 to 4; they are the same.

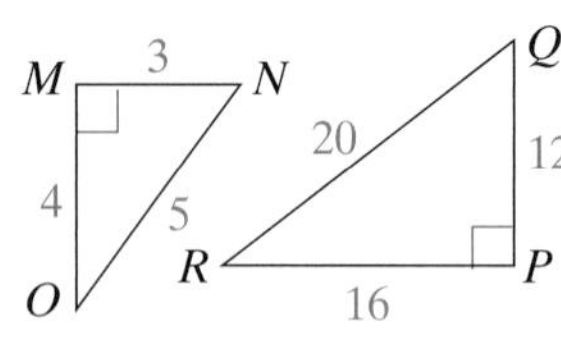

GPS Guided Problem Solving

Using Rates and Proportions

MG 1.3 Use measures expressed as rates to solve problems. *Develop*

You can use unit rates to write and solve equations involving ratios.

The table below shows data for the time it takes to make copies on a new photocopy machine. Use this data to find the amount of time it would take to copy 1,000 pages.

Time (minutes)	25	50	150	250	75
Number of Pages	875	1,750	5,250	8,750	2,625

What You Might Think	What You Might Write
What do I know? What do I want to find out?	I know how long it takes to copy certain numbers of pages. I want to find the amount of time it would take to copy 1,000 pages.
How can I find the unit rate?	To find the unit rate, I divide time by the number of pages. For the first column, the unit rate is $\frac{25 \text{ min}}{875 \text{ pages}} \approx 0.029$ min/page. The unit rate is the same for all the data, so the unit rate is about 0.029 min/page.
How can I use the unit rate in an equation to find how long it takes to make copies?	The unit rate multiplied by the number of copies c will give the time t it will take to make a certain number of copies. So my equation is $t = 0.029c$; $t = 0.029(1{,}000)$; $t = 29$
How long does it take to copy 1,000 pages?	It takes 29 min to copy 1,000 pages.

Think It Through

1. **Number Sense** How do you know if 29 min is reasonable? See margin. (*Hint*: Compare it to the time it takes to make 1,750 copies.)
2. Can you use the proportion $\frac{c}{t} = \frac{0.029}{1}$ for the situation above? Explain. No; $\frac{c}{t} = \frac{1}{0.029}$.
3. How long would it take you to copy 750 pages? 2,000 pages? about 22 min; 58 min

GPS Guided Problem Solving

Using Rates and Proportions

Students read a guided real-world problem to develop problem solving and reasoning skills. In the left-hand column, they read questions they could ask themselves to make sense of the problem. In the right-hand column, they read the steps for setting up and solving equations used to describe the situation.

Guided Instruction

Have students work through the problem, rather than just read it. Have them identify any steps that are unclear or that don't match their own work.

Error Prevention!

Students might not know which unit rate to use. Help them understand the meaning of unit rate by calculating both $\frac{25 \text{ min}}{875 \text{ pages}}$ and $\frac{875 \text{ pages}}{25 \text{ min}}$. 0.029 min/page, 35 pages/min

Discuss the difference between the two ratios, and the meaning of each. The first ratio is the number of minutes to copy one page; the second ratio is the number of pages that can be copied in one min. Ask: *Why is 0.029 min/page used in this problem?* The unit rate 0.029 minutes per page helps you find the time it takes to copy any number of pages. *If the problem asked for the number of pages that could be printed in 500 minutes, which unit rate would be more useful?* 35 pages/min

Alternative Method

Ask students how they would set up the problem using a proportion instead of a unit rate. Sample: $\frac{25 \text{ min}}{875 \text{ pages}} = \frac{t}{1{,}000 \text{ pages}}$

Teaching Tip
Have students ask themselves the same or similar questions as in the example as they work through the Exercises.

Connection to Economics
Encourage students to research data on businesses they know at the National Better Business Bureau Web site. Have them compare rates of compliments and rates of complaints for these businesses.

Universal Access

Auditory Learners
To help students keep track of values they are comparing, have them describe the unit ratios aloud. For example, "25 minutes per 875 pages, or about 0.029 minutes per page, or 0.029 minutes to copy one page."

Exercises

Solve each problem. For Exercises 4 and 5, answer parts (a) and (b) first.

4. Data from the Council of Better Business Bureaus show that in one year customers filed about 28,000 complaints about cellular phones. About how many complaints is this per week? **about 538 complaints/wk**
   a. What are you trying to find?
   b. Use the diagram below to write a proportion for this situation.

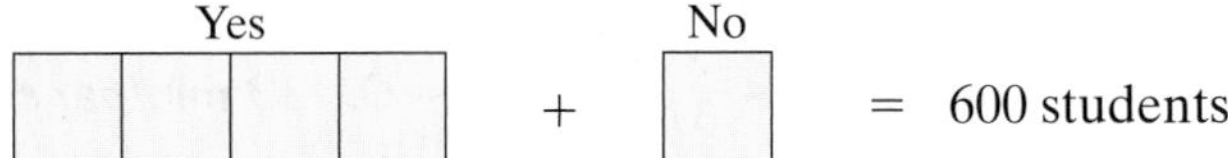

5. In an opinion poll, 600 teenagers were asked if basic money management skills should be taught in high school. The ratio of yes to no votes was 4 to 1. How many students voted yes and how many voted no? **480 students voted yes; 120 voted no.**
   a. Suppose someone says that 4 students voted yes and 1 voted no. Is that the best answer? Explain.
   b. Use the diagram below to write an equation for this situation.

Yes + No = 600 students

6. The graph at the right shows the enrollment in American Sign Language classes in various years. Compared to the number of students in 1995, how many times greater was the number of students that enrolled in American Sign Language classes in 2002? **about 14 times**

7. In a study of 6,349 public libraries, the average spending per person in the community one year was $30.32. Suppose you live in a community of 25,000 people and the annual budget is $437,500 for the library. Is this above or below the average found in the study? Explain. **Below; according to the study, your community would need to spend $758,000.**

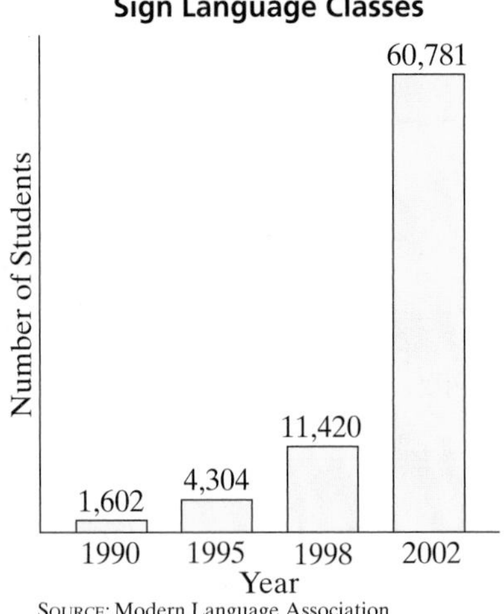

Using a Variable

You can solve many problems by using a variable to represent an unknown quantity. Use the variable to write an equation.

EXAMPLE

You have a copy of your company logo that is 3.8 cm long and 2 cm wide. You need an enlarged copy of the logo that is 6 cm long. How wide must the enlarged copy be?

You can use the diagrams at the right to help visualize which side length you are trying to find.

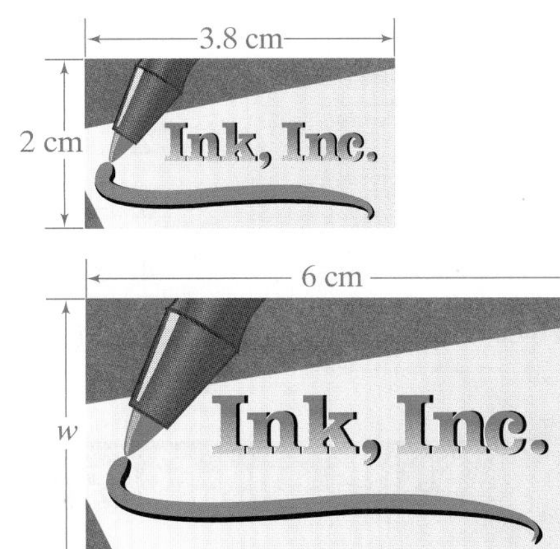

Let w = the width of the enlarged copy.

Set up a proportion to find w.

$\frac{6}{w} = \frac{3.8}{2}$ ← length / ← width

$2 \cdot 6 = 3.8 \cdot w$ ← Write the cross products.

$12 = 3.8w$ ← Multiply.

$\frac{12}{3.8} = \frac{3.8w}{3.8}$ ← Division Property of Equality

$3.2 \approx w$ ← Simplify.

The width of the enlargement should be about 3.2 cm.

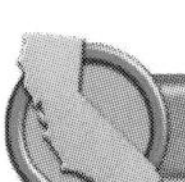

Multiple Choice Practice

MG 1.3 **1.** A family is on a 400-mi road trip. They have already driven 220 mi in 4 h. If they continue driving at this rate, about how long will it take them to drive the entire 400 mi? C

(A) 2 h (B) 3 h (C) 7 h (D) 8 h

AF 1.1 **2.** A map is 15.5 in. wide and 20 in. long. The map is enlarged so it is 32 in. long. Which proportion can you use to find the new width? B

(A) $\frac{15.5}{20} = \frac{32}{x}$ (C) $\frac{15.5}{32} = \frac{x}{20}$

(B) $\frac{15.5}{x} = \frac{20}{32}$ (D) $\frac{15.5}{x} = \frac{32}{20}$

AF 1.1 **3.** A carpenter can build 3 tables in 5 h. Which equation can he use to find the time t it will take him to make 18 tables? D

(A) $t = 5 \cdot 18$ (C) $t = 3 \cdot 18$

(B) $t = 15 \cdot 18$ (D) $t = 5 \cdot 6$

Using a Variable

This feature shows students the advantages of using a variable to solve problems involving an unknown quantity.

Guided Instruction

Teaching Tip
Point out that any lower-case letter can be used to represent an unknown quantity. However, emphasize that selecting easy-to-recall letters, such as *h* for *height* or *w* for *width,* makes good sense.

Universal Access

Visual Learners
Encourage students to draw and label diagrams to help them keep track of corresponding quantities that are proportional to each other.

Chapter 6 Review

Vocabulary Review

English and Spanish Audio Online

conversion factor (p. 226)
cross products (p. 236)
dimensional analysis (p. 227)
equivalent ratios (p. 217)

proportion (p. 235)
rate (p. 220)
ratio (p. 216)
unit rate (p. 220)

Academic Vocabulary
classify (p. 225)
contrast (p. 225)
define (p. 225)

Go Online PHSchool.com
For: Vocabulary Quiz
Visit: PHSchool.com
Web Code: axj-0651

Choose the correct vocabulary term to complete each sentence.

1. You can use a(n) _?_ to compare a part to a part. ratio
2. The _?_ for 45 mi in 1.5 h is 30 mi/h. unit rate
3. A(n) _?_ is an equation stating that two ratios are equal. proportion
4. You can use a(n) _?_ to convert 3.4 mi to feet. conversion factor
5. A(n) _?_ is a ratio of quantities measured in different units. rate

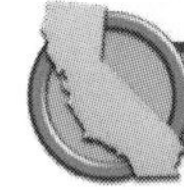

Skills and Concepts

Lesson 6-1

- To write ratios

Foundational Standard

A **ratio** compares two quantities by division. To write a ratio in simplest form, divide both numbers by their GCD. **Equivalent ratios** name the same number.

A jar contains 8 tacks, 15 bolts, and 23 nails. Write each ratio in three ways.

6. bolts to nails
   15 to 23; $\frac{15}{23}$; 15 : 23
7. nails to tacks
   23 to 8; $\frac{23}{8}$; 23 : 8
8. bolts to total items
   15 to 46; $\frac{15}{46}$; 15 : 46

Write each ratio in simplest form.

9. 8 to 32 1 to 4
10. $\frac{18}{30}$ $\frac{3}{5}$
11. 24 ft : 8 ft 3 ft : 1 ft
12. $\frac{45 \text{ boys}}{54 \text{ girls}}$ $\frac{5 \text{ boys}}{6 \text{ girls}}$

Lesson 6-2

- To find and use rates and unit rates

AF 4.2, MG 1.3

A **rate** is a ratio that compares quantities measured in different units. To find a **unit rate,** divide the numerator by the denominator.

Find each unit rate.

13. \$42 for 1.5 h \$28/h
14. 826 mi in 14 h 59 mi/h
15. 150 km per 24 L 6.25 km/L
16. One loaf of bread costs \$3.09 for 32 oz. Another costs \$1.40 for 24 oz. Which is the better buy? 24 oz
17. A travel agency offers a trip for 5 nights for \$600. Another company offers a trip for 7 nights for \$845. Which trip is the better buy? 5 nights for \$600

Chapter 6 Review

California Resources

Standards Mastery
- Math Companion
- Standards Review Transparencies
- Standards Review and Practice Workbook
- Progress Monitoring Assessments

Math Intervention
- Skills Review and Practice Workbook
- Math XL

Universal Access Resources
- Student Workbook
  - Vocabulary and Study Skills
  - Guided Problem Solving
- All-in-One Teaching Resources
  - Reteaching
  - Enrichment
- Spanish Practice Workbook L3
- Spanish Vocabulary and Study Skills 2A-F L3
- English/Spanish Glossary EL
- Multilingual Handbook EL
- Interactive Textbook Audio Glossary
- Online Vocabulary Quiz

Online at PHSchool.com

Spanish Vocabulary/Study Skills EL

Vocabulary/Study Skills L3

6F: Vocabulary Review For use with the Chapter Review

Vocabulary and Study Skills

Study Skill Take notes while you study. They will provide you with a helpful outline when you study for a quiz or test.

Complete the crossword puzzle. For help, use the glossary in your textbook.

ACROSS

1. a fraction whose numerator is greater than or equal to its denominator
3. a number that makes an equation true
5. fractions or decimals that name the same amount
7. a number that can be used to indicate part of a whole
9. a whole number greater than one with more than two factors
11. the top number in a fraction

DOWN

2. a whole number with only two factors—one and itself
4. factors that are the same for two or more numbers
6. one of two numbers whose product is 1
8. operations that undo one another
10. the bottom number in a fraction

Lesson 6-3

- To convert units and use dimensional analysis

MG 1.3

21. 15,840 ft/h
22. 256 oz/ft
23. $18/h
24. $.08/oz
25. 4,181,760 ft/day
26. $\frac{4}{15}$ pt/s

You use a **conversion factor** to convert units of measure. To check the reasonableness of a solution, you can use **dimensional analysis** to determine the correct units.

Convert each measure.

18. 880 in. = ■ ft $73\frac{1}{3}$ ft **19.** $2\frac{1}{2}$ gal = ■ c 40 c **20.** 12,000 lb = ■ t 6 t

Find each unit rate in the given units. 21–26. See left.

21. 3 mi/h = ■ ft/h

22. 16 lb/ft = ■ oz/ft

23. $.30/min = $■/h

24. $1.25/lb = $■/oz

25. 33 mi/h = ■ ft/day

26. 2 gal/min = ■ pt/s

27. A painting job takes 36 person-hours to complete. If 4 people work on the job, how many hours does it take? Use dimensional analysis to check the reasonableness of your answer. 9 h

Lesson 6-4

- To solve multi-step rate problems

AF 4.2, MG 1.3

To find a total distance for a problem involving more than one rate, first find the distance traveled at each rate. Then add the distances. To find average speed, divide the total distance traveled by the total amount of time.

28. A delivery truck travels at a rate of 25 mi/h for 0.5 h. Then it travels at a rate of 45 mi/h for 1.25 h. What is the total distance that the truck travels? 68.75 mi

29. The wind blows at a rate of 5 mi/h for 3 h. Then it blows at a rate of 12 mi/h for 8 h. What is the average speed of the wind over the 11-h time period? 10.1 mi/h

30. You run 2 mi in 16 min. At the same rate, how long will it take you to run 5 mi? 40 min

Lesson 6-5

- To identify and solve proportions

MG 1.3

31. no; $\frac{2}{5} \neq \frac{1}{3}$
32. yes; $\frac{6}{16} = \frac{21}{56}$
33. yes; $\frac{15}{9} = \frac{5}{3}$
34. no; $\frac{3}{8} \neq \frac{9}{16}$

A **proportion** is an equation stating that two ratios are equal. To solve a proportion, you can write the **cross products** and then solve.

Do the ratios form a proportion? Explain. 31–34. See left.

31. $\frac{2}{5}, \frac{1}{3}$ **32.** $\frac{6}{16}, \frac{21}{56}$ **33.** $\frac{15}{9}, \frac{5}{3}$ **34.** $\frac{3}{8}, \frac{9}{16}$

Solve each proportion.

35. $\frac{4}{5} = \frac{x}{20}$ 16 **36.** $\frac{4}{a} = \frac{18}{9}$ 2 **37.** $\frac{45}{6} = \frac{30}{t}$ 4 **38.** $\frac{b}{16} = \frac{9}{2}$ 72

39. Use the exchange rate 0.7822 euros = $1 to find the number of euros you receive for exchanging $50. 39.11 euros

Alternative Assessment L4

Alternative Assessment Form C

Chapter 6

CHILI NIGHT

Your family moved recently. Before the move you used to help your parents out by making dinner every Wednesday night. One of your favorite dishes to prepare was chili, which you made by adding water and several fresh ingredients to Montana Martha's Chili Mix. Now, however, you live in a part of the country where Montana Martha's Chili Mix is not sold. But you have a plan to change that. Your first step was asking 240 people in your new town how often they eat chili. The circle graph shows the results of your survey.

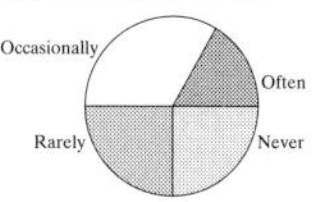

Show all of your work on a separate sheet of paper.

1. How many of the 240 people in your survey said they never eat chili?
2. Of the people who said they eat chili often, $\frac{3}{4}$ said they would be interested in trying Montana Martha's Chili Mix. What fraction of the survey group is this?

You think that grocery store managers will be more likely to carry Montana Martha's Chili Mix if you give them a sample of chili made from it. You have two packages left. You need to make a lot of chili to give away, but you want to save some of the mix to make a small batch for yourself.

3. You decide to use $1\frac{1}{2}$ packages of mix to make a large batch of chili for store managers to taste. The basic recipe calls for adding $\frac{2}{3}$ cup of water to each package. How much water will you need for $1\frac{1}{2}$ packages of mix?

Spanish Quarter 2 Test—Forms A, B EL

Quarter 2 Test—Forms D, E L2

Quarter 2 Test—Forms A, B L3

Quarter 2 Test Form A

Chapters 4–6

1. Use mental math to determine whether 22,645 is divisible by 9.
2. Use a factor tree to find the prime factorization of 120. Write your answer using exponents.
3. Find the GCF of 24, 72, and 96.
4. If you were to plot the fractions $\frac{3}{12}$ and $\frac{1}{4}$ on the same number line, where would they be in relation to each other?
5. Write a fraction with a denominator of 18 that is equivalent to $\frac{2}{3}$.
6. Write $\frac{44}{6}$ as a mixed number.
7. Find the LCM of 18 and 30.
8. Order the mixed numbers from least to greatest. $3\frac{4}{7}, 3\frac{8}{15}, 3\frac{1}{2}$
9. Fill in the ___?___ with <, >, or =. $\frac{23}{9}$ ___?___ $2\frac{10}{18}$
10. Write 0.135 as a fraction in simplest form.
11. Write $6\frac{7}{20}$ as a decimal.
12. Write six and two fifths as a decimal.
13. The sum of two decimals is 1.2. One of the decimals is twice the other. What are the two decimals?
14. Round $11\frac{7}{12}$ to the nearest whole number.
15. Estimate $7\frac{4}{5} + 9\frac{1}{12}$ by first rounding to the nearest whole number.
16. Add. Write your answer in simplest form. $\frac{3}{20} + \frac{7}{20} - \frac{2}{20}$
17. Explain how you would add the fractions $\frac{1}{2}$ and $\frac{3}{4}$.
18. Sean rode his bicycle $4\frac{1}{4}$ miles on Saturday and $5\frac{7}{8}$ miles on Sunday. How many miles did he ride during the weekend?
19. Add. Write your answer in simplest form. $11\frac{1}{2} + 3\frac{4}{5} + 6\frac{1}{3}$
20. There are two boards leaning against the wall. The first board is $3\frac{5}{8}$ meters long and the second is $4\frac{1}{4}$ meters long. How much longer is the second board?

California Resources

Standards Mastery
- Teacher Center ExamView CD-ROM
- Math XL
- Progress Monitoring Assessments
- Online Chapter Test at PHSchool.com

Math Intervention
- Skills Review and Practice Workbook

Online at PHSchool.com

Universal Access Resources
- Chapter Test
- Alternative Assessment
- Spanish Chapter Test
- Spanish Alternative Assessment
- Teacher Center ExamView CD-ROM
  - Special Needs Test
  - Special Needs Practice Banks
  - Foundational Standards Practice Banks
- Online Chapter Test at www.PHSchool.com
- All-In-One Teaching Resources
  - Cumulative Review L3
- Spanish Assessment Resources
  - Cumulative Review 

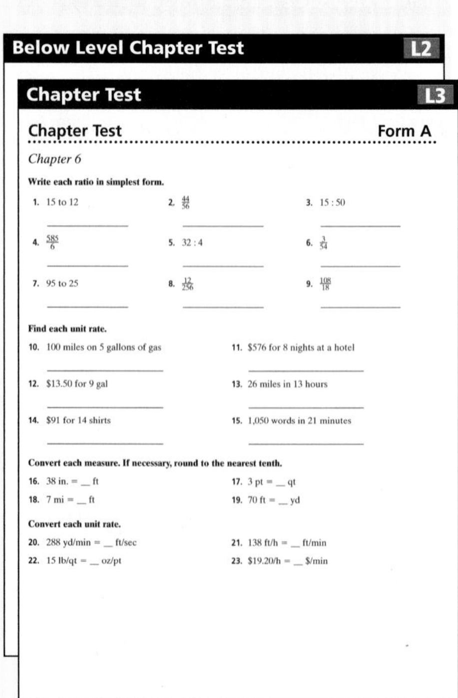

Below Level Chapter Test L2

Chapter Test L3

Chapter Test Form A

Chapter 6

Write each ratio in simplest form.

1. 15 to 12
2. $\frac{44}{56}$
3. 15 : 50
4. $\frac{585}{6}$
5. 32 : 4
6. $\frac{3}{54}$
7. 95 to 25
8. $\frac{12}{256}$
9. $\frac{108}{18}$

Find each unit rate.

10. 100 miles on 5 gallons of gas
11. $576 for 8 nights at a hotel
12. $13.50 for 9 gal
13. 26 miles in 13 hours
14. $91 for 14 shirts
15. 1,050 words in 21 minutes

Convert each measure. If necessary, round to the nearest tenth.

16. 38 in. = __ ft
17. 3 pt = __ qt
18. 7 mi = __ ft
19. 70 ft = __ yd

Convert each unit rate.

20. 288 yd/min = __ ft/sec
21. 138 ft/h = __ ft/min
22. 15 lb/qt = __ oz/pt
23. $19.20/h = __ $/min

Chapter 6 Test

Go Online PHSchool.com For: Online chapter test Web Code: axa-0652

You have 3 nickels, 11 dimes, and 5 quarters in your pocket. Write each ratio in three ways.
1–4. See margin.

1. nickels to quarters
2. dimes to nickels
3. dimes to all coins
4. quarters to dimes
5. Use the figure below. Write the ratio of the number of shaded squares to the number of unshaded squares in simplest form. $\frac{2}{3}$ or 2 : 3 or 2 to 3

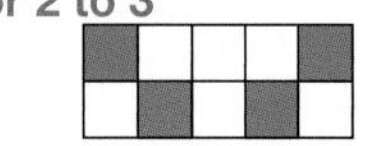

Write each ratio in simplest form.

6. 16 : 60 4 : 15
7. $\frac{54}{6}$ $\frac{9}{1}$
8. $\frac{3}{18}$ $\frac{1}{6}$
9. 6 : 8 3 : 4
10. 24 to 3 8 to 1
11. 14 : 48 7 : 24

Find each unit rate.

12. 200 yd in 5 min 40 yd/min
13. 30 gal in 24 h 1.25 gal/h
14. 700 lb in 25 ft 28 lb/ft
15. $2.50 for 10 oz $.25/oz
16. 35 oz in 7 min 5 oz/min
17. 0.5 cm in $\frac{1}{2}$ h 1 cm/h
18. A car can travel 28 mi on 1 gal of gasoline. How far can the car travel on 8 gal? 224 mi
19. A 6-oz bottle of juice costs $.96. An 8-oz bottle costs $1.12. Which size bottle is the better buy? 8-oz

Convert each measure. If necessary, round to the nearest tenth.

20. 9 c = ▪ qt 2.3
21. 25 in. = ▪ ft 2.1
22. 3 mi = ▪ ft 15,840
23. 4 oz = ▪ lb 0.3
24. A building project takes 55 person-hours to complete. If 5 people work on the job, how long will it take? Use dimensional analysis to check the reasonableness of your answer. 11 h

Convert each unit rate.

25. $33/h = $▪/min 0.55
26. 3 ft/s = ▪ yd/min 60
27. 21 lb/gal = ▪ oz/qt 84
28. 3 mi/h = ▪ ft/s 4.4
29. **Writing in Math** The ratio of girls to boys in a science class is 5 to 6. Can there be 15 boys in the class? Explain. See margin.
30. A bird flies at a rate of 25 mi/h for 2.5 h. Then the bird flies at a rate of 44 mi/h for 3 h. Find the total distance the bird flies. 194.5 mi
31. A car travels 65 mi/h for 2.4 h. Then it travels 35 mi/h for 1.5 h. What is the car's average speed over the total distance? about 53.5 mi/h
32. The distance a spring stretches varies directly with the weight applied to it. A 4-oz weight stretches a spring 5 in. How far will a 6-oz weight stretch the spring? 7.5 in.

Do the ratios form a proportion? Explain.

33. $\frac{5}{3}, \frac{15}{9}$ yes; $\frac{15}{9} = \frac{5}{3}$
34. $\frac{3}{4}, \frac{4}{5}$ no; $\frac{3}{4} \neq \frac{4}{5}$
35. $\frac{8}{12}, \frac{12}{8}$ no; $\frac{8}{12} \neq \frac{12}{8}$
36. $\frac{24}{6}, \frac{48}{12}$ yes; $\frac{24}{6} = \frac{48}{12}$

Solve each proportion.

37. $\frac{4}{5} = \frac{x}{25}$ 20
38. $\frac{6}{4} = \frac{9}{m}$ 6
39. $\frac{a}{25} = \frac{3}{10}$ 7.5
40. $\frac{3}{7} = \frac{6}{n}$ 14
41. $\frac{w}{5} = \frac{30}{15}$ 10
42. $\frac{25}{c} = \frac{100}{4}$ 1
43. A grocery store sells 6 lb of apples for $4. How much will 8 lb of apples cost? Round your answer to the nearest cent. $5.33
44. You read 12 pages of a book in 15 min. At the same rate, how many pages can you read in 45 min? 36 pgs

Some questions require you to use rates and convert units to solve a problem. Use the tips as guides to answer the question at the right.

Mario reads 72 pages of a book in 1 week. If he reads at the same rate for 15 days, about how many pages can he read?

Ⓐ 12 Ⓒ 154
Ⓑ 82 Ⓓ 1,080

Tip 1
Use dimensional analysis to check the reasonableness of the solution.

Tip 2
15 days is about 2 weeks, so the number of pages read should be about 2 times 72.

Think It Through

First, convert 1 week to 7 days. Then find a unit rate: $\frac{72 \text{ pages}}{7 \text{ days}} \approx 10.3$ pages/day. Multiply the unit rate by 15 days to find the answer. $10.3 \cdot 15 = 154.5 \approx 154$. The correct answer is choice C.

Vocabulary Review

As you solve problems, you must understand the meanings of mathematical terms. Match each term with its mathematical meaning.

A. ratio II
B. proportion IV
C. conversion factor III
D. rate I

I. a ratio that compares quantities measured in different units
II. a comparison of two quantities by division
III. a rate that is equal to 1
IV. an equation stating that two ratios are equal

Read each question. Then write the letter of the correct answer on your paper.

1. Andrea needs to buy wood trim. The hardware store has trim that is 0.375 in. wide. What is the width of the trim expressed as a fraction? (Lesson 4-4) C
   Ⓐ $\frac{1}{375}$ in. Ⓒ $\frac{3}{8}$ in.
   Ⓑ $\frac{1}{8}$ in. Ⓓ $\frac{375}{100}$ in.

2. Claudia is typing a 500-word paper. She can type 28 words per minute. About how long will it take her to type the paper? (Lesson 6-2) B
   Ⓐ 14 min Ⓒ 28 min
   Ⓑ 18 min Ⓓ 500 min

3. Which description matches the expression $\frac{n}{3} + 5$? (Lesson 1-3) D
   Ⓐ five more than three times a number
   Ⓑ three times a number increased by five
   Ⓒ five less than a number divided by three
   Ⓓ the sum of five and a number divided by three

California Resources

Standards Mastery
- Teacher Center ExamView CD-ROM
- Math XL
- Progress Monitoring Assessments
- Online Chapter Test at PHSchool.com

Math Intervention
- Skills Review and Practice Workbook

Universal Access Resources
- Teacher Center ExamView CD-ROM
  - Special Needs Test
  - Special Needs Practice Banks
  - Foundational Standards Practice Banks
- Online Chapter Test at www.PHSchool.com
- All-In-One Teaching Resources
  - Cumulative Review L3
- Spanish Assessment Resources
  - Cumulative Review L3

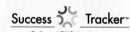

Success Tracker™
Online at PHSchool.com

4. Trevor bought 24 bottles of juice for $6.99. Which proportion can you use to find x, the cost of 18 bottles of juice? (Lesson 6-5) B

   A $\frac{x}{24} = \frac{18}{6.99}$
   B $\frac{24}{6.99} = \frac{18}{x}$
   C $\frac{6.99}{x} = \frac{18}{24}$
   D $\frac{x}{6.99} = \frac{24}{18}$

5. Mark is walking 10 mi for a fundraiser. He can walk 1.5 mi in 23 min. At this rate, about how long will it take Mark to complete the walk for the fundraiser? (Lesson 6-4) A

   A 2.5 h　　C 3 h
   B 2.75 h　　D 3.3 h

6. Sam's car traveled 64.5 mi on $2\frac{1}{2}$ gal of gasoline. At this rate, about how many gallons of gasoline would the car need to travel 100 mi? (Lesson 6-4) C

   A 2.6 gal　　C 4 gal
   B 3 gal　　D 6.4 gal

7. You need $1\frac{3}{4}$ c of sugar for one batch of cookies. Which expression can be used to find the amount of sugar you need for b batches of cookies? (Lesson 5-3) B

   A $b + 1\frac{3}{4}$
   B $1\frac{3}{4} \cdot b$
   C $1\frac{3}{4} \div b$
   D $b - 1\frac{3}{4}$

8. The wind blows 15 mi/h for 3.5 h. Then it blows 2 mi/h for 1.5 h. What is the average speed of the wind over the 5-h time period? (Lesson 6-4) B

   A 2 mi/h　　C 52.5 mi/h
   B 11.1 mi/h　　D 55.5 mi/h

9. Emma's heart beats about 150 times per minute when she is jogging. At this rate, about how many times will her heart beat in 1 h? (Lesson 6-2) C

   A 150　　C 9,000
   B 4,500　　D 15,000

10. On her math quizzes, Ms. Moran assumes that 5 problems should take 2 min to solve. One quiz has 18 problems. Which proportion can you use to find x, the time needed for the quiz? (Lesson 6-5) D

   A $\frac{2}{18} = \frac{5}{x}$
   B $\frac{x}{5} = \frac{18}{2}$
   C $\frac{5}{18} = \frac{x}{2}$
   D $\frac{x}{18} = \frac{2}{5}$

11. The ratio of children to teachers at a preschool is 8 to 1. Each day, 32 children attend the preschool. How many teachers work at the preschool each day? (Lesson 6-1) B

   A 1　　C 8
   B 4　　D 32

12. Julia drives 180 mi in 3 h. At this rate, how long will it take her to drive 300 mi? (Lesson 6-4) B

   A 4 h　　C 6 h
   B 5 h　　D 7 h

13. You mow a neighbor's lawn in 3 h and earn $15.75. What is your unit rate of pay? (Lesson 6-2) C

   A $4.00/h　　C $5.25/h
   B $5.00/h　　D $7.50/h

14. Which fraction is equivalent to 7.35? (Lesson 4-4) D

   A $\frac{7}{35}$　　C $\frac{35}{7}$
   B $\frac{7}{20}$　　D $\frac{147}{20}$

Spanish Cumulative Review EL

Cumulative Review L3

Cumulative Review

Chapters 1–6

Multiple choice. Choose the letter of the best answer.

1. Which price yields the lowest unit price?
   A. $1.30 for 2 oz
   B. $3.90 for 8 oz
   C. $5.20 for 1 lb
   D. $24.75 for 5 lb
2. Convert 0.625 to a fraction in simplest form.
   A. $\frac{2}{3}$　B. $\frac{63}{100}$
   C. $\frac{5}{8}$　D. $\frac{6}{50}$
3. To qualify for a keyboarding job, Karen needs to type 95 words per minute. She timed herself at 450 words for 5 minutes. What is her rate in comparison to the required rate?
   A. She types 5 words per minute faster.
   B. She types exactly the required rate.
   C. She types 5 words per minute too slow.
   D. She types 15 words per minute too slow.
4. Solve the proportion. $\frac{33}{y} = \frac{22}{8}$
   A. 6
   B. $7\frac{1}{2}$
   C. 9
   D. 12
5. Which price yields the lowest unit price?
   A. $3.25 for 2 qt
   B. $3.75 for 3 qt
   C. $4.25 for 1 gal
   D. $15.00 for 3 gal 1 qt
6. Solve $\frac{6}{11} = \frac{12}{x}$.
   A. 132　B. 126
   C. 22　D. 6.5
7. Find the sum. $0.46 + 0.58 + 0.05$
   A. 0.89
   B. 1.19
   C. 1.09
   D. 0.99
8. The thread on a spool is 30 meters long. Which is NOT an equivalent length?
   A. 0.03 km
   B. 3,000 cm
   C. 30,000 mm
   D. 0.3 km
9. A bucket full of water has sprung a leak. After each hour, the water is $\frac{2}{3}$ as high as the previous hour. After 2 hours, the water level is 12 in. How high was the water level before the leak?
   A. 18 in.　B. 27 in.
   C. 36 in　D. 44 in.
10. Amy ran 4 miles at 6 miles per hour and another 4 miles at 3 miles per hour. What was her average speed?
   A. 4 mi/h　B. 4.5 mi/h
   C. 5 mi/h　D. 5.5 mi/h

15. Water flows from a pipe at a rate of 6 c/min for 5 min. Then it flows at a rate of 4 c/min for 11 min. What is the total volume of water that flows from the pipe? (Lesson 6-4) C

(A) 4 c (B) 16 c (C) 74 c (D) 79 c

16. You can knit 5 in. of a sweater in 1 h. How much of the sweater can you knit in 2.5 h? (Lesson 6-2) A

(A) 12.5 in. (B) 24 in. (C) 60 in. (D) 250 in.

17. The table below shows the growth for four plants.

Plant	Growth
A	10 in. in 15 days
B	2 in. in 1 week
C	5 in. in 10 days
D	7 in. in 1 week

Which plant grew the fastest? (Lesson 6-2) D

(A) Plant A (B) Plant B (C) Plant C (D) Plant D

18. Which fraction is equivalent to -1.52? (Lesson 4-4) A

(A) $-\frac{38}{25}$ (B) $-\frac{1}{52}$ (C) $\frac{1}{152}$ (D) $\frac{38}{25}$

19. You run 4 mi/h for 30 min. Then you run 6 mi/h for 20 min. What is the total distance you run? (Lesson 6-4) B

(A) 0.5 mi (B) 4 mi (C) 6.4 mi (D) 10 mi

20. Which decimal is equivalent to $1\frac{7}{8}$? (Lesson 4-4) C

(A) 1.78 (B) 1.87 (C) 1.875 (D) 17.8

21. The distance a spring stretches varies directly with the force applied to it. A 4-lb weight stretches a spring 13 in. Which weight will stretch the spring 26 in.? (Lesson 6-4) C

(A) 2-lb (B) 4-lb (C) 8-lb (D) 26-lb

22. Which fraction is equivalent to 2.6? (Lesson 4-4) B

(A) $\frac{2}{6}$ (B) $\frac{13}{5}$ (C) $\frac{30}{10}$ (D) $\frac{26}{5}$

23. A student buys a bottle of water for \$1.50 and 3 avocados. The total cost for the items is \$4.35. Which equation can be used to find the cost of each avocado? (Lesson 3-4) C

(A) $1.50 + 3 = 4.35x$
(B) $1.50x + 3 = 4.35$
(C) $1.50 + 3x = 4.35$
(D) $x + 1.50 + 3 = 4.35$

Standards Reference Guide

California Content Standard	Item Number(s)
NS 1.5	1, 14, 18, 20, 22
AF 1.1	3, 4, 7, 10, 23
AF 4.2	5, 6, 8, 12, 15, 19, 21
MG 1.3	2, 9, 11, 13, 16, 17

For additional review and practice, see the *California Standards Review and Practice Workbook* or go online to use the

Visit: PHSchool.com, **Web Code:** axq-9045

Chapter 7 Applications of Percents

Chapter at a Glance

Lesson Titles, Objectives, and Features		California Content Standards
7-1 Fractions, Decimals, and Percents • To find equivalent forms of fractions, decimals, and percents		Find decimal and percent equivalents for common fractions. ***Foundational (Gr5 NS 1.2)***
	NS 1.3	Convert fractions to decimals and percents and use these representations in estimations, computations, and applications.
7-2 Finding a Percent of a Number • To find a percent of a number and to estimate percents **Mathematical Reasoning:** Percents Greater Than 100%		Calculate given percentages of quantities. ***Foundational (Gr6 NS 1.4)***
	NS 1.3	Convert fractions to decimals and percents and use these representations in estimations, computations, and applications.
	MR 2.7	Indicate the relative advantages of exact and approximate solutions to problems and give answers to a specified degree of accuracy.
	MR 3.2	Note the method of deriving the solution and demonstrate a conceptual understanding of the derivation by solving similar problems.
7-3 Percents and Proportions • To use proportions to solve percent problems		Use proportions to solve problems. Use cross-multiplication as a method for solving such problems. ***Foundational (Gr6 NS 1.3)***
	NS 1.3	Convert fractions to decimals and percents and use these representations in estimations, computations, and applications.
7-4 Percent of Change • To find percent of change **Mathematical Reasoning:** Checking for Reasonableness **Vocabulary Builder:** High-Use Academic Words	**NS 1.3**	Convert fractions to decimals and percents and use these representations in estimations, computations, and applications.
	MR 3.1	Evaluate the reasonableness of the solution in the context of the original situation.
7-5 Applications of Percent • To find markup and discount **7-5b Activity Lab:** Simple Interest		Solve problems involving discounts at sales. ***Foundational (Gr6 NS 1.4)***
		Solve problems involving interest earned. ***Foundational (Gr6 NS 1.4)***
	NS 1.3	Convert fractions to decimals and percents and use these representations in estimations, computations, and applications.
	MR 3.2	Note the method of deriving the solution and demonstrate an understanding of the derivation by solving similar problems.

California Content Standards
NS Number Sense
AF Algebra and Functions
MG Measurement and Geometry
MR Mathematical Reasoning

Correlations to Standardized Tests

All content for these tests is contained in *Prentice Hall Math, Algebra Readiness.* This chart reflects coverage in this chapter only.

	7-1	7-2	7-3	7-4	7-5
Terra Nova CAT6 (Level 18)					
Number and Number Relations	✔	✔	✔	✔	✔
Computation and Numerical Estimation	✔	✔	✔	✔	✔
Operation Concepts	✔	✔	✔	✔	✔
Measurement					
Geometry and Spatial Sense					
Data Analysis, Statistics, and Probability		✔		✔	✔
Patterns, Functions, Algebra	✔	✔	✔	✔	✔
Problem Solving and Reasoning	✔	✔	✔	✔	✔
Communication	✔	✔	✔	✔	✔
Decimals, Fractions, Integers, Percent	✔	✔	✔	✔	✔
Order of Operations					
Algebraic Operations					
Terra Nova CTBS (Level 18)					
Decimals, Fractions, Integers, Percents	✔	✔	✔	✔	✔
Order of Operations, Numeration, Number Theory	✔	✔	✔	✔	✔
Data Interpretation				✔	✔
Measurement					
Geometry					
ITBS (Level 14)					
Number Properties and Operations	✔	✔	✔	✔	✔
Algebra	✔	✔	✔	✔	✔
Geometry					
Measurement					
Probability and Statistics					
Estimation		✔			
SAT10 (Adv 1 Level)					
Number Sense and Operations	✔	✔	✔	✔	✔
Patterns, Relationships, and Algebra	✔	✔	✔	✔	✔
Data, Statistics, and Probability		✔			✔
Geometry and Measurement					
NAEP					
Number Sense, Properties, and Operations	✔	✔	✔	✔	✔
Measurement					
Geometry and Spatial Sense					
Data Analysis, Statistics, and Probability					
Algebra and Functions					

CAT6 California Achievement Test, 6th Ed.
SAT10 Stanford Achievement Test, 10th Ed.
CTBS Comprehensive Test of Basic Skills
NAEP National Assessment of Educational Progress 2005 Mathematics Objectives
ITBS Iowa Test of Basic Skills, Form M

California Math Background

Focus on the California Content Standards

- As early as grade 5, students began to investigate the concept of percent. They interpreted percents as part of a hundred, found decimal and percent equivalents for common fractions, and computed a given percent of a whole number (**NS 1.2**).
- Grade 6 expanded students' experiences with percents as they calculated given percentages of quantities, and solved problems involving discounts at sales, interest earned, and tips (**NS 1.4**).
- Lessons 7-1 and 7-2 in this chapter will be especially helpful to students who struggle with the foundations needed to be successful with percents.

7-1 Fractions, Decimals, and Percents

California Content Standards **NS 1.3**

Math Understandings

- A percent expresses parts per 100. The percent symbol, %, means "per 100" or "$\frac{}{100}$."
- You can represent a percent in different but related ways, such as a ratio, a fraction, and a decimal.
- You can rewrite a decimal that names hundredths directly as the equivalent percent.
- The word "of" usually indicates multiplication in the statement of a problem.

A **percent** is a ratio that compares a number to 100. To write a percent as a fraction, you can write it as a fraction with a denominator of 100 and simplify. To write a percent as a decimal, move the decimal point two places to the left and remove the percent sign.

7-2 Finding a Percent of a Number

California Content Standards **NS 1.3, MR 2.7, MR 3.2**

Math Understandings

- Knowing the fraction equivalent of common percents can help you use mental math to calculate with them.

You can find a given percent of a number by rewriting the percent as either a decimal or a fraction and then multiplying.

Example: Find 36% of 112. $0.36 \times 112 = 40.32$

Here are the fraction equivalents of common percents.

Percent	10%	20%	25%	50%	75%
Fraction	$\frac{1}{10}$	$\frac{1}{5}$	$\frac{1}{4}$	$\frac{1}{2}$	$\frac{3}{4}$
Decimal	0.1	0.2	0.25	0.5	0.75

You can estimate percents in daily transactions such as paying sales tax and figuring the tip on a restaurant bill.

Example: Estimate a 15% tip on $14.

First find 10% of $14 ($1.40). Then add half of that amount ($.70) which is 5%. A 15% tip of $14 is $1.40 × $.70, or $2.10.

7-3 Percents and Proportions

California Content Standards NS 1.3

Math Understandings

- Percent problems involve a part, a percent, and a whole.
- If you know two of the three quantities, you can find the missing one by using either a proportion or an equation.
- You can write a proportion in different but equivalent ways.
- When you find a percent that is greater than 100%, the part will be greater than the whole.

You can write and solve the proportion $\frac{\text{part}}{\text{whole}} = \frac{\text{percent}}{100}$ to find the missing part, percent, or whole.

Example: Find 300% of 180.

$\frac{n}{180} = \frac{300}{100}$
$100n = 300 \cdot 180$
$100n = 54{,}000$
$n = 540$

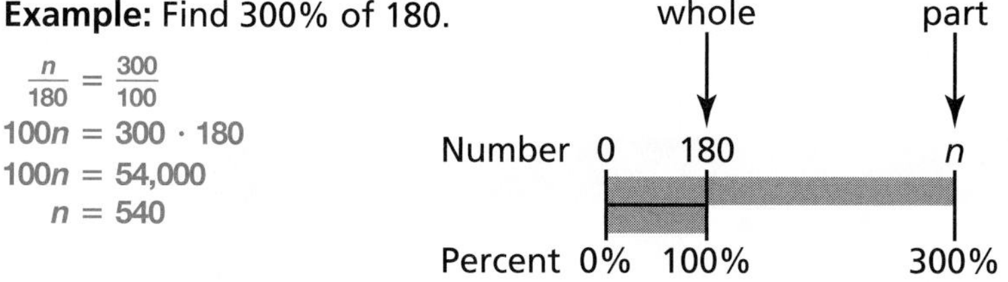

Percents and Proportions		
Finding the Part What number is 20% of 25? $\frac{n}{25} = \frac{20}{100}$	**Finding the Whole** 5 is 20% of what number? $\frac{5}{w} = \frac{20}{100}$	**Finding the Percent** 5 is what percent of 25? $\frac{5}{25} = \frac{p}{100}$

7-4 Percent of Change

California Content Standards NS 1.3, MR 3.1

Math Understandings

- A percent of change may be an increase or a decrease.
- The percent of change is a ratio, expressed as a percent. It compares the amount of change to the original amount. The amount of change is the difference between the original amount and the amount that results after the change.

The percent a quantity increases or decreases from its original amount is the **percent of change**.

$$\text{percent of change} = \frac{\text{amount of change}}{\text{original amount}}$$

7-5 Applications of Percent

California Content Standards NS 1.3, MR 3.2

Math Understandings

- A common percent decrease is a discount. The corresponding percent increase is a markup.

Markup is the amount of increase in price. Markup is added to a store's cost of an item to arrive at the **selling price**. The percent of increase in the price of an item is called the percent of markup. The amount by which the price of an item on sale is reduced is called the **discount**. The regular price of an item minus the discount equals the **sale price** of the item.

$$\text{percent of change} = \frac{\text{amount of change}}{\text{original amount}}$$

$$\text{percent of markup} = \frac{\text{markup}}{\text{store's cost}}$$

$$\text{percent of discount} = \frac{\text{discount}}{\text{regular price}}$$

Professional Development

Additional Professional Development Opportunities

Math Background notes for Chapter 7: Every lesson has a Math Background in the PLAN section.

In-Service On Demand
Prentice Hall offers free video-based tutorials to support you. Visit PHSchool.com/inserviceondemand.

Pearson Achievement Solutions
Pearson Achievement Solutions, a Pearson Education company, offers comprehensive, facilitated professional development designed to help teachers improve student achievement. To learn more, please visit pearsonachievementsolutions.com.

Chapter 7 Resources

	7-1	7-2	7-3	7-4	7-5	For the Chapter
Print Resources						
L3 Practice	●	●	●	●	●	
L3 Guided Problem Solving	●	●	●	●	●	
L2 Reteaching	●	●	●	●	●	
L4 Enrichment	●	●	●	●	●	
L3 Vocabulary and Study Skills	●	●	●	●	●	●
L3 Daily Puzzles	●	●	●	●	●	
L3 Activity Labs	●	●	●	●	●	
L3 Checkpoint Quiz		●		●		
L3 Chapter Project						●
L2 Below Level Chapter Test						●
L3 Chapter Test						●
L4 Alternative Assessment						●
L3 Cumulative Review						●
Spanish Resources EL						
L3 Practice	●	●	●	●	●	
L3 Vocabulary and Study Skills	●		●		●	●
L3 Checkpoint Quiz		●		●		
L2 Below Level Chapter Test						●
L3 Chapter Test						●
L4 Alternative Assessment						●
L3 Cumulative Review						●
Transparencies						
Check Skills You'll Need	●	●	●	●	●	
Additional Examples	●	●	●	●	●	
California Daily Review	●	●	●	●	●	
Classroom Aid						
Student Edition Answers	●	●	●	●	●	●
Lesson Quiz	●	●	●	●	●	
Technology						
California Student Center Online	●	●	●	●	●	●
California Student Center CD-ROM	●	●	●	●	●	●
Success Tracker™ Online Math Intervention	●	●	●	●	●	●
California Teacher Center: ExamView CD-ROM	●	●	●	●	●	●
California Teacher Center: Planning CD-ROM	●	●	●	●	●	●
California Teacher Center: Presentations CD-ROM and online	●	●	●	●	●	●
MindPoint Quiz Show	●	●	●	●	●	●
Prentice Hall Web Site: PHSchool.com	●	●	●	●	●	●

Also available:

California Standards Mastery
- Standards Review Transparencies
- Standards Review and Practice Workbook
- Progress Monitoring Assessments
- Math Companion
- Math*XL*

California Intervention Resources
- Skills Review and Practice Workbook
- Success Tracker™ Online Math Intervention

Other Resources
- Multilingual Handbook
- Spanish Student Edition
- Solution Key
- Math Notes Study Folder

Where You Can Use the Lesson Resources

Here is a suggestion, following the four-step teaching plan, for how you can incorporate Universal Access Resources into your teaching.

	Instructional Resources L3	Universal Access Resources
1. Plan		
Preparation Read the Math Background in the Teacher's Edition to connect this lesson with students' previous experience. **Starting Class** **Check Skills You'll Need** Assign these exercises from the Math Companion to review prerequisite skills. Review the full text of the student expectations and objectives covered in this lesson. **New Vocabulary** Help students pre-read the lesson by pointing out the new terms introduced in the lesson.	**California Math Background** **Math Understandings** **Transparencies & Presentations CD-ROM** Check Skills You'll Need California Daily Review **Resources** Vocabulary and Study Skills **Math Companion**	**Spanish Support** EL Vocabulary and Study Skills
2. Teach		
L3 **Guided Instruction** Use the Activity Labs to build conceptual understanding. Teach each Example. Use the Teacher's Edition side column notes for specific teaching tips, including Error Prevention notes. Use the Additional Examples found in the side column (and on transparency and PowerPoint) as an alternative presentation for the content. After each Example, assign the California Standards Check exercises for that Example to get an immediate assessment of student understanding. Utilize the support in the Math Companion to assist students with each Standards Check. Use the Closure activity in the Teacher's Edition to help students attain mastery of lesson content.	**Student Edition** Activity Lab **Resources** Math Companion Activity Lab **Transparencies & Presentations CD-ROM** Additional Examples Classroom Aids **Teacher Center: ExamView CD-ROM**	**Teacher's Edition** Every lesson includes suggestions for working with students who need special attention. L1 Special Needs L2 Below Level L4 Advanced Learners EL English Learners **Resources** **Multilingual Handbook** **Math Companion**
3. Practice		
Assignment Guide **Check Your Understanding** Use these questions from the Math Companion to check students' understanding before you assign homework. **Homework Exercises** Assign homework from these leveled exercises in the Assignment Guide. **A** Practice by Example **B** Apply Your Skills **C** Challenge California Multiple-Choice Practice and Mixed Review **Homework Quick Check** Use these key exercises to quickly check students' homework.	**Transparencies & Presentations CD-ROM** Student Answers **Resources** Math Companion Practice Guided Problem Solving Vocabulary and Study Skills Activity Lab Daily Puzzles **Teacher Center: ExamView CD-ROM** **Math *XL***	**Spanish Support** EL Practice EL Vocabulary and Study Skills **Resources** L4 Enrichment
4. Assess & Reteach		
Lesson Quiz Assign the Lesson Quiz to assess students' mastery of the lesson content. **Checkpoint Quiz** Use the Checkpoint Quiz to assess student progress over several lessons.	**Transparencies & Presentations CD-ROM** Lesson Quiz **Resources** Checkpoint Quiz	**Resources** L2 Reteaching EL Checkpoint Quiz Success Tracker™ **Teacher Center: ExamView CD-ROM**

KEY L1 Special Needs L2 Below Level L3 For All Students L4 Advanced, Gifted EL English Learners

Applications of Percents

Answers are in the back of the textbook.

For math intervention, direct students to:

Solving One-Step Equations
Lessons 3-1, 3-2, 3-3

Equivalent Forms of Rational Numbers
Lesson 4-4

Multiplying Rational Numbers
Lesson 5-3

Proportions
Lesson 6-5

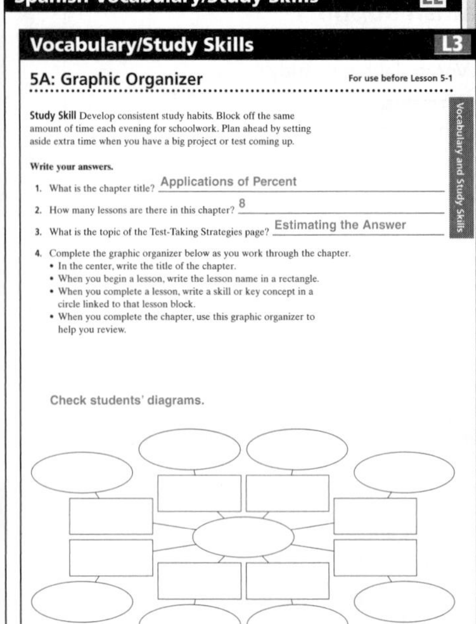

Spanish Vocabulary/Study Skills EL

Vocabulary/Study Skills L3

5A: Graphic Organizer For use before Lesson 5-1

Study Skill Develop consistent study habits. Block off the same amount of time each evening for schoolwork. Plan ahead by setting aside extra time when you have a big project or test coming up.

Write your answers.

1. What is the chapter title? Applications of Percent
2. How many lessons are there in this chapter? 8
3. What is the topic of the Test-Taking Strategies page? Estimating the Answer
4. Complete the graphic organizer below as you work through the chapter.
   - In the center, write the title of the chapter.
   - When you begin a lesson, write the lesson name in a rectangle.
   - When you complete a lesson, write a skill or key concept in a circle linked to that lesson block.
   - When you complete the chapter, use this graphic organizer to help you review.

Check students' diagrams.

Vocabulary and Study Skills

Applications of Percent

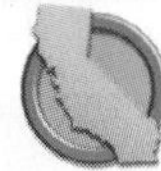

What You've Learned

California Content Standards

NS 1.2 Add, subtract, multiply, and divide rational numbers and take positive rational numbers to whole-number powers.

AF 4.2 Solve multistep problems involving rate, average speed, distance, and time or a direct variation.

MG 1.3 Use measures expressed as rates and measures expressed as products to solve problems; and use dimensional analysis to check the reasonableness of the answer.

to the lesson in green.

Solving One-Step Equations (Lesson 3-3)

Solve each equation.

1. $16 = 0.8p$ 20
2. $2m = 31.82$ 15.91
3. $0.32x = 76$ 237.5
4. $95v = 166.25$ 1.75

Finding Equivalent Forms of Rational Numbers (Lesson 4-3)

Write each fraction in simplest form.

5. $\frac{50}{100}$ $\frac{1}{2}$
6. $\frac{25}{40}$ $\frac{5}{8}$
7. $\frac{6}{72}$ $\frac{1}{12}$
8. $\frac{36}{64}$ $\frac{9}{16}$

Multiplying Rational Numbers (Lesson 5-3)

Find each product.

9. $\frac{3}{10} \cdot 100$ 30
10. $15 \cdot \frac{17}{30}$ 8.5
11. $160 \cdot \frac{5}{8}$ 100

Solving Proportions (Lesson 6-5)

Solve each proportion.

12. $\frac{7}{12} = \frac{21}{n}$ 36
13. $\frac{k}{45} = \frac{10}{225}$ 2
14. $\frac{18}{t} = \frac{27}{48}$ 32
15. $\frac{1}{4} = \frac{25}{y}$ 100
16. $\frac{5}{3} = \frac{z}{11.4}$ 19
17. $\frac{h}{76} = \frac{9}{8}$ 85.5

What You'll Learn Next

California Content Standards

NS 1.3 Convert fractions to decimals and percents and use these representations in estimations, computations, and applications.

MR 2.7 Indicate the relative advantages of exact and appropriate solutions to problems and give answers to a specified degree of accuracy.

▲ Flower sales in California make up about 73% of the total cut-flower sales in the United States.

New Vocabulary

English and Spanish Audio Online

- discount (p. 273)
- markup (p. 272)
- percent (p. 252)
- percent of change (p. 266)
- selling price (p. 272)

Academic Vocabulary
- calculate (p. 271)
- estimate (p. 271)
- support (p. 271)

California Content Standards for Chapter 7

Number Sense
NS 1.3

Mathematical Reasoning
MR 2.7, MR 3.1, MR 3.2

Chapter 7 Overview

In this chapter, students learn about percents; explore the relationships among fractions, decimals, and percents; and solve a variety of percent problems using different methods. They estimate percents and find percents using proportions and equations. They apply their understanding of percent to real-world situations as they find discounts and markups.

Activating Prior Knowledge

In this chapter, as students work with percents, they build on their knowledge of ratios and rates and of writing and solving proportions. They draw upon their prior understanding of the relationship between fractions and decimals. Ask questions such as:

- *A player has made 7 out of 10 free throw attempts. If she continues to shoot at that rate, how many free throws can she expect to make in 200 attempts?* 140 free throws
- *What is the value of x in the proportion* $\frac{4}{x} = \frac{88}{11}$? 0.5
- *Limes are 4 for \$1 at the store. What would two dozen limes cost?* \$6

7-1

1. Plan

California Content Standards

Find decimal and percent equivalents for common fractions. ***Foundational***

NS 1.3 Convert fractions to decimals and percents and use these representations in estimations, computations, and applications. ***Develop***

California Math Background

A *percent* is a ratio that compares a number to 100. Percents, fractions, and decimals can all represent parts of a whole. You can convert between percents, fractions, and decimals by using the definition of percent as $\frac{\text{part}}{\text{whole}} = \frac{\text{percent}}{100}$.

To write a decimal as a percent, move the decimal point two places to the right and write the percent sign. To convert a fraction to a percent, divide the numerator by the denominator and convert the resulting decimal to a percent.

More Math Background: p. 250C

Lesson Planning and Resources

See p. 250E for a list of the resources that support this lesson.

PRESENTATION CD-ROM
CD, Online, or Transparencies

Bell Ringer Practice

Check Skills You'll Need
Use student page, transparency, or PowerPoint.
See Math Companion.

California Standards Review
Use transparency or PowerPoint.

GO for Help: Math Companion

7-1 Fractions, Decimals, and Percents

Check Skills You'll Need

Do this in your **Math Companion.**

Vocabulary

- percent

Use your **Math Companion** *to build your vocabulary.*

California Content Standards

Foundational Standard Find decimal and percent equivalents for common fractions.
NS 1.3 Convert fractions to decimals and percents and use these representations in estimations, computations, and applications. ***Develop***

What You'll Learn . . . and Why

Math Times
Math Test Scores Go Up by 12%

You will learn to find equivalent forms of fractions, decimals, and percents. Newspapers use fractions, decimals, and percents to report data. You can convert numbers from one form to another to compare the data.

A **percent** is a ratio that compares a number to 100. The model below shows 41 out of 100 squares shaded. You can represent the shaded part of the model with a fraction, a decimal, or a percent.

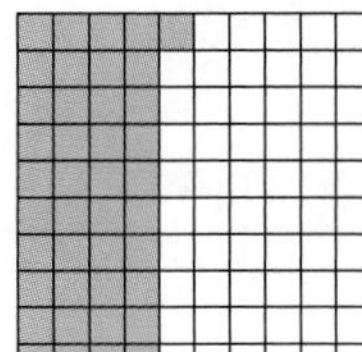

Fraction: $\frac{41}{100}$

Decimal: 0.41

Percent: 41%

Percents can be between 1% and 100%, greater than 100%, or less than 1%. To write a percent as a fraction, write the percent as a fraction with a denominator of 100. Then simplify the fraction.

Online active math

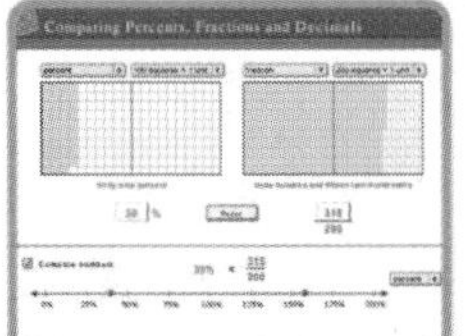

For: Comparing Numbers Activity
Use: Interactive Textbook, 7-1

EXAMPLE Writing Percents as Fractions

1 Write 36% as a fraction. Write your answer in simplest form.

$36\% = \frac{36}{100}$ ← **Write the percent as a fraction with a denominator of 100.**

$= \frac{9}{25}$ ← **Write the fraction in simplest form.**

CA Standards Check 1 *Go to your* **Math Companion** *for help.*

1. Write each percent as a fraction in simplest form.
   a. 56% $\frac{14}{25}$ **b.** 4% $\frac{1}{25}$ **c.** 25% $\frac{1}{4}$

Universal Access Solutions for All Learners

Special Needs L1
Students often incorrectly use the idea that you can write every decimal number as a number over 100 to convert to a percent. For example, this works with 0.07, but for 0.5 they need to write $\frac{50}{100}$. Show examples of how to rewrite a decimal as a percent.

Below Level L2
Make sure students understand that x% is $\frac{x}{100}$. Ask: *Why can you write 36% as $\frac{36}{100}$?* Sample: Percent is a comparison to 100, so 36% is 36 to 100, or $\frac{36}{100}$.

You can use a proportion to convert a fraction to a percent.

EXAMPLE Writing a Fraction as a Percent

Relate MATH YOU KNOW... ... *to* ALGEBRA

Write a fraction equivalent to $\frac{6}{25}$.

$$\frac{6}{25} \overset{\times 4}{=} \frac{24}{100}$$ ← Multiply the numerator and the denominator by 4.

2 **Guided Problem Solving** According to a school newspaper article, 6 out of every 25 students at the school bring their lunch to school. Write $\frac{6}{25}$ as a percent.

$\frac{6}{25} = \frac{p}{100}$ ← Write a proportion. Percents have 100 in the denominator.

$\frac{6}{25} \overset{\times 4}{=} \frac{24}{100}$ ← Find the fraction with a denominator of 100 equal to $\frac{6}{25}$.

$\frac{6}{25} = \frac{24}{100} = 24\%$ ← Write using a percent symbol.

CA Standards Check 2 *Go to your* **Math Companion** *for help.*

2. Write each fraction as a percent.

a. $\frac{11}{20}$ 55% **b.** $\frac{7}{10}$ 70%

To write a decimal as a percent, write the decimal as a fraction with a denominator of 100.

EXAMPLE Writing a Decimal as a Percent

3 Write 0.076 as a percent.

Problem Solving Tip

To write a decimal as a percent, you can move the decimal point two places to the right.

$0.076 = \frac{76}{1{,}000}$ ← Write the decimal as a fraction.

$= \frac{76 \div 10}{1{,}000 \div 10}$ ← Divide the numerator and denominator by 10.

$= \frac{7.6}{100}$ ← Write an equivalent fraction with a denominator of 100.

$= 7.6\%$ ← Write as a percent.

CA Standards Check 3 *Go to your* **Math Companion** *for help.*

3. Write each decimal as a percent.

a. 0.52 52% **b.** 0.05 5% **c.** 0.5 50%

Check Your Understanding *Homework prep is in your* **Math Companion.**

2. Teach

Guided Instruction

Example 2

Have students list the factors of 100. 1, 2, 4, 5, 10, 20, 25, 50, 100

Error Prevention!

Watch for students who incorrectly move the decimal point to the left instead of to the right when they convert decimals to percents.

PRESENTATION CD-ROM CD, Online, or Transparencies

Additional Examples

1 Write 4% as a fraction in simplest form. $\frac{1}{25}$

2 Write $\frac{7}{20}$ as a percent. 35%

3 Write each decimal as a percent.

a. 0.16 16%

b. 0.03 3%

Closure

- *Explain how to write a percent as a fraction.* Sample: Remove the % symbol. Use the resulting number as the numerator and 100 as the denominator of a fraction. Reduce the fraction to simplest terms.
- *Explain how to write a fraction as a percent.* Sample: Write the fraction as an equivalent fraction with 100 as the denominator. The numerator will be the percent.
- *Explain how to write a decimal as a percent.* Sample: Write the decimal number as a fraction with 100 as the denominator. The numerator will be the percent.

Advanced Learners L4	**English Learners** EL
What percent is 50% of 60% of a number? 30% of the number If you increase the original price of an item by 25%, by what percent do you need to reduce the new price to obtain the original price? 20%	Ask students to *describe* what happens to the decimal point when you multiply a decimal by 100. Ask them to *predict* what might happen if they divided by 100.

3. Practice

Assignment Guide

Check Your Understanding

See Math Companion.

Homework Exercises

A Practice by Example	1–26
B Apply Your Skills	27–43
C Challenge	44
California Multiple-Choice Practice	45–47
Mixed Review	48–50

Homework Quick Check

To check students' understanding of key skills and concepts, go over Exercises 3, 12, 20, 33, 36, 40.

Universal Access Resources

Adapted Practice 7-1 L1

Practice 7-1 Fractions, Decimals, and P L3

Write each percent as a fraction in simplest form.

1. 46% ______ 2. 17% ______ 3. 90% ______ 4. 5% ______

Write each decimal as a percent.

5. 0.02 ______ 6. 0.45 ______ 7. 0.4 ______ 8. 1.92 ______

Write each fraction as a percent.

9. $\frac{3}{5}$ ______ 10. $\frac{7}{10}$ ______ 11. $\frac{13}{25}$ ______ 12. $\frac{17}{20}$ ______

The table shows the fraction of students who participated in extracurricular activities from 1965 to 2000. Complete the table by writing each fraction as a percent.

Students' Extracurricular Choices

Year	1965	1970	1975	1980	1985	1990	1995	2000
Student participation (fraction)	$\frac{3}{4}$	$\frac{8}{10}$	$\frac{17}{20}$	$\frac{39}{50}$	$\frac{21}{25}$	$\frac{19}{25}$	$\frac{87}{100}$	$\frac{9}{10}$
Student participation (percent)								

Write each fraction or decimal as a percent. Write the percent (without the percent sign) in the puzzle.

Across	Down
1. $\frac{3}{5}$	1. $\frac{13}{20}$
2. $\frac{1}{5}$	2. 0.25
3. 0.55	3. $\frac{1}{2}$
5. 0.23	4. $\frac{3}{20}$
6. $\frac{7}{20}$	5. 0.24
7. 0.17	6. $\frac{3}{10}$
9. 0.4	7. 0.1
10. $\frac{9}{25}$	8. $\frac{4}{25}$

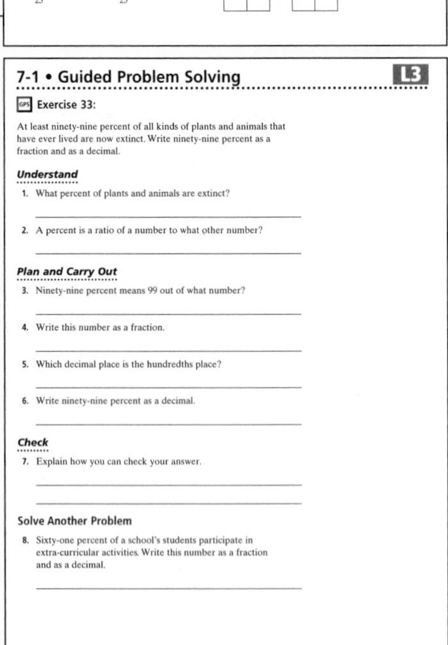
7-1 • Guided Problem Solving L3

Exercise 33:

At least ninety-nine percent of all kinds of plants and animals that have ever lived are now extinct. Write ninety-nine percent as a fraction and as a decimal.

Understand

1. What percent of plants and animals are extinct? ______
2. A percent is a ratio of a number to what other number? ______

Plan and Carry Out

3. Ninety-nine percent means 99 out of what number? ______
4. Write this number as a fraction. ______
5. Which decimal place is the hundredths place? ______
6. Write ninety-nine percent as a decimal. ______

Check

7. Explain how you can check your answer. ______

Solve Another Problem

8. Sixty-one percent of a school's students participate in extra-curricular activities. Write this number as a fraction and as a decimal. ______

Standards Practice

GO for Help: MathXL NS 1.3

A Practice by Example

Example 1 (page 252)

Write each percent as a fraction in simplest form.

1. 70% $\frac{7}{10}$

$70\% = \frac{70}{100}$

$= \blacksquare$

Guided Practice This exercise has been started for you!

GO for Help

2. 88% $\frac{22}{25}$ 3. 5% $\frac{1}{20}$ 4. 33% $\frac{33}{100}$
5. 14% $\frac{7}{50}$ 6. 15% $\frac{3}{20}$ 7. 75% $\frac{3}{4}$
8. 18% $\frac{9}{50}$ 9. 2% $\frac{1}{50}$ 10. 42% $\frac{21}{50}$

Example 2 (page 253)

Write each fraction as a percent.

11. $\frac{2}{5}$ 40%

$\frac{2}{5} = \frac{p}{100}$

$= \frac{\blacksquare}{100}$

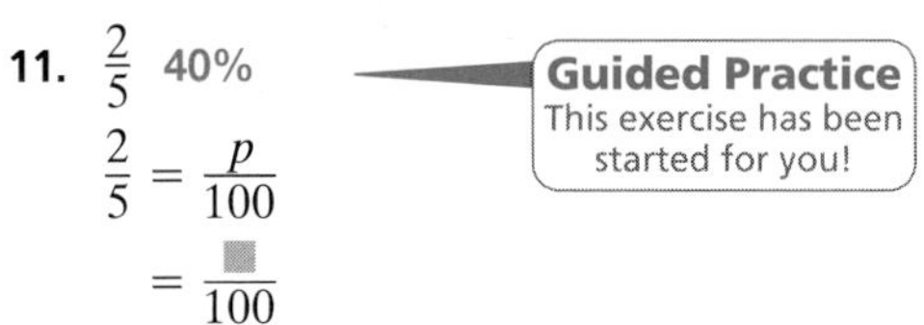

Homework Video Tutor

For: Examples 1–3
Visit: PHSchool.com
Web Code: axe-0701

12. $\frac{3}{4}$ 75% 13. $\frac{24}{25}$ 96% 14. $\frac{7}{20}$ 35% 15. $\frac{45}{50}$ 90%

16. Three of every five students who tried out for a play made the cast. Write $\frac{3}{5}$ as a percent. 60%

Example 3 (page 253)

Write each decimal as a percent.

17. 0.36 36%

$0.36 = \frac{36}{100}$

$= \blacksquare\%$

18. 0.17 17% 19. 0.003 0.3% 20. 0.98 98%
21. 0.9 90% 22. 0.44 44% 23. 0.00007 0.007%
24. 5.4 540% 25. 0.22 22% 26. 0.047 4.7%

B Apply Your Skills

27. **Guided Problem Solving** The table below shows the results of a student survey about lunch. What percent of students did *not* choose tacos as their favorite food? Round to the nearest percent. 93%

Favorite Food	Hamburgers	Tacos	Sandwiches	Pizza
Number of Students	45	7	19	34

- How many students were surveyed?
- How many students *did* choose tacos as their favorite food?

SCAFFOLDED **Problem Solving**

A bag contains 9 quarters, 4 dimes, and 12 nickels.

28. How many coins are there in all? 25 coins
29. What fraction of the coins are dimes? $\frac{4}{25}$
30. What percent of the coins are dimes? 16%
31. What percent of the coins are quarters or nickels? 84%
32. What percent of the coins are *not* nickels? 52%

GPS 33. At least ninety-nine percent of all kinds of plants and animals that have ever lived are now extinct. Write ninety-nine percent as a fraction and as a decimal. $\frac{99}{100}$, 0.99

34. Use the fuel gauge at the right. What percent of the tank is full? 75%

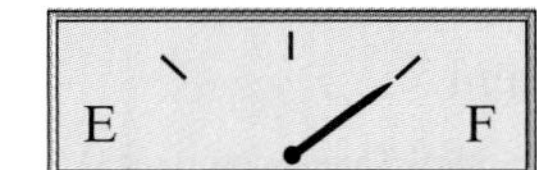

35.  **Writing in Math** Explain why 0.09 is different from 0.09%. See left.

35. 0.09% is equal to 0.0009, which is not the same as 0.09.

Write the letter of the point on the number line that represents each number.

36. 0.4 B
37. 60% C
38. $\frac{5}{6}$ D
39. 18% A

Write each percent as a fraction in simplest form.

40. 105% $\frac{21}{20}$
41. 220% $\frac{11}{5}$
42. $22\frac{2}{9}\%$ $\frac{2}{9}$
43. $66\frac{2}{3}\%$ $\frac{2}{3}$

C Challenge

44. On average, about 60% of an adult's body weight is water. About how many pounds of a 135-lb person are water? 81 lb

Multiple Choice Practice and Mixed Review

For California Standards Tutorials, visit PHSchool.com. Web Code: axq-9045

NS 1.3 45. Write $\frac{19}{20}$ as a percent. D

Ⓐ 0.95% Ⓑ $\frac{19}{20}\%$ Ⓒ 19% Ⓓ 95%

AF 4.2 46. A jogger ran 8 mi/h for 1 h and 7.5 mi/h for $\frac{1}{2}$ h. How far did the jogger run in all? B

Ⓐ 15.5 mi Ⓑ 11.75 mi Ⓒ 11.5 mi Ⓓ 1.5 mi

AF 4.2 47. Yolanda earns $12 for baby-sitting for 3 h. How much will she earn in 4 h? C

Ⓐ $48 Ⓑ $36 Ⓒ $16 Ⓓ $4

Lesson 4-2 **Find the GCD of each pair of numbers.**

48. 15 and 39 3
49. 75 and 100 25
50. 18 and 54 18

GO Online Lesson Quiz Visit: PHSchool.com Web Code: axa-0701

Alternative Assessment

Each student in a pair writes several percents. Partners exchange papers and write each other's percents as decimals and fractions in simplest form. Next, partners write several fractions and decimals, exchange papers, and write each other's fractions and decimals as percents.

California Resources

Standards Mastery
- Standards Review Transparencies
- Standards Review and Practice Workbook
- Math Companion

Math Intervention
- Skills Review and Practice Workbook
- Math XL

4. Assess & Reteach

PRESENTATION CD-ROM
CD, Online, or Transparencies
Lesson Quiz

Write each percent as a decimal and as a fraction in simplest form.

1. 60% 0.60; $\frac{3}{5}$
2. 38% 0.38; $\frac{19}{50}$

Write each decimal or fraction as a percent.

3. 0.05 5%
4. $\frac{3}{20}$ 15%

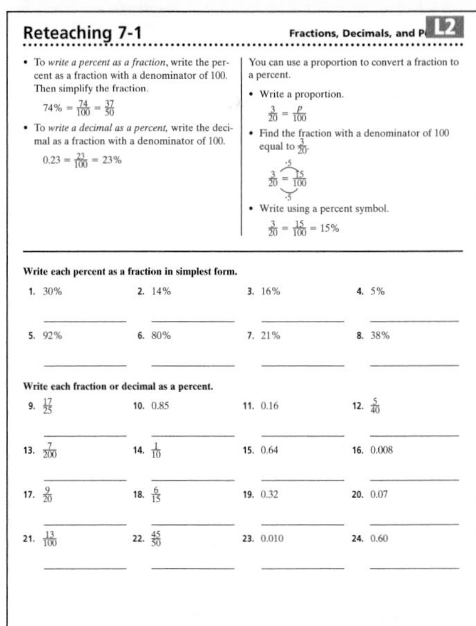

Reteaching 7-1 Fractions, Decimals, and P L2

- To *write a percent as a fraction*, write the percent as a fraction with a denominator of 100. Then simplify the fraction.
  $74\% = \frac{74}{100} = \frac{37}{50}$
- To *write a decimal as a percent*, write the decimal as a fraction with a denominator of 100.
  $0.23 = \frac{23}{100} = 23\%$

You can use a proportion to convert a fraction to a percent.

- Write a proportion.
  $\frac{3}{20} = \frac{p}{100}$
- Find the fraction with a denominator of 100 equal to $\frac{3}{20}$.
  $\frac{3 \cdot 5}{20 \cdot 5} = \frac{15}{100}$
- Write using a percent symbol.
  $\frac{3}{20} = \frac{15}{100} = 15\%$

Write each percent as a fraction in simplest form.

1. 30% 2. 14% 3. 16% 4. 5%
5. 92% 6. 80% 7. 21% 8. 38%

Write each fraction or decimal as a percent.

9. $\frac{17}{25}$ 10. 0.85 11. 0.16 12. $\frac{5}{40}$
13. $\frac{7}{200}$ 14. $\frac{1}{10}$ 15. 0.64 16. 0.008
17. $\frac{9}{20}$ 18. $\frac{6}{15}$ 19. 0.32 20. 0.07
21. $\frac{13}{100}$ 22. $\frac{45}{50}$ 23. 0.010 24. 0.60

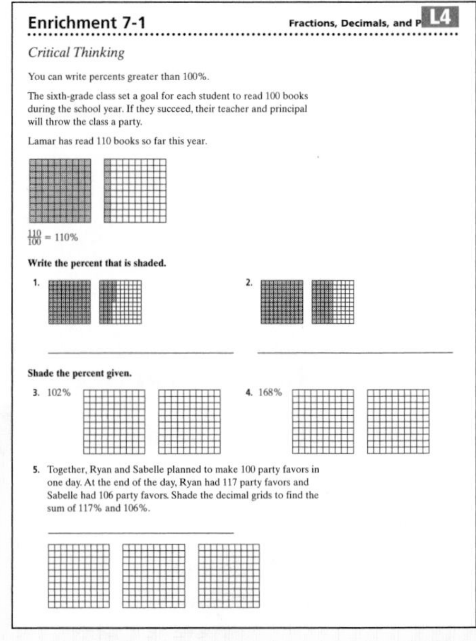

Enrichment 7-1 Fractions, Decimals, and P L4

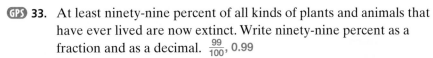

Critical Thinking

You can write percents greater than 100%.

The sixth-grade class set a goal for each student to read 100 books during the school year. If they succeed, their teacher and principal will throw the class a party.

Lamar has read 110 books so far this year.

$\frac{110}{100} = 110\%$

Write the percent that is shaded.

1.
2.

Shade the percent given.

3. 102%
4. 168%
5. Together, Ryan and Sabelle planned to make 100 party favors in one day. At the end of the day, Ryan had 117 party favors and Sabelle had 106 party favors. Shade the decimal grids to find the sum of 117% and 106%.

7-2

1. Plan

California Content Standards

Calculate given percentages of quantities. ***Foundational***

NS 1.3 Convert fractions to decimals and percents and use these representations in estimations, computations, and applications. ***Develop***

MR 2.7 Indicate the relative advantages of exact and approximate solutions to problems and give answers to a specified degree of accuracy.

California Math Background

In real-life situations, it is sometimes useful to estimate the percent of a number by multiplying by the percent in decimal form. If the percent is close to a known common fraction, multiplying the fraction by a number works well. To estimate a 15% tip, using the sum of 10% and 5% is a helpful method.

More Math Background: p. 250C

Lesson Planning and Resources

See p. 250E for a list of the resources that support this lesson.

PRESENTATION CD-ROM
CD, Online, or Transparencies
Bell Ringer Practice

Check Skills You'll Need
Use student page, transparency, or PowerPoint.
See Math Companion.

California Standards Review
Use transparency or PowerPoint.

7-2 Finding a Percent of a Number

Check Skills You'll Need

Do this in your **Math Companion.**

Vocabulary

Review:
- percent

Use your **Math Companion** *to build your vocabulary.*

California Content Standards

Foundational Standard Calculate given percentages of quantities.
NS 1.3 Convert fractions to decimals and percents and use these representations in estimations, computations, and applications. ***Develop***
MR 2.7 Indicate the relative advantages of exact and approximate solutions to problems and give answers to a specified degree of accuracy. ***Develop***

What You'll Learn . . . and Why

You will learn to find a percent of a number and to estimate percents. You can estimate percents to find the tip for a restaurant bill.

To find the percent of a number, multiply. For example, to find 22% of 250, you can write 22% as a fraction or a decimal, and then multiply by 250.

EXAMPLE Finding a Percent

Vocabulary Tip
The word *of* usually tells you to multiply.

1 Find 22% of 250.

Method 1 Write the percent as a decimal.

$22\% = 0.22$ ← **Write the percent as a decimal.**

$0.22 \cdot 250 = 55$ ← **Multiply.**

Method 2 Write the percent as a fraction.

$22\% = \frac{22}{100} = \frac{11}{50}$ ← **Write the percent as a fraction in simplest form.**

$\frac{11}{50} \cdot 250 = \frac{11}{\cancel{50}_1} \cdot \frac{\cancel{250}^5}{1}$ ← **Divide 50 and 250 by their GCD, 50.**

$= 55$ ← **Multiply.**

So 22% of 250 is 55.

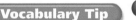

CA Standards Check 1 *Go to your* **Math Companion** *for help.*

1. Find each percent.
   a. 20% of 40 **8**
   b. 12% of 91 **10.92**
   c. 18% of 121 **21.78**

Universal Access Solutions for All Learners

Special Needs L1	**Below Level** L2
Ask students to draw pictures or use grids to represent the percents shown in the table. They can refer to these visual representations when estimating percents.	Have students find and say aloud quantities such as 25% of 8 (2), 50% of 48 (24), 75% of 100 (75), and so on.

Study Tip

Memorizing the values in the table at the right can help you find percents quickly.

The percents in the table below are often used in real-world situations. You can use these percents and their equivalent fractions and decimals to estimate percents.

Equivalent Expressions for Estimating Percents

Percent	10%	20%	25%	50%	75%	80%
Fraction	$\frac{1}{10}$	$\frac{1}{5}$	$\frac{1}{4}$	$\frac{1}{2}$	$\frac{3}{4}$	$\frac{4}{5}$
Decimal	0.1	0.2	0.25	0.5	0.75	0.8

You can estimate a percent to find the tip for a restaurant bill quickly.

Relate MATH YOU KNOW... ...*to* NEW IDEAS

EXAMPLE Estimating a Percent

Estimate $0.1 \cdot 28.85$.

$0.1 \cdot 28.85 \approx 0.1 \cdot 30$ ← **Round 28.85 to 30.**

$= 3$ ← **Multiply.**

So $0.1 \cdot 28.85$ is about 3.

2 Guided Problem Solving You and a friend go out for dinner. Use mental math to estimate a 15% tip for the bill at the right.

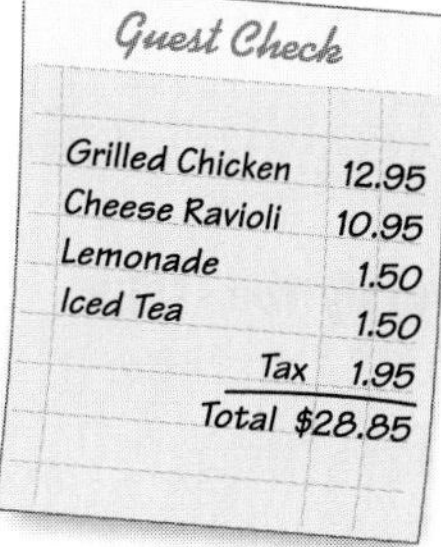

Guest Check
Grilled Chicken 12.95
Cheese Ravioli 10.95
Lemonade 1.50
Iced Tea 1.50
Tax 1.95
Total $28.85

What You Think

The bill is about \$30. I know 10% of 30 is $\frac{1}{10}$ of 30, or 3. Then 5% of 30 is half of 3, or 1.5. A 15% tip is about \$3.00 plus \$1.50, or \$4.50.

Why It Works

15% of $30 = 0.15 \cdot 30$ ← **Rewrite 15% as 0.15.**

$= (0.10 + 0.05) \cdot 30$ ← **Rewrite 0.15 as 0.10 + 0.05.**

$= 0.10(30) + 0.05(30)$ ← **Distributive Property**

$= 3 + 1.50$ ← **Multiply.**

$= 4.50$ ← **Add.**

A 15% tip for a \$28.85 bill is about \$4.50.

CA Standards Check 2 *Go to your* **Math Companion** *for help.*

2. Estimate a 15% tip for each restaurant bill.

a. \$72.10 about \$10.80 b. \$51.47 about \$7.50 c. \$15.80 about \$2.40

Check Your Understanding *Homework prep is in your* **Math Companion.**

2. Teach

Guided Instruction

Error Prevention!

Watch for students who do not write the percent as a decimal or a fraction before they multiply.

Example 2

Review the fraction equivalents for common percents found in the table. It is helpful to have students commit to memory the fractions for such common percents. You may want to add $33\frac{1}{3}\%$ $\left(\frac{1}{3}\right)$ and $66\frac{2}{3}\%$ $\left(\frac{2}{3}\right)$ to the table as well.

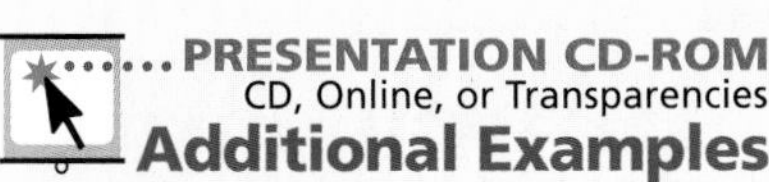
PRESENTATION CD-ROM CD, Online, or Transparencies

Additional Examples

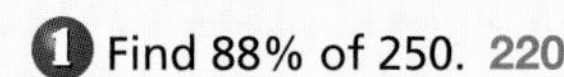
1 Find 88% of 250. 220

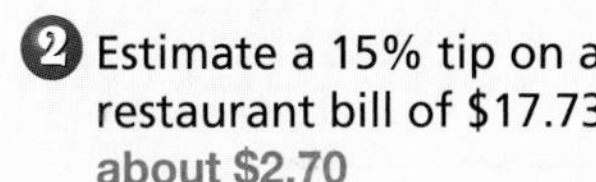
2 Estimate a 15% tip on a restaurant bill of \$17.73. about \$2.70

Closure

- *How do compatible numbers help you estimate a percent using fractions or decimals?* Both the percent and the number it will be multiplied by can be rounded off to compatible values to make mental computation possible. It is also helpful to round off the percent to a familiar fraction or decimal that is close to the original percent.

Advanced Learners L4

Which is a better deal, having a \$5 discount applied before sales tax or after? Justify your answer. before is better: $(\$10 - \$5) \cdot 1.05 = \$5.25$; after: $(\$10 \cdot 1.05) - \$5 = \$5.50$

English Learners EL

Students talk through how 15% becomes the decimals 0.10 and 0.05 in Example 2. For instance, they rename the percent as $\frac{15}{100}$ and say "15 hundredths." Then they rewrite $\frac{15}{100}$ as $\frac{10}{100}$ and $\frac{5}{100}$. Have them add the fractions to check that their sum is $\frac{15}{100}$.

3. Practice

Assignment Guide

Check Your Understanding
See Math Companion.

Homework Exercises

A Practice by Example	1–18
B Apply Your Skills	19–34
C Challenge	35
California Multiple-Choice Practice	36–37
Mixed Review	38–41

Homework Quick Check
To check students' understanding of key skills and concepts, go over Exercises 2, 9, 20, 24, 29, 30.

Universal Access Resources

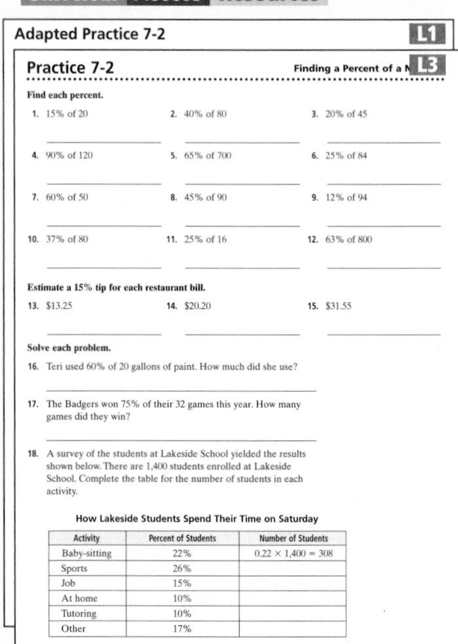
Adapted Practice 7-2 L1

Practice 7-2 Finding a Percent of a N L3

Find each percent.

1. 15% of 20
2. 40% of 80
3. 20% of 45
4. 90% of 120
5. 65% of 700
6. 25% of 84
7. 60% of 50
8. 45% of 90
9. 12% of 94
10. 37% of 80
11. 25% of 16
12. 63% of 800

Estimate a 15% tip for each restaurant bill.

13. $13.25
14. $20.20
15. $31.55

Solve each problem.

16. Teri used 60% of 20 gallons of paint. How much did she use?
17. The Badgers won 75% of their 32 games this year. How many games did they win?
18. A survey of the students at Lakeside School yielded the results shown below. There are 1,400 students enrolled at Lakeside School. Complete the table for the number of students in each activity.

How Lakeside Students Spend Their Time on Saturday

Activity	Percent of Students	Number of Students
Baby-sitting	22%	0.22 × 1,400 = 308
Sports	26%	
Job	15%	
At home	10%	
Tutoring	10%	
Other	17%	

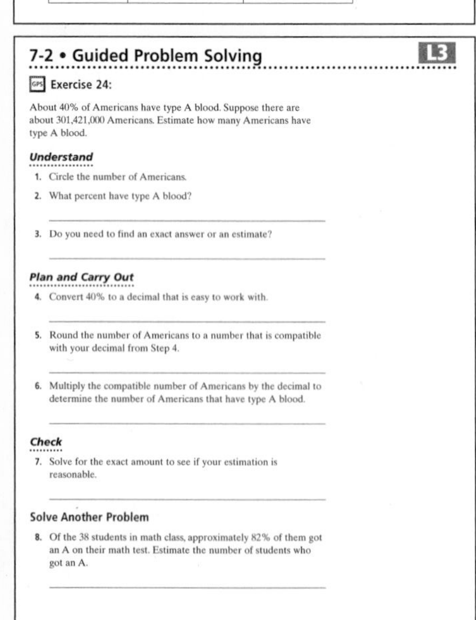
7-2 • Guided Problem Solving L3

GPS Exercise 24:

About 40% of Americans have type A blood. Suppose there are about 301,421,000 Americans. Estimate how many Americans have type A blood.

Understand

1. Circle the number of Americans.
2. What percent have type A blood?
3. Do you need to find an exact answer or an estimate?

Plan and Carry Out

4. Convert 40% to a decimal that is easy to work with.
5. Round the number of Americans to a number that is compatible with your decimal from Step 4.
6. Multiply the compatible number of Americans by the decimal to determine the number of Americans that have type A blood.

Check

7. Solve for the exact amount to see if your estimation is reasonable.

Solve Another Problem

8. Of the 38 students in math class, approximately 82% of them got an A on their math test. Estimate the number of students who got an A.

Standards Practice

GO for Help: *MathXL*

NS 1.3, MR 2.7

A Practice by Example

Example 1 (page 256)

Find each percent.

1. 42% of 70
$42\% = 0.42$
$42\% \text{ of } 70 = 0.42 \cdot 70$ 29.4

Guided Practice This exercise has been started for you!

GO for Help

2. 8% of 210 16.8
3. 70% of 185 129.5
4. 11% of 600 66
5. 15% of 90 13.5
6. 65% of 240 156
7. 7% of 50 3.5

Example 2 (page 257)

Estimate a 15% tip for each restaurant bill.

8. $9.85
$9.85 \approx 10$ about $1.50
$10\% \text{ of } 10 = 1;\ 5\% \text{ of } 10 = 0.50$

Guided Practice This exercise has been started for you!

9. $12.63 about $1.95
10. $18.20 about $2.70
11. $27.55 about $4.20
12. $31.49 about $4.80
13. $86.96 about $13.20
14. $46.15 about $6.90
15. $9.15 about $1.35
16. $51.74 about $7.50
17. $112.09 about $16.50
18. You decide to leave your waiter a 20% tip. Your dinner costs $46.51. Estimate the tip. about $9.40

Homework Video Tutor

For: Examples 1–2
Visit: PHSchool.com
Web Code: axe-0702

B Apply Your Skills

19. **Guided Problem Solving** You earn $240 for your first paycheck. You pay 22% of it in taxes. You decide to put 40% of the remaining money into savings. How much money will you have left to spend? $112.32
    - The amount you pay in taxes is ■. The money remaining after taxes is ■.
    - Write an expression to find the amount put into savings.

The results of a survey of 200 boys and 200 girls are shown at the right.

20. How many boys surf? 74 boys
21. How many girls surf? 66 girls
22. How many boys swim? 124 boys
23. How many girls swim? 152 girls
24. (GPS) About 40% of Americans have type A blood. Suppose there are about 301,421,000 Americans. Estimate how many Americans have type A blood. about 120,000,000 Americans

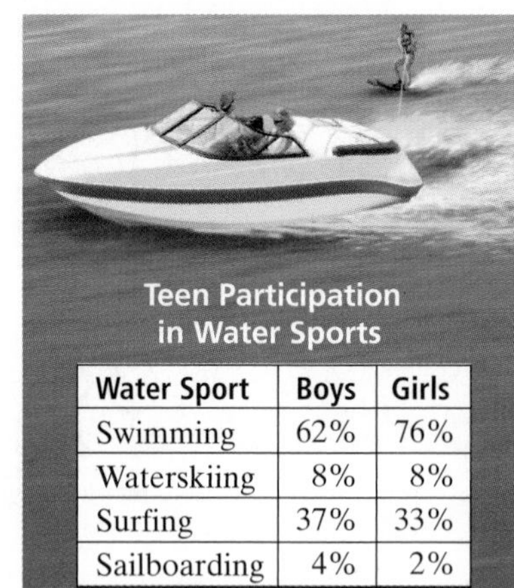

Teen Participation in Water Sports

Water Sport	Boys	Girls
Swimming	62%	76%
Waterskiing	8%	8%
Surfing	37%	33%
Sailboarding	4%	2%

SCAFFOLDED
Problem Solving

The ad shows sale prices at a store.

Back-to-school sale!
30% off
This weekend only!
Long-sleeve T-shirts $14.89
Watches $32.49
Backpacks $29.99
Jeans $32.99
Sneakers $45.99

25. If you buy a watch, about how much do you save? about $9.75

26. If you buy a long-sleeved T-shirt and a backpack, about how much do you save? about $13.46

27. Estimate the discounted price of a pair of jeans. about $23.00

28. Another store is selling sneakers for $33.95. Which store has a better deal on sneakers? Explain. See left.

29. Writing in Math Explain why it is helpful to estimate with percents even when you are finding the exact answer. See left.

28. Back-to-school sale is better because $0.70 \cdot 45.99 = 32.20$.

29. Estimates help check that the answer is reasonable.

Number Sense **Use <, =, or > to complete each statement.**

30. 85% ■ $\frac{5}{6}$ >

31. 15% of 24 ■ 20% of 18 =

32. 10% of 156 ■ 1% of 1,025 >

33. 9% of 57 ■ 5% of 47 >

34. Omar finishes a 50-mi bike race in 5 h. His brother bikes 20% faster than Omar. How long does Omar's brother take to finish the race? 4 h 10 min or $4\frac{1}{6}$ h

35. A store offers a 60% discount. Suppose you buy a book bag and save $20.97. How much did the bag originally cost? $34.95

Multiple Choice Practice and Mixed Review

For California Standards Tutorials, visit PHSchool.com. Web Code: axq-9045

NS 1.3, MR 2.7

36. In a recent city election, 66.7% of the registered voters in the city voted. If there were 717,449 registered voters in the city, about how many people voted in the election? C

Ⓐ 48,000,000 Ⓒ 480,000
Ⓑ 1,200,000 Ⓓ 240,000

NS 2.1

37. Ashley's class is using a microscope to study an insect. The insect is $8.2 \cdot 10^{-4}$ m long. Which number is equivalent to $8.2 \cdot 10^{-4}$? B

Ⓐ 0.000082 Ⓒ 82,000
Ⓑ 0.00082 Ⓓ 820,000

Lesson 6-1 **Write each ratio in simplest form.**

38. $\frac{10}{45}$ $\frac{2}{9}$ **39.** 36 : 90 2 : 5 **40.** 18 to 21 6 to 7 **41.** $\frac{100}{150}$ $\frac{2}{3}$

Online Lesson Quiz Visit: PHSchool.com Web Code: axa-0702

4. Assess & Reteach

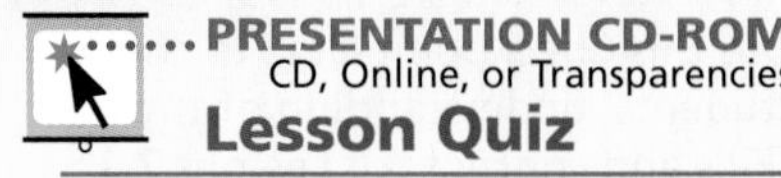

Lesson Quiz

1. Find 81% of 110. 89.1
2. Use fractions to estimate 74% of 38. $\frac{3}{4} \cdot 40 = 30$
3. Estimate a 15% tip on $8.15. $0.1(8) + 0.1(4) = 0.8 + 0.4 = \$1.20$

Reteaching 7-2 Finding a Percent of a N... L2

You can find 70% of 90 using different methods.

① Write the percent as a fraction in simplest form.
$70\% = \frac{70}{100} = \frac{7}{10}$
② Multiply by the fraction.
$\frac{7}{10} \times \frac{90}{1} = \frac{630}{10} = 63$
70% of 90 = 63.

① Write the percent as a decimal.
70% = 0.70
② Multiply.
$0.70 \cdot 90 = 63$
70% of 90 = 63.

Find each percent.

1. 45% of 60
2. 60% of 160
3. 90% of 80
4. 35% of 60
5. 40% of 60
6. 85% of 300
7. 22% of 500
8. 37% of 400
9. 25% of 100
10. 70% of 70
11. 75% of 40
12. 80% of 50
13. 24% of 80
14. 45% of 90

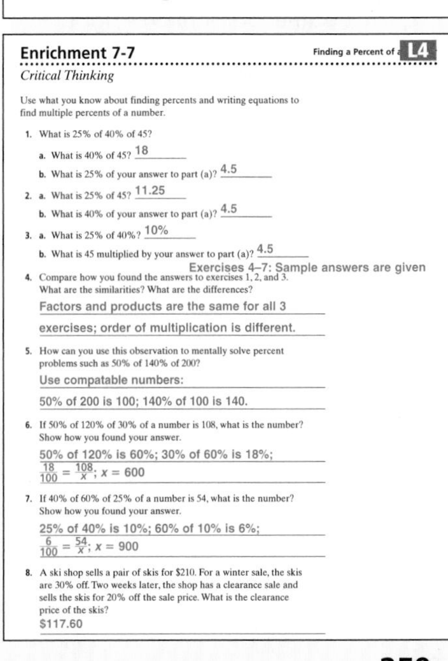

Enrichment 7-7 Finding a Percent of a... L4

Critical Thinking

Use what you know about finding percents and writing equations to find multiple percents of a number.

1. What is 25% of 40% of 45?
   a. What is 40% of 45? 18
   b. What is 25% of your answer to part (a)? 4.5
2. a. What is 25% of 45? 11.25
   b. What is 40% of your answer to part (a)? 4.5
3. a. What is 25% of 40%? 10%
   b. What is 45 multiplied by your answer to part (a)? 4.5

Exercises 4–7: Sample answers are given

4. Compare how you found the answers to exercises 1, 2, and 3. What are the similarities? What are the differences?
   Factors and products are the same for all 3 exercises; order of multiplication is different.
5. How can you use this observation to mentally solve percent problems such as 50% of 140% of 200?
   Use compatable numbers: 50% of 200 is 100; 140% of 100 is 140.
6. If 50% of 120% of 30% of a number is 108, what is the number? Show how you found your answer.
   50% of 120% is 60%; 30% of 60% is 18%; $\frac{18}{100} = \frac{108}{x}$; $x = 600$
7. If 40% of 60% of 25% of a number is 54, what is the number? Show how you found your answer.
   25% of 40% is 10%; 60% of 10% is 6%; $\frac{6}{100} = \frac{54}{x}$; $x = 900$
8. A ski shop sells a pair of skis for $210. For a winter sale, the skis are 30% off. Two weeks later, the shop has a clearance sale and sells the skis for 20% off the sale price. What is the clearance price of the skis?
   $117.60

Alternative Assessment

One student in a pair writes five percents on separate slips of paper while the partner does the same with whole numbers greater than 20. Students place the slips face down in two stacks. Together they draw a percent and a whole number from each stack. Then they work together to find the percent of the number.

California Resources

Standards Mastery
- Standards Review Transparencies
- Standards Review and Practice Workbook
- Math Companion

Math Intervention
- Skills Review and Practice Workbook
- Math XL

Checkpoint Quiz

Use this Checkpoint Quiz to check students' understanding of the skills and concepts of Lessons 7-1 through 7-2.

All in One Resources

- Checkpoint Quiz 1

Mathematical Reasoning

Percents Greater Than 100%

Students learn to work with percents that are greater than 100%.

Guided Instruction

Begin by describing this situation: If the price of an item doubles, it costs 200% of its original price. So, percents can be greater than 100%. Ask: *How can you represent 200% using a 10-by-10 grid model?* Completely shade two grid models.

Review converting percents to decimals and decimals to percents. To help students who confuse which way to move the decimal point, have them think of the percent sign as ÷ 100. When they remove the %, the decimal point moves left. When they insert the %, the decimal point moves right.

Error Prevention!

Encourage students to check their answers for reasonableness. Ask: *Is 150% of 60 going to be greater than or less than 60?* greater than

Mathematical Reasoning

For Use With Lesson 7-2

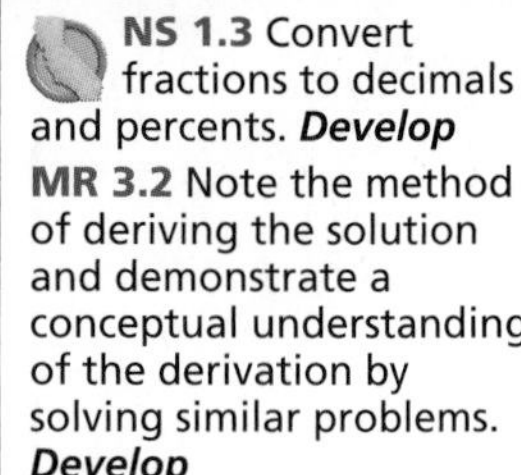

NS 1.3 Convert fractions to decimals and percents. ***Develop***
MR 3.2 Note the method of deriving the solution and demonstrate a conceptual understanding of the derivation by solving similar problems. ***Develop***

Percents Greater Than 100%

A number that is more than 100% of a number is greater than the original number.

100% + 5% = 105%

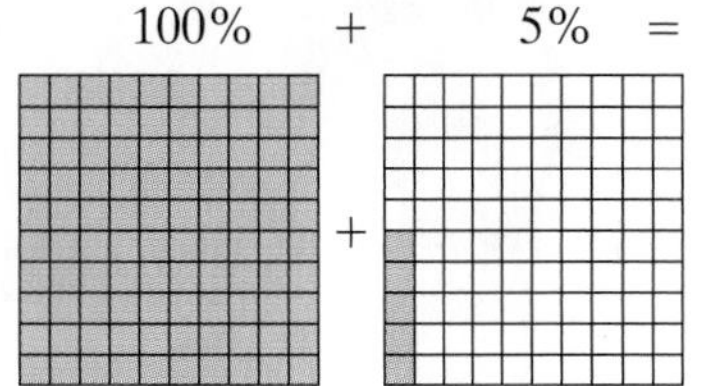

Finding percents greater than 100% is similar to finding percents between 1% and 100%.

1. Find 5% and 100% of 60. 3; 60
2. Use your answers from Exercise 1 to find 105% of 60. 63
3. What decimal is equivalent to 105%? How can you use this to find 105% of 60? 1.05; multiply 1.05 times 60
4. **Writing in Math** Describe two different methods you can use to find 115% of a number. See above right.
5. This month's heating bill is 130% of last month's bill. Last month's bill was $46. Find the cost of this month's bill. $59.80

4. Multiply the number by the decimal equivalent of 115% or multiply the number by the decimal equivalent of 15% and add the result to the original number.

Checkpoint Quiz 1

Lessons 7-1 through 7-2

Write each fraction as a percent.

1. $\frac{2}{4}$ 50%
2. $\frac{1}{10}$ 10%
3. $\frac{3}{8}$ 37.5%
4. $\frac{15}{16}$ 93.75%
5. $\frac{10}{25}$ 40%
6. $\frac{9}{10}$ 90%

Find each percent.

7. 3% of 26 0.78
8. 2% of 2 0.04
9. 20% of 58 11.6
10. 12% of 8 0.96
11. You and your family go to a restaurant for dinner. The bill is $45.67. Estimate a 15% tip on the restaurant bill. about $6.90

GO for Help: Math Companion

7-3 Percents and Proportions

Check Skills You'll Need

Do this in your **Math Companion.**

Vocabulary

Review:
- proportion
- cross products

Use your **Math Companion** *to build your vocabulary.*

California Content Standards

Foundational Standard Use proportions to solve problems. Use cross-multiplication as a method for solving such problems.

NS 1.3 Convert fractions to decimals and percents and use these representations in estimations, computations, and applications. ***Develop***

What You'll Learn . . . and Why

You will learn to use proportions to solve percent problems. Percents and proportions can help you understand the relationship between the size of a section and the size of a whole group, such as an orchestra.

You can use a diagram to show the relationship between a part and a whole. You can use the diagram below to find 45% of 32.

	part	whole
Number 0	n	32
Percent 0%	45%	100%

$\frac{n}{32} = \frac{45}{100}$ ← The part n corresponds to 45%. ← The whole 32 corresponds to 100%.

EXAMPLE Finding Part of a Whole

Relate MATH YOU KNOW... ...*to* ALGEBRA

Find the cross products of $\frac{n}{32} = \frac{45}{100}$.

$100n = 45 \cdot 32$

1 Find 45% of 32.

$\frac{n}{32} = \frac{45}{100}$ ← Write a proportion.

$100n = 45 \cdot 32$ ← Write the cross products.

$100n = 1{,}440$ ← Simplify.

$\frac{100n}{100} = \frac{1{,}440}{100}$ ← Isolate the variable. Use the Division Property of Equality.

$n = 14.4$ ← Simplify.

CA Standards Check 1

Go to your **Math Companion** *for help.*

1. Use a proportion to find each percent.
   a. 74% of 95 — 70.3
   b. 40% of 32 — 12.8
   c. 63% of 180 — 113.4

Universal Access Solutions for All Learners

Special Needs L1	**Below Level** L2
Many students frequently make errors setting up proportions. Have students use a diagram, like those used in the Examples, to set up their proportions until they can set up the correct proportions without the diagram.	Have students make a rough estimate of the answer first as an aid to catching errors in setting up a proportion.

7-3

1. Plan

California Content Standards

Use proportions to solve problems. Use cross-multiplication as a method for solving such problems. ***Foundational***

NS 1.3 Convert fractions to decimals and percents and use these representations in estimations, computations, and applications. ***Develop***

Professional Development

California Math Background

One way to find a percent of a number is to find a portion of the number that is proportional to the percent. For example, calculating 45% of 16.8 involves solving the following proportion for x: $\frac{45}{100} = \frac{x}{16.8}$. The same is true for percents greater than 100: 245% of 16.8 equals x in the proportion $\frac{245}{100} = \frac{x}{16.8}$. If the portion and the percent of the whole that it represents are known, another proportion can be used to find the whole. For instance, if 3.1 is 67% of a number, the number can be found by solving for x in the following proportion: $\frac{67}{100} = \frac{3.1}{x}$.

More Math Background: p. 250C

Lesson Planning and Resources

See p. 250E for a list of the resources that support this lesson.

PRESENTATION CD-ROM
CD, Online, or Transparencies

Bell Ringer Practice

Check Skills You'll Need
Use student page, transparency, or PowerPoint.
See Math Companion.

California Standards Review
Use transparency or PowerPoint.

2. Teach

Guided Instruction

Suggest that students say aloud to themselves, as they begin a problem, the basic proportion: *part divided by the whole equals percent divided by 100.* This strategy helps auditory learners and reminds all students that they need to identify the part, the whole, and the percent in each problem.

Review the fraction equivalents for common percents such as 10%, 20%, 25%, 50%, and 75%.

Error Prevention!

The vocabulary associated with percents may be a source of some confusion. The part of the whole has sometimes been called the *percentage.* Use the words *part* and *whole* for clarity, but make sure students understand that in percent problems, the part may be greater than the whole.

PRESENTATION CD-ROM CD, Online, or Transparencies

Additional Examples

1. Use a proportion to find 60% of 45. 27; $\frac{n}{45} = \frac{60}{100}$

2. Suppose 11,550 students make up 14% of a city's population. What is the population of the city? 82,500 people

3. 26 is what percent of 80? 32.5%

If you know the percent of the whole a part represents, you can find the whole amount.

EXAMPLE Finding a Whole Amount

2 Guided Problem Solving The 27 violinists make up 36% of the musicians in an orchestra. How many musicians are in the orchestra?

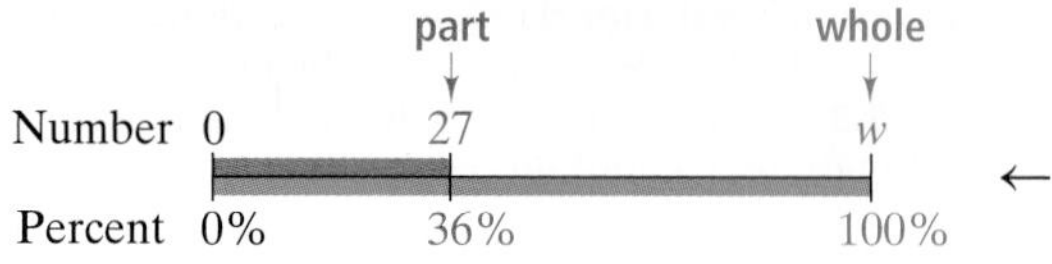

← A diagram can help you understand a problem.

Problem Solving Tip

Before solving a problem, check to make sure you set up the proportion correctly.

$\frac{27}{w} = \frac{36}{100}$ ← Write a proportion.

$100 \cdot 27 = 36w$ ← Write the cross products.

$\frac{2{,}700}{36} = \frac{36w}{36}$ ← Isolate the variable. Use the Division Property of Equality.

$75 = w$ ← Simplify.

There are 75 musicians in the orchestra.

CA Standards Check 2 *Go to your* **Math Companion** *for help.*

2. The 110 students who attend an after-school program make up 40% of the students in the school. How many students are in the school? 275 students

You can also use a proportion to find a percent.

EXAMPLE Finding a Percent

3 What percent of 200 is 105?

		part	whole
Number	0	105	200
Percent	0%	p%	100%

← A diagram can help you understand the problem.

Online active math

For: Percents and Proportions Activity
Use: Interactive Textbook, 7-3

$\frac{105}{200} = \frac{p}{100}$ ← Write a proportion.

$\frac{105}{200} = \frac{p}{100}$ (÷ 2, ÷ 2) ← Use number sense to find a common divisor.

$52.5\% = p$ ← Divide 105 by 2 to find p.

CA Standards Check 3 *Go to your* **Math Companion** *for help.*

3. **a.** What percent of 50 is 36? 72% **b.** What percent of 40 is 16? 40%

Advanced Learners L4	**English Learners** EL
Students calculate very large and small percents such as these: *What is 1,245% of 83?* 1,033.35 *What percent is 0.125 of 6.25?* 2% *0.935 is 18.7% of what number?* 5	Make sure students understand the difference between "cross products" and products of two fractions. Use an example to show that cross products can be found only when two fractions are **equal** to each other. Compare this with an example of two fractions multiplied.

You can use the following proportion to solve percent problems.

$$\frac{\text{part}}{\text{whole}} = \text{percent (written as a fraction)}$$

Take Note — **Percents and Proportions**

Finding the Part	Finding the Whole	Finding the Percent
What number is 20% of 25?	5 is 20% of what number?	What percent of 25 is 5?
$\frac{n}{25} = \frac{20}{100}$	$\frac{5}{w} = \frac{20}{100}$	$\frac{5}{25} = \frac{p}{100}$

More Than One Way

A hair dryer costs \$22. The sales tax rate is 7.25%. Find the amount of sales tax.

I can multiply 22 by the decimal equivalent of 7.25%.

$$\begin{aligned} 7.25\% \text{ of } 22 &= 0.0725 \cdot 22 && \leftarrow \textbf{Write 7.25\% as a decimal.} \\ &= 1.595 && \leftarrow \textbf{Multiply.} \\ &\approx 1.60 \end{aligned}$$

The sales tax is about \$1.60.

I can use a proportion.

$$\begin{aligned} \frac{n}{22} &= \frac{7.25}{100} && \leftarrow \textbf{Write a proportion.} \\ 100n &= 7.25 \cdot 22 && \leftarrow \textbf{Write the cross products.} \\ 100n &= 159.5 && \leftarrow \textbf{Simplify.} \\ \frac{100n}{100} &= \frac{159.5}{100} && \leftarrow \textbf{Divide each side by 100.} \\ n &= 1.595 && \leftarrow \textbf{Simplify.} \\ &\approx 1.60 \end{aligned}$$

The sales tax is about \$1.60.

Choose a Method

A bike costs \$195.99 plus 6% sales tax. Find the amount of sales tax. Describe your method and explain why you chose it.
\$11.76; check students' work.

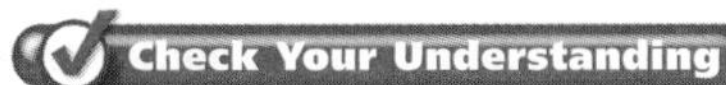

Homework prep is in your **Math Companion.**

Guided Instruction

Some students find using the definition of percent helps them set up the correct proportion. Students write $\frac{\text{part}}{\text{whole}} = \frac{\text{percent}}{100}$ and substitute the given numbers for each term. The remaining term in the proportion becomes the variable.

Error Prevention!

Emphasize that the problem must be in the form of a proportion to cross multiply. Ask students to identify both examples (such as $\frac{4}{a} = \frac{b}{5}$) and counterexamples (such as $\frac{4}{a} + 1 = \frac{b}{5}$).

Also point out that, in the proportion $\frac{\text{part}}{\text{whole}} = \frac{\text{percent}}{100}$, the percent is written, for example, as 30 and not as 30%. The % symbol has already been written by $\frac{\blacksquare}{100}$.

Alternative Method

Show students how to use four index cards to set up the proportion in Example 3. Write 105, 200, *p*, and 100 on four separate cards. Arrange the cards to form the proportion. Then students can regroup the cards to show the cross-multiplication.

Closure

- *How can you use a proportion to find a part of a whole?* **Sample: Set up a proportion using the formula $\frac{\text{percent}}{100} = \frac{\text{part}}{\text{whole}}$. Substitute for the percent and the whole; solve for the unknown part using cross products.**

3. Practice

Assignment Guide

Check Your Understanding

See Math Companion.

Homework Exercises

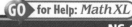

A Practice by Example	1–18
B Apply Your Skills	19–31
C Challenge	32
California Multiple-Choice Practice	33–34
Mixed Review	35–38

Homework Quick Check

To check students' understanding of key skills and concepts, go over Exercises 4, 9, 15, 20, 25, 30, 31.

Universal Access Resources

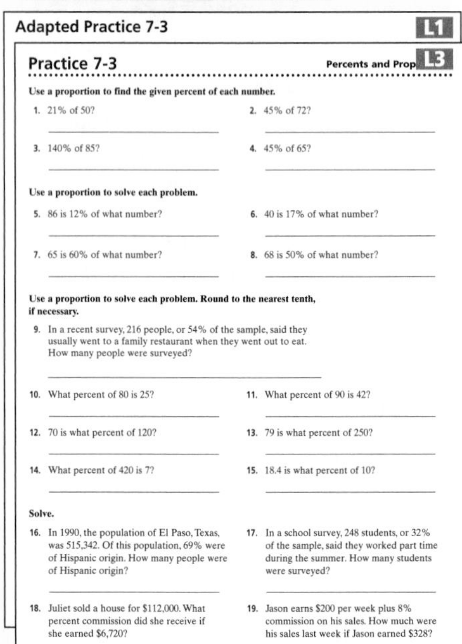

Adapted Practice 7-3 L1

Practice 7-3 — Percents and Prop[ortions] L3

Use a proportion to find the given percent of each number.

1. 21% of 50?
2. 45% of 72?
3. 140% of 85?
4. 45% of 65?

Use a proportion to solve each problem.

5. 86 is 12% of what number?
6. 40 is 17% of what number?
7. 65 is 60% of what number?
8. 68 is 50% of what number?

Use a proportion to solve each problem. Round to the nearest tenth, if necessary.

9. In a recent survey, 216 people, or 54% of the sample, said they usually went to a family restaurant when they went out to eat. How many people were surveyed?
10. What percent of 80 is 25?
11. What percent of 90 is 42?
12. 70 is what percent of 120?
13. 79 is what percent of 250?
14. What percent of 420 is 7?
15. 18.4 is what percent of 10?

Solve.

16. In 1990, the population of El Paso, Texas, was 515,342. Of this population, 69% were of Hispanic origin. How many people were of Hispanic origin?
17. In a school survey, 248 students, or 32% of the sample, said they worked part time during the summer. How many students were surveyed?
18. Juliet sold a house for $112,000. What percent commission did she receive if she earned $6,720?
19. Jason earns $200 per week plus 8% commission on his sales. How much were his sales last week if Jason earned $328?

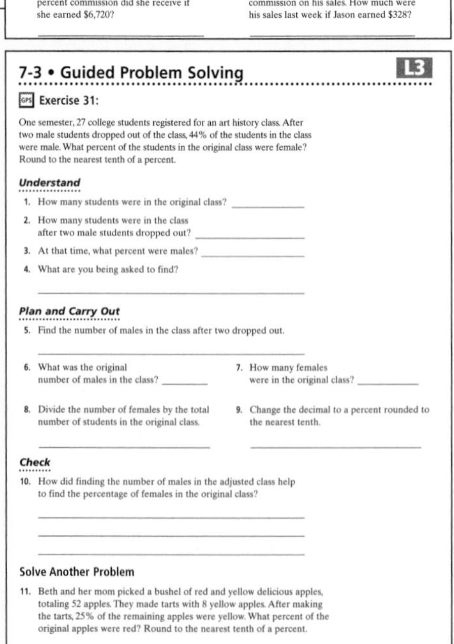

7-3 • Guided Problem Solving L3

GPS Exercise 31:

One semester, 27 college students registered for an art history class. After two male students dropped out of the class, 44% of the students in the class were male. What percent of the students in the original class were female? Round to the nearest tenth of a percent.

Understand

1. How many students were in the original class? ______
2. How many students were in the class after two male students dropped out? ______
3. At that time, what percent were males? ______
4. What are you being asked to find?

Plan and Carry Out

5. Find the number of males in the class after two dropped out.
6. What was the original number of males in the class? ______
7. How many females were in the original class? ______
8. Divide the number of females by the total number of students in the original class.
9. Change the decimal to a percent rounded to the nearest tenth.

Check

10. How did finding the number of males in the adjusted class help to find the percentage of females in the original class?

Solve Another Problem

11. Beth and her mom picked a bushel of red and yellow delicious apples, totaling 52 apples. They made tarts with 8 yellow apples. After making the tarts, 25% of the remaining apples were yellow. What percent of the original apples were red? Round to the nearest tenth of a percent.

GO for Help: MathXL

Standards Practice NS 1.3

A Practice by Example

Example 1 (page 261)

Use a proportion to find the given percent of each number.

1. 80% of 72 57.6

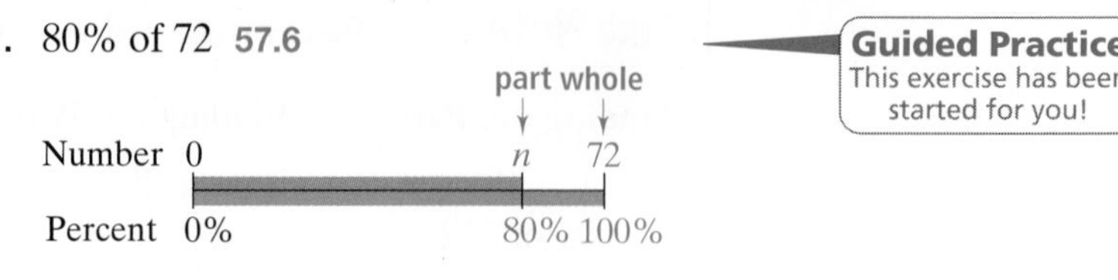

2. 3% of 48 1.44
3. 60% of 55 33
4. 38% of 50 19
5. 12% of 46 5.52
6. 26% of 65 16.9
7. 345% of 24 82.8

Example 2 (page 262)

Use a proportion to solve each problem.

8. 3 is 60% of what number? 5

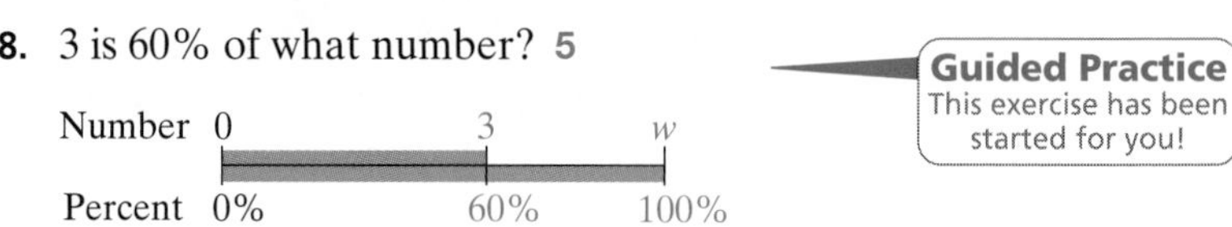

For: Examples 1–3
Visit: PHSchool.com
Web Code: axe-0703

9. 6 is 80% of what number? 7.5
10. 74 is 32% of what number? 231.25
11. 38 is 4% of what number? 950
12. 120 is 48% of what number? 250
13. In a school, 140 students with brown hair make up about 56% of the eighth-graders. About how many students are in the eighth grade? about 250 students

Example 3 (page 262)

Use a proportion to solve each problem.

14. What percent of 25 is 16? 64%

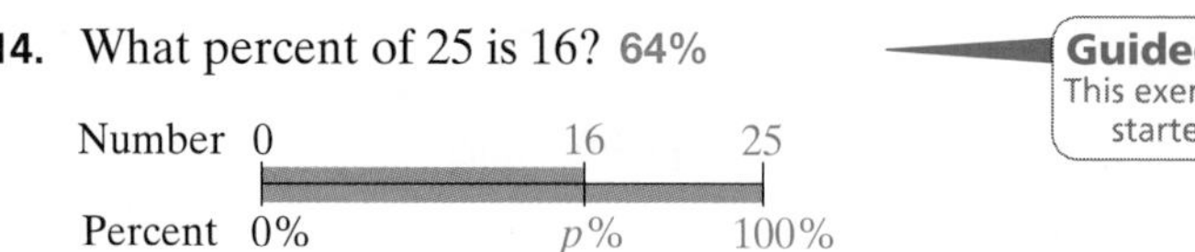

15. What percent of 300 is 12? 4%
16. 20 is what percent of 60? $33\frac{1}{3}\%$
17. What percent of 64 is 24? 37.5%
18. 18 is what percent of 45? 40%

B Apply Your Skills

19. **Guided Problem Solving** In an election with two candidates, the winner received about 72.2% of the 214,082 votes cast. By how many votes did the winning candidate win? 95,052 votes
    - Begin by finding the number of votes cast for the winner.

    Words: $\frac{\text{\% of winner's votes}}{\text{total \% of votes}} = \frac{\text{number of votes cast for winning candidate}}{\text{total number of votes cast}}$

    Proportion: $\frac{72.2}{100} = \frac{x}{\blacksquare}$

20. The Library of Congress has almost 5 million maps. Maps make up just 3.85% of the library's entire collection of items. How many items does the Library of Congress have? about 130,000,000 items

SCAFFOLDED
Problem Solving

30. Answers may vary. Sample: Multiply the number by 0.13 or set up a proportion with the fraction $\frac{13}{100}$.

The table at the right shows the rate of sales tax in a few states.

State	Sales-Tax Rate
Kansas	5.3%
California	7.25%
Virginia	5%

21. What is the rate of sales tax in Virginia? 5%
22. How much tax would you pay on an $899 television in Virginia? $44.95
23. Including sales tax, what is the total price of an $899 television in Virginia? $943.95
24. Including tax, how much more is the total price of an $899 television in California than in Kansas? $17.53

Use a proportion to solve each problem.

25. Find 0.025% of 120. 0.03
26. Find 1,342% of 5,678. 76,198.76
27. 99.6 is 200% of what number? 49.8
28. 1.8 is 30% of what number? 6

Indiana

UNITED STATES

Rhode Island

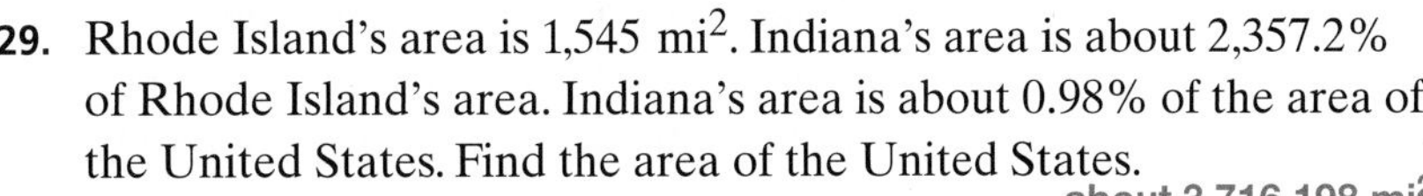

29. Rhode Island's area is 1,545 mi^2. Indiana's area is about 2,357.2% of Rhode Island's area. Indiana's area is about 0.98% of the area of the United States. Find the area of the United States. about 3,716,198 mi^2
30. **Writing in Math** Explain two ways you can find 13% of a number. See above left.

GPS 31. One semester, 27 college students registered for an art history class. After two male students dropped out of the class, 44% of the students in the class were male. What percent of the students in the original class were female? Round to the nearest tenth of a percent. 51.9%

C Challenge

32. What percent of a centimeter is a meter? 10,000%

Multiple Choice Practice and Mixed Review

For California Standards Tutorials, visit PHSchool.com. Web Code: axq-9045

NS 1.3

33. A quality-control inspector found that 3 out of every 45 radios produced on his assembly line were defective. About what percent of the radios were NOT defective? C
    - (A) 7%
    - (B) 67%
    - (C) 93%
    - (D) 135%

MG 3.3

34. The triangle at the right is a right triangle. What is the length of the hypotenuse? D

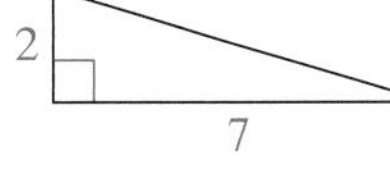

    - (A) $\sqrt{5}$
    - (B) $\sqrt{9}$
    - (C) $\sqrt{45}$
    - (D) $\sqrt{53}$

GO for Help **Lesson 7-1**

Write each fraction as a percent.

35. $\frac{3}{5}$ 60%
36. $\frac{16}{25}$ 64%
37. $\frac{9}{5}$ 180%
38. $\frac{2}{3}$ $66\frac{2}{3}$%

GO Online Lesson Quiz Visit: PHSchool.com Web Code: axa-0703

4. Assess & Reteach

PRESENTATION CD-ROM
CD, Online, or Transparencies

Lesson Quiz

1. Find 25% of 160. 40
2. 45 is 75% of what number? 60
3. What percent 68 is of 80? 85%

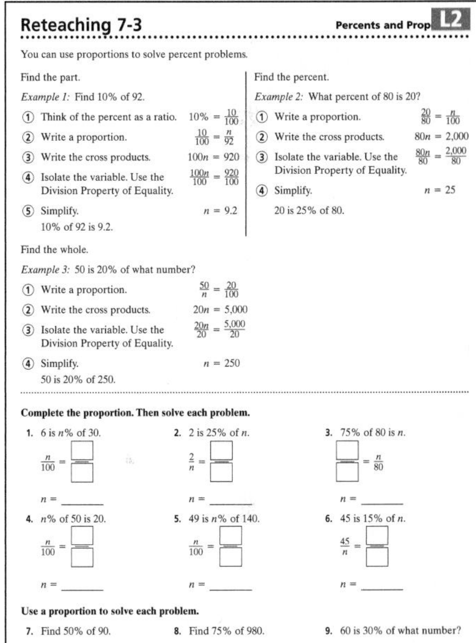

Reteaching 7-3 Percents and Prop L2

You can use proportions to solve percent problems.

Find the part.

Example 1: Find 10% of 92.

1. Think of the percent as a ratio. $10\% = \frac{10}{100}$
2. Write a proportion. $\frac{10}{100} = \frac{n}{92}$
3. Write the cross products. $100n = 920$
4. Isolate the variable. Use the Division Property of Equality. $\frac{100n}{100} = \frac{920}{100}$
5. Simplify. $n = 9.2$

10% of 92 is 9.2.

Find the percent.

Example 2: What percent of 80 is 20?

1. Write a proportion. $\frac{20}{80} = \frac{n}{100}$
2. Write the cross products. $80n = 2{,}000$
3. Isolate the variable. Use the Division Property of Equality. $\frac{80n}{80} = \frac{2{,}000}{80}$
4. Simplify. $n = 25$

20 is 25% of 80.

Find the whole.

Example 3: 50 is 20% of what number?

1. Write a proportion. $\frac{50}{n} = \frac{20}{100}$
2. Write the cross products. $20n = 5{,}000$
3. Isolate the variable. Use the Division Property of Equality. $\frac{20n}{20} = \frac{5{,}000}{20}$
4. Simplify. $n = 250$

50 is 20% of 250.

Complete the proportion. Then solve each problem.

1. 6 is n% of 30. $\frac{n}{100} = \frac{\square}{\square}$ $n =$ ______
2. 2 is 25% of n. $\frac{2}{n} = \frac{\square}{\square}$ $n =$ ______
3. 75% of 80 is n. $\frac{\square}{\square} = \frac{n}{80}$ $n =$ ______
4. n% of 50 is 20. $\frac{n}{100} = \frac{\square}{\square}$ $n =$ ______
5. 49 is n% of 140. $\frac{n}{100} = \frac{\square}{\square}$ $n =$ ______
6. 45 is 15% of n. $\frac{45}{n} = \frac{\square}{\square}$ $n =$ ______

Use a proportion to solve each problem.

7. Find 50% of 90.
8. Find 75% of 980.
9. 60 is 30% of what number?

Enrichment 7-3 Percents and Prop L4

Decision Making

Your company is giving bonuses to employees. You need to decide how much money to distribute and how that money should be allocated. Here are some facts:

- The company made $100,000 in profit this year. However, not all of the money can be given to employees—some of it is needed to keep the company in business.
- The company will keep 45% for operating expenses and place an additional 7% in a fund for emergencies.
- Another 20% has been budgeted for new equipment and building repair.
- The rest can be distributed to its employees.
- The 16 employees earn salaries from $15,000 to $75,000. The total yearly payroll is $560,000.

1. What percent of the profit can be paid as bonuses? ______
2. How much money can be paid as bonuses? ______
3. What will be each employee's bonus if everyone is paid the same amount? ______
4. What percent of the total payroll is the bonus amount? ______
5. Logan earns $40,000. What would his bonus be if it were determined using the percent of salary method? ______
6. Chris earns $15,000. What would his bonus be if it were determined using the percent of salary method? ______
7. How would you prefer the bonuses to be allocated if you made a high salary? Explain. ______
8. What salary would you have to earn to receive the same bonus under both methods of allocation? ______
9. How would you allocate the bonuses? Why did you choose that way? ______

Alternative Assessment

Have students write three different percent problems modeled after those in the Examples, but with different numbers. Then have them trade papers with a partner and solve.

California Resources

Standards Mastery
- Standards Review Transparencies
- Standards Review and Practice Workbook
- Math Companion

Math Intervention
- Skills Review and Practice Workbook
- Math XL

7-4

1. Plan

California Content Standards

NS 1.3 Convert fractions to decimals and percents and use these representations in estimations, computations, and applications. ***Develop***

California Math Background

The *percent of change* is the percent a quantity increases or decreases from its original amount. To find the percent of change, you find the amount of change and divide it by the original amount.

More Math Background: p. 250C

Lesson Planning and Resources

See p. 250E for a list of the resources that support this lesson.

...PRESENTATION CD-ROM
CD, Online, or Transparencies

Bell Ringer Practice

Check Skills You'll Need
Use student page, transparency, or PowerPoint.
See Math Companion.

California Standards Review
Use transparency or PowerPoint.

7-4 Percent of Change

Check Skills You'll Need

Do this in your **Math Companion.**

Vocabulary

- percent of change

Use your **Math Companion** *to build your vocabulary.*

California Content Standards

NS 1.3 Convert fractions to decimals and percents and use these representations in estimations, computations, and applications. ***Develop, Master***

What You'll Learn . . . and Why

You will learn to find percent of change. You can use percent of change to describe how much an amount, such as the number of U.S. representatives for a state, increases or decreases over time.

A **percent of change** is the percent a quantity increases or decreases from its original amount. Use a proportion to find a percent of change.

$$\frac{\text{amount of change}}{\text{original amount}} = \frac{\text{percent of change}}{100}$$

EXAMPLE Finding a Percent of Increase

1 North Carolina had 12 seats in the U.S. House of Representatives in the 1990s. After the 2000 census, North Carolina had 13 seats. Find the percent of increase in the number of representatives.

$13 - 12 = 1$ ← **Find the amount of change.**

$\frac{1}{12} = \frac{p}{100}$ ← **Write a proportion. Let p = percent of change.**

$100 \cdot 1 = 12p$ ← **Write the cross products.**

$\frac{100}{12} = \frac{12p}{12}$ ← **Division Property of Equality**

$8.3 \approx p$ ← **Simplify.**

The number of North Carolina representatives increased by about 8%.

CA Standards Check 1 *Go to your* **Math Companion** *for help.*

1. In 2000, California increased its number of U.S. representatives from 52 to 53. Find the percent of increase. about 2%

Universal Access Solutions for All Learners

Special Needs L1

Use the data from Example 2. On a number line on the board, draw a line segment from 0 ft to 20 ft 10 in. and another from 20 ft 10 in. to 28 ft 2.19 in. Have students compare the lengths of the two line segments.

Below Level L2

Have students practice by solving percent of increase problems such as these:

50 to 75 50% 50 to 90 80%
50 to 100 100% 50 to 125 150%

When working with different units of measure, convert all measures to the same unit.

EXAMPLE Converting Units

Relate MATH YOU KNOW... ...*to* ALGEBRA

How many inches are in 20 ft?

$20\ \cancel{ft} \cdot \frac{12\ \text{in.}}{1\ \cancel{ft}} = 240\ \text{in.}$ ← **Multiply by the conversion factor.**

2 **Guided Problem Solving** In the 1896 Olympic Games, the winner of the men's long jump jumped 20 ft 10 in. In a recent Olympic Games, an athlete jumped 28 ft 2.19 in. to win the men's long jump. Find the percent of increase in the length of the winning long jump.

$20\ \text{ft}\ 10\ \text{in.} = 20\ \cancel{ft} \cdot \frac{12\ \text{in.}}{1\ \cancel{ft}} + 10\ \text{in.} = 250\ \text{in.}$

$28\ \text{ft}\ 2.19\ \text{in.} = 28\ \cancel{ft} \cdot \frac{12\ \text{in.}}{1\ \cancel{ft}} + 2.19\ \text{in.} = 338.19\ \text{in.}$

Write measures in the same units.

Problem Solving Tip

Before you find the percent of change, decide whether the change is an increase or a decrease.

amount of change $= 338.19 - 250 = 88.19$ ← **Find the amount of change.**

$\frac{88.19}{250} = \frac{p}{100}$ ← **Write the proportion. Let *p* be the percent of increase.**

$100 \cdot 88.19 = 250p$ ← **Write the cross products.**

$\frac{8{,}819}{250} = \frac{250p}{250}$ ← **Division Property of Equality**

$35.276 = p$ ← **Simplify.**

The length of the winning long jump increased by about 35%.

CA Standards Check 2 *Go to your* **Math Companion** *for help.*

2. A girl was 4 ft 9 in. tall last year. This year she is 5 ft tall. Find the percent of increase in her height. Round to the nearest tenth. about 5.3%

EXAMPLE Finding a Percent of Decrease

3 Find the percent of decrease from 70 to 63.

$70 - 63 = 7$ ← **Find the amount of decrease.**

$\frac{7}{70} = \frac{p}{100}$ ← **Write a proportion. Let *p* be the percent of decrease.**

$100 \cdot 7 = 70 \cdot p$ ← **Write the cross products.**

$10 = p$ ← **Isolate *p*.**

The percent of decrease is 10%.

CA Standards Check 3 *Go to your* **Math Companion** *for help.*

3. Find each percent of decrease.

a. 120 to 84 30% **b.** 324 to 243 25%

Check Your Understanding *Homework prep is in your* **Math Companion.**

2. Teach

Guided Instruction

Example 1

Be sure students understand the difference between the *amount of change* and the *percent of change*. Amount of change is found by subtraction and refers to the number of seats (or individuals). The percent of change is found by solving the proportion and refers to the percent of increase in the number of seats, which relates a part to a whole (the number of new seats to the original number of seats).

Error Prevention!

Encourage students to make a note, when planning their solution, of whether a change is an increase or decrease.

...PRESENTATION CD-ROM
CD, Online, or Transparencies

Additional Examples

1 Three years ago, Max's comic book was worth \$9. Now it is worth \$13. Find the percent of increase in value. 44%

2 Andre changed the height of his basketball hoop from 8 ft 4 in. to 9 ft 2 in. Find the percent of increase. 10%

3 Find the percent of decrease from 95 to 57. 40%

Closure

- *Explain the difference between percent of increase and percent of decrease.* Sample: Percent of increase shows a change in a quantity that is growing larger, while percent of decrease shows a change in a quantity that is growing smaller.

Advanced Learners L4	**English Learners** EL
A storeowner buys three dozen T-shirts for \$185.75. He wants to sell the T-shirts at a 45% profit. What is the price of each shirt if sales tax is 5.5%? \$7.89	Elicit the fact that although *decrease* and *increase* are opposites, they both are changes in percent.

3. Practice

Assignment Guide

Check Your Understanding
See Math Companion.

Homework Exercises

A Practice by Example	1–20
B Apply Your Skills	21–33
C Challenge	34
California Multiple-Choice Practice	35–36
Mixed Review	37–38

Homework Quick Check
To check students' understanding of key skills and concepts, go over Exercises 3, 10, 15, 22, 25, 26, 33.

Universal Access Resources

Adapted Practice 7-4 **L1**

Practice 7-4 — Percent of Change **L3**

Find each percent of increase. Round to the nearest tenth, if necessary.

1. 15 to 20 ______
2. 86 to 120 ______
3. 17 to 34 ______
4. 27 to 38 ______
5. 8 to 10 ______
6. 43 to 86 ______
7. The amount won in harness racing in 1991 was $1.238 million. In 1992, the amount was $1.38 million. What was the percent of increase?
8. 14 lb 4 oz to 18 lb 2 oz ______
9. 2 ft 10 in. to 8 ft 6 in. ______
10. 12 min 8 s to 16 min 4 sec ______
11. 4 yd to 6 yd 2 ft ______

Find each percent of decrease. Round to the nearest tenth, if necessary.

12. 18 to 10 ______
13. 10 to 7.5 ______
14. 32 to 24 ______
15. 40 to 10 ______
16. 100 to 23 ______
17. 846 to 240 ______

Solve.

18. In 1995, the price of a laser printer was $1,299. In 2002, the price of the same type of printer had dropped to $499. Find the percent of decrease.

______

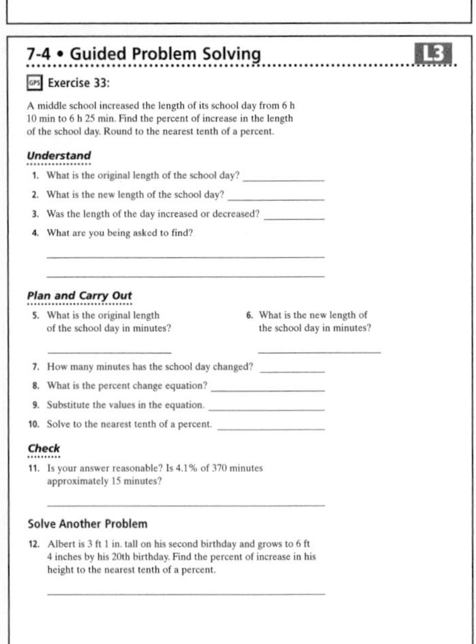

7-4 • Guided Problem Solving **L3**

GPS Exercise 33:

A middle school increased the length of its school day from 6 h 10 min to 6 h 25 min. Find the percent of increase in the length of the school day. Round to the nearest tenth of a percent.

Understand

1. What is the original length of the school day? ______
2. What is the new length of the school day? ______
3. Was the length of the day increased or decreased? ______
4. What are you being asked to find?

______

Plan and Carry Out

5. What is the original length of the school day in minutes? ______
6. What is the new length of the school day in minutes? ______
7. How many minutes has the school day changed? ______
8. What is the percent change equation? ______
9. Substitute the values in the equation. ______
10. Solve to the nearest tenth of a percent. ______

Check

11. Is your answer reasonable? Is 4.1% of 370 minutes approximately 15 minutes?

______

Solve Another Problem

12. Albert is 3 ft 1 in. tall on his second birthday and grows to 6 ft 4 inches by his 20th birthday. Find the percent of increase in his height to the nearest tenth of a percent.

______

Standards Practice

GO for Help: *MathXL* — NS 1.3

A Practice by Example

Example 1 (page 266)

Find each percent of increase. Round to the nearest tenth, if necessary.

Guided Practice This exercise has been started for you!

1. 60 to 75
   $75 - 60 = 15$
   $\frac{15}{60} = \frac{p}{100}$ 25%
2. 88 to 89 1.1%
3. 135 to 200 48.1%
4. 12 to 18 50%
5. 2 to 7 250%
6. 12 to 63 425%
7. 120 to 240 100%

GO for Help

8. A worker earning $7 per hour receives a raise. She now earns $8.05 per hour. Find the percent of increase in her hourly rate of pay. 15%

Example 2 (page 267)

Find each percent of change. Round to the nearest tenth, if necessary.

Guided Practice This exercise has been started for you!

9. 36 ft 3 in. to 37 ft 6 in. 3.4%
   36 ft 3 in. = $36 \text{ ft} \cdot \frac{12 \text{ in.}}{1 \text{ ft}} + 3 \text{ in.} = \blacksquare$
   37 ft 6 in. = $37 \text{ ft} \cdot \frac{12 \text{ in.}}{1 \text{ ft}} + 6 \text{ in.} = \blacksquare$
10. 16 lb 4 oz to 20 lb 1 oz 23.5%
11. 15 ft 6 in. to 8 ft 10 in. 43.0%
12. 9 min 10 s to 14 min 2 s 53.1%
13. 6 yd to 4 yd 2 ft 22.2%
14. A baby weighed 7 lb 3 oz at birth. Four months later, the baby weighed 13 lb 5 oz. Find the percent of increase in the baby's weight. Round to the nearest tenth. 85.2%

Homework Video Tutor

For: Examples 1–3
Visit: PHSchool.com
Web Code: axe-0704

Example 3 (page 267)

Find each percent of decrease. Round to the nearest tenth, if necessary.

15. 190 to 183 3.7%
16. 15 to 10 33.3%
17. 205 to 164 20%
18. 87 to 51 41.4%
19. 52 to 1 98.1%
20. 368 to 275 25.3%

B Apply Your Skills

21. **Guided Problem Solving** Over the course of 5 years, the annual precipitation for a city dropped from 65 cm to 47 cm. What is the average percent of change in the amount of precipitation for 1 year?
    - What was the amount of change in the precipitation over 5 years?
    - What was the average amount of change over 1 year? about 5.5%
22. **Error Analysis** The number of students enrolled in a school has increased from 1,938 to 2,128. A student calculates the percent of increase. His work is shown at the right. Explain the student's mistake. The student did not divide by the original amount, 1,938.

   ~~2,128 − 1,938 = 190~~
   ~~190 ÷ 2,128 ≈ 0.089~~
   ~~0.089 = 8.9%~~

SCAFFOLDED
Problem Solving

23. Fresno, 335,983 increase; Los Angeles, 1,724,462 increase
24. Fresno, about 366.5% increase; Los Angeles, about 87.5% increase
25. Answers may vary. Sample: Exercise 23 better describes which city's population changed by more people. Exercise 24 better describes which city's population changed by a greater percent of its original population.
26. 585.7% increase
27. 75% decrease
28. 1,048.3% increase
29. 75% decrease
30. 9,185.7% increase
31. 86.7% decrease

Use the table below for Exercises 23–25.

City	1950 Population	2000 Population
Fresno, CA	91,669	427,652
Los Angeles, CA	1,970,358	3,694,820

23. Find the change in population in each city from 1950 to 2000. State whether the change is an increase or a decrease. See left.

24. Find the percent of change in each city from 1950 to 2000. See left.

25. **Writing in Math** Does your answer to Exercise 23 or Exercise 24 better describe the population change for each city? Explain. See left.

Find each percent of change. Round to the nearest tenth of a percent, if necessary. Label your answer *increase* or *decrease*. 26–31. See below left.

26. 1.4 to 9.6
27. 0.8 to 0.2
28. 8.7 to 99.9
29. 5 to $1\frac{1}{4}$
30. $\frac{7}{5}$ to 130
31. $610\frac{1}{3}$ to 81

32. In 1996, there were 41 classical music radio stations. In 2005, there were 28 classical stations. Find the percent of decrease. Round to the nearest tenth. 31.7%

GPS 33. A middle school increased the length of its school day from 6 h 10 min to 6 h 25 min. Find the percent of increase in the length of the school day. Round to the nearest tenth of a percent. 4.1%

Challenge

34. Three weeks ago, a sunflower plant was 1 ft 3 in. tall. Since then, its height has increased by $213\frac{1}{3}\%$. Find the current height of the sunflower in feet and inches. 3 ft 11 in.

Multiple Choice Practice and Mixed Review

For California Standards Tutorials, visit PHSchool.com. Web Code: axq-9045

NS 1.3

35. The population of Marisa's town increased by 3% from last year to this year. If 30,000 people lived in the town last year, how many people live there this year? C

Ⓐ 900 Ⓑ 9,000 Ⓒ 30,900 Ⓓ 39,000

MG 3.3

36. Luke uses the Pythagorean Theorem and finds that the distance across a fish pond is $\sqrt{7}$ m. Which whole number is closest to $\sqrt{7}$? B

Ⓐ 2 Ⓑ 3 Ⓒ 4 Ⓓ 5

Lesson 6-2

Find each unit rate.

37. 6 gal for \$13.50
$2.25 per gal

38. 142 mi on 5 gal of gasoline
28.4 mi per gal

Visit: PHSchool.com Web Code: axa-0704

4. Assess & Reteach

PRESENTATION CD-ROM
CD, Online, or Transparencies

Lesson Quiz

Round to the nearest whole percent.

1. 81 people attended last year's annual picnic, and 93 people attended this year's picnic. What is the percent of increase? about 15%
2. The speed limit on a highway was 55 miles per hour last year. This year, the speed limit was increased to 65 miles per hour. What is the percent increase in the speed limit? 18%
3. The population in Arthur County, Nebraska, dropped from 462 in 1990 to 444 in 2000. What was the percent of decrease? about 4%

Alternative Assessment

One student in a pair chooses a number and the partner chooses another number. Then students work together to compute the corresponding percent of increase and the percent of decrease associated with these numbers.

California Resources

Standards Mastery
- Standards Review Transparencies
- Standards Review and Practice Workbook
- Math Companion

Math Intervention
- Skills Review and Practice Workbook
- Math XL

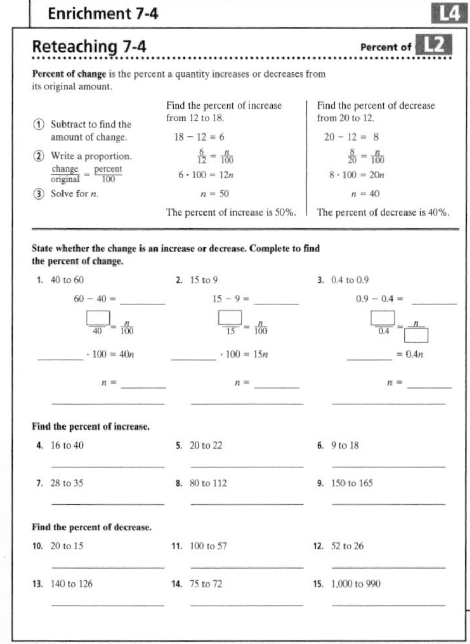

Enrichment 7-4 L4

Reteaching 7-4 Percent of L2

Percent of change is the percent a quantity increases or decreases from its original amount.

	Find the percent of increase from 12 to 18.	Find the percent of decrease from 20 to 12.
① Subtract to find the amount of change.	$18 - 12 = 6$	$20 - 12 = 8$
② Write a proportion. $\frac{\text{change}}{\text{original}} = \frac{\text{percent}}{100}$	$\frac{6}{12} = \frac{n}{100}$; $6 \cdot 100 = 12n$	$\frac{8}{20} = \frac{n}{100}$; $8 \cdot 100 = 20n$
③ Solve for n.	$n = 50$	$n = 40$
	The percent of increase is 50%.	The percent of decrease is 40%.

State whether the change is an increase or decrease. Complete to find the percent of change.

1. 40 to 60
$60 - 40 =$ ____
$\frac{\square}{40} = \frac{n}{100}$
____ $\cdot 100 = 40n$
$n =$ ____
____

2. 15 to 9
$15 - 9 =$ ____
$\frac{\square}{15} = \frac{n}{100}$
____ $\cdot 100 = 15n$
$n =$ ____
____

3. 0.4 to 0.9
$0.9 - 0.4 =$ ____
$\frac{\square}{0.4} = \frac{n}{\square}$
____ $= 0.4n$
$n =$ ____
____

Find the percent of increase.

4. 16 to 40
5. 20 to 22
6. 9 to 18
7. 28 to 35
8. 80 to 112
9. 150 to 165

Find the percent of decrease.

10. 20 to 15
11. 100 to 57
12. 52 to 26
13. 140 to 126
14. 75 to 72
15. 1,000 to 990

Checkpoint Quiz

Use this Checkpoint Quiz to check students' understanding of the skills and concepts of Lessons 7-3 through 7-4.

All in One Resources

- Checkpoint Quiz 2

Mathematical Reasoning

Checking for Reasonableness

Students learn to check their solutions for reasonableness when solving percent-of-change problems.

Guided Instruction

Explain to students that when they solve problems involving percent of change, they should be sure to check that a solution makes sense. If the context of the problem indicates percent increase, for example, they should make sure that the solution is greater than the original value. If the context of the problem indicates percent decrease, they should make sure that the solution is less than the original value.

Mathematical Reasoning

For Use With Lesson 7-4

NS 1.3 Convert fractions to decimals and percents and use these representations in computations. ***Develop***
MR 3.1 Evaluate the reasonableness of the solution in the context of the original situation. ***Develop***

Checking for Reasonableness

When you solve problems involving percent of change, be sure to check whether your solution makes sense in the context of the problem.

In 2000, Mexico had about 65,540,000 hectares of forest. In 2005, the amount of forest had decreased by about 1.99%. Find the number of acres of forest in 2005.

1. **Reasoning** A student's solution is shown below. Why is the student's solution not reasonable in the context of the situation? See right.

~~0.0199 · 65,540,000 = 1,304,246~~

~~Mexico had about 1,304,246 hectares of forest in 2005.~~

2. Find the number of hectares of forest in 2005. 64,235,754 hectares

1. The amount of forest in 2005 should be 98.01% of the amount in 2000. The student's solution is far less than 98.01% of the amount in 2000.

Checkpoint Quiz 2

Lessons 7-3 through 7-4

Use a proportion to solve each problem.

1. 20.5 is 40% of what number? 51.25
2. What percent of 320 is 16? 5%
3. Find 3% of 26. 0.78
4. 0.08 is 32% of what number? 0.25
5. In a survey, 65% of 180 dancers said they prefer modern dance. How many of the dancers prefer modern dance? 117 dancers

Find each percent of change. Round to the nearest tenth of a percent, if necessary. Label your answer *increase* or *decrease*.

6. 14 to 154 1,000% increase
7. 427 to 420 1.6% decrease
8. 2 to 0.4 80% decrease
9. 123 to 456 270.7% increase
10. At a track meet, a shot-putter's first throw was 36 ft 3 in. long. The shot-putter's second throw was 37 ft 6 in. long. Find the percent of increase in the length of the throws. Round to the nearest tenth of a percent. 3.4%

270

Vocabulary Builder

High-Use Academic Words

High-use academic words are words that you will see often in textbooks and on tests. These words are not math vocabulary terms, but knowing them will help you to succeed in mathematics.

Direction Words

Some words tell what to do in a problem. I need to understand what these words are asking so that I give the correct answer.

Word	Meaning
Estimate	To find an approximate answer
Calculate	To find an exact answer by computing
Support	To explain or prove using logic or examples

Exercises

1. Estimate your age in days. 1–2. Check students' work.
2. Calculate your age in days.
3. Support the statement "Your birthday will never fall on the same day of the week in two consecutive years." See above right.

3. Answers may vary. Sample: There are 365 or 366 days in a year and 7 days in a week. $\frac{365}{7} = 52$ R1 $\frac{366}{7} = 52$ R2 So each year a date falls on a different day of the week than it did in the previous year.

4. Estimate the total you pay if you leave a 15% tip for a lunch bill of \$29.42. about \$4.50

Use the table at the right for Exercises 5–6.

5. Calculate the cost of a game plus sales tax at the rate of 8%. \$57.51
6. Is \$200 enough to purchase a tax-free monitor if you have a coupon for 10% off the regular price? Support your answer. Yes. 90% of \$219.95 is \$197.96.

Home Arcade

Equipment	Price (\$)
Controller	\$29.95
Game	\$53.25
Monitor	\$219.95

7. **Word Knowledge** Think about the word *express*.
   a. Choose the letter for how well you know the word.
      A. I know its meaning.
      B. I've seen it, but I don't know its meaning.
      C. I don't know it.
   b. **Research** Look up and write the definition of *express*.
   c. Use the word in a sentence involving mathematics. Check students' work.

Vocabulary Builder

High-Use Academic Words

Students define and use three academic words: *estimate, calculate,* and *support.* These words are not exclusively mathematical terms, but they are commonly used in the study of mathematics.

Guided Instruction

Have students describe the meaning of each listed word in their own words. Brainstorm examples to illustrate their understanding of the words.

Universal Access

Visual Learners

After students complete the Exercises, draw a simple circle graph on the chalkboard. Divide the circle into 4 different-sized parts. Label the graph: "Students' Favorite Pets." Tell students the graph represents the results of a survey that shows the percents of students who chose cats, dogs, birds, or none of these as their favorite pet.

Ask: *What is wrong with this circle graph?* Sample: The parts are missing labels.

Have a volunteer write percents in the parts. Percents must total 100%. Let students decide which animal name to put in each section.

7-5

1. Plan

California Content Standards

Solve problems involving discounts at sales. ***Foundational***

NS 1.3 Convert fractions to decimals and percents and use these representations in estimations, computations, and applications. ***Develop***

California Math Background

With markups and discounts, the percent of markup or discount involves the same ratio as percent of change: amount of change to original amount. For markups, the original amount is the original cost the store had to pay.

More Math Background: p. 250C

Lesson Planning and Resources

See p. 250E for a list of the resources that support this lesson.

PRESENTATION CD-ROM
CD, Online, or Transparencies

Bell Ringer Practice

Check Skills You'll Need
Use student page, transparency, or PowerPoint.
See Math Companion.

California Standards Review
Use transparency or PowerPoint.

7-5 Applications of Percent

Check Skills You'll Need

Do this in your **Math Companion.**

Vocabulary

- markup
- selling price
- discount

Use your **Math Companion** *to build your vocabulary.*

California Content Standards

Foundational Standard Solve problems involving discounts at sales.

NS 1.3 Convert fractions to decimals and percents and use these representations in estimations, computations, and applications. ***Develop, Master***

What You'll Learn . . . and Why

You will learn to find markup and discount. Stores use a percent of discount to find the sale price of items.

Markup is the amount of increase in price. Markup is added to the store's cost for the item to determine the **selling price,** the price the store charges. The percent of markup is a percent of increase.

$$\frac{\text{amount of markup}}{\text{original cost}} = \frac{\text{percent of markup}}{100}$$

EXAMPLE Finding a Percent of Markup

Store's cost + Markup = Selling price

1 An electronics store orders sets of walkie-talkies for \$14.85 each. The store sells each set for \$19.90. What is the percent of markup?

$19.90 - 14.85 = 5.05$ ← Find the amount of markup.

$\frac{5.05}{14.85} = \frac{m}{100}$ ← Write a proportion. Let m = percent of markup.

$5.05 \cdot 100 = 14.85m$ ← Write the cross products.

$\frac{505}{14.85} = \frac{14.85m}{14.85}$ ← Division Property of Equality

$34 \approx m$ ← Simplify.

The percent of markup is about 34%.

CA Standards Check 1 *Go to your* **Math Companion** *for help.*

1. Find each percent of markup. Round to the nearest percent, if necessary.
   a. \$17.95 marked up to \$35.79 99%
   b. \$42 marked up to \$65 55%

Universal Access Solutions for All Learners

Special Needs L1
Help students draw double number lines for Examples 1–3, with one of them showing percents 0–150%. Highlight the distance that corresponds to the percent students are trying to find.

Below Level L2
Remind students that the amount of increase and the percent of increase are not the same. Ask: *A store buys an item for \$4 and sells it for \$6. Is \$2 the percent of increase or the markup?* the markup

The difference between the original price and the sale price of an item is called a **discount.** The percent of discount is a percent of decrease.

$$\frac{\text{amount of discount}}{\text{original cost}} = \frac{\text{percent of discount}}{100}$$

EXAMPLE Finding a Percent of Discount

2 During a clearance sale, a keyboard that normally sells for \$49.99 is discounted to \$34.99. What is the percent of discount?

$49.99 - 34.99 = 15.00$ ← Find the amount of discount.

$\frac{15}{49.99} = \frac{d}{100}$ ← Write a proportion. Let d be the percent of discount.

$15 \cdot 100 = 49.99d$ ← Write the cross products.

$\frac{1{,}500}{49.99} = \frac{49.99d}{49.99}$ ← Division Property of Equality

$30 \approx d$ ← Simplify.

The percent of discount for the keyboard is about 30%.

CA Standards Check 2 *Go to your* **Math Companion** *for help.*

2. Find the percent of discount of a \$24.95 novel on sale for \$14.97. 40%

You can use the percent of discount to find the sale price of an item.

EXAMPLE Finding a Sale Price

Relate MATH YOU KNOW...

Find 30% of 259.98.

$30\% = 0.30$ ← Write the percent as a decimal.

$0.30 \cdot 259.98 \approx 77.99$ ← Multiply.

...to NEW IDEAS

3 **Guided Problem Solving** A furniture store is having a 30%-off sale. What is the sale price of a table that regularly costs \$259.98?

Find the discount first: 30% of \$259.98 equals the discount.

$0.3 \cdot 259.98 \approx 77.99$ ← Multiply to find the discount. Round to the nearest hundredth.

Then subtract to find the sale price.

$259.98 - 77.99 = 181.99$ ← regular price − discount = sale price

The sale price is \$181.99.

Problem Solving Tip

Remember that when an item is discounted, the sale price is less than the regular price.

CA Standards Check 3 *Go to your* **Math Companion** *for help.*

3. An item that regularly sells for \$182.75 is on sale for 45% off. Find the sale price to the nearest cent. \$100.51

Check Your Understanding *Homework prep is in your* **Math Companion.**

Advanced Learners L4	**English Learners** EL
What is a store's profit on a gold necklace that cost \$226, is marked up 50%, and is discounted 15%? \$62.15	Students write *markup = increase* and *discount = decrease* on index cards. They practice saying the words and connecting them so that they use them interchangeably when appropriate.

2. Teach

Guided Instruction

Teaching Tip

To make sure that students understand the vocabulary of sales, ask them to explain *cost, selling price,* and *markup* in their own words.

Career Note

Have students name careers in which finding markups and discounts would be helpful.

Error Prevention!

Students might confuse markup with discount. Emphasize that the storeowner uses the markup to find the *selling price,* the amount the store will charge for the item. The owner uses the discount to find the *sale price,* the amount a customer will pay after the regular price is reduced or discounted.

...PRESENTATION CD-ROM CD, Online, or Transparencies

Additional Examples

1. Find the percent of markup for a stapler costing the school store \$2.10 and selling for \$3.36. 60%
2. Find the percent of discount for a \$74.99 tent that is discounted to \$48.75. 35%
3. A shoe store advertises a 35%-off sale. What is the sale price of shoes that regularly cost \$94.99? \$61.74

Closure

- *Explain the difference between markup and discount.* Sample: Markup is added to the store's cost; discount is subtracted from the selling price for the customer.

3. Practice

Assignment Guide

Check Your Understanding
See Math Companion.

Homework Exercises

A Practice by Example	1–21
B Apply Your Skills	22–30
C Challenge	31
California Multiple-Choice Practice	32–34
Mixed Review	35–38

Homework Quick Check
To check students' understanding of key skills and concepts, go over Exercises 3, 10, 17, 23, 28, 30.

Universal Access Resources

Adapted Practice 7-5 L1

Practice 7-5 Applications of P... L3

Find each percent of markup. Round to the nearest percent if necessary.

1. \$10.00 marked up to \$16.00
2. \$12.50 marked up to \$18.75
3. \$21.00 marked up to \$42.00
4. \$25.86 marked up to \$43.96
5. \$47.99 marked up to \$124.77
6. \$87.90 marked up to \$158.22

Find each percent of discount. Round to the nearest percent if necessary.

7. \$55 discounted to \$45.83
8. \$25.50 discounted to \$17.59
9. \$19.95 discounted to \$11.40
10. \$95 discounted to \$76.00

Find each sale price. Round to the nearest cent.

11. regular price: \$10.00 discount rate: 10%
12. regular price: \$12.00 discount rate: 15%
13. regular price: \$20.95 discount rate: 15%
14. regular price: \$32.47 discount rate: 20%
15. regular price: \$42.58 discount rate: 30%
16. regular price: \$53.95 discount rate: 35%

7-5 • Guided Problem Solving L3

GPS **Exercise 23:**

DVDs are on sale for 40% off the regular price of \$22.99. Your friend has \$45 to spend. How many DVDs can your friend buy at the reduced price?

Understand

1. What is the original price of the DVDs? ______
2. What is the percent of discount? ______
3. How much does your friend have to spend? ______
4. What is it that you are being asked to find?

Plan and Carry Out

5. What is the sale price of each DVD? ______
6. Divide \$45 by the sale price.
7. To determine how many DVDs can be purchased, why can you not leave the answer as a decimal?
8. How many DVDs can be purchased? ______

Check

9. If you multiply the number of DVDs by the sale price, what is the total? Is it less than \$45? Could you purchase another DVD?

Solve Another Problem

10. Ethan goes to a book fair at his school on the last day. The three books that he wants originally costs \$4.99 each, but are marked down 35%. If his mom gave him \$10 to spend, could he afford to buy all three books?

Standards Practice

GO for Help: MathXL NS 1.3

A Practice by Example

Example 1 (page 272)

GO for Help

Homework Video Tutor

For: Examples 1–3
Visit: PHSchool.com
Web Code: axe-0705

Find each percent of markup. Round to the nearest percent, if necessary.

1. \$26 marked up to \$39
   $39 - 26 = 13$
   $\frac{13}{26} = \frac{m}{100}$ 50%

Guided Practice This exercise has been started for you!

2. \$125 marked up to \$168.75 35%
3. \$75 marked up to \$90 20%
4. \$22 marked up to \$33 50%
5. \$15 marked up to \$60 300%
6. \$45.50 marked up to \$75.99 67%
7. \$.15 marked up to \$.75 400%
8. A video game costs a store \$20. If the store sells the game for \$33, what is the percent of markup? 65%

Example 2 (page 273)

Find each percent of discount. Round to the nearest percent, if necessary.

9. \$70 discounted to \$53
   $70 - 53 = 17$
   $\frac{17}{70} = \frac{d}{100}$ 24%

Guided Practice This exercise has been started for you!

10. \$9 discounted to \$4 56%
11. \$10 discounted to \$7 30%
12. \$480 discounted to \$300 38%
13. \$20 discounted to \$12 40%
14. \$39 discounted to \$25 36%
15. \$13.99 discounted to \$9.99 29%
16. A package of poster board usually sells for \$8.40. This week the package is on sale for \$6.30. What is the percent of discount? 25%

Example 3 (page 273)

Find each sale price. Round to the nearest cent.

17. regular price: \$16.99
    percent of discount: 55% \$7.65
18. regular price: \$77.00
    percent of discount: 5% \$73.15
19. regular price: \$82
    percent of discount: 35% \$53.30
20. regular price: \$63.50
    percent of discount: 20% \$50.80
21. A nursery has a 25%-off sale. Find the sale price of a \$215 tree. \$161.25

B Apply Your Skills

22. **Guided Problem Solving** A store buys bags for \$5.25 and marks them up 80%. Find the sale price of the bags after a 30% discount. \$6.62
    - What is 80% of \$5.25?
    - What is 30% of the selling price?

GPS 23. DVDs are on sale for 40% off the regular price of \$22.99. Your friend has \$45 to spend. How many DVDs can your friend buy at the reduced price? 3 DVDs

SCAFFOLDED
Problem Solving

A travel agency offers the trip advertised at the right. There is a 10% service fee.

NEW
YORK
CITY
$550
plus
10% service fee
NOW
30%
OFF

24. If you do not get 30% off the price, how much will you pay for a service fee? $55
25. Your friend purchases the trip before the 30%-off sale. Find the total cost of your friend's trip, including the service fee. $605
26. You purchase the trip and get 30% off. How much do you pay for the trip, including the service fee? $423.50
27. **Reasoning** Will you pay less if the agency adds the service fee and then subtracts the discount, or if the agency subtracts the discount and then adds the service fee? Explain. No difference; the final cost is $423.50 either way.

Find each selling price. Round to the nearest cent.

28. store's price: $71.99
percent of markup: $66\frac{2}{3}\%$
$119.98
29. store's price: $364.38
percent of markup: $37\frac{1}{2}\%$
$501.02

30. Answers may vary. Sample: Divide the selling price by 1 plus the percent of markup written in decimal form.

30.  **Writing in Math** Write a general rule for finding a store's cost for an item if you know the selling price and the percent of markup. See left.

C Challenge

31. A storeowner buys a case of 144 pens for $28.80. Tax and shipping cost an additional $8.64. He sells the pens for $.59 each. What is the percent of markup per pen? 126.9%

Multiple Choice Practice and Mixed Review

For California Standards Tutorials, visit PHSchool.com. Web Code: axq-9045

NS 1.3 32. Emily saw a dress she liked for $60. The following week, the dress was on sale for $45. By what percent was the dress discounted? B

A 1.3% B 25% C 33% D 75%

Alg1 2.0 33. The area of a square is 275 ft^2. Which is closest to the side length of the square? D

A 15.8 ft B 16.1 ft C 16.4 ft D 16.6 ft

AF 4.2 34. Ty drove 50 mi/h for 45 min. Elaine drove 65 mi/h for 30 min. What is the difference between the distances traveled by Ty and Elaine? A

A 5 mi B 15 mi C 32.5 mi D 37.5 mi

GO for Help **Lesson 6-5**

Solve each proportion.

35. $\frac{3}{8} = \frac{t}{24}$ 9
36. $\frac{k}{234} = \frac{4}{5}$ 187.2
37. $\frac{16}{25} = \frac{9.6}{n}$ 15
38. $\frac{10}{f} = \frac{3.4}{8.5}$ 25

GO Online Lesson Quiz Visit: PHSchool.com Web Code: axa-0705

4. Assess & Reteach

PRESENTATION CD-ROM
CD, Online, or Transparencies

Lesson Quiz

1. A pair of shoes costs the store $40. The store sells them for $65. What is the percent markup? 62.5%
2. A school service club sells calendars. Each calendar costs the club $5.50. The club marks up the price 80%. What is the selling price of each calendar? $9.90
3. A sweater regularly sells for $49. It is on sale for 20% off. What is the sale price? $39.20
4. You buy a baseball cap for $13. This price is 35% off the regular price. Find the regular price. $20.00

Alternative Assessment

One student in a pair chooses a number and the partner chooses a percent. Then students work together to compute the corresponding selling price and sale price associated with these numbers.

California Resources

Standards Mastery
- Standards Review Transparencies
- Standards Review and Practice Workbook
- Math Companion

Math Intervention
- Skills Review and Practice Workbook
- Math XL

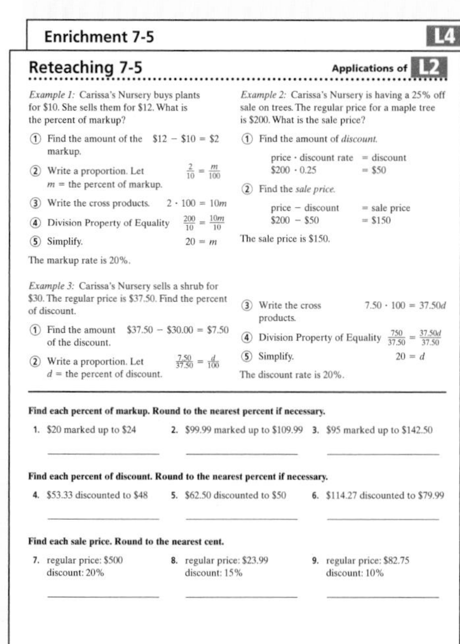
Enrichment 7-5 L4

Reteaching 7-5 Applications of L2

Example 1: Carissa's Nursery buys plants for $10. She sells them for $12. What is the percent of markup?

① Find the amount of the markup. $\$12 - \$10 = \$2$
② Write a proportion. Let m = the percent of markup. $\frac{2}{10} = \frac{m}{100}$
③ Write the cross products. $2 \cdot 100 = 10m$
④ Division Property of Equality $\frac{200}{10} = \frac{10m}{10}$
⑤ Simplify. $20 = m$

The markup rate is 20%.

Example 2: Carissa's Nursery is having a 25% off sale on trees. The regular price for a maple tree is $200. What is the sale price?

① Find the amount of *discount.*
price · discount rate = discount
$200 · 0.25 = $50
② Find the *sale price.*
price − discount = sale price
$200 − $50 = $150

The sale price is $150.

Example 3: Carissa's Nursery sells a shrub for $30. The regular price is $37.50. Find the percent of discount.

① Find the amount of the discount. $\$37.50 - \$30.00 = \$7.50$
② Write a proportion. Let d = the percent of discount. $\frac{7.50}{37.50} = \frac{d}{100}$
③ Write the cross products. $7.50 \cdot 100 = 37.50d$
④ Division Property of Equality $\frac{750}{37.50} = \frac{37.50d}{37.50}$
⑤ Simplify. $20 = d$

The discount rate is 20%.

Find each percent of markup. Round to the nearest percent if necessary.

1. $20 marked up to $24
2. $99.99 marked up to $109.99
3. $95 marked up to $142.50

Find each percent of discount. Round to the nearest percent if necessary.

4. $53.33 discounted to $48
5. $62.50 discounted to $50
6. $114.27 discounted to $79.99

Find each sale price. Round to the nearest cent.

7. regular price: $500
discount: 20%
8. regular price: $23.99
discount: 15%
9. regular price: $82.75
discount: 10%

Activity Lab

Simple Interest

Students learn what simple interest is and how to calculate it using the formula $I = p \cdot r \cdot t$.

Guided Instruction

Explain to students that interest is the amount of money paid for the use of money. They can use the formula $I = p \cdot r \cdot t$ to calculate simple interest. In this formula, I represents the amount of interest, p represents the principal, or original amount of money, r represents the interest rate per year, and t represents the time in years. Walk students through the example and make sure they understand and can distinguish between the concepts of *principal, interest,* and *interest rate.*

7-5b Activity Lab

Simple Interest

Foundational Standard Solve problems involving interest earned.

NS 1.3 Convert fractions to decimals and percents and use these representations in estimations, computations, and applications. ***Master***

Interest is the amount of money paid for the use of money. Interest is calculated at a certain percentage rate called the interest rate. *Principal* is the original amount deposited or borrowed. *Simple interest* is interest calculated only on the principal.

You can use the following formula to find simple interest. I is the interest, p is the principal, r is the interest rate per year expressed as a decimal, and t is the time in years.

$$I = p \cdot r \cdot t$$

EXAMPLE Finding Simple Interest

A student deposits \$200 in a bank account. The simple interest rate is $6\frac{1}{2}\%$ per year. Find the interest the account earns in 4 years.

$I = p \cdot r \cdot t$ ← Use the simple interest formula.

$= 200 \cdot 0.065 \cdot 4$ ← Substitute. Write $6\frac{1}{2}\%$ as a decimal.

$= 52$ ← Multiply.

In 4 years, the interest earned is \$52.

Exercises

Find the simple interest on a principal of \$300 at each rate.

1. $4\frac{1}{4}\%$ interest per year for 2 years \$25.50
2. 6% interest per year for 4 years \$72.00
3. $3\frac{1}{2}\%$ interest per year for 5 years \$52.50
4. 5.6% interest per year for 6 years \$100.80
5. You deposit \$3,500 in an account. Find the interest earned in 5 years at a simple interest rate of $7\frac{1}{2}\%$ per year. \$1,312.50
6. **Reasoning** A bank offers two types of accounts. One account pays 1.3% simple interest per year and has no monthly maintenance fee. The other account pays 2% simple interest per year but charges a \$1 monthly maintenance fee. Into which account would you prefer to deposit \$747 for one year? Explain.

   6. The account paying 1.3%; the account balance would be \$756.71 compared to \$749.94.
7. You borrow \$300 at a simple interest rate of 4% per year. You make no payments for 2 years. How much do you owe after 2 years? \$324

GPS Guided Problem Solving

Practice Solving Problems

A sign over a rack reads "40% or more off." A sweater on the rack shows a sale price of \$20 and a regular price of \$36. Should the sweater be on the sale rack? Explain.

NS 1.3 Convert fractions to decimals and percents. ***Develop***
MR 3.2 Note the method of deriving the solution and demonstrate an understanding of the derivation by solving similar problems. ***Develop***

What You Might Think	What You Write
What do I know? What do I want to find out?	I know the regular price of the sweater is \$36 and the sale price is \$20. I want to find the percent of discount.
How can I find the amount of the discount?	To find the amount of the discount, I subtract the sale price from the regular price. The amount of the discount is $\$36 - \$20 = \$16$.
How can I use the discount in a proportion to find the percent of discount?	The discount divided by the regular price is equal to the percent of discount. $\frac{\text{amount of discount}}{\text{regular price}} = \frac{\text{percent of discount}}{100}$ $\frac{16}{36} = \frac{d}{100}$ $100 \cdot 16 = 36d$ $\frac{1{,}600}{36} = \frac{36d}{36}$ $44.4 \approx d$
Should the sweater be on the sale rack?	The sweater should be on the sale rack because $44.4\% > 40\%$. The percent of discount on the sweater is greater than 40%.

Think It Through

1. **Reasoning** Could you have solved the problem by dividing the sale price by the regular price? Explain. 1–3. See margin.
2. Does a 25% discount cancel a 25% markup? Explain.
3. Suppose the sweater was discounted by 20% and then discounted by another 20%. Should the sweater still be on the sale rack?

Practice Solving Problems

Students must be able to extract important information from word problems in order to successfully solve the problems. This feature helps students analyze word problems and extract relevant information.

Guided Instruction

Have a volunteer read the introductory paragraph and question. Ask questions such as:

- *What is the question that must be answered?* Should the sweater be on the sale rack?
- *What specifically do you need to find out to answer the question?* whether the sale price of the sweater is 40% or more of its original price

Teaching Tip
Have a volunteer read aloud the questions in the *What You Might Think* column. Have a second volunteer answer by reading the text in the *What You Write* column. Call attention to the fact that the answer is an explanation in the form of a complete sentence. Have students work through the problem, rather than just read it. Have them identify any steps that they don't understand or that don't match their own work.

Error Prevention!

Review the percent of discount equation by relating it to the percent of change.

$\text{percent of change} = \frac{\text{amount of change}}{\text{original amount}}$

$\text{percent of discount} = \frac{\text{discount}}{\text{regular price}}$

Exercises

Have students work in pairs to complete Exercises 1–3. Then have partners share with the class what they were thinking as they wrote each step. Elicit the fact that there is often more than one way to arrive at the solution of a problem.

Alternatively, have students work independently. Then have them form groups in which members share and evaluate their answers. Students should make adjustments in their work based on their group discussion.

Exercises

Solve each problem. For Exercises 4–5, answer parts (a) and (b) first.

4. Spending by federal, state, and local sources for pre-K–12 public school instruction in one year was $245.2 billion. This was a 3.9% increase from the year before. About how much was the total spending the year before? about $236 billion

a. What percent of the spending for the previous year is $245.2 billion?

b. Write a proportion, where x equals the spending in the previous year.

5. New Jersey spends y% more than the national average of $8,287 per student. Use the table below to find y. about 56.6%

Per Pupil Spending

State	Amount
New Jersey	$12,981
New York	$12,930
District of Columbia	$12,801
Vermont	$11,128
Connecticut	$10,788
Massachusetts	$10,693

SOURCE: U.S. Census Bureau. Go to **PHSchool.com** for an update. Web Code: axg-9041

a. How much more did New Jersey spend than the national average?

b. Find the percent of increase for New Jersey.

6. By approximately what percent did the average price of a gallon of milk decrease during the year? about 2.2%

7. Between what two months was the greatest percent of decrease in the average price of a gallon of milk? May and June

8. During August, the price of a gallon of milk in Seattle was about 6.9% higher than in Boston. The price of milk in Boston was about 4.5% higher than in Cleveland. The price of milk in Cleveland was $2.92 per gallon. What was the price of a gallon of milk in Seattle? $3.26

U.S. Retail Prices for Reduced Fat (2%) Milk

Month	Price per Gallon	Month	Price per Gallon
January	$3.24	July	$3.18
February	$3.22	August	$3.18
March	$3.22	September	$3.18
April	$3.22	October	$3.17
May	$3.21	November	$3.18
June	$3.19	December	$3.17

Estimating the Answer

Estimating answers may help you find answers, check an answer, or eliminate one or more answer choices.

EXAMPLES

1 A student collects baseball cards. The student bought one card in the collection for \$12.07. Five years later, the card was worth \$15.98. Find the percent of increase in the value of the baseball card.

Ⓐ 3.91% Ⓑ 24.5% Ⓒ 32.4% Ⓓ 39.1%

Since the beginning value is near \$12, and the ending value is near \$16, the amount of change is about \$4. Using the percent of change proportion, you can estimate the percent of increase.

Since $\frac{P}{100} \approx \frac{4}{12} = \frac{1}{3}$, $P = 33\frac{1}{3}\%$.

You can eliminate answer choices A, B, and D, which are not close to $33\frac{1}{3}\%$. The correct answer is choice C.

2 In an election, the winning candidate received 88% of the votes. If 558 students voted, how many voted for the winning candidate?

Ⓐ 521 Ⓑ 491 Ⓒ 469 Ⓓ 387

You can estimate the answer by finding 90% of 560. Since $0.9 \cdot 560 = 560 - (560 \cdot 0.1) = 504$, the correct answer is choice B.

Multiple Choice Practice

Estimate to solve each problem.

NS 1.3 **1.** A football kicker made 21 field goal attempts in one season and was successful about 73% of the time. How many goals did he make? B

Ⓐ 20 Ⓑ 15 Ⓒ 12 Ⓓ 5

NS 1.3 **2.** Which percent is closest to $\frac{78}{643}$? B

Ⓐ 10% Ⓑ 12.5% Ⓒ 20% Ⓓ $33\frac{1}{3}\%$

NS 1.3 **3.** You and a friend have a \$23.04 restaurant bill. If you want to leave a 15% tip, about how much should you leave for a tip? C

Ⓐ \$2.50 Ⓑ \$3 Ⓒ \$3.50 Ⓓ \$4

Estimating the Answer

This strategy shows students how to estimate calculations involving percents.

Guided Instruction

Example 1
In this Example, students round to find compatible numbers to estimate the correct answer. Watch for students who try to find what percent \$4 is of \$16 rather than of \$12, the original price.

Exercises
Suggest to students that they can try different numbers as compatible numbers. There is more than one way to come to the correct answer. Remind students that if they have difficulty on a standardized multiple-choice test, they should eliminate the most obvious incorrect answers first.

Chapter 7 Review

Chapter 7 Review

California Resources

Standards Mastery
- Math Companion
- Standards Review Transparencies
- Standards Review and Practice Workbook
- Progress Monitoring Assessments

Math Intervention
- Skills Review and Practice Workbook
- Math XL

Universal Access Resources
- Student Workbook
  - Vocabulary and Study Skills
  - Guided Problem Solving
- All-in-One Teaching Resources
  - Reteaching
  - Enrichment
- Spanish Practice Workbook L3
- Spanish Vocabulary and Study Skills 2A-F L3
- English/Spanish Glossary EL
- Multilingual Handbook EL
- Interactive Textbook Audio Glossary
- Online Vocabulary Quiz

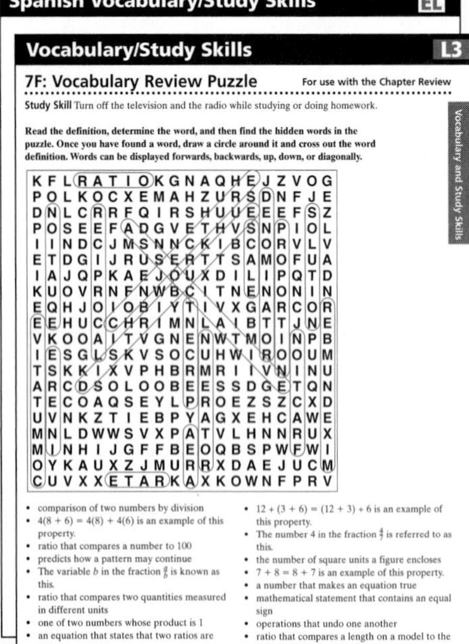

Spanish Vocabulary/Study Skills EL

Vocabulary/Study Skills L3

7F: Vocabulary Review Puzzle For use with the Chapter Review

Study Skill Turn off the television and the radio while studying or doing homework.

Read the definition, determine the word, and then find the hidden words in the puzzle. Once you have found a word, draw a circle around it and cross out the word definition. Words can be displayed forwards, backwards, up, down, or diagonally.

```
K F L R A T I O K G N A Q H E J Z V O G
P O L K O C X E M A H Z U R S D N F J E
D N L C R R F Q I R S H U U E E E F S Z
P O S E E F A D G V E T H V S N P I O L
I I N D C J M S N N C K I B C O R V L V
E T D G I J R U S E R T T S A M O F U A
I A J Q P K A E J O U X D I L I P Q T D
K U O V R N F N W B C I T N E N O N I N
E Q H J O I O B I Y T I V X G A R C O R
E E H U C C H R I M N L A I B T T J N E
V K O O A I T V G N E N W T M O I N P B
I E S G L S K V S O C U H W I R O O U M
T S K K I X V P H B R M R I I V N I N U
A R C D S O L O O B E E S S D G E T Q N
T E C O A Q S E Y L P R O E Z S Z C X D
U V N K Z T I E B P Y A G X E H C A W E
M N L D W W S V X P A T V L H N N R U X
M I N H I J G F F B E O Q B S P W F W I
O Y K A U X Z J M U R R X D A E J U C M
C U V X X E T A R K A X K O W N F P R V
```

- comparison of two numbers by division
- 4(8 + 6) = 4(8) + 4(6) is an example of this property.
- ratio that compares a number to 100
- predicts how a pattern may continue
- The variable b in the fraction $\frac{a}{b}$ is known as this.
- ratio that compares two quantities measured in different units
- one of two numbers whose product is 1
- an equation that states that two ratios are equal
- a number that describes a part of a set of a part of a whole that is divided into equal parts
- 12 + (3 + 6) = (12 + 3) + 6 is an example of this property.
- The number 4 in the fraction $\frac{4}{7}$ is referred to as this.
- the number of square units a figure encloses
- 7 + 8 = 8 + 7 is an example of this property.
- a number that makes an equation true
- mathematical statement that contains an equal sign
- operations that undo one another
- ratio that compares a length on a model to the actual length of a real object
- shows the sum of a whole number and a fraction

Vocabulary Review

English and Spanish Audio Online

discount (p. 273)
markup (p. 272)
percent (p. 252)
percent of change (p. 266)
selling price (p. 272)

Academic Vocabulary
calculate (p. 271)
estimate (p. 271)
support (p. 271)

For: Vocabulary Quiz
Visit: PHSchool.com
Web Code: axj-0751

Choose the correct vocabulary term to complete each sentence.

1. _?_ is the amount by which a store increases the price of an item. markup
2. A(n) _?_ is a ratio that compares a number to 100. percent
3. The amount by which the price of an item on sale is reduced is the _?_. discount
4. The percent a quantity increases or decreases from its original amount is called a(n) _?_. percent of change

Skills and Concepts

Lesson 7-1

- To find equivalent forms of fractions, decimals, and percents

NS 1.3

A **percent** is a ratio that compares a number to 100. You can write fractions and decimals as percents.

Write each fraction as a percent.

5. $\frac{7}{8}$ 87.5% **6.** $\frac{9}{12}$ 75% **7.** $\frac{5}{16}$ 31.25%

8. $\frac{21}{25}$ 84% **9.** $\frac{1}{5}$ 20% **10.** $\frac{2}{3}$ $66\frac{2}{3}\%$

Write each percent as a fraction in simplest form.

11. 30% $\frac{3}{10}$ **12.** 56% $\frac{14}{25}$ **13.** 25% $\frac{1}{4}$

14. 12% $\frac{3}{25}$ **15.** 9% $\frac{9}{100}$ **16.** 27% $\frac{27}{100}$

Write each decimal as a percent.

17. 0.35 35% **18.** 0.025 2.5% **19.** 0.173 17.3%

20. 0.04 4% **21.** 0.56 56% **22.** 0.1 10%

23. On a math test, a student received a grade of 135 points out of 150 total points. Write the grade as a percent. 90%

24. A school library has about 12,500 books. About 7,900 of the books are nonfiction. About what percent of the books in the library are nonfiction? about 63%

Lesson 7-2

- To find a percent of a number and to estimate percents

NS 1.3, MR 2.7

To find a percent of a number, multiply. In some situations, such as finding the tip on a restaurant bill, it is helpful to estimate percents.

Find each percent.

25. 15% of 28 4.2 **26.** 4% of 235 9.4 **27.** 98% of 3 2.94

28. 29% of 150 43.5 **29.** 8% of 10 0.8 **30.** 76% of 45 34.2

31. There are 200 students in your class, and 30% of them joined the school band. How many students in your class joined the band? 60 students

32. Your friends go out to lunch. The restaurant bill comes to $23.58. Estimate a 15% tip on the bill. about $3.60

Lesson 7-3

- To use proportions to solve percent problems

NS 1.3

You can solve a percent problem using a proportion.

$$\frac{\text{part}}{\text{whole}} = \frac{p}{100}$$

Use a proportion to solve each problem.

33. 85% of what number is 170? 200 **34.** What percent of 2 is 0.8? 40%

35. Find 150% of 12. 18 **36.** 26% of what number is 39? 150

37. The 12 students on the tennis team make up about 7.5% of the eighth-grade students in a middle school. How many students are in the eighth grade? about 160 students

Lessons 7-4, 7-5

- To find percent of change
- To find markup and discount

NS 1.3

You can find the **percent of change** p using a proportion.

$$\frac{\text{amount of change}}{\text{original amount}} = \frac{p}{100}$$

Percent of **markup** is an example of a percent of increase. Percent of **discount** is an example of a percent of decrease.

Find each percent of change. Round to the nearest tenth of a percent, if necessary. Label your answer *increase* or *decrease*.

38–43. See left.

38. 90 to 75 **39.** 3.5 to 4.2 **40.** 120 to 138

41. 300 to 420 **42.** 80.5 to 22.5 **43.** 108 to 90

38. 16.7% decrease
39. 20% increase
40. 15% increase
41. 40% increase
42. 72.0% decrease
43. 16.7% decrease

44. A store's cost for a jacket is $35.00. The selling price of the jacket is $38.50. Find the percent of markup on the jacket. 10%

45. A store is having a 20%-off sale. Find the sale price of a video game system that regularly costs $249.99. $199.99

Alternative Assessment L4

Alternative Assessment Form C

Chapter 7

SAVING FOR COLLEGE

Michelle has to make a presentation to parents, advocating savings accounts to help pay for their children's college. She knows that interest rates change all the time. Michelle created this table to give parents an idea of how much different amounts of money would be worth after a year at different simple interest rates.

1. Copy and complete the table.

	1%	2%	3%	4%	5%	6%	7%	8%	9%
$1,000	$1,010	$1,020	$1,030						
$2,000	$2,020	$2,040							
$3,000	$3,030								
$4,000									
$5,000									
$6,000									
$7,000									
$8,000									
$9,000									

2. Suppose Michelle had written the interest rates in the table as decimals rather than percents. What decimals would appear?
3. How can you use the table to find the amount after one year if $1,000 is invested at $1\frac{1}{2}$%? If $5,000 is invested at $8\frac{1}{2}$%?
4. How can you use the table to find the amount after one year if $1,500 is invested at 1%? If $6,500 is invested at 6%?
5. How can you use the table to find the amount after one year if $1,000 is invested at 10%? If $5,000 is invested at 12%?
6. Use the information in the table to write a general formula for calculating the amount saved (S) after 1 year in terms of the interest rate (R) and the initial amount invested (I).

California Resources

Standards Mastery
- Teacher Center ExamView CD-ROM
- Math XL
- Progress Monitoring Assessments
- Online Chapter Test at PHSchool.com

Math Intervention
- Skills Review and Practice Workbook

Online at PHSchool.com

Universal Access Resources
- Chapter Test
- Alternative Assessment
- Spanish Chapter Test
- Spanish Alternative Assessment
- Teacher Center ExamView CD-ROM
  - Special Needs Test
  - Special Needs Practice Banks
  - Foundational Standards Practice Banks
- Online Chapter Test at www.PHSchool.com
- All-In-One Teaching Resources
  - Cumulative Review L3
- Spanish Assessment Resources
  - Cumulative Review 

Below Level Chapter Test L2

Chapter Test L3

Chapter Test Form A

Chapter 7

Compare. Use >, <, or =.

1. $\frac{7}{8}$ ___ 0.875 2. 0.8% ___ 0.8 3. $\frac{2}{7}$ ___ 0.24

Write each fraction as a percent. Round to the nearest tenth of a percent if necessary.

4. $\frac{9}{13}$ ______ 5. $\frac{34}{9}$ ______ 6. $\frac{1}{146}$ ______

Write each percent as a fraction.

7. 45% ______ 8. 28% ______ 9. 6% ______

Find each percent.

10. 47% of 84 11. 30% of \$34.78 12. 5% of 500

13. A soccer goalie saved 85% of 315 goal attempts in one season. About how many saves did the goalie successfully make during the season?

Estimate each percent. Explain how you made your estimate and why.

14. 26.5% of 212 15. 48% of 375 16. 31.5% of 81

Write a proportion for each model. Solve for *n*.

17. Number 0, 42, 80; Percent 0%, *n*%, 100%

18. Number 0, 36, *n*; Percent 0%, 80%, 100%

Chapter 7 Test

Go Online PHSchool.com **For:** Online chapter test **Web Code:** axa-0752

Compare. Use <, =, or >.

1. $\frac{5}{8}$ ■ 0.625 =
2. $\frac{5}{6}$ ■ 85% <
3. $\frac{1}{3}$ ■ 0.34 <
4. 0.6% ■ 0.6 <

Write each fraction as a percent. Round to the nearest tenth of a percent, if necessary.

5. $\frac{1}{10}$ 10%
6. $\frac{3}{15}$ 20%
7. $\frac{5}{6}$ 83.3%
8. $\frac{11}{25}$ 44%
9. $\frac{27}{35}$ 77.1%
10. $\frac{3}{14}$ 21.4%
11. $\frac{7}{8}$ 87.5%
12. $\frac{1}{7}$ 14.3%
13. $\frac{2}{9}$ 22.2%

Write each percent as a fraction.

14. 25% $\frac{1}{4}$
15. 6% $\frac{3}{50}$
16. 98% $\frac{49}{50}$
17. 14% $\frac{7}{50}$
18. 75% $\frac{3}{4}$
19. 2% $\frac{1}{50}$
20. 49% $\frac{49}{100}$
21. 80% $\frac{4}{5}$
22. 5% $\frac{1}{20}$

Find each percent.

23. 5% of 200 10
24. 80% of 8 6.4
25. 2% of 50 1
26. 36% of 9 3.24

27. About 13% of a school's 782 students walk to school. About how many students walk to school? about 102 students

28. Suppose 86% of 50 people at a law firm enjoy their jobs. How many people like their jobs? 43 people

Estimate each percent. Explain how you made your estimate and why. 29–34. See margin.

29. 15% of \$61.51
30. 76% of 48
31. 50% of 29
32. 20% of \$23.87

Write a proportion for each model. Solve for *n*.

33. 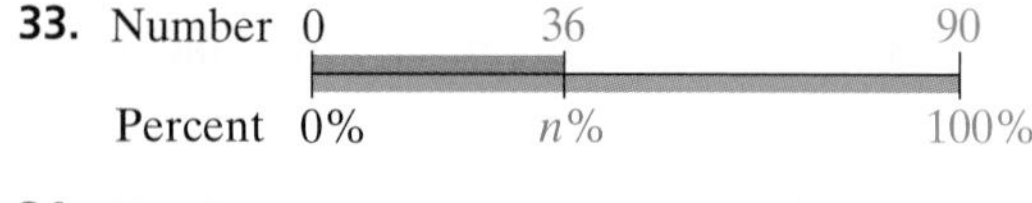

34. Number 0, 17, *n*; Percent 0%, 85%, 100%

Use a proportion to solve each problem.

35. Find 37% of 134. 49.58
36. Find 2% of 70. 1.4
37. Find 5% of 150. 7.5
38. Find 99% of 350. 346.5
39. What percent of 76 is 19? 25%
40. 350% of what number is 21,000? 6,000

41. A skateboard is priced at \$49.95 in a state that charges 5.5% sales tax. How much sales tax would you pay on the skateboard? \$2.75

Find each percent of change. Round to the nearest tenth of a percent, if necessary. Label your answer *increase* or *decrease*. 42–47. See margin.

42. 99 to 163
43. 13 to 1
44. 158 to 24
45. 613 to 655
46. 4.15 to 4.55
47. 64,379 to 302

48. Last year, a student earned \$6.00 per hour baby-sitting. This year he earns \$6.75 per hour. Find the percent of increase in his pay. 12.5% increase

49. A bicycle store pays \$29.62 for a helmet. The store sells the helmet for \$39.99. Find the percent of markup. 35% markup

50. **Writing in Math** The Drama Club bought T-shirts for \$4 and sold them for \$5. A student claims that the percent of markup is 20% because \$1 is 20% of \$5. Explain the student's error and find the correct percent of markup. See margin.

Find the sale price of each item after each discount. Round to the nearest cent.

51. regular price: \$90.00
discount: 33% \$60.30

52. regular price: \$145.99
discount: 25% \$109.49

53. regular price: \$16.50
discount: 40% \$9.90

Standards Mastery Cumulative Practice

Some questions require you to identify an equation or expression that represents a situation. Use the tips as guides for how to approach solving the problem.

An electronics store is selling a DVD player at a 15% discount. If the sales tax is 5%, which of the following expressions can be used to find the final cost of a DVD player with an original price of $145.95?

(A) $145.95 \cdot 0.85 \cdot 0.05$
(B) $145.95 \cdot 0.15 \cdot 0.05$
(C) $145.95 \cdot 0.85 \cdot 1.05$
(D) $145.95 \cdot 0.05 \cdot 1.05$

Tip 1
Try to write an expression for the final cost of the DVD player before looking at the answer choices.

Tip 2
Estimate the final cost and see which answer choice is closest to your estimate.

Think It Through
Multiply the original price by 0.85 to find the price after taking off 15%. Multiply by 1.05 to determine the discounted price with the 5% sales tax included. The correct answer is choice C.

Vocabulary Review

As you solve problems, you must understand the meanings of mathematical terms. Match each term with its mathematical meaning.

A. discount II
B. markup III
C. proportion I
D. percent IV

I. an equation stating that two ratios are equal
II. the amount the price of a sale item is reduced
III. the amount of increase in price
IV. a ratio that compares a number to 100

Read each question. Then write the letter of the correct answer on your paper.

1. A class took a career survey. Based on the results, 47.5% of the class would like a career in business. If there are 124 students in the class, about how many would like a career in business? (Lesson 7-2) B

   (A) 48 students (C) 77 students
   (B) 59 students (D) 124 students

2. Jade wants to purchase a new car for $16,000 plus a 7% sales tax. Which equation can be used to find the total cost t of the car? (Lesson 7-2) D

   (A) $t = 16{,}000 + 0.07$
   (B) $t = 16{,}000 \cdot 0.07$
   (C) $t = 16{,}000 \cdot (1 - 0.07)$
   (D) $t = 16{,}000 + (0.07 \cdot 16{,}000)$

3. In a class of 28 students, 4 students are left-handed, and the rest are right-handed. About what percent of the class is right-handed? (Lesson 7-1) D

   (A) 4% (B) 14% (C) 28% (D) 86%

California Resources

Standards Mastery
- Teacher Center ExamView CD-ROM
- Math XL
- Progress Monitoring Assessments
- Online Chapter Test at PHSchool.com

Math Intervention
- Skills Review and Practice Workbook

Universal Access Resources
- Teacher Center ExamView CD-ROM
  - Special Needs Test
  - Special Needs Practice Banks
  - Foundational Standards Practice Banks
- Online Chapter Test at www.PHSchool.com
- All-In-One Teaching Resources
  - Cumulative Review L3
- Spanish Assessment Resources
  - Cumulative Review L3

4. Which of the following is the reciprocal of $\frac{2}{7}$? (Lesson 5-4) D

   Ⓐ $-\frac{7}{2}$ Ⓒ 1
   Ⓑ $-\frac{2}{7}$ Ⓓ $\frac{7}{2}$

5. At a grocery store, 5 lb of potatoes cost \$4. How many pounds of potatoes can you buy with \$10? (Lesson 6-4) D

   Ⓐ 1.25 lb Ⓒ 8 lb
   Ⓑ 2.5 lb Ⓓ 12.5 lb

6. What is 0.36 written as a fraction in simplest form? (Lesson 4-4) C

   Ⓐ $\frac{36}{100}$ Ⓒ $\frac{9}{25}$
   Ⓑ $\frac{18}{50}$ Ⓓ $\frac{36}{1{,}000}$

7. At an animal shelter, 60% of the animals are dogs. Only 8% of the dogs weigh less than 15 lb. The shelter has 48 animals. Which expression can be used to find the number of dogs that weigh less than 15 lb? (Lesson 7-3) B

   Ⓐ $48 - 15 + 60 - 8$
   Ⓑ $48 \cdot \frac{60}{100} \cdot \frac{8}{100}$
   Ⓒ $48 \cdot 0.6 \cdot 0.8$
   Ⓓ $(48 - 15) \cdot (60 - 8)$

8. A construction company agreed to add a 120-ft^2 room to a house for \$15,000. The owners of the house would like the room to be 30% larger. If the price of the new room is proportional to the number of square feet, how much more will the larger room cost? (Lesson 6-5) B

   Ⓐ \$500 Ⓒ \$10,500
   Ⓑ \$4,500 Ⓓ \$19,500

9. Which of the following is NOT a rational number? (Lesson 4-4) B

   Ⓐ 8.9 Ⓒ $1.\overline{453}$
   Ⓑ $\sqrt{19}$ Ⓓ $\frac{3}{7}$

10. While at the store, Morgan saw a shampoo bottle that said, "Contains 20% more—Free!" If the larger bottle contains 15.6 oz of shampoo, how many ounces does the regular-size bottle contain? (Lesson 7-3) C

    Ⓐ 2.6 oz
    Ⓑ 3.12 oz
    Ⓒ 13 oz
    Ⓓ 18.7 oz

11. There are 15 c of sand at the bottom of a large hourglass. You flip the hourglass to make the sand pour down. After 5 min, 2 c have poured down. Which proportion can NOT be used to find the time *t* it takes for the sand to pour down completely? (Lesson 6-6) A

    Ⓐ $\frac{t}{15} = \frac{2}{5}$ Ⓒ $\frac{5}{2} = \frac{t}{15}$
    Ⓑ $\frac{15}{2} = \frac{t}{5}$ Ⓓ $\frac{2}{5} = \frac{15}{t}$

12. Pedro buys buttons in bulk and gets 100 buttons for \$5. How much will it cost for him to buy 2,000 buttons? (Lesson 6-4) C

    Ⓐ \$10,000 Ⓒ \$100
    Ⓑ \$200 Ⓓ \$.05

13. Which number is the opposite of $-\frac{2}{5}$? (Lesson 2-1) B

    Ⓐ $\frac{5}{2}$ Ⓒ $-\frac{2}{5}$
    Ⓑ $\frac{2}{5}$ Ⓓ $-\frac{5}{2}$

14. Which fraction is equivalent to 0.72? (Lesson 4-4) A

    Ⓐ $\frac{18}{25}$ Ⓒ $\frac{72}{1{,}000}$
    Ⓑ $\frac{35}{50}$ Ⓓ $\frac{1}{72}$

15. A student has a newspaper route. It takes the student 0.75 h to deliver 75 newspapers. At this rate, how long will it take the student to deliver 100 newspapers? (Lesson 6-3) A

    Ⓐ 60 min Ⓒ 25 min
    Ⓑ 45 min Ⓓ 15 min

Spanish Cumulative Review EL

Cumulative Review L3

Cumulative Review

Chapter 7

Multiple Choice: Choose the letter of the best answer.

1. In one high school, 75% of the graduates went on to college. If there were 1,000 graduates, how many went on to college?

   A. 0.75 graduate B. 7.5 graduates
   C. 75 graduates D. 750 graduates

2. Solve $\frac{8}{30} = \frac{n}{6}$.

   A. 48 B. 40
   C. 22.5 D. 1.6

3. Estimate 20% of \$8,950.

   A. \$18
   B. \$180
   C. \$1,800
   D. \$18,000

4. What is the absolute value of -5^2?

   A. −25 B. −10
   C. 10 D. 25

5. Of the 900 students in one school, 585 went on to college after graduation. What percent is this?

   A. 150% B. 90%
   C. 65% D. 58.5%

6. 75 is 15% of what number?

   A. 11.25 B. 50
   C. 200 D. 500

7. Before the year-end sale, one used car was priced at \$9,995. During the sale, the car was marked down to \$8,496. By what percent was the car marked down?

8. The admission charge at the zoo is \$3.75 per person. What is the total admission charge for a group of 28 people?

   A. \$31.75
   B. \$37.50
   C. \$105.00
   D. \$24.25

9. Simplify $\sqrt{6400}$.

   A. 80
   B. 320
   C. 800
   D. 3,200

10. Convert 0.04 to a fraction in simplest form.

    A. $\frac{4}{10}$
    B. $\frac{4}{100}$
    C. $\frac{1}{25}$
    D. $\frac{2}{50}$

11. School lunch costs \$3.35. If Megan buys lunch 25 times, how much money will she spend?

    A. \$3.60
    B. \$21.65
    C. \$83.75
    D. \$335.00

12. 24 cups is how many quarts?

    A. 2 qt B. 4 qt

16. One month, a car dealership sells 25 cars. The next month the dealership sells 31 cars. Find the percent of increase in the number of cars sold by the dealership. **(Lesson 7-4)** C

Ⓐ 6% Ⓒ 24%
Ⓑ 19% Ⓓ 31%

17. Simplify $\sqrt{8{,}100}$. **(Lesson 3-5)** D

Ⓐ 4,500 Ⓒ 450
Ⓑ 900 Ⓓ 90

18. Lola buys a bag of peanuts for \$2.50 and 3 boxes of crackers. She spends a total of \$6.55. Which equation can be used to find c, the cost of each box of crackers? **(Lesson 3-4)** B

Ⓐ $6.55 + 3c = 2.50$
Ⓑ $2.50 + 3c = 6.55$
Ⓒ $6.55 - 2.50 = c$
Ⓓ $2.50 + \frac{c}{3} = 6.55$

19. Gaspar is 4 ft 7 in. tall. He grows 2 in. each year. How long will it take him to reach a height of 5 ft 1 in.? **(Lesson 6-3)** D

Ⓐ 1 yr Ⓒ 2.5 yr
Ⓑ 2 yr Ⓓ 3 yr

20. Which of the following is NOT equivalent to 0.56? **(Lesson 4-4)** D

Ⓐ $\frac{56}{100}$ Ⓒ $\frac{14}{25}$
Ⓑ $\frac{112}{200}$ Ⓓ $\frac{23}{50}$

21. Suppose 56% of college students are women. What fraction of college students are women? **(Lesson 7-1)** D

Ⓐ $\frac{7}{125}$ Ⓒ $\frac{14}{50}$
Ⓑ $\frac{14}{100}$ Ⓓ $\frac{14}{25}$

22. A store is advertising 30% off all items. If a purse regularly sells for \$45, what is the sale price of the purse? **(Lesson 7-5)** B

Ⓐ \$13.50 Ⓒ \$58.50
Ⓑ \$31.50 Ⓓ \$150.00

23. Which of the following is NOT equivalent to a repeating decimal? **(Lesson 4-4)** D

Ⓐ $\frac{1}{3}$ Ⓑ $\frac{5}{9}$ Ⓒ $\frac{5}{6}$ Ⓓ $\frac{19}{20}$

24. Mrs. Lopez owns stock worth \$25 per share. After she sells 30 shares of the stock, the total value of her stock is \$4,250. Which of the following equations can be used to find k, the number of shares she owned before the sale? **(Lesson 3-4)** C

Ⓐ $4{,}250 - 30 = 25k$
Ⓑ $25k - 30 = 4{,}250$
Ⓒ $25(k - 30) = 4{,}250$
Ⓓ $25(k + 30) = 4{,}250$

25. Elijah bought three books that cost \$5.99 each. At the register, the cashier took 15% off the cost of the books. What was the total cost of the books, not including sales tax? **(Lesson 7-2)** B

Ⓐ \$2.70 Ⓒ \$17.97
Ⓑ \$15.27 Ⓓ \$20.67

Standards Reference Guide

California Content Standard	Item Number(s)
NS 1.3	1, 3, 10, 16, 21, 22, 25
NS 1.5	6, 9, 14, 20, 23
AF 1.1	2, 7, 11, 18, 24
AF 4.2	5, 8, 12, 15, 19
Alg1 2.0	4, 13, 17

For additional review and practice, see the *California Standards Review and Practice Workbook* or go online to use the

Visit: PHSchool.com, **Web Code:** axq-9045

Chapter 8 Linear Functions and Graphing

Chapter at a Glance

Lesson Titles, Objectives, and Features	California Content Standards
8-1 Graphing in the Coordinate Plane • To graph points in a coordinate plane	Use coordinate grids to represent points. ***Foundational (Gr4 MG 2.0)*** Identify and graph ordered pairs in the four quadrants of the coordinate plane. ***Foundational (Gr5 AF 1.1)*** **AF 3.3** Graph linear functions.
8-2 Length in the Coordinate Plane • To find lengths of line segments in the coordinate plane **8-2b Activity Lab:** Graphs of Right Triangles	Understand that the length of a horizontal line segment equals the difference of the *x*-coordinates. ***Foundational (Gr4 MG 2.2)*** Understand that the length of a vertical line segment equals the difference of the *y*-coordinates. ***Foundational (Gr4 MG 2.3)*** **MG 3.3** Know and understand the Pythagorean Theorem and use it to find the lengths of line segments.
8-3a Activity Lab: Tables and Equations **8-3 Functions** • To evaluate and write function rules	Understand that an equation such as $y = 3x + 5$ is a prescription for determining a second number when a first number is given. ***Foundational (Gr4 AF 1.5)*** **AF 1.1** Use variables and appropriate operations to write an equation.
8-4 Graphing Linear Functions • To graph linear functions **8-4b Activity Lab:** Systems of Linear Equations	Draw points corresponding to linear relationships on graph paper. ***Foundational (Gr4 MG 2.1)*** **AF 3.3** Graph linear functions. **AF 3.4** Plot the values of quantities whose ratios are always the same. Fit a line to the plot.
8-5 Slope • To find the slope of a line **8-5b Activity Lab:** Parallel and Perpendicular Lines **Algebraic Thinking:** Using Slope to Graph	**AF 3.3** Graph linear functions, noting that the vertical change per unit of horizontal change is always the same, and know that the ratio is called the slope of a graph. **AF 3.4** Plot the values of quantities whose ratios are always the same. Fit a line to the plot and understand that the slope of the line equals the ratio of the quantities.
8-6 Direct Variation • To graph direct variations **Math Reasoning:** Using a Graph to Estimate	**AF 3.3** Graph linear functions. **AF 3.4** Plot the values of quantities whose ratios are always the same. Fit a line to the plot and understand that the slope of the line equals the ratio of the quantities. **AF 4.2** Solve multistep problems involving a direct variation.

California Content Standards
NS Number Sense
AF Algebra and Functions
MG Measurement and Geometry
MR Mathematical Reasoning

Correlations to Standardized Tests

All content for these tests is contained in *Prentice Hall Math, Algebra Readiness*. This chart reflects coverage in this chapter only.

	8-1	8-2	8-3	8-4	8-5	8-6
Terra Nova CAT6 (Level 18)						
Number and Number Relations	✓	✓	✓	✓	✓	✓
Computation and Numerical Estimation	✓	✓	✓	✓	✓	✓
Operation Concepts	✓	✓	✓	✓	✓	
Measurement						
Geometry and Spatial Sense	✓	✓		✓	✓	✓
Data Analysis, Statistics, and Probability						
Patterns, Functions, and Algebra	✓	✓	✓	✓	✓	✓
Problem Solving and Reasoning	✓	✓	✓	✓	✓	✓
Communication	✓	✓	✓	✓	✓	✓
Decimals, Fractions, Integers, and Percent	✓	✓	✓	✓	✓	✓
Order of Operations						
Algebraic Operations		✓	✓	✓	✓	✓
Terra Nova CTBS (Level 18)						
Decimals, Fractions, Integers, Percents	✓	✓	✓	✓	✓	✓
Order of Operations, Numeration, Number Theory	✓	✓	✓	✓	✓	
Data Interpretation						
Measurement						
Geometry		✓				✓
ITBS (Level 14)						
Number Properties and Operations	✓	✓	✓	✓	✓	✓
Algebra		✓	✓	✓	✓	✓
Geometry	✓	✓		✓	✓	✓
Measurement						
Probability and Statistics						
Estimation						✓
SAT10 (Adv 1 Level)						
Number Sense and Operations	✓	✓	✓	✓	✓	✓
Patterns, Relationships, and Algebra		✓	✓	✓	✓	✓
Data, Statistics, and Probability						
Geometry and Measurement	✓	✓		✓	✓	✓
NAEP						
Number Sense, Properties, and Operations	✓	✓	✓		✓	✓
Measurement						
Geometry and Spatial Sense	✓	✓		✓	✓	✓
Data Analysis, Statistics, and Probability						
Algebra and Functions	✓	✓	✓	✓	✓	✓

CAT6 California Achievement Test, 6th Ed. **CTBS** Comprehensive Test of Basic Skills **ITBS** Iowa Test of Basic Skills, Form M
SAT10 Stanford Achievement Test, 10th Ed. **NAEP** National Assessment of Educational Progress 2005 Mathematics Objectives

California Math Background

Focus on the California Content Standards

- Linear equations are an important area of study in algebra. Experiences with representing locations on a graph began in grade 4 when students identified the relative positions of fractions, mixed numbers, and positive decimals on a number line (**NS 1.9**). The work with number lines continued in grade 5 (**NS 1.5**), with positive and negative integers. Students also graphed ordered pairs in the four quadrants of the coordinate plane (**AF 1.4**).
- In grade 7, students graphed linear functions and noted the slope (**AF 3.3**). They also explored applications of slope by plotting values of quantities whose ratios are always the same (such as feet to inches) (**AF 3.4**).

8-1 Graphing in the Coordinate Plane

California Content Standards **AF 3.3**

Math Understandings

- You can name any point on a coordinate plane by an ordered pair of numbers, and you can graph any ordered pair of real numbers as a point on the plane.
- An ordered pair (x, y) is ordered because you always name the horizontal coordinate first. If you reverse the order, you change the location of the point that the pair names.

You can use a coordinate system to name points in a plane.

The **coordinate plane** is formed by the intersection of two number lines. The plane is divided into four regions, called **quadrants.** The **origin** is the place where the two number lines intersect. An **ordered pair** is a pair of numbers that describes the location of a point in a coordinate plane.

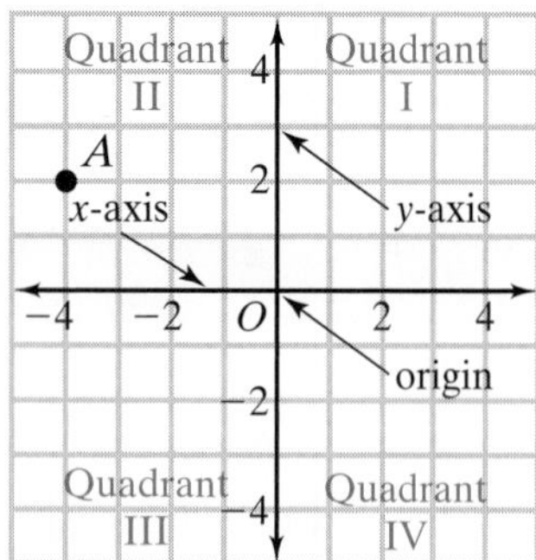

In the graph, point A has the coordinates $(-4, 2)$. The ***x*-coordinate** (-4 for point A) tells the number of horizontal units a point is from O. The ***y*-coordinate** (2 for point A) tells the number of vertical units a point is from O.

8-2 Length in the Coordinate Plane

California Content Standards **MG 3.3**

Math Understandings

- The length of a horizontal line segment equals the difference of the x-coordinates of its endpoints.
- The length of a vertical line segment equals the difference of the y-coordinates of its endpoints.
- You can use the Pythagorean Theorem to find the length of line segments in the coordinate plane.

In a right triangle, the two shortest sides are legs. The longest side, which is opposite the right angle, is the hypotenuse. The Pythagorean Theorem, $a^2 + b^2 = c^2$ relates the lengths of the legs (a and b) and hypotenuse (c) of any right triangle.

8-3 Functions

California Content Standards **AF 1.1**

Math Understandings

- Some quantities are mathematically related in a special way: for each value of one quantity, there is a unique value for the related quantity.

The **function** is a relationship that assigns exactly one output value to each input value. A **function rule** is an equation that describes a function.

Example: Make a table of input/output pairs for $d = \$.05c$.

Input c	6	12	24
Output d	\$.30	\$.60	\$1.20

8-4 Graphing Linear Functions

California Content Standards AF 3.3, AF 3.4

Math Understandings

- You can represent the relationship between two quantities using a table, a rule, or a graph.

A **function** is a rule that assigns exactly one output value to each input value. You can show a function relationship on a coordinate plane by graphing the input (x) on the horizontal axis and the output (y) on the vertical axis. When the points you graph for a function lie along a line, this type of function is a **linear function**.

Example: Make a table and graph the function $y = x - 1$.

Input	−2	0	2	4
Output	−3	−1	1	3

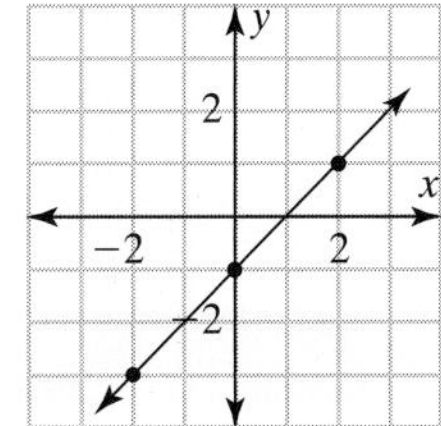

Any ordered pair that makes an equation true is a **solution** of the equation. The graph of an equation is the graph of all the points with coordinates that are solutions of the equation.

8-5 Slope

California Content Standards AF 3.3, AF 3.4

Math Understandings

- A line that rises from left to right has a positive slope; a line that falls from left to right has a negative slope.
- A vertical line has an undefined slope; a horizontal line has a slope of zero.
- Linear data have the same ratio for $\frac{\text{change in } y}{\text{change in } x}$ between any two points.
- The graph of a linear equation has a constant slope.
- To determine the slope, use any pair of points on a line.

Slope is a number indicating the steepness, or ratio of vertical change to horizontal change, of a line.

Slope of a Line
slope $= \frac{\text{change in } y\text{-coordinates}}{\text{change in } x\text{-coordinates}}$ ← **rise** / ← **run**

Example: The data in the table below are linear. Find the slope.

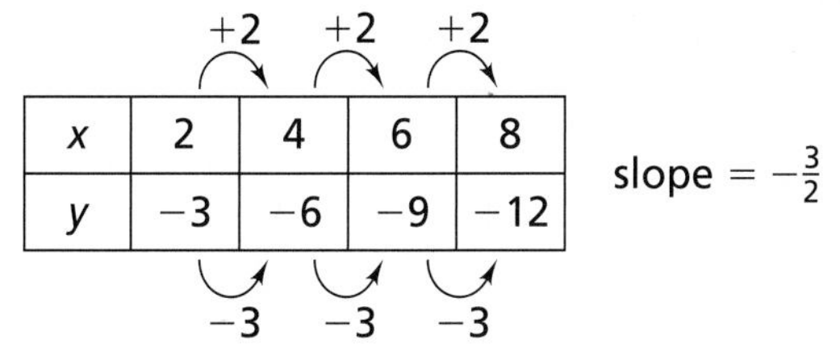

x	2	4	6	8
y	−3	−6	−9	−12

slope $= -\frac{3}{2}$

8-6 Direct Variation

California Content Standards AF 3.3, AF 3.4, AF 4.2

Math Understandings

- A **direct variation** is a linear function in the form $y = kx$, where $k \neq 0$.
- The variable y is said to vary directly with x; that is, the quantities represented by the variables have a constant ratio.
- When a direct variation is graphed, the slope of the graph is equal to the ratio of the two quantities.

Professional Development

Additional Professional Development Opportunities

Math Background notes for Chapter 8: Every lesson has a Math Background in the PLAN section.

In-Service On Demand
Prentice Hall offers free video-based tutorials to support you. Visit PHSchool.com/inserviceondemand.

Pearson Achievement Solutions
Pearson Achievement Solutions, a Pearson Education company, offers comprehensive, facilitated professional development designed to help teachers improve student achievement. To learn more, please visit pearsonachievementsolutions.com.

Chapter 8 Resources

	8-1	8-2	8-3	8-4	8-5	8-6	For the Chapter
Print Resources							
L3 Practice	●	●	●	●	●	●	
L3 Guided Problem Solving	●	●	●	●	●	●	
L2 Reteaching	●	●	●	●	●	●	
L4 Enrichment	●	●	●	●	●	●	
L3 Vocabulary and Study Skills	●	●	●	●	●	●	●
L3 Daily Puzzles	●	●	●	●	●	●	
L3 Activity Labs	●	●	●	●	●	●	
L3 Checkpoint Quiz			●			●	
L3 Chapter Project							●
L2 Below Level Chapter Test							●
L3 Chapter Test							●
L4 Alternative Assessment							●
L3 Cumulative Review							●
Spanish Resources EL							
L3 Practice	●	●	●	●	●	●	
L3 Vocabulary and Study Skills	●		●	●		●	●
L3 Checkpoint Quiz			●			●	
L2 Below Level Chapter Test							●
L3 Chapter Test							●
L4 Alternative Assessment							●
L3 Cumulative Review							●
Transparencies							
Check Skills You'll Need	●	●	●	●	●	●	
Additional Examples	●	●	●	●	●	●	
California Daily Review	●	●	●	●	●	●	
Classroom Aid	●	●	●	●	●	●	
Student Edition Answers	●	●	●	●	●	●	●
Lesson Quiz	●	●	●	●	●	●	
Technology							
California Student Center Online	●	●	●	●	●	●	●
California Student Center CD-ROM	●	●	●	●	●	●	●
Success Tracker™ Online Math Intervention	●	●	●	●	●	●	●
California Teacher Center: ExamView CD-ROM	●	●	●	●	●	●	●
California Teacher Center: Planning CD-ROM	●	●	●	●	●	●	●
California Teacher Center: Presentations CD-ROM and online	●	●	●	●	●	●	●
MindPoint Quiz Show	●	●	●	●	●	●	●
Prentice Hall Web Site: PHSchool.com	●	●	●	●	●	●	●

Also available:

California Standards Mastery
- Standards Review Transparencies
- Standards Review and Practice Workbook
- Progress Monitoring Assessments
- Math Companion
- Math*XL*

California Intervention Resources
- Skills Review and Practice Workbook
- Success Tracker™ Online Math Intervention

Other Resources
- Multilingual Handbook
- Spanish Student Edition
- Solution Key
- Math Notes Study Folder

Where You Can Use the Lesson Resources

Here is a suggestion, following the four-step teaching plan, for how you can incorporate Universal Access Resources into your teaching.

	Instructional Resources L3	Universal Access Resources
1. Plan		
Preparation Read the Math Background in the Teacher's Edition to connect this lesson with students' previous experience. **Starting Class** **Check Skills You'll Need** Assign these exercises from the Math Companion to review prerequisite skills. Review the full text of the student expectations and objectives covered in this lesson. **New Vocabulary** Help students pre-read the lesson by pointing out the new terms introduced in the lesson.	**California Math Background** **Math Understandings** **Transparencies & Presentations CD-ROM** Check Skills You'll Need California Daily Review **Resources** Vocabulary and Study Skills **Math Companion**	**Spanish Support** EL Vocabulary and Study Skills
2. Teach		
L3 **Guided Instruction** Use the Activity Labs to build conceptual understanding. Teach each Example. Use the Teacher's Edition side column notes for specific teaching tips, including Error Prevention notes. Use the Additional Examples found in the side column (and on transparency and PowerPoint) as an alternative presentation for the content. After each Example, assign the California Standards Check exercises for that Example to get an immediate assessment of student understanding. Utilize the support in the Math Companion to assist students with each Standards Check. Use the Closure activity in the Teacher's Edition to help students attain mastery of lesson content.	**Student Edition** Activity Lab **Resources** Math Companion Activity Lab **Transparencies & Presentations CD-ROM** Additional Examples Classroom Aids **Teacher Center: ExamView CD-ROM**	**Teacher's Edition** Every lesson includes suggestions for working with students who need special attention. L1 Special Needs L2 Below Level L4 Advanced Learners EL English Learners **Resources** **Multilingual Handbook** **Math Companion**
3. Practice		
Assignment Guide **Check Your Understanding** Use these questions from the Math Companion to check students' understanding before you assign homework. **Homework Exercises** Assign homework from these leveled exercises in the Assignment Guide. **A** Practice by Example **B** Apply Your Skills **C** Challenge **California** Multiple-Choice Practice and Mixed Review **Homework Quick Check** Use these key exercises to quickly check students' homework.	**Transparencies & Presentations CD-ROM** Student Answers **Resources** Math Companion Practice Guided Problem Solving Vocabulary and Study Skills Activity Lab Daily Puzzles **Teacher Center: ExamView CD-ROM** **Math *XL***	**Spanish Support** EL Practice EL Vocabulary and Study Skills **Resources** L4 Enrichment
4. Assess & Reteach		
Lesson Quiz Assign the Lesson Quiz to assess students' mastery of the lesson content. **Checkpoint Quiz** Use the Checkpoint Quiz to assess student progress over several lessons.	**Transparencies & Presentations CD-ROM** Lesson Quiz **Resources** Checkpoint Quiz	**Resources** L2 Reteaching EL Checkpoint Quiz Success Tracker™ **Teacher Center: ExamView CD-ROM**

KEY L1 Special Needs L2 Below Level L3 For All Students L4 Advanced, Gifted EL English Learners

Linear Functions and Graphing

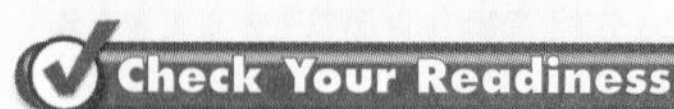

Answers are in the back of the textbook.

For math intervention, direct students to:

Subtracting Integers
Lesson 2-3

Dividing Integers
Lesson 2-5

Positive Exponents
Lesson 2-6

Fractions, Decimals, and Percents
Lesson 7-1

Spanish Vocabulary/Study Skills EL

Vocabulary/Study Skills L3

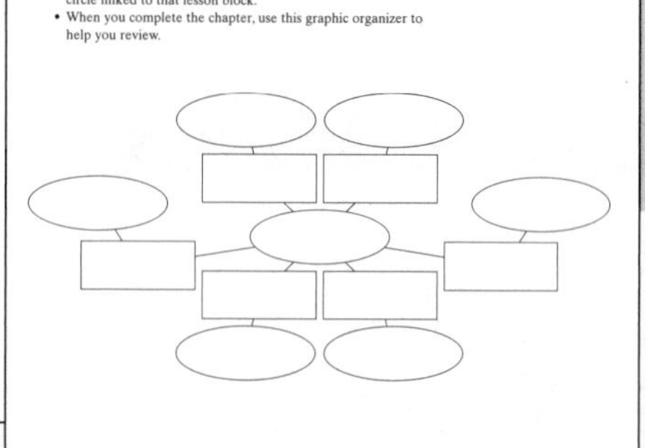

8A: Graphic Organizer — For use before Lesson 8-1

Study Skill It is important that you fully understand the basic concepts in each chapter before moving on to more complex material. Be sure to ask questions when you are not comfortable with the material you have learned.

Write your answers.

1. What is the chapter title? ______
2. How many lessons are there in this chapter? ______
3. What is the topic of the Test-Taking Strategies page? ______
4. Complete the graphic organizer below as you work through the chapter.
   - In the center, write the title of the chapter.
   - When you begin a lesson, write the lesson name in a rectangle.
   - When you complete a lesson, write a skill or key concept in a circle linked to that lesson block.
   - When you complete the chapter, use this graphic organizer to help you review.

CHAPTER 8

Linear Functions and Graphing

What You've Learned

California Content Standards

NS 1.2 Add, subtract, multiply, and divide rational numbers and take positive rational numbers to whole-number powers.

AF 2.1 Interpret positive whole-number powers as repeated multiplication. Simplify expressions that include exponents.

NS 1.3 Convert fractions to decimals and percents and use these representations in estimations, computations, and applications.

Check Your Readiness

for Help to the lesson in green.

Subtracting Integers (Lesson 2-3)

Find each difference.

1. $12 - (-8)$ 20
2. $-3 - 4$ −7
3. $7 - 9$ −2
4. $-5 - (-4)$ −1
5. $4 - 8$ −4
6. $-2 - (-5)$ 3

Dividing Integers (Lesson 2-5)

Find each quotient.

7. $\frac{35}{-7}$ −5
8. $\frac{-72}{12}$ −6
9. $\frac{-54}{-9}$ 6
10. $\frac{-40}{5}$ −8
11. $\frac{-24}{-6}$ 4
12. $\frac{63}{-21}$ −3

Positive Exponents (Lesson 2-6)

Simplify each expression.

13. $3^2 + 4^2$ 25
14. $5^2 - 2^2$ 21
15. $9^2 + (-10)^2$ 181

Fractions, Decimals, and Percents (Lesson 7-1)

Write each fraction as a percent.

16. $\frac{1}{4}$ 25%
17. $\frac{5}{8}$ 62.5%
18. $\frac{22}{33}$ 66.7%
19. $\frac{18}{12}$ 150%

▲ You can express the frequency of drumbeats as a linear function of time.

What You'll Learn Next

California Content Standards

AF 3.3 Graph linear functions, noting that the vertical change per unit of horizontal change is always the same and know that the ratio is called the slope of a graph.

AF 3.4 Plot the values of quantities whose ratios are always the same. Fit a line to the plot and understand that the slope of the line equals the ratio of the quantities.

New Vocabulary

English and Spanish Audio Online

- **coordinate plane (p. 288)**
- **direct variation (p. 316)**
- **function (p. 298)**
- **function rule (p. 298)**
- **linear function (p. 303)**
- **ordered pair (p. 288)**
- **origin (p. 288)**
- **quadrants (p. 288)**
- **slope (p. 310)**
- **slope of a line (p. 310)**
- **solution (p. 303)**
- ***x*-axis (p. 288)**
- ***x*-coordinate (p. 288)**
- ***y*-axis (p. 288)**
- ***y*-coordinate (p. 288)**

California Content Standards for Chapter 8

Algebra and Functions
AF 1.1, AF 3.3, AF 3.4, AF 4.2

Mathematical Reasoning
MR 1.1, MR 2.3, MR 2.4, MR 3.2

Measurement and Geometry
MG 3.3

Chapter 8 Overview

In this chapter, students learn to graph points and find lengths of line segments in a coordinate plane. They also learn to evaluate and write function rules, graph linear functions, find the slope of a line, and graph direct variations.

Activating Prior Knowledge

In this chapter, students build on their knowledge of writing and solving one-step and two-step equations to write and evaluate functions. They build on their knowledge of rational numbers by learning to graph points and find lengths in a coordinate place, and they put this together by graphing functions and direct variations in the coordinate plane. They build on their knowledge of ratios to understand slope.

Ask questions such as:

- *Explain what a ratio is.* a comparison of two quantities by division
- *What is the solution to the equation* $x + 5 = 12$? $x = 7$

8-1

1. Plan

California Content Standards

Use coordinate grids to represent points. ***Foundational***

Identify and graph ordered pairs in the four quadrants of the coordinate plane. ***Foundational***

AF 3.3 Graph linear functions.

California Math Background

The *coordinate plane* is a grid created by a horizontal number line and a vertical number line—the *x*-axis and *y*-axis, respectively. These number lines intersect at the *origin,* designated by the ordered pair (0, 0). Ordered pairs, such as (0, 0) and (3, −2), are used to locate points in the coordinate plane. The first number in the pair is the *x*-coordinate and the second number is the *y*-coordinate. The *x*-coordinate describes a point's location to the left or right of the origin. The *y*-coordinate describes a point's location up or down from the origin.

More Math Background: p. 286C

Lesson Planning and Resources

See p. 286E for a list of the resources that support this lesson.

PRESENTATION CD-ROM
CD, Online, or Transparencies

Bell Ringer Practice

Check Skills You'll Need
Use student page, transparency, or PowerPoint.
See Math Companion.

California Standards Review
Use transparency or PowerPoint.

8-1 Graphing in the Coordinate Plane

Check Skills You'll Need

Do this in your **Math Companion.**

Vocabulary
- coordinate plane
- *y*-axis
- *x*-axis
- quadrants
- origin
- ordered pair
- *x*-coordinate
- *y*-coordinate

Use your **Math Companion** *to build your vocabulary.*

Vocabulary Tip

The plural of *axis* is *axes.*

California Content Standards

Foundational Standard Use coordinate grids to represent points.
Foundational Standard Identify and graph ordered pairs in the four quadrants of the coordinate plane.
Prepares for **AF 3.3** Graph linear functions.

What You'll Learn . . . and Why

You will learn to graph points in a coordinate plane. Mapmakers use a coordinate grid system for maps. The coordinate plane is another type of grid system. You can use coordinates to find and describe locations.

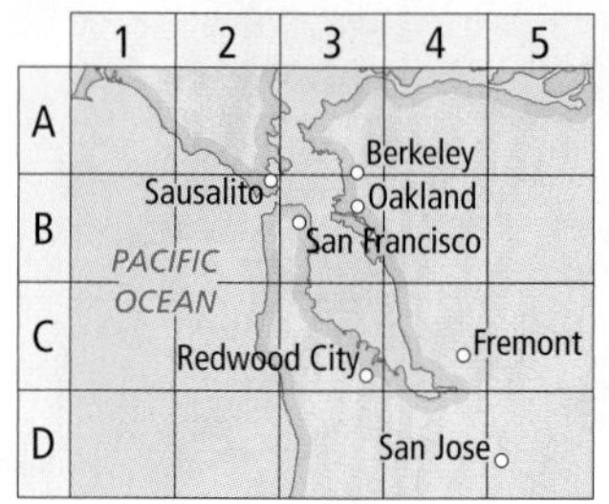

A **coordinate plane** is a grid formed by the intersection of two number lines. You can use a coordinate plane to locate and name points.

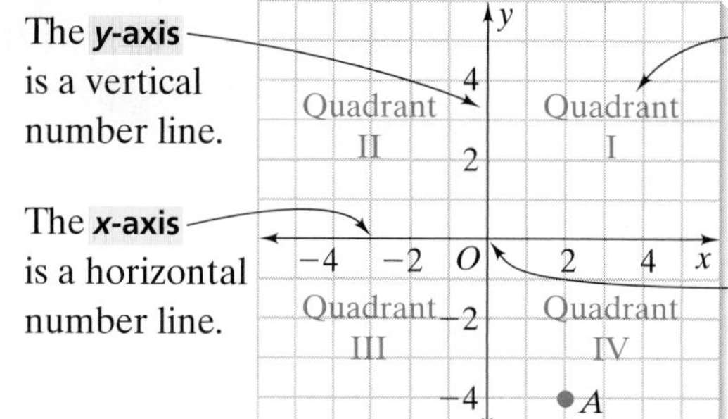

An **ordered pair** (x, y) gives the coordinates of a point's location. In the graph above, point A has coordinates $(2, -4)$. The origin has coordinates $(0, 0)$.

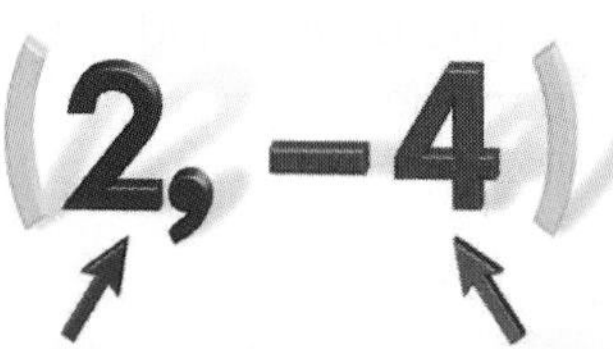

The **x-coordinate** shows the position to the right or left of the *y*-axis.

The **y-coordinate** shows the position above or below the *x*-axis.

Universal Access Solutions for All Learners

Special Needs L1	**Below Level** L2
Give students blank copies of a coordinate grid. Have them highlight the negative parts of the *x*- and *y*-axes in one color. Then have them highlight the positive parts in a different color.	Have students graph these points in a coordinate plane. Have them connect the points in order. Ask: *What is the figure?* (4, 3), (−3, 3), (4, −3), (−3, −3) rectangle

To find the coordinates of a point on a coordinate plane, first find the x-coordinate and y-coordinate. Then write them as an ordered pair.

EXAMPLE Finding Points on a Coordinate Plane

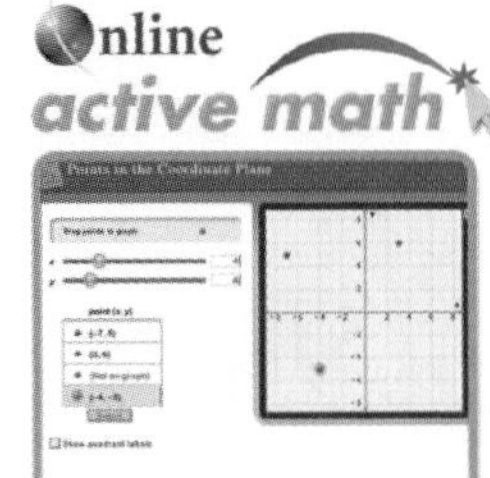

For: Coordinate Plane Activity
Use: Interactive Textbook, 8-1

1 A student draws a map of certain locations using the point labeled "Home" as the origin. Identify the coordinates of the library.

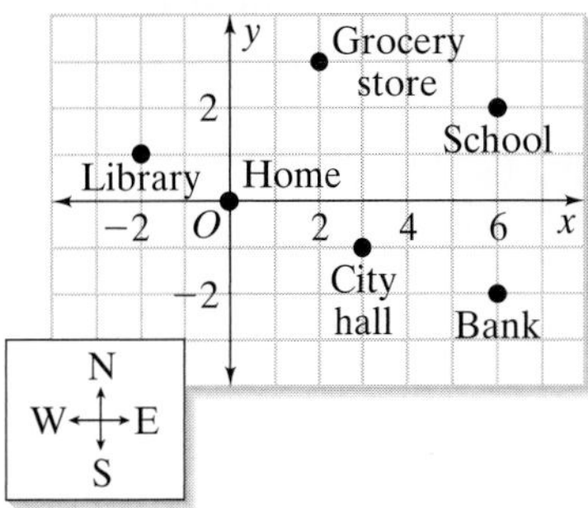

The library is 2 units to the left of the y-axis. So the x-coordinate is -2.

The library is 1 unit above the x-axis. So the y-coordinate is 1.

The library is located at $(-2, 1)$.

CA Standards Check 1 *Go to your* **Math Companion** *for help.*

1. Identify the coordinates of each building in the map above.
   a. School (6, 2) b. Bank (6, −2) c. Grocery store (2, 3)

You can graph a point when you know its coordinates. Remember that the x- and y-axes are number lines. Move right from the origin to graph a positive x-coordinate and left from the origin to graph a negative x-coordinate. Move up from the origin to graph a positive y-coordinate and down from the origin to graph a negative y-coordinate.

EXAMPLE Graphing Ordered Pairs

Relate **MATH YOU KNOW...**

Graph $2\frac{1}{2}$ on a number line.

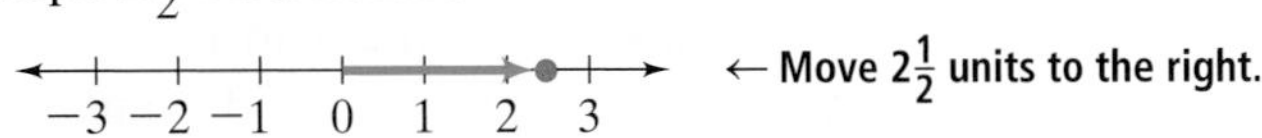

2 Graph point $A\left(2\frac{1}{2}, -3\right)$ on a coordinate plane.

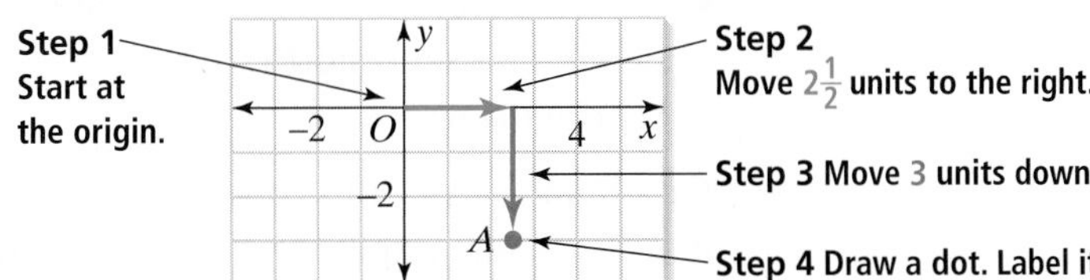

CA Standards Check 2 *Go to your* **Math Companion** *for help.*

2. Graph each point on the same coordinate plane. 2a–c. See margin.
   a. $B(-4, -4)$ b. $C\left(-3, -1\frac{1}{2}\right)$ c. $D(-3, 2)$

Check Your Understanding *Homework prep is in your* **Math Companion.**

2. Teach

Guided Instruction

Example 1
Have students locate coordinates by using their fingers to trace the corresponding horizontal and vertical lines to meet at the coordinates of the point.

Additional Examples

Use the coordinate grid for item 1.

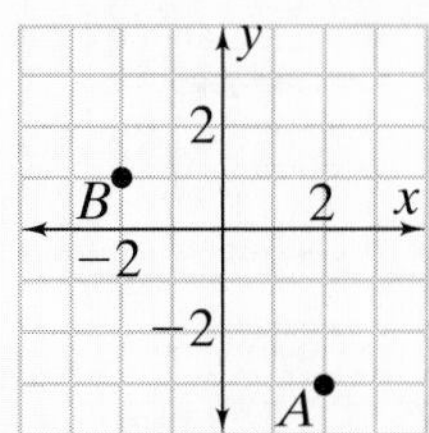

1 Identify the coordinates of each point.
a. A (2, −3) b. B (−2, 1)

2 Graph $P\left(-3, 2\frac{1}{2}\right)$ on a coordinate plane.

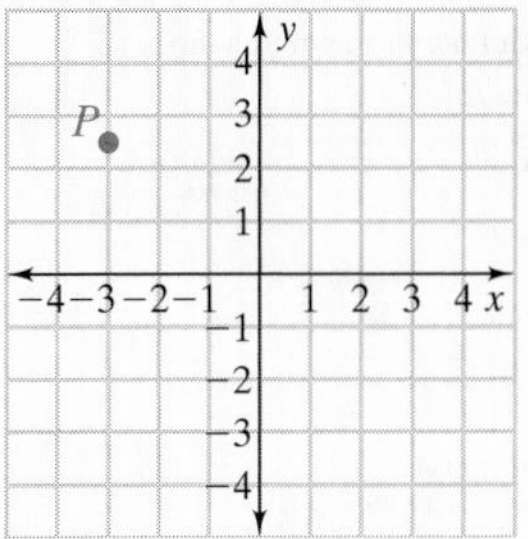

Closure

- *What is the origin in the coordinate plane?* (0, 0), the point where the two axes intersect
- *Which number comes first in an ordered pair?* the x-coordinate, the number of horizontal units from the origin

Advanced Learners L4	**English Learners** EL
A square has coordinates (3, 3) and (−3, −3). What are the missing coordinates? (−3, 3), (3, −3)	Relate terms used for a coordinate plane to their meaning. For example, quadrant has the root *quad.* Connect this to *quadrilaterals* so students see that *quad* is related to the number 4. Another example is *ordered pairs,* which must be written in a particular *order.*

3. Practice

Assignment Guide

Check Your Understanding

See Math Companion.

Homework Exercises

A Practice by Example 1–19
B Apply Your Skills 20–35
C Challenge 36
California Multiple-Choice Practice 37–39
Mixed Review 40–42

Homework Quick Check

To check students' understanding of key skills and concepts, go over Exercises 3, 13, 21, 22, 23, 30.

Universal Access Resources

Adapted Practice 8-1 L1

Practice 8-1 Graphing in the Coordinat L3

In which quadrant or on which axis is each point located?

1. (−3, −2) 2. (7, 0) 3. (4, 0) 4. (−3, −9)

Identify the coordinates of each point in the graph at the right.

5. J ____ 6. E ____
7. D ____ 8. A ____
9. G ____ 10. C ____

Graph each point on the same coordinate plane.

11. A (8, −4) 12. B (−4, 8)
13. C (4, 8) 14. D (−8, −4)
15. E (8, 4) 16. F (−4, −8)

17. A taxi begins at (4, −3). It travels 3 blocks west and 5 blocks north to pick up a customer. What are the customer's coordinates?

18. A moving truck fills up a shipment at an old address, at (−2, 1). It travels 7 blocks south and 6 blocks east to the new address. What is the location of the new address?

Use the coordinate plane at the right.

19. Graph four points on the coordinate plane so that when the points are connected in order, the shape is a rectangle. List the coordinates of the points.

20. Graph four points on the coordinate plane so that when the points are connected in order, the shape is a parallelogram that is not a rectangle. List the coordinates of the points.

8-1 • Guided Problem Solving L3

GPS Exercise 23:

Geometry A symmetrical four-pointed star has eight corner points. Seven of the points are (−1, 1), (0, 3), (1, 1), (3, 0), (1, −1), (0, −3), and (−1, −1). What are the coordinates of the missing point?

Understand

1. What does *symmetrical* mean?
2. What is a good way to set up the problem visually?

Plan and Carry Out

3. What point is symmetrical to (−1, 1) over the y-axis?
4. What point is symmetrical to (−1, −1) over the y-axis?
5. What point is symmetrical to (3, 0) over the y-axis?
6. What is the missing point?

Check

7. Does the point (−3, 0) form a four-point star with the other seven points?

Solve Another Problem

8. A five-pointed star that is symmetrical over the y-axis has ten corner points. Eight of the points are (−1, 1), (0, 3), (1, 1), (3, 1), (1, −1), (0, −1), (−2, −3), and (−3, 1). What are the coordinates of the missing points?

Standards Practice

GO for Help: MathXL

A Practice by Example

Example 1 (page 289)

GO for Help

Identify the coordinates of each point in the graph below.

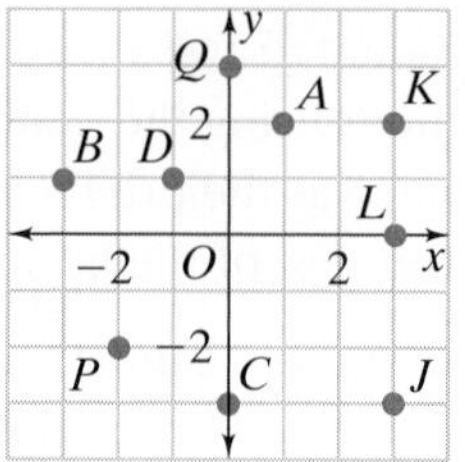

Homework Video Tutor

For: Examples 1–2
Visit: PHSchool.com
Web Code: axe-0801

1. A (1, 2)
Point A is one unit to the right of the y-axis and two units above the x-axis.

Guided Practice: This exercise has been started for you!

2. B (−3, 1) 3. C (0, −3) 4. D (−1, 1) 5. J (3, −3)
6. K (3, 2) 7. L (3, 0) 8. P (−2, −2) 9. Q (0, 3)

Example 2 (page 289)

Graph each point on the same coordinate plane. 10–19. See margin.

10. $A(4, -5)$
Start at the origin. Move 4 units to the right. Then move 5 units down.

Guided Practice: This exercise has been started for you!

11. $B(3, 4)$ 12. $C(5, 0)$ 13. $D(0, -3)$
14. $E\left(-5, 1\frac{1}{2}\right)$ 15. $F\left(-\frac{5}{2}, -4\right)$ 16. $G(-2, 0)$
17. $H(6, 2)$ 18. $I(-1, 2.5)$ 19. $J(-0.5, 4)$

B Apply Your Skills

20. **Guided Problem Solving** You are at the park shown in the map at the right. You move 5 units north and 2 units west. At which building do you arrive? school

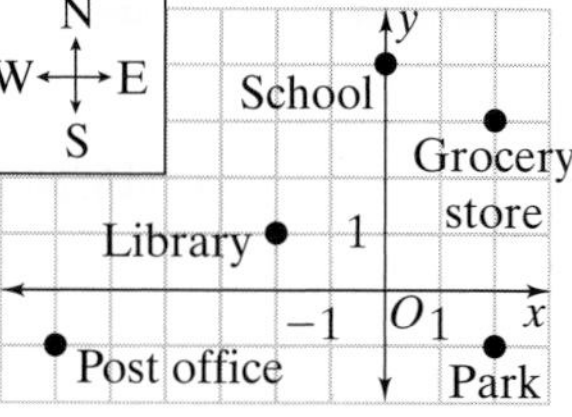

- What are the coordinates of the park?
- Which direction on the coordinate plane represents north? Which represents west?

21. Graph and connect the points (3, 2), (−2, 2), (−2, 7), and (3, 2) in order. Then graph and connect the points (3, −2), (−2, −2), (−2, −7), and (3, −2) in order. How are the two figures related? See margin.

22. **Writing in Math** What do all the points on the y-axis have in common? Explain. Their x-coordinate is 0.

GPS 23. A symmetrical four-pointed star has eight corner points. Seven of the points are (−1, 1), (0, 3), (1, 1), (3, 0), (1, −1), (0, −3), and (−1, −1). What are the coordinates of the missing point? (−3, 0)

SCAFFOLDED
Problem Solving

Use the map at the right. Maps of Earth use a coordinate system to describe locations. The longitude of a location is its x-coordinate. The latitude of a location is its y-coordinate.

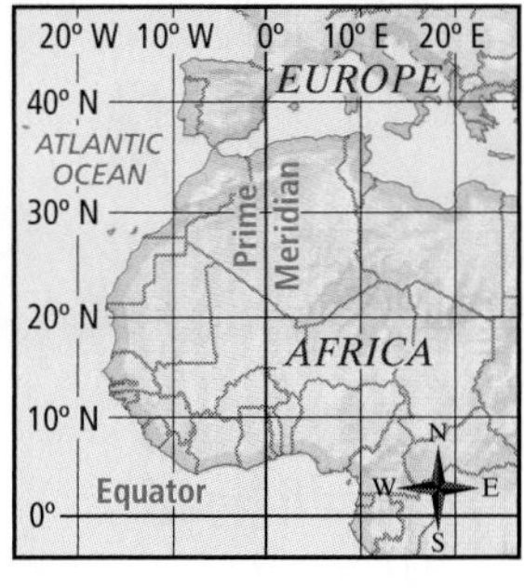

24. What is the latitude of the equator? 0°

25. A traveler is at 20° N, 10° W. On which continent is the traveler located? Africa

26. Name a possible longitude and latitude for the location of a traveler in Europe. Answers may vary. Sample: 20° E, 45° N

27. You are at 35° N, 15° W. Where are you located? in the Atlantic Ocean

28. (2, 0), (2, 1), (4, 1), (4, 0), (6, 2), (5, 2), (5, 4), (6, 4), (4, 6), (4, 5), (2, 5), (2, 6), (0, 4), (1, 4), (1, 2), (0, 2)

28. Quilt designers often use coordinate grids to design patterns. Identify the coordinates of the corners in the pattern shown at the right. See left.

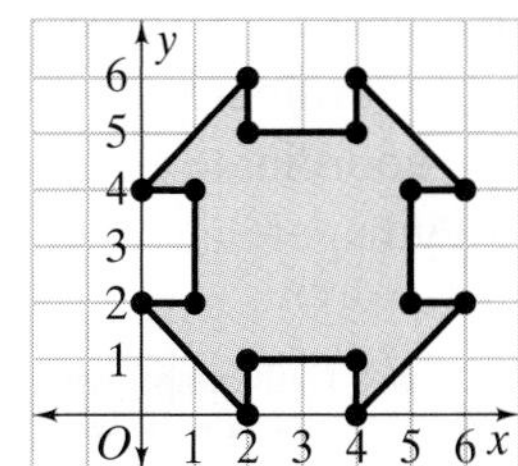

29. On a coordinate plane, draw two different rectangles, both with sides of length 3 and 5 and a corner at $(-1, 3)$. See margin.

In which quadrant or on which axis is each point located?

30. $(-2, -2)$ III **31.** $(0, 4)$ y-axis **32.** $(-1, 9)$ II **33.** $(n, 0)$ x-axis

34. (x, y) if $x > 0$ and $y < 0$ IV **35.** (x, y) if $x > 0$ and $y > 0$ I

Challenge

36. A parallelogram has vertices at (3, 2), (2, 5), and (6, 5). Find three possible points for the fourth vertex. (−1, 2); (7, 2); (5, 8)

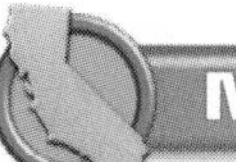

Multiple Choice Practice and Mixed Review

For California Standards Tutorials, visit PHSchool.com. Web Code: axq-9045

AF 4.2

37. A recipe for 10 oz of fondue requires 8 oz of cheese. How much cheese do you need to make 36 oz of fondue? B

Ⓐ 8 oz
Ⓑ 28.8 oz
Ⓒ 36 oz
Ⓓ 48.5 oz

AF 1.1

38. Which expression is equivalent to $3^4 \cdot 5^2$? D

Ⓐ $3 \cdot 4 \cdot 5 \cdot 2$
Ⓑ $3 \cdot 4 + 5 \cdot 2$
Ⓒ $(3 + 4)(5 + 2)$
Ⓓ $3 \cdot 3 \cdot 3 \cdot 3 \cdot 5 \cdot 5$

NS 1.2

39. At a yard sale, you pay $17.25 for 5 books. The price of each book is the same. What is the price of one book? B

Ⓐ $3.25 Ⓑ $3.45 Ⓒ $5.00 Ⓓ $12.25

for Help

Lesson 3-2 **Solve each equation.**

40. $b - 6 = 10$ 16 **41.** $k - 1 = 24$ 25 **42.** $n - (-4) = 40$ 36

Online Lesson Quiz Visit: PHSchool.com Web Code: axa-0801

Alternative Assessment

Using all four quadrants, each student in a pair plots six points and labels the points A through F. Partners exchange papers and name the coordinates of each point.

California Resources

Standards Mastery

- Standards Review Transparencies
- Standards Review and Practice Workbook
- Math Companion

Math Intervention

- Skills Review and Practice Workbook
- Math XL

4. Assess & Reteach

PRESENTATION CD-ROM
CD, Online, or Transparencies

Lesson Quiz

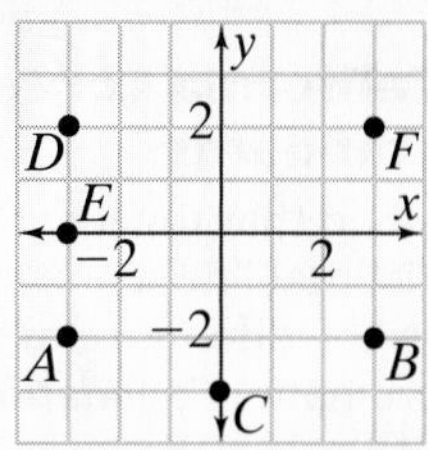

Find the coordinates of each point.

1. A (−3, −2) **2.** F (3, 2)

Name each point with the given coordinates.

3. (−3, 2) D **4.** (0, −3) C

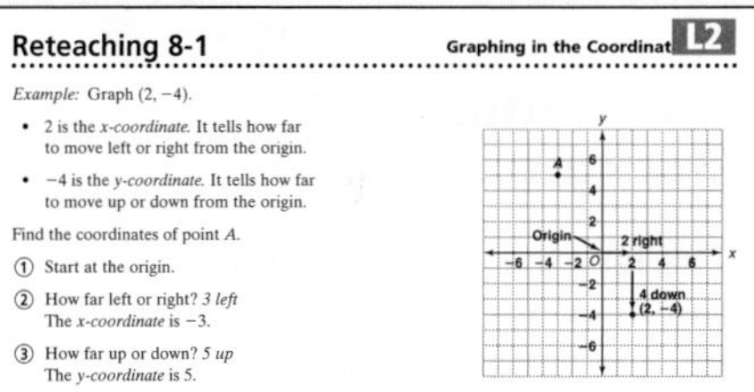

Reteaching 8-1 Graphing in the Coordinat L2

Example: Graph (2, −4).

- 2 is the *x-coordinate.* It tells how far to move left or right from the origin.
- −4 is the *y-coordinate.* It tells how far to move up or down from the origin.

Find the coordinates of point A.

① Start at the origin.
② How far left or right? *3 left*
The *x-coordinate* is −3.
③ How far up or down? *5 up*
The *y-coordinate* is 5.

The coordinates of point A are (−3, 5).

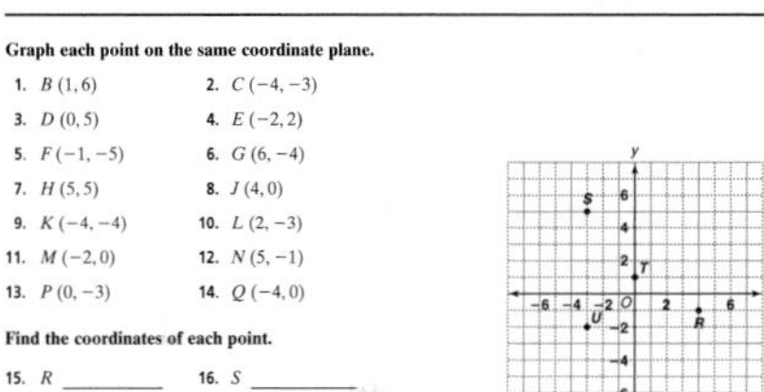

Graph each point on the same coordinate plane.

1. B (1, 6) 2. C (−4, −3)
3. D (0, 5) 4. E (−2, 2)
5. F (−1, −5) 6. G (6, −4)
7. H (5, 5) 8. J (4, 0)
9. K (−4, −4) 10. L (2, −3)
11. M (−2, 0) 12. N (5, −1)
13. P (0, −3) 14. Q (−4, 0)

Find the coordinates of each point.

15. R ________ 16. S ________
17. T ________ 18. U ________

Look at the coordinate grid above.

19. If you travel 7 units down from S, at which point will you be located?

____

20. If you travel 4 units right from T and 2 units down, at which point will you be located?

____

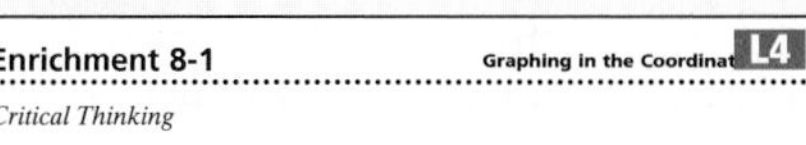

Enrichment 8-1 Graphing in the Coordinat L4

Critical Thinking

One item that Cheryl had to find on a treasure hunt was located at the point (3, 4) on the map. When Cheryl got there, she realized she had the map upside down. How many units left, right, up, and down on the map should Cheryl walk to find the correct location?

1. Mark (3, 4) on the coordinate plane. Label it A.
2. Turn this page upside down. Imagine that the graph was scaled in the usual way. Then mark (3, 4). Label it B.
3. Turn your page to original position. Follow the grid lines to mark the shortest path between the B and A.

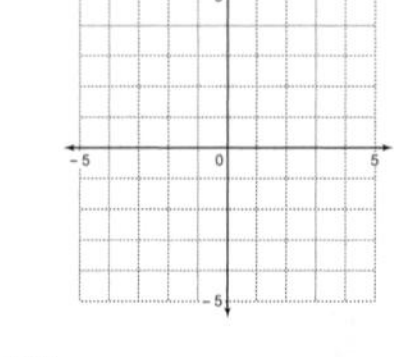

4. Does your path go up or down? How many units?

____

5. Does your path go left or right? How many units?

____

6. Are there other paths that you could choose? Explain.

____

7. What is the relationship between the number of units the path takes and the original coordinates?

____

8. One item that Norm had to find on a treasure hunt was located at the point (–2, 5) on the map. When Norm got there, he realized he had the map upside down. How many units left, right, up, and down on the map should Norm walk to find the correct location?

____

GO for Help: Math Companion

8-2

1. Plan

California Content Standards

Understand that the length of a horizontal line segment equals the difference of the x-coordinates. ***Foundational***

Understand that the length of a vertical line segment equals the difference of the y-coordinates. ***Foundational***

MG 3.3 Know and understand the Pythagorean Theorem and use it to find the lengths of line segments. ***Develop, Master***

California Math Background

The length of a horizontal line segment on a coordinate plane is the difference of the x-coordinates. The length of a vertical line segment on a coordinate plane is the difference of the y-coordinates. You can use the Pythagorean Theorem to find the lengths of other line segments on a coordinate plane.

More Math Background: p. 286C

Lesson Planning and Resources

See p. 286E for a list of the resources that support this lesson.

...PRESENTATION CD-ROM
CD, Online, or Transparencies

Bell Ringer Practice

Check Skills You'll Need
Use student page, transparency, or PowerPoint.
See Math Companion.

California Standards Review
Use transparency or PowerPoint.

8-2 Length in the Coordinate Plane

Check Skills You'll Need

Do this in your **Math Companion.**

Vocabulary

Review:
- x-coordinate
- y-coordinate
- Pythagorean Theorem

Use your **Math Companion** *to build your vocabulary.*

California Content Standards

Foundational Standard Understand that the length of a horizontal line segment equals the difference of the x-coordinates.

Foundational Standard Understand that the length of a vertical line segment equals the difference of the y-coordinates.

MG 3.3 Know and understand the Pythagorean theorem and use it to find the lengths of line segments. ***Develop, Master***

What You'll Learn . . . and Why

You will learn to find lengths of line segments in the coordinate plane. Archeologists use grids to record the locations of objects they find. You can use the coordinates of the objects to find the distances between them.

The length of a horizontal line segment equals the positive difference of the x-coordinates of its endpoints. The length of a vertical line segment equals the positive difference of the y-coordinates of its endpoints.

EXAMPLE Finding the Lengths of Line Segments

1 **a.** Find the length of the horizontal line segment with endpoints $M(-3, 2)$ and $N(1, 2)$.

length of $\overline{MN} = 1 - (-3)$ ← **Find the difference of the x-coordinates.**

$= 4$ ← **Simplify.**

b. Find the length of the vertical line segment with endpoints $E(1, 3)$ and $F(1, -2)$.

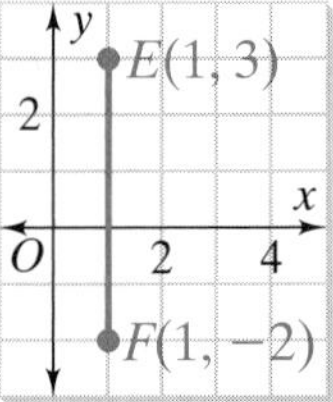

length of $\overline{EF} = 3 - (-2)$ ← **Find the difference of the y-coordinates.**

$= 5$ ← **Simplify.**

Vocabulary Tip

You name a line segment after its endpoints. For example, $\overline{MN}$ is the segment with endpoints M and N.

CA Standards Check 1

Go to your **Math Companion** *for help.*

1. Find the length of the line segment with the given endpoints.

a.

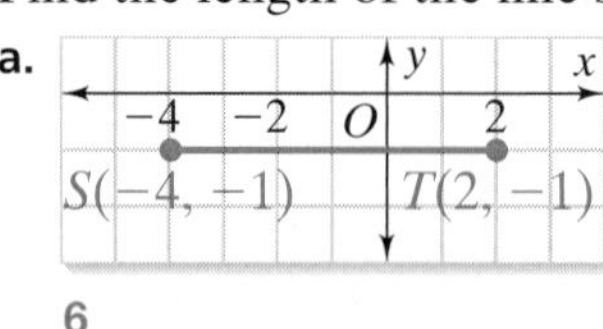

6

b.

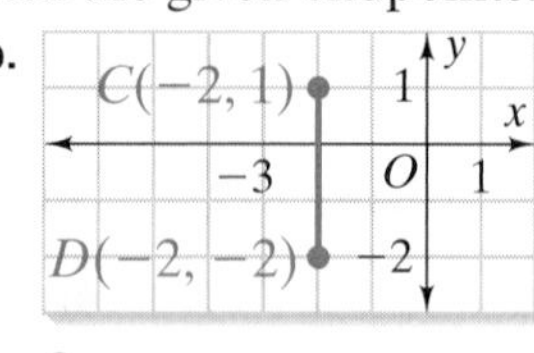

3

Universal Access Solutions for All Learners

Special Needs L1	**Below Level** L2
For Example 1, suggest that students use two colored pencils, one for writing the x-coordinates and the other for writing the y-coordinates. As they subtract, the colors of the digits should match.	For Example 1, suggest that students plot the points on a coordinate plane and then count the blocks to find the length of the line. Relate this method to the method presented in Example 1.

You can use the Pythagorean Theorem to find the length of line segments in the coordinate plane.

Relate **MATH YOU KNOW...**

EXAMPLE Finding Distance in the Coordinate Plane

Find the length of the hypotenuse of a right triangle with legs of length 5 m and 6 m to the nearest meter.

$a^2 + b^2 = c^2$ ← **Use the Pythagorean Theorem.**

$5^2 + 6^2 = c^2$ ← **Substitute.**

$25 + 36 = c^2$ ← **Simplify.**

$61 = c^2$ ← **Add.**

$\sqrt{61} = c$ ← **Find the square root of each side.**

$8 \approx c$

The hypotenuse is about 8 m long.

... to **ALGEBRA**

2 Guided Problem Solving An archeologist finds a pottery shard 5 m north of a well, and a necklace 6 m east of the well. To the nearest meter, what is the distance between the pottery shard and the necklace?

Graph the three locations on a coordinate plane. Place the well at the origin. You can draw a right triangle connecting the three points. The lengths of the legs are 5 m and 6 m.

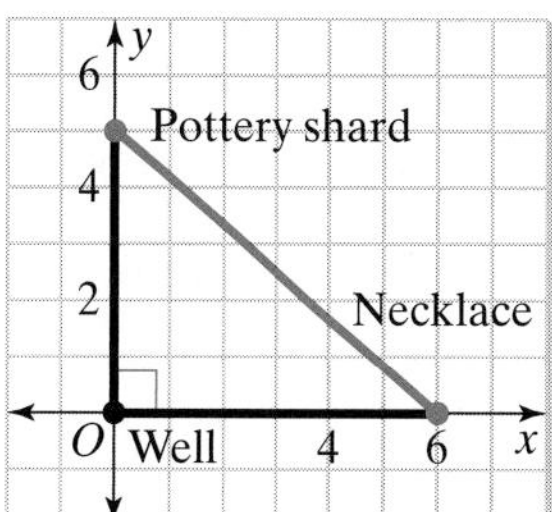

The distance between the pottery shard and the necklace is the length of the hypotenuse of the triangle. Use the Pythagorean Theorem to find the length of the hypotenuse.

$a^2 + b^2 = c^2$ ← **Use the Pythagorean Theorem.**

$5^2 + 6^2 = c^2$ ← **Substitute the lengths of the legs.**

$25 + 36 = c^2$ ← **Simplify.**

$61 = c^2$ ← **Add.**

$\sqrt{61} = c$ ← **Find the square root of each side.**

$8 \approx c$

The distance between the pottery shard and the necklace is about 8 m.

CA Standards Check 2 *Go to your* **Math Companion** *for help.*

2. An archeologist finds a cooking pot 4 m west of a fire pit and an arrowhead 6 m south of the fire pit. To the nearest meter, what is the distance between the cooking pot and the arrowhead?
about 7 m

Homework prep is in your **Math Companion.**

2. Teach

Guided Instruction

Example 1
Remind students that distance is always positive in the coordinate plane. If they get a negative result from subtracting coordinates, they can take its absolute value to find the distance.

Ask: *What is the result if you subtract the x-coordinates in a different order, such as* $(-3) - 1$ *instead of* $1 - (-3)$? The result is -4, but the distance is still 4.

Additional Examples

1 a. Find the length of the vertical line segment with endpoints $W(2, -9)$ and $Z(2, -2)$. 7

b. Find the length of the horizontal line segment with endpoints $Q(2, -7)$ and $R(8, -7)$. 6

2 The mall is 5 miles north of the library. The roller skating rink is 12 miles east of the library. To the nearest mile, how far is the mall from the roller skating rink? 13 miles

Closure

- *How do you find the length of a horizontal line segment?* Find the difference of the x-coordinates.
- *How do you find the length of a vertical line segment?* Find the difference of the y-coordinates.
- *How do you find the length of a line segment that is neither horizontal nor vertical?* Make a right triangle and use the Pythagorean Theorem.

Advanced Learners L4
Right triangle *ABC*'s hypotenuse has endpoints $A(-2, 1)$ and $C(1, -2)$. Find the two possible pairs of coordinates for point *B* if the legs of the triangle both have length 3. $(-2, -2)$ and $(1, 1)$

English Learners EL
In problems requiring the use of the Pythagorean Theorem, make sure students can identify and label the origin, the legs, and the hypotenuse as they would be drawn on a coordinate plane. Ask: *Which length are you trying to find? Is that a leg or the hypotenuse?*

3. Practice

Assignment Guide

Check Your Understanding
See Math Companion.

Homework Exercises

A	Practice by Example	1–11
B	Apply Your Skills	12–18
C	Challenge	19
California Multiple-Choice Practice		20–22
Mixed Review		23–26

Homework Quick Check
To check students' understanding of key skills and concepts, go over Exercises 2, 7, 11, 17, 18.

Universal Access Resources

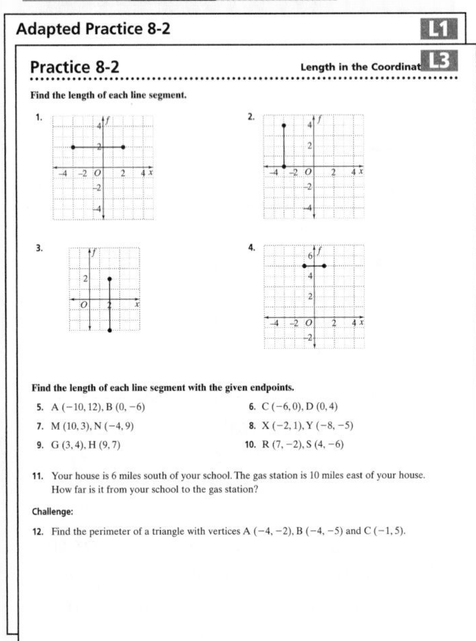

Adapted Practice 8-2 L1

Practice 8-2 Length in the Coordinate Plane L3

Find the length of each line segment.

Find the length of each line segment with the given endpoints.

5. A (−10, 12), B (0, −6)
6. C (−6, 0), D (0, 4)
7. M (10, 3), N (−4, 9)
8. X (−2, 1), Y (−8, −5)
9. G (3, 4), H (9, 7)
10. R (7, −2), S (4, −6)
11. Your house is 6 miles south of your school. The gas station is 10 miles east of your house. How far is it from your school to the gas station?

Challenge:
12. Find the perimeter of a triangle with vertices A (−4, −2), B (−4, −5) and C (−1, 5).

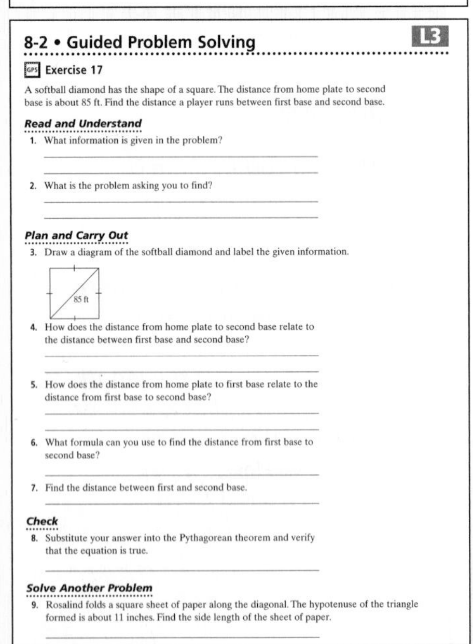

8-2 • Guided Problem Solving L3

Exercise 17

A softball diamond has the shape of a square. The distance from home plate to second base is about 85 ft. Find the distance a player runs between first base and second base.

Read and Understand
1. What information is given in the problem?
2. What is the problem asking you to find?

Plan and Carry Out
3. Draw a diagram of the softball diamond and label the given information.
4. How does the distance from home plate to second base relate to the distance between first base and second base?
5. How does the distance from home plate to first base relate to the distance from first base to second base?
6. What formula can you use to find the distance from first base to second base?
7. Find the distance between first and second base.

Check
8. Substitute your answer into the Pythagorean theorem and verify that the equation is true.

Solve Another Problem
9. Rosalind folds a square sheet of paper along the diagonal. The hypotenuse of the triangle formed is about 11 inches. Find the side length of the sheet of paper.

Standards Practice

GO for Help: MathXL — MG 3.3

A Practice by Example

Example 1 (page 292)

GO for Help

Homework Video Tutor
For: Examples 1–2
Visit: PHSchool.com
Web Code: axe-0802

Find the length of the line segment with the given endpoints.

1. 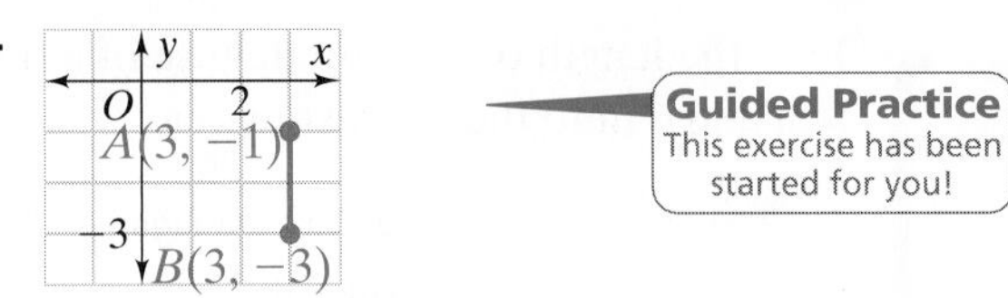

Guided Practice: This exercise has been started for you!

length of $\overline{AB} = -1 - (-3) = ■$ 2

2. 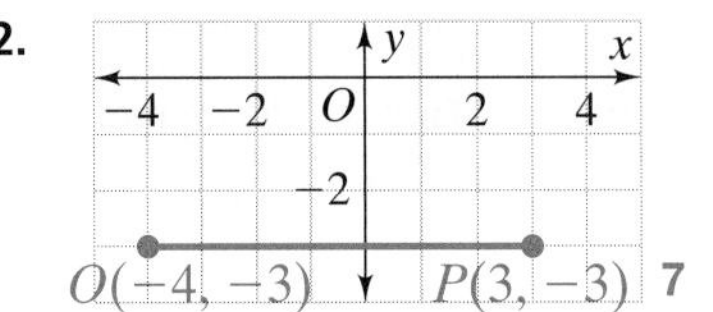
7

3. 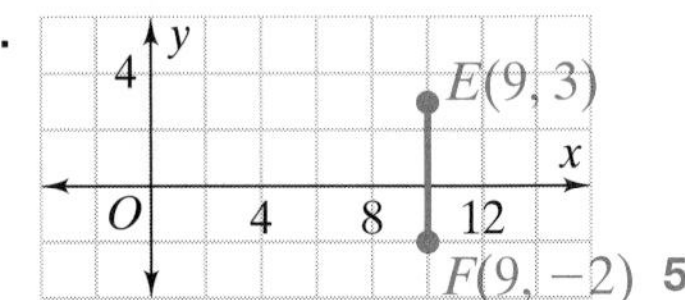
5

4. 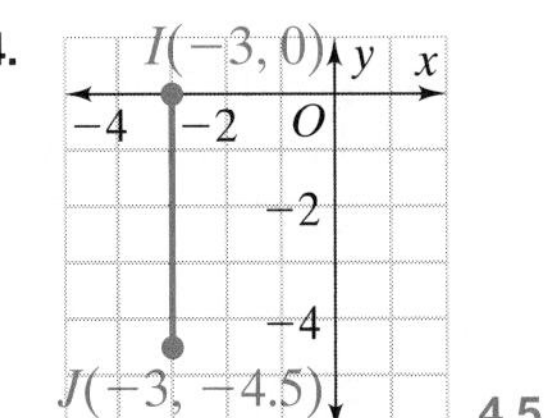
4.5

5. 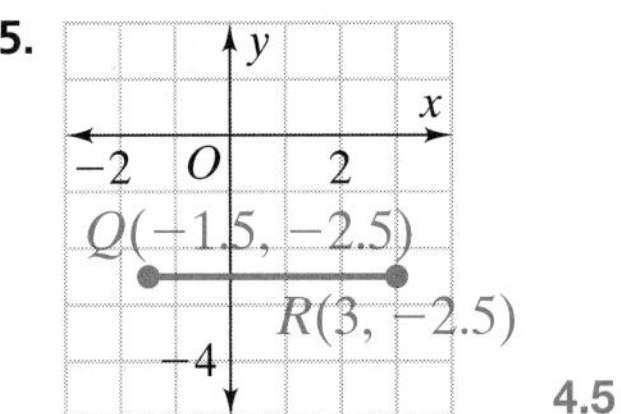
4.5

Example 2 (page 293)

Find the length of the line segment with the given endpoints.

6. $G(0, 3), H(4, 0)$

Guided Practice: This exercise has been started for you!

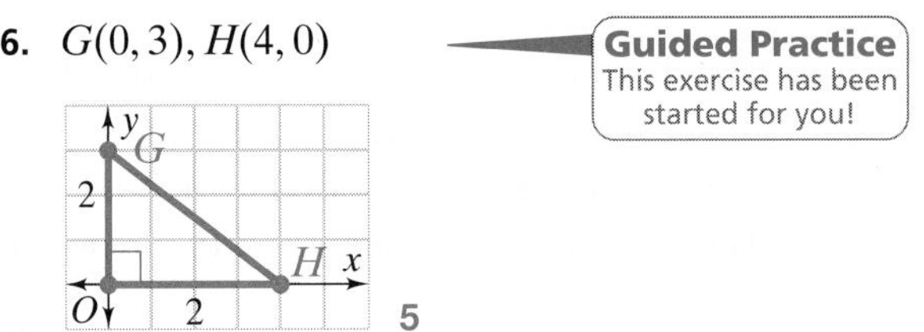
5

7. $A(0, 5),\ B(12, 0)$ 13
8. $U(-4,\ 0),\ V(0, -3)$ 5
9. $M(0, -7),\ N(-9, 0)$ about 11
10. $C(15, 0), D(0, 9)$ about 17
11. Your school is 3 mi south of your house. The grocery store is 5 mi east of your house. To the nearest mile, how far is your school from the grocery store? about 6 mi

B Apply Your Skills

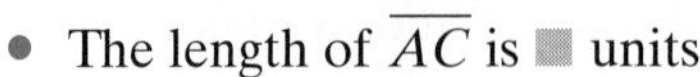

12. **Guided Problem Solving** Find the length of the hypotenuse of the triangle at the right to the nearest tenth. 7.1
    - The length of $\overline{AC}$ is ■ units.
    - The length of $\overline{BC}$ is ■ units.
    - Use the Pythagorean Theorem to find the length of $\overline{AB}$.

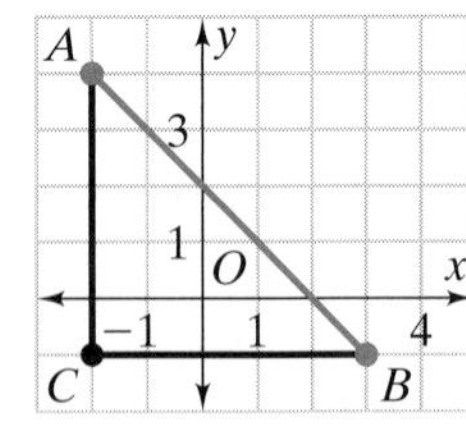

SCAFFOLDED **Problem Solving**

Use the graph at the right. 13–14. See margin.

13. Copy the coordinate plane. Draw a right triangle with hypotenuse $\overline{AB}$ and legs parallel to the x- and y-axes.

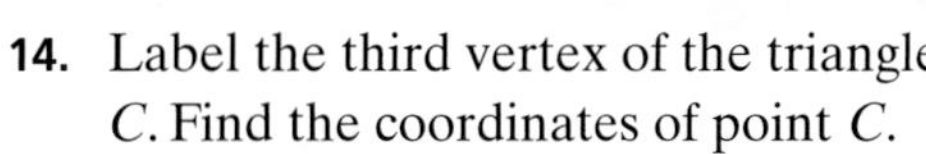

14. Label the third vertex of the triangle C. Find the coordinates of point C.

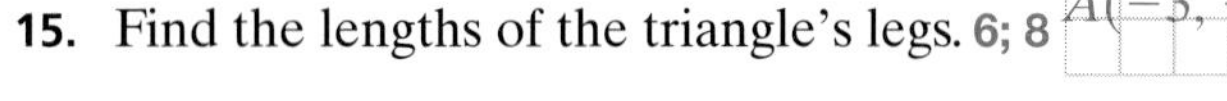

15. Find the lengths of the triangle's legs. 6; 8

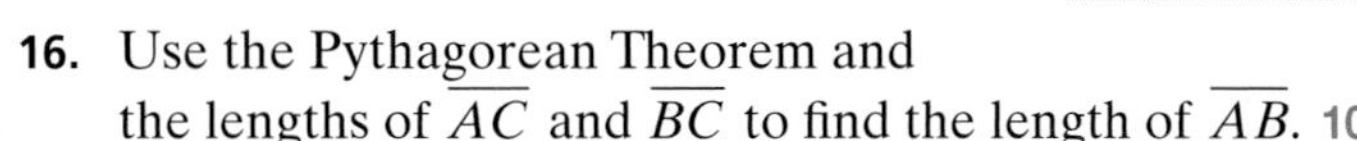

16. Use the Pythagorean Theorem and the lengths of $\overline{AC}$ and $\overline{BC}$ to find the length of $\overline{AB}$. 10

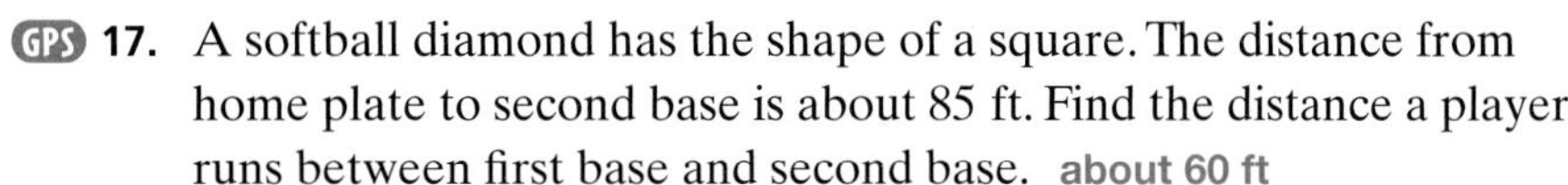

GPS **17.** A softball diamond has the shape of a square. The distance from home plate to second base is about 85 ft. Find the distance a player runs between first base and second base. about 60 ft

18. Writing in Math The graph at the right shows the temperature over time as a block of ice melts. Describe how you can find the amount of time the block of ice spent at a temperature of 32°F. See left.

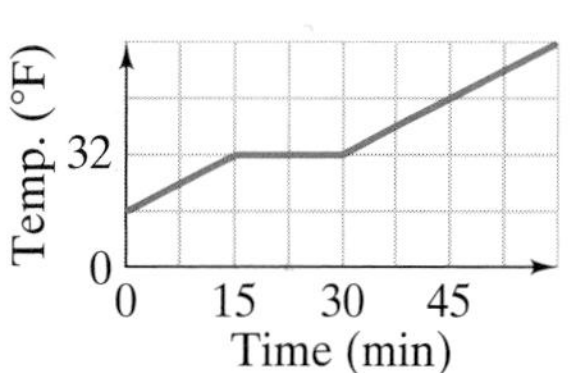

18. Find the length of the horizontal segment at 32°F by finding the difference between the time the ice reached 32°F and the time when the temperature first rose above 32°F: 30 min − 15 min = 15 min.

Challenge

19. Find the perimeter of a triangle with vertices $A(-3, -3)$, $B(5, 3)$, and $C(7, -6)$. about 29

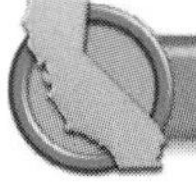

Multiple Choice Practice and Mixed Review

For California Standards Tutorials, visit PHSchool.com. Web Code: axq-9045

MG 3.3 **20.** Find the length of the hypotenuse of the triangle at the right. C

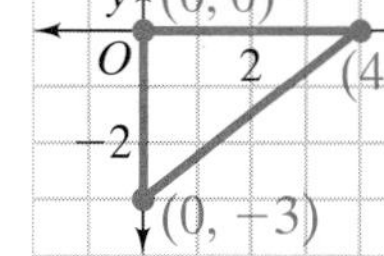

Ⓐ 3 Ⓒ 5
Ⓑ 4 Ⓓ 25

NS 1.5 **21.** Convert 0.78 to a fraction. B

Ⓐ $\frac{1}{78}$ Ⓑ $\frac{39}{50}$ Ⓒ $\frac{7}{8}$ Ⓓ $\frac{78}{1}$

AF 4.1 **22.** Alejandro wants to buy a digital audio player for \$124. His mother will pay $\frac{1}{3}$ of the cost. Alejandro has \$32.74. Use an equation to find how much more money he needs to make the purchase. B

Ⓐ \$8.59 Ⓒ \$60.84
Ⓑ \$49.93 Ⓓ \$74.07

Lesson 6-5 **Solve each proportion.**

23. $\frac{3}{8} = \frac{t}{24}$ 9

24. $\frac{k}{234} = \frac{4}{5}$ 187.2

25. $\frac{16}{25} = \frac{9.6}{n}$ 15

26. $\frac{10}{f} = \frac{3.4}{8.5}$ 25

Online Lesson Quiz Visit: PHSchool.com Web Code: axa-0802

4. Assess & Reteach

PRESENTATION CD-ROM
CD, Online, or Transparencies

Lesson Quiz

1. Graph the points $A(2, 1)$ and $B(-3, 1)$. Find the length of the line segment with endpoints A and B on the same coordinate plane. See graph below; 5.

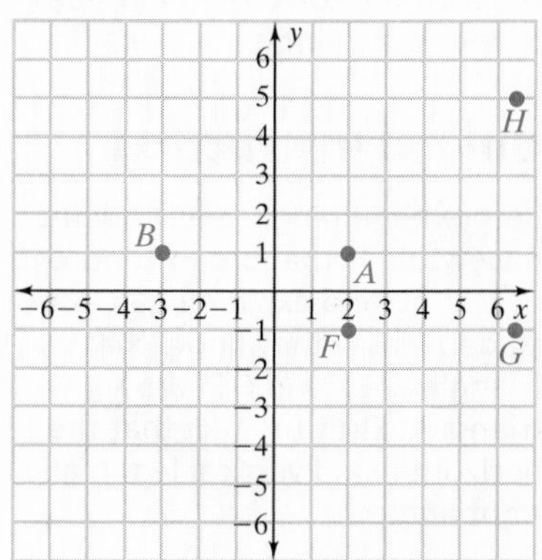

2. a. Graph the points $F(2, -1)$, $G(6.5, -1)$, and $H(6.5, 5)$ on the same coordinate plane. See graph above.

b. Find the length of the hypotenuse of $\triangle FGH$. 7.5 units

3. On a soccer field, one goalpost is 25 yards west of a second goalpost. The gymnasium is 20 yards north of the second goalpost. How far is the gymnasium from the first goalpost? 32 yards

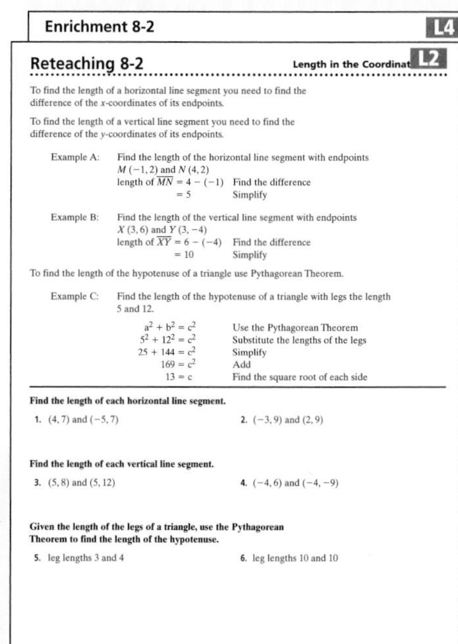

Enrichment 8-2 L4

Reteaching 8-2 Length in the Coordinate Plane L2

To find the length of a horizontal line segment you need to find the difference of the x-coordinates of its endpoints.

To find the length of a vertical line segment you need to find the difference of the y-coordinates of its endpoints.

Example A: Find the length of the horizontal line segment with endpoints $M(-1, 2)$ and $N(4, 2)$
length of $\overline{MN} = 4 - (-1)$ Find the difference
$= 5$ Simplify

Example B: Find the length of the vertical line segment with endpoints $X(3, 6)$ and $Y(3, -4)$
length of $\overline{XY} = 6 - (-4)$ Find the difference
$= 10$ Simplify

To find the length of the hypotenuse of a triangle use Pythagorean Theorem.

Example C: Find the length of the hypotenuse of a triangle with legs the length 5 and 12.
$a^2 + b^2 = c^2$ Use the Pythagorean Theorem
$5^2 + 12^2 = c^2$ Substitute the lengths of the legs
$25 + 144 = c^2$ Simplify
$169 = c^2$ Add
$13 = c$ Find the square root of each side

Find the length of each horizontal line segment.

1. (4, 7) and (−5, 7)
2. (−3, 9) and (2, 9)

Find the length of each vertical line segment.

3. (5, 8) and (5, 12)
4. (−4, 6) and (−4, −9)

Given the length of the legs of a triangle, use the Pythagorean Theorem to find the length of the hypotenuse.

5. leg lengths 3 and 4
6. leg lengths 10 and 10

Alternative Assessment

Each pair of students draws a right triangle with horizontal and vertical legs and with each of its endpoints in different quadrants. They list the coordinates of the endpoints. They then find the length of the hypotenuse.

California Resources

Standards Mastery

- Standards Review Transparencies
- Standards Review and Practice Workbook
- Math Companion

Math Intervention

- Skills Review and Practice Workbook
- Math XL

Activity Lab

Graphs of Right Triangles

Students use the Pythagorean Theorem to find the hypotenuse lengths of two triangles. They determine whether the two triangles are similar by finding ratios of the corresponding sides of the two triangles.

Guided Instruction

Before beginning, have students review the Pythagorean Theorem by stating and explaining it. Ask students how they know that triangles *ABC* and *DEF* are right triangles. Elicit the fact that the horizontal and vertical legs make right angles.

Checkpoint Quiz

Use this Checkpoint Quiz to check students' understanding of the skills and concepts of Lessons 8-1 through 8-2.

All in One Resources

- Checkpoint Quiz 1

8-2b Activity Lab

Graphs of Right Triangles

MG 3.3 Know and understand the Pythagorean theorem and use it to find the length of the missing side of a right triangle. ***Master***

MR 2.4 Test conjectures by using deductive reasoning. ***Introduce***

Use the right triangles $\triangle ABC$ and $\triangle DEF$ shown below.

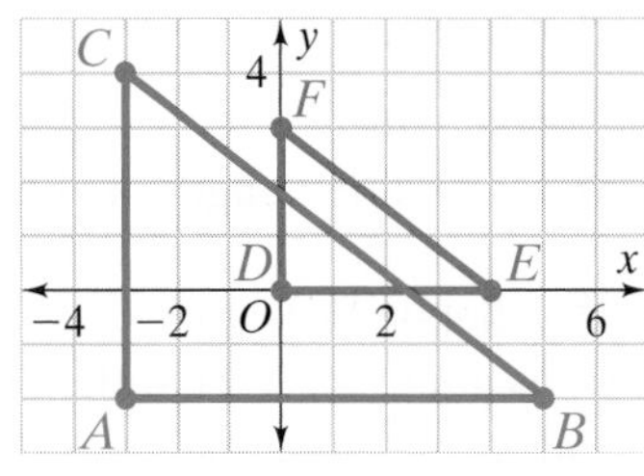

1. $A(-3, -2)$, $B(5, -2)$, $C(-3, 4)$, $D(0, 0)$, $E(4, 0)$, $F(0, 3)$

1. Identify the coordinates of each point. See above right.
2. Find the lengths of $\overline{AB}$, $\overline{AC}$, $\overline{DE}$, and $\overline{DF}$. 8; 6; 4; 3
3. Use the Pythagorean Theorem to find the lengths of $\overline{BC}$ and $\overline{EF}$. 10; 5
4. Find the ratios $\frac{\text{length of }\overline{AB}}{\text{length of }\overline{DE}}$, $\frac{\text{length of }\overline{AC}}{\text{length of }\overline{DF}}$, and $\frac{\text{length of }\overline{BC}}{\text{length of }\overline{EF}}$. $\frac{8}{4}$; $\frac{6}{3}$; $\frac{10}{5}$
5. **Reasoning** Two triangles are similar when the lengths of their corresponding sides are in proportion. Is $\triangle ABC$ similar to $\triangle DEF$? yes

Checkpoint Quiz 1

Lessons 8-1 through 8-2

Identify the coordinates of each point in the graph at the right.

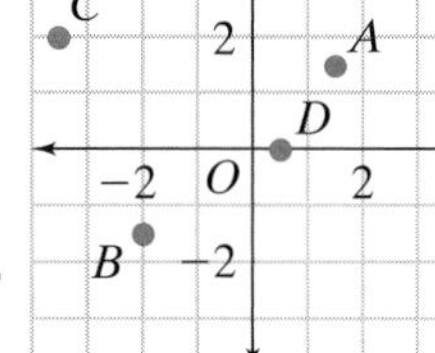

1. A (1.5, 1.5)
2. B (−2, −1.5)
3. C (−3.5, 2)
4. D (0.5, 0)

Graph each point on the same coordinate grid. 5–8. See margin.

5. $E(6, 1)$
6. $F(4, -3)$
7. $G(0, 2)$
8. $H(-5, -3.5)$

Find the length of the line segment with the given endpoints.

9. $I(-4, 2)$, $J(3, 2)$ 7
10. $M(-8, 3.5)$, $N(-8, -4)$ 7.5
11. $Q(0, 4)$, $R(3, 0)$ 5

8-3a Activity Lab

Tables and Equations

AF 1.1 Use variables and appropriate operations to write an equation. ***Develop***
MR 1.1 Analyze problems by identifying relationships and observing patterns. ***Develop***

Words, data tables, and equations are three different ways to express the same information. You can use one representation to generate another representation.

ACTIVITY

For Exercises 1 and 2, copy and complete each table. Then describe the pattern and write an equation to represent the situation.

1. The table below shows how the earnings of a lifeguard change with the number of hours she works. 180; 360; earnings increase \$60 for every four hours worked; $e = 15h$.

Hours	0	4	8	12	24
Earnings (\$)	0	60	120	■	■

2. The table below shows how the total cost of food for a cookout changes with the number of guests. 90; 225; 900; the cost increases \$22.50 for every three guests; $c = 7.5g$.

Guests	6	9	12	30	120
Cost (\$)	45	67.5	■	■	■

3. The students in the skateboarding club at Orchard Middle School had a concert that raised money to build a new skate park. The club began with 180 tickets to sell. Every day, they sold 9 tickets.
   a. Copy and complete the table below.

Number of Days	0	1	2	3	■
Tickets Remaining	■	■	■	■	0

Number of Days	0	1	2	3	20
Tickets Remaining	180	171	162	153	0

   b. Use the data in the table to write an equation relating the number of days the club has been selling tickets to the number of tickets remaining. Let x be the number of days and y be the number of tickets. $y = 180 - 9x$
   c. Use the data in the table to make a graph showing how the number of tickets remaining changes with the number of days the club has been selling tickets. Use the x-axis for the number of days and the y-axis for the number of tickets.
   See margin.

Activity Lab

Tables and Equations

In this activity, students practice showing the same information using words, tables, and equations. The final exercise challenges students to represent the data in Exercise 3 on a graph.

Guided Instruction

Exercise 1
Ask:
- *Does the table give the amount a lifeguard earns in 1 hour (the unit rate)?* no
- *Will you need this information?* You can use the unit rate of \$15 per hour or the rate of \$60 for every 4 hours to complete the table.

Exercise 3c
Remind students that the graph intervals on the x- and y-axes must be equal.

8-3

1. Plan

California Content Standards

Understand that an equation such as $y = 3x + 5$ is a prescription for determining a second number when a first number is given. *Foundational*

AF 1.1 Use variables and appropriate operations to write an equation. *Develop*

California Math Background

A **function** is a relationship between two or more quantities. The value of the function (output) depends on the value of the input. Functions can be represented numerically (as in an input/output table), graphically, symbolically (as in an equation, also called a **function rule**), or verbally (as in a problem that describes a situation).

More Math Background: p. 286C

Lesson Planning and Resources

See p. 286E for a list of the resources that support this lesson.

PRESENTATION CD-ROM
CD, Online, or Transparencies

Bell Ringer Practice

Check Skills You'll Need
Use student page, transparency, or PowerPoint.
See Math Companion.

California Standards Review
Use transparency or PowerPoint.

8-3 Functions

Check Skills You'll Need

Do this in your **Math Companion.**

Vocabulary
- function
- function rule

Use your **Math Companion** *to build your vocabulary.*

California Content Standards

Foundational Standard Understand that an equation such as $y = 3x + 5$ is a prescription for determining a second number when a first number is given.
AF 1.1 Use variables and appropriate operations to write an equation. *Develop*

What You'll Learn . . . and Why

You will learn to evaluate and write function rules. You can use a function to describe how one value depends on another, such as how the total refund you receive depends on the number of drink containers you return.

A **function** is a relationship that assigns exactly one output value to each input value. A **function rule** is an equation that describes a function. The function rule below shows the relationship between the number of containers c you return and the total refund r you receive.

EXAMPLE Evaluating a Function Rule

1 Complete the table of input-output pairs for the function rule $r = 0.04c$. Here r represents the refund in dollars and c represents the number of containers you return with a four-cent refund.

Input c (number of containers)	Output r (dollars)	
6	■	← $0.04 \cdot 6 = 0.24$
12	■	← $0.04 \cdot 12 = 0.48$
24	■	← $0.04 \cdot 24 = 0.96$

CA Standards Check 1 *Go to your* **Math Companion** *for help.*

1. In another state, the refund value of a drink container is \$.10. Use the function rule $r = 0.1c$. Make a table of input-output pairs to show the total refunds for 5, 10, and 15 containers. See left.

1.

c	r
5	\$.50
10	\$1.00
15	\$1.50

Universal Access Solutions for All Learners

Special Needs L1	Below Level L2
Students visualize examples through drawings of the example and by writing the accompanying function. Students draw the fish in Example 2 and place dollar values under each group.	Students draw and label familiar relationships that can be expressed as functions. For example, the perimeter of a square depends on the length of its sides.

Vocabulary Tip

You can use any letter to name a function, just as you can use any letter as a variable. For example, $T(c)$ is a function of the variable c. You read $T(c)$ as "T of c."

Function notation is a shorter way of writing verbal descriptions. In function notation you use an expression such as $f(x)$, where x is the input variable, for the output variable, instead of using y.

output → $T(c) = 0.04c$ ← input

To evaluate a function rule, substitute the input value for the variable inside the parentheses. Then simplify. Notice that $T(2)$ does *not* mean the product of T and 2. It means the output of the function when the input is 2.

EXAMPLE Using Function Notation

Relate MATH YOU KNOW...

Suppose you go to the store and buy several fish at \$2.35 each. Write an equation to represent the total cost for buying n fish.

Words total cost = \$2.35 times number of fish

Let n = the number of fish.

Let c = the total cost.

...*to* ALGEBRA

Equation $c = \$2.35 \cdot n$

2. Suppose you go to the store and buy several fish at \$2.35 each. Use function notation to show the relationship between the total cost and the number of fish you buy. Then find the cost of three fish.

Words total cost = \$2.35 times number of fish

Let n = the number of fish.

Let $f(n)$ = the total cost.

Function $f(n) = \$2.35 \cdot n$

$f(n) = 2.35n$ ← **Write the function rule.**

$f(3) = 2.35 \cdot 3$ ← **Substitute the number of fish for n.**

$= 7.05$ ← **Multiply.**

The function rule $f(n) = 2.35n$ shows the relationship between the total cost and the number of fish. The total cost of three fish is \$7.05.

CA Standards Check 2 *Go to your* **Math Companion** *for help.*

2. You start with \$15. You earn more money baby-sitting. Use function notation to show the relationship between the total amount of money you have and the amount of money you earn baby-sitting. Then find the total amount of money you have after earning \$26 baby-sitting. See left.

2. Let b = the amount of money you earn babysitting. Let $f(b)$ = the total amount of money you have. $f(b) = 15 + b$; \$41.00

Check Your Understanding *Homework prep is in your* **Math Companion.**

2. Teach

Guided Instruction

Error Prevention!

Students often mistake function notation ($f(x)$) for multiplication (f times x). Help students remember its meaning by reading: "f of x" or "f as a function of x" or "the value of the function f."

Additional Examples

1. Complete the table for $p = 4s$.

Input s	3	5	7	9
Output p	12	20	28	36

2. Use function notation to show the relationship between the total number of tires and the number of cars. Then find the number of cars for 20 tires. $f(t) = \frac{t}{4}$; 5 cars

Closure

- *What is a function?* a relationship that assigns exactly one output value to each input value
- *How can you use function notation to write a function rule?* Write an equation in the form $y =$ but use $f(x)$ for y, the output, and x for the input.

Universal Access Solutions for All Learners

Advanced Learners L4
Students use function notation to write expressions for the perimeter of a regular triangle, a pentagon, and an octagon. $f(s) = 3s$; $5s$; $8s$

English Learners EL
In previous lessons, students read $f(n)$ as "the product of f and n" or "f times the number n." Here they need to read it as a function, "the value of the function f at the input n."

3. Practice

Assignment Guide

Check Your Understanding
See Math Companion.

Homework Exercises

A Practice by Example	1–16
B Apply Your Skills	17–23
C Challenge	24
California Multiple-Choice Practice	25–27
Mixed Review	28–30

Homework Quick Check
To check students' understanding of key skills and concepts, go over Exercises 1, 7, 15, 20, 22.

Universal Access Resources

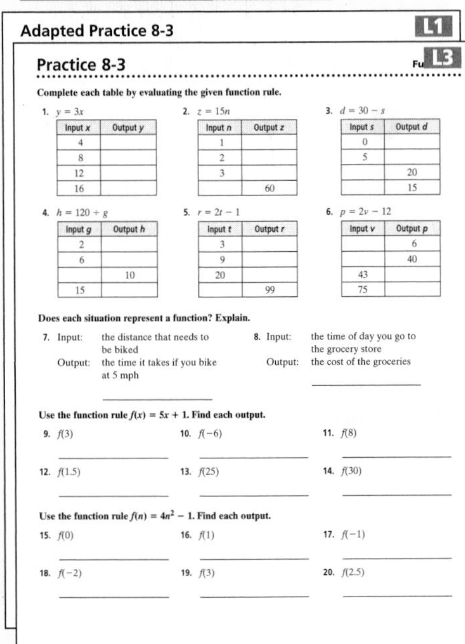

Adapted Practice 8-3 L1

Practice 8-3 L3

Complete each table by evaluating the given function rule.

1. $y = 3x$

Input x	Output y
4	
8	
12	
16	

2. $z = 15n$

Input n	Output z
1	
2	
3	
	60

3. $d = 30 - s$

Input s	Output d
0	
5	
	20
	15

4. $h = 120 \div g$

Input g	Output h
2	
6	
	10
15	

5. $r = 2t - 1$

Input t	Output r
3	
9	
20	
	99

6. $p = 2v - 12$

Input v	Output p
	6
	40
43	
75	

Does each situation represent a function? Explain.

7. Input: the distance that needs to be biked
Output: the time it takes if you bike at 5 mph

8. Input: the time of day you go to the grocery store
Output: the cost of the groceries

Use the function rule $f(x) = 5x + 1$. Find each output.

9. $f(3)$ 10. $f(-6)$ 11. $f(8)$

12. $f(1.5)$ 13. $f(25)$ 14. $f(30)$

Use the function rule $f(n) = 4n^2 - 1$. Find each output.

15. $f(0)$ 16. $f(1)$ 17. $f(-1)$

18. $f(-2)$ 19. $f(3)$ 20. $f(2.5)$

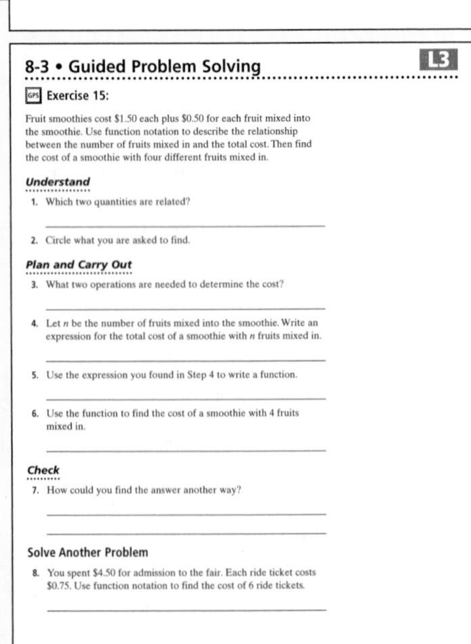

8-3 • Guided Problem Solving L3

GPS Exercise 15:

Fruit smoothies cost \$1.50 each plus \$0.50 for each fruit mixed into the smoothie. Use function notation to describe the relationship between the number of fruits mixed in and the total cost. Then find the cost of a smoothie with four different fruits mixed in.

Understand

1. Which two quantities are related?
2. Circle what you are asked to find.

Plan and Carry Out

3. What two operations are needed to determine the cost?
4. Let n be the number of fruits mixed into the smoothie. Write an expression for the total cost of a smoothie with n fruits mixed in.
5. Use the expression you found in Step 4 to write a function.
6. Use the function to find the cost of a smoothie with 4 fruits mixed in.

Check

7. How could you find the answer another way?

Solve Another Problem

8. You spent \$4.50 for admission to the fair. Each ride ticket costs \$0.75. Use function notation to find the cost of 6 ride tickets.

Standards Practice AF 1.1

A Practice by Example

Example 1 (page 298)

for Help

For: Examples 1–2
Visit: PHSchool.com
Web Code: axe-0803

Complete each table by evaluating the given function rule.

1. $h = s + 4$

s	−5	8	12	31
h	■	■	■	■

−1 12 16 35

2. $y = 7x$

x	−2	0	3	11
y	■	■	■	■

−14 0 21 77

3. $p = 0.25m$

m	−8	−6	2	4
p	■	■	■	■

−2 −1.5 0.5 1

4. $b = 4a - 3$

a	−3	−1	5	12
b	■	■	■	■

−15 −7 17 45

5. Copy and complete the table of input-output pairs for the function rule $t = \frac{n}{11}$. The variable t represents the number of teams in a hockey league. The variable n represents the number of people signed up for the league.

Input n (number of people)	Output t (number of teams)	
44	■	4
132	■	12
165	■	15

Example 2 (page 299)

Use the function rule $f(x) = 2x + 3$. Find each output.

6. $f(0)$
$f(0) = 2 \cdot 0 + 3$
$= ■$ 3

7. $f(-2)$ −1
8. $f(2)$ 7
9. $f(10)$ 23
10. $f(-3.5)$ −4
11. $f(-12)$ −21
12. $f(26)$ 55
13. $f(13.25)$ 29.5
14. $f(-16.7)$ −30.4

GPS 15. Fruit smoothies cost \$1.50 each plus \$.50 for each fruit mixed into the smoothie. Use function notation to describe the relationship between the number of fruits mixed in and the total cost. Then find the cost of a smoothie with 4 different fruits mixed in. \$3.50

16. A library charges a fine of \$.25 for each day a book is overdue. Use function notation to describe the relationship between the total fine and the number of days a book is overdue. Then find the total fine for a book that is 6 days overdue. \$1.50

B Apply Your Skills

17. **Guided Problem Solving** Paintbrushes cost \$1.79 each. Use function notation to show the total cost as a function of the number of paintbrushes you buy. Use the rule to find the cost of 5, 16, and 27 brushes. \$8.95; \$28.64; \$48.33
   - Let p represent the number of paintbrushes and $f(p)$ represent the total cost.
   - Evaluate the function rule for $p = 5$, 16, and 27.

SCAFFOLDED
Problem Solving

18. 240; the gallons of water used to wash 6 loads of laundry
19. Let n = the number of loads of laundry. Let $f(n)$ = the number of gallons of water. $f(n) = 40n$
20. The number of loads n is the domain because it is the input.

Use the function $w = 40n$, where w is the number of gallons of water used by a washing machine and n is the number of loads of laundry.

18. Find the value of w when $n = 6$. What does this represent? See left.
19. Rewrite the function $w = 40n$ using function notation. Identify the variables you use. See left.
20. **Writing in Math** The *domain* of a function is all possible input values. The *range* of a function is all possible output values. Which variable in your function represents the domain? Explain. See left.
21. The input variable is also called the *independent variable*. The output variable is the *dependent variable*, because it depends on the input variable. Which is the dependent variable in your function? $f(n)$

Copy and complete each table. Then write a rule for the function.

22.

Input	Output	
3	5	
4	6	
5	7	
6	■	8
7	■	9

$f(n) = n + 2$

23.

Input	Output	
10	2	
15	3	
20	4	
25	■	5
30	■	6

$f(n) = \frac{n}{5}$

C Challenge

24. You start a cookie business. You know that the oven and materials will cost \$600. You decide to charge \$.75 for each cookie. The function $p = 0.75c - 600$ relates profit p to c, the number of cookies that you sell. How many cookies do you have to sell to break even? 800 cookies

Multiple Choice Practice and Mixed Review

For California Standards Tutorials, visit PHSchool.com. Web Code: axq-9045

AF 1.1

25. You buy shirts for \$9 each. You have a coupon for \$2 off your total purchase. Which function models this situation? D
    - (A) $f(s) = 9$
    - (B) $f(s) = 2s + 9$
    - (C) $f(s) = 9 + s$
    - (D) $f(s) = 9s - 2$

AF 4.2

26. Tim drives his car 140 mi in 4 h. If he continues to travel at the same rate, how far will Tim drive in 7 h? C
    - (A) 35 mi
    - (B) 140 mi
    - (C) 245 mi
    - (D) 1,680 mi

AF 4.1

27. Audrey bought a box of cereal and some bananas for \$4.69. If the cereal cost \$3.99 and the bananas were on sale for \$.28 per pound, how many pounds of bananas did Audrey buy? C
    - (A) 0.42 lb
    - (B) 2.2 lb
    - (C) 2.5 lb
    - (D) 4.2 lb

for Help Lesson 7-2

Find each percent.

28. 25% of 84 21
29. 45% of 19 8.55
30. 72% of 143 102.96

Online Lesson Quiz Visit: PHSchool.com Web Code: axa-0803

Alternative Assessment

Each student in a pair makes a table of values for a function. Partners exchange tables and use function notation to write their partner's function rule.

California Resources

Standards Mastery
- Standards Review Transparencies
- Standards Review and Practice Workbook
- Math Companion

Math Intervention
- Skills Review and Practice Workbook
- Math XL

4. Assess & Reteach

PRESENTATION CD-ROM
CD, Online, or Transparencies
Lesson Quiz

1. A photocopy costs \$.08. Use the function rule $c = \$0.08n$. Make a table of input/output pairs to show the cost for 5, 10, and 15 copies.

Input n	5	10	15
Output c	\$.40	\$.80	\$1.20

Evaluate items 2 and 3 for the function rule $f(x) = 40 - 2x$.

2. $f(12)$ 16
3. $f(-12)$ 64
4. Suppose peaches cost \$.99 per pound. Write a function rule to describe the relationship between the total cost and the number of pounds of peaches you buy. Sample: $C(p) = 0.99p$

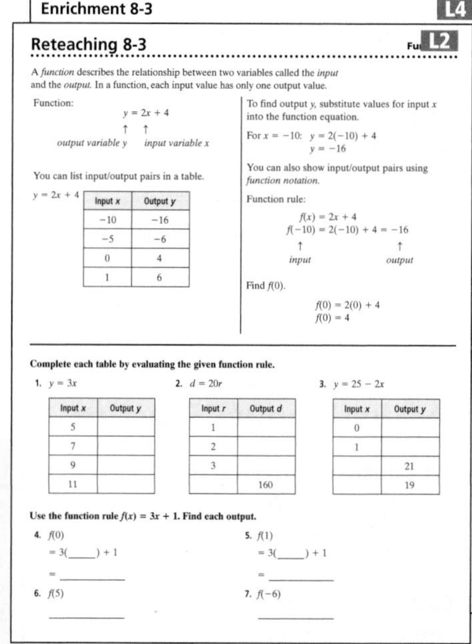
Enrichment 8-3 L4

Reteaching 8-3 Fu L2

A *function* describes the relationship between two variables called the *input* and the *output*. In a function, each input value has only one output value.

Function:

$y = 2x + 4$

output variable y ↑ ↑ input variable x

You can list input/output pairs in a table.

$y = 2x + 4$

Input x	Output y
−10	−16
−5	−6
0	4
1	6

To find output y, substitute values for input x into the function equation.

For $x = -10$: $y = 2(-10) + 4$
$y = -16$

You can also show input/output pairs using *function notation*.

Function rule:

$f(x) = 2x + 4$
$f(-10) = 2(-10) + 4 = -16$
↑ input ↑ output

Find $f(0)$.

$f(0) = 2(0) + 4$
$f(0) = 4$

Complete each table by evaluating the given function rule.

1. $y = 3x$

Input x	Output y
5	
7	
9	
11	

2. $d = 20r$

Input r	Output d
1	
2	
3	
	160

3. $y = 25 - 2x$

Input x	Output y
0	
1	
	21
	19

Use the function rule $f(x) = 3x + 1$. Find each output.

4. $f(0)$
   $= 3(\_\_\_\_) + 1$
   $= \_\_\_\_$
5. $f(1)$
   $= 3(\_\_\_\_) + 1$
   $= \_\_\_\_$
6. $f(5)$
   ____
7. $f(-6)$
   ____

8-4

1. Plan

California Content Standards

Draw points corresponding to linear relationships on graph paper. *Foundational*

AF 3.3 Graph linear functions. *Introduce*

AF 3.4 Plot the values of quantities whose ratios are always the same. Fit a line to the plot. *Introduce*

California Math Background

A table can be used to show input and output values for a particular function. The input and output values in a table can be graphed as ordered pairs on a coordinate grid. The input is graphed on the horizontal axis and the output on the vertical axis. If the graphed points lie along a line, the function is called a *linear function*. Functions can also be expressed using algebraic equations. Thus, functions can be expressed in tables, graphs, word rules, and algebraic rules.

More Math Background: p. 286C

Lesson Planning and Resources

See p. 286E for a list of the resources that support this lesson.

PRESENTATION CD-ROM
CD, Online, or Transparencies

Bell Ringer Practice

Check Skills You'll Need
Use student page, transparency, or PowerPoint.
See Math Companion.

California Standards Review
Use transparency or PowerPoint.

8-4 Graphing Linear Functions

Check Skills You'll Need

Do this in your **Math Companion.**

Vocabulary

- solution
- linear equation
- linear function

Use your **Math Companion** *to build your vocabulary.*

California Content Standards

Foundational Standard Draw points corresponding to linear relationships on graph paper.

AF 3.3 Graph linear functions. ***Introduce***

AF 3.4 Plot the values of quantities whose ratios are always the same. Fit a line to the plot. ***Introduce***

What You'll Learn . . . and Why

You will learn to graph linear functions. You can use a graph to represent a function, such as the relationship between the amount of cat food left in a feeder and the number of days that have passed since you filled the cat feeder.

You can use a table of values to make a graph. Use the horizontal axis for the input values and the vertical axis for the output values.

EXAMPLE Making a Graph From a Table

1 Suppose you save \$3 each week. Use the table at the right to make a graph of the relationship between number of weeks x and total savings in dollars y.

Number of Weeks, x	0	1	2
Total Savings in dollars, y	0	3	6

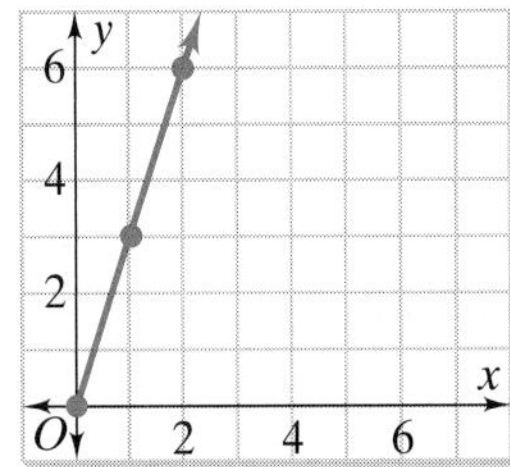

← **First plot the points. Use the horizontal axis for the number of weeks. Use the vertical axis for the total savings.**

← **Then connect the points with a line.**

CA Standards Check 1 *Go to your* **Math Companion** *for help.*

1. Use the table at the right. Make a graph of the relationship between hours worked x and dollars earned y.
See margin.

Hours Worked, x	1	2	3
Dollars Earned, y	7	14	21

Universal Access Solutions for All Learners

Special Needs L1
Pair students who might have difficulty graphing functions with students who can draw. One partner can make the table, while the other student graphs the values.

Below Level L2
Demonstrate that the graph of $y = -\frac{3}{4}x + 5$ remains a line, although a different line, if the 5 is changed to some other value.

Any ordered pair that makes an equation true is a **solution** of the equation. For example, (2, 6) is a solution of $y = 3x$ because $6 = 3 \cdot 2$. An equation or function rule with two variables may have many solutions.

You can show the solutions of an equation or function rule with a graph. An equation with solutions that lie on a line is called a **linear equation.** A function rule with solutions that lie on a line is called a **linear function.**

Relate MATH YOU KNOW...

EXAMPLE Graphing a Linear Function

Graph the point (16, 4) on a coordinate grid.

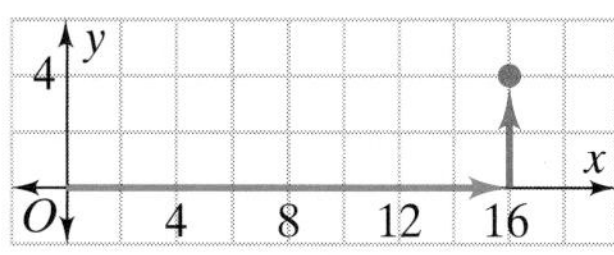

← Start at the origin. Move 16 units to the right. Then move 4 units up.

... to ALGEBRA

2 **Guided Problem Solving** Jerrod keeps track of how much dry food is in his cat's feeder. Graph the linear function $y = -\frac{1}{2}x + 12$, where y represents the cups of food left in the feeder and x represents the number of days since he filled the 12-c feeder.

Step 1 Make a table.

x	$y = -\frac{1}{2}x + 12$	(x, y)
0	$-\frac{1}{2}(0) + 12 = 12$	(0, 12)
4	$-\frac{1}{2}(4) + 12 = 10$	(4, 10)
9	$-\frac{1}{2}(9) + 12 = 7\frac{1}{2}$	$(9, 7\frac{1}{2})$
16	$-\frac{1}{2}(16) + 12 = 4$	(16, 4)

Substitute several values of x into the equation and find the corresponding y values.

Then write the solutions to the equation as ordered pairs (x, y).

Step 2 Graph the ordered pairs and draw a line through the points.

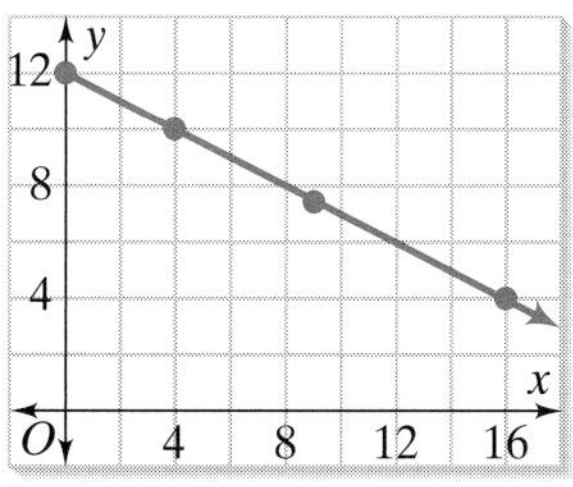

Online active math

For: Graphing Functions Activity
Use: Interactive Textbook, 8-4

CA Standards Check 2 *Go to your* **Math Companion** *for help.*

2. Graph the linear function $y = 5x + 50$, where y represents the temperature of a chemical solution in degrees Fahrenheit after x minutes. See margin.

2. Teach

Guided Instruction

Example 1

Ask:

- *How do the x-values change as you move down the table?* increase by 1
- *How do the y-values change?* increase by 3
- *If this pattern continues, what would be the next ordered pair in the table?* (3, 9)

Example 2

Help students understand that y depends on the value of x. Elicit the fact that students substitute values for x (input) to find the corresponding y-values (output).

Error Prevention!

In a real-world situation, students need to consider not only coordinates that are solutions to the equation, but values that are reasonable for the situation. Ask: *Why would you **not** choose negative values for x in Example 2?* There cannot be a negative number of days.

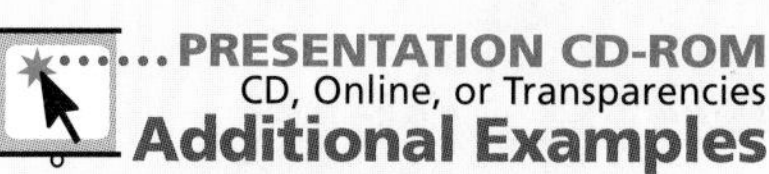

PRESENTATION CD-ROM
CD, Online, or Transparencies

Additional Examples

1 Suppose you buy a bag of food for your pet dog every week. Use the table below to make a graph of the cost of the dog food.

Number of Weeks	1	2	3	4	w
Cost of Dog Food	4	8	12	16	c

Advanced Learners L4

The input integers for a function rule are 0, 4, and 8. The outputs are 2, 10, and 18. Write an equation for the function rule. $y = 2x + 2$

English Learners EL

Students may be comfortable mentally calculating the answer for the *Choose a Method* example because the numbers are small integers. Stress that the tables and graphs also allow them to make predictions, whether the numbers are easy or hard to mentally calculate.

Additional Examples

2 Graph the linear equation $y = -x + 3$, where y represents the pressure inside a deflating balloon after x seconds.

Seconds	0	1	2	3
Pressure	3	2	1	0

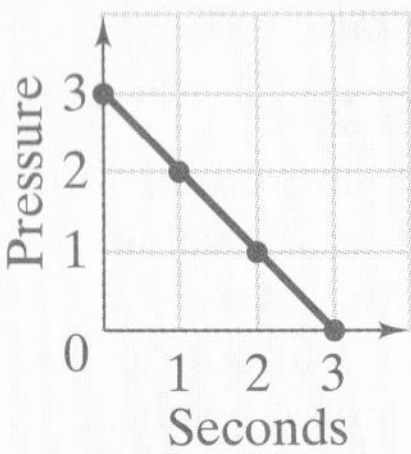

Closure

- *How do you graph a linear equation in two variables?* **Sample: Make a table of values by choosing several x-values, substituting them into the equation, and simplifying. Graph the resulting ordered pairs and connect them in a straight line.**

More Than One Way

A plant is 4 cm tall and grows 2 cm per day. Predict how tall the plant will be after 8 days.

Jasmine's Method

I can make a table of data.

Height of Plant

Days Passed	0	1	2	3	4	5	6	7	8
Height (cm)	4	6	8	10	12	14	16	18	20

After 8 days, the plant will be 20 cm tall.

Kevin's Method

I can make a graph. Let x represent the number of days that have passed. Let y represent the height of the plant.

I can make a table of solutions.

Height of Plant

Days Passed, x	1	2	3
Height, y	6	8	10

Three points on the graph are (1, 6), (2, 8), and (3, 10).

I can plot the points and draw a line through them. Then I can use the graph to find the height y when $x = 8$.

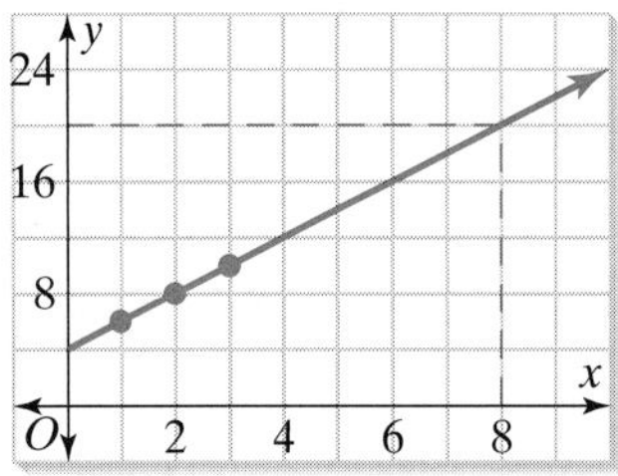

After 8 days, the plant will be 20 cm tall.

Choose a Method

You eat 10 servings of cereal from a 20-oz box. If each serving of cereal is 1 oz, how much cereal is left? Describe your method and explain why you chose it. **10 oz; check students' work.**

Check Your Understanding *Homework prep is in your* **Math Companion.**

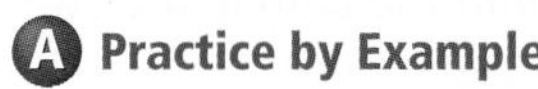

Standards Practice

GO for Help: MathXL

AF 3.3, AF 3.4

3. Practice

A Practice by Example

Example 1 (page 302)

1–13. See back of book.

Graph the values in each table. Then connect the points with a line.

1.

Input	2	4	5	10
Output	1	2	2.5	5

Guided Practice: This exercise has been started for you!

Plot the points (2, 1), (4, 2), (5, 2.5), and (10, 5) on a coordinate plane.

GO for Help

2.

Input	−1	0	2	5
Output	4	5	7	10

3.

Input	−3	0	1	4
Output	3	0	−1	−4

Homework Video Tutor

For: Examples 1–3
Visit: PHSchool.com
Web Code: axe-0803

4. Use the table at the right. Make a graph of the relationship between the number of pizzas x delivered and the delivery earnings y.

Number of Pizzas	5	10	15
Earnings (dollars)	15	25	35

Example 2 (page 303)

Graph each linear function.

5. $y = x + 2$
When $x = 0$, $y = 0 + 2 = 2$.
When $x = 1$, $y = 1 + 2 = \blacksquare$.

Guided Practice: This exercise has been started for you!

6. $y = x - 2$
7. $y = 2x$
8. $y = 4x - 5$
9. $y = 1.5x + 0.5$
10. $y = -3x$
11. $y = -\frac{3}{4}x + 3$

12. For a certain repair, an auto shop charges a \$20 fee for materials plus \$40 per hour for labor. Graph the linear function $y = 40x + 20$, where y represents the total cost and x represents the hours of labor.

B Apply Your Skills

13. **Guided Problem Solving** A woman makes necklaces and sells them at a jewelry show. She pays \$10.00 to rent a table at the show and makes \$20.25 for each necklace she sells. Write a function for the money she earns and graph the function.
   - What is the input variable? What is the output variable?
   - Write a function and use it to find ordered pairs.

GPS 14. The height of a burning candle depends on how long the candle has been burning. For one type of candle, the function $h = 8 - \frac{1}{2}t$ gives the candle's height h (in centimeters) as a function of the time t the candle has burned (in hours).
   a. Graph the function. See left.
   b. What was the original height of the candle? 8 cm
   c. What is the greatest amount of time the candle can burn? 16 h

14a.

Assignment Guide

Check Your Understanding

See Math Companion.

Homework Exercises

A	Practice by Example	1–12
B	Apply Your Skills	13–21
C	Challenge	22
California Multiple-Choice Practice		23–25
Mixed Review		26–29

Homework Quick Check

To check students' understanding of key skills and concepts, go over Exercises 2, 7, 14, 21.

Universal Access Resources

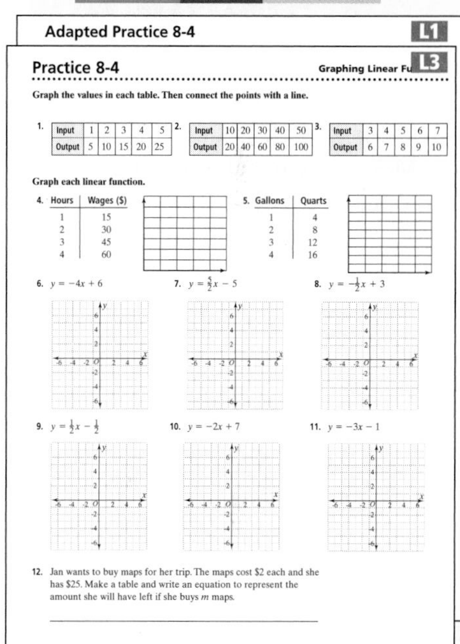

Adapted Practice 8-4 L1

Practice 8-4 Graphing Linear Fu L3

Graph the values in each table. Then connect the points with a line.

1.

Input	1	2	3	4	5
Output	5	10	15	20	25

2.

Input	10	20	30	40	50
Output	20	40	60	80	100

3.

Input	3	4	5	6	7
Output	6	7	8	9	10

Graph each linear function.

4.

Hours	Wages (\$)
1	15
2	30
3	45
4	60

5.

Gallons	Quarts
1	4
2	8
3	12
4	16

6. $y = -4x + 6$
7. $y = \frac{5}{2}x - 5$
8. $y = -\frac{1}{2}x + 3$
9. $y = \frac{1}{2}x - \frac{1}{2}$
10. $y = -2x + 7$
11. $y = -3x - 1$

12. Jan wants to buy maps for her trip. The maps cost \$2 each and she has \$25. Make a table and write an equation to represent the amount she will have left if she buys m maps.

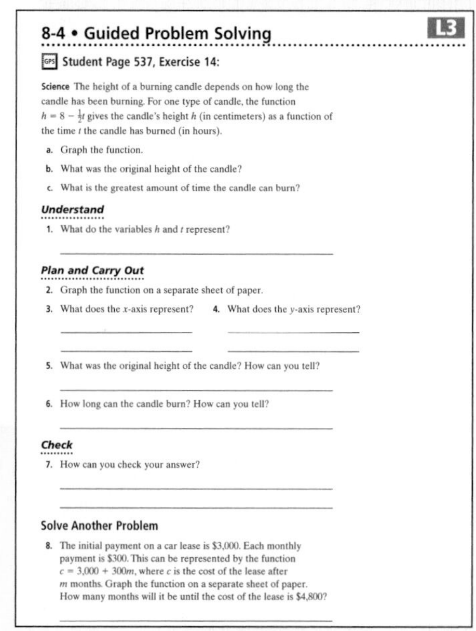

8-4 • Guided Problem Solving L3

GPS Student Page 537, Exercise 14:

Science The height of a burning candle depends on how long the candle has been burning. For one type of candle, the function $h = 8 - \frac{1}{2}t$ gives the candle's height h (in centimeters) as a function of the time t the candle has burned (in hours).

a. Graph the function.
b. What was the original height of the candle?
c. What is the greatest amount of time the candle can burn?

Understand

1. What do the variables h and t represent?

Plan and Carry Out

2. Graph the function on a separate sheet of paper.
3. What does the x-axis represent?
4. What does the y-axis represent?
5. What was the original height of the candle? How can you tell?
6. How long can the candle burn? How can you tell?

Check

7. How can you check your answer?

Solve Another Problem

8. The initial payment on a car lease is \$3,000. Each monthly payment is \$300. This can be represented by the function $c = 3{,}000 + 300m$, where c is the cost of the lease after m months. Graph the function on a separate sheet of paper. How many months will it be until the cost of the lease is \$4,800?

4. Assess & Reteach

PRESENTATION CD-ROM
CD, Online, or Transparencies

Lesson Quiz

1. Complete the table and graph the function.
   Output = Input · (–4)

Input	–3	0	6
Output	12	0	–24

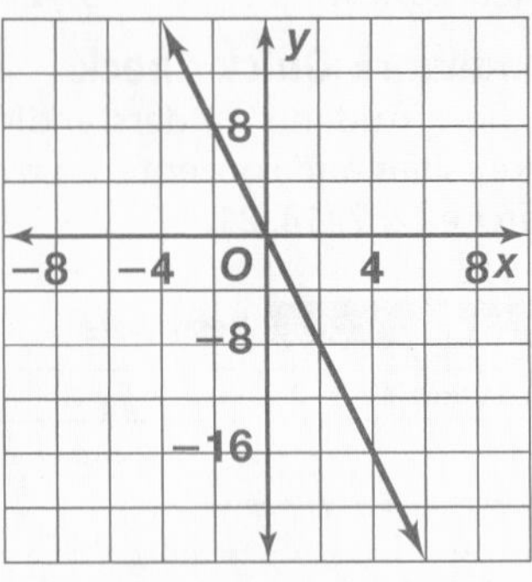

2. Make a table and graph the function $y = \frac{x}{2} - 1$.

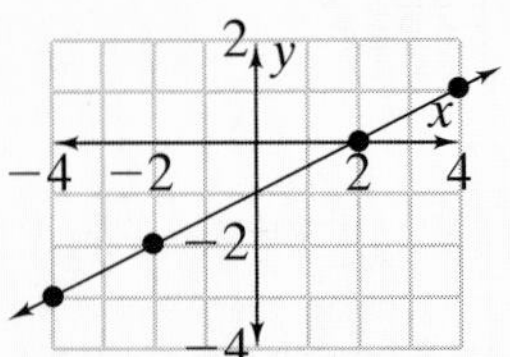

Input	–2	0	2	4
Output	–2	–1	0	1

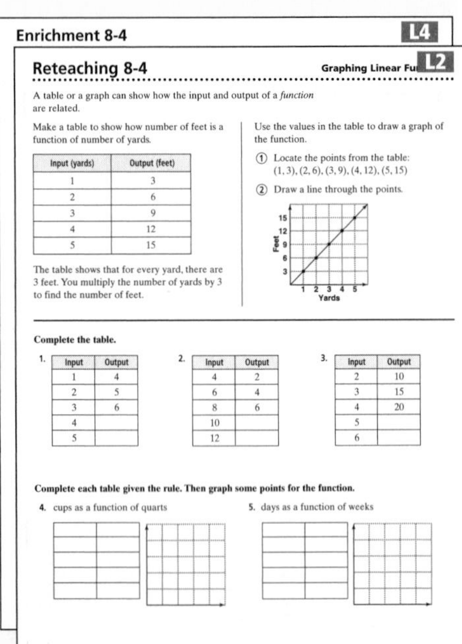

Enrichment 8-4 L4

Reteaching 8-4 Graphing Linear Fu L2

A table or a graph can show how the input and output of a *function* are related.

Make a table to show how number of feet is a function of number of yards.

Input (yards)	Output (feet)
1	3
2	6
3	9
4	12
5	15

The table shows that for every yard, there are 3 feet. You multiply the number of yards by 3 to find the number of feet.

Use the values in the table to draw a graph of the function.

① Locate the points from the table: (1, 3), (2, 6), (3, 9), (4, 12), (5, 15)

② Draw a line through the points.

Complete the table.

1.

Input	Output
1	4
2	5
3	6
4	
5	

2.

Input	Output
4	2
6	4
8	6
10	
12	

3.

Input	Output
2	10
3	15
4	20
5	
6	

Complete each table given the rule. Then graph some points for the function.

4. cups as a function of quarts

5. days as a function of weeks

SCAFFOLDED
Problem Solving

A club sells calendars for $4 each. It spends $20 on film plus $2 to make each calendar.

15. Write a function for the total income, or amount the club makes, from selling x calendars. $y = 4x$
16. Write a function for the total cost of making x calendars. $y = 2x + 20$
17. Graph the two functions on the same coordinate plane. See margin.
18. Use your graph to find the total income from selling 15 calendars. $60.00
19. How many calendars does the club need to sell for the total income to be greater than the total cost? 11 or more calendars
20. How much profit does the club earn from making and selling 15 calendars? (*Hint*: profit = total income – total cost) $10.00
21. **Writing in Math** Four of the five points below are solutions of the same linear equation. Which one is not? Explain. A; all the other points are on the same line.
    $A(2, 1)$ $B(0, -4)$ $C(1, -2)$ $D(4, 4)$ $E(3, 2)$

C Challenge
22. Graph $3x + 2y = 7$. Is $3x + 2y = 7$ a linear equation? See margin.

Multiple Choice Practice and Mixed Review

For California Standards Tutorials, visit PHSchool.com. Web Code: axq-9045

AF 3.3
23. Which of the following is a graph of the function $y = 2x - 1$? A

A
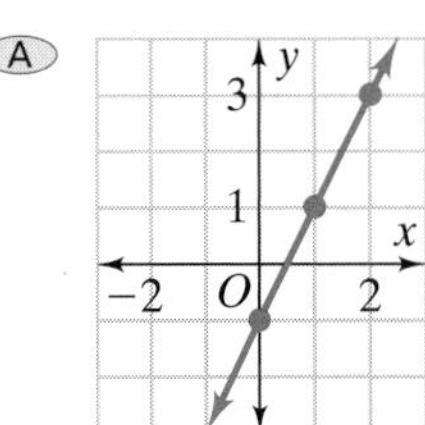

C
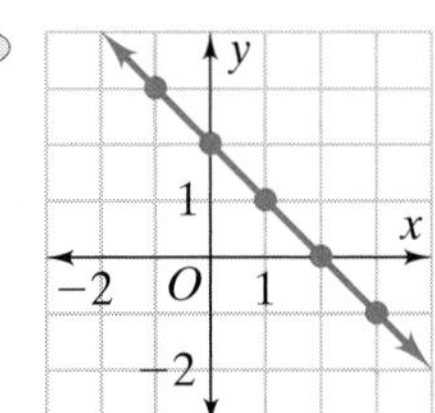

B
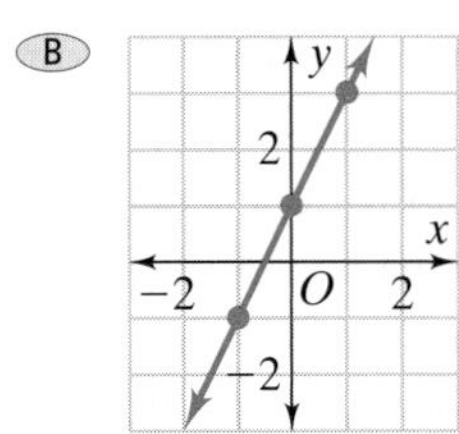

D
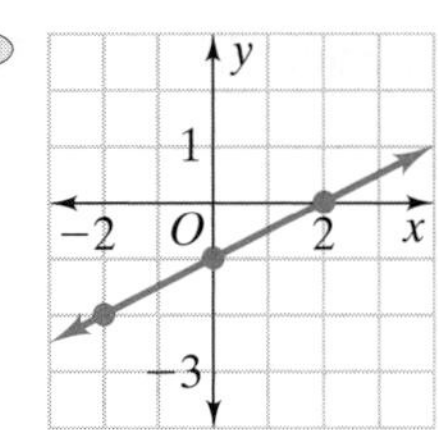

Alg1 2.0
24. Which integer is the opposite of –18? D
    A –81 B –18 C 0 D 18

MG 1.3
25. You earn $7.25 per hour. How much do you earn for working 8.5 h? D
    A $7.25 B $8.50 C $15.75 D $61.63

Lesson 8-1
Graph each point on the same coordinate plane. 26–29. See margin.

26. (2, 7) 27. (0, –3) 28. (–4, –1) 29. (1, 2.5)

Visit: PHSchool.com **Web Code:** axa-0804

Alternative Assessment

Each student in a pair writes a linear function such as $y = 2x - 3$. Partners exchange papers and make a table and graph of their partner's function rule.

California Resources

Standards Mastery
- Standards Review Transparencies
- Standards Review and Practice Workbook
- Math Companion

Math Intervention
- Skills Review and Practice Workbook
- Math XL

8-4b Activity Lab

Systems of Linear Equations

Two or more linear equations form a **system of linear equations.**

AF 1.1 Use variables and appropriate operations to write a system of equations. ***Develop***
AF 3.3 Graph linear functions. ***Develop***

EXAMPLE

The student council sells T-shirts each year as a fundraiser. It spends \$5 on each plain T-shirt plus \$30 on decorating materials. The T-shirts sell for \$10.50 each. Write a system of equations to represent the income and expenses of the student council.

Words income is \$10.50 times number of T-shirts sold

Let y = income.

Let x = the number of T-shirts sold.

Income Equation $y = 10.5 \cdot x$

The equation $y = 10.5x$ represents the income.

Words expenses are \$5 times number of T-shirts sold plus \$30

Let y = expenses.

Let x = the number of T-shirts sold.

Expenses Equation $y = 5 \cdot x + 30$

The equation $y = 5x + 30$ represents the expenses.

The system of equations $\begin{cases} y = 10.5x \\ y = 5x + 30 \end{cases}$ represents the income and expenses.

Exercises

1. Two hot-air balloons are in the air. Balloon A is at an altitude of 1,000 ft and rising at the rate of 100 ft/min. Balloon B is at 2,500 ft and descending 200 ft/min. Write a system of equations to represent the altitudes of the balloons. **Let y = altitude in feet. Let x = time in minutes. Balloon A: $y = 100x + 1000$ Balloon B: $y = 2500 - 200x$**

2. The solution of a system of linear equations is the point where the graphs of the two equations intersect. Graph the two equations from Exercise 1 on the same coordinate plane. Find the solution to this system. **(5, 1,500**

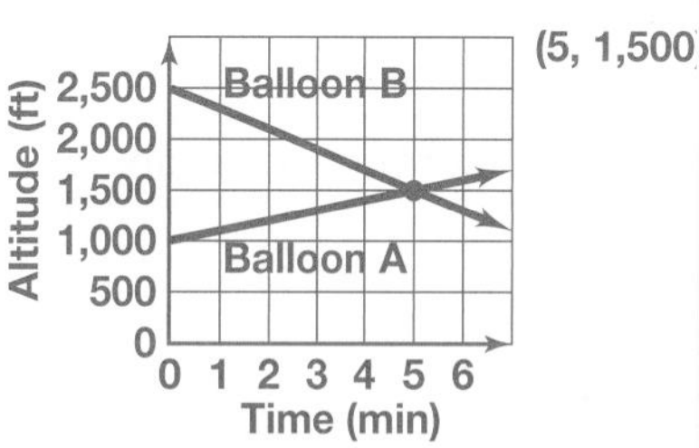

3. **Reasoning** In the situation in Exercise 1, what does the point of intersection represent? **The intersection (5, 1,500) represents the time (5 min) at which the balloons are at the same altitude (1,500 m).**

Activity Lab

Systems of Linear Equations

Students learn to write a system of linear equations. In Exercise 2, they graph a system of linear equations in the same coordinate plane and find the solution of the system.

Guided Instruction

Exercise 1

Explain that one equation represents balloon A's altitude and the other equation represents balloon B's altitude.

Exercise 2

Ask:

- *Which balloon is changing altitude more quickly?* **balloon B**
- *Name the coordinates of the point where the two lines intersect.* **(5, 1500)**

Linear Functions

Students read a guided real-world problem to develop problem-solving and reasoning skills. In the left-hand column, they read questions they could ask themselves to make sense of the problem. In the right-hand column, they read the steps for setting up and solving equations used to describe the situation.

Guided Instruction

Have students work through the problem, rather than just read. Have them identify any steps that are unclear or that don't match their own work.

Exercise 3
Remind students that the slope of a line is the ratio of the vertical change to the horizontal change.

AF 3.3 Graph linear functions, noting that the vertical change per unit of horizontal change is always the same. ***Develop***
MR 2.3 Estimate unknown quantities graphically and solve for them by using logical reasoning and arithmetic and algebraic techniques. ***Develop***

Linear Functions

For each rental plan, represent the relationship between the number of miles (from 20 to 45) and the cost of a one-day rental. Use a linear function, a table of ordered pairs, and a graph (using the same coordinate plane). What conclusions can you draw about these plans?

What You Might Think

What do I know? What do I want to find out?

How can I write a function rule for each plan?

How can I make a table and graph?

What conclusions can be stated?

What You Might Write

Plan 1 costs $15 plus $.25 per mile. Plan 2 costs $8 plus $.45 per mile. I want to compare the two plans using function rules, tables, and graphs.

Let m = the number of miles driven.Let
Let C = the cost of the rental in dollars.

Plan 1: $C_1 = \$.25m + 15$

Plan 2: $C_2 = \$.45m + 8$

I can use the function rule to get data points for the table. Then I can graph those points.

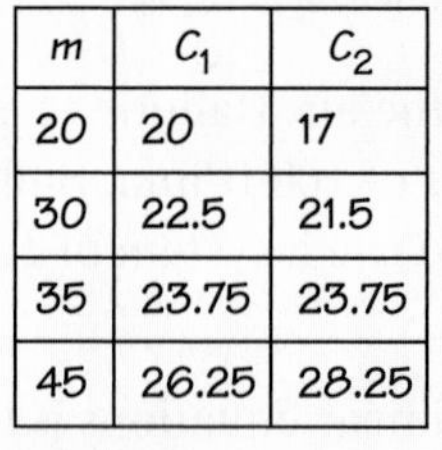

m	C_1	C_2
20	20	17
30	22.5	21.5
35	23.75	23.75
45	26.25	28.25

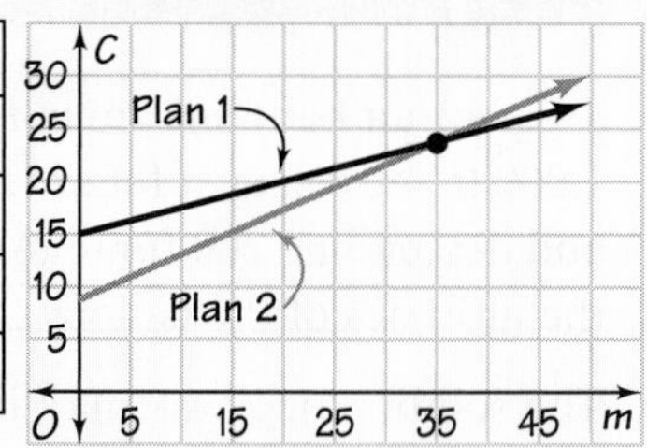

The lines intersect at (35, 23.75). Plan 2 is better if you drive less than 35 miles; otherwise, Plan 1 is better.

Guided Instruction

Teaching Tip
Have students ask themselves the same or similar questions as in the example as they work through the Exercises.

Think It Through

1. Could you have used other values for m in the table? Explain.
2. How was the conclusion arrived at? Are there other conclusions?

1. Yes; the function rule works for any positive number.
2. The conclusion was made by using a table and graph; there are no other conclusions.

Exercises

Solve each problem. For Exercises 3 and 4, answer parts (a) and (b) first.

3. Assume the relationship between the year and number of senior citizens is a linear function. Use the data at the right to predict the number of senior citizens in the United States in 2020.
   a. Using the ordered pairs in the graph as endpoints, make a line graph showing years and number of senior citizens.
   b. Use your graph to estimate the number of senior citizens in 2020. about 53 million senior citizens

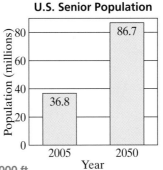

U.S. Senior Population

Year	Population (millions)
2005	36.8
2050	86.7

4. A certain airplane can climb 3,000 ft for every mile it travels horizontally. If it maintains this rate of ascent, how far will the plane have traveled horizontally when it reaches 5 mi in altitude? 15,000 ft
   a. What is the rate of ascent in feet per mile?
   b. Let m be the number of miles traveled horizontally and A be the altitude. Write a function rule relating the number of miles traveled and the altitude. Be sure to use the correct units.

5. Student council members are raising funds by selling hats. They take a survey to see how many students will buy the hats at different prices. The results are below.

Price (dollars)	2	4	6	8	10	12
Number of Buyers	400	325	250	175	100	25

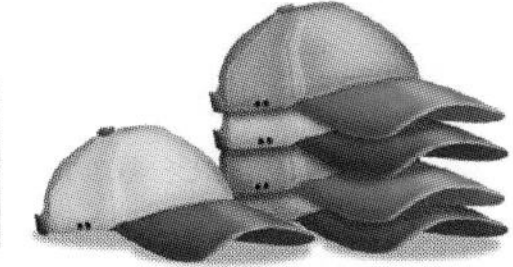

Graph the data. Use the graph to estimate the number of hats that will be sold at \$5. See margin.

6. A county landfill already contains 20,000 t of trash. It is gaining 500 t per month. How many months will it be until the landfill contains 50,000 t of trash? Write a function rule and make a graph to solve the problem. 60 mo

8-5

1. Plan

California Content Standards

AF 3.3 Graph linear functions, noting that the vertical change per unit of horizontal change is always the same, and know that the ratio is called the slope of a graph. ***Introduce, Develop***

AF 3.4 Plot the values of quantities whose ratios are always the same. Fit a line to the plot and understand that the slope of the line equals the ratio of the quantities. ***Introduce, Develop***

California Math Background

A ratio expresses the relationship between two values. For a line in the coordinate plane, the steepness of the line is expressed by a ratio. The ratio of the line's rise (the vertical change in a line) to its run (its horizontal change) is called *slope*. The slope for any given line is constant. To find the slope of a line, divide the line's rise by its run. Given a value for slope, you can draw a line with that slope through a given point.

More Math Background: p. 286C

Lesson Planning and Resources

See p. 286E for a list of the resources that support this lesson.

...PRESENTATION CD-ROM CD, Online, or Transparencies

Bell Ringer Practice

Check Skills You'll Need
Use student page, transparency, or PowerPoint.
See Math Companion.

California Standards Review
Use transparency or PowerPoint.

8-5 Slope

Check Skills You'll Need

Do this in your **Math Companion.**

Vocabulary
- slope
- slope of a line

Use your **Math Companion** *to build your vocabulary.*

California Content Standards

AF 3.3 Graph linear functions, noting that the vertical change per unit of horizontal change is always the same and know that the ratio is called the slope of a graph. ***Introduce, Develop***

AF 3.4 Plot the values of quantities whose ratios are always the same. Fit a line to the plot and understand that the slope of the line equals the ratio of the quantities. ***Introduce, Develop***

What You'll Learn . . . and Why

You will learn to find the slope of a line. You can use slope to describe the steepness of an incline, such as a skateboard ramp. The steepness of a ramp is the ratio of the vertical change to the horizontal change, or the ratio of the rise to the run.

Slope is a ratio that describes steepness.

$$\text{slope} = \frac{\text{vertical change}}{\text{horizontal change}} \begin{array}{l}\leftarrow \text{rise} \\ \leftarrow \text{run}\end{array}$$

Slope describes the steepness of lines in the coordinate plane. For any two points on a line, the ratio of rise to run is the same.

Online active math

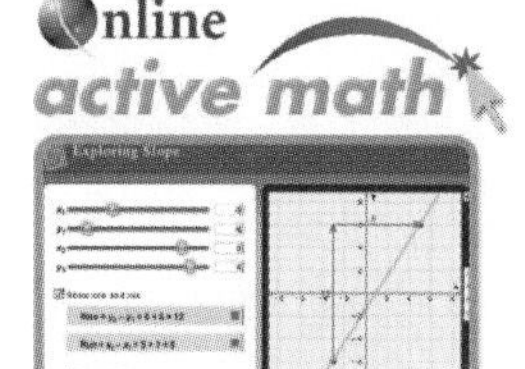

For: Exploring Slope Activity
Use: Interactive Textbook, 8-5

Take Note Slope of a Line

$$\textbf{slope of a line} = \frac{\text{change in } y\text{-coordinates}}{\text{change in } x\text{-coordinates}} \begin{array}{l}\leftarrow \text{rise} \\ \leftarrow \text{run}\end{array}$$

The slope of a line can be positive, negative, zero, or undefined. A line that goes upward from left to right has positive slope. A line that goes downward from left to right has negative slope. A horizontal line has a slope of 0. The slope of a vertical line is undefined because you cannot divide by 0.

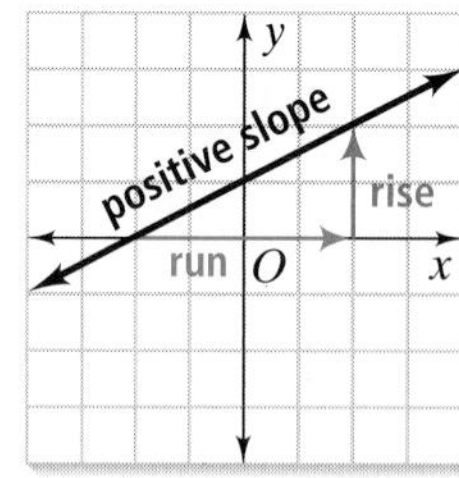

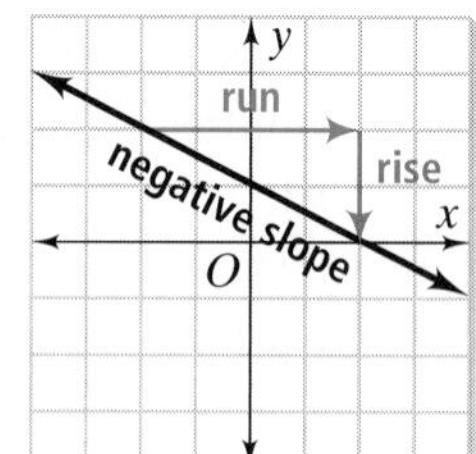

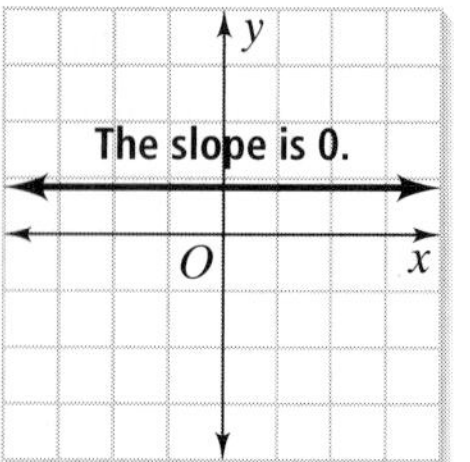

Universal Access Solutions for All Learners

Special Needs L1	**Below Level** L2
Students trace lines with zero slope, positive slope, and negative slope in the air with their fingers. They also use their forearms to show a line that is not very steep and then one that is very steep.	Review the rules for subtraction of positive and negative integers. Have students find the rise and run with simple pairs of coordinates, such as (0, 2) and (4, 6). rise: 4, run: 4

EXAMPLE Finding the Slope of a Line

1 Find the slope of the line in the graph below.

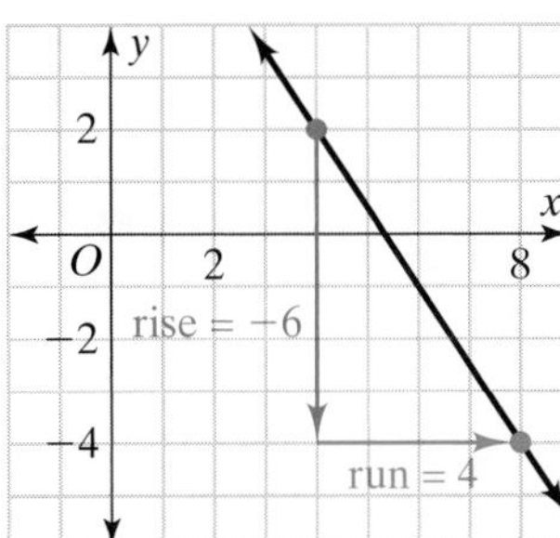

$$\text{slope} = \frac{\text{rise}}{\text{run}}$$

$= \frac{-6}{4}$ ← **Substitute the rise and run.**

$= -\frac{3}{2}$ ← **Simplify.**

The slope of the line is $-\frac{3}{2}$.

Problem Solving Tip

When describing slope, you do not need to simplify an improper fraction as a mixed number.

CA Standards Check 1 *Go to your* **Math Companion** *for help.*

1. Find the slope of each line.

a. 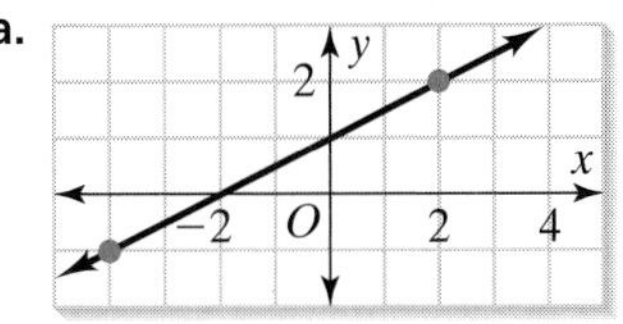

$\frac{1}{2}$

b. 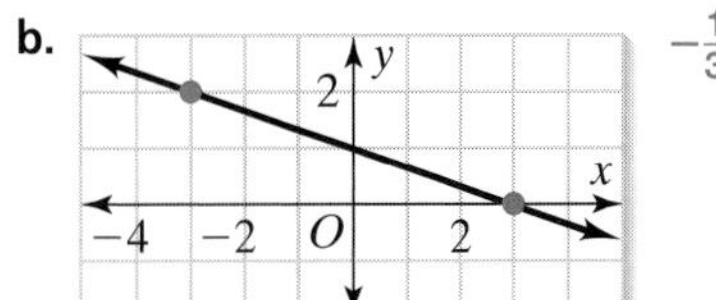

$-\frac{1}{3}$

You can use the coordinates of any two points on a line to find its slope. The vertical change is the difference of the y-coordinates. The horizontal change is the difference of the x-coordinates.

EXAMPLE Using Coordinates to Find Slope

Relate **MATH YOU KNOW...**

Evaluate the expression $\frac{b-d}{a-c}$ for $a = 5$, $b = -3$, $c = 2$, and $d = 1$.

$\frac{b-d}{a-c} = \frac{-3-1}{5-2}$ ← **Substitute the values into the expression.**

$= -\frac{4}{3}$ ← **Simplify.**

...to **ALGEBRA**

2 Find the slope of the line that contains the points $A(2, 1)$ and $B(5, -3)$.

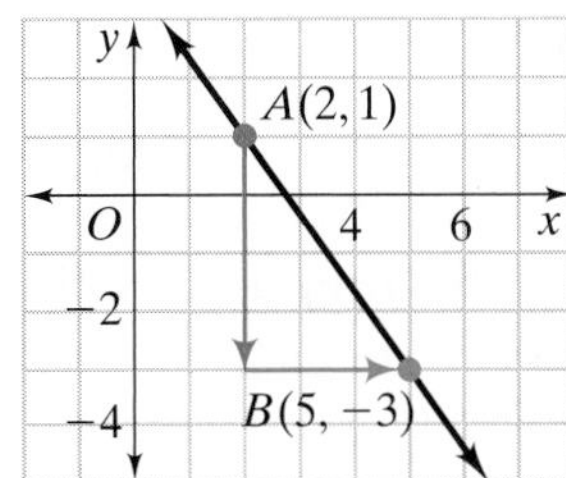

$$\text{slope} = \frac{\text{change in } y\text{-coordinates}}{\text{change in } x\text{-coordinates}}$$

$= \frac{-3-1}{5-2}$ ← **Subtract coordinates of *A* from coordinates of *B*.**

$= -\frac{4}{3}$ ← **Simplify.**

CA Standards Check 2 *Go to your* **Math Companion** *for help.*

2. Find the slope of the line that contains each pair of points.

a. (3, 1) and (3, −2) undefined **b.** (−5, −7) and (2, 4) $\frac{11}{7}$

Check Your Understanding *Homework prep is in your* **Math Companion.**

311

Advanced Learners L4	**English Learners** EL
Challenge students to think of relationships that would yield lines with positive slopes (increasing speed and distance) and negative slopes (value depreciation).	Have students use index cards to draw and label examples of a positive, negative, zero, and undefined slope. They might also draw and label examples for the terms *rise* and *run*.

2. Teach

Guided Instruction

Example 1

Students may forget to write the negative sign for a line with a negative slope. Remind them that if a line goes downward from left to right, its slope is negative. If a line goes upward from left to right, its slope is positive. Draw both a positive-slope line and a negative-slope line on the board. Write "+" and "−" to indicate each line's slope.

Error Prevention!

Make it clear that when students find the change in y by subtracting one y-coordinate from the other, they must follow the same order of subtraction for the x-coordinates.

PRESENTATION CD-ROM
CD, Online, or Transparencies

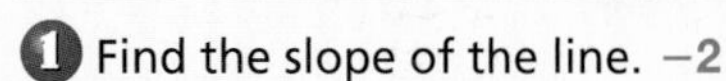
Additional Examples

1 Find the slope of the line. −2

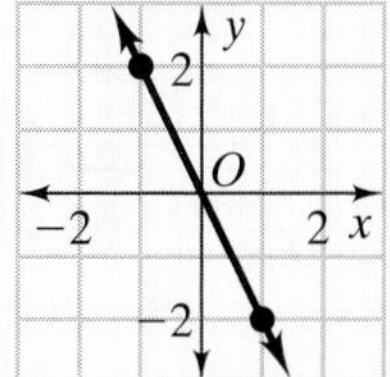

2 Find the slope of the line that contains the points (1, 3) and (−2, 2). $\frac{1}{3}$

Closure

- *What is the slope of a line?* Sample: Slope is the ratio of the vertical change to horizontal change, or rise over run.
- *What is the rise of a line?* The rise is its vertical change.
- *What is the run of a line?* The run is its horizontal change.

3. Practice

Assignment Guide

Check Your Understanding
See Math Companion.

Homework Exercises

A Practice by Example	1–12
B Apply Your Skills	13–21
C Challenge	22
California Multiple-Choice Practice	23–25
Mixed Review	26–28

Homework Quick Check
To check students' understanding of key skills and concepts, go over Exercises 2, 9, 18, 19, 20.

Universal Access Resources

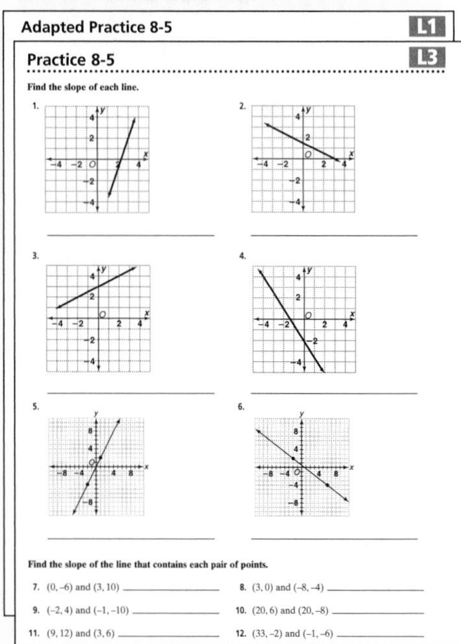

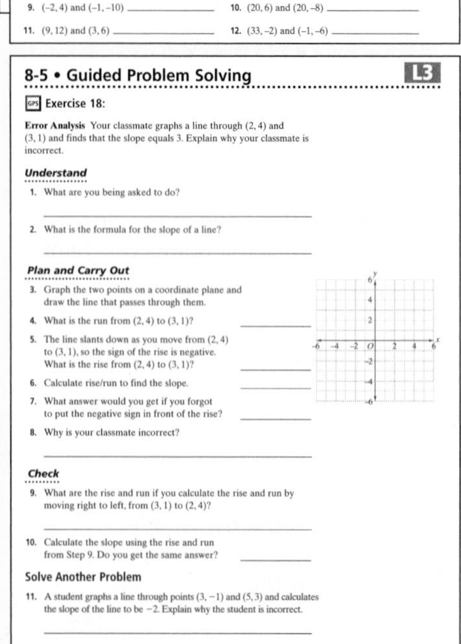

Standards Practice

GO for Help: MathXL

AF 3.3, AF 3.4

A Practice by Example

Example 1 (page 311)

Homework Video Tutor

For: Examples 1–2
Visit: PHSchool.com
Web Code: axe-0805

Find the slope of each line.

1. 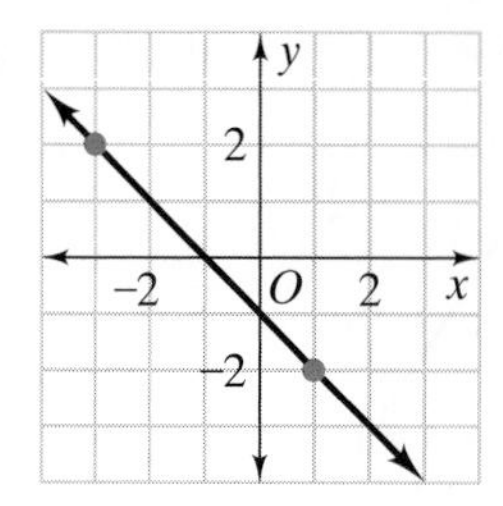 -1

Guided Practice: This exercise has been started for you!

The rise is 4. The run is −4.

2. 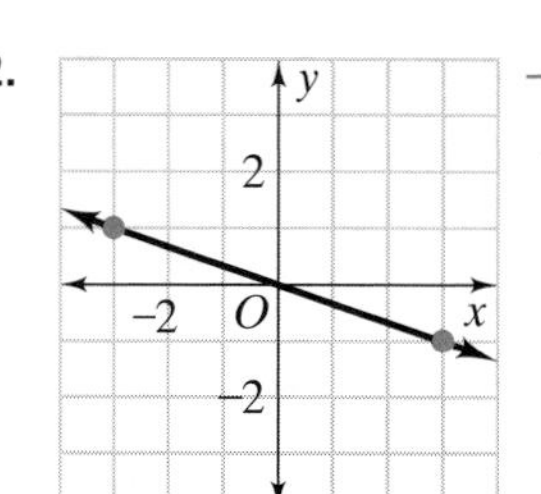 $-\frac{1}{3}$

3. 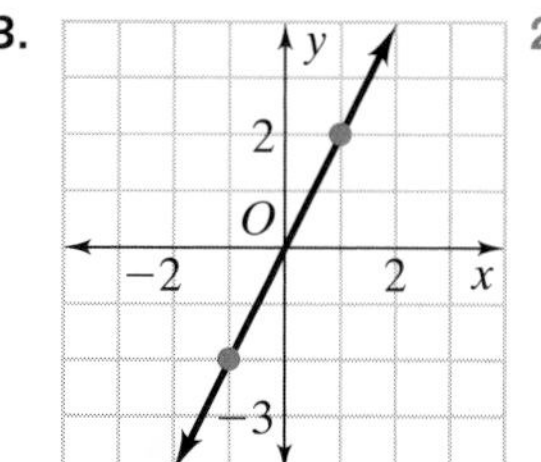 2

4. 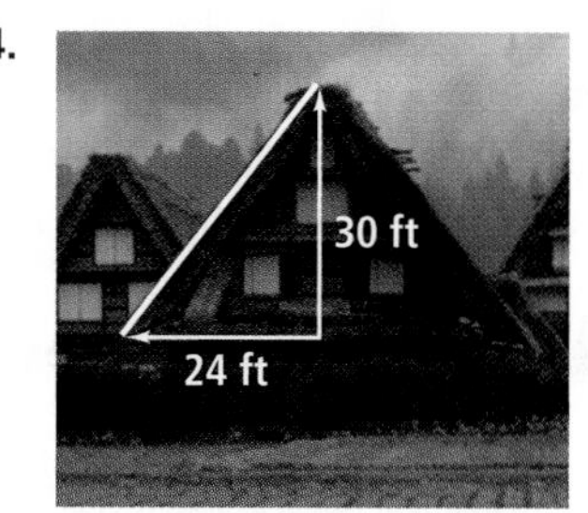 $\frac{5}{4}$

5. 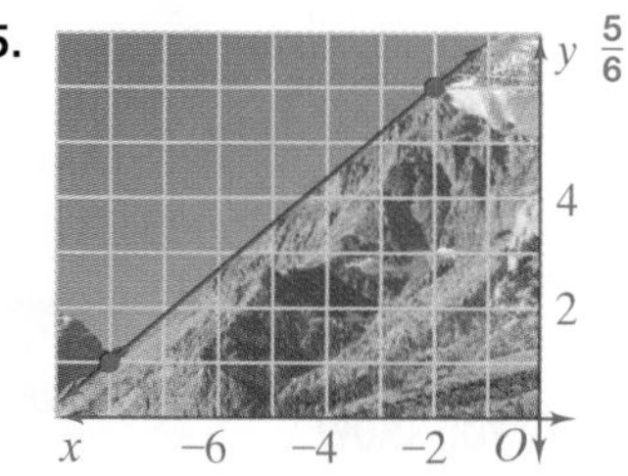 $\frac{5}{6}$

Example 2 (page 311)

Find the slope of the line that contains each pair of points.

6. (−2, 2) and (2, 0)
slope $= \frac{0-2}{2-(-2)} = \blacksquare$ $-\frac{1}{2}$

Guided Practice: This exercise has been started for you!

7. (1, −2) and (5, −3) $-\frac{1}{4}$

8. (−2, 3) and (−3, 1) 2

9. (4, −1) and (−4, 1) $-\frac{1}{4}$

10. (1.5, 10) and (−1, −3) $\frac{26}{5}$

11. (5, −2.4) and (5, 4.8) undefined

12. (14, 18) and (−12, −3) $\frac{21}{26}$

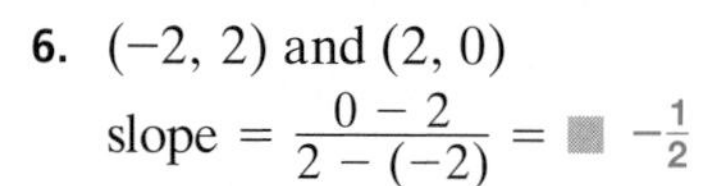

B Apply Your Skills

13. **Guided Problem Solving** The graph at the right shows the amount of rice y a store has in stock at time x. Use the slope to describe how the amount of rice changes over time.
- Find the slope of the line.
- How is the rate of change related to the slope? −5; the supply of rice decreases by 5 lb/wk.

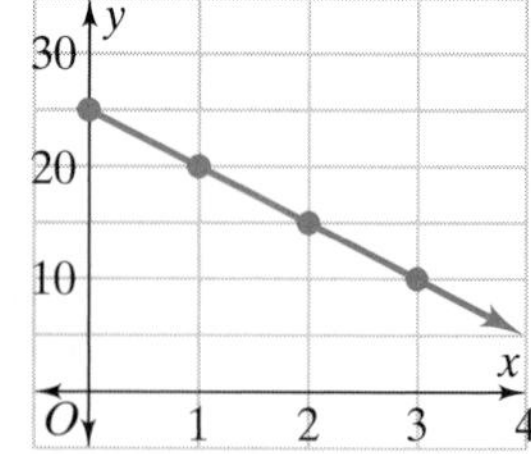

SCAFFOLDED
Problem Solving

The graph at the right shows the value of a car for the first eight years of ownership.

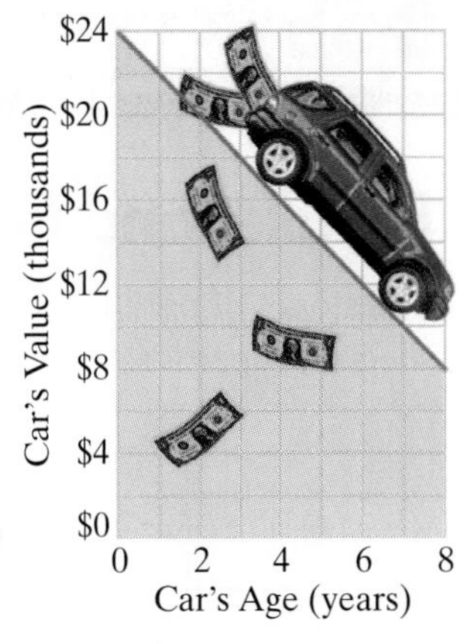

14. What was the value of the car when it was new? $24,000

15. What was the value of the car when it was six years old? $12,000

16. What is the slope of the graph? −2000

17. What does the slope of the graph tell you about the relationship between the age of the car and its value? See above left.

18. **Error Analysis** Your classmate graphs a line through (2, 4) and (3, 1) and finds that the slope equals 3. Explain why your classmate is incorrect. See above left.

19. **Writing in Math** The graph of a function contains the points (4, 2), (5, −1), and (6, −2). Is the function a linear function? Explain. See above left.

20. **Reasoning** Draw a horizontal line containing the point (1, 3). Use two points on the line to show that the slope of the line equals 0. See above left.

21. The function rule $y = \frac{1}{12}x$ describes the relationship between inches and feet. State which variable represents feet and which variable represents inches. Then graph the function and find its slope. See margin.

Challenge

22. Determine whether the following statement is *true* or *false*. If two lines have the same slope, their equations describe the same line. false

17. The value of the car decreases $2,000/yr.

18. Your classmate forgot to use the same ordered pair first for rise and for run. Correct slope is −3.

19. No; the ratio of rise to run is not the same for each pair of points.

20. 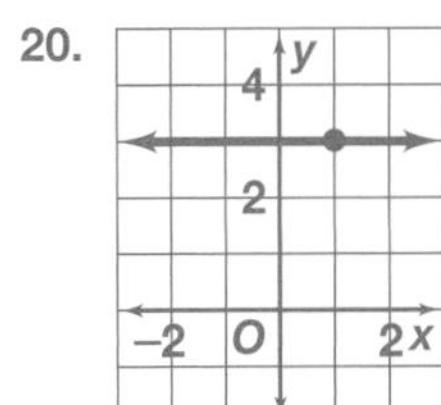

Answers may vary. Sample: Since (1, 3) and (2, 3) are both points on the line, the slope is $\frac{3-3}{2-1}$, or $\frac{0}{1}$, which is equal to 0.

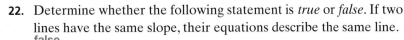

Multiple Choice Practice and Mixed Review

For California Standards Tutorials, visit PHSchool.com. Web Code: axq-9045

AF 3.3

23. Find the slope of the line that contains the points (4, 7) and (0, −1). D

Ⓐ −2 Ⓑ $\frac{1}{2}$ Ⓒ $\frac{3}{2}$ Ⓓ 2

NS 1.2

24. At the end of March, Melissa's bank account balance was $54. She deposited $75 each month in April, May, June, and July. She also made a car payment of $94 in each of those months. What was Melissa's bank account balance at the end of July? A

Ⓐ −$22 Ⓑ −$12 Ⓒ $76 Ⓓ $130

Alg1 2.0

25. A farmer has 35 mi^2 of land in the shape of a square. Which distance is closest to the measure of each side of the farmer's land? A

Ⓐ 6 mi Ⓑ 9 mi Ⓒ 18 mi Ⓓ 36 mi

for Help

Lesson 8-4 **Graph each linear function.** 26–28. See margin.

26. $y = 2x - 2$
27. $y = \frac{1}{4}x + \frac{1}{2}$
28. $y = -3x + 4$

Online Lesson Quiz Visit: PHSchool.com Web Code: axa-0805

Alternative Assessment

Have students work in pairs to complete Exercises 1–5. Partners work together to copy each line on graph paper. Students then use red pencil to draw and label the run and blue pencil to draw and label the rise. They then express the slope as a fraction in simplest form.

California Resources

Standards Mastery
- Standards Review Transparencies
- Standards Review and Practice Workbook
- Math Companion

Math Intervention
- Skills Review and Practice Workbook
- Math XL

4. Assess & Reteach

PRESENTATION CD-ROM
CD, Online, or Transparencies

Lesson Quiz

Find the slope of each line.

1. 2

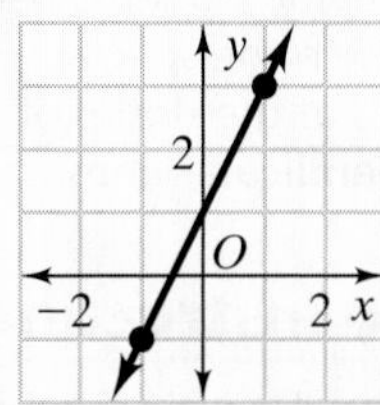

2. the line that passes through the points (1, 3) and (2, 6) 3

3. the line that passes through the points (−3, 4) and (3, −5) $-\frac{3}{2}$

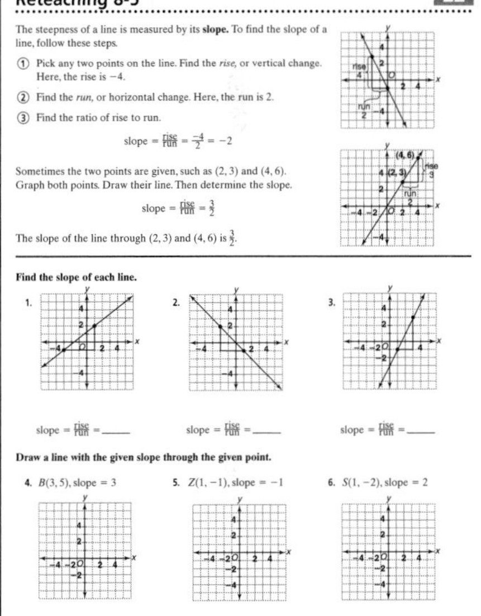
Reteaching 8-5 L2

The steepness of a line is measured by its **slope.** To find the slope of a line, follow these steps.

① Pick any two points on the line. Find the *rise*, or vertical change. Here, the rise is −4.
② Find the *run*, or horizontal change. Here, the run is 2.
③ Find the ratio of rise to run.

slope = $\frac{rise}{run} = \frac{-4}{2} = -2$

Sometimes the two points are given, such as (2, 3) and (4, 6). Graph both points. Draw their line. Then determine the slope.

slope = $\frac{rise}{run} = \frac{3}{2}$

The slope of the line through (2, 3) and (4, 6) is $\frac{3}{2}$.

Find the slope of each line.

1. slope = $\frac{rise}{run}$ = ____
2. slope = $\frac{rise}{run}$ = ____
3. slope = $\frac{rise}{run}$ = ____

Draw a line with the given slope through the given point.

4. B(3, 5), slope = 3
5. Z(1, −1), slope = −1
6. S(1, −2), slope = 2

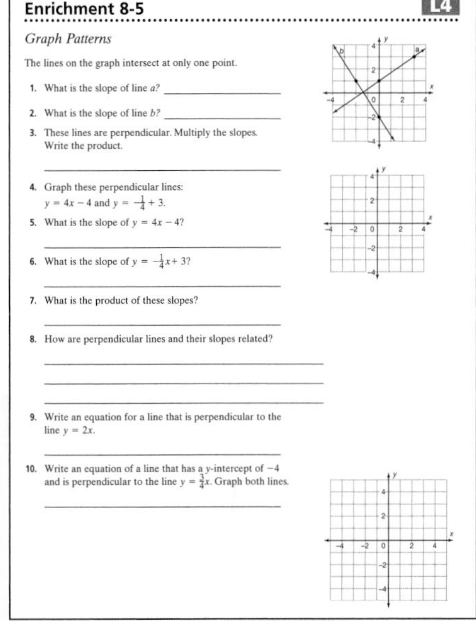
Enrichment 8-5 L4

Graph Patterns

The lines on the graph intersect at only one point.

1. What is the slope of line *a*? ____
2. What is the slope of line *b*? ____
3. These lines are perpendicular. Multiply the slopes. Write the product. ____
4. Graph these perpendicular lines: $y = 4x - 4$ and $y = -\frac{1}{4}x + 3$.
5. What is the slope of $y = 4x - 4$? ____
6. What is the slope of $y = -\frac{1}{4}x + 3$? ____
7. What is the product of these slopes? ____
8. How are perpendicular lines and their slopes related? ____
9. Write an equation for a line that is perpendicular to the line $y = 2x$. ____
10. Write an equation of a line that has a y-intercept of −4 and is perpendicular to the line $y = \frac{3}{4}x$. Graph both lines. ____

Activity Lab

Parallel and Perpendicular Lines

In this activity, students become familiar with the special properties of the slopes of parallel and perpendicular lines.

Guided Instruction

Review the definitions of *parallel* and *perpendicular.* Review the steps for finding the slope of a line.

Exercises

Have students work independently on the Exercises. When they are finished, have them work in pairs. Each student graphs his or her partner's answers to Exercises 7–9 as a check.

314

8-5b Activity Lab

AF 3.3 Graph linear functions, noting that the vertical change per unit of horizontal change is always the same and know that the ratio is called the slope of the graph. ***Develop***

Parallel and Perpendicular Lines

The slopes of parallel and perpendicular lines have special properties.

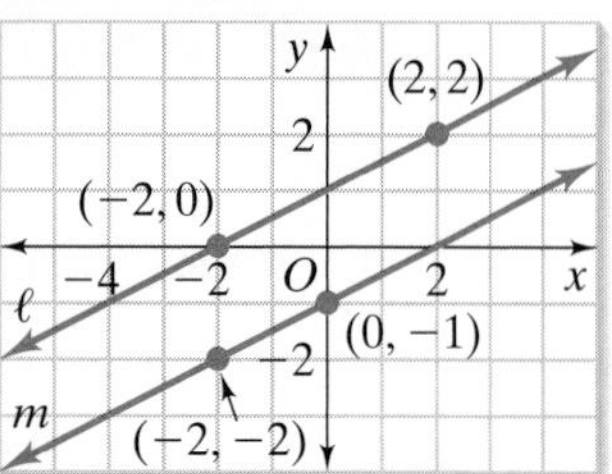

slope of $\ell = \frac{2-0}{2-(-2)} = \frac{2}{4} = \frac{1}{2}$

slope of $m = \frac{-1-(-2)}{0-(-2)} = \frac{1}{2}$

Parallel lines have the same slope.

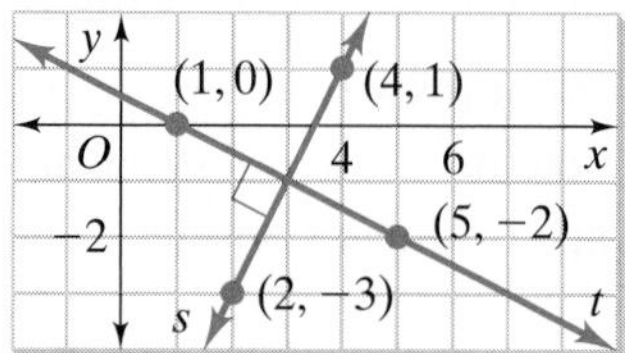

slope of $s = \frac{1-(-3)}{4-2} = \frac{4}{2} = \frac{2}{1}$

slope of $t = \frac{-2-0}{5-1} = \frac{-2}{4} = -\frac{1}{2}$

product of slopes $= \frac{2}{1} \cdot \left(-\frac{1}{2}\right) = -1$

The product of the slopes of perpendicular lines is −1.

EXAMPLE

Line AB has slope $\frac{1}{3}$. Find the slope of a line that is parallel to $\overleftrightarrow{AB}$ and the slope of a line that is perpendicular to $\overleftrightarrow{AB}$.

A line parallel to $\overleftrightarrow{AB}$ has a slope of $\frac{1}{3}$.

Let m represent the slope of a line perpendicular to $\overleftrightarrow{AB}$.

$\frac{1}{3} \cdot m = -1$ ← **The product of the slopes of perpendicular lines is −1.**

$m = -3$ ← **Multiply each side by 3, the multiplicative inverse of $\frac{1}{3}$, to isolate the variable.**

A line perpendicular to $\overleftrightarrow{AB}$ has a slope of −3.

Exercises

Are lines with the given slopes *parallel, perpendicular,* or *neither*?

1. $\frac{2}{3}, -\frac{3}{2}$ perpendicular
2. $5, -5$ neither
3. $\frac{3}{4}, \frac{4}{3}$ neither

4. $\frac{1}{12}, -12$ perpendicular
5. $\frac{3}{9}, \frac{1}{3}$ parallel
6. $\frac{2}{7}, \frac{12}{42}$ parallel

Find the slope of a line parallel to $\overleftrightarrow{PQ}$ and a line perpendicular to $\overleftrightarrow{PQ}$.

7. $P(1, 2)$, $Q(3, 4)$ 1; −1
8. $P(-5, 1)$, $Q(-1, 2)$ $\frac{1}{4}$; −4
9. $P(3, -2)$, $Q(-2, 1)$ $-\frac{3}{5}$; $\frac{5}{3}$

Algebraic Thinking

For Use With Lesson 8-5

Using Slope to Graph 1–6. See margin.

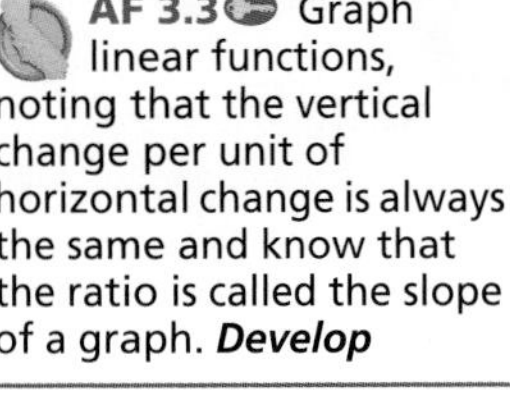

AF 3.3 Graph linear functions, noting that the vertical change per unit of horizontal change is always the same and know that the ratio is called the slope of a graph. ***Develop***

A linear function contains the point $A(-2, 4)$ and has a slope of $-\frac{1}{2}$.

1. Graph the point $A(-2, 4)$ on a coordinate plane.
2. What does the slope of the graph tell you about the vertical change and horizontal change of the graph of the function?
3. Use the ratio of the vertical change and horizontal change of the function to find another point B on the graph of the function.
4. Draw a line through points A and B. This is the graph of the function.
5. Use your line to name another point on the graph of the function.
6. **Reasoning** Is the point $(8, -1)$ a solution of the linear function? Explain.

Checkpoint Quiz 2

Lessons 8-3 through 8-5

Use the function rule $f(x) = -3x - 2$. Find each output.

1. $f(-1)$ 1
2. $f(5)$ −17
3. $f(0)$ −2
4. $f(-10)$ 28
5. At a grocery store, potatoes cost \$.99 per pound. Complete the function rule $C(p) = \underline{\ ?\ }$ to describe the relationship between the total cost $C(p)$ and p, the number of pounds of potatoes you buy. $C(p) = 0.99p$

Graph each linear function. 6–8. See margin.

6. $y = 4x$
7. $y = -2x + 4$
8. $y = 2.5x - 7$

Find the slope of each line in the graph at the right.

9. line a 0
10. line b $\frac{3}{2}$
11. line c −1
12. **Number Sense** Explain which hill is steeper: a hill with a rise of 5 ft and a run of 3 ft or a hill with a rise of 3 ft and a run of 5 ft. See margin.

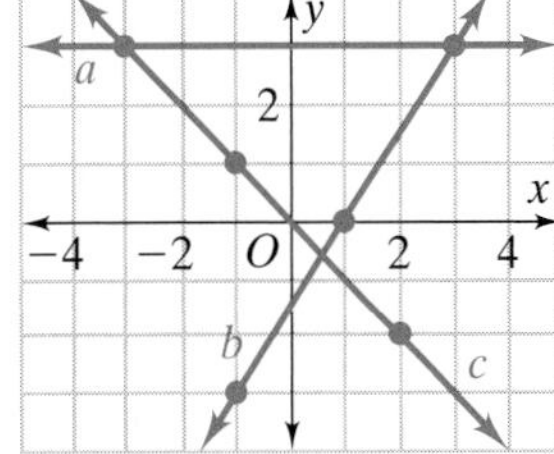

Algebraic Thinking

Using Slope to Graph

Students learn to graph a line using one pair of coordinates and the slope.

Guided Instruction

Remind students that only two points are needed to graph a line. In this example, one point is given. The second point can be found using the slope. Review that when *slope* is given, the numerator represents vertical change (*rise*) and the denominator represents horizontal change (*run*). Remind them that when slope is negative, the line travels downward as it moves to the right.

Step 3
If needed, students can draw a triangle to find the second point. Starting at the given point, draw a line moving to the right and equal to the length of the run. Then draw a line downward and equal to the length of the rise. Connect this second point to the first one to draw the line.

Use this Checkpoint Quiz to check students' understanding of the skills and concepts of Lessons 8-3 through 8-5.

All in One Resources

- Checkpoint Quiz 2

8-6

1. Plan

California Content Standards

AF 3.3 Graph linear functions. ***Master***

AF 3.4 Plot the values of quantities whose ratios are always the same. Fit a line to the plot and understand that the slope of the line equals the ratio of the quantities. ***Develop, Master***

AF 4.2 Solve multistep problems involving a direct variation. ***Develop***

California Math Background

A direct variation is a relationship between two quantities whose ratio, or proportion, is always the same. Direction variation is expressed as a linear function in the form $y = kx$, where $k \neq 0$. You can use a graph to show the relationship between two quantities that vary directly. The slope of the graph is equal to the ratio of the two quantities.

More Math Background: p. 286C

Lesson Planning and Resources

See p. 286E for a list of the resources that support this lesson.

PRESENTATION CD-ROM
CD, Online, or Transparencies

Bell Ringer Practice

Check Skills You'll Need
Use student page, transparency, or PowerPoint.
See Math Companion.

California Standards Review
Use transparency or PowerPoint.

8-6 Slope and Direct Variation

Check Skills You'll Need

Do this in your **Math Companion.**

Vocabulary

- direct variation

Use your **Math Companion** *to build your vocabulary.*

California Content Standards

AF 3.3 Graph linear functions. ***Master***

AF 3.4 Plot the values of quantities whose ratios are always the same. Fit a line to the plot and understand that the slope of the line equals the ratio of the quantities. ***Develop, Master***

AF 4.2 Solve multistep problems involving a direct variation. ***Develop***

What You'll Learn . . . and Why

You will learn the relationship between slope and direct variation. You can use slope to describe the relationship between two quantities whose ratio is always the same, such as the number of oranges you squeeze and the amount of orange juice you make.

A linear function in which the ratio of two quantities is always the same is called a **direct variation.** The slope of the graph of a direct variation is equal to the ratio of the two quantities.

EXAMPLE Identifying a Direct Variation

1 The relationship between the number of pounds of oranges squeezed x and the ounces of orange juice made y is a linear function. The table shows some solutions to the function. Is the function a direct variation?

Pounds of Oranges, x	0	1	2
Ounces of Juice, y	0	8	16

First find the ratio of the two quantities: $\frac{\text{ounces of juice}}{\text{pounds of oranges}} = \frac{8}{1} = 8.$

Then find the slope of the graph using two points from the table.

$$\text{slope} = \frac{\text{change in } y\text{-coordinates}}{\text{change in } x\text{-coordinates}} = \frac{8 - 0}{1 - 0} = 8$$

The slope of the line is equal to the ratio of the two quantities. So the function is a direct variation.

CA Standards Check 1 *Go to your* **Math Companion** *for help.*

1. Is the linear function in the table a direct variation? Explain. See left.

x	0	5	25
y	1.25	9	40

1. No; the slope equals $\frac{31}{20}$. This is not equal to the ratio of the two quantities, because the ratio of x and y is not always the same.

Universal Access Solutions for All Learners

Special Needs L1
Have students pair up to graph the functions. The student in the pair who is less able to graph works on the function table. The other student graphs the data from the table. Have each student find the slope independently, using either the graph or the table.

Below Level L2
Students draw and label familiar relationships that can be expressed as direct variations. For example, the cost of apples might vary directly with the number of apples purchased.

You can use the linear function $y = kx$, where $k \neq 0$, to represent a direct variation. The variables x and y are said to vary directly with each other.

Relate MATH YOU KNOW... ...to ALGEBRA

EXAMPLE Slope and Direct Variation

Find the slope of a line that contains the points (1, 1.5) and (2, 3).

$$\text{slope} = \frac{\text{change in } y\text{-coordinates}}{\text{change in } x\text{-coordinates}}$$ ← Use the formula for slope.

$$= \frac{3 - 1.5}{2 - 1}$$ ← Substitute the x-coordinates and y-coordinates into the formula.

$$= \frac{1.5}{1} = 1.5$$ ← Simplify.

2 Guided Problem Solving A store sells granola in bulk for $1.50 per pound. Graph the relationship between the amount of granola purchased x and the total cost y. Find the slope of the line and explain what it represents.

Make a table to find solutions of the direct variation. Then graph the points on a coordinate plane.

Problem Solving Tip

The graph of a direct variation always includes the origin.

Pounds of Granola, x	0	1	2	3
Cost in Dollars, y	0	1.50	3	4.50

← Make a table.

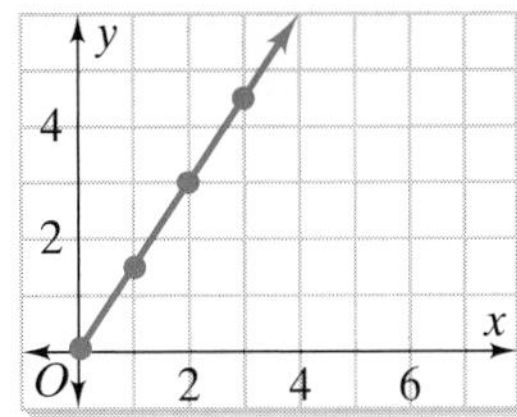

← Plot the points. Connect them with a line.

Use two points to find the slope of the line.

$$\text{slope} = \frac{\text{change in } y\text{-coordinates}}{\text{change in } x\text{-coordinates}}$$ ← Use the formula for slope.

$$= \frac{3 - 1.5}{2 - 1}$$ ← Use the points (2, 3) and (1, 1.5) to find the slope of the line.

$$= \frac{1.5}{1}$$ ← Simplify.

$$= 1.5$$

The slope of the line represents the unit cost of the granola, which is $1.50 per pound.

CA Standards Check 2 *Go to your* **Math Companion** *for help.*

2. Graph the relationship between yards and feet. Use the x-axis for yards and the y-axis for feet. Find the slope of the line and explain what the slope represents. See margin.

Homework prep is in your **Math Companion.**

2. Teach

Guided Instruction

If needed, review the definition of *function* and explain that a direct variation is a type of linear function.

Example 2

Explain that because slope is a ratio, it represents the relationship between the two quantities.

PRESENTATION CD-ROM
CD, Online, or Transparencies

Additional Examples

1 The number of miles traveled by car varies directly with the number of gallons of gas used. Use the variation $m = 27g$, where g is gallons of gas and m is miles driven. Find the total miles the car can travel on 4 gallons of gas.

2 Amber earns $7 per hour. Graph the relationship between the number of hours Amber works and the amount she earns. Find the slope of the line and explain what it represents.

Input (h)	0	1	2	3	4
Output ($)	0	7	14	21	28

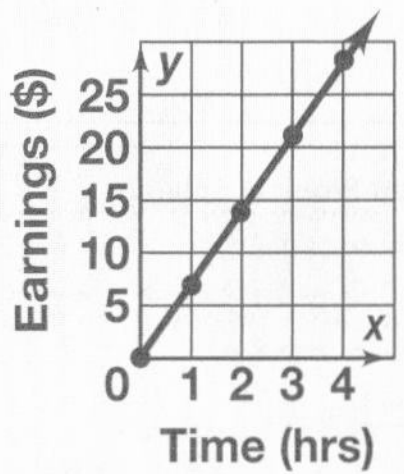

The slope is 7, which represents the amount Amber earns each hour.

Closure

- *What is a direct variation?* a linear function in the form $y = kx$, where $k \neq 0$

Advanced Learners L4

Have students graph $y = x$, $y = 3x$, $y = 5x$, and $y = 6x$. Ask them to compare the graphs and explain the difference. Each line gets steeper because the slopes increase.

English Learners EL

Relate terms to their meanings. For example, connect *variation* to *vary,* which means "to change." Help students see that in this case, one quantity increases, or *varies,* as a *direct* result of an increase in the other quantity.

3. Practice

Assignment Guide

Check Your Understanding

See Math Companion.

Homework Exercises

A Practice by Example	1–13
B Apply Your Skills	14–22
C Challenge	23
California Multiple-Choice Practice	24–25
Mixed Review	26–29

Homework Quick Check

To check students' understanding of key skills and concepts, go over Exercises 4, 9, 13, 16.

Universal Access Resources

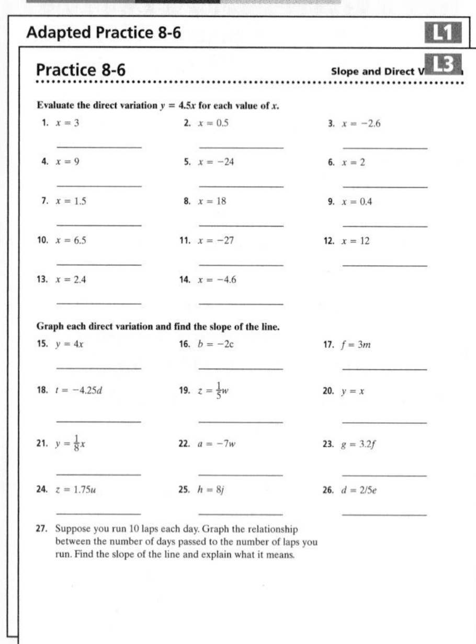

Adapted Practice 8-6 L1

Practice 8-6 L3 Slope and Direct V

Evaluate the direct variation $y = 4.5x$ for each value of x.

1. $x = 3$
2. $x = 0.5$
3. $x = -2.6$
4. $x = 9$
5. $x = -24$
6. $x = 2$
7. $x = 1.5$
8. $x = 18$
9. $x = 0.4$
10. $x = 6.5$
11. $x = -27$
12. $x = 12$
13. $x = 2.4$
14. $x = -4.6$

Graph each direct variation and find the slope of the line.

15. $y = 4x$
16. $b = -2c$
17. $f = 3m$
18. $t = -4.25d$
19. $z = \frac{1}{5}w$
20. $y = x$
21. $y = \frac{1}{8}x$
22. $a = -7w$
23. $g = 3.2f$
24. $z = 1.75u$
25. $h = 8j$
26. $d = 2/5e$
27. Suppose you run 10 laps each day. Graph the relationship between the number of days passed to the number of laps you run. Find the slope of the line and explain what it means.

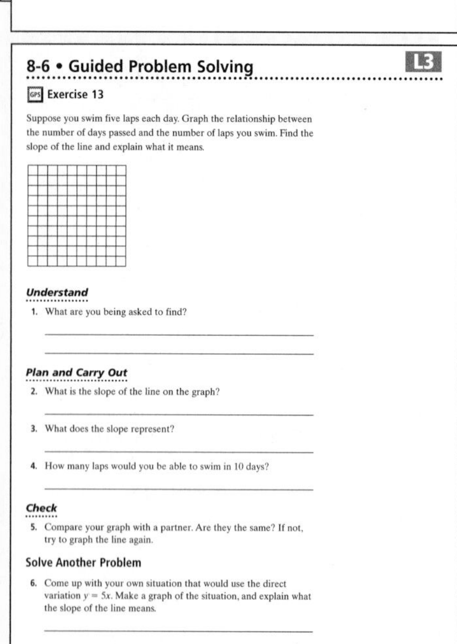

8-6 • Guided Problem Solving L3

GPS Exercise 13

Suppose you swim five laps each day. Graph the relationship between the number of days passed and the number of laps you swim. Find the slope of the line and explain what it means.

Understand

1. What are you being asked to find?

Plan and Carry Out

2. What is the slope of the line on the graph?
3. What does the slope represent?
4. How many laps would you be able to swim in 10 days?

Check

5. Compare your graph with a partner. Are they the same? If not, try to graph the line again.

Solve Another Problem

6. Come up with your own situation that would use the direct variation $y = 5x$. Make a graph of the situation, and explain what the slope of the line means.

Standards Practice

GO for Help: MathXL

AF 3.3, AF 3.4, AF 4.2

A Practice by Example

Determine whether the linear function in each table is a direct variation. Explain. 1–5. See below left.

Example 1 (page 316)

For: Examples 1–2
Visit: PHSchool.com
Web Code: axe-0806

Guided Practice: This exercise has been started for you!

1.

x	0	1	2	3
y	0	2.3	4.6	6.9

ratio of quantities $= \frac{2.3}{■}$

slope $= \frac{2.3 - 0}{1 - 0} = ■$

2.

x	5	7	10
y	15	17	20

3.

x	0	2	3	4
y	0	3.5	5.25	7

4.

Hours, x	1	2	3
Miles, y	15	20	25

5.

Cups, x	0	32	64	96
Gallons, y	0	2	4	6

Example 2 (page 317)

1. Yes; slope = ratio of y to $x = 2.3$
2. No; slope = 1 but the ratio of x and y is not always the same.
3. Yes; slope = ratio of y to $x = 1.75$
4. No; slope = 5 but the ratio of miles to hours is not always the same.
5. Yes; slope = ratio of gallons to cups $= \frac{1}{16}$

Graph each direct variation and find the slope of the line. 6–13. See back of boo

Guided Practice: This exercise has been started for you!

6. $y = 6x$
Two points on the line are $(0, 0)$ and $(2, 12)$. The slope of the line is ■.
7. $b = 2.5a$
8. $y = -x$
9. $t = -4p$
10. $c = \frac{3}{2}m$
11. $z = -\frac{1}{3}w$
12. $f = -3.25e$
13. (GPS) Suppose you swim five laps each day. Graph the relationship between the number of days passed x and the number of laps you swam y. Find the slope of the line and explain what it represents.

B Apply Your Skills

14. **Guided Problem Solving** The graph at the right shows the relationship between the pounds of lunchmeat purchased x and the total cost y. How much does the lunchmeat cost per pound? $5.00/lb
    - What is the slope of the graph?
    - What does the slope represent?

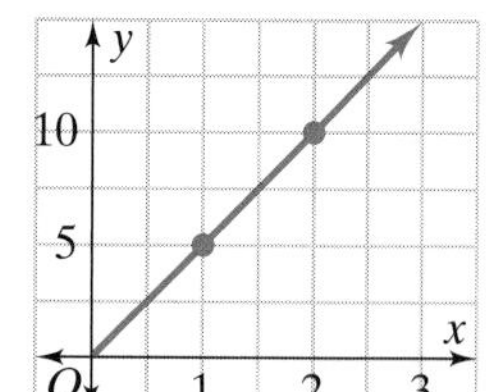

15. **Reasoning** Is the relationship between inches and yards a direct variation? Explain. See left.
16. **Writing in Math** Explain why the graph of a direct variation always includes $(0, 0)$. See left.

15. Yes; it can be represented by the direct variation $y = \frac{1}{36}x$, where y is length in yards and x is length in inches.
16. When $x = 0$, and the direct variation is $y = kx$, the value of k does not matter because $k(0) = 0$, so $y = 0$.

SCAFFOLDED
Problem Solving

Use the graph at the right.

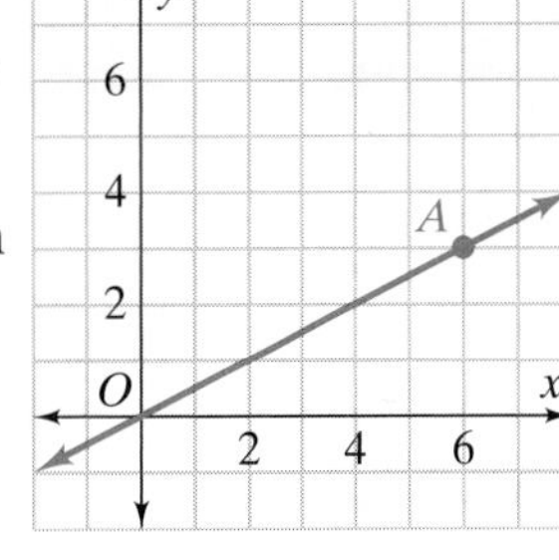

17. Identify the coordinates of point A. (6, 3)

18. Substitute the x-coordinate and y-coordinate of A into the direct variation formula $y = kx$. Solve for k. $\frac{1}{2}$

19. Use the value of k you found in Exercise 18 to write a function rule for the graph in the form $y = kx$. $y = \frac{1}{2}x$

20. Use your function rule to find the value of y when $x = 12$. 6

21. Find the slope of the line. What do you notice about the slope of the line and the value of k? $\frac{1}{2}$; the slope is the same as k.

22. **Reasoning** How can you use the slope of the graph of a direct variation to write a function rule for the direct variation? Substitute the slope for k in the function $y = kx$.

23.

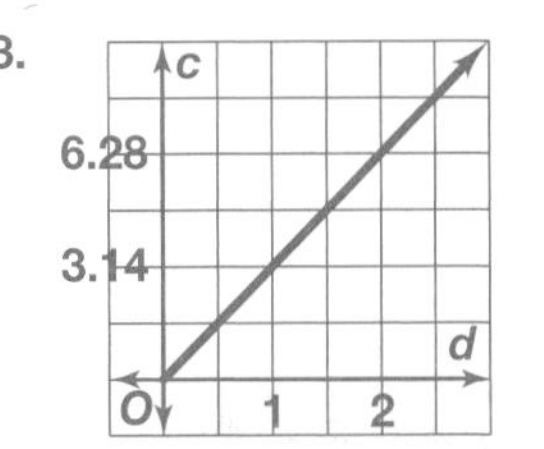

The slope, π, represents the ratio of the circumference of a circle to its diameter.

Challenge

23. The relationship between the diameter d and circumference C of a circle is given by the direct variation $C = \pi d$. Graph the function. Use 3.14 for π. Explain what the slope of the graph represents. See above left.

Multiple Choice Practice and Mixed Review

For California Standards Tutorials, visit PHSchool.com. Web Code: axq-9045

AF 3.4

24. Peaches are on sale for \$2.50 per pound. Which graph shows the relationship between the number of pounds of peaches purchased and the total cost? B

A
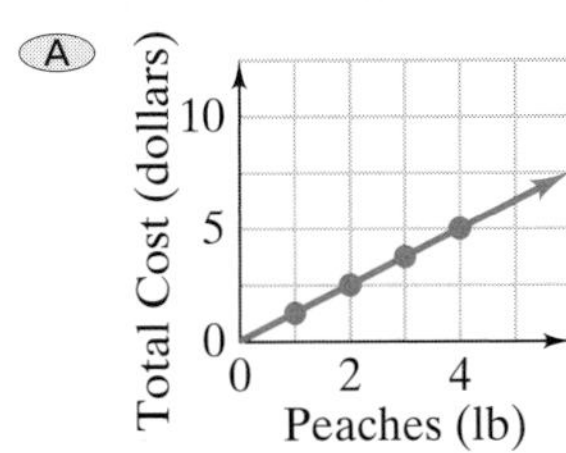

C
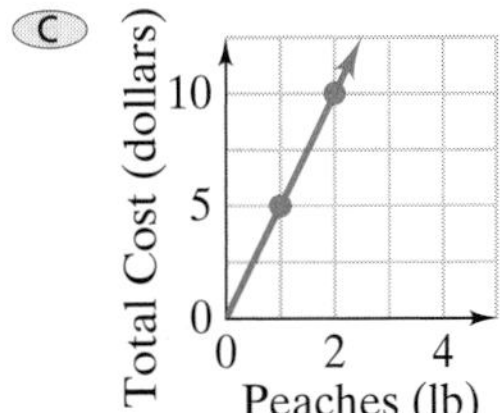

B
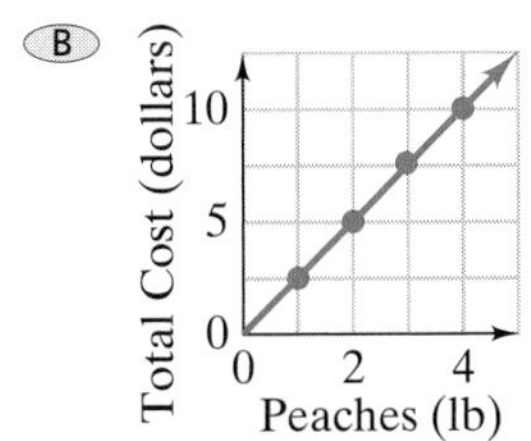

D
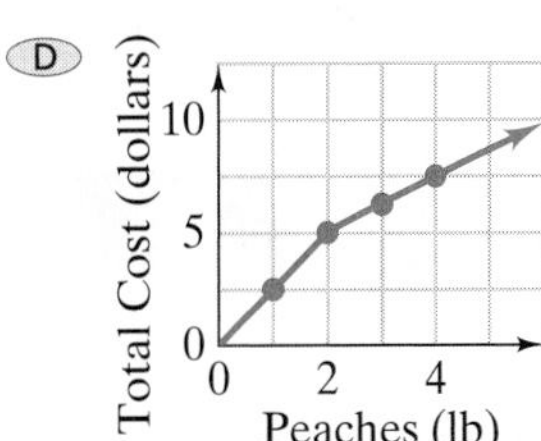

Alg1 2.0

25. Which value is a square root of 25? C

Ⓐ −25 Ⓑ 2.5 Ⓒ 5 Ⓓ 625

Lesson 5-3

Use the function rule $f(x) = 2x + 5$. Find each output.

26. $f(2)$ 9 **27.** $f(-3)$ −1 **28.** $f(27)$ 59 **29.** $f\left(\frac{4}{5}\right)$ $\frac{33}{5}$

GO Online Lesson Quiz Visit: PHSchool.com Web Code: axa-0806

Alternative Assessment

Each student in a pair writes a direct variation in the form $y = kx$, where $k \neq 0$, and makes a table of its values. Then the students swap papers, graph their partners' direct variation, and find the slope.

California Resources

Standards Mastery

- Standards Review Transparencies
- Standards Review and Practice Workbook
- Math Companion

Math Intervention

- Skills Review and Practice Workbook
- Math XL

4. Assess & Reteach

PRESENTATION CD-ROM
CD, Online, or Transparencies

Lesson Quiz

1. Christine makes \$8 per hour babysitting. The amount of money she earns varies directly with the number of hours she works. Use the direct variation $e = 8h$, where h is the number of hours worked and e is the amount of money earned. Find how much Christine will make if she works 14 hours in one week. \$112

2. One kilogram is equivalent to about 2.2 pounds. Graph the relationship between pounds and kilograms. Find the slope of the line and explain what it represents.

Kilograms	1	2	3	4
Pounds	2.2	4.4	6.6	8.8

The slope is 2.2. It represents the number of kilograms per pound.

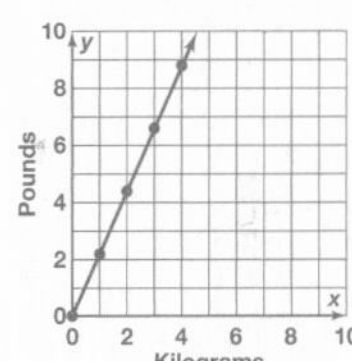

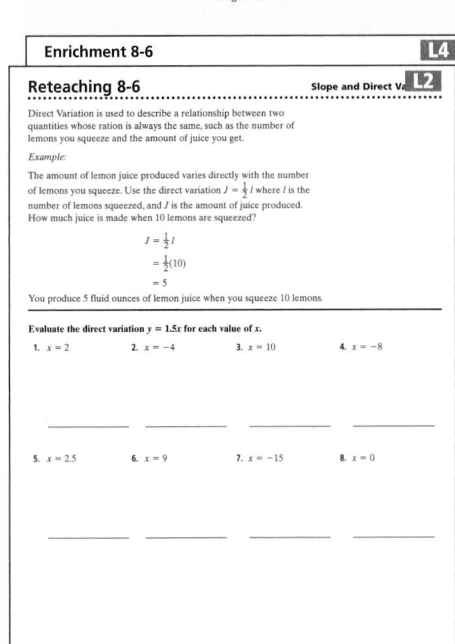

Enrichment 8-6 L4

Reteaching 8-6 Slope and Direct Va L2

Direct Variation is used to describe a relationship between two quantities whose ration is always the same, such as the number of lemons you squeeze and the amount of juice you get.

Example:

The amount of lemon juice produced varies directly with the number of lemons you squeeze. Use the direct variation $J = \frac{1}{2}l$ where l is the number of lemons squeezed, and J is the amount of juice produced. How much juice is made when 10 lemons are squeezed?

$$J = \frac{1}{2}l$$
$$= \frac{1}{2}(10)$$
$$= 5$$

You produce 5 fluid ounces of lemon juice when you squeeze 10 lemons.

Evaluate the direct variation $y = 1.5x$ for each value of x.

1. $x = 2$ 2. $x = -4$ 3. $x = 10$ 4. $x = -8$

5. $x = 2.5$ 6. $x = 9$ 7. $x = -15$ 8. $x = 0$

Mathematical Reasoning

Using a Graph to Estimate

Students learn how to use a graph to estimate unknown quantities and to use direct variations to find exact answers algebraically.

Guided Instruction

Explain to students that some real-world problems require only approximate solutions while others require exact solutions. When input and output values are small integers, it is convenient to mentally calculate solutions, but when values are large or very precise, graphing and solving algebraic equations allow you to find solutions.

AF 4.2 Solve multistep problems involving rate, average speed, distance, and time or a direct variation. ***Develop***
MR 2.3 Estimate unknown quantities graphically and solve for them by using logical reasoning and arithmetic and algebraic techniques. ***Develop***

Using a Graph to Estimate

You can use a graph to estimate unknown quantities. To find an exact answer, you can solve an equation algebraically.

EXAMPLE

Suppose you burn about 257 Cal during 1 h of walking. The total number of Calories c you burn by walking for h hours is given by the direct variation $c = 257h$. Find the number of hours you need to walk to burn 600 Cal.

First estimate graphically. Make a table and graph the function. Find the point on the graph that represents 600 Cal burned.

Hours, h	Number of Calories, c
1	257
2	514
3	771

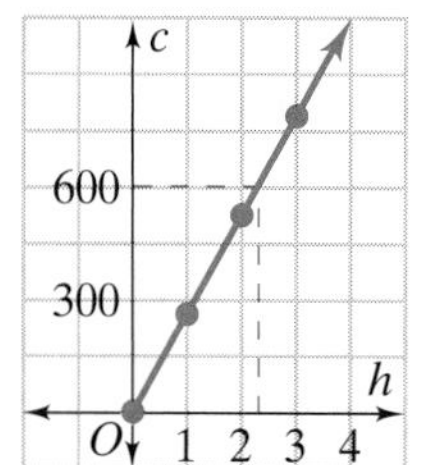

The graph shows that you need to walk for about 2.25 h to burn 600 Cal.

Now use the direct variation to find the exact answer algebraically.

$y = 257x$ ← Use the direct variation.

$600 = 257x$ ← Substitute 600 Cal for y.

$\frac{600}{257} = \frac{257x}{257}$ ← Isolate the variable. Use the Division Property of Equality.

$2.3 \approx x$ ← Simplify. Round to the nearest tenth.

You need to walk for about 2.3 h. This is close to the estimate of 2.25 h.

Exercises

1. The deeper a scuba diver descends, the more pressure the diver feels. The function $p = 1 + 0.03x$ represents the approximate pressure p in atmospheres at x feet below sea level. Use a graph to estimate the depth at which a diver feels a pressure of 1.5 atmospheres. **about 17 ft below sea level**
2. Use the function from Exercise 1 to find algebraically the depth where the pressure is 1.5 atmospheres. **$16\frac{2}{3}$ ft below sea level**

Using a Graph

You can use a graph to answer some questions. Be sure to draw your graph accurately enough to find the exact solution.

EXAMPLE

At a fair, 4 balloons cost $2. How much do 7 balloons cost?

Ⓐ $.50 Ⓒ $3.50
Ⓑ $2 Ⓓ $9

Let x represent the number of balloons. Let y represent the total cost. You know it costs $0 to buy 0 balloons and $2 to buy 4 balloons. Plot the points (0, 0) and (4, 2) on a coordinate plane. Connect the points with a line. Find the point that represents 7 balloons.

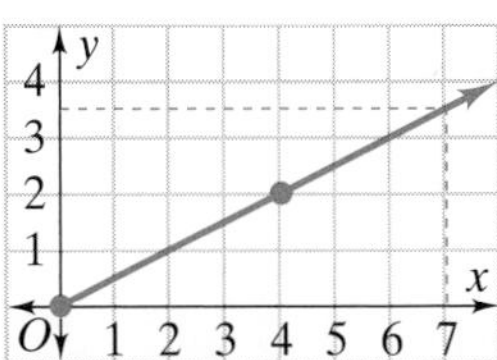

The graph shows that the cost is $3.50 for 7 balloons. The correct answer is choice C.

Multiple Choice Practice

Use a graph to solve each of the following.

AF 3.4 **1.** The relationship between the side length s of a square and its perimeter P is given by the function $P = 4s$. Find the perimeter of a square with sides of length 3 cm. D

Ⓐ 3 cm Ⓒ 7 cm
Ⓑ 4 cm Ⓓ 12 cm

AF 4.2 **2.** In 2 h, 3 mm of rain falls. At that rate, how much rain will fall in 6 h? C

Ⓐ 1.5 mm Ⓒ 9 mm
Ⓑ 3 mm Ⓓ 10.5 mm

AF 4.2 **3.** You can buy 4 pens for $3.00. How much will it cost if you buy 9 pens? D

Ⓐ $.50 Ⓒ $6.00
Ⓑ $.75 Ⓓ $6.75

Using a Graph

Students learn how to use a graph to find solutions to questions.

Guided Instruction

Explain that it is best to use graph paper if it is available because it makes the graph more accurate. Also, review the importance of making sure that the intervals on the x- and y-axes are even.

Example

Ask:

- *Why is it possible to graph a line if only one pair of coordinates is given?* **The graph of the given linear function has to begin at (0, 0) because 0 balloons will cost $0. Therefore, the origin provides the second pair of coordinates.**

Chapter 8 Review

California Resources

Standards Mastery
- Math Companion
- Standards Review Transparencies
- Standards Review and Practice Workbook
- Progress Monitoring Assessments

Math Intervention
- Skills Review and Practice Workbook
- Math XL

Universal Access Resources
- Student Workbook
  - Vocabulary and Study Skills
  - Guided Problem Solving
- All-in-One Teaching Resources
  - Reteaching
  - Enrichment
- Spanish Practice Workbook L3
- Spanish Vocabulary and Study Skills 2A-F L3
- English/Spanish Glossary EL
- Multilingual Handbook EL
- Interactive Textbook Audio Glossary
- Online Vocabulary Quiz

Online at PHSchool.com

Spanish Vocabulary/Study Skills EL

Vocabulary/Study Skills L3

8F: Vocabulary Review For use with the Chapter Review

Study Skill Taking short breaks can help you stay focused. Every 30 minutes, take a 5-minute break, then return to studying.

I. Match the term in Column A with its definition in Column B.

Column A	Column B
1. quadrant	A. the second coordinate in an ordered pair
2. origin	B. a vertical number line
3. y-axis	C. any one of the four sections into which the coordinate plane is divided
4. x-coordinate	D. the point where the x-axis and the y-axis intersect, indicated by the ordered pair (0, 0)
5. solution	E. an equation that describes a function
6. function rule	F. any ordered pair that makes an equation true
7. y-coordinate	G. the first coordinate in an ordered pair

II. Match the term in Column A with its definition in Column B.

Column A	Column B
1. slope	A. two or more linear equations
2. coordinate plane	B. an equation whose solutions all lie on a line
3. ordered pair	C. a relationship that assigns exactly one output value to each input value
4. linear equation	D. ratio that describes steepness of a line
5. function	E. a horizontal number line
6. x-axis	F. gives the coordinates of the location of a point
7. system of linear equations	G. a grid formed by the intersection of two number lines

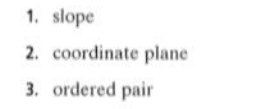

Vocabulary Review

English and Spanish Audio Online

coordinate plane (p. 288)
direct variation (p. 316)
function (p. 298)
function rule (p. 298)
linear equation (p. 303)
linear function (p. 303)
ordered pair (p. 288)
origin (p. 288)
quadrants (p. 288)
slope (p. 310)
slope of a line (p. 310)
solution (p. 303)
***x*-axis** (p. 288)
***x*-coordinate** (p. 288)
***y*-axis** (p. 288)
***y*-coordinate** (p. 288)

For: Vocabulary Quiz
Visit: PHSchool.com
Web Code: axj-0851

Choose the correct vocabulary term to complete each sentence.

1. A function whose points lie on a line is a(n) __?__. linear function
2. The coordinate plane is divided into four __?__. quadrants
3. A(n) __?__ is any value that makes an equation true. solution
4. The x-axis and the y-axis intersect at the __?__. origin
5. A(n) __?__ is a relationship that assigns exactly one output value to each input value. function

Skills and Concepts

Lessons 8-1, 8-2

- To graph points in a coordinate plane
- To find lengths of line segments in the coordinate plane

Foundational Standard, MG 3.3

An **ordered pair** describes the location of a point on a **coordinate plane.** The first number is the ***x*-coordinate**. The second is the ***y*-coordinate.**

You can use the Pythagorean Theorem to find the length of a line segment in the coordinate plane.

Identify the coordinates of each point in the graph at the right.

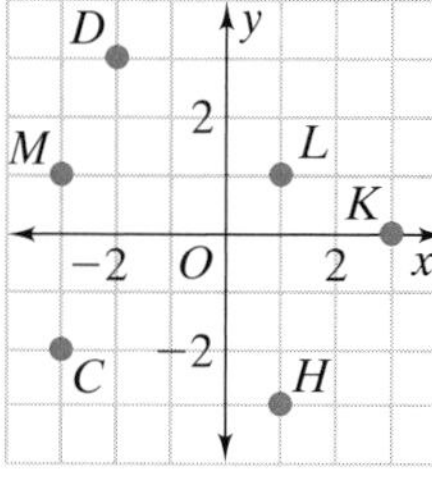

6. C (−3, −2)
7. D (−2, 3)
8. H (1, −3)
9. K (3, 0)
10. L (1, 1)
11. M (−3, 1)

Graph each point on the same coordinate plane.
12–15. See left.

12–15.
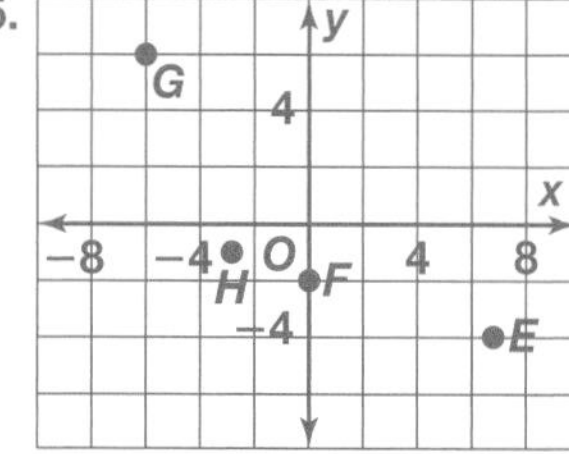

12. $E(7, -4)$
13. $F(0, -2)$
14. $G(-6, 6)$
15. $H(-3, -1)$

Find the length of the line segment with the given endpoints.

16. $A(7, 8)$, $B(-3, 8)$ 10
17. $M(0, 8)$, $N(6, 0)$ 10
18. $Q(-5, 0)$, $R(0, 12)$ 13

Alternative Assessment L4

Alternative Assessment — Form C

Chapter 8

HIT THE SLOPES

Did you ever consider the fun that you can have on a mountain? Going up mountains is fun for hikers. Going down mountains is fun for skiers.

Show all of your work on a separate sheet of paper.

1. The steeper a mountain is, the harder it is to climb up or down. Look at these two mountain profiles and decide which one looks harder to climb. Explain.

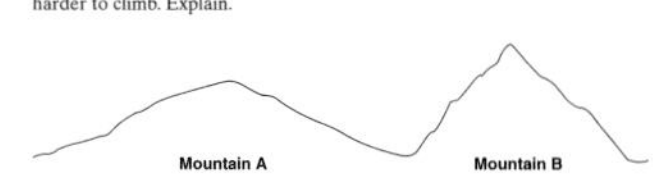

2. Ski resorts mark their trails with symbols that show the levels of difficulty of the trails. Circles represent the easiest trails, squares represent somewhat harder trails, and diamonds represent the most difficult. The map below shows several trails at Mount Ski. Choose one circle trail, one square trail, and one diamond trail. Circle the trails you choose and give them each an appropriate name.

3. Copy the chart below. Draw the profile of each of your three trails in the chart. (A profile of a ski trail shows how steep it is.) A sample profile of the beginner trail appears on the chart.

Profile Chart		
Type of trail	Name	Profile
Beginner	Easy as Pie	

Lesson 8-3

- To evaluate and write function rules

AF 1.1

A **function** is a relationship that assigns exactly one output value to each input value. A **function rule** is an equation that describes a function. In function notation, $f(3)$ represents the output of a function f when the input is 3.

Use the function rule $f(x) = 4x - 7$. Find each output.

19. $f(3)$ 5 **20.** $f(0)$ −7 **21.** $f(-5)$ −27 **22.** $f\left(\frac{1}{2}\right)$ −5

23. $f(8.5)$ 27 **24.** $f\left(-\frac{4}{9}\right)$ $-8\frac{7}{9}$ **25.** $f(21)$ 77 **26.** $f(-13)$ −59

Lesson 8-4

- To graph linear functions

AF 3.3, AF 3.4

When the values in an ordered pair make an equation with two variables true, the ordered pair is a **solution** of the equation. A **linear function** is a function whose solutions lie on a line. To graph a linear function, graph several solutions and draw a line through the points.

Graph each linear function. 27–32. See margin.

27. $y = x + 3$ **28.** $y = \frac{1}{4}x - 1$

29. $y = -2x + 1$ **30.** $y = -\frac{2}{3}x$

31. $y = -7x + \frac{1}{2}$ **32.** $y = 2.5x - 3$

Lesson 8-5

- To find the slope of a line

AF 3.3, AF 3.4

Slope is a ratio that describes steepness. It is the ratio of vertical change to horizontal change. The **slope of a line** is equal to the change in y-coordinates divided by the change in x-coordinates.

Find the slope of the line that contains each pair of points.

33. $(1, 2)$ and $(-3, 2)$ 0 **34.** $(5, 1)$ and $(0, -7)$ $\frac{8}{5}$

35. $(-4, 9)$ and $(10, 6)$ $-\frac{3}{14}$ **36.** $(8, -2)$ and $(-2, 8)$ −1

Lesson 8-6

- To understand the relationship between slope and direct variation

AF 3.3, AF 3.4, AF 4.2

A **direct variation** is a linear function in the form $y = kx$, where $k \neq 0$. The variables x and y are said to vary directly with each other.

Evaluate the direct variation $y = \frac{2}{5}x$ for each value of x.

37. $x = 5$ 2 **38.** $x = -2$ $-\frac{4}{5}$ **39.** $x = 15$ 6

40. $x = -6.5$ $-2\frac{3}{5}$ **41.** $x = \frac{7}{8}$ $\frac{7}{20}$ **42.** $x = -\frac{10}{12}$ $-\frac{1}{3}$

43. One gallon contains four quarts. Graph the relationship between gallons and quarts. Use the x-axis for gallons and the y-axis for quarts. Find the slope of the graph and explain what it represents. See margin.

California Resources

Standards Mastery
- Teacher Center ExamView CD-ROM
- Math XL
- Progress Monitoring Assessments
- Online Chapter Test at PHSchool.com

Math Intervention
- Skills Review and Practice Workbook

Online at PHSchool.com

Universal Access Resources
- Chapter Test
- Alternative Assessment
- Spanish Chapter Test
- Spanish Alternative Assessment
- Teacher Center ExamView CD-ROM
  - Special Needs Test
  - Special Needs Practice Banks
  - Foundational Standards Practice Banks
- Online Chapter Test at www.PHSchool.com
- All-In-One Teaching Resources
  - Cumulative Review L3
- Spanish Assessment Resources
  - Cumulative Review 

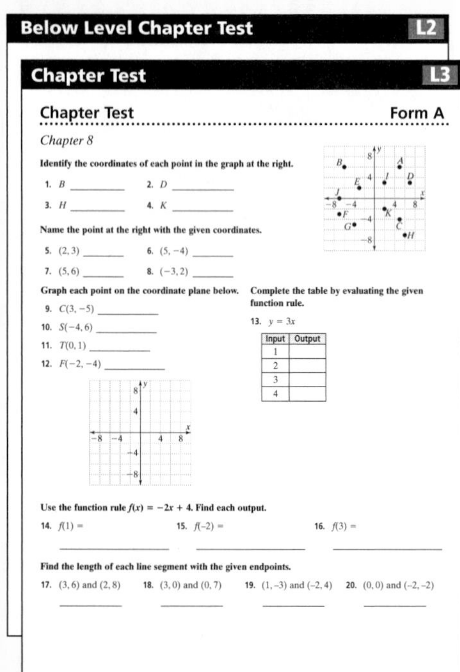

Below Level Chapter Test L2

Chapter Test L3

Chapter Test — Form A

Chapter 8

Identify the coordinates of each point in the graph at the right.

1. B ______ 2. D ______
3. H ______ 4. K ______

Name the point at the right with the given coordinates.

5. (2, 3) ______ 6. (5, −4) ______
7. (5, 6) ______ 8. (−3, 2) ______

Graph each point on the coordinate plane below.

9. C(3, −5) ______
10. S(−4, 6) ______
11. T(0, 1) ______
12. F(−2, −4) ______

Complete the table by evaluating the given function rule.

13. $y = 3x$

Input	Output
1	
2	
3	
4	

Use the function rule $f(x) = -2x + 4$. Find each output.

14. $f(1) =$ 15. $f(-2) =$ 16. $f(3) =$

Find the length of each line segment with the given endpoints.

17. (3, 6) and (2, 8) 18. (3, 0) and (0, 7) 19. (1, −3) and (−2, 4) 20. (0, 0) and (−2, −2)

Chapter 8 Test

Go Online PHSchool.com — **For:** Online chapter test **Web Code:** axa-0852

1–14. See margin.

Identify the coordinates of each point in the graph below.

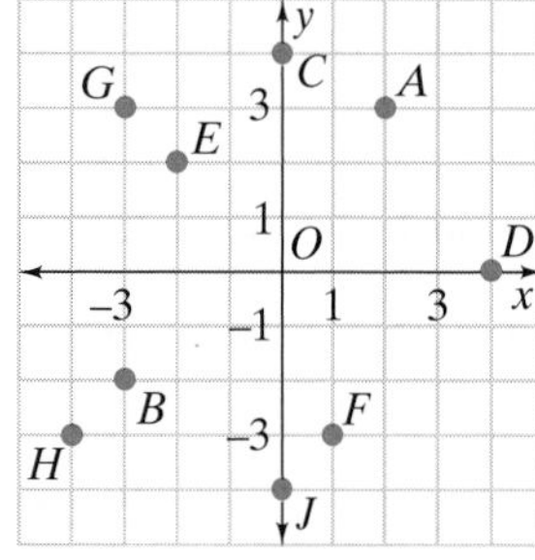

1. A 2. B 3. C 4. D
5. E 6. F 7. H 8. J

Graph each point on the same coordinate plane.

9. $M(4, -2)$ 10. $N(0, 5)$
11. $P(-3, 2)$ 12. $Q(-2, -3)$
13. $R(-1, 3.5)$ 14. $S(-5, 0)$

Find the length of the line segment with the given endpoints.

15. $(-7, 2), (-7, 4)$ 2
16. $(12, 4), (-1, 4)$ 13
17. $(4.5, 3), (-6, 3)$ 10.5
18. $(4, 0), (0, -3)$ 5
19. $(-8, -9), (12, -9)$ 20
20. $(0, 2.5), (6, 0)$ 6.5
21. A movie theater is 12 mi north of your house. A grocery store is 5 mi west of your house. How far is the movie theater from the grocery store? 13 mi

Use the function rule $f(x) = -3x + 5$. Find each output.

22. $f(4)$ −7
23. $f(0)$ 5
24. $f(-3)$ 14
25. $f(3.5)$ −5.5
26. $f(-2.75)$ 13.25
27. $f(12)$ −31
28. Suppose your neighbor is 5 years younger than you. Write a function rule to describe the relationship between your age a and your neighbor's age $f(a)$. $f(a) = a - 5$

29–34. See margin.

29. Graph the values in the table below. Then connect the points with a line.

x	−3	0	3	9
y	6	3	0	−6

Graph each linear function.

30. $y = x - 3$
31. $y = 2x + 8$
32. $y = -2.5x - 2$
33. $y = \frac{1}{2}x - 1\frac{1}{2}$
34. **Writing in Math** Which is steeper, a line with a slope of 7 or a line with a slope of −10? Explain.

Find the slope of each line.

35. 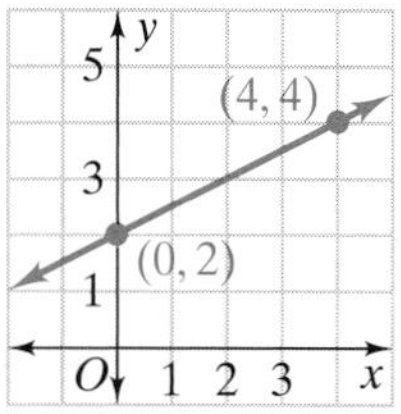 (graph: points (0, 2) and (4, 4); axis labels y, 5, 3, 1, O, 1, 2, 3, x) $\frac{1}{2}$

36. 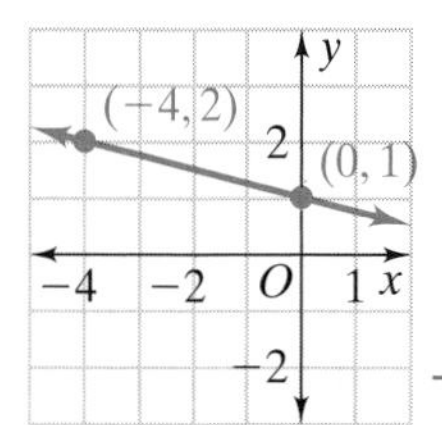

$-\frac{1}{4}$

Find the slope of the line that contains each pair of points. 37–42. See margin.

37. $(-4, 10)$ and $(6, 13)$
38. $(2, 3)$ and $(9, -3)$
39. $(5, 7)$ and $(-12, 4)$
40. $(1, -1)$ and $(5, 6)$
41. $(12, -3)$ and $(8, -9)$
42. $(-3, 4)$ and $(2, 7)$

Evaluate the direct variation $y = -3x$ for each value of x.

43. $x = 5$ −15
44. $x = -7$ 21
45. $x = -4\frac{1}{2}$ $13\frac{1}{2}$
46. $x = 9.2$ −27.6
47. $x = -0.2$ 0.6
48. $x = \frac{1}{3}$ −1
49. A nickel's mass is about 5 g. Graph the relationship between the number of nickels x and the total mass in grams y. Find the slope of the graph and explain what it represents. See margin.

Standards Mastery Cumulative Practice

Some questions require you to find the slope of a line. Use the tips as guides to answer the question at the right.

Find the slope of a line that contains the points $(-7, 2)$ and $(5, 4)$.

(A) $-\frac{1}{6}$ (C) $\frac{1}{6}$

(B) $\frac{1}{12}$ (D) $\frac{6}{1}$

Tip 1
You can find the slope using the formula or by graphing the points and counting the rise and run.

Tip 2
When you use the formula for the slope of a line, the first *y*-coordinate you substitute for the rise and the first *x*-coordinate you substitute for the run must belong to the same point.

Think It Through

Substitute the *x*- and *y*-coordinates into the formula for slope:

$$\text{slope} = \frac{\text{change in } y\text{-coordinates}}{\text{change in } x\text{-coordinates}}$$

$$= \frac{4 - 2}{5 - (-7)}$$

$$= \frac{2}{12} = \frac{1}{6}$$

The correct answer is choice C.

California Resources

Standards Mastery
- Teacher Center ExamView CD-ROM
- Math XL
- Progress Monitoring Assessments
- Online Chapter Test at PHSchool.com

Math Intervention
- Skills Review and Practice Workbook

Universal Access Resources
- Teacher Center ExamView CD-ROM
  - Special Needs Test
  - Special Needs Practice Banks
  - Foundational Standards Practice Banks
- Online Chapter Test at www.PHSchool.com
- All-In-One Teaching Resources
  - Cumulative Review L3
- Spanish Assessment Resources
  - Cumulative Review L3

Success Tracker™
Online at PHSchool.com

Vocabulary Review

As you solve problems, you must understand the meanings of mathematical terms. Match each term with its mathematical meaning.

A. linear function IV
B. origin II
C. quadrants I
D. slope III

I. the four regions of the coordinate plane
II. the intersection point of the *x*- and *y*-axes
III. a ratio that describes steepness
IV. a function whose graph is a straight line

Read each question. Then write the letter of the correct answer on your paper.

1. Megan gets a 15-min break for every 3 h of work. She works 5 h. How much break time should Megan have? (Lesson 6-4) C

   (A) 17 min (C) 25 min
   (B) 23 min (D) 75 min

2. A band raises money by selling school sweatshirts. For each sweatshirt sold, the band earns $2. Which function describes the relationship between the number of sweatshirts *n* sold and the band's total earnings $f(n)$? (Lesson 8-3) A

   (A) $f(n) = 2n$ (C) $f(n) = 2 + n$
   (B) $f(n) = \frac{1}{2}n$ (D) $f(n) = 2n - 2$

3. Which graph represents the function with values shown in the table below? **(Lesson 8-4) A**

x	−1	0	2
y	−2	−1	1

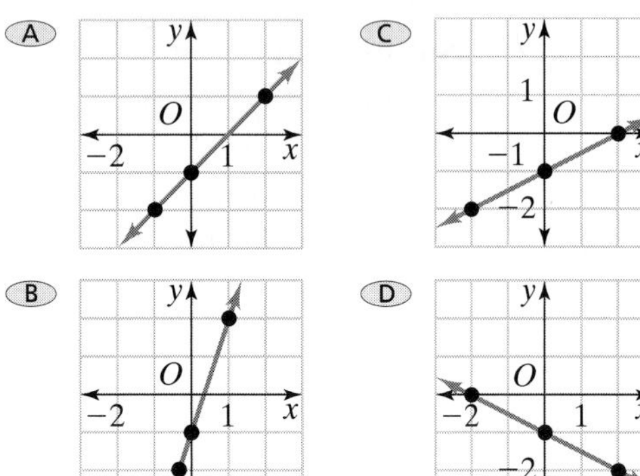

4. What is the length of the line segment with endpoints (−3, 0) and (0, 4)? **(Lesson 8-2) B**

Ⓐ 3 units Ⓒ 7 units
Ⓑ 5 units Ⓓ 25 units

5. A ream of paper usually contains 500 sheets. If 5 reams cost \$20, what is the cost of 50 reams of paper? **(Lesson 6-4) C**

Ⓐ \$20 Ⓒ \$200
Ⓑ \$100 Ⓓ \$500

6. In a basketball game, both teams have five players on the court at a time. Which function describes the relationship between the number of games *n* being played in a gym at one time and the total number of people playing $T(n)$? **(Lesson 8-3) B**

Ⓐ $T(n) = 5n$
Ⓑ $T(n) = 10n$
Ⓒ $T(n) = n + 5$
Ⓓ $T(n) = \frac{n}{5}$

7. What is the slope of the line that contains the points (−2, 5) and (4, −3)? **(Lesson 8-5) B**

Ⓐ −2 Ⓒ $-\frac{3}{4}$
Ⓑ $-\frac{4}{3}$ Ⓓ $\frac{3}{4}$

8. What is the length of the line segment with endpoints (0, 5) and (12, 0)? **(Lesson 8-2) C**

Ⓐ 5 units Ⓒ 13 units
Ⓑ 7 units Ⓓ 144 units

9. If you spend \$100 at a certain store, you get a \$10 gift card. At the same rate, how much do you have to spend to get a \$25 gift card? **(Lesson 6-4) D**

Ⓐ \$25 Ⓒ \$125
Ⓑ \$100 Ⓓ \$250

10. One quart contains four cups. Which graph shows the relationship between cups and quarts? **(Lesson 8-6) C**

Ⓐ
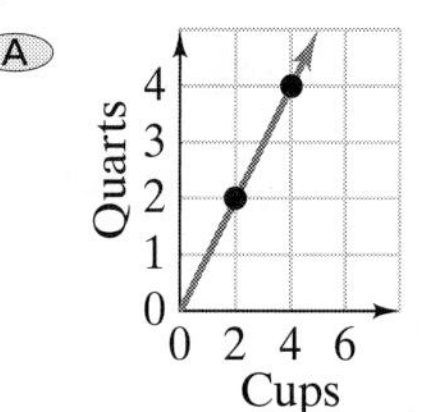

Ⓒ
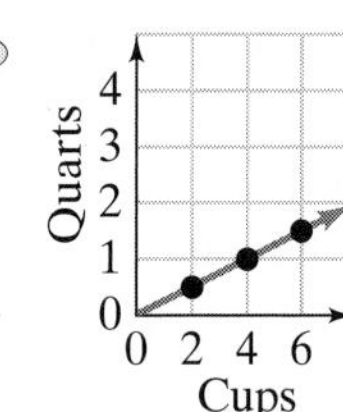

Ⓑ
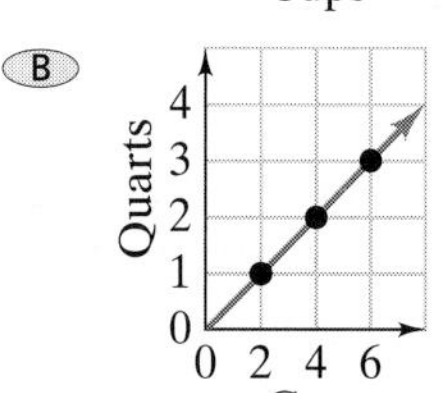

Ⓓ
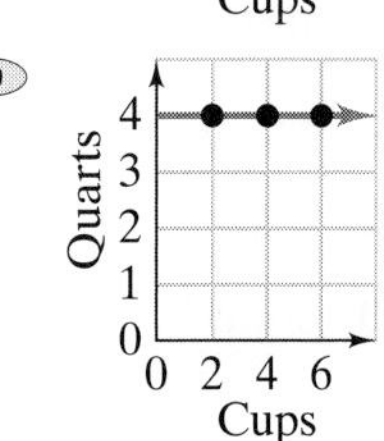

11. Which statement is true? **(Lesson 8-5) C**

Ⓐ Slope is the ratio of run to rise.
Ⓑ The slope of a line is always positive.
Ⓒ The slope is the same between any two points on a line.
Ⓓ The slope of a vertical line is 0.

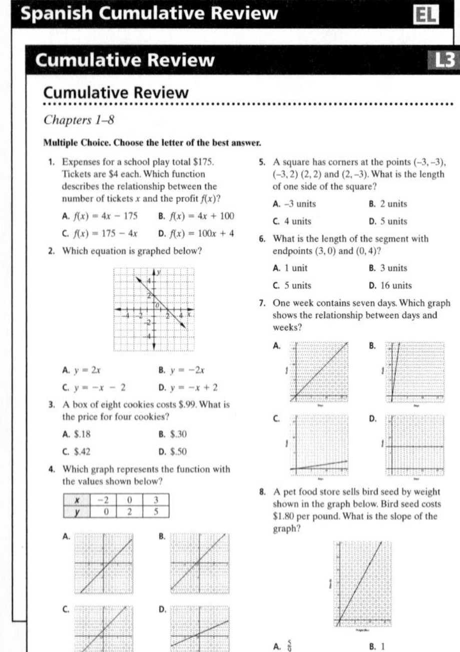

Spanish Cumulative Review EL

Cumulative Review L3

Cumulative Review

Chapters 1–8

Multiple Choice. Choose the letter of the best answer.

1. Expenses for a school play total \$175. Tickets are \$4 each. Which function describes the relationship between the number of tickets *x* and the profit $f(x)$?
   A. $f(x) = 4x - 175$ B. $f(x) = 4x + 100$
   C. $f(x) = 175 - 4x$ D. $f(x) = 100x + 4$
2. Which equation is graphed below?
   A. $y = 2x$ B. $y = -2x$
   C. $y = -x - 2$ D. $y = -x + 2$
3. A box of eight cookies costs \$.99. What is the price for four cookies?
   A. \$.18 B. \$.30
   C. \$.42 D. \$.50
4. Which graph represents the function with the values shown below?

x	−2	0	3
y	0	2	5

   A. B. C. D.
5. A square has corners at the points (−3, −3), (−3, 2) (2, 2) and (2, −3). What is the length of one side of the square?
   A. −3 units B. 2 units
   C. 4 units D. 5 units
6. What is the length of the segment with endpoints (3, 0) and (0, 4)?
   A. 1 unit B. 3 units
   C. 5 units D. 16 units
7. One week contains seven days. Which graph shows the relationship between days and weeks?
   A. B. C. D.
8. A pet food store sells bird seed by weight shown in the graph below. Bird seed costs \$1.80 per pound. What is the slope of the graph?
   A. $\frac{5}{9}$ B. 1
   C. 1.8 D. 27

12. Which graph represents the linear function $y = -\frac{1}{2}x - 1$? (Lesson 8-4) C

Ⓐ 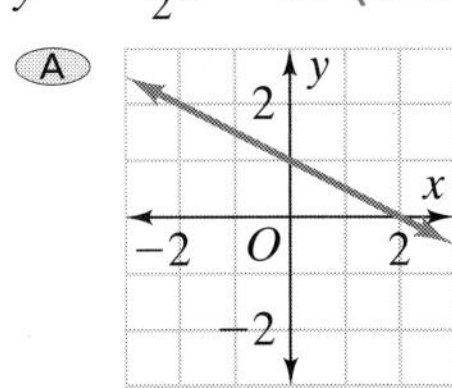
Ⓒ 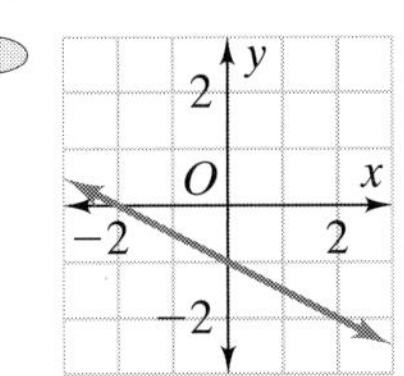
Ⓑ 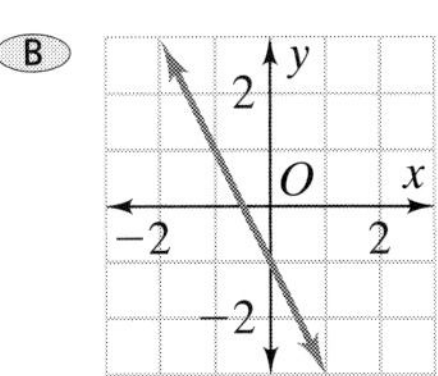
Ⓓ 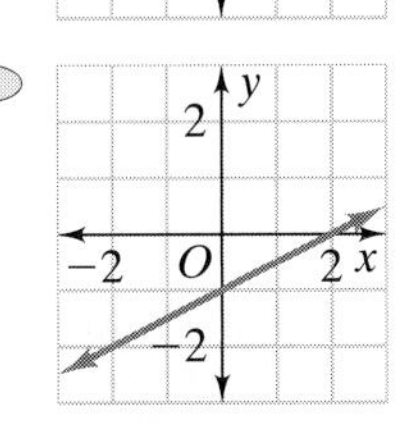

13. What is the length of the hypotenuse of a right triangle with vertices at $(-1, -2)$, $(2, -2)$, and $(2, 2)$? (Lesson 8-2) C

Ⓐ 3 units Ⓒ 5 units
Ⓑ 4 units Ⓓ 9 units

14. A jeweler sells rings based on their mass as shown in the graph below. In the graph, x represents the mass, and y represents the price. A ring costs \$22.50 per gram. What is the slope of the graph? (Lesson 8-6) C

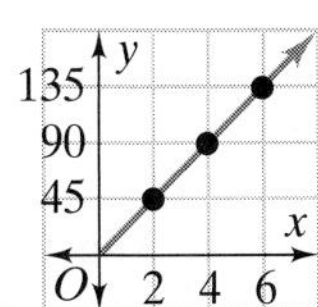

Ⓐ $\frac{2}{45}$ Ⓒ 22.5
Ⓑ 1 Ⓓ $\frac{135}{1}$

15. Ms. Coffey pays \$.20 for each gallon of water she uses. Which function describes the relationship between the gallons of water g she uses and the total bill $c(g)$? (Lesson 8-3) B

Ⓐ $c(g) = \frac{3}{5}g$ Ⓒ $c(g) = 0.2 + g$
Ⓑ $c(g) = 0.2g$ Ⓓ $c(g) = g$

16. Green beans are on sale for \$1.25 per pound. Which graph shows the relationship between the number of pounds of green beans you buy and the total cost? (Lesson 8-6) D

Ⓐ 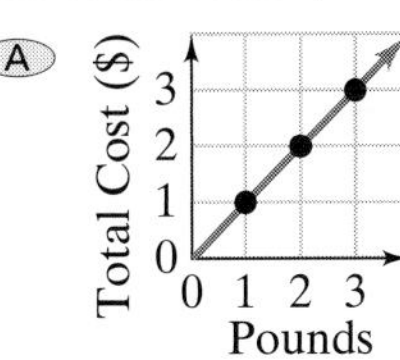
Ⓒ 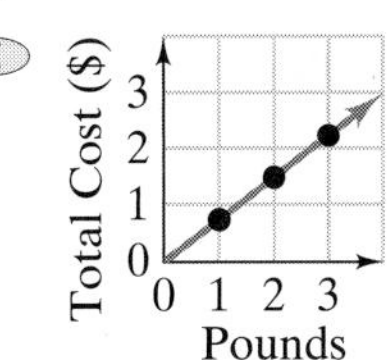
Ⓑ 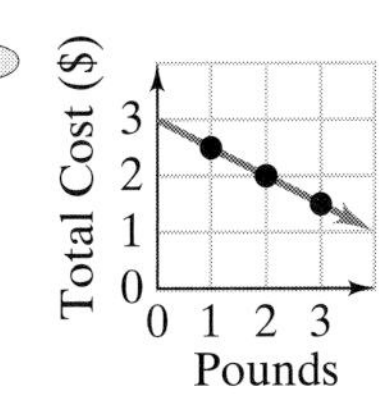
Ⓓ 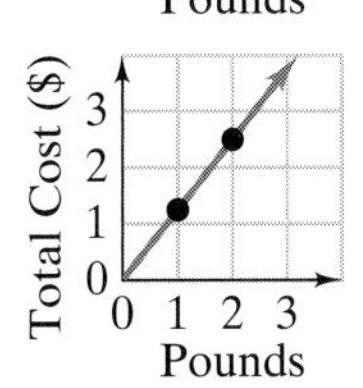

Standards Reference Guide

California Content Standard	Item Number(s)
AF 1.1	2, 6, 15
AF 3.3	3, 7, 11, 12
AF 3.4	10, 14, 16
AF 4.2	1, 5, 9
MG 3.3	4, 8, 13

For additional review and practice, see the *California Standards Review and Practice Workbook* or go online to use the

Visit: PHSchool.com, **Web Code:** axq-9045

Inequalities

Chapter at a Glance

Lesson Titles, Objectives, and Features	California Content Standards	
9-1 Writing Inequalities • To write and test inequalities	**AF 1.1**	Use variables and appropriate operations to write an inequality or system of inequalities that represents a verbal description.
9-2 Solving Inequalities by Adding or Subtracting • To solve inequalities by adding or subtracting **Vocabulary Builder:** Writing Inequalities	**AF 1.1**	Use variables and appropriate operations to write an inequality or system of inequalities that represents a verbal description.
	AF 4.1	Solve two-step linear inequalities in one variable. ***(Prepares for)***
9-3 Solving Inequalities by Dividing • To solve inequalities by dividing **Mathematical Reasoning:** Inequalities and Negative Numbers	**AF 1.1**	Use variables and appropriate operations to write an inequality that represents a verbal description.
	AF 4.1	Solve two-step linear inequalities in one variable. ***(Prepares for)***
9-4 Solving Inequalities by Multiplying • To solve inequalities by multiplying **Mathematical Reasoning:** Everyday Inequalities	**AF 1.1**	Use variables and appropriate operations to write an inequality that represents a verbal description.
	AF 4.1	Solve two-step linear inequalities in one variable. ***(Prepares for)***
	MR 3.3	Develop generalizations of the results obtained and the strategies used and apply them to new problem situations.
9-5 Solving Two-Step Inequalities • To solve two-step inequalities **9-5b Activity Lab:** Systems of Inequalities	**AF 1.1**	Use variables and appropriate operations to write an inequality that represents a verbal description.
	AF 4.1	Solve two-step linear inequalities in one variable over the rational numbers, interpret the solution or solutions in the context from which they arose, and verify the reasonableness of the results.
	MR 2.6	Support solutions with evidence in both verbal and symbolic work.

California Content Standards
NS Number Sense
AF Algebra and Functions
MG Measurement and Geometry
MR Mathematical Reasoning

Correlations to Standardized Tests

All content for these tests is contained in *Prentice Hall Math, Algebra Readiness.* This chart reflects coverage in this chapter only.

	9-1	9-2	9-3	9-4	9-5
Terra Nova CAT6 (Level 18)					
Number and Number Relations	✔	✔	✔	✔	✔
Computation and Numerical Estimation	✔	✔	✔	✔	✔
Operation Concepts		✔	✔	✔	✔
Measurement					
Geometry and Spatial Sense					
Data Analysis, Statistics, and Probability					
Patterns, Functions, Algebra	✔	✔	✔	✔	✔
Problem Solving and Reasoning	✔	✔	✔	✔	✔
Communication	✔	✔	✔	✔	✔
Decimals, Fractions, Integers, Percent	✔	✔	✔	✔	✔
Order of Operations					✔
Algebraic Operations	✔	✔	✔	✔	✔
Terra Nova CTBS (Level 18)					
Decimals, Fractions, Integers, Percents	✔	✔	✔	✔	✔
Order of Operations, Numeration, Number Theory	✔	✔	✔	✔	✔
Data Interpretation					
Measurement					
Geometry					
ITBS (Level 14)					
Number Properties and Operations	✔	✔	✔	✔	✔
Algebra	✔	✔	✔	✔	✔
Geometry					
Measurement					
Probability and Statistics					
Estimation					
SAT10 (Adv 1 Level)					
Number Sense and Operations	✔	✔	✔	✔	✔
Patterns, Relationships, and Algebra	✔	✔	✔	✔	✔
Data, Statistics, and Probability					
Geometry and Measurement					
NAEP					
Number Sense, Properties, and Operations	✔	✔	✔	✔	✔
Measurement					
Geometry and Spatial Sense					
Data Analysis, Statistics, and Probability					
Algebra and Functions					

CAT6 California Achievement Test, 6th Ed. **CTBS** Comprehensive Test of Basic Skills **ITBS** Iowa Test of Basic Skills, Form M
SAT10 Stanford Achievement Test, 10th Ed. **NAEP** National Assessment of Educational Progress 2005 Mathematics Objectives

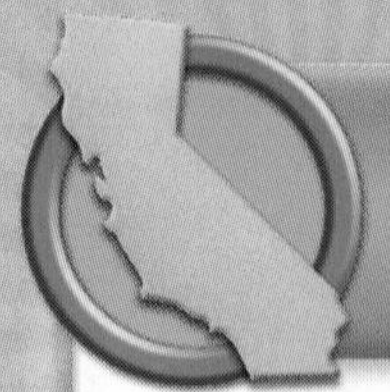

California Math Background

Focus on the California Content Standards

- Standards in grades 3 through 7 provided opportunities for students to work with inequality relationships. So, careful assessment of computation skills as well as conceptual understanding of inequalities is important to planning for this chapter.
- The Number Sense and Algebra and Functions standards in grade 3 had students comparing and ordering whole numbers (**NS 1.2**), and selecting symbols, operations, and properties to represent and solve simple number relationships (**AF 1.0**). Students ordered and compared various forms of rational numbers and placed them on a number line (Grade 6, **NS 1.1**).

9-1 Writing Inequalities

California Content Standards **AF 1.1**

Math Understandings

- We can use special symbols to describe how two numbers or expressions are related to each other.

A mathematical sentence that contains one of the following symbols is an **inequality**.

$<$ is less than	$>$ is greater than
$\leq$ is less than or equal to	$\geq$ is greater than or equal to
$\neq$ is not equal to	

The **solution of an inequality** is any value that makes the inequality true. The graph of an inequality shows that an inequality can have many solutions. A closed circle indicates that a value *is* included. An open circle indicates that a value is *not* included.

Example: Write an inequality for the verbal description "The height h is less than 8 feet."

$h < 8$

9-2 Solving Inequalities by Adding or Subtracting

California Content Standards **AF 1.1**

Math Understandings

- To solve an inequality, you can use a process that is similar to the one used to solve an equation.
- When the only operations you use to solve an inequality are addition and subtraction, the procedure is the same as it is for solving an equation.

Addition and Subtraction Properties of Inequalities

When you add or subtract the same number on each side of an inequality, the relationship between the two sides does not change.

Arithmetic	Algebra
Because $8 < 12$, $8 + 3 < 12 + 3$ and $8 - 4 < 12 - 4$.	If $a < b$, then $a + c < b + c$ and $a - c < b - c$.
Because $10 > 7$, $10 + 5 > 7 + 5$ and $10 - 2 > 7 - 2$.	If $a > b$, then $a + c > b + c$ and $a - c > b - c$.

To solve an inequality by adding or subtracting, use inverse operations to get the variable alone on one side of the inequality symbol.

Example: Solve $x - 7 > 3$.

$$x - 7 > 3$$
$$x - 7 + 7 > 3 + 7 \leftarrow \text{Add 7 to each side.}$$
$$x > 10 \quad \leftarrow \text{Simplify.}$$

9-3 Solving Inequalities by Dividing

California Content Standards **AF 1.1**

Math Understandings

- The steps for solving one-step and two-step inequalities are much the same as those for solving equations.
- Dividing both sides of an inequality by a positive number does not change the direction of the inequality sign, but dividing by a negative number changes the direction of the inequality sign.

Division Property of Inequality	
Because $9 > 6, \frac{9}{3} > \frac{6}{3}.$	If $a > b$ and $c > 0$, then $\frac{a}{c} > \frac{b}{c}.$
Because $15 < 20, \frac{15}{5} < \frac{20}{5}.$	If $a < b$ and $c > 0$, then $\frac{a}{c} < \frac{b}{c}.$
Because $16 > 12, \frac{16}{-4} < \frac{12}{-4}.$	If $a > b$ and $c < 0$, then $\frac{a}{c} < \frac{b}{c}.$
Because $10 < 18, \frac{10}{-2} > \frac{18}{-2}.$	If $a < b$ and $c < 0$, then $\frac{a}{c} > \frac{b}{c}.$

Example: Solve $-8b \geq -24$

$$-8b \geq -24$$
$$\frac{-8b}{-8} \leq \frac{-24}{-8}$$
$$b \leq \blacksquare$$

9-4 Solving Inequalities by Multiplying

California Content Standards **AF 1.1**

Math Understandings

- There is one very important difference between the operations you use to solve an equation and to solve an inequality: multiplying or dividing by a negative number reverses the sign of the inequality.

Multiplication Property of Inequality	
Because $9 > 5$, $9 \cdot 2 > 5 \cdot 2$.	If $a > b$ and $c > 0$, then $a \cdot c > b \cdot c$.
Because $3 < 6$, $3 \cdot 4 < 6 \cdot 4$.	If $a < b$ and $c > 0$, then $a \cdot c < b \cdot c$.
Because $7 > 4$, $7 \cdot (-2) < 4 \cdot (-2)$.	If $a > b$ and $c < 0$, then $a \cdot c < b \cdot c$.
Because $2 < 8$, $2 \cdot (-3) > 8 \cdot (-3)$.	If $a < b$ and $c < 0$, then $a \cdot c > b \cdot c$.

Example: Solve $2 < \frac{x}{-3}$.

$$(-3)(2) > \left(\frac{x}{-3}\right)(-3)$$
$$-6 > x$$

9-5 Solving Two-Step Inequalities

California Content Standards **AF 1.1, AF 4.1**

Math Understandings

- A two-step inequality is an inequality that contains two operations.
- Solving a two-step inequality is similar to solving a two-step equation.

To solve a two-step inequality, isolate the variable. Multiplying or dividing by a negative number changes the direction of the inequality symbol.

Example: Solve $\frac{1}{3}x - 5 \leq 7$.

$$\frac{1}{3}x - 5 + 5 \leq 7 + 5 \quad \leftarrow \text{Addition Property of Equality}$$
$$\frac{1}{3}x \leq 12 \quad \leftarrow \text{Simplify.}$$
$$\frac{3}{1} \cdot \frac{1}{3}x \leq 12 \cdot \frac{3}{1} \quad \leftarrow \text{Divide by } \tfrac{1}{3} \text{ by multiplying by } \tfrac{3}{1}\text{, the reciprocal of } \tfrac{1}{3}.$$
$$x \leq 36 \quad \leftarrow \text{Simplify.}$$

Professional Development

Additional Professional Development Opportunities

Math Background notes for Chapter 9: Every lesson has a Math Background in the PLAN section.

In-Service On Demand
Prentice Hall offers free video-based tutorials to support you. Visit PHSchool.com/inserviceondemand.

Pearson Achievement Solutions
Pearson Achievement Solutions, a Pearson Education company, offers comprehensive, facilitated professional development designed to help teachers improve student achievement. To learn more, please visit pearsonachievementsolutions.com.

Chapter 9 Resources

	9-1	9-2	9-3	9-4	9-5	For the Chapter
Print Resources						
L3 Practice	●	●	●	●	●	
L3 Guided Problem Solving	●	●	●	●	●	
L2 Reteaching	●	●	●	●	●	
L4 Enrichment	●	●	●	●	●	
L3 Vocabulary and Study Skills	●	●	●	●	●	●
L3 Daily Puzzles	●	●	●	●	●	
L3 Activity Labs	●	●	●	●	●	
L3 Checkpoint Quiz		●		●		
L3 Chapter Project						●
L2 Chapter Test						●
L3 Chapter Test						●
L4 Alternative Assessment						●
L3 Cumulative Review						●
Spanish Resources EL						
L3 Practice	●	●	●	●	●	
L3 Vocabulary and Study Skills	●	●	●	●	●	●
L3 Checkpoint Quiz		●		●		
L2 Below Level Chapter Test						●
L3 Chapter Test						●
L4 Alternative Assessment						●
L3 Cumulative Review						●
Transparencies						
Check Skills You'll Need	●	●	●	●	●	
Additional Examples	●	●	●	●	●	
California Daily Review	●	●	●	●	●	
Classroom Aid				●		
Student Edition Answers	●	●	●	●	●	●
Lesson Quiz	●	●	●	●	●	
Technology						
California Student Center Online	●	●	●	●	●	●
California Student Center CD-ROM	●	●	●	●	●	●
Success Tracker™ Online Math Intervention	●	●	●	●	●	●
California Teacher Center: ExamView CD-ROM	●	●	●	●	●	●
California Teacher Center: Planning CD-ROM	●	●	●	●	●	●
California Teacher Center: Presentations CD-ROM and online	●	●	●	●	●	●
MindPoint Quiz Show	●	●	●	●	●	●
Prentice Hall Web Site: PHSchool.com	●	●	●	●	●	●

Also available:

California Standards Mastery
- Standards Review Transparencies
- Standards Review and Practice Workbook
- Progress Monitoring Assessments
- Math Companion
- Math*XL*

California Intervention Resources
- Skills Review and Practice Workbook
- Success Tracker™ Online Math Intervention

Other Resources
- Multilingual Handbook
- Spanish Student Edition
- Solution Key
- Math Notes Study Folder

Where You Can Use the Lesson Resources

Here is a suggestion, following the four-step teaching plan, for how you can incorporate Universal Access Resources into your teaching.

	Instructional Resources L3	Universal Access Resources
1. Plan		
Preparation Read the Math Background in the Teacher's Edition to connect this lesson with students' previous experience. **Starting Class** **Check Skills You'll Need** Assign these exercises from the Math Companion to review prerequisite skills. Review the full text of the student expectations and objectives covered in this lesson. **New Vocabulary** Help students pre-read the lesson by pointing out the new terms introduced in the lesson.	**California Math Background** **Math Understandings** **Transparencies & Presentations CD-ROM** Check Skills You'll Need California Daily Review **Resources** Vocabulary and Study Skills **Math Companion**	**Spanish Support** EL Vocabulary and Study Skills
2. Teach		
L3 **Guided Instruction** Use the Activity Labs to build conceptual understanding. Teach each Example. Use the Teacher's Edition side column notes for specific teaching tips, including Error Prevention notes. Use the Additional Examples found in the side column (and on transparency and PowerPoint) as an alternative presentation for the content. After each Example, assign the California Standards Check exercises for that Example to get an immediate assessment of student understanding. Utilize the support in the Math Companion to assist students with each Standards Check. Use the Closure activity in the Teacher's Edition to help students attain mastery of lesson content.	**Student Edition** Activity Lab **Resources** Math Companion Activity Lab **Transparencies & Presentations CD-ROM** Additional Examples Classroom Aids **Teacher Center: ExamView CD-ROM**	**Teacher's Edition** Every lesson includes suggestions for working with students who need special attention. L1 Special Needs L2 Below Level L4 Advanced Learners EL English Learners **Resources** **Multilingual Handbook** **Math Companion**
3. Practice		
Assignment Guide **Check Your Understanding** Use these questions from the Math Companion to check students' understanding before you assign homework. **Homework Exercises** Assign homework from these leveled exercises in the Assignment Guide. A Practice by Example B Apply Your Skills C Challenge California Multiple-Choice Practice and Mixed Review **Homework Quick Check** Use these key exercises to quickly check students' homework.	**Transparencies & Presentations CD-ROM** Student Answers **Resources** Math Companion Practice Guided Problem Solving Vocabulary and Study Skills Activity Lab Daily Puzzles **Teacher Center: ExamView CD-ROM** **Math *XL***	**Spanish Support** EL Practice EL Vocabulary and Study Skills **Resources** L4 Enrichment
4. Assess & Reteach		
Lesson Quiz Assign the Lesson Quiz to assess students' mastery of the lesson content. **Checkpoint Quiz** Use the Checkpoint Quiz to assess student progress over several lessons.	**Transparencies & Presentations CD-ROM** Lesson Quiz **Resources** Checkpoint Quiz	**Resources** L2 Reteaching EL Checkpoint Quiz Success Tracker™ **Teacher Center: ExamView CD-ROM**

KEY L1 Special Needs L2 Below Level L3 For All Students L4 Advanced, Gifted EL English Learners

Inequalities

Inequalities

Answers are in the back of the textbook.

For math intervention, direct students to:

Adding Integers
Lesson 2-2

Solving One-Step Equations
Lesson 3-1

Solving Two-Step Equations
Lessons 3-1, 3-2, 3-3

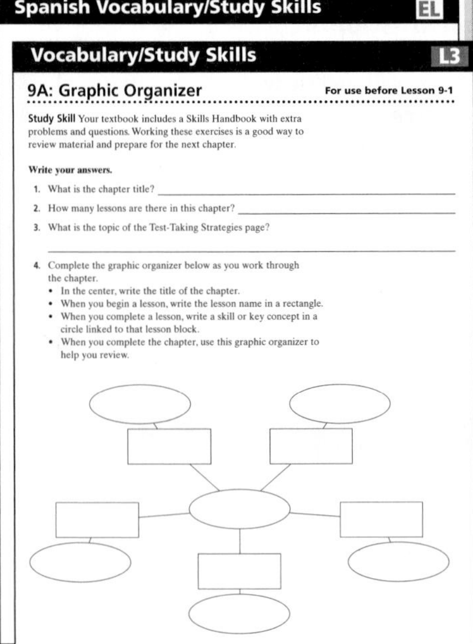

Spanish Vocabulary/Study Skills EL

Vocabulary/Study Skills L3

9A: Graphic Organizer — For use before Lesson 9-1

Study Skill Your textbook includes a Skills Handbook with extra problems and questions. Working these exercises is a good way to review material and prepare for the next chapter.

Write your answers.

1. What is the chapter title? ______
2. How many lessons are there in this chapter? ______
3. What is the topic of the Test-Taking Strategies page? ______
4. Complete the graphic organizer below as you work through the chapter.
   - In the center, write the title of the chapter.
   - When you begin a lesson, write the lesson name in a rectangle.
   - When you complete a lesson, write a skill or key concept in a circle linked to that lesson block.
   - When you complete the chapter, use this graphic organizer to help you review.

What You've Learned

California Content Standards

NS 1.2 Add, subtract, multiply, and divide rational numbers.

AF 1.3 Simplify numerical expressions by applying properties of rational numbers and justify the process used.

AF 3.3 Graph linear functions, noting that the vertical change per unit of horizontal change is always the same and that the ratio is called the slope of the graph.

for Help to the lesson in green.

Adding Integers (Lesson 2-2)

Find each sum.

1. $5 + (-3)$ 2
2. $32 + 9$ 41
3. $-9 + (-2)$ −11
4. $-14 + 14$ 0
5. $3 + (-4)$ −1
6. $-32 + (-1)$ −33
7. $2 + 9 + (-8)$ 3
8. $7 + (-13) + (-2)$ −8
9. $-1 + (-1) + 1$ −1

Solving One-Step Equations (Lesson 3-1)

Solve each equation.

10. $c + 9 = 34$ 25
11. $a + 5 = -8$ −13
12. $y + 15 = 28$ 13
13. $b + 21 = -11$ −31
14. $14 + z = 266$ 252
15. $t + 25 = 5$ −20

Solving Two-Step Equations (Lesson 3-4)

Solve each equation.

16. $3r - 9 = 18$ 9
17. $-6 + 2w = 135$ 70.5
18. $20 = -7x + 6$ −2
19. $12.5 - 3e = -2.5$ 5
20. $5k - 2.6 = 28$ 6.12
21. $10m + 54 = 32$ −2.2

 California Content Standards for Chapter 9

Algebra and Functions
AF 1.1, AF 4.1

Chapter 9 Overview

In this chapter students learn to write, test, and solve inequalities. They expand on their knowledge of solving equations to solve both one- and two-step inequalities.

Activating Prior Knowledge

In this chapter, students build on and extend their knowledge of writing and solving one- and two-step equations. Ask questions such as:

- *How do you solve the equation $x - 2 = 4$ for x?* Add 2 to both sides of the equation.
- *How do you solve the equation $3x + 2 = 8$ for x?* Subtract 2 from both sides of the equation; then divide both sides of the equation by 3.
- *How can you verify that your solution to an equation is correct?* Substitute the solution for *x* in the original equation and simplify.

▲ African elephants can travel as fast as 25 mi/h and cover as much as 19 mi per day.

What You'll Learn Next

California Content Standards

AF 1.1 Write an inequality or a system of inequalities that represents a verbal description.

AF 4.1 Solve two-step linear inequalities in one variable over the rational numbers, interpret the solution or solutions in the context from which they arose, and verify the reasonableness of the results.

New Vocabulary

English and Spanish Audio Online

- **Addition Property of Inequality (p. 334)**
- **Division Property of Inequality (p. 340)**
- **inequality (p. 330)**
- **Multiplication Property of Inequality (p. 344)**
- **solution of an inequality (p. 331)**
- **Subtraction Property of Inequality (p. 334)**
- **system of inequalities (p. 331)**

9-1

1. Plan

California Content Standards

AF 1.1 Use variables and appropriate operations to write an inequality or system of inequalities that represents a verbal description. ***Develop***

California Math Background

An equation is a mathematical sentence with an equal sign, =. An *inequality* is a mathematical sentence that contains one of five symbols: <, >, ≤, ≥, or ≠.

The *solution of an inequality* is any number that makes the inequality true. An inequality may have many solutions. You can graph an inequality on a number line. An open circle indicates that the endpoint is not included and is used with < or >. A closed circle indicates that the endpoint is included and is used with ≤ or ≥.

More Math Background: p. 328C

Lesson Planning and Resources

See p. 328E for a list of the resources that support this lesson.

... PRESENTATION CD-ROM
CD, Online, or Transparencies

Bell Ringer Practice

Check Skills You'll Need
Use student page, transparency, or PowerPoint.
See Math Companion.

California Standards Review
Use transparency or PowerPoint.

GO for Help: Math Companion

9-1 Writing Inequalities

Check Skills You'll Need

Do this in your **Math Companion.**

Vocabulary

- inequality
- system of inequalities
- solution of an inequality

Use your **Math Companion** *to build your vocabulary.*

California Content Standards

AF 1.1 Use variables and appropriate operations to write an inequality or system of inequalities that represents a verbal description. ***Develop***

What You'll Learn . . . and Why

You will learn to write and test inequalities. You can use an inequality to describe the minimum age required to apply for a job.

An **inequality** is a mathematical sentence that contains <, >, ≤, ≥, or ≠. Some inequalities, such as $x < 3$ and $x \geq 3$, contain a variable.

You can graph inequalities on a number line. Use a closed circle to graph ≤ or ≥. Use an open circle to graph < or >.

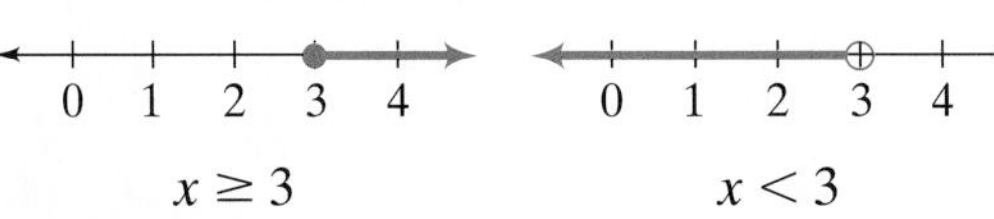

$x \geq 3$ $\quad$ $x < 3$

EXAMPLE Writing an Inequality

Relate **MATH YOU KNOW...**

Write an expression for the verbal description "The price is $4."

$p = 4$

... *to* ALGEBRA

1 Write an inequality for the verbal description "The price p is more than $4."

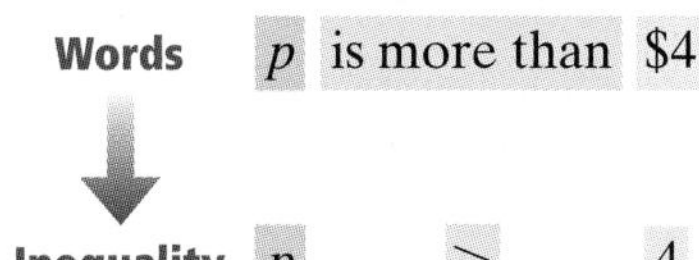

The inequality is $p > 4$. The graph of the inequality is shown below.

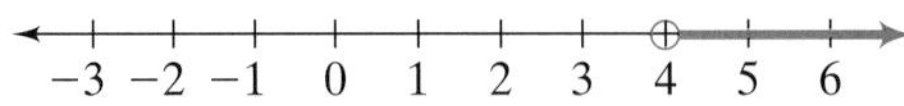

CA Standards Check 1

Go to your **Math Companion** *for help.*

1. Write an inequality for each verbal description.

a. A time t is at least 7.8 s. $\quad t \geq 7.8$

b. The wage w is less than $9. $\quad w < 9$

Universal Access Solutions for All Learners

Special Needs L1	**Below Level** L2
If students have difficulty writing inequalities, ask them to draw a number line and point out where the solutions for a given situation would lie.	Read several sets of true/false exercises like these. 2 > 8 false $\quad$ −2 > 8 false 2 > −8 true $\quad$ −2 > −8 true

Some real-world situations involve more than one inequality. Two or more inequalities form a **system of inequalities**.

EXAMPLE Writing a System of Inequalities

2 During a recent storm, the wind speed was greater than 52 mi/h but less than 75 mi/h. Write a system of inequalities to represent this situation.

Let w = the wind speed in mi/h.

wind speed was greater than 52 mi/h: $w > 52$

wind speed was less than 75 mi/h: $w < 75$

The system is: $\begin{cases} w > 52 \\ w < 75 \end{cases}$

Vocabulary Tip

You can use a brace, {, to show that two equations or inequalities form a system.

CA Standards Check 2 *Go to your* **Math Companion** *for help.*

2. Write a system of inequalities for each situation. 2a–b. See left.

a. The price of a room at a motel is at least \$75 and at most \$125.

b. An airplane flies at an altitude greater than 28,000 ft but less than 35,000 ft.

2a. $\begin{cases} p \geq 75 \\ p \leq 125 \end{cases}$

2b. $\begin{cases} a > 28{,}000 \\ a < 35{,}000 \end{cases}$

A **solution of an inequality** is any number that makes the inequality true.

EXAMPLE Identifying Solutions of an Inequality

3 **Guided Problem Solving** You must be at least 14 years old to apply for a job at a supermarket. Write an inequality and use it to determine which students listed in the table can apply.

Name	Age
Sally	$15\frac{1}{2}$ yr
Dean	14 yr
Kelsey	$13\frac{3}{4}$ yr

Words student's age is at least 14 yr

Let a = the student's age in years.

Inequality $a \geq 14$

Decide whether the inequality is true or false for each person.

Sally: $15\frac{1}{2} \geq 14$ true

Dean: $14 \geq 14$ true

Kelsey: $13\frac{3}{4} \geq 14$ false

Sally and Dean may apply for jobs.

Problem Solving Tip

You can use the graph of an inequality to help you find its solutions.

CA Standards Check 3 *Go to your* **Math Companion** *for help.*

3. Ian's age is 14 yr 9 mo. Can he apply for a job at the supermarket? yes

Check Your Understanding *Homework prep is in your* **Math Companion.**

2. Teach

Guided Instruction

Example 1

For Standards Check 1, discuss *at least 7.8* to make sure that students understand what *at least* means mathematically. Ask:

- *Does 7.8 make the sentence true?* yes
- *Does 7.9 make the sentence true?* yes
- *Does 7.7 make the sentence true?* no *Explain.* Sample: The number has to be equal to or greater than 7.8.

PRESENTATION CD-ROM CD, Online, or Transparencies

Additional Examples

1 Write an inequality for the verbal expression "The distance d is more than 90 feet." $d > 90$

2 A health insurance company offers a special plan for patients who are at least 30 years old and less than 55 years old. Write a system of inequalities for this situation. $\begin{cases} a \geq 30 \\ a < 55 \end{cases}$

3 Students who bring 3.5 pounds or more of recyclable aluminum get into the Environment Dance free. Which students can attend free: Ben (3.35 lb), Rinaldo (2.75 lb), Juanita (3.75 lb)? Juanita

Closure

- *What is an inequality?* a mathematical sentence that contains $<$, $>$, $\leq$, or $\geq$
- Explain what a solution of an inequality is. any number that makes the inequality true

Advanced Learners L4	**English Learners** EL
Have students write sentences about everyday experiences that can be described by inequalities. Sample: I ride my bike at least 5 miles each week.	Read inequality statements, including some with variables, and have students write them as you read them. Make sure they translate the words *greater than, less than, greater than or equal to,* and *less than or equal to* into the correct symbols.

Assignment Guide

Check Your Understanding
See Math Companion.

Homework Exercises

A Practice by Example	1–13
B Apply Your Skills	14–27
C Challenge	28
California Multiple-Choice Practice	29–30
Mixed Review	31–34

Homework Quick Check
To check students' understanding of key skills and concepts, go over Exercises 3, 8, 12, 15, 24, 25.

Universal Access Resources

Adapted Practice 9-1 L1

Practice 9-1 Writing Ineq L3

Write an inequality for each verbal description.

1. A number y is less than 6. ______
2. A quantity w is at most 5. ______
3. The weight w of a chicken is less than 8.2 pounds. ______
4. The distance d is greater than 4.2 miles. ______

Write a system of inequalities for each situation.

5. The number of people on an elevator is greater than 2 but less than 6. ______
6. The length of a book must be at least 100 pages but less than 250 pages. ______
7. The temperature in a cooler should be greater than 0° F but less than 32° F. ______
8. The weight of a package to ship express must be at least 2 pounds but less than 5 pounds. ______

Write and use an inequality to solve each problem.

Student	Height
Adrian	36 inches
Odette	4 feet 4 inches
Julia	42 inches
Simon	4 feet 6 inches
Kyle	4 feet 2 inches

9. To ride the newest roller coaster at an amusement park you must be at least 52 inches tall. Who can ride the roller coaster? ______
10. You must be less than 48 inches tall to ride the junior swings. Who can ride the junior swings? ______

Write whether each inequality is *true* or *false*.

11. $-3 \leq 4$ ______
12. $|-2| < 2$ ______
13. $-3^2 < (-3)^2$ ______
14. $6 \geq 4 - (-4)$ ______

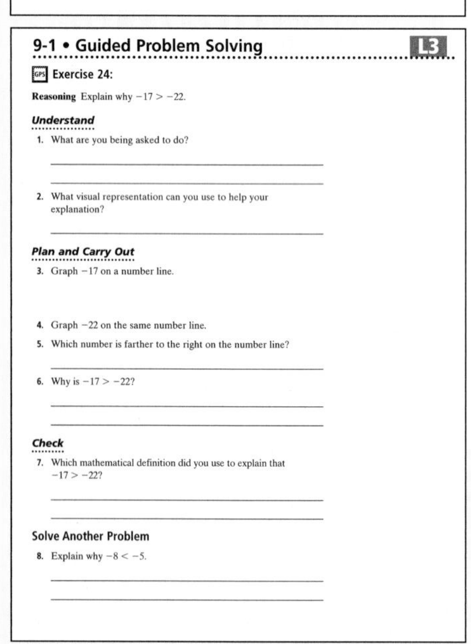

9-1 • Guided Problem Solving L3

GPS **Exercise 24:**

Reasoning Explain why $-17 > -22$.

Understand

1. What are you being asked to do? ______
2. What visual representation can you use to help your explanation? ______

Plan and Carry Out

3. Graph -17 on a number line.
4. Graph -22 on the same number line.
5. Which number is farther to the right on the number line? ______
6. Why is $-17 > -22$? ______

Check

7. Which mathematical definition did you use to explain that $-17 > -22$? ______

Solve Another Problem

8. Explain why $-8 < -5$. ______

Standards Practice

GO for Help: MathXL

AF 1.1

A Practice by Example

Example 1 (page 330)

Write an inequality for each verbal description.

1. The rate r is at most \$35/h. Use ≤ to represent "at most."
   r ■ 35 $r \leq 35$

Guided Practice
This exercise has been started for you!

GO for Help

2. A number k is not positive. $k \leq 0$
3. The quantity q is at most 4. $q \leq 4$
4. The number d is at least a 12. $d \geq 12$
5. The height h is less than 5.6 ft. $h < 5.6$
6. The distance x is less than 20 mi. $x < 20$
7. The cost c is more than \$8. $c > 8$

Example 2 (page 331)

Write a system of inequalities for each situation. 8–11. See below left.

8. The number of people on the bus is greater than 4 and less than 28.
9. The length of a student's essay must be at least 300 words but no more than 500 words.
10. The temperature should be less than 80°F but at least 70°F.
11. To be in the super heavyweight class, an Olympic wrestler must weigh at least 100 kg but no more than 130 kg.

Homework Video Tutor

For: Examples 1–3
Visit: PHSchool.com
Web Code: axe-0901

Example 3 (page 331)

Write and use an inequality to solve each problem.

12. Use the table at the right. A horse is considered a pony if its height at the shoulders is less than 14.2 hands. A hand is equal to 4 in. Which horses are ponies? Mazy, Rex, Simon

Horse	Height
Mazy	14.0 hands
Cinnamon	15.3 hands
Rex	12.1 hands
Tina	14.3 hands
Simon	13.2 hands

13. You must be at least 13 years old to rent a certain video game. From the following list of students, who may rent the game? Cara, Monique, Sierra

    Carl (12 yr 9 mo), Cara (15 yr 4 days), Monique (13 yr), Hector (8 yr 11 mo), Sierra (14 yr 2 mo)

8–11. Variables may vary. Samples are given.

8. $\begin{cases} p > 4 \\ p < 28 \end{cases}$

9. $\begin{cases} w \geq 300 \\ w \leq 500 \end{cases}$

10. $\begin{cases} t < 80 \\ t \geq 70 \end{cases}$

11. $\begin{cases} w \geq 100 \\ w \leq 130 \end{cases}$

B Apply Your Skills

14. **Guided Problem Solving** Write an inequality for "6 is less than 9 more than a number n." $6 < 9 + n$
    - Translate the words into symbols.
      Words: 6 is less than 9 more than a number n.
      Inequality: 6 < ■ + ■

Write whether each inequality is *true* or *false*.

15. $-2 \leq 2$ true
16. $|-5| < 5$ false
17. $-4^2 < (-4)^2$ true
18. $5 \geq 3 - (-2)$ true

SCAFFOLDED
Problem Solving

19. 45 mi/h
20. $s < 45$
21. $\begin{cases} s \geq 45 \\ s \leq 65 \end{cases}$
22. Yes; the speed is less than 65 mi/h and greater than 45 mi/h.

The sign at the right is posted on a highway.

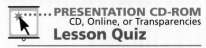

19. What is the minimum speed on the highway?
20. Write an inequality that represents the speed of a car going slower than the minimum limit.
21. Write a system of inequalities to represent the speed of a car obeying the speed limits.
22. A police officer observes a vehicle moving at 63 mi/h. Is the vehicle's driver obeying the speed limits? Explain.

23. According to a manufacturer's guidelines, a bag of pretzels is defective if it does *not* weigh from 8.9 oz to 9.2 oz. Use the table at the right. Which bags of pretzels are defective? B

Bag	Weight
A	9.0 oz
B	8.7 oz
C	9.1 oz
D	8.9 oz

24. Answers may vary. Sample: −17 is to the right of −22 on a number line.

25. Answers may vary. Sample: They are alike in that both make the statement true. They are different in that an equation usually has just one solution while an inequality can have many solutions.

GPS 24. **Reasoning** Explain why $-17 > -22$.

25. **Writing in Math** How are the solution of an inequality and the solution of an equation alike? How are they different? See left.

Identify an integer that is a solution for each system of inequalities.

26. $\begin{cases} -3 \leq x \\ x < 0 \end{cases}$ −1, − 2, or −3

27. $\begin{cases} 1 \geq y \\ -2 < y \end{cases}$ −1, 0, or 1

C Challenge

28. If $a \geq 9$ and $9 \geq b$, then a ■ b. Complete the statement using $<$, $>$, $\leq$, or $\geq$. Give an example to support your answer.
$\geq$; $a = 10$, $b = 0$

Multiple Choice Practice and Mixed Review

For California Standards Tutorials, visit PHSchool.com. Web Code: axq-9045

AF 1.1 29. A student plans to read at least 45 min per day. Which inequality represents this situation? C

Ⓐ $r > 45$ Ⓑ $r < 45$ Ⓒ $r \geq 45$ Ⓓ $r \leq 45$

MG 3.3 30. Find the width x of the kite below to the nearest inch. C

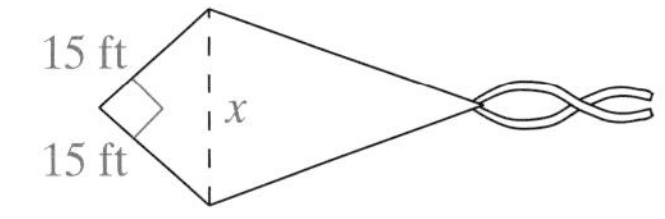

Ⓐ 12 in. Ⓑ 17 in. Ⓒ 21 in. Ⓓ 30 in.

for Help

Lesson 7-2 **Estimate a 15% tip for each restaurant bill.**

31. \$28.55
about \$4.50

32. \$64.82
about \$9.90

33. \$13.97
about \$2.10

34. \$108.16
about \$16.20

Online Lesson Quiz Visit: PHSchool.com Web Code: axa-0901

Alternative Assessment

Each partner writes an inequality such as $x > -8$ or $n \geq 7$. Partners exchange papers, write a verbal description that fits the inequality, and check each other's work.

California Resources

Standards Mastery
- Standards Review Transparencies
- Standards Review and Practice Workbook
- Math Companion

Math Intervention
- Skills Review and Practice Workbook
- Math XL

4. Assess & Reteach

PRESENTATION CD-ROM
CD, Online, or Transparencies
Lesson Quiz

Write an inequality for each verbal statement.

1. A dog weighs less than 25 pounds. $d < 25$
2. You must be at least 18 to vote. $v \geq 18$
3. Tell which numbers are solutions of $x \geq -4$: −6, −4, −2, 0, 2.
−4, −2, 0, 2

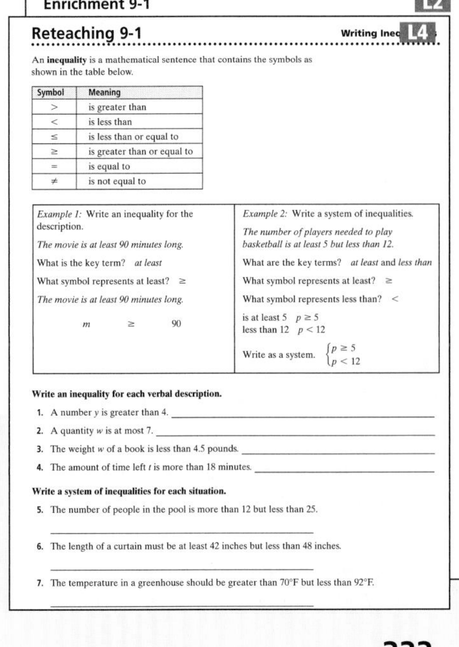
Enrichment 9-1 L2

Reteaching 9-1 Writing Ine[...] L4

An **inequality** is a mathematical sentence that contains the symbols as shown in the table below.

Symbol	Meaning
$>$	is greater than
$<$	is less than
$\leq$	is less than or equal to
$\geq$	is greater than or equal to
$=$	is equal to
$\neq$	is not equal to

Example 1: Write an inequality for the description.

The movie is at least 90 minutes long.

What is the key term? *at least*

What symbol represents at least? $\geq$

The movie is at least 90 minutes long.

$m \quad \geq \quad 90$

Example 2: Write a system of inequalities.

The number of players needed to play basketball is at least 5 but less than 12.

What are the key terms? *at least* and *less than*

What symbol represents at least? $\geq$

What symbol represents less than? $<$

is at least 5 $p \geq 5$
less than 12 $p < 12$

Write as a system. $\begin{cases} p \geq 5 \\ p < 12 \end{cases}$

Write an inequality for each verbal description.

1. A number y is greater than 4. ______
2. A quantity w is at most 7. ______
3. The weight w of a book is less than 4.5 pounds. ______
4. The amount of time left t is more than 18 minutes. ______

Write a system of inequalities for each situation.

5. The number of people in the pool is more than 12 but less than 25.
______
6. The length of a curtain must be at least 42 inches but less than 48 inches.
______
7. The temperature in a greenhouse should be greater than 70°F but less than 92°F.
______

9-2

1. Plan

California Content Standards

AF 1.1 Use variables and appropriate operations to write an inequality that represents a verbal description. ***Develop***

AF 4.1 Solve two-step linear inequalities in one variable.

California Math Background

Solving an inequality involves the same basic strategy used for solving an equation: Isolate the variable. The method is the same as that used with equations. That is, you use inverse operations to "undo" the addition or subtraction.

More Math Background: p. 328C

Lesson Planning and Resources

See p. 328E for a list of the resources that support this lesson.

PRESENTATION CD-ROM
CD, Online, or Transparencies

Bell Ringer Practice

Check Skills You'll Need
Use student page, transparency, or PowerPoint.
See Math Companion.

California Standards Review
Use transparency or PowerPoint.

9-2 Solving Inequalities by Adding or Subtracting

Check Skills You'll Need

Do this in your **Math Companion.**

Vocabulary

- Addition Property of Inequality
- Subtraction Property of Inequality

Use your **Math Companion** *to build your vocabulary.*

California Content Standards

AF 1.1 Use variables and appropriate operations to write an inequality that represents a verbal description. ***Develop***

Prepares for **AF 4.1** Solve two-step linear inequalities in one variable.

What You'll Learn . . . and Why

You will learn to solve inequalities by adding or subtracting. You can use inequalities to find how many people can fit safely on buses, which have limits on the number of people they can hold.

You can solve inequalities using properties similar to those you use to solve equations. The model below shows that if you add 3 to each side of the inequality $-3 < 2$, the resulting inequality, $0 < 5$, is also true.

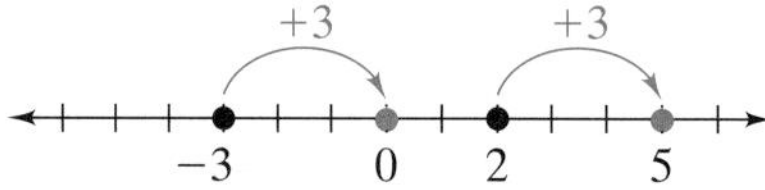

To solve an inequality, use properties to isolate the variable.

Vocabulary Tip

You can think of the $\geq$ symbol as $>$ and $=$ combined. You can think of the $\leq$ symbol as $<$ and $=$ combined.

Take Note — **Addition and Subtraction Properties of Inequality**

When you add or subtract the same number on each side of an inequality, the relationship between the two sides does not change.

Arithmetic	Algebra
Since $10 > 7$, $10 + 5 > 7 + 5$, and $10 - 2 > 7 - 2$.	If $a > b$, then $a + c > b + c$, and $a - c > b - c$.
Since $8 < 12$, $8 + 3 < 12 + 3$, and $8 - 4 < 12 - 4$.	If $a < b$, then $a + c < b + c$, and $a - c < b - c$.

Note: The addition and subtraction properties of inequality also apply to $\leq$ and $\geq$.

Universal Access Solutions for All Learners

Special Needs L1
Students *test out* their solutions to inequality statements with several numbers. This will help them understand that the solution to an inequality can represent more than one number.

Below Level L2
Write inequalities like the following. Have students write the inverse operation on each side.

$t + 3 < 10$ $t + 3 - 3 < 10 - 3$
$x - 7 \leq 9$ $x - 7 + 7 \leq 9 + 7$

Relate MATH YOU KNOW...

...*to* ALGEBRA

EXAMPLE Solving an Inequality by Adding

Solve $q - 7 = -2$.

$q - 7 + 7 = -2 + 7$ ← Isolate the variable. Use the Addition Property of Equality.

$q = 5$ ← Simplify.

1 Solve $q - 7 < -2$.

$q - 7 + 7 < -2 + 7$ ← Isolate the variable. Use the Addition Property of Inequality.

$q < 5$ ← Simplify.

Check

Step 1 Check whether your answer is a solution to the related equation.

$q - 7 = 2$ ← Write the related equation.

$5 - 7 \stackrel{?}{=} -2$ ← Substitute 5 for *q*.

$-2 = -2$ ✔

Step 2 Check the inequality symbol by substituting into the inequality.

$4 - 7 < -2$ ← Substitute a number less than 5 for *q* into the inequality.

$-3 < -2$ ✔

Quick Tip

An inequality sometimes has an infinite number of solutions. You cannot check them all. Instead, check your computations and the direction of the inequality symbol.

CA Standards Check 1 *Go to your* **Math Companion** *for help.*

1. a. Solve $1 \le u - 4$. $u \ge 5$ **b.** Solve $y - 3 < 10$. $y < 13$

EXAMPLE Solving an Inequality by Subtracting

2 **Guided Problem Solving** A bus can carry at most 76 students. If 19 students are on the bus, how many more can board the bus?

Words	students already on bus	plus	students remaining	is at most	76
	Let s = the number of students remaining.				
Inequality	19	+	s	$\le$	76

$19 + s \le 76$

$19 - 19 + s \le 76 - 19$ ← Isolate the variable. Use the Subtraction Property of Inequality.

$s \le 57$ ← Simplify.

At most, 57 more students can board the bus.

Vocabulary Tip

You can also write the solutions of an inequality in the form $\{s: s \le 14\}$.

CA Standards Check 2 *Go to your* **Math Companion** *for help.*

2. A theater can hold at most 300 people. So far, 89 tickets have been sold for a play. Write and solve an inequality to find how many more tickets can be sold. $s \le 211$

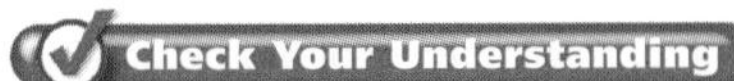

Check Your Understanding *Homework prep is in your* **Math Companion.**

2. Teach

Guided Instruction

Example 1

Some students better understand the process when it is shown vertically.

$$\begin{array}{rcr} q - 7 & < & -2 \\ +7 & = & +7 \\ \hline q & < & 5 \end{array}$$

Error Prevention!

Emphasize that you must perform the *same* operation on both sides of an inequality in order to rewrite it as an equivalent inequality.

...PRESENTATION CD-ROM
CD, Online, or Transparencies

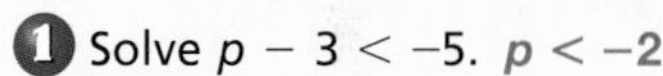

Additional Examples

1 Solve $p - 3 < -5$. $p < -2$

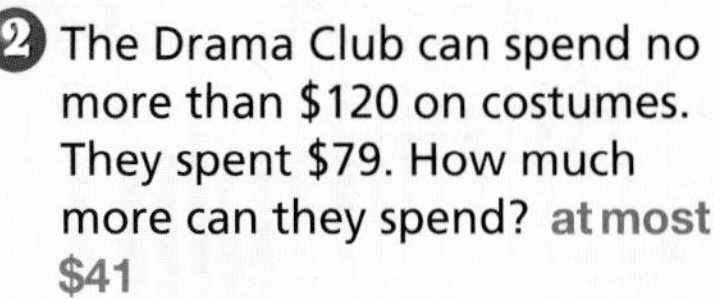

2 The Drama Club can spend no more than $120 on costumes. They spent $79. How much more can they spend? at most $41

Closure

- Explain how to solve inequalities by adding or subtracting. Sample: Isolate the variable. If a number has been added to the variable, subtract that number from each side. If a number has been subtracted from the variable, add that number to each side.

Advanced Learners L4

Find possible integer values for a *and* b *in the inequality* $n \div a \le b$ *that would yield a solution of* $n \le -8$. Samples:

$a = 1, b = -8; a = 2, b = -4;$
$a = 4, b = -2; a = 8, b = -1$

English Learners EL

Help students connect words to symbols to develop linguistic flexibility. For example, the solution to Example 1 might be read as *n is less than 5*. The solution to Example 2 is translated as *at most, 57 more students*.

3. Practice

Assignment Guide

Check Your Understanding

See Math Companion.

Homework Exercises

A	Practice by Example	1–17
B	Apply Your Skills	18–36
C	Challenge	37
California Multiple-Choice Practice		38–39
Mixed Review		40–42

Homework Quick Check

To check students' understanding of key skills and concepts, go over Exercises 2, 15, 19, 25, 34, 36.

Universal Access Resources

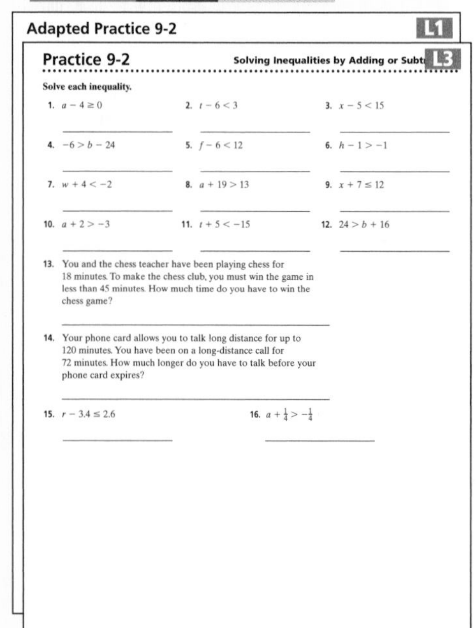
Adapted Practice 9-2 L1

Practice 9-2 Solving Inequalities by Adding or Subtr[acting] L3

Solve each inequality.

1. $a - 4 \geq 0$
2. $t - 6 < 3$
3. $x - 5 < 15$
4. $-6 > b - 24$
5. $f - 6 < 12$
6. $h - 1 > -1$
7. $w + 4 < -2$
8. $a + 19 > 13$
9. $x + 7 \leq 12$
10. $a + 2 > -3$
11. $t + 5 < -15$
12. $24 > b + 16$
13. You and the chess teacher have been playing chess for 18 minutes. To make the chess club, you must win the game in less than 45 minutes. How much time do you have to win the chess game?
14. Your phone card allows you to talk long distance for up to 120 minutes. You have been on a long-distance call for 72 minutes. How much longer do you have to talk before your phone card expires?
15. $r - 3.4 \leq 2.6$
16. $a + \frac{1}{4} > -\frac{1}{4}$

9-2 • Guided Problem Solving L3

GPS Exercise 36:

Banking A bank offers free checking for accounts with a balance greater than \$500. You have a balance of \$516.46 and you write a check for \$26.47. Write an inequality to represent how much you would need to deposit to have free checking.

Understand

1. What does your balance have to be in order to get free checking?
2. Circle the information you need to know.
3. What do you need to find?

Plan and Carry Out

4. Write an inequality to represent the given situation, where d represents the deposit.
5. Simplify and solve the inequality.
6. How much should the deposit be?

Check

7. If you deposit \$10.01, will you have free checking? Why?

Solve Another Problem

8. Most packages contain a nutritional analysis based on an average intake of 2,000 calories. You are trying to follow this guideline and have 580 calories for breakfast and 642 calories for lunch. What number of calories can you have for dinner?

Standards Practice

AF 1.1

A Practice by Example

Example 1 (page 335)

For: Examples 1–2
Visit: PHSchool.com
Web Code: axe-0902

Solve each inequality.

1. $g - 2 \leq -8$
   $g - 2 + 2 \leq -8 + 2$
   $g \leq$ ■ $g \leq -6$

   Guided Practice This exercise has been started for you!

2. $x - 8 > 18$ $x > 26$
3. $m - 1 < -3$ $m < -2$
4. $1 > a - 3$ $a < 4$
5. $y - 5 \geq 11$ $y \geq 16$
6. $p - 9 < -9$ $p < 0$
7. $4 < q - 2$ $q > 6$
8. $17 \leq n - 10$ $n \geq 27$
9. $b - 4 \geq -6$ $b \geq -2$

Example 2 (page 335)

Solve each inequality.

10. $h + 8 < -13$
    $h + 8 -$ ■ $< -13 -$ ■
    $h < -21$

    Guided Practice This exercise has been started for you!

11. $4 \geq n + 3$ $n \leq 1$
12. $r + 9 > 4$ $r > -5$
13. $x + 12 \leq 1$ $x \leq -11$
14. $1 < 3 + t$ $t > -2$
15. $w + 1 < 2$ $w < 1$
16. $u + 10 \leq 0$ $u \leq -10$
17. Your parents give you \$35 for a scooter that costs at least \$100. Write and solve an inequality to find the amount of money you have to save to buy the scooter. $s \geq 65$

B Apply Your Skills

18. **Guided Problem Solving** During the summer months, a town restricts the water each household uses to 250 gal of water per day. One day, a family uses 50 gal for bathing, 27 gal for laundry, and 25 gal for cleaning. How many gallons can the family use to water the garden? $w \leq 148$
    - How much water is used for bathing, laundry, and cleaning?
    - Write and solve an inequality for the total water usage. Use a variable to represent the amount of water *not* used.

Solve each inequality. 19–24. See left.

19. $w - \frac{1}{4} > -\frac{3}{4}$
20. $j + 6.2 \geq \frac{1}{5}$
21. $a - 1\frac{4}{5} < 3\frac{7}{10}$
22. $b + \frac{5}{4} \leq -17$
23. $8.7 < m + 9\frac{2}{5}$
24. $-\frac{11}{15} \geq t - 1.75$
25. **Writing in Math** Explain how you know that $4 + x > 4 + x$ has no solutions. See left.
26. Beef is well done when the internal temperature is at least 170°F. A steak is 109°F. Write and solve an inequality to find how many degrees the temperature must rise for the beef to be well done. at least 61°F

19. $w > -\frac{1}{2}$
20. $j \geq -6$
21. $a < 5\frac{1}{2}$
22. $b \leq -18\frac{1}{4}$
23. $m > -0.7$
24. $t \leq 1\frac{1}{60}$
25. Answers may vary. Sample: A number cannot be greater than itself.

SCAFFOLDED
Problem Solving

Use the inequality $1.2 < x < 6.9$ to answer each question.

27. Is 7 a solution to the inequality? no

28. What is the greatest integer that is a solution of the inequality? 6

29. What is the least integer that is a solution of the inequality? 2

30. How many integers are solutions of the inequality? 5

31. Which graph below shows the solutions of the inequality? B

(A) 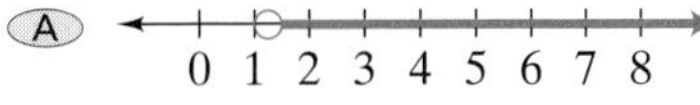
0 1 2 3 4 5 6 7 8

(C) 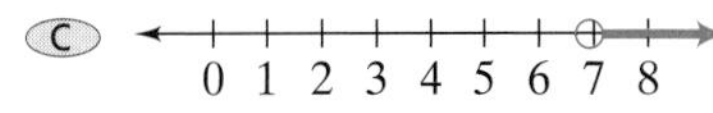
0 1 2 3 4 5 6 7 8

(B) 0 1 2 3 4 5 6 7 8

(D) 0 1 2 3 4 5 6 7 8

Reasoning **Write > or < to make each statement true.**

32. If $x > y$ and $y > z$, then x ■ z. >

33. If $a > b$, then b ■ a. <

Write an inequality for each graph.

34. −3 −2 −1 0 1 2 3
$x > -1$

35. −3 −2 −1 0 1 2 3
$x \leq 0$

GPS **36.** A bank offers free checking for accounts with a balance greater than \$500. You have a balance of \$516.46, and you write a check for \$26.47. Write and solve an inequality to find how much you would need to deposit to have free checking. $d > \$10.01$

C Challenge

37. Solve the inequality $2(y + a) > a$ for y. $y > -\frac{a}{2}$

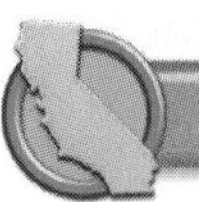

Multiple Choice Practice and Mixed Review

For California Standards Tutorials, visit PHSchool.com. Web Code: axq-9045

AF 1.1

38. Which inequality represents the verbal description, "Fifteen plus a number is greater than 10"? D

(A) $15 + n \leq 10$
(B) $15 + n < 10$
(C) $15 + n \geq 10$
(D) $15 + n > 10$

MG 1.3

39. The table at the right shows the weights and costs of three different bags of dog food. Which bag contains the least expensive dog food per pound? B

(A) Red
(B) Blue
(C) Green
(D) Yellow

Bag	Weight (lb)	Cost
Red	30.0	\$30.00
Blue	25.0	\$16.00
Green	14.9	\$11.92
Yellow	9.8	\$8.33

for Help **Lesson 5-2**

Find each difference. Write your answer in simplest form.

40. $\frac{1}{5} - \frac{2}{9}$ $-\frac{1}{45}$

41. $\frac{3}{4} - \frac{1}{3}$ $\frac{5}{12}$

42. $\frac{1}{2} - \frac{7}{11}$ $-\frac{3}{22}$

Online Lesson Quiz Visit: PHSchool.com Web Code: axa-0902

337

4. Assess & Reteach

PRESENTATION CD-ROM
CD, Online, or Transparencies
Lesson Quiz

Solve each inequality.

1. $q - 5 \geq 8$ $q \geq 13$

2. $r + 10 < 4$ $r < -6$

3. $6 + x \leq 21$ $x \leq 15$

4. A lamp can use lightbulbs of up to 75 watts. The lamp is using a 45-watt bulb. At most, how many watts are available for brighter light? 30 watts

Alternative Assessment

Ask students to write four different inequalities. Two inequalities should be solved by adding and two by subtracting. Students then exchange papers with a partner, who solves each inequality. Have partners discuss their results.

California Resources

Standards Mastery
- Standards Review Transparencies
- Standards Review and Practice Workbook
- Math Companion

Math Intervention
- Skills Review and Practice Workbook
- Math XL

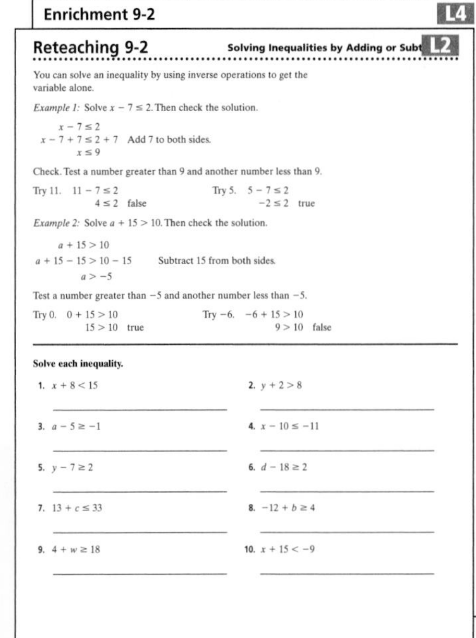

Enrichment 9-2 L4

Reteaching 9-2 Solving Inequalities by Adding or Subt L2

You can solve an inequality by using inverse operations to get the variable alone.

Example 1: Solve $x - 7 \leq 2$. Then check the solution.

$x - 7 \leq 2$
$x - 7 + 7 \leq 2 + 7$ Add 7 to both sides.
$x \leq 9$

Check. Test a number greater than 9 and another number less than 9.

Try 11. $11 - 7 \leq 2$; $4 \leq 2$ false
Try 5. $5 - 7 \leq 2$; $-2 \leq 2$ true

Example 2: Solve $a + 15 > 10$. Then check the solution.

$a + 15 > 10$
$a + 15 - 15 > 10 - 15$ Subtract 15 from both sides.
$a > -5$

Test a number greater than −5 and another number less than −5.

Try 0. $0 + 15 > 10$; $15 > 10$ true
Try −6. $-6 + 15 > 10$; $9 > 10$ false

Solve each inequality.

1. $x + 8 < 15$ ____
2. $y + 2 > 8$ ____
3. $a - 5 \geq -1$ ____
4. $x - 10 \leq -11$ ____
5. $y - 7 \geq 2$ ____
6. $d - 18 \geq 2$ ____
7. $13 + c \leq 33$ ____
8. $-12 + b \geq 4$ ____
9. $4 + w \geq 18$ ____
10. $x + 15 < -9$ ____

Use this Checkpoint Quiz to check students' understanding of the skills and concepts of Lessons 9-1 through 9-2.

All in One Resources

- Checkpoint Quiz 1

Vocabulary Builder

Writing Inequalities

Students write sentences using phrases such as *less than, more than, at most,* and *no fewer than.* Then students translate their sentences into inequalities.

Guided Instruction

Make sure that students understand the differences among the phrases *less than, at most, greater than,* and *at least.* Use examples to demonstrate the differences. Ask: *Which of the following statements are satisfied by $10?*

- Jim has less than $10.
- Karen needs at most $10.
- Meg needs more than $10.
- Jillian has at least $10.

Connection to Language Arts
Have students identify other words or phrases that would translate into each inequality symbol. Some examples are *younger than* (for $<$), *taller than* (for $>$), *no older than* (for $\leq$), and *as heavy as* (for $\geq$).

Vocabulary Builder

Writing Inequalities

AF 1.1 Use variables and operations to write an inequality that represents a verbal description. ***Develop***

The table below lists some common verbal descriptions used in real-world situations that you can represent with inequalities.

Symbol	Verbal Description
$<$	• less than, fewer than
$>$	• greater than, more than
$\leq$	• less than or equal to • at most, no greater than • as much as, no more than
$\geq$	• greater than or equal to • at least, no less than • as little as, no fewer than

1. Write a sentence for each word phrase in the table. Then translate each sentence into an inequality. Check students' work.

Checkpoint Quiz 1

Lessons 9-1 through 9-2

Write an inequality for each verbal description.

1. The distance d is at most 50 mi. $d \leq 50$
2. The time t is less than 30 min. $t < 30$
3. The cost c is at least \$12.99. $c \geq 12.99$
4. 30 lb is greater than the weight w. $30 > w$
5. A student's test score must be at least 80% but no more than 89%. Write a system of inequalities for this situation. $\begin{cases} t \geq 0.80 \\ t \leq 0.89 \end{cases}$

Solve each inequality.

6. $4 + e \geq 10$ $e \geq 6$
7. $r - 12 < 2$ $r < 14$
8. $k - 3 \leq 42$ $k \leq 45$
9. $9 + m > 27.5$ $m > 18.5$
10. A truck weighs 28,500 lb. The total weight limit for the truck is 64,000 lb. What is the weight of the maximum load the truck can carry? 35,500 lb

For Use With Lesson 9-3

Inequalities and Negative Numbers

NS 1.2 Add, subtract, multiply, and divide rational numbers. ***Develop***

MR 2.4 Make and test conjectures by using both inductive and deductive reasoning. ***Develop***

Solving inequalities is similar to solving equations. However, multiplying or dividing each side of an inequality by a negative number changes the relationship in the inequality.

ACTIVITY

Start with the inequality $6 < 12$.

Simplify each expression. Then replace each ■ with <, =, or >.

1. $6 \cdot 3$ ■ $12 \cdot 3$ $18 < 36$
2. $6 \cdot 2$ ■ $12 \cdot 2$ $12 < 24$
3. $6 \cdot 1$ ■ $12 \cdot 1$ $6 < 12$
4. $\frac{6}{3}$ ■ $\frac{12}{3}$ $2 < 4$
5. $\frac{6}{2}$ ■ $\frac{12}{2}$ $3 < 6$
6. $\frac{6}{1}$ ■ $\frac{12}{1}$ $6 < 12$
7. **Patterns** Make a conjecture about what happens to the direction of the inequality symbol as you multiply or divide each side of the inequality by a positive number.
   7. When you multiply or divide an inequality by a positive number, the direction of the inequality does not change.
8. Test your conjecture by multiplying each side of the inequality $-5 < -3$ by 4. $-20 < -12$; this is true and the conjecture holds.

Simplify each expression. Then replace each ■ with <, =, or >.

9. $6 \cdot (-1)$ ■ $12 \cdot (-1)$ $-6 > -12$
10. $6 \cdot (-2)$ ■ $12 \cdot (-2)$ $-12 > -24$
11. $6 \cdot (-3)$ ■ $12 \cdot (-3)$ $-18 > -36$
12. $\frac{6}{-1}$ ■ $\frac{12}{-1}$ $-6 > -12$
13. $\frac{6}{-2}$ ■ $\frac{12}{-2}$ $-3 > -6$
14. $\frac{6}{-3}$ ■ $\frac{12}{-3}$ $-2 > -4$
15. **Patterns** Make a conjecture about what happens to the direction of the inequality symbol as you multiply or divide each side of the inequality by a negative number.
    15. When you multiply or divide an inequality by a negative number, the direction of the inequality symbol changes.
16. Test your conjecture by multiplying each side of the inequality $-5 < -3$ by -4. $20 > 12$; this is true and the conjecture holds.
17. **Reasoning** Suppose a is larger than b. Replace each ■ with <, =, or >.
    a. $2a$ ■ $2b$ >
    b. $-2a$ ■ $-2b$ <

Mathematical Reasoning

Inequalities and Negative Numbers

Students compare quantities and use inequality symbols to make true statements. They observe their results and begin to notice that multiplying or dividing by a negative number changes the direction of the inequality.

Guided Instruction

Visual Learners

To help students obtain accurate results, have them make a large number line with tick marks from −36 to 36. Ask students to find each pair of numbers on the number line to verify their comparisons.

Error Prevention!

For Exercise 17, have students who are not comfortable making a symbolic comparison reason about the same question using a few numerical examples. Then ask them to describe the pattern they notice and make the transition to describing that pattern in terms of any two numbers *a* and *b*.

9-3

1. Plan

California Content Standards

AF 1.1 Use variables and appropriate operations to write an inequality that represents a verbal description. ***Develop***

California Math Background

The steps involved in solving an equation and solving an inequality both end in isolating the variable on one side (either side). However, there is a key difference in the process of solving an inequality: multiplying or dividing each side of an inequality by a negative number reverses the direction of the inequality.

More Math Background: p. 328C

Lesson Planning and Resources

See p. 328E for a list of the resources that support this lesson.

PRESENTATION CD-ROM
CD, Online, or Transparencies

Bell Ringer Practice

Check Skills You'll Need
Use student page, transparency, or PowerPoint.
See Math Companion.

California Standards Review
Use transparency or PowerPoint.

GO for Help: Math Companion

9-3 Solving Inequalities by Dividing

Check Skills You'll Need

Do this in your **Math Companion.**

Vocabulary

- Division Property of Inequality

Use your **Math Companion** *to build your vocabulary.*

California Content Standards

AF 1.1 Write an inequality that represents a verbal description. ***Develop***
Prepares for **AF 4.1** Solve two-step linear inequalities in one variable.

What You'll Learn . . . and Why

You will learn to solve inequalities by dividing. You can use inequalities to help find the minimum number of hours a car trip will take.

When you divide an inequality by a positive number, the direction of the inequality sign does not change. The number line below shows the effect of dividing an inequality by a negative number.

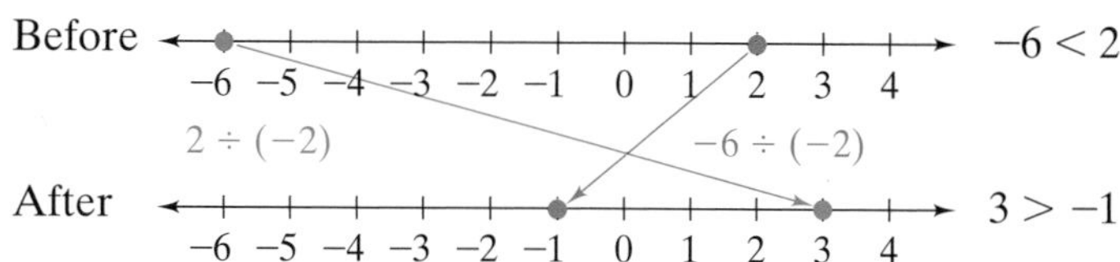

When the inequality $-6 < 2$ is divided by -2, the result is $3 > -1$. Notice that the direction of the inequality is reversed.

Take Note **Division Property of Inequality**

When you divide each side of an inequality by a positive number, do not change the direction of the inequality sign. When you divide each side of an inequality by a negative number, *reverse* the direction of the inequality sign.

Arithmetic	Algebra
Since $6 > 5$, $\frac{6}{2} > \frac{5}{2}$.	If $a > b$, and $c > 0$, then $\frac{a}{c} > \frac{b}{c}$.
Since $4 < 10$, $\frac{4}{2} < \frac{10}{2}$.	If $a < b$, and $c > 0$, then $\frac{a}{c} < \frac{b}{c}$.
Since $6 > 5$, $\frac{6}{-2} < \frac{5}{-2}$.	If $a > b$, and $c < 0$, then $\frac{a}{c} < \frac{b}{c}$.
Since $4 < 10$, $\frac{4}{-2} > \frac{10}{-2}$.	If $a < b$, and $c < 0$, then $\frac{a}{c} > \frac{b}{c}$.

Note: The Division Property of Inequality also applies to $\leq$ and $\geq$.

Universal Access Solutions for All Learners

Special Needs L1	**Below Level** L2
For Example 1, ask students to use a number line and show jumps in increment of 60 until they get close to 210. Each jump represents 1 hour. It takes 3 jumps to get to 180, and you need another partial jump to get to 210, so 3.5 hours makes sense.	Have students fill in the blank for several exercises like these. $-3t > -24$ $5w \leq -15$ t □ 8 < w □ -3 ≤

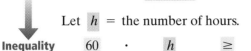

EXAMPLE Dividing by a Positive Number

1 **Guided Problem Solving** Michael and his family plan to drive to his aunt's house, which is 210 mi away. His parents drive 60 mi/h. At least how many hours should Michael's family plan for the trip?

Study Tip

When writing inequalities, be sure to use the correct inequality symbol to represent phrases such as "is at least."

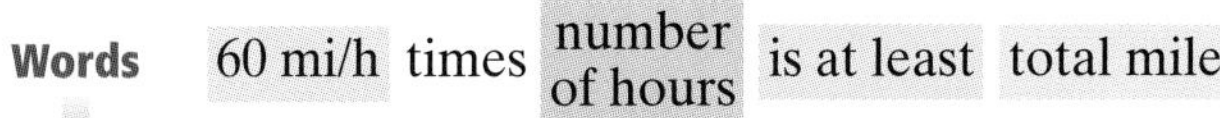

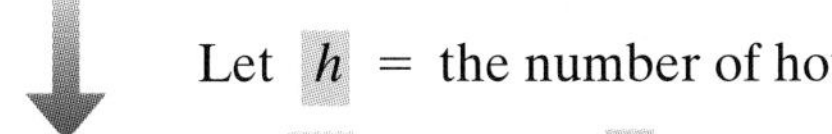

Inequality $60 \cdot h \geq 210$

$60h \geq 210$

$\frac{60h}{60} \geq \frac{210}{60}$ ← **Division Property of Inequality**

$h \geq 3.5$ ← **Simplify.**

Michael's family should plan for at least 3 h and 30 min.

CA Standards Check 1 *Go to your* **Math Companion** *for help.*

1. A hotel elevator has a weight limit of 2,000 lb. Suppose the average weight of a passenger is 160 lb. How many passengers can the elevator safely hold? at most 12 passengers

Recall that a negative number is the opposite of a positive number. So when you divide each side of an inequality by a negative number, remember to reverse the direction of the inequality sign.

EXAMPLE Dividing by a Negative Number

Relate **MATH YOU KNOW...**

Solve $-3y = -27$.

$\frac{-3y}{-3} = \frac{-27}{-3}$ ← **Isolate the variable. Use the Division Property of Equality.**

$y = 9$ ← **Simplify.**

2 Solve $-3y \leq -27$.

$-3y \leq -27$

$\frac{-3y}{-3} \geq \frac{-27}{-3}$ ← **Isolate the variable. Use the Division Property of Inequality. Reverse the direction of the inequality symbol.**

$y \geq 9$ ← **Simplify.**

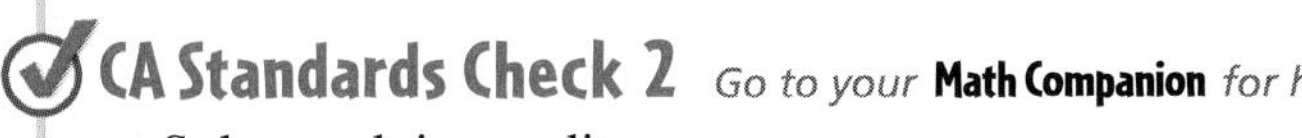

2. Solve each inequality.

a. $-2p \geq 34$ $p \leq -17$ **b.** $-8m < -24$ $m > 3$

Check Your Understanding *Homework prep is in your* **Math Companion.**

2. Teach

Guided Instruction

Example 2

Most students probably are aware that the rules for solving inequalities are very similar to the rules for solving equations. Focus their attention on the difference. Ask:

- *Why do you divide each side by −3?* to undo the multiplication by −3
- *Why do you reverse the direction of the inequality symbol?* You have divided each side by a negative number.

Error Prevention!

Watch for students who reverse the direction of the inequality whenever they see a negative number, even if the number by which they multiply or divide each side is positive.

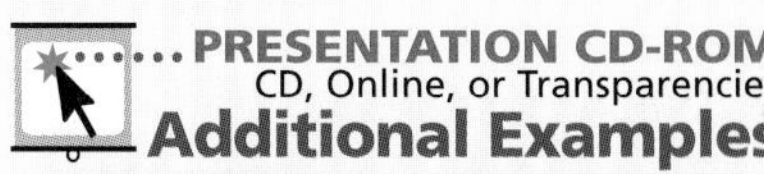

Additional Examples

1 A woodworker makes a profit of \$30 on each picture frame sold. How many frames must she sell to make a profit of at least \$500? 17 frames

2 Solve $-5b \leq 15$. $b \geq -3$

Closure

- *What is the difference between dividing an inequality by a number greater than zero and dividing an inequality by a number less than zero?* Dividing an inequality by a negative number reverses the direction of the inequality symbol.

Advanced Learners L4	**English Learners** EL
Solve each inequality. $2y > y$ all positive numbers $2y < y$ all negative numbers	Have students test out and explain why the inequality sign changes direction when you divide by a negative integer. Use $3 < 5$ as an example. If you divide each side by −1, then the inequality becomes $-3 > -5$. Have them write other examples and explain them to you.

3. Practice

Assignment Guide

Check Your Understanding
See Math Companion.

Homework Exercises
A	Practice by Example	1–23
B	Apply Your Skills	24–36
C	Challenge	37
California Multiple-Choice Practice		38–40
Mixed Review		41–43

Homework Quick Check
To check students' understanding of key skills and concepts, go over Exercises 3, 14, 26, 32, 36.

Universal Access Resources

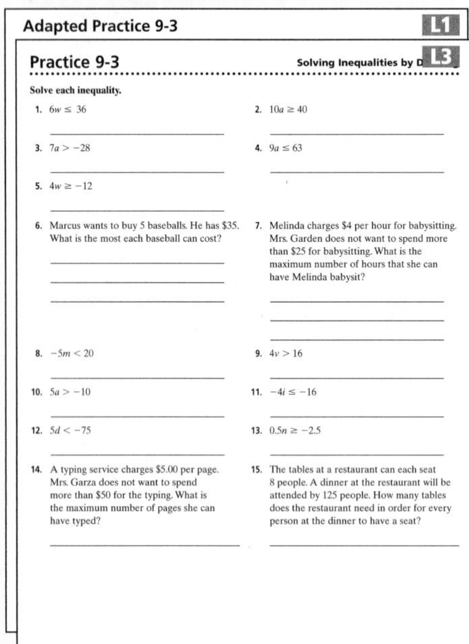

Adapted Practice 9-3 L1

Practice 9-3 Solving Inequalities by Dividing L3

Solve each inequality.

1. $6w \le 36$
2. $10a \ge 40$
3. $7a > -28$
4. $9a \le 63$
5. $4w \ge -12$
6. Marcus wants to buy 5 baseballs. He has \$35. What is the most each baseball can cost?
7. Melinda charges \$4 per hour for babysitting. Mrs. Garden does not want to spend more than \$25 for babysitting. What is the maximum number of hours that she can have Melinda babysit?
8. $-5m < 20$
9. $4v > 16$
10. $5a > -10$
11. $-4i \le -16$
12. $5d < -75$
13. $0.5n \ge -2.5$
14. A typing service charges \$5.00 per page. Mrs. Garza does not want to spend more than \$50 for the typing. What is the maximum number of pages she can have typed?
15. The tables at a restaurant can each seat 8 people. A dinner at the restaurant will be attended by 125 people. How many tables does the restaurant need in order for every person at the dinner to have a seat?

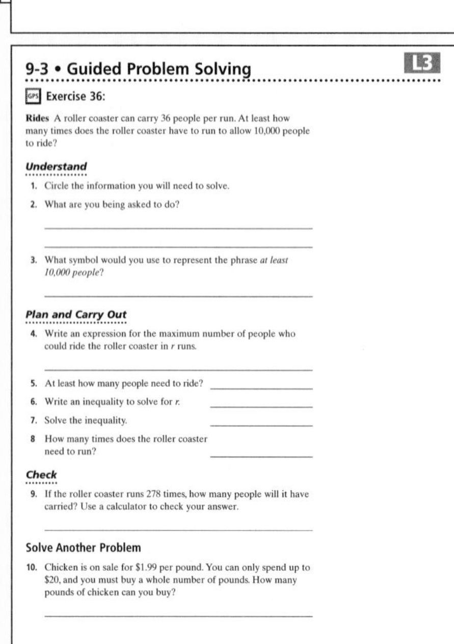

9-3 • Guided Problem Solving L3

Exercise 36:

Rides A roller coaster can carry 36 people per run. At least how many times does the roller coaster have to run to allow 10,000 people to ride?

Understand

1. Circle the information you will need to solve.
2. What are you being asked to do?
3. What symbol would you use to represent the phrase *at least 10,000 people*?

Plan and Carry Out

4. Write an expression for the maximum number of people who could ride the roller coaster in *r* runs.
5. At least how many people need to ride?
6. Write an inequality to solve for *r*.
7. Solve the inequality.
8. How many times does the roller coaster need to run?

Check

9. If the roller coaster runs 278 times, how many people will it have carried? Use a calculator to check your answer.

Solve Another Problem

10. Chicken is on sale for \$1.99 per pound. You can only spend up to \$20, and you must buy a whole number of pounds. How many pounds of chicken can you buy?

Standards Practice

GO for Help: MathXL

AF 1.1

A Practice by Example

Example 1 (page 341)

Solve each inequality.

1. $5c < 10$
   $\frac{5c}{5} < \frac{10}{5}$
   $c < \blacksquare$ $c < 2$

Guided Practice This exercise has been started for you!

2. $-20 \le 4y$ $y \ge -5$
3. $6w \ge -54$ $w \ge -9$
4. $3p > 36$ $p > 12$
5. $-27 \le 9n$ $n \ge -3$
6. $6x > 48$ $x > 8$
7. $2h < 16$ $h < 8$
8. $15d \le 135$ $d \le 9$
9. $6 \ge 2y$ $y \le 3$
10. $9k < 85.5$ $k < 9.5$

For: Examples 1–2
Visit: PHSchool.com
Web Code: axe-0903

11. A photo album page can hold as many as six photographs. You have 296 photographs. How many pages do you need? at least 50 pages
12. The daily special at a restaurant costs \$4.89. The math club has \$23.50 in its treasury. How many daily specials can the club buy? at most 4 specials

Example 2 (page 341)

Solve each inequality.

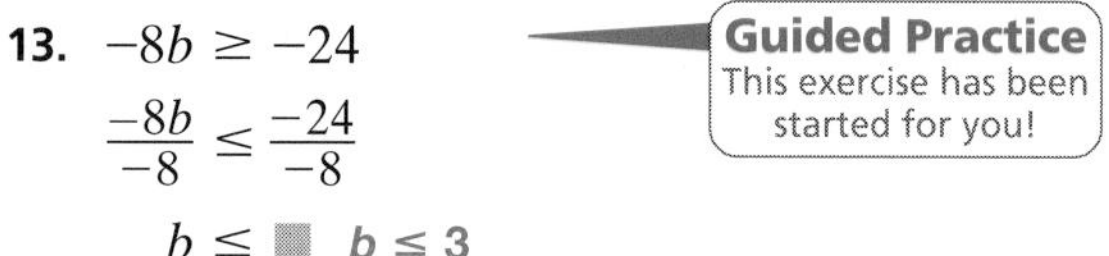

13. $-8b \ge -24$
    $\frac{-8b}{-8} \le \frac{-24}{-8}$
    $b \le \blacksquare$ $b \le 3$

Guided Practice This exercise has been started for you!

14. $-5w \le 30$ $w \ge -6$
15. $-10d \ge -75$ $d \le 7.5$
16. $10 > -2t$ $t > -5$
17. $-4.5p \le 22.5$ $p \ge -5$
18. $-7y < -42.7$ $y > 6.1$
19. $53.95 \ge -8.3q$ $q \ge -6.5$
20. $-9h \le 81.9$ $h \ge -9.1$
21. $-12f < 360$ $f > -30$
22. $-0.5g > 16$ $g < -32$
23. $64 \ge -8y$ $y \ge -8$

B Apply Your Skills

24. **Guided Problem Solving** A forklift can safely carry as much as 6,000 lb. A case of paint weighs 70 lb. At most, how many cases of paint can the forklift safely carry at one time? 85 cases
    - Use number sense: How much do 100 cases weigh?
    - Write and solve an inequality to find *c*, the number of cases the forklift can carry.
25. **Reasoning** Which number is not a solution of $x < -3$ or $-x < 3$? -3
26. **Writing in Math** Explain how solving $5x < 20$ is different from solving $-5x < 20$. See above left.
27. **Error Analysis** A student solves the inequality $5n > -25$. He says the solution is $n < -5$. Explain the student's error. See above left.

26. To solve $-5x < 20$, you divide both sides by -5, so you reverse the direction of the inequality symbol.

27. The student switched the direction of the inequality sign. The answer should be $n > -5$.

SCAFFOLDED
Problem Solving

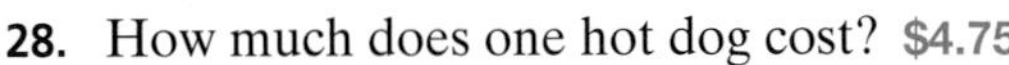

Use the drawing at the right for Exercises 28–31. You have $15.

28. How much does one hot dog cost? $4.75

29. Use the inequality $4.75h \leq 15$ to find at most how many hot dogs you can buy. 3 hot dogs

30. If you buy only peanuts, at most how many bags can you buy? 12 bags

31. You buy two hot dogs.
a. How many bags of peanuts can you buy? 4 bags
b. How much money do you have left? $.50

32–35. See left.

Algebra **What values of a and b make each inequality true?**

32. $-ab > 0$ **33.** $ab < 0$

34. $a^2b > 0$ **35.** $\frac{a}{b} > 0$

32. a and b must have opposite signs.
33. a and b must have opposite signs.
34. a can be positive or negative, but b must be positive.
35. a and b must have the same sign, and $b \neq 0$.

GPS **36.** A roller coaster can carry 36 people per run. At least how many times does the roller coaster have to run to allow 10,000 people to ride? at least 278 times

Challenge

37. A student solved $\frac{a}{b} > 2$ for a and got the solution $a > 2b$. Is the student's answer correct for all values of b? Explain. No; the solution is true for $b > 0$ only. $b < 0$, then $a < 2b$.

Multiple Choice Practice and Mixed Review

For California Standards Tutorials, visit PHSchool.com. Web Code: axq-9045

AF 1.1 **38.** A day-care center must have at least 1 teacher for every group of 5 two-year-olds. Suppose there are 19 two-year-olds enrolled. Which inequality represents t, the number of teachers needed? D

(A) $5 \cdot 19 \leq t$ (B) $\frac{5}{t} \leq 19$ (C) $5t \leq 19$ (D) $\frac{19}{5} \leq t$

AF 4.1 **39.** Solve $4c - 9 = 13$. C

(A) 22 (B) 18 (C) 5.5 (D) 1

AF 2.1 **40.** Which of the following is equivalent to $\frac{3}{4} \cdot \frac{3}{4} \cdot \frac{3}{4} \cdot \frac{3}{4} \cdot \frac{3}{4}$? B

(A) $5 \cdot \frac{3}{4}$ (B) $\left(\frac{3}{4}\right)^5$ (C) $\left(\frac{3}{4}\right)^{-5}$ (D) $\frac{3}{4} \div 5$

for Help Lesson 9-2 **Solve each inequality.**

41. $y + 3 \leq 29$ $y \leq 26$ **42.** $a - 7 > 15$ $a > 22$ **43.** $w - 6 \geq 9$ $w \geq 15$

Online Lesson Quiz Visit: PHSchool.com Web Code: axa-0903

4. Assess & Reteach

PRESENTATION CD-ROM CD, Online, or Transparencies

Lesson Quiz

Solve each inequality.

1. $9c \leq -36$ $c \leq -4$
2. $-7r \geq 14$ $r \leq -2$
3. Leroy's class is having a cookie sale to raise money for a class trip. They will sell homemade cookies for $1.50 each. If they earn at least $200, a local business will match the amount they earn. At least how many cookies do they need to sell to get the local company to match their cookie-sale earnings? 134 cookies

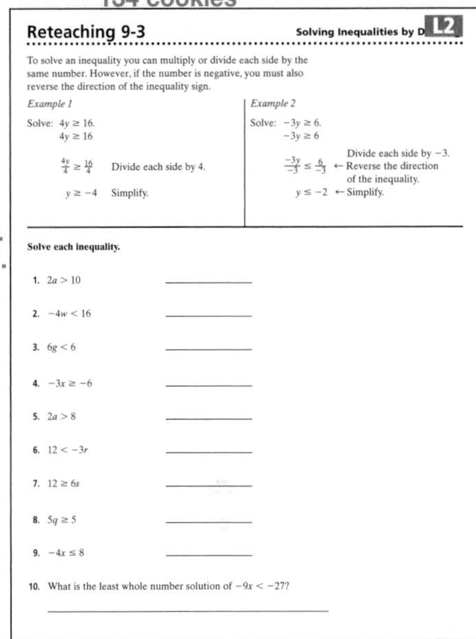

Reteaching 9-3 Solving Inequalities by D L2

To solve an inequality you can multiply or divide each side by the same number. However, if the number is negative, you must also reverse the direction of the inequality sign.

Example 1

Solve: $4y \geq 16$.
$4y \geq 16$
$\frac{4y}{4} \geq \frac{16}{4}$ Divide each side by 4.
$y \geq -4$ Simplify.

Example 2

Solve: $-3y \geq 6$.
$-3y \geq 6$
$\frac{-3y}{-3} \leq \frac{6}{-3}$ ← Divide each side by −3. Reverse the direction of the inequality.
$y \leq -2$ ← Simplify.

Solve each inequality.

1. $2a > 10$ ________
2. $-4w < 16$ ________
3. $6g < 6$ ________
4. $-3x \geq -6$ ________
5. $2a > 8$ ________
6. $12 < -3r$ ________
7. $12 \geq 6s$ ________
8. $5q \geq 5$ ________
9. $-4x \leq 8$ ________
10. What is the least whole number solution of $-9x < -27$?

____

Enrichment 9-3 Solving Inequalities by D L4

Critical Thinking

Many companies throughout the United States and Europe have been rating their customer management performance through a benchmark program. This program measures the average performance of customer satisfaction in various different categories.

The table to the right shows the average scores a computer company has received so far this year in their Information and Technology department. How does the company need to score in *managing customer information* to achieve an overall average score greater than 40?

Information and Technology	Average Score
Acquiring customer information	49
Managing customer information	?
Current system functions	32
Developing new systems	52

Source: http://www.qci.co.uk/Home_page.asp

1. Write an inequality to represent the overall score that the company wants to achieve.
____
2. What operations do you use to find an average?
____
3. Let x represent the score of managing customer information. Write an inequality that represents the desired average of the Information and Technology department.
____
4. Solve the inequality in Step 3. ________
5. Based on the other scores in the table, do you think the company can achieve their goal? Explain why or why not.
____
____
6. To be awarded a national certificate of achievement, the computer company must have an overall average in their Information and Technology Department of no less than 51.
   a. Write and solve an inequality to find what the company must score in managing customer information to achieve the certificate.
   ____
   b. Based on the other scores in the table, do you think the company can achieve the certificate? Explain why or why not.
   ____
   ____

Alternative Assessment

Each student in a pair writes a word problem similar to those in Exercises 11–12. Students then exchange problems and challenge each other to write an inequality for the problem and solve the inequality.

California Resources

Standards Mastery
- Standards Review Transparencies
- Standards Review and Practice Workbook
- Math Companion

Math Intervention
- Skills Review and Practice Workbook
- Math XL

9-4

1. Plan

California Content Standards

AF 1.1 Use variables and appropriate operations to write an inequality that represents a verbal description. ***Develop***

AF 4.1 Solve two-step linear inequalities in one variable.

California Math Background

The *rules* for solving equations and inequalities refer to the properties of equality and inequality. In Lesson 9-2, the addition and subtraction rules for inequalities were essentially the same as those for equations. In this lesson, the exposition demonstrates that the multiplication rule for inequalities differs from the rule for equations in an important way: When multiplying each side of an inequality by a negative number, the direction of the inequality must be reversed.

More Math Background: p. 328C

Lesson Planning and Resources

See p. 328E for a list of the resources that support this lesson.

PRESENTATION CD-ROM
CD, Online, or Transparencies

Bell Ringer Practice

Check Skills You'll Need
Use student page, transparency, or PowerPoint.
See Math Companion.

California Standards Review
Use transparency or PowerPoint.

9-4 Solving Inequalities by Multiplying

Check Skills You'll Need

Do this in your **Math Companion.**

Vocabulary

- Multiplication Property of Inequality

Use your **Math Companion** *to build your vocabulary.*

California Content Standards

AF 1.1 Use variables and appropriate operations to write an inequality that represents a verbal description. ***Develop***

Prepares for **AF 4.1** Solve two-step linear inequalities in one variable.

What You'll Learn . . . and Why

You will learn to solve inequalities by multiplying. Event planners use inequalities to calculate how many people can attend an event.

Solving inequalities by multiplying is similar to solving inequalities by dividing. Multiplying by a positive number does not change the direction of the inequality sign.

The number line below shows that multiplying by a negative number does reverse the direction of the inequality sign.

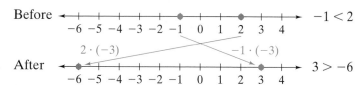

Before: number line from −6 to 4 with points at −1 and 2; $-1 < 2$

$2 \cdot (-3)$ $\quad -1 \cdot (-3)$

After: number line from −6 to 4 with points at −6 and 3; $3 > -6$

Take Note — Multiplication Property of Inequality

When you multiply each side of an inequality by a positive number, do not change the direction of the inequality sign. When you multiply each side of an inequality by a negative number, *reverse* the direction of the inequality sign.

Arithmetic	Algebra
Since $6 > 2$, $6 \cdot 3 > 2 \cdot 3$.	If $a > b$, and $c > 0$, then $a \cdot c > b \cdot c$.
Since $3 < 6$, $3 \cdot 4 < 6 \cdot 4$.	If $a < b$, and $c > 0$, then $a \cdot c < b \cdot c$.
Since $6 > 2$, $6 \cdot (-3) < 2 \cdot (-3)$.	If $a > b$, and $c < 0$, then $a \cdot c < b \cdot c$.
Since $3 < 6$, $3 \cdot (-2) > 6 \cdot (-2)$.	If $a < b$, and $c < 0$, then $a \cdot c > b \cdot c$.

Note: The Multiplication Property of Inequality also applies to $\leq$ and $\geq$.

Universal Access — Solutions for All Learners

Special Needs L1
Have students draw a picture to represent the situation in CA Standards Check 1. To visualize the minimum length of the rope, they should draw 7 sections of rope and label each section 2.4 ft.

Below Level L2
Review the rules for multiplying signed numbers. Use the rules below.

$+ \cdot + = +$ $\quad - \cdot - = +$ $\quad + \cdot - = -$ $\quad - \cdot + = -$

For: Solving Inequalities Activity
Use: Interactive Textbook, 9-4

EXAMPLE Multiplying by a Positive Number

1 **Guided Problem Solving** A reception hall has 14 tables that can hold 8 people each. Write and solve an inequality to find the number of people, at most, a couple can have attend their wedding at the reception hall.

Words: number of people attending / 14 tables — is at most — 8 people per table

Let n = the number of people attending.

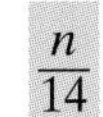

Inequality: $\frac{n}{14}$ $\leq$ 8

$$\frac{n}{14} \leq 8$$

$$14 \cdot \frac{n}{14} \leq 8 \cdot 14$$ ← **Isolate the variable. Use the Multiplication Property of Inequality.**

$$n \leq 112$$ ← **Simplify.**

The couple can have at most 112 people attend the wedding.

CA Standards Check 1 *Go to your* **Math Companion** *for help.*

1. A carpenter has some rope. He cuts the rope into 7 pieces, each of which is at least 2.4 ft long. Write and solve an inequality to find how much rope the carpenter has. **at least 16.8 ft**

When you multiply an inequality by a negative number, remember to reverse the direction of the inequality sign.

EXAMPLE Multiplying by a Negative Number

Relate MATH YOU KNOW... ...*to* ALGEBRA

Solve $-3c > 9$.

$$\frac{-3c}{-3} < \frac{9}{-3}$$ ← **Use the Division Property of Inequality. Reverse the inequality sign.**

$$c > -3$$ ← **Simplify.**

2 Solve $\frac{c}{-3} < 9$.

$$\frac{c}{-3} < 9$$

$$-3 \cdot \frac{c}{-3} > 9 \cdot (-3)$$ ← **Use the Multiplication Property of Inequality. Reverse the inequality sign.**

$$c > -27$$ ← **Simplify.**

CA Standards Check 2 *Go to your* **Math Companion** *for help.*

2. Solve each inequality.

a. $\frac{b}{-4} \geq 1$ **$b \leq -4$**

b. $\frac{k}{-5} < -4$ **$k > 20$**

Check Your Understanding *Homework prep is in your* **Math Companion.**

2. Teach

Guided Instruction

Teaching Tip
In preparation for Example 2 (multiplying by a negative number), ask students to verify that the inequality written in each step is equivalent to the inequality in the previous step, that is, it has exactly the same solution, even though the form has changed.

Error Prevention!

When solving an inequality that involves multiplying by a negative number, some students may write the negative multiplier in one step and fail to reverse the symbol until the second step. Ask students to check that each step they write as they solve an inequality expresses an equivalent inequality. This means that the *same* step that shows multiplying or dividing by a negative number must also show reversing the inequality.

PRESENTATION CD-ROM
CD, Online, or Transparencies

Additional Examples

1 For a field trip, a science teacher reserved 5 vans that can each carry 7 students. Write and solve an inequality that can be used to find how many students, at most, can attend the field trip. **$\frac{n}{5} \leq 7$, $n \leq 35$**

2 Solve $\frac{y}{-4} > 3$. **$y < -12$**

Closure

- How do the Multiplication and Division Properties of Inequality differ from the Multiplication and Division Properties of Equality? **When you multiply or divide each side of an inequality by a negative number, the direction of the inequality symbol is reversed.**

Advanced Learners L4
Students write an informal explanation for a friend about why the inequality sign must be reversed when multiplying or dividing by a negative number.

English Learners EL
Read inequality statements and have students write them using math notation as you read them. Make sure they translate the words for *greater than, less than, greater than or equal to,* and *less than or equal to* into the correct symbols.

3. Practice

Assignment Guide

Check Your Understanding

See Math Companion.

Homework Exercises

A	Practice by Example	1–21
B	Apply Your Skills	22–36
C	Challenge	37
California Multiple-Choice Practice		38–40
Mixed Review		41–43

Homework Quick Check

To check students' understanding of key skills and concepts, go over Exercises 3, 13, 23, 25, 33.

Universal Access Resources

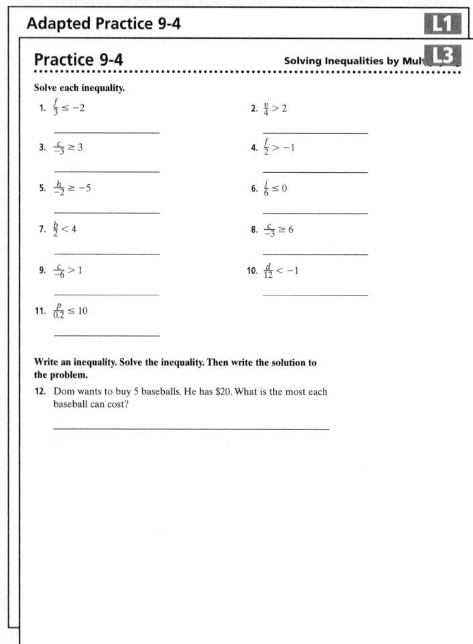
Adapted Practice 9-4 L1

Practice 9-4 — Solving Inequalities by Mult... L3

Solve each inequality.

1. $\frac{f}{3} \le -2$
2. $\frac{v}{4} > 2$
3. $\frac{c}{-3} \ge 3$
4. $\frac{f}{2} > -1$
5. $\frac{h}{-2} \ge -5$
6. $\frac{j}{6} \le 0$
7. $\frac{b}{2} < 4$
8. $\frac{c}{-3} \ge 6$
9. $\frac{c}{-6} > 1$
10. $\frac{d}{12} < -1$
11. $\frac{p}{0.2} \le 10$

Write an inequality. Solve the inequality. Then write the solution to the problem.

12. Dom wants to buy 5 baseballs. He has \$20. What is the most each baseball can cost?

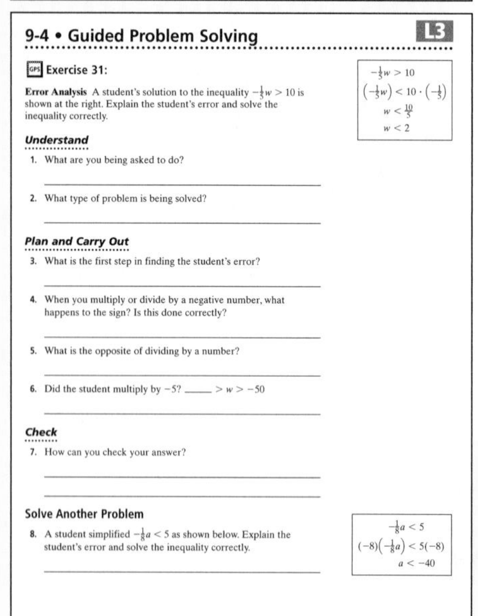
9-4 • Guided Problem Solving L3

GPS Exercise 31:

Error Analysis A student's solution to the inequality $-\frac{1}{5}w > 10$ is shown at the right. Explain the student's error and solve the inequality correctly.

$-\frac{1}{5}w > 10$
$\left(-\frac{1}{5}w\right) < 10 \cdot \left(-\frac{1}{5}\right)$
$w < \frac{10}{5}$
$w < 2$

Understand

1. What are you being asked to do?
2. What type of problem is being solved?

Plan and Carry Out

3. What is the first step in finding the student's error?
4. When you multiply or divide by a negative number, what happens to the sign? Is this done correctly?
5. What is the opposite of dividing by a number?
6. Did the student multiply by −5? _____ $> w > -50$

Check

7. How can you check your answer?

Solve Another Problem

8. A student simplified $-\frac{1}{8}a < 5$ as shown below. Explain the student's error and solve the inequality correctly.

$-\frac{1}{8}a < 5$
$(-8)\left(-\frac{1}{8}a\right) < 5(-8)$
$a < -40$

Standards Practice

GO for Help: *MathXL* — AF 1.1

A Practice by Example

Example 1 (page 345)

Solve each inequality.

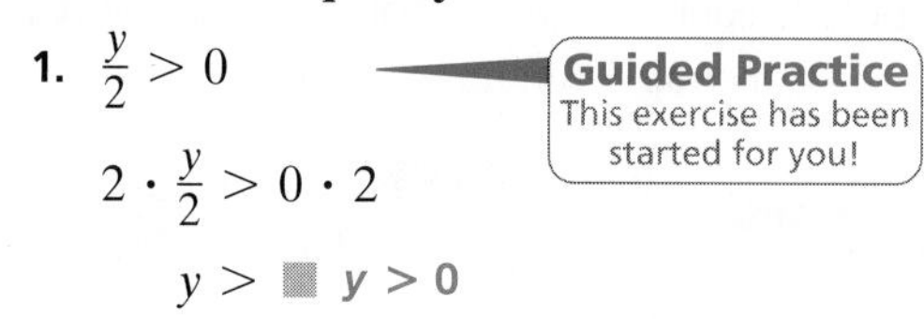
1. $\frac{y}{2} > 0$

$2 \cdot \frac{y}{2} > 0 \cdot 2$

$y > \blacksquare$ $y > 0$

Guided Practice: This exercise has been started for you!

GO for Help

2. $-18 \le \frac{x}{2}$ $x \ge -36$
3. $\frac{p}{5} < -3$ $p < -15$
4. $\frac{k}{4} \ge 6$ $k \ge 24$
5. $\frac{w}{7} \le -5$ $w \le -35$
6. $-8 < \frac{v}{7}$ $v > -56$
7. $\frac{x}{4} > -20$ $x > -80$
8. $9 < \frac{z}{5}$ $z > 45$
9. $\frac{s}{10} \le -10$ $s \le -100$
10. $-1 \ge \frac{u}{6}$ $u \le -6$
11. A baseball league organizer wants 14 teams in the league. Each team must have at least 20 players. Write and solve an inequality to find the number of players that need to sign up for the league. at least 280 players

Homework Video Tutor

For: Examples 1–2
Visit: PHSchool.com
Web Code: axe-0904

Example 2 (page 345)

Solve each inequality.

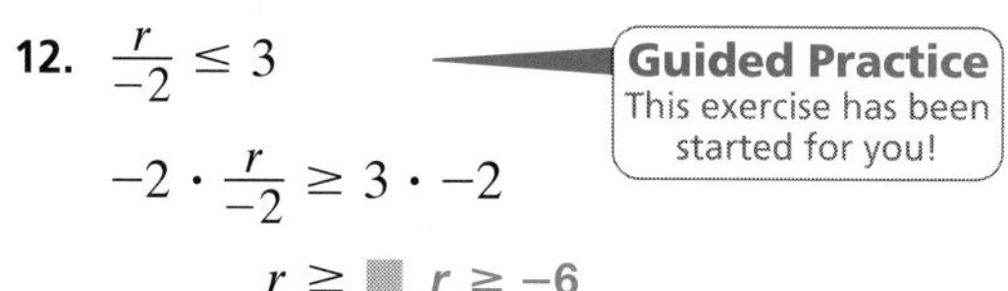
12. $\frac{r}{-2} \le 3$

$-2 \cdot \frac{r}{-2} \ge 3 \cdot -2$

$r \ge \blacksquare$ $r \ge -6$

Guided Practice: This exercise has been started for you!

13. $\frac{z}{-12} < -8$ $z > 96$
14. $-20 \ge \frac{b}{-7}$ $b \ge 140$
15. $6 < \frac{x}{-5}$ $x < -30$
16. $\frac{c}{-5} \le -2$ $c \ge 10$
17. $\frac{p}{-8} < 2.1$ $p > -16.8$
18. $9 > \frac{m}{-6}$ $m > -54$
19. $\frac{s}{-10} \ge 1.5$ $s \le -15$
20. $18 \le \frac{h}{-2}$ $h \le -36$
21. $\frac{t}{-8} < -8$ $t > 64$

B Apply Your Skills

22. **Guided Problem Solving** A trio of musicians performs nightly. Each member would like to earn at least \$65 per performance. How much money does the trio need to earn for each performance? at least \$195
    - How many people are in a trio?
    - Write and solve an inequality to find how much the trio needs to earn for each performance.
23. **Writing in Math** Explain how to solve $\frac{2}{3}d \le 7$. Justify each step.

23. Answers may vary. Sample: Multiply each side of the inequality by $\frac{3}{2}$.

Write an inequality for each word phrase. Then solve the inequality.

24. A number n divided by −9 is less than 10. $\frac{n}{-9} < 10$; $n > -90$
25. (GPS) The quotient of a number x and 5 is at least −8. $\frac{x}{5} \ge -8$; $x \ge -40$
26. A number w divided by 5.5 is at most 7.8. $\frac{w}{5.5} \le 7.8$; $w \le 42.9$

SCAFFOLDED
Problem Solving

Use the system of inequalities shown below for Exercises 27–31.

$$\begin{cases} -5y \le 35 \\ y - 1 \le 8 \end{cases}$$

27. Solve $-5y \le 35$. $y \ge -7$

28. Graph your solution on a number line. See left.

29. Solve $y - 1 \le 8$. Graph your solution on the same number line used in Exercise 27. See left.

30. A solution to a system of inequalities makes both inequalities true. Make a conjecture about which part of your graph is the solution to this system of inequalities.

31. Use your graph to write your solution to this system of inequalities in the form $a \le y \le b$. $-7 \le y \le 9$

28. −7 −3 1 5 9

29. $y \le 9$; −7 −3 1 5 9

30. The part of the number line that is common to each graph.

32. The student multiplied each side by $-\frac{1}{5}$ instead of dividing; $w < -50$.

32. **Error Analysis** A student's solution to the inequality $-\frac{1}{5}w > 10$ is shown at the right. Explain the student's error and solve the inequality correctly.

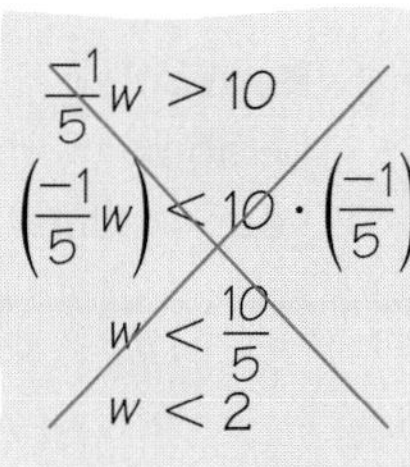

Solve each inequality.

33. $\frac{3}{5}k \le 9.6$ $k \le 16$

34. $\frac{7}{10}g > 2\frac{1}{2}$ $g > 3\frac{4}{7}$

35. $13.75 \le -\frac{9}{16}j$ $j \le -24\frac{4}{9}$

36. $-6\frac{2}{3} < -\frac{1}{3}a$ $a < 20$

C Challenge

37. Solve $2q - 6 < 20$. $q < 13$

Multiple Choice Practice and Mixed Review

For California Standards Tutorials, visit PHSchool.com. Web Code: axq-9045

AF 1.1

38. Which inequality represents the verbal description, "The quotient of a number p and 3 is at most 10"? B

Ⓐ $3p \le 10$ Ⓑ $\frac{p}{3} \le 10$ Ⓒ $3p < 10$ Ⓓ $\frac{p}{3} < 10$

NS 1.5

39. Which of the following is a rational number? D

Ⓐ $\sqrt{3}$ Ⓑ $\sqrt{5}$ Ⓒ $\sqrt{7}$ Ⓓ $\sqrt{9}$

NS 1.3

40. Which is equivalent to $\frac{3}{8}$? D

Ⓐ $\frac{3}{8}\%$ Ⓑ 0.375% Ⓒ 3.75% Ⓓ 37.5%

GO for Help Lesson 9-3

Solve each inequality.

41. $6x \le 18$ $x \le 3$

42. $9 > 3r$ $r < 3$

43. $25m \ge 125$ $m \ge 5$

Online Lesson Quiz Visit: PHSchool.com Web Code: axa-0904

Alternative Assessment

Ask students to write four different inequalities. The inequalities should be solved by multiplying. Students then trade papers with a partner who solves each inequality. Have students discuss their results.

California Resources

Standards Mastery
- Standards Review Transparencies
- Standards Review and Practice Workbook
- Math Companion

Math Intervention
- Skills Review and Practice Workbook
- Math XL

4. Assess & Reteach

PRESENTATION CD-ROM
CD, Online, or Transparencies
Lesson Quiz

Solve each inequality.

1. $\frac{5}{6} > 30$ $s > 180$
2. $\frac{x}{-3} < 7$ $x > -21$
3. Anthony has 4 cases that can each hold up to 12 CDs. Write and solve an inequality to find how many CDs, at most, Anthony can store in the cases. $\frac{n}{12} \cdot 4$, $n \le 48$

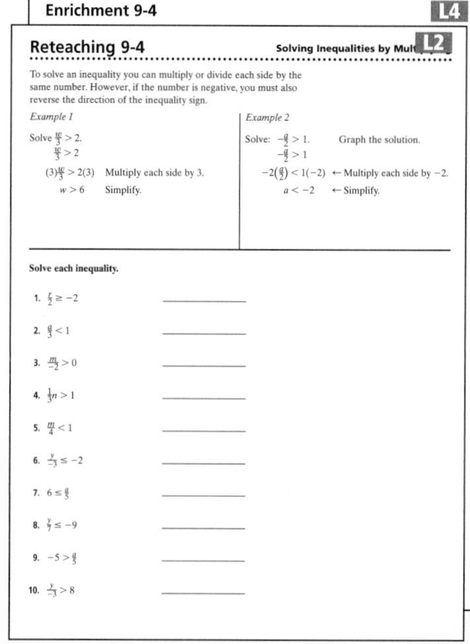

Checkpoint Quiz

Use this Checkpoint Quiz to check students' understanding of the skills and concepts of Lessons 9-3 through 9-4.

All in One Resources

- Checkpoint Quiz 2

Mathematical Reasoning

Everyday Inequalities

Students write and graph inequalities to solve an everyday scheduling problem.

Guided Instruction

Explain to students that they can solve some problems easily by graphing two inequalities on the same number line. For Exercise 1, have students read the question carefully; make sure they write an inequality that represents the time the concert ends, rather than the given start time. For Exercises 1 and 2, ask students to describe the graph they created. Ask how they can use the graph to answer Exercise 3.

Mathematical Reasoning

For Use With Lesson 9-4

AF 1.1 Use variables and operations to write an inequality that represents a verbal description. ***Develop***

MR 3.3 Develop generalizations of the results obtained and the strategies used and apply them to new problem situations. ***Develop***

Everyday Inequalities

Understanding the solutions of inequalities can help you make decisions.

Suppose you and your friend plan to go to a concert. The concert starts at 9:00 P.M. and will be at least an hour and a half long.

1. Write and graph an inequality that represents the time t the concert will be over. $t \geq 10{:}30$;

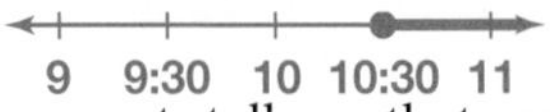

2. On the night of the concert, your parents tell you that you must be home before 10:00 P.M. The inequality $t < 10$ represents the time at which you must be home. Graph this inequality on the number line from Exercise 1.

3. **Reasoning** Is it possible for you to go to the entire concert and to be home by the time your parents would like? Use your graph in your explanation. See above right.

3. No. Answers may vary. Sample: The graph shows that the concert will end after the time your parents want you home.

Checkpoint Quiz 2

Lessons 9-3 through 9-4

Solve each inequality.

1. $4g > 16$ $g > 4$
2. $\frac{d}{3} \leq -3$ $d \leq -9$
3. $64 \leq 8x$ $x \geq 8$
4. $\frac{k}{-6} < 10$ $k > -60$
5. $-5t \geq 25$ $t \leq -5$
6. $1.5 \geq \frac{x}{-2}$ $x \geq -3$
7. $3d \geq -9$ $d \geq -3$
8. $60p \leq 6$ $p \leq \frac{1}{10}$
9. $-15 > \frac{s}{-3}$ $s > 45$

Write and solve an inequality to solve each problem.

10. A shuttle bus can carry 36 people per run. At least how many times does the shuttle bus have to run to carry 1,000 people to their destination? at least 28 times

11. You and six of your friends want to make a group donation to a local homeless shelter. Each person can afford to donate as much as \$23.50. How much can your group afford to donate? at most \$164.50

348

9-5 Solving Two-Step Inequalities

Check Skills You'll Need

Do this in your **Math Companion.**

Vocabulary

Review:

- inequality
- properties of inequality

Use your **Math Companion** *to build your vocabulary.*

California Content Standards

AF 1.1 Use variables and appropriate operations to write an inequality that represents a verbal description. ***Develop, Master***

AF 4.1 Solve two-step linear inequalities in one variable over the rational numbers, interpret the solution or solutions in the context from which they arose, and verify the reasonableness of the results. ***Develop, Master***

What You'll Learn . . . and Why

You will learn to solve two-step inequalities. You can use a two-step inequality to find how many items you can buy, given a budget.

A two-step inequality is an inequality that contains two operations. Solving a two-step inequality is similar to solving a two-step equation.

EXAMPLE Solving a Two-Step Inequality

Relate **MATH YOU KNOW...**

Solve $-2x - 3 = -7$.

$-2x - 3 + 3 = -7 + 3$ ← **Addition Property of Equality**

$-2x = -4$ ← **Simplify.**

$\frac{-2x}{-2} = \frac{-4}{-2}$ ← **Isolate the variable. Use the Division Property of Inequality.**

$x = 2$ ← **Simplify.**

. . . to **ALGEBRA**

1 Solve $-2x - 3 > -7$.

$-2x - 3 > -7$

$-2x - 3 + 3 > -7 + 3$ ← **Addition Property of Inequality**

$-2x > -4$ ← **Simplify.**

$\frac{-2x}{-2} < \frac{-4}{-2}$ ← **Use the Division Property of Inequality. Reverse the direction of the inequality sign.**

$x < 2$ ← **Simplify.**

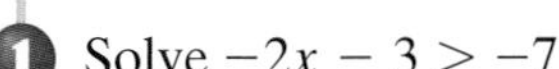

CA Standards Check 1

Go to your **Math Companion** *for help.*

1. Solve each inequality.

a. $\frac{m}{6} - 4 > 14$

$m > 108$

b. $-3x + 7 \leq 10$

$x \geq -1$

Universal Access Solutions for All Learners

Special Needs L1

Before students complete CA Standards Check 1, review the process of solving two-step equations. Ensure that students use the same operation on each side of the equation.

Below Level L2

Ask: *When do you not need to reverse the sign of an inequality?* when adding or subtracting any number and when multiplying or dividing by positive numbers

9-5

1. Plan

California Content Standards

AF 1.1 Use variables and appropriate operations to write an inequality that represents a verbal description. ***Develop***

AF 4.1 Solve two-step linear inequalities in one variable over the rational numbers, interpret the solution or solutions in the context from which they arose, and verify the reasonableness of the results. ***Develop***

Professional Development

California Math Background

Solving two-step inequalities follows the same procedures for isolating the variable as solving two-step equations. Always bear in mind the significant difference that multiplying or dividing by a negative number reverses the direction of the inequality symbol.

More Math Background: p. 328C

Lesson Planning and Resources

See p. 328E for a list of the resources that support this lesson.

PRESENTATION CD-ROM CD, Online, or Transparencies

Bell Ringer Practice

Check Skills You'll Need

Use student page, transparency, or PowerPoint.

See Math Companion.

California Standards Review

Use transparency or PowerPoint.

2. Teach

Guided Instruction

Example 1
Have students graph the solution to Example 1. Explain that all of the values on the graph will satisfy the original inequality. Demonstrate this by having students choose several values to substitute into the original inequality.

Error Prevention!

To focus attention on the essential difference involved in solving inequalities, have students draw a circle around the inequality sign in any step in which they reverse it.

Additional Examples

1. Solve $-5x - 2 > -12$ $x < 2$
2. You have $50 to spend on books that cost $7 each and one bookcase that costs $29. How many books can you buy? 3 books

Just as you have done with equations, you can use estimation to check the reasonableness of your answer when you solve two-step inequalities.

EXAMPLE Writing Two-Step Inequalities

2 Guided Problem Solving A student has his photo taken and wants to order copies of it. He wants to buy a large copy and some wallet-size copies. The prices are shown below.

The student has $20 to spend. At most, how many wallet-size photos can he order?

Write an inequality to represent the situation. Then solve the inequality.

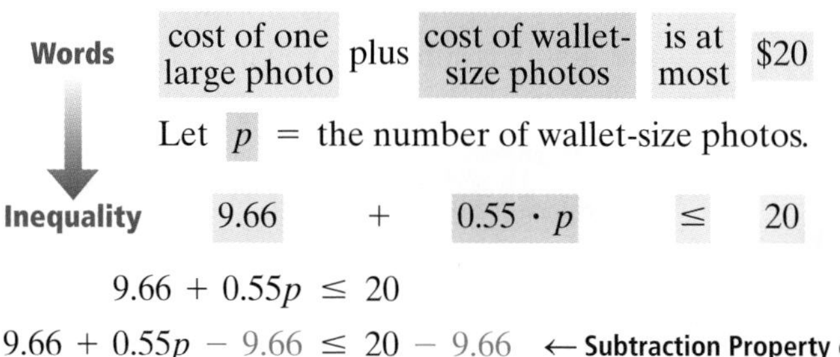

Words
cost of one large photo
plus
cost of wallet-size photos
is at most
$20
Let p = the number of wallet-size photos.
Inequality
9.66
+
0.55 · p
≤
20

$$9.66 + 0.55p \leq 20$$

$$9.66 + 0.55p - 9.66 \leq 20 - 9.66 \quad \leftarrow \text{Subtraction Property of Inequality}$$

$$0.55p \leq 10.34 \quad \leftarrow \text{Simplify.}$$

$$\frac{0.55p}{0.55} \leq \frac{10.34}{0.55} \quad \leftarrow \text{Isolate the variable. Use the Division Property of Inequality.}$$

$$p \leq 18.8 \quad \leftarrow \text{Simplify.}$$

Since the student cannot order 0.8 of a photo, the student can order 18 or fewer wallet-size photos.

Check for Reasonableness A large photo costs about $10 and wallet-size photos cost about $.50 each. $10 + 18 \cdot 0.50 = 10 + 9 = 19$. Since 19 is close to 20, the answer is reasonable.

CA Standards Check 2 *Go to your* **Math Companion** *for help.*

2. You have $15 to spend on school supplies. You need to buy a three-ring binder and some folders. The binder costs $5.99 and each folder costs $1.99. How many folders can you buy? 4 or fewer folders

Advanced Learners L4	**English Learners** EL
Have students solve CA Standards Check 1a in two ways: by performing the multiplication first and by performing the addition first. Ask students to discuss which method they prefer and why.	Help students understand the importance of units in the answer to each exercise. For Example 2, explain that the answer is the number of wallet-sized photographs, so the answer must be a whole number.

More Than One Way

Solve $\frac{1}{3}x - 5 \leq 7$.

Michelle's Method

I will add first. Then I will divide by $\frac{1}{3}$.

$\frac{1}{3}x - 5 + 5 \leq 7 + 5$ ← Addition Property of Equality

$\frac{1}{3}x \leq 12$ ← Simplify.

$\frac{3}{1} \cdot \frac{1}{3}x \leq 12 \cdot \frac{3}{1}$ ← Divide by $\frac{1}{3}$ by multiplying by $\frac{3}{1}$, the reciprocal of $\frac{1}{3}$.

$x \leq 36$ ← Simplify.

Eric's Method

I will multiply each side by 3 so my equation only contains integers.

$3 \cdot \frac{1}{3}x - 3 \cdot 5 \leq 7 \cdot 3$ ← Multiply each term by 3.

$x - 15 \leq 21$ ← Simplify.

$x - 15 + 15 \leq 21 + 15$ ← Addition Property of Inequality

$x \leq 36$ ← Simplify.

Choose a Method

Solve $\frac{4}{5}y + 3 > 15$. Describe your method and explain why you chose it. $y > 15$; check students' work.

Closure

- *When is solving a two-step inequality different from solving a two-step equation?* When you use a negative number to multiply or divide each side of the inequality, you must reverse the inequality symbol.

for Help: MathXL

Standards Practice

AF 1.1, AF 4.1

A Practice by Example

Example 1 (page 349)

for Help

Solve each inequality.

1. $2x - 4 < 8$
   $2x - 4 + 4 < 8 + 4$
   $2x < 12$
   $x < 6$

Guided Practice: This exercise has been started for you!

2. $3y + 1 < -7$ $\quad y < -2\frac{2}{3}$
3. $-5w + 8 \geq 13$ $\quad w \leq -1$
4. $\frac{a}{8} - 7 > -8$ $\quad a > -8$
5. $\frac{k}{5} + 2 > 6$ $\quad k > 20$
6. $30 > 12 + 2b$ $\quad b < 9$
7. $-2 + \frac{m}{3} \leq -11$ $\quad m \leq -27$
8. $5 \geq -4d + 9$ $\quad d \geq 1$
9. $-7 \geq 5 - 2g$ $\quad g \geq 6$
10. $5 + 5m > 5$ $\quad m > 0$

3. Practice

Assignment Guide

Check Your Understanding
See Math Companion.

Homework Exercises

A Practice by Example	1–20
B Apply Your Skills	21–37
C Challenge	38
California Multiple-Choice Practice	39–41
Mixed Review	42–44

Homework Quick Check
To check students' understanding of key skills and concepts, go over Exercises 2, 11, 22, 24, 31, 37.

Universal Access Resources

Adapted Practice 9-5 L1

Practice 9-5 — Solving Two-Step Ineq[…] L3

Solve each inequality.

1. $6x + 5 \le -19$
2. $2x + 12 < 24$
3. $15x - 9 > 21$
4. $5x - 11 \ge -36$
5. $18x - 6 \ge 84$
6. $9x + 2.3 > -10.3$
7. $11x + 4 \le -29$
8. $8x + 15 < 71$
9. $\frac{1}{2}x + 3 < 5$
10. $\frac{x}{6} - 7 \le 3$
11. $\frac{1}{4}x + 10 > -7$
12. $\frac{x}{9} - 15 \ge 5$
13. $12x + 7 \ge 139$
14. $3x - 8 \le 55$
15. $7x - 5.8 > 13.1$
16. $4x + 13 < 61$
17. $\frac{x}{8} - 7 > -12$
18. $\frac{1}{5}x + 8 < -2$
19. $\frac{n}{11} + 2 \le 6$
20. $\frac{x}{7} - 9 \ge -4$
21. $20n - 2 \le 138$
22. $10x - 3 \ge -83$
23. $8x - 3.2 > 37.6$
24. $12x - 10 > -130$
25. $\frac{w}{10} - 11 > 6$
26. $\frac{1}{3}x + 3 < -9$
27. $\frac{u}{12} + 4 \le 8$

Write and solve an inequality to answer each question.

28. A drama club's production of "Oklahoma!" is going to cost \$1,250 to produce. How many tickets will they need to sell for \$8 each in order to make a profit of at least \$830?
29. A pet store is selling hamsters for \$3.50 each if you purchase a cage for \$18.25. You have at most \$30 you can spend. How many hamsters can you buy?

9-5 • Guided Problem Solving L3

GPS Exercise 31:

Your parents are having a 100th birthday party for your greatgrandmother. The hall costs \$400 to rent. The meal costs \$20 per person. The decorations cost \$75. Your parents budgeted no more than \$2000 in all. How many people can attend the party?

Understand

1. What does the hall cost?
2. What does each meal cost?
3. What do the decorations cost?
4. Underline what you are being asked to do.

Plan and Carry Out

5. What will determine how many people can come?
6. Write an inequality for what you know, where x represents the number of people who can attend.
7. Combine the like terms.
8. Subtract \$475 from each side.
9. What do you need to do to isolate the variable x?
10. Solve the inequality.
11. How many people can attend the party?

Check

12. Does the answer make sense? Does the answer check?

Solve Another Problem

13. Your parents have given you \$125 to take when you go skiing. The bus trip costs \$25 and ski rental costs \$30. The cost to ski is \$12.00 per hour. How many hours can you plan on skiing?

Example 2 (page 350)

Homework Video Tutor
For: Examples 1–2
Visit: PHSchool.com
Web Code: axe-0905

Solve each inequality.

11. $-12 - 4n \le 0$ $n \ge -3$
12. $23 - 2x \le -9$ $x \ge 16$
13. $17p - 34 > 306$ $p > 20$
14. $-11z - 6 > 335$ $z < -31$
15. $5 - \frac{t}{9} < 4$ $t > 9$
16. $13 - \frac{a}{6} < 29$ $a > -96$
17. $4r + 7 \ge 15$ $r \ge 2$
18. $\frac{s}{-2} - 19 \le 1$ $s \ge -40$

19. Basic cable television costs \$21.99 per month. There is a \$10.50 charge for each premium channel. Your parents budget no more than \$60 per month for cable service. Write and solve an inequality to find how many premium channels your family can order. 3 or fewer

20. You have at most 20 c of flour. You make a batch of bread that uses 12 c of flour. A batch of muffins uses $3\frac{1}{2}$ c. Write and solve an inequality to find how many batches of muffins you can make. 2 or fewer

B Apply Your Skills

21. **Guided Problem Solving** A student is running a 13-mi race. She wants to finish with a time under 2 h. After 5 mi, 52 min have elapsed. To reach her goal, what must the student's average time per mile be for the remainder of the race? at least 8.5 min/mi
    - **Make a Plan** Find the number of miles and the time the student has left to reach her goal. Write and solve an inequality to find the average time per mile.
    - **Carry Out the Plan** How many minutes are in 2 h?

Error Analysis **Explain the error made in solving each inequality.**

22. $-3w - 4 < 5$
    $-3w < 9$
    $w < -3$

23. 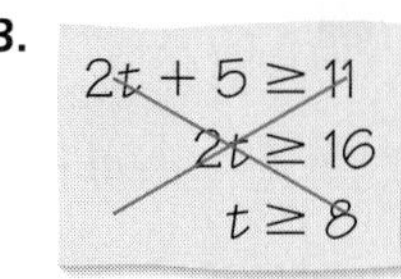

The student added 5 to each side instead of subtracting 5.

Solve each inequality. 24–30. See left.

24. $\frac{t}{-2} - 0.8 \ge 1$
25. $2.5j - 3\frac{1}{10} > 1.4$
26. $1\frac{1}{5} \le 3x - 1\frac{4}{5}$
27. $0.7 - 2.5g \ge 8\frac{2}{10}$
28. $15 < -5(h + 1)$
29. $-(b - 4) \ge 11$

30. Solve $2(x - 8) < 52$. Justify each step.

31. (GPS) Your parents are having a hundredth birthday party for your great-grandmother. The hall costs \$400 to rent. The meal costs \$20 per person. The decorations cost \$75. Your parents budgeted no more than \$2,000 in all. How many people can attend the party? 76 or fewer people

32. **Estimation** You have \$25 to spend at the bookstore. You want to buy a travel guide for \$13.95 and some novels that cost \$2.99 each. Is 3 a reasonable estimate for the number of novels you can buy? Explain. See left.

22. The student did not change the direction of the inequality.
24. $t \le -3.6$
25. $j > 1.8$
26. $x \ge 1$
27. $g \le -3$
28. $h < -4$
29. $b \le -7$
30. Justifications may vary. Sample: $2(x - 8) < 52$; Div. Prop. of Ineq.: $x - 8 < 26$. Add. Prop. of Ineq.: $x < 34$.
32. Yes; \$13.95 is about \$14, and \$2.99 is about \$3. 3 is a solution to the inequality $3(3) + 14 \le 25$, but 4 is not a solution.

SCAFFOLDED
Problem Solving

A teacher's grading policy is shown at the right.

Grading Policy	
Test Average	Grade
90–100	A
80–89	B
70–79	C
60–69	D
59 or below	F

33. What is the minimum test average a student needs for an A? 90

34. Write an inequality that represents the test average needed for an A. $t \geq 90$

35. One student has scored 87, 92, and 85 on the first three tests of the semester. What grade does the student receive? B

36. There are four tests in the semester. Write and solve an inequality to find the score the student needs on the fourth test to earn an A. 96

37. **Writing in Math** Describe how the process of solving $-3v - 9 = 12$ is different from solving $-3v - 9 < 12$. See above left.

37. Answers may vary. Sample: The process is the same except the direction of the inequality sign is reversed when you divide by -3.

C Challenge

38. Solve $2z + z - 9 > 30$. $z > 13$

Multiple Choice Practice and Mixed Review

For California Standards Tutorials, visit PHSchool.com. Web Code: axq-9045

AF 1.1 **39.** Chandra's calling plan has a monthly fee of \$17 plus \$.05 per minute for long-distance calls. She budgets no more than \$25 per month for her telephone bill. Which inequality can be used to find how many minutes she can talk long distance each month? A

Ⓐ $17 + 0.05x \leq 25$
Ⓑ $17 + 0.05x < 25$
Ⓒ $17 + 0.05x \geq 25$
Ⓓ $17 + 0.05x > 25$

AF 4.1 **40.** Solve $\frac{k}{-4} + 3 \leq -1$. D

Ⓐ $k \leq 16$ Ⓑ $k \leq -8$ Ⓒ $k \geq -8$ Ⓓ $k \geq 16$

MG 3.3 **41.** The stated size of a computer monitor is based on the length of the diagonal of the screen. If the height of a screen is 9.75 in. and the width is 12.75 in., which is the best estimate of the stated size of the monitor? C

Ⓐ 8.5 in. Ⓑ 15 in. Ⓒ 16 in. Ⓓ 22 in.

Lesson 9-1

Write an inequality for each verbal description.

42. You must be at least 17 years old to donate blood. $a \geq 17$

43. The delivery truck makes more than 85 stops each day. $s > 85$

44. On a certain street, a car's speed should not exceed 35 mi/h. $s \leq 35$

Online Lesson Quiz Visit: PHSchool.com **Web Code:** axa-0905

4. Assess & Reteach

PRESENTATION CD-ROM
CD, Online, or Transparencies
Lesson Quiz

Solve.

1. $3x - 11 > 10$ $x > 7$
2. $\frac{r}{-4} - 5 \geq -2$ $r \leq 28$
3. You want to order one large photo of yourself for \$8.95 and some small photos for your friends. The small photos cost \$.75 each. You have \$25 to spend. Write an inequality you can use to find how many small photos you can order. Then solve it. $0.75p + 8.95 \leq 25$; $p \leq 21.4$; 21 or fewer small photos

Alternative Assessment

Have students choose an integer. Then have them set it less than $5n - 1$ and solve the resulting inequality for n.

California Resources

Standards Mastery

- Standards Review Transparencies
- Standards Review and Practice Workbook
- Math Companion

Math Intervention

- Skills Review and Practice Workbook
- Math XL

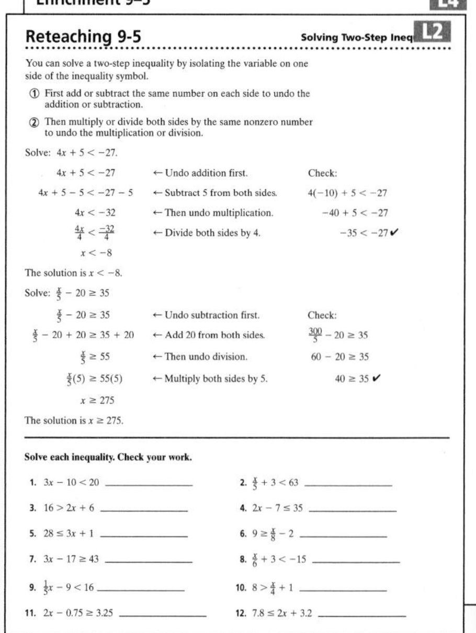

Enrichment 9–5 L4

Reteaching 9-5 Solving Two-Step Ineq L2

You can solve a two-step inequality by isolating the variable on one side of the inequality symbol.

① First add or subtract the same number on each side to undo the addition or subtraction.

② Then multiply or divide both sides by the same nonzero number to undo the multiplication or division.

Solve: $4x + 5 < -27$.

		Check:
$4x + 5 < -27$	← Undo addition first.	
$4x + 5 - 5 < -27 - 5$	← Subtract 5 from both sides.	$4(-10) + 5 < -27$
$4x < -32$	← Then undo multiplication.	$-40 + 5 < -27$
$\frac{4x}{4} < \frac{-32}{4}$	← Divide both sides by 4.	$-35 < -27$ ✔
$x < -8$		

The solution is $x < -8$.

Solve: $\frac{x}{5} - 20 \geq 35$

		Check:
$\frac{x}{5} - 20 \geq 35$	← Undo subtraction first.	
$\frac{x}{5} - 20 + 20 \geq 35 + 20$	← Add 20 from both sides.	$\frac{300}{5} - 20 \geq 35$
$\frac{x}{5} \geq 55$	← Then undo division.	$60 - 20 \geq 35$
$\frac{x}{5}(5) \geq 55(5)$	← Multiply both sides by 5.	$40 \geq 35$ ✔
$x \geq 275$		

The solution is $x \geq 275$.

Solve each inequality. Check your work.

1. $3x - 10 < 20$ ________
2. $\frac{x}{5} + 3 < 63$ ________
3. $16 > 2x + 6$ ________
4. $2x - 7 \leq 35$ ________
5. $28 \leq 3x + 1$ ________
6. $9 \geq \frac{x}{8} - 2$ ________
7. $3x - 17 \geq 43$ ________
8. $\frac{x}{6} + 3 < -15$ ________
9. $\frac{1}{5}x - 9 < 16$ ________
10. $8 > \frac{x}{4} + 1$ ________
11. $2x - 0.75 \geq 3.25$ ________
12. $7.8 \leq 2x + 3.2$ ________

GPS Guided Problem Solving

Practice Solving Problems

Students practice solving problems by first analyzing each step necessary to solve a problem. They then follow the steps to write and graph two inequalities. Students compare the inequalities and check the reasonableness of their answers.

Guided Instruction

Explain to students how the phrase *between 2,000 and 3,000 calories* can be translated into two inequalities. Demonstrate the relationship by using a simple example such as *between 3 and 7 students.* Ask:

- *What inequality represents the least number of students?* $x > 3$
- *What inequality represents the greatest number of students?* $x < 7$
- *What numbers are solutions of this system of inequalities?* 4, 5, and 6

GPS Guided Problem Solving

Practice Solving Problems

AF 1.1 Use variables and operations to write an inequality that represents a verbal description. ***Develop***
MR 2.6 Support solutions with evidence in both verbal and symbolic work. ***Develop***

Art wants to eat between 2,000 and 3,000 Calories per day. He consumes 610 Calories for breakfast and has two bowls of soup for lunch. Each bowl contains 335 Calories. How many Calories can Art consume at dinner?

What You Might Think	What You Might Write
What do I know? What do I want to find out?	Art consumed 610 Cal + 2 · 335 Cal. So he has consumed 1,280 total Calories. I want to find how many more Calories he can eat to consume more than 2,000 Cal and fewer than 3,000 Cal for the day.
What inequalities can I write?	Let C = the number of Calories Art can eat. I will write two inequalities. One will represent eating more than 2,000 Cal, and the other will represent eating fewer than 3,000 Cal.
How can I find the number of Calories he can consume for dinner?	$C + 1{,}280 > 2{,}000$ $C + 1{,}280 - 1{,}280 > 2{,}000 - 1{,}280$ $C > 720$ $C + 1{,}280 < 3{,}000$ $C + 1{,}280 - 1{,}280 < 3{,}000 - 1{,}280$ $C < 1{,}720$
I'll use a graph to show the range of Calories for dinner.	Graph the two inequalities on one number line. 700 900 1,100 1,300 1,500 1,700 The overlapping region represents the range for dinner Calories. He can consume between 720 and 1,720 Cal.

Think It Through

1–3. See right.

1. Is the answer reasonable? Explain.
2. **Reasoning** Why do you need two inequalities for this problem?
3. Would the answer differ if Anthony wanted to consume more than 3,000 Cal? Support your answer with a graph.

1. Yes; Art consumed about 1,300 Cal before dinner. If he consumes about 700 Cal more, then the total is about 2,000 Cal. If he consumes about 1,700 Cal more, then the total is about 3,000 Cal.
2. You need one inequality for the least number of Calories and one inequality for the greater number of Calories.
3. Yes;

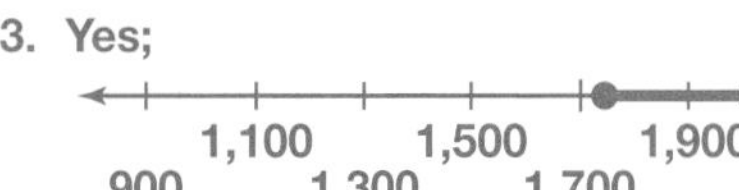

Exercises

Solve each problem. For Exercise 4, answer parts (a) and (b) first.

4. A college estimates that about 30% of accepted applicants will choose to attend. The college would like to have between 4,500 and 7,000 new students to attend next year. How many applicants should the college accept to meet this goal? between 15,000 and 23,333 applicants
   a. Let a = the number of accepted applicants. Let $0.3a$ represent the number of accepted applicants who choose to attend the college. Write and solve two inequalities to represent the number of applicants the college hopes will attend.
   b. Graph your solutions from part (a) on a number line to find the number of applicants the college should accept.

5. The slope, or pitch, of the roof in the diagram is $\frac{3}{12}$. The slope indicates that each time the horizontal distance changes by 12 in., the vertical distance changes by 3 in. Use the diagram to find the length x. about 16.5 ft

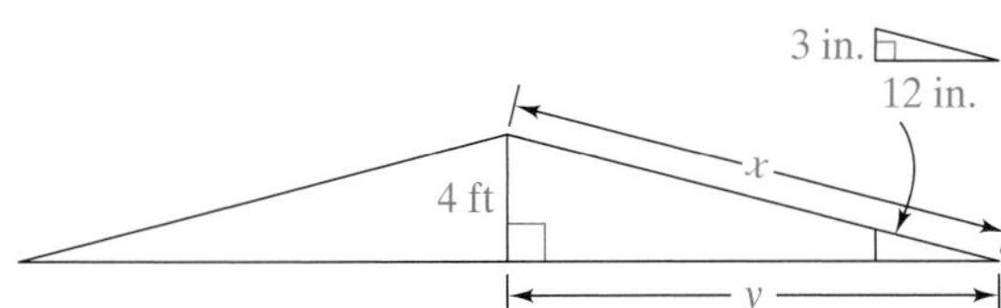

6. Two students begin weightlifting. One student starts with a 3-lb hand weight and increases the weight by 2 lb per month. The other student starts with a 5-lb hand weight and increases the weight by 1 lb per month. Write and graph two equations to find when the students will be lifting the same weight.

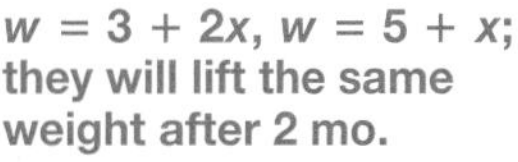
$w = 3 + 2x$, $w = 5 + x$; they will lift the same weight after 2 mo.

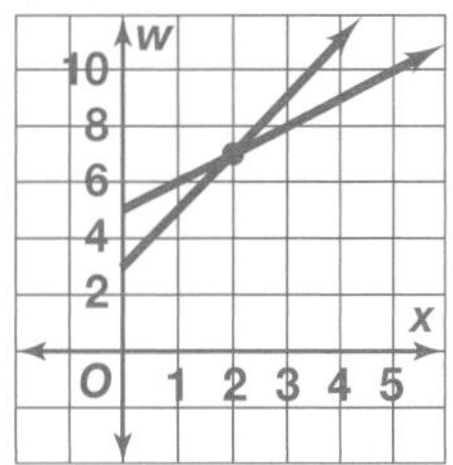

Error Prevention!

Some students may not calculate the correct number of Calories that Anthony consumes for breakfast and lunch. Make sure that students multiply 335 by 2 (to account for the two bowls of soup) and add the product to 610 (the number of Calories consumed for breakfast).

Exercises

Have students work independently on Exercises 3–5. Then, in pairs, have students compare answers and describe the techniques they used to solve each problem.

Universal Access

English Learners EL

Ask:

- *What are Calories and why are they important?* The term *Calorie* refers to the amount of chemical energy found in a piece of food. When we eat, our bodies transform the food's chemical energy into energy we can use to move and stay warm.

Activity Lab

Systems of Inequalities

Students learned to write systems of inequalities earlier in the chapter. In this activity, students graph systems of inequalities and use the graphs to determine whether a system has no solution, one solution, or many solutions.

Guided Instruction

Review the process of graphing inequalities. Ask students to:

- *Describe the graph of the inequality* $x > 3$. a ray on a number line, pointing to the right, with an open circle at 3
- *Describe the graph of the inequality* $x \leq -2$. a ray on a number line, pointing to the left, with a closed circle at −2

Activity

Have students work in pairs for Exercises 1–5. One student can draw the graph while the other student uses the graph to determine the solutions to the system. Have students work independently on Exercises 6–9 and then discuss their responses in small groups.

Alternative Method

Some students may find it easier to first graph each inequality on its own number line and then combine the two graphs to form the graph of the system.

9-5b Activity Lab

AF 1.1 Use variables and appropriate operations to write a system of inequalities. ***Develop***

MR 2.6 Support solutions with evidence in both verbal and symbolic work. ***Develop***

Systems of Inequalities

You have learned to write systems of inequalities from a verbal description. The solutions to a system of inequalities are the solutions shared by both inequalities in the system.

You can use the graph of a system of inequalities to determine whether the system has no solution, one solution, or many solutions.

ACTIVITY

1. Write a system of inequalities from the following verbal description: A number is less than 5 and greater than −3. $x < 5$, $x > -3$
2. Graph both inequalities on the same number line.

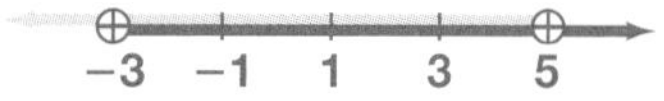

3. The overlapping region on a graph indicates the solutions to a system of inequalities. Find the solutions to the system you graphed in Exercise 2. $-3 < x < 5$
4. Graph $x > 5$ and $x < -3$ on the same number line.

5. What are the solutions of the system? no solution
$$\begin{cases} x > 5 \\ x < -3 \end{cases}$$
6. How many solutions does the following system have? Use a graph to support your answer. One; $x = 5$; check students' graphs.
$$\begin{cases} x \leq 5 \\ x \geq 5 \end{cases}$$
7. Explain how the solutions to the following systems differ.
$$\begin{cases} x > -3 \\ x > 5 \end{cases} \qquad \begin{cases} x > -3 \\ x < 5 \end{cases}$$
8. **Error Analysis** Two students solve the following system.
$$\begin{cases} x > 5 \\ x \leq 5 \end{cases}$$
Consuela says the solution to the system is 5. Jeanne says the system has no solution. Which student is correct? Explain.
9. **Writing in Math** Explain how you can use the graph of a system of inequalities to show the number of solutions to the system.

7. Answers may vary. Sample: The solution to the first system is $x > 5$. The solution to the second system is the set of numbers between −3 and 5.

8. Jeanne; the system has no solution since the graph of the system does not have an overlapping region.

9. Answers may vary. Sample: The solution is the set that is common to the two graphs.

Answering the Question Asked

When answering a multiple-choice question, be sure to answer the question asked. Eliminate answer choices that are not related to the question that is asked. Read the question carefully and check that you have answered it.

EXAMPLE

1 You have \$10 to spend at the arcade. You buy a drink for \$1.25. Each game you play costs \$.30. Which inequality represents the greatest number of games you can play?

Ⓐ $1.25 + 0.3g \leq 10$
Ⓑ $1.25 + 0.3g = 10$
Ⓒ $1.25 + 0.3g \geq 10$
Ⓓ $1.25 + 0.3g \neq 10$

The question asks for the inequality that represents the greatest number of games you can play with your \$10. Eliminate choice B because it is an equation. Since the most you can spend is \$10, 10 must be greater than what you spend. So the correct answer choice is choice A.

Multiple Choice Practice

AF 4.1 **1.** Which number is NOT a solution to the inequality $6x - 7 < 11$? A

Ⓐ 6 Ⓑ 3 Ⓒ −3 Ⓓ −6

NS 1.2 **2.** The table at the right shows the scores contestants received on a game show. What was the combined score of the blue team? B

Player	Team	Score
Liang	Red	50
Yvonne	Red	25
Carlos	Blue	−5
Tate	Blue	60

Ⓐ 5 Ⓒ 60
Ⓑ 55 Ⓓ 65

AF 4.2 **3.** A customer buys 3 lb of deli meat for \$17.97. At that rate, what is the cost of 2 lb of meat? C

Ⓐ \$5.99 Ⓑ \$8.99 Ⓒ \$11.98 Ⓓ \$17.97

AF 1.1 **4.** To join a health club, you must pay a joining fee plus a monthly fee. You can use the equation $c = 50 + 39.99m$ to find the cost c of a membership for m months. What is the monthly fee? A

Ⓐ \$39.99 Ⓑ \$50 Ⓒ $\$c$ Ⓓ $\$m$

Answering the Question Asked

This feature alerts students to the importance of reading test questions carefully to make sure that they answer the question asked. It points out the importance of recognizing that some of the answer choices are distractors.

Guided Instruction

Teaching Tip
Students may know that some answer choices on tests are there to catch common mathematical errors. Discuss that other choices are included because they are correct given a *misreading* of the question asked. Stress the importance of reading carefully to avoid this trap. Point out that choice B can easily be eliminated because it is an equation, not an inequality.

Chapter 9 Review

California Resources

Standards Mastery
- Math Companion
- Standards Review Transparencies
- Standards Review and Practice Workbook
- Progress Monitoring Assessments

Math Intervention
- Skills Review and Practice Workbook
- Math XL

Universal Access Resources
- Student Workbook
  - Vocabulary and Study Skills
  - Guided Problem Solving
- All-in-One Teaching Resources
  - Reteaching
  - Enrichment
- Spanish Practice Workbook L3
- Spanish Vocabulary and Study Skills 2A-F L3
- English/Spanish Glossary EL
- Multilingual Handbook EL
- Interactive Textbook Audio Glossary
- Online Vocabulary Quiz

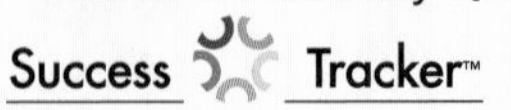

Online at PHSchool.com

Spanish Vocabulary/Study Skills EL

Vocabulary/Study Skills L3

9F: Vocabulary Review For use with the Chapter Review

Study Skill Review notes that you have taken in class as soon as possible to clarify any points you missed and to refresh your memory.

Circle the word that best completes the sentence.

1. A (*variable, expression*) is a letter that stands for a number.
2. An (*expression, equation*) is a mathematical statement with an equal sign.
3. A (*solution, sentence*) is a value for a variable that makes an equation true.
4. To solve an equation, use (*inverse, variable*) operations.
5. A mathematical statement that contains $<$ or $>$ is called an (*equation, inequality*).
6. The statement $4 + (9 + 3) = (4 + 9) + 3$ is an example of the (*Commutative Property of Addition, Associative Property of Addition*).
7. The (*opposite, absolute value*) of 15 is -15.
8. The (*mean, median*) is the middle number in a data set when the data is arranged from least to greatest.
9. You can use the (*commutative, identity*) property to change the order in an expression.
10. The statement $a + 0 = a$ is an example of the (*Identity Property of Zero, Identity Property of Multiplication*).
11. The (*absolute value, opposite*) of a number is its distance from 0 on a number line.
12. (*Rational numbers, Integers*) are the set of whole numbers, their opposites, and zero.
13. Two numbers whose sum is 0 are (*additive, opposite*) inverses.
14. A(n) (*outlier, range*) is a data value that is much greater or less than the other values in the data set.
15. Using the (*distributive property, order of operations*), you can calculate that $12 + 5 \cdot 2$ equals 22.

Chapter 9 Review

Vocabulary Review

English and Spanish Audio Online

Addition Property of Inequality (p. 334)
Division Property of Inequality (p. 340)
inequality (p. 330)
Multiplication Property of Inequality (p. 344)
solution of an inequality (p. 331)
Subtraction Property of Inequality (p. 334)
system of inequalities (p. 331)

Go Online PHSchool.com
For: Vocabulary Quiz
Visit: PHSchool.com
Web Code: axj-0951

Choose the correct vocabulary term to complete each sentence.

1. An (equation, inequality) is a mathematical sentence that contains $<, >, \leq, \geq$, or $\neq$. inequality
2. When you use the (Addition Property of Inequality, Division Property of Inequality), you may need to reverse the direction of the inequality sign. Div. Prop. of Ineq.
3. Two or more inequalities form a (system of inequalities, solution of an inequality). system of inequalities
4. To solve the inequality $x - 5 < 7$, use the (Addition Property of Inequality, Multiplication Property of Inequality). Add. Prop. of Ineq.
5. A (solution of an inequality, system of inequalities) is any number that makes the inequality true. solution of an inequality

Skills and Concepts

Lesson 9-1
- To write and test inequalities

AF 1.1

An **inequality** is a mathematical sentence that contains $<, >, \leq, \geq$, or $\neq$. Two or more inequalities form a **system of inequalities.** The **solution of an inequality** is any number that makes an inequality true.

Write an inequality for each verbal description.

6. The volume v is at least 35 cm^3. $v \geq 35$
7. The ticket t costs at most \$10. $t \leq 10$
8. The race r is less than 5 miles. $r < 5$
9. The cost c is greater than \$53. $c > 53$
10. A typical dairy cow produces at least 9 gal of milk and less than 11 gal of milk each day. Write a system of inequalities to represent this situation. $\begin{cases} c \geq 9 \\ c < 11 \end{cases}$
11. Give three integers that are solutions to the inequality $5 \geq d$. Answers may vary. Sample: 4, 3, 2

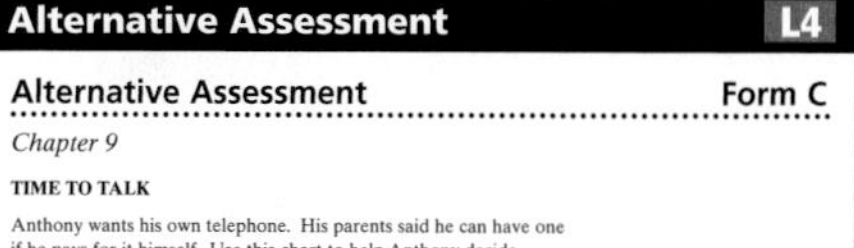

Alternative Assessment L4

Alternative Assessment — Form C

Chapter 9

TIME TO TALK

Anthony wants his own telephone. His parents said he can have one if he pays for it himself. Use this chart to help Anthony decide whether he can afford his own phone.

Telephone Company Charges	
Installation:	$42
Deposit:	$50
Basic Monthly Charge:	$8

Show all of your work on a separate sheet of paper.

1. To earn money, Anthony mows lawns for $4 per hour. First, he wanted to find the least number of hours needed to pay for the installation and deposit. He wrote this inequality:

   $4h \geq 42 + 50$

   Describe what each term in this inequality represents. Then solve for *h*.
2. Next Anthony wanted to find the least number of hours he would have to work to pay his basic monthly charge. He wrote this inequality:

   $4h \geq 8$

   Describe what each term in this inequality represents and solve the inequality for *h*.
3. Anthony has two out-of-state friends whom he would like to call. He discovered the following about long-distance calls:
   - The phone company charges one price for the first minute and then a lower price per minute for every minute thereafter.
   - If a customer talks for any part of a minute, he or she is charged for the whole minute.
   - Rates vary according to the time of day.

Anthony looked up the rates to the two cities where his friends live. He used this information to make the price chart shown on the next page. (*n* represents the number of minutes after the first minute.)

Lesson 9-2

- To solve inequalities by adding or subtracting

AF 1.1

Solving inequalities is similar to solving equations. You can solve an inequality by using the addition and subtraction properties of inequality.

Solve each inequality.

12. $g - 7 > 12$ $g > 19$

13. $u + 3 \leq 5$ $u \leq 2$

14. $4 + t \geq -7$ $t \geq -11$

15. $h + 7 > -15$ $h > -22$

16. $x - 8 > 14$ $x > 22$

17. $22 \leq y + 23$ $y \geq -1$

18. You have $15 to spend on souvenirs. You buy a visor for $7.99. Write and solve an inequality to find how much more money you can spend. $7.01 or less

Lessons 9-3, 9-4

- To solve inequalities by dividing
- To solve inequalities by multiplying

AF 1.1

When you multiply or divide an inequality by a positive number, the relationship between the two sides does not change. When you multiply or divide an inequality by a negative number, you must reverse the direction of the inequality symbol.

Solve each inequality.

19. $4x < -12$ $x < -3$

20. $-17y > 34$ $y < -2$

21. $-6a > -42$ $a < 7$

22. $-9m \leq 27$ $m \geq -3$

23. $\frac{w}{8} \leq 16$ $w \leq 128$

24. $\frac{c}{-2} > 10$ $c < -20$

25. $\frac{z}{-4} < -3$ $z > 12$

26. $\frac{p}{5} \geq -3$ $p \geq -15$

27. The Spanish club is having a dinner to raise money. Each ticket costs $5. The club wants to raise at least $650. At least how many tickets does the club need to sell to reach its goal? at least 130 tickets

Lesson 9-5

- To solve two-step inequalities

AF 1.1, AF 4.1

Solving two-step inequalities is similar to solving two-step equations.

Solve each inequality.

28. $3j - 5 < 19$ $j < 8$

29. $5 - 4m > -2.6$ $m \leq 1.9$

30. $-1 > \frac{e}{5} + 3$ $e < -20$

31. $\frac{v}{-12} + 15 \leq 15$ $v \geq 0$

32. A Web site offers video games for $14.50 each. There is a shipping charge of $6 for all orders. You can spend as much as $50. How many games can you buy? 3 or fewer games

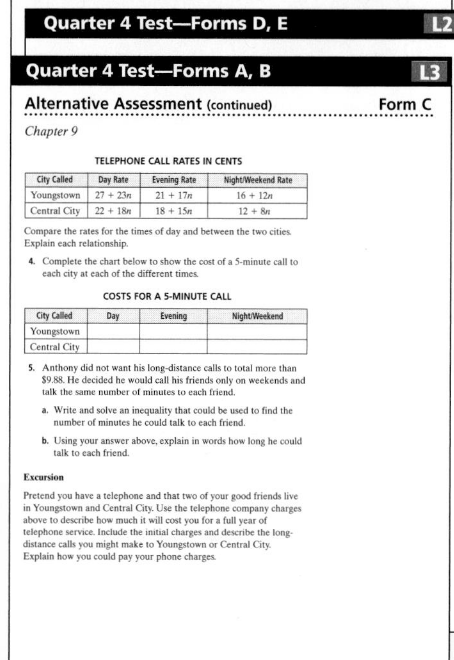

Spanish Quarter 4 Test—Forms A, B EL

Quarter 4 Test—Forms D, E L2

Quarter 4 Test—Forms A, B L3

Alternative Assessment (continued) — Form C

Chapter 9

TELEPHONE CALL RATES IN CENTS

City Called	Day Rate	Evening Rate	Night/Weekend Rate
Youngstown	27 + 23*n*	21 + 17*n*	16 + 12*n*
Central City	22 + 18*n*	18 + 15*n*	12 + 8*n*

Compare the rates for the times of day and between the two cities. Explain each relationship.

4. Complete the chart below to show the cost of a 5-minute call to each city at each of the different times.

COSTS FOR A 5-MINUTE CALL

City Called	Day	Evening	Night/Weekend
Youngstown			
Central City			

5. Anthony did not want his long-distance calls to total more than $9.88. He decided he would call his friends only on weekends and talk the same number of minutes to each friend.
   a. Write and solve an inequality that could be used to find the number of minutes he could talk to each friend.
   b. Using your answer above, explain in words how long he could talk to each friend.

Excursion

Pretend you have a telephone and that two of your good friends live in Youngstown and Central City. Use the telephone company charges above to describe how much it will cost you for a full year of telephone service. Include the initial charges and describe the long-distance calls you might make to Youngstown or Central City. Explain how you could pay your phone charges.

California Resources

Standards Mastery
- Teacher Center ExamView CD-ROM
- Math XL
- Progress Monitoring Assessments
- Online Chapter Test at PHSchool.com

Math Intervention
- Skills Review and Practice Workbook

Success Tracker™
Online at PHSchool.com

Universal Access Resources
- Chapter Test
- Alternative Assessment
- Spanish Chapter Test
- Spanish Alternative Assessment
- Teacher Center ExamView CD-ROM
  - Special Needs Test
  - Special Needs Practice Banks
  - Foundational Standards Practice Banks
- Online Chapter Test at www.PHSchool.com
- All-In-One Teaching Resources
  - Cumulative Review L3
- Spanish Assessment Resources
  - Cumulative Review L3

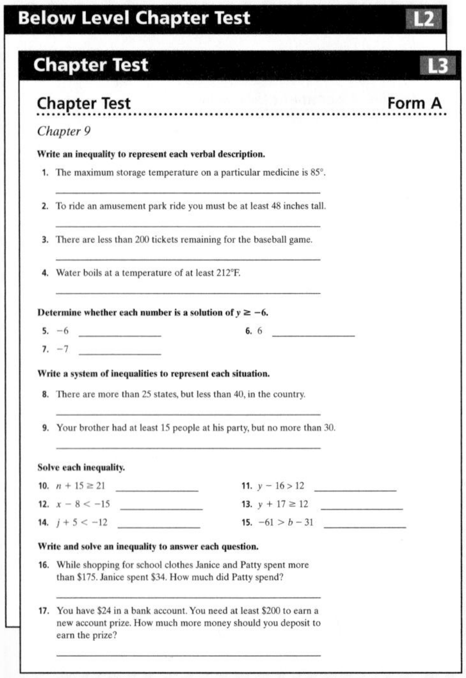
Below Level Chapter Test L2

Chapter Test L3

Chapter Test Form A

Chapter 9

Write an inequality to represent each verbal description.

1. The maximum storage temperature on a particular medicine is 85°. ____
2. To ride an amusement park ride you must be at least 48 inches tall. ____
3. There are less than 200 tickets remaining for the baseball game. ____
4. Water boils at a temperature of at least 212°F. ____

Determine whether each number is a solution of $y \geq -6$.

5. -6 ____ 6. 6 ____
7. -7 ____

Write a system of inequalities to represent each situation.

8. There are more than 25 states, but less than 40, in the country. ____
9. Your brother had at least 15 people at his party, but no more than 30. ____

Solve each inequality.

10. $n + 15 \geq 21$ ____ 11. $y - 16 > 12$ ____
12. $x - 8 < -15$ ____ 13. $y + 17 \geq 12$ ____
14. $j + 5 < -12$ ____ 15. $-61 > b - 31$ ____

Write and solve an inequality to answer each question.

16. While shopping for school clothes Janice and Patty spent more than \$175. Janice spent \$34. How much did Patty spend? ____
17. You have \$24 in a bank account. You need at least \$200 to earn a new account prize. How much more money should you deposit to earn the prize? ____

Chapter 9 Test

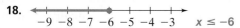

Go Online PHSchool.com **For:** Online chapter test **Web Code:** axa-0952

Write an inequality to represent each verbal description.

1. A driver's age a must be at least 16 years. $a \geq 16$
2. The game's duration g is at most 3 h. $g \leq 3$
3. The maximum weight w that a truck can haul is less than 20,000 lb. $w < 20{,}000$
4. The length of your essay e must be at least 4 pages. $e \geq 4$

Determine whether each number is a solution of the inequality $c \leq -8$.

5. 8 no
6. -7 no
7. -8 yes

Write a system of inequalities to represent each situation. 8–9. See margin.

8. The number of people attending is between 350 and 525.
9. To be in the Open division of the road race, you must be between 20 and 39 years old.

Solve each inequality.

10. $18 > w + 3$ $w < 15$
11. $y - 12 > -7$ $y > 5$
12. $n + 12 \geq 15$ $n \geq 3$
13. $m - 8 \leq -17$ $m \leq -9$
14. $t + 22 < 14$ $t < -8$
15. $10 < e - 14$ $e > 24$

Write and solve an inequality to answer each question.

16. A ferry can safely transport at most 220 people. There are already 143 people aboard. How many more people can the ferry take aboard? 77 or fewer people
17. You have \$59 in a bank account. You need at least \$200 to avoid bank fees. How much more money should you deposit to avoid a bank fee? \$141 or more

Write an inequality for each graph.

18. 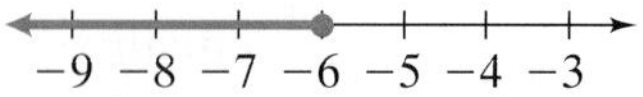

$x \leq -6$

19. 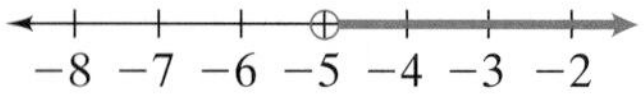

$x > -5$

20. **Writing in Math** Is -9 a solution to the inequality $d \leq -9$? Explain. yes; $-9 = -9$

Solve each inequality.

21. $\frac{z}{3} \leq 5$ $z \leq 15$
22. $-4s \geq 64$ $s \leq -16$
23. $3m < 12$ $m < 4$
24. $-2t \geq -3$ $t \leq 1.5$
25. $\frac{b}{-4} \leq 16$ $b \geq -64$
26. $9c > -81$ $c > -9$
27. $3.5x > 10.5$ $x > 3$
28. $\frac{w}{4.4} \leq -12.3$ $w \leq -54.12$

Write and solve an inequality to answer each question.

29. When a number is multiplied by -3, the result is at least 15. What is the greatest value the number can have? -5
30. A sports drink costs \$1.49 per bottle. At most, how many bottles can you buy if you have \$12? 8 bottles

Solve each inequality.

31. $3m - 8 < 4$ $m < 4$
32. $-2t + 8 \geq 5$ $t \leq 1.5$
33. $5 + 4b \leq 21$ $b \leq 4$
34. $7 - 9c > 88$ $c < -9$
35. $2w + 7 \geq 31$ $w \geq 12$
36. $\frac{k}{-5} - 12 > 13$ $k < -125$
37. $\frac{d}{8} - 10 \leq -15$ $d \leq -40$
38. $-6h + 25 > 61$ $h < -6$
39. You have \$15 to buy a sketch pad and some pens. The sketch pad you want costs \$11, and pens cost \$.40 each. Write and solve an inequality. What maximum number of pens can you buy? 10 or fewer pens

Cumulative Practice

Some questions require you to choose the inequality or system of inequalities that represents a situation. Use the tips as guides for how to approach solving the problem.

You want to buy a poster and make copies of a flier for a school concert. The poster is $6.00, and each copy is $.09. You can spend at most $10. Which inequality can be used to represent c, the number of copies you can make?

(A) $10 + 0.09c \leq 6$
(B) $10 + 0.09c \geq 6$
(C) $0.09c + 6 \leq 10$
(D) $0.09c + 6 \geq 10$

Tip 1
Look for a key phrase, such as "at most," that indicates which inequality symbol should be used.

Tip 2
Think about which expression represents the total cost of the items.

Think It Through
Express the cost of c copies as $0.09c$. The total cost of the poster and the copies is $6 + 0.09c$. This must be less than $10.00, so use the inequality symbol $\leq$. The correct answer is choice C.

Vocabulary Review

As you solve problems, you must understand the meanings of mathematical terms. Match each term with its mathematical meaning.

III	**A.** equation	**I.**	an equation stating that two ratios are equal
IV	**B.** inequality	**II.**	made up of two or more inequalities
II	**C.** system of inequalities	**III.**	a mathematical sentence with an equal sign
I	**D.** proportion	**IV.**	a mathematical sentence that contains $<$, $>$, $\leq$, $\geq$, or $\neq$

Read each question. Then write the letter of the correct answer on your paper.

1. Which fraction is equivalent to 0.625? (Lesson 4-4) B
   (A) $\frac{1}{2}$ (C) $\frac{11}{16}$
   (B) $\frac{5}{8}$ (D) $\frac{3}{4}$

2. Write an expression for the verbal description "three more than a number n is at least 27." (Lesson 9-1) C
   (A) $3 + n < 27$
   (B) $3 + n = 27$
   (C) $3 + n \geq 27$
   (D) $3 + n \leq 27$

3. A linear function of g has a value of 10 when $g = 2$. The function has a value of 20 when $g = 4$. What is the value of the function when $g = 6$? (Lesson 8-5) D
   (A) 15 (B) 20 (C) 25 (D) 30

California Resources

Standards Mastery
- Teacher Center ExamView CD-ROM
- Math XL
- Progress Monitoring Assessments
- Online Chapter Test at PHSchool.com

Math Intervention
- Skills Review and Practice Workbook

Universal Access Resources
- Teacher Center ExamView CD-ROM
  - Special Needs Test
  - Special Needs Practice Banks
  - Foundational Standards Practice Banks
- Online Chapter Test at www.PHSchool.com
- All-In-One Teaching Resources
  - Cumulative Review L3
- Spanish Assessment Resources
  - Cumulative Review L3

Success Tracker™
Online at PHSchool.com

4. What is the slope of the line below? **(Lesson 8-5) B**

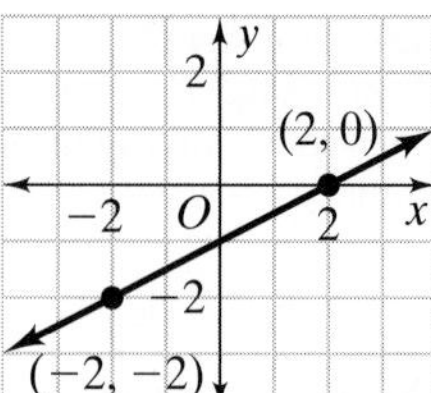

Ⓐ 0 Ⓑ $\frac{1}{2}$ Ⓒ 2 Ⓓ 4

5. Which of the following shows the solution set to the inequality $-3x + 2 < 5$? **(Lesson 9-5) D**

Ⓐ $\{x: x < 1\}$
Ⓑ $\{x: x < -1\}$
Ⓒ $\{x: x > 1\}$
Ⓓ $\{x: x > -1\}$

6. Simplify 5^{-3}. **(Lesson 5-7) C**

Ⓐ -125 Ⓑ $-\frac{1}{125}$ Ⓒ $\frac{1}{125}$ Ⓓ 125

7. Which of the following graphs shows the linear function $y = \frac{1}{3}x$? **(Lesson 8-4) A**

Ⓐ 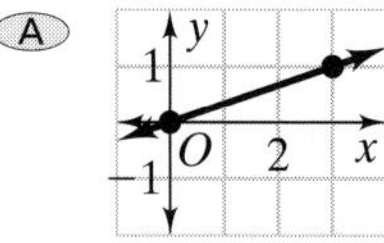

Ⓒ 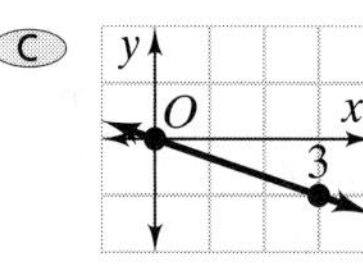

Ⓑ 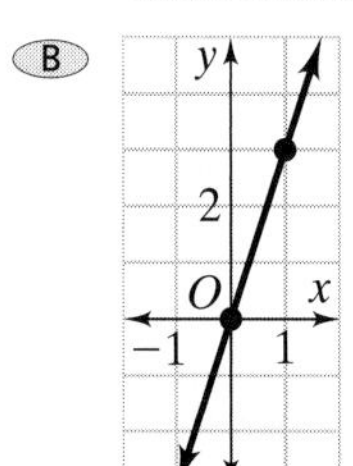

Ⓓ 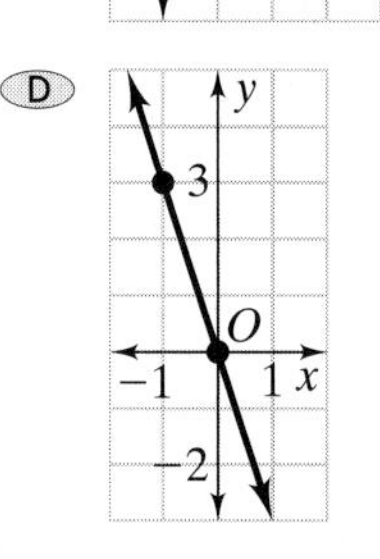

8. Which number is NOT a solution to the inequality $6 - 2w > 2$? **(Lesson 9-5) D**

Ⓐ -4 Ⓑ -2 Ⓒ 0 Ⓓ 2

9. Gaspar is 55 in. tall. He grows 2 in. each year. Which equation can be used to find the number of years y it will take him to reach a height of 61 in.? **(Lesson 3-4) C**

Ⓐ $2y + 61 = 55$ Ⓑ $55 + \frac{y}{2} = 61$ Ⓒ $55 + 2y = 61$ Ⓓ $61 + \frac{y}{2} = 55$

10. At least 26 students must sign up for a painting class or it will be canceled. So far, 11 students have signed up. Which inequality best represents n, the number of additional students who must sign up to prevent the class from being canceled? **(Lesson 9-2) A**

Ⓐ $n \geq 15$ Ⓑ $n \leq 15$ Ⓒ $n \geq 37$ Ⓓ $n \leq 37$

11. Kwami takes 0.4 tons of newspaper to the recycling plant. Which fraction is NOT equivalent to 0.4? **(Lesson 4-4) C**

Ⓐ $\frac{2}{5}$ Ⓑ $\frac{4}{10}$ Ⓒ $\frac{6}{14}$ Ⓓ $\frac{8}{20}$

12. Which function is graphed below? **(Lesson 8-4) D**

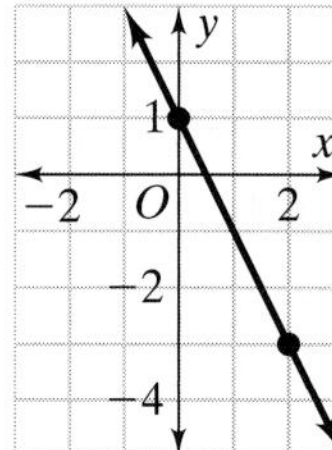

Ⓐ $y = 2x + 1$ Ⓑ $y = x - 2$ Ⓒ $y = 0.5x - 1$ Ⓓ $y = -2x + 1$

13. On a rainy day, a student goes to the video store to rent a video game and some movies. The student has $15 to spend. The game costs $4.95 and each movie costs $3.99. At most, how many movies can the student rent? **(Lesson 9-5) B**

Ⓐ 1 Ⓑ 2 Ⓒ 3 Ⓓ 4

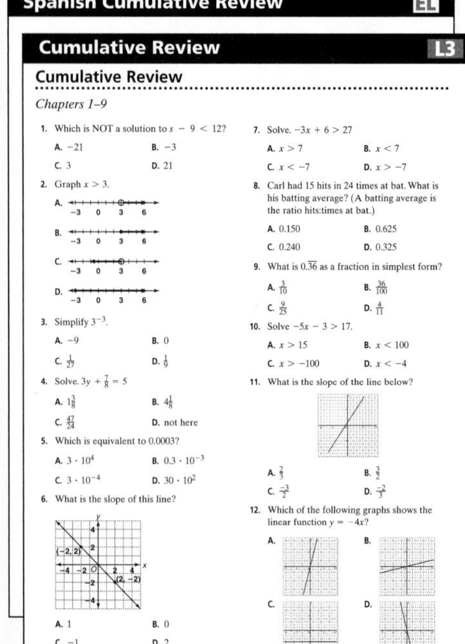

Spanish Cumulative Review EL

Cumulative Review L3

Cumulative Review

Chapters 1–9

1. Which is NOT a solution to $s - 9 < 12$?
   A. −21 B. −3 C. 3 D. 21
2. Graph $x > 3$.
   A. B. C. D.
3. Simplify 3^{-3}.
   A. −9 B. 0 C. $\frac{1}{27}$ D. $\frac{1}{9}$
4. Solve. $3y + \frac{7}{8} = 5$
   A. $1\frac{3}{8}$ B. $4\frac{1}{8}$ C. $\frac{47}{24}$ D. not here
5. Which is equivalent to 0.0003?
   A. $3 \cdot 10^4$ B. $0.3 \cdot 10^{-3}$ C. $3 \cdot 10^{-4}$ D. $30 \cdot 10^2$
6. What is the slope of this line?
   A. 1 B. 0 C. −1 D. 2
7. Solve. $-3x + 6 > 27$
   A. $x > 7$ B. $x < 7$ C. $x < -7$ D. $x > -7$
8. Carl had 15 hits in 24 times at bat. What is his batting average? (A batting average is the ratio hits:times at bat.)
   A. 0.150 B. 0.625 C. 0.240 D. 0.325
9. What is $0.\overline{36}$ as a fraction in simplest form?
   A. $\frac{3}{10}$ B. $\frac{36}{100}$ C. $\frac{9}{25}$ D. $\frac{4}{11}$
10. Solve $-5x - 3 > 17$.
    A. $x > 15$ B. $x < 100$ C. $x > -100$ D. $x < -4$
11. What is the slope of the line below?
    A. $\frac{2}{3}$ B. $\frac{3}{2}$ C. $\frac{-3}{2}$ D. $\frac{-2}{3}$
12. Which of the following graphs shows the linear function $y = -4x$?
    A. B. C. D.

14. A plant cell is about 0.000000001 m wide. Which of the following is equivalent to 0.000000001? **(Lesson 5-7) D**

Ⓐ 10^9 Ⓒ 10^{-8}

Ⓑ 10^8 Ⓓ 10^{-9}

15. According to the graph below, how much does each bagel cost? **(Lesson 8-6) B**

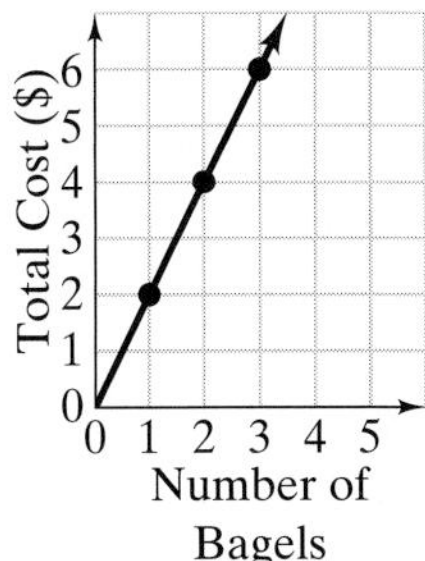

Ⓐ $1.00 Ⓒ $3.00

Ⓑ $2.00 Ⓓ $4.00

16. Kyla wants to buy some fish for her aquarium. She buys 1 guppie for $2.30 and some goldfish for $.75 each. She has $9.00 to spend. At most, how many goldfish can Kyla buy? **(Lesson 9-5) C**

Ⓐ 10 goldfish Ⓒ 8 goldfish

Ⓑ 9 goldfish Ⓓ 7 goldfish

17. Which of the following is NOT a rational number? **(Lesson 4-4) A**

Ⓐ $\sqrt{2}$ Ⓒ $0.\overline{33}$

Ⓑ $\frac{1}{6}$ Ⓓ $\sqrt{25}$

18. What is the slope of the linear function below? **(Lesson 8-5) C**

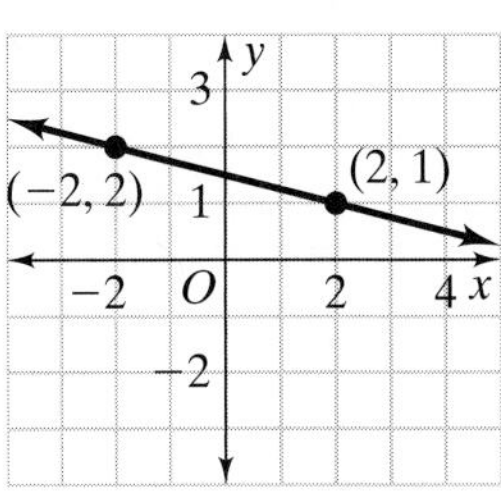

Ⓐ 4 Ⓑ $\frac{1}{4}$ Ⓒ $-\frac{1}{4}$ Ⓓ −4

19. There are 4 quarts in a gallon. Which graph shows this relationship? **(Lesson 8-6) C**

Ⓐ

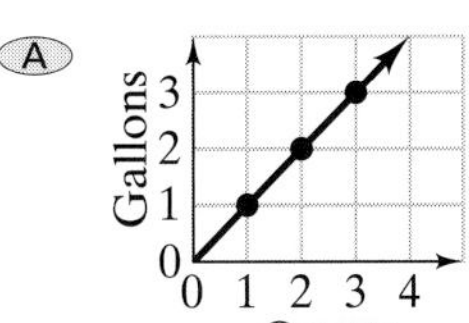

Ⓒ

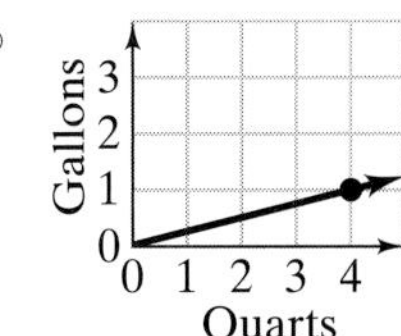

Ⓑ

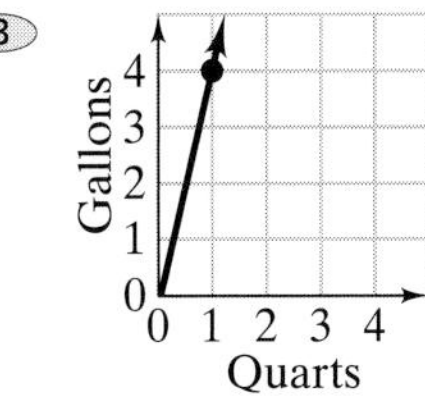

Ⓓ

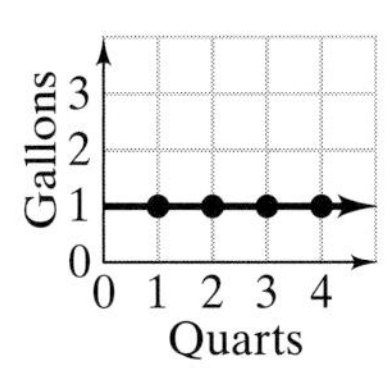

Standards Reference Guide

California Content Standard	Item Number(s)
NS 1.5	1, 11, 17
NS 2.1	6, 14
AF 1.1	2, 9, 10
AF 4.1	5, 8, 13, 16
AF 3.3	3, 4, 7, 12, 18
AF 3.4	15, 19

For additional review and practice, see the *California Standards Review and Practice Workbook* or go online to use the

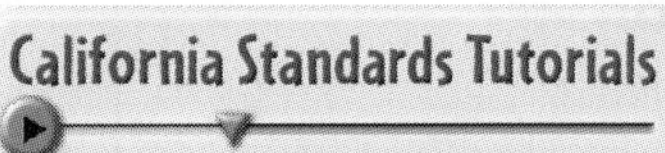

Visit: PHSchool.com, **Web Code:** axq-9045

Chapter 10 Exponents and Equations

Chapter at a Glance

Lesson Titles, Objectives, and Features	California Content Standards
10-1 Properties of Exponents • To multiply and divide expressions with exponents	**NS 2.1** Multiply and divide expressions involving exponents with a common base. **AF 2.1** Simplify and evaluate expressions that include exponents. **Alg1 2.0** Understand the rules of exponents.
10-2 Power Rules • To use power rules	**NS 2.1** Multiply and divide expressions involving exponents with a common base. **AF 2.1** Simplify and evaluate expressions that include exponents. **Alg1 2.0** Understand the rules of exponents.
10-3 Exploring Roots • To simplify expressions with roots **Vocabulary Builder:** Square Roots and Cube Roots	**Alg1 2.0** Understand and use such operations as taking a root.
10-4a Activity Lab: Modeling Expressions **10-4 Simplifying Algebraic Expressions** • To simplify algebraic expressions **Algebraic Thinking:** Writing Expressions	**AF 1.1** Use variables and appropriate operations to write an expression. **Alg1 4.0** Simplify expressions before solving linear equations in one variable. **MR 2.5** Use a variety of methods, such as diagrams and models, to explain mathematical reasoning.
10-5a Activity Lab: Modeling Multi-Step Equations **10-5 Solving Multi-Step Equations** • To solve multi-step equations **Mathematical Reasoning:** Justifying Each Step	**Alg1 4.0** Simplify expressions before solving linear equations in one variable. **Alg1 5.0** Solve multistep problems, including word problems, involving linear equations in one variable and provide justification for each step. **MR 2.6** Support solutions with evidence in both verbal and symbolic work.
10-6 Solving Equations with Variables on Both Sides • To solve equations with variables on both sides **Algebraic Thinking:** Using Equation Language	**Alg1 4.0** Simplify expressions before solving linear equations in one variable. **Alg1 5.0** Solve multistep problems, including word problems, involving linear equations in one variable and provide justification for each step.

California Content Standards
NS Number Sense
AF Algebra and Functions
MG Measurement and Geometry
MR Mathematical Reasoning

Correlations to Standardized Tests

All content for these tests is contained in *Prentice Hall Math, Algebra Readiness.* This chart reflects coverage in this chapter only.

	10-1	10-2	10-3	10-4	10-5	10-6
Terra Nova CAT6 (Level 18)						
Number and Number Relations	✔	✔	✔			
Computation and Numerical Estimation	✔		✔		✔	✔
Operation Concepts	✔	✔	✔	✔	✔	✔
Measurement						
Geometry and Spatial Sense						
Data Analysis, Statistics, and Probability						
Patterns, Functions, Algebra	✔	✔	✔	✔	✔	✔
Problem Solving and Reasoning	✔	✔	✔	✔	✔	✔
Communication	✔	✔	✔	✔	✔	✔
Decimals, Fractions, Integers, Percent						
Order of Operations			✔			
Algebraic Operations	✔	✔	✔	✔	✔	✔
Terra Nova CTBS (Level 18)						
Decimals, Fractions, Integers, Percents	✔	✔	✔	✔	✔	✔
Order of Operations, Numeration, Number Theory	✔	✔	✔			
Data Interpretation						
Measurement						
Geometry						
ITBS (Level 14)						
Number Properties and Operations	✔	✔	✔	✔	✔	✔
Algebra	✔	✔	✔	✔	✔	✔
Geometry						
Measurement						
Probability and Statistics						
Estimation	✔	✔	✔	✔		
SAT10 (Adv 1 Level)						
Number Sense and Operations	✔	✔	✔	✔	✔	✔
Patterns, Relationships, and Algebra	✔	✔	✔	✔	✔	✔
Data, Statistics, and Probability						
Geometry and Measurement						
NAEP						
Number Sense, Properties, and Operations	✔	✔	✔	✔	✔	✔
Measurement						
Geometry and Spatial Sense						
Data Analysis, Statistics, and Probability						
Algebra and Functions	✔	✔	✔	✔	✔	✔

CAT6 California Achievement Test, 6th Ed.
CTBS Comprehensive Test of Basic Skills
ITBS Iowa Test of Basic Skills, Form M
SAT10 Stanford Achievement Test, 10th Ed.
NAEP National Assessment of Educational Progress 2005 Mathematics Objectives

California Math Background

Focus on the California Content Standards

- Students' experiences with exponents have links to content standards in grades 5 through 7.
- In grade 5, for example, students computed positive integer powers of nonnegative integers using the concept of repeated multiplication (**NS 1.3**). In grade 6, students solved problems using the correct order of operations, including exponents (**AF 1.4**).
- Grade 7 Standards **NS 1.0**, **NS 1.1**, and **NS 1.2** provide opportunities for students to investigate scientific notation and raise rational numbers to whole-number powers. More importantly, **NS 2.0** and **2.3** introduce students to the laws of exponents as they multiply, divide, and simplify rational numbers by using exponent rules.

10-1 Properties of Exponents

California Content Standards **NS 2.1, AF 2.1, Alg1 2.0**

Math Understandings

- To multiply two powers with the same base, you keep the common base and add the exponents to find the new exponent.
- To divide two powers with the same base, you keep the common base and subtract the exponent of the divisor from the exponent of the dividend to find the new exponent.

Multiplying Powers With the Same Base	
To multiply numbers or variables with the same base, add the exponents.	
Arithmetic	**Algebra**
$3^2 \cdot 3^7 = 3^{(2+7)} = 3^9$	$a^m \cdot a^n = a^{(m+n)}$

Dividing Powers With the Same Base	
To divide nonzero numbers or variables with the same nonzero base, subtract the exponents.	
Arithmetic	**Algebra**
$\frac{8^5}{8^3} = 8^{(5-3)} = 8^2$	$\frac{a^m}{a^n} = a^{(m-n)}$, where $a \neq 0$

10-2 Power Rules

California Content Standards **NS 2.1, AF 2.1, Alg1 2.0**

Math Understandings

- To raise a power to a power, you multiply the exponents.
- To raise a product to a power, you raise each factor to the power.

$$(4^3)^2 = 4^3 \cdot 4^3 \quad \leftarrow \text{Write two factors of } 4^3.$$
$$= 4^{(3+3)} \quad \leftarrow \text{Use the rules for multiplying powers.}$$
$$= 4^6 \quad \leftarrow \text{Simplify the exponent.}$$

You can use power rules to raise numbers in scientific notation to a power.

Example: $(2.3 \times 10^4)^3 = 2.3^3 \times 10^{(4 \times 3)} = 2.3^3 \times 10^{12}$

10-3 Exploring Roots

California Content Standards **Alg1 2.0**

Math Understandings

- The nth root of a number is a number that when multiplied by itself n times is equal to the original number.
- If n is an even number, it has two n^{th} roots; if n is odd, it has one n^{th} root.

$$\sqrt[4]{10{,}000}$$
$$\blacksquare \cdot \blacksquare \cdot \blacksquare \cdot \blacksquare = 10{,}000$$

Like parentheses, the radical symbol is a grouping symbol. When simplifying expressions with roots, you must first simplify the terms under the radical symbol.

Example: $3 + 2\sqrt{68 - 4} = 3 + 2\sqrt{64} = 3 + 2(8) = 19$

10-4 Simplifying Algebraic Expressions

California Content Standards **AF 1.1, Alg1 4.0**

Math Understandings

- The terms of an algebraic expression are separated by plus and minus signs.
- You can combine only like terms by addition or subtraction.
- There is an understood coefficient of 1 in front of a variable that does not have any numeric coefficient, so you can write b as $1b$ and $-c$ as $-1c$.

In an algebraic expression, a **term** is a number, a variable, or the product of a number and one or more variables. **Like terms** have exactly the same variable factors. The Distributive Property justifies combining like terms such as: $4a + 5a = (4 + 5)a$, or $9a$.

Example: $3ab - 2a + 4ab - ab$ has 4 terms while $14abc$ has 1 term. In the expression $3ab - 2a + 4ab - ab$, the terms $3ab$, $4ab$, and $-ab$ are like terms, and you can combine them so that the expression becomes $6ab - 2a$.

10-5 Solving Multi-Step Equations

California Content Standards **Alg1 4.0, Alg1 5.0**

Math Understandings

- At every step in the process of solving an equation, the new equation must be equivalent to the original equation, that is, it has the same solution.
- Before solving an equation, it is often necessary to simplify one or both sides of an equation by combining like terms or using the Distributive Property.

It is sometimes possible to use division to simplify equations, rather than using the Distributive Property.

Example: Solve the equation $3(5 + x) = 27$.

$$\frac{3(5 + x)}{3} = \frac{27}{3}$$
$$5 + x = 9$$
$$x = 4$$

10-6 Solving Equations With Variables on Both Sides

California Content Standards **Alg1 4.0, Alg1 5.0**

Math Understandings

- When an equation has variables on both sides, you must bring all the variable terms to one side of the equation to solve it.
- When you solve an equation, before you apply inverse operations to each side of the equation, simplify as much as you can on both sides.

When you solve an equation to find the solution to a real-world problem, always make sure that the solution is a reasonable one.

Professional Development

Additional Professional Development Opportunities

Math Background notes for Chapter 10: Every lesson has a Math Background in the PLAN section.

In-Service On Demand
Prentice Hall offers free video-based tutorials to support you. Visit PHSchool.com/inserviceondemand.

Pearson Achievement Solutions
Pearson Achievement Solutions, a Pearson Education company, offers comprehensive, facilitated professional development designed to help teachers improve student achievement. To learn more, please visit pearsonachievementsolutions.com.

Chapter 10 Resources

	10-1	10-2	10-3	10-4	10-5	10-6	For the Chapter
Print Resources							
L3 Practice	●	●	●	●	●	●	
L3 Guided Problem Solving	●	●	●	●	●	●	
L2 Reteaching	●	●	●	●	●	●	
L4 Enrichment	●	●	●	●	●	●	
L3 Vocabulary and Study Skills	●	●	●	●	●	●	●
L3 Daily Puzzles	●	●	●	●	●	●	
L3 Activity Labs	●	●	●	●	●	●	
L3 Checkpoint Quiz			●		●		
L3 Chapter Project							●
L2 Below Level Chapter Test							●
L3 Chapter Test							●
L4 Alternative Assessment							●
L3 Cumulative Review							●
Spanish Resources EL							
L3 Practice	●	●	●	●	●	●	
L3 Vocabulary and Study Skills	●		●	●	●	●	●
L3 Checkpoint Quiz			●		●		
L2 Below Level Chapter Test							●
L3 Chapter Test							●
L4 Alternative Assessment							●
L3 Cumulative Review							●
Transparencies							
Check Skills You'll Need	●	●	●	●	●	●	
Additional Examples	●	●	●	●	●	●	
California Daily Review	●	●	●	●	●	●	
Classroom Aid	●	●	●		●	●	
Student Edition Answers	●	●	●	●	●	●	●
Lesson Quiz	●	●	●	●	●	●	
Technology							
California Student Center Online	●	●	●	●	●	●	●
California Student Center CD-ROM	●	●	●	●	●	●	●
Success Tracker™ Online Math Intervention	●	●	●	●	●	●	●
California Teacher Center: ExamView CD-ROM	●	●	●	●	●	●	●
California Teacher Center: Planning CD-ROM	●	●	●	●	●	●	●
California Teacher Center: Presentations CD-ROM and online	●	●	●	●	●	●	●
MindPoint Quiz Show	●	●	●	●	●	●	●
Prentice Hall Web Site: PHSchool.com	●	●	●	●	●	●	●

Also available:

California Standards Mastery
- Standards Review Transparencies
- Standards Review and Practice Workbook
- Progress Monitoring Assessments
- Math Companion
- Math*XL*

California Intervention Resources
- Skills Review and Practice Workbook
- Success Tracker™ Online Math Intervention

Other Resources
- Multilingual Handbook
- Spanish Student Edition
- Solution Key
- Math Notes Study Folder

Where You Can Use the Lesson Resources

Here is a suggestion, following the four-step teaching plan, for how you can incorporate Universal Access Resources into your teaching.

	Instructional Resources L3	Universal Access Resources
1. Plan		
Preparation Read the Math Background in the Teacher's Edition to connect this lesson with students' previous experience. **Starting Class** **Check Skills You'll Need** Assign these exercises from the Math Companion to review prerequisite skills. Review the full text of the student expectations and objectives covered in this lesson. **New Vocabulary** Help students pre-read the lesson by pointing out the new terms introduced in the lesson.	**California Math Background** **Math Understandings** **Transparencies & Presentations CD-ROM** Check Skills You'll Need California Daily Review **Resources** Vocabulary and Study Skills **Math Companion**	**Spanish Support** EL Vocabulary and Study Skills
2. Teach		
L3 **Guided Instruction** Use the Activity Labs to build conceptual understanding. Teach each Example. Use the Teacher's Edition side column notes for specific teaching tips, including Error Prevention notes. Use the Additional Examples found in the side column (and on transparency and PowerPoint) as an alternative presentation for the content. After each Example, assign the California Standards Check exercises for that Example to get an immediate assessment of student understanding. Utilize the support in the Math Companion to assist students with each Standards Check. Use the Closure activity in the Teacher's Edition to help students attain mastery of lesson content.	**Student Edition** Activity Lab **Resources** Math Companion Activity Lab **Transparencies & Presentations CD-ROM** Additional Examples Classroom Aids **Teacher Center: ExamView CD-ROM**	**Teacher's Edition** Every lesson includes suggestions for working with students who need special attention. L1 Special Needs L2 Below Level L4 Advanced Learners EL English Learners **Resources** **Multilingual Handbook** **Math Companion**
3. Practice		
Assignment Guide **Check Your Understanding** Use these questions from the Math Companion to check students' understanding before you assign homework. **Homework Exercises** Assign homework from these leveled exercises in the Assignment Guide. **A** Practice by Example **B** Apply Your Skills **C** Challenge **California** Multiple-Choice Practice and Mixed Review **Homework Quick Check** Use these key exercises to quickly check students' homework.	**Transparencies & Presentations CD-ROM** Student Answers **Resources** Math Companion Practice Guided Problem Solving Vocabulary and Study Skills Activity Lab Daily Puzzles **Teacher Center: ExamView CD-ROM** **Math *XL***	**Spanish Support** EL Practice EL Vocabulary and Study Skills **Resources** L4 Enrichment
4. Assess & Reteach		
Lesson Quiz Assign the Lesson Quiz to assess students' mastery of the lesson content. **Checkpoint Quiz** Use the Checkpoint Quiz to assess student progress over several lessons.	**Transparencies & Presentations CD-ROM** Lesson Quiz **Resources** Checkpoint Quiz	**Resources** L2 Reteaching EL Checkpoint Quiz Success Tracker™ **Teacher Center: ExamView CD-ROM**

KEY L1 Special Needs L2 Below Level L3 For All Students L4 Advanced, Gifted EL English Learners

Exponents and Equations

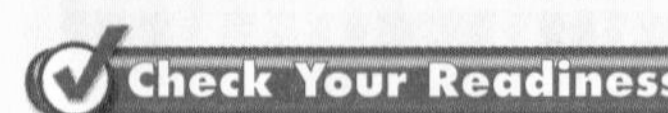

Answers are in the back of the textbook.

For math intervention, direct students to:

Positive Exponents
Lesson 2-6

Properties of Numbers
Lesson 1-5

The Distributive Property
Lesson 1-6

Solving Two-Step Equations
Lesson 3-4

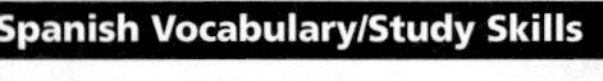

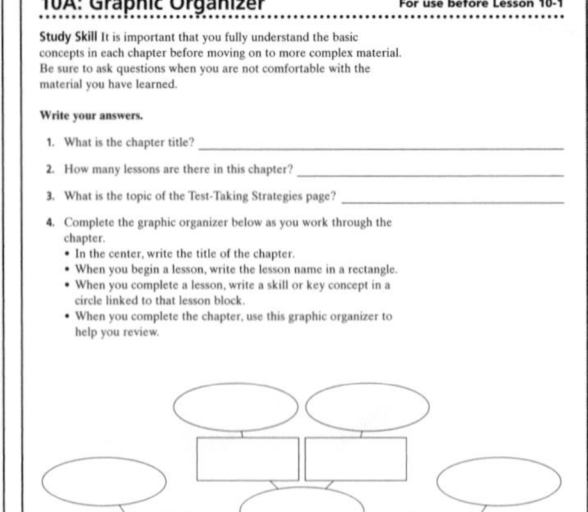

Vocabulary/Study Skills L3

10A: Graphic Organizer For use before Lesson 10-1

Study Skill It is important that you fully understand the basic concepts in each chapter before moving on to more complex material. Be sure to ask questions when you are not comfortable with the material you have learned.

Write your answers.

1. What is the chapter title? ______
2. How many lessons are there in this chapter? ______
3. What is the topic of the Test-Taking Strategies page? ______
4. Complete the graphic organizer below as you work through the chapter.
   - In the center, write the title of the chapter.
   - When you begin a lesson, write the lesson name in a rectangle.
   - When you complete a lesson, write a skill or key concept in a circle linked to that lesson block.
   - When you complete the chapter, use this graphic organizer to help you review.

CALIFORNIA CHECK SYSTEM CHAPTER 10

Exponents and Equations

What You've Learned

California Content Standards

NS 1.2 Add, subtract, multiply, and divide rational numbers and take positive rational numbers to whole-number powers.

AF 1.3 Simplify numerical expressions by applying the properties of rational numbers and justify the process used.

AF 4.1 Solve two-step linear equations in one variable, interpret the solution or solutions in the context from which they arose, and verify the reasonableness of the results.

Check Your Readiness

for Help to the lesson in green.

Positive Exponents (Lesson 2-6)

Simplify each expression.

1. 4^2 16
2. $(-4)^2$ 16
3. -4^2 −16
4. $-(-2)^5$ 32
5. 10^2 100
6. 10^3 1,000

Properties of Numbers (Lesson 1-5)

Name the property that each equation illustrates. 7–10. See right.

7. $x + 7 = 7 + x$
8. $42 \cdot m \cdot 6 = 42 \cdot 6 \cdot m$
9. $19 + (4 + d) = (19 + 4) + d$
10. $56z + 0 = 56z$

7. Comm. Prop. of Add.
8. Comm. Prop. of Mult.
9. Assoc. Prop. of Add.
10. Ident. Prop. of Add.

The Distributive Property (Lesson 1-6)

Simplify each expression.

11. $5(c - 3)$ 5c − 15
12. $-2(w + 8)$ −2w − 16
13. $(-5 + a)2$ −10 + 2a
14. $-9(6 - t)$ −54 + 9t
15. $(4 - b)11$ 44 − 11b
16. $-1(x - 2)$ −x + 2

Solving Two-Step Equations (Lesson 3-4)

Solve each equation.

17. $3x + 7 = -5$ −4
18. $8m - 3 = 9$ 1.5
19. $-f + 2 = -13$ 15

California Content Standards for Chapter 10

Number Sense
NS 2.1

Algebra and Functions
AF 1.1, AF 2.1

Mathematical Reasoning
MR 2.5, MR 2.6, MR 3.3

Algebra I
Alg1 2.0, Alg1 4.0, Alg1 5.0

Chapter 10 Overview

In this chapter, students learn to multiply and divide expressions with exponents, use power rules, and simplify expressions with roots. Students also learn to simplify algebraic expressions and solve multi-step equations, including equations with variables on both sides of the equal sign.

Activating Prior Knowledge

In this chapter, students build on their knowledge of expressions with exponents and square roots, as well as their experience simplifying and solving equations, including using the order of operations. Ask:

- *How can you simplify* $(-2)^3$? $(-2)(-2)(-2) = -8$
- *Simplify* $-2(x + 4)$. $-2x + 8$
- *Solve the equation* $4x - 3 = 9$. $4x = 12$; $x = 3$

What You'll Learn Next

▲ You can use the radius of Earth and the rules of exponents to find the surface area of Earth.

California Content Standards

Alg1 2.0 Understand and use such operations as taking a root. Understand and use the rules of exponents.

Alg1 4.0 Simplify expressions before solving linear equations in one variable.

Alg1 5.0 Solve multistep problems, including word problems, involving linear equations in one variable and provide justification for each step.

New Vocabulary

English and Spanish Audio Online

- *n*th roots (p. 374)
- term (p. 380)
- like terms (p. 380)

Academic Vocabulary
- consecutive (p. 390)

10-1

1. Plan

California Content Standards

NS 2.1 Multiply and divide expressions involving exponents with a common base. ***Develop***

AF 2.1 Simplify and evaluate expressions that include exponents. ***Develop***

Alg1 2.0 Understand the rules of exponents. ***Introduce***

California Math Background

Two exponential expressions with different exponents can be combined only when the bases are identical. So x^3 and y^2 cannot be combined unless you have values for the variables.

On the other hand, x^3 and x^2 can be multiplied (or divided) by adding (or subtracting) the exponents. But the quantities x^3 and x^2 cannot be added or subtracted.

More Math Background: p. 364C

Lesson Planning and Resources

See p. 364E for a list of the resources that support this lesson.

PRESENTATION CD-ROM
CD, Online, or Transparencies

Bell Ringer Practice

Check Skills You'll Need
Use student page, transparency, or PowerPoint.
See Math Companion.

California Standards Review
Use transparency or PowerPoint.

10-1 Properties of Exponents

Check Skills You'll Need

Do this in your **Math Companion.**

Vocabulary

Review:
- exponent
- power

Use your **Math Companion** *to build your vocabulary.*

California Content Standards

NS 2.1 Multiply and divide expressions involving exponents with a common base. ***Develop***
AF 2.1 Simplify and evaluate expressions that include exponents. ***Develop***
Alg1 2.0 Understand the rules of exponents. ***Introduce***

What You'll Learn . . . and Why

You will learn to multiply and divide expressions with exponents. Scientists use expressions with exponents to make calculations involving large numbers, such as the distance between the sun and a comet.

You can write expressions like $3^2 \cdot 3^4$ using a single exponent.

$$3^2 \cdot 3^4 = (3 \cdot 3)(3 \cdot 3 \cdot 3 \cdot 3) = 3^6$$

The two factors of 3 together with the four factors of 3 give a total of six factors of 3. Notice that the exponent 6 is equal to the sum of the exponents 2 and 4. This suggests the following property.

Take Note **Multiplying Powers With the Same Base**

To multiply numbers or variables with the same base, add the exponents.

Arithmetic	Algebra
$4^2 \cdot 4^7 = 4^{(2+7)} = 4^9$	$a^m \cdot a^n = a^{(m+n)}$

EXAMPLE **Multiplying Expressions with Exponents**

Vocabulary Tip
Remember that $x = x^1$.

1 Write the expression $(-2)^3 \cdot (-2)^5$ using a single exponent.

$$(-2)^3 \cdot (-2)^5 = (-2)^{(3+5)} \quad \leftarrow \text{Add the exponents.}$$
$$= (-2)^8 \quad \leftarrow \text{Simplify the exponent.}$$

CA Standards Check 1 *Go to your* **Math Companion** *for help.*

1. Write each expression using a single exponent.
   a. $6^{-2} \cdot 6^3$ 6^1 or 6 **b.** $(-4) \cdot (-4)^7$ $(-4)^8$ **c.** $m^1 \cdot m^{11}$ m^{12}

Universal Access Solutions for All Learners

Special Needs L1	**Below Level** L2
Remind students **not** to add the base when they multiply powers with the same base. They should add the exponents but keep the base the same, for example, $3^3 \times 3^2 = (3 \times 3 \times 3) \times (3 \times 3) = 3 \times 3 \times 3 \times 3 \times 3 = 3^5$.	Have students review the vocabulary for powers by naming the parts of 2^5 and finding the value. 2 is the base; 5 is the exponent; the value is 32.

You can divide powers with the same base by writing out all the factors.

$$\frac{7^5}{7^3} = \frac{\cancel{7}^1 \cdot \cancel{7}^1 \cdot \cancel{7}^1 \cdot 7 \cdot 7}{{}_1\cancel{7} \cdot {}_1\cancel{7} \cdot {}_1\cancel{7}} = \frac{7 \cdot 7}{1} = 7^2$$

Notice that the exponent 2 is equal to the difference of the exponents 5 and 3. This suggests the following property.

Take Note **Dividing Powers With the Same Base**

To divide nonzero numbers or variables with the same nonzero base, subtract the exponents.

Arithmetic	Algebra
$\frac{8^7}{8^2} = 8^{(7-2)} = 8^5$	$\frac{a^m}{a^n} = a^{(m-n)}$, where $a \neq 0$

EXAMPLE Dividing Expressions With Exponents

Relate **MATH YOU KNOW...**

Use the formula time $= \frac{\text{distance}}{\text{rate}}$ to find the time it takes to travel 7 mi at 8 mi/h.

$$\text{time} = \frac{7 \text{ mi}}{8 \text{ mi/h}}$$
$$= 0.875 \text{ h}$$

... to **ALGEBRA**

2 **Guided Problem Solving** The distance between the sun and a comet is about 2.79×10^8 mi. Light travels about 1.1×10^7 mi/min. Use the formula time $= \frac{\text{distance}}{\text{rate}}$ to estimate how many minutes sunlight takes to reach the comet.

$\text{time} = \frac{\text{distance}}{\text{speed}}$ ← **Use the formula for time.**

$= \frac{2.79 \times 10^8}{1.1 \times 10^7}$ ← **Substitute.**

$= \frac{2.79}{1.1} \times \frac{10^8}{10^7}$ ← **Write as a product of two quotients.**

$= \frac{2.79}{1.1} \times 10^1$ ← **Subtract the exponents.**

$\approx 2.54 \times 10^1$ ← **Divide.**

$= 25.4$ ← **Simplify.**

Sunlight takes about 25 min to reach the comet.

CA Standards Check 2 *Go to your* **Math Companion** *for help.*

2. The distance between the sun and Earth is about 9.3×10^7 mi. Light travels about 1.1×10^7 mi/min. Estimate to the nearest minute how long sunlight takes to reach Earth. **about 8 min**

Homework prep is in your **Math Companion.**

2. Teach

Guided Instruction

Error Prevention!

Use Example 1 to show that, when powers having the same base are multiplied, the base, including its sign, does not change.

In Example 2, remind students that subtracting exponents is the method for dividing powers, and that the numerical bases are *not* divided.

PRESENTATION CD-ROM CD, Online, or Transparencies

Additional Examples

1 Write the expression using a single exponent.
$(-3^2) \cdot (-3)^4$ $(-3)^6$

2 The distance between the sun and Jupiter is about 4.84×10^8 miles. Light travels at about 1.1×10^7 miles per minute. Use the formula time $= \frac{\text{distance}}{\text{speed}}$ to estimate how long it takes sunlight to reach Jupiter. Write your answer in standard form.
44 minutes

Closure

- *How do you multiply powers with the same base?* Add the exponents.
- *How do you divide powers with the same base?* Subtract the exponents.

Advanced Learners L4	**English Learners** EL
Students prove that $\frac{2^3}{2^5} = 2^{-2}$. $\frac{2^3}{2^5} = \frac{2 \cdot 2 \cdot 2}{2 \cdot 2 \cdot 2 \cdot 2 \cdot 2} = \frac{1}{2 \cdot 2} = 2^{-2}$	Remind students that *inverse operations* undo each other. Show by an example that if exponents are added when powers with the same base are multiplied, they must be subtracted when powers with the same base are divided since multiplication and division are inverse operations.

3. Practice

Assignment Guide

Check Your Understanding
See Math Companion.

Homework Exercises
A Practice by Example 1–21
B Apply Your Skills 22–39
C Challenge 40
California Multiple-Choice Practice 41–43
Mixed Review 44–45

Homework Quick Check
To check students' understanding of key skills and concepts, go over Exercises 2, 15, 23, 32, 33, 34.

Universal Access Resources

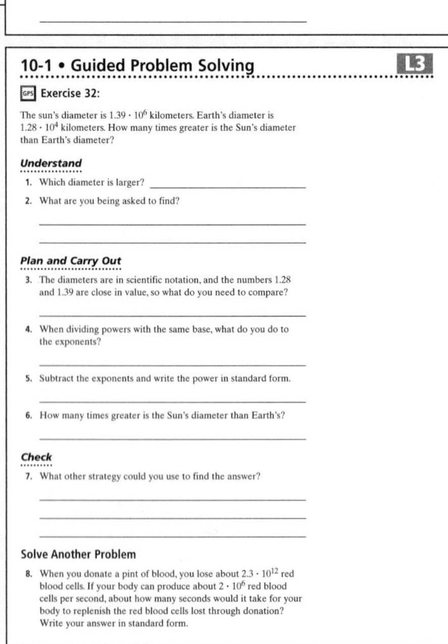

Adapted Practice 10-1 L1

Practice 10-1 — Properties of Ex[ponents] L3

Write each expression using a single exponent.

1. $3^2 \cdot 3^5$ 2. $1^3 \cdot 1^4$ 3. $a^1 \cdot a^2$
4. $(-y)^3 \cdot (-y)^2$ 5. $(3x) \cdot (3x)$ 6. $4.5^8 \cdot 4.5^2$
7. $3^3 \cdot 3 \cdot 3^4$ 8. $3^x \cdot 3^y$ 9. $5^2 \cdot 5 \cdot 5^3$
10. $\frac{4^4}{4}$ 11. $\frac{8^6}{8^4}$ 12. $\frac{(-3)^{12}}{(-3)^8}$
13. $\frac{8^4}{8^0}$ 14. $\frac{1^{18}}{1^{15}}$ 15. $\frac{7^4}{7}$
16. $\frac{(-4)^8}{(-4)^4}$ 17. $\frac{10^{12}}{10^9}$ 18. $\frac{5^a}{5^b}$
19. $\frac{g^{15}}{g^9}$ 20. $\frac{x^{16}}{x^7}$ 21. $\frac{v^{25}}{v^{20}}$

Simplify.

22. $\frac{12x^6}{4x^2}$ 23. $\frac{3y^5}{2y} + \frac{5y^3}{2y}$ 24. $\frac{25x^9}{5x^{-2}}$

25. The Sahara is a desert of about 3.5 million square miles. There are about $2.79 \cdot 10^7$ square feet in a square mile. About how many square feet does the Sahara cover? Write your answer in scientific notation.

10-1 • Guided Problem Solving L3

GPS **Exercise 32:**

The sun's diameter is $1.39 \cdot 10^6$ kilometers. Earth's diameter is $1.28 \cdot 10^4$ kilometers. How many times greater is the Sun's diameter than Earth's diameter?

Understand

1. Which diameter is larger?
2. What are you being asked to find?

Plan and Carry Out

3. The diameters are in scientific notation, and the numbers 1.28 and 1.39 are close in value, so what do you need to compare?
4. When dividing powers with the same base, what do you do to the exponents?
5. Subtract the exponents and write the power in standard form.
6. How many times greater is the Sun's diameter than Earth's?

Check

7. What other strategy could you use to find the answer?

Solve Another Problem

8. When you donate a pint of blood, you lose about $2.3 \cdot 10^{12}$ red blood cells. If your body can produce about $2 \cdot 10^6$ red blood cells per second, about how many seconds would it take for your body to replenish the red blood cells lost through donation? Write your answer in standard form.

Standards Practice

GO for Help: MathXL

NS 2.1, AF 2.1, Alg1 2.0

A Practice by Example

GO for Help Example 1 (page 366)

Homework Video Tutor
For: Examples 1–2
Visit: PHSchool.com
Web Code: axe-1001

Write each expression using a single exponent.

1. $y^3 \cdot y^5$
$y^3 \cdot y^5 = y^{(3+5)}$
$= y^{\blacksquare}$ y^8

Guided Practice This exercise has been started for you!

2. $d^{10} \cdot d^{100}$ d^{110}
3. $3.4^3 \cdot 3.4^{10}$ 3.4^{13}
4. $12^5 \cdot 12^{50}$ 12^{55}
5. $4.5^{10} \cdot 4.5^{10}$ 4.5^{20}
6. $(-5)^5 \cdot (-5)$ $(-5)^6$
7. $0.4^6 \cdot 0.4^2$ 0.4^8
8. $x \cdot x^0$ x^1 or x
9. $(-4)^7 \cdot (-4)^9$ $(-4)^{16}$
10. $23^5 \cdot 23^{14}$ 23^{19}

Example 2 (page 367)

Write each expression using a single exponent.

11. $\frac{a^6}{a^4}$
$\frac{a^6}{a^4} = a^{(6-4)}$
$= a^{\blacksquare}$ a^2

Guided Practice This exercise has been started for you!

12. $\frac{x^9}{x^5}$ x^4
13. $\frac{c^7}{c^2}$ c^5
14. $\frac{(-1)^5}{(-1)^4}$ $(-1)^1$ or -1
15. $\frac{23^{12}}{23^8}$ 23^4
16. $\frac{(-2)^3}{(-2)^3}$ $(-2)^0$ or 1
17. $\frac{(-7)^{99}}{(-7)^{98}}$ $(-7)^1$ or -7
18. $\frac{k^8}{k^{-2}}$ k^{10}
19. $\frac{6^7}{6^1}$ 6^6
20. $\frac{135^{10}}{135^1}$ 135^9

21. The distance from the sun to Saturn is about 8.88×10^8 mi. The speed of light is about 1.1×10^7 mi/min. Use the formula time $= \frac{\text{distance}}{\text{rate}}$ to estimate to the nearest minute how long sunlight takes to reach Saturn. about 81 min

B Apply Your Skills

22. **Guided Problem Solving** China has about 1.3×10^9 people. One of the world's smallest nations, the Marshall Islands, has a population of just 5.9×10^4 people. How many times as great as the Marshall Islands' population is China's population? about 22,034
- **Make a Plan** Write a ratio comparing China's population to the Marshall Islands' population.
- **Carry Out the Plan** Divide using the properties of exponents. Simplify.

Complete each equation.

23. $\frac{4^{\blacksquare}}{4^2} = 4^{10}$ 12
24. $j^6 \cdot j^{\blacksquare} = j^4$ -2
25. $2b^{(-3)} \cdot 3b^6 = 6b^{\blacksquare}$ 3

26. **Open-Ended** Give three different ways to write 4^{12} as the product of two powers. Answers may vary. Sample: $4 \cdot 4^{11}$, $4^2 \cdot 4^{10}$, $4^5 \cdot 4^7$

SCAFFOLDED **Problem Solving**

27. Simplify $\frac{10}{2}$. 5

28. Write $\frac{x^5}{x^2}$ using a single exponent. x^3

29. Simplify $\frac{10x^5}{2x^2}$. $5x^3$

30. Simplify $\frac{10x^5}{2x^2} + \frac{6x^3}{2x^2}$. $5x^3 + 3x$

31. Simplify $\frac{6x^5 - 12x^2}{3x^2}$. $2x^3 - 4$

GPS 32. The sun's diameter is 1.39×10^6 kilometers. Earth's diameter is 1.28×10^4 kilometers. How many times greater is the sun's diameter than Earth's diameter? about 108.6 times greater

33. Answers may vary. Sample: You can add exponents only when the bases are the same.

33. **Writing in Math** Explain why you cannot write $5^3 \cdot 7^9$ as $(35)^{12}$. See left.

Write each expression using a single exponent.

34. $4^x \cdot 4^t$ 4^{x+t}

35. $3^m \cdot 3^n$ 3^{m+n}

36. $1.5^8 \cdot 1.5^t$ 1.5^{8+t}

37. $\frac{5^r}{5^d}$ 5^{r-d}

38. $2^3 \cdot 2 \cdot 2^8$ 2^{12}

39. $\frac{5^{2t} \cdot 4^{3c}}{5^t \cdot 4^{2c}}$ $5^t \cdot 4^c$

C Challenge

40. Simplify $\frac{4m^9 + 6m^6 + 2m^3}{2m^3}$. $2m^6 + 3m^3 + 1$

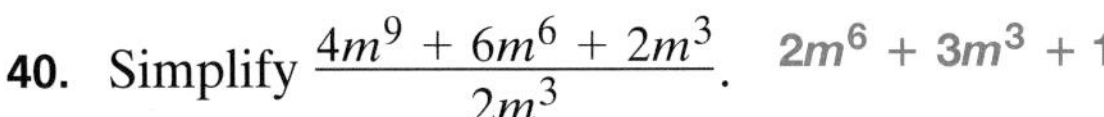

Multiple Choice Practice and Mixed Review

For California Standards Tutorials, visit PHSchool.com. Web Code: axq-9045

NS 2.1

41. Which expression has the same value as $\frac{5^2 \cdot 5^7}{5^3}$? D

   (A) 5^3 (B) 5^4 (C) 5^5 (D) 5^6

AF 4.1

42. Lola's monthly charge for downloading music can be found using the equation $c = 8.95 + 0.95s$, where s represents the number of songs she downloaded that month. If she downloads 23 songs in a month, what is the charge on her bill? B

   (A) \$9.90 (B) \$30.80 (C) \$32.90 (D) \$206.80

AF 1.1

43. In a class, there are $2\frac{1}{2}$ times as many people who have siblings as people who do not. If m people in the class have siblings, which expression can be used to find the number of people who do not? B

   (A) $2\frac{1}{2}m$ (B) $m \div 2\frac{1}{2}$ (C) $2\frac{1}{2} \div m$ (D) $2\frac{1}{2} + m$

GO for Help Lesson 7-3

Use a proportion to solve each problem. Round to the nearest hundredth, if necessary.

44. What percent of 58 is 17? 29.31%

45. What is 12.5% of 34.50? 4.31

Online Lesson Quiz Visit: PHSchool.com Web Code: axa-1001

369

Alternative Assessment

Each student in a pair writes a number in scientific notation. Then partners together find the quotient of their numbers.

California Resources

Standards Mastery

- Standards Review Transparencies
- Standards Review and Practice Workbook
- Math Companion

Math Intervention

- Skills Review and Practice Workbook
- Math XL

4. Assess & Reteach

PRESENTATION CD-ROM
CD, Online, or Transparencies

Lesson Quiz

1. Write $(-8)^4 \cdot (-8)^5$ using a single exponent. $(-8)^9$
2. Write $\frac{9^7}{9^4}$ using a single exponent. 9^3
3. Jupiter's diameter is about 1.43×10^5 kilometers. Earth's diameter is about 1.28×10^4 kilometers. How many times greater is Jupiter's diameter than Earth's diameter? Round the answer to the nearest tenth. 11.2 times greater

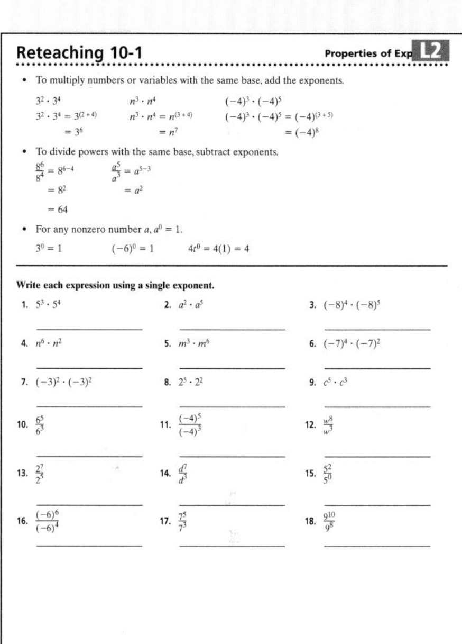

Reteaching 10-1 Properties of Exp L2

- To multiply numbers or variables with the same base, add the exponents.

$3^2 \cdot 3^4$ $n^3 \cdot n^4$ $(-4)^3 \cdot (-4)^5$

$3^2 \cdot 3^4 = 3^{(2+4)} = 3^6$ $n^3 \cdot n^4 = n^{(3+4)} = n^7$ $(-4)^3 \cdot (-4)^5 = (-4)^{(3+5)} = (-4)^8$

- To divide powers with the same base, subtract exponents.

$\frac{8^6}{8^4} = 8^{6-4} = 8^2 = 64$ $\frac{a^5}{a^3} = a^{5-3} = a^2$

- For any nonzero number a, $a^0 = 1$.

$3^0 = 1$ $(-6)^0 = 1$ $4t^0 = 4(1) = 4$

Write each expression using a single exponent.

1. $5^3 \cdot 5^4$
2. $a^2 \cdot a^5$
3. $(-8)^4 \cdot (-8)^5$
4. $n^6 \cdot n^2$
5. $m^3 \cdot m^6$
6. $(-7)^4 \cdot (-7)^2$
7. $(-3)^2 \cdot (-3)^2$
8. $2^5 \cdot 2^2$
9. $c^5 \cdot c^3$
10. $\frac{6^5}{6^3}$
11. $\frac{(-4)^5}{(-4)^3}$
12. $\frac{w^8}{w^3}$
13. $\frac{2^7}{2^5}$
14. $\frac{d^7}{d^3}$
15. $\frac{5^2}{5^0}$
16. $\frac{(-6)^6}{(-6)^4}$
17. $\frac{7^5}{7^3}$
18. $\frac{9^{10}}{9^8}$

Enrichment 10-1 Properties of Exp L4

Critical Thinking

Arrange each of the following numbers from greatest to least. Explain your answer.

a. $1.24 \cdot 10^{-3}$ b. $2.24 \cdot 10^{-2}$ c. $1.89 \cdot 10^{-4}$ d. $2.6 \cdot 10^{-2}$

1. Are these numbers written in standard or scientific notation?
2. Which of the numbers are positive?
3. Compare 10^{-4} and 10^{-3}. Which number is greater?
4. How can you use the exponents to compare powers of ten?
5. Compare $1.6 \cdot 10^{-2}$ and $2.6 \cdot 10^{-2}$. Which number is greater?
6. When the powers of 10 of two numbers written in scientific notation are the same, how can you compare the numbers?
7. Use your insights from Exercises 2, 4, and 6 to order the numbers.
8. How could you have found the answer using a different method?
9. Arrange these numbers from least to greatest.

   a. $1.9 \cdot 10^{-3}$ b. $2.5 \cdot 10^{-4}$ c. $1.2 \cdot 10^{-2}$ d. $2.8 \cdot 10^{-4}$

10-2

1. Plan

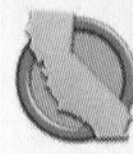

California Content Standards

NS 2.1 Multiply and divide expressions involving exponents with a common base. ***Develop, Master***

AF 2.1 Simplify and evaluate expressions that include exponents. ***Master***

Alg1 2.0 Understand the rules of exponents. ***Develop***

California Math Background

Since $a^3 \cdot a^3$ is a^6, it follows that $(a^3)^2$ is a^6. This example illustrates the rule that exponents are multiplied in order to raise a power to a power. Applying this rule means that $(2^3a^4)^2$ can be simplified to 2^6a^8 or $54a^8$.

More Math Background: p. 364C

Lesson Planning and Resources

See p. 364E for a list of the resources that support this lesson.

PRESENTATION CD-ROM CD, Online, or Transparencies

Bell Ringer Practice

Check Skills You'll Need
Use student page, transparency, or PowerPoint.
See Math Companion.

California Standards Review
Use transparency or PowerPoint.

10-2 Power Rules

Check Skills You'll Need

Do this in your **Math Companion.**

Vocabulary

Review:
- exponent
- power

Use your **Math Companion** *to build your vocabulary.*

California Content Standards

NS 2.1 Multiply and divide expressions involving exponents with a common base. ***Develop, Master***
AF 2.1 Simplify and evaluate expressions that include exponents. ***Master***
Alg1 2.0 Understand the rules of exponents. ***Develop***

What You'll Learn . . . and Why

You will learn to use power rules. You can use power rules to find the surface area of large objects, such as the moon.

You can use the rules for multiplying exponents to simplify an expression such as $(4^3)^2$.

$$(4^3)^2 = 4^3 \cdot 4^3 \quad \leftarrow \text{Write two factors of } 4^3.$$
$$= 4^{(3+3)} \quad \leftarrow \text{Use the rules for multiplying powers.}$$
$$= 4^6 \quad \leftarrow \text{Simplify the exponent.}$$

Since $6 = 3 \cdot 2$, $(4^3)^2 = 4^{(3 \cdot 2)} = 4^6$. This result suggests the following rule.

Vocabulary Tip

The word *power* can be used in two ways. The expression a^n is a power. You can also read a^n as "*a* to the *n*th power."

Take Note — Raising a Power to a Power

To raise a power to a power, multiply the exponents.

Arithmetic	Algebra
$(2^5)^3 = 2^{(5 \cdot 3)} = 2^{15}$	$(a^m)^n = a^{(m \cdot n)}$

EXAMPLE Raising a Power to a Power

1 Write $(3^{-4})^5$ using a single exponent.

$$(3^{-4})^5 = 3^{(-4 \cdot 5)} \quad \leftarrow \text{Multiply the exponents.}$$
$$= 3^{-20} \quad \leftarrow \text{Simplify the exponent.}$$
$$= \frac{1}{3^{20}} \quad \leftarrow \text{Write with a positive exponent.}$$

CA Standards Check 1 *Go to your* **Math Companion** *for help.*

1. Write each expression using a single exponent.
   a. $(5^3)^{-2}$ $\frac{1}{5^6}$ **b.** $(12^{-3})^{-2}$ 12^6

Universal Access Solutions for All Learners

Special Needs L1	**Below Level** L2
Suggest that students recall the rules for $x^a \cdot x^b$ and $(x^a)^b$ by writing out the factors for $x^2 \cdot x^3$ and $(x^2)^3$. $(x \cdot x) \cdot (x \cdot x \cdot x)$ or x^5 and $(x \cdot x) \cdot (x \cdot x) \cdot (x \cdot x)$ or x^6	Write in factored form and find the value of 2^5, $(-2)^5$, and -2^5. $2 \cdot 2 \cdot 2 \cdot 2 \cdot 2 = 32$; $-2 \cdot -2 \cdot -2 \cdot -2 \cdot -2 = 32$; $-(2 \cdot 2 \cdot 2 \cdot 2 \cdot 2) = -32$

You can raise a product to a power using repeated multiplication.

$(2w)^3 = (2w) \cdot (2w) \cdot (2w)$ ← Write out the factors of the power.

$= 2 \cdot 2 \cdot 2 \cdot w \cdot w \cdot w$ ← Use the Commutative Property of Multiplication to rearrange the factors.

$= 2^3 \cdot w^3$ ← Write the factors as a product.

$= 8w^3$ ← Simplify.

Notice that $(2w)^3 = 2^3w^3$. This result suggests the following rule.

Take Note **Raising a Product to a Power**

To raise a product to a power, raise each factor to the power.

Arithmetic	Algebra
$(3 \cdot 5)^2 = 3^2 \cdot 5^2$	$(ab)^m = a^mb^m$

EXAMPLE Raising a Product to a Power

Relate **MATH YOU KNOW...**

Write $6 \cdot 6 \cdot x \cdot x \cdot x$ using exponents.

...to ALGEBRA

$6 \cdot 6 \cdot x \cdot x \cdot x = 6^2x^3$ ← 6 is a factor 2 times and x is a factor 3 times.

2 The radius of the moon is about 1.08×10^3 mi. Use the formula S.A. $= 4\pi r^2$ to find the surface area of the moon. Use 3.14 for π.

S.A. $= 4\pi r^2$

$= 4 \cdot 3.14 \cdot (1.08 \times 10^3)^2$ ← Substitute into the formula.

$= 4 \cdot 3.14 \cdot 1.08^2 \times (10^3)^2$ ← Raise the product to a power.

$= 4 \cdot 3.14 \cdot 1.1664 \times 10^6$ ← Raise the power to a power.

$\approx 14.65 \times 10^6$ ← Multiply.

$= 14{,}650{,}000$ ← Simplify.

The surface area of the moon is about 14,650,000 mi^2.

Check for Reasonableness The radius of the moon is about 1,100 mi. Round 3.14 to 3. Then $4 \cdot 3 \cdot (1{,}100)^2 = 12 \cdot 1{,}210{,}000 = 14{,}520{,}000$, which is close to 14,650,000. The answer is reasonable.

CA Standards Check 2 *Go to your* **Math Companion** *for help.*

2. Use the formula S.A. $= 4\pi r^2$ to find the surface area of each object. Use 3.14 for π.

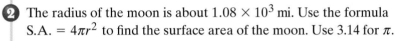

   a. plant cell: radius 4×10^{-6} m about 2×10^{-10} m^2

   b. Saturn: radius 3.6×10^4 mi about 1.63×10^{10} mi^2

Check Your Understanding *Homework prep is in your* **Math Companion.**

2. Teach

Guided Instruction

To illustrate the concept behind the rule for raising a power to a power, write out the factors for Example 1.

$(3^{-4})^5$

$= 3^{-4} \cdot 3^{-4} \cdot 3^{-4} \cdot 3^{-4} \cdot 3^{-4}$

$= 3^{(-4) + (-4) + (-4) + (-4) + (-4)}$

$= 3^{-20}$

Ask students to show other examples.

Error Prevention!

Prepare students for algebra and help them distinguish between the meaning of $(ab)^2$ and $(a + b)^2$ by having them find the value for these two expressions using $a = 3$ and $b = 4$. For $a = 3$ and $b = 4$, $(ab)^2$ has a value of $(12)^2$ or 144, while $(a + b)^2$ has a value of $(7)^2$ or 49.

Additional Examples

1. Write each expression using a single exponent.

   a. $(5^{-2})^3$ 5^{-6}

   b. $(8^{-4})^{-5}$ 8^{20}

2. Use the formula for the area of a circle, $A = \pi r^2$, to find the area of a circle with a radius of 4×10^{-2} m. Use 3.14 for the value of π. 5.024×10^{-3} m^2

Closure

- *What is the difference between multiplying two powers and raising a power to a power?* Sample: To multiply two powers, such as x^2 and x^3, you add the exponents to get x^5. To raise a power to a power, such as $(x^2)^3$, you multiply the exponents to get x^6.
- *How do you raise a product to a power?* Sample: Raise each factor to the power and simplify.

Advanced Learners L4	**English Learners** EL
Write −340,000 in scientific notation. $-(3.4 \times 10^5)$	Review the words *power, exponent,* and *product.* Ask students to demonstrate the differences among finding the product of powers, raising a power to a power, and raising a product to a power.

3. Practice

Assignment Guide

Check Your Understanding
See Math Companion.

Homework Exercises

A Practice by Example	1–28
B Apply Your Skills	29–49
C Challenge	50
California Multiple-Choice Practice	51–53
Mixed Review	54–56

Homework Quick Check
To check students' understanding of key skills and concepts, go over Exercises 5, 18, 30, 36, 42, 48.

Universal Access Resources

Practice 10-2 Powe[r Rules] L2

Write each expression using one base and one exponent.

1. $(5^3)^{-6}$
2. $(-9^4)^{-2}$
3. $(d^5)^6$
4. $(8^{-3})^{-9}$
5. $(4^{-3})^{-4}$
6. $(y^8)^{-6}$
7. $(v^9)^6$
8. $(k^{-7})^{-5}$
9. $(n^3)^5$
10. $((a^2)^2)^2$

Simplify each expression.

11. $(xyz)^6$
12. $(10^2 \cdot x^7)^3$
13. $(7y^8)^2$
14. $(3^2 \cdot 3^1 \cdot 3^5)^2$
15. $(x \cdot 10^{-2})^3$
16. $((x^5)y^4)^8$

Use >, =, or < to complete each statement.

17. $7^3 \cdot 7^3$? $(7^3)^3$
18. $(6^{-2} \cdot 6^5)^3$? $(6^3)^2$
19. $(4^6)^0$? $4^6 \cdot 4^{-6}$
20. Find the area of a square whose side is 3×10^4 millimeters. Write the answer in scientific notation.
21. As of October 29, 2002 the Ijen volcano had an active crater with a radius of 1,100 ft. Using the formula for a circle $A = \pi r^2$ and 3.14 for π, what is the area of the crater?

Reteaching 10-2 Powe[r Rules] L4

The expression x^n is a power. It can also be read as x to the nth power.

Raising a Power to a Power

To raise a power to a power, multiply exponents.

Arithmetic:
$(2^4)^6$
$= 2^{(4 \cdot 6)}$ ← Multiply the exponents.
$= 2^{24}$ ← Simplify the exponent.

Algebra:
$(a^x)^y$
$= a^{(x \cdot y)}$ ← Multiply the exponents.
$= a^{xy}$ ← Simplify the exponent.

$(x^{-3})^{-5}$
$= x^{(-3 \cdot -5)}$ ← Multiply the exponents.
$= x^{15}$ ← Simplify the exponent.

Raising a Product to a Power

To raise a product to a power, raise each factor to the power.

Arithmetic:
$(4 \cdot 7)^2$
$= 4^2 \cdot 7^2$ ← Raise each factor to the power.

Algebra:
$(xy)^a$
$= x^a y^a$ ← Raise each factor to the power.

$(4a^2)^3$
$= 4^3(a^2)^3$ ← Raise each factor to the power.
$= 4^3 a^6$ ← Multiply the exponents.
$= 64a^6$ ← Simplify.

Write each expression using a single exponent.

1. $(6^2)^{-4}$
2. $(y^6)^{-5}$
3. $(7^{-4})^{-5}$
4. $(x^b)^c$
5. $(5^9)^3$
6. $(a^{-3})^{-8}$

Simplify each expression.

7. $(ht)^n$
8. $(5v)^2$
9. $(7p^4)^2$
10. $(3d^4f^2)^3$
11. $(k^5j^4)^3$
12. $(2s^7u^6)^4$

Use <, =, or > to complete each statement.

13. 2^5 ☐ $(2^3)^2$
14. $(5^{-4})^2$ ☐ 5^{-8}
15. $(6 \cdot 4)^2$ ☐ 10^2

Standards Practice

GO for Help: MathXL

NS 2.1, AF 2.1, Alg1 2.0

A Practice by Example

Example 1 (page 370)

For: Examples 1–2
Visit: PHSchool.com
Web Code: axe-1002

Write each expression using a single exponent.

1. $(3^3)^7$
$(3^3)^7 = 3^{(3 \cdot 7)}$
$= 3^{\blacksquare}$ 3^{21}

Guided Practice This exercise has been started for you!

2. $(9^2)^{-5}$ $\frac{1}{9^{10}}$
3. $(h^2)^2$ h^4
4. $(y^{-3})^{-4}$ y^{12}
5. $(w^{-2})^{-6}$ w^{12}
6. $(7^2)^9$ 7^{18}
7. $(p^{-2})^{-1}$ p^2
8. $(r^2)^3$ r^6
9. $(10^5)^{-2}$ $\frac{1}{10^{10}}$
10. $(d^7)^3$ d^{21}
11. $(9^2)^2$ 9^4
12. $(v^{-1})^{-6}$ v^6
13. $(2^{-3})^3$ $\frac{1}{2^9}$

Example 2 (page 371)

Simplify each expression.

14. $(3x)^2$
$(3x)^2 = 3^2 \cdot x^2$
$= \blacksquare x^2$ $9x^2$

Guided Practice This exercise has been started for you!

15. $(y \cdot y^2)^5$ y^{15}
16. $(2p^2)^4$ $16p^8$
17. $(a^2b^3)^4$ a^8b^{12}
18. $(abc)^5$ $a^5b^5c^5$
19. $(10x^5)^2$ $100x^{10}$
20. $(9^2w)^2$ 9^4w^2
21. $(3 \cdot 5a)^2$ $225a^2$
22. $(g^3h^4)^6$ $g^{18}h^{24}$
23. $(4t^5y^2)^3$ $64t^{15}y^6$
24. $(3 \times 10^5)^3$ 27×10^{15}
25. $(5 \times 10^2)^{-5}$ $5^{-5} \times 10^{-10}$
26. $(2.1 \times 10^4)^2$ 4.41×10^8
27. Find the area of a square whose side is 7.1×10^3 cm. 5.041×10^7 cm^2
28. Find the area of a circle with a radius of 4×10^{-6} in. Use the formula $A = \pi r^2$ and 3.14 for π. 5.024×10^{-11} in.^{2}

B Apply Your Skills

29. **Guided Problem Solving** Einstein's famous equation states that $E = mc^2$. E represents energy, m represents mass, and c represents the speed of light. Find the amount of energy (in joules) of a peanut with a mass of 8.4×10^{-3} kg. Use $c = 3.0 \times 10^8$ m/s. 7.56×10^{14} joules
- Substitute the values into the equation.
- Use power rules to simplify the exponents.

Use <, =, or > to complete each statement.

30. $5^5 \blacksquare (5^3)^2$ <
31. $8^2 \cdot 8^6 \blacksquare (8^2)^2$ >
32. $(5^3)^0 \blacksquare 5^3 \cdot 5^{-3}$ =
33. $(7^{-3} \cdot 7^5)^3 \blacksquare (7^2)^6$ <
34. $4^5 \cdot 4^6 \blacksquare (4^5)^6$ <
35. $(-3^4)^2 \blacksquare ((-3)^4)^2$ =
36. **Writing in Math** How is multiplying powers with the same base different from raising a power to a power? See left.

36. Answers may vary. Sample: When multiplying powers with the same base, you add the powers. When raising a power to a power, you multiply the powers.

SCAFFOLDED
Problem Solving

40. Answers may vary. Sample: Raise both the numerator and the denominator to the power of p: $\left(\frac{a^m}{b^n}\right)^p = \frac{a^{mp}}{b^{np}}$.

48. No; $(2 + 3)^2 = 25$ and $2^2 + 3^2 = 13$. You cannot raise a sum to a power by raising each addend to the power.

49. The student who got $x^2 \cdot x^2 = x^4$; when you multiply two numbers with the same base you add the powers.

37. Simplify 3^4. 81

38. Simplify $\left(\frac{3}{x}\right)^4$. $\frac{81}{x^4}$

39. Simplify $\left(\frac{3}{7x^3}\right)^4$. $\frac{81}{7^4x^{12}}$

40. **Reasoning** Make a conjecture about how to simplify $\left(\frac{a^m}{b^n}\right)^p$. See above left.

41. Use your conjecture to simplify $\left(\frac{k^3}{w^2}\right)^5$. $\frac{k^{15}}{w^{10}}$

Simplify each expression.

42. $(2 \cdot 2^2 \cdot 2^3)^2$ 2^{12}

43. $(3^{-2} \cdot 3^{-1} \cdot 3^0)^{-3}$ 3^9

44. $((5^2)^3)^2$ 5^{12}

45. $(y \cdot y^5 \cdot y^{10})^2$ y^{32}

46. $(a \cdot 10^{-1})^5$ $\frac{a^5}{10^5}$

47. $((m^3)^2)^4$ m^{24}

GPS 48. **Reasoning** Does $(2 + 3)^2 = 2^2 + 3^2$? Explain. See above left.

49. **Error Analysis** Which student simplified $x^2 \cdot x^2$ correctly? Explain. See above left.

$x^2 \cdot x^2 = 2x^2$ $x^2 \cdot x^2 = x^4$

Challenge

50. Arrange the numbers below from least to greatest.
2^{222}, $(2^{22})^2$, $(4)^{4^4}$, $(4^4)^{44}$ $(2^{22})^2$, 2^{222}, $(4^4)^{44}$, $(4)^{4^4}$

Multiple Choice Practice and Mixed Review

For California Standards Tutorials, visit PHSchool.com. Web Code: axq-9045

Alg1 2.0

51. Which of the following has the same value as $(6^5)^4$? B

(A) 6^{54} (B) 6^{20} (C) 6^9 (D) 6^1

AF 4.2

52. In 40 min, Alex can pick 3 qt of berries. If four people work at that rate, how long will they take to pick 15 qt? B

(A) 30 min (C) 160 min
(B) 50 min (D) 200 min

NS 1.3

53. An interior designer saved \$29 on a pair of window blinds. If the sale price was 20% off the regular price, what was the regular price of the blinds? B

(A) \$345 (C) \$69
(B) \$145 (D) \$36

GO for Help Lesson 7-1

Write each percent as a fraction in simplest form.

54. 20% $\frac{1}{5}$

55. $33\frac{1}{3}$% $\frac{1}{3}$

56. 1.75% $\frac{7}{400}$

Online Lesson Quiz Visit: PHSchool.com Web Code: axa-1002

4. Assess & Reteach

PRESENTATION CD-ROM
CD, Online, or Transparencies

Lesson Quiz

1. Write $(9^{-3})^8$ using a single exponent. 9^{-24}

2. Simplify $(2a^6)^3$. $8a^{18}$

3. Find the area of a circle whose radius is 5×10^{-7} m. Use 3.14 for π. 7.85×10^{-13} m^2

Alternative Assessment

Each student in a pair writes an exponential expression. Partners exchange papers. Then each student raises his or her partner's expression to the seventh power and simplifies the expression.

California Resources

Standards Mastery
- Standards Review Transparencies
- Standards Review and Practice Workbook
- Math Companion

Math Intervention
- Skills Review and Practice Workbook
- Math XL

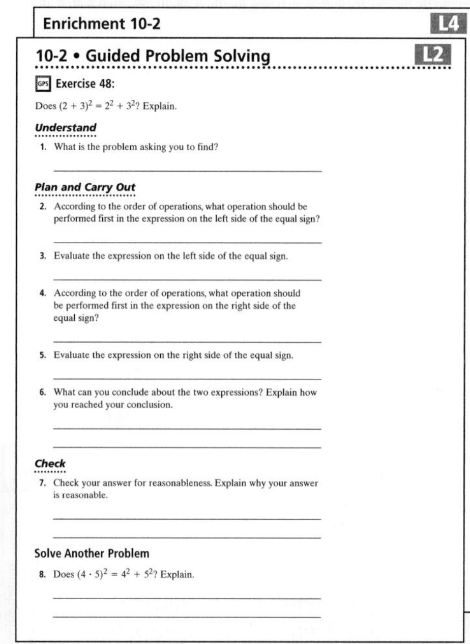

Enrichment 10-2 L4

10-2 • Guided Problem Solving L2

GPS Exercise 48:

Does $(2 + 3)^2 = 2^2 + 3^2$? Explain.

Understand

1. What is the problem asking you to find?

Plan and Carry Out

2. According to the order of operations, what operation should be performed first in the expression on the left side of the equal sign?

3. Evaluate the expression on the left side of the equal sign.

4. According to the order of operations, what operation should be performed first in the expression on the right side of the equal sign?

5. Evaluate the expression on the right side of the equal sign.

6. What can you conclude about the two expressions? Explain how you reached your conclusion.

Check

7. Check your answer for reasonableness. Explain why your answer is reasonable.

Solve Another Problem

8. Does $(4 \cdot 5)^2 = 4^2 + 5^2$? Explain.

10-3

1. Plan

California Content Standards

Alg1 2.0 Understand and use such operations as taking a root. ***Develop***

California Math Background

The square root of a number is a number that, when multiplied by itself, is equal to the original number. Numbers also have other roots, such as cube roots and fourth roots. A root is represented by a radical sign: $\sqrt[n]{x}$. The radical symbol can contain an expression or be a part of an expression.

More Math Background: p. 364C

Lesson Planning and Resources

See p. 364E for a list of the resources that support this lesson.

PRESENTATION CD-ROM
CD, Online, or Transparencies

Bell Ringer Practice

Check Skills You'll Need
Use student page, transparency, or PowerPoint.
See Math Companion.

California Standards Review
Use transparency or PowerPoint.

GO for Help: Math Companion

10-3 Exploring Roots

Check Skills You'll Need

Do this in your **Math Companion.**

Vocabulary

- *n*th roots

Use your **Math Companion** *to build your vocabulary.*

California Content Standards

Alg1 2.0 Understand and use such operations as taking a root. ***Develop***

What You'll Learn . . . and Why

You will learn to simplify expressions with roots. You can use roots to evaluate formulas and to find measures such as the radius of a model of Earth.

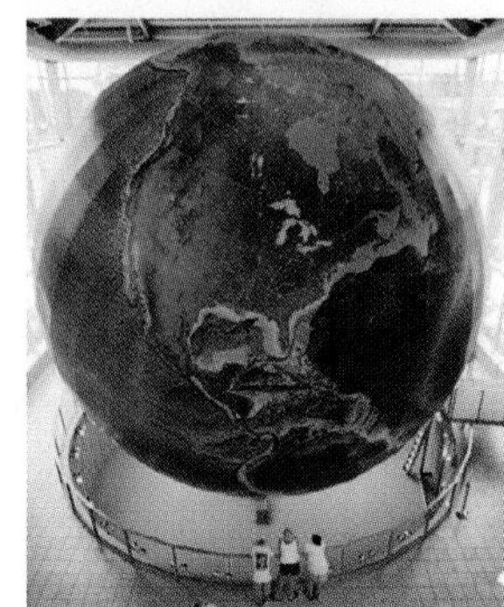

Recall that the square root of a number is a number that when multiplied by itself is equal to the original number. You can find other roots of numbers, including cube roots and the fourth roots.

$3^2 = 9 \Rightarrow \sqrt{9} = 3$ ← square root

$3^3 = 27 \Rightarrow \sqrt[3]{27} = 3$ ← cube root

$3^4 = 81 \Rightarrow \sqrt[4]{81} = 3$ ← fourth root

This pattern suggests the following definition.

Vocabulary Tip

For square roots, you can use $\sqrt{\ }$ instead of $\sqrt[2]{\ }$.

Take Note **Roots**

For any real numbers a and b, and any positive integer n, if $a^n = b$, then a is an **nth root** of b.

Arithmetic	Algebra
Since $4^3 = 64$, $\sqrt[3]{64} = 4$.	If $a^n = b$, then $\sqrt[n]{b} = a$.

The symbol $\sqrt[n]{\ }$ is a radical sign. Recall that $\sqrt{\ }$ represents the square root. The symbol $\sqrt[3]{\ }$ represents a cube root, $\sqrt[4]{\ }$ represents a fourth root, and $\sqrt[5]{\ }$ represents a fifth root.

Universal Access Solutions for All Learners

Special Needs L1	**Below Level** L2
Students can work together to create a chart of the squares, cubes, and fourth powers of integers from 1 to 5. When necessary, they can refer to the chart for help in simplifying roots.	Students review the order of operations by simplifying expressions such as $6 + 3(4 - 2)$ 12 and $6 \times 3 + (4 - 8)$ 14.

Recall that a number has two square roots: one positive square root and one negative square root. A number also has two fourth roots: one positive and one negative.

A number has just one third root. If the number is negative, the third root is also negative. If the number is positive, the third root is positive.

EXAMPLE Finding Roots of a Number

Relate **MATH YOU KNOW...**

Find the two square roots of 81.

$9 \cdot 9 = 81$
$(-9) \cdot (-9) = 81$ **Find each number that when multiplied by itself equals 81.**

The square roots of 81 are 9 and −9.

... to **ALGEBRA**

1 Simplify $\sqrt[3]{-125}$.

Since −125 is negative, the cube root will also be negative.

$(-5)^3 = (-5) \cdot (-5) \cdot (-5) = -125$ ← **Find the number that when raised to the third power equals −125.**

So $\sqrt[3]{-125} = -5$.

CA Standards Check 1 *Go to your* **Math Companion** *for help.*

1. Simplify each expression.

a. $\sqrt[4]{256}$ 4 **b.** $\sqrt[3]{-1}$ −1 **c.** $\sqrt{1{,}296}$ 36

A radical sign ($\sqrt{\ }$) is a type of grouping symbol. When you simplify expressions with roots, follow the order of operations and simplify under the radical sign first. Then evaluate the root.

EXAMPLE Simplifying Expressions With Roots

2 Simplify $5 \cdot 3 + \sqrt[4]{80 + 1}$.

$5 \cdot 3 + \sqrt[4]{80 + 1} = 5 \cdot 3 + \sqrt[4]{81}$ ← **Work inside grouping symbols.**
$= 5 \cdot 3 + 3$ ← **Simplify the root.**
$= 15 + 3$ ← **Multiply.**
$= 18$ ← **Add.**

CA Standards Check 2 *Go to your* **Math Companion** *for help.*

2. Simplify each expression.

a. $6 \cdot \sqrt[4]{-5 + 6} - 7$ −1 **b.** $\sqrt{8 - 4} + \sqrt[3]{-125}$ −3

Check Your Understanding *Homework prep is in your* **Math Companion.**

2. Teach

Guided Instruction

Example 1
Ask: *What number, when raised to the third power, equals −125?* If necessary, review the rules for multiplying integers, and the values of 2^3, 3^3, 4^3, 5^3, and 6^3.

Error Prevention!

In Example 2, remind students that the radical sign functions as a grouping symbol, like parentheses, in the order of operations. Make sure students begin by simplifying the expression under the radical sign.

PRESENTATION CD-ROM
CD, Online, or Transparencies

Additional Examples

1 Simplify $\sqrt[3]{-64}$. −4

2 Simplify $3 + 2 \cdot \sqrt{50 - 14}$. 15

Closure

- *What is the nth root of a number?* a number that, when multiplied by itself *n* times, is equal to the original number
- *What is the first step in simplifying an expression containing roots?* Simplify the expression under the radical sign.

Advanced Learners L4
Explain why the equation $x^n = b$, where n is an even number and b is any positive number, always has two solutions. Sample answer: The product of an even number of negative factors is positive, so the equation always has both a positive and a negative solution.

English Learners EL
Have students write mathematical expressions for word phrases such as *the cube root of negative eight* and *the fourth root of 81*. Then have them write word phrases for roots and expressions used in the lesson.

3. Practice

Assignment Guide

Check Your Understanding
See Math Companion.

Homework Exercises

A Practice by Example	1–24
B Apply Your Skills	25–38
C Challenge	39
California Multiple-Choice Practice	40–42
Mixed Review	43–45

Homework Quick Check
To check students' understanding of key skills and concepts, go over Exercises 2, 15, 26, 27, 34.

Universal Access Resources

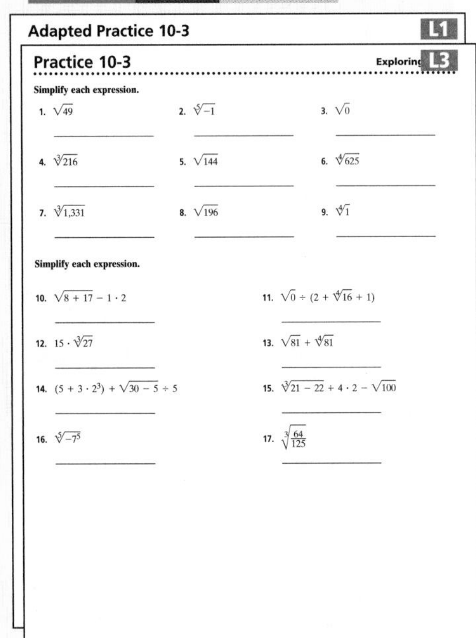

Adapted Practice 10-3 L1

Practice 10-3 Exploring L3

Simplify each expression.

1. $\sqrt{49}$
2. $\sqrt[5]{-1}$
3. $\sqrt{0}$
4. $\sqrt[3]{216}$
5. $\sqrt{144}$
6. $\sqrt[4]{625}$
7. $\sqrt[3]{1{,}331}$
8. $\sqrt{196}$
9. $\sqrt[4]{1}$

Simplify each expression.

10. $\sqrt{8 + 17} - 1 \cdot 2$
11. $\sqrt{0} \div (2 + \sqrt[4]{16} + 1)$
12. $15 \cdot \sqrt[3]{27}$
13. $\sqrt{81} + \sqrt[4]{81}$
14. $(5 + 3 \cdot 2^3) + \sqrt{30 - 5} \div 5$
15. $\sqrt[3]{21 - 22} + 4 \cdot 2 - \sqrt{100}$
16. $\sqrt[5]{-7^5}$
17. $\sqrt[3]{\frac{64}{125}}$

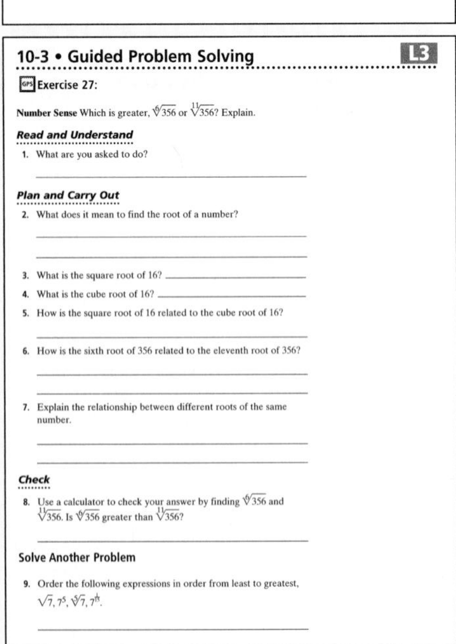

10-3 • Guided Problem Solving L3

GPS Exercise 27:

Number Sense Which is greater, $\sqrt[6]{356}$ or $\sqrt[11]{356}$? Explain.

Read and Understand

1. What are you asked to do?

Plan and Carry Out

2. What does it mean to find the root of a number?
3. What is the square root of 16? ______
4. What is the cube root of 16? ______
5. How is the square root of 16 related to the cube root of 16?
6. How is the sixth root of 356 related to the eleventh root of 356?
7. Explain the relationship between different roots of the same number.

Check

8. Use a calculator to check your answer by finding $\sqrt[6]{356}$ and $\sqrt[11]{356}$. Is $\sqrt[6]{356}$ greater than $\sqrt[11]{356}$?

Solve Another Problem

9. Order the following expressions in order from least to greatest, $\sqrt{7}, 7^5, \sqrt[5]{7}, 7^{\frac{1}{5}}$.

Standards Practice
Alg1 2.0

A Practice by Example

Example 1 (page 375)

Simplify each expression.

1. $\sqrt[4]{10{,}000}$
   $\blacksquare \cdot \blacksquare \cdot \blacksquare \cdot \blacksquare = 10{,}000$ 10

Guided Practice This exercise has been started for you!

2. $\sqrt[3]{-8}$ −2
3. $\sqrt{16}$ 4
4. $\sqrt[4]{16}$ 2
5. $\sqrt[5]{32}$ 2
6. $\sqrt[3]{0}$ 0
7. $\sqrt{121}$ 11
8. $\sqrt[3]{-1}$ −1
9. $\sqrt[4]{625}$ 5
10. $\sqrt{169}$ 13
11. $\sqrt[3]{1{,}000}$ 10
12. $\sqrt[3]{-1{,}331}$ −11
13. $\sqrt[4]{1}$ 1

GO for Help

For: Examples 1–2
Visit: PHSchool.com
Web Code: axe-1003

Example 2 (page 375)

Simplify each expression.

14. $3 + \sqrt[3]{8 \cdot 8}$
    $3 + \sqrt[3]{8 \cdot 8} = 3 + \sqrt[3]{64}$
    $= 3 + \blacksquare$ 7

Guided Practice This exercise has been started for you!

15. $\sqrt{5 + 20} - 6 \cdot 3$ −13
16. $9 \cdot \sqrt[3]{-8}$ −18
17. $\sqrt[5]{1} \cdot (3 + 2)$ 5
18. $\sqrt[4]{9^2} + 2$ 5
19. $(-1)^2 - \sqrt[3]{8 \cdot 0}$ 1
20. $\sqrt{64} + \sqrt[3]{64}$ 12
21. $(-3)^2 - \sqrt{17 - 8}$ 6
22. $(-9 + 5 \cdot 3) \div \sqrt[3]{-8}$ −3
23. $\frac{5 \cdot 4}{10} - \sqrt[3]{0}$ 2
24. $\sqrt{16} - \sqrt{4} + \sqrt[3]{-27}$ −1

B Apply Your Skills

25. **Guided Problem Solving** The photo at the beginning of this lesson shows Eartha, one of the largest models of Earth. The volume of Eartha is about 503,187,513.6 in.^{3}. Use the formula $V = \frac{4}{3}\pi r^3$ to find the radius of Eartha to the nearest half inch. Use 3.14 for π. 493.5 in.
    - Substitute the given values for V and π into the formula.
    - You need to isolate r. What is the inverse of raising a number to the third power?

26. **Writing in Math** A positive number has two square roots, one positive and one negative. Why does a positive number only have one cube root? See left.

26. Answers may vary. Sample: The product of three neg. numbers is neg.

GPS 27. **Number Sense** Which is greater, $\sqrt[6]{356}$ or $\sqrt[11]{356}$? Explain.
$\sqrt[6]{356}$; six factors are needed to make 356 instead of 11 factors.

SCAFFOLDED
Problem Solving

28. Simplify $\sqrt[4]{3^4}$. 3

29. Simplify $(3^4)^{\frac{1}{4}}$ by multiplying the exponents. 3

30. Simplify $\sqrt{5^2}$ and $(5^2)^{\frac{1}{2}}$. 5, 5

31. Simplify $\sqrt[3]{2^3}$ and $(2^3)^{\frac{1}{3}}$. 2, 2

32. **Reasoning** Make a conjecture about the relationship between taking the nth root of a number and raising a number to the $\frac{1}{n}$th power. Conjectures may vary. Sample: $\sqrt[n]{a} = a^{\frac{1}{n}}$.

33. Use your conjecture to simplify $(-27)^{\frac{1}{3}}$. −3

Simplify each expression.

34. $(3 \cdot 2^4)^2 - \sqrt[3]{16 - 8} \cdot 5$ 2,294

35. $\sqrt[4]{(3 + 2)^4} + 6 \cdot 7 - 5^2$ 22

36. $\left(\frac{2}{3}\right)^3 + \sqrt{10 - 3^0}$ $3\frac{8}{27}$

37. $\sqrt[5]{15 - 16} \cdot 6 \div (4 - 2)$ −3

38. **Reasoning** Explain why $\sqrt[3]{-8}$ has one real root but $\sqrt{-64}$ has no real roots. See left.

38. Answers may vary. Sample: $-2 \cdot -2 \cdot -2 = -8$, but the square of a real number is always positive.

C Challenge

39. Simplify $\sqrt[4]{\frac{81}{625}}$. $\frac{3}{5}$

Multiple Choice Practice and Mixed Review

For California Standards Tutorials, visit PHSchool.com. Web Code: axq-9045

Alg1 2.0

40. Simplify $\sqrt[3]{125} + \sqrt{4}$. D

Ⓐ 129
Ⓑ $45\frac{2}{3}$
Ⓒ 9
Ⓓ 7

NS 1.3

41. Lorna has 60 stamps in her stamp collection. If 30% of the stamps are U.S. stamps, which of the following represents the fraction of Lorna's stamps that are U.S. stamps? B

Ⓐ $\frac{1}{12}$
Ⓑ $\frac{3}{10}$
Ⓒ $\frac{1}{3}$
Ⓓ $\frac{1}{2}$

NS 2.1

42. Simplify $\left(\frac{2}{5}\right)^{-2} \cdot \left(\frac{2}{5}\right)^6$. C

Ⓐ $\left(\frac{5}{2}\right)^{-8}$
Ⓑ $\left(\frac{2}{5}\right)^{-8}$
Ⓒ $\left(\frac{2}{5}\right)^4$
Ⓓ $\left(\frac{5}{2}\right)^4$

Lesson 10-2

Simplify each expression.

43. $(3v^3)^2$ $9v^6$

44. $(2r)^5$ $32r^5$

45. $(w^3b^2)^7$ $w^{21}b^{14}$

Online Lesson Quiz Visit: PHSchool.com Web Code: axa-1003

Alternative Assessment

Each student uses repeated multiplication to write a root that can be simplified and then writes an expression containing the root. Students exchange papers with a partner and simplify each other's expressions.

California Resources

Standards Mastery

- Standards Review Transparencies
- Standards Review and Practice Workbook
- Math Companion

Math Intervention

- Skills Review and Practice Workbook
- Math XL

4. Assess & Reteach

PRESENTATION CD-ROM
CD, Online, or Transparencies

Lesson Quiz

Simplify each expression.

1. $\sqrt{225}$ 15
2. $\sqrt[3]{-27}$ −3
3. $4 \cdot \sqrt[3]{90 + 5 \cdot 7}$ 20
4. $\sqrt{36 + 45} - 8$ 1

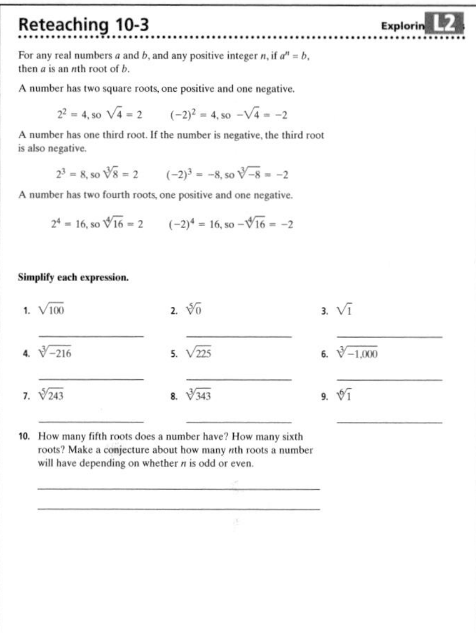

Reteaching 10-3 Explorin L2

For any real numbers a and b, and any positive integer n, if $a^n = b$, then a is an nth root of b.

A number has two square roots, one positive and one negative.

$2^2 = 4$, so $\sqrt{4} = 2$ $(-2)^2 = 4$, so $-\sqrt{4} = -2$

A number has one third root. If the number is negative, the third root is also negative.

$2^3 = 8$, so $\sqrt[3]{8} = 2$ $(-2)^3 = -8$, so $\sqrt[3]{-8} = -2$

A number has two fourth roots, one positive and one negative.

$2^4 = 16$, so $\sqrt[4]{16} = 2$ $(-2)^4 = 16$, so $-\sqrt[4]{16} = -2$

Simplify each expression.

1. $\sqrt{100}$
2. $\sqrt[5]{0}$
3. $\sqrt{1}$
4. $\sqrt[3]{-216}$
5. $\sqrt{225}$
6. $\sqrt[3]{-1{,}000}$
7. $\sqrt[5]{243}$
8. $\sqrt[3]{343}$
9. $\sqrt[6]{1}$
10. How many fifth roots does a number have? How many sixth roots? Make a conjecture about how many nth roots a number will have depending on whether n is odd or even.

Enrichment 10-3 Explorin L4

Patterns in Algebra

Use your calculator to find the roots of each integer below. Round your answer to the nearest thousandth.

n	$\sqrt{n}$	$\sqrt[3]{n}$	$\sqrt[4]{n}$	$\sqrt[5]{n}$
0				
1				
−1				
2				
−2				
8				
−8				
16				
−16				
32				
−32				
64				
−64				

1. What conjecture can you make about any positive root of a negative number?
2. What conjecture can you make about any root of 0? What is the tenth root of 0? the hundredth root? the nth root?
3. What conjecture can you make about any root of 1? What is the tenth root of 1? the hundredth root? the nth root?

Vocabulary Builder

Square Roots and Cube Roots

Students use geometric models for the area of a square and the volume of a cube to help them understand the concepts of square roots and cube roots.

Guided Instruction

Before beginning the activity, remind students of the formulas for finding the area of a parallelogram and the volume of a rectangular prism. Show students that since squares and cubes are special types of parallelograms and prisms in which all of the side lengths are equal, the formulas $A = s^2$ and $V = s^3$ can be used to represent their areas and volumes, respectively.

Checkpoint Quiz

Use this Checkpoint Quiz to check students' understanding of the skills and concepts of Lessons 10-1 through 10-3.

All in One Resources

- Checkpoint Quiz 1

Vocabulary Builder

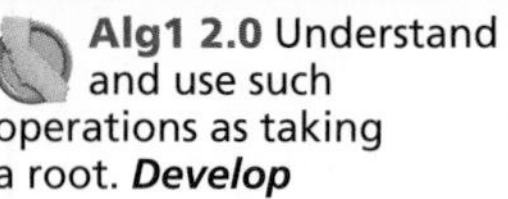

Alg1 2.0 Understand and use such operations as taking a root. ***Develop***

Square Roots and Cube Roots

You can use geometry to understand some of the vocabulary used in algebra. **1–4. See right.**

1. Use the formula $A = s^2$ to find the side length of each square below.

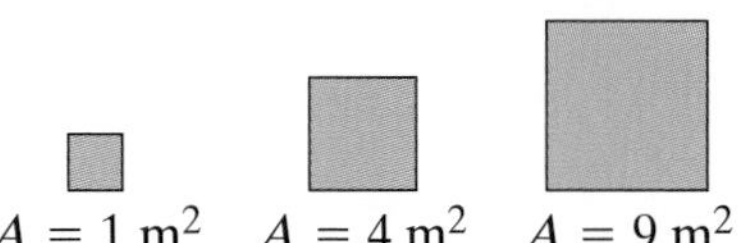

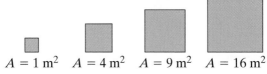

$A = 1\text{ m}^2$ $A = 4\text{ m}^2$ $A = 9\text{ m}^2$ $A = 16\text{ m}^2$

2. **Reasoning** Why is $\sqrt{n}$ called the *square* root of n?
3. Use the formula $V = s^3$ to find the side length of each cube below.

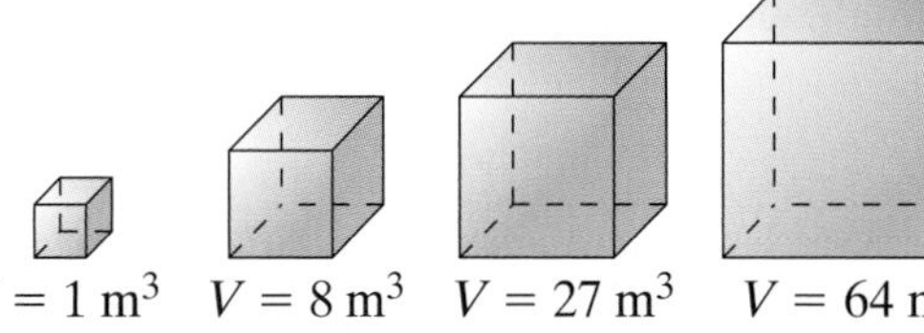

$V = 1\text{ m}^3$ $V = 8\text{ m}^3$ $V = 27\text{ m}^3$ $V = 64\text{ m}^3$

4. **Reasoning** Why is $\sqrt[3]{n}$ called the *cube* root of n?

Answers:

1. 1 m, 2 m, 3 m, 4 m
2. Answers may vary. Sample: When you raise a number to the second power, it represents the area of a square.
3. 1 m, 2 m, 3 m, 4 m
4. Answers may vary. Sample: When you raise a number to the third power, it represents the volume of a cube.

Checkpoint Quiz 1

Lessons 10-1 through 10-3

Write each expression using a single exponent.

1. $4.7^6 \cdot 4.7^{15}$ 4.7^{21}
2. $(-4)^2 \cdot (-4)^7$ $(-4)^9$
3. $(t^{12})^{-5}$ t^{-60}
4. $\frac{m^{10}}{m^2}$ m^8
5. $\frac{6^5}{6^3}$ 6^2
6. $(8^3)^7$ 8^{21}

Simplify each expression.

7. $(4a)^2$ $16a^2$
8. $(x^2y^4)^3$ x^6y^{12}
9. $\sqrt[4]{16}$ 2
10. $\sqrt[3]{-1}$ –1
11. $3 + \sqrt{5 \cdot 20}$ 13
12. $\sqrt[3]{128 - 3} - 8 \cdot 2$ –11

378

10-4a Activity Lab

Modeling Expressions

Alg1 2.0 Simplify expressions before solving linear equations in one variable. ***Introduce***

MR 2.5 Use a variety of methods, such as diagrams and models, to explain mathematical reasoning. ***Develop***

Two students from Garth School bicycled to a game. Three buses of students also went to the game. From Greenly School, four students on bicycles and two buses went to the game. Each bus carried the same number of students. You can model this situation with a diagram.

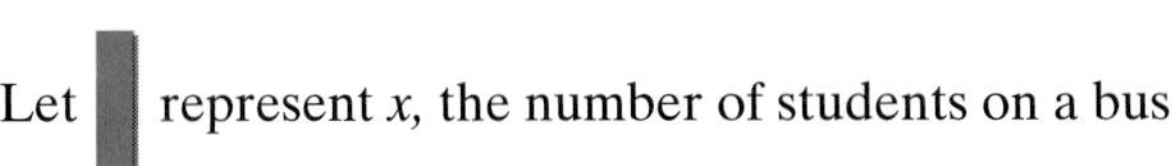

Let ▌ represent x, the number of students on a bus.

Let □ represent a student arriving by bicycle.

The diagrams below model the total number of students at the game.

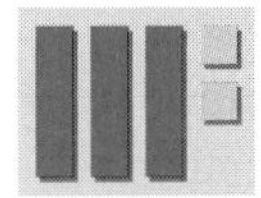

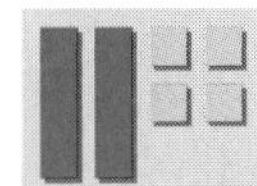

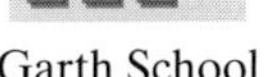

Garth School   Greenly School

Exercises

1. Write two algebraic expressions, one for the number of students from Garth School who went to the game and one for the number of students from Greenly School who went to the game. $3x + 2$, $2x + 4$
2. **a.** How many buses were there in all at the game? 5
   b. How many students rode bicycles to the game? 6
3. Use your answers to Exercise 2 to write an algebraic expression that represents the total number of students from the two schools who went to the game. $5x + 6$
4. **Reasoning** How are your algebraic expressions in Exercise 1 related to your algebraic expression in Exercise 3?

4. The sum of the two expressions in Exercise 1 equals the expression in Exercise 3.

Copy and complete the algebraic expression for each diagram.

5. 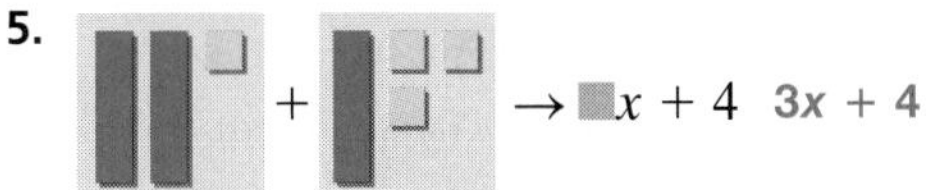 $\rightarrow$ ■$x + 4$ $3x + 4$

6. 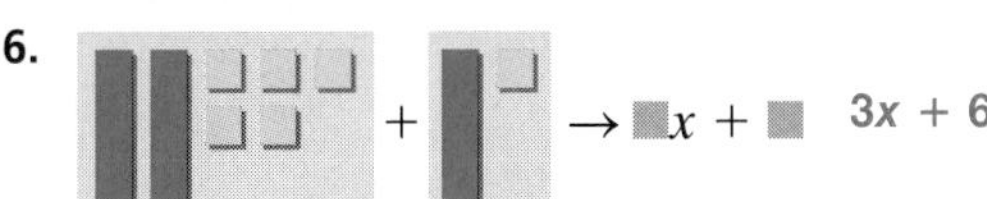 $\rightarrow$ ■$x +$ ■ $3x + 6$

7. A student wrote the equation $3x + 2 + 5x + 1 =$ ■$x + 3$. What number should the student use to fill in the blank? Justify your reasoning. 8; the sum of $3x$ and $5x$ is $8x$.

Activity Lab

Modeling Expressions

Students use diagrams to model expressions that can be generated from real-world problems. This activity prepares students to simplify expressions and solve equations with more than one variable term.

Guided Instruction

Error Prevention!

Before beginning the activity, have students use the diagram symbols to convince themselves that the length of the x-symbol is not an exact multiple of the unit symbol. The x-symbol is representing an unknown number rather than a specific length.

Connection to Algebra
Many students are not accustomed to expressing quantities symbolically because they are used to finding numerical answers. Explain that algebra provides a way of thinking about quantities and expressing the relationships between them even when we don't know their values.

Universal Access
Visual Learners
Have students make a chart with three columns wide enough to accommodate the diagrams. Label the columns Garth School, Greenleaf School, and Granville School. Have students draw the corresponding symbols in each column. They could also write "x" and "1" underneath each symbol to remind themselves what each symbol represents.

10-4

1. Plan

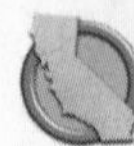

California Content Standards

AF 1.1 Use variables and appropriate operations to write an expression that represents a verbal description. ***Develop***

Alg1 4.0 Simplify expressions before solving linear equations in one variable. ***Introduce***

California Math Background

The terms of an algebraic expression are separated by either + or − signs. Thus the entire expression $(6 + p)(32)$ consists of only one term, while the expression inside the first parentheses contains two terms.

More Math Background: p. 364C

Lesson Planning and Resources

See p. 364E for a list of the resources that support this lesson.

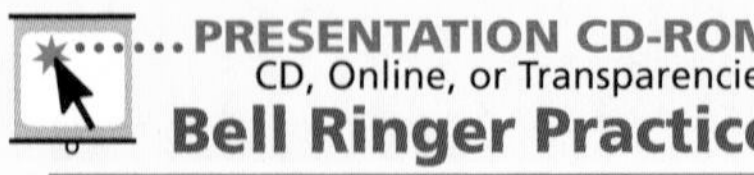

PRESENTATION CD-ROM CD, Online, or Transparencies

Bell Ringer Practice

Check Skills You'll Need
Use student page, transparency, or PowerPoint.
See Math Companion.

California Standards Review
Use transparency or PowerPoint.

GO for Help: Math Companion

10-4 Simplifying Algebraic Expressions

Check Skills You'll Need

Do this in your **Math Companion.**

Vocabulary
- term
- like terms

Use your **Math Companion** *to build your vocabulary.*

California Content Standards

AF 1.1 Use variables and appropriate operations to write an expression that represents a verbal description. ***Develop***

Alg1 4.0 Simplify expressions before solving linear equations in one variable. ***Introduce***

What You'll Learn . . . and Why

You will learn to simplify algebraic expressions. You can use algebraic expressions to represent the total cost when you buy multiple items, such as supplies for a picnic. Simplifying expressions first can make calculations easier.

An expression may have one or more terms. A **term** is a number, a variable, or the product of a number and one or more variables. **Like terms** are terms that have exactly the same variable factors.

Vocabulary Tip

Expressions with only numbers are always like terms.

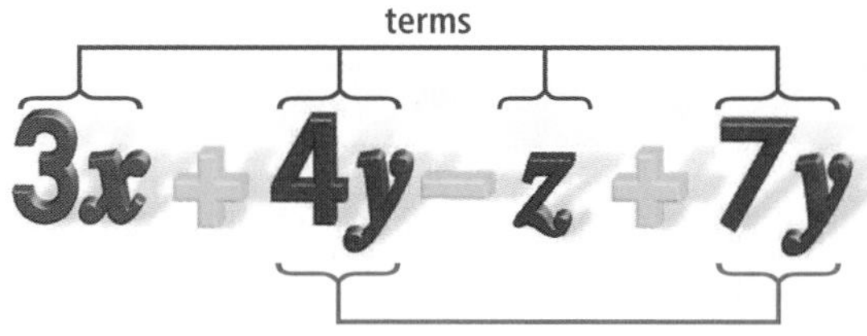

Often a variable does not have a number in front of it. In this case, there is an understood "1" in front of the variable. For example, b is the same as $1b$ and $-a$ is the same as $-1a$.

When you add or subtract like terms, you are combining like terms.

EXAMPLE Combining Like Terms

1 Combine like terms in the expression $5m + 9m + m$.

$5m + 9m + m = 5m + 9m + 1m$ ← **Rewrite *m* as 1*m*.**

$= (5 + 9 + 1)m$ ← **Distributive Property**

$= 15m$ ← **Combine like terms by adding.**

CA Standards Check 1 *Go to your* **Math Companion** *for help.*

1. Combine like terms.

a. $2t + t - 17t$ $-14t$ **b.** $-x - 7x$ $-8x$

Universal Access Solutions for All Learners

Special Needs L1	**Below Level** L2
Give students a copy of Examples 2 and 3. Before they simplify, have students use a colored pencil or pen to circle the like terms in each expression.	Review the rules for multiplying signed numbers, especially the product of two negatives, as shown below. + · + = + − · − = + + · − = − − · + = −

EXAMPLE Writing and Simplifying Expressions

2 **Guided Problem Solving** Garrick buys 5 fruit drinks for a class picnic. Tanya buys 8 fruit drinks for the picnic. Macy buys 13 fruit drinks for the picnic. Write and simplify an algebraic expression to represent the total cost of the drinks.

Words $5\left(\text{cost of one drink}\right)$ plus $8\left(\text{cost of one drink}\right)$ plus $13\left(\text{cost of one drink}\right)$

Let d = the cost of one fruit drink.

Expression $5d \quad + \quad 8d \quad + \quad 13d$

$$5d + 8d + 13d = (5 + 8 + 13)d \quad \leftarrow \text{Distributive Property}$$
$$= 26d \quad \leftarrow \text{Simplify.}$$

The expression $26d$ represents the total cost of the drinks.

CA Standards Check 2 *Go to your* **Math Companion** *for help.*

2. In one trip to a hardware store, you buy 16 wooden boards. On a second trip, you buy 10 more boards. Write and simplify an algebraic expression to represent the total cost of the boards. $26c$

When you use the Distributive Property with subtraction, remember to distribute the negative sign.

EXAMPLE Distributing and Simplifying

Relate **MATH YOU KNOW...**

Simplify $-3(c + 5)$.

$$-3(c + 5) = -3c + (-15) \quad \leftarrow \text{Distributive Property}$$
$$= -3c - 15 \quad \leftarrow \text{Simplify.}$$

... to **ALGEBRA**

3 Simplify $8c - 3(c + 5)$.

$$8c - 3(c + 5) = 8c + (-3)(c + 5) \quad \leftarrow \text{Add the opposite of } 3(c + 5).$$
$$= 8c + [-3c + (-3) \cdot 5] \quad \leftarrow \text{Distributive Property}$$
$$= 8c + (-3c) - 15 \quad \leftarrow \text{Simplify.}$$
$$= [8 + (-3)]c - 15 \quad \leftarrow \text{Distributive Property}$$
$$= 5c - 15 \quad \leftarrow \text{Simplify.}$$

CA Standards Check 3 *Go to your* **Math Companion** *for help.*

3. Simplify each expression.

a. $11 - 2(b + 1)$ $9 - 2b$ **b.** $4(2f + 1) - 3f$ $5f + 4$

Check Your Understanding *Homework prep is in your* **Math Companion.**

2. Teach

Guided Instruction

Visual Learners
In Example 3, have students draw one arrow from the −3 to the c term and another arrow from the −3 to the 5 to emphasize that the multiplier is distributed to each term in the parentheses.

PRESENTATION CD-ROM
CD, Online, or Transparencies

Additional Examples

1 Combine like terms in the expression $8p + 13p + p$. $22p$

2 Carlos buys 6 tubes of paint to make an art project. Shauna buys 8 tubes of paint. Define and use variables to represent the total cost. $6t + 8t = 14t$

3 Simplify the expression $7t - 2(t - 3)$ $5t + 6$

Closure

- *When can you combine terms?* when they are like terms

Advanced Learners L4	**English Learners** EL
Ask: *When is it possible to find a single value for the expression* $3x + 4y$*?* when you have values to substitute for both x and y	Students read terms, such as $5d$ in Example 2, out loud to make sure they understand the meaning of the terms. For example, they should read this term as *5 times the cost of a fruit drink,* not *5 fruit drinks.*

3. Practice

Assignment Guide

Check Your Understanding
See Math Companion.

Homework Exercises

A	Practice by Example	1–25
B	Apply Your Skills	26–40
C	Challenge	41
California Multiple-Choice Practice		42–43
Mixed Review		44–47

Homework Quick Check
To check students' understanding of key skills and concepts, go over Exercises 6, 14, 21, 32, 38, 39.

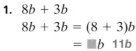

Universal Access Resources

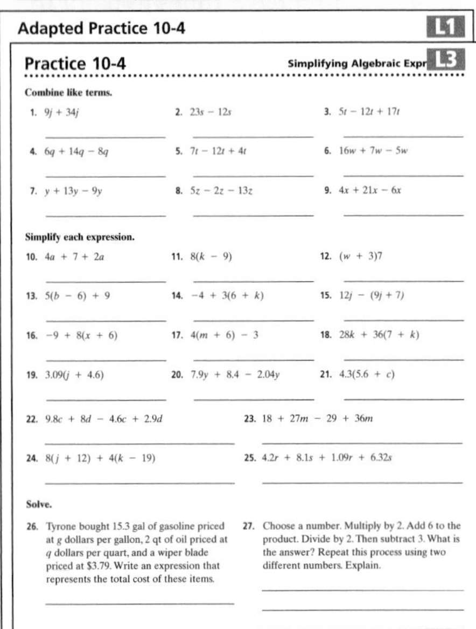

Adapted Practice 10-4 L1

Practice 10-4 Simplifying Algebraic Expr L3

Combine like terms.

1. $9j + 34j$
2. $23s - 12s$
3. $5t - 12t + 17t$
4. $6q + 14q - 8q$
5. $7t - 12t + 4t$
6. $16w + 7w - 5w$
7. $y + 13y - 9y$
8. $5z - 2z - 13z$
9. $4x + 21x - 6x$

Simplify each expression.

10. $4a + 7 + 2a$
11. $8(k - 9)$
12. $(w + 3)7$
13. $5(b - 6) + 9$
14. $-4 + 3(6 + k)$
15. $12j - (9j + 7)$
16. $-9 + 8(x + 6)$
17. $4(m + 6) - 3$
18. $28k + 36(7 + k)$
19. $3.09(j + 4.6)$
20. $7.9y + 8.4 - 2.04y$
21. $4.3(5.6 + c)$
22. $9.8c + 8d - 4.6c + 2.9d$
23. $18 + 27m - 29 + 36m$
24. $8(j + 12) + 4(k - 19)$
25. $4.2r + 8.1s + 1.09r + 6.32s$

Solve.

26. Tyrone bought 15.3 gal of gasoline priced at g dollars per gallon, 2 qt of oil priced at q dollars per quart, and a wiper blade priced at $3.79. Write an expression that represents the total cost of these items.
27. Choose a number. Multiply by 2. Add 6 to the product. Divide by 2. Then subtract 3. What is the answer? Repeat this process using two different numbers. Explain.

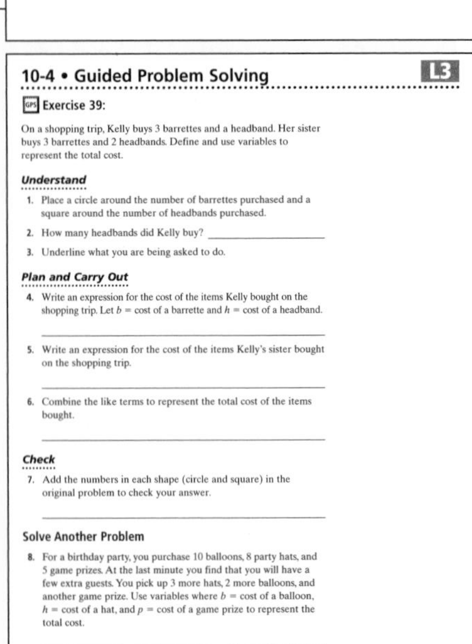

10-4 • Guided Problem Solving L3

GPS **Exercise 39:**

On a shopping trip, Kelly buys 3 barrettes and a headband. Her sister buys 3 barrettes and 2 headbands. Define and use variables to represent the total cost.

Understand

1. Place a circle around the number of barrettes purchased and a square around the number of headbands purchased.
2. How many headbands did Kelly buy? ______
3. Underline what you are being asked to do.

Plan and Carry Out

4. Write an expression for the cost of the items Kelly bought on the shopping trip. Let b = cost of a barrette and h = cost of a headband.
5. Write an expression for the cost of the items Kelly's sister bought on the shopping trip.
6. Combine the like terms to represent the total cost of the items bought.

Check

7. Add the numbers in each shape (circle and square) in the original problem to check your answer.

Solve Another Problem

8. For a birthday party, you purchase 10 balloons, 8 party hats, and 5 game prizes. At the last minute you find that you will have a few extra guests. You pick up 3 more hats, 2 more balloons, and another game prize. Use variables where b = cost of a balloon, h = cost of a hat, and p = cost of a game prize to represent the total cost.

Standards Practice

GO for Help: MathXL

AF 1.1, Alg1 4.0

A Practice by Example

Example 1 (page 380)

Combine like terms.

1. $8b + 3b$
   $8b + 3b = (8 + 3)b$
   $= \blacksquare b$ **11b**

Guided Practice This exercise has been started for you!

GO for Help

2. $9r + 22r$ **31r**
3. $34x - 3x$ **31x**
4. $19z - 24z + 6z$ **z**
5. $-25t + 21t - 7t$ **−11t**
6. $-13d - 17d + 32d$ **2d**
7. $-6a + a + 28a$ **23a**
8. $29f - f + 6f$ **34f**
9. $j - 4j - 15j$ **−18j**
10. $-2m + 5m - 6m$ **−3m**

Example 2 (page 381)

Simplify each expression.

11. $3a + 2 + a$
    $3a + 2 + a = 3a + a + 2$
    $= (3 + 1)a + 2$ **4a + 2**

Guided Practice This exercise has been started for you!

Homework Video Tutor

For: Examples 1–3
Visit: PHSchool.com
Web Code: axe-1004

12. $2x + 1 + 3x$ **5x + 1**
13. $q + 4q - 3$ **5q − 3**
14. $5n - 6 + 4n + 3$ **9n − 3**
15. $2 - 3y - 8 + y$ **−6 − 2y**
16. $9 - 7t + 1 + 4t$ **10 − 3t**
17. $3d - d + 8 - 9d$ **−7d + 8**
18. For the summer, Tai buys 3 T-shirts. Her brother buys 4 T-shirts. Her sister buys 5 T-shirts. Write and simplify an algebraic expression to represent the total cost of the T-shirts. **12c**

Example 3 (page 381)

Simplify each expression.

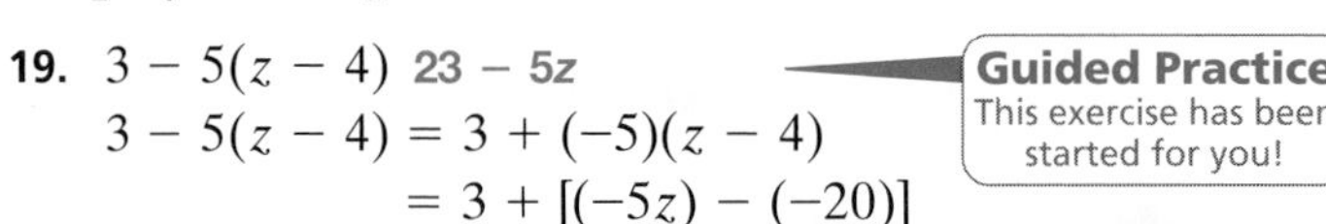

19. $3 - 5(z - 4)$ **23 − 5z**
    $3 - 5(z - 4) = 3 + (-5)(z - 4)$
    $= 3 + [(-5z) - (-20)]$

Guided Practice This exercise has been started for you!

20. $7(t + 8.5) - 5t$ **2t + 59.5**
21. $-8(m + 2) - 19m$ **−27m − 16**
22. $4.3(5.6 + c) + 9c$ **13.3c + 24.08**
23. $-5b - 2(b - 1)$ **−7b + 2**
24. $16h - 4(h + 3) - 4h$ **8h − 12**
25. $\frac{1}{2}(6p + 8) - 7 + 2p$ **5p − 3**

B Apply Your Skills

26. **Guided Problem Solving** Simone drove to the mall and back home. Then she drove 10 mi to a market and back. The next day, she made two trips from home to the mall. Write and simplify an algebraic expression to represent the total distance Simone traveled.
    - **Draw a diagram** Show the trips between the mall, the market, and home.

    - What quantity do you need to represent with a variable? **Let d = distance to the mall. 6d + 20**

SCAFFOLDED
Problem Solving

27. Let t = cost of 1 lb of turkey; $6t$.
28. Let s = cost of 1 lb of cole slaw; $3s$.
29. Let c = cost of 1 lb of cheese; $4c$.
30. $6t + 3s + 4c$

You buy 6 lb of turkey, 3 lb of cole slaw, and 4 lb of cheese for a party.
27–30. See left.

27. Define and use a variable to represent the cost of the turkey.
28. Define and use a variable to represent the cost of the cole slaw.
29. Define and use a variable to represent the cost of the cheese.
30. Use your expressions from Exercises 27–29 to write an expression to represent the total cost of the food.
31. You buy another 4 lb of turkey, 2 lb of cole slaw, and 3 lb of cheese for the party. Write and simplify an expression to represent the total cost of all of the food for the party. $10t + 5s + 7c$

Simplify each expression.

32. $7b + 5 - 9b + c$ $-2b + c + 5$
33. $x + 2(x - y)$ $3x - 2y$
34. $(5x + y) - (4x - 9)$ $x + y + 9$
35. $3(t - 14) - 5(t + 12)$ $-2t - 102$
36. $9(a + 1.4b) + 8(b - 16a)$ $-119a + 20.6b$
37. $4.2x + 8.1y + 1.8y - 2.1x$ $2.1x + 9.9y$
38. **Writing in Math** One way to organize a music collection is by categories of music. Explain how combining like terms is similar to organizing a music collection by categories. See left.
39. GPS On a shopping trip, Kelly buys 3 barrettes and a headband. Her sister buys 3 barrettes and 2 headbands. Define and use variables to represent the total cost. See left.
40. **Reasoning** Does $5a + 5b = 10ab$? Explain. No; a and b are not like terms and cannot be combined.

38. Answers may vary. Sample: Similar categories of music are grouped together, and like terms are grouped together.
39. Let b = cost of 1 barrette and h = cost of 1 headband; $6b + 3h$.

Challenge

41. Solve $3r + 4 - 7r = 28$. -6

Multiple Choice Practice and Mixed Review

For California Standards Tutorials, visit PHSchool.com. Web Code: axq-9045

Alg1 4.0

42. Expand and simplify $5(3w - 7) + 9w$. D

  Ⓐ $17w - 7$ Ⓑ $15w - 35 + 9w$ Ⓒ $17w - 35$ Ⓓ $24w - 35$

AF 3.3

43. Which graph contains all the points represented by the coordinate pairs in the table at the right? B

x	-1	$-\frac{1}{2}$	1
y	-3	-2	1

Ⓐ
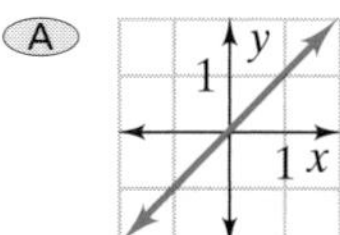

Ⓑ
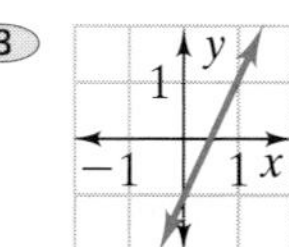

Ⓒ
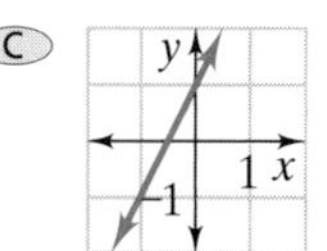

Ⓓ
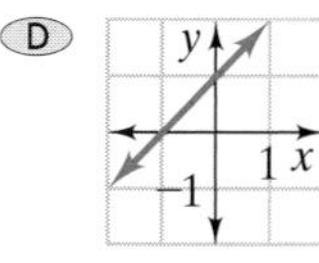

Lesson 10-1

Write each expression using a single exponent.

44. $5^2 \cdot 5^{13}$ 5^{15}
45. $f^{-2} \cdot f^9$ f^7
46. $\frac{3^8}{3^5}$ 3^3
47. $\frac{x^4}{x^3} \cdot x^5$ x^6

Online Lesson Quiz Visit: PHSchool.com Web Code: axa-1004

4. Assess & Reteach

PRESENTATION CD-ROM
CD, Online, or Transparencies

Lesson Quiz

Simplify each expression.

1. $-13c + c$ $-12c$
2. $4y - 7 + 8y$ $12y - 7$
3. $1 - 6(b - 9)$ $-6b + 55$
4. Karen buys 4 boxes of cereal at the grocery store. Her brother, David, buys 2 boxes of cereal. Define and use variables to represent the total cost. Let c = the cost of a box of cereal. Then $6c$ represents the total cost.

Alternative Assessment

Write a term on the board such as $12z$. Several students take turns writing like terms under it. Then other students write unlike terms in a different place on the board.

California Resources

Standards Mastery

- Standards Review Transparencies
- Standards Review and Practice Workbook
- Math Companion

Math Intervention

- Skills Review and Practice Workbook
- Math XL

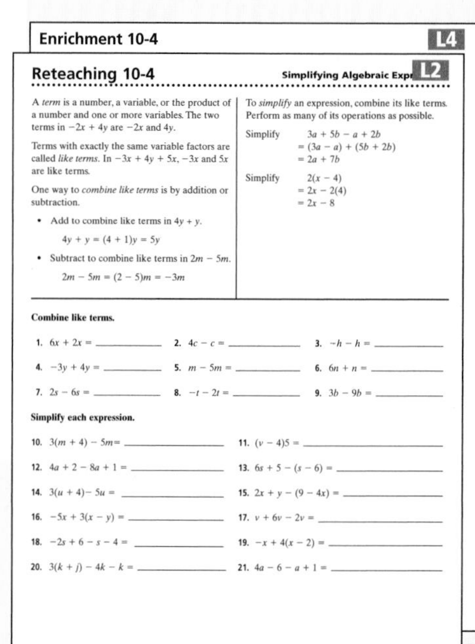

Enrichment 10-4 L4

Reteaching 10-4 Simplifying Algebraic Expr... L2

A *term* is a number, a variable, or the product of a number and one or more variables. The two terms in $-2x + 4y$ are $-2x$ and $4y$.

Terms with exactly the same variable factors are called *like terms*. In $-3x + 4y + 5x$, $-3x$ and $5x$ are like terms.

One way to *combine like terms* is by addition or subtraction.

- Add to combine like terms in $4y + y$.
  $4y + y = (4 + 1)y = 5y$
- Subtract to combine like terms in $2m - 5m$.
  $2m - 5m = (2 - 5)m = -3m$

To *simplify* an expression, combine its like terms. Perform as many of its operations as possible.

Simplify $3a + 5b - a + 2b$
$= (3a - a) + (5b + 2b)$
$= 2a + 7b$

Simplify $2(x - 4)$
$= 2x - 2(4)$
$= 2x - 8$

Combine like terms.

1. $6x + 2x =$ ______
2. $4c - c =$ ______
3. $-h - h =$ ______
4. $-3y + 4y =$ ______
5. $m - 5m =$ ______
6. $6n + n =$ ______
7. $2s - 6s =$ ______
8. $-t - 2t =$ ______
9. $3b - 9b =$ ______

Simplify each expression.

10. $3(m + 4) - 5m =$ ______
11. $(v - 4)5 =$ ______
12. $4a + 2 - 8a + 1 =$ ______
13. $6s + 5 - (s - 6) =$ ______
14. $3(u + 4) - 5u =$ ______
15. $2x + y - (9 - 4x) =$ ______
16. $-5x + 3(x - y) =$ ______
17. $v + 6v - 2v =$ ______
18. $-2s + 6 - s - 4 =$ ______
19. $-x + 4(x - 2) =$ ______
20. $3(k + j) - 4k - k =$ ______
21. $4a - 6 - a + 1 =$ ______

Algebraic Thinking

Writing Expressions

In this activity, students perform specific sequences of operations—here called "number tricks"—on their own ages. Then they write algebraic expressions representing their answers and compare these to their ages to understand how the tricks work.

Guided Instruction

Activity

For each trick, ask students to describe the relationship between the "secret" age and the number that results after Step 6. Ask:

- *What happens when you let* x *be the age, perform the operations on* x*, and then simplify the polynomial?* **Sample: When you simplify the polynomial, the answer has the same relationship to the number you started with, such as 1 more for the first number trick and 1 less for the second number trick.**
- *What would you have to do to make up your own number trick so you would divide the last number by 2 to guess the correct age?* **Sample: Use operations on the variable that, when simplified, give the result 2*x*. When this expression is divided by 2, the result will be *x*.**

AF 1.1 Use variables and appropriate operations to write an expression that represents a verbal description. ***Develop***

Writing Expressions

ACTIVITY

William enjoys number tricks. Below is a number trick he uses to guess his friends' ages.

Number Trick 1

1. Start with your age.	4. Multiply the result by 2.
2. Multiply your age by 3.	5. Subtract 2 from the result.
3. Add 4 to the result.	6. Divide the result by 6. Tell me your answer.

1. How is your age related to the result in Step 6? How is William able to tell his friends' ages from the answer they tell him? **1. Your age is one less than the answer; William subtracts one from the answer.**
2. Let x be your age. Use x to write an algebraic expression for the answer you get in Step 6. $x + 1$

Here is another number trick William uses to guess his friends' ages.

Number Trick 2

1. Start with your age.	4. Multiply the result by 2.
2. Multiply your age by 4.	5. Add 4 to the result.
3. Subtract 6 from the result.	6. Divide the result by 8. Tell me your answer.

3. How is your age related to the result in Step 6? How is William able to tell his friends' ages from the answer they tell him? **3. Your age is one more than the answer; William adds one to the answer.**
4. Let x be your age. Use x to write an algebraic expression for the answer you get in Step 6. $x - 1$

Exercises

1–3. Check students' work.

1. Write instructions for another number trick with six steps. Trade tricks with a partner.
2. How does the number you chose for Step 1 in your partner's trick compare to the result in Step 6?
3. Use x to write an algebraic expression for the answer in Step 6 of your partner's trick.

10-5a Activity Lab

Modeling Multi-Step Equations

You can use diagrams to model and solve multi-step equations.

Alg1 4.0 Simplify expressions before solving linear equations in one variable. ***Develop***
MR 2.5 Use a variety of methods, such as models, to explain mathematical reasoning. ***Develop***

ACTIVITY

Use a diagram to solve $4x + 4 - x = 10$.

Model the equation. → 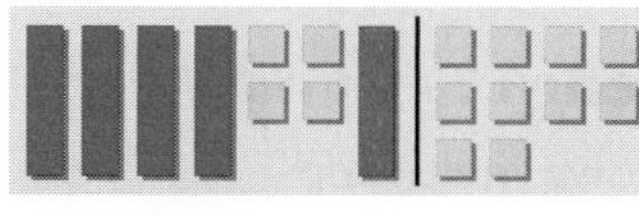 $4x + 4 - x = 10$

Redraw the diagram so the x's are together and the units are together. → 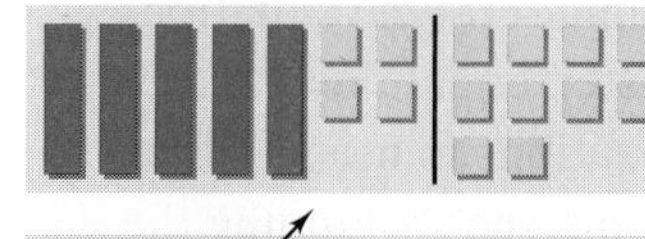 $4x - x + 4 = 10$

Remove the zero pair. Simplify. → 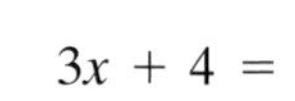 $3x + 4 = 10$

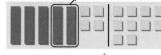

Remove 4 units from each side. → 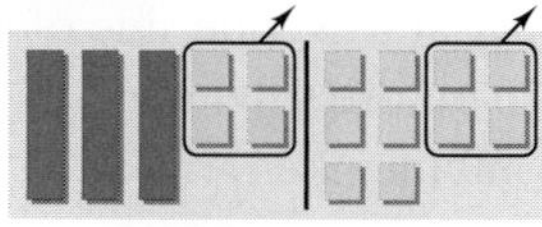 $3x + 4 - 4 = 10 - 4$

Simplify. → 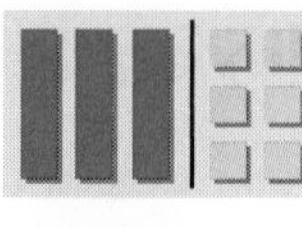 $3x = 6$

Divide each side into 3 equal groups. → 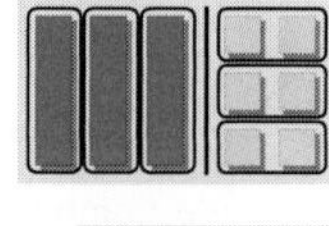 $\frac{3x}{3} = \frac{6}{3}$

Simplify. → 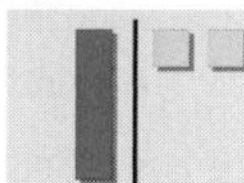 $x = 2$

Exercises

Use a diagram to solve each equation.

1. $6x + 3 - 5x = 12$ 9
2. $x + 3x - 5 = 3$ 2
3. $3x + 2 + 6x = 11$ 1

4. **Reasoning** Which property justifies why you can rewrite $4x + 4 - x = 10$ as $4x - x + 4 = 10$? Comm. Prop. of Add.

Activity Lab

Modeling Multi-Step Equations

By using diagrams, students can gain a concrete understanding of what an equation is and what it means to find its solution.

Guided Instruction

Have students draw a vertical line through each diagram to better visualize the idea of two sides of an equation. Show students that rectangles representing negative x and positive x can be combined to form zero pairs.

Error Prevention!

Remind students that the size of the bar used to represent x in a diagram is not related to its value (for example, some students might think the value of x is greater than 1 because the bar is larger than a unit square).

Help students resist the urge to move the unit squares from one side of the equation to the other. Remind them that each side is equivalent and that what is done to one side must be done to the other side.

10-5

1. Plan

California Content Standards

Alg1 4.0 Simplify expressions before solving linear equations in one variable. ***Develop***

Alg1 5.0 Solve multistep problems, including word problems, involving linear equations in one variable and provide justification for each step. ***Introduce***

California Math Background

Equations are made up of numbers, operations, and expressions with variables. Simplifying, by combining like terms and using the Distributive Property, can be part of the process of solving an equation.

More Math Background: p. 364C

Lesson Planning and Resources

See p. 364E for a list of the resources that support this lesson.

...PRESENTATION CD-ROM
CD, Online, or Transparencies
Bell Ringer Practice

Check Skills You'll Need
Use student page, transparency, or PowerPoint.
See Math Companion.

California Standards Review
Use transparency or PowerPoint.

10-5 Solving Multi-Step Equations

Check Skills You'll Need
Do this in your **Math Companion.**

Vocabulary
Review:
- like terms
- Distributive Property

Use your **Math Companion** *to build your vocabulary.*

California Content Standards

Alg1 4.0 Simplify expressions before solving linear equations in one variable. ***Develop***

Alg1 5.0 Solve multistep problems, including word problems, involving linear equations in one variable and provide justification for each step. ***Introduce***

What You'll Learn . . . and Why

You will learn to solve multi-step equations. You can model some situations with one- and two-step equations. You need multi-step equations to model more complicated problems, such as finding the number of canned goods needed to reach the goal for a food drive.

You need to simplify at least one side of a multi-step equation before solving it. To simplify, you combine like terms.

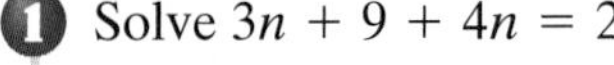

EXAMPLE Simplifying Before Solving an Equation

1 Solve $3n + 9 + 4n = 2$.

$3n + 9 + 4n = 2$

$3n + 4n + 9 = 2$ ← Commutative Property

$7n + 9 = 2$ ← Combine like terms.

$7n + 9 - 9 = 2 - 9$ ← Subtraction Property of Equality

$7n = -7$ ← Simplify.

$\frac{7n}{7} = \frac{-7}{7}$ ← Isolate the variable. Use the Division Property of Equality.

$n = -1$ ← Simplify.

Check $3n + 9 + 4n = 2$

$3(-1) + 9 + 4(-1) \stackrel{?}{=} 2$ ← Substitute −1 for *n*.

$2 = 2$ ✔ ← The solution checks.

CA Standards Check 1 *Go to your* **Math Companion** *for help.*

1. Solve each equation.

a. $-15 = 5b + 12 - 2b + 6$ −11 **b.** $9 = 8w + 45 - 12w$ 9

Universal Access Solutions for All Learners

Special Needs L1	**Below Level** L2
When working on More Than One Way, providing a number line may help students subtract the decimal numbers 8.3 and 14.5 correctly.	Have students, before writing any steps, say aloud what has been done to the variable and what operation will undo that.

You can use the Distributive Property to simplify an expression in an equation.

EXAMPLE Using the Distributive Property

Relate **MATH YOU KNOW...** *... to* **ALGEBRA**

Simplify $24(3 + a)$ using the Distributive Property.

$$24(3 + a) = 24 \cdot 3 + 24a \quad \leftarrow \text{Distributive Property}$$
$$= 72 + 24a \quad \leftarrow \text{Simplify.}$$

2 **Guided Problem Solving** Your class hopes to collect 120 canned goods for a food drive at your school. During the first week of the drive, the 24 students in your class bring an average of 3 canned goods each. For your class to reach its goal, how many more canned goods does each student need to bring?

Write an equation to describe the situation.

Words	24 students	times	(3 cans per student	+	additional cans per student)	=	120 cans

Let a = the number of additional canned goods.

Expression	24	$\cdot$	(3	+	a)	=	120

$$24(3 + a) = 120$$
$$24 \cdot 3 + 24a = 120 \quad \leftarrow \text{Distributive Property}$$
$$72 + 24a = 120 \quad \leftarrow \text{Simplify.}$$
$$72 - 72 + 24a = 120 - 72 \quad \leftarrow \text{Subtraction Property of Equality}$$
$$24a = 48 \quad \leftarrow \text{Simplify.}$$
$$\frac{24a}{24} = \frac{48}{24} \quad \leftarrow \text{Division Property of Equality}$$
$$a = 2 \quad \leftarrow \text{Simplify.}$$

Each student needs to bring 2 additional canned goods.

Check for Reasonableness Round 24 to 25. The class collected about $25 \cdot 3$, or 75, canned goods. They need to collect about 50 more, or about 2 more per student. The answer is reasonable.

Problem Solving Tip

Be sure to answer the question asked. You need to find the additional number of canned goods each student needs to bring, not the total number.

CA Standards Check 2 *Go to your* **Math Companion** *for help.*

2. Your class goes to an amusement park. Admission is \$10 for each student and \$15 for each chaperone. The total cost is \$380. There are 12 girls in your class and 6 chaperones on the trip. How many boys are in your class? 17 boys

2. Teach

Guided Instruction

Teaching Tip

Explain that students can save time and work if they form the habit of first examining the equation for terms that can be combined or simplified before using any further steps to isolate the variable.

Example 2

Have students ensure that the equation they write makes sense with the question being asked. Ask:

- *What does the variable* a *represent?* the number of additional cans
- *What does the product* $24(3 + a)$ *represent?* the total number of cans collected by the 24 students

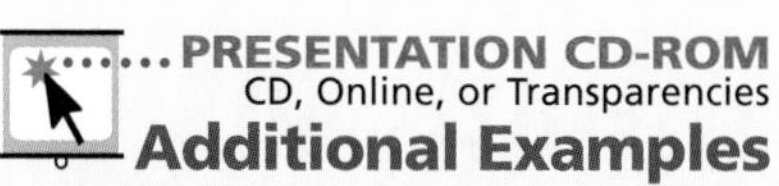

... PRESENTATION CD-ROM
CD, Online, or Transparencies

Additional Examples

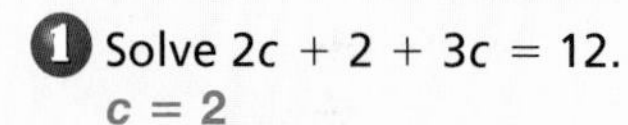

1. Solve $2c + 2 + 3c = 12$. $c = 2$
2. Eight cheerleaders set a goal of selling 424 boxes of cards to raise money. After two weeks, each cheerleader has sold 28 boxes. How many more boxes must each cheerleader sell? 25 boxes

Advanced Learners L4

Students write and solve a problem similar to Example 2. Sample: The yearbook printing costs are \$2,280. If 120 students pay an average of \$15, how much more per student must be collected? \$4

English Learners EL

For Example 2, review the meaning of the word *average* and the words *per student.* Make sure students know they are finding the number of cans *each* of the 24 students still has to collect, not the total number the class still has to collect.

Closure

- *When can you simplify before solving an equation?* Sample: when you can combine like terms on either side of the equation or use the Distributive Property

You can also use division to simplify equations. The models below show one way to simplify the equation $2(x + 1) = 12$. First divide each side by 2, grouping the numbers and variables into two equal groups. Then remove one group from each side. The simplified equation is $x + 1 = 6$. You can then solve for x.

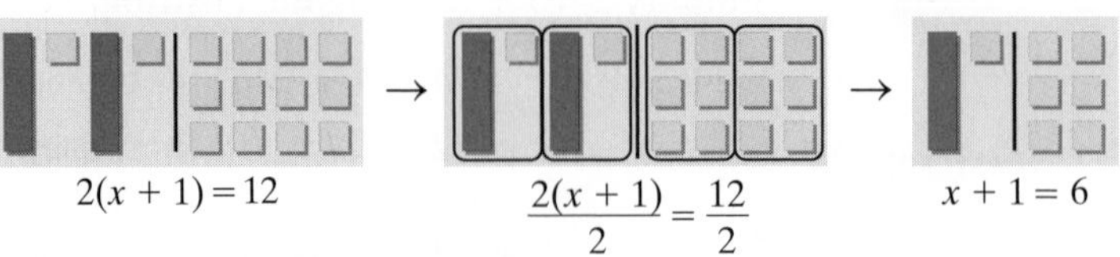

$2(x + 1) = 12$ → $\frac{2(x + 1)}{2} = \frac{12}{2}$ → $x + 1 = 6$

More Than One Way

Solve the equation $5(2.9 + k) = 8.3$.

Michelle's Method

I'll use the Distributive Property to eliminate the parentheses.

$5(2.9 + k) = 8.3$

$5 \cdot 2.9 + 5k = 8.3$ ← **Distributive Property**

$14.5 + 5k = 8.3$ ← **Simplify.**

$14.5 - 14.5 + 5k = 8.3 - 14.5$ ← **Subtraction Property of Equality**

$5k = -6.2$ ← **Simplify.**

$\frac{5k}{5} = \frac{-6.2}{5}$ ← **Division Property of Equality**

$k = -1.24$ ← **Simplify.**

Daryl's Method

I'll use division to eliminate the parentheses.

$5(2.9 + k) = 8.3$

$\frac{5(2.9 - k)}{5} = \frac{8.3}{5}$ ← **Division Property of Equality**

$2.9 + k = 1.66$ ← **Simplify.**

$2.9 - 2.9 + k = 1.66 - 2.9$ ← **Subtraction Property of Equality**

$k = -1.24$ ← **Simplify.**

Choose a Method

Solve $3(m - 6.5) = 27$. Describe your method and explain why you chose it. 15.5; check students' work.

Check Your Understanding *Homework prep is in your* **Math Companion.**

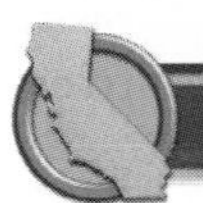

Standards Practice

GO for Help: MathXL

Alg1 4.0, Alg1 5.0

A Practice by Example

Example 1 (page 386)

GO for Help

Homework Video Tutor

For: Examples 1–2
Visit: PHSchool.com
Web Code: axe-1005

Solve each equation. Check the solution.

1. $5h + 2 - h = 22$
$5h - h + 2 = 22$
$4h + 2 = 22$
$4h + 2 - 2 = 22 - 2$ 5

Guided Practice This exercise has been started for you!

2. $-8 = z + 3z$ −2

3. $56 = -4t + 5 + 7t$ 17

4. $3b + b - 8 = 4$ 3

5. $3a + 12 - 6a = -9$ 7

6. $21 = 6 - x - 4x$ −3

7. $2m + 8 - 4m = 28$ −10

8. $-3y + 4 + 5y = -6$ −5

9. $78 = 3c + 12 - c + 4$ 31

Example 2 (page 387)

Solve each equation. Justify each step.

10. $36 = 3(w + 5)$
$36 = 3w + 3 \cdot 5$
$36 = 3w + 15$ 7

Guided Practice This exercise has been started for you!

11. $4(m + 3) = -32$ −11

12. $14 = 2(s + 5)$ 2

13. $40 = 5(d - 2)$ 10

14. $2(z - 1) = 16$ 9

15. $-2(x - 9) = -24$ 21

16. $7(4 + t) = -84$ −16

17. You want to buy 4 lb of Cortland apples and some Gala apples. Each variety of apple cost \$1.20/lb. You can spend \$7.20. How many pounds of Gala apples can you buy? 2 lb

B Apply Your Skills

18. Guided Problem Solving You mailed three identical letters weighing more than 1 oz each. Mailing each letter cost \$.39 for the first ounce, plus \$.24 for each additional ounce. Each letter required \$1.59 postage. How much did each letter weigh? 6 oz

- **Make a Plan** Write and solve an equation to solve for x, the number of additional ounces.
- **Check the Answer** Be sure you answer the question asked.

Solve each equation. Justify each step.

19. $15 = -3(c - 1) + 9$ −1

20. $2(1.5n + 4) - 6n = -7$ 5

21. $2(z - 20) + 3z = 10$ 10

22. $5s - 2 + 3(s - 11) = 5$ 5

GPS **23.** An employee earns \$7.00 per hour for the first 35 hours worked in a week and \$10.50 for every hour over 35. One week's paycheck (before deductions) was for \$308.00. How many hours did the employee work? 41 h

3. Practice

Assignment Guide

Check Your Understanding
See Math Companion.

Homework Exercises

A	Practice by Example	1–17
B	Apply Your Skills	18–32
C	Challenge	33
California Multiple-Choice Practice		34–36
Mixed Review		37–39

Homework Quick Check
To check students' understanding of key skills and concepts, go over Exercises 2, 13, 19, 23, 30, 32.

Universal Access Resources

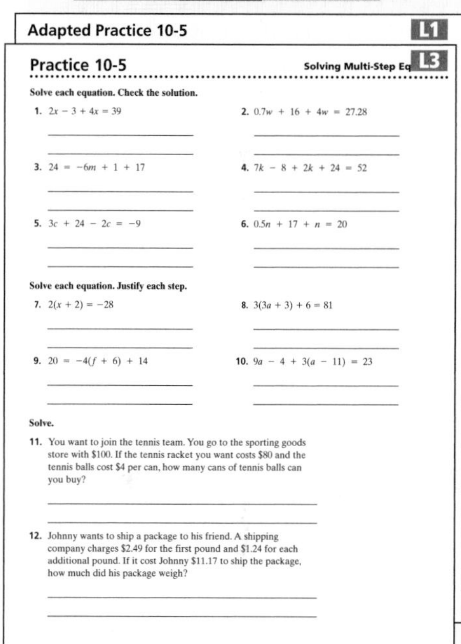

Adapted Practice 10-5 L1

Practice 10-5 Solving Multi-Step Eq L3

Solve each equation. Check the solution.

1. $2x - 3 + 4x = 39$
2. $0.7w + 16 + 4w = 27.28$
3. $24 = -6m + 1 + 17$
4. $7k - 8 + 2k + 24 = 52$
5. $3c + 24 - 2c = -9$
6. $0.5n + 17 + n = 20$

Solve each equation. Justify each step.

7. $2(x + 2) = -28$
8. $3(3a + 3) + 6 = 81$
9. $20 = -4(f + 6) + 14$
10. $9a - 4 + 3(a - 11) = 23$

Solve.

11. You want to join the tennis team. You go to the sporting goods store with \$100. If the tennis racket you want costs \$80 and the tennis balls cost \$4 per can, how many cans of tennis balls can you buy?
12. Johnny wants to ship a package to his friend. A shipping company charges \$2.49 for the first pound and \$1.24 for each additional pound. If it cost Johnny \$11.17 to ship the package, how much did his package weigh?

10-5 • Guided Problem Solving L3

GPS Exercise 23:

An employee earns \$7.00 an hour for the first 35 hours worked in a week and \$10.50 for every hour over 35. One week's paycheck (before deductions) was for \$308.00. How many hours did the employee work?

Understand

1. How much per hour does the employee make for the first 35 hours?
2. How much per hour does the employee make after 35 hours of work?
3. How much was the week's paycheck? ______
4. What is it you are asked to find? ______

Plan and Carry Out

5. Write an equation for this situation. Multiply the hourly rate by 35 hours. Add the overtime rate multiplied by an unknown, x. Set this sum equal to the total amount of the check.
6. Solve for x, the number of overtime hours the employee worked.
7. What do you have to do to find the total hours worked?
8. How many total hours did the employee work? ______

Check

9. Does the answer check? Is 35 times \$7 plus the overtime hours equal to the total check?

Solve Another Problem

10. A college student has a long-distance phone card. The phone card rate for the first 100 minutes is 12 cents per minute and then goes to 15 cents per minute after that. If the student had a long distance charge of \$21, how many total minutes did the student talk?

4. Assess & Reteach

PRESENTATION CD-ROM
CD, Online, or Transparencies

Lesson Quiz

Solve the following equations.

1. $2m + 4 - 8m = 28$ $m = -4$
2. $2(f - 1) + f = 37$ $f = 13$
3. $4.5(4x - 12) = 144$ $x = 11$
4. Jasmine earns a certain amount per hour for the first 40 hours worked in a week. Each hour she works over 40 in one week, she earns an additional $4.50 per hour. If Jasmine works 46 hours one week, and earned $383.50 that week, how much does she earn per hour for the first 40 hours? $7.75 per hour

Enrichment 10-5 L4

Reteaching 10-5 Solving Multi-Step Equ[ations] L2

Combining like terms can help solve equations.

Solve: $5n + 6 + 3n = 22$
$5n + 3n + 6 = 22$ ← Commutative Property of Addition
$8n + 6 = 22$ ← Combine like terms.
$8n + 6 - 6 = 22 - 6$ ← Subtraction Property of Equality
$8n = 16$ ← Simplify.
$\frac{8n}{8} = \frac{16}{8}$ ← Division Property of Equality
$n = 2$ ← Simplify.

Check: $5n + 6 + 3n = 22$
$5(2) + 6 + 3(2) \stackrel{?}{=} 22$ ← Substitute 2 for n.
$22 = 22$ ✔ ← The solution checks.

Sometimes you need to distribute a term in order to simplify.

Solve: $4(x + 2) = 28$
$4x + 4 \cdot 2 = 28$ ← Distributive Property
$4x + 8 = 28$ ← Simplify.
$4x + 8 - 8 = 28 - 8$ ← Subtraction Property of Equality
$4x = 20$ ← Simplify.
$\frac{4x}{4} = \frac{20}{4}$ ← Division Property of Equality
$x = 5$ ← Simplify.

Solve each equation. Check the solution.

1. $a - 4a = 36$ $a =$ ______	2. $3b - 5 - 2b = 5$ $b =$ ______	3. $5n + 4 - 8n = -5$ $n =$ ______
4. $12k + 6 = 10$ $k =$ ______	5. $3(x - 4) = 15$ $x =$ ______	6. $y - 8 + 2y = 10$ $y =$ ______
7. $3(s - 10) = 36$ $s =$ ______	8. $-15 = p + 4p$ $p =$ ______	9. $2g + 3g + 5 = 0$ $g =$ ______
10. $6c + 4 - c = 24$ $c =$ ______	11. $3(x - 2) = 15$ $x =$ ______	12. $4y + 9 - 7y = -6$ $y =$ ______
13. $4(z - 2) + z = -13$ $z =$ ______	14. $24 = -2(b - 3) + 8$ $b =$ ______	15. $17 = 3(g + 3) - g$ $g =$ ______

SCAFFOLDED
Problem Solving

When you count by ones from any integer, you are counting consecutive integers. For example, 23, 24, and 25 are consecutive integers.

24. Let n be an integer. Write algebraic expressions for the next two consecutive integers. $n + 1, n + 2$
25. Use your expressions to write an algebraic expression for the sum of n and the next two consecutive integers. $3n + 3$
26. Suppose the sum of three consecutive integers is 48. Write an equation to find n, the first integer. $3n + 3 = 48$
27. Solve your equation for n. 15
28. Use the value of n and your expressions from Exercise 24 to find the next two consecutive integers. 16, 17
29. The sum of three consecutive integers is -255. Write and solve an equation to find the integers. $-86, -85, -84$

Write an equation for each diagram. Then find the unknown lengths.

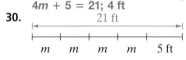

30. $4m + 5 = 21$; 4 ft

21 ft

m m m m 5 ft

31. $3y + 505 = 1{,}000$; 165 in.

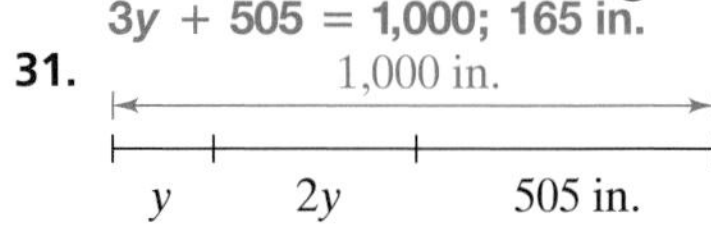

32. **Writing in Math** To solve $5y - 2 - 3y = 8$, can you start by adding 2 to each side? Justify your reasoning. Yes; Add. Prop. of Eq.: $5y - 2 - 3y + 2 = 8 + 2$.

C Challenge

33. Solve $1.5 - 0.25(a + 4) = 3 + 3(0.05 - 0.5a)$. 2.12

Multiple Choice Practice and Mixed Review

For California Standards Tutorials, visit PHSchool.com. Web Code: axq-9045

Alg1 5.0

34. Two classes went to the zoo. Admission was $5 per person. The total cost was $200. One class had 19 people. Solve the equation $5(n + 19) = 200$ to find n, the number of people in the other class. B

    (A) 10 (B) 21 (C) 36 (D) 105

NS 1.3

35. During the softball season, Maggie got a hit 5 times out of every 12 times at bat. Which percent represents Maggie's success at getting hits? C

    (A) 2.4% (B) 29.4% (C) 41.7% (D) 70.6%

MG 3.3

36. Tony leaves his house and bikes west 3.3 mi to the movie theater. He then turns south and bikes 4.1 mi to the pet store. About how far is the pet store from Tony's house? B

    (A) 3.8 mi (B) 5.3 mi (C) 7.4 mi (D) 27.7 mi

Lesson 3-4 **Solve each equation.**

37. $\frac{n}{4} - 1 = 10$ 44
38. $\frac{x}{-5} - 7 = 8$ -75
39. $\frac{a}{8} + 12 = -4$ -128

Visit: PHSchool.com **Web Code:** axa-1005

California Resources

Standards Mastery
- Standards Review Transparencies
- Standards Review and Practice Workbook
- Math Companion

Math Intervention
- Skills Review and Practice Workbook
- Math XL

Alternative Assessment

Students each write an expression that contains two like terms, with the variable n, and two constants. Then they set their expression equal to 24 and solve the equation.

Mathematical Reasoning

For Use With Lesson 10-5

Justify Each Step

You use the properties of numbers and equality to solve equations. Supporting your solutions with justification for each step will help you avoid reasoning mistakes.

Alg1 5.0 Solve multistep problems involving linear equations and provide justification for each step. ***Develop***
MR 2.6 Support solutions with evidence in both verbal and symbolic work. ***Develop***

1. **Error Analysis** A student correctly solved the equation below but gave incorrect justifications for some of the steps. Give a correct justification for each step.

Step	Justification
$11x + 5 - 4x = -30$	
$11x - 4x + 5 = -30$	Associative Property
$7x + 5 = -30$	Simplify.
$7x + 5 - 5 = -30 - 5$	Multiplication Property of Equality
$7x = -35$	Simplify.
$\frac{7x}{7} = \frac{-35}{7}$	Addition Property of Equality
$x = -5$	Simplify.

2. Solve the equation $9(y + 7) - 44 = 73$. Justify each step. See above.

1. Comm. Prop. of Add.; Simplify; Subt. Prop. of Eq.; Simplify; Div. Prop. of Eq.; Simplify
2. $9(y + 7) - 44 = 73$; Dist. Prop.: $9y + 63 - 44 = 73$; Simplify: $9y + 19 = 73$; Subtr. Prop. of Eq.: $9y = 54$; Div. Prop. of Eq.: $y = 6$

Checkpoint Quiz 2

Lessons 10-4 through 10-5

Simplify each expression.

1. $-3m + 4 - 5m$ $-8m + 4$
2. $1.7(g - 0.5) - 6.4$ $1.7g - 7.25$
3. $2h - 4(h - 5)$ $-2h + 20$
4. $28 - 10(a - 14) + 7a$ $168 - 3a$

Solve each equation.

5. $-3.5 - 4f + 2.5f = 10$ -9
6. $-z - (z - 6) = 8$ -1
7. $-1 = 4.5(x - 3) - 2x$ 5
8. $-7t + 16t + 4 = -14$ -2
9. Your class hopes to collect 1,200 returnable bottles to raise money for a field trip. During the first week, the 24 students in the class collect an average of 34 bottles each. How many more bottles should each student in the class collect? 16 bottles

Mathematical Reasoning

Justify Each Step

Students learn how justifying the steps used to solve an equation can help them understand equations and avoid mistakes when simplifying and solving equations.

Guided Instruction

Before beginning, ask students to list some properties used when solving equations. Review the properties of numbers, such as the Associative Properties, the Commutative Properties, and the Distributive Property, as well as the Addition, Subtraction, Multiplication, and Division Properties of Equality.

Checkpoint Quiz

Use this Checkpoint Quiz to check students' understanding of the skills and concepts of Lessons 10-4 through 10-5.

All in One Resources

- Checkpoint Quiz 2

10-6

1. Plan

California Content Standards

Alg1 4.0 Simplify expressions before solving linear equations in one variable. ***Develop***

Alg1 5.0 Solve multistep problems, including word problems, involving linear equations in one variable and provide justification for each step. ***Develop***

California Math Background

When solving an equation, it is often necessary to first simplify expressions on each side by combining like terms. Some equations have variables on both sides of the equal sign. Before you can solve these equations, all of the terms containing variables must be isolated on one side of the equation.

More Math Background: p. 364C

Lesson Planning and Resources

See p. 364E for a list of the resources that support this lesson.

PRESENTATION CD-ROM
CD, Online, or Transparencies
Bell Ringer Practice

Check Skills You'll Need
Use student page, transparency, or PowerPoint.
See Math Companion.

California Standards Review
Use transparency or PowerPoint.

10-6 Solving Equations With Variables on Both Sides

Check Skills You'll Need

Do this in your **Math Companion.**

Vocabulary

Review:
- term
- like terms
- Distributive Property

Use your **Math Companion** *to build your vocabulary.*

California Content Standards

Alg1 4.0 Simplify expressions before solving linear equations in one variable. ***Develop***
Alg1 5.0 Solve multistep problems, including word problems, involving linear equations in one variable and provide justification for each step. ***Develop***

What You'll Learn . . . and Why

You will learn to solve equations with variables on both sides. You can use an equation with variables on both sides to find how long it takes two plants growing at different rates to reach the same height.

To solve an equation with variables on both sides, bring all the variable terms to one side of the equation.

EXAMPLE Variables on Both Sides

1 Solve $7 + 3h = -1 - 5h$.

$7 + 3h = -1 - 5h$

$7 + 3h + 5h = -1 - 5h + 5h$ ← Addition Property of Equality

$7 + 8h = -1$ ← Combine like terms.

$7 - 7 + 8h = -1 - 7$ ← Subtraction Property of Equality

$8h = -8$ ← Simplify.

$\frac{8h}{8} = \frac{-8}{8}$ ← Division Property of Equality

$h = -1$ ← Simplify.

Check $7 + 3h = -1 - 5h$

$7 + 3(-1) \stackrel{?}{=} -1 - 5(-1)$ ← Substitute –1 for h into the equation.

$7 + (-3) \stackrel{?}{=} -1 - (-5)$ ← Multiply.

$4 = 4$ ✔ ← The solution checks.

Quick Tip

You can also solve equations with variables on both sides by moving all of the variables to the right side.

CA Standards Check 1 *Go to your* **Math Companion** *for help.*

1. Solve each equation.

a. $9m = 3m + 24$ 4 **b.** $7b - 2 = b + 10$ 2

Universal Access Solutions for All Learners

Special Needs L1	**Below Level** L2
Provide students with copies of Examples 1 and 2 in this lesson. Have students circle the terms with variables on both sides of each equation, and underline the constants. Then ask them to combine the like terms.	Give students the equation $3p - 2 = 4p + 9 + 7p$. Ask: *On which side of the equation do you want to isolate the variable? Why?* $3p$ is on the left, $4p$ and $7p$ are on the right; right side because $4p + 7p = 11p$ is greater than $3p$.

You may need to use the Distributive Property to simplify an equation before you can bring the variable terms to one side.

EXAMPLE Using the Distributive Property

Relate MATH YOU KNOW...

A plant grows 1.5 cm per day. Find the height of the plant after 4 days.

$$\text{height} = 1.5\,\frac{\text{cm}}{\text{day}} \cdot 4\ \text{days} \quad \leftarrow \textbf{Multiply the rate by the amount of time.}$$

$$= 6\ \text{cm} \quad \leftarrow \textbf{Simplify.}$$

...to ALGEBRA

2 **Guided Problem Solving** A gardener is growing two plants. Plant A grows 1.5 cm per day. The gardener plants Plant B one day after he plants Plant A. Plant B grows 2 cm per day. How many days after Plant A was planted will the two plants be the same height?

Problem Solving Tip

Plant B has been growing one less day than Plant A. So when Plant A has been growing for *d* days, Plant B has been growing for $d - 1$ days.

Write an equation for the height of each plant.

height of Plant A = $1.5\,\frac{\text{cm}}{\text{day}}$ · the number of days

height of Plant B = $2\,\frac{\text{cm}}{\text{day}}$ · (the number of days − one day)

Then set the height equations equal to each other.

height of Plant A = height of Plant B

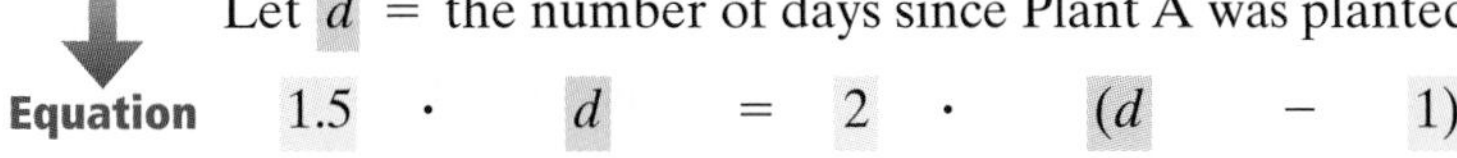

Words $1.5\,\frac{\text{cm}}{\text{day}}$ · the number of days = $2\,\frac{\text{cm}}{\text{day}}$ · (the number of days − one day)

Let *d* = the number of days since Plant A was planted.

Equation 1.5 · *d* = 2 · (*d* − 1)

$1.5d = 2(d - 1)$

$1.5d = 2d - 2$ ← **Distributive Property**

$1.5d - 2d = 2d - 2d - 2$ ← **Subtraction Property of Equality**

$-0.5d = -2$ ← **Combine like terms.**

$\frac{-0.5d}{-0.5} = \frac{-2}{-0.5}$ ← **Division Property of Equality**

$d = 4$ ← **Simplify.**

The plants will be the same height 4 days after Plant A was planted.

CA Standards Check 2 *Go to your* **Math Companion** *for help.*

2. You run $\frac{1}{2}$ lap/min. Your friend runs $\frac{2}{3}$ lap/min. Your friend starts running 5 min after you start. How long after you start running have you and your friend run the same number of laps? 20 min

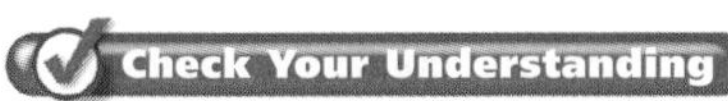

Homework prep is in your **Math Companion.**

2. Teach

Guided Instruction

Example 2
Review dimensional analysis with students. Have students use dimensional analysis to check the reasonableness of the equation representing the height of each plant:

$$\frac{\text{cm}}{\text{day}} \times \text{number of days} = \text{cm}$$

After students solve the equations, ask them to check their work by substituting their solutions into the two original equations.

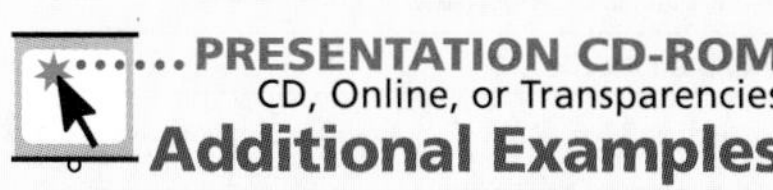

Additional Examples

1 Solve $9 + 2p = -3 - 4p$. $p = -2$

2 Each week you set aside $18 for a stereo and put the remainder of your weekly pay in a savings account. After 7 weeks, the amount you place in the savings account is 4.2 times your total weekly pay. How much do you earn each week? $45

Closure

- *Explain the steps for solving an equation with variables on both sides of the equal sign.* Sample Answer: First simplify each side of the equation by combining like terms and, if necessary, using the Distributive Property. Then bring all of the terms that contain variables to one side of the equation.

Advanced Learners L4
Students solve equations with more than one variable term on each side, such as
$6n + 2 + 3n = 4(n - 1) + 4n$. $n = -6$

English Learners EL
For a quick assessment of students' understanding, have them write examples of the following math concepts as you say them: *variable expression, constant, like terms, distributive property, inverse operations.*

3. Practice

Assignment Guide

Check Your Understanding
See Math Companion.

Homework Exercises

A Practice by Example	1–17
B Apply Your Skills	18–27
C Challenge	28
California Multiple-Choice Practice	29–30
Mixed Review	31–32

Homework Quick Check
To check students' understanding of key skills and concepts, go over Exercises 6, 14, 20, 27.

Universal Access Resources

Adapted Practice 10-6 L1

Practice 10-6 Solving Equations with Variables on Bot L3

Solve each equation. Check the solution.

1. $12y = 2y + 40$
2. $6c + 24 = 4c - 18$
3. $0.5m + 6.4 = 4.9 - 0.1m$
4. $14b = 16b + 32$
5. $7y = y - 42$
6. $0.7p + 4.6 = 7.3 - 0.2p$

Solve each equation. Justify each step.

7. $12j = 16(j - 8)$
8. $9(d - 4) = 5d + 8$
9. $6(f + 5) = 2f - 8$
10. $4 = -2(4.5p + 25)$

Solve.

11. Jace owns twice as many DVDs as Louis. Bo has sixty fewer DVDs than five times Louis's collection. If Jace and Bo have the same amount of DVDs, how many DVDs are in Louis's collection?
12. Deborah has two paintings in her portfolio and paints three more each week. Kai has twelve paintings in her portfolio and paints two more each week. After how many weeks will Deborah and Kai have the same number of paintings?

10-6 • Guided Problem Solving L3

GPS **Exercise 20:**

Efren leaves home at 9 A.M. and walks 4 mi/h. His brother Gregory leaves half an hour later and runs 8.5 mi/h in the same direction as Efren. Predict the time at which Gregory will catch up to Efren.

Understand

1. What is the distance formula? ______
2. What can you say about the distance each boy will have traveled when Gregory catches up to Efren? ______

Plan and Carry Out

3. Write an expression for the distance Gregory travels per hour. Let h stand for time in hours. ______
4. Write an expression for the distance Efren travels per hour plus the distance he will have traveled when Gregory leaves the house. ______
5. Write an equation setting the distance expressions in Steps 3 and 4 equal. ______
6. Solve for h. Use your answer to estimate the time at which Gregory will catch up to Efren. ______

Check

7. Solve the expressions in Steps 3 and 4 for your value of h. Are the distances equal? ______

Solve Another Problem

8. Roshonda begins riding her bike home from school at 3:00 P.M., traveling 12 mi/h. James leaves school in a bus a quarter of an hour later and travels 35 mi/h in the same direction. At about what time will James catch up to Roshonda?

Standards Practice

GO for Help: MathXL

Alg1 4.0, Alg1 5.0

A Practice by Example

Solve each equation. Check the solution.

Example 1 (page 392)

GO for Help

1. $2 + 14z = -8 + 9z$

   $2 + 14z = -8 + 9z$

   $2 + 14z - 9z = -8 + 9z - 9z$

   $2 + \blacksquare z = -8$ **−2**

   Guided Practice: This exercise has been started for you!

2. $22 + 2x = 37 + 6 + x$ **21**
3. $-8 - 5y = 12 - 9y$ **5**
4. $6d + 1 = 15 - d$ **2**
5. $18 - t = 3t$ **4.5**
6. $5m - 5.5 = 17 + 2m$ **7.5**
7. $19.5 + 3p = 7.5p - 25.5$ **10**
8. $3.5a - 4.2 = 4.7a$ **−3.5**
9. $-7.2 + 3w - 5w = -3.5w$ **4.8**

Homework Video Tutor

For: Examples 1–2
Visit: PHSchool.com
Web Code: axe-1006

Example 2 (page 393)

Solve each equation. Justify each step.

10. $-k = 9(k - 10)$

    $-k = 9k - 9 \cdot 10$

    $-k = 9k - \blacksquare$ **9**

    Guided Practice: This exercise has been started for you!

11. $7m = 9(m + 4)$ **−18**
12. $8(4 - a) = 2a$ **3.2**
13. $3(f + 11) = -7.5 - 6f$ **−4.5**
14. $8 - 3(p - 4) = 2p$ **4**
15. $5(2c - 8) = 35c - 5c$ **−2**
16. $138 + 8y = 4(3y + 58)$ **−23.5**
17. A freight train leaves a station and travels east at a rate of 40 mi/h. A passenger train leaves the station an hour later and travels west at a rate of 60 mi/h. How long after the freight train leaves the station will the two trains be the same distance from the station? **3 h**

B Apply Your Skills

18. **Guided Problem Solving** A chef and his assistant are making ravioli. The assistant can make 2 ravioli per minute and the chef can make 5 ravioli per minute. The chef starts making ravioli $\frac{1}{4}$ h after the assistant. How long after the assistant starts making ravioli have they both made the same number of ravioli? **25 min**
    - Which quantity will you represent with a variable?
    - Write an equation. Set the number of ravioli the chef makes equal to the number of ravioli the assistant makes.
19. At Video Shack, movie rentals cost \$3.99 each. The cost of renting three movies and one video game is \$.11 less than the cost of renting five video games. How much does renting a video game cost? **\$3.02**
20. GPS Efren leaves home at 9 A.M. and walks 4 mi/h. His brother Gregory leaves half an hour later and runs 8.5 mi/h in the same direction as Efren. Predict the time at which Gregory will catch up to Efren. **about 9:57 A.M.**

SCAFFOLDED
Problem Solving

A solution to a system of equations is a pair of x and y values that make both equations true. Use this system: $\begin{cases} y = 3x \\ y = -x + 4 \end{cases}$

21. Graph the system of equations in the same coordinate plane. See left.
22. Identify the point where the two lines intersect. (1, 3)
23. How is the equation $3x = -x + 4$ related to the system of equations? See left.
24. Solve the equation $3x = -x + 4$. 1
25. Evaluate $y = 3x$ for the value of x you found in Exercise 24. 3
26. Compare the values of x and y you found in Exercises 24 and 25 to the x- and y-coordinates you found in Exercise 22. What do you notice? They are the same.
27. **Writing in Math** Explain how to solve an equation with the same variable on both sides. See left.

C Challenge

28. Solve $\frac{3}{4} + 2(x - 0.5) = 3x - 0.4$. 0.15

21.

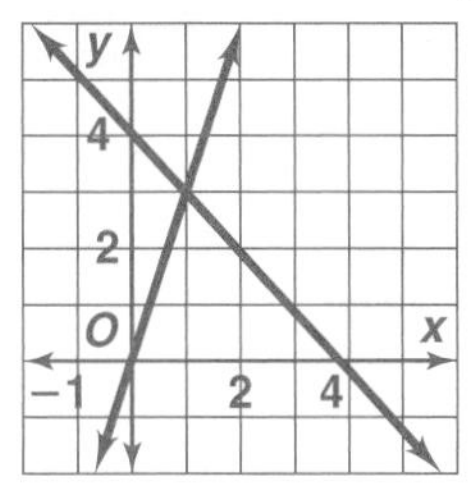

23. Answers may vary. Sample: If you substitute $y = 3x$ into the equation $y = -x + 4$ for y, you get $3x = -x + 4$.

27. Answers may vary. Sample: Bring all the variable terms to one side of the equation and use the properties of equality to isolate the variable.

Multiple Choice Practice and Mixed Review

For California Standards Tutorials, visit PHSchool.com. Web Code: axq-9045

Alg1 5.0

29. The side of a square is $2x + 8$ in. long. The perimeter of the square is $20x + 8$ in. How many inches long is the side of the square? B

(A) 2 in. (B) 12 in. (C) 24 in. (D) 48 in.

MG 1.3

30. Which fabric store's prices are based on a constant unit price? C

(A) **Materials Unlimited**

Yards	Total Price
2	\$10
4	\$18
6	\$27
8	\$32

(B) **Haley's Fabric**

Yards	Total Price
2	\$8
4	\$18
6	\$28
8	\$38

(C) **The Fab Store**

Yards	Total Price
2	\$9
4	\$18
6	\$27
8	\$36

(D) **We R Fabric**

Yards	Total Price
2	\$10
4	\$18
6	\$27
8	\$35

Lesson 10-5

Solve each equation.

31. $6q + 3 - 4q = 9$ 3
32. $7(x + 1) = 34$ $3\frac{6}{7}$

Online Lesson Quiz Visit: PHSchool.com Web Code: axa-1006

395

4. Assess & Reteach

PRESENTATION CD-ROM
CD, Online, or Transparencies
Lesson Quiz

Solve each equation.

1. $4(3u - 1) = 20$ 2
2. $5t - 4 = t - 8$ −1
3. $3(k - 8) = -k$ 6

Alternative Assessment

Have students write an expression involving the variable x. Then have them set it equal to $10x - 2$ and solve the equation.

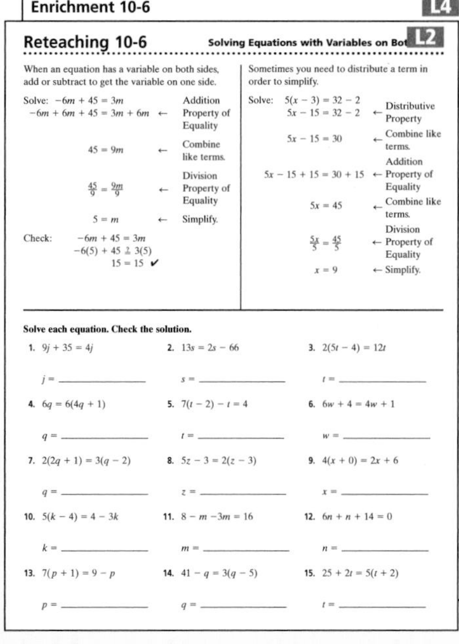

Enrichment 10-6 L4

Reteaching 10-6 Solving Equations with Variables on Bot L2

When an equation has a variable on both sides, add or subtract to get the variable on one side.

Solve: $-6m + 45 = 3m$
$-6m + 6m + 45 = 3m + 6m$ ← Addition Property of Equality
$45 = 9m$ ← Combine like terms.
$\frac{45}{9} = \frac{9m}{9}$ ← Division Property of Equality
$5 = m$ ← Simplify.

Check: $-6m + 45 = 3m$
$-6(5) + 45 \stackrel{?}{=} 3(5)$
$15 = 15$ ✔

Sometimes you need to distribute a term in order to simplify.

Solve: $5(x - 3) = 32 - 2$
$5x - 15 = 32 - 2$ ← Distributive Property
$5x - 15 = 30$ ← Combine like terms.
$5x - 15 + 15 = 30 + 15$ ← Addition Property of Equality
$5x = 45$ ← Combine like terms.
$\frac{5x}{5} = \frac{45}{5}$ ← Division Property of Equality
$x = 9$ ← Simplify.

Solve each equation. Check the solution.

1. $9j + 35 = 4j$ $j =$ ______
2. $13s = 2s - 66$ $s =$ ______
3. $2(5t - 4) = 12t$ $t =$ ______
4. $6q = 6(4q + 1)$ $q =$ ______
5. $7(t - 2) - t = 4$ $t =$ ______
6. $6w + 4 = 4w + 1$ $w =$ ______
7. $2(2q + 1) = 3(q - 2)$ $q =$ ______
8. $5z - 3 = 2(z - 3)$ $z =$ ______
9. $4(x + 0) = 2x + 6$ $x =$ ______
10. $5(k - 4) = 4 - 3k$ $k =$ ______
11. $8 - m - 3m = 16$ $m =$ ______
12. $6n + n + 14 = 0$ $n =$ ______
13. $7(p + 1) = 9 - p$ $p =$ ______
14. $41 - q = 3(q - 5)$ $q =$ ______
15. $25 + 2t = 5(t + 2)$ $t =$ ______

California Resources

Standards Mastery
- Standards Review Transparencies
- Standards Review and Practice Workbook
- Math Companion

Math Intervention
- Skills Review and Practice Workbook
- Math XL

Writing Equations

Students read a guided real-world problem to develop problem-solving and reasoning skills. In the left column, they read questions they could ask themselves to make sense of the problem. In the right column, they read the steps for setting up and solving equations used to describe the situation.

Guided Instruction

Have students work through the problem, rather than just read it. Have them identify any steps they don't understand or that don't match their own work.

Alg1 5.0 Solve multistep problems, including word problems, involving linear equations. ***Develop***

MR 3.3 Develop generalizations of the results obtained and the strategies used and apply them to new problem situations. ***Develop***

Writing Equations

Mr. and Mrs. Smith have two children, ages 4 and 8. They are trying to decide whether to buy day passes or a yearly membership to the aquarium. With how many single-day visits would it be less expensive for the Smiths to have a yearly membership?

What You Might Think	What You Might Write
What do I know? What do I want to find out?	I know single-day tickets are \$21.95 for adults and \$10.95 for children. Two adult tickets → $2 \cdot \$21.95 = \$43.90$. Two child tickets → $2 \cdot \$10.95 = \$21.90$. A yearly membership is \$175. I want to find when a yearly membership would be less expensive.
What equation can I write?	Let d = the number of visits. Then the total cost of d visits is $43.90d + 21.90d$.
When will the cost of single-day tickets equal the cost of a yearly membership?	$43.90d + 21.90d = 175$ $65.80d = 175$ $d \approx 2.66$ Since you cannot have 2.66 visits, round the answer up to 3. So for three or more visits it would be less expensive to have the yearly membership.
Is the answer reasonable?	The cost for single-day tickets is about \$40 + \$20 or \$60. $3 \cdot \$60 = \$180$. So 3 visits is a reasonable answer.

Think It Through

1. **Reasoning** Can an answer to this problem be 2 visits? Explain.

2. Can you use the following equation to solve this problem? Explain.

$$21.95d + 21.95d + 10.95d + 10.95d = 175$$

1. No; two single-day visits cost $131.60, which is less expensive than a yearly membership.
2. Yes; $21.95d + 21.95d$ equals $43.90d$, and $10.95d + 10.95d$ equals $21.90d$.

Exercises

Solve each problem. For Exercises 3 and 4, answer parts (a) and (b) first.

3. The cost of a membership at a health club last year was 75% of the cost at the club this year. This year's membership costs $20 more than last year's membership. Find the cost of a membership last year and the cost of a membership this year. $60; $80
   a. Let x = the cost of last year's membership. Write an expression for the cost of this year's membership.
   b. Represent the cost of last year's membership as $0.75(x + 20)$. To find the value of x, solve $x = 0.75(x + 20)$.

4. A camp counselor buys granola bars and juice drinks for the campers. She decides to buy three times as many drinks as granola bars. Predict how many of each she can buy on a budget of $24. 10 granola bars, 30 juice drinks

   a. Let x = the number of granola bars the counselor buys and let $3x$ = the number of juice drinks she buys. What is the cost of x granola bars? The cost of $3x$ juice drinks?
   b. Use your answers to part (a) to write and solve an equation to find how many of each the camp leader can buy.

5. In a random survey of adults and children, children were found to eat 23% more snacks between meals each year than adults. Altogether, the adults and children in this survey ate 3,000 snacks between meals in one year. About how many snacks did the children in this survey eat in one year? (*Hint:* Let x = the number of between-meal snacks the adults in this survey ate in one year.) about 1,654

Error Prevention!

Students might tend to round 2.66 up to 3 by habit. Ask: *What does 2.66 represent?* the value of d for which the cost of annual membership equals the cost of purchasing day passes *Why is 3 not a useful answer?* because 2.66 is the number of visits below which (1 or 2) it is better for the Smiths to purchase day passes, and above which (3 or more) it is better for them to purchase a yearly membership

Alternative Method

Guide students toward writing the equation by having them start with a sentence. Sample: (2 adults)(Cost of adult ticket)(number of visits) + (2 children)(Cost of 2 child tickets)(number of visits) = cost of yearly membership

Teaching Tip

Have students ask themselves questions that are the same as or similar to those in the Example as they work through the Exercises.

Connection to Health and Nutrition

Discuss the food pyramid, including types of foods that are healthy between-meal snacks. Have students research nutrition information on these foods, such as suggested daily servings, vitamin, protein, sugar, or fat content, and ingredients.

Using Equation Language

Students use equation language to model and solve real-world puzzles. Students practice writing equations from verbal descriptions and finding solutions to the equations.

Guided Instruction

Show students that each of the given clues can be represented by an equation. Explain that to find the solution to the puzzle, students must find values that satisfy all the equations.

Error Prevention!

Make sure that students write the correct equation for each clue. In Exercise 1, some students may be tempted to reverse the variables in clues 2 and 3. For example, in clue 2, students may incorrectly subtract 4 from the number of California quarters to find the number of Maryland quarters. Have students choose values that satisfy their equations and then refer to the original clues to make sure that the values make sense.

Using Equation Language

Equations describe real-world situations. Solve the puzzles below using equation language.

ACTIVITY

A class makes puzzles with quarters that honor the 50 U.S. states. For each puzzle, find the number of quarters from each of three states. **1–4. See margin.**

1. Martin's Puzzle

Clue 1 10 quarters from California, Maryland, or Florida

Clue 2 4 fewer California quarters than Maryland quarters

Clue 3 3 times as many Maryland quarters as Florida quarters

2. Sara's Puzzle

Clue 1 6 Indiana quarters

Clue 2 2 more Kentucky quarters than Tennessee quarters

Clue 3 12 quarters from Indiana, Kentucky, or Tennessee

3. Joaquin's Puzzle

Clue 1 $\frac{1}{2}$ are Ohio quarters.

Clue 2 18 quarters from Ohio, Texas, or Tennessee

Clue 3 Twice as many Tennessee quarters as Texas quarters

4. Donelle's Puzzle

Clue 1 15 quarters from Maine, Louisiana, or Idaho

Clue 2 1 fewer Maine quarters than Louisiana quarters

Clue 3 1 more Maine quarters than Idaho quarters

5–7. Check students' work.

5. Make a puzzle by choosing quarters from three states. Then write clues. Include the total number of quarters as a clue.
6. Exchange puzzles with another student. Solve the puzzle.
7. **Writing in Math** How did you solve Joaquin's puzzle? Explain.

Drawing a Diagram

The problem-solving strategy *Draw a Diagram* may help you answer questions using given information.

EXAMPLE

Three cars, A, B, and C, are parked in that order in the same row of a parking lot, as shown at the right. The distance between B and C is twice the distance between A and B. The distance between A and C is 3 m more than the distance between B and C. Find the distance between B and C.

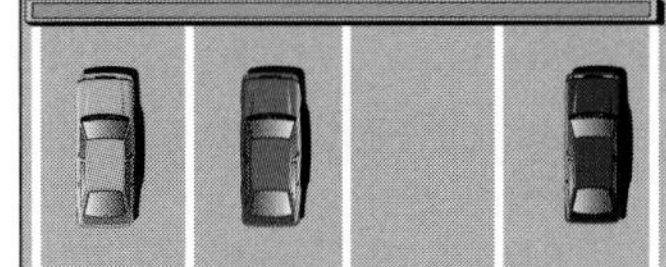

Ⓐ 3 m Ⓑ 5 m Ⓒ 6 m Ⓓ 9 m

You can draw a diagram to model the situation. Let points A, B, and C represent the cars. Let x be the distance between A and B.

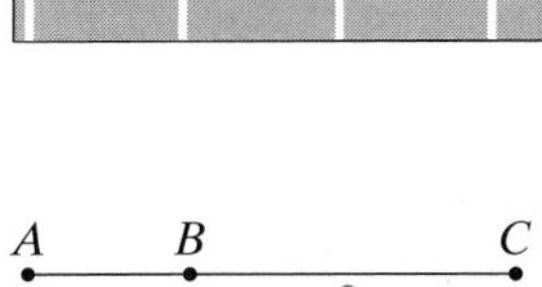

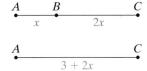

$x + 2x = 3 + 2x$ ← **Use the picture to write an equation.**

$3x = 3 + 2x$ ← **Combine like terms.**

$3x - 2x = 3 + 2x - 2x$ ← **Subtraction Property of Equality**

$x = 3$ ← **Simplify.**

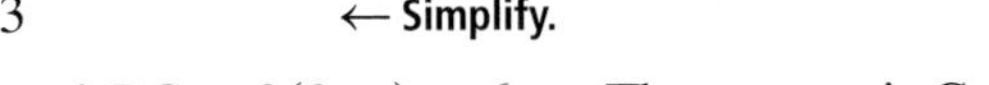

So $AB = 3$ m and $BC = 2(3\text{ m}) = 6$ m. The answer is C.

Multiple Choice Practice

Alg1 5.0 **1.** Joe's house (J), Kate's house (K), and Lin's house (L) are located along a straight road in that order. The distance from K to L is 4 times the distance from J to K. The distance from J to L is 36 yd more than 3 times the distance from J to K. What is the distance from J to K? **B**

Ⓐ 24 yd Ⓑ 18 yd Ⓒ 12 yd Ⓓ 4.5 yd

Alg1 5.0 **2.** Logan and Julie climbed different hills. Julie climbed 28 yd less than twice the height Logan climbed. They climbed a total of 95 yd. How far did each person climb? **A**

Ⓐ Logan climbed 41 yd and Julie climbed 54 yd.
Ⓑ Logan climbed 54 yd and Julie climbed 41 yd.
Ⓒ Logan climbed $22\frac{1}{3}$ yd and Julie climbed $72\frac{2}{3}$ yd.
Ⓓ Logan climbed 28 yd and Julie climbed 56 yd.

Drawing a Diagram

Students learn to use diagrams to help visualize problems. They can use diagrams to help write and solve equations.

Guided Instruction

Example

Ask:

- *What expressions can represent the relationship, "The distance between B and C is twice the distance between A and B"?* **x can represent the distance from A to B, and $2x$ can represent the distance from B to C.**

Ask:

- *What expression can represent the relationship, "The distance between A and C is three more than the distance between B and C"?* **Since $2x$ represents the distance from B to C, the expression $2x + 3$ can represent the distance from A to C.**

Use the diagram to show students how they can create an equation by comparing the two expressions that represent the distance between *A* and *C*.

Chapter 10 Review

Chapter 10 Review

California Resources

Standards Mastery
- Math Companion
- Standards Review Transparencies
- Standards Review and Practice Workbook
- Progress Monitoring Assessments

Math Intervention
- Skills Review and Practice Workbook
- Math XL

Universal Access Resources
- Student Workbook
  - Vocabulary and Study Skills
  - Guided Problem Solving
- All-in-One Teaching Resources
  - Reteaching
  - Enrichment
- Spanish Practice Workbook L3
- Spanish Vocabulary and Study Skills 2A-F L3
- English/Spanish Glossary EL
- Multilingual Handbook EL
- Interactive Textbook Audio Glossary
- Online Vocabulary Quiz

Online at PHSchool.com

Spanish Vocabulary/Study Skills EL

Vocabulary/Study Skills L3

10F: Vocabulary Review Puzzle For use with the Chapter Review

Study Skill Turn off the television and radio when studying.

Find each of the words below in the Word Search. Circle the word and cross it off the Word List. Words can be displayed forwards, backwards, up, down, or diagonally.

variable	absolute value	integer	exponent
inequality	equation	additive inverse	inverse
isolate	like terms	solution	

```
L F E E T P U O M O I I H H H R D K W V
I B T F C C S P R R J N H E I E O B C M
K M A G T J L B X P X T X A E L S T F I
E A V V E Z Y S C I O E B O B O J Z J N
T B L L P A D L S E J G M L L O T D N E
E S Q W C K K C T U O E H U K G N V F Q
R O F C Y N R L Z S L R T N S L Z M X U
M L W A D D I T I V E I N V E R S E G A
S U G N R E U I V E O U C M V B A I H L
W T T R R C M O Q N D U V S T M E S L I
R E M Q N N S Y V N L V S I I G X U I T
P V E O M G W A B N Z Y P M I O P S E Y
D A A V Z Y R K A W S D I N K U O A D C
O L B G Q I B I L I C U V Y Q L N U O Z
H U J A A K D I Q U W E I M A L E F N T
K E J B R E N L W T R I F T L D N V W P
T R L R M Q H N S S L D E H E R T K F W
S E E D E W A R E J I R O N G E E W V Y
W T K H T R F F C A R H F U W J K Y F V
E Q U A T I O N T Q N H G H M U N C W C
```

Vocabulary Review

English and Spanish Audio Online

nth roots (p. 374)
term (p. 380)
like terms (p. 380)

Academic Vocabulary
consecutive (p. 390)

For: Vocabulary Quiz
Visit: PHSchool.com
Web Code: axj-1051

Choose the correct vocabulary term to complete each sentence.

1. __?__ have the same variables. Like terms
2. A(n) __?__ is a number, a variable, or the product of a number and a variable. term
3. A number a is a(n) __?__ of b if $a^n = b$. nth root

Skills and Concepts

Lesson 10-1
- To multiply and divide expressions with exponents

NS 2.1, AF 2.1, Alg1 2.0

To multiply numbers with the same base, add the exponents. To divide numbers with the same base, subtract the exponents.

Write each expression using a single exponent.

4. $8^{10} \cdot 8^9$ 8^{19}
5. $(-3)^4 \cdot (-3)^6$ $(-3)^{10}$
6. $2.6^{12} \cdot 2.6^{12}$ 2.6^{24}
7. $f^4 \cdot f^{-2}$ f^2
8. $d^{-8} \cdot d^{13}$ d^5
9. $(4 \times 10^5)(6 \times 10^3)$ 24×10^8

Write each expression using a single exponent.

10. $\frac{5^{10}}{5^7}$ 5^3
11. $\frac{(-8)^{12}}{(-8)^2}$ $(-8)^{10}$
12. $\frac{76^{11}}{76^5}$ 76^6
13. $\frac{1.8^6}{1.8^5}$ 1.8
14. $\frac{m^4}{m^2}$ m^2
15. $\frac{y^9}{y^9}$ 1
16. The diameter of a golf ball is 4.267×10^{-3} m. The diameter of a basketball is 2.388×10^{-1} m. How many times as great as the diameter of a golf ball is the diameter of a basketball? about 56

Lesson 10-2
- To use power rules

NS 2.1, AF 2.1, Alg1 2.0

To raise a power to a power, multiply the powers. To raise a product to a power, raise each factor to the power.

Write each expression using a single exponent.

17. $(5^5)^4$ 5^{20}
18. $(9^2)^{20}$ 9^{40}
19. $(8^{-2})^{-3}$ 8^6
20. $(a^{-4})^2$ $\frac{1}{a^8}$
21. $(x^{20})^{-1}$ $\frac{1}{x^{20}}$
22. $(2^{10})^{-10}$ $\frac{1}{2^{100}}$
23. $(333^{33})^3$ 333^{99}
24. $(w^5)^0$ w^0

Simplify each expression.

25. $(4x)^2$ $16x^2$
26. $(2n)^3$ $8n^3$
27. $(4 \times 10^9)^2$ 16×10^{18}
28. $(ab^5)^4$ a^4b^{20}
29. $(kmg)^4$ $k^4m^4g^4$
30. $(3a^{-4})^2$ $\frac{9}{a^8}$
31. $(w^5x^{-5})^2$ $\frac{w^{10}}{x^{10}}$
32. $(2x^3y)^0$ 1

Lesson 10-3
- To simplify expressions with roots

Alg1 2.0

You can find roots of numbers other than the square roots. If $a^n = b$, then a is an ***n*th root** of b.

Simplify each expression.

33. $\sqrt[4]{16}$ 2
34. $\sqrt[6]{1{,}000{,}000}$ 10
35. $\sqrt[5]{-1}$ –1
36. $\sqrt{9} + \sqrt[3]{-27}$ 0
37. $6 \cdot \sqrt[4]{25 - 9}$ 12
38. $\sqrt{9} + \sqrt{9 \cdot 4} + 9$ 18
39. The surface area of a sphere is 1.1304×10^4 in.^{2}. Use the formula S.A. $= 4\pi r^2$ to find the radius of the sphere. Use 3.14 for π. 30 in.

Lesson 10-4
- To simplify algebraic expressions

AF 1.1, Alg1 4.0

The parts of an algebraic expression are **terms. Like terms** have exactly the same variable factors. You simplify an expression by combining like terms.

Simplify each expression.

40. $4 - 3(f - 1)$ $7 - 3f$
41. $3(a + 2) + 5$ $3a + 11$
42. $8x + 6x - 4 - 2x$ $12x - 4$
43. $9(y - 2) + y - 7$ $10y - 25$
44. $15c + 12c - 4c + 3$ $23c + 3$
45. $-(t + 3 - 4t) + 6t$ $9t - 3$
46. Four classes go on a field trip. Let x represent the cost for each student. One class has 25 students. Another class has 15 students. The other two classes have 21 students each. Write and simplify an expression to represent the total cost of the field trip. $82x$

Lessons 10-5, 10-6
- To solve multi-step equations
- To solve equations with variables on both sides

Alg1 4.0, Alg1 5.0

When simplifying an equation, combine like terms. If an equation has variables on both sides, use the addition or subtraction property of equality to bring all the variable terms to one side.

Solve each equation.

47. $18 = 2(3k + 1) - k$ $3\frac{1}{5}$
48. $3(c + 4) - 7 = -10$ –5
49. $4a + 3 - a = -7 + 2 + a$ –4
50. $2b - 8 = -b + 7$ 5
51. $5c + 3 - 3(12 + c) = 12$ 22.5
52. $3(d + 4) = 2(3d - 3)$ 6
53. Marsha buys 3 lb of cheddar cheese and some Swiss cheese. Both cheeses cost \$4.50 per pound. The total cost is \$24.75. How many pounds of Swiss cheese does Marsha buy? 2.5 lb

Alternative Assessment L4

Alternative Assessment Form C

Chapter 10

SPACE TRAVEL

Imagine that you have a one-person space pod that you can use to fly yourself around the solar system. Take a look at the table below and start planning your trip.

Show all of your work on a separate sheet of paper.

Average Distances in the Solar System

From	To	Distance
Earth	the Sun	$1.496 \cdot 10^8$ km
Mars	the Sun	$2.28 \cdot 10^8$ km
Mars	Jupiter	$5.50 \cdot 10^8$ km

1. First you fly from Earth to the surface of the Sun (your space pod is fireproof!). Use the formula speed = d/t, where d is distance and t is time, to calculate how long it will take you to make the trip. Your pod travels at about half the speed of light, or $1.499 \cdot 10^5$ kilometers per second.
2. Oops! One of your engines blew! Looks like you can only travel at about a quarter of the speed of light, or $7.495 \cdot 10^4$ km/s. How long will it take you to make the entire trip now?
3. Now you leave the Sun to fly to Mars. If it takes you $7.625 \cdot 10^2$ seconds to travel there, how fast are you flying?
4. One more stop! You leave Mars for Jupiter, the next planet out. You travel there at half the speed of light, and it takes you $3.67 \cdot 10^3$ seconds to get there. How far must you travel?

Spanish Quarter 4 Test—Forms A, B L3

Quarter 4 Test—Forms D, E L2

Quarter 4 Test—Forms A, B L3

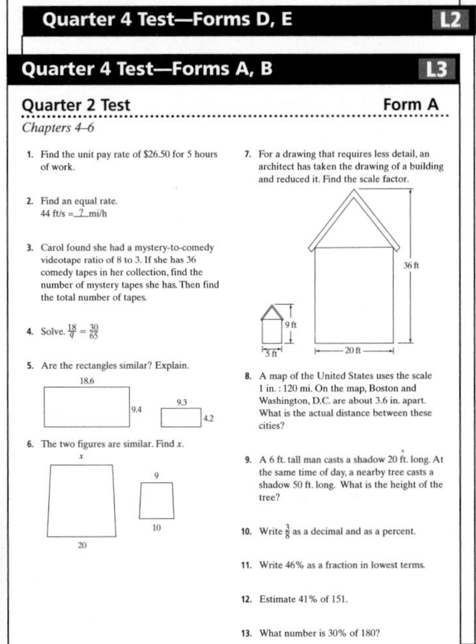

Quarter 2 Test Form A

Chapters 4–6

1. Find the unit pay rate of \$26.50 for 5 hours of work.
2. Find an equal rate.
44 ft/s = ? mi/h
3. Carol found she had a mystery-to-comedy videotape ratio of 8 to 3. If she has 36 comedy tapes in her collection, find the number of mystery tapes she has. Then find the total number of tapes.
4. Solve. $\frac{18}{q} = \frac{30}{65}$
5. Are the rectangles similar? Explain.
6. The two figures are similar. Find x.
7. For a drawing that requires less detail, an architect has taken the drawing of a building and reduced it. Find the scale factor.
8. A map of the United States uses the scale 1 in. : 120 mi. On the map, Boston and Washington, D.C. are about 3.6 in. apart. What is the actual distance between these cities?
9. A 6 ft. tall man casts a shadow 20 ft. long. At the same time of day, a nearby tree casts a shadow 50 ft. long. What is the height of the tree?
10. Write $\frac{3}{8}$ as a decimal and as a percent.
11. Write 46% as a fraction in lowest terms.
12. Estimate 41% of 151.
13. What number is 30% of 180?

California Resources

Standards Mastery
- Teacher Center ExamView CD-ROM
- Math XL
- Progress Monitoring Assessments
- Online Chapter Test at PHSchool.com

Math Intervention
- Skills Review and Practice Workbook

Online at PHSchool.com

Universal Access Resources
- Chapter Test
- Alternative Assessment
- Spanish Chapter Test
- Spanish Alternative Assessment
- Teacher Center ExamView CD-ROM
  - Special Needs Test
  - Special Needs Practice Banks
  - Foundational Standards Practice Banks
- Online Chapter Test at www.PHSchool.com
- All-In-One Teaching Resources
  - Cumulative Review L3
- Spanish Assessment Resources
  - Cumulative Review L3

Below Level Chapter Test L2

Chapter Test L3

Chapter Test Form A

Chapter 10

Write each expression using a single exponent.

1. $10^8 \cdot 10^7$
2. $w^6 \cdot w^3$
3. $(3^4)^5$
4. $h^{25} \cdot h^0$
5. $\frac{12^9}{12^5}$
6. $\frac{m^7}{m^3}$
7. $(-7)^3 \cdot (-7)$
8. $\frac{(1.4)^5}{(1.4)^3}$

Simplify each expression.

9. $(xyz^2)^3$
10. $(7 \cdot 10^{-4})^{-2}$
11. $(3a^4)^3$
12. $(8x^2y^3z)^4$
13. $\sqrt[5]{-1}$
14. $5 \cdot \sqrt[3]{-125}$
15. $\sqrt[3]{8} + \sqrt{81} - \sqrt[4]{4^2}$
16. $\sqrt{10{,}000}$

Simplify each expression.

17. $(ab^4)^{11}$
18. $(8y^2)^3$
19. A hummingbird flaps its wings $1.5 \cdot 10^3$ times per minute. How many times would it flaps its wings if it could stay airborne for one week?
20. A star is 6.3 light-years from earth. If one light-year is $5.87 \cdot 10^{12}$ miles, how many miles from earth is the star?

Chapter 10 Test

Go Online PHSchool.com **For:** Online chapter test **Web Code:** axa-1052

Write each expression using a single exponent.

1. $10^7 \cdot 10^6$ 10^{13}
2. $a^5 \cdot a^2$ a^7
3. $3.4^3 \cdot 3.4^6$ 3.4^9
4. $(-h)^5 \cdot (-h)^8$ $(-h)^{13}$
5. $2^3 \cdot 2^6 \cdot 2^5$ 2^{14}
6. $r^3 \cdot r^6 \cdot r^5$ v^{14}
7. $t^{23} \cdot t^0$ t^{23}
8. $\frac{(-3)^5}{(-3)^2}$ $(-3)^3$
9. $\frac{14^8}{14^4}$ 14^4
10. $\frac{c^6}{c^2}$ c^4
11. The human eye blinks about 4.2×10^6 times each year. About how many years old is a person who has blinked 5.88×10^7 times? 14 yr

Write each expression using a single exponent.

12. $(4^3)^2$ 4^6
13. $(9^5)^8$ 9^{40}
14. $(10^4)^{-6}$ $\frac{1}{10^{24}}$
15. $(7^2)^5$ 7^{10}
16. $(a^4)^{12}$ a^{48}
17. $(n^{-7})^{-1}$ n^7

Simplify each expression.

18. $(3b)^2$ $9b^2$
19. $(9x^3)^4$ 9^4x^{12}
20. $(h^4w^3)^6$ $h^{24}w^{18}$
21. $(4tp^7)^{-2}$ $\frac{1}{4^2t^2p^{14}}$
22. $(9 \times 10^2)^8$ $9^8 \times 10^{16}$
23. $(5.2 \times 10^5)^{-6}$ $5.2^{-6} \times 10^{-30}$
24. Find the area of a square whose side length is 4.3×10^4 cm. 1.849×10^9 cm^2
25. **Writing in Math** Explain why you multiply the exponents when you raise a power to a power. Use the expression $(a^2)^3$ in your explanation. See margin.

Simplify each expression.

26. $\sqrt[4]{81}$ 3
27. $\sqrt[3]{8}$ 2
28. $\sqrt[3]{1{,}000}$ 10
29. $\sqrt[4]{625}$ 5
30. $\sqrt[4]{1} + \sqrt{121}$ 12
31. $73 - \sqrt[3]{125}$ 68
32. Find the radius of a sphere that has a volume of 113.04 m^3. Use the formula $V = \frac{4}{3}\pi r^3$. Use 3.14 for π. 3 m

Simplify each expression.

33. $9 - 4r - 7$ $2 - 4r$
34. $5 + (-12t) + 8t$ $5 - 4t$
35. $2(3m - 5) + 6$ $6m - 4$
36. $-4(7a + 2a) - 5$ $-36a - 5$
37. $4v + 17 - 9v$ $17 - 5v$
38. $13s - (-6 - 4s)$ $17s + 6$
39. Write and simplify an expression for the perimeter of the rectangle below. $6x - 6$

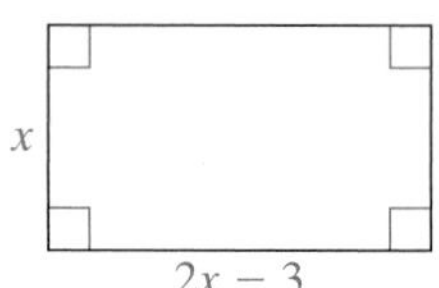

Solve each equation.

40. $4z - 5 + 2z = -30$ $-4\frac{1}{6}$
41. $6c - 4c + 5 = 9$ 2
42. $-2m - 9 + m = 27$ -36
43. $\frac{r}{-5} + r - 3 = 14$ $21\frac{1}{4}$
44. $-3(h + 7) = -18$ -1
45. $5 = 3(4 - b) + 2$ 3
46. You cut a 5-ft piece of ribbon into two pieces. The longer piece is 9 times as long as the shorter piece. How long is the shorter piece of ribbon? 0.5 ft

Solve each equation.

47. $x + 7 = 18 - 2x$ $3\frac{2}{3}$
48. $2 + y = -7 + 2y$ 9
49. $\frac{a}{-2} = 2.5 - 3a$ 1
50. $6 + 2d = 3d - 4$ 10
51. $5t - 1 = 7t - 5$ 2
52. $2(c + 1) = c - 7$ -9
53. A cricket bat weighs 42 oz. Together, two cricket balls and a cricket bat weigh the same as eight cricket balls plus 9 oz. How much does a cricket ball weigh? $5\frac{1}{2}$ oz
54. You swim across a lake at a rate of 2 ft/s. Your friend starts swimming 10 s after you start. She swims at a rate of 2.5 ft/s. How many seconds after you start swimming does your friend catch up to you? 50 s

Standards Mastery

Cumulative Practice

Read each question. Then write the letter of the correct answer on your paper.

1. What is the solution set to the inequality $\frac{x}{3} + 12 \geq 15$? (Lesson 9-5) C
   - A $\{x: x \geq 1\}$
   - B $\{x: x \leq 1\}$
   - C $\{x: x \geq 9\}$
   - D $\{x: x \leq 9\}$

2. Which graph is best represented by the equation $y = \frac{2}{3}x - \frac{1}{2}$? (Lesson 8-4) D

   A 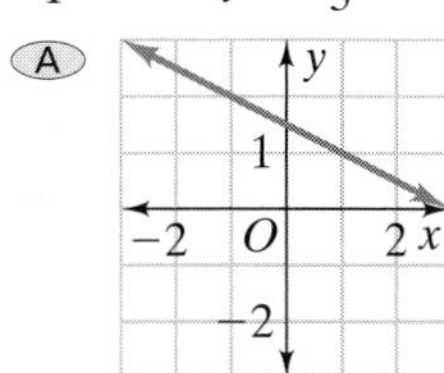

   C 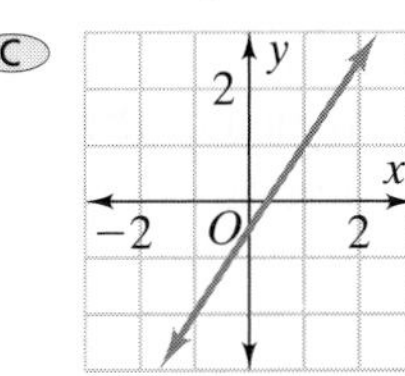

   B 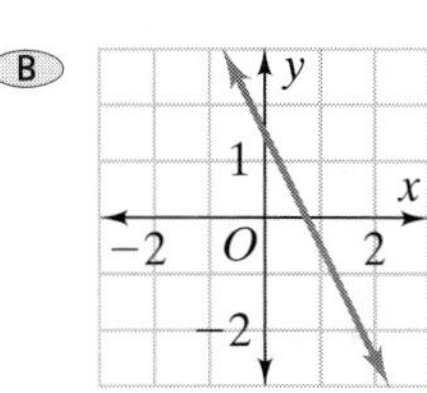

   D 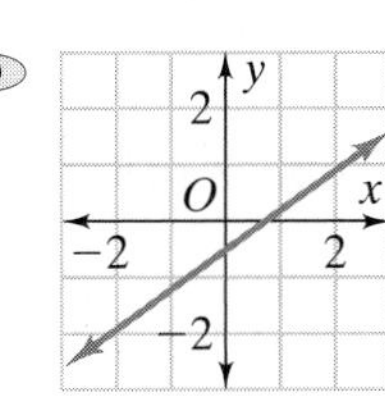

3. Simplify $3 + \sqrt{25} - \sqrt[3]{8}$. (Lesson 10-3) B
   - A 5.17
   - B 6
   - C 10
   - D 12.83

4. For every \$100 you spend at a store, you receive a \$10 gift card. How much do you need to spend at the store to receive a \$40 gift card? (Lesson 6-4) B
   - A \$40
   - B \$400
   - C \$4,000
   - D \$40,000

5. Which of the following is equal to $\frac{3}{4}$? (Lesson 4-4) A
   - A 0.75
   - B $1.\overline{33}$
   - C $1.\overline{66}$
   - D 1.75

6. The graph shows the relationship between miles driven m and the number of gallons of gasoline g used. Which statement is true about the slope of the line? (Lesson 8-6) B

   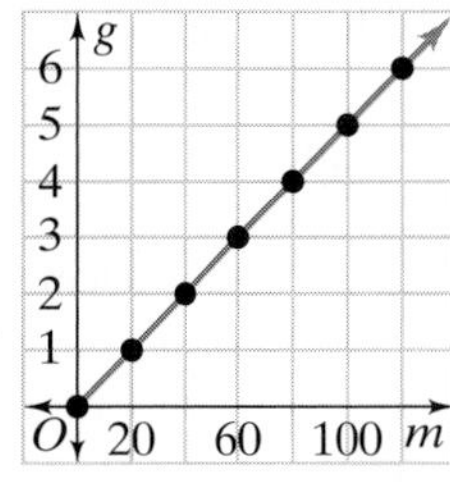

   - A The slope represents the number of gallons of gas remaining in the car's tank.
   - B The slope represents the ratio of the number of gallons of gas used to the number of miles driven.
   - C The slope represents the number of gallons of gas used.
   - D The slope represents the number of miles driven.

7. Ramon and three friends order 4 drinks and 2 pizzas. The pizzas cost \$9.99 each. The total is \$29.98. What was the cost of each drink? (Lesson 3-4) C
   - A \$10.00
   - B \$3.50
   - C \$2.50
   - D \$.75

8. Which expression is equivalent to $(h^2)^4$? (Lesson 10-2) C
   - A h^2
   - B h^6
   - C h^8
   - D h^{16}

9. An ad in the newspaper costs \$52 plus \$2.50 for each line of the ad. How many lines long is an ad that costs \$69.50? (Lesson 3-4) A
   - A 7 lines
   - B 8 lines
   - C 9 lines
   - D 10 lines

10. Rachel is making three aprons for a school play. Each apron uses $2\frac{1}{4}$ yd of fabric. If Rachel has 7.5 yd of fabric, how much will be left after she makes the aprons? (Lesson 5-3) B
    - A 0.3 yd
    - B 0.75 yd
    - C 5.25 yd
    - D 9.75 yd

California Resources

Standards Mastery
- Teacher Center ExamView CD-ROM
- Math XL
- Progress Monitoring Assessments
- Online Chapter Test at PHSchool.com

Math Intervention
- Skills Review and Practice Workbook

Universal Access Resources
- Teacher Center ExamView CD-ROM
  - Special Needs Test
  - Special Needs Practice Banks
  - Foundational Standards Practice Banks
- Online Chapter Test at www.PHSchool.com
- All-In-One Teaching Resources
  - Cumulative Review L3
- Spanish Assessment Resources
  - Cumulative Review L3

Success Tracker™
Online at PHSchool.com

11. In the graph of a linear function, which of the following is equal to the slope? (Lesson 8-5) B

(A) $\dfrac{\text{horizontal change}}{\text{vertical change}}$

(B) $\dfrac{\text{vertical change}}{\text{horizontal change}}$

(C) vertical change

(D) horizontal change

12. Harry's Health Club costs $19 per month plus an $80 joining fee. Fiona's Fitness Club costs $35 per month. After how many months will the cost to be a member be the same at both clubs? (Lesson 9-5) D

(A) 2 mo (C) 4 mo
(B) 3 mo (D) 5 mo

13. The equation $c = 17t + 5$ models the total cost c of a tomato garden, where t is the cost of each tomato plant. Find the cost of each plant if the total cost is $13.50. (Lesson 3-4) B

(A) $.25 (C) $.75
(B) $.50 (D) $1.00

14. Which of the following could be the side lengths of a right triangle? (Lesson 3-7) A

(A) 3 m, 4 m, 5 m
(B) 5 m, 7 m, 9 m
(C) 2 m, 5 m, 11 m
(D) 7 m, 12 m, 13 m

15. Which of the following is equivalent to $3^4 \cdot 3^2$? (Lesson 10-1) A

(A) 3^6 (C) 9^6
(B) 3^8 (D) 9^8

16. Which expression is equivalent to $4(3r - 7) + 5(2 - r)$? (Lesson 10-4) C

(A) $12r - 7 + 10 - r$
(B) $12r - 28 + 5r$
(C) $7r - 18$
(D) $11r - 18$

17. What is the length of $\overline{LK}$ in the graph below? (Lesson 8-2) D

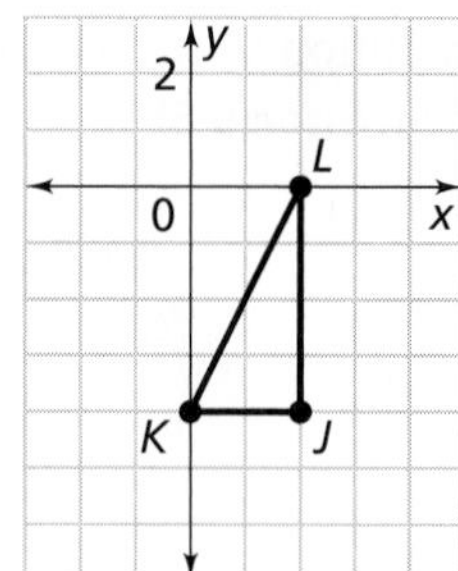

(A) 2 (C) 4
(B) $\sqrt{6}$ (D) $\sqrt{20}$

18. Which of the following expressions demonstrates the Commutative Property of Multiplication? (Lesson 1-5) C

(A) $3(5 - x) = 15 - 3x$
(B) $3 \cdot 5 = 5 + 5 + 5$
(C) $3 \cdot 5 = 5 \cdot 3$
(D) $3 \cdot (5 \cdot 7) = (3 \cdot 5) \cdot 7$

19. For a fruit salad, Miranda bought 1.5 lb of cantaloupe, $\frac{2}{3}$ lb strawberries, and 2 lb of apples. What was the total weight of the fruit Miranda bought? (Lesson 5-1) B

(A) $3\frac{2}{3}$ lb (C) $4\frac{1}{3}$ lb
(B) $4\frac{1}{6}$ lb (D) 5 lb

20. Parking at a meter costs $.25 for 15 min. How much will it cost to park for 2.5 h? (Lesson 6-4) C

(A) $3.75 (C) $2.50
(B) $3.50 (D) $2.00

21. What value makes the equation $2x + 16 = -4x + 4$ true? (Lesson 10-6) B

(A) −20 (C) 2
(B) −2 (D) 20

22. Which fraction is equal to 1.8? (Lesson 4-4) A

(A) $\frac{9}{5}$ (C) $\frac{5}{8}$
(B) $\frac{8}{5}$ (D) $\frac{5}{9}$

Spanish Cumulative Review EL

Cumulative Review L3

Cumulative Review

Chapters 1–10

Multiple Choice. Choose the letter of the best answer.

1. Solve $16 + k = 5(k - 2) - 2k$.
A. 13 B. 9 C. 7 D. 3

2. Four oranges cost $.99. What is the price for three oranges?
A. $.25 B. $.33 C. $.45 D. $.74

3. A piece of glass is 12.25 inches long. A glass cutter needs to shave 2.5 inches off of one end. How long will the glass be once the glass cutter is finished?
A. 4.9 in. B. 9.75 in. C. 10.2 in. D. 14.75 in.

4. Write 44 pens out of 200 pens as a decimal and a fraction in simplest form.
A. 0.22, $\frac{22}{100}$
B. 0.33, $\frac{33}{100}$
C. 0.22, $\frac{11}{50}$
D. 0.2, $\frac{22}{100}$

5. Suppose $\frac{3}{4}$ of the area of a garden is flowers. Zinnias cover $\frac{1}{8}$ of the flower area. What fraction of the garden is zinnias?
A. $\frac{8}{12}$ B. $\frac{15}{32}$ C. $\frac{20}{24}$ D. $\frac{20}{32}$

6. Evaluate $5a^2 - 10a$ for $a = -2$.
A. 40 B. 10 C. 0 D. −10

7. Which of the following properties is demonstrated by this equation? $7(x + y) = 7x + 7y$
A. the addition property of equality
B. the multiplication property of equality
C. the distributive property
D. the identity property

8. Solve $6y - 12 = 0$.
A. 0 B. 6 C. 12 D. 2

9. Mark and two friends mowed lawns this summer and made $1,125. At the end of the summer, they divided their total earnings equally. Mark had enough money to buy a bicycle and deposit $250 in the bank. How much did Mark pay for his new bicycle?
A. $875 B. $625 C. $292 D. $125

10. Twelve more than twice a number is −8. What is the number?
A. −16 B. −10 C. 2 D. 12

23. The diagram shows two perpendicular sidewalks at a school. Students take a shortcut between points A and B. Which is closest to the length of the shortcut? (Lesson 3-6) C

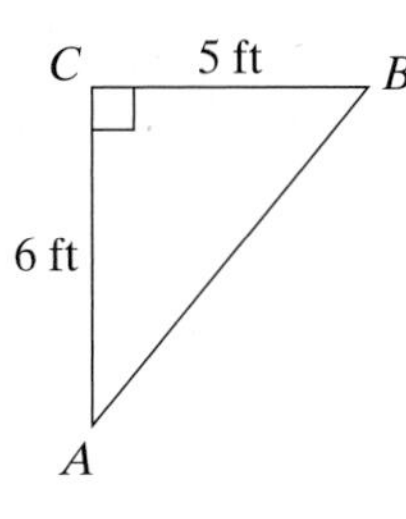

- (A) 3 ft
- (B) 5 ft
- (C) 8 ft
- (D) 11 ft

24. Which value is closest to 5? (Lesson 3-5) D

- (A) $\sqrt{2}$
- (B) $\sqrt{5}$
- (C) $\sqrt{21}$
- (D) $\sqrt{26}$

25. A player receives 300 points for completing each level of a video game. Let n represent the number of levels completed and let p represent the total number of points earned. Which graph represents this relationship? (Lesson 8-4) B

(A)

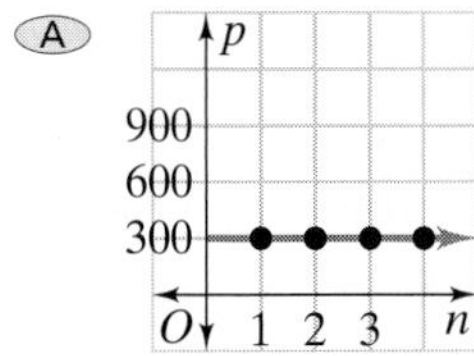

(B)

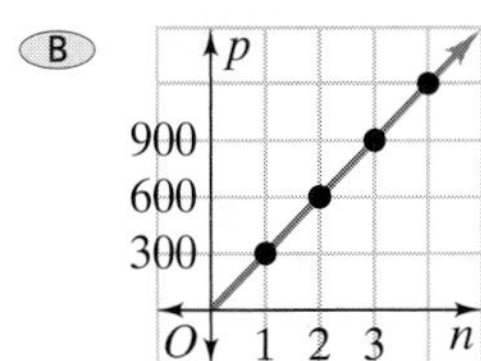

(C)

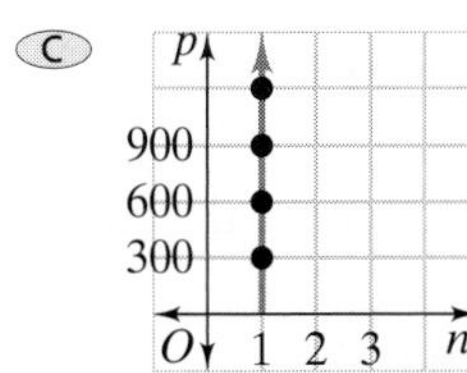

(D)

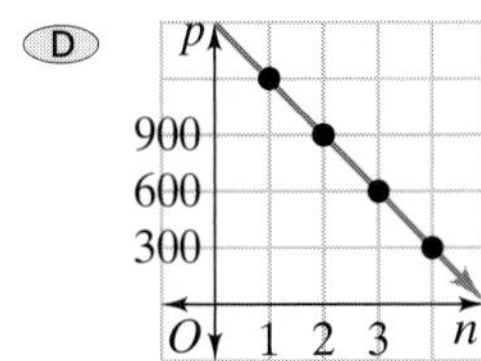

26. A student simplified the expression $3(x - 2) + 12$ as shown below. Which property did the student use in Step 1? (Lesson 10-4) D

Step 1: $3(x - 2) + 12 = 3x - 6 + 12$
Step 2: $= 3x + 6$

- (A) Commutative Property of Multiplication
- (B) Associative Property of Multiplication
- (C) Identity Property of Multiplication
- (D) Distributive Property

27. Which of the following stores has the lowest price per box of juice? (Lesson 6-2) C

- (A) Corner Store: 4 boxes for \$1.52
- (B) Joe's Grocery: 10 boxes for \$3.60
- (C) Fast Mart: 8 boxes for \$2.80
- (D) Mandy's Market: 5 boxes for \$1.85

28. Which expression is equivalent to $5w + 9$? (Lesson 10-4) C

- (A) $5(w + 2) - w - 1$
- (B) $5(w + 4)$
- (C) $6(w + 2) - w - 3$
- (D) $6(w - w + 3)$

29. Raul bikes $3\frac{1}{2}$ mi to a movie. Then he bikes 2.75 mi to the mall and 5 mi home. How many miles does he bike in all? (Lesson 5-1) C

- (A) $10\frac{1}{4}$ mi
- (B) $10\frac{3}{4}$ mi
- (C) $11\frac{1}{4}$ mi
- (D) $11\frac{3}{4}$ mi

30. What is the slope of the line below? (Lesson 8-5) D

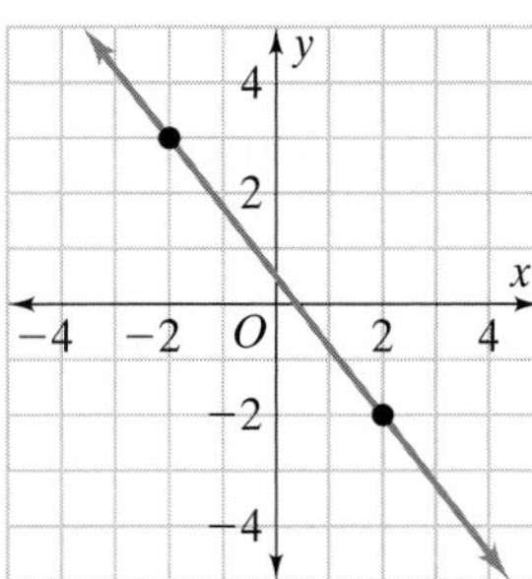

- (A) $\frac{5}{4}$
- (B) $\frac{4}{5}$
- (C) $-\frac{4}{5}$
- (D) $-\frac{5}{4}$

31. Which of the following numbers is NOT a rational number? (Lesson 4-4) B

(A) $\sqrt{0.81}$
(B) $\sqrt{0.\overline{66}}$
(C) 0.81
(D) $0.\overline{66}$

32. Grapes are on sale. Grace buys 3 lb for \$3.75. Which graph shows the relationship between the number of pounds of grapes bought x and the total cost y? (Lesson 8-6) C

(A)
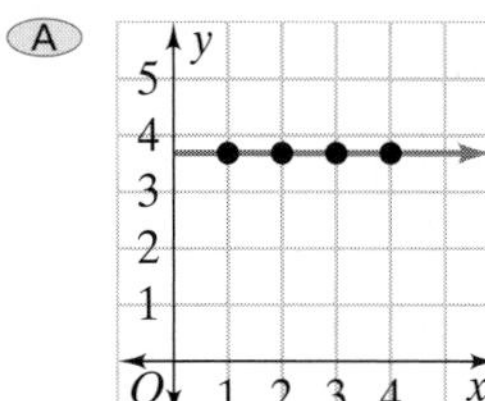

(B)
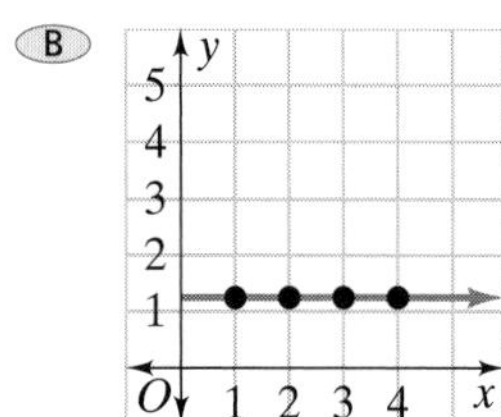

(C)
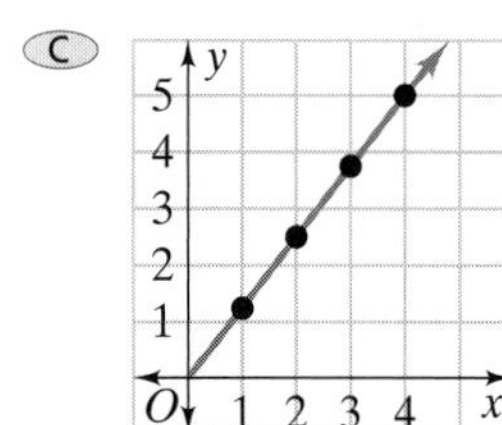

(D)
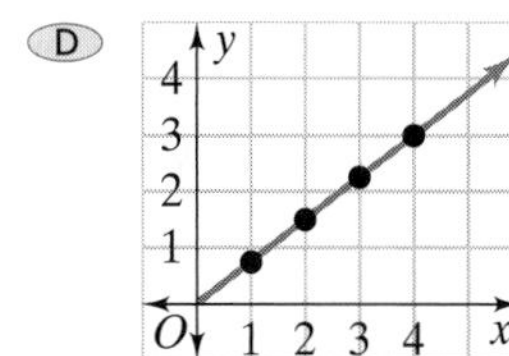

33. Which expression demonstrates the Identity Property of Addition? (Lesson 1-5) B

(A) $y + 1 = 1 + y$
(B) $y + 0 = y$
(C) $(y + 0) + 1 = y + (0 + 1)$
(D) $1(y + 1) = y + 1$

34. Mary Jo paid \$27.75 for 3 basketball tickets and \$21.50 for 2 football tickets. Which statement is true about these prices? (Lesson 6-4) D

(A) One basketball ticket costs the same as one football ticket.
(B) One basketball ticket costs \$.75 less than one football ticket.
(C) One basketball ticket costs \$1.25 less than one football ticket.
(D) One basketball ticket costs \$1.50 less than one football ticket.

35. Which value makes the equation $12h - 7 = -3h + 38$ true? (Lesson 10-6) A

(A) 3
(B) 5
(C) 7
(D) 9

36. Which number is NOT a solution to the inequality $4t - 7 \geq 9$? (Lesson 9-5) A

(A) 3
(B) 4
(C) 5
(D) 6

37. The table below shows costs for DVD rentals. Which statement is supported by the data? (Lesson 6-4) B

Number of DVDs	Rental Cost
1	\$3
2	\$5
3	\$6
4	\$7

(A) As you rent fewer DVDs, the cost per DVD decreases.
(B) As you rent fewer DVDs, the cost per DVD increases.
(C) As you rent more DVDs, the cost per DVD stays the same.
(D) As you rent more DVDs, the cost per DVD increases.

38. What is the length of $\overline{TW}$ in the graph below? (Lesson 8-2) C

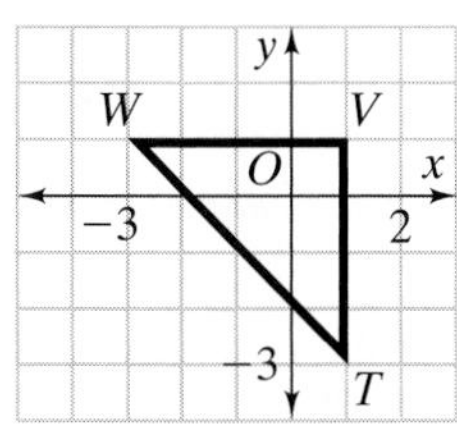

Ⓐ $\sqrt{8}$ Ⓒ $\sqrt{32}$
Ⓑ 2 Ⓓ 4

39. On a typing test, Lana typed 900 words in 5 min. Sierra typed 980 words in 7 min. Which of the following statements is true? (Lesson 6-4) C

Ⓐ Lana's average typing rate was 67 words per min faster than Sierra's average rate.
Ⓑ Sierra's average typing rate was 80 words per min faster than Lana's average rate.
Ⓒ Lana's average typing rate was 40 words per min faster than Sierra's average rate.
Ⓓ Lana's average typing rate was the same as Sierra's average rate.

40. The graph shows the relationship between the number of hours worked h and Gomez Plumbing's total bill b in dollars. What is the ratio of the total bill to the number of hours worked? (Lesson 8-6) D

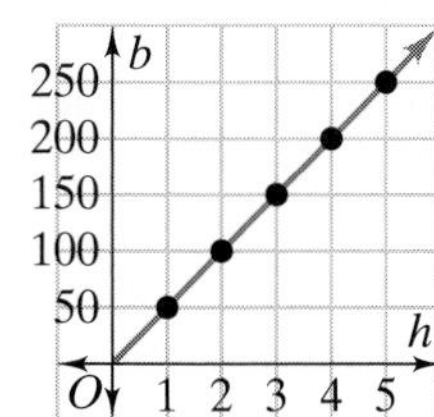

Ⓐ $\frac{150}{1}$ Ⓑ $\frac{100}{1}$ Ⓒ $\frac{250}{3}$ Ⓓ $\frac{50}{1}$

41. Which expression is equivalent to $3p + 5p + p - 2p + 4$? (Lesson 10-4) C

Ⓐ $11p$ Ⓒ $7p + 4$
Ⓑ $10p$ Ⓓ $6p + 4$

42. Anita has \$15. She plans to save \$6 per week. How long will it take her to save \$45? (Lesson 3-4) C

Ⓐ 9 wk Ⓒ 5 wk
Ⓑ 7.5 wk Ⓓ 3 wk

Standards Reference Guide

California Content Standard	Item Number(s)
NS 1.2	10, 19, 29
NS 1.5	5, 22, 31
AF 1.3	18, 26, 33
AF 3.3	2, 11, 30
AF 3.4	6, 25, 32, 40
AF 4.1	1, 7, 9, 12, 13, 36, 42
AF 4.2	4, 20, 34
MG 1.3	27, 37, 39
MG 3.3	14, 17, 23, 38
Alg1 2.0	3, 8, 15, 24
Alg1 4.0	16, 28, 41
Alg1 5.0	12, 21, 35

For additional review and practice, see the *California Standards Review and Practice Workbook* or go online to use the

Visit: PHSchool.com, **Web Code:** axq-9045

Chapter 1 Variables and Algebraic Expressions

Suppose your class is planning to honor someone special in the community or to congratulate a winning team. You need to decide when and where you will hold the event, how you will decorate, and what entertainment and refreshments you will provide. You may also need to decide how to raise funds for the celebration.

Plan a Celebration Your chapter project is to plan a celebration. You must decide how much it will cost and how much money each member of the class must raise. Your plan should include a list of supplies for the event and their costs.

For: Information to help you complete your project
Web Code: axd-0161

Chapter 2 Integers and Exponents

Would you go swimming in 32° water? Is −2° a good temperature setting for a home freezer? The answer to both questions is "That depends!"

Are you using the Celsius or Fahrenheit scale? Water at 32°C feels like a bath! As for a freezer, −2°C is barely below freezing, while −2°F is a deep freeze! People living in North America use both the Fahrenheit and the Celsius scales, so it pays to know the difference.

Prepare a Report For the chapter project, you will examine weather data for a state or region of your choice. Your final project will be a report on temperature data, using both scales.

Go Online
PHSchool.com

For: Information to help you complete your project
Web Code: axd-0261

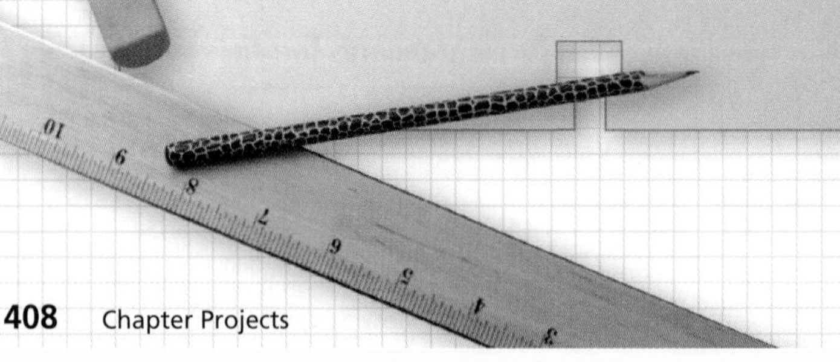

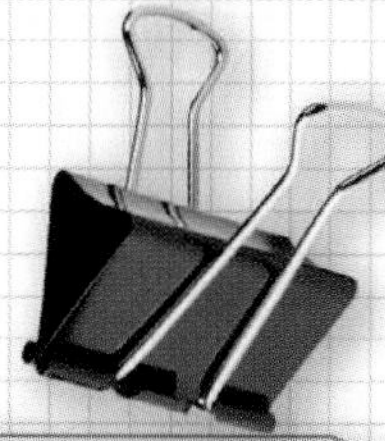

Chapter 3 Equations and Applications

Think about a historic building, such as one of the ancient pyramids or the Eiffel Tower. How many pieces of stone do you think were needed for the bottom of a pyramid compared to the top? Many buildings use mathematical patterns in their designs.

Building a Fort For this project, you will build a model of a simple fort. You will record the amounts of materials needed for each course, or layer of blocks. You will look for patterns and write equations to describe the patterns.

For: Information to help you complete your project
Web Code: axd-0361

Chapter 4 Rational Numbers

In Malcolm's daydream, he floats in the air on his way to a slam dunk. In reality, he tosses pieces of paper into a wastebasket. He makes some shots, and he misses others.

Compare Basketball Statistics Your project will be to record and compare baskets attempted and baskets made by the players on your own imaginary basketball team. You can shoot baskets with a real basketball on a real court, or you can toss pieces of paper into a wastebasket.

Go Online PHSchool.com
For: Information to help you complete your project
Web Code: axd-0461

Chapter Projects

SEEing is Believing

Chapter 5 Rational Number Operations

Have you ever conducted a science experiment? Scientists perform experiments to determine whether an idea is correct or incorrect. You can determine whether something is correct or not in math class, too.

Design a Demonstration You will learn ways to add fractions and mixed numbers with unlike denominators, but can you show that these techniques really work? Your goal is to show that they do by giving several demonstrations.

Go Online PHSchool.com
For: Information to help you complete your project
Web Code: axd-0561

CRACK IT and Cook It!

Chapter 5 Rational Number Operations

Eating a hearty breakfast is a great way to start any day! You are probably familiar with pouring a bowl of cereal, making toast, or maybe even scrambling eggs. But have you ever made an omelet? An omelet recipe can be simple—eggs, water, and maybe some salt or pepper. However, you can add other ingredients to this basic recipe to suit your taste. A cheese omelet is delicious. So is a bacon-and-tomato omelet. You might also add mushrooms, onions, and peppers.

Create a Recipe Put on your chef's hat. In this chapter project, you will write and name your own recipe for an omelet. Your final project will be a recipe that can feed everyone in your class.

Go Online PHSchool.com
For: Information to help you complete your project
Web Code: axd-0561

Chapter 6 Rates and Proportions

How much should a pizza cost? Many restaurants sell pizzas in a variety of sizes and types, with many different kinds of toppings. Do restaurants base their prices on what they think their customers will be willing to pay for different sizes? Or do they take a mathematical approach and figure their costs using area formulas?

Set Prices for a Product For the chapter project, you will investigate prices for a product that is available in many sizes. You will look for patterns in the prices and describe the patterns mathematically. Then you will use this analysis to decide on prices for new products. Your final project will be a written proposal for setting pizza prices.

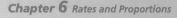

For: Information to help you complete your project
Web Code: axd-0661

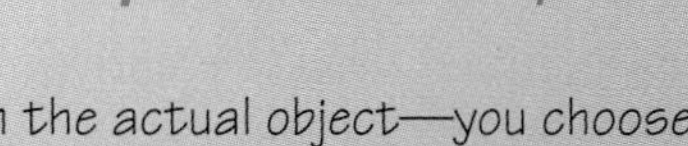

Chapter 6 Rates and Proportions

Mount Rushmore is an example of a scale model that is larger than the objects on which it is based—much larger! Other types of scale models, such as toy trains, dollhouses, and other toys, are smaller than the objects on which they are based.

Build a Scale Model For the chapter project, you will build your own scale model. First, you will choose an object to model. Use your imagination! Your model can be larger or smaller than the actual object—you choose the scale. Then you will select building materials and assemble the model. Your final project will be to present the model to your class, explaining the scale and how you chose the item to model.

For: Information to help you complete your project
Web Code: axd-0661

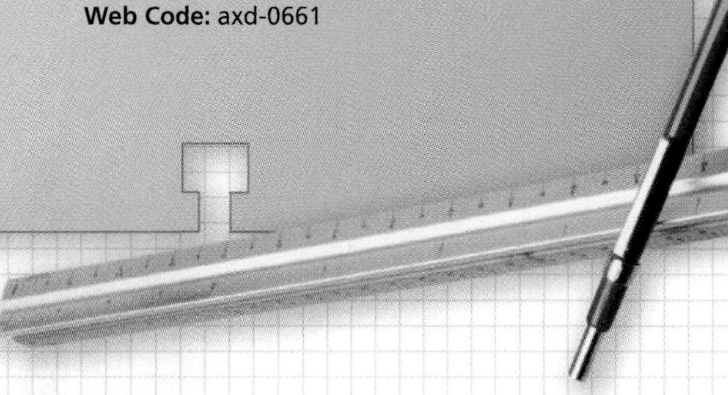

Chapter Projects

411

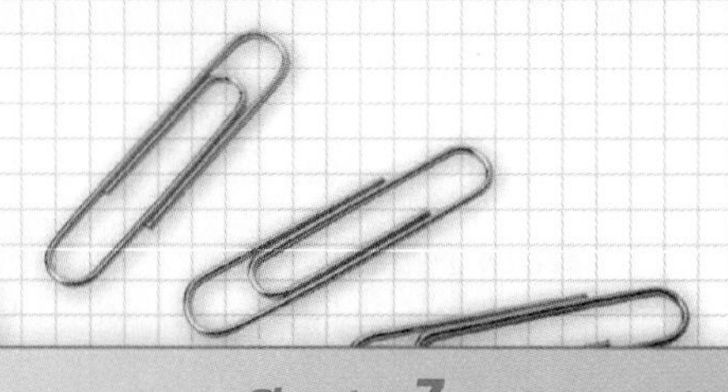

Invest in a WINNER

Chapter 7 Applications of Percent

You've won! You entered a quiz contest thinking you didn't have a chance, and now you're $5,000 richer! You are looking for a way to double your money in five years. Is that possible?

Explore Ways to Invest Money For the chapter project, you will explore different investments, looking for the best one for your money. Your final project will be to prepare an oral and visual presentation describing your investment choice.

Go Online
PHSchool.com
For: Information to help you complete your project
Web Code: axd-0761

Step Right UP!

Chapter 8 Linear Functions and Graphing

Have you ever been to a carnival or fair? "Hit the bull's-eye and win a prize!" Is it skill? Or is it luck?

Design a Game Suppose your class is putting on a fair to raise money for a class trip. For the chapter project, you will invent a game in which a ball rolls down a ramp and comes to rest in a target area of your own design. Does a bull's-eye score 10, or maybe 100? Can the players vary the slope of the ramp? You decide, since you make up the rules! Your final project will be the game, along with written rules to play by.

Go Online
PHSchool.com
For: Information to help you complete your project
Web Code: axd-0861

WORKING for a Cause

Chapter 9 Inequalities

Have you ever participated in a fundraiser? Schools and sports clubs often use fundraisers as a way to pay for such things as equipment, trips, and camps. You have probably purchased candy bars, magazines, or wrapping paper to help a friend or group raise money.

Plan a Fundraiser In this chapter project, you will plan a fundraiser. You will choose a cause or charity, decide how much money you would like to raise, and determine the type of event to hold or the type of product to sell. As part of your final project, you will present a fundraising plan to your class.

For: Information to help you complete your project
Web Code: axd-0961

One Small STEP

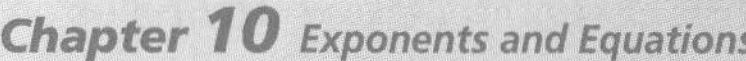

Chapter 10 Exponents and Equations

"That's one small step for man; one giant leap for mankind." In July of 1969, Neil Armstrong was the first man to touch the moon's surface. Since then, space travel has expanded, with new missions being launched almost monthly.

Can you imagine what the space program will be like in 30 more years? How about in 100 years? Take a small step into the future. Pretend you are a travel agent—one who specializes in space travel!

Create a brochure For the chapter project, you will collect information about two planets, including travel between them, and calculate the approximate distance from Earth to each of them. Your final project will be to design a space-travel brochure that includes interesting and enticing information about travel between the planets.

For: Information to help you complete your project
Web Code: axd-1061

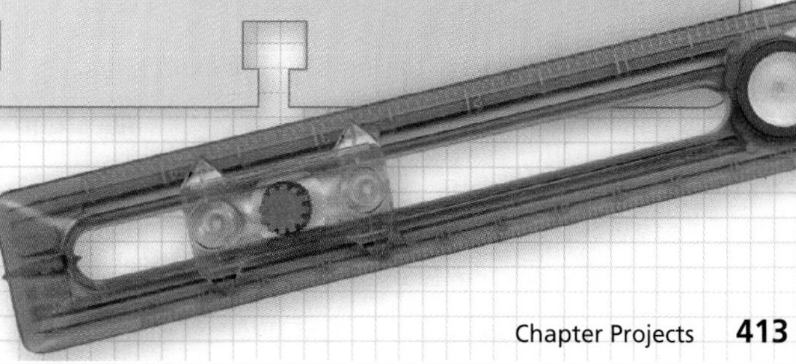

Chapter Projects

CHAPTER 1 Extra Practice

Skills

Lesson 1-1 Simplify each expression.

1. $2 + 6 \cdot 3 + 1$ 21
2. $(14 + 44) \div 2$ 29
3. $3 + 64 \div -10$ −3.4
4. $1.44 + 56 \div 4$ 15.44
5. $30 - 5 + 4 \cdot 3.2$ 37.8
6. $(27 - 9) \div 3$ 6
7. $5.4 \cdot 8 + 4 \div 2$ 45.2
8. $(9 - 1 \cdot 3) \div 2$ 3

Lesson 1-2 Evaluate each expression for $n = 9$.

9. $n - 7$ 2
10. $3n - 5$ 22
11. $22 - 2n$ 4
12. $4n \div 6$ 6

Evaluate each expression for $x = 3.2$.

13. $2x + 5$ 11.4
14. $3x + 18$ 27.6
15. $4 - x$ 0.8
16. $(13 - x) \div 5$ 1.96

Lesson 1-3 Write an expression for each word phrase.

17. 1 less than b $b - 1$
18. p times 2 $2p$
19. 4 more than b $b + 4$
20. n divided by 2 $n \div 2$
21. 13 less than q $q - 13$
22. the sum of v and 18 $v + 18$
23. 7 subtracted from m $m - 7$
24. 9 minus d $9 - d$
25. the quotient of x and 4 $x \div 4$

Lesson 1-4 Estimate. Use rounding or compatible numbers.

26. $5.32 \cdot 2.01$ about 10
27. $15.348 - 7.92$ about 7
28. $22.961 \div 3.6$ about 6
29. $728.6 + 36.09$ about 765
30. $97 + 22 + 48$ about 170
31. $207 \div 51$ about 4
32. $94 - 32 - 41$ about 20
33. $69 \cdot 7$ about 490

Lesson 1-5 Name the property each equation illustrates.

34. $2(11) + 2(4) = 2(11 + 4)$ Dist. Prop.
35. $(3 + 4) + 5 = 3 + (4 + 5)$ Assoc. Prop. of Add.
36. $2n + p = p + 2n$ Comm. Prop. of Add.
37. $(3 + m)(-7) = (-7)(3 + m)$ Comm. Prop. of Mult.
38. $(12 \cdot 5) \cdot 100 = 12 \cdot (5 \cdot 100)$ Assoc. Prop. of Mult.
39. $c + 0 = c$ Ident. Prop. of Add.

Lesson 1-6 Simplify each expression.

40. $(n + 14)(18)$ $18n + 252$
41. $(m + 4)8$ $8m + 32$
42. $3(p - 7)$ $3p - 21$
43. $5(2 - k)$ $10 - 5k$

Use the Distributive Property to simplify each expression.

44. $7 \cdot 78$ 546
45. $3 \cdot 19$ 57
46. $6 \cdot 66$ 396
47. $4 \cdot 47$ 188

Word Problems

Lesson 1-1

48. A group of 28 students and 3 teachers goes to the theater. Each student pays $12. The school pays an additional $4 per student and $16 per adult. Find the total cost of the trip. $496

Lesson 1-2

49. A company selling T-shirts charges $45 to create a design it will print on shirts. Each T-shirt costs $3. You can use the expression $3x + 45$ to find the cost of an order, where x stands for the number of T-shirts. How much does it cost to order 350 T-shirts? $1,095

Lesson 1-3

50. A paddleboat rents for $10 plus $8 per hour. How much does it cost to rent a paddleboat for *h* hours? Draw a model and write an expression for the situation. $10 + $8*h*

Lesson 1-4

51. You spend $546 on school lunches for the school year. There are about 180 days of school in the school year. About how much do you spend on lunch each day? about $3

Lesson 1-5

52. What is the total number of instruments in the orchestra shown in the table at the right? 56 instruments

53. The monthly rate for a 3-year subscription to an online music service is $10. What is the total cost for 3 years? $360

Orchestra

Instrument	Number
Violin	29
Viola	13
Bass	2
Cello	12

Lesson 1-6 **Use the Distributive Property to find each total cost.**

54. 3 loaves of bread at $1.99 each $5.97

55. 6 cans of tuna at $.97 each $5.82

56. 4 bags of berries at $1.98 each $7.92

57. 5 boxes of rice at $2.95 each $14.75

Extra Skills and Word Problems

415

CHAPTER 2

Extra Practice

Skills

Lesson 2-1 Find the least integer in each list.

1. 3, −1, 0, −2 −2
2. 4, −8, −5, 2 −8
3. −6, 8, 7, −8 −8
4. −1, −8, 0, 1 −8

Compare. Write <, =, or >.

5. −7 ■ 7 <
6. 32 ■ $|-32|$ =
7. $|-9|$ ■ −3 >
8. $|-8|$ ■ $|-6|$ >

Evaluate each expression for the given value.

9. $|4d|$ for $d = 71$ 284
10. $32 + |b|$ for $b = -9$ 41
11. $4|s|$ for $s = -5$ 20
12. $|m|$ for $m = -12$ 12

Lesson 2-2 Find each sum.

13. −14 + 28 14
14. −72 + (−53) −125
15. −3 + 1 −2
16. −6 + 4 −2
17. −4 + (−5) −9
18. −2 + 6 4
19. −3 + (−5) −8
20. −38 + (−38) −76

Lesson 2-3 Find each difference.

21. −27 − (−27) 0
22. −8 − (−5) −3
23. 15 − (−8) 23
24. 99 − (−101) 200
25. 21 − (−15) 36
26. −23 − (−23) 0
27. 6 − 18 −12
28. 12 − (−5) 17

Lesson 2-4 Find each product.

29. −8 · 5 −40
30. −4 · (−9) 36
31. −3 · 4 −12
32. −15 · (−5) 75
33. 2 · (−7) · 5 −70
34. −9 · 8 · (−2) 144
35. −4 · (−2) · (−2) −16
36. −7 · (−2) · 4 56

Lesson 2-5 Find each quotient.

37. 93 ÷ (−3) −31
38. −48 ÷ (−2) 24
39. −12 ÷ 6 −2
40. −80 ÷ −16 5
41. 16 ÷ −8 −2
42. −50 ÷ 5 −10
43. −54 ÷ −9 6
44. −120 ÷ 3 −40

Lesson 2-6 Simplify each expression.

45. $7 + 5^2$ 32
46. $(6 - 2)^3 \cdot 3$ 192
47. 8^3 512
48. $9^2 + 2^2$ 85

Evaluate each expression for the given value.

49. $-3x^2 - (-8)$ for $x = 5$ −67
50. $2r^2 + 6r + 3$ for $r = -6$ 39

Word Problems

Lesson 2-1

51. A teacher asks 15 students to estimate an answer to a question. The answers are 1, 5, 5, 6, 7, 8, 10, and 12. The correct estimate is 7. The teacher wants to calculate how far off the estimates were by finding the absolute value of the difference between each estimate and the answer. Which estimate was off by the most? 1

Lesson 2-2

52. A football team gains 6 yd on one play and loses 11 yd on the next play. What is the result of the two plays? a loss of 5 yd

53. A stock worth $34 at the beginning of the day lost $15 in value by the end of the day. What was the price at the end of the day? $19

Lesson 2-3

54. A balloon is floating 47 ft above a lake. The bottom of the lake is 128 ft below the surface. How high above the lake bottom is the balloon? 175 ft

Lesson 2-4

55. A fishing line sinks at 4 in./s. Find the change in depth of the fishing line after 30 s. −120 in.

56. The temperature drops 5°F/h. Find the change in temperature after 3 h. −15°F

Lesson 2-5

57. Over five months, a horse loses 15 lb. Find the rate of change in pounds per month. −3 lb/month

58. During a 3-day sale, the price of a sweater decreases by $42. Find the rate of change in dollars per day. −$14/day

Lesson 2-6

59. The formula for the area of a square is $A = s^2$. What is the area of a square whose sides measure 12 cm? 144 cm^2

Extra Skills and Word Problems

Extra Skills and Word Problems

CHAPTER 3

Extra Practice

Skills

Lesson 3-1 Solve each equation.

1. $b + 4 = 7.7$ 3.7
2. $c + 3.5 = 7.5$ 4
3. $-12 = m + 8$ -20
4. $x + 10 = 10$ 0

Lesson 3-2 Solve each equation.

5. $n - 1.7 = 8$ 9.7
6. $8.4 = s - 0.2$ 8.6
7. $x - 6 = -15$ -9
8. $1.5 = m - 3.2$ 4.7

Lesson 3-3 Solve each equation.

9. $15t = 600$ 40
10. $62 = 2b$ 31
11. $x \div 5 = 2.5$ 12.5
12. $a \div 0.05 = 140$ 7
13. $\frac{b}{7} = 9$ 63
14. $-3w = 360$ -120
15. $144 = 6k$ 24
16. $20 = \frac{h}{-10}$ -200

Lesson 3-4 Solve each equation.

17. $2a + 8 = 26$ 9
18. $3c + 2.5 = 29.5$ 9
19. $5b - 13 = 17$ 6
20. $7.5d - 7 = 53$ 8
21. $6n + 3 = 21$ 3
22. $10 = \frac{m}{5} + 2$ 40
23. $-b + 2 = -\frac{1}{2}$ 2.5
24. $7g - 4 = 10$ 2

Lesson 3-5 Find the square roots of each number.

25. 36 6, -6
26. 64 8, -8
27. 169 13, -13
28. 484 22, -22

Lesson 3-6 Find the length of the hypotenuse of each right triangle if *a* and *b* represent the lengths of the two legs.

29. $a = 10$, $b = 24$ 26
30. $a = 7$, $b = 13$ $\sqrt{218} \approx 14.8$
31. $a = 6$, $b = 11$ $\sqrt{157} \approx 12.5$
32. $a = 1.2$, $b = 1.6$ 2

Lesson 3-7 Find the missing leg length.

33. $a = 21$, $b = ■$, $c = 35$ 28
34. $a = ■$, $b = 9$, $c = 15$ 12
35. $a = 7$, $b = ■$, $c = 25$ 24
36. $a = ■$, $b = 7.5$, $c = 12.5$ 10
37. $a = 23$, $b = ■$, $c = 44$ $\sqrt{1,407} \approx 37.5$
38. $a = ■$, $b = 50$, $c = 76$ $\sqrt{3,276} \approx 57.2$

Determine whether the given lengths can be sides of a right triangle. Explain.

39. 5 ft, 12 ft, 13 ft
yes; $5^2 + 12^2 = 13^2$
40. 15 cm, 35 cm, 40 cm
no; $15^2 + 35^2 \neq 40^2$
41. 2.0 in., 2.1 in., 2.9 in.
yes; $2.0^2 + 2.1^2 = 2.9^2$

Word Problems

Lesson 3-1

42. Between 7:30 A.M. and 8:00 A.M. the number of students in a school increased by 73. There were 152 students in the school at 8:00 A.M. How many students were in school at 7:30 A.M.? **79 students**

Lesson 3-2

43. The height of the female giraffe in a zoo is 14.1 ft. The female is 3.2 ft shorter than the male giraffe. Write and solve an equation to find the male's height. **17.3 ft**

Lesson 3-3

44. The area of the Pacific Ocean is about 64,000,000 mi^2. This area is about twice the area of the Atlantic Ocean. Find the approximate area of the Atlantic Ocean. **32,000,000 mi^2**

Lesson 3-4

45. Claudia bought 3 movie passes and a large box of popcorn. The total cost was $33.49. The popcorn cost $4.99. How much did each movie pass cost? **$9.50**

46. You deliver boxes weighing 20 lb each to a business on the sixth floor of a building. The elevator has a weight limit of 1,500 lb. Your weight is 180 lb. How many boxes can you load on the elevator? Use b for the number of boxes. Use the equation $20b + 180 = 1{,}500$. **66 boxes**

Lesson 3-5

47. A square has an area of 240.25 in.^{2}. What is the length of each side? **15.5 in.**

Lesson 3-6

48. A support wire is attached to the top of a 60-m tower. It meets the ground 25 m from the base of the tower. How long is the support wire? **65 m**

Lesson 3-7

49. A tree forms a right angle with the ground. If you place the base of a 12-ft ladder 3 ft from the tree, how high up the tree will it reach? **about 11.6 ft**

Extra Skills and Word Problems

1. Composite; the factors are 1, 2, 3, 4, 6, 8, and 24.
2. Composite; the factors are 1, 7, 7, and 49.
3. Prime; the only factors are 1 and 7.
4. Composite; the factors are 1, 3, 9, 27, and 81.
5. Prime; the only factors are 1 and 37.
6. Prime; the only factors are 1 and 29.

CHAPTER 4 Extra Practice

Skills

Lesson 4-1 **Is each number prime or composite? Explain.** 1–6. See margin.

1. 24 **2.** 49 **3.** 7 **4.** 81 **5.** 37 **6.** 29

Find the prime factorization of each number.

7. 64 2^6 **8.** 72 $2^3 \cdot 3^2$ **9.** 132 $2^2 \cdot 3 \cdot 11$ **10.** 180 $2^2 \cdot 3^2 \cdot 5$ **11.** 255 $3 \cdot 5 \cdot 17$ **12.** 324 $2^2 \cdot 3^4$

Lesson 4-2 **Use prime factorization to find the GCD of each pair of numbers.**

13. 7, 15 1 **14.** 4, 18 2 **15.** 22, 121 11

16. 17, 51 17 **17.** 42, 165 3 **18.** 18, 60 6

Lesson 4-3 **Write two fractions equivalent to each fraction.** 19–24. Answers may vary. Samples are given.

19. $\frac{6}{60}$ $\frac{1}{10}, \frac{2}{20}$ **20.** $\frac{3}{5}$ $\frac{6}{10}, \frac{9}{15}$ **21.** $\frac{27}{36}$ $\frac{3}{4}, \frac{6}{8}$ **22.** $\frac{40}{50}$ $\frac{4}{5}, \frac{8}{10}$ **23.** $\frac{3}{4}$ $\frac{6}{8}, \frac{30}{40}$ **24.** $\frac{42}{70}$ $\frac{6}{10}, \frac{3}{5}$

Write each fraction in simplest form.

25. $\frac{20}{25}$ $\frac{4}{5}$ **26.** $\frac{7}{77}$ $\frac{1}{11}$ **27.** $\frac{40}{48}$ $\frac{5}{6}$ **28.** $-\frac{15}{35}$ $-\frac{3}{7}$ **29.** $\frac{36}{63}$ $\frac{4}{7}$ **30.** $-\frac{9}{42}$ $-\frac{3}{14}$

Lesson 4-4 **Write each decimal as a fraction in simplest form.**

31. 0.24 $\frac{6}{25}$ **32.** 0.36 $\frac{9}{25}$ **33.** 0.65 $\frac{13}{20}$

34. 0.125 $\frac{1}{8}$ **35.** 0.225 $\frac{9}{40}$ **36.** 0.625 $\frac{5}{8}$

Write each fraction as a decimal. Round to three decimal places, if necessary.

37. $\frac{4}{5}$ 0.8 **38.** $-\frac{9}{10}$ −0.9 **39.** $\frac{14}{3}$ 4.667 **40.** $-\frac{2}{3}$ −0.667 **41.** $\frac{4}{11}$ 0.364 **42.** $\frac{13}{8}$ 1.625

Lesson 4-5 **Order each set of numbers from least to greatest.**

43. $\frac{4}{7}, \frac{4}{5}, \frac{4}{9}$ $\frac{4}{9}, \frac{4}{7}, \frac{4}{5}$ **44.** $\frac{6}{16}, \frac{7}{16}, \frac{5}{16}$ $\frac{5}{16}, \frac{6}{16}, \frac{7}{16}$

45. $\frac{2}{3}, \frac{5}{6}, \frac{7}{12}$ $\frac{7}{12}, \frac{2}{3}, \frac{5}{6}$ **46.** $\frac{3}{4}, \frac{4}{6}, \frac{7}{9}$ $\frac{4}{6}, \frac{3}{4}, \frac{7}{9}$

Compare each pair of numbers. Use <, =, or >.

47. $\frac{7}{8}$ ■ $\frac{2}{3}$ > **48.** $\frac{3}{5}$ ■ $\frac{7}{9}$ < **49.** $\frac{25}{40}$ ■ $\frac{5}{8}$ = **50.** $\frac{5}{6}$ ■ $\frac{8}{9}$ <

Word Problems

Lesson 4-1

51. A photographer arranges 126 students for a class picture. Each row has the same number of students. What numbers of rows can he make?
1, 2, 3, 6, 7, 9, 14, 18, 21, 42, 63, or 126 rows

Lesson 4-2

52. On a field day, 84 girls and 78 boys are divided into teams. Each team has the same number of girls and the same number of boys. At most, how many teams are possible? 6 teams

53. Two frogs hop around a circular track that is 60 in. around. First the larger frog jumps 13 in. and then the smaller frog jumps 11 in. If they take turns jumping, how many inches from the start will they be when they are once again at the same point? 30 in.

Lesson 4-3

54. You have 20 homework problems. You finish 15 of them while you are at the library. In simplest form, what fraction of the problems do you have left to do at home? $\frac{1}{4}$

55. A framer uses an inch ruler marked in sixteenths to measure the frame at the right. What is the measure of the height of the frame to the nearest sixteenth of an inch? $32\frac{10}{16}$ in.

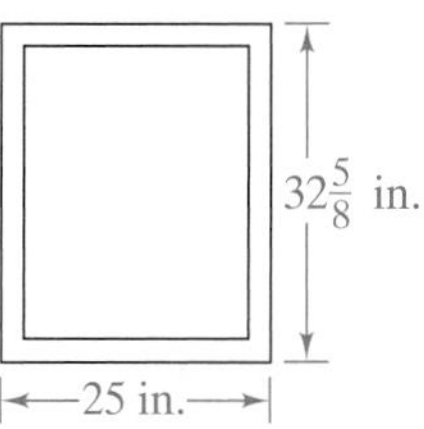

Lesson 4-4

56. The red volleyball team won 4 out of 9 matches. The blue team won 5 out of 12 matches. Which team has the better record? Explain. the red team; $\frac{4}{9} > \frac{5}{12}$

57. A bag of beads for a craft project weighs 6 oz. The project uses 5 bags. Express the total weight of the beads in pounds as a decimal. 1.875

Lesson 4-5

58. Two students are measuring the amount of water in two liquids. One student finds that $\frac{10}{17}$ of the first liquid is water. The other finds that 0.6 of the second liquid is water. Which of the two liquids has the greater fraction of water? the second liquid

59. Arrange the side lengths of the triangle in order from least to greatest. Explain your reasoning. $1\frac{3}{16}$, $1\frac{7}{32}$, $1\frac{1}{4}$

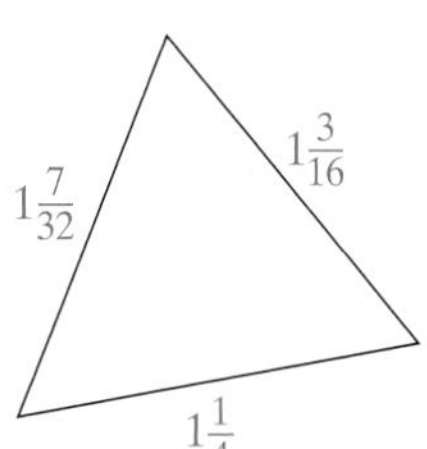

Extra Skills and Word Problems

421

CHAPTER 5

Extra Practice

Skills

Lesson 5-1 Find each sum.

1. $\frac{5}{8}+\frac{1}{8}$ $\frac{3}{4}$
2. $\frac{11}{12}+\frac{5}{12}$ $1\frac{1}{3}$
3. $\frac{5}{6}+\frac{2}{3}$ $1\frac{1}{2}$
4. $\frac{3}{5}+\frac{5}{8}$ $1\frac{9}{40}$
5. $6\frac{2}{3}+1\frac{1}{2}$ $8\frac{1}{6}$
6. $5\frac{7}{8}+1\frac{3}{4}$ $7\frac{5}{8}$
7. $8\frac{1}{4}+3\frac{1}{3}$ $11\frac{7}{12}$
8. $7\frac{3}{10}+3\frac{1}{4}$ $10\frac{11}{20}$

Lesson 5-2 Find each difference.

9. $\frac{4}{5}-\frac{2}{5}$ $\frac{2}{5}$
10. $\frac{7}{8}-\frac{3}{8}$ $\frac{1}{2}$
11. $\frac{7}{16}-\frac{1}{4}$ $\frac{3}{16}$
12. $\frac{3}{4}-\frac{5}{12}$ $\frac{1}{3}$
13. $7\frac{3}{8}-1\frac{2}{3}$ $5\frac{17}{24}$
14. $11\frac{1}{6}-2\frac{3}{4}$ $8\frac{5}{12}$
15. $7\frac{5}{6}-2\frac{1}{10}$ $5\frac{11}{15}$
16. $6\frac{1}{3}-2\frac{1}{4}$ $4\frac{1}{12}$

Lesson 5-3 Find each product.

17. $\frac{1}{2}\cdot\frac{2}{3}$ $\frac{1}{3}$
18. $\frac{1}{3}\cdot\frac{1}{5}$ $\frac{1}{15}$
19. $\frac{7}{8}\cdot\frac{3}{4}$ $\frac{21}{32}$
20. $\frac{6}{7}\cdot 42$ 36

Simplify each expression.

21. $\left(\frac{1}{5}\right)^3$ $\frac{1}{125}$
22. $\left(-\frac{5}{8}\right)^2$ $\frac{25}{64}$
23. $\left(\frac{1}{4}\right)^4$ $\frac{1}{256}$
24. $\left(\frac{2}{7}\right)^2$ $\frac{4}{49}$

Lesson 5-4 Find each quotient.

25. $2\div\frac{4}{5}$ $2\frac{1}{2}$
26. $\frac{2}{3}\div\frac{2}{5}$ $1\frac{2}{3}$
27. $\frac{1}{4}\div\frac{1}{5}$ $1\frac{1}{4}$
28. $\frac{4}{11}\div 8$ $\frac{1}{22}$

Lesson 5-5 Solve each equation.

29. $x+6\frac{4}{9}=8\frac{1}{9}$ $1\frac{2}{3}$
30. $n+4\frac{1}{2}=5$ $\frac{1}{2}$
31. $m-5\frac{3}{4}=10\frac{1}{2}$ $16\frac{1}{4}$
32. $p-8\frac{1}{3}=9\frac{1}{4}$ $17\frac{7}{12}$

Lesson 5-6 Solve each equation.

33. $4x=\frac{1}{8}$ $\frac{1}{32}$
34. $7c=\frac{14}{15}$ $\frac{2}{15}$
35. $-\frac{3}{4}w=12$ -16
36. $\frac{1}{3}y=15$ 45

Lesson 5-7 Simplify each expression.

37. 2^{-5} $\frac{1}{32}$
38. $(-9)^{-2}$ $\frac{1}{81}$
39. $\left(\frac{3}{8}\right)^{-3}$ $\frac{512}{27}$
40. $\left(\frac{1}{5}\right)^{-4}$ 625

Word Problems

Lesson 5-1

41. You buy two goldfish. One goldfish weighs $\frac{1}{6}$ oz. The other goldfish weighs $\frac{1}{3}$ oz. What is the combined weight of the goldfish? $\frac{1}{2}$ oz

Lesson 5-2

42. A small room has a floor space that measures $48\frac{3}{4}$ ft^2. In one corner of the room a cabinet will be set. The rest of the room will be carpeted. If the cabinet takes up $4\frac{2}{3}$ ft^2, how much carpeting is needed? $44\frac{1}{12}$ ft^2

Lesson 5-3

43. Find the perimeter of a square whose sides measure $4\frac{7}{8}$ in. $19\frac{1}{2}$ in.

44. A bag of nuts weighs $2\frac{1}{4}$ oz. A chef uses $3\frac{1}{2}$ bags to make a recipe. How many ounces of nuts are used in the recipe? $7\frac{7}{8}$ oz

Lesson 5-4

45. You bake an apple pie. The recipe calls for eight sliced apples. You cut the apples into eighths. How many pieces of apple do you have? 64 pieces

46. The price of one technology stock rises $71\frac{5}{8}$ points in $7\frac{1}{2}$ h. Find the number of points gained per hour during that time. $9\frac{11}{20}$ points/h

Lesson 5-5

47. A piece of poster board is $2\frac{3}{4}$ ft long. You shorten the length by $\frac{1}{2}$ ft. How long is the shortened poster board? $2\frac{1}{4}$ ft

48. Theresa has 200 yd of ribbon. She needs $1\frac{1}{6}$ yd of ribbon to make a bow. How many bows can she make? 171 bows

Lesson 5-6

49. Pedro bikes $3\frac{1}{3}$ times as far as Pat, and Pat bikes $\frac{1}{5}$ as far as Jen. If Pedro bikes 8 mi per day, how far does Jen bike? 12 mi

Lesson 5-7

50. One millimeter equals 10^{-4} m. Simplify 10^{-4}. $\frac{1}{10{,}000}$ or 0.0001

Extra Skills and Word Problems

Extra Skills and Word Problems

CHAPTER 6

Extra Practice

Skills

Lesson 6-1 Write two different ratios equivalent to each ratio. 1–4. Answers may vary. Samples are given.

1. $\frac{30}{60}$ $\frac{1}{2}$, $\frac{3}{6}$
2. 5 : 15 1 : 3, 10 : 30
3. 13 to 52 1 to 4, 2 to 8
4. 18 to 72 1 to 4, 26 to 104

Write each ratio in simplest form.

5. 4 : 28 1 : 7
6. $\frac{27}{9}$ $\frac{3}{1}$
7. $\frac{30}{45}$ $\frac{2}{3}$
8. 12 to 8 3 to 2

Lesson 6-2 Find each unit rate.

9. 240 mi on 8 gal 30 mi/gal
10. \$3.50 for 10 oz \$.35/dozen
11. 450 mi in 9 h 50 mi/h
12. \$18 for 12 cans \$1.50/can

Find the better buy for each pair of products.

13. Cereal: 12 oz for \$2.99; 16 oz for \$3.59 16 oz
14. Rice: 8 oz for \$1.95; 12 oz for \$2.99 8 oz
15. Shampoo: 10.2 oz for \$5.98; 16 oz for \$9.95 10.2 oz

Lesson 6-3 Convert each measurement.

16. 4 ft = ■ yd $1\frac{1}{3}$
17. 48 oz = ■ lb 3
18. 32 qt = ■ gal 8
19. 8,000 lb = ■ t 4
20. 10 lb = ■ oz 160
21. ■ ft = 60 in. 5
22. 64 c = ■ pt 32
23. 9 mi = ■ ft 47,520
24. 12 h = ■ min 720

Lesson 6-4 Find each total distance.

25. 20 mi/h for 7 h and 35 mi/h for 12 h 560 mi
26. 22 m/s for 20 s and 78 m/s for 8 s 1,064 m

Lesson 6-5 Do the ratios form a proportion? Explain.

27. $\frac{11}{18}, \frac{22}{32}$ no; $\frac{11}{18} \neq \frac{22}{32}$
28. $\frac{15}{27}, \frac{5}{9}$ yes; $\frac{15}{27} = \frac{5}{9}$
29. $\frac{30}{4}, \frac{15}{2}$ yes; $\frac{30}{4} = \frac{15}{2}$
30. $\frac{3}{8}, \frac{4}{10}$ no; $\frac{3}{8} \neq \frac{4}{10}$
31. $\frac{7}{19}, \frac{21}{34}$ no; $\frac{7}{19} \neq \frac{21}{34}$
32. $\frac{11}{2}, \frac{55}{10}$ yes; $\frac{11}{2} = \frac{55}{10}$

Solve each proportion.

33. $\frac{4}{7} = \frac{x}{21}$ 12
34. $\frac{3}{x} = \frac{18}{9}$ 1.5
35. $\frac{x}{10} = \frac{8}{15}$ $5\frac{1}{3}$
36. $\frac{3}{5} = \frac{2}{x}$ $3\frac{1}{3}$
37. $\frac{29}{x} = \frac{14}{7}$ 14.5
38. $\frac{9}{36} = \frac{x}{120}$ 30

Word Problems

Lesson 6-1

39. Seven out of 21 students at a school do not like horror movies. Write the ratio, in simplest form, of students who like horror movies to students who dislike horror movies. 2 to 1 or $\frac{2}{1}$ or 2 : 1

40. A family has 10 pets. Three of the pets are cats, one of the pets is a turtle, and the rest of the pets are fish. Write the ratio, in simplest form, of the number of fish to the total number of pets. 3 to 5 or $\frac{3}{5}$ or 3 : 5

Lesson 6-2

41. You baby-sit for four hours and earn $22.00. How much money do you make each hour? $5.50

42. A 12-oz bottle of liquid detergent costs $3.99. A 25.4-oz bottle of the same liquid detergent costs $7.49. Find the unit cost of each bottle. Which bottle of liquid detergent is the better buy? $.33; $.29; 25.4 oz

Lesson 6-3

43. In parts of Alaska, moose cause traffic jams. An adult moose weighs about 1,000 lb. How many tons does an adult moose weigh? 0.5 tons

44. The world's fastest elevators are located in a building in Taiwan. At top speed, the elevators can go as fast as 37.6 mi/h. What is the rate in feet per second? about 55 ft/s

Lesson 6-4

45. You pay $1.08 to make 18 copies of a report. At that rate, how much would you pay for 40 copies? $2.40

46. A plant grows 3 in. per week for 2 weeks and then grows 1 in. per week for the next 2 weeks. What is the plant's average rate of growth over the 4 weeks? 2 in./wk

Lesson 6-5

47. Florence can knit 3 scarves in 7 days. Write and solve a proportion to find how long it will take her to knit 10 scarves for a school fundraiser. $23\frac{1}{3}$ days

48. On a particular day, the exchange rate for dollars to German marks was 0.5582. How many German marks would you receive in exchange for 350 dollars? 195.37 marks

Extra Skills and Word Problems

Extra Skills and Word Problems

CHAPTER 7

Extra Practice

Skills

Lesson 7-1 Write each percent as a fraction in simplest form.

1. 42% $\frac{21}{50}$
2. 96% $\frac{24}{25}$
3. 80% $\frac{4}{5}$
4. 87% $\frac{87}{100}$

Write each fraction or decimal as a percent.

5. $\frac{3}{20}$ 15%
6. $\frac{22}{25}$ 88%
7. 0.004 0.4%
8. 0.3 30%

Lesson 7-2 Find each percent.

9. 20% of 80 16
10. 15% of 22.5 3.375
11. 50% of 86 43
12. 90% of 100 90

Estimate a 15% tip for each restaurant bill. 13–16. Answers may vary. Samples are given.

13. $15.50 $2.40
14. $27.89 $4.20
15. $33.07 $4.95
16. $52.31 $7.80

Lesson 7-3 Use a proportion to solve each problem.

17. 6% of 51 is what number? 3.06
18. 117% of 22 is what number? 25.74
19. 1.95 is 2.5% of what number? 78
20. 145 is 15% of what number? $966\frac{2}{3}$
21. What percent of 5 is 0.4? 8%
22. What percent of 20 is 43? 215%

Lesson 7-4 Find each percent of change. Round to the nearest tenth, if necessary. Label your answer *increase* or *decrease*.

23. 16 to 20 25% increase
24. 95 to 45 52.6% decrease
25. 1 to 4 300% increase
26. 13 ft 5 in. to 17 ft 4 in. 29.2% increase
27. 8 qt 3 pt to 6 qt 6 pt 5.3% decrease
28. 10 lb 4 oz to 14 lb 1 oz 37.2% increase

Lesson 7-5 Find each percent of markup. Round to the nearest percent, if necessary.

29. $43 marked up to $57.19 33%
30. $24.50 markup up to $34.79 42%

Find each percent of discount. Round to the nearest percent, if necessary.

31. $20 discounted to $16 20%
32. $62.00 discounted to $50.84 18%

Find each sale price. Round to the nearest cent.

33. regular price: $14.49; percent of discount: 6% $13.62
34. regular price: $28; percent of discount: 11% $24.92

Word Problems

Lesson 7-1

Household Pets

Animal	Number of Students
Bird	3
Cat	35
Dog	42
Rabbit	8

35. The table on the right shows the results of a survey asking students what pets they have at home. What percent of students have a dog at home? about 48%

36. You answer 29 questions correctly on a 40-question test. What percent of your answers are correct? 72.5%

Lesson 7-2

37. Hector made 80% of his free throws. He attempted 200 free throws. How many free throws did Hector make? 160

38. A restaurant's appetizers are $\frac{1}{3}$ off on Thursdays. Your bill for appetizers comes to $17.25. If you base your tip on the cost before the discount, how much should you leave for a 15% tip? $3.88

Lesson 7-3

39. The area of Iowa is about 55,869 mi^2. Missouri's area is about 123.3% of Iowa's area. What is the area of Missouri? about 68,886 mi^2

40. Suppose a car salesperson makes a $3\frac{1}{2}$% commission on each car sold. What is the salesperson's commission on a $34,288 car? $1,199.98

Lesson 7-4

41. If the cost of a dozen eggs rises from $.99 to $1.34, what is the percent of increase? 35.4%

42. A television is on sale for $449.95. This is $30 off the original price. Find the percent of discount. 6.3%

Lesson 7-5

43. Daniel ordered a shipment of $18.00 sunglasses for his store. He marked them up 50%. After a few weeks, he marked them down to $22.95. What was the percent of discount? 15%

44. You buy a camera for 20% off the regular price of $89.99, plus a 7% sales tax. Find the price of the camera. $77.03

Extra Skills and Word Problems

5–8.
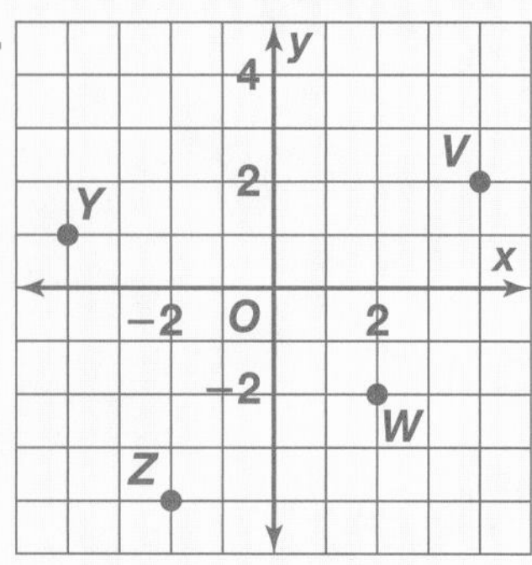

17.
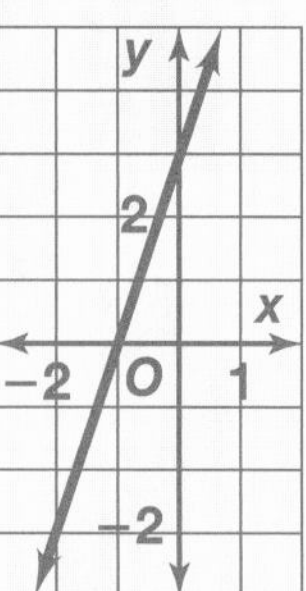

18.
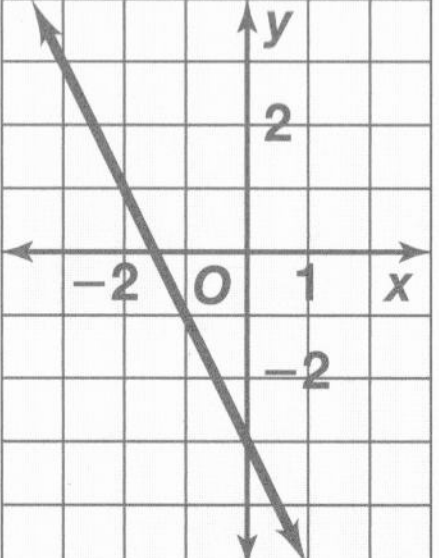

19.
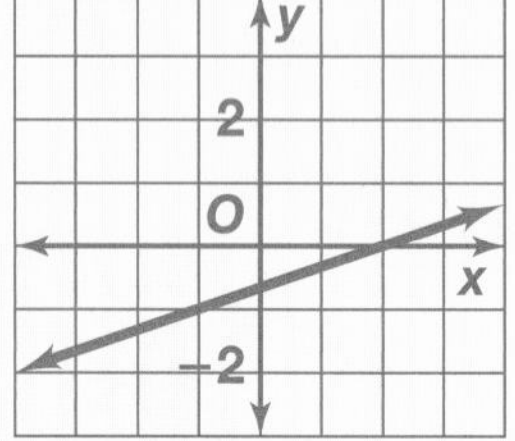

20.
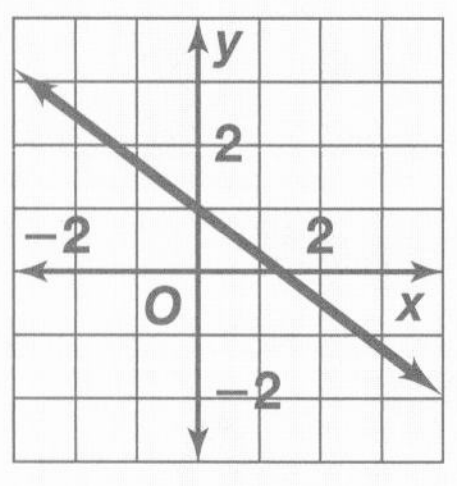

CHAPTER 8 Extra Practice

Skills

Lesson 8-1 Identify the coordinates of each point in the graph at the right.

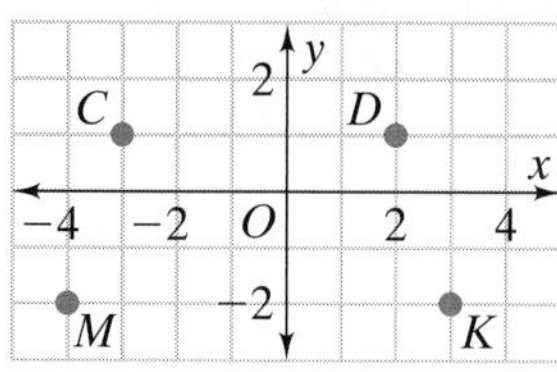

1. C (−3, 1) 2. D (2, 1)
3. K (3, −2) 4. M (−4, −2)

Graph each point on the same coordinate plane. 5–8. See margin.

5. $V(4, 2)$ 6. $W(2, -2)$ 7. $Y(-4, 1)$ 8. $Z(-2, -4)$

Lesson 8-2 Find the length of the line segment with the given endpoints.

9. $C(-3, 0)$, $D(0, 4)$ 5
10. $E(2, 3)$, $F(2, 7)$ 4
11. $G(0, 12)$, $H(5, 0)$ 13
12. $I(5, -4)$, $J(12, -4)$ 7

Lesson 8-3 Use the function rule $f(x) = 2x - 1$. Find each output.

13. $f(1)$ 1 14. $f(0)$ −1 15. $f(-3)$ −7 16. $f\left(\frac{1}{2}\right)$ 0

Lesson 8-4 Graph each linear function. 17–20. See margin.

17. $y = 3x + 3$ 18. $y = -2x - 3$ 19. $y = \frac{1}{3}x - \frac{2}{3}$ 20. $y = -\frac{3}{4}x + 1$

Lesson 8-5 Find the slope of the line that contains each pair of points.

21. (2, 5) and (4, 9) 2 22. (−2, 10) and (6, −2) $-\frac{3}{2}$ 23. (−1, 0) and (5, 10) $\frac{5}{3}$

Lesson 8-6 Determine whether the linear function in each table is a direct variation. Explain.

24.

x	0	4	6	10
y	0	2	3	5

Yes; slope = ratio of y to $x = \frac{1}{2}$.

25.

x	0	5	9	15
y	7	12	16	22

No; the ratio of y to x is not constant.

26.

x	−3	1	2.5	8
y	15	−1	−7	−29

No; the ratio of y to x is not constant.

27.

x	−5	0	4	7	20
y	2.5	0	−2	−3.5	−10

Yes; slope = ratio of y to $x = -\frac{1}{2}$.

Graph each direct variation and find the slope of the line. 28–31. See back of book.

28. $k = \frac{5}{8}\ell$ 29. $m = -1.25n$ 30. $p = 3q$ 31. $r = -\frac{1}{2}s$

Word Problems

Lesson 8-1

32. Your cousin is at (−5, −2). He walks 3 blocks west and 1 block south to the park. Identify the coordinates of the park. **(−8, −3)**

Lesson 8-2

33. The library is 5 mi north of your house. The post office is 6 mi east of your house. To the nearest mile, how far is the library from the post office? **8 mi**

Lesson 8-3

34. A taxicab ride costs \$1.50 plus \$2.00 for every mile traveled. Use function notation to describe the relationship between the number of miles traveled and the total cost. Then find the cost of a taxicab ride of 12 mi. **$f(x) = 2x + 1.5$ where x is the number of miles and $f(x)$ is the total cost; \$25.50.**

Lesson 8-4

35. A uniform company sells name patches for uniforms. The company charges \$2 per patch plus a handling fee of \$5 for each order. The function $p = 2n + 5$ shows how price p relates to the number of patches n. Make a table and graph the function. **See margin.**

36. A country's population is currently about 20 million. The population increases by about 1.2 million people per year. The equation for the population p in millions after y years is $p = 1.2y + 20$. Graph the equation and predict how many people there will be in 19 yr. **See margin.**

Lesson 8-5

37. The slope of a piece of land is its grade. If the grade of a piece of land is 12%, what is its slope? **0.12**

38. Suppose a wheelchair ramp has a slope of $\frac{1}{15}$. If it reaches a doorway that is 2 ft above ground level, how far from the doorway does the ramp begin? **30 ft**

Lesson 8-6

39. The amount of money you earn varies directly with the number of hours you work. Suppose you earn \$4 per hour. Graph the relationship between the number of hours you work and the amount of money you earn. Find the slope of the line and explain what it represents. **See margin.**

35.

n	0	1	2	3
p	5	7	9	11

36.

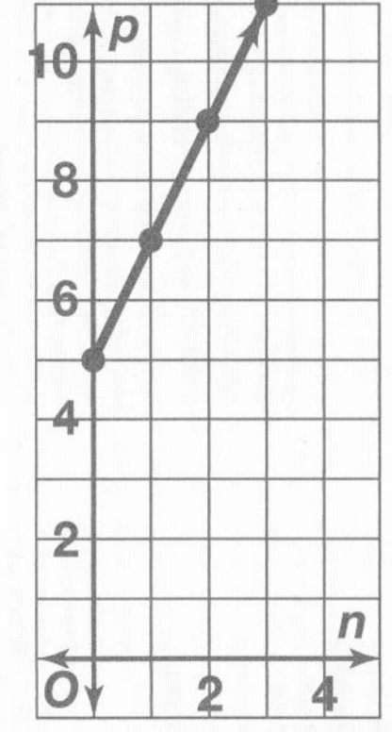

about 42.8 million

39.

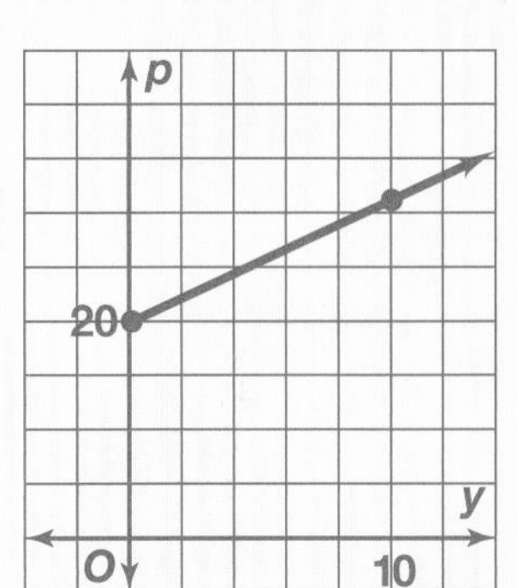

Slope is \$4/h; it is your hourly wage.

CHAPTER 9

Extra Practice

Skills

Lesson 9-1 Write an inequality for each verbal description.

1. The temperature stayed below 0°C. $t < 0$
2. You must bring at least \$5 to cover the cost of lunch. $b \geq 5$
3. The paintings for display can be a maximum of 12 in. wide. $w \leq 12$

Write a system of inequalities for each situation.

4. The delivery truck makes more than 85 stops but less than 100 stops each day. $s > 85, s < 100$
5. The number of people on the train is greater than 125 but less than 300. $p > 125, p < 300$

Lesson 9-2 Solve each inequality.

6. $x - 2 \leq 10$ $x \leq 12$
7. $f + 21 \geq 12$ $f \geq -9$
8. $p - 1 > -1$ $p > 0$
9. $r + 7 < -3$ $r < -10$
10. $a - 9 \leq 1$ $a \leq 10$
11. $m + 4 < 16$ $m < 12$

Lesson 9-3 Solve each inequality.

12. $3y \geq 33$ $y \geq 11$
13. $4d > -36$ $d > -9$
14. $7p \leq -35$ $p \leq -5$
15. $-4n < 28$ $n > -7$
16. $26 \geq -2.5t$ $t \geq -10.4$
17. $8q > 72$ $q > 9$

Lesson 9-4 Solve each inequality.

18. $\frac{p}{7} < -2$ $p < -14$
19. $\frac{a}{-8} \leq -7$ $a \geq 56$
20. $\frac{q}{-6} < 3.1$ $q > -18.6$
21. $\frac{x}{3} > 0$ $x > 0$
22. $\frac{z}{-1} \geq -11$ $z \leq 11$
23. $\frac{m}{9} \geq -5$ $m \geq -45$

Lesson 9-5 Solve each inequality.

24. $3w - 5 \leq -11$ $w \leq -2$
25. $8 + 4d > 12$ $d > 1$
26. $\frac{r}{-4} - 3 > -6$ $r < 12$
27. $8 - \frac{b}{5} > 13$ $b < -25$
28. $5 - 4m \geq -2.6$ $m \leq 1.9$
29. $-1 > \frac{e}{5} + 3$ $e < -20$

Word Problems

Lesson 9-1 **Use the table at the right.**

Law Enforcement Hiring Requirements

Level	Federal	Local
U.S. Citizen	Yes	Yes
Age (years)		
Minimum	21	20
Maximum	36	None

SOURCE: *Occupational Outlook Handbook*

30. Officers in local law enforcement must meet certain requirements at the time of hire. Write an inequality showing the usual age requirement for local law enforcement officers. $a \geq 20$

31. The requirements for federal law enforcement officers are different from those for local law enforcement officers. Write an inequality showing the maximum age for federal law enforcement officers. $a \leq 36$

Lesson 9-2

32. You spent $12.50 on groceries. When you got home, you had at least $25 in your wallet. At least how much money did you have before you went shopping? at least $37.50

Lesson 9-3

33. For your party, you plan a game where each player needs three spoons. You buy a box of 50 spoons. At most, how many people can play the game? 16 people

34. There are 47 children going to a birthday party at a family entertainment center. If a minivan can transport at most 6 children, how many vans are needed to transport all the children? at least 8 vans

Lesson 9-4

35. When a number is divided by −3, the result is not more than 15. What is the number? at least −45

Lesson 9-5

36. You have $25 to spend at an amusement park. Admission to the park is $5 per person, and tickets for rides cost $1.75 each. At most, how many rides can you go on? 11 rides

37. Angelica sells magazines. She earns $30 per day plus $2 for each magazine subscription sold. Angelica would like to earn a minimum of $65 per day. How many magazine subscriptions must she sell per day to earn at least $65? at least 18 subscriptions

Extra Skills and Word Problems

CHAPTER 10 Extra Practice

Skills

Lesson 10-1 **Write each expression using a single exponent.**

1. $4^8 \cdot 4^{10}$ 4^{18}
2. $(-9)^2 \cdot (-9)^4$ $(-9)^6$
3. $3.2^8 \cdot 3.2^3$ 3.2^{11}
4. $7^5 \cdot 7^3$ 7^8
5. $\frac{4^7}{4^5}$ 4^2
6. $\frac{8.1^{15}}{8.1^{12}}$ 8.1^3
7. $\frac{(654)^{20}}{(654)^1}$ 654^{19}
8. $\frac{2^9}{2^3}$ 2^6

Lesson 10-2 **Simplify each expression.**

9. $(a^4)^7$ a^{28}
10. $(z^2)^9$ z^{18}
11. $(2x^7)^3$ $8x^{21}$
12. $(w^3x^5)^7$ $w^{21}x^{35}$
13. $(3n)^3$ $27n^3$
14. $(2a)^4$ $16a^4$
15. $(2 \times 10^5)^0$ 1
16. $(3 \times 10^5)^2$ 9×10^{10}

Lesson 10-3 **Simplify each expression.**

17. $\sqrt[3]{64}$ 4
18. $\sqrt[4]{1}$ 1
19. $\sqrt[3]{216}$ 6
20. $\sqrt[3]{1{,}000}$ 10
21. $\sqrt{53 - 4} \cdot 6$ 42
22. $(-24 + 8 \cdot 2) \div \sqrt[6]{64}$ -4
23. $\sqrt[3]{1{,}000} + \sqrt{49} \cdot \sqrt[5]{8 \cdot 4}$ 24

Lesson 10-4 **Simplify each expression.**

24. $6x + 4 - 3x$ $3x + 4$
25. $7(h - 5)$ $7h - 35$
26. $2(y + 1) + 5$ $2y + 7$
27. $-5 + 3p - p$ $2p - 5$
28. $13q + 91 - 13q$ 91
29. $-(8z + 2z - 1)$ $-10z + 1$
30. $47 - 11r - 7r$ $47 - 18r$
31. $-15b - (23 - 9b)$ $-6b - 23$
32. $-14w - 2w + 17$ $-16w + 17$

Lesson 10-5 **Solve each equation. Check the solution.**

33. $16 = -(2 - 2b)$ 9
34. $123 = 9y + 4 - 7y$ 59.5
35. $4(2.2d - 1) - 0.8d = 23$ 3.375
36. $9g - 4g + 25 = 10$ -3
37. $-10 = 2w + 16 + 11w$ -2
38. $5x - 2 + 3x = 30$ 4

Lesson 10-6 **Solve each equation. Check the solution.**

39. $k = 1.5(7 - k)$ 4.2
40. $-8(3a - 5) = 56a$ 0.5
41. $30 - 5(p - 10) = 11p$ 5
42. $5(d + 2) = 25 + 2d$ 5
43. $5s - 2 = 3(s - 11) - 5$ -18
44. $19 - 2k = 4(k + 1) - k$ 3

Word Problems

Lesson 10-1

45. The distance between the sun and Mars is about 1.4×10^8 mi. Light travels about 1.1×10^7 mi/min. Estimate how long sunlight takes to reach Mars. about 13 min

Lesson 10-2

46. Find the volume of a cylinder with a radius of 6.3×10^3 cm and a height of 30 cm. Use the formula $V = \pi r^2 h$ and 3.14 for π. about 3.7×10^9 cm^3

Lesson 10-3

47. A cone has a volume of 5,890 ft^3 and a height of 25 ft. Use the formula $V = \frac{1}{3}\pi r^2 h$ and 3.14 for π to find the radius to the nearest foot. 15 ft

Lesson 10-4

48. Seth bought lunch three times and breakfast twice last week. This week Seth bought lunch four times and breakfast once. Define and use variables to represent the total cost. Let ℓ = cost for a lunch and b = cost for a breakfast; total cost = $7\ell + 3b$.

49. An art class is painting a mural on the side of the school building. They plan to use a rectangular area that is $(3x + 5)$ ft long and $8x$ ft wide. Write and simplify an expression for the perimeter of the completed mural. $(22x + 10)$ ft

Lesson 10-5

50. You buy 5 lb of Bartlett pears and some Bosc pears. Both varieties of pears cost \$1.09 per pound. The total cost is \$10.36. About how many pounds of Bosc pears did you buy? about 5 lb

Lesson 10-6

51. One mobile phone plan costs \$29.94 per month plus \$.10 for each text message sent. Another plan costs \$32.99 per month plus \$.05 for each text message sent. For what number of text messages will the monthly bill for both plans be the same? 61 messages

Extra Skills and Word Problems

Place Value

Each digit in a whole number or a decimal has both a place and a value. The value of any place is one tenth the value of the place to its left. The chart below can help you read and write decimals. It shows the place and value of the number 2,401,262,830.750191.

billions	hundred millions	ten millions	millions	hundred thousands	ten thousands	thousands	hundreds	tens	ones	.	tenths	hundredths	thousandths	ten-thousandths	hundred-thousandths	millionths
2	4	0	1	2	6	2	8	3	0	.	7	5	0	1	9	1

EXAMPLE

a. What is the value of the digit 8 in the number above?

The digit 8 is in the hundreds place. So its value is 8 hundreds.

b. Write 2.006 in words.

The digit 6 is in the thousandths place. The answer is two and six thousandths.

c. Write five and thirty-four ten-thousandths as a decimal.

Ten-thousandths is 4 places to the right of the decimal point. So the decimal will have 4 places after the decimal point. The answer is 5.0034.

Exercises

Use the chart above. Write the value of each digit.

1. the digit 9 hundred-thousandths
2. the digit 7 tenths
3. the digit 5 hundredths
4. the digit 6 ten thousands
5. the digit 4 hundred millions
6. the digit 3 tens

Write a decimal for the given words.

7. forty-one ten-thousandths 0.0041
8. eighteen and five hundred four thousandths 18.504
9. eight millionths 0.000008
10. seven and sixty-three hundred-thousandths 7.00063
11. twelve thousandths 0.012
12. sixty-five and two hundred one thousandths 65.201

Write each decimal in words.

13. 0.06 six hundredths
14. 4.7 four and seven tenths
15. 0.00011 eleven hundred-thousandths
16. 0.9 nine tenths
17. 0.012 twelve thousandths
18. 0.000059 fifty-nine millionths
19. 0.0042 forty-two ten-thousandths
20. 6.029186 six and twenty-nine thousand one hundred eighty-six millionths

Comparing and Ordering Decimals

To compare two decimals, use the symbols < (is less than), = (is equal to), or > (is greater than). When you compare, start at the left and compare the digits.

EXAMPLE 1

Use <, =, or > to compare the decimals.

a. 0.1 ■ 0.06

1 tenth > 0 tenths, so 0.1 > 0.06

b. 2.4583 ■ 2.48

5 hundredths < 8 hundredths, so 2.4583 < 2.48

c. 0.30026 ■ 0.03026

3 tenths > 0 tenths, so 0.30026 > 0.03026

EXAMPLE 2

Draw number lines to compare the decimals.

a. 0.1 ■ 0.06

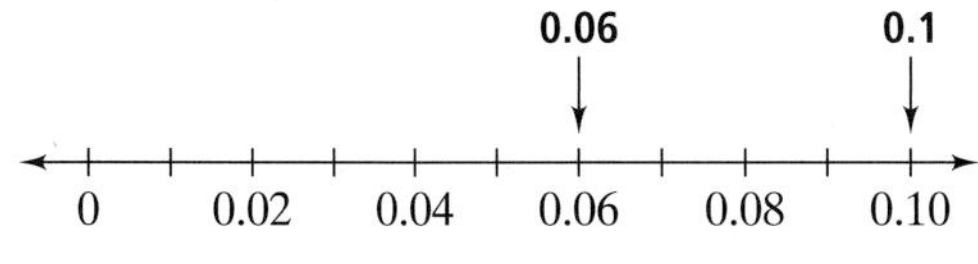

0.1 > 0.06

b. 2.4583 ■ 2.48

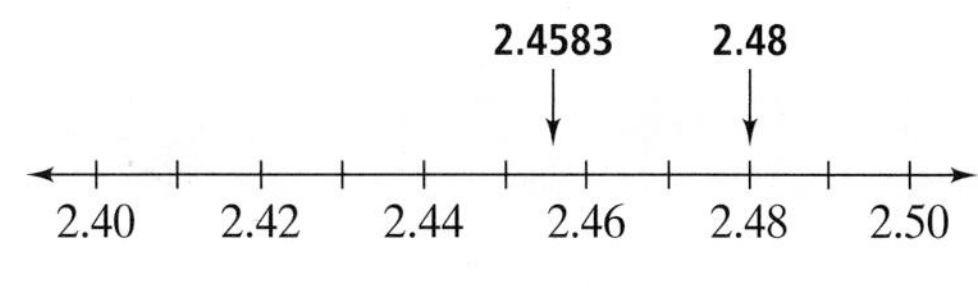

2.4583 < 2.48

Exercises

Use <, =, or > to compare the decimals. Draw number lines if you wish.

1. 0.003 ■ 0.02 <
2. 84.2 ■ 842 <
3. 0.162 ■ 0.106 >
4. 0.0659 ■ 0.6059 <
5. 2.13 ■ 2.99 <
6. 3.53 ■ 3.529 >
7. 2.01 ■ 2.010 =
8. 0.00072 ■ 0.07002 <
9. 0.458 ■ 0.4589 <
10. 8.627 ■ 8.649 <
11. 0.0019 ■ 0.0002 >
12. 0.19321 ■ 0.19231 >

Write the decimals in order from least to greatest.

13. 2.31, 0.231, 23.1, 0.23, 3.21
0.23, 0.231, 2.31, 3.21, 23.1

14. 1.02, 1.002, 1.2, 1.11, 1.021
1.002, 1.02, 1.021, 1.11, 1.2

15. 0.02, 0.002, 0.22, 0.222, 2.22
0.002, 0.02, 0.22, 0.222, 2.22

16. 55.5, 555.5, 55.555, 5.5555
5.5555, 55.5, 55.555, 555.5

17. 7, 7.3264, 7.3, 7.3246, 7.0324
7, 7.0324, 7.3, 7.3246, 7.3264

18. 0.0101, 0.0099, 0.011, 0.00019
0.00019, 0.0099, 0.0101, 0.011

19. 0.8, 0.83, 0.08, 0.083, 0.082
0.08, 0.082, 0.083, 0.8, 0.83

20. 4.6, 4.61, 4.601, 4.602, 4.6002, 4.62
4.6, 4.6002, 4.601, 4.602, 4.61, 4.62

Skills Handbook

Rounding

When you round to a particular place, look at the digit to the right of that place. If it is 5 or more, the digit in the place you are rounding to will increase by 1. If it is less than 5, the digit in the place you are rounding to will stay the same.

EXAMPLE

a. Round 1.627 to the nearest whole number.

The digit to the right of the units place is 6, so 1.627 rounds up to 2.

b. Round 12,034 to the nearest thousand.

The digit to the right of the thousands place is 0, so 12,034 rounds down to 12,000.

c. Round 2.7195 to the nearest hundredth.

The digit to the right of the hundredths place is 9, so 2.7195 rounds up to 2.72.

d. Round $0.060\underline{5}21$ to the place of the underlined digit.

The digit to the right of $\underline{5}$ is 2, so 0.060521 rounds down to 0.0605.

Exercises

Round to the nearest thousand.

1. 105,099 105,000 **2.** 10,400 10,000 **3.** 79,527,826 79,528,000 **4.** 79,932 80,000 **5.** 4,312,349 4,312,000

Round to the nearest whole number.

6. 135.91 136 **7.** 3.001095 3 **8.** 96.912 97 **9.** 101.167 101 **10.** 299.9 300

Round to the nearest tenth.

11. 82.01 82.0 **12.** 4.67522 4.7 **13.** 20.397 20.4 **14.** 399.95 400.0 **15.** 129.98 130.0

Round to the nearest hundredth.

16. 13.458 13.46 **17.** 96.4045 96.40 **18.** 0.699 0.70 **19.** 4.234 4.23 **20.** 12.09531 12.10

Round to the place of the underlined digit.

21. $7.0\underline{6}15$ 7.06 **22.** $\underline{5}.77125$ 6 **23.** $1{,}5\underline{2}2$ 1,520 **24.** $0.919\underline{5}2$ 0.9195 **25.** $4.\underline{2}43$ 4.2

26. $2\underline{3}6.001$ 240 **27.** $\underline{3}52$ 400 **28.** $3.4953\underline{6}6$ 3.49537 **29.** $8.\underline{0}7092$ 8.1 **30.** $\underline{0}.6008$ 1

31. $\underline{9}18$ 900 **32.** $7{,}\underline{7}35$ 7,700 **33.** $25.66\underline{0}47$ 25.660 **34.** $9\underline{8}3{,}240{,}631$ 980,000,000 **35.** $\underline{2}7$ 30

436

Adding Whole Numbers

When you add, line up the digits in the correct columns. Begin by adding the ones. You may need to regroup from one column to the next.

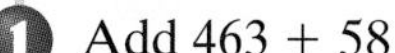

1 Add 463 + 58.

Step 1

```
   1
 463
+ 58
----
   1
```

Step 2

```
  11
 463
+ 58
----
  21
```

Step 3

```
  11
 463
+ 58
----
 521
```

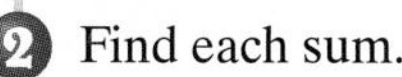

2 Find each sum.

a. 962 + 120

```
  962
+ 120
-----
1,082
```

b. 25 + 9 + 143

```
   1
  25
   9
+143
----
 177
```

c. 3,887 + 1,201

```
  1
  3,887
+ 1,201
-------
  5,088
```

Exercises

Find each sum.

1. 45 + 31 76 **2.** 56 + 80 136 **3.** 25 + 16 41 **4.** 43 + 29 72 **5.** 66 + 78 144 **6.** 87 + 35 122

7. 81 + 312 393 **8.** 406 + 123 529 **9.** 207 + 72 279 **10.** 480 + 365 845 **11.** 217 + 347 564 **12.** 675 + 329 1,004

13. 2,051 + 843 2,894 **14.** 786 + 4,109 4,895 **15.** 5,227 + 1,527 6,754 **16.** 3,104 + 2,698 5,802 **17.** 5,337 + 1,812 7,149 **18.** 4,282 + 7,518 11,800

19. 78 + 56 134 **20.** 35 + 96 131 **21.** 105 + 71 176 **22.** 29 + 342 371 **23.** 654 + 103 757

24. 286 + 42 328 **25.** 55 + 77 132 **26.** 242 + 83 325 **27.** 32 + 68 100 **28.** 108 + 13 121

29. 589 + 318 907 **30.** 642 + 975 1,617 **31.** 2,308 + 451 2,759 **32.** 976 + 4,035 5,011

33. 8,228 + 1,024 9,252 **34.** 5,417 + 2,391 7,808 **35.** 6,470 + 9,828 16,298 **36.** 7,121 + 5,359 12,480

Skills Handbook

437

Subtracting Whole Numbers

When you subtract, line up the digits in the correct columns. Begin by subtracting the ones. Rename if the bottom digit is greater than the top digit. You may need to rename more than once.

EXAMPLE

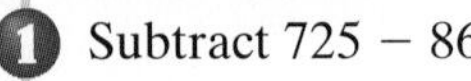

1 Subtract 725 − 86.

Step 1	Step 2	Step 3
115 7~~2~~~~5~~ − 86 9	11 6~~1~~15 ~~7~~~~2~~~~5~~ − 86 39	11 6~~1~~15 ~~7~~~~2~~~~5~~ − 86 639

EXAMPLE

2 Find each difference.

a. 602 − 174	**b.** 625 − 273	**c.** 5,002 − 1,247
9 51~~0~~12 ~~6~~~~0~~~~2~~ − 174 428	512 ~~6~~~~2~~5 − 273 352	9 9 41~~0~~1~~0~~12 ~~5~~,~~0~~~~0~~~~2~~ − 1,247 3,755

Exercises

Find each difference.

1. 81 − 37 44 **2.** 59 − 23 36 **3.** 41 − 19 22 **4.** 83 − 25 58 **5.** 99 − 78 21 **6.** 87 − 31 56

7. 707 − 361 346 **8.** 680 − 47 633 **9.** 240 − 63 177 **10.** 881 − 391 490 **11.** 517 − 287 230 **12.** 973 − 529 444

13. 7,411 − 583 6,828 **14.** 3,789 − 809 2,980 **15.** 6,508 − 2,147 4,361 **16.** 8,000 − 5,274 2,726 **17.** 3,003 − 1,998 1,005 **18.** 8,282 − 4,118 4,164

19. 78 − 19 59 **20.** 231 − 99 132 **21.** 901 − 65 836 **22.** 629 − 382 247 **23.** 918 − 133 785

24. 800 − 435 365 **25.** 403 − 122 281 **26.** 973 − 228 745 **27.** 721 − 119 602 **28.** 522 − 146 376

29. 642 − 223 419 **30.** 427 − 193 234 **31.** 444 − 345 99 **32.** 988 − 489 499 **33.** 601 − 425 176

Multiplying Whole Numbers

When you multiply by a one-digit number, multiply the one-digit number by each digit in the other number.

EXAMPLE

1 Multiply 294 × 7.

Step 1 Multiply 7 by the ones digit.

$$\begin{array}{r} {}^{2} \\ 294 \\ \times\ 7 \\ \hline 8 \end{array}$$

Step 2 Multiply 7 by the tens digit.

$$\begin{array}{r} {}^{6\,2} \\ 294 \\ \times\ 7 \\ \hline 58 \end{array}$$

Step 3 Multiply 7 by the hundreds digit.

$$\begin{array}{r} {}^{6\,2} \\ 294 \\ \times\ \ 7 \\ \hline 2{,}058 \end{array}$$

When you multiply by a two-digit number, first multiply by the ones. Then multiply by the tens. Add the products. Remember, 0 times any number is equal to 0.

EXAMPLE

2 Multiply 48 × 327.

Step 1 Multiply the ones.

$$\begin{array}{r} {}^{2\,5} \\ 327 \\ \times\ 48 \\ \hline 2{,}616 \end{array}$$

Step 2 Multiply the tens.

$$\begin{array}{r} {}^{1\,2} \\ 327 \\ \times\ 48 \\ \hline 2616 \\ +\ 1308 \\ \hline \end{array}$$

Step 3 Add the products.

$$\begin{array}{r} 327 \\ \times\ 48 \\ \hline 2616 \\ +\ 1308 \\ \hline 15{,}696 \end{array}$$

Exercises

Find each product.

1. 81 × 3 243
2. 47 × 2 94
3. 58 × 6 348
4. 678 × 5 3,390
5. 412 × 7 2,884
6. 326 × 4 1,304
7. 7 × 45 315
8. 62 × 3 186
9. 213 × 4 852
10. 8 × 177 1,416
11. 673 × 9 6,057
12. 25 × 46 1,150
13. 62 × 88 5,456
14. 808 × 60 48,480
15. 409 × 70 28,630
16. 915 × 27 24,705
17. 312 × 53 16,536
18. 415 × 76 31,540
19. 500 × 80 40,000
20. 320 × 47 15,040
21. 562 × 18 10,116
22. 946 × 37 35,002
23. 76 × 103 7,828
24. 32 × 558 17,856
25. 371 × 84 31,164
26. 505 × 40 20,200
27. 620 × 19 11,780

Skills Handbook

Skills Handbook

1. 73 R2
2. 41 R7
3. 93 R1
4. 67 R5
5. 29
6. 211 R3
7. 1,197
8. 724 R4
9. 429 R2
10. 627 R5
11. 227 R13
12. 72 R5
13. 68 R17
14. 71 R6
15. 98 R20
16. 84 R8
17. 47 R11
18. 48 R17
19. 25
20. 57
21. Check students' work.

Dividing Whole Numbers

Division is the opposite of multiplication. So you multiply the divisor by your estimate for each digit in the quotient. Then subtract. You repeat this step until you have a remainder that is less than the divisor.

EXAMPLE

Divide $23\overline{)1,178}$.

Step 1 Estimate the quotient.

$1,178 \div 23$ ← **The dividend is 1,178. The divisor is 23.**

↓ ↓

$1,200 \div 20 = 60$ ← **Round 1,178 to the nearest hundred. Round 23 to the nearest ten.**

Step 2

```
     6      ← Try 6 tens.
23)1178
  -138      ← 6 × 23 = 138
              You cannot
              subtract, so
              6 tens is
              too much.
```

Step 3

```
     5      ← Try 5 tens.
23)1178
  -115      ← 5 × 23 = 115
     2      ← Subtract.
```

Step 4

```
    51 R5
23)1178
  -115↓
     28     ← Bring down 8.
    -23     ← 1 × 23 = 23
      5     ← Subtract. The
              remainder is 5.
```

Step 5 Check your answer.

First compare your answer to the estimate. Since 51 R5 is close to 60, the answer is reasonable.

Then find $51 \times 23 + 5$.

Exercises

Find each quotient. Check your answer. 1–21. See margin.

1. $9\overline{)659}$	**2.** $9\overline{)376}$	**3.** $3\overline{)280}$	**4.** $8\overline{)541}$	**5.** $8\overline{)232}$
6. $1,058 \div 5$	**7.** $3,591 \div 3$	**8.** $5,072 \div 7$	**9.** $1,718 \div 4$	**10.** $3,767 \div 6$
11. $3,872 \div 17$	**12.** $19\overline{)1,373}$	**13.** $27\overline{)1,853}$	**14.** $4,195 \div 59$	**15.** $41\overline{)4,038}$
16. $2,612 \div 31$	**17.** $34\overline{)1,609}$	**18.** $1,937 \div 40$	**19.** $54\overline{)1,350}$	**20.** $1,824 \div 32$

21. **Writing in Math** Describe how to estimate a quotient. Use the words *dividend* and *divisor* in your description.

Zeros in Quotients

When you divide, after you bring down a digit you must write a digit in the quotient. In this example, the second digit in the quotient is 0.

EXAMPLE

Find $19\overline{)5{,}823}$.

Step 1

Estimate the quotient.

$$\begin{array}{ccccc} 5{,}823 & \div & 19 & & \\ \downarrow & & \downarrow & & \\ 5{,}800 & \div & 20 & = & 290 \end{array}$$

Step 2

$$\begin{array}{r} 3 \\ 19\overline{)5{,}823} \\ \underline{-\,5\,7} \\ 1 \end{array}$$

Step 3

$$\begin{array}{r} 30 \\ 19\overline{)5{,}823} \\ \underline{-\,5\,7} \\ 12 \\ \underline{-\,0} \\ 12 \end{array}$$

Step 4

$$\begin{array}{r} 306 \text{ R9} \\ 19\overline{)5{,}823} \\ \underline{-\,5\,7} \\ 12 \\ \underline{-\,0} \\ 123 \\ \underline{-\,114} \\ 9 \end{array}$$

Step 5

Check your answer.
Since 306 is close to 290, the answer is reasonable.
Find $306 \times 19 + 9$.

Exercises

Find each quotient.

1. $7\overline{)212}$ 30 R2 **2.** $9\overline{)367}$ 40 R7 **3.** $3\overline{)271}$ 90 R1 **4.** $8\overline{)485}$ 60 R5 **5.** $6\overline{)483}$ 80 R3

6. $34\overline{)1{,}371}$ 40 R11 **7.** $19\overline{)1{,}335}$ 70 R5 **8.** $62\overline{)1{,}881}$ 30 R21 **9.** $54\overline{)1{,}094}$ 20 R14 **10.** $41\overline{)3{,}710}$ 90 R20

11. $282 \div 4$ 70 R2 **12.** $143 \div 7$ 20 R3 **13.** $181 \div 3$ 60 R1 **14.** $400 \div 8$ 50 **15.** $365 \div 9$ 40 R5

16. $1{,}008 \div 5$ 201 R3 **17.** $3{,}018 \div 6$ 503 **18.** $4{,}939 \div 7$ 705 R4 **19.** $1{,}682 \div 4$ 420 R2 **20.** $3{,}647 \div 6$ 607 R5

21. $2{,}488 \div 31$ 80 R8 **22.** $3{,}372 \div 67$ 50 R22 **23.** $1{,}937 \div 48$ 40 R17 **24.** $4{,}165 \div 59$ 70 R35 **25.** $1{,}686 \div 82$ 20 R46

Skills Handbook

Adding and Subtracting Decimals

You add or subtract decimals just as you do whole numbers. Line up the decimal points and then add or subtract. If you wish, you can use zeros to make the columns even.

EXAMPLE

Find each sum or difference.

a. 37.6 + 8.431

$$\begin{array}{r} 37.6 \\ +\ 8.431 \\ \hline \end{array} \rightarrow \begin{array}{r} 37.600 \\ +\ 8.431 \\ \hline 46.031 \end{array}$$

b. 8 − 4.593

$$\begin{array}{r} 8. \\ -\ 4.593 \\ \hline \end{array} \rightarrow \begin{array}{r} 8.000 \\ -\ 4.593 \\ \hline 3.407 \end{array}$$

c. 8.3 + 2.99 + 17.5

$$\begin{array}{r} 8.3 \\ 2.99 \\ +\ 17.5 \\ \hline \end{array} \rightarrow \begin{array}{r} 8.30 \\ 2.99 \\ +\ 17.50 \\ \hline 28.79 \end{array}$$

Exercises

Find each sum or difference.

1. 39.7 − 36.03 3.67

2. 1.08 − 0.9 0.18

3. 6.784 + 0.528 7.312

4. 5.01 − 0.87 4.14

5. 13.02 + 23.107 36.127

6. 8.634 + 1.409 10.043

7. 2.1 − 0.5 1.6

8. 8.23 − 3.1 5.13

9. 1.05 + 12.9 13.95

10. 2.60 + 23.107 25.707

11. 0.1 + 58.21 + 1.9 60.21

12. 12.2 + 3.06 + 0.5 15.76

13. 9.42 + 3.6 + 21.003 34.023

14. 15.22 + 7.4 + 8.125 30.745

15. 3.7 + 20.06 + 16.19 39.95

16. 12.22 + 9.8 + 2.375 24.395

17. 76.39 − 8.47 67.92

18. 8.7 + 17.03 25.73

19. 32.403 + 12.06 44.463

20. 20.5 + 11.45 31.95

21. 8.9 − 4.45 4.45

22. 1.245 + 5.8 7.045

23. 3.9 + 6.57 10.47

24. 14.81 − 8.6 6.21

25. 11.9 − 2.06 9.84

26. 3.45 + 4.061 7.511

27. 8.29 + 4.3 12.59

28. 7.06 − 4.235 2.825

29. 5.002 − 3.45 1.552

30. 6.8 + 3.57 10.37

31. 0.23 + 0.091 0.321

32. 0.5 − 0.18 0.32

33. 8.3 + 2.99 + 17.52 28.81

34. 9.5 + 12.32 + 6.4 28.22

35. 4.521 + 1.8 + 3.07 9.391

36. 57 + 0.6327 + 189.007 246.6397

37. 741 + 6.08 + 0.0309 747.1109

38. 0.045 + 16.32 + 8.6 24.965

39. 4.27 + 6.18 + 0.91 11.36

40. 3.856 + 14.01 + 1.72 19.586

41. 11.45 + 3.79 + 23.861 39.101

Multiplying Decimals

Multiply decimals as you would whole numbers. Then place the decimal point in the product. To do this, add the number of decimal places in the factors.

EXAMPLE

1 Multiply 0.068 × 2.3.

Step 1 Multiply decimals without the decimal point.

$$\begin{array}{r} 0.068 \\ \times\ 2.3 \\ \hline \end{array} \qquad \begin{array}{r} 68 \\ \times\ 23 \\ \hline 204 \\ +\ 1360 \\ \hline 1564 \end{array}$$

Step 2 Place the decimal point.

$$\begin{array}{rl} 0.068 & \leftarrow \text{three decimal places} \\ \times\ 2.3 & \leftarrow \text{one decimal place} \\ \hline 204 & \\ +\ 1360 & \\ \hline 0.1564 & \leftarrow \text{four decimal places} \end{array}$$

EXAMPLE

2 Find each product.

a. 3.12 × 0.9

$$\begin{array}{r} 3.12 \\ \times\ 0.9 \\ \hline 2.808 \end{array}$$

b. 5.75 × 42

$$\begin{array}{r} 5.75 \\ \times\ 42 \\ \hline 1150 \\ +\ 23000 \\ \hline 241.50 \end{array}$$

c. 0.964 × 0.28

$$\begin{array}{r} 0.964 \\ \times\ 0.28 \\ \hline 7712 \\ +\ 19280 \\ \hline 0.26992 \end{array}$$

Exercises

Multiply.

1. 1.48 × 3.6 5.328
2. 191.1 × 3.4 649.74
3. 0.05 × 43 2.15
4. 0.27 × 5 1.35
5. 1.36 × 3.8 5.168

6. 6.23 × 0.21 1.3083
7. 0.512 × 0.76 0.38912
8. 0.04 × 7 0.28
9. 0.136 × 8.4 1.1424
10. 3 × 0.05 0.15

11. 2.07 × 1.004 2.07828
12. 0.12 × 61 7.32
13. 3.2 × 0.15 0.48
14. 0.74 × 0.23 0.1702

15. 0.42 × 98 41.16
16. 6.3 × 85 535.5
17. 45 × 0.028 1.26
18. 76 × 3.3 250.8

19. 8.003 × 0.6 4.8018
20. 42.2 × 0.9 37.98
21. 0.6 × 30.02 18.012
22. 0.05 × 11.8 0.59

Skills Handbook

Skills Handbook

443

Zeros in a Product

When you multiply with decimals, you may have to write one or more zeros to the left of a product before you can place the decimal point.

EXAMPLE 1

Multiply 0.06×0.015.

Step 1 Multiply.

$$\begin{array}{r} 0.015 \\ \times\ 0.06 \\ \hline 90 \end{array}$$

Step 2 Place the decimal point.

$$\begin{array}{r} 0.015 \\ \times\ 0.06 \\ \hline 0.00090 \end{array}$$

- 0.015 ← **three decimal places**
- × 0.06 ← **two decimal places**
- 0.00090 ← **The product should have five decimal places, so you must write three zeros before placing the decimal point.**

EXAMPLE 2

a. 0.02×1.3

$$\begin{array}{r} 1.3 \\ \times\ 0.02 \\ \hline 0.026 \end{array}$$

b. 0.012×2.4

$$\begin{array}{r} 2.4 \\ \times\ 0.012 \\ \hline 48 \\ +\ 240 \\ \hline 0.0288 \end{array}$$

c. 0.022×0.051

$$\begin{array}{r} 0.051 \\ \times\ 0.022 \\ \hline 102 \\ +\ 1020 \\ \hline 0.001122 \end{array}$$

Exercises

Multiply.

1. 0.03×0.9 **0.027**

2. 0.06×0.5 **0.03**

3. 2.4×0.03 **0.072**

4. 7×0.01 **0.07**

5. 0.05×0.05 **0.0025**

6. 0.016×0.12 **0.00192**

7. 0.031×0.08 **0.00248**

8. 0.03×0.2 **0.006**

9. 0.27×0.033 **0.00891**

10. 0.014×0.25 **0.0035**

11. 0.003×0.55 **0.00165**

12. 0.01×0.74 **0.0074**

13. 0.47×0.08 **0.0376**

14. 0.76×0.1 **0.076**

15. 0.3×0.27 **0.081**

16. 0.19×0.05 **0.0095**

17. 0.018×0.04 **0.00072**

18. 0.43×0.2 **0.086**

19. 0.03×0.03 **0.0009**

20. 4.003×0.02 **0.08006**

21. 0.5×0.08 **0.04**

22. 0.06×0.7 **0.042**

23. 0.3×0.24 **0.072**

24. 0.67×0.09 **0.0603**

25. 3.02×0.006 **0.01812**

26. 0.31×0.08 **0.0248**

27. 0.14×0.05 **0.007**

28. 0.07×0.85 **0.0595**

Dividing Decimals by Whole Numbers

When you divide a decimal by a whole number, the decimal point in the quotient goes directly above the decimal point in the dividend. You may need extra zeros to place the decimal point.

EXAMPLE

1 Divide 2.432 ÷ 32.

Step 1 Divide.

$$\begin{array}{r} 76 \\ 32\overline{)2.432} \\ -\,2\ 24 \\ \hline 192 \\ -\,192 \\ \hline 0 \end{array}$$

Step 2 Place the decimal point.

$$\begin{array}{r} 0.076 \\ 32\overline{)2.432} \\ -2\ 24 \\ \hline 192 \\ -192 \\ \hline 0 \end{array}$$

← **You need two extra zeros to get the decimal point in the correct place.**

EXAMPLE

2 **a.** 37.6 ÷ 8

$$\begin{array}{r} 4.7 \\ 8\overline{)37.6} \\ -\,32 \\ \hline 5\ 6 \\ -\,5\ 6 \\ \hline 0 \end{array}$$

b. 39.33 ÷ 69

$$\begin{array}{r} 0.57 \\ 69\overline{)39.33} \\ -\,34\ 5 \\ \hline 4\ 83 \\ -\,4\ 83 \\ \hline 0 \end{array}$$

c. 4.482 ÷ 54

$$\begin{array}{r} 0.083 \\ 54\overline{)4.482} \\ -\,4\ 32 \\ \hline 162 \\ -\,162 \\ \hline 0 \end{array}$$

Exercises

Divide.

1. 17.92 ÷ 7 2.56
2. 16.5 ÷ 5 3.3
3. 6.984 ÷ 9 0.776
4. 91.44 ÷ 6 15.24
5. 35.16 ÷ 4 8.79
6. 8.848 ÷ 56 0.158
7. 2.42 ÷ 22 0.11
8. 1,723.8 ÷ 26 66.3
9. 17.52 ÷ 2 8.76
10. 37.14 ÷ 6 6.19
11. 0.1352 ÷ 8 0.0169
12. 0.0324 ÷ 9 0.0036
13. 0.0882 ÷ 6 0.0147
14. 0.8682 ÷ 6 0.1447
15. 12.342 ÷ 22 0.561
16. 29.792 ÷ 32 0.931
17. 22.568 ÷ 26 0.868
18. 11.340 ÷ 36 0.315
19. 45.918 ÷ 18 2.551
20. 79.599 ÷ 13 6.123
21. 0.0672 ÷ 48 0.0014
22. 171.031 ÷ 53 3.227
23. 79.53 ÷ 11 7.23
24. 3.2 ÷ 8 0.4
25. 0.378 ÷ 5 0.0756
26. 9.76 ÷ 32 0.305
27. 0.133 ÷ 7 0.019
28. 61.915 ÷ 35 1.769

Skills Handbook

445

Multiplying and Dividing by Powers of Ten

You can use shortcuts to multiply or divide by powers of ten.

When you multiply by...	Move the decimal point ...	When you divide by...	Move the decimal point ...
10,000	4 places to the right.	10,000	4 places to the left.
1,000	3 places to the right.	1,000	3 places to the left.
100	2 places to the right.	100	2 places to the left.
10	1 place to the right.	10	1 place to the left.
0.1	1 place to the left.	0.1	1 place to the right.
0.01	2 places to the left.	0.01	2 places to the right.
0.001	3 places to the left.	0.001	3 places to the right.

EXAMPLE

1 Multiply.

a. 0.7×0.001

Move the decimal point three places to the left. 0.000.7

$0.7 \times 0.001 = 0.0007$

b. 0.934×100

Move the decimal point two places to the right. 0.93.4

$0.934 \times 100 = 93.4$

EXAMPLE

2 Divide.

a. $0.605 \div 100$

Move the decimal point two places to the left. 0.00.605

$0.605 \div 100 = 0.00605$

b. $0.38 \div 0.001$

Move the decimal point three places to the right. 0.380.

$0.38 \div 0.001 = 380$

Exercises

Multiply or divide.

1. $10{,}000 \times 0.056$ **560** **2.** 0.001×0.09 **0.00009** **3.** 5.2×10 **52** **4.** $0.03 \times 1{,}000$ **30**

5. $236.7 \div 0.1$ **2,367** **6.** $45.28 \div 10$ **4.528** **7.** $0.9 \div 1{,}000$ **0.0009** **8.** $1.07 \div 0.01$ **107**

9. 100×0.08 **8** **10.** $1.03 \times 10{,}000$ **10,300** **11.** $4.7 \div 10$ **0.47** **12.** $203.05 \div 0.01$ **20,305**

Dividing Decimals by Decimals

To divide by a decimal divisor, multiply it by the smallest power of ten that will make the divisor a whole number. Then multiply the dividend by that same power of ten.

EXAMPLE

Find each quotient.

a. $3.348 \div 6.2$

Multiply by 10.

$$\begin{array}{r} 0.54 \\ 6.2.\overline{)3.3.48} \\ -3\,1\,0 \\ \hline 2\,48 \\ -2\,48 \\ \hline 0 \end{array}$$

b. $2.4885 \div 0.35$

Multiply by 100.

$$\begin{array}{r} 7.11 \\ 0.35.\overline{)2.48.85} \\ -2\,45 \\ \hline 3\,8 \\ -3\,5 \\ \hline 35 \\ -35 \\ \hline 0 \end{array}$$

c. $0.0576 \div 0.012$

Multiply by 1,000.

$$\begin{array}{r} 4.8 \\ 0.012.\overline{)0.057.6} \\ -48 \\ \hline 9\,6 \\ -9\,6 \\ \hline 0 \end{array}$$

Skills Handbook

Exercises

Divide.

1. $268.8 \div 3.2$ 84
2. $123.5 \div 1.9$ 65
3. $135.6 \div 0.3$ 452
4. $170.2 \div 2.3$ 74
5. $252.8 \div 7.9$ 32
6. $10.26 \div 5.7$ 1.8
7. $71.53 \div 2.3$ 31.1
8. $16.12 \div 3.1$ 5.2
9. $24.18 \div 7.8$ 3.1
10. $14.49 \div 6.3$ 2.3
11. $134.42 \div 5.17$ 26
12. $89.96 \div 3.46$ 26
13. $160.58 \div 5.18$ 31
14. $106.59 \div 6.27$ 17
15. $62.4 \div 3.9$ 16
16. $260.4 \div 8.4$ 31
17. $316.8 \div 7.2$ 44
18. $162.4 \div 2.9$ 56
19. $1.512 \div 0.54$ 2.8
20. $3.225 \div 0.43$ 7.5
21. $2.484 \div 0.69$ 3.6
22. $511.5 \div 5.5$ 93
23. $0.992 \div 0.8$ 1.24
24. $4.53 \div 0.05$ 90.6
25. $3.498 \div 0.06$ 58.3
26. $59.2 \div 0.8$ 74
27. $2.198 \div 0.07$ 31.4
28. $14.28 \div 0.7$ 20.4
29. $1.98 \div 0.5$ 3.96
30. $26.36 \div 0.04$ 659
31. $3.922 \div 7.4$ 0.53
32. $23.52 \div 0.98$ 24
33. $71.25 \div 7.5$ 9.5
34. $114.7 \div 3.7$ 31
35. $0.832 \div 0.52$ 1.6
36. $1.125 \div 0.09$ 12.5
37. $9.666 \div 2.7$ 3.58
38. $1.456 \div 9.1$ 0.16
39. $0.4374 \div 1.8$ 0.243

Skills Handbook

447

Zeros in Decimal Division

When you are dividing by a decimal, sometimes you need to use extra zeros in the dividend or the quotient, or both.

EXAMPLE

1 Divide 0.045 ÷ 3.6.

Step 1 Multiply by 10.

$3.6\overline{)0.045}$ → $36\overline{)0.45}$

Step 2 Divide.

$$\begin{array}{r} 125 \\ 36\overline{)0.4500} \\ -36 \\ \hline 90 \\ -72 \\ \hline 180 \\ -180 \\ \hline 0 \end{array}$$

Step 3 Place the decimal point.

$$\begin{array}{r} 0.0125 \\ 36\overline{)0.4500} \\ -36 \\ \hline 90 \\ -72 \\ \hline 180 \\ -180 \\ \hline 0 \end{array}$$

EXAMPLE

2 Find each quotient.

a. 0.4428 ÷ 8.2

Multiply by 10.

$$\begin{array}{r} 0.054 \\ 8.2\overline{)0.4428} \end{array}$$

b. 0.00434 ÷ 0.07

Multiply by 100.

$$\begin{array}{r} 0.062 \\ 0.07\overline{)0.00434} \end{array}$$

c. 0.00306 ÷ 0.072

Multiply by 1,000.

$$\begin{array}{r} 0.0425 \\ 0.072\overline{)0.0030600} \end{array}$$

Exercises

Divide.

1. 0.0023 ÷ 0.05 0.046
2. 0.000162 ÷ 0.02 0.0081
3. 0.009 ÷ 0.12 0.075
4. 0.021 ÷ 2.5 0.0084
5. 0.0019 ÷ 0.2 0.0095
6. 0.9 ÷ 0.8 1.125
7. 0.000175 ÷ 0.07 0.0025
8. 0.142 ÷ 0.04 3.55
9. 0.0017 ÷ 0.02 0.085
10. 0.003 ÷ 0.6 0.005
11. 0.0105 ÷ 0.7 0.015
12. 0.034 ÷ 0.05 0.68
13. 0.00056 ÷ 0.16 0.0035
14. 0.0612 ÷ 7.2 0.0085
15. 0.217 ÷ 3.1 0.07
16. 0.052 ÷ 0.8 0.065
17. 0.000924 ÷ 0.44 0.0021
18. 0.05796 ÷ 0.63 0.092
19. 0.00123 ÷ 8.2 0.00015
20. 0.0954 ÷ 0.09 1.06
21. 0.0084 ÷ 1.4 0.006
22. 0.259 ÷ 3.5 0.074
23. 0.00468 ÷ 0.52 0.009
24. 0.104 ÷ 0.05 2.08
25. 0.00063 ÷ 0.18 0.0035
26. 0.011 ÷ 0.25 0.044
27. 0.3069 ÷ 9.3 0.033
28. 0.00045 ÷ 0.3 0.0015

Mixed Numbers and Improper Fractions

A fraction, such as $\frac{10}{7}$, in which the numerator is greater than or equal to the denominator, is an improper fraction. You can write an improper fraction as a mixed number that shows the sum of a whole number and a fraction.

Sometimes it is necessary to do the opposite and write a mixed number as an improper fraction.

EXAMPLE

a. Write $\frac{11}{5}$ as a mixed number.

$$\frac{11}{5} \rightarrow \begin{array}{r} 2 \\ 5\overline{)11} \\ -10 \\ \hline 1 \end{array}$$

2 ← **whole number**

1 ← **remainder**

$\frac{11}{5} = 2\frac{1}{5}$ ← **whole number +** $\frac{\textbf{remainder}}{\textbf{denominator}}$

b. Write $2\frac{5}{6}$ as an improper fraction.

$2\frac{5}{6} = 2 + \frac{5}{6}$

$= \frac{12}{6} + \frac{5}{6}$ ← **Write 2 as** $\frac{12}{6}$**.**

$= \frac{12 + 5}{6}$ ← **Add the numerators.**

$= \frac{17}{6}$

$2\frac{5}{6} = \frac{17}{6}$ ← **Simplify.**

Exercises

Write each improper fraction as a mixed number.

1. $\frac{7}{5}$ $1\frac{2}{5}$	**2.** $\frac{9}{2}$ $4\frac{1}{2}$	**3.** $\frac{13}{4}$ $3\frac{1}{4}$	**4.** $\frac{21}{5}$ $4\frac{1}{5}$	**5.** $\frac{13}{10}$ $1\frac{3}{10}$
6. $\frac{49}{5}$ $9\frac{4}{5}$	**7.** $\frac{21}{8}$ $2\frac{5}{8}$	**8.** $\frac{13}{7}$ $1\frac{6}{7}$	**9.** $\frac{17}{5}$ $3\frac{2}{5}$	**10.** $\frac{49}{6}$ $8\frac{1}{6}$
11. $\frac{17}{4}$ $4\frac{1}{4}$	**12.** $\frac{5}{2}$ $2\frac{1}{2}$	**13.** $\frac{27}{5}$ $5\frac{2}{5}$	**14.** $\frac{12}{9}$ $1\frac{1}{3}$	**15.** $\frac{30}{8}$ $3\frac{3}{4}$
16. $\frac{37}{12}$ $3\frac{1}{12}$	**17.** $\frac{8}{6}$ $1\frac{1}{3}$	**18.** $\frac{19}{12}$ $1\frac{7}{12}$	**19.** $\frac{45}{10}$ $4\frac{1}{2}$	**20.** $\frac{15}{12}$ $1\frac{1}{4}$
21. $\frac{11}{2}$ $5\frac{1}{2}$	**22.** $\frac{20}{6}$ $3\frac{1}{3}$	**23.** $\frac{34}{8}$ $4\frac{1}{4}$	**24.** $\frac{21}{9}$ $2\frac{1}{3}$	**25.** $\frac{42}{4}$ $10\frac{1}{2}$

Write each mixed number as an improper fraction.

26. $1\frac{1}{2}$ $\frac{3}{2}$	**27.** $2\frac{2}{3}$ $\frac{8}{3}$	**28.** $1\frac{1}{12}$ $\frac{13}{12}$	**29.** $3\frac{1}{5}$ $\frac{16}{5}$	**30.** $2\frac{2}{7}$ $\frac{16}{7}$
31. $4\frac{1}{2}$ $\frac{9}{2}$	**32.** $2\frac{7}{8}$ $\frac{23}{8}$	**33.** $1\frac{2}{9}$ $\frac{11}{9}$	**34.** $5\frac{1}{5}$ $\frac{26}{5}$	**35.** $4\frac{7}{9}$ $\frac{43}{9}$
36. $9\frac{1}{4}$ $\frac{37}{4}$	**37.** $2\frac{3}{8}$ $\frac{19}{8}$	**38.** $7\frac{7}{8}$ $\frac{63}{8}$	**39.** $1\frac{5}{12}$ $\frac{17}{12}$	**40.** $3\frac{3}{7}$ $\frac{24}{7}$
41. $6\frac{1}{2}$ $\frac{13}{2}$	**42.** $3\frac{1}{10}$ $\frac{31}{10}$	**43.** $4\frac{6}{7}$ $\frac{34}{7}$	**44.** $8\frac{1}{8}$ $\frac{65}{8}$	**45.** $6\frac{1}{3}$ $\frac{19}{3}$

Skills Handbook

449

Adding and Subtracting Fractions With Like Denominators

When you add or subtract fractions with the same denominator, add or subtract the numerators and then write the answer over the denominator.

EXAMPLE

1 Add or subtract. Write the answers in simplest form.

a. $\frac{5}{8} + \frac{7}{8}$

$$\frac{5}{8} + \frac{7}{8} = \frac{5 + 7}{8} = \frac{12}{8} = 1\frac{4}{8} = 1\frac{1}{2}$$

b. $\frac{11}{12} - \frac{2}{12}$

$$\frac{11}{12} - \frac{2}{12} = \frac{11 - 2}{12} = \frac{9}{12} = \frac{3}{4}$$

To add or subtract mixed numbers, add or subtract the fractions first. Then add or subtract the whole numbers.

EXAMPLE

2 Add or subtract. Write the answers in simplest form.

a. $3\frac{4}{6} + 2\frac{5}{6}$

$$\begin{array}{r} 3\frac{4}{6} \\ +\ 2\frac{5}{6} \\ \hline 5\frac{9}{6} \end{array} = 5 + 1 + \frac{3}{6} = 6\frac{1}{2}$$

b. $6\frac{1}{4} - 1\frac{3}{4}$

$$\begin{array}{rcr} 6\frac{1}{4} & & 5\frac{5}{4} \\ -1\frac{3}{4} & \rightarrow & -1\frac{3}{4} \\ \hline & & 4\frac{2}{4} \end{array} = 4\frac{1}{2}$$

←Rewrite 6 as $5\frac{4}{4}$ and add it to $\frac{1}{4}$.

Exercises

Add or subtract. Write the answers in simplest form.

1. $\frac{4}{5} + \frac{3}{5}$ $1\frac{2}{5}$
2. $\frac{2}{6} - \frac{1}{6}$ $\frac{1}{6}$
3. $\frac{2}{7} + \frac{2}{7}$ $\frac{4}{7}$
4. $\frac{7}{8} + \frac{2}{8}$ $1\frac{1}{8}$
5. $1\frac{2}{5} - \frac{1}{5}$ $1\frac{1}{5}$

6. $\frac{3}{6} - \frac{1}{6}$ $\frac{1}{3}$
7. $\frac{6}{8} - \frac{3}{8}$ $\frac{3}{8}$
8. $\frac{2}{9} + \frac{1}{9}$ $\frac{1}{3}$
9. $\frac{4}{5} - \frac{1}{5}$ $\frac{3}{5}$
10. $\frac{5}{9} + \frac{7}{9}$ $1\frac{1}{3}$

11. $9\frac{1}{3} - 8\frac{1}{3}$ 1
12. $8\frac{6}{7} - 4\frac{2}{7}$ $4\frac{4}{7}$
13. $3\frac{1}{10} + 1\frac{3}{10}$ $4\frac{2}{5}$
14. $2\frac{2}{9} + 3\frac{4}{9}$ $5\frac{2}{3}$

15. $4\frac{5}{12} - 3\frac{1}{12}$ $1\frac{1}{3}$
16. $9\frac{5}{9} + 6\frac{7}{9}$ $16\frac{1}{3}$
17. $5\frac{7}{8} + 2\frac{3}{8}$ $8\frac{1}{4}$
18. $4\frac{4}{7} - 2\frac{1}{7}$ $2\frac{3}{7}$

19. $9\frac{3}{4} + 1\frac{3}{4}$ $11\frac{1}{2}$
20. $8\frac{2}{3} - 4\frac{1}{3}$ $4\frac{1}{3}$
21. $8\frac{7}{10} + 2\frac{3}{10}$ 11
22. $1\frac{4}{5} + 3\frac{3}{5}$ $5\frac{2}{5}$

23. $7\frac{1}{5} - 2\frac{3}{5}$ $4\frac{3}{5}$
24. $4\frac{1}{3} - 1\frac{2}{3}$ $2\frac{2}{3}$
25. $4\frac{3}{8} - 3\frac{5}{8}$ $\frac{3}{4}$
26. $5\frac{1}{12} - 2\frac{7}{12}$ $2\frac{1}{2}$

Table 1 Measures

Metric	Customary
Length	**Length**
10 millimeters (mm) = 1 centimeter (cm) 100 cm = 1 meter (m) 1,000 m = 1 kilometer (km)	12 inches (in.) = 1 foot (ft) 36 in. = 1 yard (yd) 3 ft = 1 yd 5,280 ft = 1 mile (mi) 1,760 yd = 1 mi
Area	**Area**
100 square millimeters (mm^2) = 1 square centimeter (cm^2) 10,000 cm^2 = 1 square meter (m^2)	144 square inches (in.^{2}) = 1 square foot (ft^2) 9 ft^2 = 1 square yard (yd^2) 4,840 yd^2 = 1 acre
Volume	**Volume**
1,000 cubic millimeters (mm^3) = 1 cubic centimeter (cm^3) 1,000,000 cm^3 = 1 cubic meter (m^3)	1,728 cubic inches (in.^{3}) = 1 cubic foot (ft^3) 27 ft^3 = 1 cubic yard (yd^3)
Mass	**Mass**
1,000 milligrams (mg) = 1 gram (g) 1,000 g = 1 kilogram (kg)	16 ounces (oz) = 1 pound (lb) 2,000 lb = 1 ton (t)
Capacity	**Capacity**
1,000 milliliters (mL) = 1 liter (L)	8 fluid ounces (fl oz) = 1 cup (c) 2 c = 1 pint (pt) 2 pt = 1 quart (qt) 4 qt = 1 gallon (gal)

Time
1 minute (min) = 60 seconds (s) 1 hour (h) = 60 min 1 day (d) = 24 h 1 year (yr) = 365 d

Table 2 Math Symbols

Symbol	Meaning	Page
$+$	plus (addition)	p. 2
$-$	minus (subtraction)	p. 2
$\times, \cdot$	times (multiplication)	p. 2
$\div, \overline{)\ }$	divide (division)	p. 2
$=$	is equal to	p. 4
$()$	parentheses for grouping	p. 5
$[]$	brackets for grouping	p. 6
ℓ	length	p. 10
w	width	p. 10
P	perimeter	p. 10
A	area	p. 17
h	height	p. 18
$\approx$	is approximately equal to	p. 20
$-a$	opposite of a	p. 46
$\ldots$	and so on	p. 46
$^\circ$	degrees	p. 46
$\lvert a \rvert$	absolute value of a	p. 46
a^n	nth power of a	p. 73
$\stackrel{?}{=}$	Is the statement true?	p. 87
$\sqrt{x}$	nonnegative square root of x	p. 107
$\triangle ABC$	triangle with vertices A, B, and C	p. 112
⦜	right angle (90°)	p. 112
$\frac{b}{a}$	reciprocal of $\frac{a}{b}$	p. 186
$a : b$, $\frac{a}{b}$	ratio of a to b	p. 216
d	distance	p. 230
r	rate	p. 230
t	time	p. 230
$\%$	percent	p. 252
(a, b)	ordered pair with x-coordinate a and y-coordinate b	p. 288
$\overline{AB}$	segment AB	p. 292
AB	length of segment $\overline{AB}$	p. 292
$f(n)$	the function value at n, f of n	p. 299
$\overleftrightarrow{AB}$	line AB	p. 314
π	pi, an irrational number approximately equal to 3.14	p. 319
C	circumference	p. 319
d	diameter	p. 319
$<$	is less than	p. 330
$>$	is greater than	p. 330
$\leq$	is less than or equal to	p. 330
$\geq$	is greater than or equal to	p. 330
$\neq$	is not equal to	p. 330
r	radius	p. 371
$\sqrt[n]{x}$	nth root of x	p. 374

Table 3 Squares and Square Roots

Number n	Square n^2	Positive Square Root $\sqrt{n}$	Number n	Square n^2	Positive Square Root $\sqrt{n}$
1	1	1.000	**51**	2,601	7.141
2	4	1.414	**52**	2,704	7.211
3	9	1.732	**53**	2,809	7.280
4	16	2.000	**54**	2,916	7.348
5	25	2.236	**55**	3,025	7.416
6	36	2.449	**56**	3,136	7.483
7	49	2.646	**57**	3,249	7.550
8	64	2.828	**58**	3,364	7.616
9	81	3.000	**59**	3,481	7.681
10	100	3.162	**60**	3,600	7.746
11	121	3.317	**61**	3,721	7.810
12	144	3.464	**62**	3,844	7.874
13	169	3.606	**63**	3,969	7.937
14	196	3.742	**64**	4,096	8.000
15	225	3.873	**65**	4,225	8.062
16	256	4.000	**66**	4,356	8.124
17	289	4.123	**67**	4,489	8.185
18	324	4.243	**68**	4,624	8.246
19	361	4.359	**69**	4,761	8.307
20	400	4.472	**70**	4,900	8.367
21	441	4.583	**71**	5,041	8.426
22	484	4.690	**72**	5,184	8.485
23	529	4.796	**73**	5,329	8.544
24	576	4.899	**74**	5,476	8.602
25	625	5.000	**75**	5,625	8.660
26	676	5.099	**76**	5,776	8.718
27	729	5.196	**77**	5,929	8.775
28	784	5.292	**78**	6,084	8.832
29	841	5.385	**79**	6,241	8.888
30	900	5.477	**80**	6,400	8.944
31	961	5.568	**81**	6,561	9.000
32	1,024	5.657	**82**	6,724	9.055
33	1,089	5.745	**83**	6,889	9.110
34	1,156	5.831	**84**	7,056	9.165
35	1,225	5.916	**85**	7,225	9.220
36	1,296	6.000	**86**	7,396	9.274
37	1,369	6.083	**87**	7,569	9.327
38	1,444	6.164	**88**	7,744	9.381
39	1,521	6.245	**89**	7,921	9.434
40	1,600	6.325	**90**	8,100	9.487
41	1,681	6.403	**91**	8,281	9.539
42	1,764	6.481	**92**	8,464	9.592
43	1,849	6.557	**93**	8,649	9.644
44	1,936	6.633	**94**	8,836	9.695
45	2,025	6.708	**95**	9,025	9.747
46	2,116	6.782	**96**	9,216	9.798
47	2,209	6.856	**97**	9,409	9.849
48	2,304	6.928	**98**	9,604	9.899
49	2,401	7.000	**99**	9,801	9.950
50	2,500	7.071	**100**	10,000	10.000

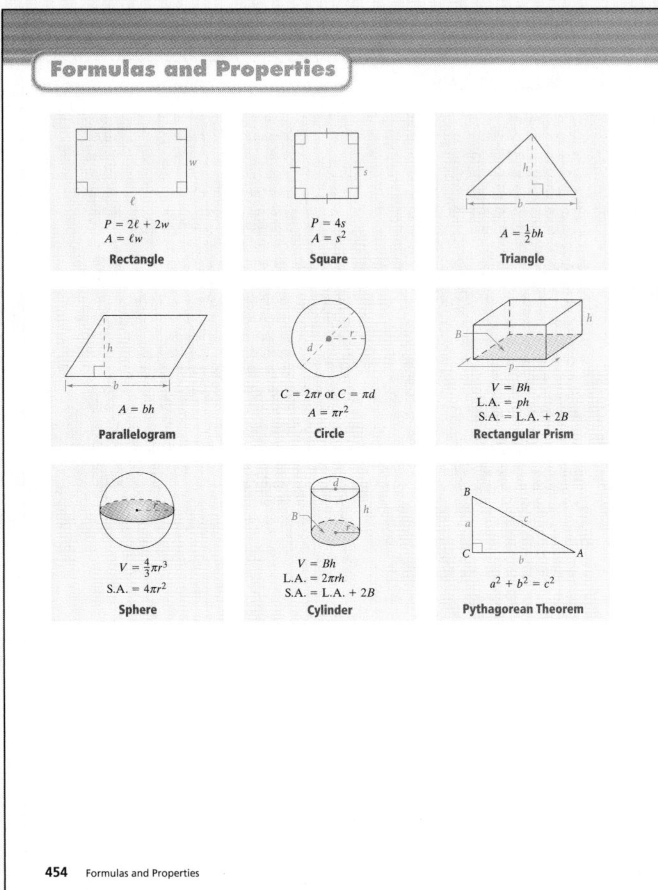

Properties of Real Numbers

Unless otherwise stated, the variables a, b, c, and d used in these properties can be replaced with any number represented on a number line.

Identity Properties

Addition $a + 0 = a$ and $0 + a = a$

Multiplication $a \cdot 1 = a$ and $1 \cdot a = a$

Commutative Properties

Addition $a + b = b + a$

Multiplication $a \cdot b = b \cdot a$

Associative Properties

Addition $(a + b) + c = a + (b + c)$

Multiplication $(a \cdot b) \cdot c = a \cdot (b \cdot c)$

Inverse Properties

Addition

$a + (-a) = 0$ and $-a + a = 0$

Multiplication

$a \cdot \frac{1}{a} = 1$ and $\frac{1}{a} \cdot a = 1$ $(a \neq 0)$

Distributive Properties

$a(b + c) = ab + ac$ $(b + c)a = ba + ca$

$a(b - c) = ab - ac$ $(b - c)a = ba - ca$

Properties of Equality

Addition If $a = b$, then $a + c = b + c$.

Subtraction If $a = b$, then $a - c = b - c$.

Multiplication If $a = b$, then $a \cdot c = b \cdot c$.

Division If $a = b$, and $c \neq 0$, then $\frac{a}{c} = \frac{b}{c}$.

Substitution If $a = b$, then b can replace a in any expression.

Reflexive $a = a$

Symmetric If $a = b$, then $b = a$.

Transitive If $a = b$ and $b = c$, then $a = c$.

Cross Products Property

$\frac{a}{c} = \frac{b}{d}$ is equivalent to $ad = bc$.

Zero-Product Property

If $ab = 0$, then $a = 0$ or $b = 0$.

Closure Property

$a + b$ is a unique real number.
ab is a unique real number.

Density Property

Between any two rational numbers, there is at least one other rational number.

Properties of Inequality

Addition If $a > b$, then $a + c > b + c$.
If $a < b$, then $a + c < b + c$.

Subtraction If $a > b$, then $a - c > b - c$.
If $a < b$, then $a - c < b - c$.

Multiplication

If $a > b$ and $c > 0$, then $ac > bc$.
If $a < b$ and $c > 0$, then $ac < bc$.
If $a > b$ and $c < 0$, then $ac < bc$.
If $a < b$ and $c < 0$, then $ac > bc$.

Division

If $a > b$ and $c > 0$, then $\frac{a}{c} > \frac{b}{c}$.
If $a < b$ and $c > 0$, then $\frac{a}{c} < \frac{b}{c}$.
If $a > b$ and $c < 0$, then $\frac{a}{c} < \frac{b}{c}$.
If $a < b$ and $c < 0$, then $\frac{a}{c} > \frac{b}{c}$.

Transitive

If $a > b$ and $b > c$, then $a > c$.

Comparative

If $a = b + c$ and $c > 0$, then $a > b$.

Properties of Exponents

For any nonzero number a and any integers m and n:

Zero Exponent $a^0 = 1$

Negative Exponent $a^{-n} = \frac{1}{a^n}$

Product of Powers $a^m \cdot a^n = a^{m+n}$

Quotient of Powers $\frac{a^m}{a^n} = a^{m-n}$

English/Spanish Illustrated Glossary

A

EXAMPLES

Absolute value (p. 46) The absolute value of a number is its distance from 0 on a number line.

Valor absoluto (p. 46) El valor absoluto de un número es su distancia del 0 en una recta numérica.

-7 is 7 units from 0, so $|-7| = 7$.

Addition Property of Equality (p. 92) The Addition Property of Equality states that if you add the same value to each side of an equation, the results are equal.

Propiedad Aditiva de la Igualdad (p. 92) La Propiedad Aditiva de la Igualdad establece que si se suma el mismo valor a cada lado de una ecuación, los resultados son iguales.

If $a = b$, then $a + c = b + c$.
Since $\frac{20}{2} = 10$, $\frac{20}{2} + 3 = 10 + 3$.

Addition Property of Inequality (p. 334) The Addition Property of Inequality states that if you add the same value to each side of an inequality, the relationship between the two sides does not change.

Propiedad Aditiva de la Desigualdad (p. 334) La Propiedad Aditiva de la Desigualdad establece que si sumas el mismo valor a cada lado de una desigualdad, la relación entre los dos lados no cambia.

If $a > b$, then $a + c > b + c$.
Since $4 > 2$, $4 + 11 > 2 + 11$.
If $a < b$, then $a + c < b + c$.
Since $4 < 9$, $4 + 11 < 9 + 11$.

Additive inverses (p. 52) Two numbers whose sum is 0 are additive inverses.

Inversos aditivos (p. 52) Dos números cuya suma es 0 son inversos aditivos.

$-a + a = 0$
$(-5) + 5 = 0$

Algebraic expression (p. 8) An algebraic expression is a mathematical phrase that contains variables, numbers, and operation symbols.

Expresión algebraica (p. 8) Una expresión algebraica es un enunciado matemático que contiene variables, números y símbolos de operaciones.

$2x - 5$ is an algebraic expression.

Area (p. 17) The area of a figure is the number of square units it encloses.

Área (p. 17) El área de una figura es el número de unidades cuadradas que contiene.

Each square equals 1 ft^2. $\ell = 6$ ft, and $w = 4$ ft, so the area is $6 \cdot 4 = 24$ ft^2.

EXAMPLES

Associative Property of Addition (p. 26) The Associative Property of Addition states that changing the grouping of the addends does not change the sum.

Propiedad Asociativa de la Suma (p. 26) La Propiedad Asociativa de la Suma establece que cambiar la agrupación de los sumandos no cambia la suma.

$(a + b) + c = a + (b + c)$
$(2 + 3) + 7 = 2 + (3 + 7)$

Associative Property of Multiplication (p. 26) The Associative Property of Multiplication states that changing the grouping of factors does not change the product.

Propiedad Asociativa de la Multiplicación (p. 26) La Propiedad Asociativa de la Multiplicación establece que cambiar la agrupación de los factores no altera el producto.

$(a \cdot b) \cdot c = a \cdot (b \cdot c)$
$(3 \cdot 4) \cdot 5 = 3 \cdot (4 \cdot 5)$

B

Base (p. 73) When a number is written in exponential form, the number that is used as a factor is the base.

Base (p. 73) Cuando un número se escribe en forma exponencial, el número que se usa como factor es la base.

$5^4 = 5 \times 5 \times 5 \times 5$
base

C

Circle (p. 319) A circle is the set of points in a plane that are all the same distance from a given point called the center.

Círculo (p. 319) Un círculo es el conjunto de puntos en un plano que están a la misma distancia de un punto dado llamado centro.

Circumference (p. 319) Circumference is the distance around a circle. You calculate the circumference of a circle by multiplying the diameter by π.

Circunferencia (p. 319) La circunferencia es la distancia alrededor de un círculo. La circunferencia de un círculo se calcula multiplicando el diámetro por π.

The circumference of a circle with a diameter of 10 cm is approximately 31.4 cm.

Common divisor (p. 136) A common divisor is a divisor that two or more numbers share.

Divisor común (p. 136) Un divisor común es un divisor que comparten dos o más números.

The common divisors of 12 and 30 are 1, 2, 3, and 6.

EXAMPLES

Commutative Property of Addition (p. 26) The Commutative Property of Addition states that changing the order of the addends does not change the sum.

Propiedad Conmutativa de la Suma (p. 26) La Propiedad Conmutativa de la Suma establece que al cambiar el orden de los sumandos no se altera la suma.

$a + b = b + a$
$3 + 1 = 1 + 3$

Commutative Property of Multiplication (p. 26) The Commutative Property of Multiplication states that changing the order of the factors does not change the product.

Propiedad Conmutativa de la Multiplicación (p. 26) La Propiedad Conmutativa de la Multiplicación establece que al cambiar el orden de los factores no se altera el producto.

$a \cdot b = b \cdot a$
$6 \cdot 3 = 3 \cdot 6$

Compatible numbers (p. 21) Compatible numbers are numbers that are easy to compute mentally.

Números compatibles (p. 21) Los números compatibles son números con los que se puede calcular mentalmente con facilidad.

Estimate $151 \div 14.6$.
$151 \approx 150$, $14.6 \approx 15$
$150 \div 15 = 10$
$151 \div 14.6 \approx 10$

Composite number (p. 133) A composite number is a whole number greater than 1 with more than two factors.

Número compuesto (p. 133) Un número compuesto es un número entero mayor que 1, que tiene más de dos factores.

24 is a composite number that has 1, 2, 3, 4, 6, 8, 12, and 24 as factors.

Conjecture (p. CA39) A conjecture is a prediction that suggests what can be expected to happen.

Conjectura (p. CA39) Una conjectura es una predicción que sugiere lo que se puede esperar que ocurra.

Every clover has three leaves.

Converse of the Pythagorean Theorem (p. 117) The converse of the Pythagorean Theorem states that if a triangle has sides of length a, b, and c, and $a^2 + b^2 = c^2$, then the triangle is a right triangle with hypotenuse of length c.

Recíproco del Teorema de Pitágoras (p. 117) El recíproco del Teorema de Pitágoras establece que si la longitud de los lados de un triángulo son a, b y c, y $a^2 + b^2 = c^2$, el triángulo es un triángulo rectángulo en la cual la hipotenusa es de longitud c.

A triangle with sides of length 4, 6, and 10 is not a right triangle, since $4^2 + 6^2 \neq 10^2$.

Conversion factor (p. 226) Rates equal to 1.

Factor de conversión (p. 226) Las razones dan igual a 1.

$\frac{3 \text{ ft}}{1 \text{ yd}}$ and $\frac{1 \text{ yd}}{3 \text{ ft}}$ are conversion factors.

EXAMPLES

Coordinate plane (p. 288) A coordinate plane is formed by the intersection of a horizontal number line called the x-axis and a vertical number line called the y-axis.

Plano de coordenadas (p. 288) Un plano de coordenadas está formado por la intersección de una recta numérica horizontal llamada eje de x y por una recta numérica vertical llamada eje de y.

Cross products (p. 236) For two ratios, the cross products are found by multiplying the denominator of one ratio by the numerator of the other ratio.

Productos cruzados (p. 236) En dos razones, los productos cruzados se hallan al multiplicar el denominador de una razón por el numerador de la otra razón.

In the proportion $\frac{2}{5} = \frac{10}{25}$, the cross products are $2 \cdot 25$ and $5 \cdot 10$.

Cube (p. 210) A cube is a rectangular prism whose faces are all squares.

Cubo (p. 210) Un cubo es un prisma rectangular cuyas caras son todas cuadrados.

D

Deductive reasoning (p. 100) A process of reasoning logically from given facts to a conclusion is called deductive reasoning.

Razonamiento deductivo (p. 100) El proceso de razonar lógicamente para llegar a una conclusión a partir de datos dados se llama razonamiento deductivo.

Dimensional analysis (p. 227) Dimensional analysis is a method of determining the proper units of measure for a quantity.

Análisis dimensional (p. 227) Análisis dimensional es el método que decide las unidades adecuadas para calcular cierta cantidad.

$\frac{\text{worker} \cdot \text{hours}}{\text{worker}} = \text{hours}$

Direct variation (p. 316) A direct variation is a linear function in which the ratio of two quantities is always the same.

Variación directa (p. 316) Una variación directa es una función en la que la razón de dos cantidades es siempre la misma.

$y = 3x$

Discount (p. 273) The amount the price of an item is reduced is called the discount.

Descuento (p. 273) La cantidad que se reduce el precio de un artículo se llama descuento.

A \$20 book is discounted by \$2.50 to sell for \$17.50.

EXAMPLES

Distributive Property (p. 30) The Distributive Property shows how multiplication affects an addition or subtraction: $a(b + c) = ab + ac$.

Propiedad distributiva (p. 30) La Propiedad Distributiva muestra cómo la multiplicatión afecta a una suma o a una resta: $a(b + c) = ab + ac$.

$2\left(3 + \frac{1}{2}\right) = 2 \cdot 3 + 2 \cdot \frac{1}{2}$
$8(5 - 3) = 8 \cdot 5 - 8 \cdot 3$

Divisible (p. 133) A number is divisible by a second whole number if the first number can be divided by the second number with a remainder of 0.

Divisible (p. 133) Un número es divisible por un segundo número entero si el primer número se puede dividir por el segundo número y el residuo es 0.

16 is divisible by 1, 2, 4, 8, and 16.

Division Property of Equality (p. 96) The Division Property of Equality states that if you divide each side of an equation by the same nonzero number, the sides remain equal.

Propiedad de División de la Igualdad (p. 96) La Propiedad de División de la Igualdad establece que si cada lado de una ecuación se divide por el mismo número distinto de cero, los dos lados se mantienen iguales.

If $a = b$ and $c \neq 0$, then $\frac{a}{c} = \frac{b}{c}$.
Since $3 \cdot 2 = 6$, $\frac{3 \cdot 2}{2} = \frac{6}{2}$.

Division Property of Inequality (p. 340) The Division Property of Inequality states that if you divide an inequality by a positive number, the direction of the inequality is unchanged. If you divide an inequality by a negative number, *reverse* the direction of the inequality sign.

Propiedad de División de la Desigualdad (p. 340) La Propiedad de División de la Desigualdad establece que si se divide una desigualdad por un número positivo, la dirección de la desigualdad no cambia. Si se divide una desigualdad por un número negativo, se *invierte* la dirección del signo de desigualdad.

If $a > b$ and $c > 0$, then $\frac{a}{c} > \frac{b}{c}$.
Since $2 > 1$ and $3 > 0$, $\frac{2}{3} > \frac{1}{3}$.
If $a < b$ and $c > 0$, then $\frac{a}{c} < \frac{b}{c}$.
Since $2 < 4$ and $3 > 0$, $\frac{2}{3} < \frac{4}{3}$.
If $a > b$ and $c < 0$, then $\frac{a}{c} < \frac{b}{c}$.
Since $2 > 1$ and $-4 < 0$, $\frac{2}{-4} < \frac{1}{-4}$.
If $a < b$ and $c < 0$, then $\frac{a}{c} > \frac{b}{c}$.
Since $2 < 4$ and $-4 < 0$, $\frac{2}{-4} > \frac{4}{-4}$.

E

Equation (p. 87) An equation is a mathematical sentence with an equal sign.

Ecuación (p. 87) Una ecuación es una oración matemática con un signo igual.

$2(3 + 5) = 16$ and $x + 10 = 8$ are examples of equations.

Equivalent fractions (p. 142) Equivalent fractions are fractions that name the same point on the number line.

Fracciones equivalentes (p. 142) Fracciones equivalentes son aquellas que señalan un mismo punto en una recta numérica.

$\frac{1}{2}$ and $\frac{25}{50}$ are equivalent fractions.

EXAMPLES

Equivalent ratios (p. 217) Equivalent ratios name the same number. Equivalent ratios written as a fractions are equivalent fractions.

Razones equivalentes (p. 217) Las razones equivalentes indican el mismo número. Las razones equivalanetes escritas como fracciones son fracciones equivalentes.

The ratios $\frac{4}{7}$ and $\frac{8}{14}$ are equivalent.

Evaluating algebraic expressions (p. 9) To evaluate an algebraic expression, replace each variable with a number. Then follow the order of operations to simplify the expression.

Evaluación de una expresión algebraica (p. 9) Para evaluar una expresión algebraica, se reemplaza cada variable con un número. Luego se sigue el orden de las operaciones para simplificar la expresión.

To evaluate the expression $3x + 2$ for $x = 4$, substitute 4 for x.
$3x + 2 = 3(4) + 2 = 12 + 2 = 14$

Expanded notation (p. 206) Expanded notation uses a sum to show the place value of each digit in a number.

Forma desarrollada (p. 206) La forma desarrollada de un número es la suma que muestra el lugar y valor de cada dígito.

4.85 can be written in expanded notation as
$(4 \cdot 10^0) + (8 \cdot 10^{-1}) + (5 \cdot 10^{-2})$.

Exponent (p. 73) An exponent tells how many times a number, or base, is used as a factor.

Exponente (p. 73) Un exponente dice cuántas veces se usa como factor un número o base.

exponent
$3^4 = 3 \times 3 \times 3 \times 3$
Read 3^4 as "three to the fourth power."

F

Factor (p. 73) A factor is a whole number that divides another whole number with a remainder of 0.

Divisor (p. 73) Un divisor es un número entero que divide a otro número entero y el residuo es 0.

1, 2, 3, 4, 6, 12, 18, and 36 are factors of 36.

Formula (p. 10) A formula is a rule that shows the relationship between two or more quantities.

Fórmula (p. 10) Una fórmula es una regla que muestra la relación entre dos o más cantidades.

The formula $P = 2\ell + 2w$ gives the perimeter of a rectangle in terms of its length and width.

Function (p. 298) A function is a relationship that assigns exactly one output value for each input value.

Función (p. 298) Una función es una relación que asigna exactamente un valor resultante a cada valor inicial.

Earned income is a function of the number of hours worked w. If you earn \$6/h, then your income can be expressed by the function $f(w) = 6w$.

EXAMPLES

Function rule (p. 298) A function rule is an equation that describes a function.

Fórmula de una función (p. 298) Una fórmula de una función es una ecuación que describe una función.

The function rule that describes the cost c of buying x movie tickets that cost \$9 each is $c = 9x$.

G

Graph of an equation (p. 302) The graph of an equation is the graph of all the points whose coordinates are solutions of the equation.

Gráfica de una ecuación (p. 302) La gráfica de una ecuación es la gráfica de todos los puntos cuyas coordenadas son soluciones a la ecuación.

The coordinates of all the points on the graph satisfy the equation $y = |x| - 1$.

Graph of an inequality (p. 330) The graph of an inequality containing a variable shows all the solutions that satisfy the inequality.

Gráfica de una desigualdad (p. 330) La gráfica de una desigualdad que contiene una variable muestra todas las soluciones que satisfacen la desigualdad.

−4 −3 −2 −1 0 1 2 3 4
The graph shows the inequality $x < 0$.

Greatest common divisor (GCD) (p. 136) The greatest common divisor of two or more numbers is the greatest common divisor shared by all the numbers.

Máximo común divisor (MCD) (p. 136) El máximo común divisor de dos o más números es el mayor divisor que los números tienen en común.

The GCD of 15 and 20 is 5.

Greatest common factor (GCF) (p. 136) The greatest common factor of two or more numbers is the greatest number that is a factor of all of the numbers.

Máximo común divisor (MCD) (p. 136) El máximo común divisor de dos o más números es el mayor número que es divisor de todos los números.

The GCF of 12 and 30 is 6.

H

Hypotenuse (p. 112) In a right triangle, the hypotenuse is the longest side, which is opposite the right angle.

Hipotenusa (p. 112) En un triángulo rectángulo, la hipotenusa es el lado más largo, que es el lado opuesto al ángulo recto.

$\overline{AC}$ is the hypotenuse of $\triangle ABC$.

I

EXAMPLES

Identity Property of Addition (p. 26) The Identity Property of Addition states that the sum of 0 and a is a.

Priopiedad de Identidad de la Suma (p. 26) La Propiedad de Identidad de la Suma establece que la suma de 0 y a es a.

$a + 0 = a$
$7 + 0 = 7$

Identity Property of Multiplication (p. 26) The Identity Property of Multiplication states that the product of 1 and a is a.

Propiedad de Identidad de la Multiplicación (p. 26) La Propiedad de Identidad de la Multiplicación establece que el producto de 1 y a es a.

$a \cdot 1 = a$
$7 \cdot 1 = 7$

Improper fraction (p. 153) An improper fraction has a numerator that is greater than or equal to its denominator.

Fracción impropia (p. 153) Una fracción impropia tiene un numerador mayor o igual que su denominador.

$\frac{24}{15}$ and $\frac{16}{16}$ are improper fractions.

Inductive reasoning (p. CA39) Making conclusions based on observed patterns is called inductive reasoning.

Razonamiento inductivo (p. CA39) Razonamiento inductivo es sacar conclusiones a partir de patrones observados.

Inequality (p. 330) An inequality is a mathematical sentence that contains $<, >, \leq, \geq$, or $\neq$.

Desigualdad (p. 330) Una desigualdad es una oración matemática que contiene los signos $<, >, \leq, \geq$, o $\neq$.

$x < -5$, $3 > 8$, $y \leq 1$, $5 \geq -11$

Integers (p. 46) Integers are the set of whole numbers and their opposites.

Enteros (p. 46) Los enteros son el conjunto de números enteros y sus opuestos.

$\ldots, -3, -2, -1, 0, 1, 2, 3, \ldots$

Interest (p. 276) Interest is the amount of money paid for the use of borrowed money.

Interés (p. 276) El interés es la cantidad de dinero que se paga por el uso del dinero prestado.

See *Simple interest*.

Interest rate (p. 276) The rate, usually expressed as a percent, used to calculate interest.

Tasa de interés (p. 276) La tasa, que generalmente se expresa como porcentaje, se usa para calcular el interés.

EXAMPLES

Inverse operations (p. 87) Inverse operations are operations that undo each other.

Operaciones inversas (p. 87) Las operaciones inversas son las operaciones que se anulan entre ellas.

Example: Addition and subtraction are inverse operations.

Isolate (p. 87) To isolate the variable means to get the variable alone on one side of an equation.

Despejar (p. 87) Despejar la variable quiere decir dejar la variable sola a un lado de la ecuación.

Example: To isolate y on one side of the equation $y - 2x = 4$, add $2x$ to each side. The equation becomes $y = 4 + 2x$.

L

Least common denominator (LCD) (p. 155) The least common denominator of two or more fractions is the least common multiple (LCM) of their denominators.

Mínimo común denominador (MCD) (p. 155) El mínimo común denominador de dos o más fracciones es el mínimo común múltiplo (MCD) de sus denominadores.

Example: The LCD of the fractions $\frac{3}{8}$ and $\frac{7}{10}$ is 40.

Least common multiple (LCM) (p. 155) The least common multiple of two numbers is the smallest number that is a multiple of both numbers.

Mínimo común múltiplo (MCM) (p. 155) El mínimo común múltiplo de dos números es el menor número que es múltiplo de ambos números.

Example: The LCM of 15 and 6 is 30.

Legs of a right triangle (p. 112) The legs of a right triangle are the two shorter sides of the triangle.

Catetos de un triángulo rectángulo (p. 112) Los catetos de un triángulo rectángulo son los dos lados más cortos del triángulo.

Example: $\overline{AB}$ and $\overline{BC}$ are the legs of $\triangle ABC$.

Like terms (p. 380) Like terms are terms with exactly the same variable factors.

Términos semejantes (p. 380) Los términos semejantes tienen exactamente las mismas variables como factores.

Example: $3b$ and $12b$ are like terms. You can combine like terms using the Distributive Property:

$$\begin{aligned} 3b + 12b &= 3 \cdot b + 12 \cdot b \\ &= (3 + 12)b \\ &= 15b \end{aligned}$$

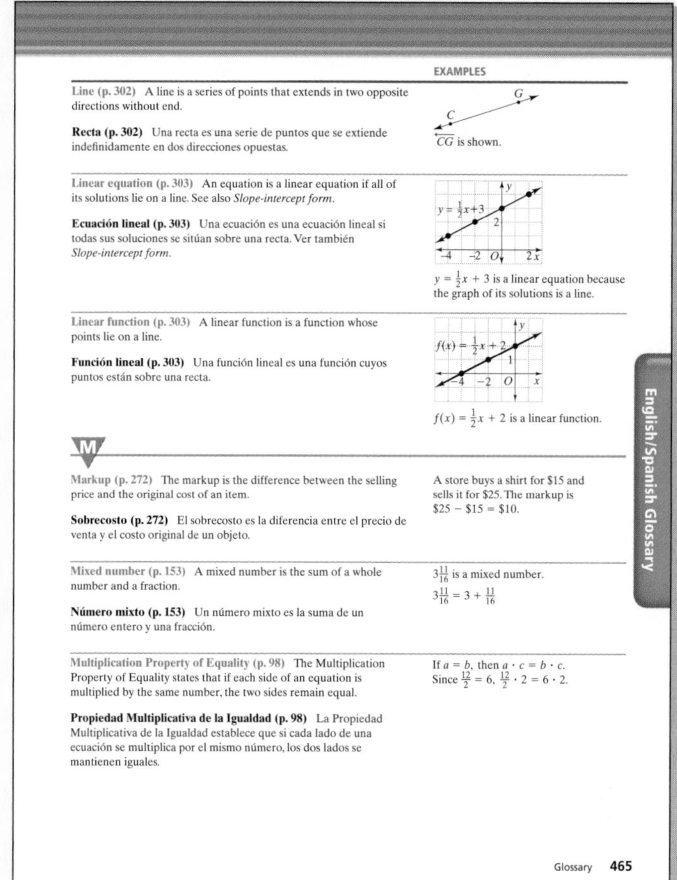

EXAMPLES

Line (p. 302) A line is a series of points that extends in two opposite directions without end.

Recta (p. 302) Una recta es una serie de puntos que se extiende indefinidamente en dos direcciones opuestas.

Example: $\overleftrightarrow{CG}$ is shown.

Linear equation (p. 303) An equation is a linear equation if all of its solutions lie on a line. See also *Slope-intercept form*.

Ecuación lineal (p. 303) Una ecuación es una ecuación lineal si todas sus soluciones se sitúan sobre una recta. Ver también *Slope-intercept form*.

Example: $y = \frac{1}{2}x + 3$ is a linear equation because the graph of its solutions is a line.

Linear function (p. 303) A linear function is a function whose points lie on a line.

Función lineal (p. 303) Una función lineal es una función cuyos puntos están sobre una recta.

Example: $f(x) = \frac{1}{2}x + 2$ is a linear function.

M

Markup (p. 272) The markup is the difference between the selling price and the original cost of an item.

Sobrecosto (p. 272) El sobrecosto es la diferencia entre el precio de venta y el costo original de un objeto.

Example: A store buys a shirt for $15 and sells it for $25. The markup is $25 − $15 = $10.

Mixed number (p. 153) A mixed number is the sum of a whole number and a fraction.

Número mixto (p. 153) Un número mixto es la suma de un número entero y una fracción.

Example: $3\frac{11}{16}$ is a mixed number.
$3\frac{11}{16} = 3 + \frac{11}{16}$

Multiplication Property of Equality (p. 98) The Multiplication Property of Equality states that if each side of an equation is multiplied by the same number, the two sides remain equal.

Propiedad Multiplicativa de la Igualdad (p. 98) La Propiedad Multiplicativa de la Igualdad establece que si cada lado de una ecuación se multiplica por el mismo número, los dos lados se mantienen iguales.

Example: If $a = b$, then $a \cdot c = b \cdot c$.
Since $\frac{12}{2} = 6$, $\frac{12}{2} \cdot 2 = 6 \cdot 2$.

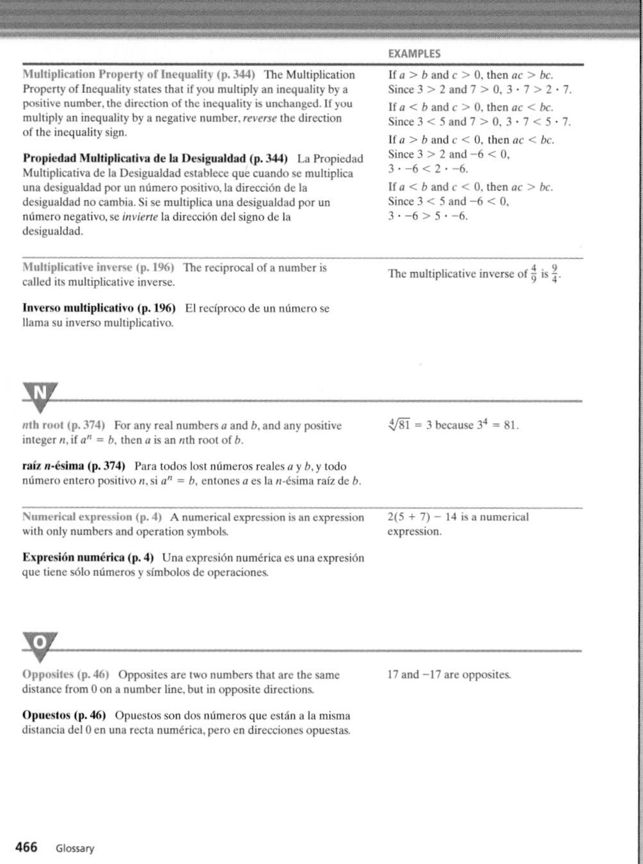

EXAMPLES

Multiplication Property of Inequality (p. 344) The Multiplication Property of Inequality states that if you multiply an inequality by a positive number, the direction of the inequality is unchanged. If you multiply an inequality by a negative number, *reverse* the direction of the inequality sign.

Propiedad Multiplicativa de la Desigualdad (p. 344) La Propiedad Multiplicativa de la Desigualdad establece que cuando se multiplica una desigualdad por un número positivo, la dirección de la desigualdad no cambia. Si se multiplica una desigualdad por un número negativo, se *invierte* la dirección del signo de la desigualdad.

Example:
If $a > b$ and $c > 0$, then $ac > bc$.
Since $3 > 2$ and $7 > 0$, $3 \cdot 7 > 2 \cdot 7$.
If $a < b$ and $c > 0$, then $ac < bc$.
Since $3 < 5$ and $7 > 0$, $3 \cdot 7 < 5 \cdot 7$.
If $a > b$ and $c < 0$, then $ac < bc$.
Since $3 > 2$ and $-6 < 0$, $3 \cdot -6 < 2 \cdot -6$.
If $a < b$ and $c < 0$, then $ac > bc$.
Since $3 < 5$ and $-6 < 0$, $3 \cdot -6 > 5 \cdot -6$.

Multiplicative inverse (p. 196) The reciprocal of a number is called its multiplicative inverse.

Inverso multiplicativo (p. 196) El recíproco de un número se llama su inverso multiplicativo.

Example: The multiplicative inverse of $\frac{4}{9}$ is $\frac{9}{4}$.

N

nth root (p. 374) For any real numbers a and b, and any positive integer n, if $a^n = b$, then a is an nth root of b.

raíz n-ésima (p. 374) Para todos lost números reales a y b, y todo número entero positivo n, si $a^n = b$, entones a es la n-ésima raíz de b.

Example: $\sqrt[4]{81} = 3$ because $3^4 = 81$.

Numerical expression (p. 4) A numerical expression is an expression with only numbers and operation symbols.

Expresión numérica (p. 4) Una expresión numérica es una expresión que tiene sólo números y símbolos de operaciones.

Example: $2(5 + 7) - 14$ is a numerical expression.

O

Opposites (p. 46) Opposites are two numbers that are the same distance from 0 on a number line, but in opposite directions.

Opuestos (p. 46) Opuestos son dos números que están a la misma distancia del 0 en una recta numérica, pero en direcciones opuestas.

Example: 17 and −17 are opposites.

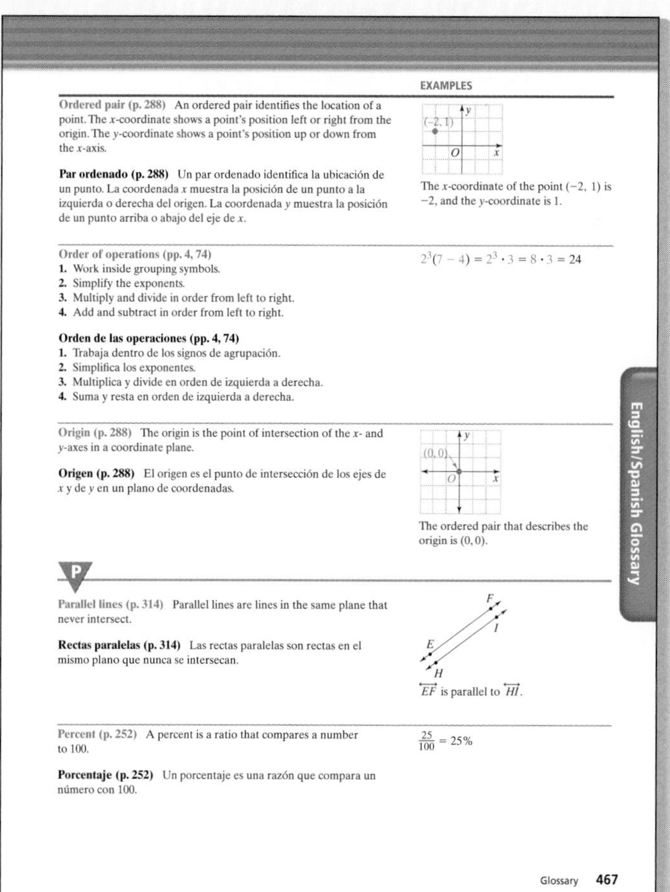

EXAMPLES

Ordered pair (p. 288) An ordered pair identifies the location of a point. The x-coordinate shows a point's position left or right from the origin. The y-coordinate shows a point's position up or down from the x-axis.

Par ordenado (p. 288) Un par ordenado identifica la ubicación de un punto. La coordenada x muestra la posición de un punto a la izquierda o derecha del origen. La coordenada y muestra la posición de un punto arriba o abajo del eje de x.

Example: The x-coordinate of the point $(-2, 1)$ is -2, and the y-coordinate is 1.

Order of operations (pp. 4, 74)
1. Work inside grouping symbols.
2. Simplify the exponents.
3. Multiply and divide in order from left to right.
4. Add and subtract in order from left to right.

Orden de las operaciones (pp. 4, 74)
1. Trabaja dentro de los signos de agrupación.
2. Simplifica los exponentes.
3. Multiplica y divide en orden de izquierda a derecha.
4. Suma y resta en orden de izquierda a derecha.

Example: $2^3(7 - 4) = 2^3 \cdot 3 = 8 \cdot 3 = 24$

Origin (p. 288) The origin is the point of intersection of the x- and y-axes in a coordinate plane.

Origen (p. 288) El origen es el punto de intersección de los ejes de x y de y en un plano de coordenadas.

Example: The ordered pair that describes the origin is (0, 0).

P

Parallel lines (p. 314) Parallel lines are lines in the same plane that never intersect.

Rectas paralelas (p. 314) Las rectas paralelas son rectas en el mismo plano que nunca se intersecan.

Example: $\overleftrightarrow{EF}$ is parallel to $\overleftrightarrow{HI}$.

Percent (p. 252) A percent is a ratio that compares a number to 100.

Porcentaje (p. 252) Un porcentaje es una razón que compara un número con 100.

Example: $\frac{25}{100} = 25\%$

EXAMPLES

Percent of change (p. 266) The percent of change is the percent a quantity increases or decreases from its original amount.

Porcentaje de cambio (p. 266) El porcentaje de cambio es el porcentaje que aumenta o disminuye una cantidad a partir de su cantidad original.

The number of employees increases from 14 to 21. The percent of change is $\frac{21 - 14}{14} = 50\%$.

Perfect square (p. 107) A perfect square is a number that is the square of an integer.

Cuadrado perfecto (p. 107) Un cuadrado perfecto es un número que es el cuadrado de un entero.

Since $25 = 5^2$, 25 is a perfect square.

Perimeter (p. 10) The perimeter of a figure is the distance around the figure.

Perímetro (p. 10) El perímetro de una figura es la distancia alrededor de la figura.

A 4 ft B
2 ft 2 ft
D 4 ft C

The perimeter of rectangle $ABCD$ is 12 ft.

Perpendicular lines (p. 314) Perpendicular lines intersect to form right angles.

Rectas perpendiculares (p. 314) Las rectas perpendiculares se intersecan para formar ángulos rectos.

$\overleftrightarrow{DE} \perp \overleftrightarrow{RS}$

Pi (p. 319) Pi (π) is the ratio of the circumference C of any circle to its diameter d.

Pi (p. 319) Pi (π) es la razón de la circunferencia C de cualquier círculo a su diámetro d.

$\pi = \frac{C}{d}$

Point (p. 288) A point is a location that has no size.

Punto (p. 288) Un punto es una ubicación que no tiene tamaño.

• A

A is a point.

Power (p. 73) A power is a number that can be expressed using a base and an exponent.

Potencia (p. 73) Una potencia es un número que se puede expresar usando una base y un exponente.

3^4, 5^2, and 2^{10} are powers.

Prime factorization (p. 133) Writing a composite number as the product of its prime factors is the prime factorization of the number.

Descomposición en factores primos (p. 133) Escribir un número compuesto como el producto de sus factores primos es la descomposición en factores primos del número.

The prime factorization of 12 is $2 \cdot 2 \cdot 3$, or $2^2 \cdot 3$.

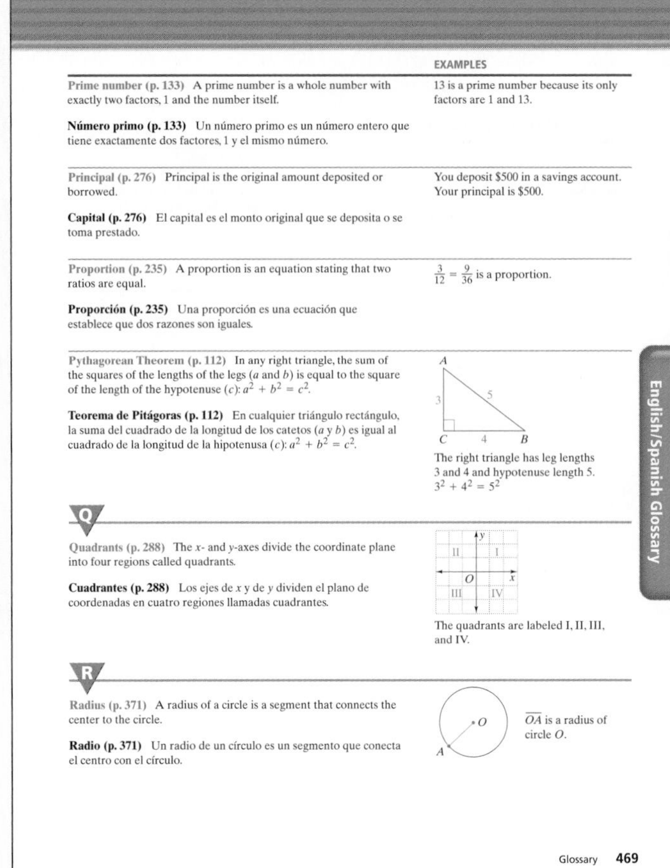

EXAMPLES

Prime number (p. 133) A prime number is a whole number with exactly two factors, 1 and the number itself.

Número primo (p. 133) Un número primo es un número entero que tiene exactamente dos factores, 1 y el mismo número.

13 is a prime number because its only factors are 1 and 13.

Principal (p. 276) Principal is the original amount deposited or borrowed.

Capital (p. 276) El capital es el monto original que se deposita o se toma prestado.

You deposit \$500 in a savings account. Your principal is \$500.

Proportion (p. 235) A proportion is an equation stating that two ratios are equal.

Proporción (p. 235) Una proporción es una ecuación que establece que dos razones son iguales.

$\frac{3}{12} = \frac{9}{36}$ is a proportion.

Pythagorean Theorem (p. 112) In any right triangle, the sum of the squares of the lengths of the legs (a and b) is equal to the square of the length of the hypotenuse (c): $a^2 + b^2 = c^2$.

Teorema de Pitágoras (p. 112) En cualquier triángulo rectángulo, la suma del cuadrado de la longitud de los catetos (a y b) es igual al cuadrado de la longitud de la hipotenusa (c): $a^2 + b^2 = c^2$.

The right triangle has leg lengths 3 and 4 and hypotenuse length 5. $3^2 + 4^2 = 5^2$

Q

Quadrants (p. 288) The x- and y-axes divide the coordinate plane into four regions called quadrants.

Cuadrantes (p. 288) Los ejes de x y de y dividen el plano de coordenadas en cuatro regiones llamadas cuadrantes.

The quadrants are labeled I, II, III, and IV.

R

Radius (p. 371) A radius of a circle is a segment that connects the center to the circle.

Radio (p. 371) Un radio de un círculo es un segmento que conecta el centro con el círculo.

$\overline{OA}$ is a radius of circle O.

English/Spanish Glossary

EXAMPLES

Rate (p. 220) A rate is a ratio that compares two quantities measured in different units.

Tasa (p. 220) Una tasa es una razón que compara dos cantidades medidas en unidades diferentes.

You read 116 words in 1 min. Your reading rate is $\frac{116 \text{ words}}{1 \text{ min}}$.

Ratio (p. 216) A ratio is a comparison of two quantities by division.

Razón (p. 216) Una razón es una comparación de dos cantidades mediante la división.

There are three ways to write a ratio: 9 to 10, 9 : 10, and $\frac{9}{10}$.

Rational number (p. 148) A rational number is any number that can be written as a quotient of two integers where the denominator is not 0.

Número racional (p. 148) Un número racional es cualquier número que puede ser escrito como cociente de dos enteros, donde el denominador es diferente de 0.

$\frac{1}{3}$, -5, 6.4, 0.666 . . . , $-2\frac{4}{5}$, 0, and $\frac{7}{3}$ are rational numbers.

Reciprocals (p. 186) Two numbers are reciprocals if their product is 1.

Recíprocos (p. 186) Dos números son recíprocos si su producto es 1.

The numbers $\frac{4}{9}$ and $\frac{9}{4}$ are reciprocals.

Rectangle (p. 10) A rectangle is a parallelogram with four right angles.

Rectángulo (p. 10) Un rectángulo es un paralelogramo que tiene cuatro ángulos rectos.

R S
H W

Repeating decimal (p. 149) A repeating decimal is a decimal that repeats the same digits without end. The repeating block can contain one digit or more than one digit.

Decimal periódico (p. 149) Un decimal periódico es un decimal que repite los mismos dígitos interminablemente. El bloque que se repite puede ser un dígito o más de un dígito.

$0.888\ldots = 0.\overline{8}$

$0.272727\ldots = 0.\overline{27}$

Right angle (p. 112) A right angle is an angle with a measure of 90°.

Ángulo recto (p. 112) Un ángulo recto es un ángulo que mide 90°.

$m\angle D = 90°$

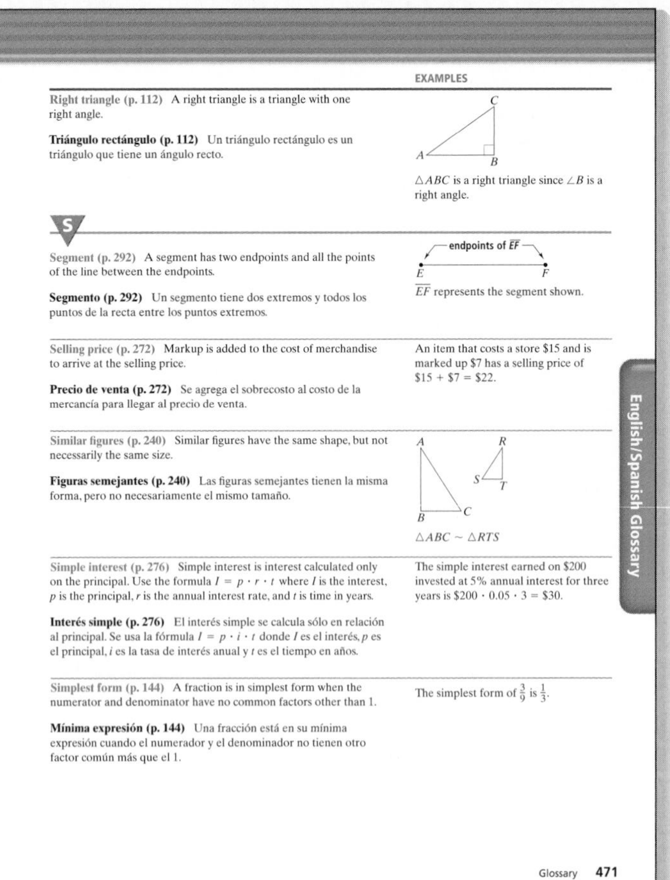

EXAMPLES

Right triangle (p. 112) A right triangle is a triangle with one right angle.

Triángulo rectángulo (p. 112) Un triángulo rectángulo es un triángulo que tiene un ángulo recto.

$\triangle ABC$ is a right triangle since $\angle B$ is a right angle.

S

Segment (p. 292) A segment has two endpoints and all the points of the line between the endpoints.

Segmento (p. 292) Un segmento tiene dos extremos y todos los puntos de la recta entre los puntos extremos.

endpoints of $\overline{EF}$

$\overline{EF}$ represents the segment shown.

Selling price (p. 272) Markup is added to the cost of merchandise to arrive at the selling price.

Precio de venta (p. 272) Se agrega el sobrecosto al costo de la mercancía para llegar al precio de venta.

An item that costs a store \$15 and is marked up \$7 has a selling price of \$15 + \$7 = \$22.

Similar figures (p. 240) Similar figures have the same shape, but not necessarily the same size.

Figuras semejantes (p. 240) Las figuras semejantes tienen la misma forma, pero no necesariamente el mismo tamaño.

$\triangle ABC \sim \triangle RTS$

Simple interest (p. 276) Simple interest is interest calculated only on the principal. Use the formula $I = p \cdot r \cdot t$ where I is the interest, p is the principal, r is the annual interest rate, and t is time in years.

Interés simple (p. 276) El interés simple se calcula sólo en relación al principal. Se usa la fórmula $I = p \cdot i \cdot t$ donde I es el interés, p es el principal, i es la tasa de interés anual y t es el tiempo en años.

The simple interest earned on \$200 invested at 5% annual interest for three years is $\$200 \cdot 0.05 \cdot 3 = \$30$.

Simplest form (p. 144) A fraction is in simplest form when the numerator and denominator have no common factors other than 1.

Mínima expresión (p. 144) Una fracción está en su mínima expresión cuando el numerador y el denominador no tienen otro factor común más que el 1.

The simplest form of $\frac{3}{9}$ is $\frac{1}{3}$.

English/Spanish Glossary

EXAMPLES

Simplify (p. 4) To simplify a numerical expression, replace it with its simplest name. | $8 + 3x - 2$ simplifies to $6 + 3x$.

Simplificar (p. 4) Para simplificar una expresión numérica, se reemplaza con su mínima expresión.

Slope (p. 310) Slope is a ratio that describes steepness.

$$\text{Slope} = \frac{\text{vertical change}}{\text{horizontal change}} = \frac{\text{rise}}{\text{run}}$$

Pendiente (p. 310) La pendiente es la razón que describe la inclinación.

$$\text{Pendiente} = \frac{\text{cambio vertical}}{\text{cambio horizontal}} = \frac{\text{elevación}}{\text{desplazamiento}}$$

Slope of a line (p. 310)

$$\text{Slope} = \frac{\text{change in } y\text{-coordinates}}{\text{change in } x\text{-coordinates}} = \frac{\text{rise}}{\text{run}}$$

Pendiente de una recta (p. 310)

$$\text{Pendiente} = \frac{\text{cambio en la coordenada } y}{\text{cambio en la coordenada } x} = \frac{\text{elevación}}{\text{desplazamiento}}$$

y, 2, O, rise: 2, run: 4, 4, x

The slope of the given line is $\frac{2}{4} = \frac{1}{2}$.

Solution (pp. 303, 331) A solution is any value (or values) that makes an equation or inequality true. | 4 is the solution of $x + 5 = 9$. 7 is a solution of $x < 15$.

Solución (pp. 303, 331) Una solución es cualquier valor (o valores) que hacen que una ecuación o una desigualdad sea verdadera.

Solution set (p. 335) The set of all solutions. | The solution set of the inequality $x + 3 < 4$ is $\{x: x < 1\}$.

Conjunto de soluciones (p. 335) Conjunto de todas las soluciones.

Sphere (p. 403) A sphere is the set of all points in space that are the same distance from a center point.

Esfera (p. 403) Una esfera es el conjunto de todos los puntos en el espacio que están a la misma distancia de un punto central.

Square (p. 108) A square is a parallelogram with four right angles and four congruent sides.

Cuadrado (p. 108) Una cuadrado es un paralelogramo que tiene cuatro ángulos rectos y cuatro lados congruentes.

Q, R, S, T, 5 cm, 5 cm, 5 cm, 5 cm

$QRST$ is a square. $\angle Q$, $\angle R$, $\angle T$, and $\angle S$ are right angles, and $\overline{QR} = \overline{RT} = \overline{TS} = \overline{SQ}$.

472 Glossary

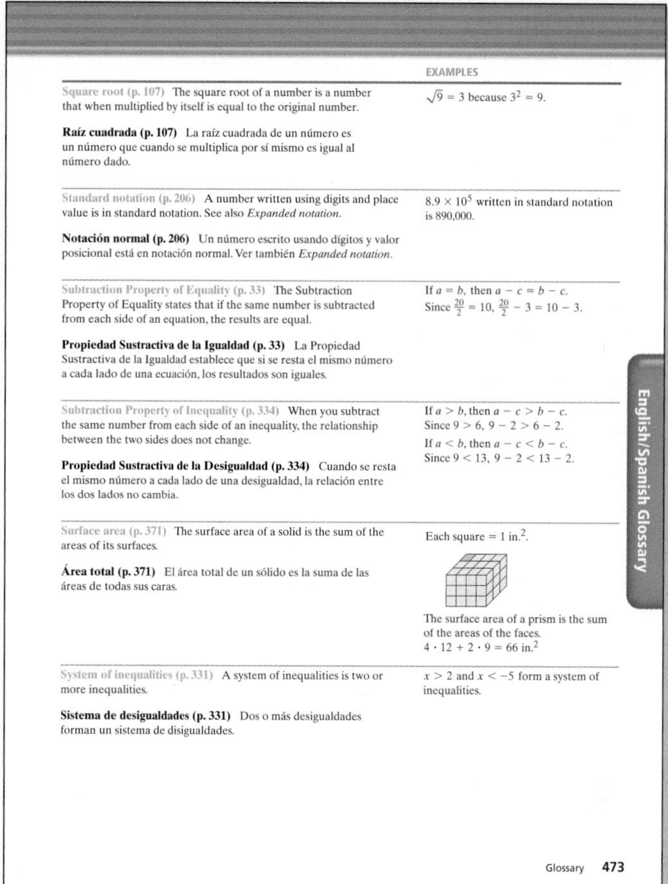

EXAMPLES

Square root (p. 107) The square root of a number is a number that when multiplied by itself is equal to the original number. | $\sqrt{9} = 3$ because $3^2 = 9$.

Raíz cuadrada (p. 107) La raíz cuadrada de un número es un número que cuando se multiplica por sí mismo es igual al número dado.

Standard notation (p. 206) A number written using digits and place value is in standard notation. See also *Expanded notation*. | 8.9×10^5 written in standard notation is 890,000.

Notación normal (p. 206) Un número escrito usando dígitos y valor posicional está en notación normal. Ver también *Expanded notation*.

Subtraction Property of Equality (p. 33) The Subtraction Property of Equality states that if the same number is subtracted from each side of an equation, the results are equal. | If $a = b$, then $a - c = b - c$. Since $\frac{20}{2} = 10$, $\frac{20}{2} - 3 = 10 - 3$.

Propiedad Sustractiva de la Igualdad (p. 33) La Propiedad Sustractiva de la Igualdad establece que si se resta el mismo número a cada lado de una ecuación, los resultados son iguales.

Subtraction Property of Inequality (p. 334) When you subtract the same number from each side of an inequality, the relationship between the two sides does not change. | If $a > b$, then $a - c > b - c$. Since $9 > 6$, $9 - 2 > 6 - 2$. If $a < b$, then $a - c < b - c$. Since $9 < 13$, $9 - 2 < 13 - 2$.

Propiedad Sustractiva de la Desigualdad (p. 334) Cuando se resta el mismo número a cada lado de una desigualdad, la relación entre los dos lados no cambia.

Surface area (p. 371) The surface area of a solid is the sum of the areas of its surfaces. | Each square = 1 in.^{2}.

Área total (p. 371) El área total de un sólido es la suma de las áreas de todas sus caras.

The surface area of a prism is the sum of the areas of the faces. $4 \cdot 12 + 2 \cdot 9 = 66$ in.^{2}

System of inequalities (p. 331) A system of inequalities is two or more inequalities. | $x > 2$ and $x < -5$ form a system of inequalities.

Sistema de desigualdades (p. 331) Dos o más desigualdades forman un sistema de disigualdades.

English/Spanish Glossary

Glossary 473

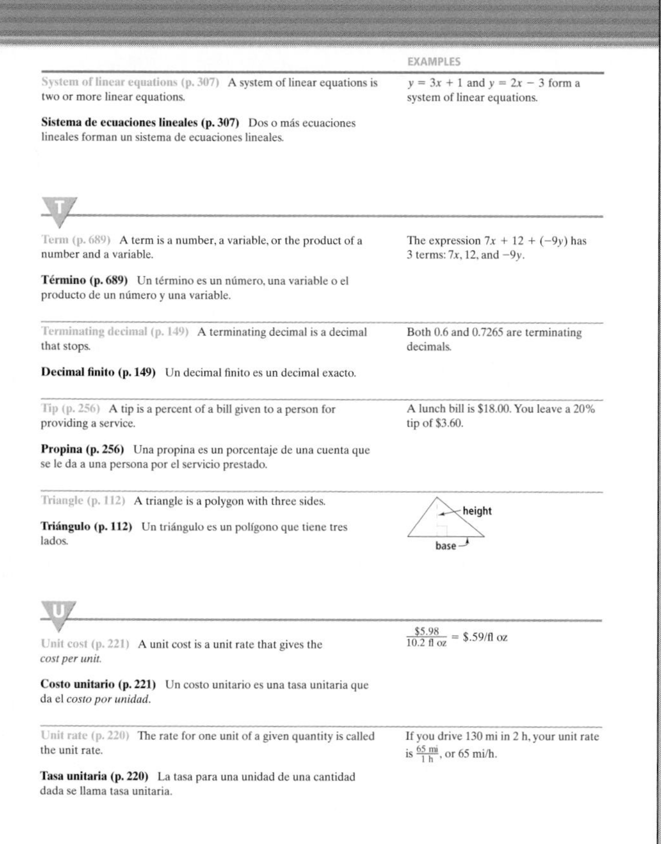

EXAMPLES

System of linear equations (p. 307) A system of linear equations is two or more linear equations. | $y = 3x + 1$ and $y = 2x - 3$ form a system of linear equations.

Sistema de ecuaciones lineales (p. 307) Dos o más ecuaciones lineales forman un sistema de ecuaciones lineales.

T

Term (p. 689) A term is a number, a variable, or the product of a number and a variable. | The expression $7x + 12 + (-9y)$ has 3 terms: $7x$, 12, and $-9y$.

Término (p. 689) Un término es un número, una variable o el producto de un número y una variable.

Terminating decimal (p. 149) A terminating decimal is a decimal that stops. | Both 0.6 and 0.7265 are terminating decimals.

Decimal finito (p. 149) Un decimal finito es un decimal exacto.

Tip (p. 256) A tip is a percent of a bill given to a person for providing a service. | A lunch bill is \$18.00. You leave a 20% tip of \$3.60.

Propina (p. 256) Una propina es un porcentaje de una cuenta que se le da a una persona por el servicio prestado.

Triangle (p. 112) A triangle is a polygon with three sides.

Triángulo (p. 112) Un triángulo es un polígono que tiene tres lados.

height, base

U

Unit cost (p. 221) A unit cost is a unit rate that gives the *cost per unit*. | $\frac{\$5.98}{10.2 \text{ fl oz}} = \$.59/\text{fl oz}$

Costo unitario (p. 221) Un costo unitario es una tasa unitaria que da el *costo por unidad*.

Unit rate (p. 220) The rate for one unit of a given quantity is called the unit rate. | If you drive 130 mi in 2 h, your unit rate is $\frac{65 \text{ mi}}{1 \text{ h}}$, or 65 mi/h.

Tasa unitaria (p. 220) La tasa para una unidad de una cantidad dada se llama tasa unitaria.

474 Glossary

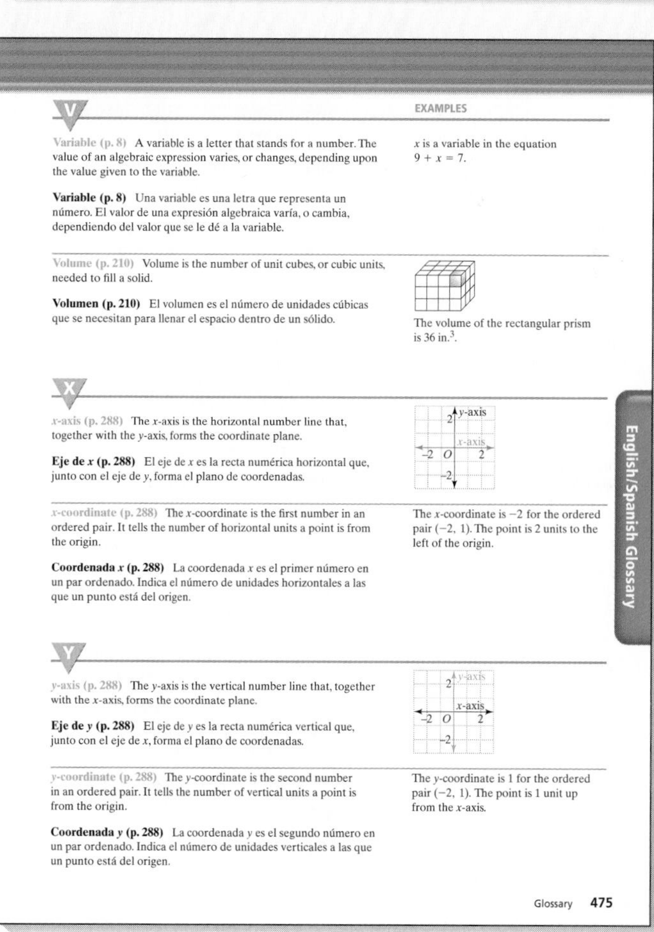

V

EXAMPLES

Variable (p. 8) A variable is a letter that stands for a number. The value of an algebraic expression varies, or changes, depending upon the value given to the variable. | x is a variable in the equation $9 + x = 7$.

Variable (p. 8) Una variable es una letra que representa un número. El valor de una expresión algebraica varía, o cambia, dependiendo del valor que se le dé a la variable.

Volume (p. 210) Volume is the number of unit cubes, or cubic units, needed to fill a solid. | The volume of the rectangular prism is 36 in.^{3}.

Volumen (p. 210) El volumen es el número de unidades cúbicas que se necesitan para llenar el espacio dentro de un sólido.

X

x-axis (p. 288) The x-axis is the horizontal number line that, together with the y-axis, forms the coordinate plane.

Eje de x (p. 288) El eje de x es la recta numérica horizontal que, junto con el eje de y, forma el plano de coordenadas.

y-axis, x-axis, 2, −2, O, 2, −2

x-coordinate (p. 288) The x-coordinate is the first number in an ordered pair. It tells the number of horizontal units a point is from the origin. | The x-coordinate is -2 for the ordered pair $(-2, 1)$. The point is 2 units to the left of the origin.

Coordenada x (p. 288) La coordenada x es el primer número en un par ordenado. Indica el número de unidades horizontales a las que un punto está del origen.

Y

y-axis (p. 288) The y-axis is the vertical number line that, together with the x-axis, forms the coordinate plane.

Eje de y (p. 288) El eje de y es la recta numérica vertical que, junto con el eje de x, forma el plano de coordenadas.

y-axis, x-axis, 2, −2, O, 2, −2

y-coordinate (p. 288) The y-coordinate is the second number in an ordered pair. It tells the number of vertical units a point is from the origin. | The y-coordinate is 1 for the ordered pair $(-2, 1)$. The point is 1 unit up from the x-axis.

Coordenada y (p. 288) La coordenada y es el segundo número en un par ordenado. Indica el número de unidades verticales a las que un punto está del origen.

English/Spanish Glossary

Glossary 475

English/Spanish Glossary

Answers to California Check System

Entry-Level Assessment pp. CA46–CA49

1. B **2.** D **3.** C **4.** C **5.** D **6.** B **7.** D **8.** A **9.** C **10.** B **11.** D **12.** B **13.** A **14.** B **15.** C **16.** D **17.** C **18.** B **19.** C **20.** C **21.** A **22.** C **23.** B **24.** D **25.** C **26.** B **27.** A **28.** C **29.** B **30.** D **31.** B **32.** A **33.** D **34.** D **35.** C **36.** A **37.** B **38.** D **39.** C **40.** A **41.** D

Chapter 1

Check Your Readiness p. 2

1. 310 **2.** 7,530 **3.** 40 **4.** 1,990 **5.** 1.2034 **6.** 0.96 **7.** 7.29 **8.** 47.3 **9.** 1.88 **10.** 10.16 **11.** 0.68 **12.** 14.7 **13.** 15.52 **14.** 0.0138 **15.** 22.53 **16.** 8.512 **17.** 5.68 **18.** 8.95 **19.** 0.092

Lesson 1-1 p. 5

CA Standards Check **1a.** 16.6 **b.** 11.7 **2.** $44.50

Lesson 1-2 pp. 8–12

CA Standards Check **1a.**

b.

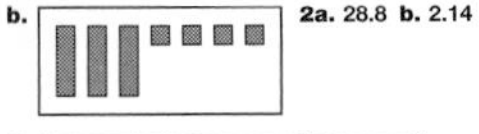

2a. 28.8 **b.** 2.14

3.

Number of Games	Expression	Amount Earned
35	$4.5 \cdot 35$	157.50
50	$4.5 \cdot 50$	225
60	$4.5 \cdot 60$	270

Checkpoint Quiz 1 **1.** 1.02 **2.** 50.82 **3.** 7.5 **4.** 6.2 **5.** $158.50 **6.** 56 **7.** 9 **8.** 23 **9.** −9.8 **10.** $54

Lesson 1-3 p. 15

CA Standards Check **1a.** $2x$ **b.** $q \div 8$ **2.** $b + 28$

Lesson 1-4 pp. 20–24

CA Standards Check **1a.** about 170 **b.** about 20 **2a.** about 400 **b.** about 14 **3.** No; the estimate is $28. This is significantly less than the cashier's estimate of $32.62, so it is not reasonable.

Checkpoint Quiz 2 **1.** $3s$ **2.** $v \div 12$ **3.** $17 - d$ **4.** $m \div 10$ **5.** $f + 4$ **6.** $14 \div q$ **7.** $168 + 35h$; $273 **8.** about 20 **9.** about 9,000 **10.** about 2 **11.** If you round each amount up to the next dollar, the total is about $23. The actual cost must be less than this.

Lesson 1-5 p. 27

CA Standards Check **1a.** Comm. Prop. of Mult. **b.** Identity Prop. of Add. **2a.** 1,300 **b.** 95 **c.** 800

Lesson 1-6 p. 31

CA Standards Check **1a.** $105 - 7h$ **b.** $6m + 18$ **2a.** $14 **b.** $118

Chapter 2

Check Your Readiness p. 44

1. 33.15 **2.** 14.76 **3.** 16.1 **4.** 80 **5.** 32 **6.** 36 **7.** 4 **8.** $a + 12$ **9.** $y \div 3.5$ **10.** $17.2t$ **11.** 117 **12.** 1,400 **13.** 59 **14.** 2,300 **15.** 11.96 **16.** 444

Lesson 2-1 pp. 46–47

CA Standards Check **1a.** 7 **b.** 3 **2.** Asia **3a.** 15 **b.** 15

Lesson 2-2 pp. 52–56

CA Standards Check **1a.** −4 **b.** 2 **2a.** −21 **b.** −31 **3a.** 18 **b.** −7

Checkpoint Quiz 1 **1.** 13 **2.** 64 **3.** 30.4 **4.** 10.5 **5.** 28 **6.** 7.2 **7.** −32 **8.** −3 **9.** −64 **10.** −6 **11.** 12°F

Lesson 2-3 p. 59

CA Standards Check **1a.** −4 **b.** 12 **2.** Alvin moved up 622 ft.

Lesson 2-4 pp. 62–63

CA Standards Check **1a.** 10 **b.** −10 **2a.** −27 **b.** 16 **3.** −20°F

Lesson 2-5 pp. 66–72

CA Standards Check **1a.** −4 **b.** 18 **c.** −4 **2.** $4 per day

Checkpoint Quiz 2 **1.** −2 **2.** 37 **3.** −352 **4.** 4 **5.** 5 **6.** 25 **7.** −53.5 **8.** −$15/day

Lesson 2-6 pp. 73–74

CA Standards Check **1a.** $6 \cdot 7^6$ **b.** $9^4 \cdot x^3$ **2a.** −64 **b.** −216 **3a.** 12 **b.** 69

Chapter 3

Check Your Readiness p. 84

1. 29 **2.** 6.6 **3.** 15.5 **4.** 3 **5.** 0 **6.** 2.3 **7.** −2 **8.** 14 **9.** −14 **10.** 15 **11.** −36 **12.** 3 **13.** −42 **14.** −36 **15.** −320 **16.** 144 **17.** 36 **18.** 8 **19.** 100,000 **20.** 1 **21.** 625 **22.** 16,807

Lesson 3-1 pp. 87–88

CA Standards Check **1a.** 4.8 **b.** 6.9 **2.** $g + 1.8 = 11.6$; 9.8 lb

Lesson 3-2 pp. 92–93

CA Standards Check **1a.** 81 **b.** 16.3 **2.** 63°F

Lesson 3-3 pp. 96–100

CA Standards Check **1a.** 40 **b.** −4 **2.** 865 cards **3a.** −40 **b.** 15

Checkpoint Quiz 1 **1.** 60 **2.** 20 **3.** 18.2 **4.** 7 **5.** 38 **6.** 2.2 **7.** 7.7 **8.** 48.6 **9.** $4.27 **10.** 3.75 mi

Lesson 3-4 pp. 102–103

CA Standards Check **1a.** 4 **b.** 9 **2a.** 9 **b.** 8 **3.** 40 min

Lesson 3-5 pp. 108–111

CA Standards Check **1a.** 6, −6 **b.** 7, −7 **2.** about 12 ft

Checkpoint Quiz 2 **1.** 5.5 **2.** −6.3 **3.** 1 **4.** −28 **5.** 1.5 **6.** 32 **7.** $1.50 **8.** 7, −7 **9.** 11, −11 **10.** 0 **11.** 8, −8 **12.** 9

Lesson 3-6 p. 113

CA Standards Check **1a.** 15 in. **b.** 34 cm **2.** $\sqrt{125}$ in.

Lesson 3-7 pp. 116–117

CA Standards Check **1.** $\sqrt{21}$ ft or about 4.6 ft **2a.** No; $15^2 + 35^2 \neq 40^2$. **b.** No; $7^2 + 6^2 \neq 15^2$.

Chapter 4

Check Your Readiness p. 130

1. four tenths **2.** thirty-seven hundredths **3.** eight hundredths **4.** two hundred five thousandths **5.** sixty-one ten-thousandths **6.** one thousand five hundred two ten-thousandths **7.** 4.02, 4.2, 4.21 **8.** 0.033, 0.3, 0.33 **9.** 6.032, 6.203, 6.302 **10.** 9.013, 9.103, 9.13 **11.** −3 **12.** −5 **13.** 9 **14.** −3 **15.** 6 **16.** −3 **17.** 3^4 **18.** $5^3 \cdot 7^2$ **19.** $2^2 \cdot 5^2 \cdot 7$ **20.** $3^4 \cdot 7 \cdot 11^3$

Lesson 4-1 pp. 132–133

CA Standards Check **1.** 1, 2, 3, 4, 6, 8, 12, 24 **2a.** Prime; 53 has only two factors, 1 and 53. **b.** Prime; 47 has only two factors, 1 and 47. **c.** Composite; 1, 3, 7, 9, 21, and 63 are factors of 63. **3a.** $3^2 \cdot 11$ **b.** $2^2 \cdot 3 \cdot 7$ **c.** $2^4 \cdot 3 \cdot 5$

Lesson 4-2 pp. 136–140

CA Standards Check **1a.** 3 **b.** 1 **c.** 14 **2.** 21 ft

Checkpoint Quiz 1 **1.** $2 \cdot 3 \cdot 7$ **2.** $2^4 \cdot 5$ **3.** 3^3 **4.** $2^3 \cdot 5^3$ **5.** 5 **6.** 24 **7.** 3 **8.** 3 **9.** 1×105; 3×35; 5×21; 7×15

Lesson 4-3 pp. 142–143

CA Standards Check **1.** Answers may vary. Samples are given. **a.** $\frac{2}{5}, \frac{6}{15}$ **b.** $\frac{10}{16}, \frac{15}{24}$ **c.** $\frac{2}{14}, \frac{3}{21}$ **2a.** $-\frac{3}{4}$ **b.** $\frac{1}{2}$ **c.** $\frac{3}{5}$ **3.** $\frac{2}{7}$

Lesson 4-4 pp. 148–152

CA Standards Check **1a.** $\frac{411}{500}$ **b.** $\frac{23}{50}$ **2a.** .273 **b.** .459

Checkpoint Quiz 2 **1.** $\frac{4}{5}$ **2.** $\frac{3}{7}$ **3.** $\frac{1}{4}$ **4.** $\frac{1}{12}$ **5.** $\frac{14}{25}$ **6.** $\frac{8}{25}$ **7.** $\frac{17}{20}$ **8.** $\frac{1}{8}$ **9.** $0.\overline{3}$ **10.** The player with 10 hits in 30 at bats has a higher average because $\frac{8}{27} < \frac{10}{30}$.

Lesson 4-5 pp. 154–155

CA Standards Check **1a.** $-\frac{7}{8}$, −0.625, $1\frac{1}{2}$, $\frac{8}{5}$, 1.61 **b.** $\frac{1}{3}$, 0.375, $1\frac{2}{3}$, 2.8, $2\frac{5}{6}$ **2a.** < **b.** > **3a.** < **b.** >

Chapter 5

Check Your Readiness p. 168

1. −13 **2.** −13 **3.** −9 **4.** −47 **5.** 18 **6.** −2 **7.** 5^4 **8.** $w^3 3^2$ **9.** p^6 **10.** 19^3 **11.** $2^2 6^2$ **12.** 10^4 **13.** 4 **14.** 2 **15.** 4 **16.** 8 **17.** $\frac{1}{2}$ **18.** $\frac{2}{5}$ **19.** $\frac{3}{4}$ **20.** $\frac{1}{11}$

Lesson 5-1 pp. 171–172

CA Standards Check **1a.** $\frac{7}{30}$ **b.** $\frac{26}{35}$ **2.** $1\frac{1}{4}$ h **3a.** 7.15 **b.** 13.85

Lesson 5-2 pp. 176–181

CA Standards Check **1a.** $-\frac{3}{20}$ **b.** $-\frac{5}{24}$ **2a.** $-\frac{5}{18}$ **b.** $\frac{2}{15}$ **3.** $1\frac{3}{8}$ lb or 1.375 lb

Checkpoint Quiz 1 **1.** $\frac{49}{80}$ **2.** $-1\frac{1}{6}$ **3.** $\frac{95}{117}$ **4.** $-\frac{1}{12}$ **5.** $\frac{17}{30}$ **6.** $\frac{1}{2}$ **7.** −1 **8.** $\frac{1}{12}$ **9.** $2\frac{1}{6}$ **10.** $\frac{11}{18}$ **11.** $6\frac{1}{10}$ ft

Lesson 5-3 pp. 182–183

CA Standards Check **1a.** $\frac{3}{10}$ **b.** $\frac{10}{63}$ **2.** $10\frac{5}{12}$ ft **3a.** $\frac{49}{100}$ **b.** $\frac{1}{81}$

Lesson 5-4 pp. 186–187

CA Standards Check **1a.** $\frac{8}{7}$ **b.** 7 **2.** $11\frac{1}{4}$ days or 11.25 days

Lesson 5-5 pp. 190–191

CA Standards Check **1a.** $\frac{7}{12}$ **b.** $-\frac{1}{4}$ **2.** $1\frac{3}{4}$ in.

Lesson 5-6 pp. 196–200

CA Standards Check **1a.** $\frac{2}{9}$ **b.** $\frac{11}{65}$ **2a.** 48 **b.** $-1\frac{1}{8}$ **3.** $2\frac{1}{3}$ in./h

Checkpoint Quiz 2 **1.** 15 **2.** $23\frac{5}{8}$ **3.** 64 **4.** $\frac{1}{6}$ **5.** $3\frac{15}{28}$ **6.** −10 **7.** $-\frac{7}{36}$ **8.** $10\frac{1}{18}$ **9.** $4\frac{2}{3}$ **10.** $10\frac{1}{2}$ **11.** 51 markers

Lesson 5-7 p. 203

CA Standards Check **1a.** 1 **b.** $\frac{1}{7}$ **2a.** 49 **b.** $7\frac{58}{81}$

Chapter 6

Check Your Readiness p. 214

1. $\frac{1}{2}$ **2.** $\frac{2}{7}$ **3.** $\frac{5}{7}$ **4.** $\frac{11}{20}$ **5.** 0.630 **6.** 0.323 **7.** 2.714 **8.** 0.514 **9.** $\frac{6}{7}$ **10.** $1\frac{23}{49}$ **11.** $3\frac{8}{9}$ **12.** $4\frac{1}{8}$ **13.** 56 **14.** $\frac{1}{4}$ **15.** $\frac{5}{6}$ **16.** $\frac{9}{16}$ **17.** $4\frac{1}{5}$ **18.** 30

Lesson 6-1 pp. 216–217

CA Standards Check **1a.** 2 to 6; $\frac{2}{6}$; 2 : 6 **b.** 2 to 4; $\frac{2}{4}$; 2 : 4 **2a–c.** Answers may vary. Samples are given. **2a.** $\frac{2}{7}$ and $\frac{20}{70}$ **b.** 4 : 1 and 24 : 6 **c.** 4 to 11 and 16 to 44 **3.** 4 to 3 or 4 : 3 or $\frac{4}{3}$

Lesson 6-2 pp. 220–224

CA Standards Check **1a.** 6.5 deliveries/h **b.** 70 Calories/serving **2a.** 250 words **b.** 1,500 words **3.** 20-oz box

Checkpoint Quiz 1 **1.** 18 to 41 and $\frac{18}{41}$ **2.** 5 : 2 or 5 to 2 or $\frac{5}{2}$ **3.** 24 to 35 **4.** $\frac{3}{1}$ **5.** 6 : 1 **6.** $\frac{5}{18}$ **7.** $12/book **8.** 12 m/s **9.** 3 gal/min **10.** 8 mi/h **11.** $2.85

Lesson 6-3 pp. 226–227

CA Standards Check **1a.** 36 oz **b.** 28 fl oz **2.** 782.2 ft/min **3.** 5 persons

Lesson 6-4 pp. 230–234

CA Standards Check **1.** 3.5 mi **2.** 14 mi/h **3a.** $38.50 **b.** $8.25

Checkpoint Quiz 2 **1.** 72 min **2.** $\frac{9}{16}$ lb or 0.5625 lb **3.** 180 in. **4.** 64 qt **5.** 30 in. **6.** 0.525 gal **7.** 7 h **8.** $7.92 **9.** 5.7 mi/h

Lesson 6-5 pp. 235–236

CA Standards Check **1a.** no; $\frac{6}{7} \neq \frac{23}{28}$ **b.** no; $\frac{16}{20} \neq \frac{74}{100}$ **2.** $22.91

Chapter 7

Check Your Readiness p. 250

1. 20 **2.** 15.91 **3.** 237.5 **4.** 1.75 **5.** $\frac{1}{2}$ **6.** $\frac{5}{8}$ **7.** $\frac{1}{12}$ **8.** $\frac{9}{16}$ **9.** 30 **10.** 8.5 **11.** 100 **12.** 36 **13.** 2 **14.** 32 **15.** 100 **16.** 19 **17.** 85.5

Lesson 7-1 pp. 252–253

CA Standards Check **1a.** $\frac{14}{25}$ **b.** $\frac{1}{25}$ **c.** $\frac{1}{4}$ **2a.** 55% **b.** 70% **3a.** 52% **b.** 5% **c.** 50%

Lesson 7-2 pp. 256–260

CA Standards Check **1a.** 8 **b.** 10.92 **c.** 21.78 **2a.** about $10.80 **b.** about $7.50 **c.** about $2.40

Checkpoint Quiz 1 **1.** 50% **2.** 10% **3.** 37.5% **4.** 93.75% **5.** 40% **6.** 90% **7.** 0.78 **8.** 0.04 **9.** 11.6 **10.** 0.96 **11.** about $6.90

Lesson 7-3 pp. 261–262

CA Standards Check **1a.** 70.3 **b.** 12.8 **c.** 113.4 **2.** 275 students **3a.** 72% **b.** 40%

Lesson 7-4 pp. 266–270

CA Standards Check **1.** about 2% **2.** about 5.3% **3a.** 30% **b.** 25%

Checkpoint Quiz 2 **1.** 51.25 **2.** 5% **3.** 0.78 **4.** 0.25 **5.** 117 dancers **6.** 1,000% increase **7.** 1.6% decrease **8.** 80% decrease **9.** 270.7% increase **10.** 3.4%

Lesson 7-5 pp. 272–273

CA Standards Check **1a.** 99% **b.** 55% **2.** 40% **3.** $100.51

Chapter 8

Check Your Readiness p. 286

1. 20 **2.** −7 **3.** −2 **4.** −1 **5.** −4 **6.** 3 **7.** −5 **8.** −6 **9.** 6 **10.** −8 **11.** 4 **12.** −3 **13.** 25 **14.** 21 **15.** 181 **16.** 25% **17.** 62.5% **18.** 66.7% **19.** 150%

Lesson 8-1 pp. 288–289

CA Standards Check **1a.** (6, 2) **b.** (6, −2) **c.** (2, 3)

2a–c.

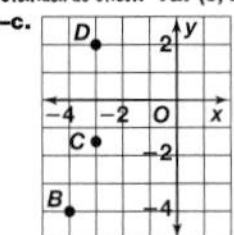

Lesson 8-2 pp. 292–296

CA Standards Check **1a.** 6 **b.** 3 **2.** about 7 m

Checkpoint Quiz 1 **1.** (1.5, 1.5) **2.** (−2, −1.5) **3.** (−3.5, 2) **4.** (0.5, 0)

5–8.

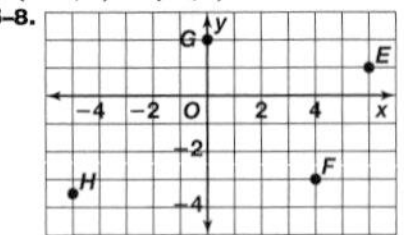

9. 7 **10.** 7.5 **11.** 5

Lesson 8-3 pp. 298–299

CA Standards Check **1.**

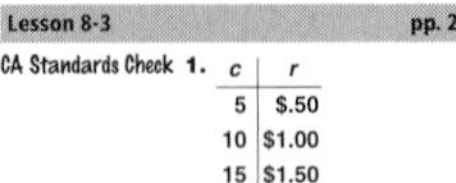

c	r
5	$.50
10	$1.00
15	$1.50

2. Let b = the amount of money you earn baby-sitting. Let $f(b)$ = the total amount of money you have. $f(b) = 15 + b$; $41.00

Lesson 8-4 pp. 302–303

CA Standards Check **1.**

2.

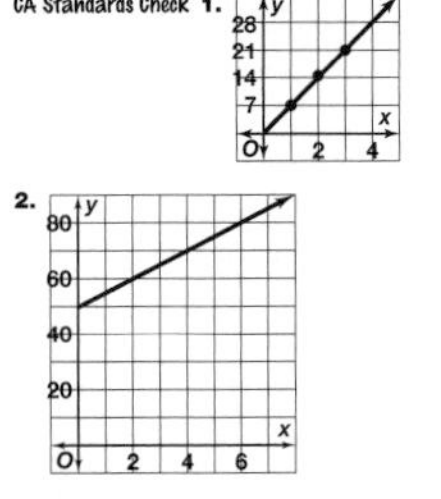

Lesson 8-5 pp. 311–315

CA Standards Check **1a.** $\frac{1}{2}$ **b.** $-\frac{1}{3}$ **2a.** undefined **b.** $\frac{11}{7}$

Checkpoint Quiz 2 **1.** 1 **2.** −17 **3.** −2 **4.** 28 **5.** $C(p) = 0.99p$ **6.**

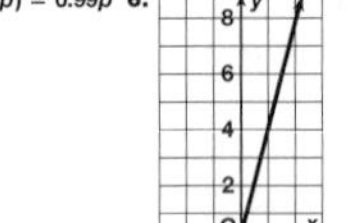

7. **8.**

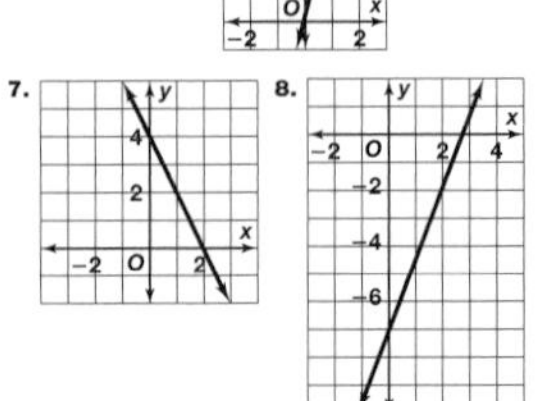

9. 0 **10.** $\frac{3}{2}$ **11.** −1 **12.** Since $\frac{5}{3} > \frac{3}{5}$, the hill with rise of 5 ft and run of 3 ft is steeper.

Lesson 8-6 — pp. 316–317

CA Standards Check **1.** No; the slope equals $\frac{31}{20}$. This is not equal to the ratio of the two quantities, because the ratio of x and y is not always the same. **2.**

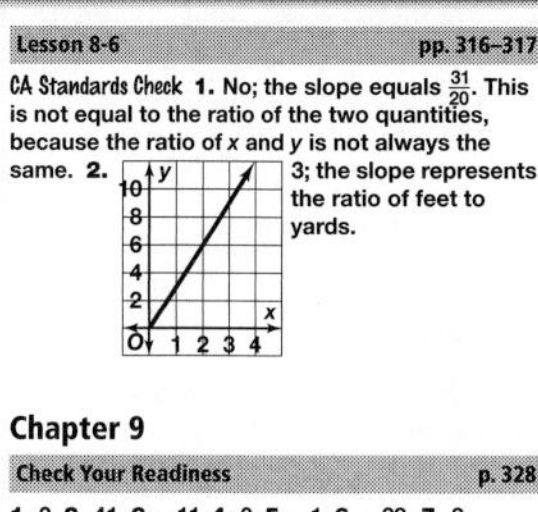

3; the slope represents the ratio of feet to yards.

Chapter 9

Check Your Readiness — p. 328

1. 2 **2.** 41 **3.** −11 **4.** 0 **5.** −1 **6.** −33 **7.** 3 **8.** −8 **9.** −1 **10.** 25 **11.** −13 **12.** 13 **13.** −31 **14.** 252 **15.** −20 **16.** 9 **17.** 70.5 **18.** −2 **19.** 5 **20.** 6.12 **21.** −2.2

Lesson 9-1 — pp. 330–331

CA Standards Check **1a.** $t \geq 7.8$ **b.** $w < 9$ **2a.** $\begin{cases} p \geq 75 \\ p \leq 125 \end{cases}$ **b.** $\begin{cases} a > 28{,}000 \\ a < 35{,}000 \end{cases}$ **3.** yes

Lesson 9-2 — pp. 335–338

CA Standards Check **1a.** $u \geq 5$ **b.** $y < 13$ **2.** $s \leq 211$

Checkpoint Quiz 1 **1.** $d \leq 50$ **2.** $t < 30$ **3.** $c \geq 12.99$ **4.** $30 > w$ **5.** $\begin{cases} t \geq 0.80 \\ t \leq 0.89 \end{cases}$ **6.** $e \geq 6$ **7.** $r < 14$ **8.** $k \leq 45$ **9.** $m > 18.5$ **10.** 35,500 lb

Lesson 9-3 — p. 341

CA Standards Check **1.** at most 12 passengers **2a.** $p \leq -17$ **b.** $m > 3$

Lesson 9-4 — p. 345–348

CA Standards Check **1.** at least 16.8 ft **2a.** $b \leq -4$ **b.** $k > 20$

Checkpoint Quiz 2 **1.** $g > 4$ **2.** $d \leq -9$ **3.** $x \geq 8$ **4.** $k > -60$ **5.** $t \leq -5$ **6.** $x \geq -3$ **7.** $d \geq -3$ **8.** $p \leq \frac{1}{10}$ **9.** $s > 45$ **10.** at least 28 times **11.** at most $164.50

Lesson 9-5 — pp. 349–350

CA Standards Check **1a.** $m > 108$ **b.** $x \geq -1$ **2.** 4 or fewer folders

Chapter 10

Check Your Readiness — p. 364

1. 16 **2.** 16 **3.** −16 **4.** 32 **5.** 100 **6.** 1,000 **7.** Comm. Prop. of Add. **8.** Comm. Prop. of Mult. **9.** Assoc. Prop. of Add. **10.** Ident. Prop. of Add. **11.** $5c - 15$ **12.** $-2w - 16$ **13.** $-10 + 2a$ **14.** $-54 + 9t$ **15.** $44 - 11b$ **16.** $-x + 2$ **17.** −4 **18.** 1.5 **19.** 15

Lesson 10-1 — pp. 366–367

CA Standards Check **1a.** 6^1 or 6 **b.** $(-4)^8$ **c.** m^{12} **2.** about 8 min

Lesson 10-2 — pp. 370–371

CA Standards Check **1a.** $\frac{1}{5^6}$ **b.** 12^6 **2a.** about 2×10^{-10} m^2 **b.** about 1.63×10^{10} mi^2

Lesson 10-3 — pp. 375–378

CA Standards Check **1a.** 4 **b.** −1 **c.** 36 **2a.** −1 **b.** −3

Checkpoint Quiz 1 **1.** 4.7^{21} **2.** $(-4)^9$ **3.** t^{-60} **4.** m^8 **5.** 6^2 **6.** 8^{21} **7.** $16a^2$ **8.** x^6y^{12} **9.** 2 **10.** −1 **11.** 13 **12.** −11

Lesson 10-4 — pp. 380–381

CA Standards Check **1a.** $-14t$ **b.** $-8x$ **2.** $26c$ **3a.** $9 - 2b$ **b.** $5f + 4$

Lesson 10-5 — pp. 386–391

CA Standards Check **1a.** −11 **b.** 9 **2.** 17 boys

Checkpoint Quiz 2 **1.** $-8m + 4$ **2.** $1.7g - 7.25$ **3.** $-2h + 20$ **4.** $168 - 3a$ **5.** −9 **6.** −1 **7.** 5 **8.** −2 **9.** 16 bottles

Lesson 10-6 — pp. 392–393

CA Standards Check **1a.** 4 **b.** 2 **2.** 20 min

480 Answers to California Check System

Selected Answers

Chapter 1

Lesson 1-1 pp. 6–7

STANDARDS PRACTICE **1.** 15 **3.** 19 **5.** 20 **7.** 35 **9.** 16.2 **11.** 72.1 **13.** 42.5 **15.** $39 **17.** First subtract the numbers in parentheses, then divide, then multiply, and finally add. **19.** 21 g **21.** 46 g **23.** 2 c **25.** $(11 - 7) \div 2 = 2$ **27.** $13 - (4.1 + 7.4) = 1.5$ **29.** 2 mm **31.** B **33.** 19,968 **35.** 1,185

Lesson 1-2 pp. 10–11

STANDARDS PRACTICE **1.** **3.** **5.** **7.** **9.**

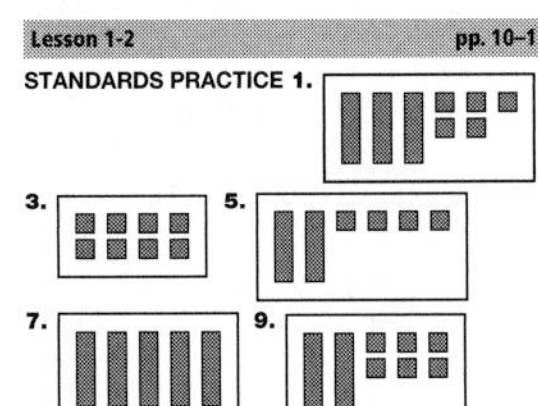

11. 13 **13.** 9 **15.** 3 **17.** 7; 9; 11 **19.** 14; 28; 42 **21.** 22 cm **23.** 90 balloons; 70 balloons **25.** C **27.** 10 h **29.** 75 **31.** 8 **33.** C **35.** 5 **37.** 15.8

Lesson 1-3 pp. 16–18

STANDARDS PRACTICE **1.** $50 + d$ **3.** $m - 5$ **5.** $14p$ **7.** $a + 6$ **9.** $21 \div w$ **11.** $n \div 9$ **13.** $w - 8$ **15.** $10h$ **17.** $m \div 3$ **19.** B **21.** A **23.** 2 gal **25.** $A \div 400$ **27.** $17.95 \cdot (A \div 400)$ **29a.** $5 + 2r$ **b.** 5 rides **31.** $35p + 105n$ **33.** $t \cdot (20 + 0.75n)$ **35.** D **37.** A **39.** 30

Lesson 1-4 pp. 22–23

STANDARDS PRACTICE **1.** about 73 **3.** about 13 **5.** about 4,000 **7.** about 220 **9.** about 4 **11.** about 5,000 **13.** about 5 **15.** No; the estimate is $93. Since the prices were all rounded up and $99.53 is more than the estimate, it is not reasonable. **17.** about $20 **19.** about 500 **21.** about 55 **23.** about 2 times longer **25.** $156.30 **27.** Yes; the total should be $272.40, not $302.40. **29.** Answers may vary. Sample: $10; the estimate is higher than the actual because the total amount was rounded up to $40. **31.** about 200 g **33.** B

Lesson 1-5 pp. 28–29

STANDARDS PRACTICE **1.** Comm. Prop. of Mult. **3.** Assoc. Prop. of Add. **5.** Assoc. Prop. of Mult. **7.** Identity Prop. of Add. **9.** 19 **11.** 33,000 **13.** 24 **15.** 37 cars **17.** = **19.** The assoc. prop. was applied but cannot be applied unless both operations are either addition or multiplication. **21.** $.40 **23.** $2.95 **25.** Yes; the total is $3.20 and she has more money than this. **27.** The comm. properties show that you can change the places of the numbers without changing the values of an expression. **29.** No; no; no; examples may vary. Sample: $9 - 3 \neq 3 - 9$ and $9 \div 3 \neq 3 \div 9$; $(12 - 4) - 2 \neq 12 - (4 - 2)$ and $(12 \div 4) \div 2 \neq 12 \div (4 \div 2)$ **31.** B **33.** about 75 **35.** about 130

Lesson 1-6 pp. 32–33

STANDARDS PRACTICE **1.** $5a + 30$ **3.** $4t + 12$ **5.** $32 + 4r$ **7.** $72 - 12f$ **9.** $7m + 70$ **11.** $2p - 1$ **13.** $88 + 4j$ **15.** 224 **17.** 136 **19.** 26.1 **21.** 39.95 **23.** 945 **25.** no **27.** $7d - 14$; 21 **29.** $162 + 18d$; 252 **31.** Answers may vary. Sample: First combine 68 and 32 to equal 100. Rewrite 99 as 100 − 1 and distribute the 6. Then add and subtract from left to right. **33.** 75 **35.** Check students' work. **37.** Step 1: Write 10.3 as 10 + 0.3.; Step 2: Dist. Prop.; Step 3: Add.; Step 4: Simplify. **39.** No; the weight will be greater than 20 lb. **41.** B **43.** Comm. Prop. of Add. **45.** Identity Prop. of Mult.

Chapter Review pp. 38–39

1. Ident. Prop. of Add. **2.** numerical expression **3.** algebraic expression **4.** variable **5.** compatible numbers **6.** 37.9 **7.** 0.8 **8.** 45.5 **9.** 16.5 **10.** 14 **11.** 4 **12.** 27 **13.** 25 **14.** $48 **15.** $x \div 12$ **16.** $2b$ **17.** $k + 3$ **18.** $s + 5$ **19.** about 8,000 **20.** about 3,000 **21.** about 10 **22.** yes **23.** Identity Prop. of Mult. **24.** Comm. Prop. of Add. **25.** Assoc. Prop. of Add. **26.** Comm. Prop. of Mult. **27.** 350 **28.** 130 **29.** 30 **30.** $3p - 21$ **31.** $8m + 32$ **32.** $10 + 5k$ **33.** 196 **34.** 17 **35.** 627

Chapter 2

Lesson 2-1 pp. 48–49

STANDARDS PRACTICE **1.** 4 **3.** 26 **5.** 200 **7.** 67 **9.** 7 **11.** −16 **13.** −45 **15.** Helium **17.** 13 **19.** 190 **21.** 18 **23.** 19,340 ft **25.** −50°C **27.** South Dakota **29.** Yes; the lowest temperature in Kansas was 2°C colder. **31.** < **33.** = **35.** No; answers may vary. Sample: If $a = -5$ and $b = 2$, $|a| > |b|$ but $a < b$. **37.** $x \leq 0$ **39.** D **41.** $15g + 30$ **43.** $7y - 112$

Lesson 2-2 pp. 54–55

STANDARDS PRACTICE **1.** 3 **3.** 6 **5.** −1 **7.** −5 **9.** −9 **11.** −60 **13.** −21 **15.** −3 **17.** 0 **19.** 1 **21.** −12 **23.** −3 **25.** 17th floor **27.** 8 floors below **29.** −2 **31.** −7 **33.** −1 **35.** No; it is true because of the Inv. Prop. of Add. **37.** C **39.** < **41.** >

Lesson 2-3 pp. 60–61

STANDARDS PRACTICE **1.** 11 **3.** −2 **5.** −58 **7.** −1,015 **9.** 4 **11.** 29 **13.** −178 **15.** 50 **17.** 45 **19.** −57 **21.** down 362 ft **23.** 80 **25.** 56 **27.** −1,250 ft **29.** Never; the sum of a number and its opposite is zero. **31.** 10 **33.** −8 **35.** Cairo, 7:45 P.M.; Honolulu, 7:45 A.M.; Los Angeles, 9:45 A.M.; Paris, 6:45 P.M.; Sydney, 3:45 A.M.; Tokyo, 2:45 A.M.; Washington, 12:45 P.M. **37.** 9:15 A.M. **39.**

−8
3 | −11
2 | 1 | −12
−6 | 8 | −7 | −5

41. A **43.** −2 **45.** −5

Lesson 2-4 pp. 64–65

STANDARDS PRACTICE **1.** 4 **3.** −14 **5.** 3 **7.** −12 **9.** −42 **11.** −99 **13.** 12 **15.** −22 **17.** 54 **19.** −45 **21.** −36 **23.** −231 **25.** −362 **27.** −48 **29.** B **31.** 40 **33.** −2 **35.** −96 **37.** 192 **39.** negative **41.** −300 **43.** 192 **45.** Positive; the product of two nonzero numbers with the same sign is positive. **47.** −3; $1 - 2 + 3 - 4 \cdot 5 - 6$ **49.** C **51.** 13 **53.** −7

Lesson 2-5 pp. 68–69

STANDARDS PRACTICE **1.** −8 **3.** 6 **5.** −72 **7.** −5 **9.** −11 **11.** −6 **13.** −9 **15.** −12 **17.** −13 **19.** 12 **21.** −$3 per day **23.** −9 ft/min **25.**

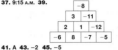

−14,580
−108 | 135
12 | −9 | −15
−4 | −3 | 3 | −5

27. 1 **29.** −10 **31.** −$6/day **33.** −500 **35.** −120 mL/day **37.** negative **39.** negative **41.** positive **43.** Negative; the sum of five negative numbers is negative; the sum divided by 5 will also be negative. **45.** D **47.** B **49.** 173

Lesson 2-6 pp. 75–76

STANDARDS PRACTICE **1.** $4^2 \cdot g^3$ **3.** $(-6)^3 \cdot 11$ **5.** $(-3)^2 \cdot j^5$ **7.** $7^2 \cdot t^3$ **9.** −32 **11.** 1,296 **13.** 81 **15.** 23 **17.** 56 **19.** 0.95 **21.** 7 **23.** 47 **25.** No; $2^2 \cdot 3^2 - 2^3 - 1 = 27$, but $2^2 \cdot (3^2 - 2^3) - 1 = 3$.
27a. $10^4 = 10{,}000$
$10^5 = 100{,}000$
b. The number of zeros is the same as the exponent.
c. $10^6 = 1{,}000{,}000$
$10^7 = 10{,}000{,}000$
$10^8 = 100{,}000{,}000$
d. n zeros **29.** 4 cells **31.** 2^8 cells **33.** 125 **35.** 68 **37.** 256 ft **39.** 5 and 6 **41.** B **43.** 36 **45.** 60

Chapter Review pp. 78–79

1. absolute value **2.** exponent; base **3.** power **4.** integers **5.** opposites **6.** 7 **7.** 24 **8.** 0 **9.** 13 **10.** −14 **11.** North America **12.** −4 **13.** −2 **14.** −13 **15.** −15 **16.** −20 **17.** 19 **18.** the fourth floor **19.** −4 **20.** 8 **21.** −11 **22.** −8 **23.** $263 **24.** −21 **25.** 48 **26.** −40 **27.** 17 **28.** −13 **29.** −7 **30.** −9 **31.** −9 ft/min **32.** $6^5 \cdot 8^3$ **33.** $4^4 \cdot t^3$ **34.** 343 **35.** 100,000 **36.** 16 **37.** 89 **38.** 13 **39.** 206 **40.** 135

Chapter 3

Lesson 3-1 pp. 89–90

STANDARDS PRACTICE **1.** 26 **3.** −11 **5.** 1.5 **7.** 9.7 **9.** 6.3 **11.** −13.8 **13.** −13.4 **15.** −11.42 **17.** −0.8 **19.** Equations may vary. Sample: $x + 6 = 1{,}762$; 1756 **21.** $5.55 **23.** No; after you subtract 27.6 from 31.8, the result will be much less than 59.4. **25.** 6 **27.** 9 **29.** $a = -5$, $b = -3$, $c = 3$ **31.** −2 and 2 **33.** −1 and 1 **35.** All values; the equation can be written as $x + 15 = x + 15$, which is true for any value of x. **37.** C **39.** 23 **41.** −54

Lesson 3-2 pp. 93–95

STANDARDS PRACTICE **1.** 23.2 **3.** 315 **5.** −35 **7.** 11.4 **9.** 4 **11.** 19 **13.** 41.5 **15.** 137.9 **17.** 5.5 **19.** 102.3°F **21.** −2.7 **23.** −13.06 **25.** −81.7 **27.** 56.5 **29.** The student should have subtracted 46 from each side rather than adding 46 to each side. **31.** $39.83 **33.** $56.90 **35.** $26 **37.** Negative; if you add 9.7 to −10.5, the result will be negative. **39.** A **41.** C **43.** −2

Lesson 3-3 pp. 98–99

STANDARDS PRACTICE **1.** 5 **3.** 1.7 **5.** 2.5 **7.** 16 **9.** 0.5 **11.** 718 cartons **13.** 108 **15.** 60 **17.** 0.42 **19.** 144 **21.** 70.525 **23.** $5.56 per week **25.** Answers may vary. Sample: Division by 0 is undefined. **27.** 6 movies **29.** $27r = 80.73$ or $80.73 \div r = 27$ **31.** $.55 **33.** −29 **35.** 42.12 **37.** 0.4096 **39.** 3 students **41.** D **43.** 4.4 **45.** 25.3

Lesson 3-4 pp. 104–106

STANDARDS PRACTICE **1.** 7 **3.** 7 **5.** 3 **7.** 28 **9.** 35 **11.** −28 **13.** −75 **15.** 75 **17.** 34 **19.** −44 **21.** −225 **23.** $22 per shirt **25.** 117.9 **27.** −19.8 **29.** 1 **31.** 11 mg **33.** output = input ÷ 3 − 8; 2, 13 **35.** A **37.** $60 + 6x = 600$; 90 h **39.** In the last step, the student should have multiplied each side by 5. **41.** 7; multiplying each side by 10 removes all the decimal numbers. **43.** A **45.** −13 **47.** −247

Lesson 3-5 pp. 109–110

STANDARDS PRACTICE **1.** 5, −5 **3.** 9, −9 **5.** 2, −2 **7.** 10, −10 **9.** 11, −11 **11.** 12, −12 **13.** 25, −25 **15.** 4 **17.** 9 **19.** 10 **21.** 7 **23.** 13 **25.** 100 **27.** about 3 ft **29.** 9 in.^{2} **31.** 5 **33.** 33 **35.** −9 **37.** Answers may vary. Sample: $5^2 = 25$ and $6^2 = 36$. Since 30 is between 25 and 36, $\sqrt{30}$ is between 5 and 6. $\sqrt{30}$ is about 5. **39.** 5 **41.** 9 **43.** 36 **45.** 2 **47.** Yes; no; explanations may vary. Sample: Since $\sqrt{1} = 1$, $\sqrt{2}$ must be greater than 1. Since $\sqrt{4} = 2$, $\sqrt{2}$ must be less than 2. **49.** 36 and 64, or 0 and 100 **51.** No integer multiplied by itself ends in 2. **53.** B **55.** 4.5 **57.** 48

Lesson 3-6 pp. 114–115

STANDARDS PRACTICE **1.** 17 in. **3.** 25 ft **5.** 10 in. **7.** 74 cm **9.** 0.5 **11.** 250 **13.** 90 **15.** 24 cm **17.** 37 in. **19.** 27 in. **21.** 7.1 cm **23.** 14.1 in. **25.** 2.3 km **27.** (right triangle with legs 1 and 2, hypotenuse $\sqrt{2}$) **29.** D **31.** 8, −8 **33.** 0.5, −0.5

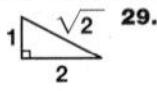

Lesson 3-7 pp. 118–119

STANDARDS PRACTICE **1.** 12 ft **3.** 24 in. **5.** 12 cm **7.** No, $1.5^2 + 2.5^2 \neq 3.5^2$. **9.** Yes, $36^2 + 15^2 = 39^2$. **11.** Yes, $75^2 + 100^2 = 125^2$. **13.** about 130 in.^{2} **15.** $(\sqrt{1})^2 + (\sqrt{2})^2 = 1 + 2 = 3$, and $(\sqrt{3})^2 = 3$, so $(\sqrt{1})^2 + (\sqrt{2})^2 = (\sqrt{3})^2$. **17.** Answers may vary. Sample: If d is the distance between the bases, write and solve the equation $d^2 + d^2 = 127.3^2$. **19.** about 90 ft **21.** 6 m^2 **23.** about 19.8 m^2 **25.** Yes; if $m = 3$, then $m^2 + (m + 1)^2 = 3^2 + 4^2 = 25$, and $(m + 2)^2 = 5^2 = 25$, so $m^2 + (m + 1)^2 = (m + 2)^2$. **27.** B **29.** B **31.** 3 **33.** 84

Chapter Review pp. 124–125

1. equation **2.** perfect square **3.** hypotenuse **4.** converse of the Pythagorean Theorem **5.** square root **6.** 5,614 **7.** 6.6 **8.** 1.4 **9.** 6.06 **10.** 30.4 **11.** 2.3 **12.** 129.7 lb **13.** $52.49 **14.** 56 **15.** −48 **16.** 10.8 **17.** 0.9 **18.** 2.5 **19.** 2 **20.** $16.68 **21.** 9, −9 **22.** 14, −14 **23.** 1, −1 **24.** 7, −7 **25.** 12, −12 **26.** 0 **27.** 7 **28.** −5 **29.** 13 **30.** 10 **31.** 8 **32.** $\sqrt{5}$ or 2.2 **33.** $\sqrt{28}$ or 5.3 **34.** about 23 ft **35.** no **36.** yes **37.** no **38.** yes

Chapter 4

Lesson 4-1 pp. 134–135

STANDARDS PRACTICE **1.** 1, 2, 4, 7, 14, 28 **3.** 1, 17 **5.** 1, 2, 3, 4, 6, 8, 12, 16, 24, 48 **7.** 1, 2, 3, 4, 6, 8, 9, 12, 16, 18, 24, 36, 48, 72, 144 **9.** 1, 2, 4, 5, 10, 20, 25, 50, 100, 125, 250, 500 **11.** 1, 59 **13.** 1, 3, 37, 111 **15.** Prime; the only factors are 1 and 19. **17.** Composite; the factors are 1, 3, 19, and 57. **19.** Composite; the factors are 1, 2, 3, 4, 6, 8, 12, 16, 24, and 48. **21.** Prime; the only factors are 1 and 73. **23.** Composite; the factors are 1, 2, 5, 10, 25, 50, 125, and 250. **25.** $2 \cdot 3 \cdot 7$ **27.** $2^4 \cdot 5^2$ **29.** $2^3 \cdot 7$ **31.** $2^5 \cdot 5$ **33.** $2 \cdot 3^2 \cdot 13$ **35.** 1 × 36; 2 × 18; 3 × 12; 4 × 9; 6 × 6 **37.** 1, 2, 3, 4, 6, 8, 12, 24 **39.** $2^2 \cdot 3$ **41.** $2 = 2$; $3 = 3$; $4 = 2^2$; $6 = 2 \cdot 3$; $8 = 2^3$; $12 = 2^2 \cdot 3$; each factor's prime factorization is a subset of the prime factorization of 24. **43.** 1,001 **45.** 850 **47.** the number itself **49.** Composite; if p is a prime number greater than 2, then p is an odd number. So $p + 1$ is an even number, and the only even number that is prime is 2. **51.** D **53.** D **55.** −13

Lesson 4-2 pp. 138–139

STANDARDS PRACTICE **1.** 2 **3.** 6 **5.** 26 **7.** 4 **9.** 3 **11.** 20 **13.** 9 **15.** 16 **17.** 31 **19.** 19 **21.** 25 groups **23.** 11 **25.** 12 **27.** 9 is not a divisor of 24. **29.** 6 **31.** $120 \div 6 = 20$; 20 paintbrushes **33.** Brand B and Brand C; 3 is a common divisor of 12 and of 15. **35.** 1; since the divisors of a prime number are 1 and itself, the only common divisor for two different prime numbers is 1. **37.** A **39.** C **41.** 16 **43.** 9

Lesson 4-3 pp. 145–146

STANDARDS PRACTICE **1–9.** Answers may vary. Samples are given. **1.** $\frac{1}{2}, \frac{6}{12}$ **3.** $\frac{12}{14}, \frac{18}{21}$ **5.** $\frac{6}{32}, \frac{9}{48}$ **7.** $\frac{1}{3}, \frac{6}{18}$ **9.** $\frac{3}{4}, \frac{30}{40}$ **11.** $\frac{5}{10}, \frac{1}{2}$ **13.** $\frac{3}{9}, \frac{10}{30}$ **15.** $\frac{2}{9}$ **17.** $\frac{1}{2}$ **19.** $\frac{1}{3}$ **21.** $\frac{2}{3}$ **23.** $-\frac{2}{7}$ **25.** $\frac{5}{13}$ **27.** $\frac{3}{5}$ **29.** $\frac{1}{3}$ **31.** $\frac{2}{3}$ **33.** $\frac{2}{3}; \frac{2}{3}; \frac{2}{3}$ **35.** $\frac{5}{7}$ **37.** yes **39.** no; $\frac{1}{3}$ **41.** 2 days **43.** A **45.** C **47.** $3 \cdot 43$ **49.** $2 \cdot 3^2 \cdot 5 \cdot 11$

Lesson 4-4 pp. 150–151

STANDARDS PRACTICE **1.** $\frac{3}{20}$ **3.** $\frac{17}{100}$ **5.** $\frac{1}{2}$ **7.** $\frac{149}{1{,}000}$ **9.** $\frac{8}{25}$ **11.** $\frac{2}{5}$ **13.** $\frac{57}{125}$ **15.** 0.444 **17.** 1.063 **19.** −1.857 **21.** 0.385 **23.** 0.543 **25.** 0.625 **27.** .333 **29.** They have the same record. **31.** *D* **33.** *C* **35.** $0.\overline{6}$; 1; $1.\overline{3}$; $1.\overline{6}$; 2; when the numerator is not a multiple of 3 **37.** 0.25 **39.** repeating **41.** .960 **43.** $\frac{26}{125} = 0.208$ **45.** C **47.** −7 **49.** 34

Lesson 4-5 pp. 156–157

STANDARDS PRACTICE **1.** $-3.13, \frac{10}{13}, \frac{15}{19}, 0.8$ **3.** $\frac{4}{9}, 0.7, 1.3, 1\frac{2}{5}$ **5.** $\frac{5}{7}, \frac{5}{6}, \frac{5}{3}, \frac{5}{2}$ **7.** $-3, -\frac{3}{7}, -0.3, \frac{1}{3}$ **9.** < **11.** > **13.** < **15.** Tim **17.** > **19.** < **21.** > **23.** < **25.** men **27.** $\frac{5}{8}, \frac{5}{7}, \frac{5}{4}, \frac{5}{3}$; when the numerators are the same, the larger the denominator is, the smaller the value of the fraction. **29.** $12\frac{9}{20}$ **31a.** $\frac{1}{2}, \frac{1}{4}, \frac{1}{8}, \frac{1}{16}$ **b.** 𝅗𝅥 ♩ ♪ 𝅘𝅥𝅯 The "open" note symbol has the greatest value. The more flags the note has, the smaller the value of the note. **33.** your friend **35.** 6 or 7 **37.** A **39.** 8 **41.** 6

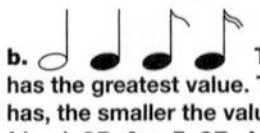

Chapter Review pp. 162–163

1. terminating decimal **2.** prime factorization **3.** simplest form **4.** equivalent fractions **5.** greatest common divisor **6.** $2^2 \cdot 7$ **7.** $2 \cdot 5^3$ **8.** $2 \cdot 3^3 \cdot 7$ **9.** $2 \cdot 139$ **10.** 1, 2, 3, 4, 6, 9, 12, 18, 36 **11.** 2 **12.** 2 **13.** 5 **14.** 8 **15.** 8 classes **16.** no; $\frac{1}{4}$ **17.** yes **18.** no; $\frac{2}{3}$ **19.** yes **20.** $\frac{11}{35}$ **21.** $\frac{49}{50}$ **22.** $\frac{14}{25}$ **23.** $\frac{41}{50}$ **24.** $\frac{33}{100}$ **25.** 0.333 **26.** 0.08 **27.** 0.367 **28.** 0.75 **29.** .247 **30.** $-\frac{25}{6}, -4, 0.54, \frac{7}{12}, 3.25$ **31.** $\frac{12}{6}, 2.07, \frac{23}{10}, 2\frac{3}{5}, 2.7$ **32.** < **33.** < **34.** =

Chapter 5

Lesson 5-1 pp. 173–174

STANDARDS PRACTICE **1.** $\frac{17}{21}$ **3.** $1\frac{1}{28}$ **5.** $\frac{37}{40}$ **7.** $1\frac{1}{132}$ **9.** $\frac{3}{4}$ **11.** $1\frac{13}{18}$ **13.** $\frac{1}{60}$ **15.** $\frac{1}{2}$ lb **17.** 2.3 **19.** 8.04 **21.** −10 **23.** $4\frac{4}{5}$ mi **25.** 13 yd **27.** $75.63 **29.** First add the whole numbers: $5 + 3 + 3 + 6 = 17$. Then add the fractions with the same denominators: $\frac{1}{3} + \frac{2}{3} = 1$ and $\frac{4}{5} + \frac{1}{5} = 1$. So $17 + 1 + 1 = 19$. **31.** −15.26 **33.** 13.21 **35.** 5.45 **37.** 0.75; 0.875; 0.9375; never; the sum will always approach 1. **39.** B **41–43.** Answers may vary. Samples are given. **41.** $\frac{2}{12}, \frac{4}{24}$ **43.** $\frac{14}{20}, \frac{28}{40}$

Lesson 5-2 pp. 178–180

STANDARDS PRACTICE **1.** $\frac{1}{12}$ **3.** $\frac{11}{35}$ **5.** $\frac{7}{20}$ **7.** $\frac{1}{3}$ **9.** $-\frac{2}{21}$ **11.** $-\frac{13}{30}$ **13.** $\frac{2}{3}$ **15.** $1\frac{5}{8}$ **17.** $\frac{6}{55}$ **19.** $-1\frac{1}{20}$ **21.** $-11\frac{25}{36}$ **23.** $3\frac{33}{40}$ **25.** $21\frac{3}{25}$ **27.** $2\frac{3}{10}$ **29.** $4\frac{5}{6}$ ft **31.** $14\frac{39}{40}$ **33.** $9\frac{17}{40}$ **35.** $9\frac{11}{40}$ **37.** 24 ft $3\frac{1}{2}$ in. **39.** 11.57 in. **41.** $2\frac{7}{12}$ in. **43.** $1\frac{5}{6}$ **45.** C **47.** $\frac{1}{125}, 0.8, 0.808, \frac{22}{25}$

Lesson 5-3 pp. 184–185

STANDARDS PRACTICE **1.** $\frac{2}{5}$ **3.** $3\frac{2}{5}$ **5.** $\frac{5}{24}$ **7.** $-\frac{1}{3}$ **9.** 1 **11.** $-\frac{4}{5}$ **13.** $\frac{22}{27}$ **15.** $\frac{11}{800}$ **17.** $11\frac{7}{8}$ **19.** 28 **21.** 5 in. by 5 in. **23.** $\frac{1}{729}$ **25.** $\frac{81}{4{,}096}$ **27.** $\frac{1}{8}$ **29.** $\frac{1}{9}$ **31.** $\frac{125}{8}$ **33.** $\frac{484}{25}$ **35.** $10\frac{7}{8}$ lb **37.** $\frac{1}{8}$ **39.** $1,017.19 **41.** No; the denominator is the product of the two denominators. **43.** 0.24 or $\frac{6}{25}$ **45.** 1.5 or $1\frac{1}{2}$ **47.** 9 nickels **49.** D **51.** $1\frac{3}{10}$ **53.** $\frac{37}{40}$

Lesson 5-4 pp. 188–189

STANDARDS PRACTICE **1.** $\frac{5}{2}$ **3.** 2 **5.** $\frac{3}{5}$ **7.** $-\frac{6}{5}$ **9.** 1 **11.** $\frac{18}{17}$ **13.** 27 **15.** $-\frac{2}{3}$ **17.** 9 **19.** $\frac{2}{31}$

21. $21\frac{1}{2}$ **23.** $20\frac{1}{4}$ **25.** 10,941,176.47 mi **27.** $\frac{1}{10}$ **29.** 5 times **31.** 2 **33.** $\frac{3}{4}$ **35.** $\frac{5}{6}$ **37.** 4.5 loaves or $4\frac{1}{2}$ loaves **39.** $2\frac{14}{25}$ **41.** B **43.** $\frac{2,401}{10,000}$

Lesson 5-5 pp. 192–193

STANDARDS PRACTICE **1.** $1\frac{17}{24}$ **3.** $\frac{38}{45}$ **5.** $-\frac{1}{4}$ **7.** $\frac{23}{45}$ **9.** $3\frac{13}{18}$ **11.** $-10\frac{5}{8}$ **13.** $1\frac{83}{330}$ **15.** $6\frac{1}{5}$ **17.** $1\frac{5}{6}$ lb **19.** $\frac{4}{15}$ **21.** $\frac{1}{12}$ **23.** Check students' work. **25.** $\frac{3}{10}$ mi **27.** $-2\frac{1}{2}$ **29.** $\frac{3}{4}$ **31.** $1\frac{5}{6}$ **33.** $\frac{5}{6}$ yd **35.** C **37.** $\frac{6}{7}$ **39.** $1\frac{4}{11}$

Lesson 5-6 pp. 198–199

STANDARDS PRACTICE **1.** $\frac{1}{36}$ **3.** $\frac{4}{15}$ **5.** $\frac{11}{90}$ **7.** $\frac{6}{55}$ **9.** 15 **11.** 16 **13.** 28 **15.** $5\frac{2}{5}$ **17.** 2 **19.** $-3\frac{3}{4}$ **21.** $\frac{5}{37}$ **23.** $-\frac{17}{46}$ **25.** $-\frac{16}{75}$ **27.** about 1,015 ft **29.** \$15 **31.** $16\frac{1}{2}$ c **33.** 31 apples **35.** $-\frac{17}{56}$ **37.** $4\frac{19}{48}$ **39.** $5\frac{2}{81}$ **41.** $\frac{6}{11}$ or $-\frac{6}{11}$ **43.** B **45.** $2\frac{4}{15}$ **47.** $21\frac{8}{9}$

Lesson 5-7 pp. 204–205

STANDARDS PRACTICE **1.** $\frac{1}{4,096}$ **3.** $\frac{1}{y^{12}}$ **5.** 1 **7.** 1 **9.** 1 **11.** 1 **13.** $\frac{4}{25}$ **15.** $\frac{4,096}{625}$ **17.** 1 **19.** $\frac{243}{32}$ **21.** $\frac{8,000}{729}$ **23.** 343 **25.** $\frac{125}{512}$ **27.** $\frac{625}{16}$ **29.** false; $4^0 = 1$ and $4^{-1} = \frac{1}{4}$ **31.** true; $2^1 \cdot 2^{-1} = 2 \cdot \frac{1}{2} = 1$ and $2^0 = 1$ **33.** The student incorrectly simplified $(-3)^4$ to be -243; $2^{-2} \cdot (-3)^4 = \frac{1}{2^2} \cdot (-3)^4 = \frac{1}{4} \cdot 81 = 20\frac{1}{4}$ **35.** $\frac{1}{16}$ **37.** 1 **39.** yes **41.** $11\frac{251}{256}$ **43.** $\frac{1}{144}$ **45.** $78\frac{17}{27}$ **47.** Any value of a where $a \neq 0$; if you simplify $\frac{a \cdot a \cdot a \cdot a \cdot a}{a \cdot a}$, you get a^3. **49.** D **51.** 45 **53.** $1\frac{17}{100}$

Chapter Review pp. 208–209

1. reciprocals **2.** multiplicative inverse **3.** exponent **4.** 1 **5.** $-\frac{13}{8}$ or $-1\frac{5}{8}$ **6.** $\frac{7}{8}$ **7.** $7\frac{14}{15}$ **8.** $-1\frac{1}{2}$ **9.** 8.45 or $8\frac{9}{20}$ **10.** $\frac{13}{15}$ mi **11.** $\frac{3}{10}$ **12.** $-\frac{2}{39}$ **13.** $4\frac{1}{54}$ **14.** $\frac{729}{1,000,000}$ **15.** $-\frac{1}{512}$ **16.** $\frac{64}{225}$ **17.** $\frac{1}{3}$ c **18.** $\frac{1}{9}$ **19.** $\frac{12}{7}$ **20.** $\frac{17}{10}$ **21.** 3 **22.** 16 **23.** $\frac{5}{11}$ **24.** $-\frac{9}{55}$ **25.** 4 **26.** $\frac{3}{7}$ **27.** $11\frac{1}{18}$ **28.** $6\frac{2}{5}$ **29.** 4 **30.** 2 **31.** $1\frac{19}{20}$ **32.** 3 pieces **33.** $\frac{1}{15,625}$

34. $\frac{1}{4,096}$ **35.** 1 **36.** $-\frac{1}{27}$ **37.** 1 **38.** $\frac{1}{144}$ **39.** $7\frac{58}{81}$ **40.** 1 **41.** $-\frac{1}{1,000,000,000}$ **42.** 64 **43.** $4\frac{19}{36}$ **44.** $-2\frac{1}{3}$

Chapter 6

Lesson 6-1 pp. 218–219

STANDARDS PRACTICE **1.** 2 to 6; $\frac{2}{6}$; 2 : 6 **3.** 5 to 6; $\frac{5}{6}$; 5 : 6 **5.** 2 to 3; $\frac{2}{3}$; 2 : 3 **7–15.** Answers may vary. Samples are given. **7.** 1 to 3 and 2 to 6 **9.** 4 : 5 and 16 : 20 **11.** 6 : 10 and 30 : 50 **13.** 18 to 14 and 36 to 28 **15.** 10 : 4 and 30 : 12 **17.** 4 : 3 **19.** $\frac{1}{3}$ **21.** $\frac{3}{2}$ **23.** $\frac{1}{13}$ **25.** 1 to 2 **27.** 20 : 10 or 20 to 10 or $\frac{20}{10}$ **29.** 2 : 3 or 2 to 3 or $\frac{2}{3}$ **31.** 1 : 3 or 1 to 3 or $\frac{1}{3}$ **33.** 2 **35.** 64 **37.** 225 **39.** 5 : 7 or 5 to 7 or $\frac{5}{7}$ **41.** 1 : 2 **43.** C **45.** $\frac{6}{35}$ **47.** $\frac{1}{10}$

Lesson 6-2 pp. 222–223

STANDARDS PRACTICE **1.** 3 gal/min **3.** 6.25 ft/s **5.** 12.5 m/s **7.** 9°F/min **9.** 45 ft **11.** 6 ft **13.** about 225 students **15.** 48 fl oz **17.** 32 oz **19.** 374 mi/h **21.** \$7.84/h **23.** \$313.60 **25.** Answers may vary. Sample: About 28 mi/gal; round 279.9 mi to 280 mi and 9.8 gal to 10 gal. Then find the unit rate $\frac{280 \text{ mi}}{10 \text{ gal}}$ or 28 mi/gal. **27.** Oscar and Monica **29.** 0.15 mi/s **31.** B **33.** $2\frac{2}{3}$ **35.** $\frac{1}{3}$

Lesson 6-3 pp. 228–229

STANDARDS PRACTICE **1.** 12 pt **3.** $2\frac{1}{12}$ h **5.** 15,840 ft **7.** 10.5 ft **9.** 1.5 gal **11.** 7.5 ft/min **13.** $1\frac{1}{3}$ cm/day **15.** 11.375 lb/yr **17.** 81 ft/h **19.** 5 persons **21.** 3 d **23.** x represents yd and y represents ft since 1 yd = 3 ft. **25.** \$9.38 **27.** 17 costumes **29.** 0.6 in./s **31.** 552 oz/ft **33.** Answers may vary. Sample: Count the number of times you blink in one minute, then multiply by $\frac{60 \text{ minutes}}{1 \text{ hour}}$, $\frac{24 \text{ hours}}{1 \text{ day}}$, and $\frac{7 \text{ days}}{1 \text{ week}}$. **35.** C **37.** C **39–41.** Answers may vary. Samples are given. **39.** $\frac{14}{24}$ and $\frac{21}{36}$ **41.** $\frac{2}{22}$ and $\frac{3}{33}$

Lesson 6-4 pp. 232–233

STANDARDS PRACTICE **1.** 250 mi **3.** 73.6 ft **5.** 2.3 mi/h **7.** 255 **9.** 88 **11.** $41\frac{2}{3}$ **13.** 30 mi **15.** 19.5 h **17.** Car A; Car A travels 135 mi and Car B travels 130 mi, so Car A travels farther.

19. 36.36 mi/h **21.** Answers may vary. Sample: average speed = total distance ÷ total time, so answer should have a unit of distance divided by a unit of time. **23.** B **25.** B **27.** 4 **29.** $\frac{11}{50}$

Lesson 6-5 pp. 238–239

STANDARDS PRACTICE **1.** no; $\frac{1}{4} \neq \frac{2}{10}$ **3.** no; $\frac{10}{20} \neq \frac{30}{40}$ **5.** yes; $\frac{42}{6} = \frac{504}{72}$ **7.** yes; $\frac{72}{27} = \frac{8}{3}$ **9.** no; $\frac{3}{2} \neq \frac{22}{16}$ **11.** 7 **13.** 9 **15.** 16 **17.** 5.4 **19.** 0.375 **21.** 19.6 in. **23.** Yes; the cross products are equal. **25.** $ay = bx$ and $bx = ay$; they are the same. **27.** −0.5 **29.** 1.62 **31.** 14 **33.** The student did not write the second rate in the correct order. It should be $\frac{3}{14} = \frac{h}{25}$. **35.** Answers may vary. Sample: x will only equal $x + z$ when z is 0. **37.** D **39.** C **41.** −1

Chapter Review pp. 244–245

1. ratio **2.** unit rate **3.** proportion **4.** conversion factor **5.** rate **6.** 15 to 23; $\frac{15}{23}$; 15 : 23 **7.** 23 to 8; $\frac{23}{8}$; 23 : 8 **8.** 15 to 46; $\frac{15}{46}$; 15 : 46 **9.** 1 to 4 **10.** $\frac{3}{5}$ **11.** 3 ft : 1 ft **12.** $\frac{5 \text{ boys}}{6 \text{ girls}}$ **13.** \$28/h **14.** 59 mi/h **15.** 6.25 km/L **16.** 24 oz **17.** 5 nights for \$600 **18.** $73\frac{1}{3}$ ft **19.** 40 c **20.** 6 t **21.** 15,840 ft/h **22.** 256 oz/ft **23.** \$18/h **24.** \$.08/oz **25.** 4,181,760 ft/day **26.** $\frac{4}{15}$ pt/s **27.** 9 h **28.** 68.75 mi **29.** 10.1 mi/h **30.** 40 min **31.** no; $\frac{2}{5} \neq \frac{1}{3}$ **32.** yes; $\frac{6}{16} = \frac{21}{56}$ **33.** yes; $\frac{15}{9} = \frac{5}{3}$ **34.** no; $\frac{3}{8} \neq \frac{9}{16}$ **35.** 16 **36.** 2 **37.** 4 **38.** 72 **39.** 39.11 euros

Chapter 7

Lesson 7-1 pp. 254–255

STANDARDS PRACTICE **1.** $\frac{7}{10}$ **3.** $\frac{1}{20}$ **5.** $\frac{7}{50}$ **7.** $\frac{3}{4}$ **9.** $\frac{1}{50}$ **11.** 40% **13.** 96% **15.** 90% **17.** 36% **19.** 0.3% **21.** 90% **23.** 0.007% **25.** 22% **27.** 93% **29.** $\frac{4}{25}$ **31.** 84% **33.** $\frac{99}{100}$, 0.99 **35.** 0.09% is equal to 0.0009, which is not the same as 0.09. **37.** C **39.** A **41.** $\frac{11}{5}$ **43.** $\frac{2}{3}$ **45.** D **47.** C **49.** 25

Lesson 7-2 pp. 258–259

STANDARDS PRACTICE **1.** 29.4 **3.** 129.5 **5.** 13.5 **7.** 3.5 **9.** about \$1.95 **11.** about \$4.20 **13.** about \$13.20 **15.** about \$1.35 **17.** about \$16.50

19. \$112.32 **21.** 66 girls **23.** 152 girls **25.** about \$9.75 **27.** about \$23.00 **29.** Estimates help check that the answer is reasonable. **31.** = **33.** > **35.** \$34.95 **37.** B **39.** 2 : 5 **41.** $\frac{2}{3}$

Lesson 7-3 pp. 264–265

STANDARDS PRACTICE **1.** 57.6 **3.** 33 **5.** 5.52 **7.** 82.8 **9.** 7.5 **11.** 950 **13.** about 250 students **15.** 4% **17.** 37.5% **19.** 95,052 votes **21.** 5% **23.** \$943.95 **25.** 0.03 **27.** 49.8 **29.** about 3,716,198 mi² **31.** 51.9% **33.** C **35.** 60% **37.** 180%

Lesson 7-4 pp. 268–269

STANDARDS PRACTICE **1.** 25% **3.** 48.1% **5.** 250% **7.** 100% **9.** 3.4% **11.** 43.0% **13.** 22.2% **15.** 3.7% **17.** 20% **19.** 98.1% **21.** about 5.5% **23.** Fresno, 335,983 increase; Los Angeles, 1,724,462 increase **25.** Answers may vary. Sample: Exercise 23 better describes which city's population changed by more people. Exercise 24 better describes which city's population changed by a greater percent of its original population. **27.** 75% decrease **29.** 75% decrease **31.** 86.7% decrease **33.** 4.1% **35.** C **37.** \$2.25 per gal

Lesson 7-5 pp. 274–275

STANDARDS PRACTICE **1.** 50% **3.** 20% **5.** 300% **7.** 400% **9.** 24% **11.** 30% **13.** 40% **15.** 29% **17.** \$7.65 **19.** \$53.30 **21.** \$161.25 **23.** 3 DVDs **25.** \$605 **27.** No difference; the final cost is \$423.50 either way. **29.** \$501.02 **31.** 126.9% **33.** D **35.** 9 **37.** 15

Chapter Review pp. 280–281

1. markup **2.** percent **3.** discount **4.** percent of change **5.** 87.5% **6.** 75% **7.** 31.25% **8.** 84% **9.** 20% **10.** $66\frac{2}{3}$% **11.** $\frac{3}{10}$ **12.** $\frac{14}{25}$ **13.** $\frac{1}{4}$ **14.** $\frac{3}{25}$ **15.** $\frac{9}{100}$ **16.** $\frac{27}{100}$ **17.** 35% **18.** 2.5% **19.** 17.3% **20.** 4% **21.** 56% **22.** 10% **23.** 90% **24.** about 63% **25.** 4.2 **26.** 9.4 **27.** 2.94 **28.** 43.5 **29.** 0.8 **30.** 34.2 **31.** 60 students **32.** about \$3.60 **33.** 200 **34.** 40% **35.** 18 **36.** 150 **37.** about 160 students **38.** 16.7% decrease **39.** 20% increase **40.** 15% increase **41.** 40% increase **42.** 72.0% decrease **43.** 16.7% decrease **44.** 10% **45.** \$199.99

Chapter 8

Lesson 8-1 pp. 290–291

STANDARDS PRACTICE **1.** (1, 2) **3.** (0, −3) **5.** (3, −3) **7.** (3, 0) **9.** (0, 3)

10–19.

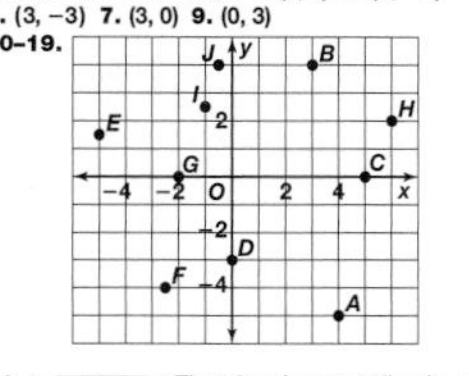

21. The triangles are reflections of each other over the x-axis.

23. (−3, 0) **25.** Africa **27.** in the Atlantic Ocean **29.** Answers may vary. Sample:

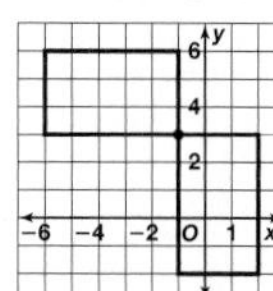

31. y-axis **33.** x-axis **35.** I **37.** B **39.** B **41.** 25

Lesson 8-2 pp. 294–295

STANDARDS PRACTICE **1.** 2 **3.** 5 **5.** 4.5 **7.** 13 **9.** about 11 **11.** about 6 mi **13–14.** Answers may vary. Sample:

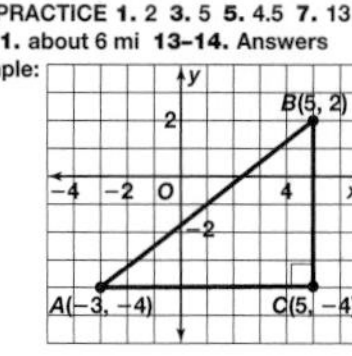

15. 6; 8 **17.** about 60 ft **19.** about 29 **21.** B **23.** 9 **25.** 15

Lesson 8-3 pp. 300–301

STANDARDS PRACTICE **1.** −1; 12; 16; 35 **3.** −2; −1.5; 0.5; 1 **5.** 4; 12; 15 **7.** −1 **9.** 23 **11.** −21 **13.** 29.5 **15.** \$3.50 **17.** \$8.95; \$28.64; \$48.33 **19.** Let n = the number of loads of laundry. Let $f(n)$ = the number of gallons of water. $f(n) = 40n$ **21.** $f(n)$ **23.** 5; 6; $f(n) = \frac{n}{5}$ **25.** D **27.** C **29.** 8.55

Lesson 8-4 pp. 305–306

STANDARDS PRACTICE **1.**

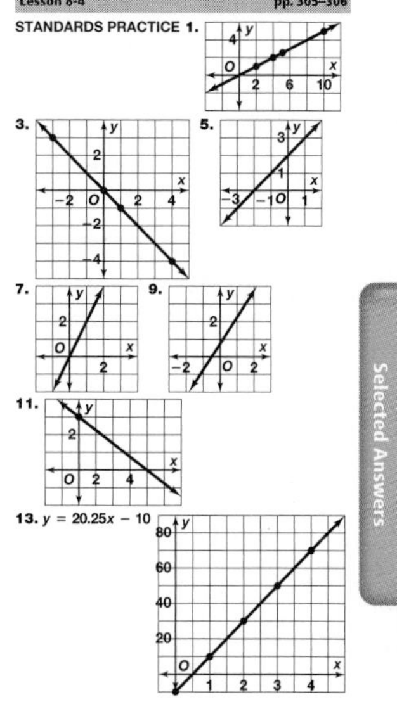

3. **5.** **7.** **9.** **11.** **13.** $y = 20.25x - 10$

15. $y = 4x$ **17.**

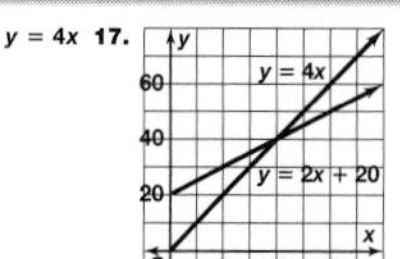

19. 11 or more calendars **21.** A; all the other points are on the same line. **23.** A **25.** D

26–29.

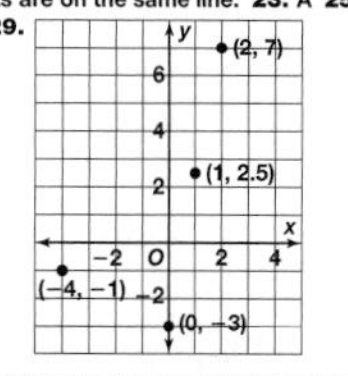

Lesson 8-5 pp. 312–313

STANDARDS PRACTICE **1.** −1 **3.** 2 **5.** $\frac{5}{6}$ **7.** $-\frac{1}{4}$ **9.** $-\frac{1}{4}$ **11.** undefined **13.** −5; the supply of rice decreases by 5 lb/wk. **15.** \$12,000 **17.** The value of the car decreases \$2,000/yr. **19.** No; the ratio of rise to run is not the same for each pair of points. **21.** x represents inches and y represents feet; $\frac{1 \text{ ft}}{12 \text{ in.}}$.

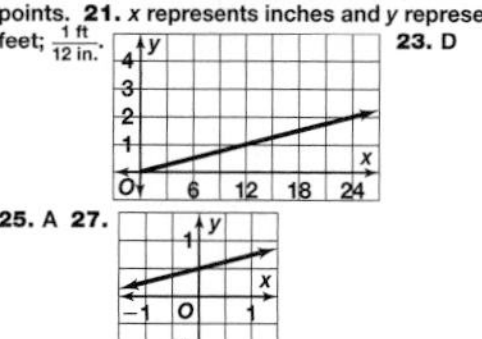

23. D **25.** A **27.**

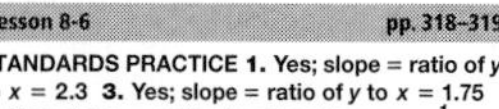

Lesson 8-6 pp. 318–319

STANDARDS PRACTICE **1.** Yes; slope = ratio of y to x = 2.3 **3.** Yes; slope = ratio of y to x = 1.75 **5.** Yes; slope = ratio of gallons to cups = $\frac{1}{16}$

7.

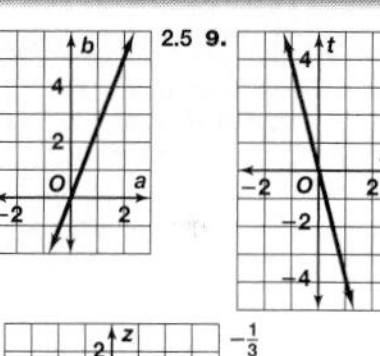

2.5 **9.** −4

11.

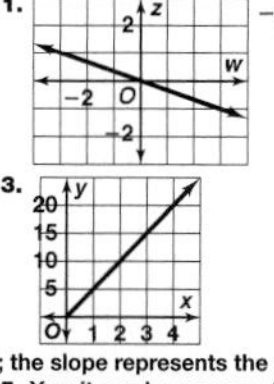

$-\frac{1}{3}$ **13.** 5; the slope represents the ratio of laps to days. **15.** Yes; it can be represented by the direct variation $y = \frac{1}{36}x$, where y is length in yards and x is length in inches. **17.** (6, 3) **19.** $y = \frac{1}{2}x$ **21.** $\frac{1}{2}$; the slope is the same as k.

23.

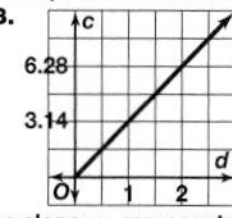

The slope, π, represents the ratio of the circumference of a circle to its diameter. **25.** C **27.** −1 **29.** $\frac{33}{5}$

Chapter Review pp. 322–323

1. linear function **2.** quadrants **3.** solution **4.** origin **5.** function **6.** (−3, −2) **7.** (−2, 3) **8.** (1, −3) **9.** (3, 0) **10.** (1, 1) **11.** (−3, 1)

12–15.

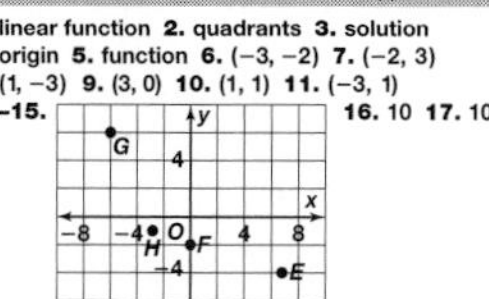

16. 10 **17.** 10

18. 13 **19.** 5 **20.** −7 **21.** −27 **22.** −5 **23.** 27
24. $-8\frac{7}{9}$ **25.** 77 **26.** −59 **27.**

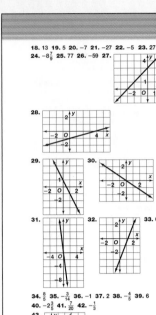

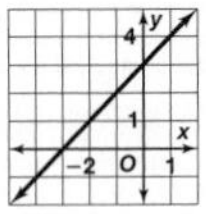

28.

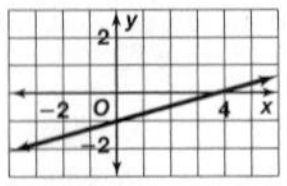

29. 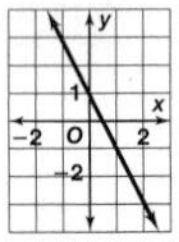 **30.**

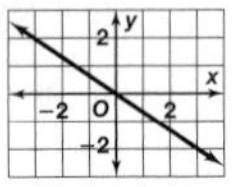

31. 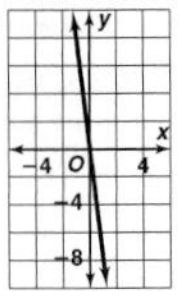 **32.** 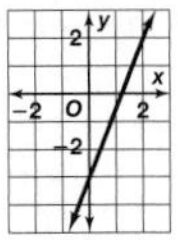 **33.** 0

34. $\frac{8}{5}$ **35.** $-\frac{3}{14}$ **36.** −1 **37.** 2 **38.** $-\frac{4}{5}$ **39.** 6
40. $-2\frac{3}{5}$ **41.** $\frac{7}{20}$ **42.** $-\frac{1}{3}$
43.

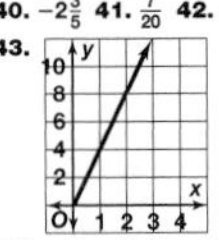

4; the slope is the ratio of quarts to gallons.

Chapter 9

Lesson 9-1 pp. 332–333

STANDARDS PRACTICE **1.** $r \le 35$ **3.** $q \le 4$ **5.** $h < 5.6$ **7.** $c > 8$ **9–11.** Variables may vary. Samples are given. **9.** $\begin{cases} w \ge 300 \\ w \le 500 \end{cases}$ **11.** $\begin{cases} w \ge 100 \\ w \le 130 \end{cases}$
13. Cara, Monique, Sierra **15.** true **17.** true **19.** 45 mi/h **21.** $\begin{cases} s \ge 45 \\ s \le 65 \end{cases}$ **23.** B
25. Answers may vary. Sample: They are alike in that both make the statement true. They are different in that an equation usually has just one solution while an inequality can have many solutions. **27.** −1, 0, or 1 **29.** C **31–33.** Answers may vary. Samples are given. **31.** about $4.50 **33.** about $2.10

Lesson 9-2 pp. 336–337

STANDARDS PRACTICE **1.** $g \le -6$ **3.** $m < -2$ **5.** $y \ge 16$ **7.** $q > 6$ **9.** $b \ge -2$ **11.** $n \le 1$ **13.** $x \le -11$ **15.** $w < 1$ **17.** $s \ge 65$ **19.** $w > -\frac{1}{2}$ **21.** $a < 5\frac{1}{2}$ **23.** $m > -0.7$
25. Answers may vary. Sample: A number cannot be greater than itself. **27.** no **29.** 2 **31.** B **33.** < **35.** $x \le 0$ **37.** $y > -\frac{a}{2}$ **39.** B **41.** $\frac{5}{12}$

Lesson 9-3 pp. 342–343

STANDARDS PRACTICE **1.** $c < 2$ **3.** $w \ge -9$ **5.** $n \ge -3$ **7.** $h < 8$ **9.** $y \le 3$ **11.** at least 50 pages **13.** $b \le 3$ **15.** $d \le 7.5$ **17.** $p \ge -5$ **19.** $q \ge -6.5$ **21.** $f > -30$ **23.** $y \ge -8$ **25.** −3
27. The student switched the direction of the inequality sign. The answer should be $n > -5$. **29.** 3 hot dogs **31a.** 4 bags **b.** $.50 **33.** a and b must have opposite signs. **35.** a and b must have the same sign, and $b \ne 0$. **37.** No; the solution is true for $b > 0$ only. If $b < 0$, then $a < 2b$. **39.** C **41.** $y \le 26$ **43.** $w \ge 15$

Lesson 9-4 pp. 346–347

STANDARDS PRACTICE **1.** $y > 0$ **3.** $p < -15$ **5.** $w \le -35$ **7.** $x > -80$ **9.** $s \le -100$ **11.** at least 280 players **13.** $z > 96$ **15.** $x < -30$ **17.** $p > -16.8$ **19.** $s \le -15$ **21.** $t > 64$
23. Answers may vary. Sample: Multiply each side of the inequality by $\frac{3}{2}$. **25.** $\frac{x}{5} \ge -8$; $x \ge -40$ **27.** $y \ge -7$
29. $y \le 9$; −7 −3 1 5 9 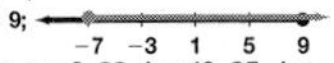
31. $-7 \le y \le 9$ **33.** $k \le 16$ **35.** $j \le -24\frac{4}{9}$ **37.** $q < 13$ **39.** D **41.** $x \le 3$ **43.** $m \ge 5$

Lesson 9-5 pp. 351–353

STANDARDS PRACTICE **1.** $x < 6$ **3.** $w \le -1$ **5.** $k > 20$ **7.** $m \le -27$ **9.** $g \ge 6$ **11.** $n \ge -3$ **13.** $p > 20$ **15.** $t > 9$ **17.** $r \ge 2$ **19.** 3 or fewer **21.** at least 8.5 min/mi **23.** The student added 5 to each side instead of subtracting 5.
25. $j > 1.8$ **27.** $g \le -3$ **29.** $b \le -7$ **31.** 76 or fewer people **33.** 90 **35.** B **37.** Answers may vary. Sample: The process is the same except the direction of the inequality sign is reversed when you divide by −3. **39.** A **41.** C **43.** $s > 85$

Chapter Review pp. 358–359

1. inequality **2.** Div. Prop. of Ineq. **3.** system of inequalities **4.** Add. Prop. of Ineq. **5.** solution of an inequality **6.** $v \ge 35$ **7.** $t \le 10$ **8.** $r < 5$ **9.** $c > 53$ **10.** $\begin{cases} c \ge 9 \\ c < 11 \end{cases}$
11. Answers may vary. Sample: 4, 3, 2 **12.** $g > 19$ **13.** $u \le 2$ **14.** $t \ge -11$ **15.** $h > -22$ **16.** $x > 22$ **17.** $y \ge -1$ **18.** $7.01 or less **19.** $x < -3$ **20.** $y < -2$ **21.** $a < 7$ **22.** $m \ge -3$ **23.** $w \le 128$ **24.** $c < -20$ **25.** $z > 12$ **26.** $p \ge -15$ **27.** at least 130 tickets **28.** $j < 8$ **29.** $m \le 1.9$ **30.** $e < -20$ **31.** $v \ge 0$ **32.** 3 or fewer games

Chapter 10

Lesson 10-1 pp. 368–369

STANDARDS PRACTICE **1.** y^8 **3.** 3.4^{13} **5.** 4.5^{20} **7.** 0.4^8 **9.** $(-4)^{16}$ **11.** a^2 **13.** c^5 **15.** 23^4 **17.** $(-7)^1$ or −7 **19.** 6^6 **21.** about 81 min **23.** 12 **25.** 3 **27.** 5 **29.** $5x^3$ **31.** $2x^3 - 4$ **33.** Answers may vary. Sample: You can add exponents only when the bases are the same. **35.** 3^{m+n} **37.** 5^{r-d} **39.** $5^t \cdot 4^c$ **41.** D **43.** B **45.** 4.31

Lesson 10-2 pp. 372–373

STANDARDS PRACTICE **1.** 3^{21} **3.** h^4 **5.** w^{12} **7.** p^2 **9.** $\frac{1}{10^{10}}$ **11.** 9^4 **13.** $\frac{1}{2^9}$ **15.** y^{15} **17.** a^8b^{12} **19.** $100x^{10}$ **21.** $225a^2$ **23.** $64t^{15}y^6$ **25.** $5^{-5} \times 10^{-10}$ **27.** 5.041×10^7 cm^2 **29.** 7.56×10^{14} joules **31.** > **33.** < **35.** = **37.** 81 **39.** $\frac{81}{7^4x^{12}}$ **41.** $\frac{k^{15}}{w^{10}}$ **43.** 3^9 **45.** y^{32} **47.** m^{24} **49.** The student who got $x^2 \cdot x^2 = x^4$; when you multiply two numbers with the same base you add the powers. **51.** B **53.** B **55.** $\frac{1}{3}$

Lesson 10-3 pp. 376–377

STANDARDS PRACTICE **1.** 10 **3.** 4 **5.** 2 **7.** 11 **9.** 5 **11.** 10 **13.** 1 **15.** −13 **17.** 5 **19.** 1 **21.** 6 **23.** 2 **25.** 493.5 in. **27.** $\sqrt[6]{356}$; six factors are needed to make 356 instead of 11 factors. **29.** 3 **31.** 2, 2 **33.** −3 **35.** 22 **37.** −3 **39.** $\frac{3}{5}$ **41.** B **43.** $9v^6$ **45.** $w^{21}b^{14}$

Lesson 10-4 pp. 382–383

STANDARDS PRACTICE **1.** $11b$ **3.** $31x$ **5.** $-11t$ **7.** $23a$ **9.** $-18j$ **11.** $4a + 2$ **13.** $5q - 3$ **15.** $-6 - 2y$ **17.** $-7d + 8$ **19.** $23 - 5z$ **21.** $-27m - 16$ **23.** $-7b + 2$ **25.** $5p - 3$
27. Let t = cost of 1 lb of turkey; $6t$. **29.** Let c = cost of 1 lb of cheese; $4c$. **31.** $10t + 5s + 7c$ **33.** $3x - 2y$ **35.** $-2t - 102$ **37.** $2.1x + 9.9y$ **39.** Let b = cost of 1 barrette and h = cost of 1 headband; $6b + 3h$. **41.** −6 **43.** B **45.** f^7 **47.** x^6

Lesson 10-5 pp. 389–390

STANDARDS PRACTICE **1.** 5 **3.** 17 **5.** 7 **7.** −10 **9.** 31 **11.** −11 **13.** 10 **15.** 21 **17.** 2 lb **19.** −1 **21.** 10 **23.** 41 h **25.** $3n + 3$ **27.** 15 **29.** −86, −85, −84 **31.** $3y + 505 = 1{,}000$; 165 in. **33.** 2.12 **35.** C **37.** 44 **39.** −128

Lesson 10-6 pp. 394–395

STANDARDS PRACTICE **1.** −2 **3.** 5 **5.** 4.5 **7.** 10 **9.** 4.8 **11.** −18 **13.** −4.5 **15.** −2 **17.** 3 h **19.** $3.02 **21.**

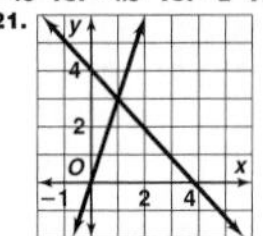

23. Answer may vary. Sample: If you substitute $y = 3x$ into the equation $y = -x + 4$ for y, you get $3x = -x + 4$. **25.** 3 **27.** Answers may vary. Sample: Bring all the variable terms to one side of the equation and use the properties of equality to isolate the variable. **29.** B **31.** 3

Chapter Review pp. 400–401

1. Like terms **2.** term **3.** nth root **4.** 8^{19} **5.** $(-3)^{10}$ **6.** 2.6^{24} **7.** f^2 **8.** d^5 **9.** 24×10^8 **10.** 5^3 **11.** $(-8)^{10}$ **12.** 76^6 **13.** 1.8 **14.** m^2 **15.** 1 **16.** about 56 **17.** 5^{20} **18.** 9^{40} **19.** 8^6 **20.** $\frac{1}{a^8}$ **21.** $\frac{1}{x^{20}}$ **22.** $\frac{1}{2^{100}}$ **23.** 333^{99} **24.** w^0 **25.** $16x^2$ **26.** $8n^3$ **27.** 16×10^{18} **28.** a^4b^{20} **29.** $k^4m^4g^4$ **30.** $\frac{9}{a^8}$ **31.** $\frac{w^{10}}{x^{10}}$ **32.** 1 **33.** 2 **34.** 10 **35.** −1 **36.** 0 **37.** 12 **38.** 18 **39.** 30 in. **40.** $7 - 3f$ **41.** $3a + 11$ **42.** $12x - 4$ **43.** $10y - 25$ **44.** $23c + 3$ **45.** $9t - 3$ **46.** $82x$ **47.** $3\frac{1}{5}$ **48.** −5 **49.** −4 **50.** 5 **51.** 22.5 **52.** 6 **53.** 2.5 lb

Additional Answers

CHAPTER 1

Lesson 1-2

pages 8–9 CA Standards Check

3.

Number of Games	Expression	Amount Earned
35	$4.5 \cdot 35$	157.50
50	$4.5 \cdot 50$	225
60	$4.5 \cdot 60$	270

pages 10–11 Standards Practice

6. 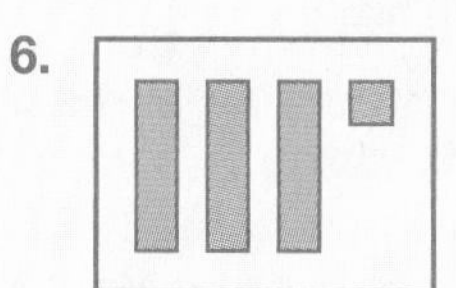

7. 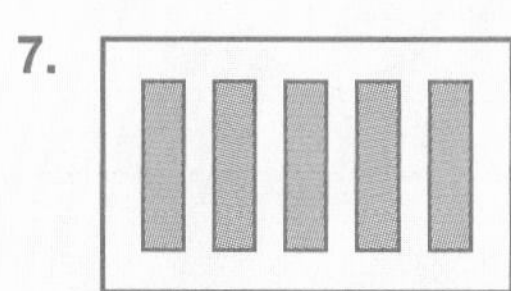

8. 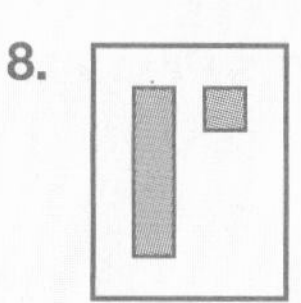

9. 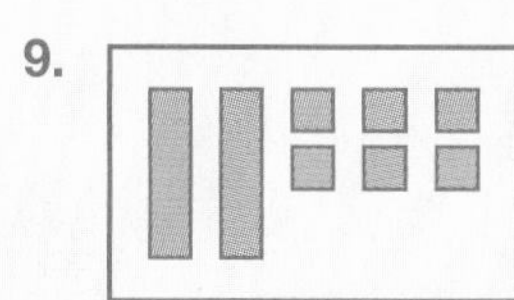

page 13 Activity Lab

1–4.

Word Phrase	Diagram 1	Diagram 2
1. Height h divided by 6	h; ? ? ? ? ? ?	h; ? ? ? ? ? ?
2. Answers may vary. Sample: 8 more than q	q 8	q 8
3. Answers may vary. Sample: 7 times r	r r r r r r r	r r r r r r r
4. 6.3 smaller than t	t; ? 6.3	t; ? 6.3

Lesson 1-4

pages 22–23 Standards Practice

15. No; the estimate is \$93. Since the prices were all rounded up and \$99.53 is more than the estimate, it is not reasonable.

16. Yes; the estimate is \$5. This is close to the actual total of \$4.69.

18. No; the estimate is \$87. Since this is significantly less than \$92.70, the estimate is not reasonable.

page 24 Checkpoint Quiz 2

11. If you round each amount up to the next dollar, the total is about \$23. The actual cost must be less than this.

CHAPTER 2

Lesson 2-1

page 51 Activity Lab

5a-c. Answers may vary. Sample:

a. To add two positive integers, add their absolute values. The result is the desired sum.

b. To add two negative integers, add their absolute values. The opposite of the result is the desired sum.

c. To add two integers with different signs, find the diff. of the absolute values. Use the sign of the number with the greater value.

Lesson 2-2

page 57 Activity Lab

5. Answers may vary. Sample:

a. To subtract a negative integer from a negative integer, add its opposite.

b. To subtract a negative integer from a positive integer, add its opposite. To subtract a positive integer from a negative integer, add its opposite.

Lesson 2-5

pages 70–71 Guided Problem Solving

2b. Answers may vary.
Sample:
$100 + (-3) + 2 = 99$
$100 + (-4) + 2 = 98$
$100 + (-5) + 2 = 97$
$100 + 2(-3) + 2 = 96$
$100 + (-3) + (-4) + 2 = 95$
$100 + 2(-3) = 94$
$100 + (-3) + (-4) = 93$
$100 + 2(-4) = 92$
$100 + (-4) + (-5) = 91$

page 80 Chapter Test

11. Answers may vary. Sample: The absolute value of a number is its distance from 0 on a number line. −5 is 5 units from 0 on a number line, so its absolute value is 5.

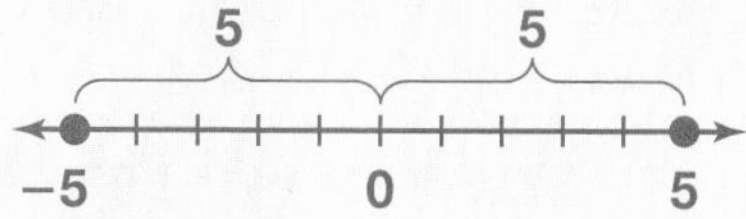

42. Answers may vary. Sample: The product of two integers is 0 when either integer is 0. The sum of two integers is 0 when the integers are add. inv. (opposites).

CHAPTER 3

page 86 Algebraic Thinking

1–4. Explanations may vary. Samples are given.

1. True; each of the numbers on the right side is 3 more than the number on the left side, so the two differences are equal.

2. False; the left side can be expressed as $800 \cdot 2$, which is not the same as the right side.

3. True; both sides can be expressed as $130 \cdot 4$.

4. False; the right side can be expressed as $38.1 + (10 + 18.2)$, or $38.1 + 28.2$, which is not the same as the left side.

Lesson 3-1

pages 89–90 Standards Practice

35. All values; the equation can be written as $x + 15 = x + 15$, which is true for any value of x.

Lesson 3-3

page 100 Mathematical Reasoning

1. Subtr. Prop. of Eq.: $p + 12.3 - 12.3 = 45 - 12.3$; Inv. Prop. of Add.: $p + 0 = 32.7$; Ident. Prop. of Add.: $p = 32.7$
2. Div. Prop. of Eq.: $15e \div 15 = 120 \div 15$; Inv. Prop. of Div.: $1 \cdot e = 8$; Ident. Prop. of Mult.:$e = 8$
3. Add. Prop. of Eq.: $67 + 9 = t - 9 + 9$; Inv. Prop. of Add.: $76 = t + 0$; Ident. Prop. of Add.: $76 = t$
4. Mult. Prop. of Eq.: $\frac{k}{4.2} \cdot 4.2 = 10 \cdot 4.2$; Inv. Prop. of Mult.: $1 \cdot k = 42$; Ident. Prop. of Mult.: $k = 42$
5. You can use the Add. Prop. of Eq. by adding -5 to each side of $h - (-5) = 245.6$. Or, you can rewrite the equation as $h + 5 = 245.6$, and then use the Subtr. Prop. of Eq. to subtract 5 from each side.

page 126 Chapter Test

23. Answers may vary. Sample: The two types of equations are the same because you isolate the variable in both types. The two types of equations are different because you can solve one using one operation, and the other you can solve using two operations.
43. The hypotenuse is the longest side of a right triangle.

CHAPTER 4

Lesson 4-1

pages 134–135 Standards Practice

1. 1, 2, 4, 7, 14, 28
2. 1, 3, 7, 21
3. 1, 17
4. 1, 2, 3, 4, 5, 6, 10, 12, 15, 20, 30, 60
5. 1, 2, 3, 4, 6, 8, 12, 16, 24, 48
6. 1, 37
7. 1, 2, 3, 4, 6, 8, 9, 12, 16, 18, 24, 36, 48, 72, 144
8. 1, 2, 3, 5, 6, 9, 10, 15, 18, 25, 30, 45, 50, 75, 90, 150, 225, 450
9. 1, 2, 4, 5, 10, 20, 25, 50, 100, 125, 250, 500
10. 1, 2, 17, 34
11. 1, 59
12. 1, 2, 4, 5, 10, 11, 20, 22, 44, 55, 110, 220
13. 1, 3, 37, 111
14. 1, 2, 3, 4, 6, 9, 12, 18, 36
15. Prime; the only factors are 1 and 19.
16. Prime; the only factors are 1 and 67.
17. Composite; the factors are 1, 3, 19, and 57.
18. Composite; the factors are 1, 7, 13, and 91.
19. Composite; the factors are 1, 2, 3, 4, 6, 8, 12, 16, 24, and 48.
20. Composite; the factors are 1, 5, and 25.
21. Prime; the only factors are 1 and 73.
22. Prime; the only factors are 1 and 101.
23. Composite; the factors are 1, 2, 5, 10, 25, 50, 125, and 250.

Lesson 4-2

page 140 Mathematical Reasoning

1. Yes; the last two digits are divisible by 4.
2. No; the last two digits are 46, which is not divisible by 4.
3. No; for a number to be divisible by 6 it must be divisible by both 2 and 3. The ones digit is 2, so it is divisible by 2. The sum of the digits is 5, which is not divisible by 3.
4. No; the sum of the digits is 3, which is not divisible by 9.
5. Yes; the ones digit is 4.
6. No; the ones digit is not 0 or 5.
7. Yes; the ones digit is 0.
8. Yes, the sum of the digits is 12, which is divisible by 3.
9. 2 and 3 are divisors of 6. Since 6 is a divisor of 54, 2 and 3 also are divisors of 54.

page 152 Checkpoint Quiz 2

10. The player with 10 hits in 30 at bats has a higher average because $\frac{8}{27} < \frac{10}{30}$.

page 153 Activity Lab

9. The denominator shows the number of parts needed to make a whole unit. For example, in the fraction $\frac{1}{4}$, it takes 4 units to make one whole. So $2\frac{1}{4}$ is equivalent to $\frac{2 \cdot 4 \text{ units}}{4}$ plus $\frac{1}{4}$.

Lesson 4-5

pages 156–157 Standards Practice

1. $-3.13, \frac{10}{13}, \frac{15}{19}, 0.8$
2. $0.03, \frac{3}{10}, 0.33, \frac{1}{3}$
3. $\frac{4}{9}, 0.7, 1.3, 1\frac{2}{5}$
4. $-4, -3.9, -\frac{2}{9}, \frac{2}{11}$
5. $\frac{5}{7}, \frac{5}{6}, \frac{5}{3}, \frac{5}{2}$
6. $\frac{1}{5}, 1\frac{1}{5}, 1.5, \frac{15}{5}$
7. $-3, -\frac{3}{7}, -0.3, \frac{1}{3}$

page 160 Vocabulary Builder

1.

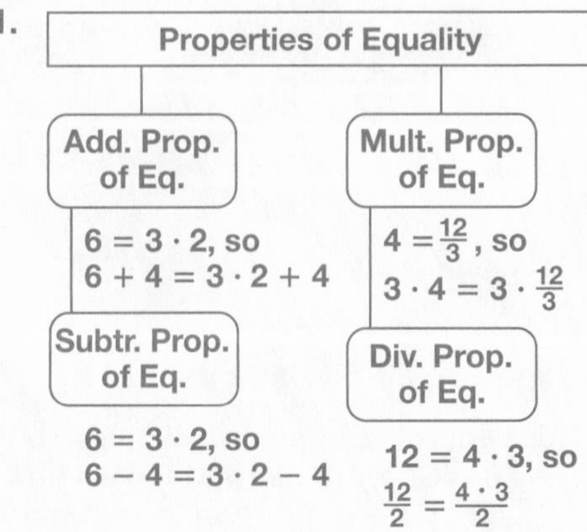

page 164 Chapter Test

18–23. Answers may vary. Samples are given.

18. $\frac{3}{9}$, $\frac{12}{36}$
19. $\frac{3}{8}$, $\frac{18}{48}$
20. $\frac{9}{10}$, $\frac{36}{40}$
21. $\frac{6}{10}$, $\frac{120}{200}$
22. $\frac{5}{14}$, $\frac{30}{84}$
23. $\frac{14}{22}$, $\frac{21}{33}$

CHAPTER 5

Lesson 5-1

pages 173–174 Standards Practice

29. First add the whole numbers: $5 + 3 + 3 + 6 = 17$. Then add the fractions with the same denominators: $\frac{1}{3} + \frac{2}{3} = 1$ and $\frac{4}{5} + \frac{1}{5} = 1$. So $17 + 1 + 1 = 19$.

Lesson 5-5

pages 194–195 Guided Problem Solving

2. Answers may vary. Sample: Each board is about 11 in. wide, so together they are about 22 in. wide. Since $36 - 22 = 14$, and $13\frac{1}{2}$ is close to 14, the answer is reasonable.

Lesson 5-7

page 206 Activity Lab

1. $(6 \cdot 10^2) + (7 \cdot 10^1) + (9 \cdot 10^0)$
2. $(4 \cdot 10^1) + (3 \cdot 10^0) + (6 \cdot 10^{-1}) + (7 \cdot 10^{-2})$
3. $(1 \cdot 10^3) + (2 \cdot 10^2) + (6 \cdot 10^0) + (4 \cdot 10^{-1})$
4. $(9 \cdot 10^0) + (3 \cdot 10^{-2})$
5. $(6 \cdot 10^0) + (2 \cdot 10^{-1}) + (3 \cdot 10^{-2}) + (6 \cdot 10^{-3}) + (7 \cdot 10^{-4})$
6. $(4 \cdot 10^3) + (5 \cdot 10^2) + (3 \cdot 10^1) + (7 \cdot 10^0) + (1 \cdot 10^{-1}) + (2 \cdot 10^{-2})$
7. $(7 \cdot 10^{-1}) + (3 \cdot 10^{-2}) + (1 \cdot 10^{-3})$
8. $(3 \cdot 10^2) + (1 \cdot 10^{-3})$

CHAPTER 6

Lesson 6-1

pages 218–219 Standards Practice

7–15. Answers may vary. Samples are given.

7. 1 to 3 and 2 to 6
8. $\frac{2}{7}$ and $\frac{40}{140}$
9. 4 : 5 and 16 : 20
10. $\frac{3}{4}$ and $\frac{15}{20}$
11. 6 : 10 and 30 : 50
12. 1 to 4 and 10 to 40
13. 18 to 14 and 36 to 28
14. $\frac{1}{2}$ and $\frac{36}{72}$
15. 10 : 4 and 30 : 12

Lesson 6-3

pages 228–229 Standards Practice

38–41. Answers may vary. Samples are given:

38. $\frac{1}{4}$ and $\frac{4}{16}$
39. $\frac{14}{24}$ and $\frac{21}{36}$
40. $\frac{3}{7}$ and $\frac{18}{42}$
41. $\frac{2}{22}$ and $\frac{3}{33}$

Lesson 6-4

pages 232–233 Standards Practice

14.

Hours	1	2	4	6	7	10
Pay (Dollars)	5	10	20	30	35	50

Lesson 6-5

pages 238–239 Standards Practice

1. no; $\frac{1}{4} \neq \frac{2}{10}$
2. yes; $\frac{1}{2} = \frac{50}{100}$
3. no; $\frac{10}{20} \neq \frac{30}{40}$
4. no; $\frac{4}{12} \neq \frac{6}{8}$
5. yes; $\frac{42}{6} = \frac{504}{72}$
6. yes; $\frac{9}{11} = \frac{63}{77}$
7. yes; $\frac{72}{27} = \frac{8}{3}$
8. no; $\frac{16}{27} \neq \frac{4}{9}$
9. no; $\frac{3}{2} \neq \frac{22}{16}$

page 246 Chapter Test

1. 3 to 5; $\frac{3}{5}$; 3 : 5
2. 11 to 3; $\frac{11}{3}$; 11 : 3
3. 11 to 19; $\frac{11}{19}$; 11 : 19
4. 5 to 11; $\frac{5}{11}$; 5 : 11
29. No; solving the proportion $\frac{5}{6} = \frac{x}{15}$ does not give a whole number of girls.

CHAPTER 7

Lesson 7-5

pages 277–278 Guided Problem Solving

1. Yes; then compare your answer to 60% of the regular price.
2. No. Explanations may vary. Sample: On a \$100 item, a 25% markup raises the price to \$125, but a 25% discount brings the price down to \$93.75.
3. No; 80% of 80% is 64%, which is only a 36% discount.

page 282 Chapter Test

29–32. Explanations may vary. Samples are given.

29. about \$9.00
30. about 36
31. about 15
32. about \$4.80
33. $\frac{36}{90} = \frac{n}{100}$; 40
34. $\frac{17}{n} = \frac{85}{100}$; 20
42. 64.6% increase
43. 92.3% decrease
44. 84.8% decrease
45. 6.9% increase
46. 9.6% increase
47. 99.5% decrease

50. Answers may vary. Sample: The student calculated the percent of markup using the selling price instead of the store's cost. The correct answer is 25% markup.

CHAPTER 8

Lesson 8-1

page 289 CA Standards Check

2a.

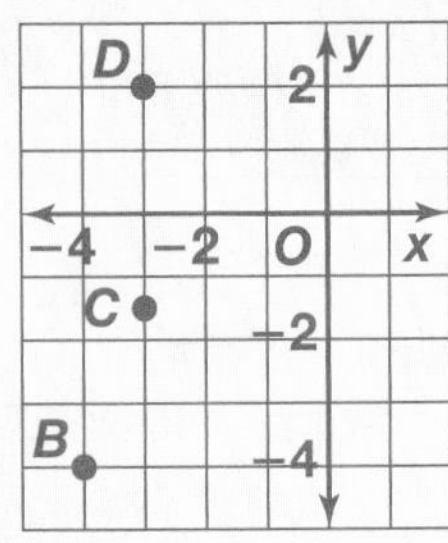

pages 290–291 Standards Practice

10–19.

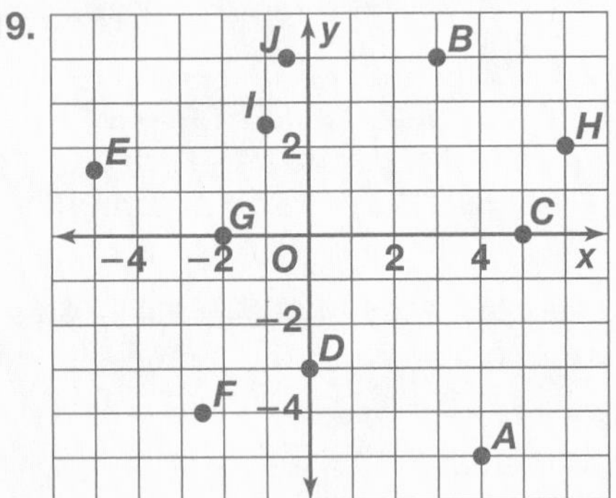

21.

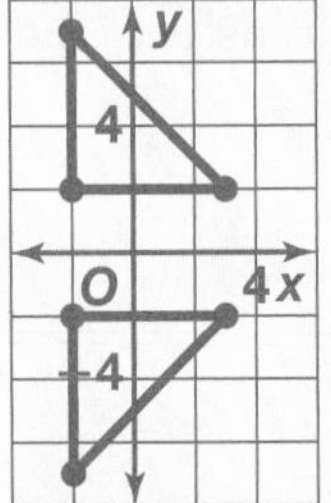

The triangles are reflections of each other over the x-axis.

29. Answers may vary. Sample:

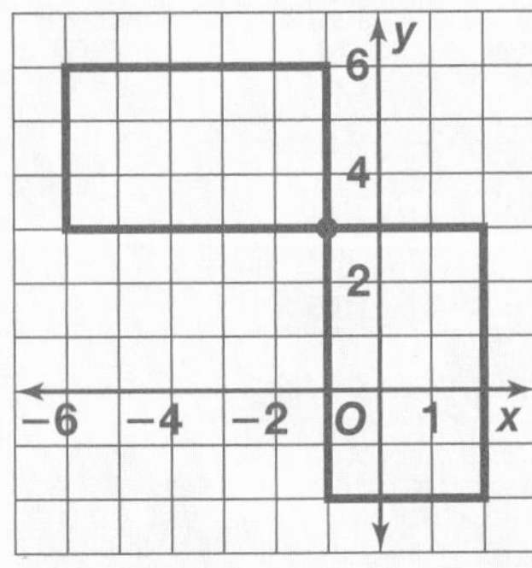

Lesson 8-2

pages 294–295 Standards Practice

13–14. Answers may vary. Sample:

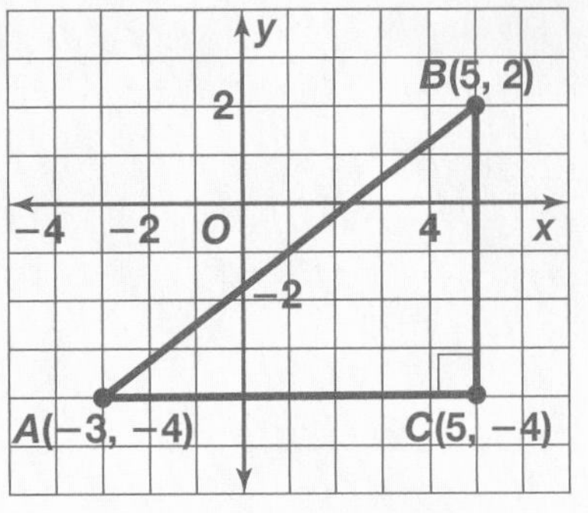

page 296 Checkpoint Quiz 1

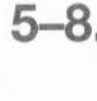

5–8.

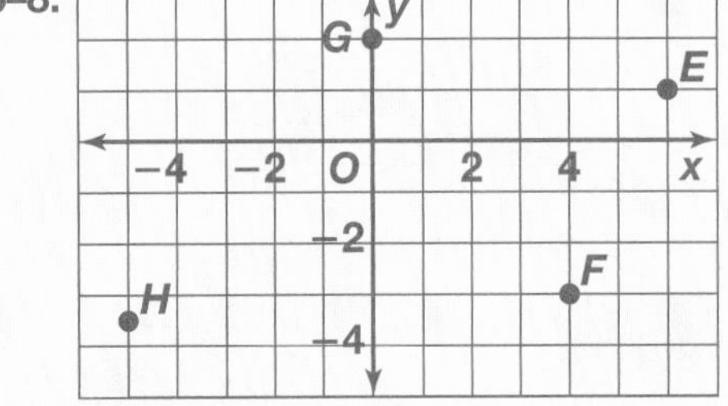

page 297 Activity Lab

3a.

Number of Days	0	1	2	3	20
Tickets Remaining	180	171	162	153	0

b. $y = 180 - 9x$

c.

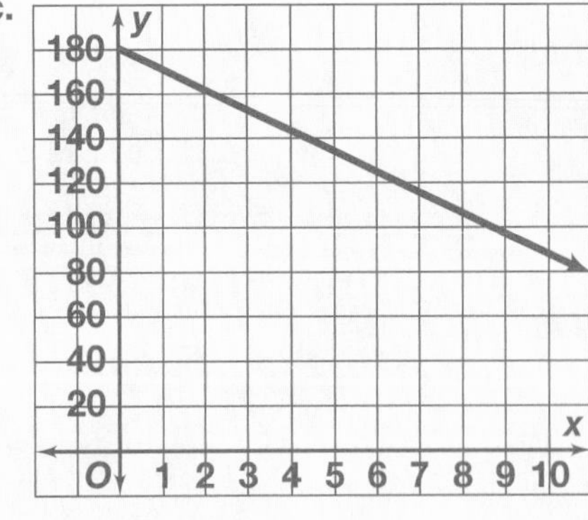

Lesson 8-4

pages 302–303 CA Standards Check

1.

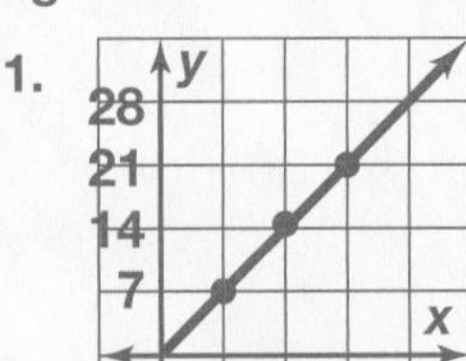

2.

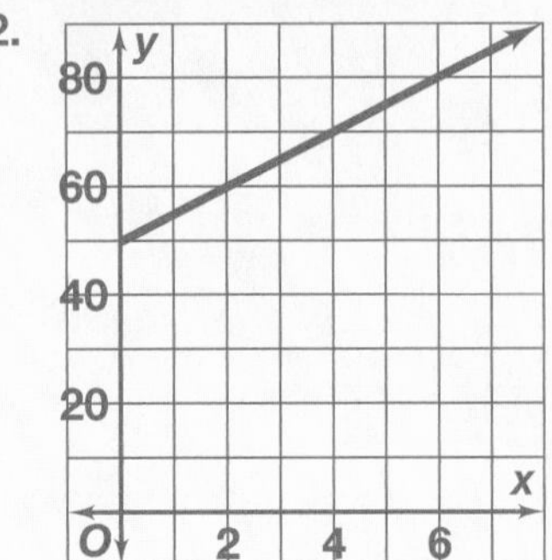

pages 305–306 Standards Practice

1.

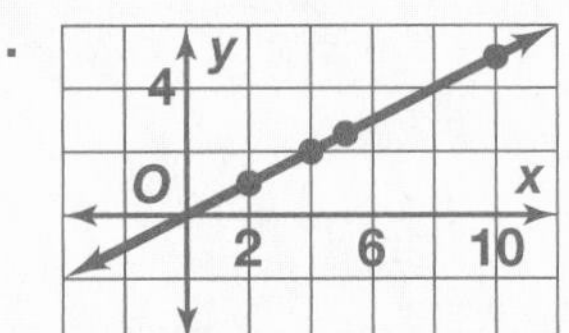

2.

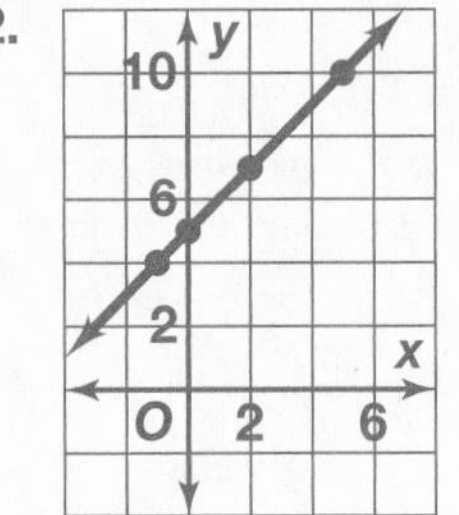

3.

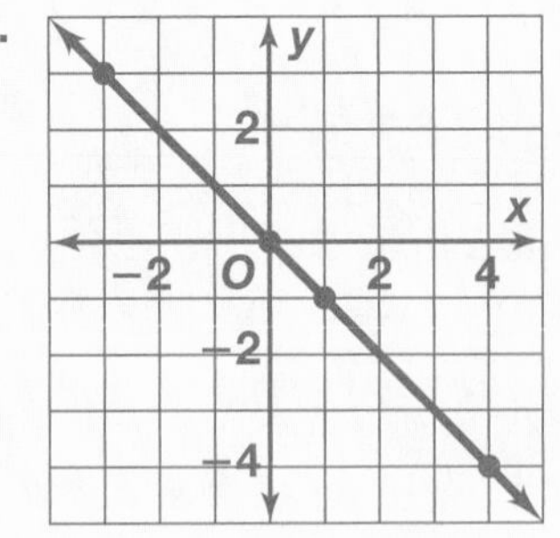

4.

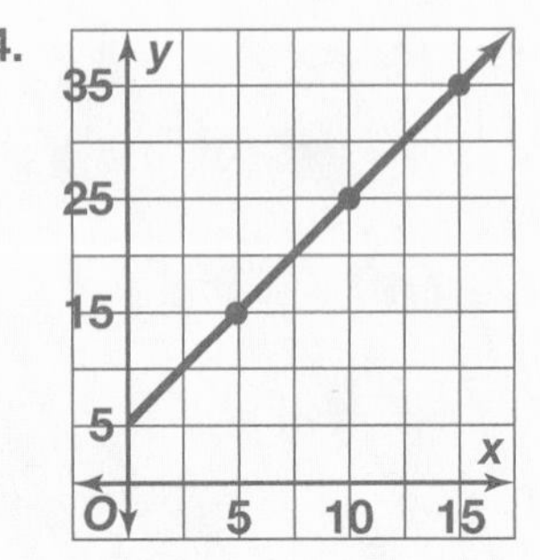

5.
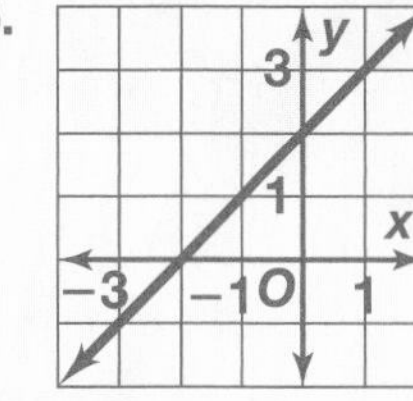

6.
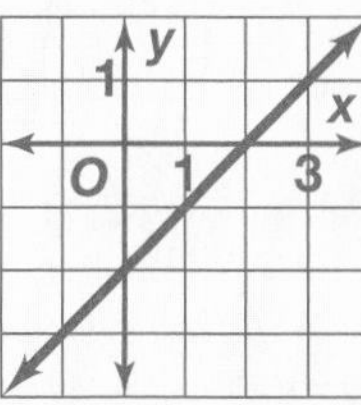

7.
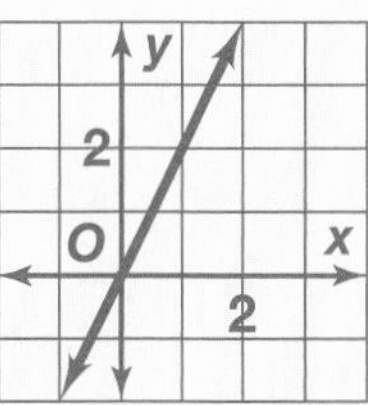

8.
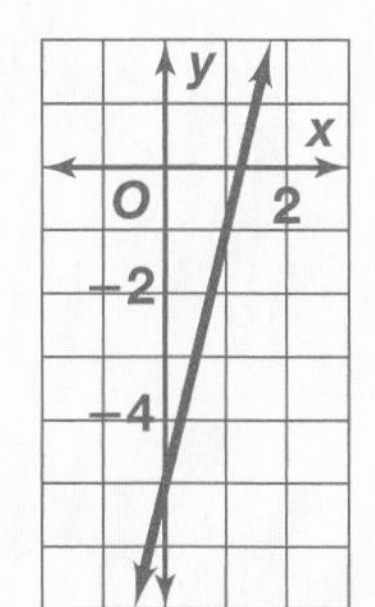

9.
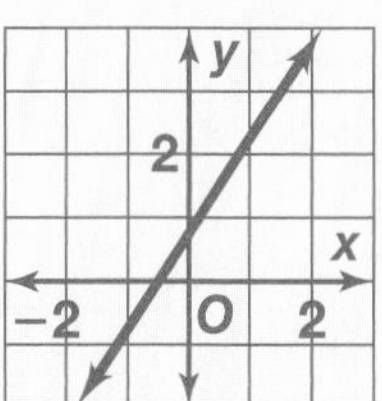

10.
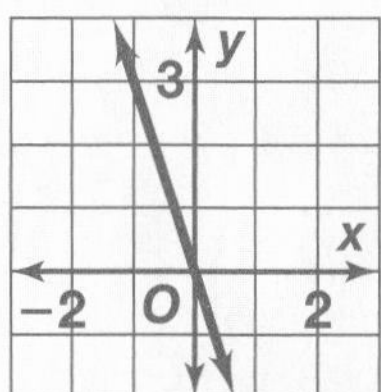

11.
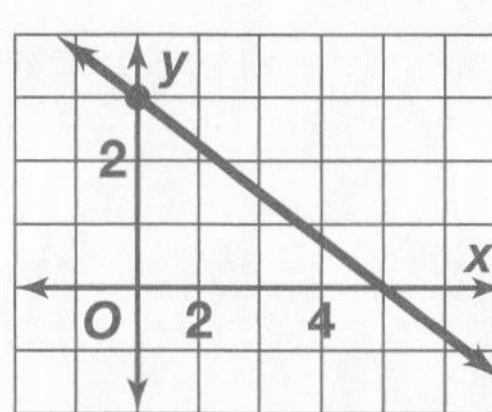

12.
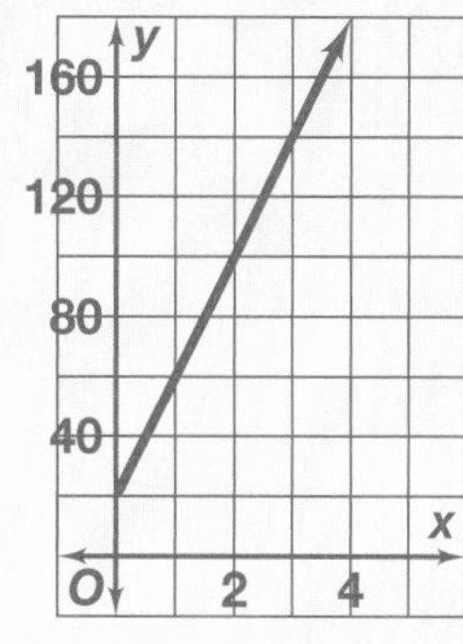

13. $y = 20.25x - 10$

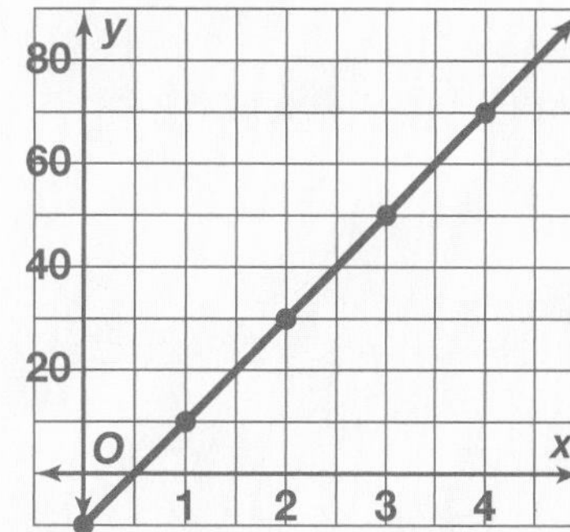

17.
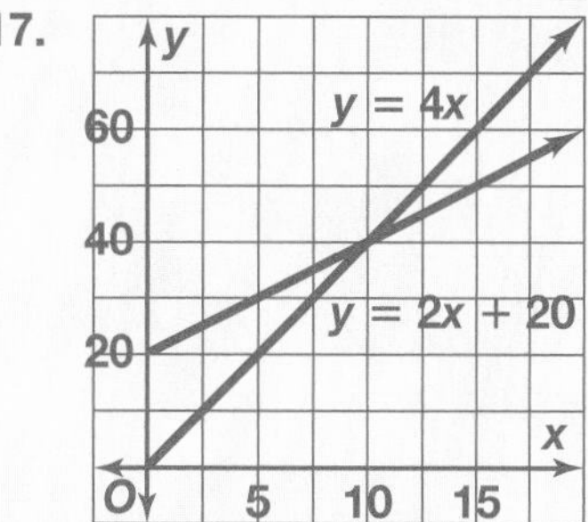

22.
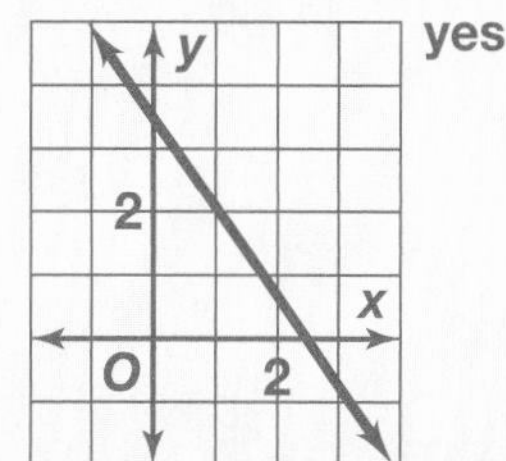

yes

26–29.
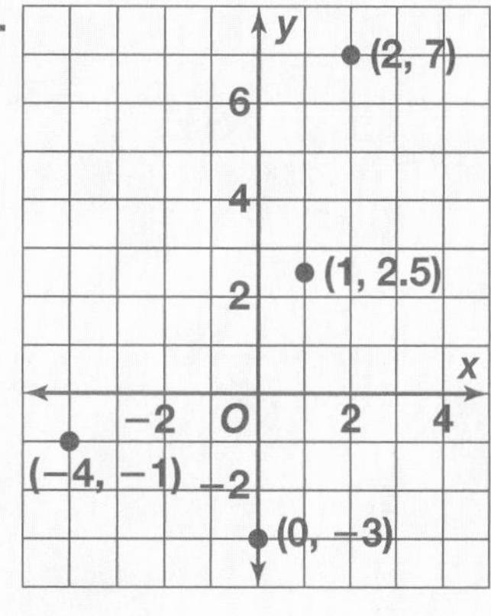

page 308–309 Guided Problem Solving

5.
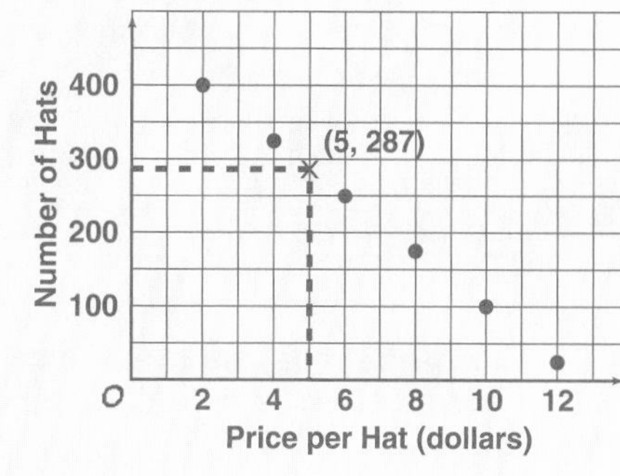

about 287

Lesson 8-5

pages 312–313 Standards Practice

21. x represents inches and y represents feets; $\frac{1 \text{ ft}}{12 \text{ in.}}$

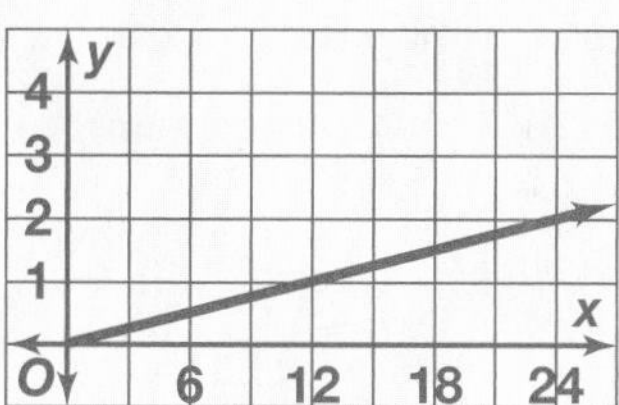

26.
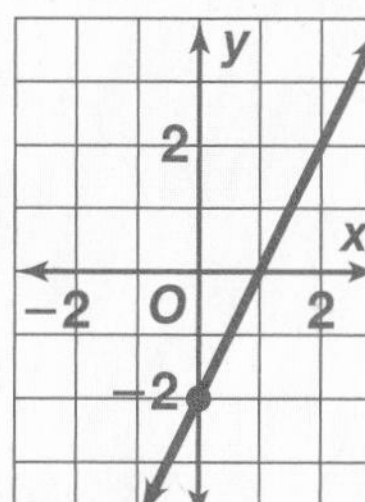

27.
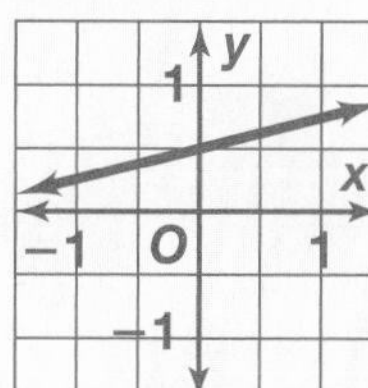

28.
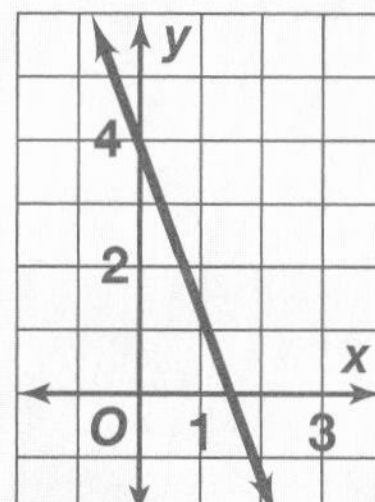

Additional Answers

page 315 Algebraic Thinking

1. 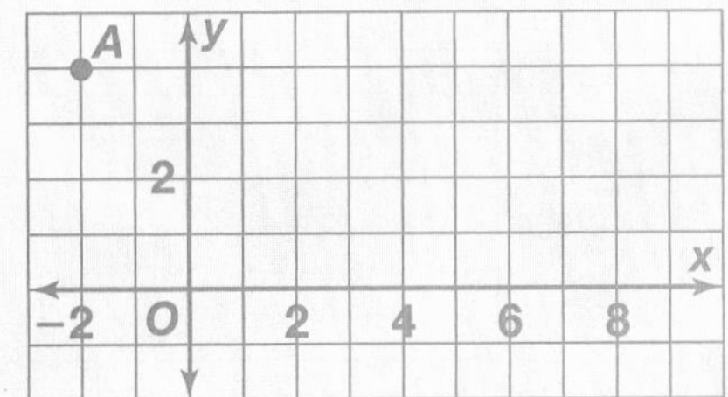

2. The slope tells you that the ratio of vertical change to horizontal change is −1 : 2.

3. Answers may vary. Sample: $B(0, 3)$

4.

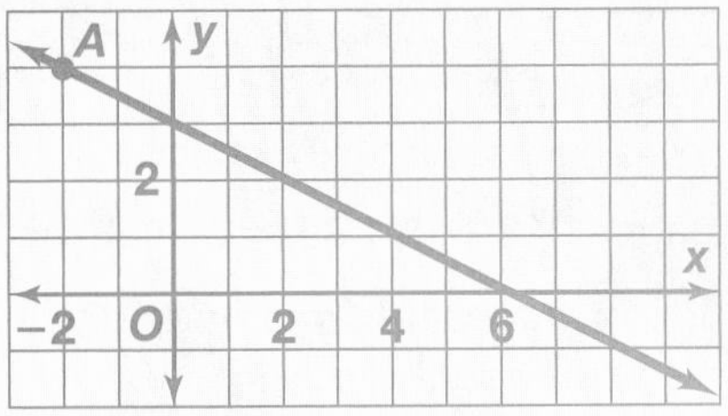

5. Answers may vary. Sample: (6, 0)

6. Yes; (8, −1) lies on the line.

page 315 Checkpoint Quiz 2

6. 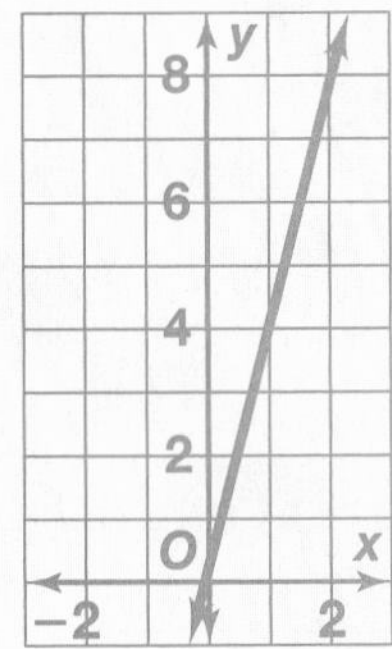

7. 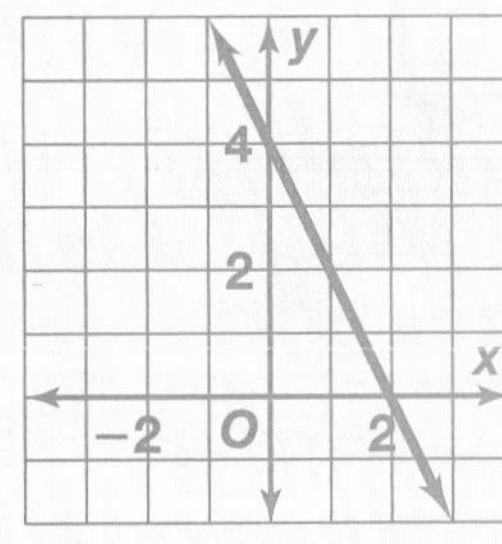

8. 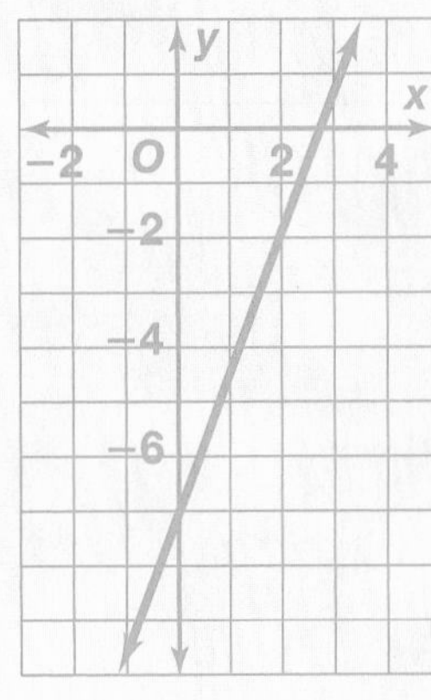

12. Since $\frac{5}{3} > \frac{3}{5}$, the hill with rise of 5 ft and run of 3 ft is steeper.

Lesson 8-6

pages 316–317 CA Standards Check

2.

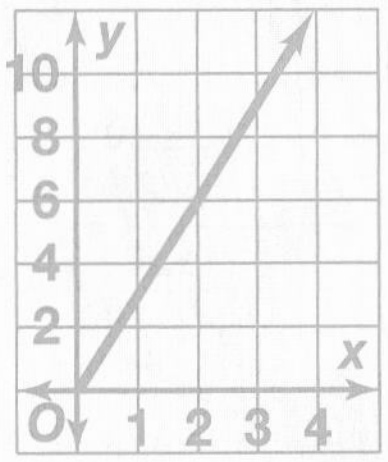

3; the slope represents the ratio of feet to yards.

pages 318–319 Standards Practice

6. 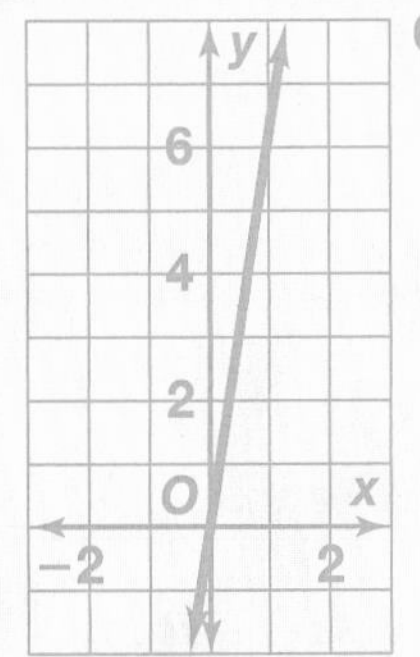 6

7. 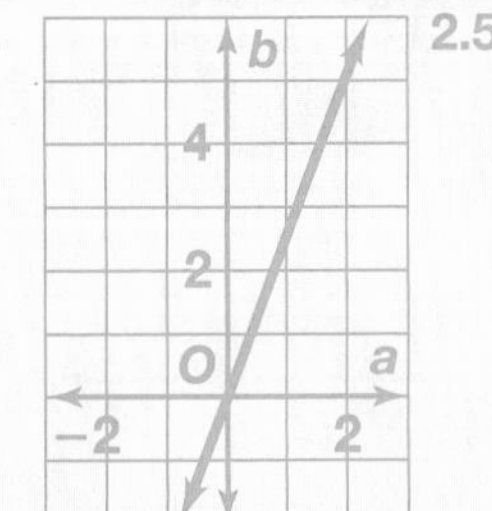 2.5

8. 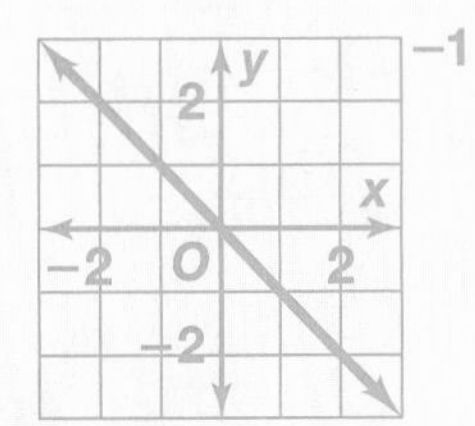 −1

9. 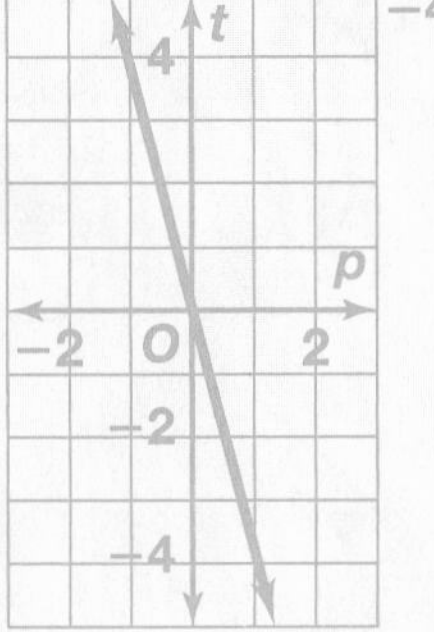 −4

10. 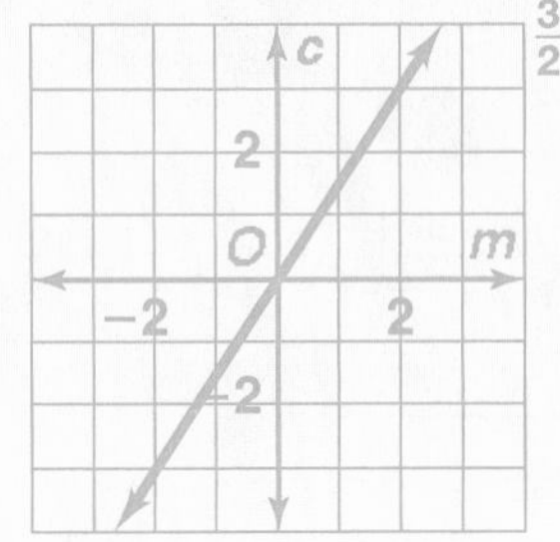 $\frac{3}{2}$

11. 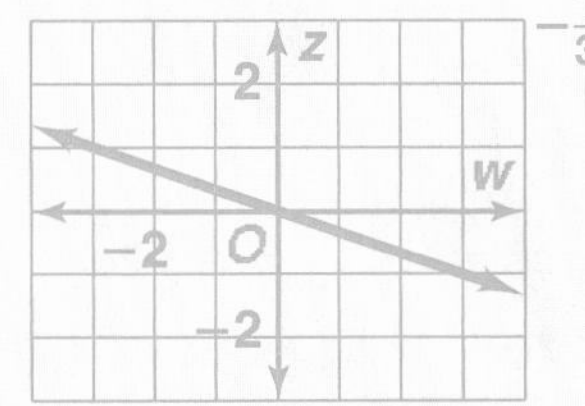 $-\frac{1}{3}$

12. 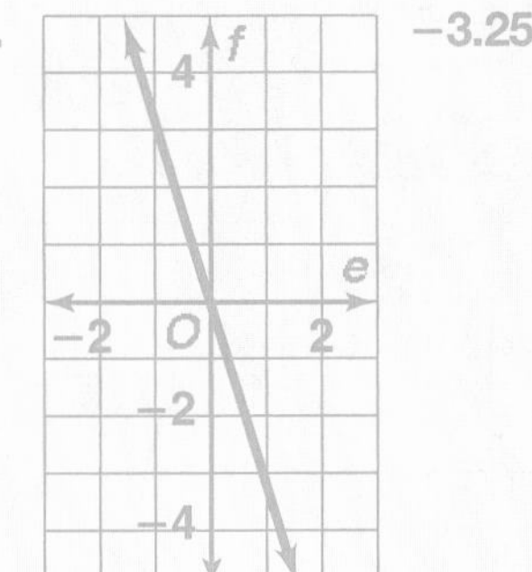 −3.25

13. 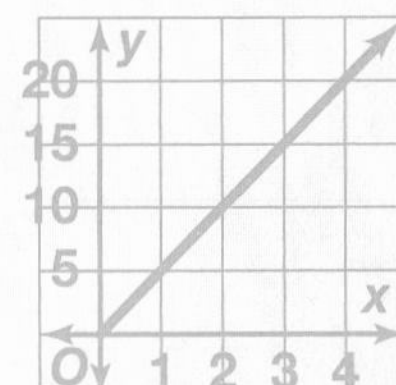

5; the slope represents the ratio of laps to days.

pages 322–323 Chapter Review

27. 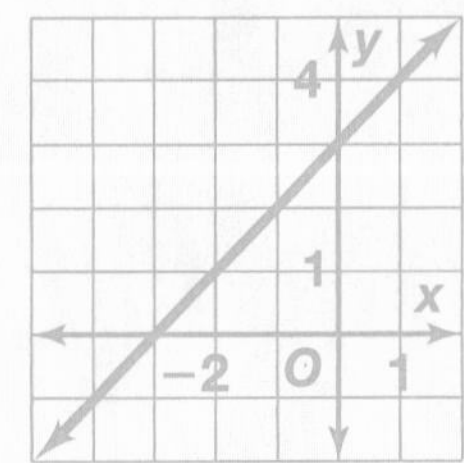

28. 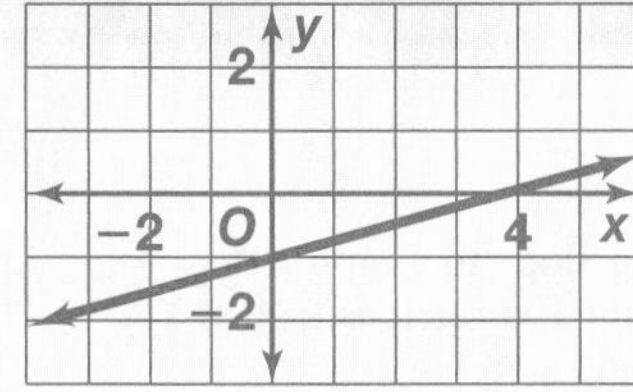

29. 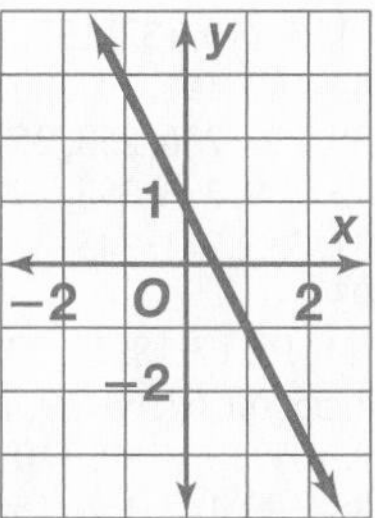

30. 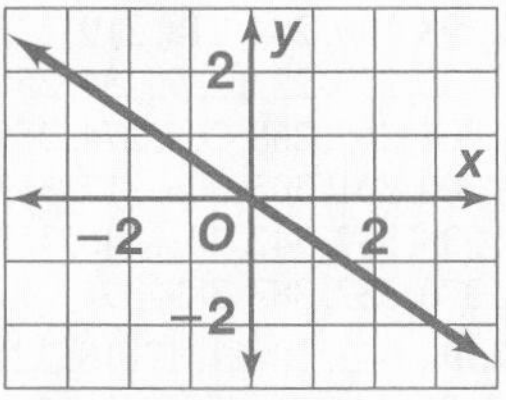

31. 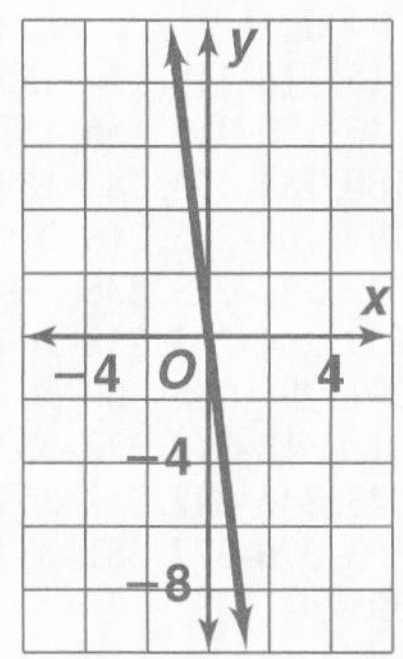

32. 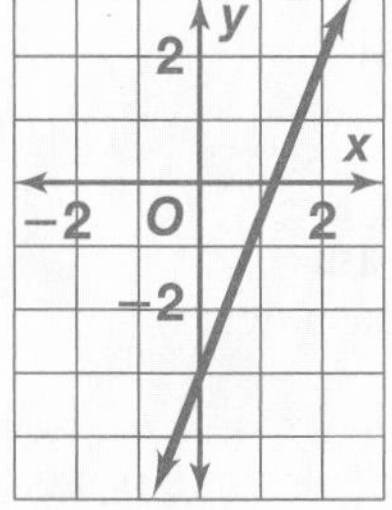

43. 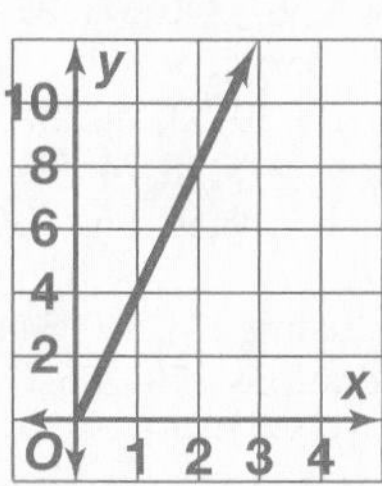

4; the slope is the ratio of quarts to gallons.

page 324 Chapter Test

29. 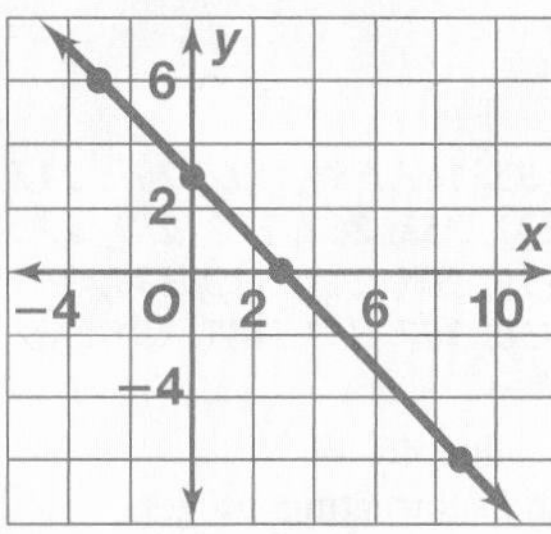

30. 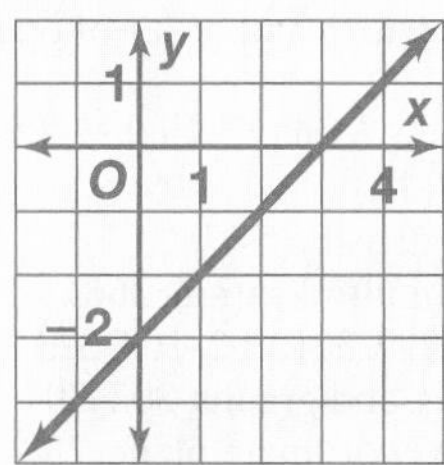

31. 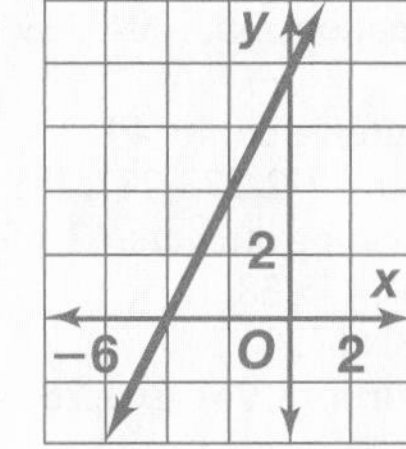

32. 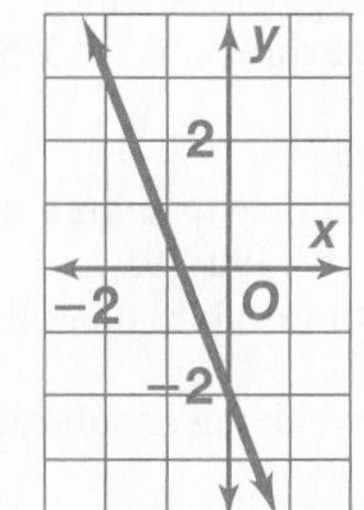

33. 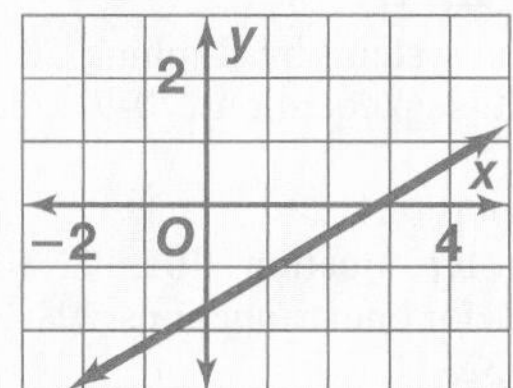

34. Slope of −10; it decreases more sharply than the line with a slope of 7 increases.

37. $\frac{3}{10}$

38. $-\frac{6}{7}$

39. $\frac{3}{17}$

40. $\frac{7}{4}$

41. $\frac{3}{2}$

42. $\frac{3}{5}$

49. 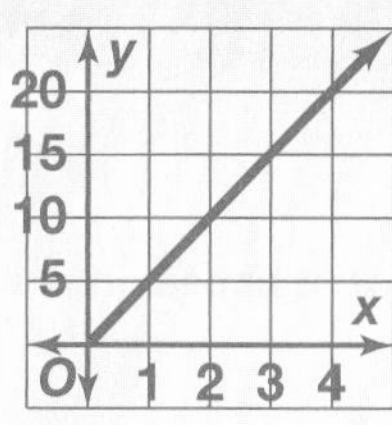

5; the slope represents the ratio of mass to number of nickels.

CHAPTER 9

page 360 Chapter Test

8. $\begin{cases} p \leq 525 \\ p \geq 350 \end{cases}$

9. $\begin{cases} a \leq 39 \\ a \geq 20 \end{cases}$

CHAPTER 10

Lesson 10-6

page 398 Algebraic Thinking

1. 2 from Florida, 6 from Maryland, 2 from California
2. 2 from Tennessee, 4 from Kentucky, 6 from Indiana
3. 9 from Ohio, 3 from Texas, 6 from Tennessee
4. 5 from Maine, 6 from Louisiana, 4 from Idaho

page 402 Chapter Test

25. Answers may vary. Sample: $(a^2)^3$ means $(a^2)(a^2)(a^2)$. The bases are the same, so add the exponents $a^{2+2+2} = a^6$.

Index

Teacher's Edition entries appear in blue type.

A

B

C

D

E

H

I

J

K

L

N

O

P

Q

R

S

T

U

V

W

X

Y

Z

Acknowledgments

Staff Credits

The people who made up the California Mathematics team—representing design services, editorial, editorial services, education technology, image services, marketing, market research, production services, publishing processes, and strategic markets—are listed below. Bold type denotes the core team members.

Dan Anderson, **Scott Andrews,** Carolyn Artin, Judith D. Buice, Kerry Cashman, Sarah Castrignano, Allison Cook, Carl Cottrell, Bob Craton, Patrick Culleton, Sheila DeFazio, Kathleen J. Dempsey, Frederick Fellows, **Suzanne Finn,** Patricia Fromkin, David J. George, **Patricia K. Gilbert,** Sandy Graff, **Ellen Welch Granter,** Richard Heater, Jayne Holman, Jennifer King, Betsy Krieble, Christopher Langley, Lisa LaVallee, Christine Lee, **Elizabeth Lehnertz,** Catherine Maglio, Cheryl Mahan, **Ann Mahoney,** Constance McCarty, **Carolyn McGuire,** Anne McLaughlin, Richard McMahon, Eve Melnechuk, Terri Mitchell, Michael Oster, Jeffrey Paulhus, Marcy Rose, Rashid Ross, Siri Schwartzman, Vicky Shen, **Dennis Slattery,** Nancy Smith, Mark Tricca, Paula Vergith, Teresa Whitney, Merce Wilczek, Joe Will, Kristin Winters, Heather Wright, Helen Young

Additional Credits: J.J. Andrews, Sarah J. Aubry, Deborah Belanger, Beth Blumberg, Casey Clark, Patty Fagan, Tom Greene, Karmyn Guthrie, Gillian Kahn, Jonathan Kier, Mary Landry, Mary Beth McDaniel, Anakin Steuart Michele, Hope Morley, Carol Roy, Jewel Simmons, Ted Smykal, Richard Sullivan, Dan Tanguay, Steve Thomas, Michael Torocsik, Alwyn Velasquez, Allison Wyss

Cover Design

Nancy Smith

Cover Photos

Building, Ted Soqui/Corbis; Artichoke, Ed Young/Corbis.

Illustration

XNR Productions

Photography

Front matter: Page CA6, Ralph A. Clevenger/Corbis; **CA7,** Jon Riley/Getty Images, Inc.; **CA8,** Frank Lane/Parfitt/Stone/Getty Images, Inc.; **CA9,** Corbis/Stock Market; **CA10,** Rob Atkins/Image Bank/Getty Images, Inc.; **CA11,** Alan Thornton/Getty Images, Inc.; **CA12,** Wilfried Krecichwost/Stone/Getty Images, Inc.; **CA13,** John Lund/Getty Images, Inc.; **CA14,** Ron Kimball/Ron Kimball Stock; **CA15,** R.D. Rubic/Precision Chromes, Inc.; **CA16,** Zefa/London/Corbis; **CA17,** Jeff Greenberg/Photo Edit; **CA29,** David McNew/Getty Images; **CA33,** David McNew/Getty Images; **CA34,** Steve Vidler/SuperStock.

Chapter One: Page 3, Galen Rowell/Corbis; **5,** Jon Riley/Stone/Getty Images, Inc.; **7,** Bob Daemmrich/Stock Boston; **12,** Steve Bronstein/The Image Bank/Getty Images, Inc.; **13,** PhotoEdit; **27,** Getty Images, Inc.; **39,** Nicholas Devore III/Bruce Coleman, Inc.; **43,** Courtesy of Cedar Point/Photo by Dan Feicht; **53,** Russ Lappa.

Chapter Two: Page 67, V.C.L./FPG/Getty Images, Inc.; **70,** Russ Lappa; **80,** VCL/Alistair Berg/Getty Images, Inc.; **85,** Michelle Bridwell/Photoedit; **97,** Pedro Coll/Superstock; **102,** The Image Works.

Chapter Three: Page 123 ml, Sinibaldi/Corbis; **126,** Tony Freeman/PhotoEdit; **128,** Poulides/Thatcher/Getty Images, Inc.; **133,** Clive Brunskill/Allsport/Getty Images, Inc.; **134,** Corbis; **140,** Doug Sokell/Visuals Unlimited; **144,** Russ Lappa; **147,** Robin L. Sachs/PhotoEdit; **148,** Stone/Getty Images, Inc.; **152,** Bob Daemmrich/Stock Boston; **155,** Michael Newman/PhotoEdit; **161,** Dave King/Dorling Kindersley; **162,** Juan Silva/Getty Images.

Chapter Four: Page 175, Steve Hamblin/Alamy; **181,** Daryl Balfour/Stone/Getty Images, Inc.; **195,** Seth Resnick/Stock Boston; **203,** Rob Atkins/Getty Images, Inc.; **205,** Jim West/The Image Works; **208,** Nancy Richmond/The Image Works; **210,** David Young-Wolff/PhotoEdit; **213,** CLOSE TO HOME ©John McPherson. Reprinted with permission of Universal Press Syndicate. All rights reserved.

Chapter Five: Page 229, Superstock; **232,** Mark Richards/Photo Edit; **236 l,** Gail Mooney/Masterfile; **241,** David Young-Wolff/PhotoEdit, Inc.; **244,** Tim Davis/Stone/Getty Images, Inc.; **248,** Myrleen Ferguson/PhotoEdit; **250,** Kenneth W. Fink/Photo Researchers, Inc.; **254,** Tom Stock/Getty Images, Inc.; **259,** Alan Thornton/Getty Images, Inc.; **261,** Robert Landau/Corbis.

Chapter Six: Page 275, Phil Klein/Corbis; **277,** SuperStock, Inc.; **284,** Wilfried Krecichwost/Getty Images, Inc.; **288,** Robert Brenner/PhotoEdit; **294,** Index Stock Imagery, Inc.; **299,** Steve McCutcheon/Visuals Unlimited; **305,** Ilan Rosen/Alamy; **306,** Aaron Stevenson/Prentice Hall; **311,** Steven Kline/Bruce Coleman, Inc.; **312 t,** Pearson Education; **312 b,** Leonard de Selva/Corbis; **314,** Frank Pedrick/The Image Works; **315,** Omni-Photo Communications, Inc.

Chapter Seven: Page 327, John Lund/Getty Images, Inc.; **337,** Frans Lanting/Minden Pictures; **341,** Andrew Syred/Science Photo Library/Photo Researchers, Inc.; **343,** Maxine Hall/Corbis; **347,** Bettmann/Corbis; **352,** Royalty-Free/Corbis; **355,** Artiga Photo/Corbis; **359,** AP Photo/Paul Sakuma.

Chapter Eight: Page 369, Mark Bacon/Alamy; **370,** Getty Images, Inc.; **374,** Chuck Savage/Corbis; **385,** Cesar Lucas Abreu/Getty Images, Inc.; **389,** Ron Kimball/Ron Kimball Stock; **392,** Lynn M. Stone.

Chapter Nine: Page 425, Craig Aurness/Corbis; **427,** Richard Megna/Fundamental Photographs; **430 l,** Getty Images, Inc.; **430 r,** Prentice Hall; **431,** C Squared Studios/PhotoDisc, Inc./Getty Images, Inc.; **435,** R.D. Rubic/Precision Chromes, Inc.; **437,** Agence Vandystadt/Getty Images, Inc.; **438,** Jose Carrillo/PhotoEdit; **441,** David Austen/Getty Images, Inc.; **442 t,** NASA; **442 b,** Reprinted by permission: Tribune Media Services; **448,** A. Ramey/Stock Boston; **454,** Michael Keller/Getty Images, Inc.; **463,** David Cannon/Getty Images; **467,** CLOSE TO HOME by John McPherson/Universal Press Syndicate; **472,** Jeff Sherman/Getty Images, Inc.

Chapter Ten: Page 485, Doug Dreyer/AP/Wide World Photos; **494,** Spencer Jones/Getty Images, Inc.; **497,** AFP/Corbis; **502,** ©ABC/Mondrian Estate/Holtzman Trust/Haags Gemeentemuseum; **505,** ©Tribune Media Services, Inc. All Rights Reserved. Reprinted with permission; **511,** David Young-Wolff/PhotoEdit; **515,** James Shaffer/PhotoEdit; **517,** Kelly-Mooney Photography/Corbis; **518,** David Young-Wolff/PhotoEdit.

Teacher's Edition

Editorial Services: Publisher's Resource Group
Production Services: datagrafix